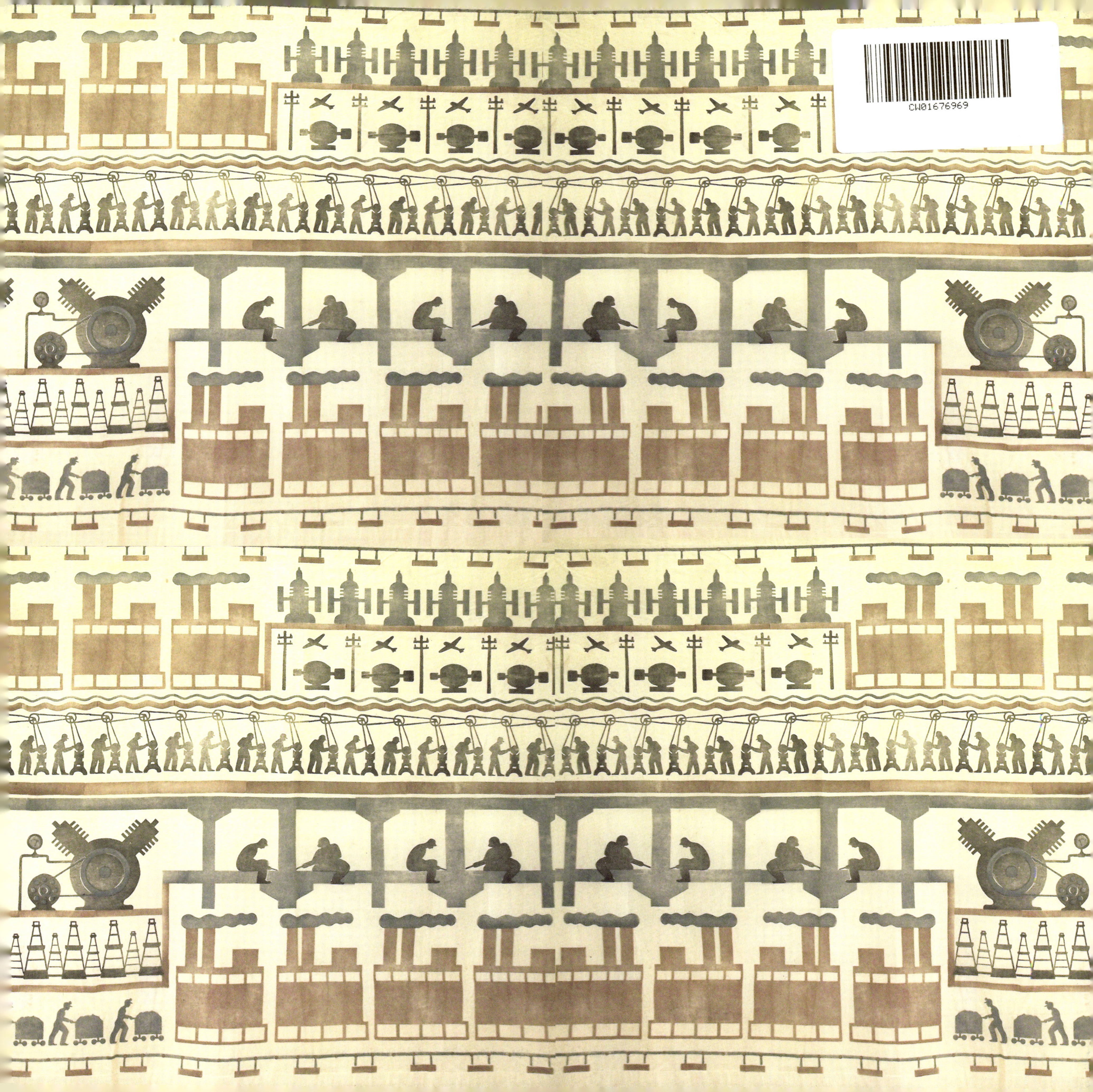

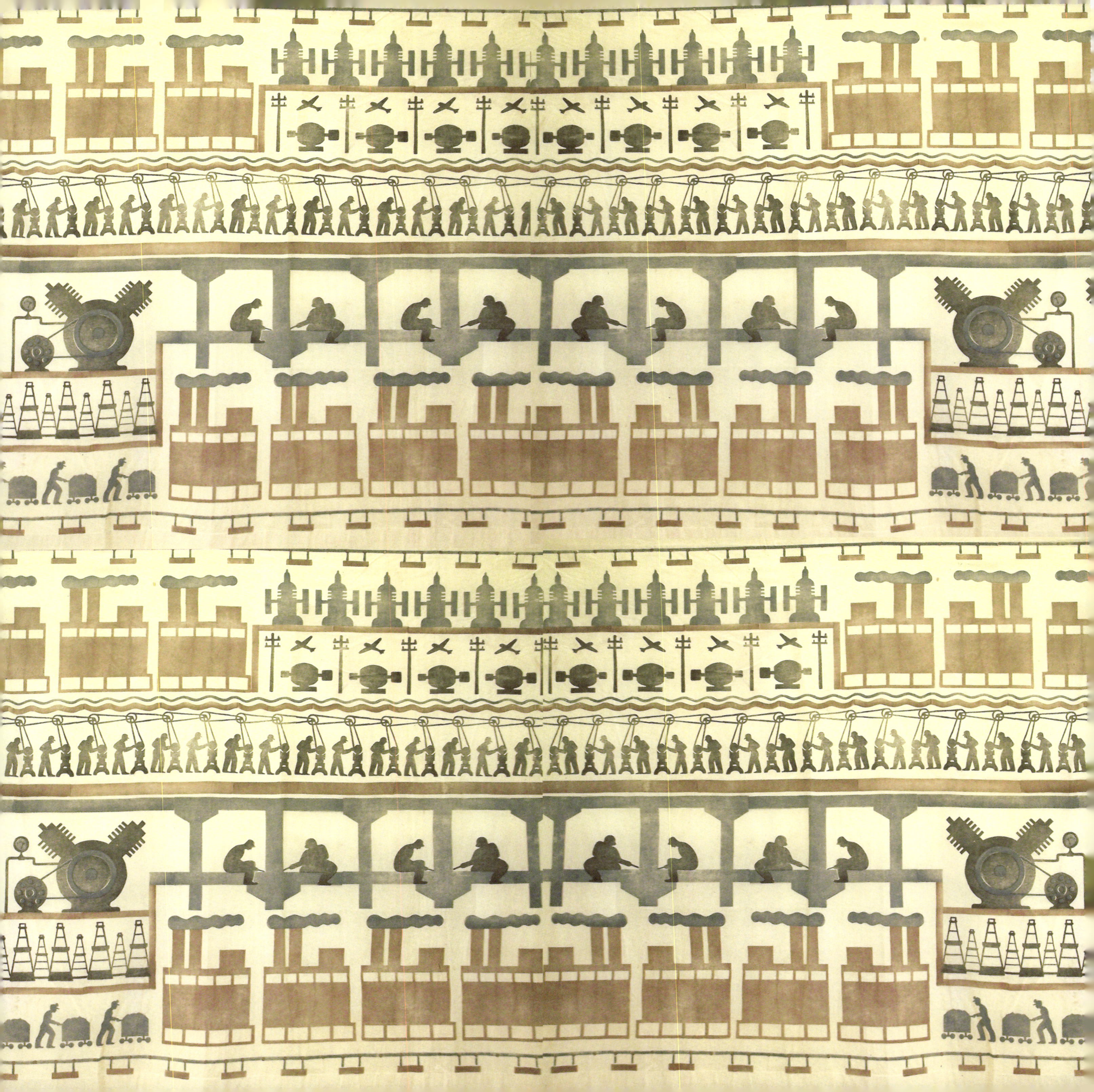

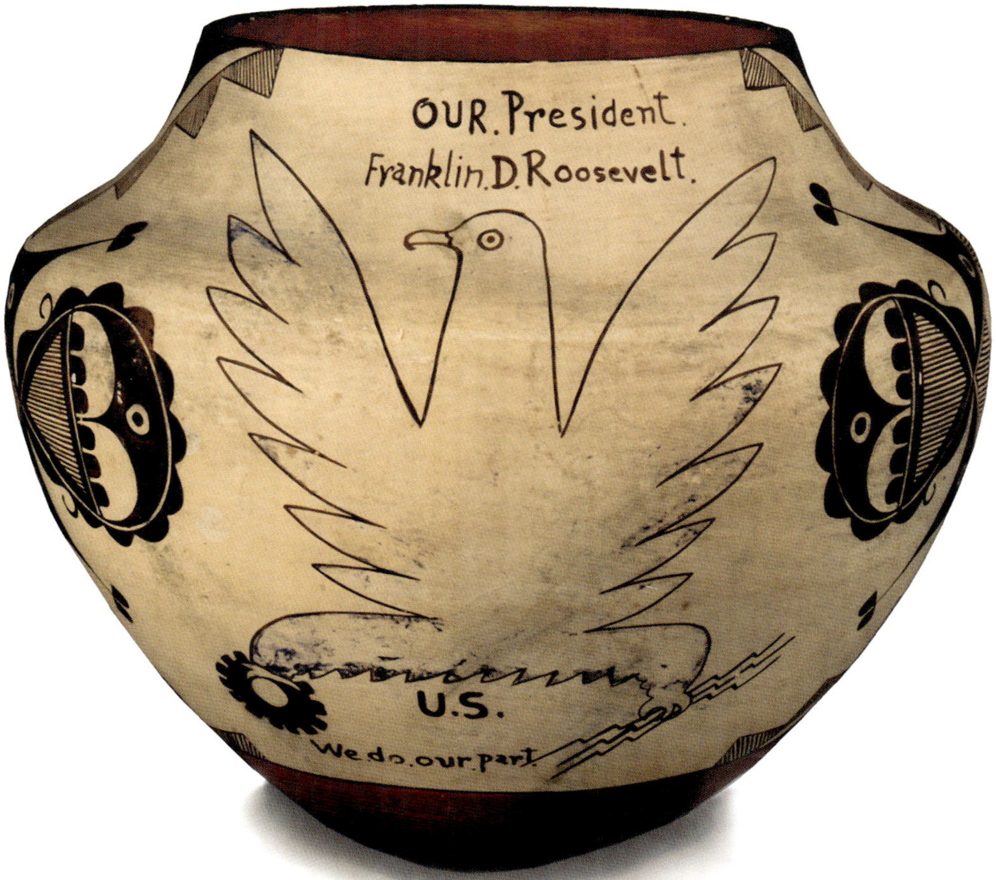

WHEN ART WORKED

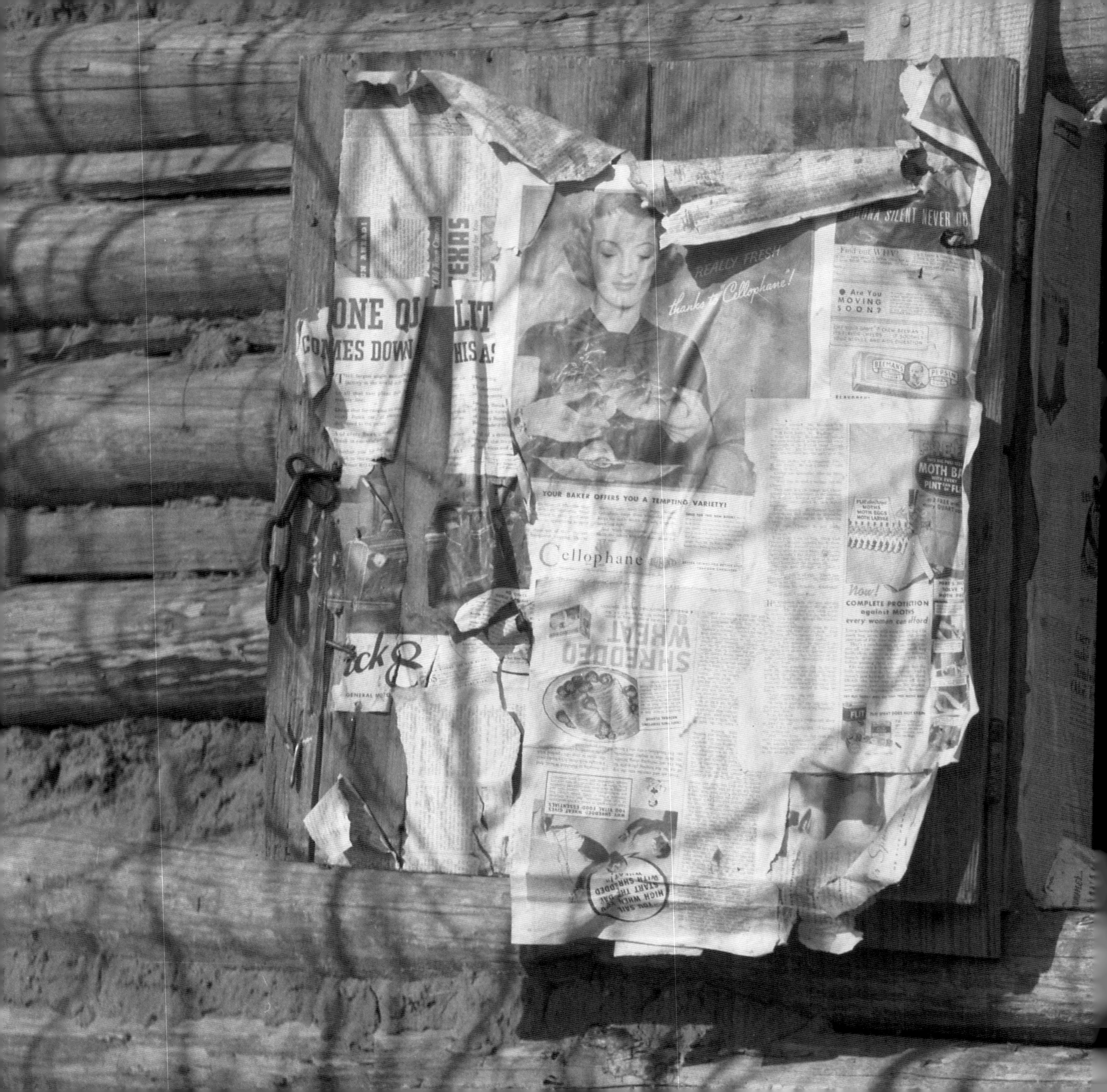

ONE QU LIT
COMES DOW HIS A
TEXAS
REALLY FRESH
thanks to "Cellophane"!
Are You MOVING SOON?
YOUR BAKER OFFERS YOU A TEMPTING VARIETY!
Cellophane
MOTH BA
Now!
COMPLETE PROTECTION against MOTHS every women can afford

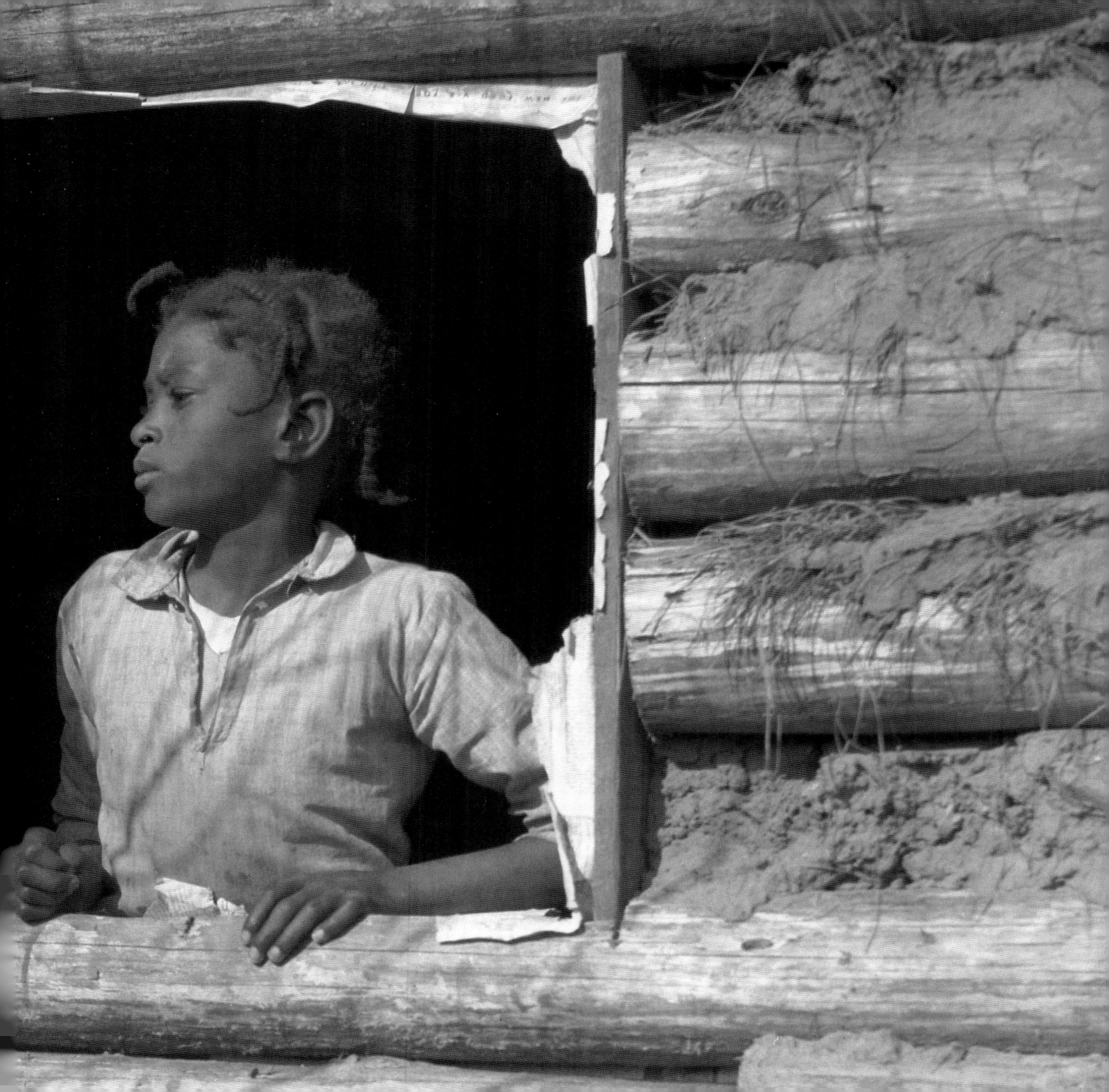

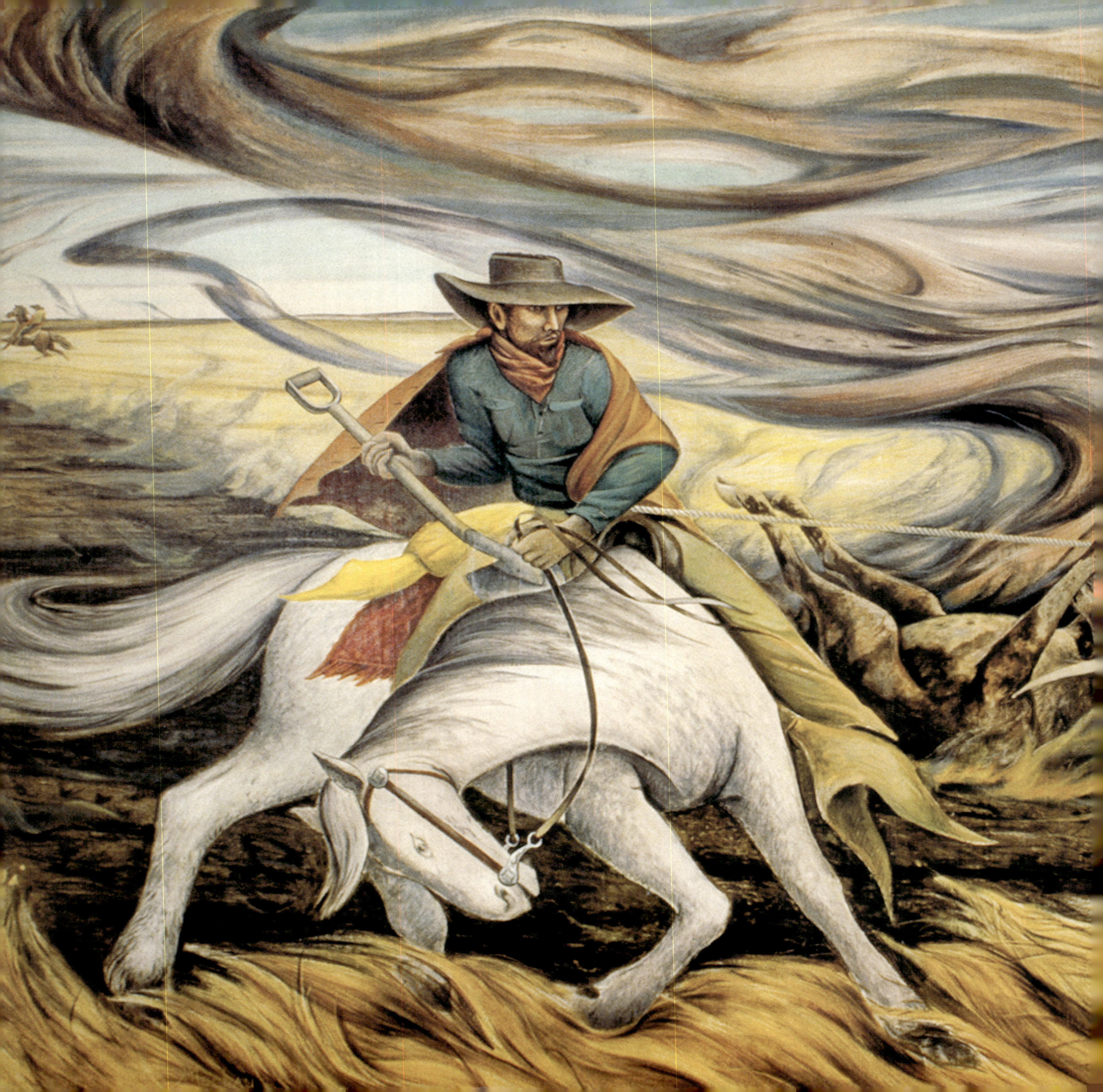

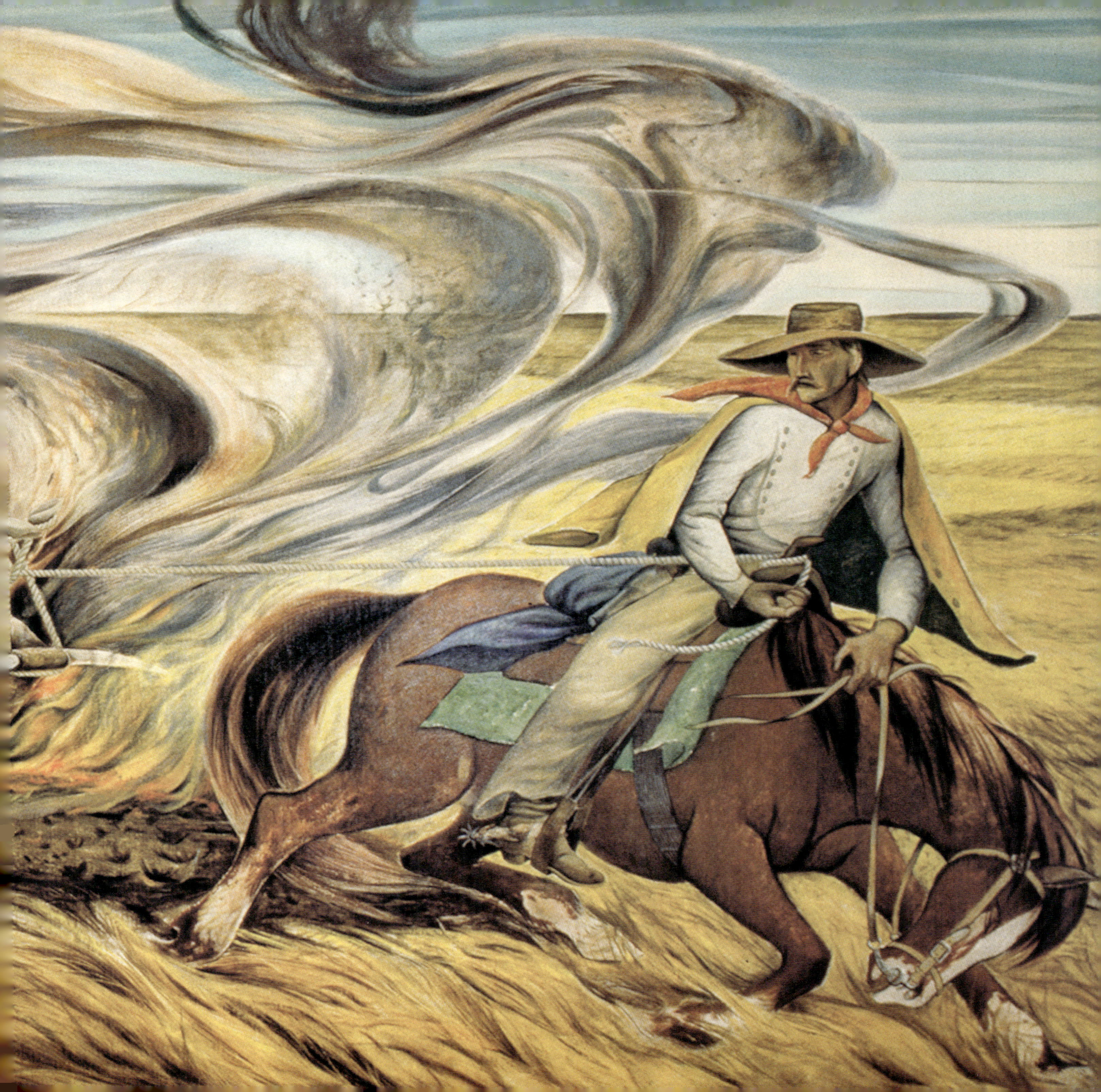

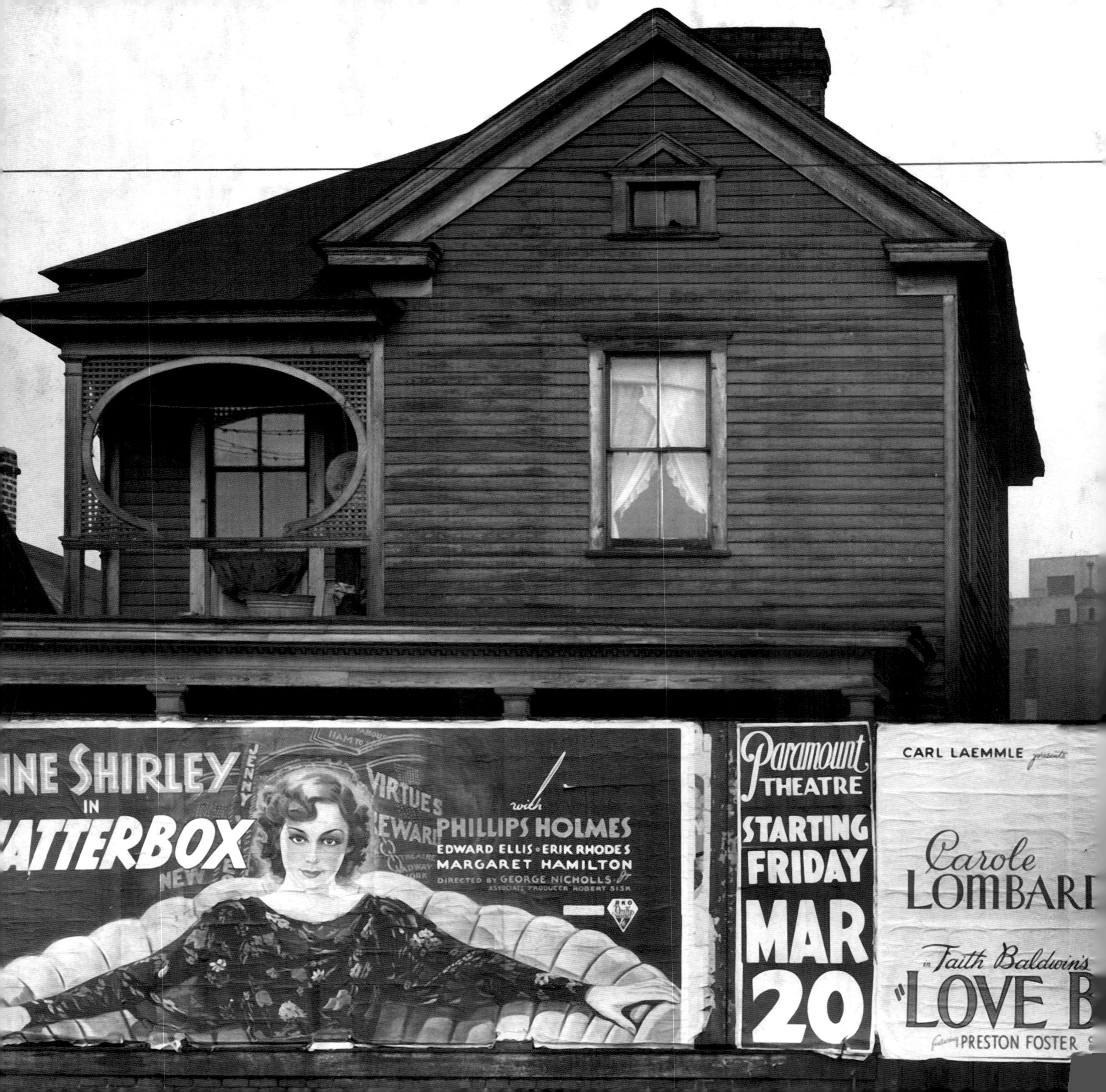
NNE SHIRLEY
IN
ATTERBOX
with
PHILLIPS HOLMES
EDWARD ELLIS • ERIK RHODES
MARGARET HAMILTON
DIRECTED BY GEORGE NICHOLLS, Jr
ASSOCIATE PRODUCER ROBERT SISK
Paramount
THEATRE
STARTING
FRIDAY
MAR
20
CARL LAEMMLE presents
Carole
LOMBAR
in Faith Baldwin's
"LOVE B
featuring PRESTON FOSTER

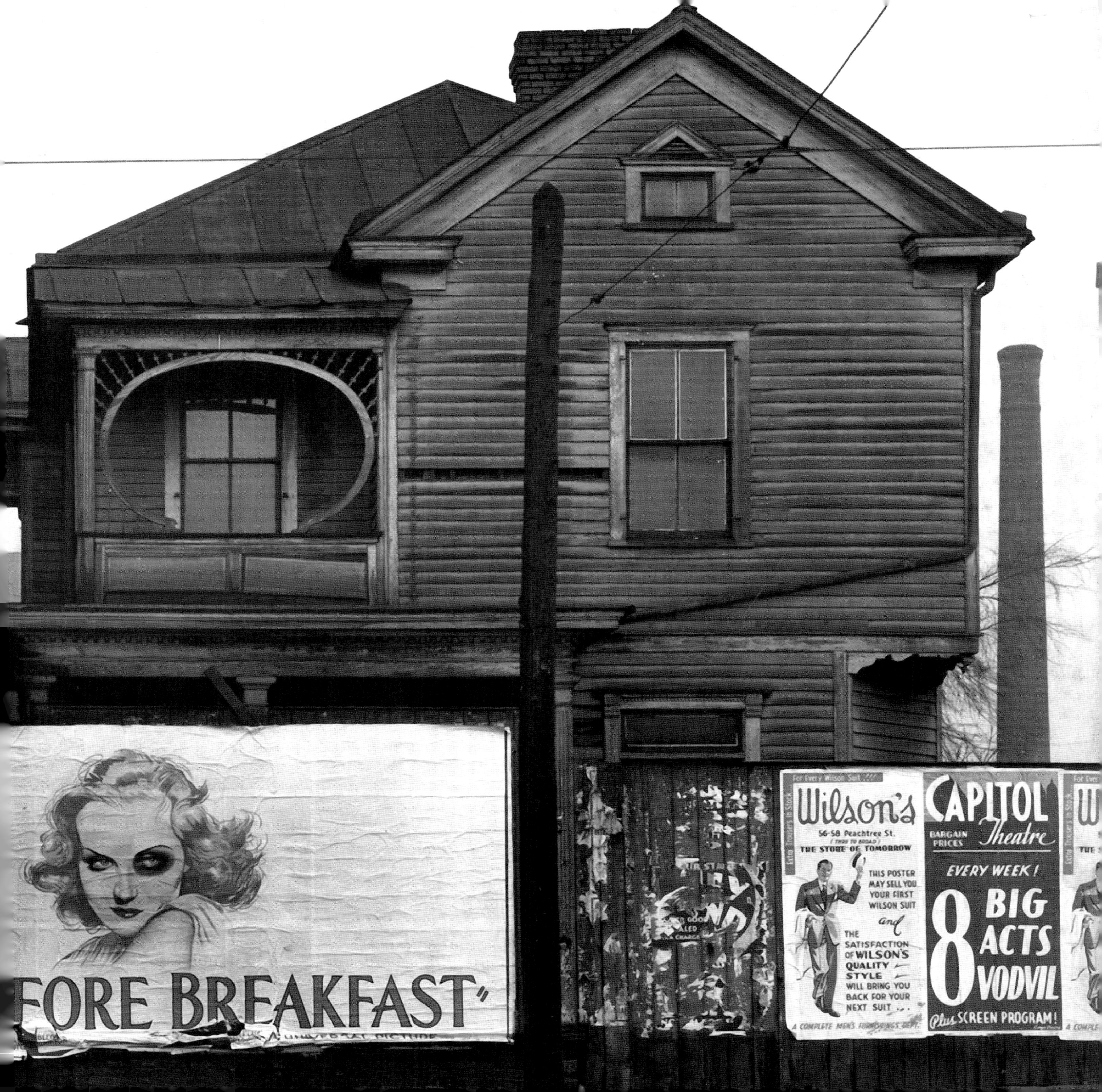
FORE BREAKFAST"
For Every Wilson Suit !!!
Extra Trousers in Stock
Wilson's
56-58 Peachtree St.
(THRU TO BROAD)
THE STORE OF TOMORROW
THIS POSTER MAY SELL YOU YOUR FIRST WILSON SUIT
and
THE SATISFACTION OF WILSON'S QUALITY STYLE WILL BRING YOU BACK FOR YOUR NEXT SUIT ...
A COMPLETE MEN'S FURNISHINGS DEPT.
CAPITOL Theatre
BARGAIN PRICES
EVERY WEEK!
8 BIG ACTS VODVIL
Plus SCREEN PROGRAM!

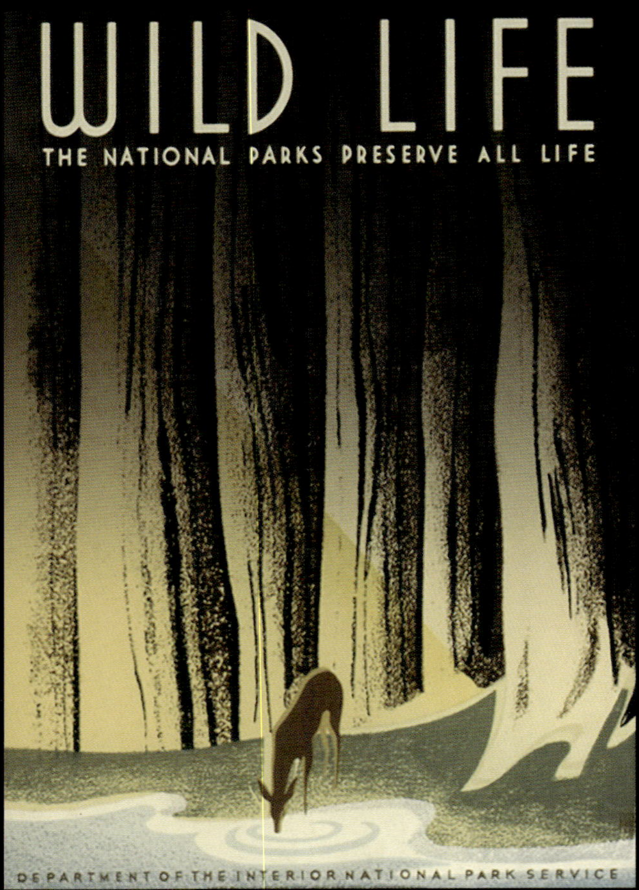
WILD LIFE
THE NATIONAL PARKS PRESERVE ALL LIFE
DEPARTMENT OF THE INTERIOR NATIONAL PARK SERVICE

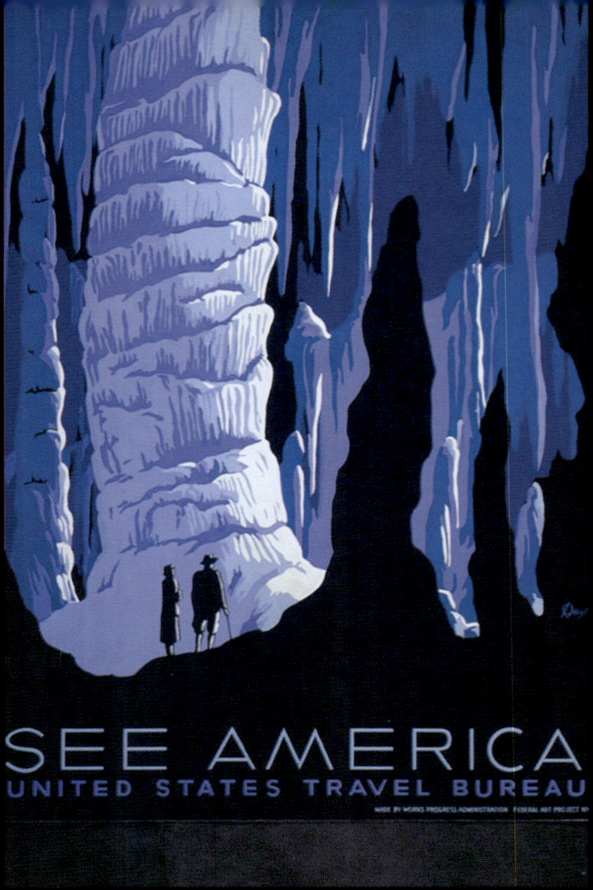
SEE AMERICA
UNITED STATES TRAVEL BUREAU

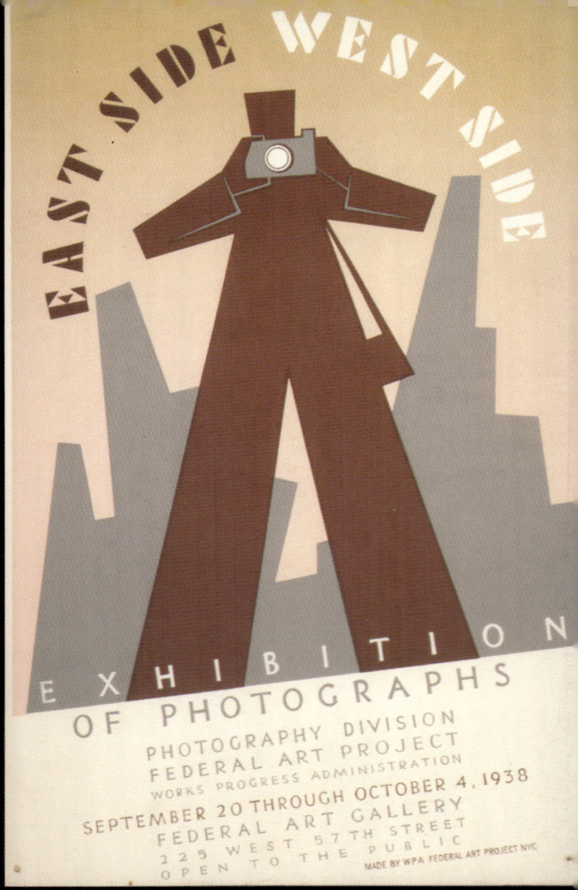
EAST SIDE WEST SIDE
EXHIBITION
OF PHOTOGRAPHS
PHOTOGRAPHY DIVISION
FEDERAL ART PROJECT
WORKS PROGRESS ADMINISTRATION
SEPTEMBER 20 THROUGH OCTOBER 4, 1938
FEDERAL ART GALLERY
225 WEST 57TH STREET
OPEN TO THE PUBLIC
MADE BY WPA FEDERAL ART PROJECT NYC

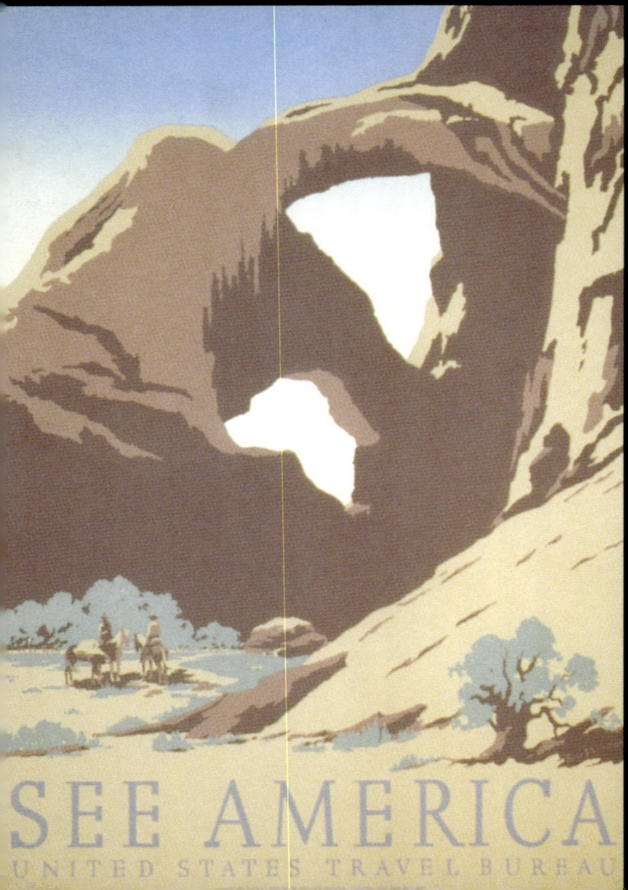
SEE AMERICA
UNITED STATES TRAVEL BUREAU

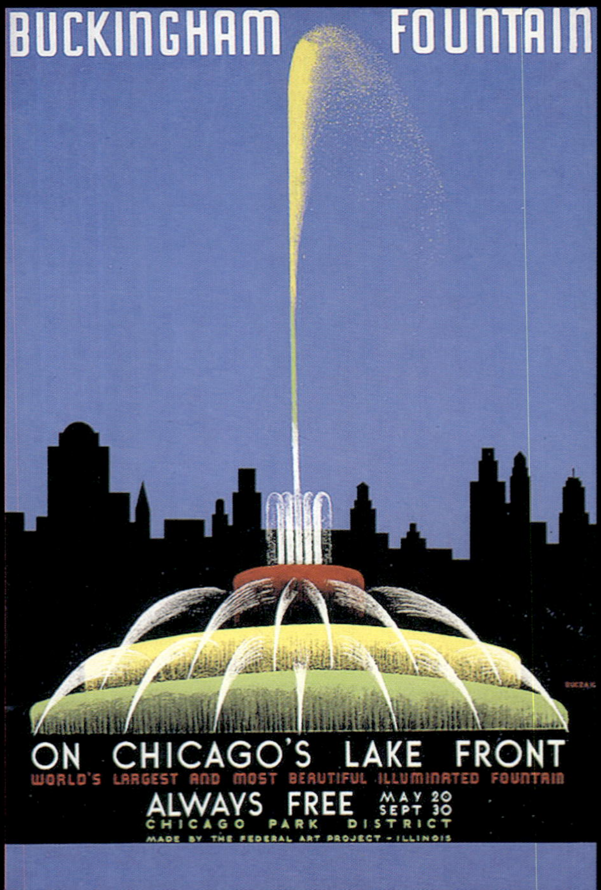
BUCKINGHAM FOUNTAIN
ON CHICAGO'S LAKE FRONT
WORLD'S LARGEST AND MOST BEAUTIFUL ILLUMINATED FOUNTAIN
ALWAYS FREE MAY 20 SEPT 30
CHICAGO PARK DISTRICT
MADE BY THE FEDERAL ART PROJECT - ILLINOIS

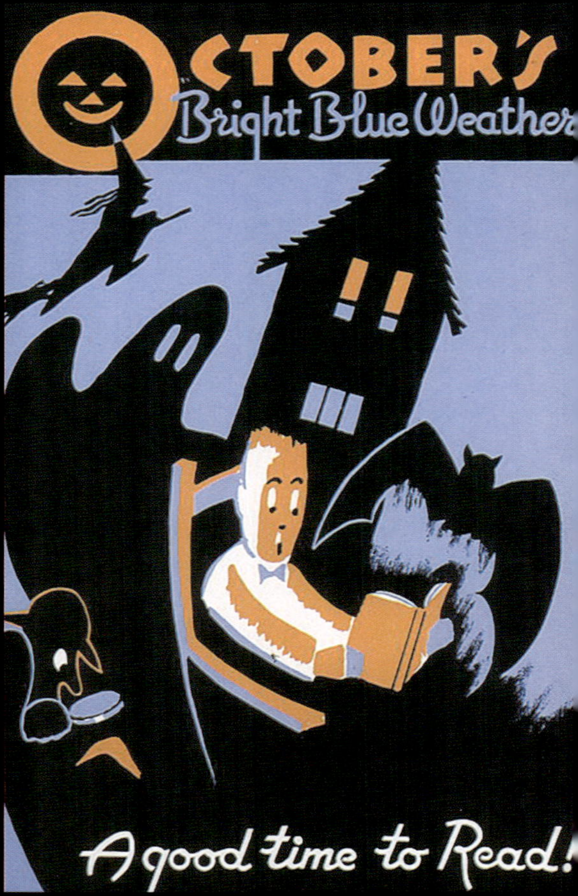
OCTOBER'S
Bright Blue Weather
A good time to Read!

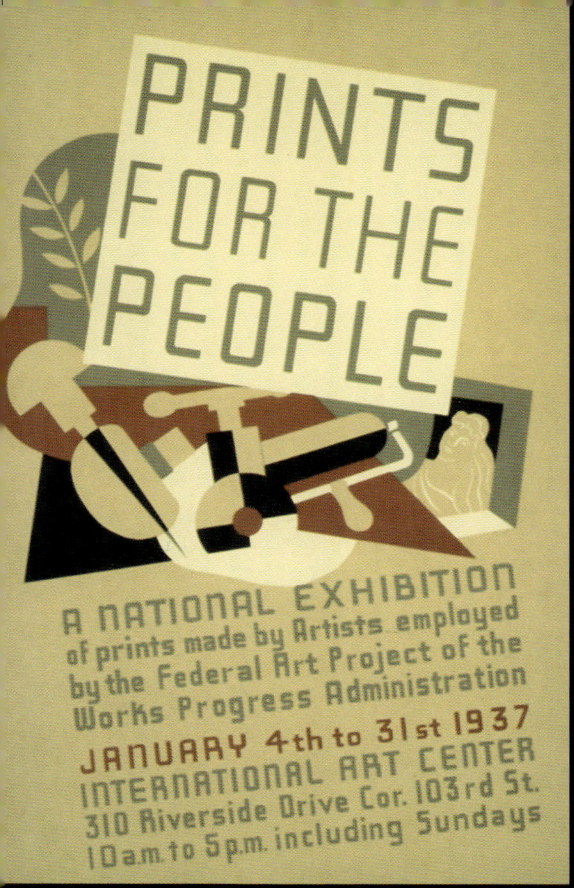
PRINTS FOR THE PEOPLE
A NATIONAL EXHIBITION
of prints made by Artists employed by the Federal Art Project of the Works Progress Administration
JANUARY 4th to 31st 1937
INTERNATIONAL ART CENTER
310 Riverside Drive Cor. 103rd St.
10 a.m. to 5 p.m. including Sundays

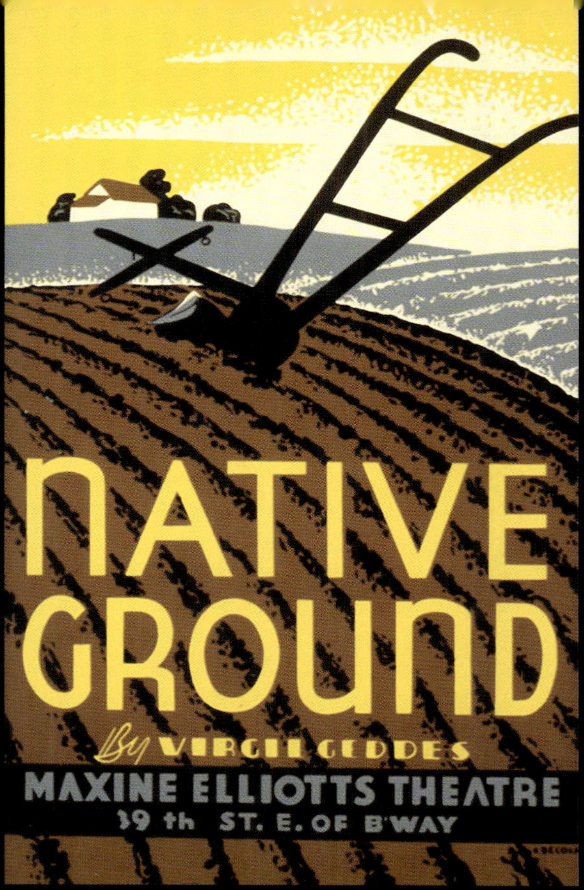
NATIVE GROUND
By VIRGIL GEDDES
MAXINE ELLIOTTS THEATRE
39 th ST. E. OF B'WAY

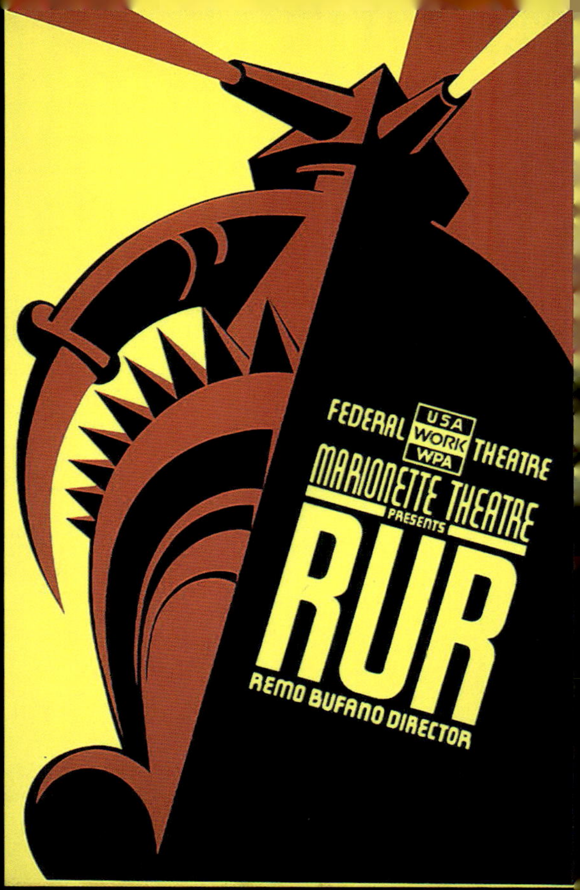
FEDERAL
USA WORK WPA
THEATRE
MARIONETTE THEATRE
PRESENTS
RUR
REMO BUFANO DIRECTOR

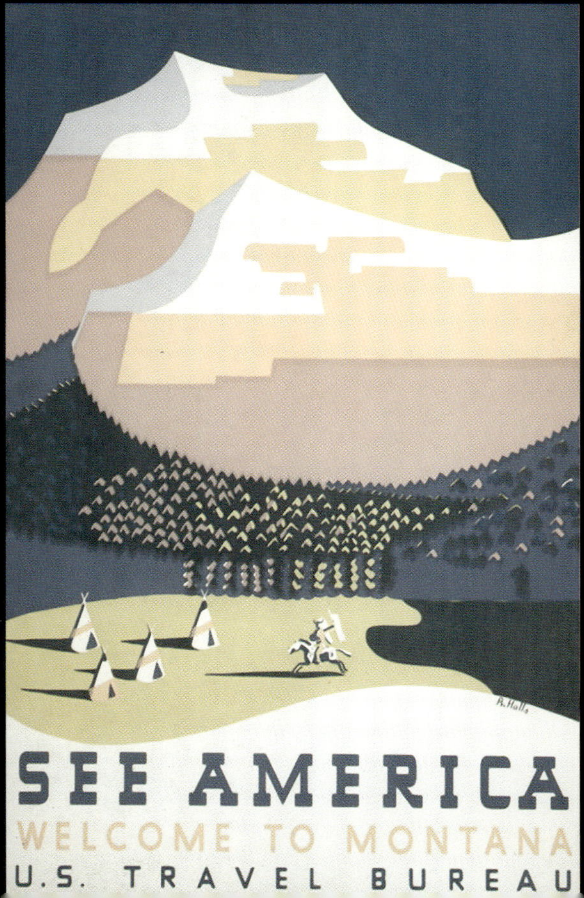
SEE AMERICA
WELCOME TO MONTANA
U.S. TRAVEL BUREAU

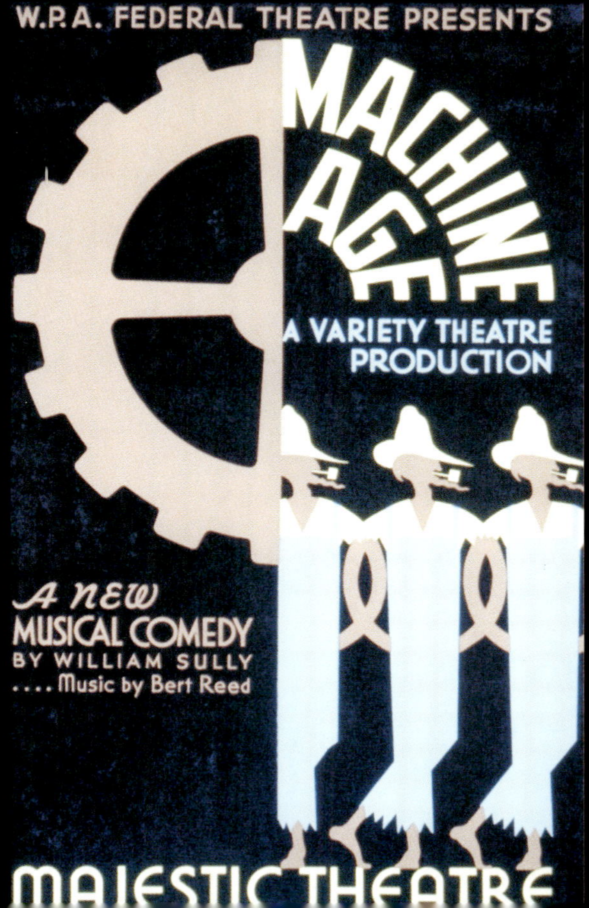
W.P.A. FEDERAL THEATRE PRESENTS
MACHINE AGE
A VARIETY THEATRE PRODUCTION
A NEW MUSICAL COMEDY
BY WILLIAM SULLY
.... Music by Bert Reed
MAJESTIC THEATRE

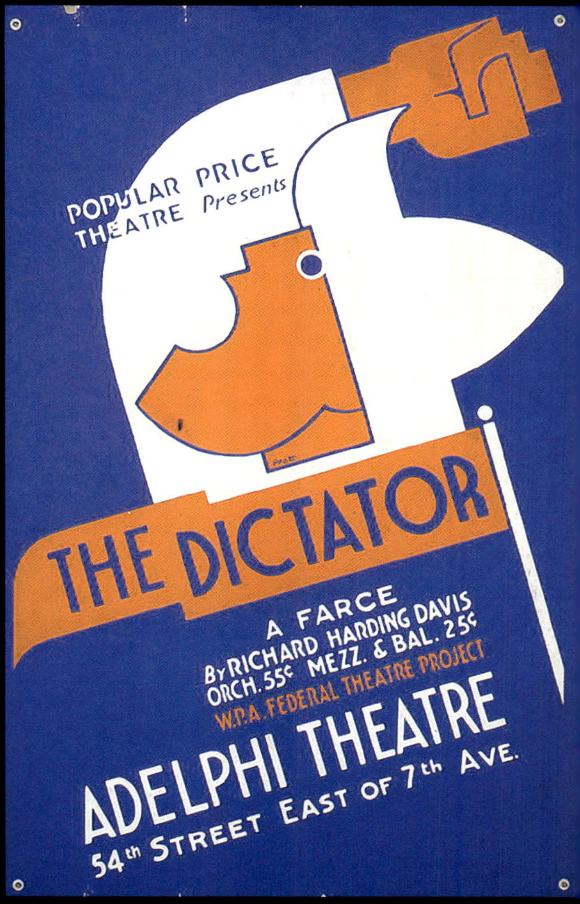
POPULAR PRICE THEATRE Presents
THE DICTATOR
A FARCE
By RICHARD HARDING DAVIS
ORCH. 55¢ MEZZ. & BAL. 25¢
W.P.A. FEDERAL THEATRE PROJECT
ADELPHI THEATRE
54th STREET EAST OF 7th AVE.

Whe
Wor

n Art

ked

Text by ROGER G. KENNEDY

An Illustrated Documentary by David Larkin

RIZZOLI
NEW YORK

First published in the United States of America in 2009
by Rizzoli International Publications, Inc.
300 Park Avenue South
New York, NY 10010
www.rizzoliusa.com

2009 2010 2011 2012 / 10 9 8 7 6 5 4 3 2 1

Distributed in the U.S. trade by Random House, New York

Printed in China

ISBN-10: 0-8478-3089-6
ISBN-13: 978-0-8478-3089-3

Library of Congress Cataloging-in-Publication Data

Kennedy, Roger G.
When art worked / text by Roger G. Kennedy.
p. cm.
"An illustrated documentary by David Larkin."
Includes bibliographical references and index.
ISBN-13: 978-0-8478-3089-3 (hardcover : alk. paper)
ISBN-10: 0-8478-3089-6 (hardcover : alk. paper)
1. Federal Art Project. 2. New Deal art. 3. Art and society—United States—History—20th century. 4. United States—Cultural policy—History—20th century. I. Larkin, David, 1936– II. Title.
N8838.K46 2009
700.1'03097309043—dc22
2009028308

Publisher's note: All attempts were made to contact copyright holders prior to publication. The publisher apologizes for any oversights and will correct these in subsequent printings.

From Roger Kennedy:

To Frances: Once Again

From David Larkin:

To the memory of Ken Sprague–artist, cartoonist, printmaker, teacher–who wanted to be a carpenter.

Acknowledgments

From Roger Kennedy:
This book was David Larkin's idea, and I thank him for permitting me to join with him in it. Tricia Levi has done all a good editor can do to make this a good book, competently, compassionately, and capaciously. Frances Kennedy read and improved—read, and improved. She also has made life joyous for the author.

Over a half century of writing for publication and learning from other people, I have accumulated thousands of obligations for good ideas, and for innumerable facts and relationships of facts. Many of these have gone into this book.

I started counting the scholars who have helped in this work and reached a total of one hundred thirty-three before I realized that I would surely leave somebody really important out in any listing from memory. So, friends and colleagues, I thank you. This book is the outcome upon which we have labored together, and it shows your thumbprints. Thank you.

I have been the beneficiary of kindness from the library staff at the Library of Congress, the Franklin D. Roosevelt Library, and the Harry S. Truman Library, the libraries of Harvard University, Stanford University, Columbia University, the George Washington University, the Smithsonian Institution, the National Gallery, the Smithsonian American Art Museum; and from the curatorial staff at the Metropolitan Museum of Art, the National Gallery of Art, the Smithsonian American Art Museum, the National Museum of the American Indian, the National Museum of American History, and the National Portrait Gallery; and from many scholars in the National Park Service, in the U.S. Forest Service, the Natural Resources Conservation Service, the Department of Justice, the Department of the Interior, the General Services Administration, the Government Accountability Office, and the Department of Defense. Thanks to you all.

From David Larkin:
I would like to thank the following people who helped my research for *When Art Worked* over the last fifteen years: Christine Savage Palmer, Sharon Klein, Herman Eberhardt, Michelle M. Frauenberger, Alexander Gillman, Ethan Carr, Sally King, Bob Clarke, Lawrence Hudetz, Michael Freeman, Paul Rocheleau, Cecelia Esposito, Steven Butler, Robin R. Cooper, Gregory Smith, Richard Gould, David Barna, David D. McKinney, Ted Spiegel, Kevin Daley, Kim D. Robins, Paul Bachortz, and Jena Pike of The Park Rapids Enterprise. I would also like to thank Elizabeth Broun, Richard Sorensen, and Leslie Green of the Smithsonian American Art Museum.

Page 1: Bowl made for President Franklin Roosevelt, by Mary Histia, 1930s
Pages 2–3: "Artelia Bendolph of Gees Bend," Arthur Rothstein, 1937
Pages 4–5: "Ranchers of the Panhandle: Fighting Prairie Fire with Skinned Steer," Frank Mechau, 1940
Pages 6–7: "Frame houses and a Billboard, Atlanta, Georgia," Walker Evans, 1936

Pages 8–9:
The Poster as Proclamation: A Collection of Posters from the Works Progress Administration (after 1939 the Work Projects Administration—WPA in either case), 1937–1940
These posters by WPA graphic artists set before the public the programs of the New Deal in its embattled final years, among them the WPA United States Travel Bureau, established in 1937 and managed, under the Federal Unemployment Relief Act of 1933, by the National Park Service. The Park Service also managed the WPA-funded National Park Service Work Camps (NPSWC), officially entitled "Emergency Conservation Work" (ECW). For simplicity in this book, as noted in the main text, the NPSWC and ECW are subsumed under the Civilian Conservation Corps (CCC), the generic name for their consolidated functions after 1937, though there were differences: CCC "boys" tended to be younger than the ECW "men."

Page 8, clockwise from top left:
"Wild Life: The National Parks Preserve All Life"
For the National Park Service
Frank S. Nicholson, 1940

"See America"
For the United States Travel Bureau
Alexander Dux, 1939

"East Side, West Side, Exhibition of Photographs"
For the Federal Art Project
Anthony Velonis, 1939

"October's Bright Blue Weather, A good time to Read!"
For the WPA/FAP
Albert M. Bender, 1940

"Buckingham Fountain"
WPA for the Chicago Park District
John Buczak, 1939

"See America, Visit the National Parks"
WPA for the United States Travel Bureau
Harry Herzog, 1940

Page 9, clockwise from top left:
"Prints for the People"
For the WPA/FAP
Richard Halls, 1937

"Native Ground, By Virgil Geddes"
WPA Federal Theatre Project
Emanuel DeColas, 1939

"RUR"
WPA Federal Theatre Project—Marionette Theatre
Charles Verschuuren, 1939

"The Dictator—A Farce by Richard Harding Davis"
For the WPA Federal Theatre Project
Herbert W. Pratt, 1941
Davis's 1904 farce was revived as an anti-Fascist play in 1941 by the Popular Price Theatre of the WPA Federal Theatre Project

"Machine Age—A New Musical Comedy"
For the WPA Federal Theatre Project
Martin Weitzman, 1937

"See America, Welcome to Montana"
For the WPA United States Travel Bureau
Richard Halls, 1938

Contents

Part One: The New Deal and The Arts

Part Two: The New Deal, The Earth, The Arts, and Three Presidents

Chapter Six

Chapter Seven

Chapter Eight

Chapter Nine

Chapter Ten

Part One

The New Deal and The Arts

Of course we will provide useful work for the needy unemployed; we prefer useful work to the pauperism of a dole.

Here and now I want to make myself clear about those who disparage their fellow citizens on the relief rolls. They say that those on relief are not merely jobless -- that they are worthless. Their solution for the relief problem is to end relief -- to purge the rolls by starvation. To use the language of the stock broker, our needy unemployed would be cared for ~~if, as and when~~ when, as, and if, some fairy godmother ~~appeared~~ should happen on the scene.

You and I will continue to refuse to accept that estimate of our unemployed fellow Americans. Your Government is still on the same side of the street with the Good Samaritan and not with those who pass by on the other side.

Again-- what of our objectives?

Of course we will continue our efforts for young men and women so that they may obtain an education and an opportunity to put it to use. Of course, we will continue our help for the crippled, for the blind, for the mothers -- our insurance for the unemployed --

FDR's draft for the "New Deal" speech accepting the Democratic Party's nomination for the presidency (see main text).

Chapter One
The Work of Art

"The real success . . . of aid to the creative ones among us, is in . . . what that does to the nation's mind . . . to coax the soul of America back to life."
(Gutson Borglum to Harry Hopkins, 1933)[1]

THIS IS A BOOK ABOUT ARTISTS AS CITIZENS. Its point of departure is Franklin Roosevelt's speech accepting the Democratic Party's nomination for president in 1932, in which he summoned his fellow citizens, including artists, to participate in a covenant of common purpose: "I pledge you, I pledge myself, to a new deal for the American people." Roosevelt's use of the lower case "new deal" is important; he was putting his stress not on that now famous phrase but upon what came before and after it in the sentence, upon the pledging president and the people he summoned to a new covenant. He was not announcing a program of princely patronage or largesse. He was, instead, inviting each of his countrymen, artists among them, to come forward in a covenant of service. Artists were among the many who needed work in 1932, and the nation needed the work artists could do.[2]

The emphasis in these pages will be upon the *work* of art in the 1930s—in the context of earlier art that had large effects upon policy in the New Deal period and upon the lasting consequences of the New Deal and its art. The subject is what artists did for their country. Three decades later, President Kennedy blazoned that concept upon the memories of the next generation in the incandescent phrases of his first inaugural address—"ask not what your country can do for you, but what you can do for your country"—echoing Roosevelt's inaugural address of 1933, which itself echoed Abraham Lincoln's second inaugural address in 1865 and the great covenanting tradition from which came Lincoln's passion for union.[3]

In 1933 Roosevelt told a suffering people: "These dark days will be worth all they cost us if they teach us that our true destiny is not to be ministered unto but to minister to ourselves and to our fellow men . . . we can not merely take but we must give as well." In 1937, in his second inaugural address, he reminded his audience of the mutual commitments made four years earlier when: "we dedicated ourselves to the fulfillment of a vision" that would redefine who was included within "we of the Republic." Thus Roosevelt evoked Gouverneur Morris's phrase "We the People of the United States" in the Preamble to the great covenant, the Constitution itself, as reaffirmed in Roosevelt's time in "our covenant with ourselves." Roosevelt often sought to place his generation's "rendezvous with destiny" within the terms of such a continuing covenant. In his third inaugural address he once again asserted that the "vitality" of mutual commitments "was written into our own Mayflower Compact, into the Declaration of Independence, into the Constitution of the United States, [and] into the Gettysburg Address . . . [gaining] stature and clarity with each generation."[4]

In 1620 the Mayflower Compact had united its signatories "mutually" in reciprocal pledges, promising "all due submission and obedience [to] . . . covenant and combine . . . for the general good." The Declaration of Independence concluded with a covenant among the "good people of these colonies" in mutual pledges of their lives, their fortunes, and their sacred honor. That was Roosevelt's tradition, John Kennedy's, and that to which Lyndon Johnson dedicated his own inaugural address, which he entitled "The Covenant."[5]

Roosevelt required more of his fellow covenanters than mutual assent. After his assertion that "we can not merely take but we must give as well," he went on to ask his fellow citizens to be "willing to sacrifice for the good of a common discipline, because without such discipline no progress is made [toward] . . . the larger purposes [that] will bind upon us all as a sacred obligation with a unity of duty hitherto evoked only in time of armed strife." Art had a place in that unity of duty, in the front line of "a disciplined attack upon our common problems."[6]

Necessity and Response

In the 1920s the affluent had danced the Charleston as the riffs of the Jazz Age mocked the miseries of the poor. Rural people had been afflicted for six years by crop failures, natural disasters, and falling farm prices. At the end of the decade, the industrial system convulsed and collapsed, and the banking and credit structure ceased to function. Extravagance and imprudence no longer exhilarated corporate headquarters. The stock market crash shook all expectations in 1929, and the second sell-off of 1931–1933 shattered them. The intoxication of the Great Euphoria of the 1920s subsided; the Great Depression settled in. Nothing seemed to function properly. Millions were out of work, out of food, out of hope. A people unprepared for deprivation suffered plagues, layoffs, strikes, lockouts, and an unrelenting dust-in-the-mouth hopelessness.

Those of us who lived through the Great Depression bear in our hearts a deep fear and a profound sense of betrayal. Since then, many of us have seen much ugliness in wartime, but the Depression permeates our nightmares. In August 2007, the eminent historian and consulting economist, Peter L. Bernstein, reminded his financial clients about the 1930s: "my most vivid memory was what men on the street looked like—unshaven, coat collars turned up, . . . shoes with newspaper inside to keep feet warm where there were holes in the soles. The husband of a friend sold apples on 72nd Street and West End Avenue." Along the Hudson River, for fifty blocks from Seventy-second Street to the abutments of the George Washington Bridge, straggled a shantytown in which hungry and destitute people inhabited boxes, crates, and tents left over from the Great War. Some of them wore their old uniforms—or what was left of them.[7]

The American experiment in government of, by, and for the people was in peril. "Fear itself" filled the hearts of the nation. Hate was ready to follow fear, as it had in Germany. The things people did failed to produce their expected outcomes. The fabric of life unraveled. Life came apart in ways no one fully understood. Yet the nation did not dissolve into chaos or civil war. Armed gangs did not take over the cities. Country people did not turn to killing one another as they did in the social cannibalism of China or Russia, nor did farmers and farm laborers join doomed but destructive insurrections. Although there was a communist menace and there was a fascist menace, democratic government was sustained. The circle was not broken. The community held together—barely.

Roosevelt was inaugurated on March 4, 1933, announcing that "with the support and understanding of the people themselves" he would end the "unjustified terror which paralyzes" and commence the "primary task" which was "to put people to work." Ten days later he sent to the Congress what he rightly assessed to be "the most drastic and far-reaching farm bill ever proposed in peacetime"—the Agricultural Adjustment Act (AAA). Then came proposals for banking and securities-law reform, and two weeks later Roosevelt moved on to conservation and the arts, calling upon Congress to set in motion programs that remained in tandem until they both became casualties of World War II.[8]

Conservation and the Arts

Conservation was a lifelong enthusiasm for Roosevelt, who consistently stated his profession to be "grower of trees," rather than "lawyer" or "landowner." The consequences of that self-definition to the nation were immense, most obviously in the work done by the agency toward which he exhibited the greatest personal enthusiasm—the Civilian Conservation Corps (see chapter four). In these pages we will

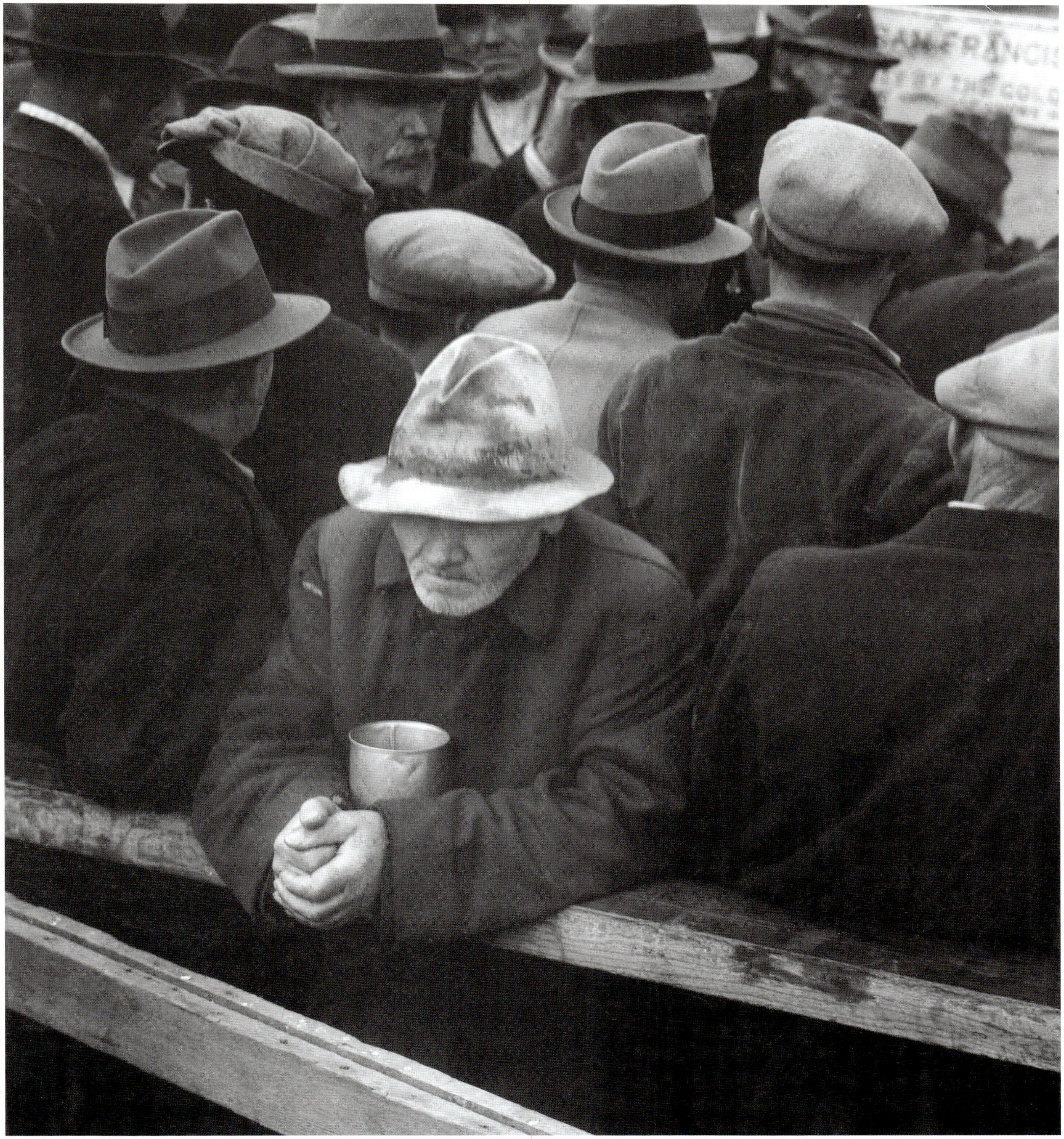

"White Angel Breadline" (detail)
Dorothea Lange, 1933

From June 1931 through September 1933 in a junk-filled lot at the foot of Telegraph Hill in San Francisco, Lois Jordan, "the white angel," operated and supported from her own pocket a soup kitchen serving as many as two thousand hungry people a day with donated food. Dorothea Lange moved from New York to San Francisco in 1918, became a fashionable portrait photographer, married the painter Maynard Dixon and moved to Berkeley. In 1935 she divorced Dixon and married the Berkeley economist Paul Schuster Taylor. He documented the lives of sharecroppers and migrant farm workers in words while she did so in pictures from 1935 through 1940 for Roy Stryker's Resettlement Administration and the Farm Security Administration (see main text).

In 1941, after the attack on Pearl Harbor, the U.S. government rounded up many Japanese Americans as "enemy aliens" and forced them into internment camps. Lange and her colleague, Ansel Adams, photographed that process so powerfully that when, in the 1990s, the nation was willing to reconsider what it had done to its citizens, their photographs helped secure an official congressional apology and some reparations.

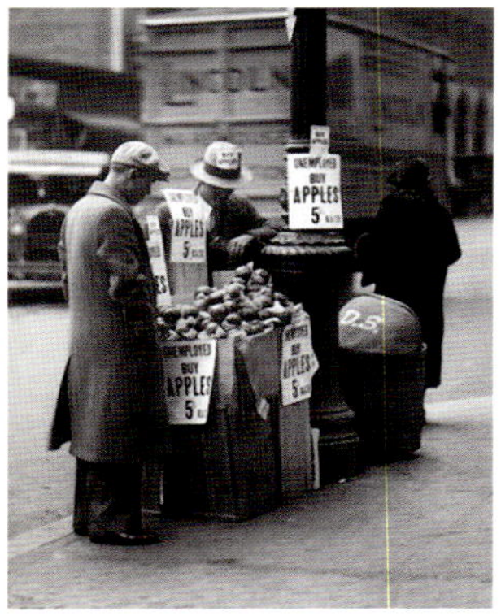

Apple sellers, 1931

Unemployed men in cities around the country sold apples—sometimes one by one, sometimes by the crate. City judges suspended sentences for selling apples without a license. However, when many of the apple shippers themselves went bankrupt, the subsidized source of apples ran out and federal public works replaced apple selling.

follow the convention of using the familiar letters "CCC" to designate the group of New Deal work programs ensuing from the letter from Roosevelt to Congress dated March 21, 1933, proposing the first of these, the Emergency Conservation Work (ECW). The Federal Unemployment Relief Act of 1933 accepted his definition of the ECW as "a civilian conservation corps to be used in simple work . . . confining itself to forestry, the prevention of soil erosion, flood control and similar projects." As in the case of his "new deal" speech (see chapter six) there were no capital letters—no CCC as yet. In the ensuing four years the ECW achieved much that went beyond forestry, the prevention of soil erosion, and flood control, and continued to do so after it was renamed the Civilian Conservation Corps in 1937.

Two hundred thousand young men were in the woods and fields by July 1933, the advance contingent of twice that number within two years, accompanied by artists and photographers to record and publicize their accomplishments. After December 1935, the National Park Service (NPS), by agreement with Harry Hopkins's Works Progress Administration (known after 1939, less boldly, as the Work Projects Administration—in either case the WPA), assumed responsibility for planning and technical services for National Park Service Work Camps (NPSWC). In the Park Service program its staff trained previously unemployed people given stipends by the WPA to learn new skilled crafts—alongside the ECW/CCC.

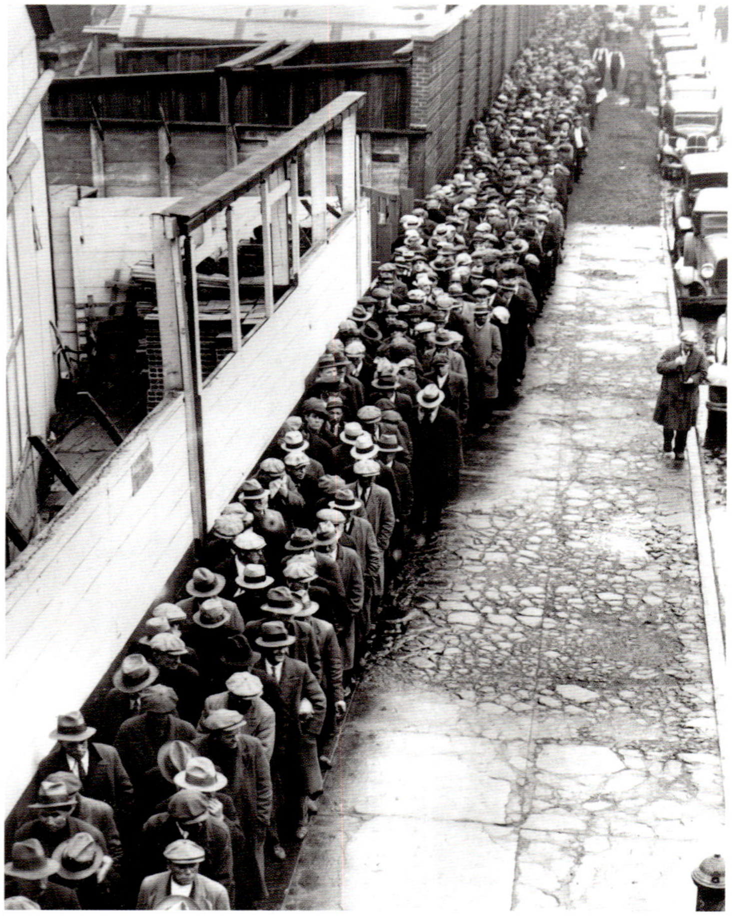

A long line of jobless and homeless men wait outside to get a free dinner. New York, 1932.

To give coherence to the conservation projects and other public works undertaken by the NPS, the NPSWC, and the ECW/CCC, Roosevelt initiated the National Planning Board, later the National Resources Planning Board (NRPB). The NRPB survived its own succession of name changes and mission redirections, all the while demonstrating how democratic government can take responsibility for outcomes. Today, the fresh effort being made to reinvigorate ecosystem-wide planning for "infrastructure" would gladden the hearts of New Deal landscape architects such as Charles W. Eliot II, who convinced Roosevelt to create the NRPB and served as its first staff director in 1933. Having worked with the National Capital Park and Planning Commission and in Boston, he sought to make the NRPB an ecologically sophisticated agency sustaining the work of "architects building a habitation for a new social order." The NRPB planners were in their ways important New Deal artists. Their inaugural experiment in ecosystem management was art achieved across an entire river basin as they worked with the Tennessee Valley Authority (TVA). It evolved into many complex industrial projects, but to its founders, conservation and taking responsibility through planning were as important as power generation. Wartime exigencies contributed to the demise of the NRPB, but it had lost its grounding by then, having moved away from land-based, regional planning and coordinated public works toward national economic planning; it lost precision, immediacy, and constituency as planning rose like a balloon into the stratosphere of macroeconomics before evaporating in the 1940s.[9]

The TVA's cluster of existing federal dams and power plants at Muscle Shoals, and the additional engineering marvels produced by it, lit and powered up the valley, while it led the way in campaigns for flood control, soil conservation, reforestation, and dispersed industrialization. In the course of planning, splendid designs were generated and illustrated in drawings that were works of art, and many of the actual structures were works of art as well. Thus the TVA, like the NRPB, CCC, the Erosion Service (later Soil Conservation Service—SCS—generally known as the Soil Service), and the non-art components of the WPA were presented to the public by artists, only a few of whom were on their payrolls. Most were employed by the WPA arts programs. A smaller but celebrated group was commissioned by the Treasury Department initially through its own relief program (TRAP) and, after October 1934, through its Procurement Division's Section on Fine Arts (the Section) or by other agencies such as the SCS.

Because the Section vied with the WPA arts programs that were financed through what became known as "Federal One," these terms are staples of the specialized literature of the period. Because their titles help not a whit in distinguishing them, this is a good place to note that Federal Project Number One became known as "Federal One" for its placement in a budget document, although thereafter it transmuted many times through a bewildering series of new names and initials.

Yet the outcome was not at all bewildering. The New Deal put art to work for the community. Its success was sufficient to induce Roosevelt to remark to Henry Morgenthau, Jr., his friend, neighbor, and Secretary of the Treasury, that "one hundred years from now my administration will be known for its art, not for its relief."[10]

There is nothing in Roosevelt's life or in his recorded opinions to suggest that he cared much for art for art's sake. He cared for art for the nation's sake. That is the import of his speech dedicating the National Gallery of Art in 1941; that is why he put his stress not upon art itself but upon art's consequences, especially upon its efficacy in enhancing the nation's sense of itself:

> A few generations ago, the people of this country were taught by their writers and their critics and their teachers to believe that art was something foreign to America and to themselves—something imported from another continent and from an age that was not theirs—something they had no part in, save to go and see it in a guarded room on holidays and Sundays. But . . . within the last few years, they have discovered that they have a part. They have seen in their own towns, in their own villages, in schoolhouses, in post offices . . . pictures painted by their sons, their neighbors—people they have known and lived beside and talked to. They have seen . . . rooms full of paintings by Americans—some of it good, some of it not good, but all of it native, human, eager and alive—all of it painted by their own kind in their own country, and painted about things they know and look at often and have touched and loved.[11]

Public support for the New Deal was rallied by art that summoned forth pride out of common experience. Often it illuminated common necessities, arousing awareness of suffering people and of suffering nature. Roosevelt in effect said to artists, as he said to many others, "go out among the people and make me do it!" Many artists responded by doing what they could with their skills to serve democratic institutions and to take responsibility for the physical circumstances within which such institutions might flourish.

In the 1960s, Presidents Kennedy and Johnson reanimated the New Deal covenant in language familiar to people who had listened to Roosevelt. At his first inaugural, Kennedy, as if taking his place in the New Deal tradition of putting art to work to strengthen the covenant, summoned to his side a poet, Robert Frost, as Roosevelt had singled out for attention a poet, Edwin Markham, while he moved toward the podium to deliver the summons to his generation in his "Rendezvous with Destiny" speech. Later—as we shall see in the final chapter—when challenged to explain some of his expedients in the face of baffling circumstances, Roosevelt urged the study of the biography by a third poet,

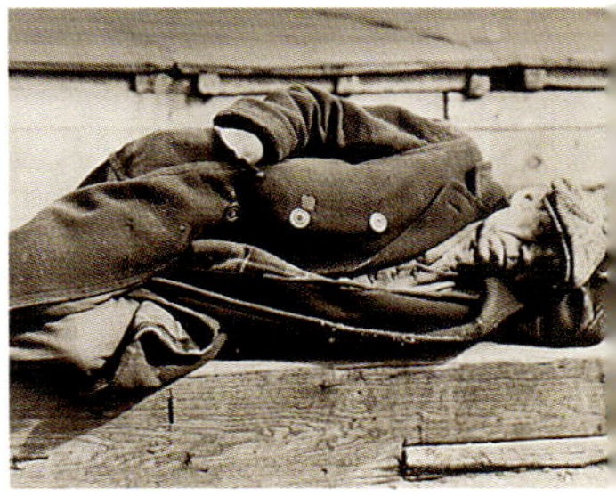

Idle man dressed in worn coat lying down on pier. Lewis W. Hine, c. 1935.

Lewis Hine studied sociology at the University of Chicago, Columbia University, and New York University, and, when he taught photography, had his classes join him in recording the arrivals of immigrants at Ellis Island in New York Harbor. From 1907 through 1917, he produced many now famous images of child labor for the National Child Labor Committee (NCLC).

In 1908 he photographed tenement conditions in Pittsburgh, and, during and after World War I, photographed American Red Cross relief work in Europe. In the 1920s, one of his "work portraits" depicting construction of the Empire State Building was taken from a gondola swinging out one thousand feet above Fifth Avenue. During the Depression, Hine photographed drought relief in the American South for the Red Cross and life in the Appalachians for the Tennessee Valley Authority (TVA). He served as chief photographer for the WPA National Research Project, recording conditions in the workforce. He died in 1940, poor and neglected, though his work is now in many famous collections.

Carl Sandburg of Abraham Lincoln, whose memorial had been dedicated with a poem by Markham.

In chapters to follow, we will observe how art worked in concert with conservation in the United States. Long before the New Deal, art had made the case for the protection of the Yosemite Valley and the Yellowstone Basin as national parks, by depicting their wonders on a grand scale. During the New Deal and since, in images of a more intimate focus, art has helped to sustain the habitat for the birds and animals of the Everglades, while increasing public understanding of the need to take responsibility for entire ecosystems. The Resettlement Administration sponsored films such as the *Plow That Broke the Plains* (1936) and *The River* (1937) by Pare Lorentz, with scores by Virgil Thompson. Poignant photographs were taken by artists of genius, and distributed to newspapers and magazines by the artist of persuasion, Roy Stryker. Among the purposes of Stryker's efforts was making the case stronger for the Tennessee Valley Authority (TVA), for the WPA, for the CCC, and for the renewal of rural life through soil conservation and resettlement through the Resettlement Administration (RA) and Farm Security Administration (FSA).

Artists as Citizens

When the Roosevelt Administration took office in 1933, its first order of business for artists and for the nation at large, was to make sure "no one starved." Next, it sought to put them to work. The national unemployment rate had been 3.2 percent of the workforce in 1929. It had become 25 percent in 1933. In many places half the willing workforce could not find work, and in some places there was no paid work at all. Artists suffered along with everybody else: "Hell," said Harry Hopkins, "they've got to eat just like other people!" The New Deal provided food, it provided work, and with the aid of art, it began to provide hope grounded in common purposes.[12]

While Roosevelt was governor of New York, the Depression was already blighting the nation. Roosevelt's schoolmate, neighbor, and kinsman, George Biddle, urged him to bring together artists and government in a covenant of public service. Roosevelt commissioned Harry Hopkins, his administrator of work-relief, to provide funds for nearly one hundred artists to brighten the walls of settlement houses under the aegis of New York City's College Art Association. Others provided drawings and paintings that were published to illustrate the work of Roosevelt's proto-civilian conservation corps. Hopkins emphasized the *corps*: the workforce. Henry Morgenthau, at the time Roosevelt's agriculture commissioner, stressed *conservation:* thousands of trees were planted and across the state eroded landscapes were restored. After 1933, the New York experience was expanded to a national scale in the New Deal's CCC, in which artists served as recorders. Other artists were recruited to create public works that carried messages that might counteract "fear itself" and thus help restore the fabric of society as a covenant of participating citizens. They did so with sufficient success to justify Biddle's writing in September 1934 that the New Deal had made "America art conscious as never before" and the artist as never before "conscious of the fact that he is of service to the community."[13]

Biddle was reinforcing what had been said by Gutzon Borglum, the celebrated sculptor of presidential monuments. In his *Roosevelt and Hopkins*, Robert E. Sherwood reported that Hopkins treasured a letter from Borglum for the rest of his life, which put in straightforward language the satisfactions they were beginning to feel from their efforts to help artists help the nation: "the real success . . . of aid to the creative ones among us, is in . . . what that does to the nation's mind . . . to coax the soul of America back to life."[14]

The arts programs of the Roosevelt Administration took two routes, in parallel and concurrently: *work relief* for unemployed artists and *commissions* for those who might make a go of it without government aid but who would aid in reinspiriting community. By the end of Roosevelt's first term, the work-relief program of the WPA was reported by *Time* magazine in March 1936, to have been able to announce "that 4,300 muralists, portrait painters, print makers, sculptors, etc. are now at work . . . on 327 projects that will cost

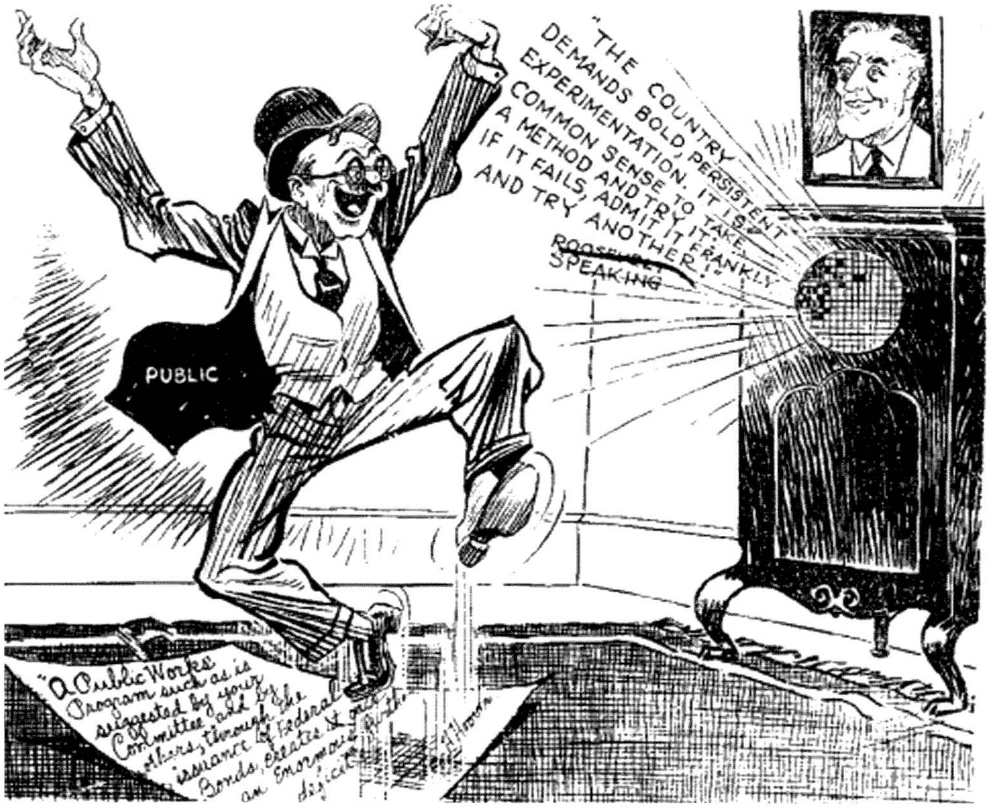

Top:
"His Stamp of Approval"
Philadelphia Record
Jerry Doyle, 1932

"The country needs and, unless I mistake its temper, the country demands bold, persistent experimentation. It is common sense to take a method and try it: if it fails, admit it frankly and try another. But above all, try something. The millions who are in want will not stand by silently forever while the things to satisfy their needs are within easy reach. We need enthusiasm, imagination, and the ability to face facts, even unpleasant ones, bravely. We need to correct, by drastic means if necessary, the faults in our economic system from which we now suffer. We need the courage of the young. Yours is not the task of making your way in the world, but the task of remaking the world which you will find before you. May every one of us be granted the courage, the faith, and the vision to give the best that is in us to that remaking!"
—Franklin Roosevelt, Oglethorpe University Commencement Address (May 22, 1932)

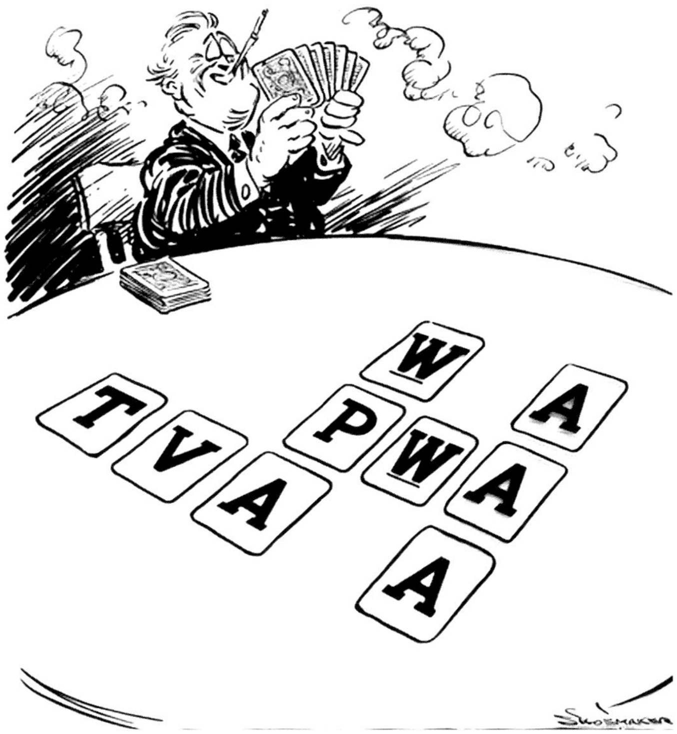

Bottom far left:
Chicago Daily News
Vaughn Shoemaker

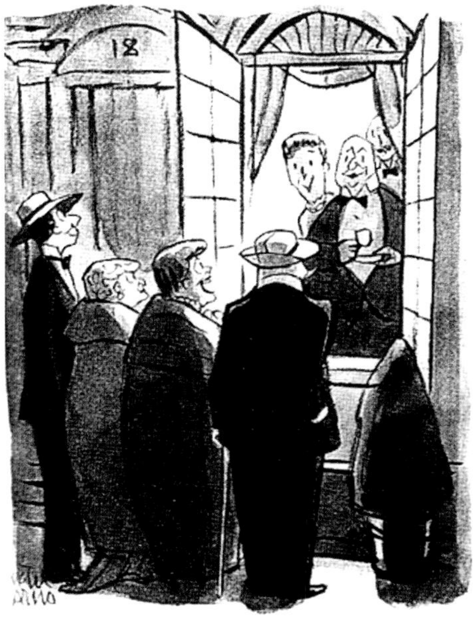

Come along. We're going to the Trans-Lux to hiss Roosevelt.

Bottom left:
New Yorker
Peter Arno,
September 26, 1936

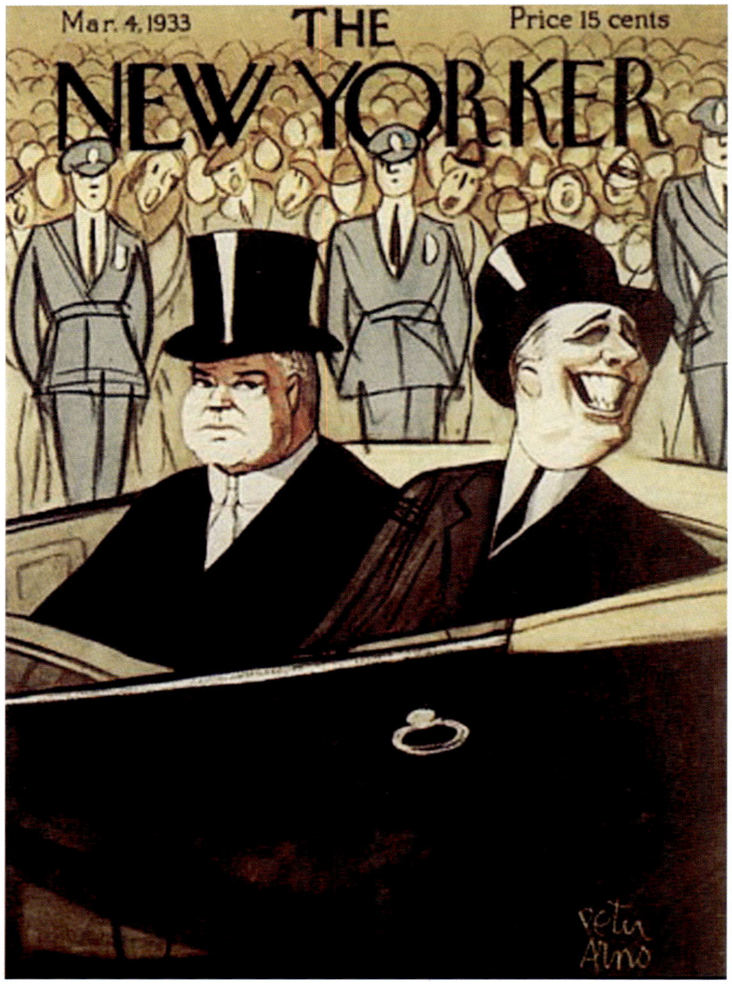

New Yorker cover
Peter Arno,
March 4, 1933
An ebullient Franklin D. Roosevelt accompanied to his 1933 inauguration by a dour, disapproving Herbert Hoover.

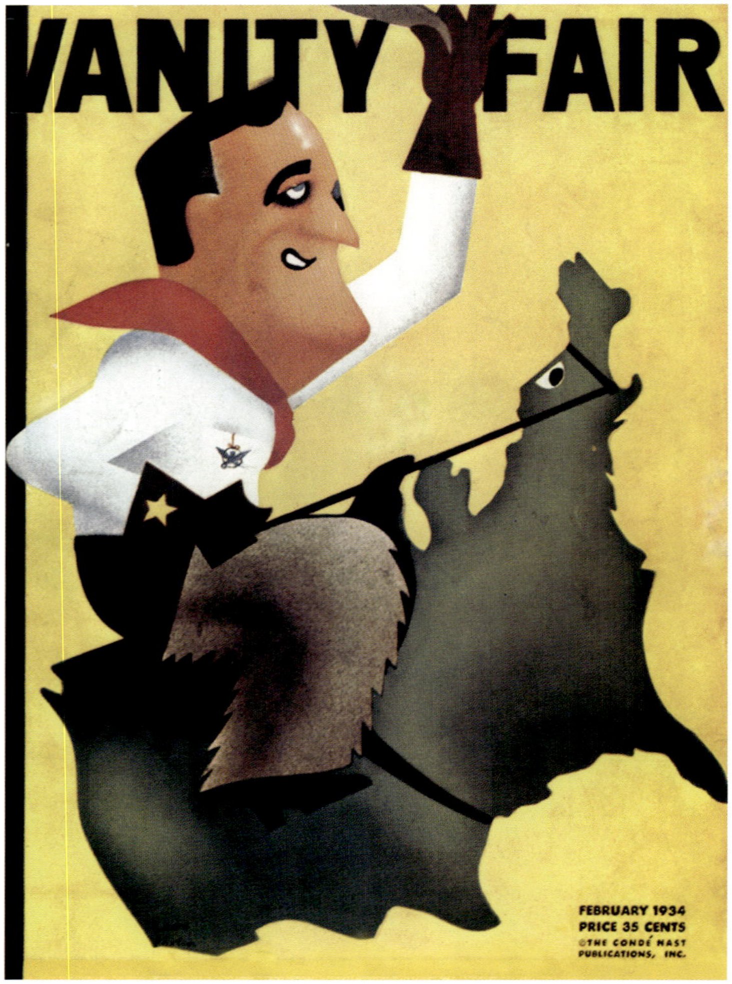

Vanity Fair cover
Leon Carlin,
February 1934

the Government $3,000,000. The Government has set up free art schools in New York City, Nashville, Raleigh, Oklahoma City, Orlando, Gainesville and Dade City, Fla., Columbus, Grand Rapids, Elizabeth and Newark, N. J., has opened art galleries in New York, Tennessee, North Carolina, South Carolina, Oklahoma, Florida, Virginia." *Time*'s punch line was: "Today there exists the greatest official interest in art, the greatest production of paintings the U.S. has ever known."[15]

Between 1933 and 1942, ten thousand artists "produced a staggering amount of work: 100,000 easel paintings, 18,000 sculptures, over 13,000 prints, and 4,000 murals, not to mention posters and photographs." They worked for an average monthly check of fifty-three dollars, ranging downward to twenty-three dollars in some southern states to avoid butting against the "prevailing wage" for employed workers. This list of accomplishments does not include works of landscape art, such as bridges, parkways, and lodges created by the CCC and the National Park Service. Nor does it enumerate plays, operas, the famous Living Newspapers (see chapter five), or motion pictures. The New Deal provided to artists a larger share of national tax revenue and more national attention than at any other period in the nation's life. In response, they served the society that nourished them more explicitly than at any other time.[16]

The great treasure houses of New Deal art are the Department of the Interior and Department of Justice buildings in Washington, D.C., both of which are glorious in murals by

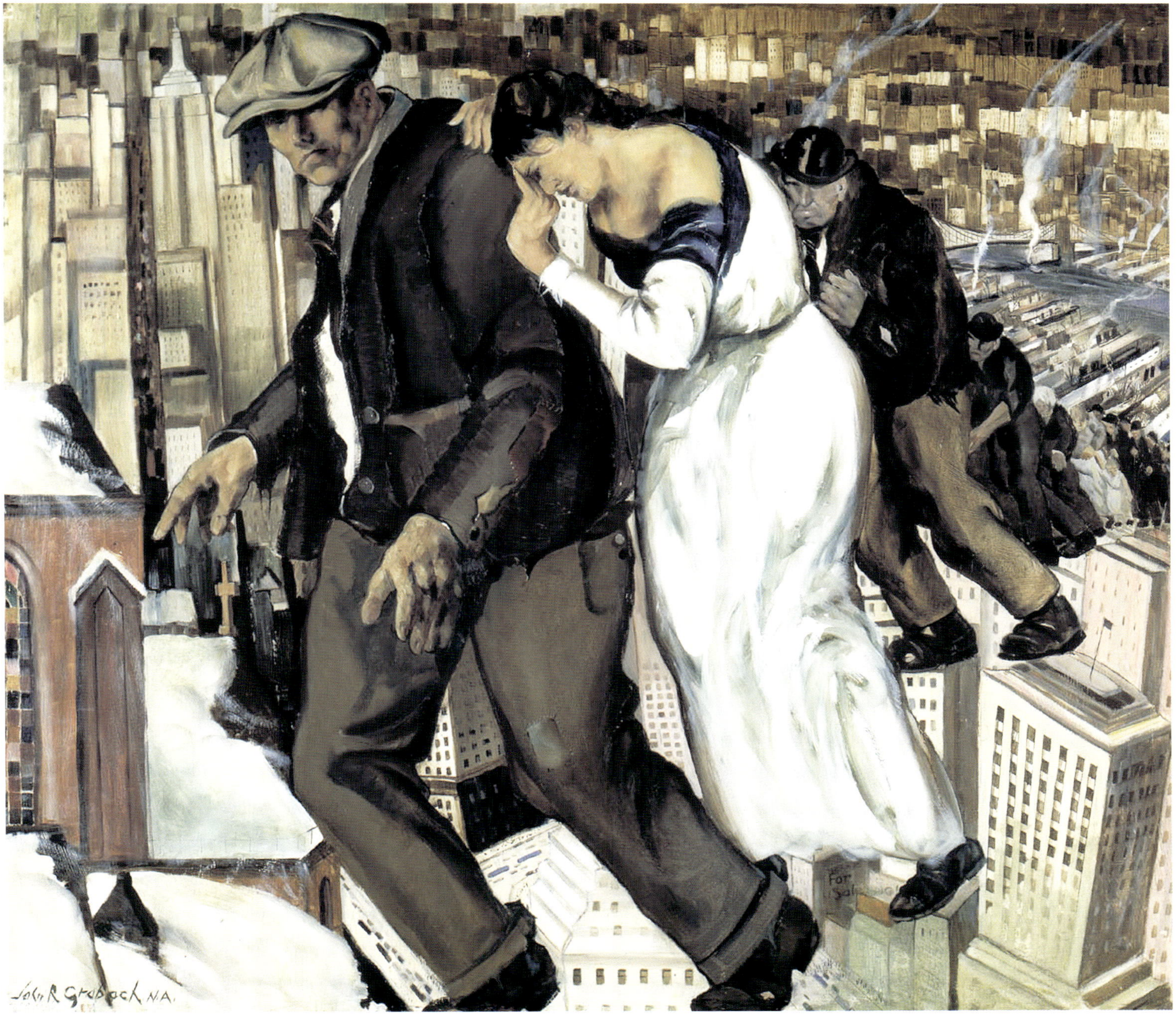

The Fifth Year
John R. Grabach, 1934
Oil on wood

John Grabach received his earliest art training from Albert Dyck and August Schwabe, in Newark, New Jersey. When he was eighteen, Grabach began working for a silverware manufacturing company in Newark, commuting to New York for night classes at the Art Students League, where he studied under Kenyon Cox, George Bridgman, and Frank Vincent Dumond. He later taught at the Newark School of Fine and Industrial Arts.

Grabach painted this image five years after the great stock market crash of 1929. It shows an endless stream of people in gray faces and threadbare clothes, rising up out of New York and trudging across the sky. The man in front looks at the viewer from under his hat, while a compassionate spirit weeps on his shoulder—a classic image derived from ancient funeral monuments, and from medieval paintings and sculpture. Augustus St-Gaudens sculpted a similar figure hovering over the doomed African American troops of the Massachusetts Fifty-Fourth Regiment in his Robert Gould Shaw Memorial.

New Deal artists. The Interior building presents so wide a range of artistic prowess in support of the Roosevelt Administration's social causes that it will have a later chapter of its own. It was Harold Ickes's command center for the Public Works Administration (PWA), for a reformed Indian policy, for national parks, and soil conservation. The Justice Department was the dynamo of remedial action under the law—often under laws passed as components of the New Deal. Some groundwork will be laid in the next few pages for the discussion in chapter three of the role of art in building constituencies for those new laws that provided new remedies and it is necessary to put on stage three principal figures in the New Deal—Harry Hopkins, Harold Ickes, and Henry Morgenthau—whose programs were advanced by art, and who made deliberate and effective use of art.

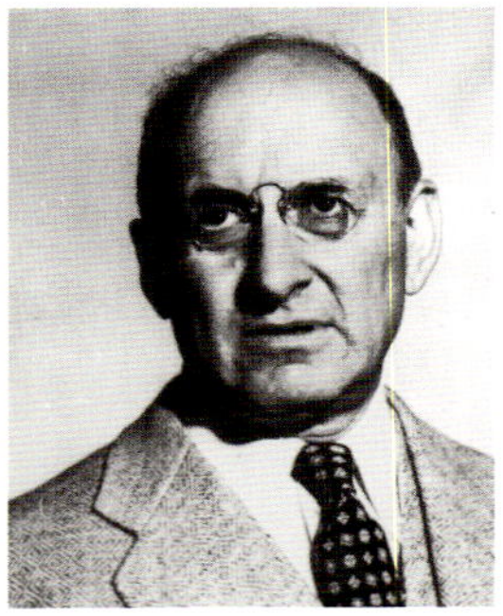

Henry Morgenthau, Jr., 1944

Morgenthau and Hopkins

Under Franklin Roosevelt's eye, three of his cabinet officers did what they could to manage the government's partnership with the arts. Harry Hopkins was a professional social worker, who evolved from Public Works Administrator into Secretary of Commerce and then into Roosevelt's chief foreign policy advisor. Secretary of the Interior Harold Ickes was a lawyer and real estate speculator from Chicago. Secretary of the Treasury Henry Morgenthau, Jr., entered the Roosevelt circle as a farming neighbor and agriculture expert. Like Ickes he had personal experience in settlement work as a young man. He had worked at Lillian Wald's Henry Street Settlement in New York; Ickes had been part of Jane Addams's circle at Hull House, in Chicago, and served as her lawyer.

Morgenthau came to the Roosevelt Administration without professional experience in finance except through exposure to the career of his father, a lawyer and real estate speculator in New York City. The senior Morgenthau worked his way through Columbia Law School, made his fortune, cultivated associations with the William Rockefeller branch of that increasingly wealthy family, tended his charities, raised campaign funds for Woodrow Wilson, and became known "as 'Uncle Henry' throughout the Democratic party" according to Arthur Schlesinger, Jr. He was small, "articulate, cocky, outgoing, and merry . . . powerful, adored, and irrepressible . . . his son's opposite," according to Schlesinger, who knew them both. As ambassador to the Ottoman Empire during World War I, Morgenthau sought to get help to the Armenian victims of holocaust, presaging his son's endeavors on behalf of the refugee Jews of Central Europe from 1938 onward.[17]

Henry Morgenthau, Jr., was "tall, heavyset, nearsighted, partly bald . . . of grave courtesy, slow in speech, often hesitant and wary in reaction, always apprehensive and not seldom gloomy but possessed of great stubbornness." His son, Henry Morgenthau III, surmised that his father "had a learning disability in the era before dyslexia was readily diagnosed, and his occasional inarticulateness caused people to underrate his basic intelligence . . . he tended toward worry and suspicion, and his government career mingled insecurity and aggressiveness. But in private relations, once he had given his confidence, he was a person of much delicacy and warmth."*

Henry Morgenthau, Jr., made no secret of his father's humble immigrant antecedents. He worked among more recent immigrants at the Henry Street Settlement, where he met his future wife, Elinor Fatman. She was cultivated, gentle, intelligent, humane, and rich. Her mother was a Lehman, daughter of one of the Lehman brothers, formerly of Montgomery, Alabama. By 1900 the Lehman brothers had become capitalized in both senses of that word as "Lehman Brothers," and were by the 1920s among the magnates, allied by marriage and financial arrangements in New York, who referred to themselves as "Our Crowd": the Altschuls, Wertheims, Kuhns, Loebs, and Strauses. The Lehmans had emigrated from Bavaria a generation ahead of the Morgenthaus and had made their way from dry goods through cotton manufacturing, cotton brokering, general brokerage, and investment banking. As attested by the Lehman Collection, set within the Lehman Wing of the Metropolitan Museum, the Lehmans were as sophisticated artistically as they were financially and politically. They were pillars of the New York liberal establishment in the New Deal period: Robert Lehman led the firm, while Herbert Lehman was governor of New York and then senator, and Irving Lehman was chief judge of the New York Court of Appeals.

The Morgenthaus' personal artistic talents were musical. Lazarus Morgenthau, the immigrant, had briefly made one of his evanescent livings as a singer. All the Henry Morgenthaus sang, and musical talent was present as well in the Fatman family; Elinor's sister sang at the Metropolitan Opera. Elinor's skills seem to have been primarily theatrical and political. While their husbands were off on the business of state and nation, Elinor Morgenthau and Eleanor Roosevelt went to the

* One might have used that sentence to describe Schlesinger himself, adding as to both him and Morgenthau the factor of kindness and generosity when helping younger and less celebrated people in their early careers.

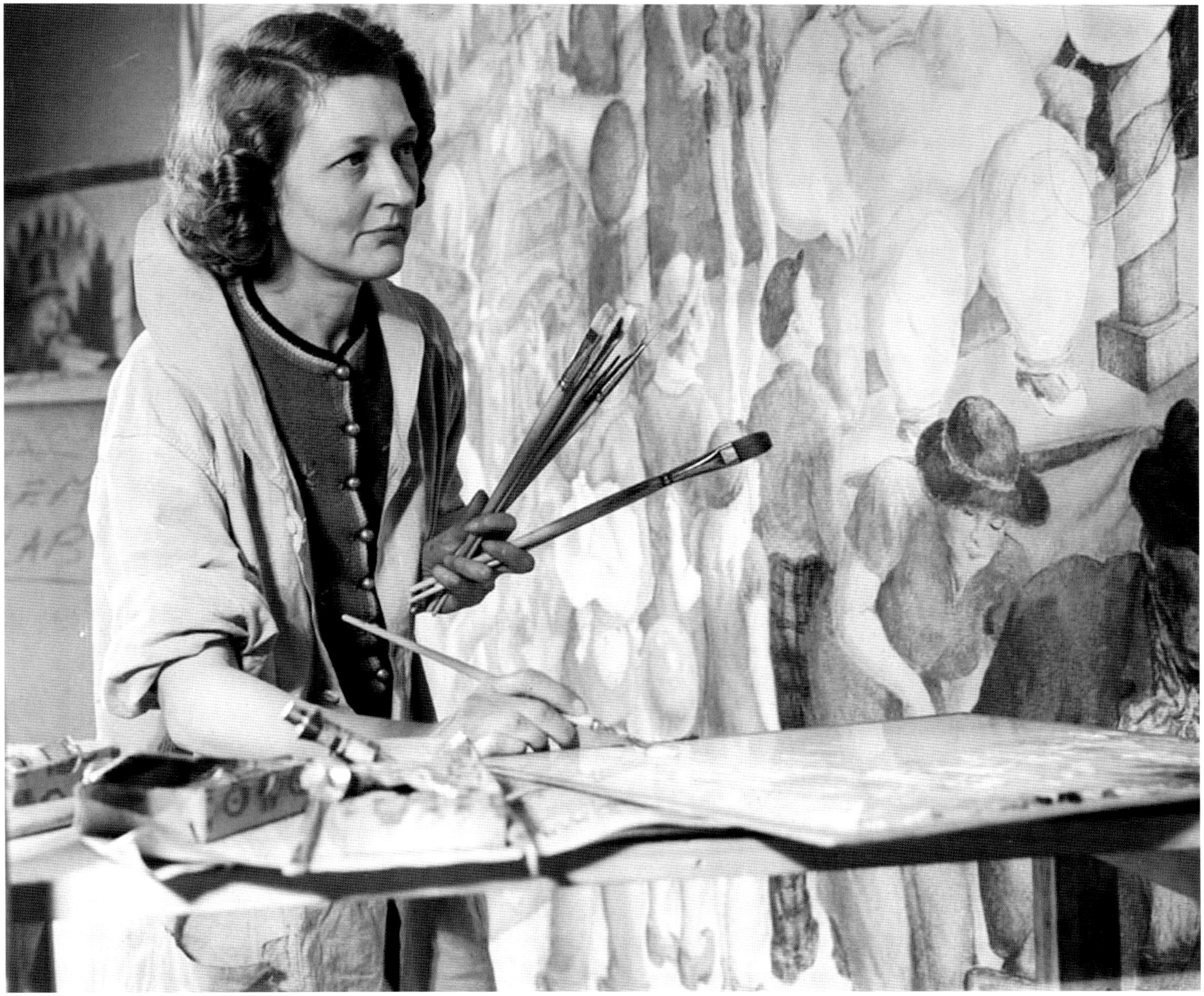

Elizabeth Deering working on a mural for the nurses' recreation lounge at Fordham Hospital, New York City. Deering was a portrait painter who joined the mural division of the WPA/FAP.
Sol Horn, 1939

theater, building a circle of friends in that profession, and accumulating the sophistication necessary to weigh in effectively in support of the WPA theater projects managed by Hopkins.

The Morgenthaus' interests in the countryside evolved after Henry Jr. invested some profits from a Bronx speculation in one thousand acres of farms and orchards in Duchess County and purchased a gentleman farmer's journal, *The American Agriculturalist*. Thereafter, he gave "farmer" as his profession, as his country neighbor Franklin Roosevelt gave his as "grower of trees." Morgenthau's ascent in public life began when Roosevelt, as Governor of New York, appointed him Chairman of the state Agricultural Advisory Committee, and then Conservation Commissioner. On the strength of his massive reforestation program in the over-timbered and overgrazed flanks of the Adirondacks,

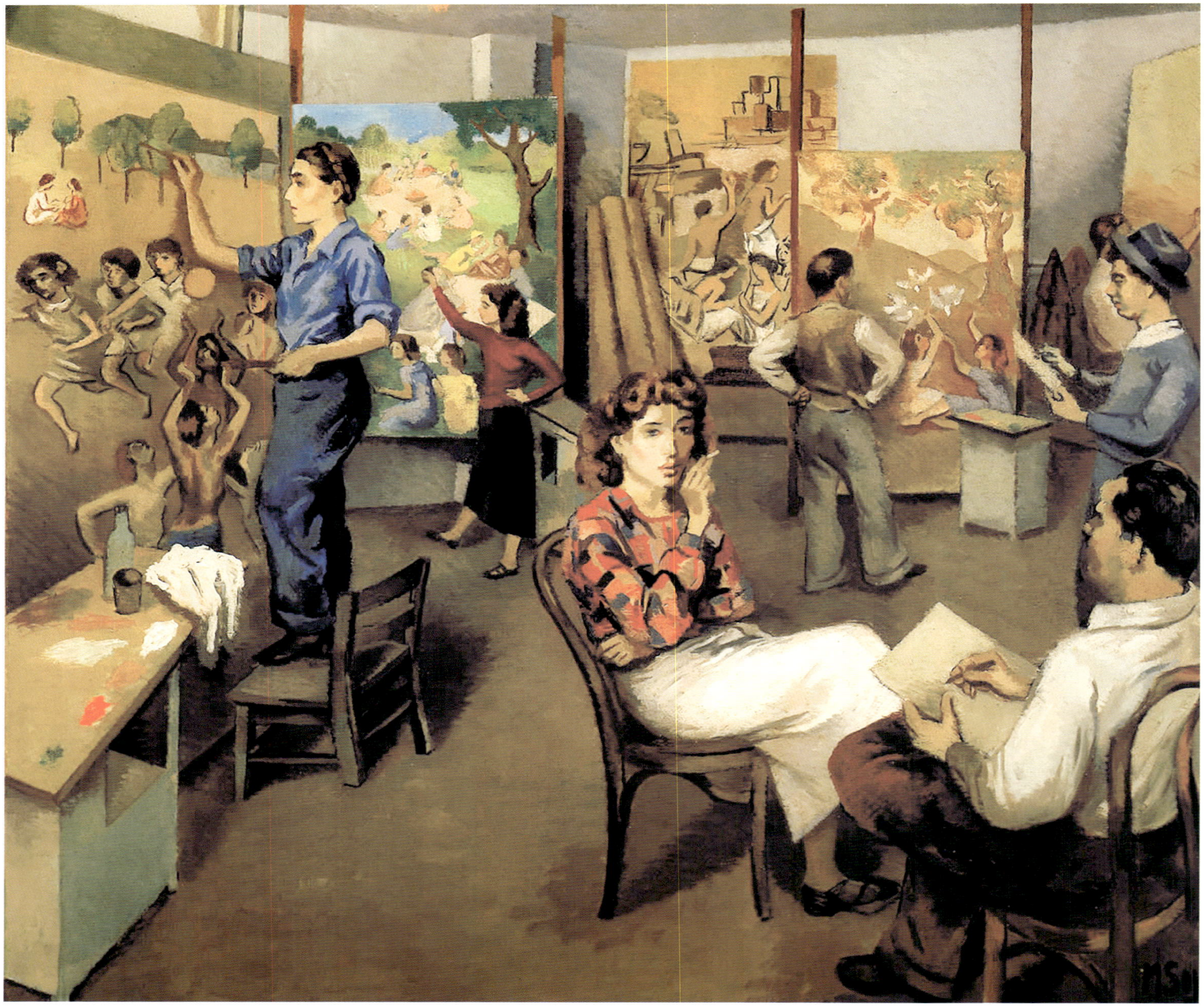

Artists in WPA
Moses Soyer, 1935

Moses Soyer and his identical twin brother, Raphael, were born in Borisoglebsk, Russia, and raised in an intellectual atmosphere fostered by their father, Abraham, a Hebrew scholar. Both brothers were WPA artists. Moses Soyer became a naturalized citizen in 1914, and after the Depression became popular both as painter and printmaker. He died in September 1974 in New York City.

he might have become Secretary of the Interior rather than Ickes, who had weaker conservation credentials. Either he or Ickes might have been chosen to administer relief, for that matter, on the basis of their settlement house experience, had Hopkins not been available. Instead, Roosevelt brought his farming friend into his administration as Chairman of the Federal Farm Board and Governor of the Farm Credit Administration.

Roosevelt moved Morgenthau along to be Undersecretary of the Treasury, and, in 1934, Secretary. In his recollections of this period, Schlesinger reported that after a stint ghostwriting articles with Morgenthau for *Collier's*, he came away "with great affection for Mr. Morgenthau, and also with enhanced respect for President Roosevelt who had so early discerned Morgenthau's solid abilities and had used them to such good effect." Those abilities were great, and Roosevelt's respect for

Morgenthau as a Secretary of the Treasury was fully earned. He was as good at his job as Ickes was at his. Roosevelt learned to trust him, and also how to "kid" him—and to use him. The dour, scrupulous, shy Morgenthau and the president were friends, to the extent that Franklin Roosevelt had friends. Morgenthau told an interviewer in 1964 that "he was very close to Roosevelt, perhaps closest of anyone in the cabinet," and that he "knew President Roosevelt in a different and more intimate way." Yet Morgenthau also conceded that Roosevelt "would never let down the bars beyond a certain point. And . . . never let anyone around him have complete assurance that he would have the job tomorrow. That gave you a sense of uneasiness, of insecurity, of his playing one person off against another." With the resentment natural to the son of a person manipulated in that way, Henry Morgenthau III concluded that "although Roosevelt would never give Morgenthau all the assurance and love he craved, there was between the two men a bond of trust and fondness that held firm to the end of Roosevelt's life."[18]

At a time when the federal government was constructing thousands of buildings, Morgenthau controlled the process of design, construction, and managing all *federal* public buildings—unless they happened to house the command posts of Ickes or Hopkins. As a result, he had a greater influence on American art than any Secretary of the Treasury other than Andrew Mellon, whose gifts to establish the National Gallery ($50 million in cash and paintings) were not made as part of his job. Elinor Morgenthau was as potent as Eleanor Roosevelt in asserting the relevance of art to the nation's life. The Secretary's loyalty, consistency, kindness, and thoughtfulness were boons to his chief, and his remarkable adaptability was necessary to keep a contentious administration together. His cool fastidiousness of speech and dress betokened propriety, a characteristic also expressed in his preferences for the kind of art that government should support. His watchword was "quality" as defined by those thought at the time to be people of taste, whose views prevailed in the Treasury arts programs, especially those of its Section on Fine Arts, as administered by Edward Bruce, who shared Morgenthau's views. Harry Hopkins had other priorities; putting people to work. And Ickes? As we shall see in the next chapter, he had his own ideas as to what "quality" might be.

Morgenthau, Hopkins, and Ickes were the three leviathan figures of the Roosevelt Administration's arts programs. Subordinate to them were Horace Albright, Ickes's Director of the National Park Service; Edward Bruce, upon whom Morgenthau relied to lead the Treasury arts programs; and Holger Cahill, who performed that duty for Hopkins and the WPA. John Collier, Ickes's Commissioner of Indian Affairs, had a status of his own, to be given some appreciation in the next chapter.

Harry Hopkins's squalid little headquarters building on Eighteenth Street contrasted with Henry Morgenthau's Treasury Department building on the other side of the White House grounds. Hopkins's has gone to the wrecking ball, and Morgenthau's palace of finance is devoid of murals or sculpture that might give evidence of the passage of the New Deal through American life. The curators of the Treasury Department have searched under subsequent plastering and remodeling for any trace of Morgenthau or Bruce's Section on Fine Arts, and have found nothing. This is passing strange, for Bruce and Morgenthau saw to it that major portions of the nation's first systematic arts program emerged from that immense, grey granite, columned and pilastered structure.

Hopkins and Relief

Grandiloquence of any sort was distasteful to Harry Hopkins. He insisted that all he sought to achieve in an arts program was to provide decent livings to artists who needed work. In practice he was willing to provide the conduit for funds moving from Ickes to Morgenthau and Bruce, but he made it clear that he found all their talk about "quality" in art to be patronizing, and worse, inhumane. Many artists needed work—any work. Hopkins was pallid, disheveled, ascerbic, brilliant, and so frail that his intimates called him by his high-school nickname, "Skinny." One observer was quoted by Schlesinger as saying of him that he gave off "a suggestion of quick cigarettes, thinning hair, dandruff, brief sarcasm, fraying suits of clothes, and a wholly understandable preoccupation" with alleviating other people's tribulations.[19]

Hopkins wrote of himself that he was "the son of a harness maker from Sioux City," and so he was—a harness maker for horse-drawn carriages, who went into that business after the rise of the automobile and was reduced to seeking an increasing quantum of his modest income from betting on bowling, with better success than that derived by his son from betting on horses. While the senior Morgenthau was growing wealthy, the elder Hopkins was not; he could not assist his son in making his way through Grinnell College and on to training in social work at Christadora House on New York's Lower East Side, not far from Lillian Wald's Henry Street.

Hopkins started plain and remained plain. The columnist Ernie Pyle visited him in his office, when he was administering the distribution of many millions of dollars, and wrote: "Mr. Hopkins, I liked you because you look like common people . . . you sit there so easy swinging forth in your swivel chair, in your blue suit and blue shirt, and your neck is sort of skinny, like poor people's necks . . . And that old office of yours, Mr. Hopkins . . . it's terrible. It's so little in the first place, and the walls are faded and water pipes run up the walls and your desk doesn't even shine. But I guess you don't care. Maybe it wouldn't look right for you to have a nice office anyway, when you're dealing in misery all the time."[20]

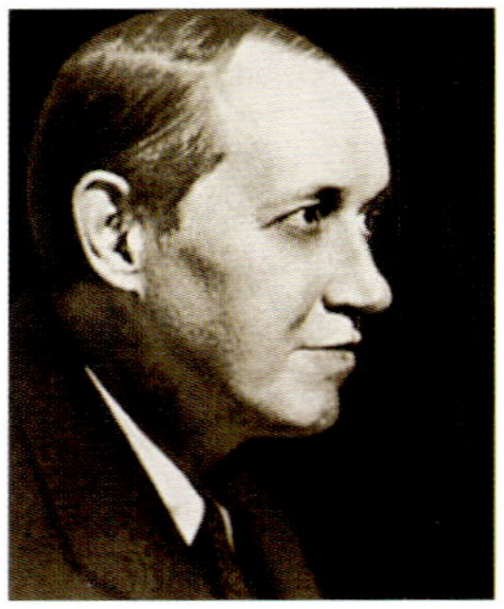
Harry Hopkins

All three—Hopkins, Morgenthau, and Ickes—were dealing with misery, and with art, as well. Each had worked to alleviate misery at retail, long before they were asked to organize government to do so at wholesale. Their differences were not in aspiration or in commitment, but in style and method. Their headquarters showed how different were those styles and methods. Morgenthau operated out of a citadel of prudence, the Treasury building. If he were to walk to reach Hopkins in his headquarters, he would pass through Roosevelt's Rose Garden, cross the White House west driveway, and traverse the vast corridors of the Old Executive Office Building to emerge onto New York Avenue just across Eighteenth Street from the monstrous glass-and-steel office building that has obliterated Hopkins's "shabby, old building."[21]

If one thinks of Hopkins as operating the national ambulance after 1933, it was a vehicle composed of parts from two vehicles placed onto the national driveway by the administration of Herbert Hoover, who had had more experience administering relief than anyone working for the New Deal, including Hopkins. Hoover failed, however, to put gas into the tank of either the Reconstruction Finance Corporation (RFC) or the PWA. After Inauguration Day 1933, they were stripped of parts to fit out Hopkins's new machine, leaving only bare chassis of each to be boarded by other New Dealers, loaded up with new programs, and driven onto byways beyond the imaginings of Hoover—including succor for artists and subsidies for the arts.

The RFC had been chartered in 1932 to make federal loans to banks, railroads, and "other institutions" (presumably insurance companies) to avert their bankruptcy. Roosevelt's RFC Chairman, Jesse Jones of Texas, made it the nation's investment bank, buying preferred stock in some financial institutions and starting new ones. Jones also created the prototypes for federal mortgage insurers (FNMA and GNMA), the Commodity Credit Corporation, the Electric Home and Farm Authority, and the Export-Import Bank. Jones contributed to the New Deal arts programs by allocating from his RFC appropriation half of the million dollars with which Harry Hopkins started his Federal Emergency Relief Administration (FERA) in May 1933, which included direct work-relief for artists through the Federal Public Works of Art Project (FERA/PWAP). While the post office murals *commissioned* by the Treasury's Section have been much discussed, the FERA and the Treasury's *relief* program (TRAP) were the immediate beneficiaries of the radiant energy released at a famous dinner with Mrs. Roosevelt. Her friend, the painter Olin Dows, is our witness to the great occasion on December 7, 1933, when the New Deal arts programs were launched—and not just those Edward Bruce continued to administer at the Treasury: "The FERA was being thought about . . . George Biddle had written [his] . . . letter to the President . . . Bruce had a meeting in his house . . . and Mrs. Roosevelt came to it and knitted all the way through the several-hours-long meeting. There were men and women from all over the country."[22]

The FERA soon became the Civil Works Administration (CWA), which, following a brief reappearance as the FERA, mutated once again in 1935 to become the WPA. In 1933, while the federal work programs were being organized, Hopkins's FERA made federal grants to the states for work-relief designed to see to it that "no one starved." Artists were among those it put to work, through the Federal Public Works of Art Project (FERA/PWAP), since, as Hopkins said, they "eat just like other people." And they produced: a painting for each congressional district, to enrich public schools, orphanages, libraries, museums, and a variety of other public buildings, while also recording the achievements of the CCC and TVA. Dows also recalled that though the Federal Public Works of Art Project only "lasted from December to June and it employed [only] about three thousand people . . . they did about ten thousand works of art . . . at a minimum workman's wage. I have a feeling that a certain number of men were in it . . . just to have work on the project . . . There were men of great distinction . . . that sent in work. Some may have needed it, but some of them did not. It got an enthusiasm from the artists . . . Painters like Reggie Marsh, after all, earned a darned good living, even in the Depression, doing *New Yorker* drawings, things like that. Yet he gave up a great deal to do that [New York] Custom House job. Now, in a sense, it's a monument to him as he'd done only one other big mural . . . Still, it took a great deal of time and thought. And, of course, the important point is that it is a very good job."[23]

(Like the King Arthur of myth, neither the PWA nor the WPA ever quite died. Both were retired into the General Services Administration in 1943 and lived on under a sequence of other names.)

Before moving to his battle station on Eighteenth Street and New York Avenue, Hopkins had established himself behind a surplus desk in a corridor of Jones's RFC Building. Although half his money and many of his early procedures came from Jones, he got the other half from Ickes. As heir to the PWA, Hoover's other anti-Depression agency, Ickes became an essential patron of artists; in a memorandum to Hopkins he endorsed their inclusion among those to be provided work relief.

And Bruce got his perch in the tree of New Deal agencies. Thereafter, charming in his orotund manner, with a smile at the door, notepaper and address book at the ready, Bruce found frequent reasons to write directly to the President, to send him trinkets, remind him of conversations, to arrange meals with Elinor Morgenthau and Eleanor Roosevelt, and to display notes from the President addressed to "Dear Ned." He wisely selected, as his assistant at the Treasury, Olin Dows, a gifted painter who turned out to be an excellent administrator as well. After seeing TRAP through its crises from 1934 onward, Dows remained with Bruce at the Treasury Section for five years, after which he went back to his own painting and writing. A little more than a year later, he went to work for the Section on a set of post office murals under the direct guidance of Roosevelt (see page 56).[24]

Bruce and Biddle were the chief promoters of "government employment of artists"; however, Ickes was not only present at the creation and necessary to it, but was also the patron of the largest single undertaking of any New Deal arts agency, his Department of the Interior building. With his help, Bruce and his group at the Treasury had become the recipients of the two streams of subvention, one from Jones's RFC and the other from Ickes's PWA, flowing with Ickes's acquiescence through Hopkins's WPA. The confluent funds then irrigated Hopkins's FERA/PWAP, and then, augmented by fresh congressional appropriations, the Treasury—both for TRAP and the Section. After 1935 Hopkins sent the stream of money previously flowing to the PWAP to the Federal Art Project (FAP), which, after many meanders, slip-sluices, and bayous, ultimately became the WPA arts program.

The New Deal was meeting necessity, while inviting the arts to make necessity humane. Dows recalled that "most of those jobs were a damn sight more interesting than most jobs artists get anyway, through regular commission channels. These were very exciting as problems." Sharing in that

A large pottery jar made for President Franklin Roosevelt by Mary Histia of Acoma Pueblo inscribed: "Our President Franklin D. Roosevelt" and "U.S. We Do Our Part," 1930s

Mary Histia's main patron was FDR. During the time of his administration until his death, he purchased all of her pottery. It was the aim of the President and Mrs. Roosevelt to see that every U.S. embassy had a piece of this truly American art form.

Opposite: Entrance to the office suite of the Secretary of the Interior

The totem poles were carved in 1939–42 by John Wallace of Hydaburg, Alaska, for ninety dollars each.

In the 1930s the Civilian Conservation Corps and the U.S. Forest Service brought twenty-one totem poles to the Haida village of Hydaburg, Alaska, five of which were restored. The remaining sixteen poles were replicated between 1939 and 1942 under the direction of the master carver John Wallace, in the Haida tradition of the carving of poles, monuments, and houseposts to record and embody the customs of the people.

"great excitement" and "missionary sense of dedication to . . . making the world a better place in which to live" were the Farm Security Administration photographers—the words quoted were those of one of the most skilled of them, Arthur Rothstein. Architects shared the New Deal fervor that Dows recalled: "[Hans] Warneke was very steamed up about his Harlem project and he did a super job. He employed a large number of sculptors." Among these was the African American Richmond Berthé, who said Dows, "did a beautiful bas relief on a stairway retaining wall . . . But what was important, and I think we were very wise in emphasizing it, was that we asked the outside artists, and expected the local artists, to get in touch with local people who were interested in the murals, the history. It worked very well. Later, I did one in my hometown and found an immense amount of interest in local history. I think the artists found it stimulating." (For Dows's hometown work, see page 58.)[25]

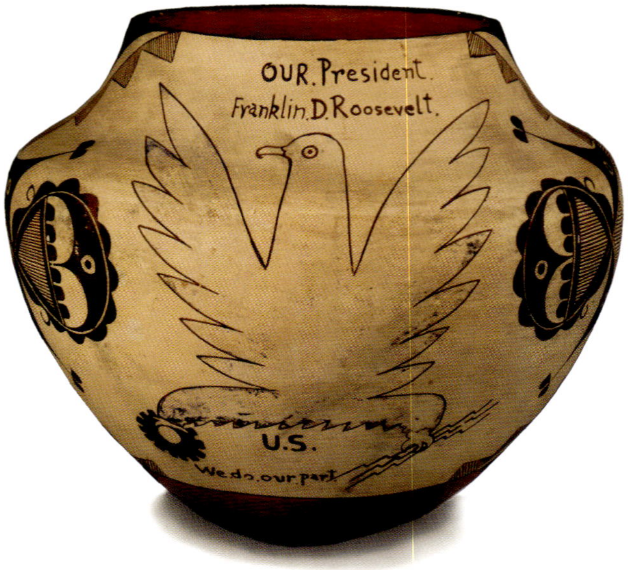

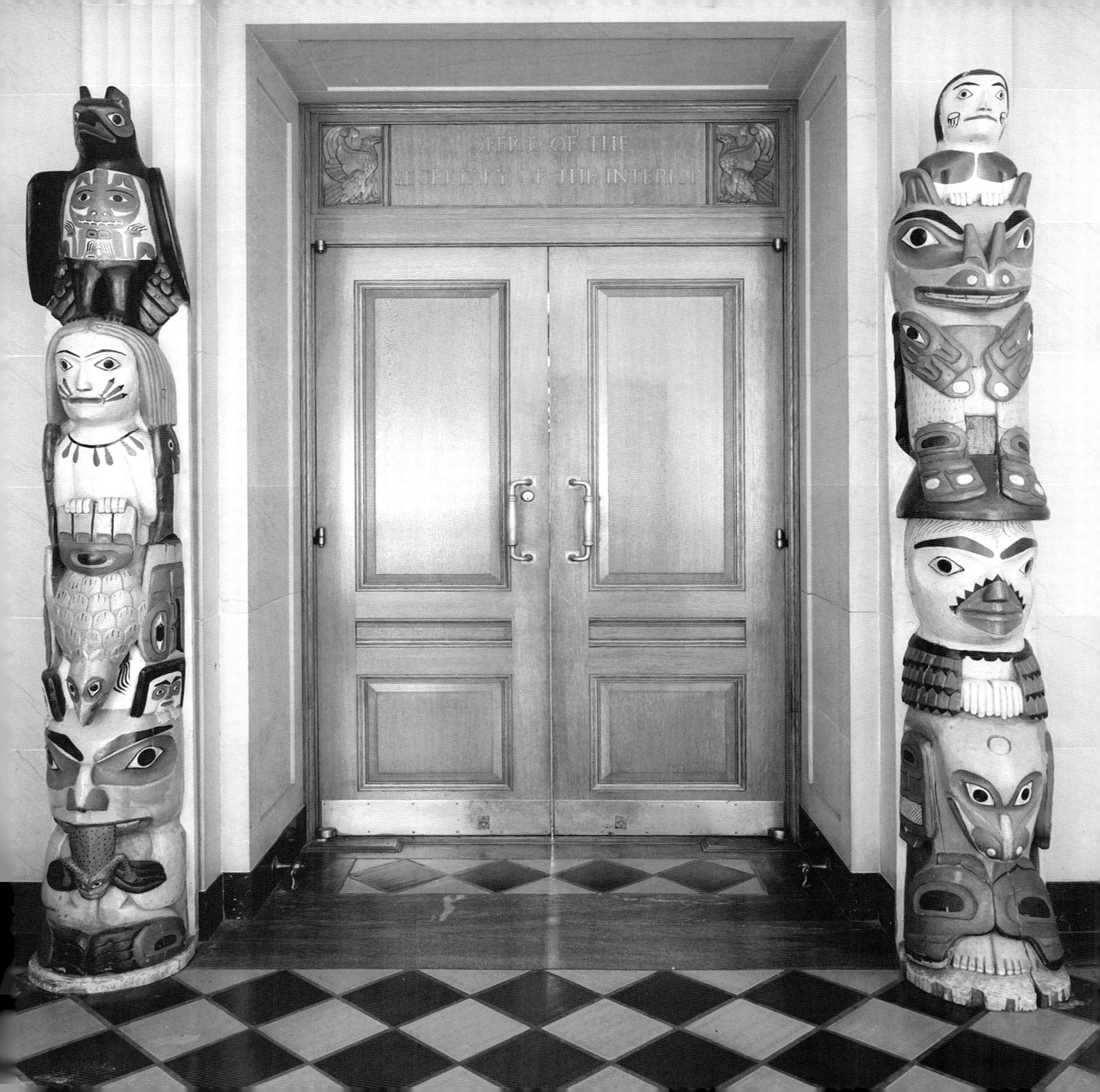
OFFICE OF THE
INTERIOR

Chapter Two

The Pursuit of Happiness, the PWA, the WPA, and the Arts

"One hundred years from now my administration will be known for its art, not for its relief."
(Franklin D. Roosevelt as quoted by Henry Morgenthau, Jr., in an interview with Erica and Lewis Rubenstein)[1]

"The New Deal was a very exciting period . . . There is no doubt Roosevelt elicited enthusiasm from us in an extraordinary way."[2]
(Olin Dows in an interview with Richard Doud in 1963)

FRANKLIN ROOSEVELT RALLIED HIS FOLLOWERS to a tradition that he proudly asserted to have commenced with the founders of the republic and to have descended to the New Deal through Abraham Lincoln who, like George Washington and Roosevelt, took seriously the implications of the "pursuit of happiness" clause of the Declaration of Independence. Its acceptance by the Continental Congress was immediate because the term "happiness" was familiar to all educated people as a process of active citizenship, honored by Aristotle, explicated by Leibnitz, and demanding in its implications. Washington would never have stooped to anything less profound. Not for him or the other founders would there be a pursuit of any smiling silliness, feckless glee, or addled acquisitive bliss of the sort offered the twenty-first century public as "happiness." The American tradition, commencing with the Declaration, has confirmed the hopes of the ages by seeking a civic order that enables people by discipline to make themselves better—more perfect—as participants in a more perfect union. As soon as the Declaration bearing that clause reached him, Washington hastened to have it "proclaimed before all the Army under my immediate Command, and have the pleasure to inform them [the Congress], that the measure seemed to have their most hearty assent." From then onward "happiness" became a legitimate objective of the common cause. Washington wrote the Congress when the future of their revolution was uncertain, "it is not with us to determine in many instances what consequences will flow from our Counsels, but yet it behooves us to adopt such, as under the smiles of a Gracious and all kind Providence will be most likely to promote our happiness." These words were so emphatic that they were cited by Ronald Reagan when under attack for support of the arts. "George Washington," wrote Reagan, "declared in 1781 that both 'arts and sciences are essential to the prosperity of the state and to the ornament and happiness of human life.'"[3]

Lincoln was Roosevelt's guide to the "pursuit of happiness clause." He had placed it at the centerpoint of his Cooper Union speech in which he made the argument that the Declaration rather than the Constitution was the rock upon which the American civil edifice was built. After assuring life and liberty, both Lincoln and Roosevelt asserted, the people's government must enable a pursuit of happiness, which meant that it must free the people from fear and from "necessity." The national union achieved by the founders, personified by Washington, given new birth by Lincoln, and reanimated in the New Deal, carried within it a related ideal: that such a union might provide conditions within which human potentiality might flower fully. Roosevelt coupled the pursuit of happiness to the doctrine of Anglo-American law that "necessitous" men cannot be "happy" because "they are not free men," making the two concepts operating principals of the New Deal. "Liberty requires opportunity to make a living" he said, "a living decent according to the standard of the time, a living which gives man not only enough to live by, but something to live for." In the depths of the Depression, artists were among the "too many" for whom "life was no longer free; liberty no longer real." A program of work-relief was required because "men could no longer follow the pursuit of happiness" on their own. Roosevelt had taken office proclaiming an intention to recruit the nation into "a loyal army willing to sacrifice for the good of a common discipline" and proclaiming the need for "broad Executive power to wage a war against the emergency, as great as the power that would be given to me if we were in fact invaded by a foreign foe."[4]

In fact, "the good of the common discipline" was often somewhat confused by local patronage considerations, such as the Congressional requirement that half the FERA appropriation go in matching grants administered by the states and localities. That took time, keeping some people—including artists—hungry longer than Hopkins thought necessary or morally defensible. So he set loose a team of picadors to prod the states for requests and matching funds for projects that would put to work as many of the unemployed as possible. "Gulping down endless rounds of black coffee and chain-smoking cigarettes," Hopkins authorized "payments of five million dollars in his first two hours in office." Still, it was not enough, or fast enough. Eight million people were out of work and out of savings.[5]

Hopkins's relief programs helped the nation get through the winter of 1933–34. By the New Deal historian William Leuchtenburg's accounting, this inefficient, cumbersome, patronage-cluttered process, further curdled by state means tests, "built or improved some 500,000 miles of roads, 40,000 schools, over 3,500 playgrounds and athletic fields, and 1,000 airports . . . renovated Montana's State Capitol Building and helped erect Pittsburgh's Cathedral of Learning . . . employed fifty thousand teachers to keep rural schools open and to teach adult education classes in the cities . . . provided enough money to put back to work every teacher on Boston's unemployed rolls . . . prehistoric mounds were excavated for

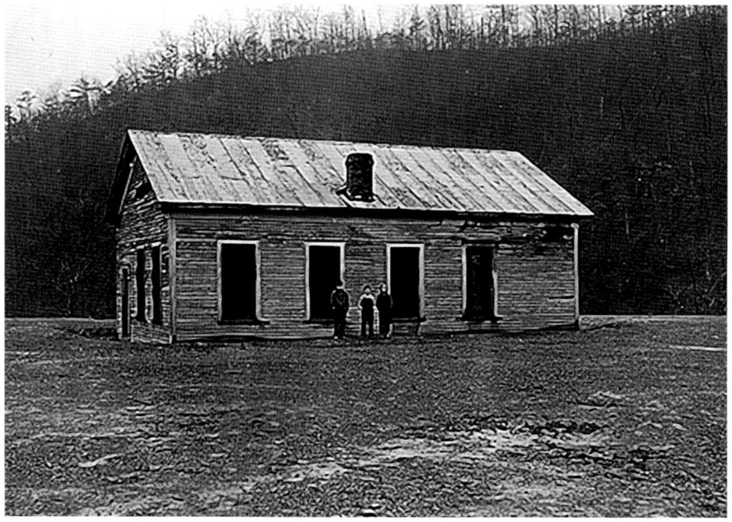

The old Abner Gap, Virginia, school replaced by the WPA with the new one shown below, 1938

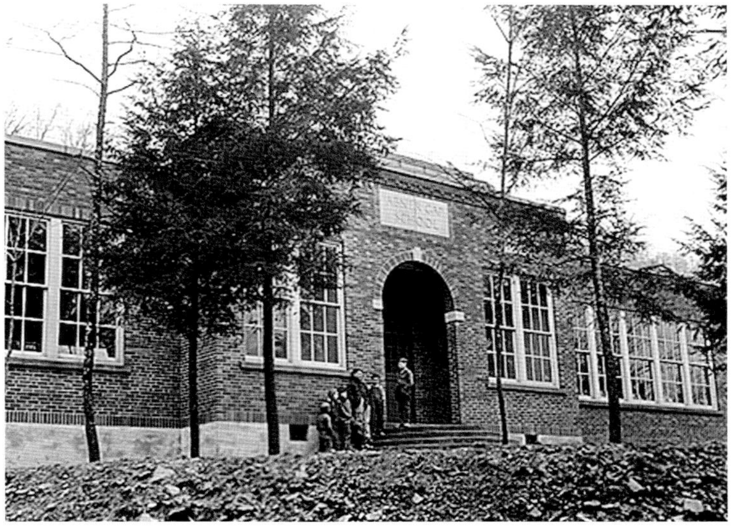

School in New Abner Gap, Virginia, 1938

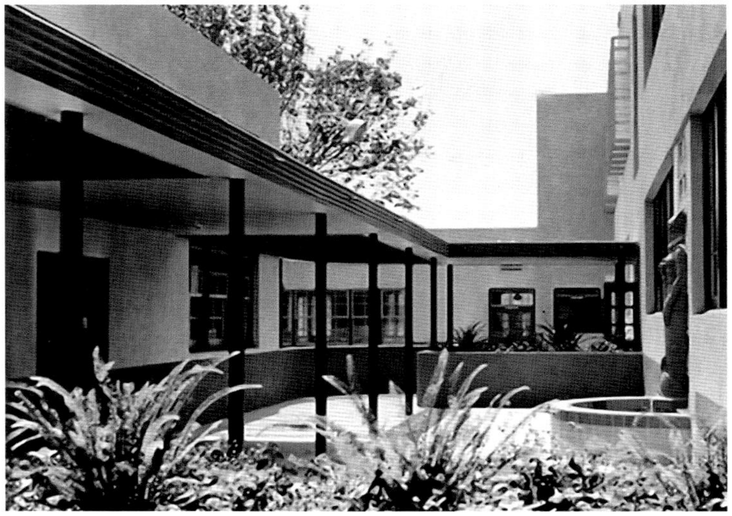

Entrance to the Washington Junior High School, an earthquake-proof structure in Long Beach, California

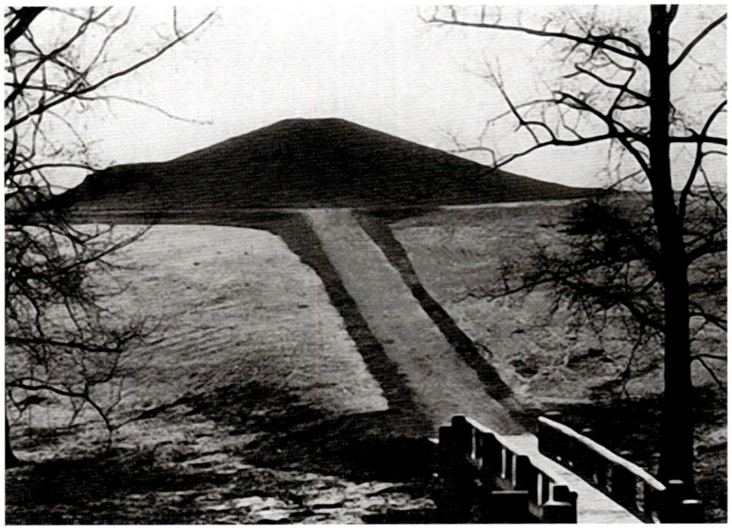

Ocmulgee Mounds restoration viewed from a distance, near Macon, Georgia; now Ocmulgee National Monument, c. 1934

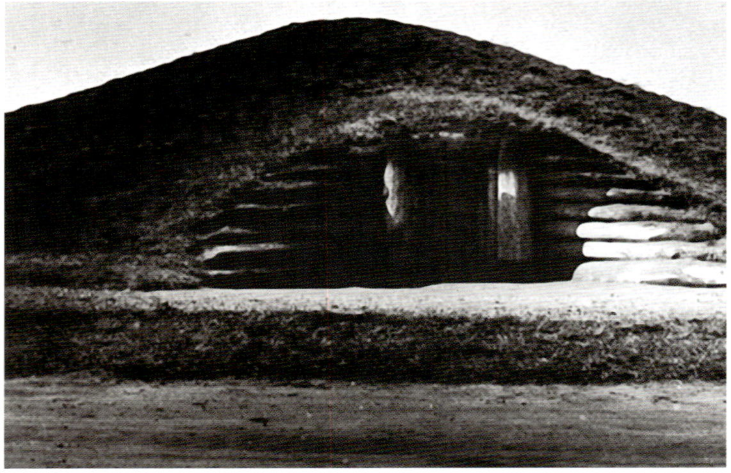

Earth lodge restored by the WPA at Ocmulgee National Monument, c. 1934

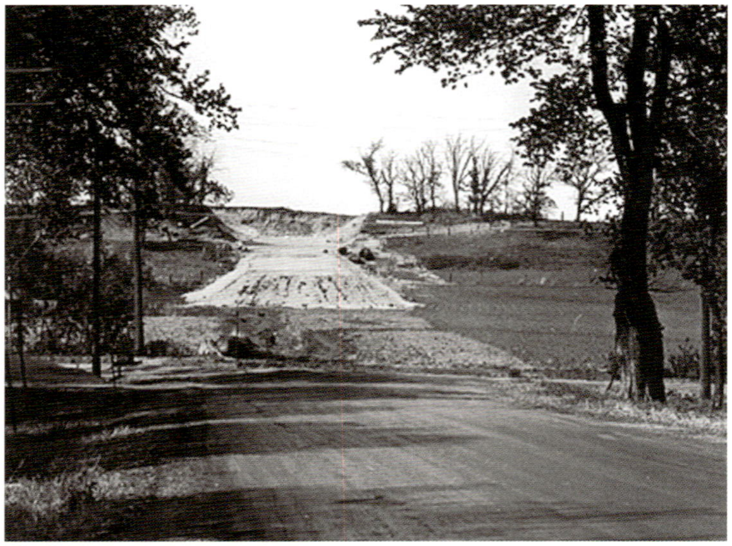

New highway construction in Minnesota, November 1933–March 1934

the Smithsonian Institution" and the Kodiak Islands were restocked with snowshoe rabbits.[6]

The arts component of all this, the FERA/PWAP, lasted barely five months, but for unemployed sculptors, painters, and printmakers it was a lifesaver—they needed not only work, but to work. And work the artists did: nearly thirty-eight hundred of them produced fifteen thousand works of art. Among them were seventy Indians, including Kiowas who painted murals for two state colleges and the state historical society in Oklahoma. In Albuquerque and Santa Fe, Indian artists painted more murals and wove rugs for state and federal buildings, including schools and hospitals.

As the first FERA dollars were running out, the President took a risk, going back to Congress for more money, telling Hopkins to create the CWA as a full-tilt federal operation, without state means tests and state patronage delays, and paying minimum wages. Hopkins put four million men and women to work—including artists—but the states bucked at the loss of control and patronage, and although Roosevelt asked for fresh appropriations, he told Hopkins to phase out the CWA and resume the old FERA patronage process. Forced to operate within that rattletrap system, Hopkins's federal staff and state committees "bailed out stranded coal towns like Dewmaine and Colp, Illinois, where 95 percent of the people were on relief; and, in the course of aiding rural areas, experimented with long-term projects such as loans to farmers and the creation of new communities through the Resettlement Administration (see chapter seven). "The FERA erected five thousand public buildings and seven thousand bridges, cleared streams, dredged rivers, . . . terraced land . . . taught over one and a half million adults to read and write, ran nursery schools for children from low-income families, and helped one hundred thousand students to attend college."[7]

However, it was becoming manifest that the Depression would not soon be over. In 1933 the stock market had gone into a sickening second free fall, and the general economy went with it. Employers were unable to rehire; they could neither raise capital nor borrow money. All hopes seemed to wither. Breadlines lengthened. Many people believed, as Harry Hopkins was informed by Lorena Hickok (his chief source of ground-truth, see chapter six) that "we're in this relief business for a long, long, time. The majority of those over 45 probably will NEVER get their jobs back." If no one was to starve, work relief would have to be sustained. The Depression—Herbert Hoover's term for a transitory phenomenon—was proving Hoover wrong. It was intractable. The nation was gripped by an economic and psychological illness deeper than depression.[8]

The so-called Second New Deal got underway in 1935, with the Social Security Act, the Banking Act, the Wealth Tax Act, the Wagner Labor Relations Act, and the Public Utility Holding Company Act. Although the public rallied to these efforts, the President's rhetoric became more pugnacious as both the New Deal and democracy came under assault from the extremes of left and right. Roosevelt told the nation he was "fighting Communism, Huey Longism, Coughlinism, Townsendism . . . to save our system."[9]

The PWA and the WPA

As work relief was salvaging the self-respect of the unemployed, Roosevelt moved toward structural change in the system, requesting—and getting—a three-part National Industrial Recovery Act (NIRA). Part one put the federal government in charge of setting maximum hours and minimum pay for industrial workers. Part two created the National Recovery Administration (NRA), which suspended antitrust laws to permit industries to agree on wages and prices under federal sponsorship. As an anti-deflationary measure it did little, but it did diminish child labor and make less dreadful the sweatshops that Ickes, Hopkins, and Morgenthau had sought to alleviate in their settlement work. Part three provided Ickes's Public Works Administration (PWA) with a $3.3 billion appropriation. Added to the grants to farmers proposed by the Agricultural Adjustment Act (AAA), this added enough spending money to keep the prime in the pump of recovery.

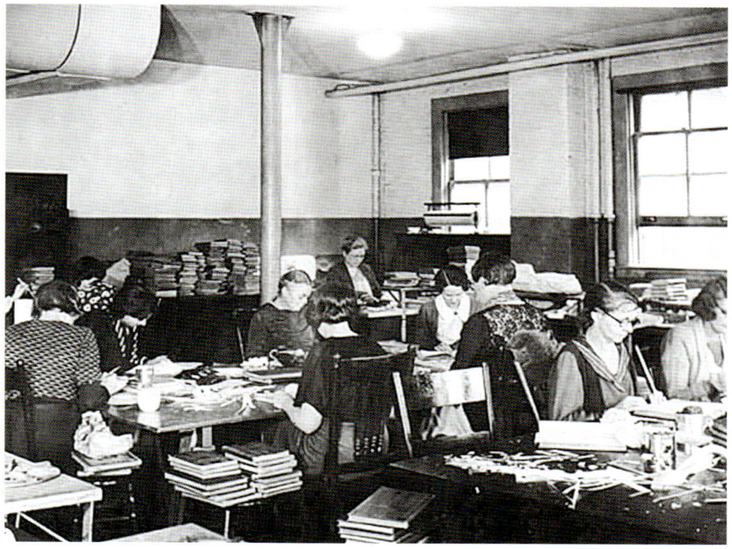

Book menders for the Seattle public schools, Seattle, Washington, 1934

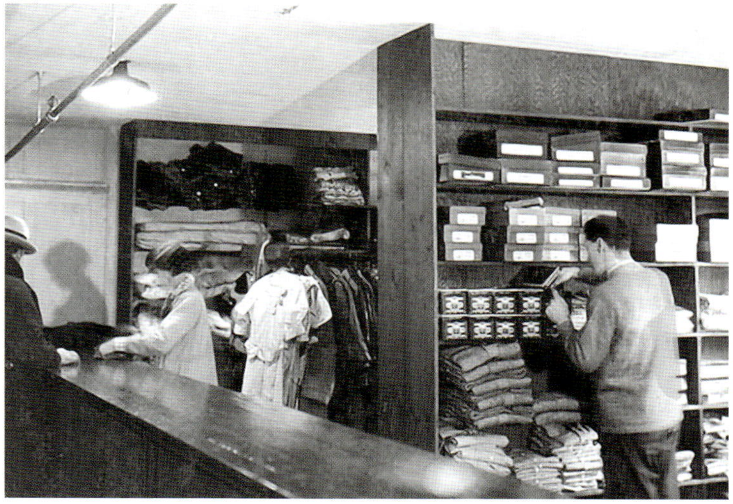

Clothing outlet interior, Seattle, Washington, 1934

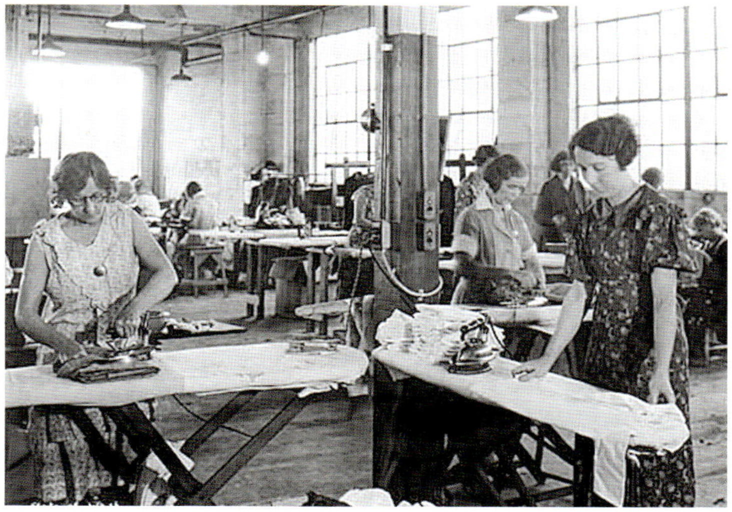

Sewing Center interior showing seamstresses pressing clothes, Seattle, Washington, 1934

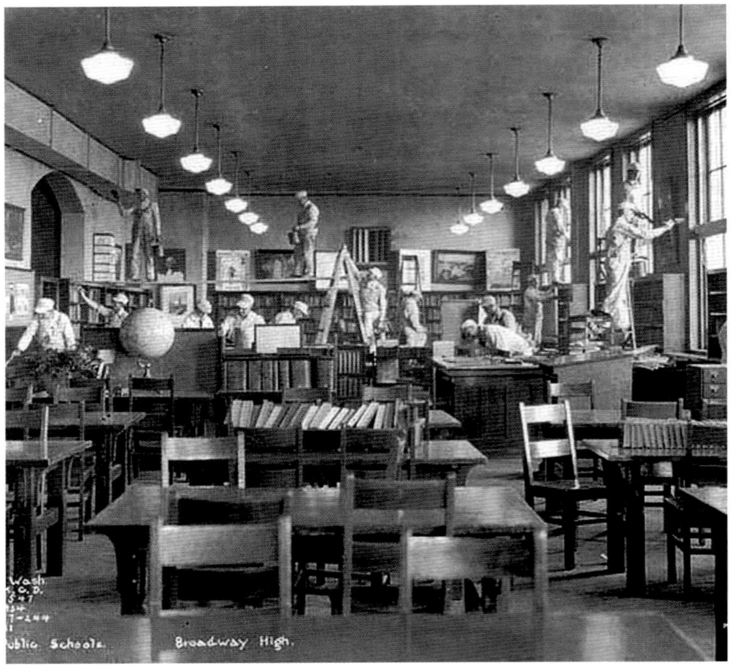

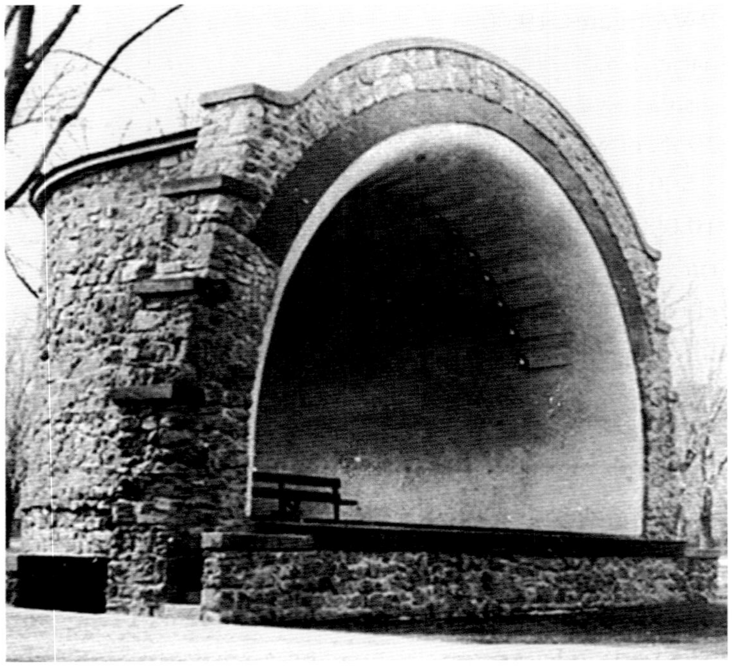

Right:
Broadway High School library interior showing painters at work, Capitol Hill neighborhood, Seattle, Washington, 1934

Far right:
Band shell, City Park, Twin Falls, Idaho, 1934

As administrator of the PWA, Ickes picked up the RFC application files Hopkins had set down when his first FERA funds ran out and invited new ones, letting the state governors know that they should change their address books under HELP, so he could start building—big. "The resultant search through the RFC records was swift and exhaustive," he wrote proudly in *Back to Work*: "Lights blazed in the Interior Building throughout most of the ensuing nights; groups of engineers and lawyers pored over the mass of documents relating to each of the hundreds of applications made to the RFC by municipalities all over the country, sifting, sorting, rejecting, approving. The building had some of the tense atmosphere of a general staff headquarters after a declaration of war. Indeed, we had declared war on depression!" Ickes treated his Interior Department building as a Pentagon, although it had six wings rather than five sides. As the PWA kept the lights on all night, Ickes converted a department of the exploitable interior into a department of conservation, celebrating that process with art arrayed throughout the building in the same way that later, in wartime, posters enhanced the morale of the armed forces.[10]

There were essential differences between Ickes's array of big schemes and Hopkins's recruitment of millions of workers into Roosevelt's "loyal army." Ickes was not running a recruiting station. His was a huge production system, measuring results by what was built, not by how many were hired. His insistence upon big projects, rather than direct employment, led him to move too slowly for those like Hopkins who advocated a PWA primarily as "an agency to distribute money." Ickes insisted that he sought to get "honest work at honest wages on honest projects, which was a great deal more difficult task than giving away money." The duty of public works, wrote Ickes in 1948, "was to build permanent and socially desirable projects that would be assets of the communities which they would serve many years in the future."[11]

"In the long run" was a phrase strung like a litany through Ickes's speeches and in his *Back to Work*. As T. H. Watkins wrote in his biography of Ickes: "It was for the long run that he wanted PWA projects built, and it was for the long run that most of them did get built, giving rise to . . . William E. Leuchtenburg's description of Ickes as 'a builder to rival Cheops.' Ickes doubtless would have enjoyed (and agreed with) the description, and not without justification. According to

PWA figures, 19,000 individual projects in 3,040 of the nation's 3,073 counties, and in all her territorial and insular possessions, had been authorized by the spring of 1935, of which more than 11,500 were completed and nearly 5,500 under construction . . . it is estimated that at least 10,000,000 persons have been directly benefited by expenditures to increase the national wealth through construction of useful public works as a substitute for direct relief . . . [S]omewhere on most of these utilitarian monuments appear the words 'Harold L. Ickes, Secretary of the Interior' as the stamp of immortality."[12]

Watkins totted up Ickes's "monuments" as follows: 583 municipal water systems . . . 622 sewerage systems, including a $42 million sewer and waste-treatment complex built for the Chicago Sanitary District; 263 hospitals, including a $2.4 million, 700-bed marine hospital in New York City supervised by the National Public Health Service; 522 schools, including a $2 million expansion of facilities at Virginia State College for Negroes; 368 street and highway projects, including $8.5 million in highway construction for the state of Wyoming alone" and "$200 million in loans to railroads, including $80 million to the Pennsylvania Railroad to electrify its line from New York to Washington, D.C., cutting its running time by forty minutes, and to build new electric locomotives in the aging shops of Ickes's old hometown of Altoona."[13]

Hopkins derided Ickes's grand, slow-moving public works, remarking to the press that "people don't eat in the long run." Ickes said of Hopkins that he was not priming the pump but "just turning on the fire-plug." Hopkins listened, grimaced, and turned away: "He bores me," he wrote. The competition between Ickes and Hopkins, and the proliferation of relief agencies under their management was, as Robert E. Sherwood admitted, baffling. And though Sherwood knew the New Deal from top to bottom as an adviser and speechwriter for the President, like "a large number of Roosevelt supporters" he found it difficult to "understand what was the difference between W.P.A. [Hopkins's fiefdom] and P.W.A. [Ickes's] and why there should have been two of them." The best explanation, he found upon reflection, was that the difference lay "between two opposed philosophies, the difference between Hopkins and Ickes. The former had the point of view of the welfare worker. The main object was to get the greatest number of people work in the shortest possible space of time . . . Ickes had the point of view of a business man . . . the best way to relieve unemployment on a long range point of view was . . . by subsidizing private enterprise with massive . . . projects. Ickes was proud of the amount of heavy, durable materials that went into the P.W.A. projects such as Bonneville Dam . . . [and his own Interior Department Building]; whereas Hopkins boasted of the small percentage of the W.P.A. dollar that went into materials and consequently the large percentage that went directly into the pockets of those on relief."[14]

Harold Ickes

Harold Ickes came from Altoona, Pennsylvania, the son of a self-denigrating woman and an alcoholic dry-goods salesman who signed his letters "your poor miserable father." According to the famous football coach Amos Alonzo Stagg, who measured Ickes in his somewhat pudgy youth, he stood 5 feet 8 inches tall and weighed 150 pounds. Already the self-described "curmudgeon" was showing signs of his chronic depressions, often "listless and melancholy," and his condition was not alleviated by a drab childhood and a straightened youth: he often "dined on bread and milk" as he worked his way through the University of Chicago. There, however, he met Anna Wilmarth, also the child of an alcoholic, but a wealthy one. After they were married, she helped him set up in a legal business and introduced him to the world of Jane Addams. It was at once a thrilling and horrifying world. Addams won the Nobel Prize for her work among the desperate and destitute. Through her, Ickes met Frances Perkins, the social worker who later became Secretary of Labor, his peer, and colleague. Perkins in turn introduced him to Franklin and Eleanor Roosevelt. By then, Ickes was a "streetside politician and habitué of the ward halls and law offices in which the protocols of Chicago's civic life were forged."

Statue of Liberty Torch Repair
The engineer is shown examining one of the openings from which the glass of the highest point of the "flame" of the torch, which is held aloft in Liberty's right hand, had broken out. The WPA constructed a replacement.

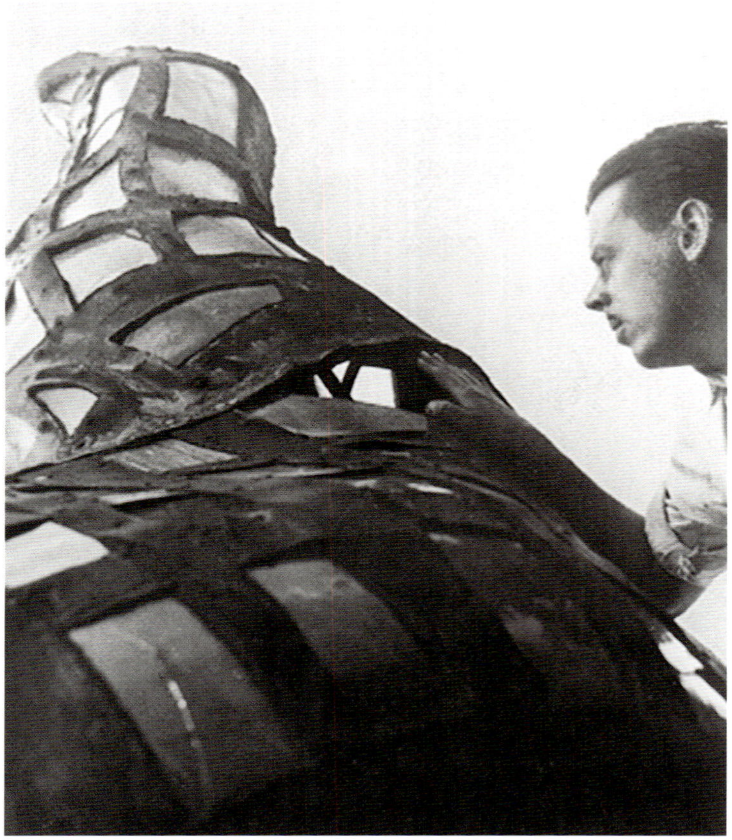

Although Robert E. Sherwood described him as a "businessman" he was a creature more interesting than that—he was a Chicago pro.[15]

Until the end of the 1920s, Ickes was a Bullmoose Republican conservationist like Secretary of Agriculture Henry Wallace, with whom Ickes had as bitter a rivalry as that with Hopkins. The struggle with Hopkins was to control relief and art as a part of relief—with Wallace it was to control conservation. During the course of their contest, the Soil Service was situated first at the Agriculture Department, then moved within Ickes's empire, and then reverted to Wallace's. Rexford Tugwell, Roy Stryker, and the photographers they famously mobilized and publicized for the Resettlement and Farm Security Administrations (RA and FSA) were within Wallace's Department of Agriculture during the entire New Deal period, though he did not show much interest in the art part of their endeavors. What mattered was that Eleanor Roosevelt did, as we shall see.

The Department of the Interior had been the department of easy pickings, although not of crops, it was the department of corrupt mining and drilling concessions deals under Grant and again under Harding. It had the Land Office/ Bureau of Land Management, which was responsible for land too dry or rocky to farm—and, oh yes, it had the National Parks. Its last period of glory lay toward the end of the nineteenth century when it was the power base for Secretary of the Interior Carl Schurz, who treated it as a Department of Conservation. Ickes longed to restore it to Schurz's glory days. Accordingly, he summoned the best artistic talent that government could hire to make his headquarters the recognizable command center for a Schurz-style department. The murals and sculpture in its stairways, corridors, niches, dining room, and auditorium—and in the apartment-size office of the Secretary with Schurz's portrait at the door—were intended to inspirit, embolden, and empower its employees to think bigger and bolder.

Sherwood had no greater fondness for Ickes than did Hopkins, and lost no occasion to sideswipe him by contrasting him to Hopkins. The "shabby old building" in which the WPA was administered expressed, he wrote, Hopkins's "natural aversion to pomp and circumstance, while, just across Eighteenth Street, Ickes—with full pomp and circumstance—was marking the spot for the cornerstone for his Interior Building." What Robert Mills and Thomas U. Walter had done for Andrew Jackson, Ickes elicited from Waddy Wood, a builder of mansions and embassies, more "modern" than Morgenthau's Treasury, and much bigger. A battalion of talent, mobilized and deployed in the war on the Depression, came to occupy sixteen acres of usable floor space within the six double baroque-moderne wings emerging back to back from a central palace—the ensemble covering two city blocks. Franklin Roosevelt laid its cornerstone using the trowel employed by George Washington for the Capitol itself, announcing that the building would be big enough to be "symbolical of the Nation's vast resources we are sworn to protect." Henry Wallace and Ickes were vying for control of the Soil Conservation Service, the Forest

Service, and other conservation agencies in the Department of Agriculture, so it was somewhat mischievous for Roosevelt to go on to say that by initiating Ickes's building he was also laying the "cornerstone for conservation policy." It was his habit to keep both Ickes and Wallace eager and nervous.[16]

Ickes's equivalent to the Pentagon, unlike either the Treasury or the Pentagon, has plenty of art to urge along its workers and to explain to visitors what those workers are doing. It is as eloquent as "architecture parlante" (self-explaining architecture) as George Washington's campaign tent, commencing its disquisition as Sherwood was writing in *Roosevelt and Hopkins* that Hopkins's "first office had been in the Federal Security Building," but that he had "fought his way out of that and continued for five years to resist all attempts to move his headquarters into new government buildings which were marbled and air conditioned." Ickes's was the first government building to have air conditioning—and, for that matter, the first to have escalators, a staff library, a gymnasium, soundproof office walls and, during his tenure, outside windows for everybody, including the Secretary, who came to occupy the largest private office of any cabinet officer—nearly six hundred square feet on the top floor of the nation's most ambitious museum of New Deal art.[17]

Harold Ickes produced projects. Harry Hopkins produced work. Both produced art. And so did Henry Morgenthau's Treasury Department, which placed art in other people's projects, under the guidance of Morgenthau's deputy for art, Edward Bruce.

Bruce, TRAP, and the Section

George Biddle was no administrator. Edward Bruce and Dows were, and Bruce an infighter to boot. Son of a Baptist preacher, he also became chief evangelist of the New Deal

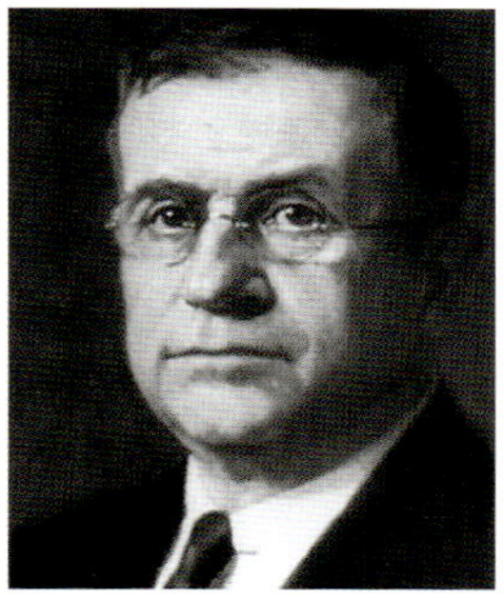

Harold Ickes

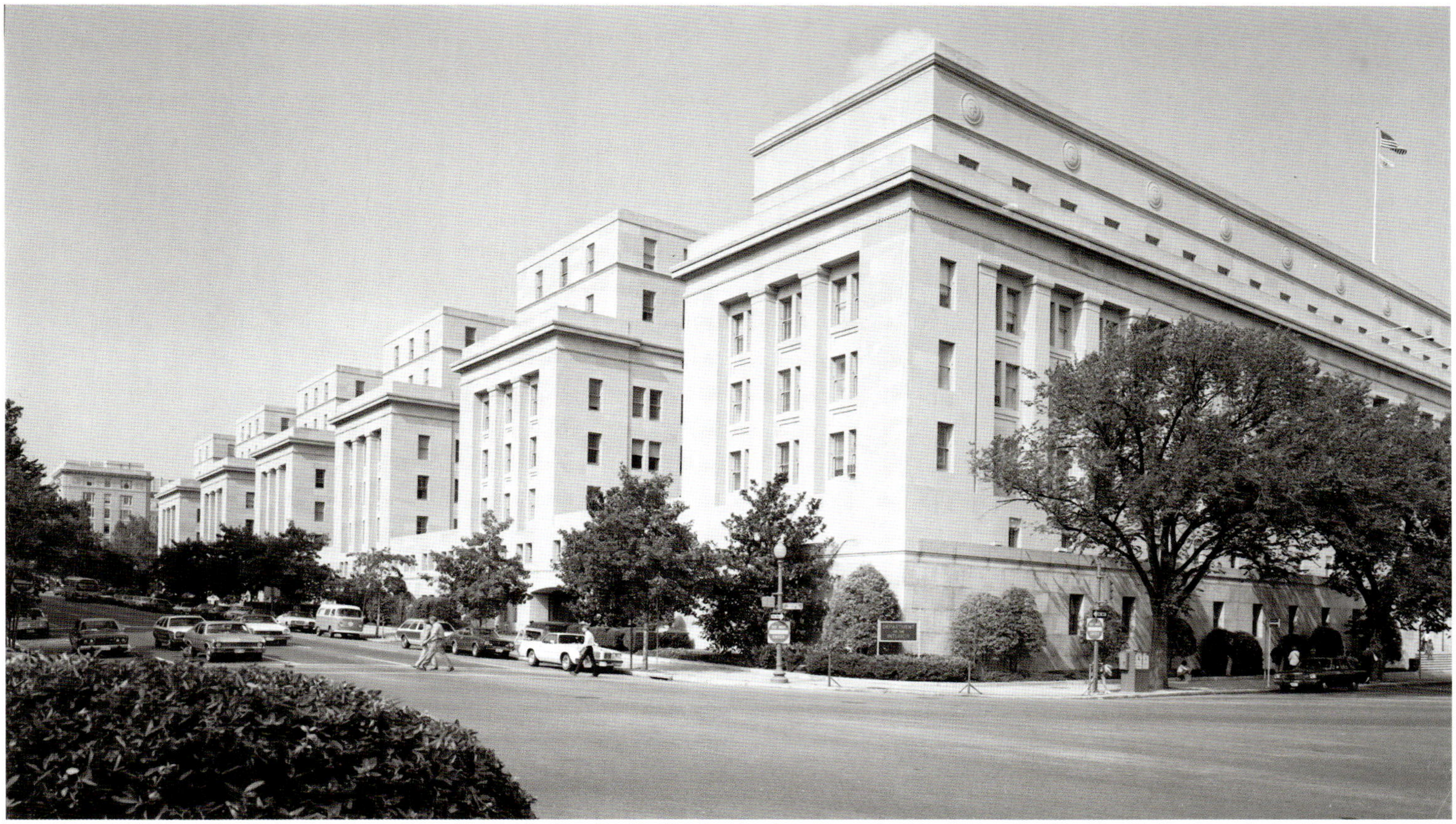

The west facade of the Interior Building

arts programs. His first career had been as a lawyer in Manila, before bigger prospects called him to a trading firm in China. It failed him and its investors, although Bruce acquired a reputation as a silver expert. He set that line of work aside for a time to study painting in Paris, where he became good enough at painting to make a living at it, and his salesmanship remained strong enough to gain him a commission to provide a mural for the San Francisco Stock Exchange. The mural remains there, although it is eclipsed as the major visitor attraction to the building by the work of Diego Rivera. Bruce's twin capacities in silver and in paint were sufficiently distinctive to bring a summons from the Treasury, which in 1933 was sorely in need of advice on both. Having given sound advice on currency matters, Bruce convinced the Morgenthaus to detail him to organize and manage the work-relief efforts of the Treasury that Hopkins had funded. Bruce had at the outset played to the President's conservation interests by proposing to siphon more money from Ickes's PWA to his office in the Treasury, to pay artists to record the endeavors of the CCC in the parks. Although Ickes kept the money for a CCC art program, Hopkins provided Bruce with money from the Emergency Relief Appropriations Act (ERAA) for a Treasury Relief Art Program (TRAP): a $530,000 grant bearing a requirement that 90 percent of the artists it employed be taken from the relief rolls. Since the CCC was important to the President, Bruce promptly asked the CCC to accept the services of thirty artists to "embellish the unusually stark walls of the CCC buildings," emboldening the CCC itself to employ nearly one hundred artists at a time, working forty hour weeks for $30 a month in cash, subsistence, clothes, health care, and shelter in the camps.[18]

Despite its centralized command structure, the artists for TRAP did some magnificent work. TRAP never employed more than 356 artists of its authorized level of 450, but over the cruel winter of 1935–36, it provided bread on the table and coal for the grate. Before it finally expired in 1939 after a total expenditure of little more than $800,000, it had delivered to the public nearly ninety murals, scores of sculptures, and 10,000 easel paintings and prints. Much of that work was of high quality, exemplified by Reginald Marsh's frescoes of New York harbor, painted on the inner shell of the rotunda of the New York Custom House.

Bruce was a formidable entrepreneur. After making a success of TRAP, he was assigned by Morgenthau to lead the Section on Fine Arts of the Procurement Division of the Treasury Department (the Section) with the purpose of providing art in federal buildings. TRAP had produced murals, but those now celebrated as "post office murals" were the glory of the Section, arising from one of its three modes of operation. Firstly, it sustained the Treasury's role as the commissioning agency for art enriching federal buildings, avoiding the worst contamination of patronage by publishing

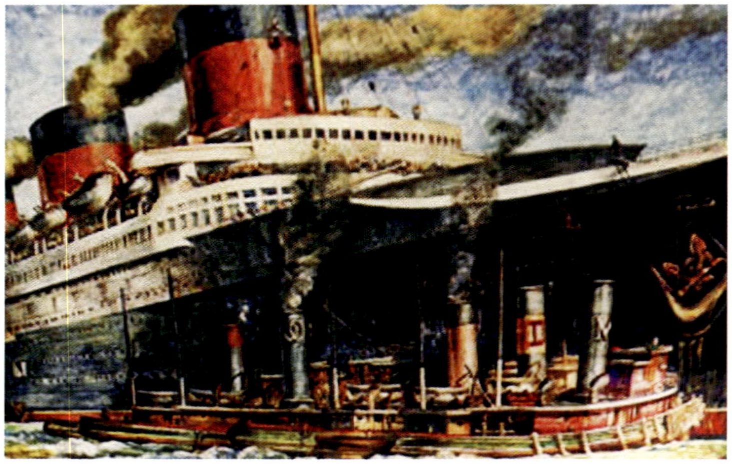

Atlantic Liner in Harbor with Tugs (Mural study, U.S. Customs House, New York, New York)

Gouache sketch by Reginald Marsh for one of his frescoes of New York Harbor, painted on the inner shell of the rotunda of the U.S. Custom House (today the National Museum of the American Indian).

notices of competitions in a bulletin that reached eighteen thousand artists by 1941. It did, however, allow exceptions to the competitive process when seeking proposals from eminent muralists for truly conspicuous commissions. Among those exceptions for which posterity may be grateful are the paintings for the Department of Justice building. At the time, Bruce apparently felt constrained to explain that more than 230 "other artists" had submitted competitive designs, of whom 62 had "received commissions in Washington" and "almost a fifth . . . got jobs."[19]

Secondly, the mural program supplied "ornamentation" for the New Deal's eleven hundred new post offices. The usual place of honor was the wall through which one would enter a postmaster's office. In most cases the "ornament" was a mural, but sometimes it was a bas-relief or an easel painting. The winners were selected by competitions whose outcomes were largely determined by local committees that were expected to favor local and regional artists, though they were informed that Bruce and his colleagues had not only the last word but quite a few words to say along the way. When the Section was instructed to "ornament" a new post office, Bruce urged the chosen artists to seek the views of community leaders who might have some experience or taste in the arts, including art educators, museum people, artists, and patrons. Following Bruce's injunction, the sculptor Alonzo Hauser executed three wood reliefs for the post office of the lumber-and-wild-rice town of Park Rapids, Minnesota: *Park Service Symbol*, *Indian*, and *Lumberjack in Setting*, after he and the postmaster, Mr. Campbell, "went to about fifteen or twenty of the leading citizens . . . the head of the Chamber of Commerce, the president of the Citizens Committee, a couple of bankers, merchants, and resort owners . . . in fact about everybody that had an active part and interest in community affairs" to talk over his plans. When the Section made a genuine effort to consult "everybody that had an active part and interest in community affairs" it was often, as in Park Rapids, effective.[20]

By and large, the federally commissioned murals in post offices, the chief federal presence in every county, were successful in community-building because, as Bruce laid out, their main objective "was to keep away from official art and to develop local cultural interests throughout the country." "One sculptor," he wrote, "explained why a realistic subject was more appropriate than a symbolic one for a Kentucky post office: 'persons entering the building would get more local pride out of a design having to do with their own activities than mythological figures which the average man does not even understand and which may give him a feeling of the majesty and might of his government, rather than a feeling of his own personal relation to it and the concern of the government towards him.'" As Marlene Park and Gerald Markowitz concluded in their study of the program: "the federal government could have chosen to make the post offices symbols of its power by decorating them with murals depicting national heroes or with emblems such as eagles, flags clutched in their talons, their wings outstretched over the postmaster's door. Instead, it chose to make the murals mirrors of local communities, stressing the primacy of the welfare of the ordinary citizen."[21]

The third mode of operation devised by Bruce and his colleagues was the "Forty-Eight States Competition." At the end of the 1930s, buffeted from one side by artists' groups proclaiming entitlement to self-expression and disdaining the lack of connoisseurship on Main Street, and, from the other side, by congressmen, senators, and pundits asserting that "modernism" and European Socialist influence were oozing out from post offices across the land, each of the then forty-eight states got a post office mural, but through the marvelous mathematics of patronage those forty-eight became sixty-four after sixteen bonus competitions.

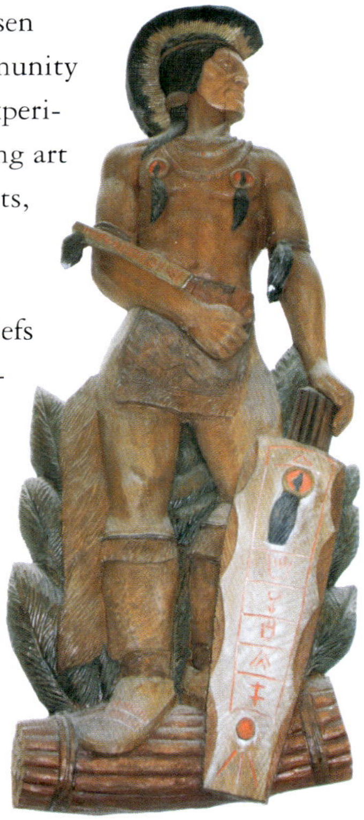

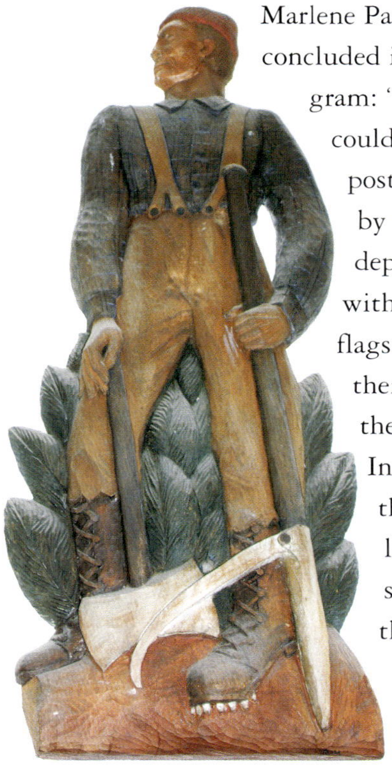

Left and below:
Indian, *Lumberjack*, and *Park Service Symbol*. Wooden reliefs for the Park Rapids Post Office, Park Rapids, Minnesota. Alonzo Hauser, 1939

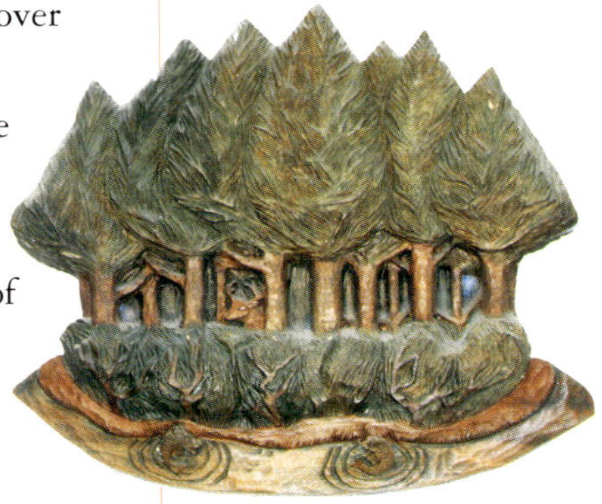

Alonzo Hauser was born in Wisconsin, studied in New York, apprenticed as a stone carver, went to Paris to study studio sculpture in 1931, and returned to work with William Zorach in New York. His public sculpture in the Twin Cities includes "The Source" in St. Paul's Rice Park, the huge Christ on the facade of the St. Paul United Church of Christ, and "The Promise of Youth" for the Veterans Service Building on the capitol grounds in St. Paul. Hauser expressed in words and life his belief that "the artist" must be an active citizen, for he "does not live to ornament existence" or merely "to decorate life." His later work shows his interest in Native American and Inuit cultures.

Soon, however, the Congress realized that local political bosses had little more to say about what art they got with the Forty-Eight States Competition than they had with TRAP, and no more than they had in the conventional methods of the Section. Winning artists were selected from 1,475 entries by juries of eminent artists, including Dows, Henry Varnum Poor, Edgar Miller, and Maurice Sterne. Honorable persons all, they tended to select works by artists they knew to be worthy (or more simply put, who they knew). Some of the eminent beneficiaries of their review were not hospitable to the suggestions of local committees, though in theory the "Forty-Eight States" process, like that of the Section, sought local opinion, and many "Forty-Eight States" winners understood the fundamental community-building purpose of the mural program. The ultimate outcome was that the communities got art, "the field" got commissions, and art got larger audiences as exhibitions of competition sketches were posted at the Corcoran Gallery in Washington and published in *Life* magazine, interspersed among somber images of the war in Europe.

Naturally enough, the works produced for TRAP, Federal One, and the Section had a generally positive tone. Their purpose was affirmation. The newly devised Social Security System, for example, received "a good review" in a mural by Ben Shahn in the building now the headquarters of the Department of Health and Human Services. (Shahn was busy on New Deal business throughout the 1930s; aside from his Social Security murals, his design for the Bronx Central Post Office triumphed over 188 competitors in a "Forty-eight States" competition, and his photographs for the Farm Security Administration and the Resettlement Administration could—and in this book do—serve as illustrations for the reports of Lorena Hickok (see p. 242). The primary assignments of TRAP and Federal One's Art Project (WPA/FAP) were providing work for the "necessitous." They did so, while also shoring up community among people and across time. "The New Deal was a very exciting period," said Dows to an interviewer in 1963: "There is no doubt Roosevelt elicited enthusiasm from us in an extraordinary way."[22]

Where the Work Was Done

In his new Department of the Interior building, Ickes had a community of his own to inspirit, the employees of that department and of a panoply of other New Deal agencies. Ordinarily both constructing the building and selecting art to give it character would have been managed by the Procurement Division of the Treasury Department, as it would today be managed by the General Services Administration. Ickes had other plans. He asked the President for authority to take building and contents out of the control of Morgenthau, even though the Treasury would provide most of the funding. Roosevelt told him to work it out with Morgenthau. In November 1934, Ickes wrote in his diary that he had written Morgenthau: "I was asking a personal favor, that it did not mean anything to him personally whether he built this building or not, but it did mean a good deal to me." Morgenthau devised a scheme permitting all Interior Department employees working on the project—construction crews, artists and designers—to be on temporary assignment to the Treasury, although taking their orders from Ickes. Roosevelt characteristically rejoiced in a contrivance that "should clear everything up."

As a hands-on patron Ickes had no peer in the New Deal hierarchy, though the standard histories of art in the New Deal are rough on him, as he was rough on nearly everybody; he was often graceless in his benefactions, inarticulate in his subtleties, and unduly critical of his colleagues. But he is gratefully remembered by many who have come to know the Department of the Interior building well. Some recall most poignantly the nine-hundred-seat auditorium in which retirement ceremonies are performed and new appointments given celebrity treatment. Those attending are provided delight and diversion by the gifts of Harold Ickes: Lewis, Clark, Sacagawea, and her child Baptiste Charbonneau, carved for us by Hans Warneke, and Ralph Stackpole's John Wesley Powell in limestone, exploring the Grand Canyon. Just outside are landscapes by William Henry Jackson that redouble Stackpole's theme of survey and exploration, and also remind us that art emerging from scouting and surveying built constituencies for national parks and for the reform of American Indian policy. Jackson is most often entered in art history texts as the photographer accompanying Thomas "Yellowstone" Moran, but he was himself a competent painter—as Moran was a competent photographer.

John Collier

The other presence felt most strongly throughout the Department of the Interior building is the spirit of John Collier. It was a surprise to Harold Ickes when Franklin Roosevelt appointed him Secretary of the Interior rather than "Indian Commissioner" (Collier's customary term for the office), since Raymond Moley, Roosevelt's aid, knew Collier but not Ickes. Both Ickes and Collier expressed gratification at the outcome, and history has justified their feelings. Collier's success in cleaning out corruption in the Bureau of Indian affairs—or, rather, making a brave beginning to cleaning it up; his abolition of the Indian schools as boot camps for forced assimilation; his protection of tribal lands and customs; and his encouragement of traditional art, secured the steady support of Ickes, and of the President and Mrs. Roosevelt, but he was capable of recruiting support from many disparate sources, perhaps because his own character and demeanor were so complex. Sometimes mystical, sometimes fussy, sometimes compassionate, sometimes ferocious, his nature was as irreducible to journalistic simplicities as was that of Ickes or that of Ickes's chief, Franklin Roosevelt. But "by golly" as Ickes would say, Collier was effective.[23]

Collier's father, an Atlanta banker, sent his son to Columbia University and on to the Collège de France, where he read Erwin Markham's *Man with a Hoe* and developed reformist ideas. He began publishing those ideas in 1908, after moving to New York and a career in journalism and social work. In 1908, he met Walter Lippmann and Herbert Croly at the Greenwich Village salon of Mabel Dodge. She was a patroness and painter, who presided over many interactions of art and Indian policy after marrying Antonio Lujan of Taos Pueblo and moving to a huge and hospitable adobe compound next to his ancestral home. Collier was one of many guests there when he was in New Mexico. Following a period in San Francisco, working among Chinese and Japanese immigrants, and thereafter in Washington, he found himself in demand negotiating the interactions of Indian, art, and land policy. His most remarkable insight was his sense that federal policy toward American Indians must be organized around saving "for the Indian, places that are all his own," reversing a long history of expropriation. By the 1930s a generation had taken power in the United States that had not experienced warfare between Indians and non-Indians; it was ready for an Indian New Deal. Roosevelt, Ickes, and Collier were able to rely upon slowly accumulating public support, and although they did not extirpate animosity against Indians, public opinion became increasingly willing to support genuine change in governmental policy toward them. Collier gave an account of his exit interview with Roosevelt in which the president told him that one achievement of his administration in which he "took great pride . . . [was] the new orientation in Indian affairs," and that he was pleased that Collier had not "merely accepted the status quo" but instead had "added to the Indians' worth and dignity by protecting their cultural values, religious freedom, and property rights."[24]

Collier's contributions to the history of conservation and art grew in importance after his partnership with the Chief of the Soil Service, Hugh Hammond Bennett in creating their project on the Navajo Reservation in 1934. It was the second project undertaken by the Soil Service. Photographs taken by artists employed by the Service showed land on the reservation so ravaged by overgrazing as to "have little present value," a message for the nation as a whole imparted with furious effect by Joe Jones's painting of an *American Farm* perched on the brink of an eroded desolation. Overgrazing on the reservation by nearly a million head of livestock had been encouraged by earlier commissioners of the Bureau of Indian Affairs. After 1934, with the backing of the President and Ickes, Collier and Bennett set about restoring the land where that was possible and provided a research station on the

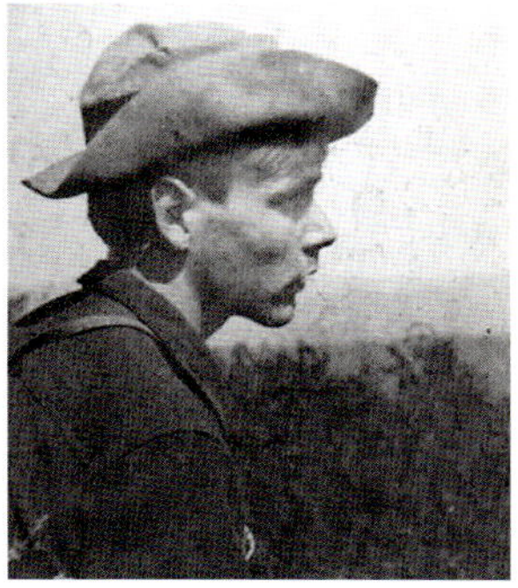

John Collier, 1907

reservation to assist the Navajo to find better ways to sustain themselves.[25]

Ickes and Collier sought every means art might provide to increase the constituency for treating Indians respectfully, situating the Indian Craft Shop at the center of the first floor to remind employees and visitors that Indian painters continue to produce work of high quality. The store has miraculously remained in its place, making its point in the quality of the goods it sells and also in its splendid murals by Allan Houser (Chiricahua Apache) and Gerald Nailor (Navajo). The main cafeteria, downstairs, is mostly a Kiowa gallery, celebrating the harvest with James Auchiah's dancers on the west wall and Stephen Mopope's on the east.

Auchiah and Mopope were two of the "Kiowa Five" of Anadarko, Oklahoma, who earned international reputations (the others were Spencer Asah, Jack Hokeah, and Monroe Tsatoke). The Five were by no means uniform in style, although they often presented starkly delineated figures, with little modeling and less shadow, against large flat planes of High Plains color, contrasting wonderfully with the European perspective of the murals by Nicolai Cikovsky for the Bureau of Reclamation. Opposite a wall of painted yuccas and desert, Cikovsky's reclamation crews are at work along irrigation ditches from which little water-courses emerge at perspective-enabling right angles. The politics of art in the Interior building tended to be subtle: visitors disposed to think of Cikovsky's work only as instructive for art classes might miss a detail conveying a current message: his work crews were desegregated, as were all those in Interior Department murals. When William Gropper painted both black and white hands on the levers being used to pry rocks out of the way of the dam-making he depicted, several congressmen sought to have the mural whitewashed, ostensibly because Gropper had also done cartoons for left-wing magazines.[26]

Ickes's and Collier's theme of the continuing vitality of American Indian cultures in American life was everywhere in the building, but it had its sanctuary on the eighth floor. Far from the hurry and bustle below, reached only by a stairway, it remains the only room in the city of equal interest to James McNeill Whistler's Peacock Room at the Freer Gallery.

The eighth-floor Indian Rooms contain mural masterpieces of Potawatomi life by Woodrow Wilson Crumbo: *Courting*, *Flute Player*, *Peyote Bird*, *Wild Horses*, *Buffalo Hunt*, and an almost abstract *Deer*. On the south and west walls are Gerald Nailor's *The Hunting Ground*, with symbols taken from sand paintings, *Preparing Yarn for Weaving*, and *Initiation Ceremony*. Allan Houser is there, too, with some of his best work: *Singing Love Songs* depicts an Apache love

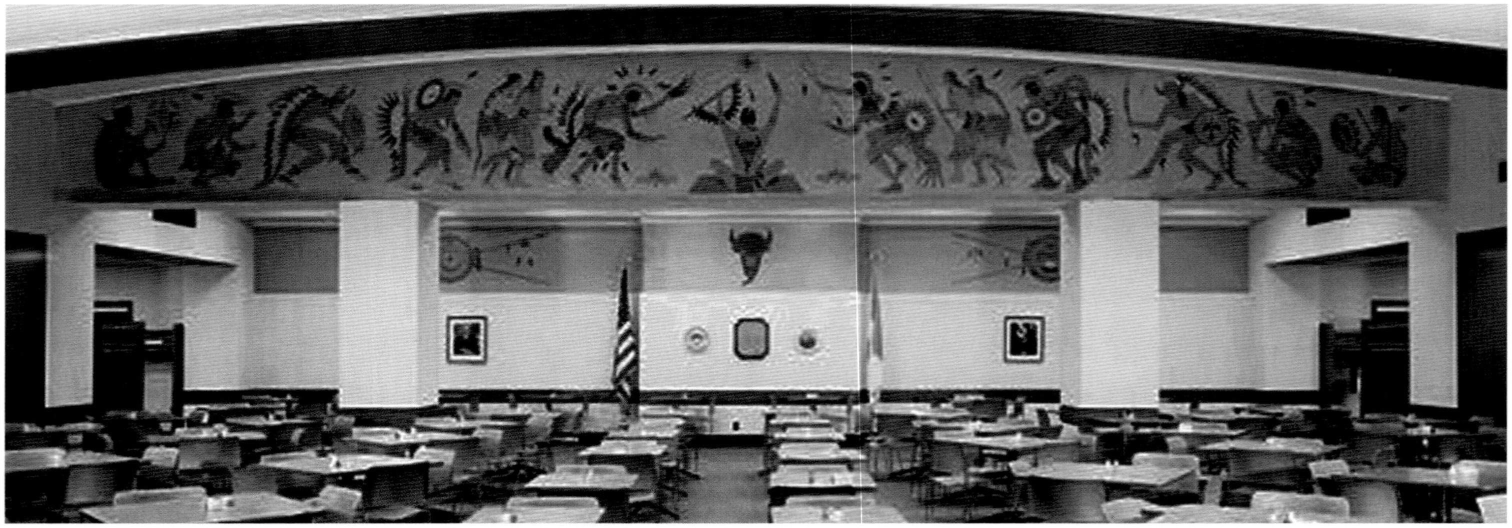

The mural *Ceremonial Dance* on the east wall of the Cafeteria of the Interior Building, Stephen Mopope, 1939

Mopope was a Kiowa—one of "The Kiowa Five." He studied at the University of Oklahoma, and his work was widely exhibited throughout the United States.

story in which the male figure is a singer wooing on horseback—courtly love on the High Plains; the others are *Apache Round Dance* and *Sacred Fire Dance.* Having honored the Apache and Navajo, this magnificent array also includes Velino Herrera's paintings of the people of the pueblos, *Buffalo Dance, Buffalo Chase, Pueblo Woman and Child, Pueblo Corn Dance, Women Making Pottery, Pueblo Girls Carrying Water,* and *Pueblo Symbols*—among them that enigmatic figure the *WPA Guide* identifies as "the sacred clown."[27]

In a third-floor corridor are David McCosh's oils of national parks and cases of objects of art held by the National Park Service. Along the Indian Commissioner's corridor is an oil by Maynard Dixon of a soldier and a robed Plains Indian entitled *Indian and Teacher* and explained by Dixon as representing an agricultural extension agent imparting wisdom about corn planting. Odd. The "student" represents a corn-planting culture thousands of years old, which introduced the crop's cultivation to the ancestors of the "teacher." Dixon was a great artist, but his own teachers had left some things out.

Ickes had urged Bruce that it would be good to show the public and the employees of the Bureau of Indian Affairs something about the systematic exclusion of Indians from the American covenant, perhaps a panel on "woods Indians being uprouted {sic} out of their native . . . {lands} and brutally driven into an arid country by the United States Army"

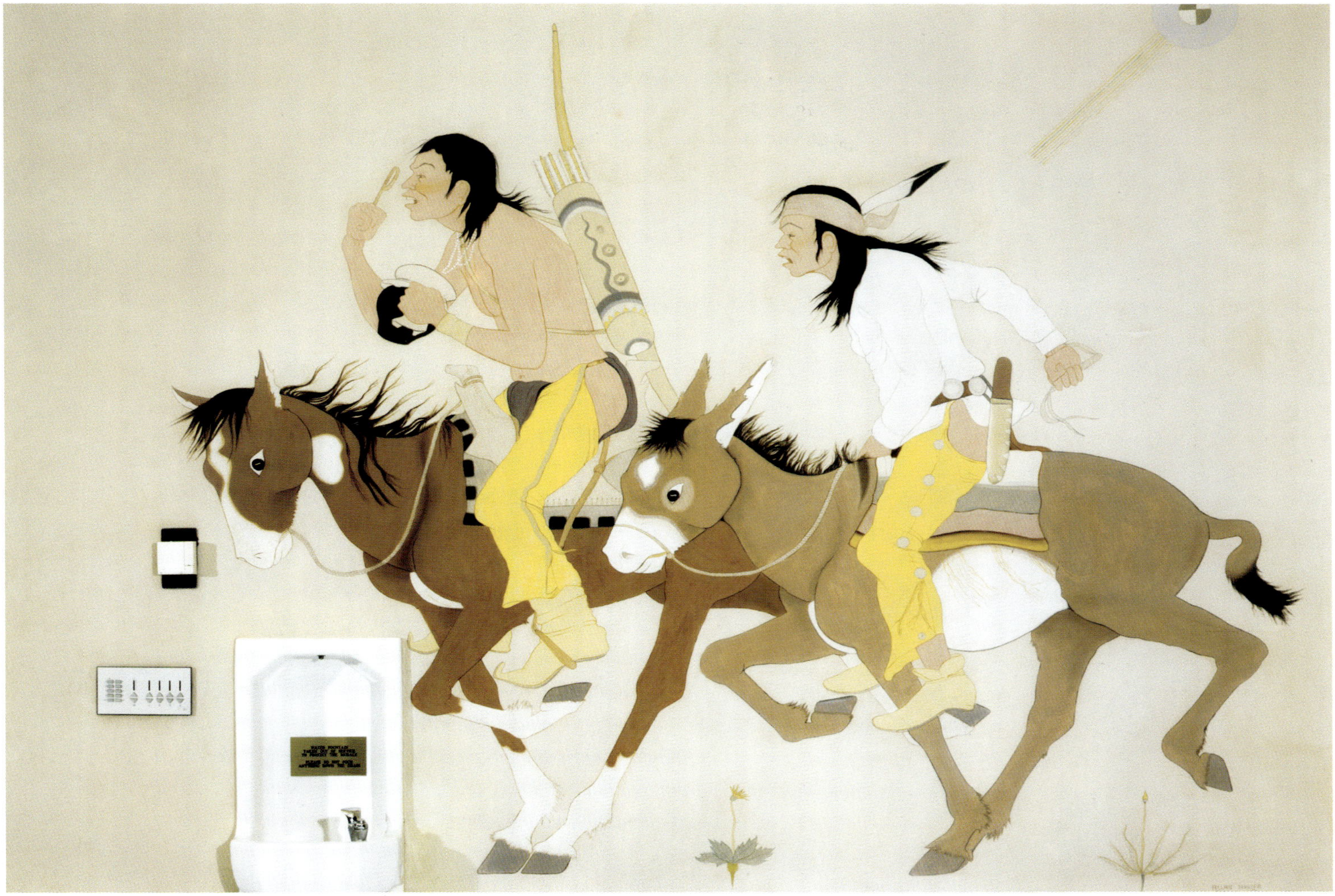

Singing Love Songs (detail)
Allan Cafran Houser, 1939

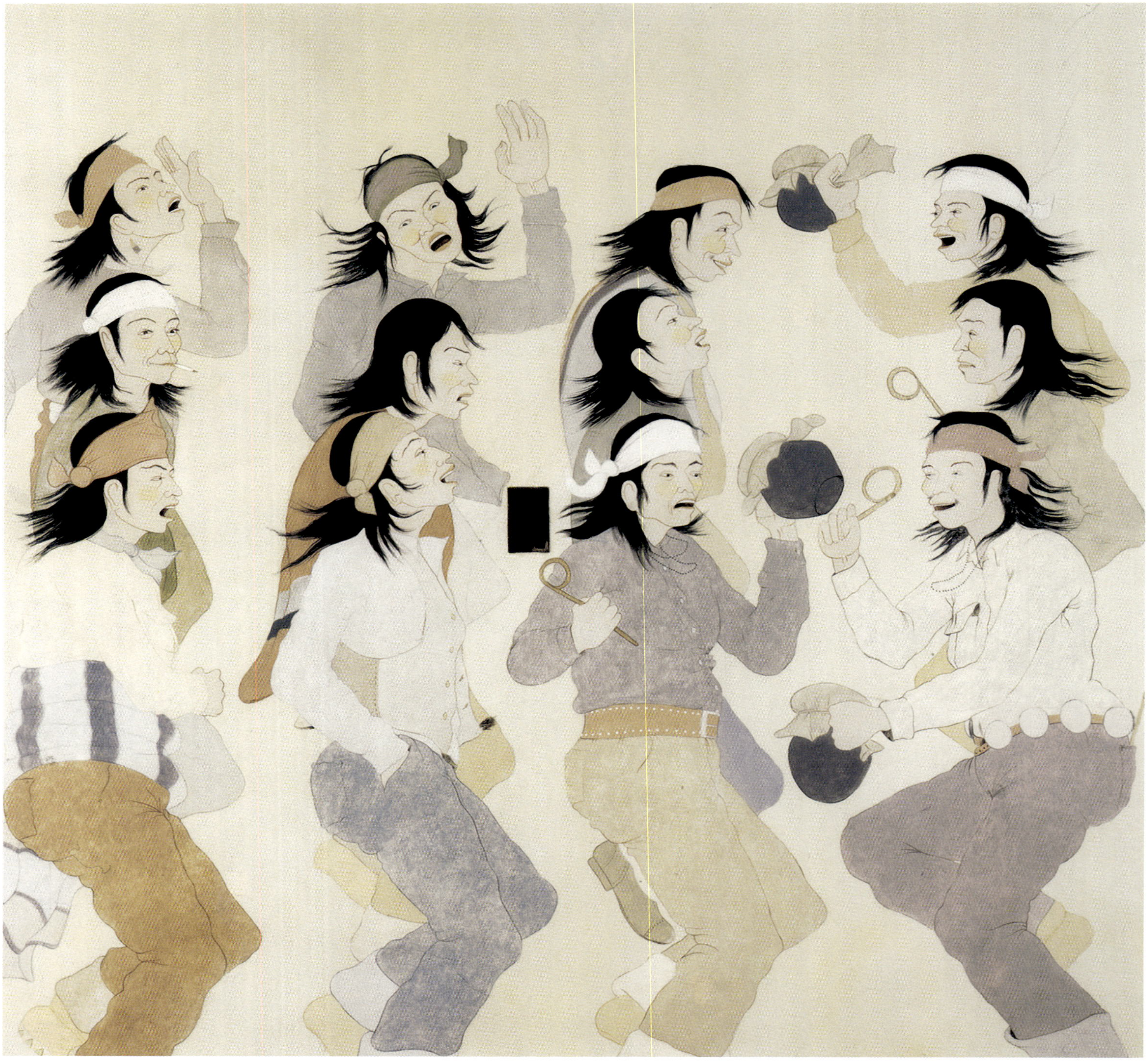

Sacred Fire Dances (detail)
Allan Cafran Houser, 1940

In 1886 the Chiricahua Apaches led by Geronimo surrendered to the U.S. Army in New Mexico and were held as prisoners of war in Florida, Alabama, and Oklahoma until their final release in 1914. Allan Cafran Houser was the first Warm Springs Chiricahua Apache child born out of captivity, in 1914. He grew up on his parents' farm in Oklahoma and began studying painting in 1934 at the Santa Fe Indian School. In 1939 and 1940 he received commissions from the Treasury Section to paint murals in the Department of the Interior in Washington, D.C. He moved to Los Angeles in 1941. In 1947 the Haskell Institute in Lawrence, Kansas, commissioned him to sculpt a memorial in marble to the Haskell students who had died in World War II. Houser taught at the Inter-Mountain Indian School in Utah and at the Institute of American Indian Arts in Santa Fe, where he created the sculpture department. He retired from teaching in 1975 and, until his death in 1994, worked in stone, bronze, and wood. He received the National Medal for the Arts in 1992 and was honored by an inaugural exhibition at the National Museum of the American Indian in 2004.

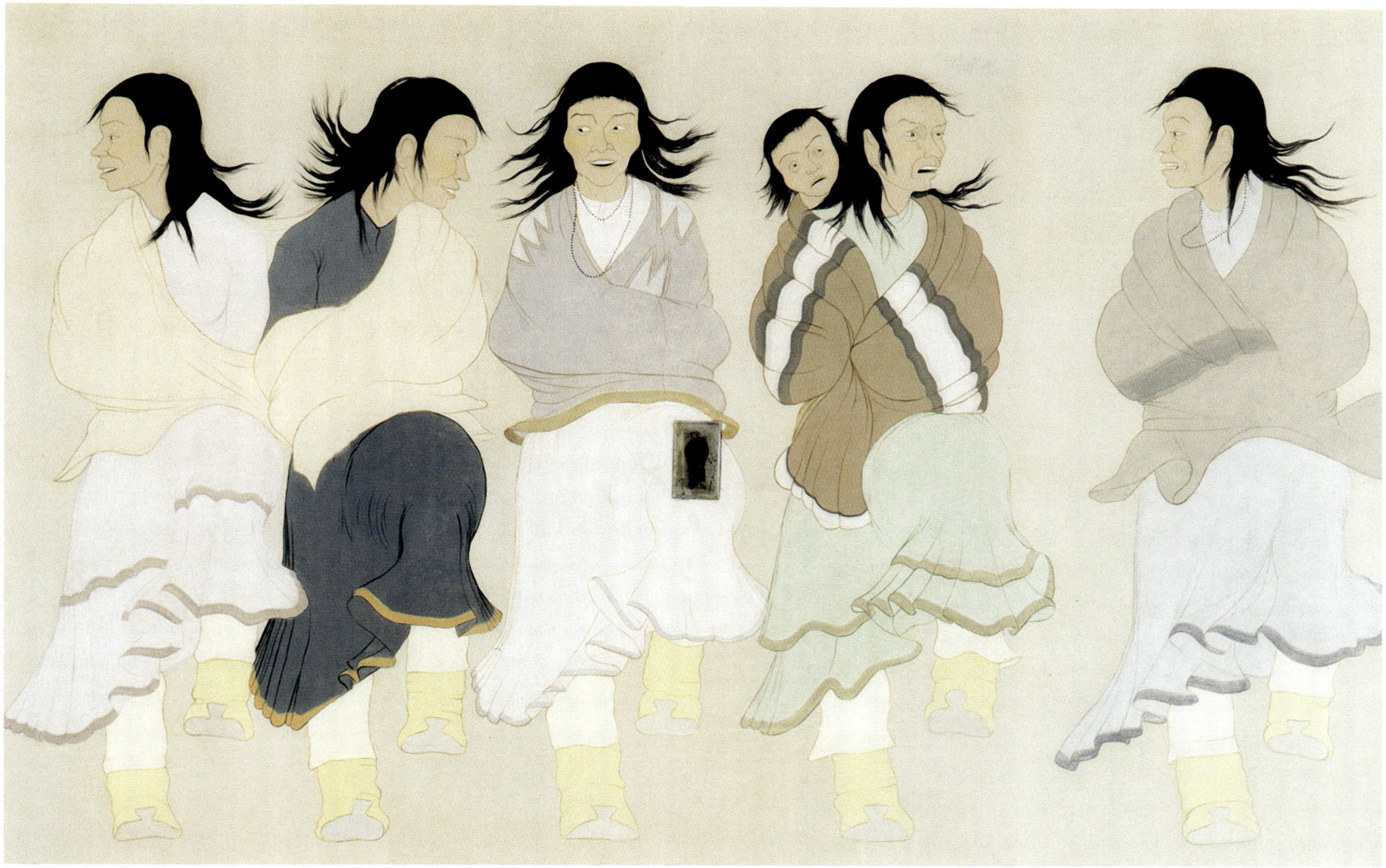

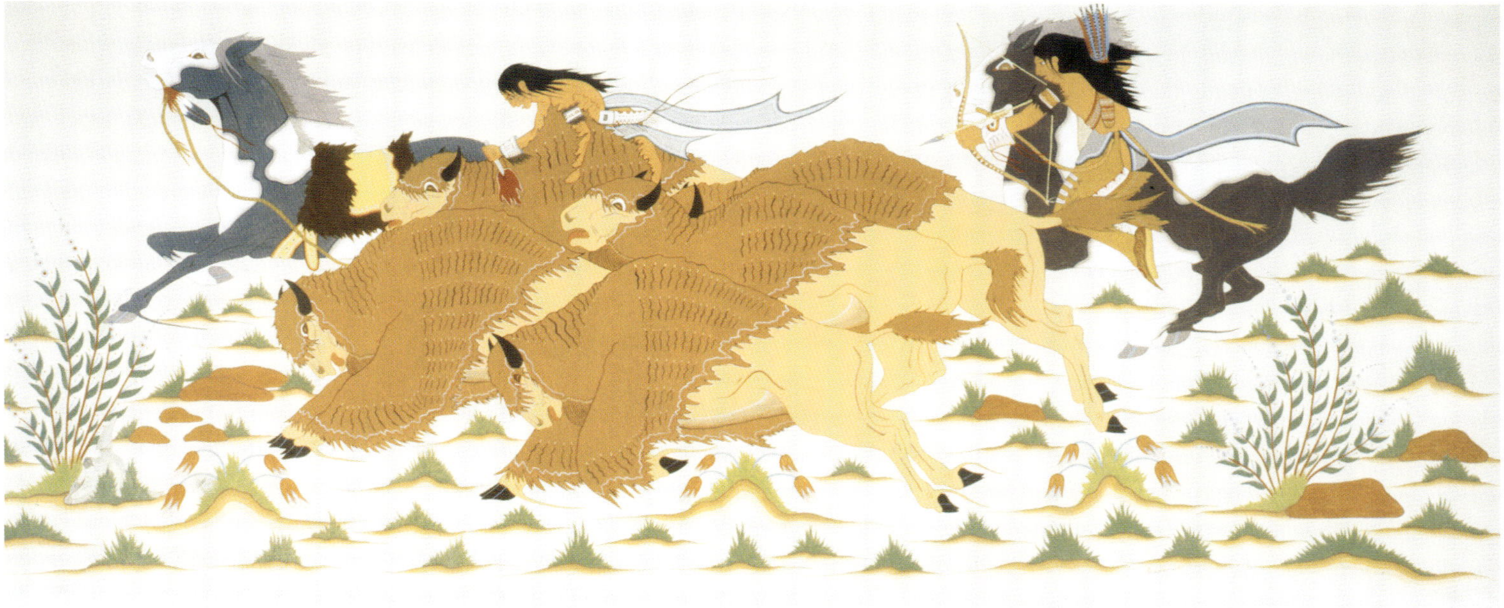

Top:
Apache Round Dance
Allan Cafran Houser, 1940

Bottom:
Buffalo Hunt
Woodrow Wilson "Woody" Crumbo, 1940

Woodrow Crumbo was born in Lexington, Oklahoma, the son of a Creek-Potawatomie mother and a French father. He attended government schools as a child, the American Indian Institute in Wichita, the University of Wichita, and the University of Oklahoma. At the age of twenty-one, he was appointed director of Indian Art at Bacone College in Muskogee, Oklahoma, where he studied Indian design and revived ancient techniques of silverwork, vegetable dying, and weaving.

Crumbo played the cedar wood flute, danced professionally and ceremonially, designed for the Douglas Corporation, and served as curator and administrator of art museums in Tulsa and El Paso. He said of his work, "[I] always painted with the desire of developing Indian art so that it may be judged on art standards rather on its value as a curio—I am attempting to record Indian customs and legends now, while they are alive, to make them a part of the great American culture before these, too, become lost, only to be fragmentarily pieced together by fact and supposition."

and another, contrasting to it, of "the more enlightened treatment of the Indian in our own day." Bruce began sputtering about how "revolting" and "ridiculous" that would be, telling colleagues that in suggesting such things Ickes showed himself to be an "utter vulgarian and ignoramous [sic]." On another occasion, Bruce warned the muralist Frank Mechau that Ickes was "extremely particular about the presentation of the American Indian and does not condone . . . any but the most friendly scenes." Mechau was working on a Section commission for the wall outside the office of Postmaster-General James A. Farley depicting among the *Dangers of the Mail* a lurid scene of Indians scalping nude white women. Mechau went ahead, and for the next seventy years his art has deepened divisions in the community, confronting the Indian employees of the Postal Service with daily reminders of hostile stereotypes, except during interludes in which the murals have been hidden from view. (The building is now the headquarters of the Environmental Protection Agency.)[28]

Secretary Ickes and "Negro Contributions"

The messages conveyed by the murals executed in the Interior building by several painters commissioned by the Section did their assigned tasks. John Steuart Curry's fifth-floor rendering of the Oklahoma Land Rush is as action-packed as a baroque tapestry of a scene from the *Iliad*. Although in Curry's adjacent panel, *The Homesteading and The Building of Barbed Wire Fences*, the new occupants are seen tranquilly establishing themselves. A little quiet contemplation of his land-rush painting suggests that it may have had an ironic subtext. The very violence of the homesteader's assault reminds us of his statement about a similar scene in which he showed his "own ideas about telling the story of pioneers coming into Kansas. I want to paint this [as a] war with nature and I want to paint the things I feel."[29]

An entire wall of the third floor of the Interior building presents Henry Varnum Poor's *Conservation of Wild Life*, which mutes the message even more, though it is there, subtly. Henry David Thoreau and Jean-Jacques Audubon appear among migrating birds, waterfalls, salt flats, and animals, in a scene of an Edenic "before," while in the implied "after," earnest departmental employees restock streams following overfishing, one must assume, and tending waterfowl to replace overhunting.

Harold Ickes saw to it that most of the art in the Interior building communicated the New Deal message. The PWA and WPA work crews depicted in its murals were integrated, although work crews generally were not in the 1930s. Ickes wanted such lessons to be taught, although that meant rejecting several of the first proposals made to him by Bruce and Bruce's deputy at the Section, Edward Rowan. For a place of honor—and teaching—close to the main first-floor staircase, Bruce and Rowan had offered a set of murals by Millard Sheets on *Air, Fire, Land,* and *Water*. The reply was that there were plenty of other places to learn about airplanes, irrigation canals, or blast furnaces. The purpose of the art was to work at emboldening employees—and who would be emboldened to work harder at anything important by exposure to such innocuous stuff? Why should murals not instead show the "advancement which has been made by the 'Negro'"? Might they not "depict Howard University . . . or the contributions which Negroes have made toward science, literature, and art?"[30]

Bruce admitted that within the Interior Department building, Ickes, was "bound to lick us," yet even there some subtleties revealed more of Bruce's view of life than Ickes's. The four murals ultimately produced by Sheets depicted all *The Negro's Contributions* as occurring in segregated settings. The panels on *The Negro's Contribution to the Social and Cultural Development of America: The Arts* did offer the departmental employee some images of Black Americans working at some dignified jobs into which their "contributions" had recently been welcomed. But "Negro art" was presented as song and dance, with a dancer fixing her garter on the way to join a banjo player for a vaudeville performance. This was as far as Sheets, Rowan, and Bruce could extend their appreciation of what black Americans had accomplished in the arts by 1939, the year of Marian Anderson's concert at the

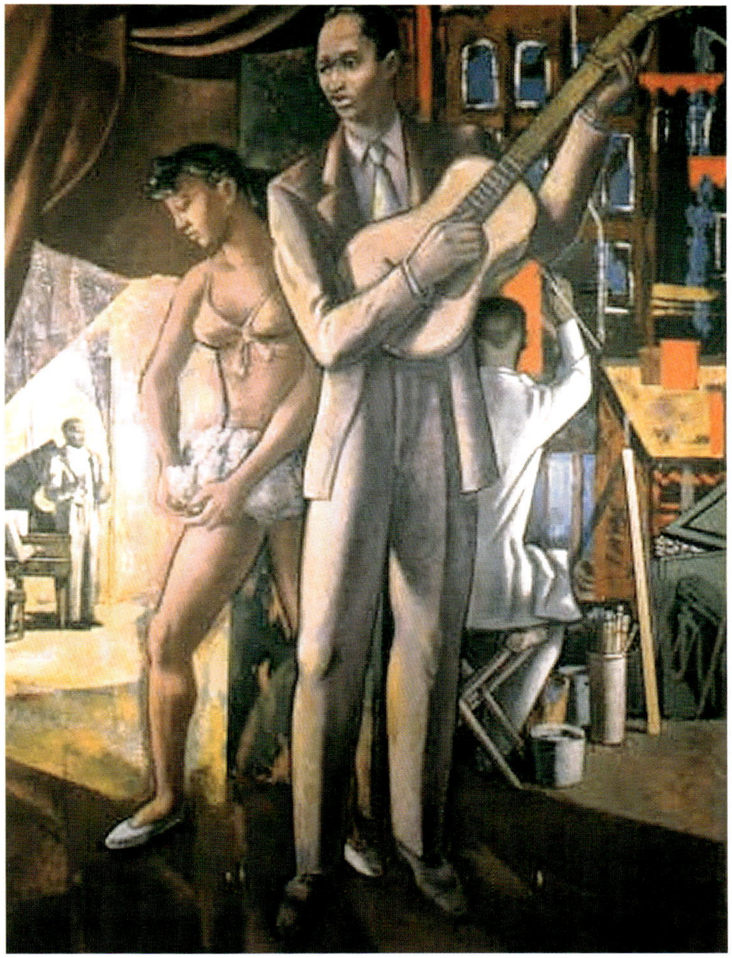

The Negro's Contribution to the Social and Cultural Development of America: The Arts

Millard Owen Sheets was commissioned to create this series of four works in 1939 by the Treasury Section; it was installed in 1948, in the time of Paul Robeson, Marian Anderson, and Duke Ellington (see main text). The Glickman statue and the Jamieson mural of Marian Anderson better represent the arts working for the New Deal.

Lincoln Memorial, three years after the success of the black *Macbeth* of the Negro Theatre Unit for the WPA, and while the career of Paul Robeson was in full flower. There were many well-known African American easel painters who might have merited a collegial nod—even generically. Sheets asserted that he had "high regard for and feeling about the Negro" and that he "had tried to show that the Negro himself will be treated sympathetically and in no way caricaturized."[31]

That satisfied neither the self-emancipating fervor of people of African descent, expressed in their own art, nor the support and respect for their efforts, expressed by Ickes and by New Deal artists, discussed in the final chapters of his book. The Roosevelt administration was more vigorous in returning to the spirit of Abraham Lincoln than any other since Reconstruction. Although it was not vigorous enough to satisfy the aspirations of Roosevelt, and far too laggard in performance to meet the standards of his wife, it did welcome the work of the arts to advance the cause of Civil Rights.

Sometimes those efforts seemed too subtle to matter much, but wherever he could, Franklin Roosevelt—like Harold Ickes—used art to show that African Americans, many of them the descendants of slaves, belonged within the American covenant, and that they, like all other citizens, should have the attention of government. For a man of Roosevelt's background, it was especially appropriate to show that those who were descended from masters and who had remained powerful and fortunate, should advance through art a tradition of justice and mercy close to home. Which brings us back to Hyde Park and Dutchess County, by way of the Justice Department.

Chapter Three

Actionable Art

"Franklin Roosevelt at Hyde Park" . . . is not just a pictorial history of my husband. It is the story of a whole era that has passed. Few people in the future will live the kind of life depicted in this book but the record will be there, and I think it is well for us to remember that out of this kind of living came great democratic leaders.
(Eleanor Roosevelt in "My Day," March 18, 1949)[1]

We need to know what kind of firm ground other men, belonging to generations before us, have found to stand on.
(John Dos Passos, 1941)[2]

Society Freed Through Justice
George Biddle, 1936

George Biddle studied painting in France and Mexico. He became a muralist, landscape painter, and a gifted social caricaturist in the Hogarthian tradition, who could mercilessly caricature the pretensions of hypocrites and opponents to social reform. He was not a "WPA artist"–he was successful on his own as a teacher, independently wealthy by Depression-era standards, was widely exhibited, and provided the illustrations for the libretto of George Gershwin's opera *Porgy and Bess*. In 1936 he was commissioned by the Treasury Department's Section on Fine Arts to paint five murals for the stair corridor of the Department of Justice Building, and in 1939 the Section selected him to do three more for the New Brunswick, New Jersey, post office–conventional Revolutionary War scenes. The Justice Department

THE MURALS AT THE ENTRANCE to the law library in the Justice Department building are strong medicine, strong enough to have required protection from those critics who regarded them as too radical in theme and not pretty enough. That protection came from a commission including Justice Harlan F. Stone of the United States Supreme Court. A man of strong opinions about the role of art in community and the role of law in democracy, Justice Stone rallied to the support of George Biddle's choice of subject: "Society Freed Through Justice—The Tenement and Sweatshop of Yesterday Can Be the Life Planned with Justice of Tomorrow." Nor was he willing to accede to demands that the "ornamentation" of the Justice Department building be without depiction of conditions requiring remedy by governmental intervention. As Stone understood, Biddle was making the point that where life is hard, justice is especially necessary.

Justice Stone "rode the circuit," as the justices did in those days, and found plenty of evidence in the cases before him that the nation needed a New Deal. Sometimes those cases were grim, illustrating the need to arouse the public to give support to judicial enforcement of laws. In other places on his circuit, Justice Stone came into communities in which constituencies were being built by art that drew people together around the themes of the affirmative New Deal. In the depressed Dust Bowl town of Big Spring, Texas, he saw a mural by Peter Hurd that confirmed art's capacity to build confidence in community action. "What a lovely composition the Hurd mural is," he wrote, "how important it is that the humble people of this country should be impressed with the fact that the artist finds beauty and dignity in their life, and one of the many things we need to be taught in this country is that our lives, however simple or humble, may be both beautiful and dignified."[3]

President Franklin Delano Roosevelt did not issue pronouncements about what he liked and disliked in art, but he showed what he hoped art might accomplish when he personally directed the architecture of the six post offices built by the New Deal along the central Hudson River and the subjects of the murals to be painted within them. It is a safe guess that he was well aware of the selection of his young friend Olin Dows to paint the murals at Rhinebeck (1940) and Hyde Park (1941). Dows was his neighbor and kinsman, and the record is clear that when Dows depicted Roosevelt in them he showed the President as the President wished to be depicted. Roosevelt also expressed strong views about the murals at Beacon (1937), Poughkeepsie (1937), Wappingers Falls (1940), and Ellenville (1942). Taken together, the New Deal murals in these six towns set forth unifying themes of the history of the region and—with remarkable inclusiveness for the time—its people.

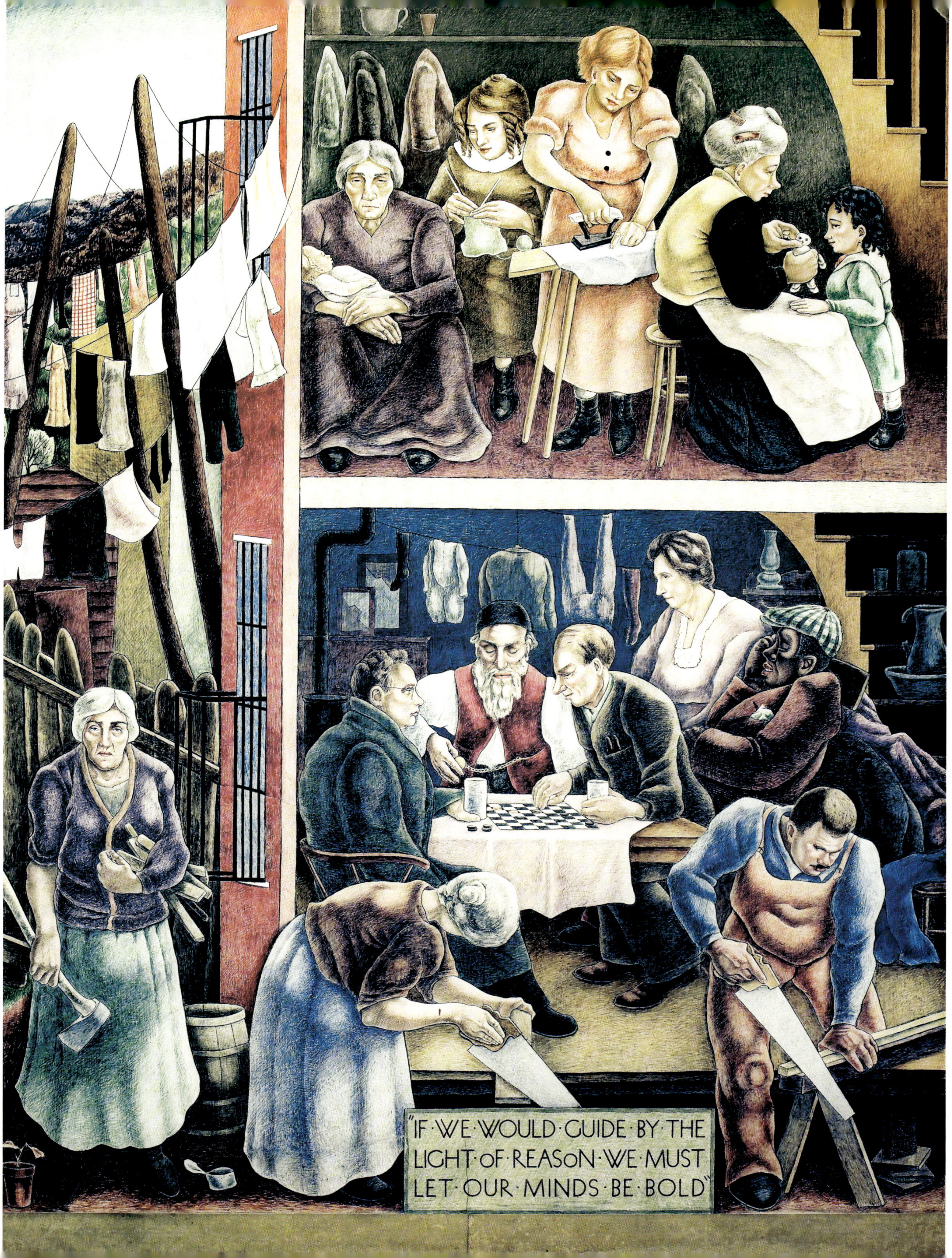

murals were not at all conventional. Their primary theme, captioned by Biddle himself, was that the sweatshops and tenements he showed in grim detail could be redeemed by justice. Though this was a thoroughly hopeful and patriotic New Deal message, it was decried as "intrinsically un-American" because Biddle's style was so manifestly influenced by that of left-wing Mexican muralists and because many of the people identifiable in his Justice Department murals were New Dealers. Biddle painted himself working a sewing machine in a sweatshop, with Secretary of Labor Frances Perkins at hand to help; the Treasury Section's assistant director is there, too, and in another is Biddle's brother Francis, soon to become Attorney General (see main text).

During World War II, Biddle served as chairman of the War Department's Art Advisory Committee and as a combat artist in Algeria, Tunisia, Sicily, and Italy (see main text).

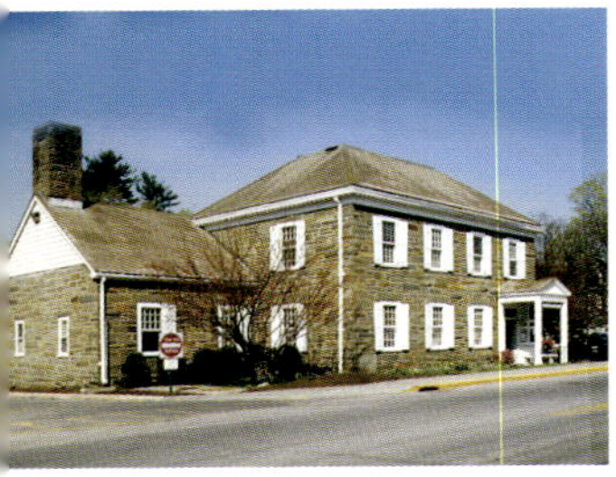

Above:
Post Office, Hyde Park, New York, 1940

Hudson River valley post office murals executed under the direct supervision of President Franklin Roosevelt (see main text) and for the Treasury Section.

Top right:
Franklin D. Roosevelt and the Hyde Park School Board reviewing plans for the Roosevelt High School
Olin Dows, 1940
Post Office, Hyde Park, New York

Middle:
Harvest festival with black young man gathering grain.
Olin Dows, 1939
Post Office, Rhinebeck, New York

Bottom:
Slaves loading ship
Olin Dows, 1940
Post Office, Rhinebeck, New York

Roosevelt chose the sites for each building and the local prototypes he wished the architecture of each to emulate. He selected their materials, directed the configuration of their stonework, checked the stain colors of their woodwork, and personally approved their working drawings as he had in 1926 when he provided instructions to the architect of the James Roosevelt Memorial Library, Henry J. Toombs. After that experience Toombs was puckish enough to substitute Roosevelt's name for his own on the drawings he gave for publication to *Life* magazine, signing himself only as "Assistant." In 1939, as Roosevelt and Dows were readying themselves for their final work together, the President instructed Rear Admiral Christian J. People, who was in charge of the work, that the post office at Wappingers Falls was to be designed according to his wishes—just like the others. The admiral had been a major figure in New Deal relief operations—and knew his client.[4]

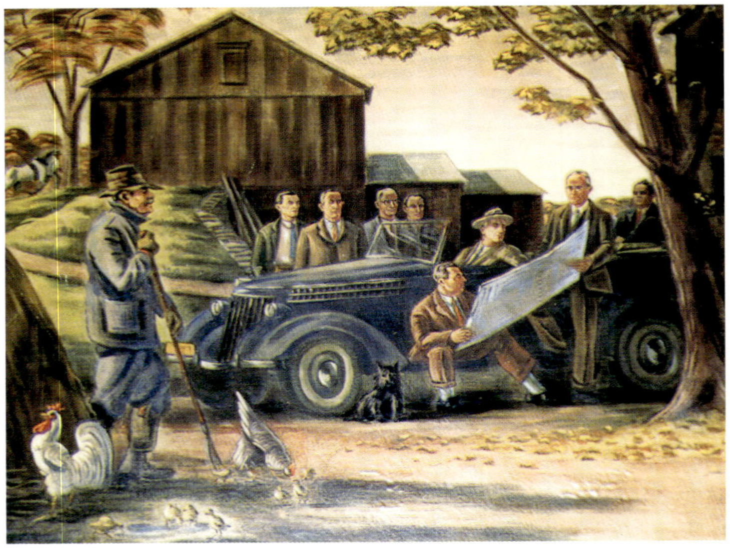

These six projects were built midway between New York City and Albany in a smiling land of great estates, dairy farms, orchards, and market villages. People like the Roosevelts and the Dows spoke of "the river" as a place of healing and recovery—as others spoke of "the Cape" or "the

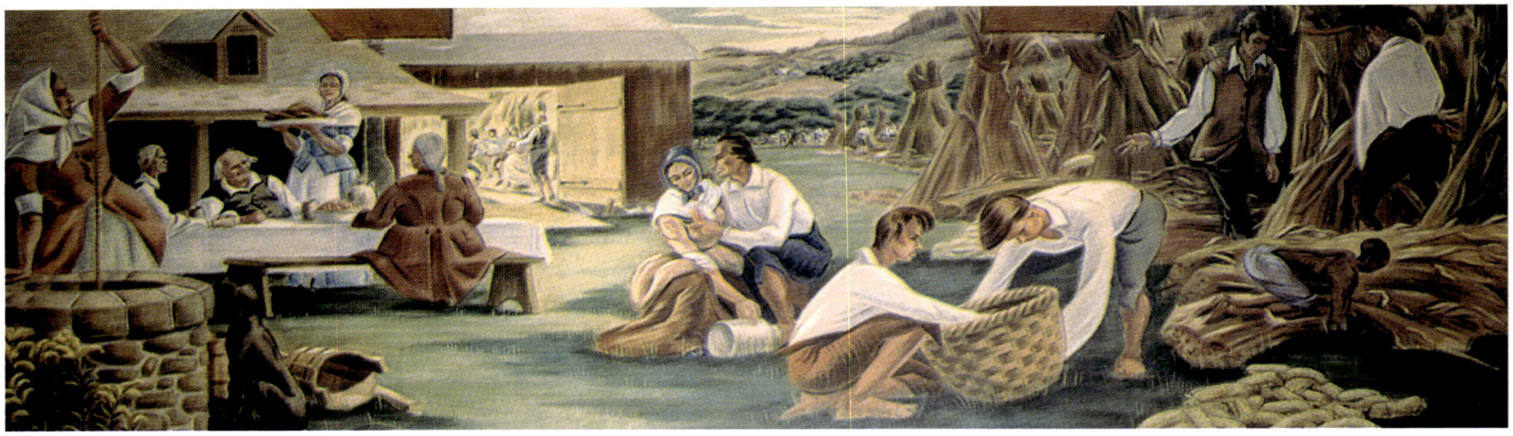

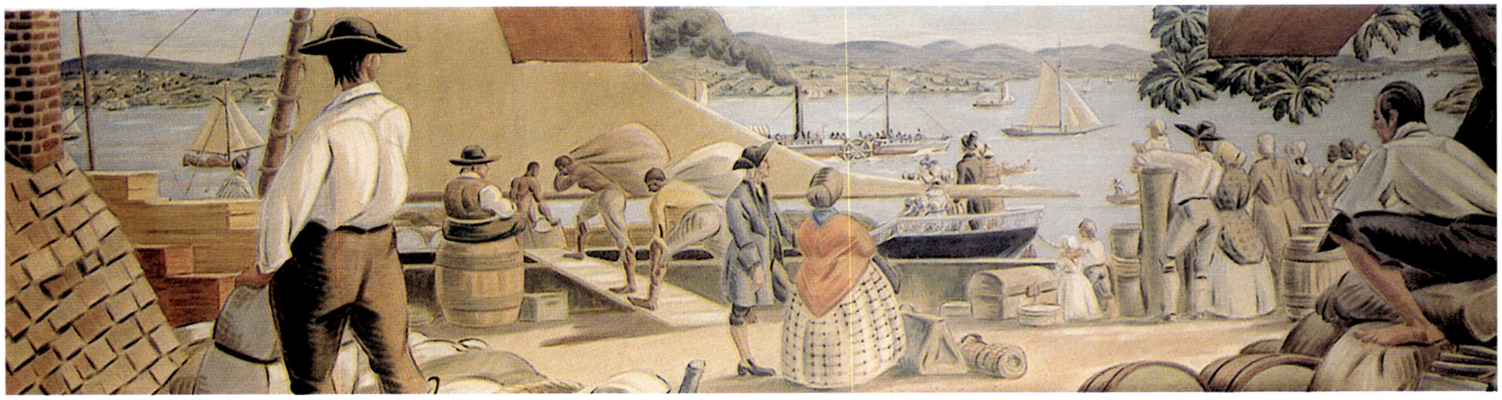

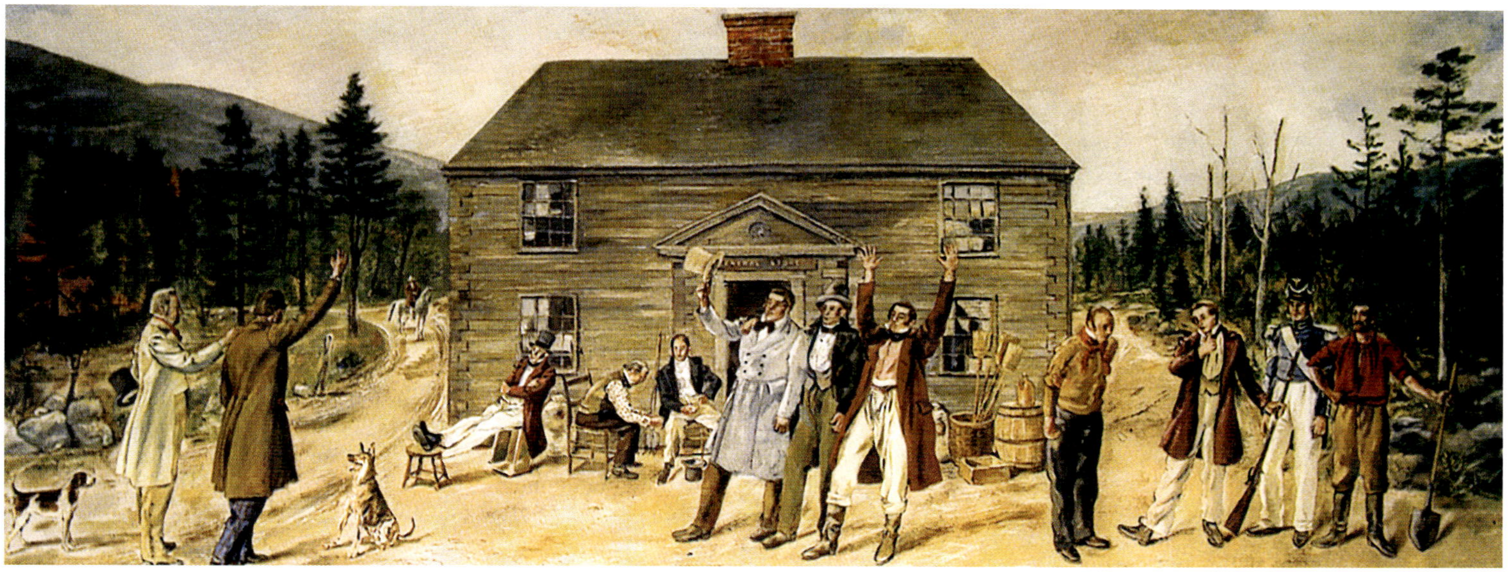

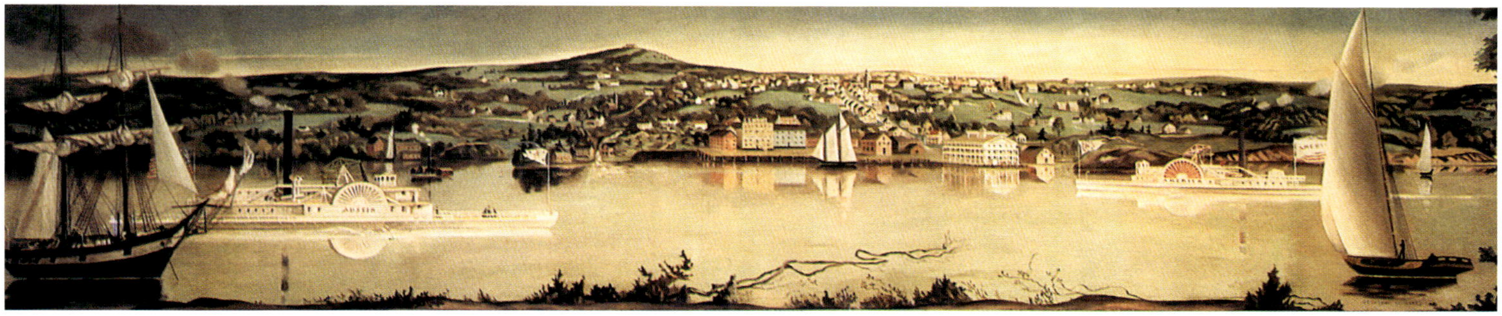

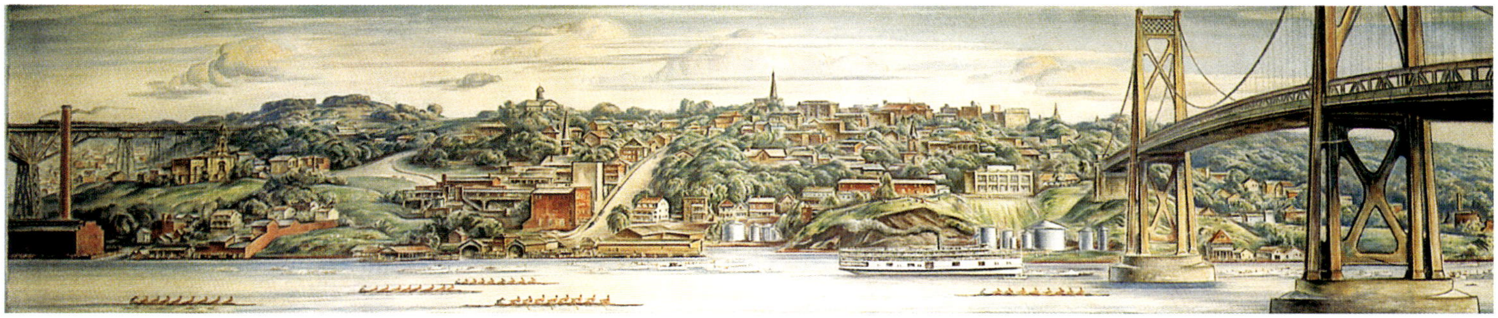

Top:
Establishment of the first post office in Ellenville, New York, 1823
Louis Bouché, 1942
Ellenville, New York

Louis Bouché was trained in Paris and painted murals for Radio City Music Hall and for the Section for the Justice Department and Interior buildings in Washington.

Middle:
View of the Village of Poughkeepsie in 1839
Georgina Klitgaard, 1940
Post Office, Poughkeepsie, New York

Georgina Klitgaard was a New York landscapist trained at Barnard College and the National Academy of Design. She painted another Hudson River valley mural for the Section in the post office at Goshen, New York. When she undertook the larger one for Poughkeepsie, she came under constant supervision from the President, who insisted upon changes in her depiction of boats on the river to make them historically accurate; in each instance he was correct.

Bottom:
Contemporary View of the Village of Poughkeepsie
Charles Rosen, 1939
For the Treasury Section: Post Office Poughkeepsie, New York
(see main text)

Charles Rosen headed the Art Students League of the New York Summer School at Woodstock, New York, and in 1937 was commissioned by TRAP—not the Section—to paint a mural for the post office at Beacon, New York.

lake." In the murals in the two post offices closest to the Roosevelt estate, and in a book of sketches published in 1949, Olin Dows depicted life at "the river" as both native sons experienced it, in the sunny years before the great wars and the Depression. Eleanor Roosevelt recalled in 1946, after her husband's death, that "life here had always a healing quality for him," characteristically proceeding to express the generous hope that its solace would also be felt by "those who come to see the surroundings in which he grew to maturity." They might quietly explore his library and his home, and pause at his grave, that "peaceful resting place behind the high hedge with flowers blooming around it." There they might come to "understand the rest and peace and strength which he had gained here and perhaps learn to come, and go away with some sense of healing and courage themselves."[5]

Healing and courage were Roosevelt's messages to the nation, not as princely or messianic gifts but as shared achievements arising from belonging and participating. Roosevelt saw to it that the Hudson Valley post office murals were not merely elegiac images of life among the proprietors of the great estates in the prewar years, for if they were merely nostalgic, like Dows's sketches of the Roosevelts' life at Hyde Park, they might only call to mind an "era that has passed," Mrs. Roosevelt wrote in her syndicated newspaper column "My Day" in 1949. "Few people in the future will live the kind of life." Because so few had lived that way even in the past, Roosevelt saw to it that Dows and the other muralists made certain that "the record" be composed to include Indians, blacks, tenants and farm laborers, along with magnates, lawn parties, and mansions. Having all these images together, Mrs. Roosevelt wrote of Dows's sketches, would help "us to remember that out of this kind of living came great democratic leaders."[6]

In the eighteenth century, "the river" had a Tidewater social structure, including slavery. Although the central Hudson Valley lies too far north for the cultivation of plantation crops such as cotton, indigo, sugar, or rice, slaves were brought to the valley by the Dutch. Some were put to work in grain fields and orchards, and some served as domestic servants in grand establishments such as those of the Livingstons. New York commenced emancipation in the 1790s—thanks largely to Alexander Hamilton, Aaron Burr, and John Jay—but some landowners were buying "fresh" slaves as late as the 1820s. Sixty or more African American families remained, invisible to some, neighbors for others, appearing in Dows's murals among the people of the community to whom art gave attention. They were part of "our community's past," a past, he wrote, that helped "shape our ideas." Many of the murals showed blacks and whites working together, and Jacobus Stoutenburgh's sons are seen working beside his slaves to clear land. A school for black children is shown in a fishing scene, a free black sexton of St. James's Church brings paint for its repair, and other blacks pick fruit. At Rhinebeck they join in husking corn, making brick, and loading ships.

The dramatic climax of Dows's murals offers an actionable past, showing what an eighteenth-century "democratic leader" might be doing in such a mixed community. Dr. Samuel Bard is shown treating a black worker who has been badly burned in a fire that has destroyed a house—probably the black man's—as the doctor's son adds light with a lantern and his son-in-law, the rector of St. James's, supports the patient and comforts his wife. The doctor was famous in the neighborhood as an abolitionist who had "shaped his ideas" about slavery as an institution full of "inherent evils" having the most "injurious effects." Dows's explanation of the panel pointed out that the son-in-law went on to become a professional shaper of ideas as the first professor of political philosophy at King's College (Columbia University).[7]

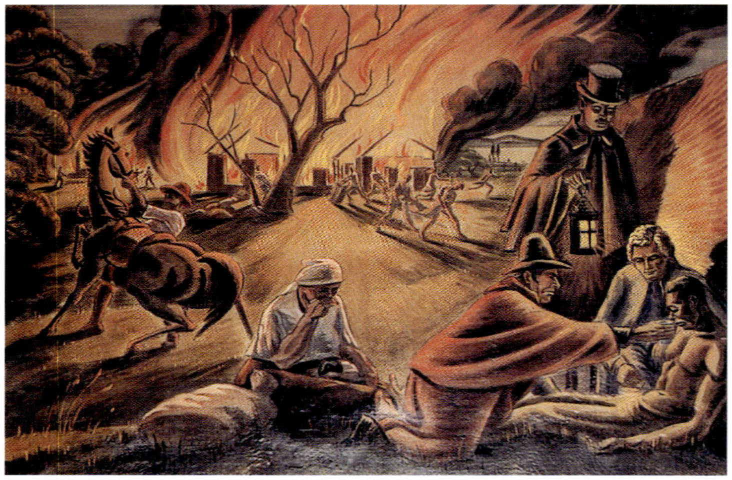

Drs. Bard and McVickar tending a black man, perhaps a slave, perhaps a freeman, injured in a fire. Olin Dows, 1940 Post Office, Hyde Park, New York

Art in Context

The land, too, needed healing. Dows showed Dr. Bard and his brother experimenting with restorative agriculture in the 1780s. In another, Roosevelt was depicted as a young man joining with his neighbor Archibald Rogers to clear land for scientific forestry. The proprietors of some of the great estates had been for many years applying German, French, and British experience to nursing land back to health after overgrazing and erosive cultivation. But needful landscapes lay on the uplands in each direction. The granite peaks and sphagnum bogs of the Adirondacks lie northwestward, scarred by lumbermen's fires and brief, unsuccessful intrusions to raise merino sheep. These mountains are not hospitable to agriculture. Their granite and chalky limestone lie too close to the surface for easy cultivation, and they can be very cold in winter. Until the 1820s, however, the mountains had been a refuge for escaping slaves and for tenants seeking escape from the rack-renting of the manor lords, whose only other recourse had been the night-riding posses, barn-burnings, and riots shown in other New Deal post office murals.

In his post office murals at Rhinebeck and Hyde Park, Dows made another point: most of the Indians of the valley were agricultural, settled people—settled for a very long time. In his scene of the arrival of Henry Hudson he showed a petroglyph to underline the point: that the truly "old settlers" and "old families" were Indians. As other murals suggested, their resistance to later, European settlers required the Dutch to build the fortress-houses that became the forms for post offices designed under Franklin Roosevelt's direction. The social order so established was still manifested in the presence of great landowners in the 1930s—of Van Rensselaers and Livingstons (who were Scottish Protestant refugees "naturalized" as Dutch citizens) and their kinsmen bearing other patronymics, such as Roosevelt, Biddle, and Olin.

The escarpment of the Hudson Highlands lies to the south, a psychological barrier to the moods and habits of the big city. In 1910, when Franklin Roosevelt took over the management of the badly eroded Hyde Park estate, the ecology was precarious but the social order seemed serene. But that, as Eleanor Roosevelt observed, was a "whole era that has passed." It lasted long enough, however, to have its quiet assurances, as she acknowledged when she noted that part of her husband's "great affection for Olin Dows . . . as well as for Olin Dows's mother" arose from their being among "the people who loved 'the river' as much as he did himself, and whose associations went far back into the lives of their forebears." Their comforts were gathered in mansions, some of them built in the effulgent eighteenth century, and some, including "Southlands," the house in which Dows grew to manhood, built in the twentieth on land owned by the family since the seventeenth. Another "family place" was Callendar House, where the twenty-year-old Olin Dows painted filigrees of academic flowers in his first mural commission, and where Franklin Roosevelt was said to have proposed marriage to his distant cousin Eleanor. "Southlands" was described by his friend Thomas Wolfe, in his novel *Of Time and the River* as a "great white house, set delicate and gleaming in frail morning light upon a noble hill that swept back from the river, and it was shaded by the silent stature of great trees, and a vast sward of velvet lawn swept round it, and morning was always there and the tender purity of light."[8]

In the depressed 1930s, some of the great houses were shuttered. Others went unpainted. The towns lost business, and jobs. When the press corps came along on the President's tour of the site of the new post office in the tired and depressed old mill town of Wappingers Falls on November 18, 1939, he suggested that their "architectural reporting" include some reference to its mural of the town when it "was a very big and very important manufacturing center . . . with cotton mills and waterpower all harnessed." One reporter with an eye for the negative noted that "Wappingers" did "not look any too prosperous." It had been six years since the first New Deal help had arrived, and no one was starving. Roosevelt replied: "It is a lot better than it used to be."[9]

The president-patron had no interest in art for its own sake or in history that had no message for present action. When he could decide among styles, he turned to an actionable historic realism, answering a national aspiration stated by the novelist John Dos Passos: "We need to know what kind of firm ground other men, belonging to generations before us, have found to stand on." Olin Dows understood that. He took the jobs because, he said, he wished to have a hand in enhancing "our sense of history . . . Great art is a living record . . . Most important it helps form and shape our beliefs" about what community is, and ought to be.[10]

Dows did not require instruction about what a community is. Throughout his career, whether painting scenes in Mexico, France, or wartime Germany, he did so with scrupulous honesty, often implying, when those scenes were ugly, the possibility of remedial action. And in his work in his "home town," he wrote, he welcomed the President's suggestions of "subjects" and "improvements" because the work was improved by Roosevelt's "extraordinary knowledge of local history"—including its shadows.[11]

Precedents in the Midwest

The New Deal mural programs for local post offices often served the restorative purpose of drawing upon local history to re-nucleate community in restored confidence. To achieve that end, the history depicted had to be accurate or it would have had no nucleating power. National history may impart a message through the symbolic or the typical, but local art must be felt to be true. The Hudson River mural program had ample precedent in the Midwest; in the 1920s and 1930s, Grant Wood led a school of muralists in Iowa, as did John Steuart Curry in Wisconsin. Sponsorship for art had been largely private, though its purposes had often been public. Country banks in Iowa and Wisconsin, as in Ohio, Indiana, Illinois, and Minnesota, housed informal museums of local and regional art, and the bank building itself became an art form. Genius ennobled commerce in the Progressive Era from 1905 until postwar "normalcy" set in. Louis Sullivan and George Grant Elmslie created one of the nation's true masterpieces at Owatonna, Minnesota; a little later Elmslie, another student of Sullivan's, William Gray Purcell, and George Maher created other jewel-box banks in nearby Winona. Their murals, terra-cotta, stained glass, bronze sculpture, and carved wood made it an adventure to get in the buggy or the gas-buggy to visit the bank. Check-cashing and depositing could be life-enriching experiences in Owatonna, Winona, Sydney, Grinnell, Columbus (Wisconsin), Mason City, LeRoy, Adams, Hector, Rhinelander, Grand Meadow, and Cedar Rapids. Extraordinarily good bank buildings were produced by other architects for Poseyville, Indiana, and Pierz, Minnesota.

The ideology inspiring this Progressive work presaged that expressed in the New Deal arts program, as art worked

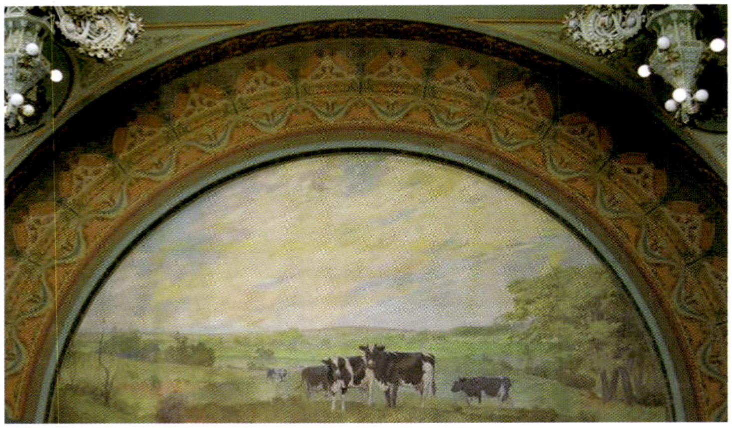

Cows in the Field
Oskar Gross, 1909
Mural in the National Farmers' Bank building in Owatonna, Minnesota

The Owatonna Bank, designed by Louis Sullivan with assistance from George Elmslie, is America's Parthenon, a masterpiece of symbiotic arts—architecture, mural painting, terra-cotta, and stained glass—set accessibly before a public that was ennobled by it. Sullivan, Elmslie, and the muralists, mosaicists, and stained-glass artisans they commissioned, anticipated the New Deal's recognition of the importance of a reciprocal relationship between artists and their communities. Oskar Gross was a Viennese portrait painter and landscapist whose two murals in the Austro-Hungarian State Buildings at the 1900 World's Fair in Paris caught the attention of Sullivan and Daniel H. Burnham. They urged him to come to the United States to work with them on murals and decoration for their buildings. The only surviving examples of that work in 2009 were a mural in a bank in Dwight, Illinois, a mosaic in a building on South Dearborn Street in Chicago, and the two murals, "Cows in the Field" and "Farming Scene," for Sullivan at Owatonna.

in and for community. The jewel-box banks functioned as the modems, switching stations, and junction boxes of the community, as the post offices did for the New Deal era. In the 1930s, when the leaders of New Deal arts programs sought local people in the grain-producing states to set the tone for post office murals, they could count on bankers who had already shown their sophisticated interest in putting the arts to work for their communities. Even amid bank failures, crop failures, and depression they were still in town, respected, and able to be of aid.

Those who created community arts and science councils often turned not only to bankers but also to the remaining local proprietors of department stores for advice and financial support. Like local banks and post offices, locally owned department stores often functioned as gathering places and their owners as patrons of art both on the premises and in their homes. The Kaufmanns of Pittsburgh come especially to mind because the magnificent murals they commissioned for their store, like the jewel-box bank murals, had the community-building role of New Deal murals in post offices. In 1926 the Kaufmanns engaged Boardman Robinson to give the mezzanine of a department store the function of a town square, as the New Deal murals provided nuclei for civic life in a thousand other cities and villages. Robinson produced *A History of Commerce*—murals in the art deco mode. They did exactly what their patrons needed and desired, making trade itself elegant in a succession of scenes of trading towns and merchant traders, with Pittsburgh as their culmination, with its construction cranes and rising buildings painted in auto-body colors. His clients were people of very high standards: they were patrons of Frank Lloyd Wright for their Pennsylvania country house, "Fallingwater," and of Wright's student Richard Neutra for their winter home in Palm Springs, California.[12]

Art and Action

The great opportunity for art to enable effective citizenship came in the 1930s. There was work to do. A sick society to be healed. A world to change in practical, lasting ways. A New Deal to advance. George Biddle's Department of Justice murals *Society Freed Through Justice* commence with circumstances requiring remedy, such as the tenement and sweatshop of yesterday, and conclude with scenes of redemption. A new home for a worker redeemed by just laws is open to a better future. Trees are being planted around it. A New Deal kind of justice is shown to justify hope and hard work. Biddle painted another believer in such hopeful prospects, his friend, Olin Dows, setting those trees into the ground. It was a courteous reminder that both Biddle and Dows were friends of Franklin Roosevelt, the "grower of trees," taking note of Dows as an active citizen of a democracy, one of those described by Biddle as the "younger artists of America . . . conscious . . . of the social revolution that our country and civilization are going through." Eleanor Roosevelt kept such friendships vigorous, often coming to encourage Biddle's work at the Justice Department when he needed reinforcement.[13]

Neither Biddle nor Dows were class- or place-bound. Biddle's Philadelphia trading family had married into the Dutchess County squirearchy, and he built a house in Croton-on-Hudson, not far from the Dows's "Southlands," but his vocation was using art to help people in tenements and sweatshops and encouraging his fellow citizens to help. In 1928 he had gone to Mexico to study among the Social Realist muralists, and came home to paint in a historic realism that was directly actionable, without any reliance upon myth, costume drama, or symbol. He painted real people in the present, not the past, with real people giving them aid. Some of these healers were "democratic leaders" whom he, Roosevelt, and Dows knew very well. The message was the same as that of Dows's, however: the favored classes bear obligations to bring justice and mercy to the poor and distressed.

In the summer of 1929 Dows followed Biddle to Mexico, where he also studied the work of Diego Rivera. He returned home to go to work for the New Deal in its first months, assisting Edward Bruce in the Treasury relief program. He was a practical person and a good administrator, and was persuaded to continue to serve Bruce and Henry Morgenthau as deputy director of TRAP from July 1935 through 1938. Then, being of independent means, he was free to go back to doing independent work. He executed the Hudson River mural commissions as a freelance painter, and then enlisted in the army in World War II. His sketches of war and desolation, drawn during front-line service, are tough and true.

Above the entrance to the Justice Department library, to the right of the Biddle murals, is a powerful painting by John Steuart Curry of a black-robed judge standing on the courthouse steps to protect a man from a lynch mob—the scene illuminated by the lights of an automobile, and therefore contemporary. In 1931 Curry had already produced a

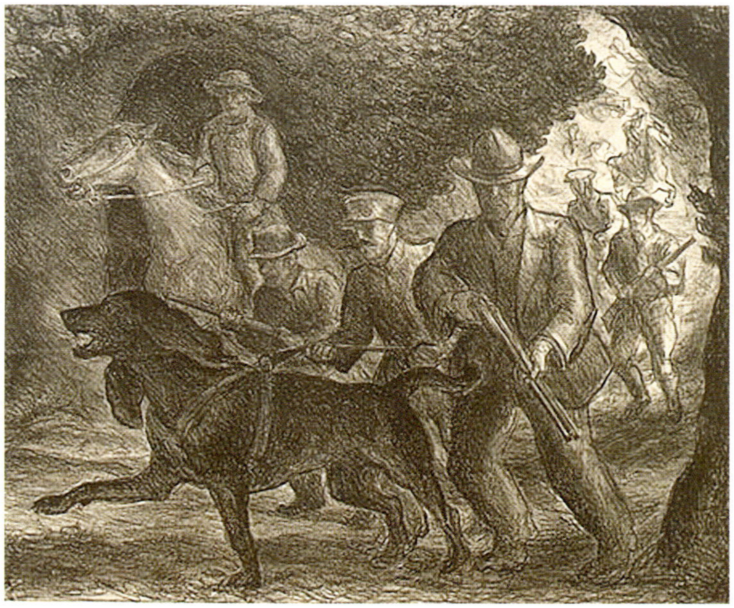

Man Hunt
John Steuart Curry, 1934

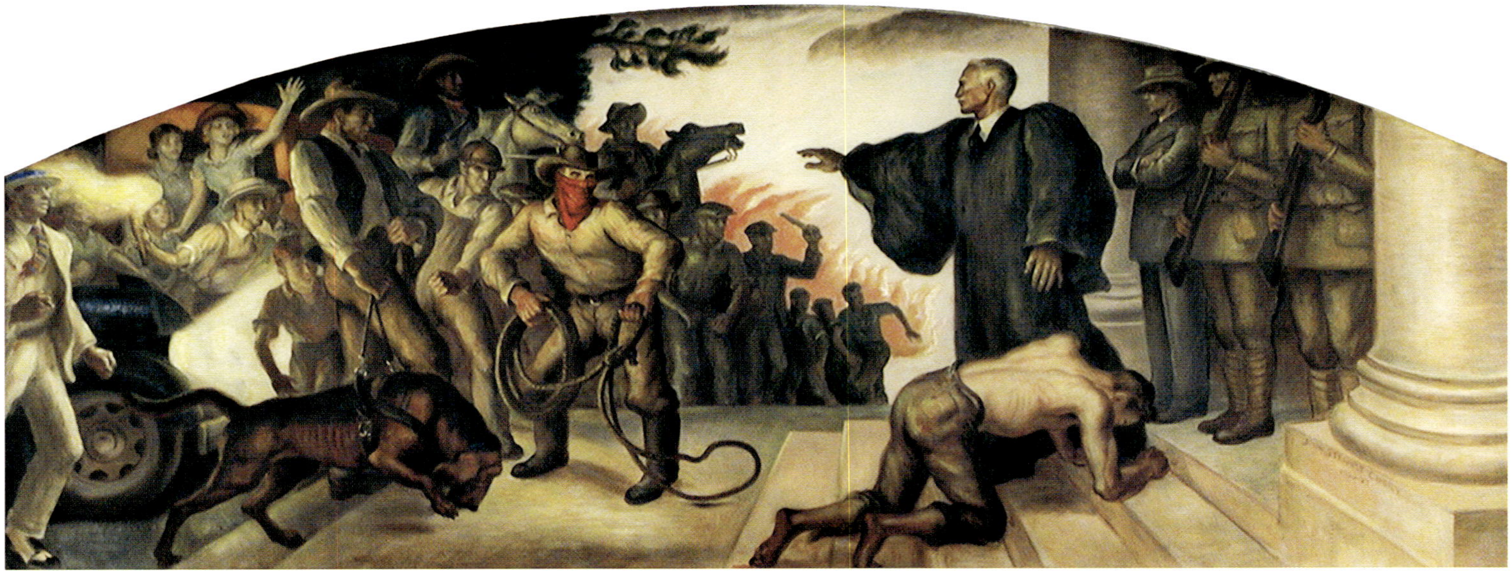

Law Versus Mob Rule
John Steuart Curry, 1936

John Steuart Curry was born and grew up in rural Kansas, studied art in Chicago and Paris, and commenced his career as an illustrator for *Boys' Life*, *Country Gentleman*, and *The Saturday Evening Post*, but by 1932 his work had been presented at the National Academy of Design, the Corcoran Gallery, the Whitney Museum, and the Metropolitan Museum of Art. During the Depression years, as artist-in-residence at the University of Wisconsin College of Agriculture, he served rural communities and struggling artists. The Treasury Section of Fine Arts rejected Curry's proposal for a mural, *Freeing of the Slaves*, for the Justice Department Building, but it was later completed for the law library of the University of Wisconsin. Curry's murals for the state house rotunda in Topeka, Kansas, were as tough and true as Thomas Hart Benton's for Jefferson City and Independence. The Kansas legislature insisted on obstructions in front of his *Tragic Prelude* showing John Brown, evoking memories of "Bloody Kansas" as a battleground between slave owners and abolitionists like Brown, and his unblinking evocation of the plagues on the frontier and the erosion caused by plowing the dust bowl. So Curry left them unfinished and unsigned. After his death, the legislature apologized and the sketches for the murals were purchased from his estate. In 1937, a big year for Curry, he was commissioned

painting of a lynch mob called *The Man Hunt* and in 1934 a lithograph of a close-up of such a mob. He was participating in the long struggle of the NAACP to secure federal enforcement of the provisions of the post–Civil War civil rights acts and amendments and to secure new legislation making lynching a federal crime. Antilynching bills were introduced sporadically throughout the early twentieth century, and President Theodore Roosevelt spoke out against lynching, although his successors did nothing against it until the New Deal. Bills making lynching a federal crime passed the House of Representatives in 1937 and 1940, but even when provided images by artists, the constituency of conscience was slow to build sufficiently to get past filibusters in the Senate. Franklin Roosevelt explained his failure to be bolder early in his administration by saying of the filibustering Southern Democrats that "If I come out for the antilynching bill now, they will block every bill I ask Congress to pass to keep America from collapsing. I just can't take that risk."[14]

Eleanor Roosevelt took her independent course at this point, sitting conspicuously for hours in the visitors' gallery of the senate chamber, "bearing witness" to express her support of the antilynching legislation being filibustered by the Southern Democrats. The most help she could secure from her husband was the creation of the Civil Rights Section of the Justice Department in 1939, which began prosecutions to combat lynching under existing law. That law was porous and the commitment of the administration was frail; the Justice Department failed to win any convictions until after World War II. In 1946 the Civil Rights Section successfully prosecuted a Florida constable for complicity in a fatal lynching, but his only penalties were a one thousand dollar fine and one year in prison. In 1947 a report entitled "To Secure These Rights" was issued by the Truman Administration—but the Southerners in the Senate were able to block antilynching legislation until public support swelled behind the alliance of Martin Luther King and Lyndon Johnson. In 1968 the Civil Rights Act was passed.

Artists had been advocates of such an outcome since 1923 when George Bellows's lithograph *The Law Is Too Slow* showed a black man being burned at the stake by a white mob. In 1929 Walter White of the NAACP used Bellows's picture as the frontispiece of his book *Rope and Faggot*. In the 1930s White made similar uses of several of Curry's works, including *The Fugitive* and *The Man Hunt*. Other artists joined: Langston Hughes and James Weldon Johnson wrote antilynching poetry and Johnson's *God's Trombones* bore a cover by Aaron Douglas in 1927, showing Christ being lynched. In 1935 two exhibitions of antilynching art were presented in New York, one organized by White and the NAACP. The other, backed by left-wing groups including the Artists' Union and the John Reed Club, was entitled "Pictures Can Fight." For his catalogue, White secured introductory essays from Erskine Caldwell and Sherwood Anderson; *The Fugitive* was on the cover. Among the seventy-seven artists who contributed works to one or both of the two exhibitions in 1935 were George Biddle, Juan Clemente Orosco, Harry Sternberg, Peggy Bacon, Isamu Naguchi, Paul Cadmus, and Reginald Marsh, whose graphic lynching picture was published in *The New Yorker.*[15]

Meanwhile other New Deal causes were being supported by artists who never received a WPA stipend or Section commission. Thomas Hart Benton, for example, supported himself on other commissions throughout the Depression years, beginning with his *America Today* murals at the New School for Social Research in 1929–30 and his series on Indiana life at the 1933 Chicago World's Fair. Benton drew upon his studies of El Greco, Tintoretto, the Mexican muralists of his own time, and regional painters of the American heartland. He did not prettify. Indiana was a hotbed of segregationist violence, and Benton showed Indiana as it was to World's Fair crowds—prowled by sheeted and hooded terrorists of the Ku Klux Klan. (After the state of Indiana boldly displayed Benton's murals in Chicago, they were installed at Indiana University in Bloomington, where they serve continue to provoke active discussion about art, history, and social policy.)

Benton was famous by 1934, when he was featured on the first cover of *Time* magazine to be in color. His *Social History of Missouri* in Jefferson City was a further act of courage. He put front and center in the state capitol Jesse James, slaves, and Tom Pendergast, while Pendergast was still the boss of Kansas City, and had the further effrontery to take up residence in Pendergast's town. In early 1960, three years after the founding of the Truman Library in Independence, Benton was working on the scaffolding of a huge mural on its wall when Truman insisted upon making comments about the work. Benton called down, "If you want to help paint, come up here." "By golly, I will," replied Truman, mounting the scaffold. He took up a brush, dipped it into Benton's blue paint, and dabbed at Benton's sky—just enough to make his point. (*America Today* is now in the atrium of the Equitable Building, in the Equitable Center, near Rockefeller Center.)

Art and Ideology

On May 9, 1933, George Biddle wrote the recently inaugurated president urging him toward federal support for the arts, not just to help artists but to mobilize them to be of aid in "the social revolution that our country and civilization are going through." Biddle informed Roosevelt that "the Mexican artists have produced the greatest national school of mural art since the Renaissance. Diego Rivera tells me that it was only possible because [President Alvaro] Obregón allowed Mexican artists . . . to express on the walls of government buildings the social ideals of the Mexican revolution." As was often the case with what Rivera told people, that was not quite a full account of the aid given his career by presidents of his own country. While a promising youth, he had been given a state pension by the despotic Diaz regime, and his studies abroad had been financed by another repressive government. Then came Obregón, who came to power by meeting popular uprisings in the streets with artillery and machine guns. After enjoying his favor, Rivera kept working on a huge commission for the presidential palace for Obregón's compatible successors. His other clients included the San Francisco Stock Exchange and both the Fords and the Rockefellers. His murals for Edsel Ford celebrated the Ford River Rouge plant and industrial Detroit with factory managers in the places of honor he reserved for Lenin when painting at home. In his later work for other audiences, he reserved those "star spots" for Mao, Stalin, and the North Koreans.[16]

As Biddle was writing Roosevelt, Rivera was at work on a mural for the RCA Building in Rockefeller Center and received a notification from the Rockefeller family's rental office that the Depression had made securing tenants for any

to execute two Interior Department murals celebrating the Oklahoma land rush and homesteading (see main text) and two more in the grand sequence of New Deal murals in the Justice Department Building: *Justice of the Plains*, *The Movement Westward*, and *Law Versus Mob Rule*, where they accompany George Biddle's tenement and sweatshop panels. Curry depicts a lynch mob of frontiersmen being confronted by a courageous judge protecting a man seeking the law's protection on the courthouse steps. Curry had produced both a painting and a set of lithographs of lynch mobs earlier. *Justice of the Plains: The Movement Westward* shows gangsters fleeing before the law, in an affirmative message like that of Curry's two Interior Department murals: the first of which illustrates cinematically the crowd rushing ahead in the first seconds after the gunshot that opened the Oklahoma Indian Territories to white squatter settlement (a great painting of a not altogether proud moment in which law, in the form of treaties with Indians, was set aside). Curry's westward-moving European-American pioneers are also proceeding into the Indian-free "empty continent" of myth. The pioneers bearing justice—at the Justice Department—are on their way, it seems, to homesteading, perhaps next door to those across town in the Interior Department: homesteading where Indian homes had been, behind barriers of barbed wire across what had been open range. (But see main text for possible subtexts.)

speculative office building difficult. The RCA Building could not bear the additional burden of a portrait of Lenin in the lobby. After Rivera refused several polite requests from Nelson Rockefeller to remove Lenin, he was told that the landlord would remove the mural.[17]

Young Mr. Rockefeller broke the news saying that "the piece is beautifully painted" but he also pointed out the obvious truth that the RCA Building was a real estate speculation and that "this mural is in a public place." That was hardly news to Rivera. Despite legitimate lamentation at the loss of what may indeed have been beautifully painted, the rental office could hardly be expected to explain why Lenin was depicted leading humankind toward what Rivera described as "a New and Better Future, . . . guiding the exploited masses toward a new social order based on the suppression of classes." By 1933 Lenin's legacy was apparent in the murderous despotism of Stalin. Roosevelt had not expressed a desire to lead a "social revolution" and gently responded to Biddle that he was all for putting artists to work, but not for encouraging "a lot of young enthusiasts painting Lenin's head on the Justice Building."[18]

Biddle understood; the recognizable people in his Justice murals were leaders of the New Deal, including his brother, Solicitor General Francis Biddle, and Secretary of Labor Frances Perkins. Those murals, like the antilynching mural of John Steuart Curry nearby, were produced by artists commissioned to celebrate the kind of justice that protects people in their rights, including the interposition of justice in the face of despots or mobs, and the uses of law to remedy economic exploitation in tenements and sweatshops. Biddle, Dows, Benton, and Curry admired the Mexican muralists as artists but not as propagandists for despots. Their respect for the art did not extend to the politics of the artists; at their best they painted with the Mexicans' verve, without their ideological implications. Benton's nine-part *America Today* for the New School for Social Research in New York eschewed party-line agit-prop, and was thus, as he commented, too apolitical to please the "radicals . . . because I didn't put Nicolai Lenin in as an American prophet."[19]

The price paid by artists for "state support" in Communist countries was that they must support the state through a slavish Socialist Realism. In capitalist-dominated arts institutions, that price was often adherence to the best-selling fashions endorsed by the market. The WPA and the Section were generally free of pressures as severe as those, however imperfect may have been their selection processes. Peer review may become cronyism in the machine politics of the intellectuals. Community endorsement can become dumbing down. Mrs. Roosevelt consoled the readers of "My Day" in 1939 with a contrast between the WPA's processes—and by implication, those of the Section—and a market-based reliance upon the preferences of a few rich or politically powerful patrons. Spreading responsibilities through committees was boring and messy, but that was better than relying only on "nobles" when "all nobles had their pet." That had been true in the Renaissance, and with a little flexibility in the meaning of "noble," it had become true again in the capitalist countries: "In the old days" she wrote, "it was sufficient for an artist to have a rich patron and then to develop under the protection of his important sponsor," and told her readers that widening the constituency led her to "wondering if the WPA arts projects may not take their place." Six years had passed since the WPA experiment had gotten underway, and it had only three more years to go. Already the President was being forced to cut away at both the WPA and the Section. Soon war accelerated that process as a hostile Congress held hearings whipping up public apprehension that the WPA was harboring left-wingers and foreign-born artists. The President's defense was that there was nothing left-wing, or Mexican or Russian, in the mass of WPA art. It was as home-grown as the writings of the Greenbackers, Populists, and Progressives who had never read Marx and Engels. When he stood in the National Gallery of Art to give its dedicatory oration, Franklin Roosevelt summarized the results of his arts program.[20]

> A few generations ago, the people of this country were taught by their writers and their critics and their teachers

to believe that art was something foreign to America and to themselves—something imported from another continent and from an age that was not theirs—something they had no part in, save to go and see it in a guarded room on holidays and Sundays. But . . . within the last few years, they have discovered that they have a part. They have seen in their own towns, in their own villages, in schoolhouses, in post offices . . . pictures painted by their sons, their neighbors—people they have known and lived beside and talked to. They have seen . . . rooms full of paintings by Americans—some of it good, some of it not good, but all of it native, human, eager and alive —all of it painted by their own kind in their own country, and painted about things they know and look at often and have touched and loved.[21]

Roosevelt and Art

As suggested earlier, Franklin Roosevelt was not interested in art as art. On the other hand—the open hand—he showed great interest in art that could make a difference in how people lived. Art worked for him if it could sustain the New Deal legacy, if it might improve what happened to the land, and if it rallied the people into the American covenant. Accordingly, he supported the art programs of Harry Hopkins's WPA, Harold Ickes's Interior Department and PWA, Rexford Tugwell's Farm Security photographers, and Henry Morgenthau's Treasury. He attended exhibitions, cut ribbons, made enthusiastic speeches, and pointed with pride at the color sketches made of traditional crafts by the WPA's Index of Design and displayed at the White House. All these were there for the press to observe, and for members of Congress coming for dinner to note as important. Roosevelt's political objectives were his artistic objectives as well. He encouraged art that encouraged "a new deal for the American people" rather than the expressionist painting of his time, which he characterized as "despondent." His personal resiliency in the face of physical infirmity required of him a quality he called "cheerfulness." This persistence in the face of adversity did not deny the reality of ugliness and evil, nor did it require abatement of that inner dissatisfaction he called "sadness." "Sadness" fueled fervor for reform; it was hopeful and active, qualities he shared with Abraham Lincoln. Despondency was subversive of his campaign against depression, psychological as well as economic. He did not encourage what he called the "decadence common to much European art"—surrealism, the art of escape, or abstract expressionism, which would leave society mired in trouble. Olin Dows was acting as Roosevelt's proxy when, as Edward Bruce's deputy at TRAP in September 1936, he urged the Artists' Coordination Committee of New York to submit "no more abstractions like the one you sent in." Since "the American Scene" should be the "general field for subject matter" of an actionable realism, there was no need to encourage "slavery to classical standards"—another term of the President's. As Eleanor Roosevelt observed, her husband particularly liked pictures in which "he could recognize people." If he could recognize people, so could other people. Then, from recognition could come relevance, and from relevance could come reform.[22]

Dows and Edward Bruce sought to guide American public art past two temptations. One was described by the social and art critic, Karal Ann Marling, as "academic art, the nymph-ridden nostalgia purveyed by the National Academy of Design." The other, she wrote, "was the modernism of the School of Paris, imported and promulgated by the Museum of Modern Art." Dows, Bruce, Holger Cahill, and Eleanor Roosevelt sought, instead, to affirm "American reality . . . the visible truths of modern life."[23]

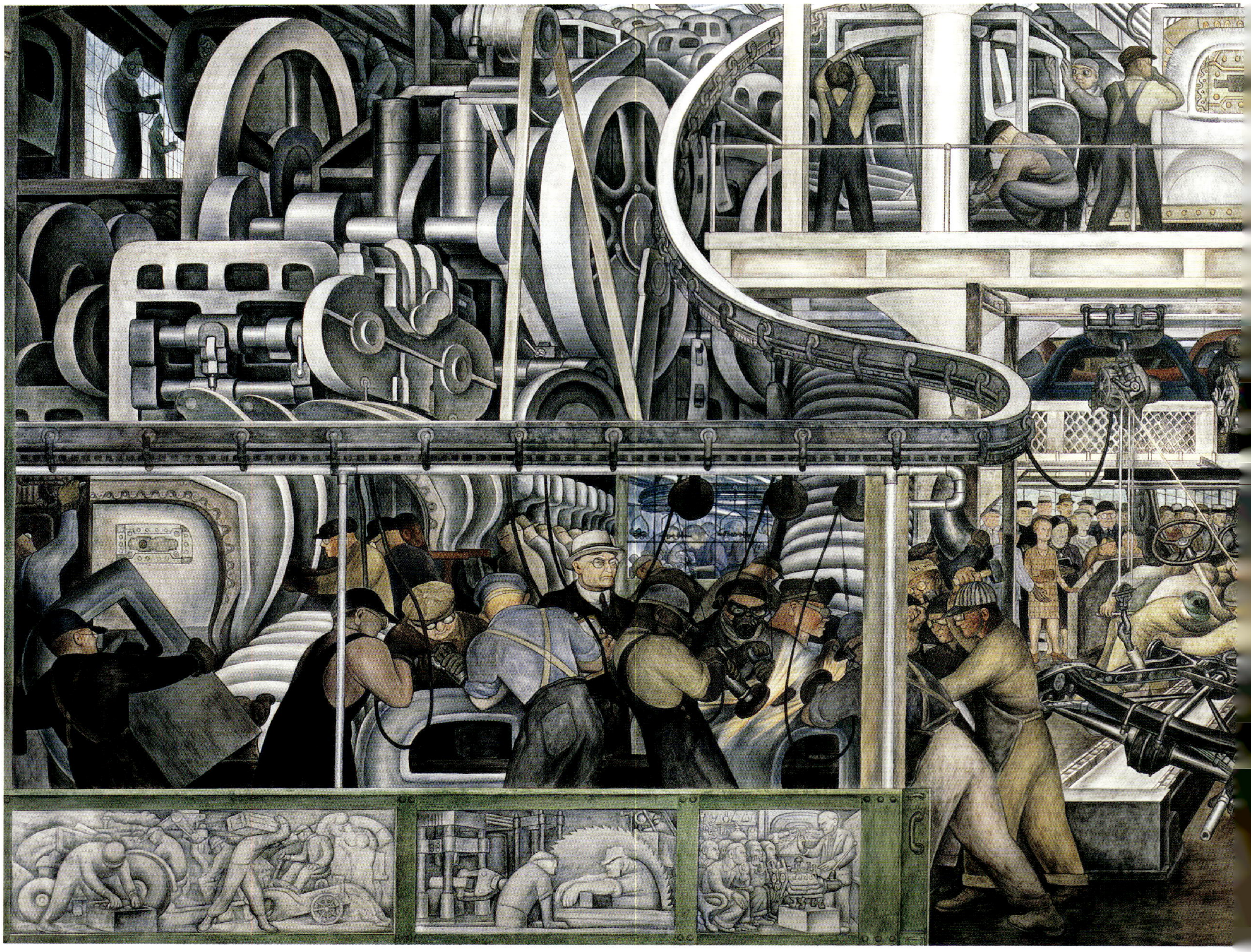

Detroit Industry (detail)
Diego Rivera, 1932
The South Wall

Many young American painters went to Mexico in the 1920s and 1930s to study the work of Diego Rivera, David Alfaro Siqueiros, and Jose Clemente Orozco, all of whom espoused Communist political views. Rivera, however, was in practice as willing to accept large commissions awarded by a succession of Mexican regimes of the extreme right, center, and non-communist left, and from industrialists, heirs of oil companies, and bankers. His major commissions in the United States came from the Fords, Rockefellers, and the San Francisco Chamber of Commerce.

Stylistically, the great Mexican muralists produced turbulent neo-baroque scenes in vehement color, seething with crowded action, largely figurative but arranged along flanges and planes derived from Native American traditions.

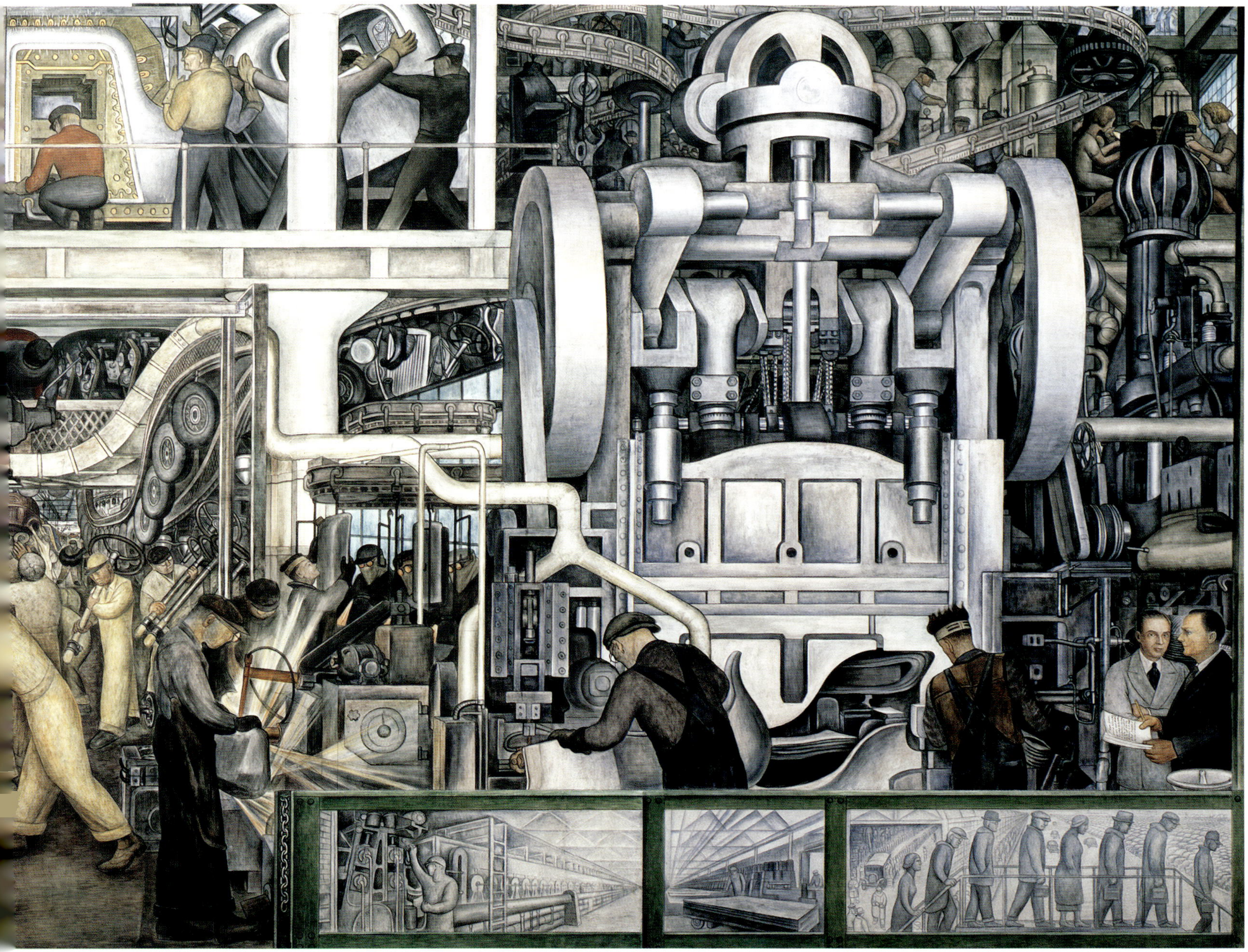

They were enormously proficient and lively in their synthesis of Mayan, Aztec, Spanish Baroque, and Italian Renaissance devices with contemporary cubist and surrealist experiments, often including cameo portraits of living and historical figures—and a great many sprockets, valves, and turbines.

The grandeur, color, and drama of the Mexican style was informative to their American students, but seldom emulated by them. George Biddle, Olin Dows, Mitchell Jamieson, and Howard Cook returned from Mexico emboldened to abandon the saccharine sentimentality of late-Victorian academic work, but none became any more Mexican in style than their contemporaries who did not study in Mexico: Thomas Hart Benton, Grant Wood, Boardman Robinson, and John Steuart Curry. All did their own work in their own way.

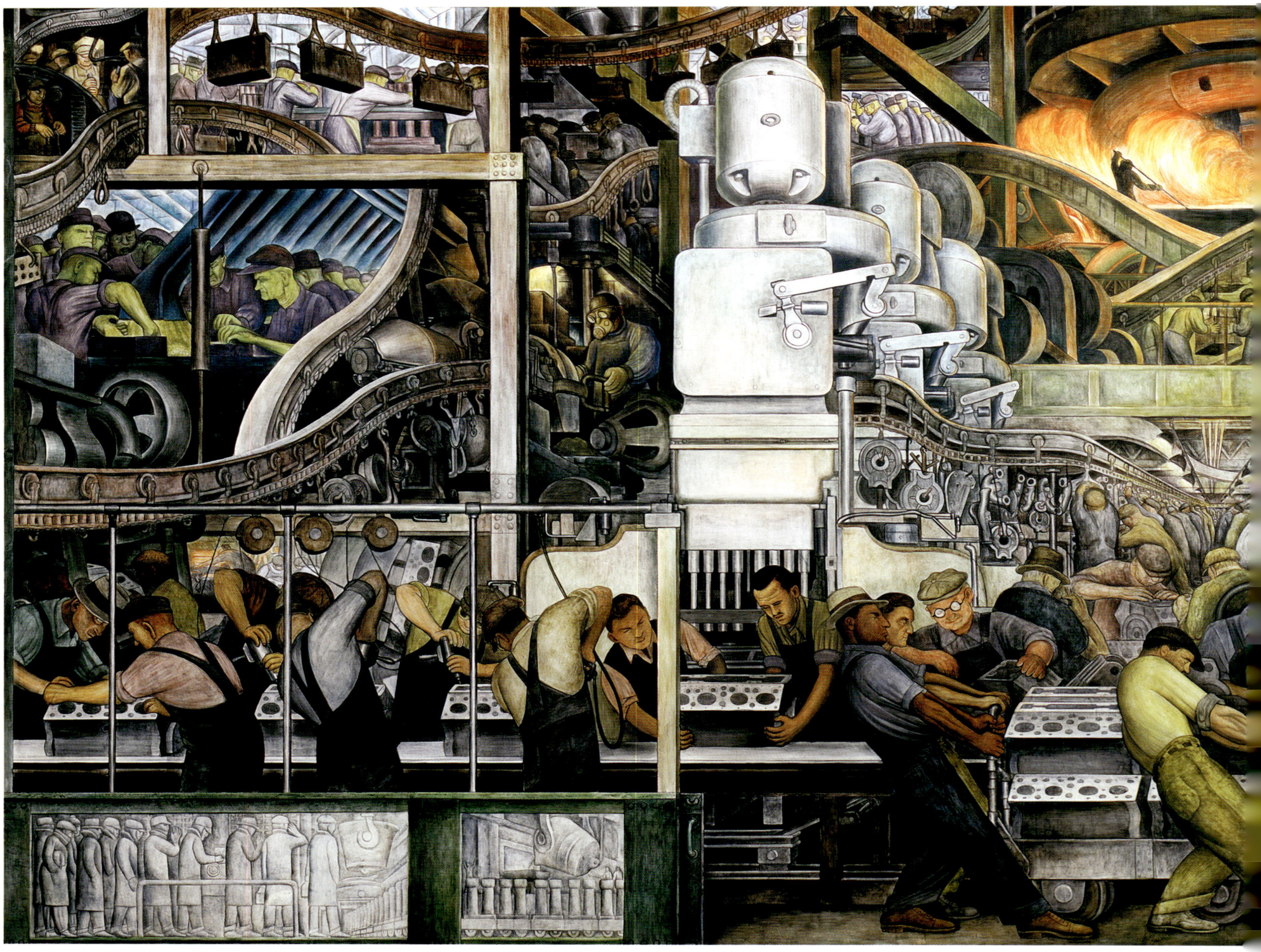

Detroit Industry (detail)
Diego Rivera, 1932
The North Wall

Diego Rivera's *Detroit Industry* murals were commissioned in 1932 by Edsel Ford and by Dr. William Valentiner, Director of the Detroit Institute of Arts. The son and heir of Henry Ford was the most powerful member of the Institute's board, and was also president of the Detroit Arts Commission. The north and south walls carry three sets of images representative of the diversity of people making up Detroit's workforce, the automobile industry, and the other industries of the city (medical, pharmaceutical, and chemical). Below these large scenes are small panels depicting daily life of happy employees at the Ford River Rouge plant, in a paean for industry and machinery. The workers and managers in the central panel of the north wall are seen producing the engine and transmission of the 1932 Ford V8. The major panel of the south wall shows them at work on the V8's exterior.

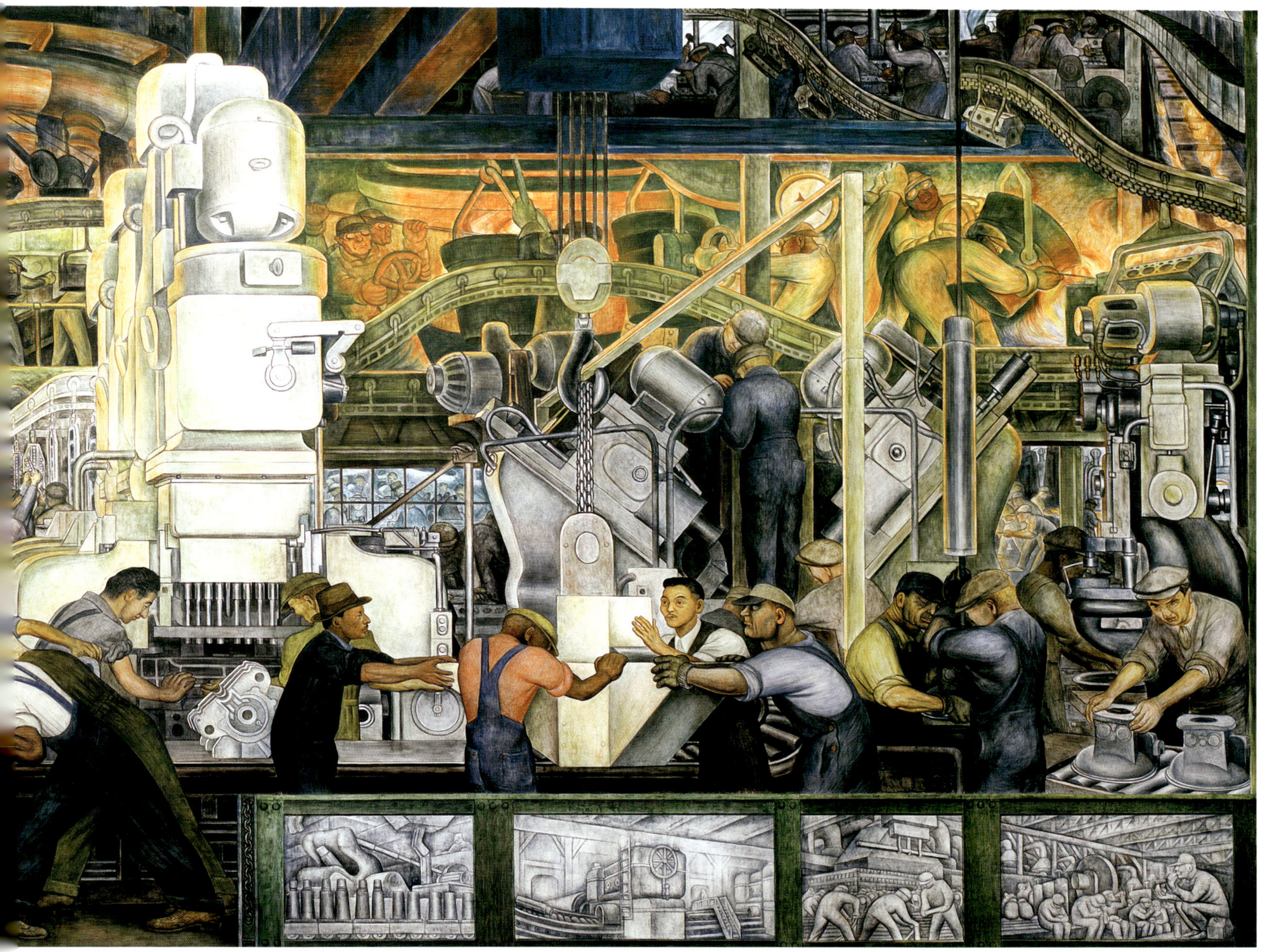

These celebrations of large-scale, production-line capitalism were produced a few months after the first new Ford Model V-8 emerged from the River Rouge plant. They offer no social commentary, no privation, and no grimness—Rivera's factory workers seem to be dancing with the machines.

Rivera's other completed commissions for capitalist clients in the United States were: *The Making of a Fresco Showing the Building of a City*, of 1931, San Francisco Art Institute; *Pan-American Unity*, of 1940, commissioned in 1940 for the Golden Gate International Exposition and moved to the Diego Rivera Theatre at the Ocean Avenue Campus of the City College of San Francisco in 1961; and, in the stairhall of the San Francisco Stock Exchange Building (1931), the star of which is Helen Wills Moody, winner of eight Wimbledon tennis titles.

The Social History of Indiana
Thomas Hart Benton

Twenty of the twenty-two tempera panels that were designed to face one another.

In 1932 Thomas Hart Benton, having studied in Paris where he became acquainted with the work of Diego Rivera, and having executed only one large commission—a set of murals for the New School for Social Research in New York—was chosen to produce a 250-foot-long set of murals of Indiana life for the 1933 Chicago World's Fair. They were not tourism-encouraging puff pieces but direct expressions of Indiana down-home decency and honest hard work—as well

Industrial Panels

The top row of panels progresses from left to right.

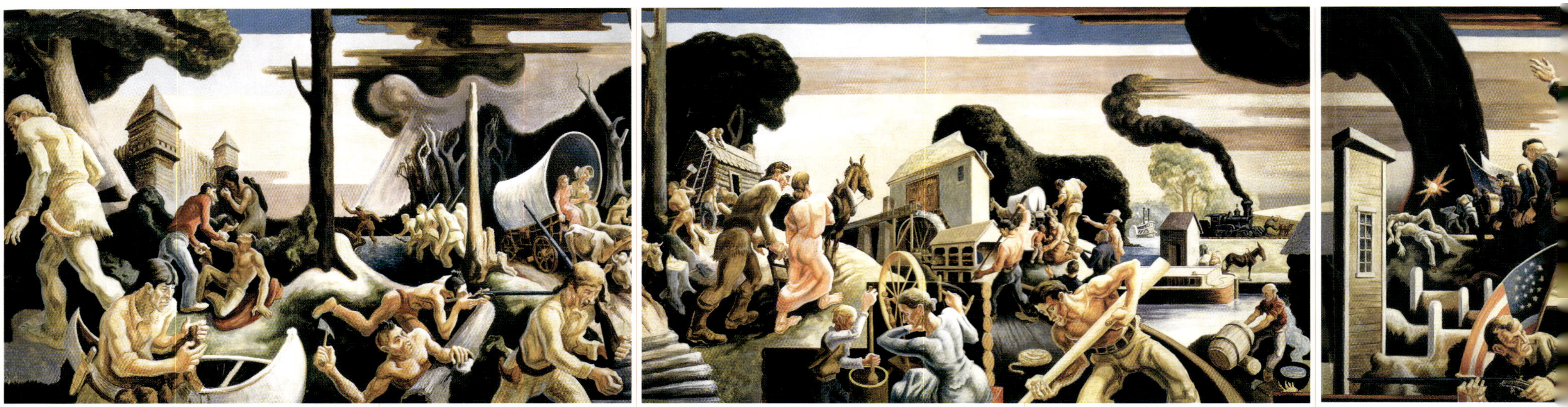

The Fur Traders | Pioneers | Home Industry | Internal Improvements | The Civil War

Cultural Panels

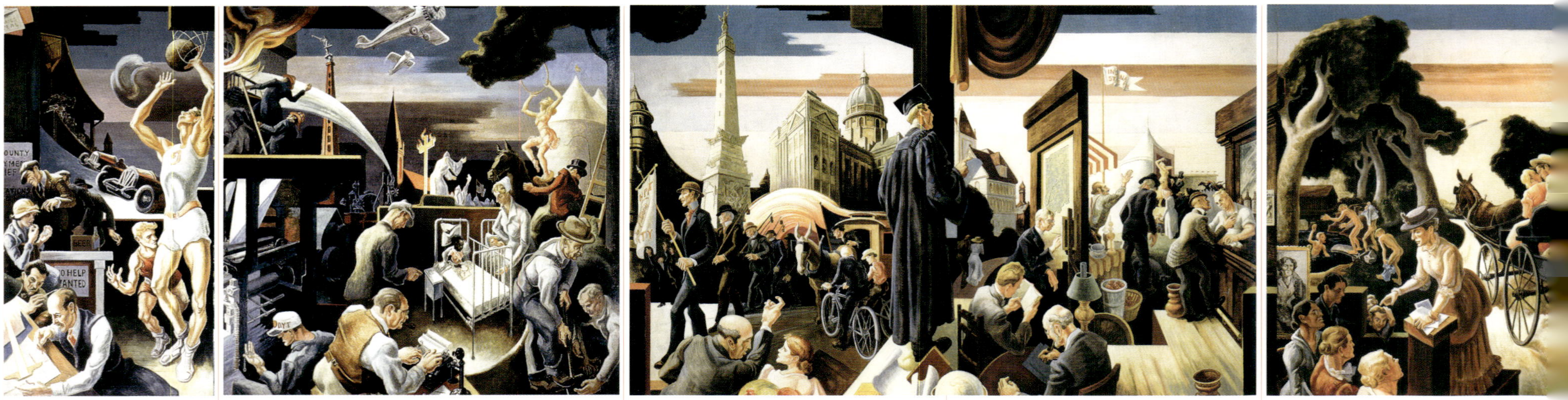

Indiana Puts Her Trust in Thought | Parks, the Circus, the Klan, the Press | Colleges and City Life | Leisure and Literature | Woman's Place

as Indiana the northern hotbed of Ku Klux Klan activity and of tawdry "carny" life juxtaposed with bible camps. The Indiana Department of Conservation was embarrassed by Benton's vehement candor, but kept the murals on display. After the Chicago Fair closed, the murals were re-installed on the Bloomington campus of Indiana University—where they remain. (See also pages 65 and 185.)

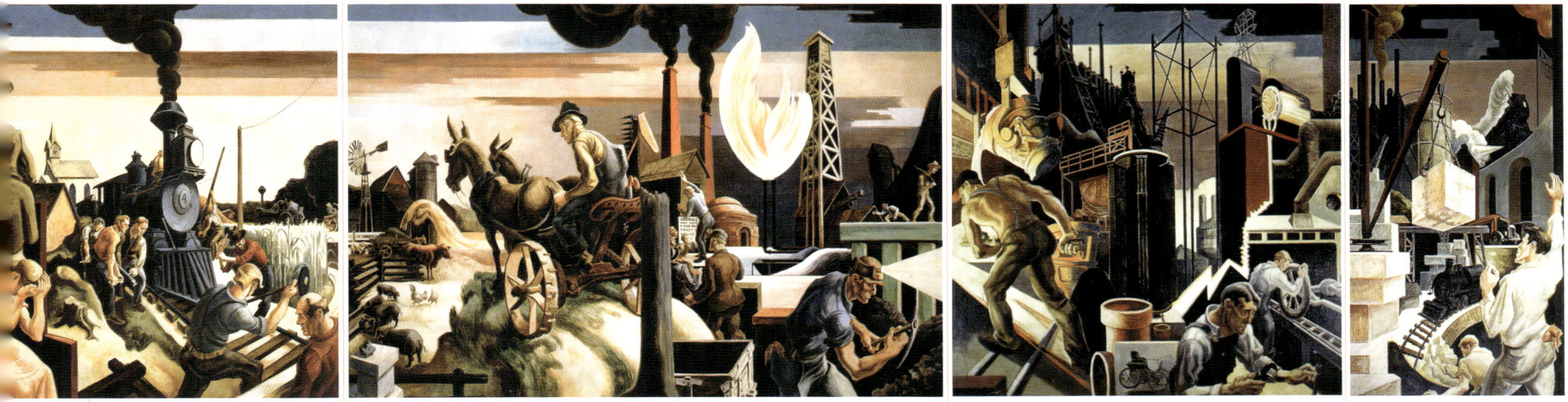

Expansion

The Farmer Up and Down

Coal, Gas, Oil , Brick

Electric Power, Motor Cars, Steel

Indiana Puts Her Trust in Work

The bottom row of panels progresses from right to left.

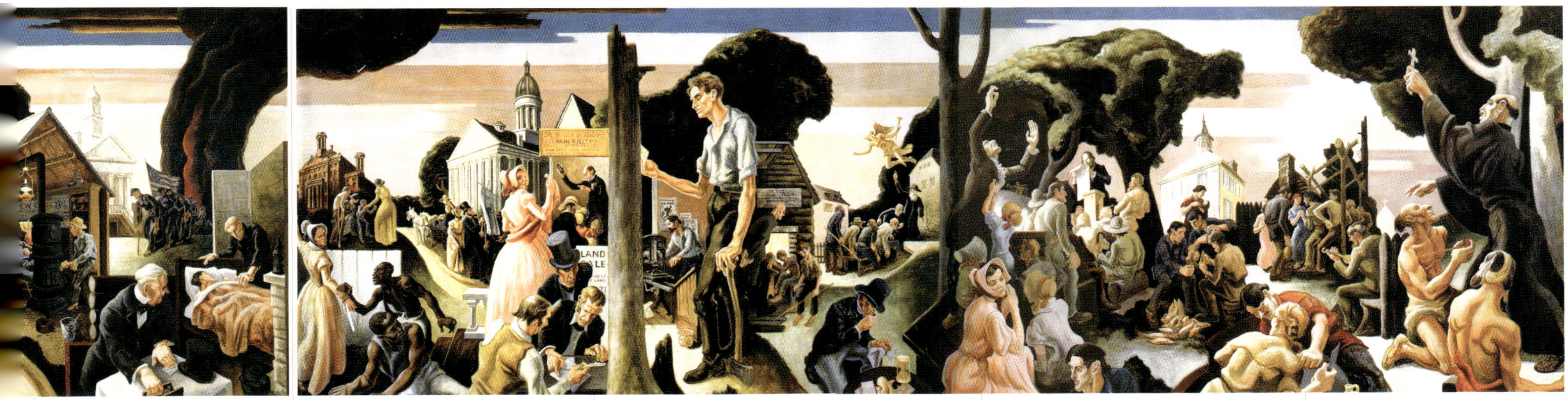

The Old Time Doctor and the Grange

Reformers and Squatters

Early Schools . . . Communities

Frontier Life

The French

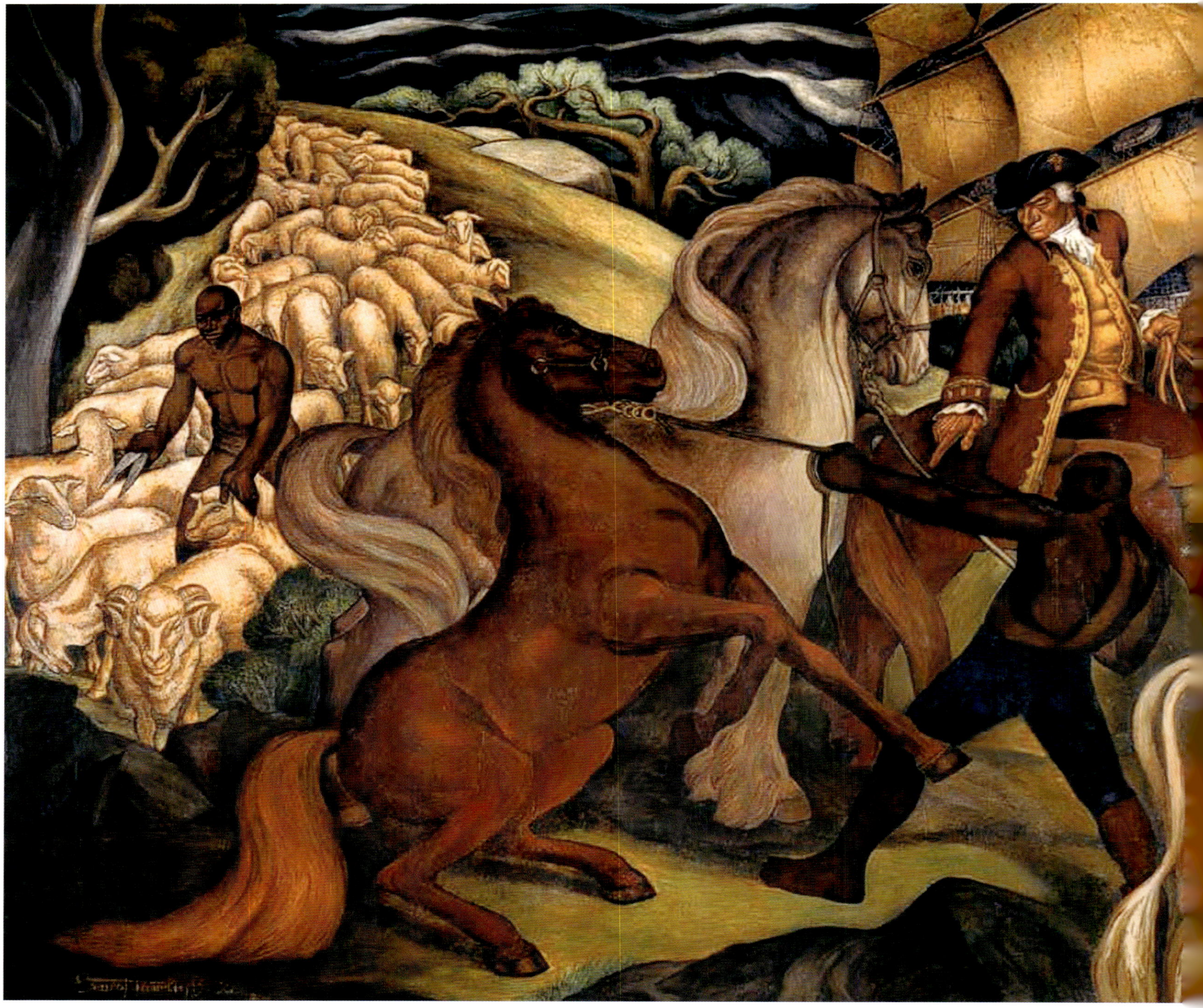

The Economic Activities of the Narragansett Planters
Ernest Hamlin Baker, 1939
Post Office, Wakefield, Rhode Island

Born in Rhode Island, Ernest Hamlin Baker became famous for eleven *Fortune Magazine* covers between 1929–41, and more than three hundred covers for *Time* magazine. He did not need government work; he executed the commission for the Section because the subject interested him. *The Economic Activities of the Narragansett Planters* was installed in the Wakefield post office in 1939, where it remained until the building was closed in 1999. In June 2003, the painting was restored and reinstalled in the Pettaquamscutt Historical Society in the Old Washington Jail, Kingston.

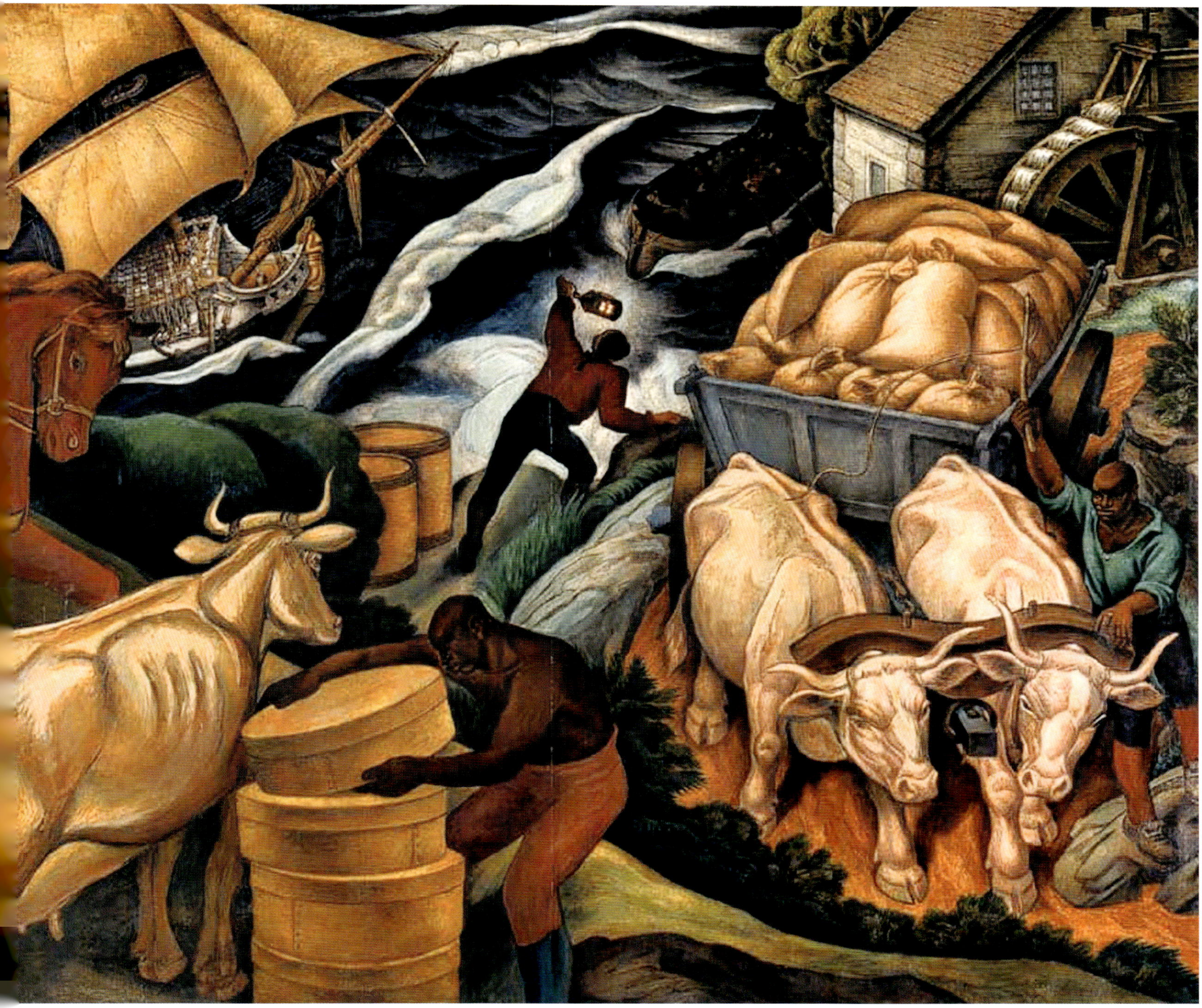

Southwest Rhode Island was known as "South County" in the eighteenth century, with a plantation culture worked by slaves of African descent, many brought by the slave traders of Bristol, Rhode Island, and Newport. Baker depicted bare-chested and heavily muscled black slaves, contrasting with the delicate frame and finery of their owner, a white Narragansett planter, and their uncovered heads with the planter's ostentatious wig and hat.

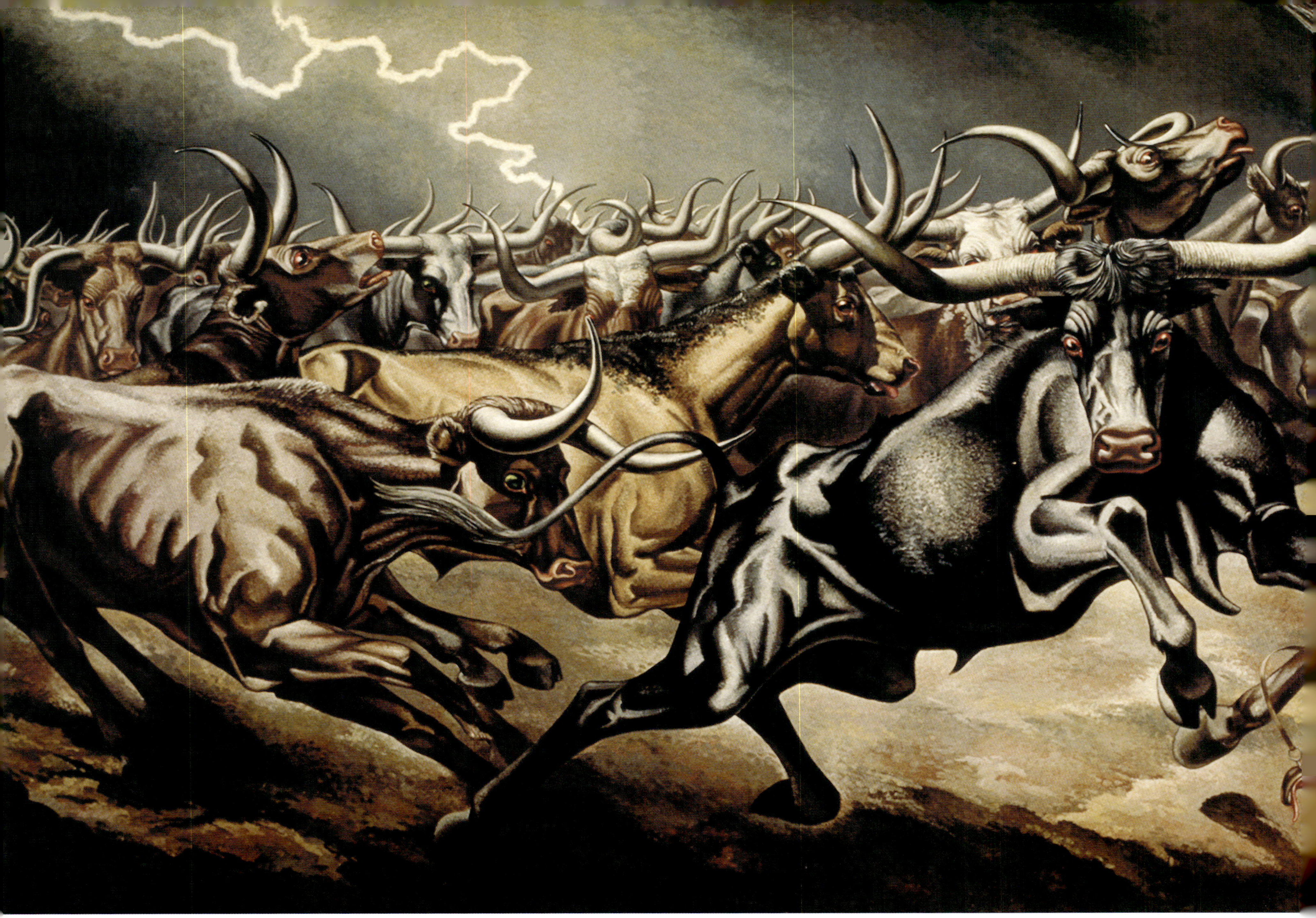

Stampede
Tom Lea, 1940
Post Office, Odessa, Texas
Moved in 1970 to the Odessa Post Office at 200 North Texas Avenue

Tom Lea was a muralist, illustrator, novelist, historian, World War II artist correspondent, and studio painter. Born in El Paso, Texas, he studied art in Chicago, Paris, and Italy, responding especially to the work of Delacroix, Della Francesca, and Signorelli. He returned into the teeth of the Depression, moved to New Mexico, and pieced out a living with commissions from the Laboratory of Anthropology, *Santa Fe Magazine*, and, when the work ran out, the WPA.

At the end of the 1930s, he secured mural commissions for the Texas Centennial celebration and for the Branigan Library in Las Cruces before Edward Bruce and the Section chose him to paint murals for the Main Post Office in Washington, D.C., for the Federal Building in El Paso, Texas, and for post offices in Pleasant Hill, Missouri, and Seymour and Odessa, Texas. His private commissions included the Burlington Railroad Station in Lacrosse, Wisconsin. When he died, he was

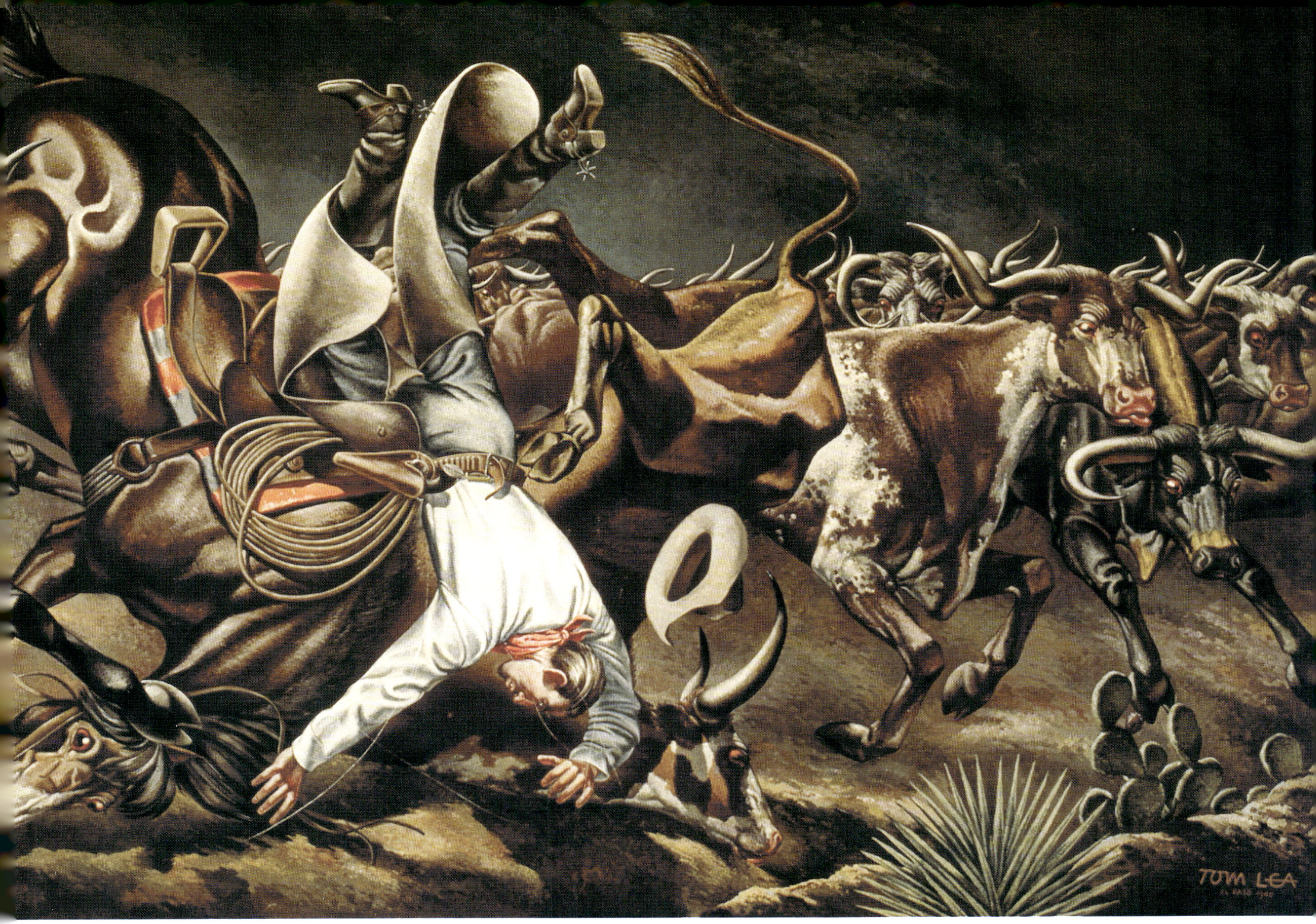

memorialized with proclamations read on the floors of the United States House of Representatives and Senate.

Two of his novels were bestsellers: *The Brave Bulls* and *The Wonderful Country*. The *New York Times* wrote of him that he "is probably the only person, dead or alive, who can say he has been threatened by Pancho Villa, interrupted by Chiang Kai-shek, and regaled by President Franklin D. Roosevelt."

Lea said of *Stampede* that "it was for a new post office at Odessa, Texas, about seventy miles from a crossing of the Pecos River. The first verse of "Little Joe the Wrangler" was easy to remember:

We was camping on the Pecos when the wind began to blow,
And we doubled up the guard to hold them tight,
When the storm came roaring from the north with thunder
And with rain,
And the herd stampeded off into the night.

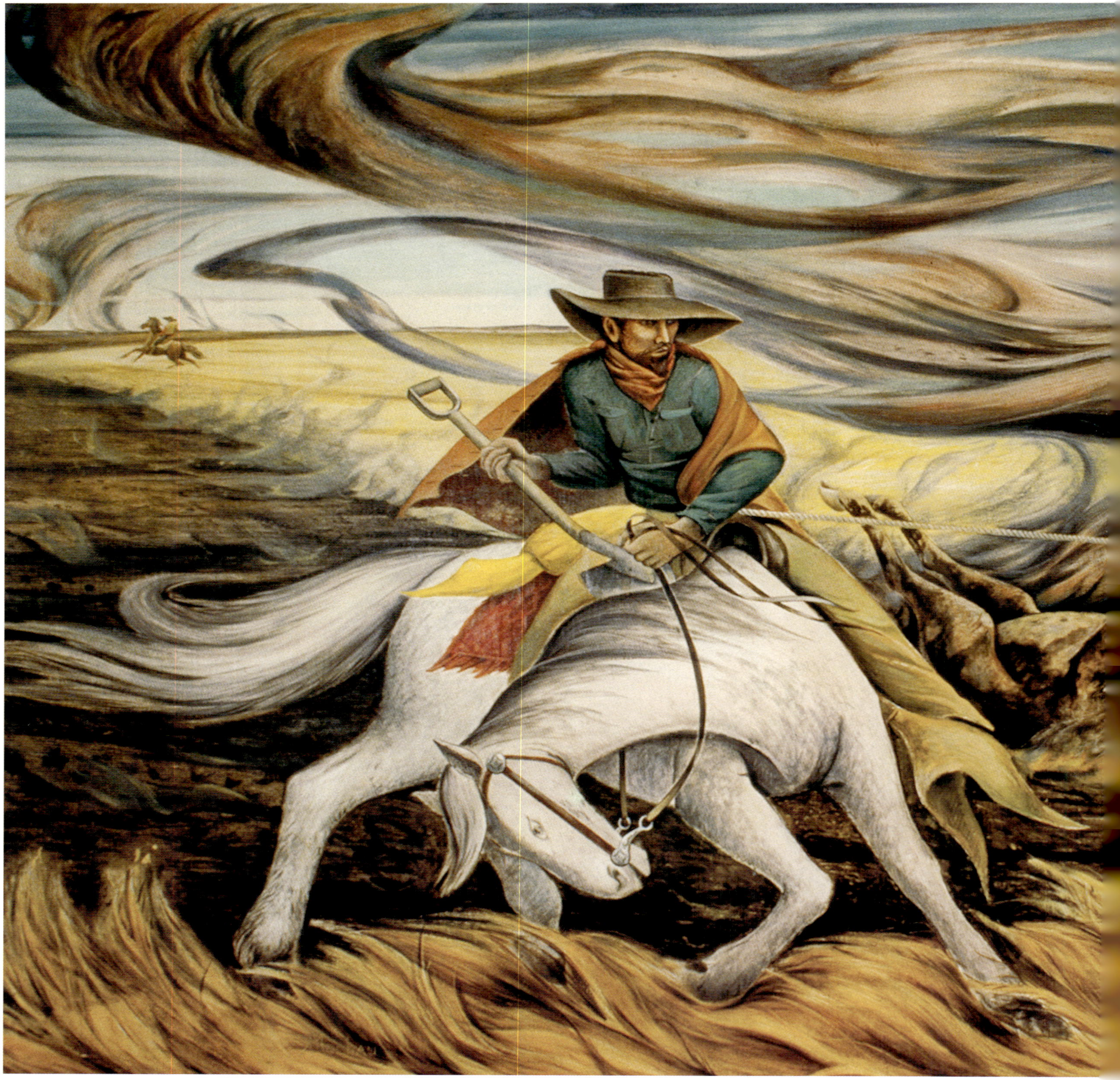

Ranchers of the Panhandle: Fighting Prairie Fire with Skinned Steer
Frank Mechau, 1940
Post Office,
Brownfield, Texas

Frank Mechau was born in 1904 in Kansas. His painting career took him to Europe, where he studied Rubens, Tintoretto, and other masters of the baroque. It was a long way from their subject matter to his in the Brownfield fire suppression mural, from courtiers' finery to a steer skin, but the sweep and swirl are in them all. In 1933, he returned to Colorado and ultimately settled in Redstone. His mural *Wild Horse Race*, *Indian Fight*, and *Pony Express* have been installed in the new Federal Courthouse in Denver.

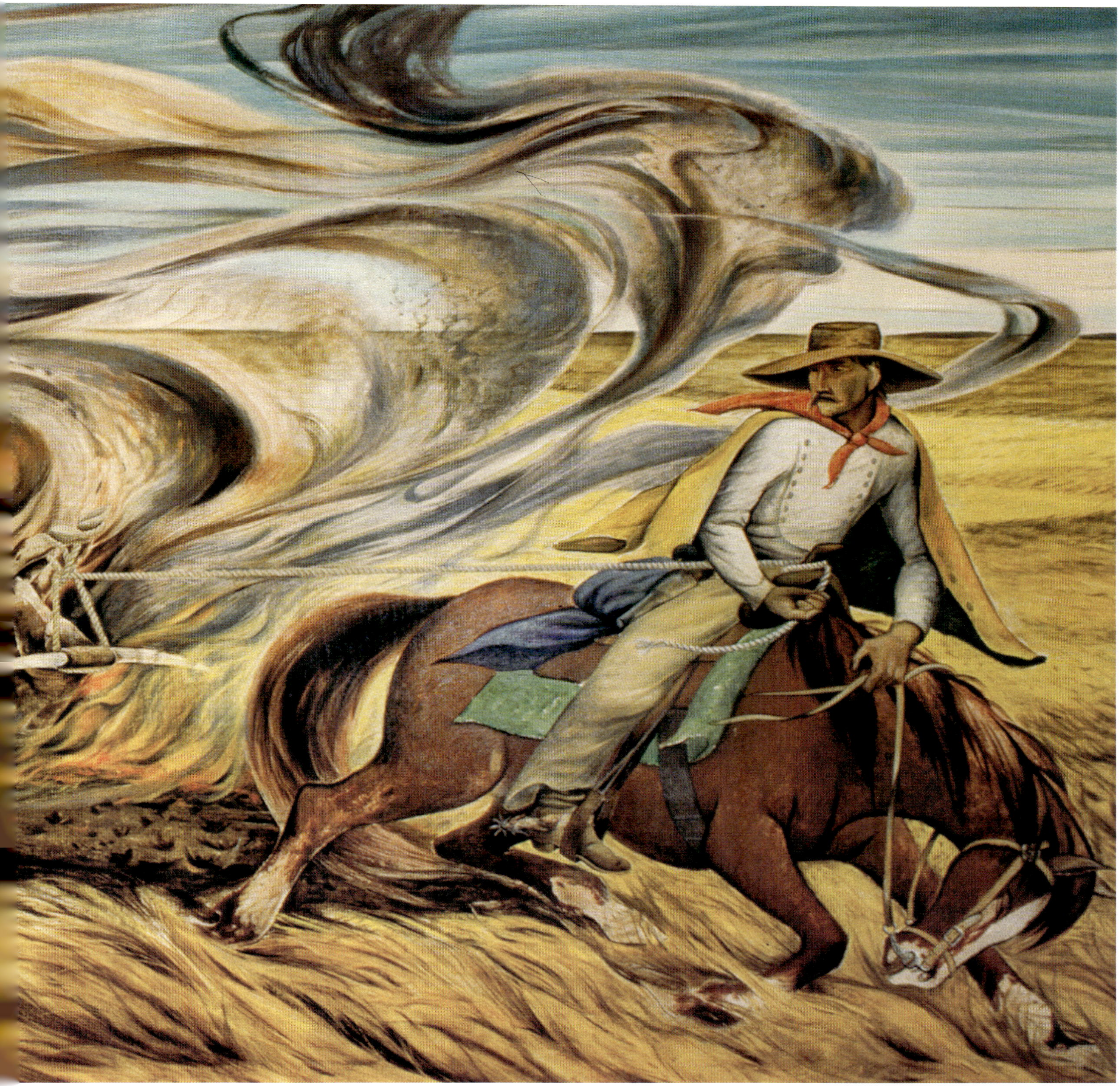

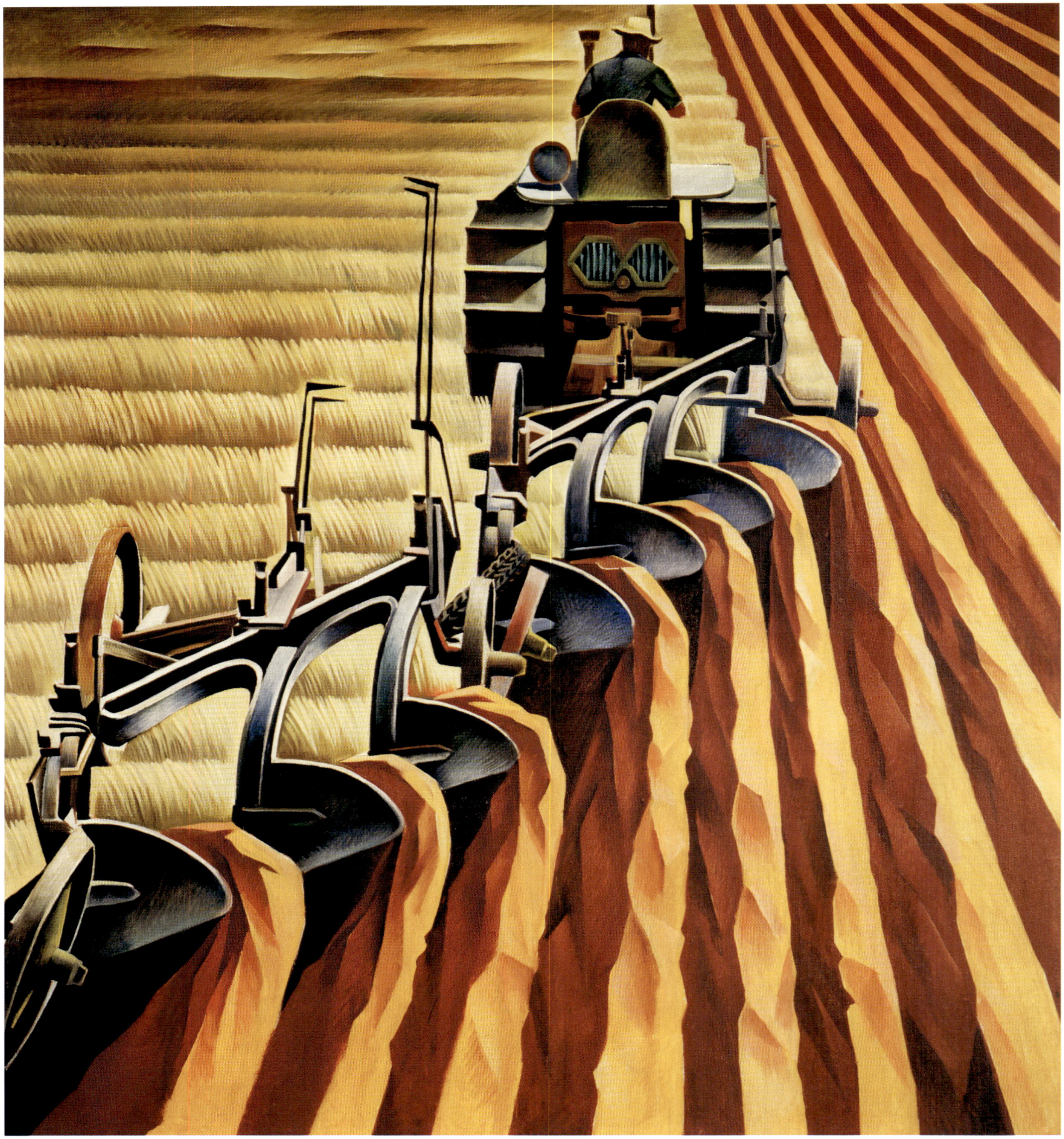

Gang Plow
Julius Woeltz, 1941

Opposite:
Disk Harrow
Julius Woeltz, 1941

Two panels from a series of murals for the Post Office, Amarillo, Texas

Julius Woeltz was born in San Antonio, Texas, and studied at the Art Institute of Chicago, in France and in Mexico, before returning to Texas to teach at the Sul Ross State Teachers College in Alpine, Texas, and the New Orleans Art School. He was also commissioned by the Treasury Section for post office murals for Elgin, Texas. Sixty-seven other post offices in Texas were provided murals by artists including Peter Hurd, Victor Arnautoff, Tom Lea, Frank Mechau, and Fletcher Martin. The murals by Woeltz shown here were two of his six panels for Amarillo.

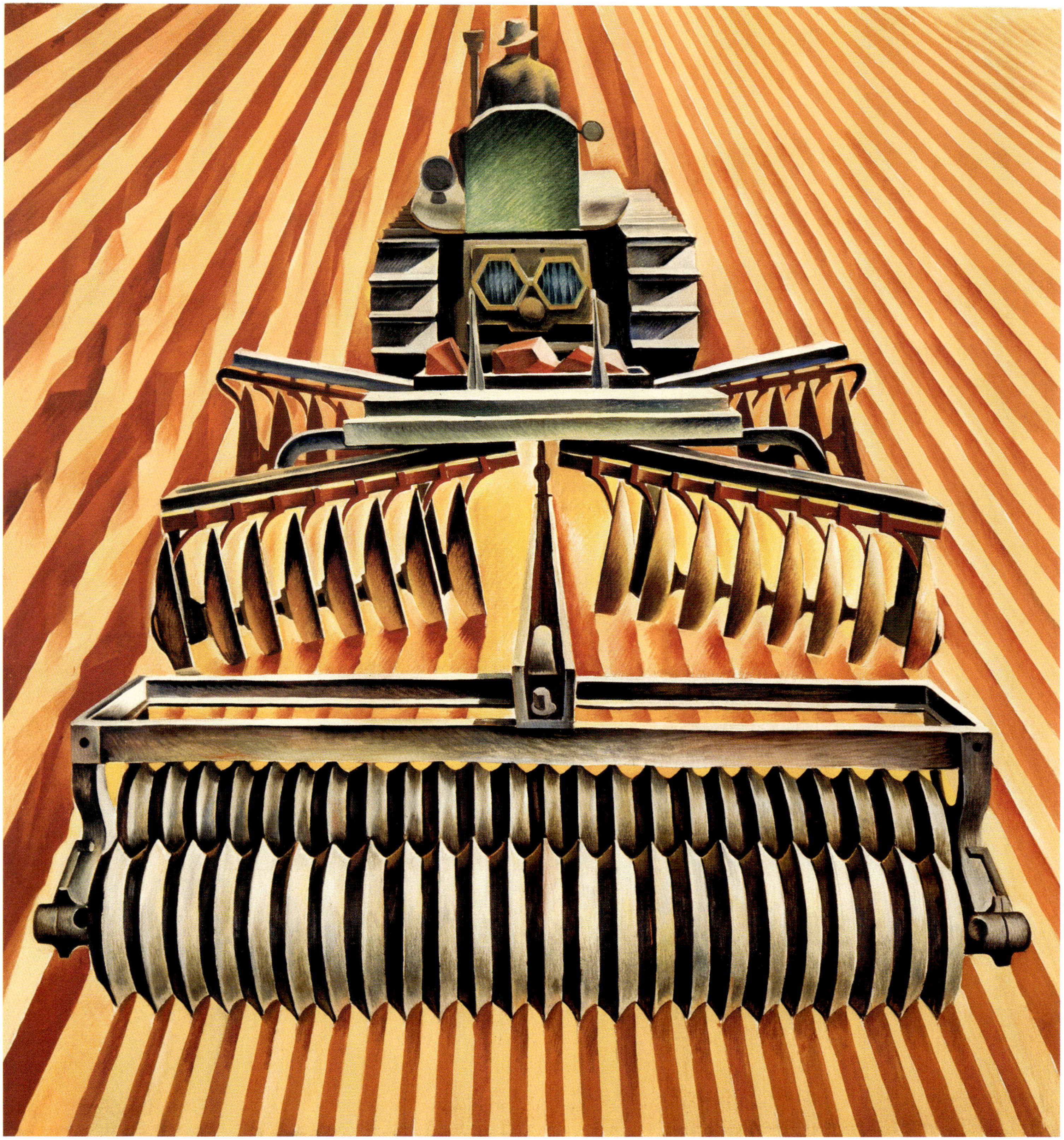

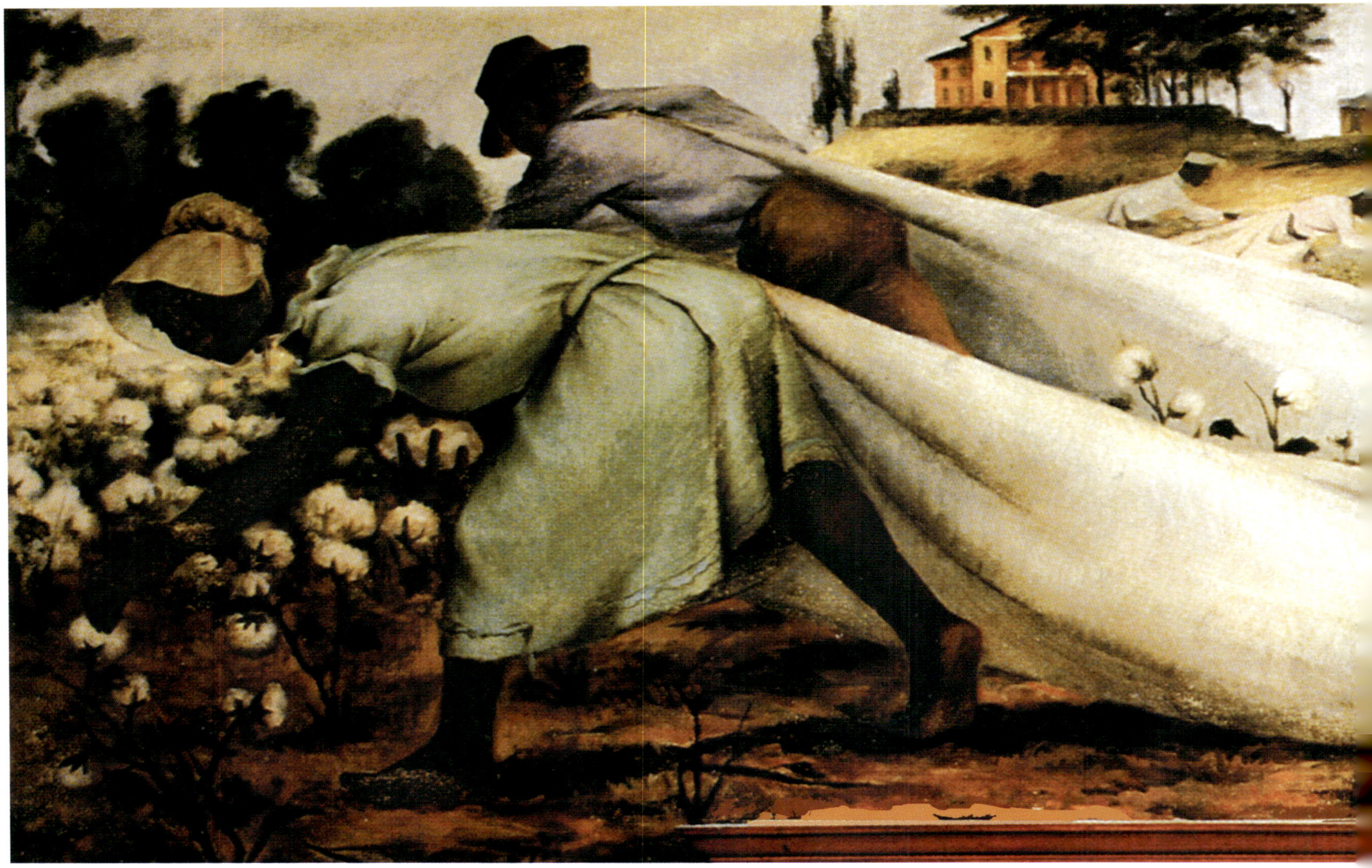

The Last Crop
Victor Mikhail Arnautoff, 1939
U.S. Postal Service Building, Linden, Texas

Like Ben Shahn (see opposite page), Victor Mikhail Arnautoff was born in the Czarist Empire—Shahn in Lithuania, Arnautoff in the Ukraine. Arnautoff arrived in San Francisco in 1925, having traveled through China and Mexico. He studied with Diego Rivera from 1929 to 1931, taught at the California School of Fine Arts, and from 1939 to 1963 at Stanford University. In 1934, he and Rivera's associate Clifford Wight presided over a group of twenty-five artists given work by the CWA/PWAP to provide murals for the Coit Tower, a memorial to volunteer firefighters. After their sketches had been approved, Arnautoff and Wight inserted references to Karl Marx, Lenin, *The Daily Worker, The Western Worker*, a Hammer and Sickle, and the motto "Workers of the World Unite!" Wight had worked with Rivera for Edsel Ford in Detroit, and on the Rockefellers' RCA Building project at the time Rivera inserted its Lenin portrait, provoking the grand controversy. In San Francisco their insertions after the approval of the designs called down upon the Coit project the wrath of the San Francisco Park Commission, which shut the doors to the tower. Picket lines appeared, as they had at Rockefeller Center. Piety contended with piety. Finally some of the interpolations disappeared and the doors opened.

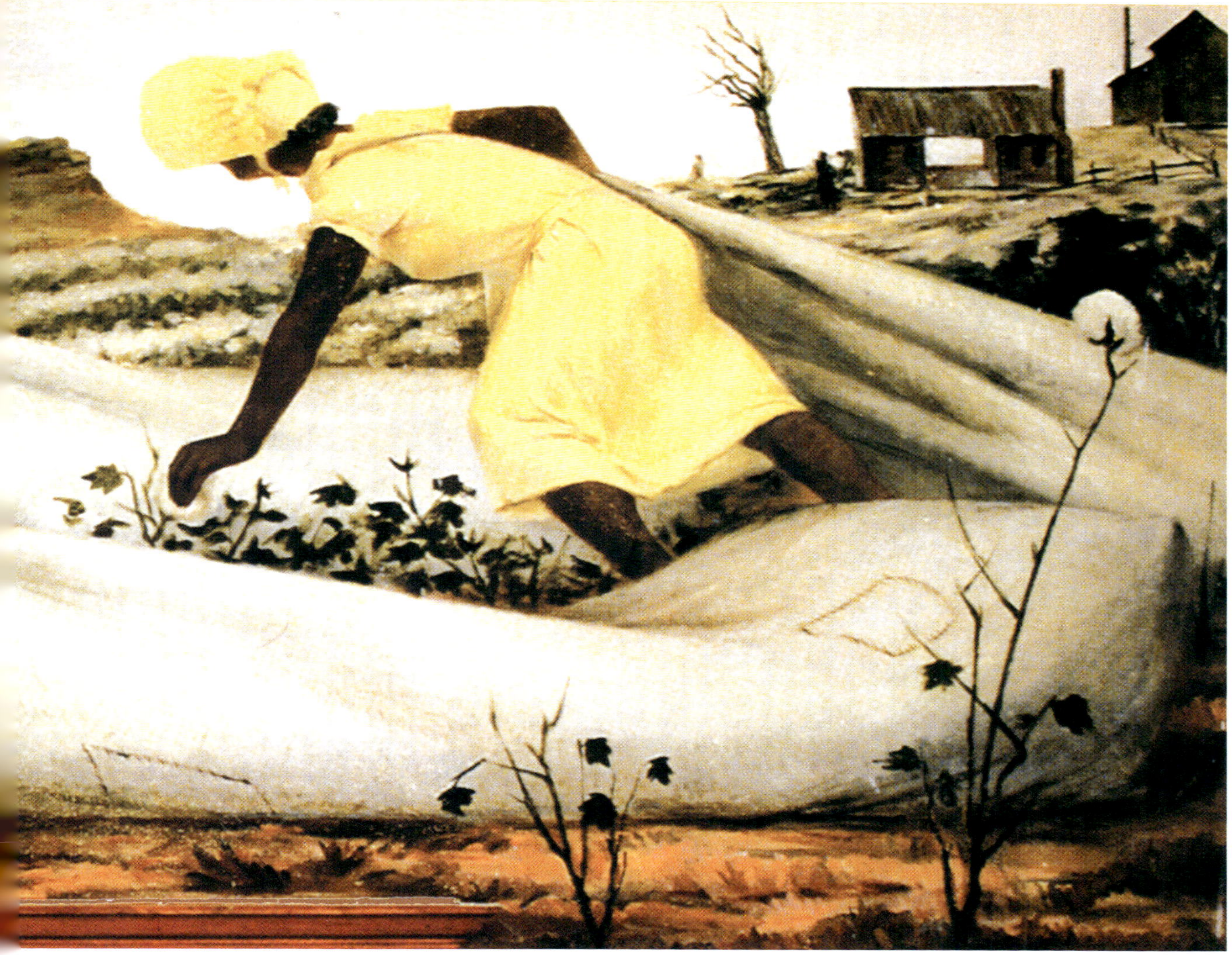

Nonetheless, the Section gave Arnautoff two further mural commissions: a post office mural for College Station, Texas, and another for the Department of Agriculture and Post Office Building in Linden, Texas, where Arnautoff depicted the privations of migrant cotton pickers and sharecroppers who harvested cotton by hand, mysteriously entitling the work *The Last Crop*. Ben Shahn photographed the cotton pickers dragging their heavy sacks of cotton bolls—and heavy they are, as the sacks accumulate great weight, and the work is often done when temperatures in the fields are over 100 degrees Fahrenheit.

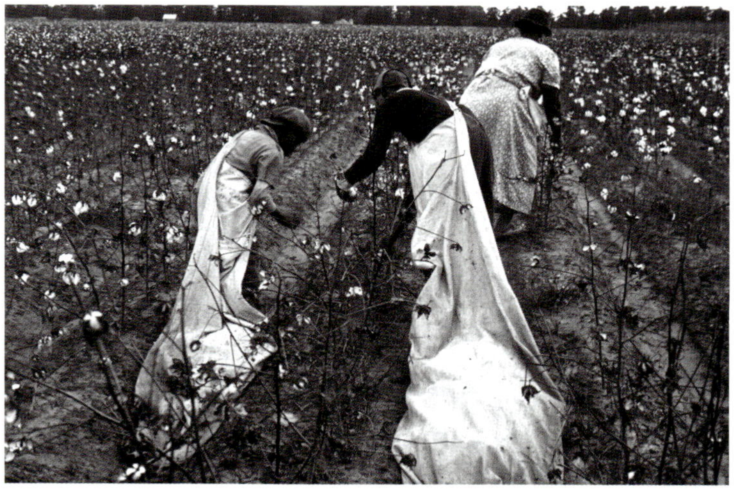

"Cotton Pickers"
Ben Shahn, 1935
Photograph

After working as a lithographer's apprentice, Ben Shahn attended New York University and the National Academy of Design. His murals for the PWAP depicted squalid working conditions among industrial workers, and his photographs of country people in drought and destitution informed the urban public of the desperate conditions among the rural poor (see main text). In 1935 he joined other photographers, including Arthur Rothstein, Carl Mydans, Russell Lee, Walker Evans, Gordon Parks, and Dorothea Lange, who were mobilized by Roy Stryker to support the work of the Resettlement Administration and its successor, the Farm Security Administration. During World War II, Shahn and many others in Stryker's crew produced posters for the Office of War Information. Shahn died in 1969.

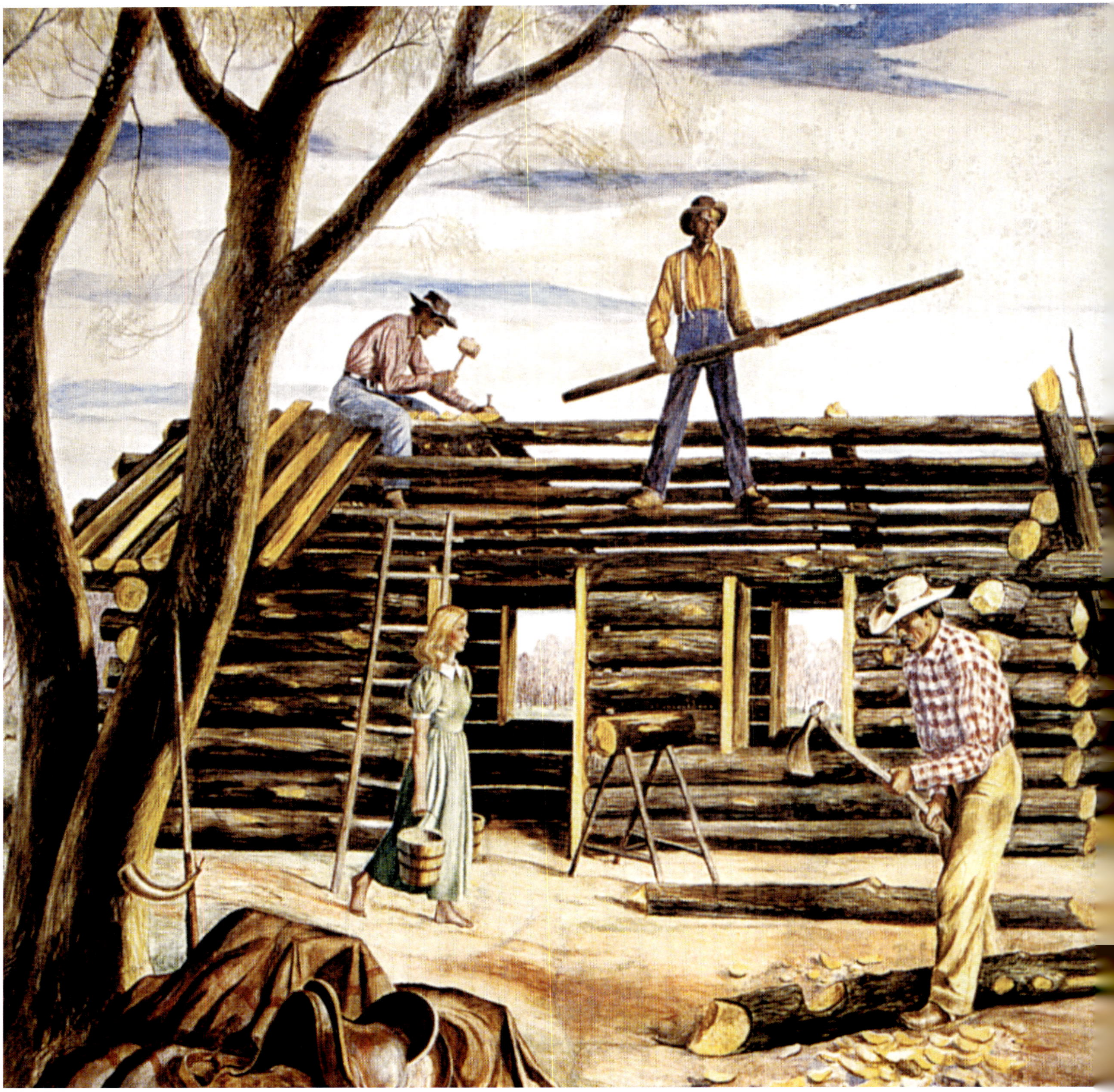

Pioneer Homebuilders
Peter Hurd, 1939
Post Office, Dallas, Texas

The mural shows pioneers raising a new home for a settler family. The model for the young girl standing with her mother under the canopy was Peter Hurd's daughter. Hurd was born in Roswell, New Mexico; his birth certificate named him Harold Hurd, Jr., however, his friends called him Pete, and in his early twenties he legally changed his name to Peter. He attended the United States Military Academy at West Point for two years, attended Haverford College, studied at the Pennsylvania Academy of the Fine Arts and with N. C. Wyeth, the patriarch of a painting family, father of Andrew and Henriette, whom Hurd married. He painted murals for the Federal Building in Alamogordo, New Mexico, and for the Public Library in Big Spring, Texas, for the Treasury Section, which drew the approbation of the circuit-riding Justice Harlan F. Stone (see page 56).

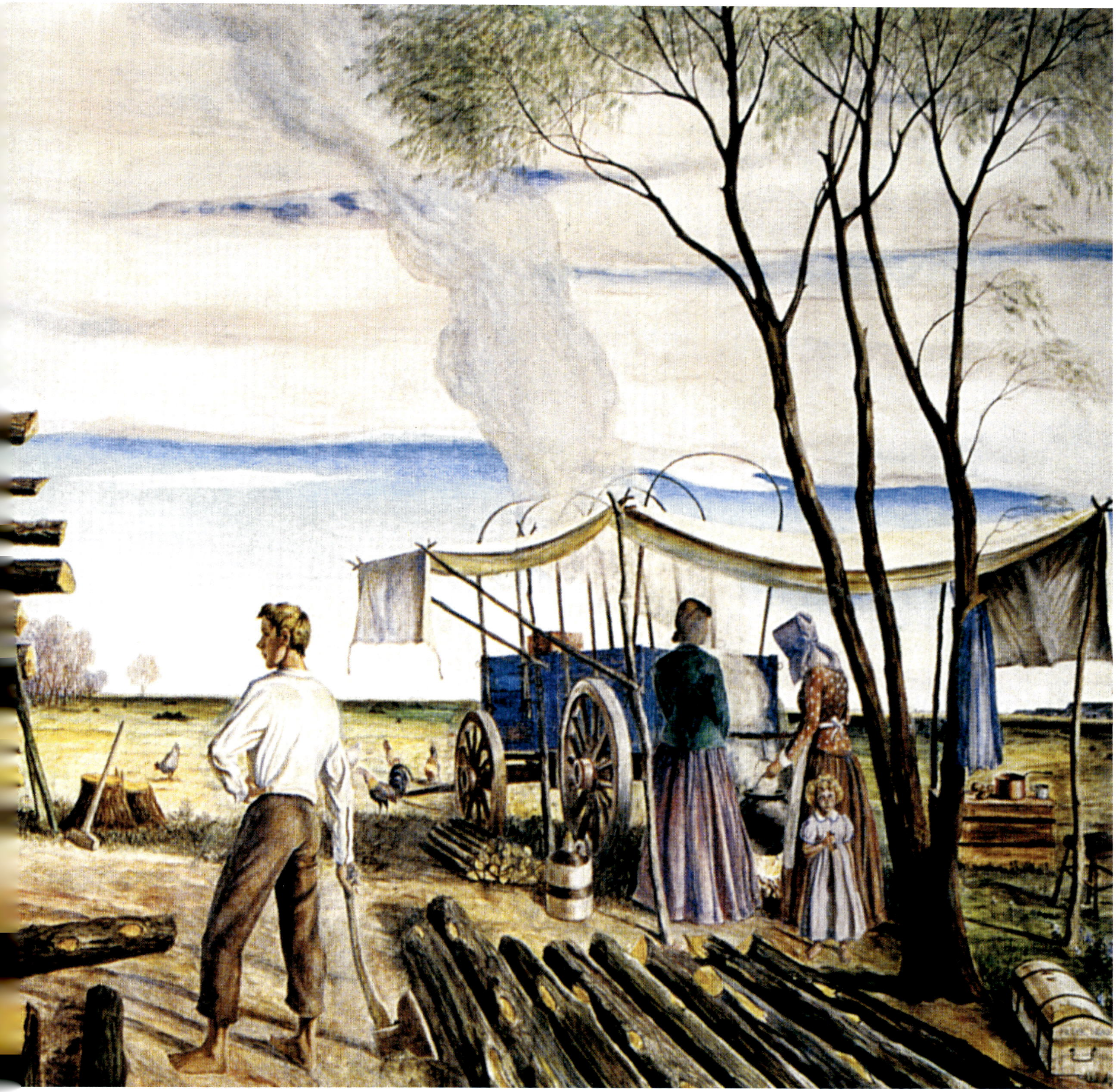

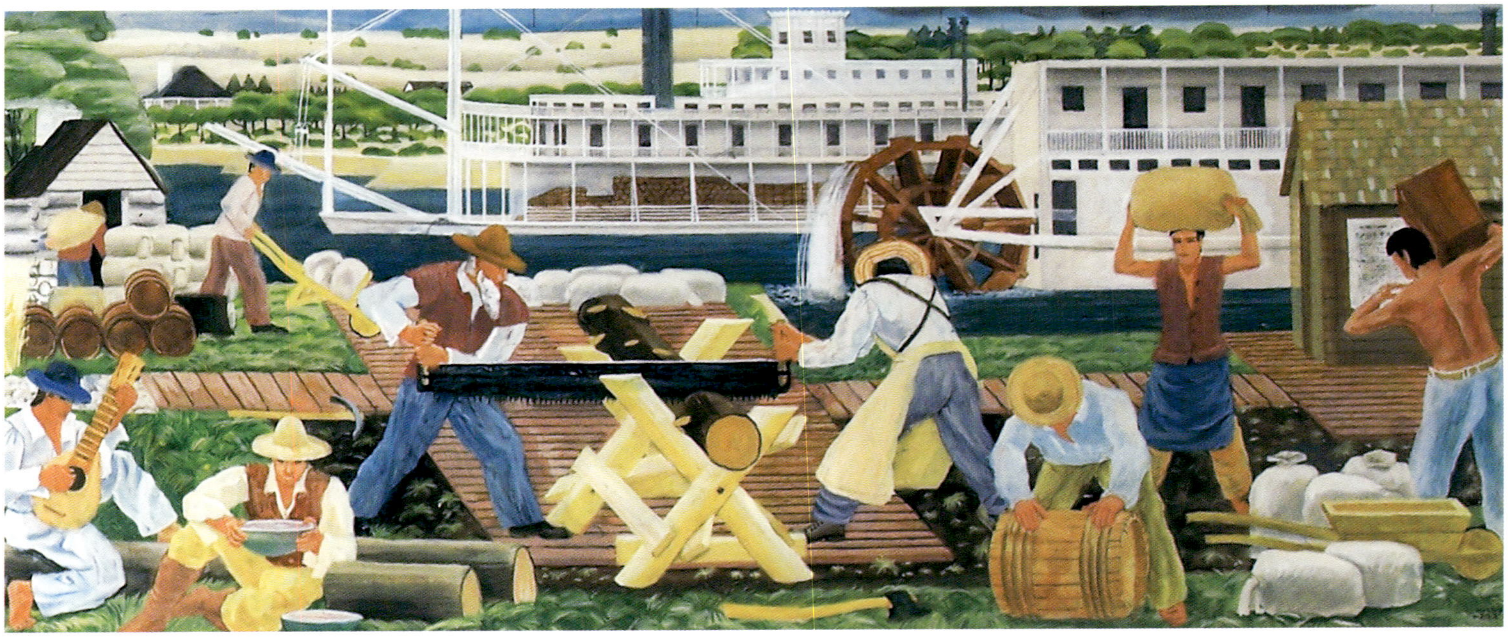

History of Southern Illinois
Karl Kelpe, 1939
Southern Illinois University,
Carbondale, Illinois

Karl Kelpe executed similar murals for the WPA/Federal Art Project for the Percy Julian School in Oak Park, Illinois. Though much of the art of the German-born Kelpe tended toward the abstract, his mural for the Southern Illinois University Library was in the illustrative "American Scene" style, depicting the growth of local industry, agriculture, and commerce. There is an affirming simplicity in all four of the works on these pages of WPA and Section art for Illinois and Indiana.

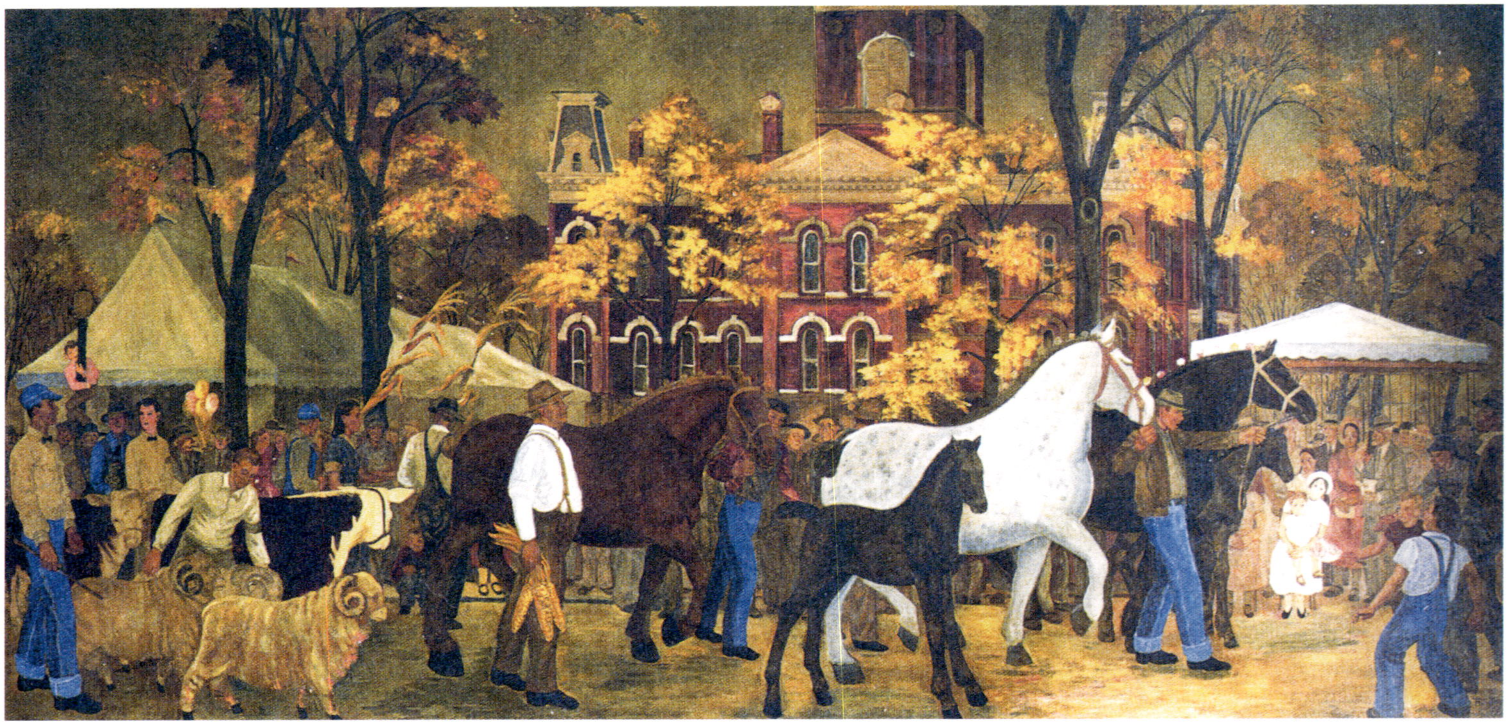

Bottom:
The Corn School
Post Office,
LaGrange, Indiana
Jessie Hull Mayer, 1941

Jessie Hull Mayer also painted murals for Culver, Indiana, in 1938, and Canton, Missouri, in 1940. She was born in Connecticut, studied at Yale under the muralist Eugene Savage, became a fine watercolorist and oil painter, and with her husband, the painter Henrik Mayer, worked mostly in Indianapolis.

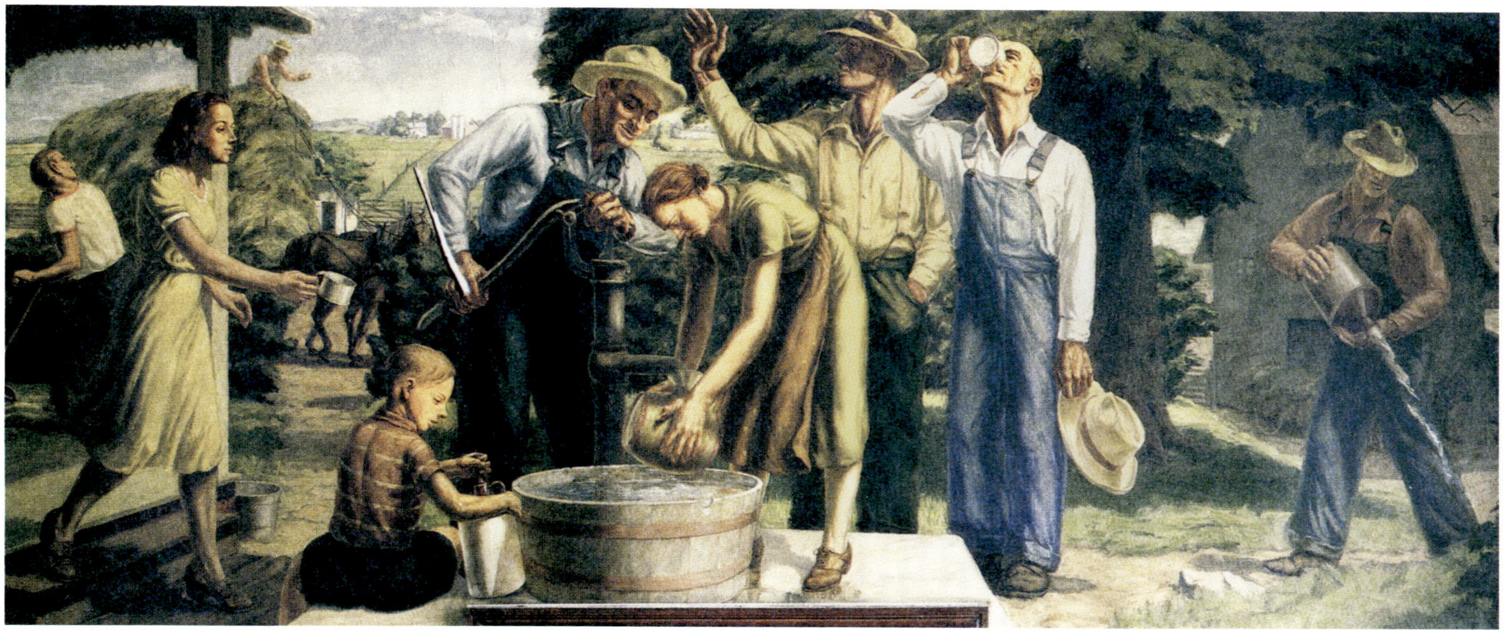

Filling the Water Jugs; Haymaking Time
Post Office, Danville, Indiana
Gail Wycoff Martin, 1939

Gail Wycoff Martin was a lithographer and painter educated at the John Herron Art School in Indianapolis and at Iowa State University. He also executed work for the WPA/FAP, and his work was acquired by the Art Institute of Chicago, Metropolitan Museum of Art, the Museum of Modern Art, and the Pennsylvania Academy of the Fine Arts.

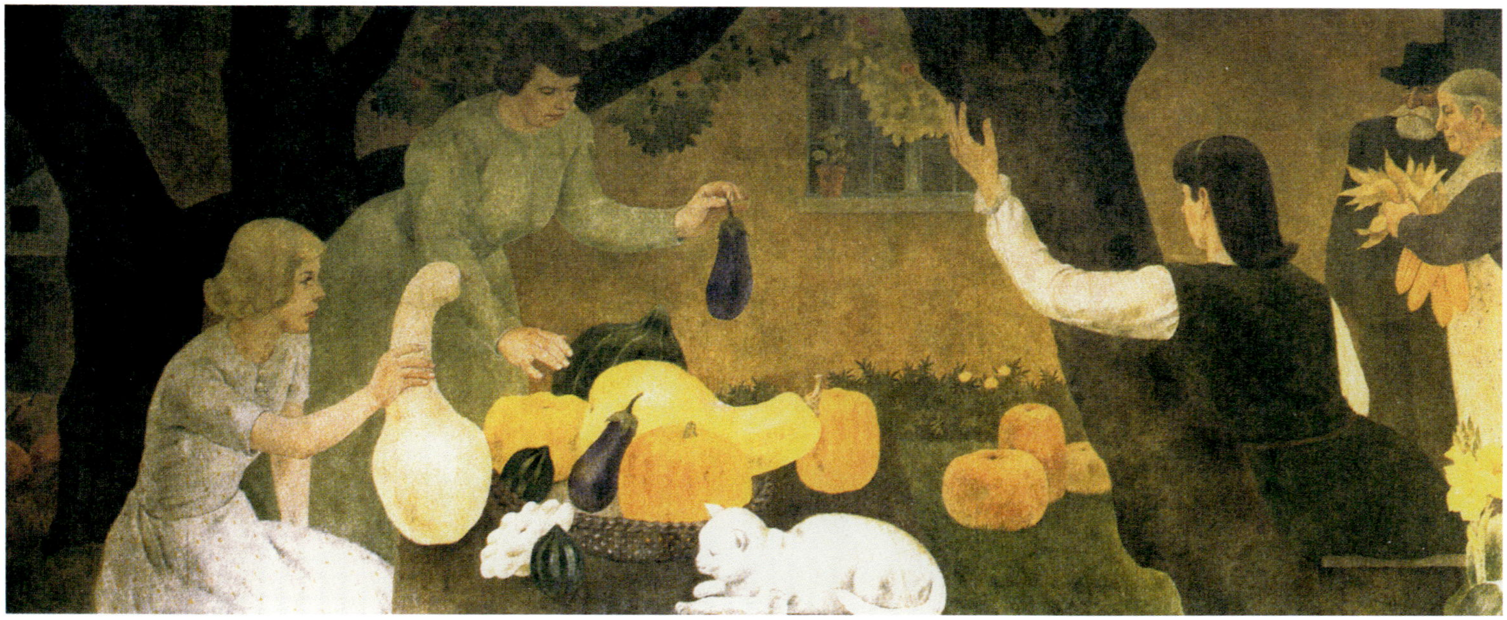

Bottom:
Preparations for Dunkirk Autumn Festival
Post Office, Dunkirk, Indiana
Frances Foy, 1941

Frances Foy was a Chicago artist who gave Dunkirk, an industrial town struggling out of the Depression, an affirming message in the Arts and Crafts style of a generation earlier. She wrote of going to the town and being impressed by the goats, the apple trees with apples still on, the glass-factory chimney, the yellow corn hung up to dry, and especially the "huge, goose-neck squashes, like gorgeous musical instruments. They are hardly natural looking." Foy often painted in light colors even when depicting scenes that social realists would have given darker hues. She received other Section post office commissions for West Allis, Wisconsin, and Gibson City and East Alton, Illinois.[24]

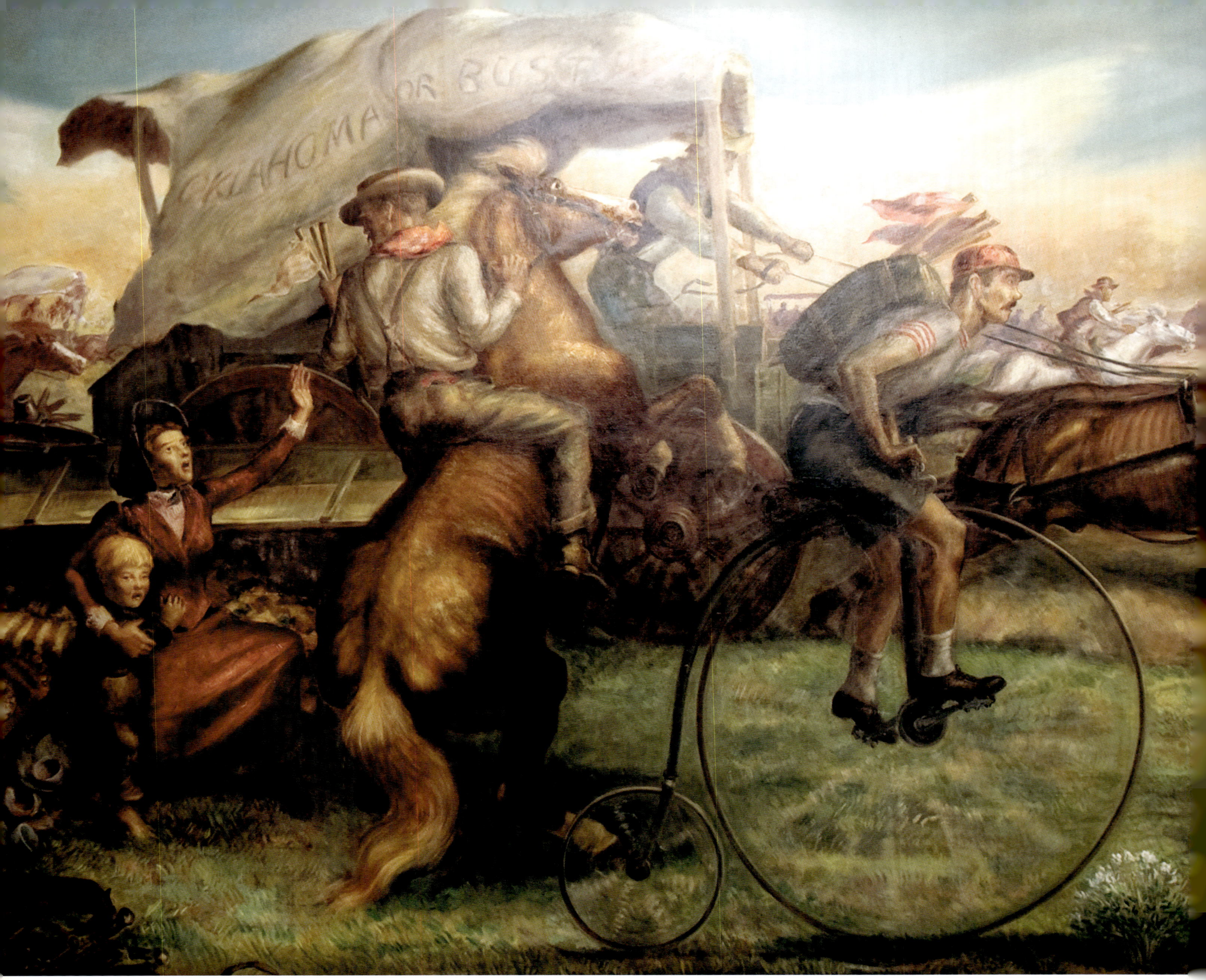
OKLAHOMA OR BUST

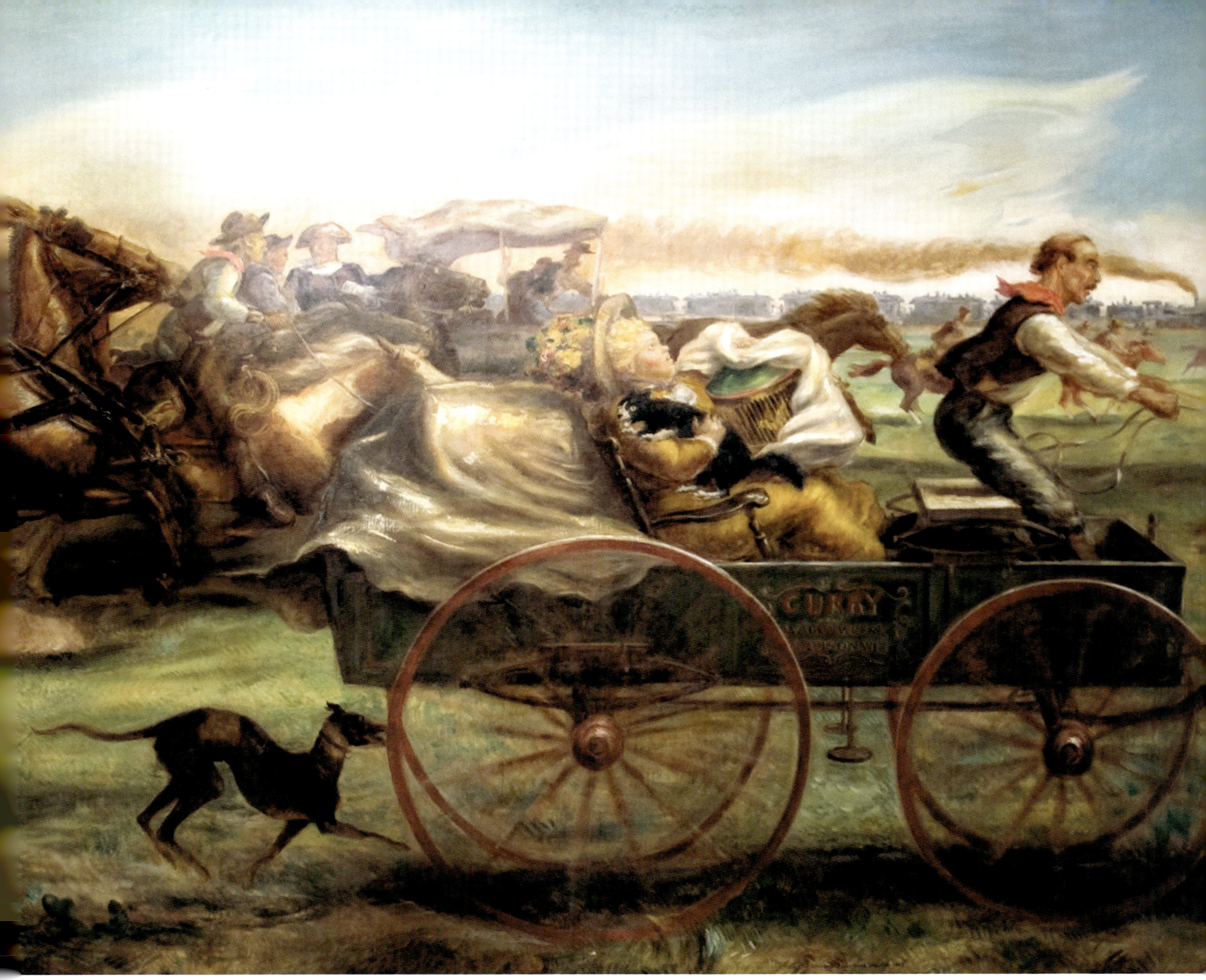

The Oklahoma Land Rush, April 22, 1889
John Steuart Curry, commissioned 1937, installed 1939

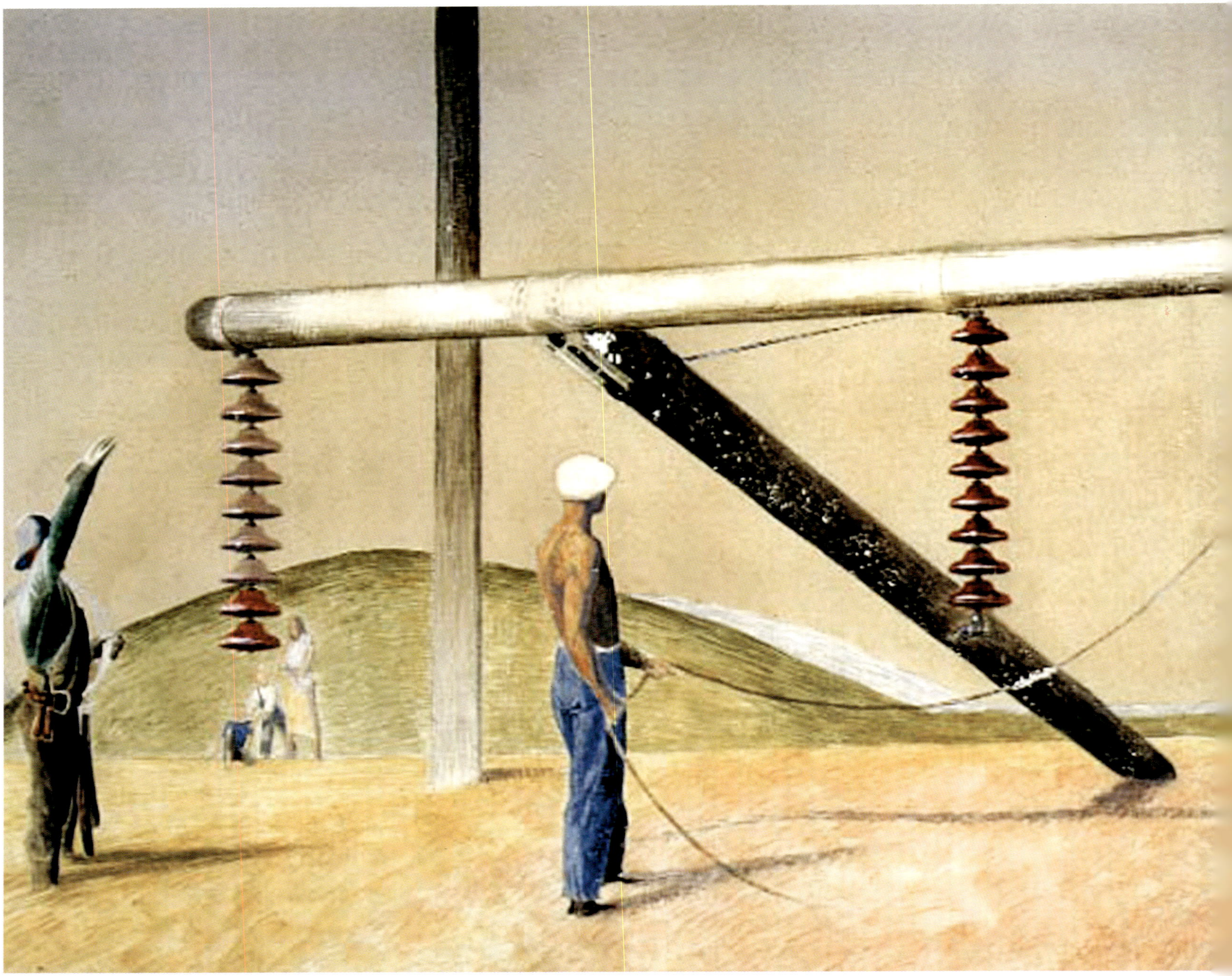

Electrification
Post Office, Lenoir City, Tennessee
David Stone Martin, 1940

David Stone Martin was born in Chicago in 1913, studied at the Art Institute of Chicago, and began his career as an assistant to Ben Shahn as Shahn was working on his murals for the 1933 Chicago World's Fair. Martin spent the remainder of the decade as art director of the Tennessee Valley Authority, served during World War II as an artist/correspondent for *Life* magazine, and gained fame for his jazz visuals on many album covers.

In the early 1930s, nine out of ten American farms had no electricity, and few had indoor plumbing. One of the New Deal's major achievements was bringing electrical power to rural parts of the country, a success most vividly demon-

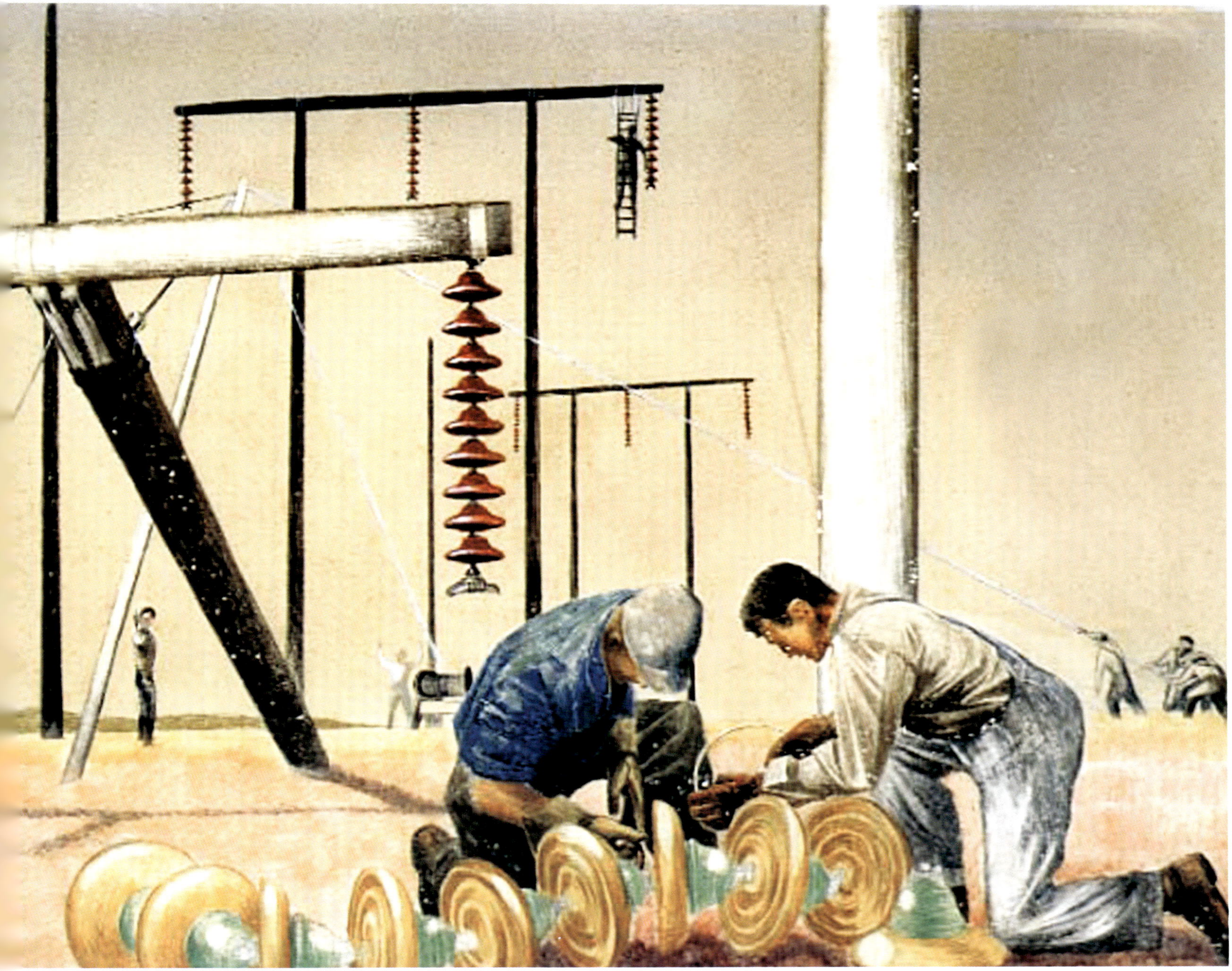

strated in the Tennessee River Valley, where the Tennessee Valley Authority (TVA) built a series of huge hydroelectric dams to provide power to the countryside.

Electrification was installed a few miles from where the TVA was constructing the Fort Loudon Dam.

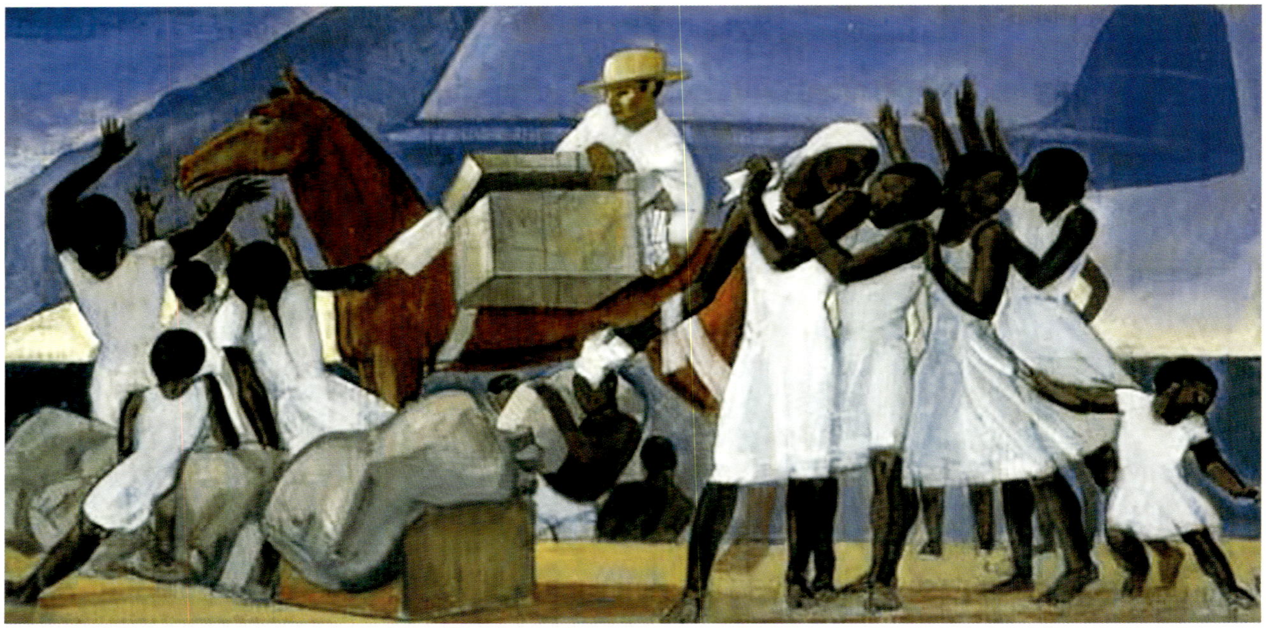

Mail Service in the Tropics (mural study, U.S. Post Office Department, Washington, D.C.) Rockwell Kent, 1936

Rockwell Kent was an artist, author, architectural draftsman, illustrator, printmaker, painter, lobsterman, ship's carpenter, dairy farmer, political activist, and master of unsparing depictions of bleak landscapes. Born in Tarrytown Heights, New York, he lived in Maine, Newfoundland, Alaska, Greenland, and the Adirondacks, and explored the waters around Tierra del Fuego in a small boat. He studied architecture at Columbia and painting under the tutelage of William Merritt Chase, Abbott Thayer, and Robert Henri. Henri encouraged him to go to Monhegan Island, Maine, where he learned to paint seascapes.

In the 1920s, Kent wrote and illustrated several books about wilderness in Alaska, along the Strait of Magellan, and Greenland. He also wrote two autobiographies, *This Is My Own* (1940) and *It's Me O Lord* (1955). Kent never belonged to the Communist Party, but in 1967 was awarded the Lenin Peace Prize, and donated paintings and eight hundred prints and drawings to the Russian people. During the Red Scare of the 1950s, after the State Department revoked his passport, Kent sued for its reinstatement and won in the United States Supreme Court.

His painting deferred little to the contemporary enthusiasm among other left-wing artists for the Mexican muralists. It was derived instead from English graphic artists such as Hogarth, Blake, the pre-Raphaelites, Aubrey Beardsley, and Americans such as Harvey Ellis. His experience as a carpenter and builder and his familiarity with tools served him well when he took up the graphic process. His blocks were beautiful in themselves, every line deliberate and under perfect control. The tones and lines in his lithography were solidly built up, subtle, and full of color. He usually made preliminary studies—old-master style—for composition or detail before starting on a print. Nothing was vague, accidental, misty, or suggestive; all was clear, clean, athletic, deliberate, and at times so austere as to become almost cold. Humanity was the hero in most of his prints, in which the human figure becomes a symbolic representation of destiny and human assertion in an inscrutable yet visible universe. There is a wondering yet exultant spirit in "Starlight," amid the terrors of "The End," and triumph in "Pinnacle."[25]

In the 1950s and 1960s, Kent was unpopular with those apprehensive of his political views, and with the increasingly

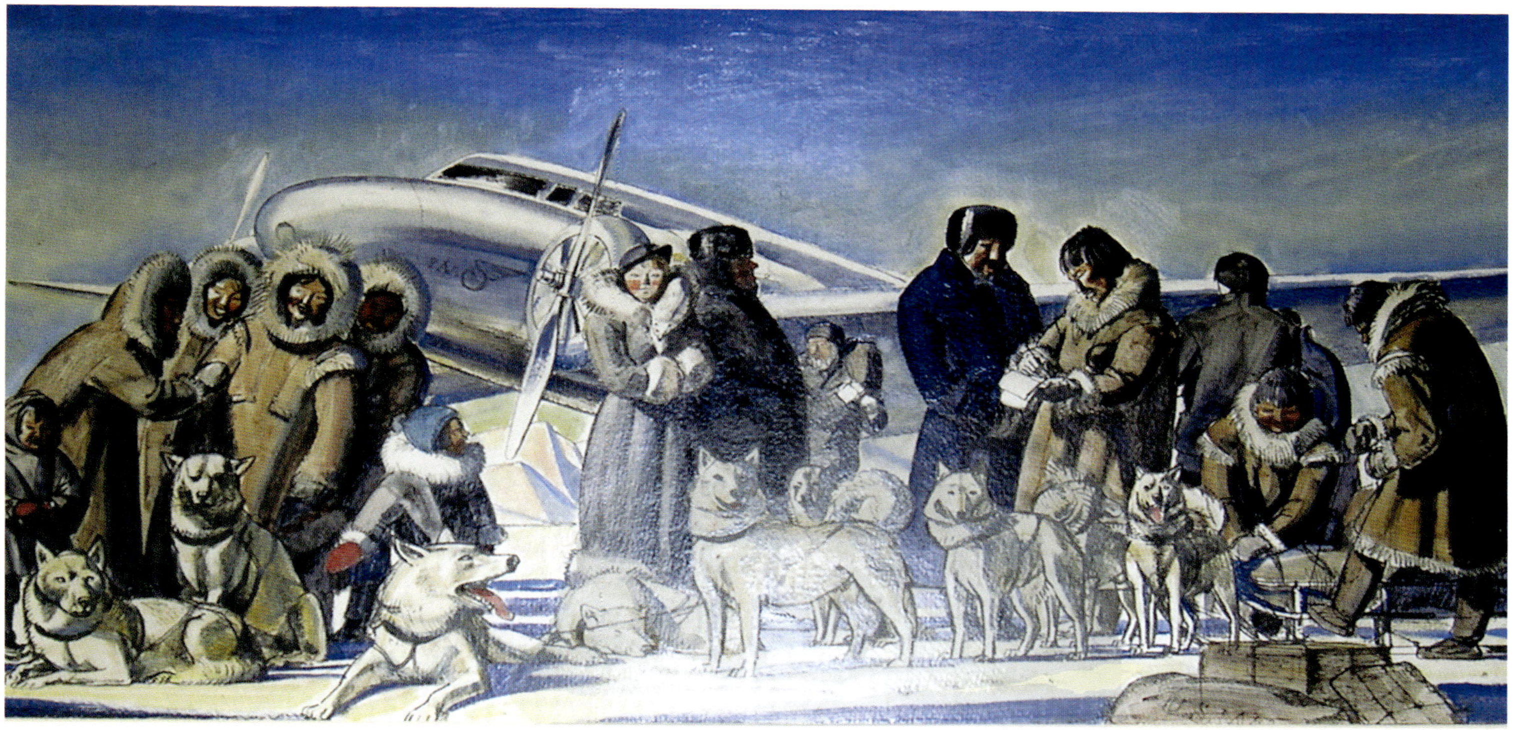

Study for U.S. Post Office Mural, Alaska
Rockwell Kent, c. 1930

dominant critics to whom art must be Post-Impressionist or non-figurative. He received his greatest popular acclaim in the 1920s and 1930s, as a printmaker and illustrator, when a survey found him to be the most widely known printmaker in the country.

Kent chose to celebrate Puerto Rico's first airmail delivery in a scene that verges on abstraction, in which the angles play off one another in a rhythmic and unified design—the horse's form appears to echo the shape of the airplane in the background. Kent smuggled into the design a political message—no head of Lenin or *Daily Worker* headline, but a letter held by a young woman in the foreground written in an Eskimo dialect that says, "To the people of Puerto Rico, our friends! Let us change chiefs. That alone can make us equal and free!" To the outcry that ensued in Congress, Kent responded: "The cause of independence in Puerto Rico needs no propaganda. Everybody knows that the majority of the people down there are in favor of it."

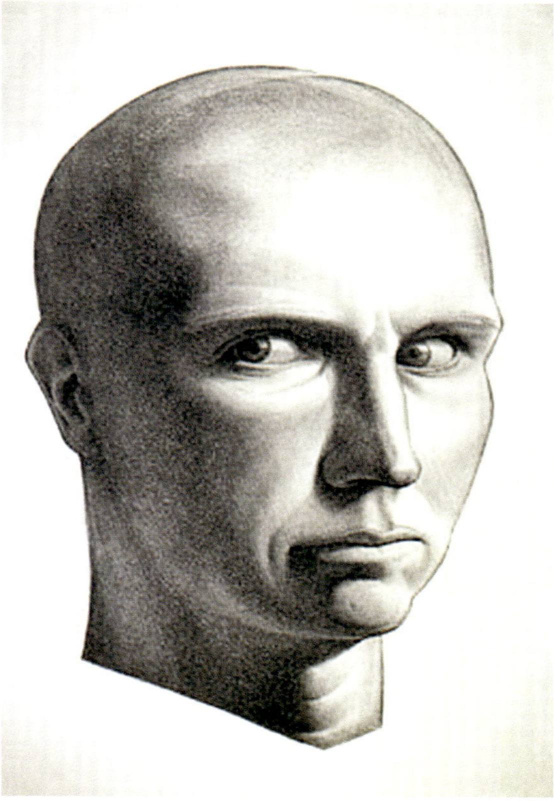

Bottom:
Self-Portrait (It's Me O Lord)
Rockwell Kent

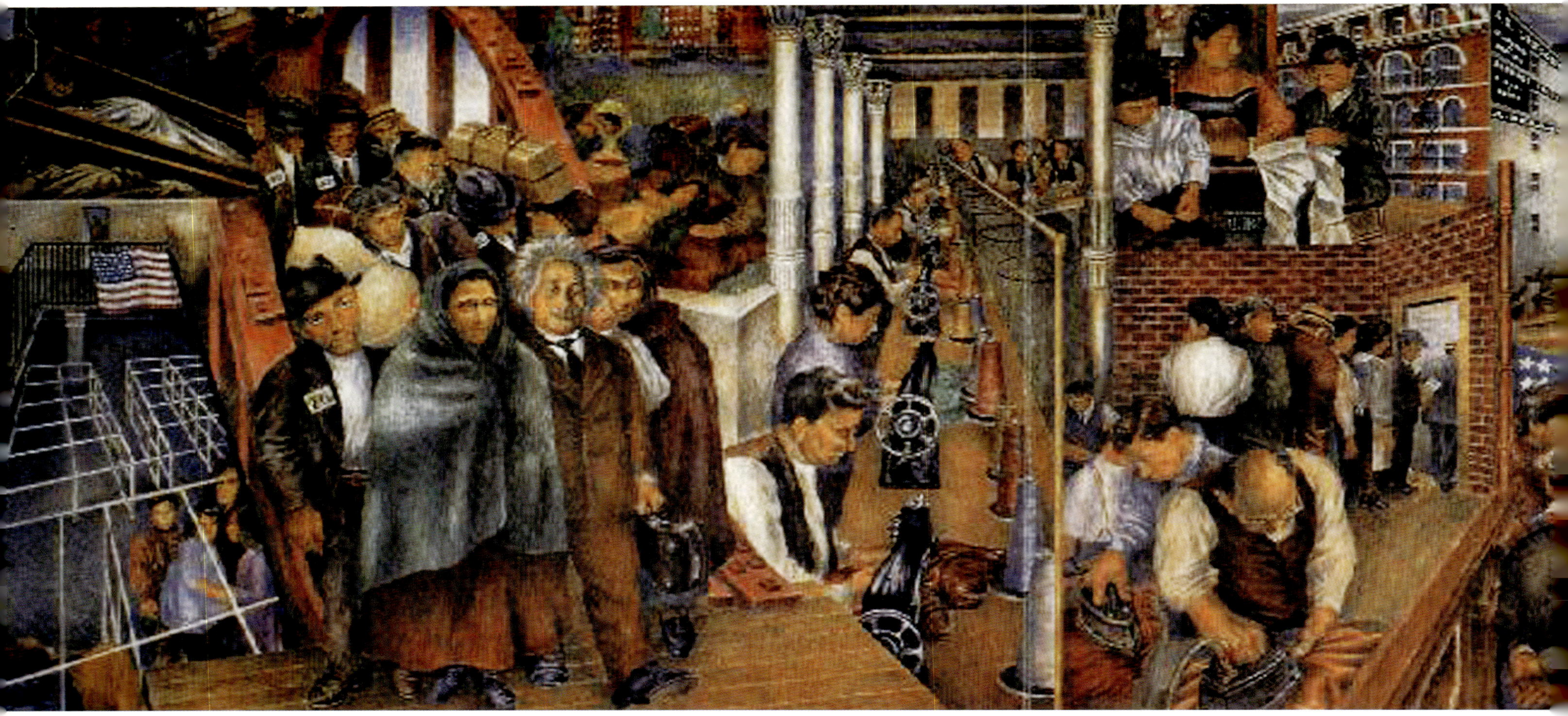

The Jersey Homesteads Mural
Ben Shahn, 1938
In the Roosevelt Public School, Roosevelt, New Jersey

Shahn created this fresco mural to commemorate the New Deal resettlement community of Jersey Homesteads, now called Roosevelt, in which he chose to live and work. It was an urban equivalent to the rural housing built by the Resettlement Administration and the Farm Security Administration, also administered by Rexford Tugwell, and for which Shahn had made photographs under the direction of Roy Stryker.

Jersey Homesteads was created to provide work-relief and housing for garment workers during the Great Depression, most of whom were Jewish immigrants from Eastern Europe. Shahn's panels depicted their ancestral places, their arrival at Ellis Island, and their planning of their cooperative community, and contrasted dark tenements and sweatshops in the city and the simple but light-filled homes and cooperative garment-factory, store, and farm in Homesteads.

Shahn was invited to create the mural by the architect Alfred Kastner, whose principal assistant was Louis Kahn. Later, the community was privatized, and the government sold off the boxlike houses.

Opposite:
When Fletcher Martin won the competition to paint a mural for Kellogg's new post office, the Section jury that awarded the commission praised his design for *Mine Rescue*, and so did Local 18 of the Mine and Smelter Workers. However, the local mine owners objected that the mural was unfair and would pain those who had lost a loved one in an accident. The Section buckled and asked Martin to redesign the mural to produce an inoffensive substitute, *Discovery*, showing two prospectors discovering a mine. Martin received other Section post office commissions in Texas and California.

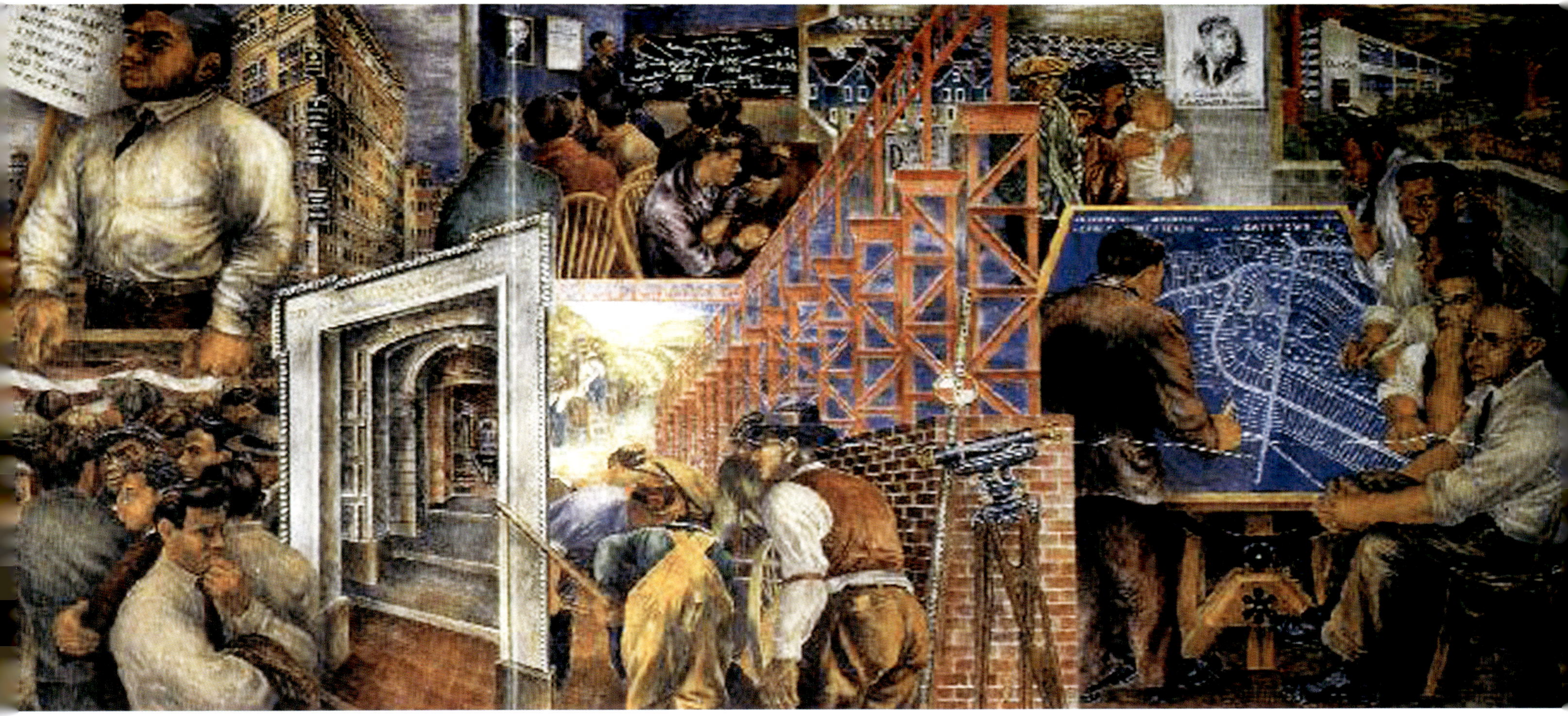

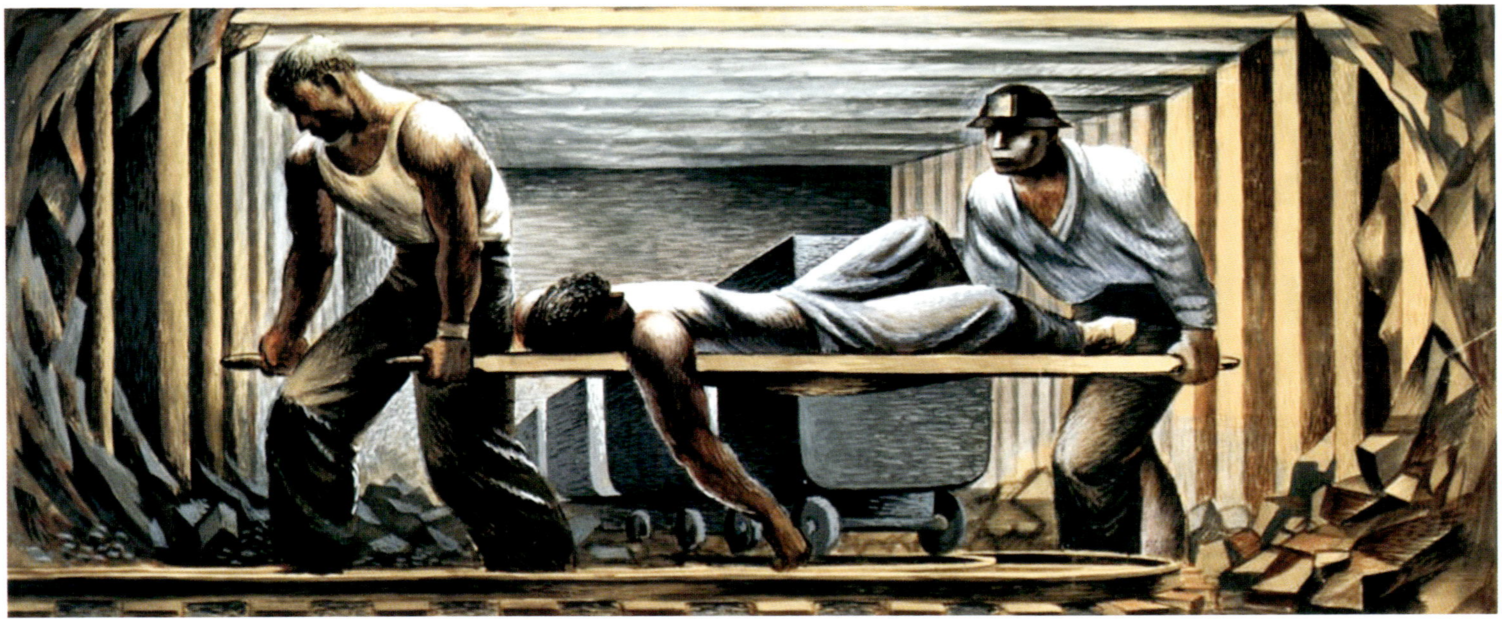

Mine Rescue
Fletcher Martin, 1939
Sketch for the Post Office,
Kellogg, Idaho

Chapter Four

Indians, Parks, the CCC, and the Arts

Then he told me–really ordered me–to "get busy . . . Suppose you do something tomorrow about this."
(National Park Service Director Horace M. Albright, recalling a discussion with President Franklin D. Roosevelt)[1]

READINESS IS A NECESSITY for fundamental and lasting reform. Both in celebration and in remonstrance, artists began in the 1820s to build constituencies for Indian policy reforms, for conservation, and to make the case for parks. In the nineteeth century, artistic science and scientific art were companions in exploring the West and Florida, providing visual and descriptive arguments for the preservation of the curious and the magnificent. During the 1920s and 1930s, photography and motion pictures extended and deepened the discussion, not only offering fresh reasons for protection but also showing what happened without it. In aid of New Deal policy, the older celebratory paintings and photographs were juxtaposed with dismaying new images: for every painting by George Catlin, Thomas Moran, Albert Bierstadt, or John Kensett that aroused the public to pride, distressing images were brought to the public in the work of photographers and filmmakers attached to the Farm Security Administration, the Tennessee Valley Authority, the CCC, and the WPA. These were admonitions, depicting what happens when public trusteeship is delinquent. Only after restoration and conservation did it become possible for art to celebrate success. There was cause for celebration by the end of the 1930s. Already, photographs could offer evidence of what had been rescued.

The arts also contributed mightily to building public support for the renewal of federal civil rights legislation, for Horace Albright's reorganization of the National Park System, for the preservation and protection of other common ground, and for John Collier's transformation of federal Indian programs. Artists had long been busy acquainting the public with Indians as individuals worthy of respect and of inclusion in the American covenant. Art had presented landscapes that deserved and required protection, celebrating magnificence. Fifty years after American Indians ceased to be a military threat, the New Deal was able to bring genuine reform to what Abraham Lincoln had, in the 1860s, called "the accursed Indian system." By the 1930s, the public was finally prepared to accept American Indians into the covenant. Religion and science provided the words—the arguments of decency and of realism—for which art had provided the pictures, of which the most immediate and telling were portraits. At last, a working majority of people was coming to think of Indians as individuals rather than as undifferentiated, skulking, and savage lurkers in the underbrush, stereotypes found in dime novels and B movies. The long, hard but successful slogging toward reform had been sustained by religious leaders who changed some hearts, as some minds were changed by the evidence of anthropologists who progressed beyond derogation of "primitive people" to an understanding of the varieties of human experience. Portraits provided faces for Indians, and John Collier—in accordance with Roosevelt's regular injunction to earnest, reforming subordinates to "go out and make me do it!"—went out and drew upon the accumulated constituency for reform.[2]

Thanks to New Deal art, reinforcing images were offered the public, some as sophisticated as Allan Houser's painting of Apaches *Singing Love Songs*, some as posed and romanticized as they appeared in the photographs of Lewis Curtis—but all of real people. Thus, on the principal fundamental to

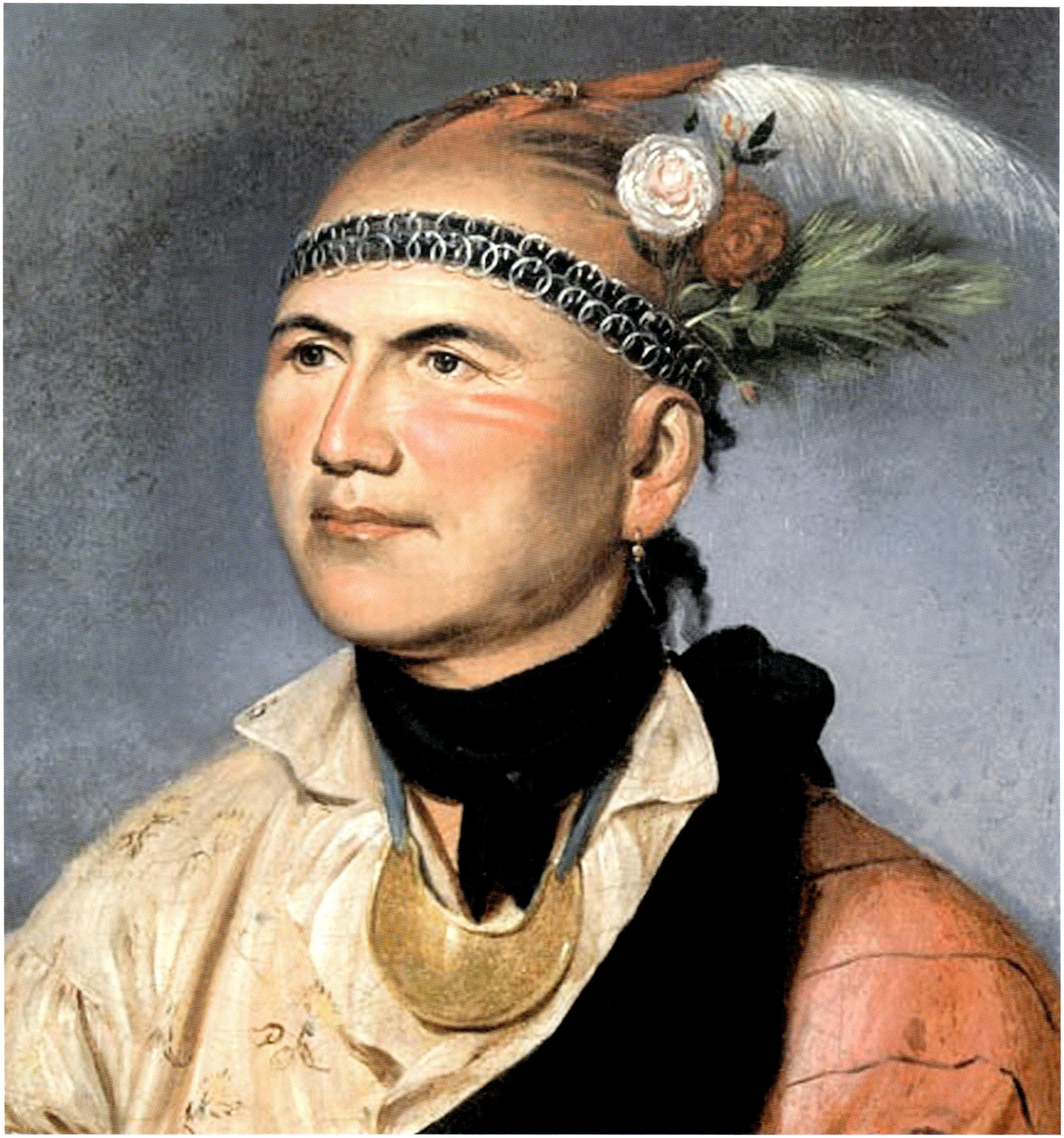

Joseph Brant
(detail)
Charles Willson Peale,
1797

Joseph Brant, or Thayendanegea, was a Mohawk war chief. He served under Sir William Johnson, the common-law husband of Brant's sister, during the Seven Years' War. He was educated in Lebanon, Connecticut, and served as an interpreter and a translator for missionary teachers. Brant sided with the Loyalists in the Revolutionary War as a captain in the British forces whose skill was admired by George Washington. After the war, Aaron Burr became Brant's friend and host in Philadelphia; Burr's daughter Theodosia and her husband were Brant's guests in his Georgian mansion in Ontario on their honeymoon. Brant offered aid to Washington in negotiating respectful treaties with the western tribes, though steadfastly opposed American invasions of the lands guaranteed those tribes by treaty. Brant was a very great man, whose presence in Independence Hall would have been approved by Washington.

portraiture that distinctiveness among people is the necessary precondition to informed respect, art contributed toward policy. As the nation learned to consider Indians as individuals, it derived useful lessons about community and about dignity in adversity. Collier wrote of "groups cooperating in order to intensify their own individualities . . . in the face of a commercialism ruthless alike toward man and the wild creatures and toward the land, the earth."[3]

Indian Portraits

Between 1820 and 1860 artists, some commissioned by government and some protected by it, depicted American Indians in their natural settings, with reverence for the people depicted. The first Indian to be the subject of a portrait by a major European artist was Joseph Brant, leader of the Mohawks, a man impossible to thrust into a background or to shrink into a stereotype. He was interviewed by James Boswell and painted by George Romney, Gilbert Stuart, and Charles Willson Peale, whose image of Brant is the only one of an Indian set among the notable white men in Independence Hall. In 1801 Aaron Burr's daughter Theodosia wrote her father from Brant's Canadian estate, where she and her husband were spending part of their honeymoon, telling him that her host was charming and courtly. Her view of Brant was confirmed by the mother and grandmother of George Catlin, who were among the prisoners he took in battle during the Revolutionary War and treated with such kindness that Catlin took as his mission in life returning kindness to American Indians. Even while earning his living as a fashionable portraitist of dowagers, magnates, and statesmen in Philadelphia, Catlin sought out visiting Indians, befriending them, and then visiting them in their homelands in order to provide "graphic delineation of . . . [their] living manners, customs, and character." He set forth from St. Louis in 1831, as had Meriwether Lewis and William Clark a quarter century earlier, with a military escort and a guide provided by Clark as General and Superintendent of Indian Affairs for Western Tribes. The guide was John Colter, another member of the expedition of 1803–6, who had explored on his own as far as the thermal extravaganza in the Yellowstone Basin known by Catlin's time as "Colter's Hell."[4]

Catlin painted Indians so assiduously that, as he said, he had been "reproachfully designated as the 'Indian loving Catlin'." "What of this?" he responded, "What have I to answer? Have I any apology to make for loving the Indians? I love the people who have always made me welcome to the best they had. I love a people who are honest without law, who have no jails and no poor-houses. I love a people who keep the commandments without ever having read them or heard them preached from the pulpit . . . . I love a people who have never fought a battle with white man except on their own ground."[5]

The Five Southern Tribes were being forced from "their own ground" westward onto the plains, where they had to compete for survival with other Indians already struggling to survive. Catlin made three hundred portraits of Indians. As many of them appear rank upon rank in the Renwick Gallery in Washington, they convey nobility undiminished by the destruction of traditional ways of life, rebuking those who called Indians "savages . . . an abuse of the word, and the people to whom it is applied." In 1872 Joseph Henry, the first Secretary of the Smithsonian Institution, provided him a studio and living quarters looking out upon a national park now known as the National Mall. By then, the Yosemite Valley had been dedicated as a park through the exertions of Frederick Law Olmsted and Abraham Lincoln (see chapter ten). Most people had forgotten that thirty years earlier Catlin had proposed a vast High Plains reservation, "preserved by some great protecting policy of government . . . in a magnificent park. . . . A nation's park, containing man and beast, in all the wild[ness] and freshness of their nature's beauty!"[6]

Like George Catlin, Seth Eastman of Brunswick, Maine, had an early affinity to Indian life. As an undergraduate at West Point he spent his vacation time among the local Indians, sketching their daily lives while broadening his skills as a scout and topographer. His first post was to topography duty at Fort Snelling, where the Minnesota River joins the

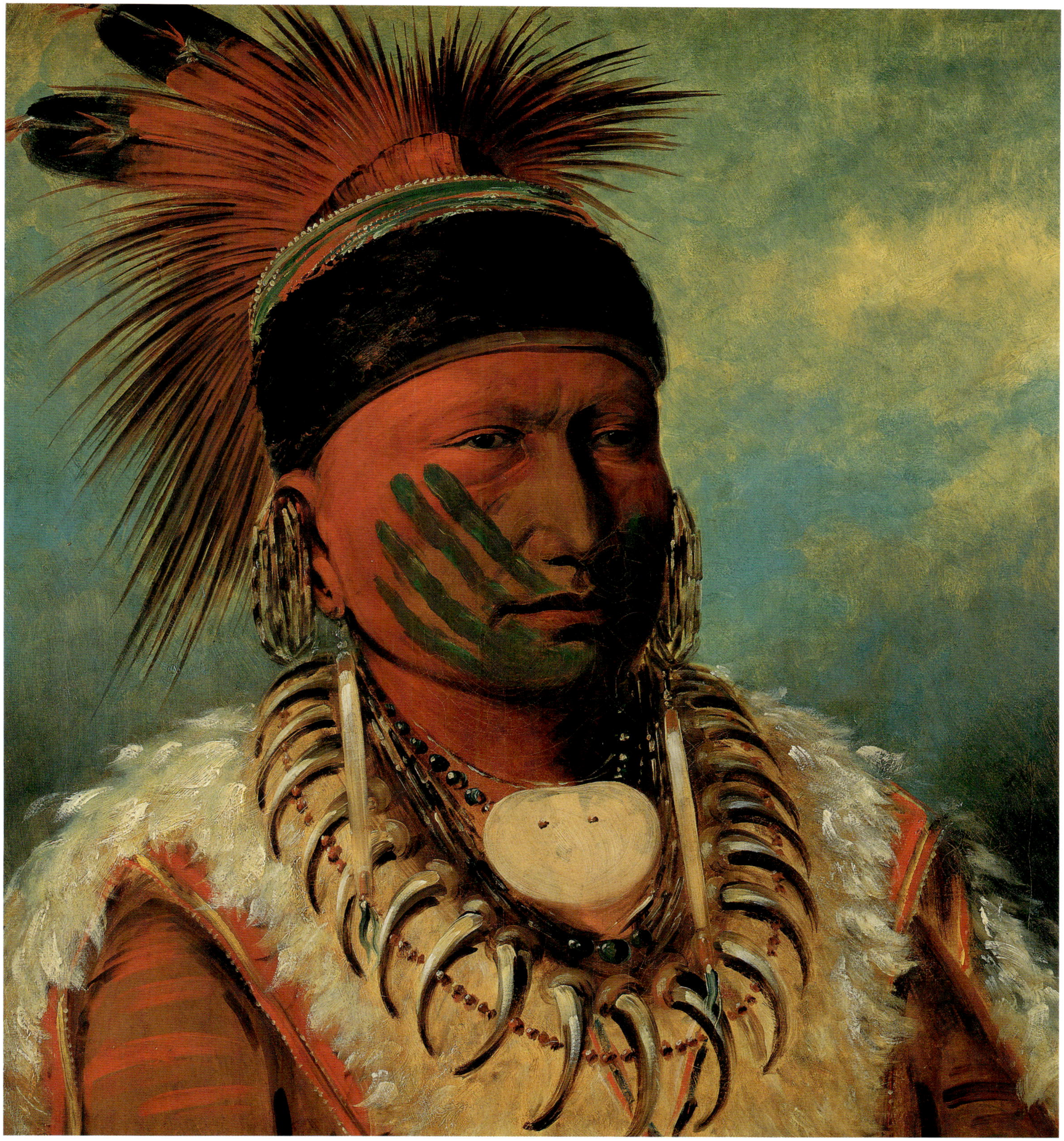

The White Cloud, Head Chief of the Iowas (detail)
George Catlin, 1844–45

Mew-hu-she-kaw, known both as White Cloud and No Heart-of-Fear, was one of several tribal chiefs of the Iowa people in the mid-nineteenth century. By the time this portrait of the younger White Cloud was painted in 1844–45, the Iowa population had dwindled from 1,400 to about 470 people. Treaties, some signed by the senior White Cloud, and laws passed to promote America's westward expansion had forced the Iowa people from their traditional territories on the plains of eastern Iowa to a small reservation in southeast Nebraska.

At this time of great crisis, White Cloud decided to raise money for the tribe by taking a small group of his people to London around 1844–45. There the American artist George Catlin had opened an exhibition of his large collection of paintings and artifacts representing American Indians. White Cloud and thirteen other Iowas wore their native costumes and performed tribal dances at Catlin's gallery and met with British dignitaries while touring London.

This portrait reflects White Cloud's stature within the Iowa tribe and his brave nature. He wears a white wolf skin over the shoulders of his deerskin shirt, strands of beads and carved conch shell tubes in his multi-pierced ears, and a headdress of deer's tail (dyed vermillion red) and eagle's quills above a fur (possibly otter) turban.

Mississippi. There he married the fifteen-year-old daughter of a Dakota chief. They had a daughter, to whom they gave the traditional name "Winona," but Eastman abandoned them, returned to West Point, arranged exhibitions of his landscapes in New York City, taught drawing, and married the daughter of a post surgeon. In 1841 he went back to Fort Snelling as its commander; his second wife wrote small books of Indian tales that were illustrated by Eastman.

Eastman was drawn back to Indian matters by Henry Schoolcraft, who needed illustrations for his six volumes of *Historical and Statistical Information Respecting the History, Condition, and Prospects of the Indian Tribes of the United States*. Schoolcraft tried to interest Catlin, failed, and turned to Eastman, who complied very competently before returning to active duty during the Civil War. The armies and battlefields were photographed by Mathew Brady and sketched by Winslow Homer, and the human effects of war distilled into verse by Walt Whitman. Eastman, a professional soldier, was the only artist brevetted a general; after the war he received full general's pay to make paintings of seventeen forts for the House Committee on Military Affairs, and a series of nine scenes of Indian life for the Committee on Indian Affairs.

He was depicting things he had actually seen, while his competitor, Charles Bird King, remained in Philadelphia executing portraits for a government-sponsored, three-volume survey of the "tribes of North America" without setting foot in Indian country. King had studied in London with Benjamin West, and it was thought a compliment to the Indians he depicted that he was chosen to record them, in or out of context.

Some of the forts painted by Seth Eastman later became parks, if something interesting had happened to them, or in them, or if there were interesting animals to be seen in and around them. Fort Jefferson, in the Dry Tortugas, the largest of them all, began to acquire celebrity status after John James Audubon sought out the tropical birds and animals around its formidable parapets. Fort Snelling was an artistic favorite after Seth Eastman demonstrated how picturesque was its site atop a limestone butte. It remains so even though the flatlands around it have been engulfed by shopping malls and the Minneapolis–St. Paul airport.

Expedition Art

Painting forts is a celebration of stasis and perdurance—take notice, they say, we are, we have been, and we will be. Painting expeditions is different. It expresses discovery, novelty, and change, but it too acquaints a public with landscapes, raising questions about what should be done with them after seeking to settle questions about who owns them. Artists were engaged to accompany European expeditions to record staking claims. Their descriptions of places discovered were important to posterity and preservation, but that was not why they were hired; although science and anthropology were served, imperial ambition came first. So art traveled at government expense, under military protection, with Sir Humphrey Gilbert's expedition to Newfoundland in 1583, with Sir Walter Raleigh's to Virginia in 1585, and with the French along the Gulf Coast and in Florida. What little is known about the ceremonial life of the Natchez Indians of Mississippi comes to us from images contributed to the visual record by artists attached as scouts to the French, as confirmed only by fragments of pottery and inferences drawn from ceremonial space bounded by mounds.

In the eighteenth century, art expanded its role, with increasing opportunities to record matters of interest to science and anthropology. Thomas Jefferson and other cognoscenti among the founders of the United States were the beneficiaries of the documentary prowess of the artists engaged by the Royal Society and the British Admiralty, who collaborated with the intelligence services organized and managed from London by the scientist and spymaster, Sir Joseph Banks. (Patrick O'Brian's Aubrey/Maturin novels are the best source of reading about Banks and his proxies.) Captain Cook had enough artists and draftsman aboard his three Pacific voyages to produce hundreds of engravings together with several thousand drawings and paintings in oil and watercolors.

In the pre-photographic age, scouting required sketching. Military academies required drawing and painting classes. Artists being the meticulous people they are, the figures they set to give scale to topography were often provided clothing and faces. Accordingly, a profession grew that might be designated in curricula as "illustrated military anthropology." Behind the figures, naturally enough, was landscape, some of it quite dramatic and painted so attractively as to merit preservation. Between the bucolic and the picturesque—the cultivated Midwest and the wild Rocky Mountains—however, lay the high, dry plains traversed by early explorers such as Zebulon Pike and Stephen Harriman Long and recorded by their complements of artists. Few were the paintings of badlands and dust storms, but those few were enough to provide warnings confirmed later in the nineteenth century when scientists sought to convince policy makers that large portions of "Indian country" were hopeless for agriculture, a basic truth later affirmed by the artists and scientists attached to the expeditions of Major John Wesley Powell. *The Grapes of Wrath* came later, but the visual reports of early artists made it easier for conservation and water policy to begin a realistic assessment of the West and to act in recognition that there was a Dust Bowl and a Great American Desert. Photography sponsored by the New Deal confirmed that recognition and encouraged policy based upon it.

From May 1819 until January 1821, Long had brought along with his blue-uniformed troopers a squad of painters, including Samuel Seymour, Titian R. Peale, and Thomas Say. Peale and Say were also botanists. Edwin James, Long's surgeon-surveyor, was also a geologist, "keeping the books" of land forms as Peale collected and illustrated specimens of flora and fauna. Long's expedition traversed the plains all the way to the Colorado Rockies, where its leaders named, and climbed, one peak for Long and another for Pike. A core of support for parks in the Rocky Mountains thus began developing among climbers. At the same time, dry-plains conservation policy gained its first constituency among those who made their way to mountainous high drama across the intervening windswept dessication that in the 1920s and 1930s became the Dust Bowl. Long returned from the Rockies across the Staked Plains, avoiding the strong Spanish garrisons in Texas and among the pueblos in New Mexico, so twenty years passed before there was another opportunity for a professional painter to depict Taos, Acoma, or the ruined missions and ancient structures now preserved as parks. Only in the 1840s could the public obtain the impressions of them conveyed by the brush of John Mix Stanley by grace of the sabers of Stephen Kearney.[7]

Like Catlin, Stanley was born on the Iroquois frontier, but he had a slower start in getting a cavalry escort to paint Indians. Apprenticed to a coach maker, he progressed to painting coaches, signs, and the exteriors of houses. Then, at Fort Snelling, he started painting Indian portraits where Eastman

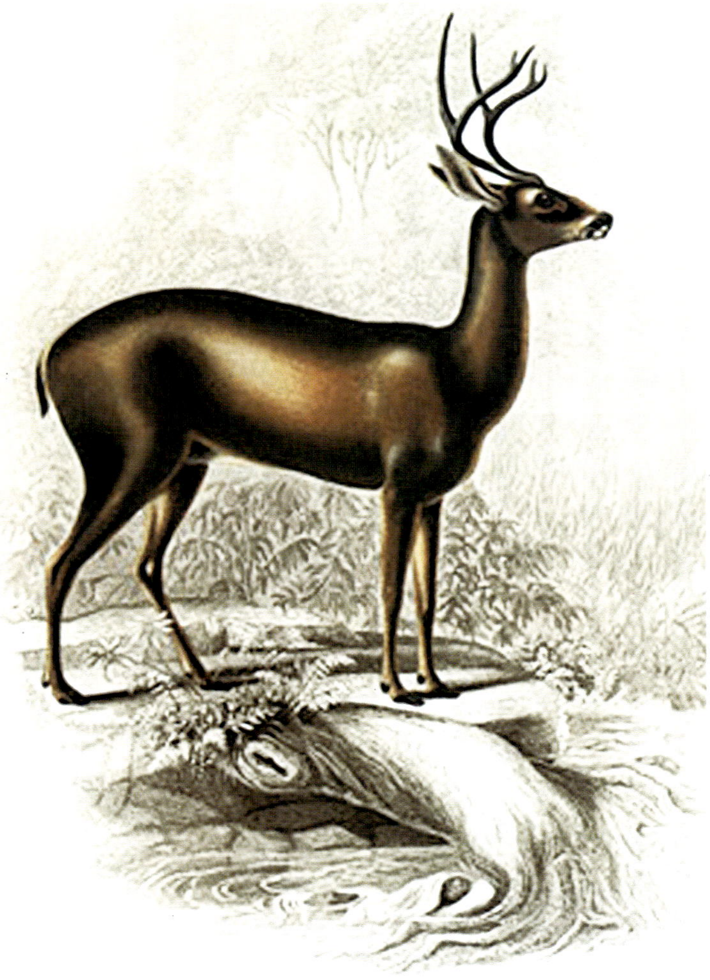

Columbian Blacktail
Titian Ramsay Peale,
c. 1830

Titian Ramsay Peale, son of Charles Willson Peale, was, like his father, a splendid painter and botanist, ornithologist, and natural historian. He accompanied the Wilkes Exploring Expedition along the shores of the Pacific Ocean and also painted and did scientific research in Florida (see main text).

Peale's *Columbian Blacktail* is an example of virtuoso lithography; his painting of volcanic action on Hawaii (not shown in these pages) is his masterpiece.

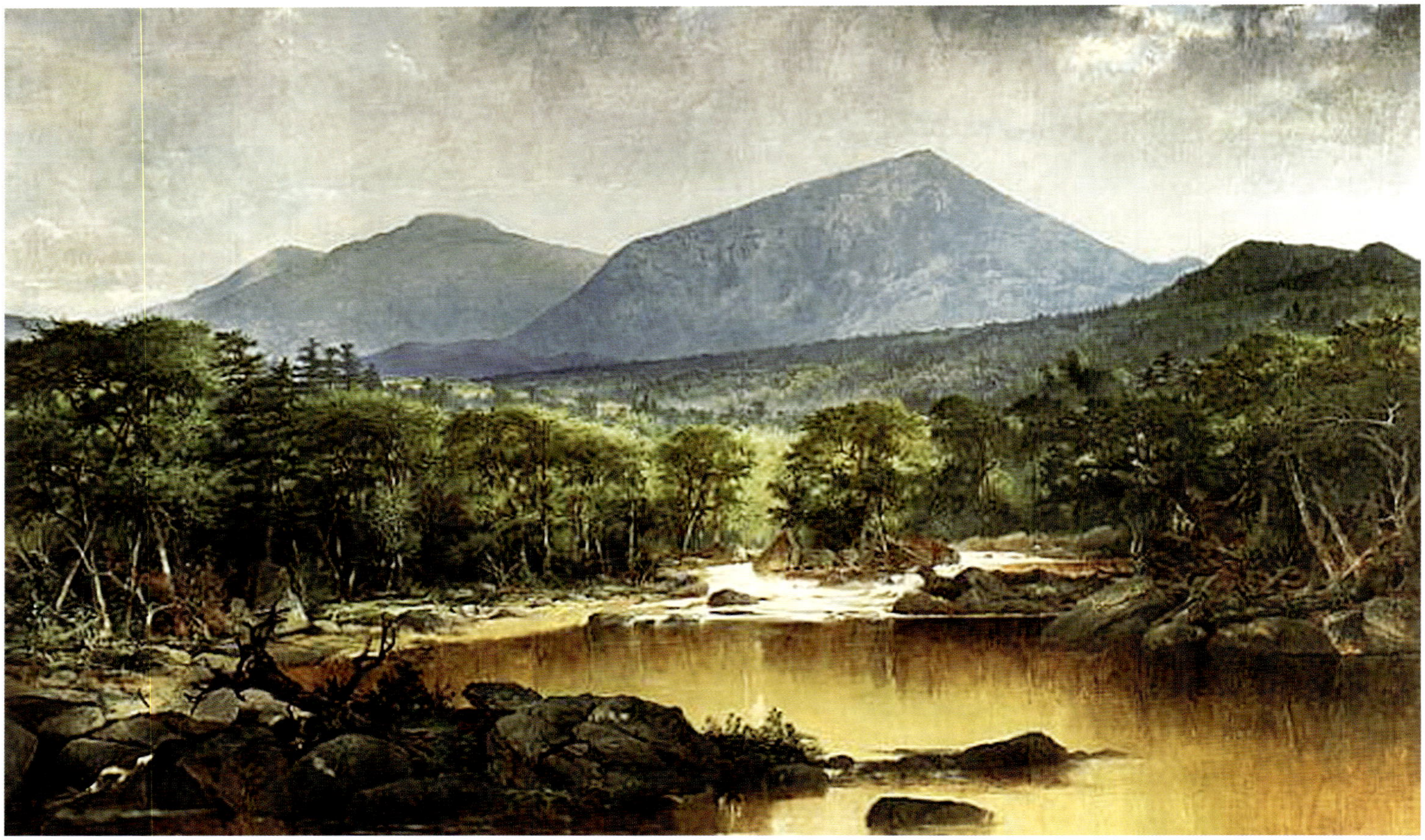

River in a Mountain Landscape (detail)
John Mix Stanley, 1840s

John Mix Stanley was born in Canandaigua, New York, apprenticed to a coach maker, then to sign painters and, ultimately, learned portraiture and landscape art. He painted in the High Plains, and along the approaches of the Rocky Mountains, illustrated here. During the Mexican War he accompanied Colonel Stephen Watts Kearney's expedition to California. He followed Titian Peale to Hawaii and spent a year painting portraits of members of the royal family. He traveled across the Isthmus of Panama in 1853, and after more Western explorations retired to Detroit, where he helped to found a forerunner of the Detroit Institute of Arts.

had painted them. Thereafter, he alternated that unprofitable labor with fashionable portraiture in New York, Philadelphia, Baltimore, and Washington. In 1843 he moved to the Indian Territory in present-day Oklahoma and painted the tribes forced to settle there, accumulating more portraits. The westward course of empire finally offered Stanley his cavalry escort when he was invited in 1846 to join Major Kearney's cross-desert cavalcade to complete the conquest of California.

Stanley went to Hawaii in 1848 and remained for two years to paint the scenery and the Hawaiian royal family. He returned to Indian country in 1853 as the official artist on the survey expedition led by General Isaac I. Stevens to explore a railroad route for the Northern Pacific Railroad from St. Paul to Puget Sound. He sketched, painted, and made some very early daguerreotype landscapes of the Glacier Park country. He returned to settle down as Catlin's neighbor in Washington, D.C., where he began a huge panorama of the West in forty-two scenes that was lost in a fire at the Smithsonian Institution along with most of his paintings, and many of Catlin's. Stanley's illustrations of the pueblo country of New Mexico and Arizona he had traversed with Kearney served as illustrations for Albert Gallatin's late-in-life prose about the region. Together, their words and pictures commenced the long process of impressing the Congress with the antiquities of the Southwest, which after sixty years produced the Antiquities Act of the Progressive Era and stimulated the restoration work of the WPA and CCC.[8]

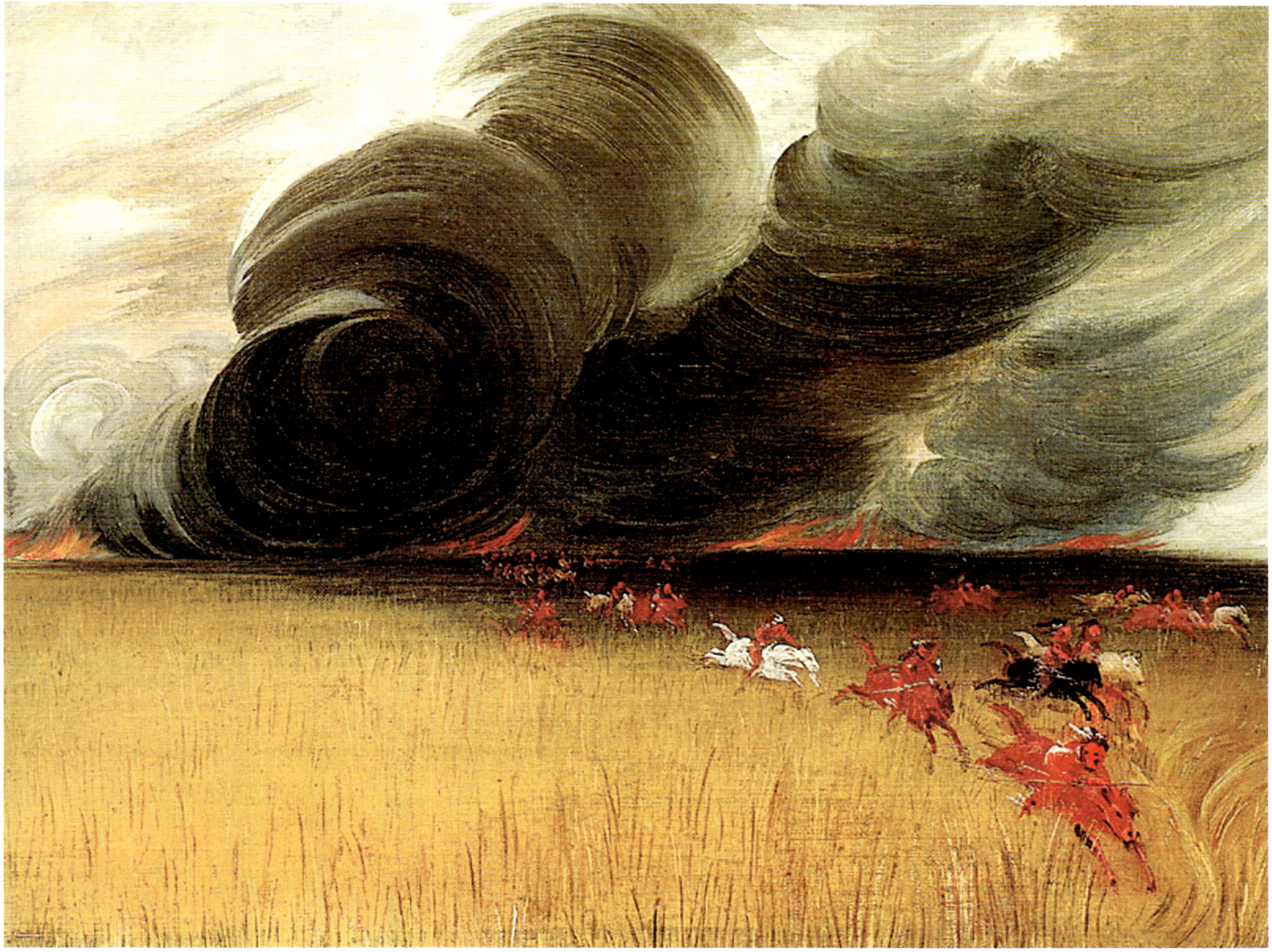

Prairie Meadows Burning (detail)
George Catlin, 1832

William Clark wrote of a prairie fire that it "went with such violence and speed as to catch a man and woman and burn them to death. Several escaped, among others a small boy who was saved by getting under a green buffalo skin."

In this work Catlin used big, broad brushstrokes and arranged his large forms like a baroque painter. The smoke in the sky billows from the left edge, driving the horsemen from middle to the lower right (see main text).

Many expedition artists, and a few of those who went west seeking the picturesque, had painted their impressions of the dry plains, but not affectionately until Worthington Whittredge arrived in the West in the 1860s. Two Hudson River artists, John Kensett and Sanford Gifford, accompanied an army under General John Pope, painting mountains magnificently, while Whittredge preferred plains: "I cared more for them than for the mountains . . . Whoever crossed the plains at that period, not withstanding its herds of buffalo and flocks of antelope, its wild horses, deer and fleet rabbits, could hardly fail to be impressed with its vastness . . . silence and . . . innocent, primitive existence."[9]

George Catlin had been similarly impressed, but it took another century for the nation as a whole to appreciate what could not and should not be farmed. Finally, the New Deal began the process by which National Grasslands were ultimately assembled from the bits and pieces of true prairie still unspoiled—remnants of the grassy vastness Catlin had proposed as a great national park. It took time. The natural parks in the National Park System had been products of a sensibility welcoming the grand and wondrous as presented in dazzling images of the West. The Yellowstone and

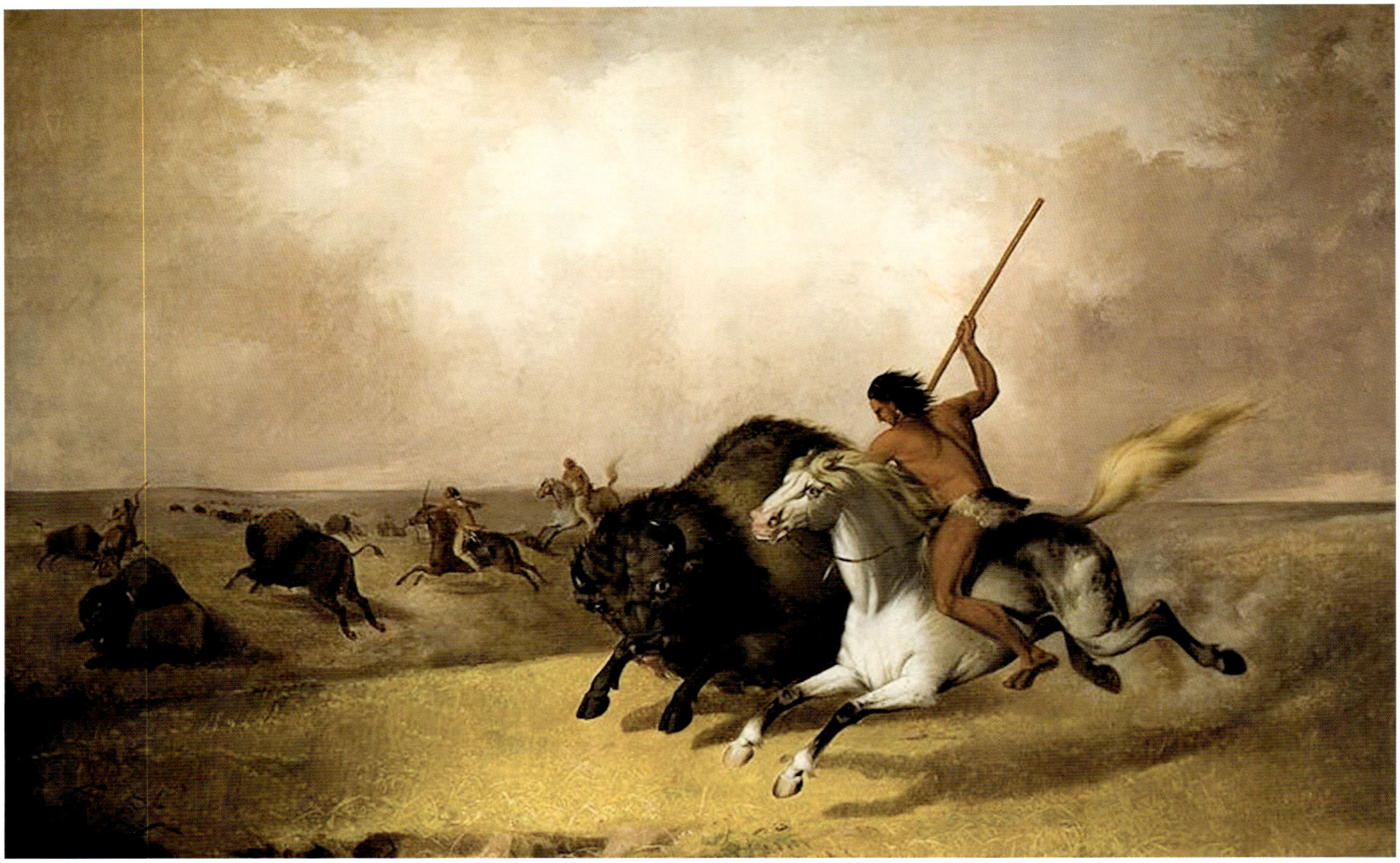

Buffalo Hunt on the Southwestern Prairies (detail)
John Mix Stanley, 1845

Stanley placed this painting of the Keechies "on the South-western Prairies" in the annotated catalogue of his portraits of North American Indians published in 1852. Perhaps then, even as now, the subject of an Indian buffalo hunt seemed so romantic as to need no further description. That same year Stanley took his collection of paintings to Washington, where they were put on display in the recently created Smithsonian Institution. They were burned in the fire in the Smithsonian Castle in January 1865 (see main text).

Yosemite valleys became familiar to millions of Americans through art centering on geysers and waterfalls. It helped that these natural wonders had been first described by the mountain men painted as muscular, ruddy, bearded, and gesturing toward something big. As Jedediah Smith, Joseph Reddeford Walker, and Thomas Fitzpatrick led emigrant trains to Oregon, artists' wagons rumbled and squeaked alongside those bearing children, chickens, and dreams of new starts where things hadn't been ruined yet. By the end of the 1830s, the glorious West was becoming a painted landscape.

Charles Preuss, a landscapist-cartographer, provided the first portable glimpses of the Wind River Range, as he accompanied John Charles Fremont on his espionage and exploration into Mexican California in 1843–44 and his two tours of the Hudson Bay Company's southern frontier in Oregon. The diaries of Preuss reveal his resentment of the swashbuckling Fremont, whose campaign-symbologist he reluctantly became. During Fremont's presidential campaign in 1856, he made unattributed use of Preuss's image of a peak in Wyoming on placards and banners. While Preuss and Fremont were in the Northwest, Catlin was on a tour of Europe with a Wild West Show and art exhibition, and Eastman was in command at Fort Snelling, French and Belgian Jesuit artists began making their contributions to America's sense of itself. Nicholas Point, S.J., enjoyed the protection of the U.S. Cavalry through Blackfoot country to the Flatheads, and provided the first pictures of an emigrant party moving toward Oregon from the east.

As discussed in the final chapter of this work, the dramatic artistry of Abraham Lincoln encouraged the Congress to give park status to the Yosemite Valley thus consummating a process in which the public had been made ready for such a grand symbolic act in wartime by the paintings of Albert Bierstadt and the photographs of Carleton Emmons Watkins. They were also fortunate in receiving cavalry cover, but their expeditions were not always government-sponsored. When Bierstadt began his career, in New Bedford, Massachusetts, he made powerful use of the daguerreotype, but his larger contributions were panoramas that provided "to the people on the Atlantic" impressions of "the sublimity of the Yosemite, and of the stateliness of the neighboring Sequoia

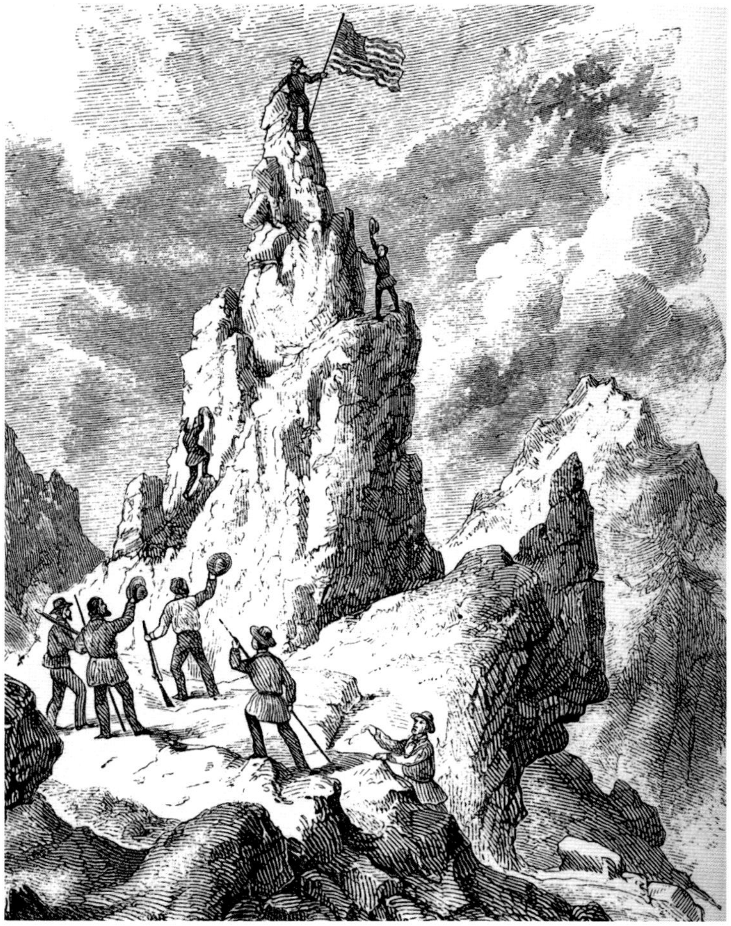

Engraving after Charles Preuss, 1843

In the journal of his western expedition of 1842, John Charles Fremont gave his account of the ascent of the peak he believed to be the highest of the Rocky Mountains: "I sprang upon the summit, and another step would have precipitated me to an immense snow field five hundred feet below . . . We mounted the barometer in the snow of the summit, and fixing a ramrod in a crevice, unfurled the national flag to wave in the breeze where never flag waved before." At 13,790 feet, Fremont Peak was not the highest in the Rocky Mountains and when, in 1856, Fremont ran against James Buchanan as the Republican Party's first presidential candidate, he was not successful in ascending to the highest office in the land, though he used this image by Preuss to adorn campaign banners and posters: he is shown planting the flag on the peak.

grove" according to Frederick Law Olmsted. Olmsted himself had been a photographer before seeking his fortune in California in 1863. He was a manager of forty-four thousand acres near Yosemite purchased at a sheriff's sale by New York investors from the estate of the bankrupt Fremont.

As Hudson River School painters were providing Eastern audiences with vast paintings of vast Western wonders, photographers were already busy with the details. Even on boulder-strewn terrain they set up their strange three-legged boxes shrouded in black, from which came portable and reproducible images of Half Dome and Bridalveil Falls. In cities along the seaboard, magazine readers scanned lithographs by Thomas A. Ayres and James Hutchings of the astonishing juxtaposition of a tranquil, nearly level valley floor and cliffs rising to Alpine crags. Later came illustrated magazines using the photographs of Watkins, Charles Leander Weed and R. H. Vance. Thus was created the constituency that in the New Deal years sustained the National Park System.[10]

Like John Kensett before him, Bierstadt had set out from the domesticated Hudson Valley to experience the West—with a cavalry escort provided by Colonel Frederick W. Lander. On his next expedition, however, a wartime shortage of cavalry escorts required him to set out for California by Overland Mail stagecoach. When it passed a wagon train near Fort Kearny, Nebraska, he had the opportunity to paint his *Emigrants Crossing the Plains* for the panoramic pageant market. He did so, thereby providing grist for his competition. Idealized pageant-paintings of how the conquest of the West was proceeding were popular at the time, some by German artists unable to journey to make first-hand observations. The most famous of their works is *Westward the Course of Empire* by Emanuel Leutze in the United States Capitol. Leutze's emigrants, animals, and wagons were in fact Bierstadt's, just as his Washington in *Washington Crossing the Delaware* was Worthington Whittredge, whom he hired as a model in Germany when Whittredge was a student there.

In the 1840s and 1850s the United States was in the midst of a German romance. Academics admired the German university system. Conservationists admired German forestry. The statements of the liberal revolutionaries of 1848 were compatible with those of American Whigs such as Henry Clay and the young Abraham Lincoln, especially after the Whigs

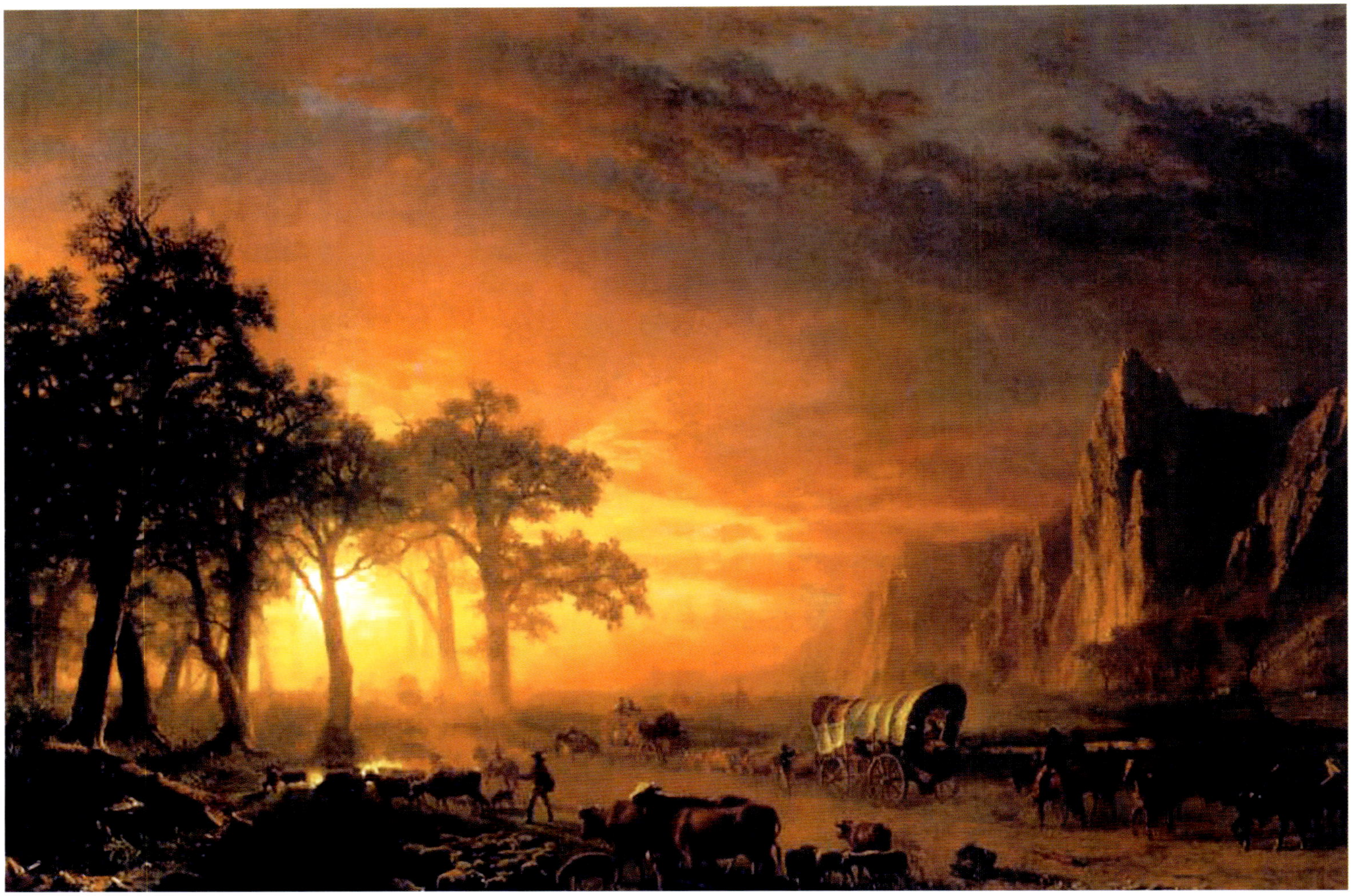

Emigrants Crossing the Plains
Albert Bierstadt, 1867

Over the course of fifty years, almost four hundred thousand people traveled the 2,170-mile route from their farms along the East Coast to Oregon Territory (see main text). In 1859 Bierstadt made the first of many trips west, joining a survey expedition led by Colonel Frederick William Lander along the Oregon Trail to California. He made his way home on his own (see main text).

were joined by a series of distinguished refugee-heroes of those revolutions. Chief among them was Carl Schurz, who campaigned for Abraham Lincoln in 1860 in German and led German-speaking troops to defend the Union and to free the slaves. German painting was for a time more important than British painting had been or French painting would become, especially in landscape and, within landscape, western panoramas. Painters trained to think of all mountains as Alp-like were among the first to bring the Rocky Mountains and the Sierras to the attention of eastern audiences and to policy makers in Congress. And scientists brought to America in the entourages of German princes, protected by order of the Army on the recommendation of the State Department, were among the first to sketch, identify, and catalogue many of the animals to be found in the West. When Prince Paul of Würtemberg wished to see the West and bring along Heinrich Baldwin Molhausen, his painter of mountains and Indians, Secretary of State John Quincy Adams sent instructions that Prince Paul and Molhausen should have protection. One never knew which European monarchs were related to which other monarchs, and the United States was contesting for territory against Spain, Britain, and Russia. And if one knew anything about science, it was important to know as well that Prince Alexander Philip Maximilian of the diminutive state of Weid, an intrepid and wealthy amateur anthropologist and botanist, had been trained by the great scientist, explorer, and geographer, Alexander von Humboldt. Prince Maximilian was interested in the West, to which he was accompanied by the Swiss Carl Bodmer, a competent landscapist and a portraitist of individual Indians.

Art and the Yellowstone

Bodmer and Prince Maximilian got up the Missouri as far as the Yellowstone River, but not all the way to its headwaters in the present national park. That honor fell to a Scottish lairdling, William Drummond Stewart. Although his artistic companion, Alfred Jacob Miller, got no farther than Jackson Hole, Miller was the first professionally trained painter to depict the Tetons. The Gore Range in central Colorado is just as spectacular, but it has not received national park status. Among the reasons for this may be that despite some early efforts by the Union Pacific to come close, they were not close to a powerful railroad that could lobby for them in the Congress; they did not shelter a rendezvous of picturesque mountainmen, as the Tetons did at Jackson Hole. The first celebrity-explorer to reach them, Lord St. George Gore (in 1854–56), came without a painter.

Alfred Jacob Miller helped bring international attention to the men and the mountains of the Tetons, a service Thomas Moran provided for the Yellowstone; John Mix Stanley, John Fery, and Julius Seyler for the Glacier; Albert Bierstadt for the Yosemite; and Moran, again, for the Grand Canyon. Lacking its recording genius, Gore's entourage only included a valet, a dog-handler, a pack of thirty-two greyhounds and eighteen foxhounds, a fly-tying specialist, arsenal attendants for his seventy-five rifles, his shotguns, his Sharps rifle, and his pistols, two wagons of fishing equipment, a "green and white linen tent, an ornamental brass bed that could be dismantled and packed quickly, a steel bathtub bearing Gore coat-of-arms, a portable iron table and iron wash stand, a complete set of pewterware, several camp stoves, a campaign chest and trunks filled with appropriate seasonal wardrobes, a fur-lined commode with removable chamber pot . . . a collection of leatherbound classics . . . a sextant, two chronometers, a refracting telescope with 6-inch lens . . . two . . . cows . . . an inflatable India rubber raft . . . 250 gallons of . . . whiskey . . . and . . . wines and liquors." Gore was there to kill animals —at least 2,500 buffalo, 1,200 elk, and 40 grizzly bears—and make an impression, which he did, leaving upon the map the Gore Range, Gore Pass, Gore Lake, Gore Canyon, Gore Mountain, Gore Creek, Gore Wilderness Area and, briefly, Gore City—but no painter, no park.[11]

Stewart had heard of the Mountain Men's annual rendezvous in Jackson Hole, and purchased white buckskins and a white horse to attend, having secured an introduction from a fellow Scot, Robert Campbell. Their first stop was the Horse Creek Rendezvous in the Green River Valley of Wyoming, attended by Jim Bridger and Thomas Fitzpatrick. Stewart went on to the Big Horn Mountains, to Taos, back north to the Wind Rivers, and then to Fort Vancouver, Washington. In the following year he went back to the rendezvous, on his own. Bridger had the misfortune of being recommended by Stewart as a guide to the despicable Lord Gore, who slaughtered so many buffalo that the cavalry had to be summoned to escort him out of the West lest he provoke an Indian war.

After inheriting his lairdship and its income, Stewart made his final foray into the American wild with his own small army of forty-five men, traveling in forty carts. Together with his whiskey, canned sardines, white buckskins and white mount, he had his artist, Alfred Miller. In New Orleans he had convinced Miller that the Indians of the West would be more interesting subjects than the brokers' wives Miller had been painting in the Crescent City. He was right; the Shoshones, Blackfeet, Snakes, and Crows painted by Miller have real character, benefiting from finesse that Miller had learned in the studio of Thomas Sully in England, at the École des Beaux Arts in Paris, and the English Life School in Rome. Miller fell ill before he could reach the Yellowstone, but later accompanied Stewart back to Scotland, where at Murthly Castle Stewart amazed the neighborhood with a half-breed Cree seneschal, a squad of Indian bodyguards, a herd of bison, and large Western canvases by Miller hung amid the armor in the Great Hall. The descendents of the bison live today in an Edinburgh Zoo.

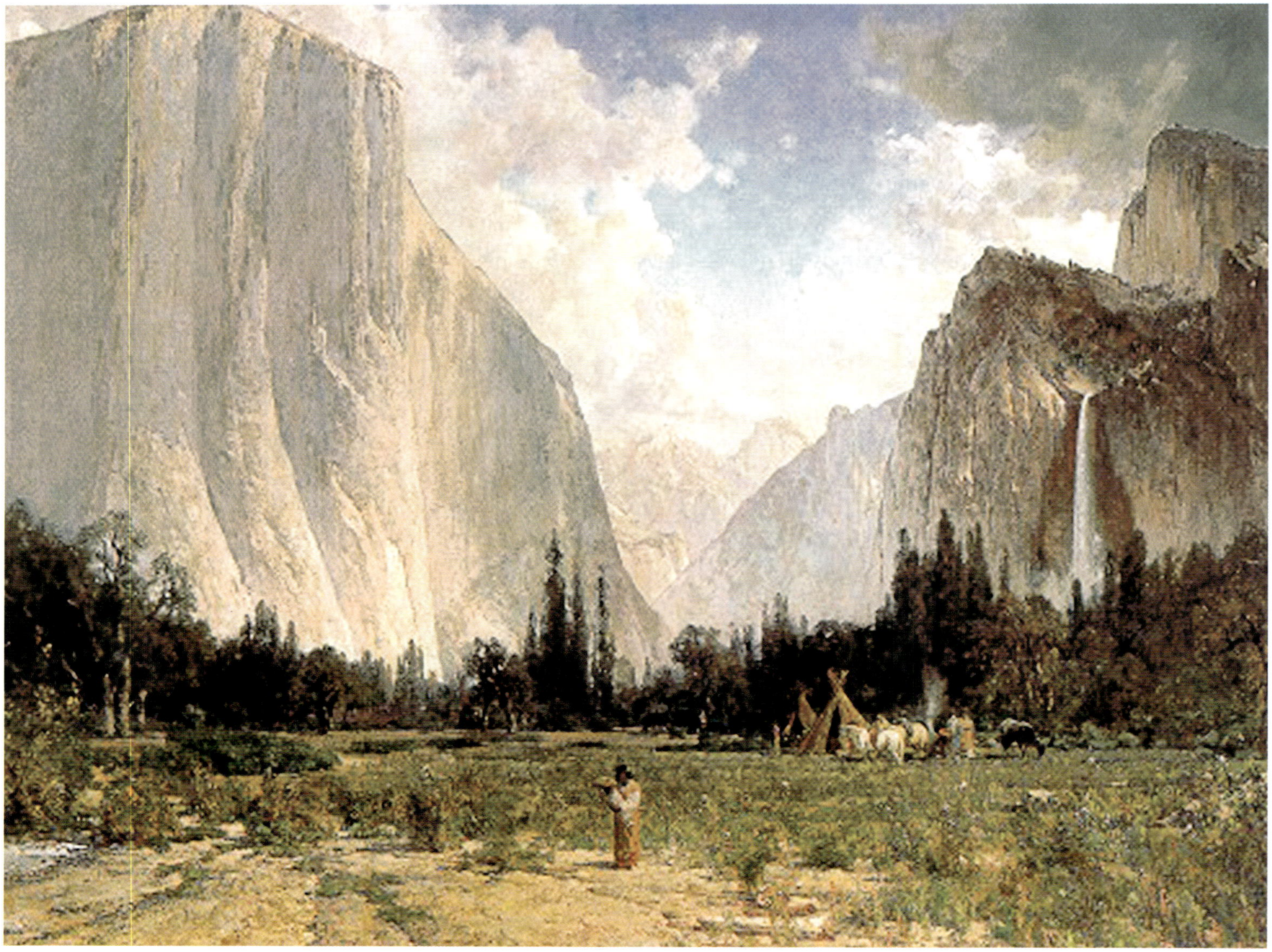

Bridal Veil Falls, Yosemite
Thomas Hill, c. 1875

Thomas Hill's enormous Yosemite panoramas were prized by San Francisco's business leaders, especially after one of his landscapes won a bronze medal at the Centennial Exposition in Philadelphia. Born in England, Hill settled in the San Francisco Bay area and often traveled to Yosemite. In 1883 he established his first summer studio at Yosemite, and in 1886 he moved to Wawona, fifteen miles southwest of the valley, where he maintained a studio and residence the rest of his life. His painting of Bridalveil Fall presents the Yosemite Valley as seen from its western entrance. On the left is El Capitan, and on the right is Bridalveil Fall. Sentinel Rock, Half Dome, and the distant peaks of the High Sierra are faintly visible. Hill's Yosemite pictures often included the American Indians who lived there. Hill's business notebook from 1884–87 notes that his clients often requested images of specific seasons, times of day, and local color, such as: "early morning," "mid-day spring time," and "sunset with Indians." Whatever his clients' motivation may have been, it became important for the public to consider such "wilderness" places as having people in them before they were "discovered."

The opportunity to be the first artists to record the geysers, seeps, steam, canyons, and waterfalls of the Yellowstone, lost to Bodmer and Miller, was captured by William Henry Jackson and Thomas Moran, who in 1871 accompanied a cavalry detachment led by Ferdinand Hayden, a surgeon turned surveyor assigned to find a route for the Northern Pacific Railroad being promoted by the financier Jay Cooke. The Northern Pacific became the primary sponsor of national park status for the Yellowstone, which lay along its route and was already being touted as a picturesque destination by Cooke's agents. They wished to display lithographs and photographs of its geysers in the Capitol as they lobbied for more troops to guard their crews and for it to become a national park. Even after Jackson showed how to make photographic images nearly two feet square, however, the impression was not overwhelming. For impact and for color, the sponsors required a painter on a grand scale. Moran was available; he had accompanied Hayden before, together with Hudson River School painters Sanford Gifford and John Frederick Kensett. The railroad assured the military authorities that Moran expected "to pay for his own expenses, and simply wishes to take advantage of your cavalry . . . for his protection."

The Northern Pacific was aware of the traffic being generated for the Central Pacific by tourists bound for Yosemite, drawn by Bierstadt's glamorous pictures; its request for cavalry protection for Moran carried the assurance "[t]hat he will surpass Bierstadt's Yosemite."[12]

Moran came to the Yellowstone impelled not only by an eager railroad but also by an enthusiasm imparted by his father, who had heard George Catlin lecture in London, and had seen both his entourage of Indians and his paintings. Catlin's passion for the American West had also been conveyed to the younger Moran at the time he was learning to be a painter. The younger Moran secured a commission from *Scribners Magazine* to illustrate an article about the Yellowstone, which he had never seen but wished to see. To finance his trip Moran placed in pawn his grand landscape, *Children of the Mountain*, an imaginary scene of the Alps he had exhibited at the Exposition Universelle in Paris in 1867. His first images of the American West showed very similar mountains, but over time they, and he, evolved. Moran settled down at Artist's Point, above the canyon of the Yellowstone, producing sketches, photographs, and watercolors which he took back to Newark, New Jersey, to compose into a "seven-by-twelve-foot panoramic" of Yellowstone Canyon, including, as a sort of thank-offering to his protector and guide, the figures of Hayden and his deputy beckoning tourists "like angels at the gates of heaven." Moran promised the railroad that "every member of Congress will see it," and after the House bought the picture, every member who entered the old Hall of Representatives could do so. Soon a bill was introduced to make the scene of the painting, and the rest of the Yellowstone Basin, into a national park.[13]

Moran's double success—selling a picture and selling an idea—was yet another instance of a new interaction of art and government. The federal "art program" of the first half of the nineteenth century had meant buying portrait-busts of founding fathers backed by pageant pictures of great events in national history to hang in the Capitol. Next, the taste of Congress turned to vast semi-symbolic imperial extravaganzas like those of Leutze, and, finally, landscapes. "Expedition art" gave the stay-at-home public glamorous impressions of the West and Florida, while laying up a store of scientific information for later generations to use in deciding what scenery and animal life acquired by the sword and depicted by pencil and brush should be kept in common ownership. Moran delighted in explaining the reciprocity between government support for art and art support for governmental action, signing his work with "(TYM)" for "Thomas Yellowstone Moran." Some obituaries described him as "father of the national parks." That he wasn't. George Washington was that first parent, as the consequence of his insistence that the national capital include parkland that is now as much part of the National Park System as the Yosemite Valley or the Yellowstone Basin. The New Deal consolidation of the system saw to that.

Science, Art, and Commerce

Moran shared the paternity of Yellowstone National Park with the Northern Pacific Railroad. Glacier National Park, promoted by the Great Northern, came along next, and then the Grand Canyon, touted by the Santa Fe and Southern Pacific, and painted on Congressional commission by Moran. His *Chasm of the Colorado* became his national calling card after he became John Wesley Powell's recording artist on explorations down the Colorado. Moran returned to the Grand Canyon in 1892, commissioned by the Santa Fe to produce a painting that became the basis for what later marketeers called "a logo," reproduced on calendars, cards, and advertisements.[14]

The New Deal's successes in conservation were enabled by a public consciousness that had been nurtured by an alliance of art, commerce, and the sciences, especially natural history. Science provided the taxonomy, art the rhetoric, and commerce the lobbying that led to the establishment of national parks in the Yosemite valley, the Yellowstone basin, the Grand Canyon, the Glacier region, and Mount Rainier, and for the preservation and recovery of substantial portions of other landscapes on the High Plains, in the Mountain West, on the Coast Range, in the Great Basin, and in interior

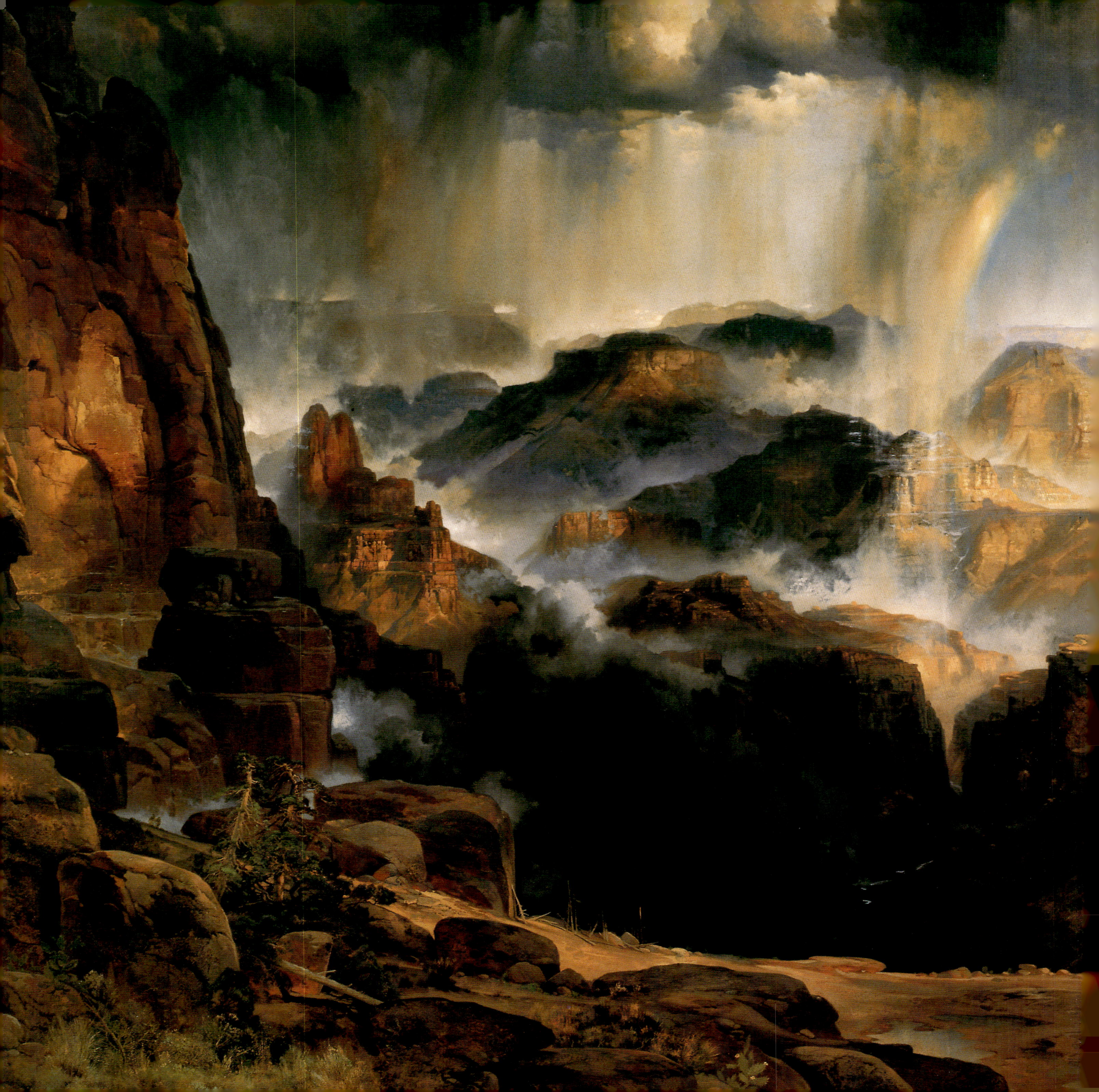

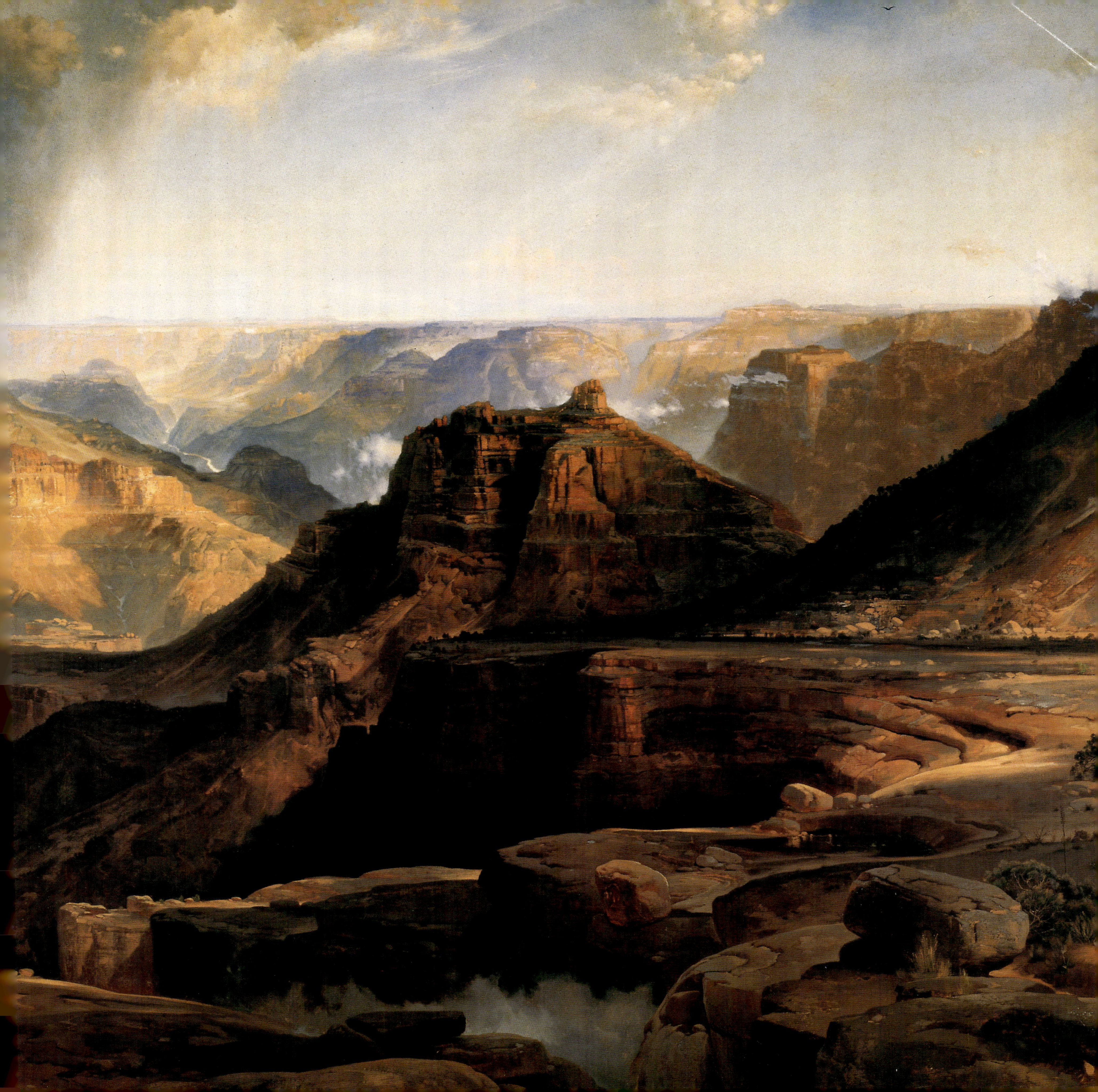

Previous pages:
Chasm of the Colorado
Thomas Moran, 1873

Thomas Moran accompanied the Powell survey of the Colorado River in 1873 and Hayden's survey of the Yellowstone region in 1871. He sold paintings of Yellowstone and of the Grand Canyon to the U.S. Congress for exhibit in the Capitol. They are now hanging beside George Catlin's Indian portraits in the Smithsonian's Renwick Gallery (see main text).

California and Florida. When commerce did not want a place protected, however, commerce often got its way: the Spiro Mounds, containing the greatest repository of portable Native American art on the continent, were dynamited by commercial pot hunters; the terraces, truncated pyramids, and plazas of thirteenth-century St. Louis made way for a warehouse complex. And the Florida Everglades have been protected only sporadically and partially. But art has done what it could, and for its exertions we should be grateful.[15]

In that good work, the Peales have been the American family that most successfully combined skills in art, in natural history, and in public presentation. Their prodigious patriarch was Charles Willson Peale, museum director, natural historian, painter, and publicist. Titian Ramsay Peale was his sixteenth child, and fourth painting son, and the one who came closest to his versatility. A first-rate natural historian and painter of statesmen, mountains, and meadowlarks, his grand occasion for drama came between 1838 and 1842 as a member of the United States Exploring Expedition led by Lieutenant Charles Wilkes. It was the nation's most ambitious expression of a determination to understand its terrestrial habitat after Jefferson's explorations of the Louisiana Purchase—and beyond—before the New Deal, setting a standard for interaction of natural history and art not again attained until the Smithsonian Institution and National Park Service came of age. Like those of the New Deal's National Resources Planning Board, the reports of Wilkes and his colleagues synthesized what might be learned about the environment by many academic disciplines and brought the wonders of the natural world to public awareness. Wilkes brought along for those tasks Titian Peale, William Brackenridge, a botanist, and the artists Alfred Agate, Joseph Drayton, and James Dwight Dana. Wilkes commanded a squadron of six ships, formidable enough to stand off the European claimants to the northwest coast of North America and Hawaii. Wilkes was to have his gun ports at the ready, for the Spaniards, Dutch, British, and Russians were present in force and resentful of the newly arrived Americans. His other orders were to describe, identify, depict, and collect scientific specimens from the Madeiras, Brazil, around South America by way of Cape Horn and the Antarctic, then to Chile, the Navigator Islands, Fiji, and New Zealand. He was to plant the flag judiciously in Hawaii, somehow gain access to Japan, survive the still piratical Malay Straights, and get home around Africa. All that, he achieved. During the nearly four years he was abroad, he collected, surveyed, and charted along sixteen hundred miles of the coast of Antarctica, described archipelagos of Pacific islands, and noted the conveniences of San Francisco Bay and Puget Sound for geopolitics and commerce. One ship and its entire crew were lost getting around the Horn of South America. Another went on the rocks with many of Peale's specimen collections as the fleet worked its way to the disputed, rocky, and storm-tossed shore at the mouth of the Columbia River claimed by Lewis and Clark; it made its circuit around Africa via the Cape of Good Hope before reaching New York in June 1842.

When on August 6, 1841, Wilkes and his colleagues landed at the mouth of the Columbia, much had happened since the dried specimens brought home by Lewis and Clark for deposit in the Peale Museum were living things. Titian Peale lacked his father's showmanship and good luck. On Hawaii, he had his chance to paint an active volcano in what is now Hawaii Volcanoes National Park, rendering lava flows as well as he had depicted hummingbirds. Ill health deprived him of his chance to paint the two North American mountains that are deservedly compared in isolated grandeur to Mount Fuji, and Mounts Shasta and Rainier, and which were observed by a detachment of Wilkes's force. They became parks only after other artists were able to present their iconic power. Much of Peale's best work was burned in the Smithsonian fire that also consumed much of the legacies of Catlin and Stanley, and the museum Peale inherited went insolvent. Like many other artistic people (including Albert Einstein and William Thornton), Peale had to support his further researches by working in a patent office.

Shasta was a favorite of painters, for a time rivaling Mont Blanc. It was painted by Agate, sketched by Dana, and after them by anybody who could get there—and by some who

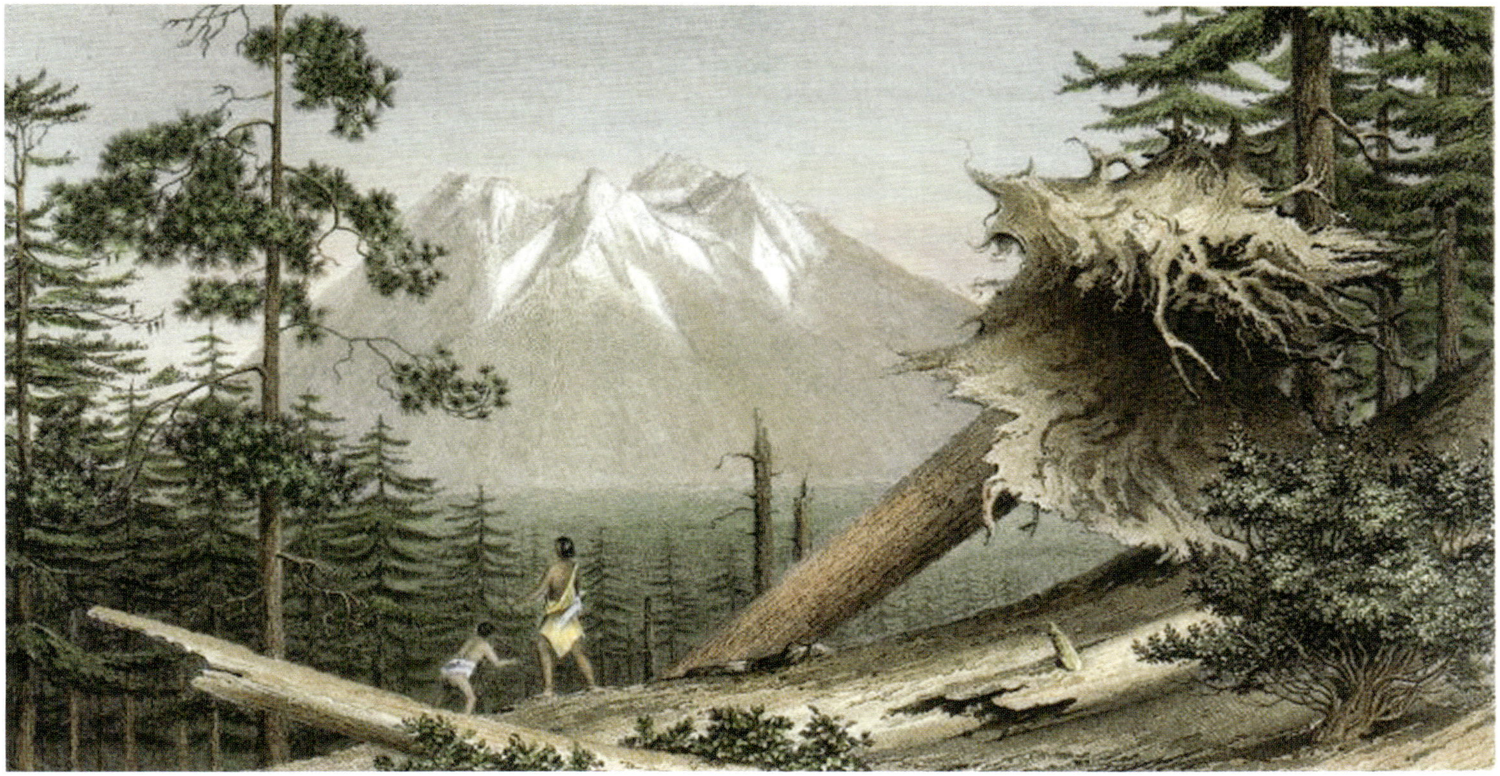

Shaste [Shasta] Peak
Steel engraving by Alfred Thomas Agate, c. 1840

Wilkes's *Narrative of the United States Exploring Expedition, 1838, 1839, 1840, 1841, 1842* was published by Congress in a limited edition of one hundred copies, many of which were sent to foreign heads of state. Wilkes was granted a special copyright on the volumes, and he privately published 1,150 more sets. Only the earliest three editions contain the engraving of Mount Shasta. Agate was a portraitist, botanical illustrator, and landscapist. He used a camera lucida, which projected the scene onto a piece of paper for purposes of tracing (see main text).

never got there. "These Shasta pictures came in all shapes and sizes, from two inch wide engravings to ten foot wide paintings . . . each decade, from 1840 to 1940, brought with it new reasons for artists to come to Mount Shasta. Scientific artists, spy artists, journalist artists, survey artists, Indian artists, visionary artists, book artists, mountain climbing artists, cartoon artists, portrait artists, landscape artists . . . over 120 noted artists." One of these, Harry Best, sent his version to Theodore Roosevelt, who displayed it in the White House after writing the donor: "I . . . shall give it the place of honor in my home. I consider the evening twilight on Mt. Shasta one of the grandest sights I have ever witnessed." (Franklin Roosevelt preferred the evening twilight on the Catskills opposite Hyde Park.)[16]

Without the attention of Titian Peale, Mount Rainier had to wait for an art-loving railroad president to bring Congressional recognition, after it was painted by a competent San Franciscan, Thomas Hill. Hill understood how successful the California railroads had been with their campaign to interest the public in the wonders of the Yosemite, reinforcing the glorious prose of John Muir and the images produced by a battalion of photographers and painters. Mount Rainier lay close to the tracks of the Northern Pacific, which had been largely responsible for bringing art and Congressional attention to the Yellowstone, and whose president in the 1890s was my great-grandfather, Edwin W. Winter. Hill's powerful images drew Winter's attention to the mountain as a potential asset in his competition with the Great Northern Railroad's "Switzerland of America" campaign to publicize the Northern Rocky Mountains. The Northern Pacific secured park status for Mount Rainier in 1899, through Winter's lobbyists in Washington and his understanding of the persuasive power of pictures. He was a friend and patron of James McNeill Whistler and an avid collector of engravings. In his enthusiastic youth in the 1870s in Chicago, he had been in the business of selling reproductions of paintings, and at the Northern Pacific he deployed artists to aid its lobbying staff.

The "empire builder" of the Great Northern was James J. Hill (unrelated to the painter Thomas Hill), whose painter son, Louis, succeeded him as president of the railroad and as a sponsor of painters, photographers, and congressional junkets. In 1910 Louis Hill secured national park status for the Glacier country along the Great Northern tracks, after the railroad's staff landscape photographer, Fred Kiser, barraged the Congress with colored pictures to illustrate the Great Northern's slogan "See America First." One of Louis Hill's sisters married the Bavarian landscapist Julius Seyler, who, before returning to Germany, painted the huge canvases of "the Switzerland of America" that appeared in many of the railroad's major station waiting rooms. James J. Hill collected French paintings; Louis Hill collected painters, among them Adolph Heinze, Joseph Scheuerle, Kathryn W. Leighton, and John Fery, who produced more than three hundred landscapes for the Great Northern's public buildings, "to sell the West to the prospective traveler."[17]

Many people were sold on a glamorous West of cowboys and mountains by the magazine illustrations of Charles Russell and Frederic Remington. Russell did not need the Great Northern's assistance, although he received it, for he was doing very nicely as a provider of pictures of the True West. Before the coming of movies and television, pictures in black and white amid columns of exceedingly colorful prose imparted a heady sense of what one might experience after a pleasant train ride into the sunset. But by the end of the 1920s, reality had obtruded. The promise of the West began blowing away in dry winds. Sometimes Great Northern and Northern Pacific had to slow their trains to a crawl through eastern Montana at noon because the dust was so heavy in the air that it seemed to be midnight.

Art, the Everglades, and California

At the other extremity of the continent lies Florida. The Everglades are not spectacular as Yosemite is spectacular, but in the nineteenth century its birds and animals were astoundingly profuse. Although much destruction has been wrought upon the Everglades since art first brought the world's attention to its wonders, the New Deal did interpose a period of reform between two long sorry epochs in which rapacity, stupidity, avarice, and heedlessness prevailed. But for the better part of a decade, the New Deal averted more damage, prevented much irreversible harm, and established a baseline to which later and better times might return. The conservation history of the Everglades records a sequence of such periods, interrupted by periods of destruction in which art, natural history, citizenship, and trusteeship were insufficient to overcome the power of predators, developers, and commercial agriculture. The protection that from time to time has been afforded the nation's subtropical treasure house has largely resulted from constituency-building through visualization of what might be lost. That has been the work of art—in conjunction with the sciences of natural history.

In the nineteenth century the nation became acquainted with the Everglades through the art of Martin Johnson Heade, John James Audubon, and—once again—Titian Peale. Peale had gone to Florida and Georgia in 1817 as an assistant to Thomas Say, of the Academy of Natural Sciences, who was doing field research for his *American Entomology*. After sending home 122 drawings and a wild turkey—the turkey for the family museum and the drawings to illustrate Say's huge work—Peale continued to do honor to Florida's wildlife as an illustrator for the *American Ornithology* of Charles Lucien (Carlo) Jules Laurent Bonaparte, 2nd Prince of Canino and Musignano, the revolutionary and scientific nephew of Napoleon. Next to arrive was John James Audubon, born on the French sugar island of Saint-Domingue (Haiti), who had his own Bonapartist associations. Audubon was a neoclassical painter whose subjects happened to be birds and mammals rather than emperors and princes—he painted marmosets and moles with the precision and panache of the Napoleonic portraits of his mentor Jacques-Louis David. So powerful were Audubon's images of Florida's birds and animals that to this day reproductions of "Audubon prints" can be found on the walls of most of the motels in South Florida. Audubon's first expedition to Florida took him to the northeastern corner of the territory in search of water birds and tropical species. He pressed on to Key West and Florida Bay, whose rookeries were pictorial but buggy, so Audubon moved to the Dry Tortugas (now the neighborhood of Fort Jefferson National Park), which offered more breezes and still more tropical birds. In the late 1830s Audubon went back to Florida to explore its west coast, securing material for his *Birds of America* and its companion volume, *The Ornithological Biography*.[18]

Martin Heade was painter of light and nature, who first came to Florida in the 1870s. He too should receive credit for Everglades protection, for his work captures the incandescent vitality of its insects, birds, and flowers better than that of any other artist. His living things seem to be as motionless as Audubon's, but they are alive! Who would willingly see the extermination of such creatures? Heade's paintings are not grand in size—indeed, he painted hummingbirds and orchids as the greatest Dutch masters painted bowls, jewels, furs, and fruit. However, he found his own railroad magnate to sponsor his work—Henry Morrison Flagler of the Florida East Coast Railroad. Flagler bought many of his pictures after Heade married and settled in St. Augustine in 1883 and began painting landscapes evoking the brooding prairielike expanse of the Everglades. Those images, like his bird and flower pictures, served the New Deal in making the Everglades the nation's largest bird sanctuary. The Congress authorized the creation of Everglades National Park on May 20, 1934, setting aside for the first time a park primarily for its wildlife rather than for its historic resonances or its scenic wonders. As late as the 1930s, millions of roseate spoonbills, cranes, and ibises reminded the imaginative that the Ohio Valley had once been like that. Until the 1850s, it had been an aviary also—as was the Red River Valley of Oklahoma and Arkansas. Flocks of more than a hundred thousand passenger pigeons had blotted out its midsummer sun. By 1900, when the sun shone upon the last wild passenger pigeon before it was shot in the Scioto Valley of Ohio—where these birds had been venerated by the Hopewell and Adena Indians in the time of Christ—the man who held it in his sights could discern its subtle beauty—bluish gray on the

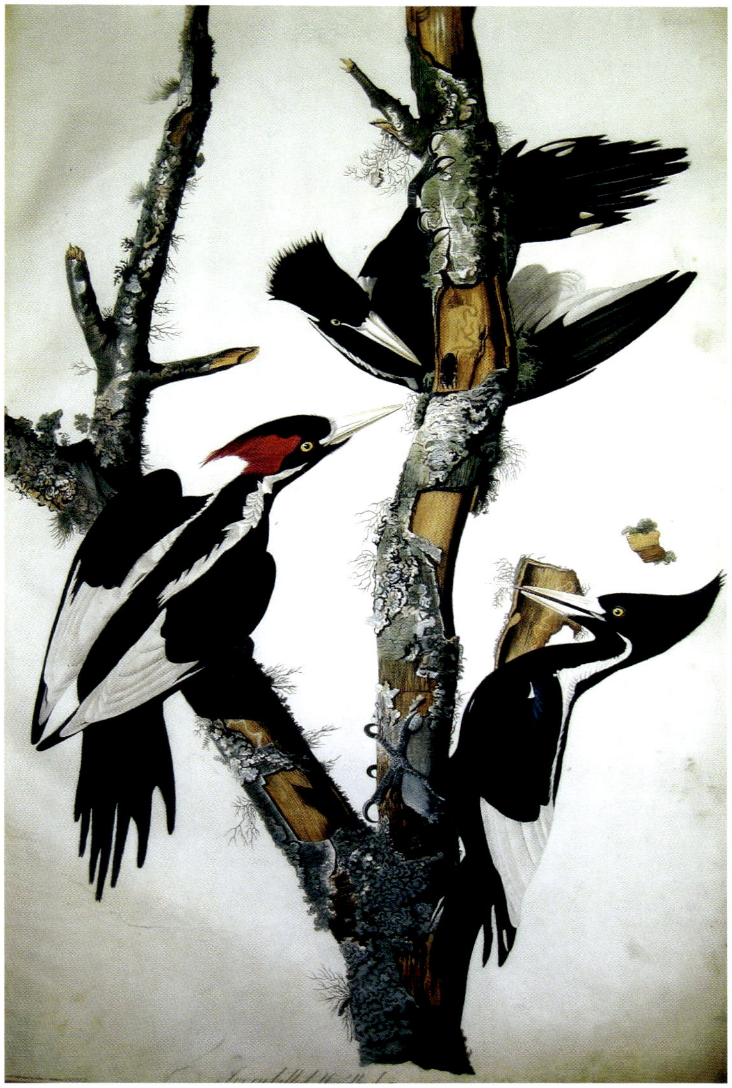

Ivory-billed Woodpecker
John James Audubon,
c. 1840

The Ivory-billed woodpecker is—or was—the largest woodpecker to live within the boundaries of the United States (a Mexican woodpecker is bigger). Audubon wrote: "I have always imagined, that in the plumage of the beautiful Ivory-billed Woodpecker, there is something very closely allied to the style of coloring of the great Van Dyke . . . So strongly indeed have these thoughts become ingrated in my mind . . . that whenever I have observed one of these birds flying from one tree to another, I have mentally exclaimed, 'There goes a Van Dyke' . . . [Its] favorite resort . . . [is] those deep morasses, overshadowed by millions of gigantic dark cypresses, spreading their sturdy moss-covered branches, as if to admonish intruding man to pause and reflect on the many difficulties which he must encounter, should he persist in venturing farther into their almost inaccessible recesses, extending for miles before him . . . [many a] massy trunk of a fallen and decaying tree, and thousands of creeping and twining plants of numberless species . . . oozing, spongy, and miry disposition . . . dismal croaking of innumerable frogs, the hissing of serpents . . . the bellowing of alligators . . . It never utters any sound whilst on wing, unless during the love-season; but at all other times, no sooner has this bird alighted than its remarkable voice is heard, at almost every leap which it makes."[i]

body, with black streaks; pinkish iridescence on the throat becoming a metallic bronze, green, and purple at the back; a rose-hued breast becoming whiter at the lower edges; and bright red on the sides, feet, and legs. Even today in the Everglades, who is not moved when a pileated woodpecker flaps by as if to remind us of its much larger departed cousins, the ivory bills, before the destruction of their habitat?[19]

The nation decided to save what was left of the Everglades after a century of art and natural history had already, so to speak, gone out and made Roosevelt "do it"—as a series of convincing writers and painters had focused attention on its small, animate wonders with eloquence as compelling as that

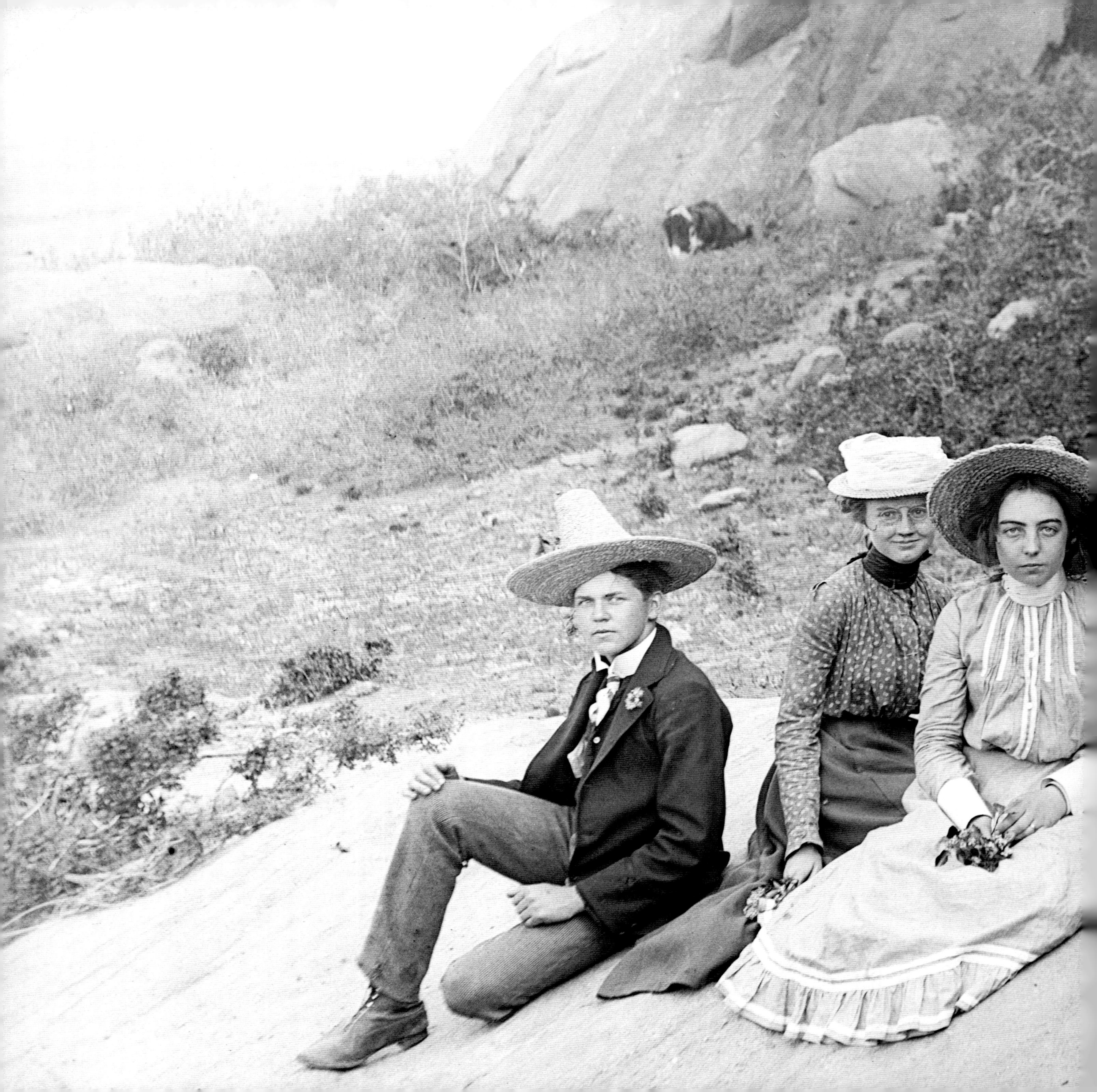

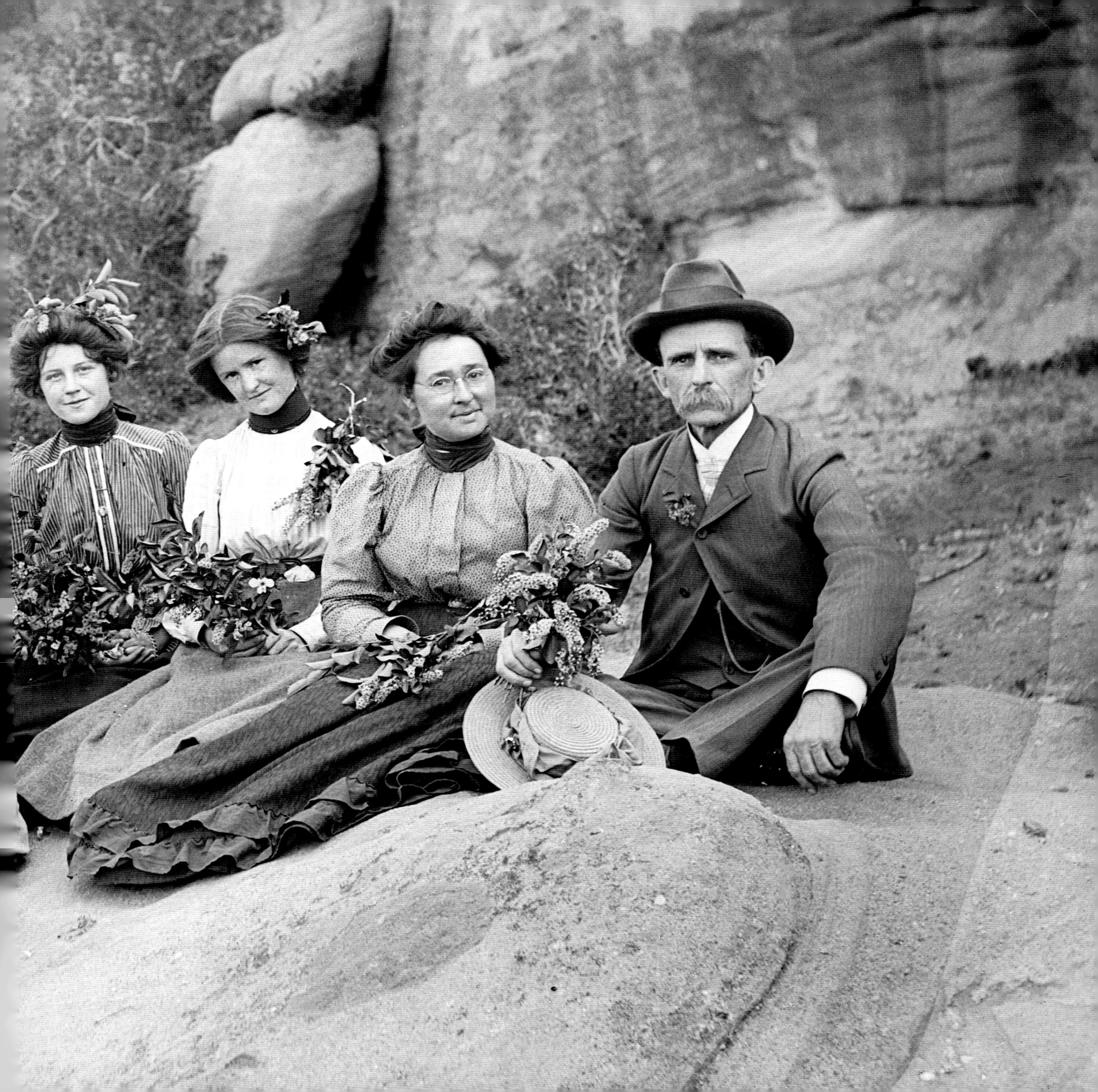

Previous pages: An excursion to Red Rocks

which had created a constituency for the mountains and waterfalls of the West. In 1934 there was a concerted effort to establish it as a national park, though by then its wildlife had suffered at the hands of the lumbering interests, the sugar interests, and of hunters answering the importunings of the makers of ladies' feathered hats. The Roosevelt Administration moved matters forward, but these powerful exploiters were able to delay the dedication of the park until 1947. The desolation wrought in the interim, and thereafter, was made worse by feckless or pernicious government interventions. After the New Deal, the conservation coalition weakened. Great careers were built in the U.S. Army Corps of Engineers, as the nation's taxpayers supported earth-moving and sluice-making that enriched a few ranchers, sugar-growers, and cotton farmers. The Everglades were laced with levees, canals, and pumping stations until half the area of the wetlands was lost. The slight eminence upstream from the Everglades was ditched and drained for sugar production, destroying the natural plumbing of the land. Misdirected engineering deprived the park of much of the water it required, and animals were deprived of the conditions necessary to their survival. Seven hundred thousand acres of farms and sugarcane fields dumped chemicals into the underground rivers flowing into the park until the neighboring cities ran low on potable drinking water. Millions of birds died, and many species went extinct in the name of progress, as Governor Napoleon Bonaparte Broward promised to create an "Empire of the Everglades" by drying out that "pestilence-ridden swamp."

Finally, in the 1990s, something like a New Deal spirit returned, largely due to the exertions of Rachel Carson and Marjorie Stoneman Douglas in the 1940s, 1950s, and 1960s. In the afterglow of the New Deal, they were able to draw upon familiar images of birds and animals to arouse sympathy for an Endangered Species Act in general, and for the Everglades in particular. Several billion dollars have subsequently been spent attempting to rectify the damage done in the dreadful interim before the voices of reform were heeded. Now, despite further delays and ineptitude, restoration is resuming. There is a long way to go. There is, however, renewed hope that the work of Titian Peale, John Jacques Audubon, and Martin Johnson Heade may not have been

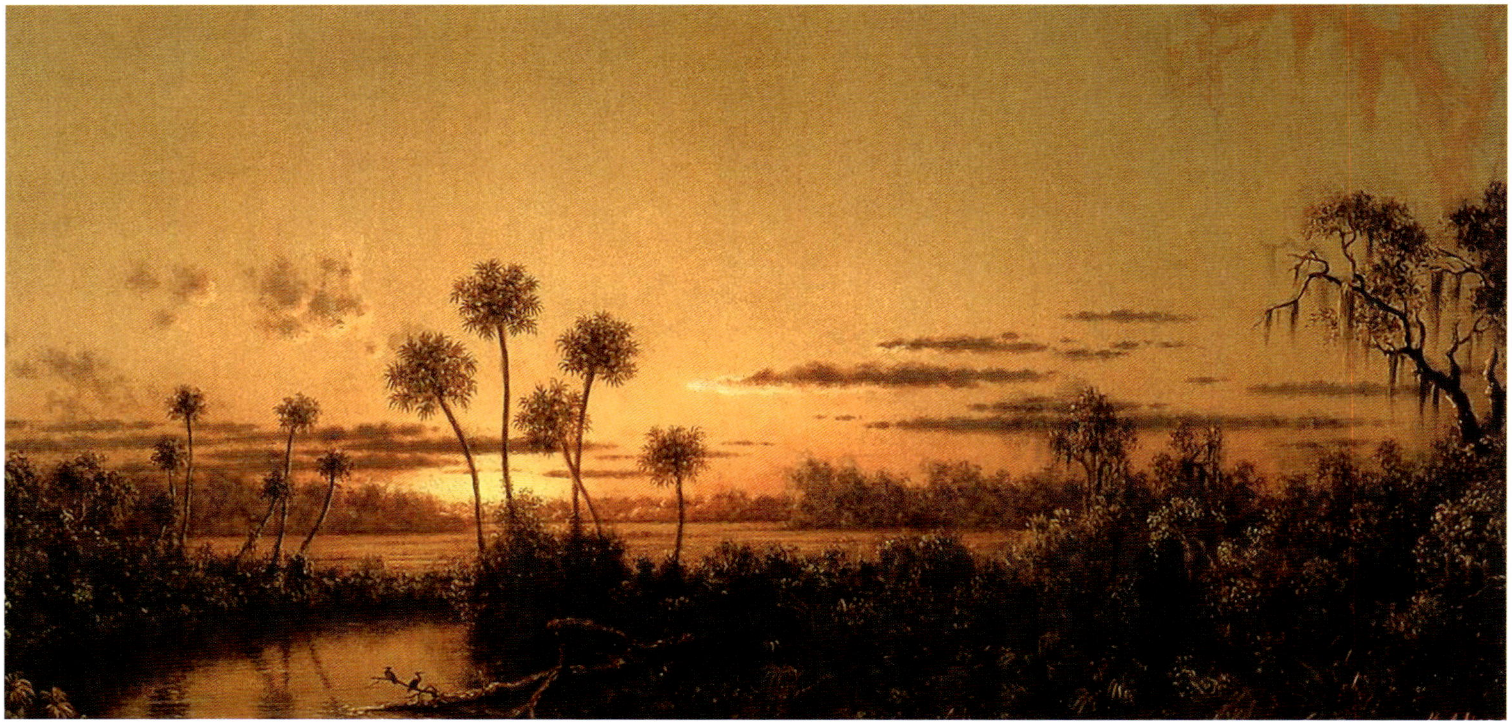

Florida River Scene Early Evening After Sunset
Martin Johnson Heade, 1887–1900

Martin Johnson Heade was born and reared in Lumberville, in Bucks County, Pennsylvania, the son of a farming lumber-mill owner. As his clientele increased in midlife he changed the spelling of his name from "Head," which was often mispronounced, to "Heade." He studied with the "primitivists" Edward and Thomas Hicks, and then with not-so-primitive artists in England and on the Continent. He lived for two years in Rome, and then in New York, Brooklyn, Philadelphia, and Boston, where he painted marshes and seascapes before three extended visits to the jungles of Brazil to paint hummingbirds and tropical plants. He returned to New England and New Jersey, painting still lifes and landscapes until 1883 when he married and moved to Saint Augustine (see main text). Heade, Titian Peale, and John James Audubon drew public attention to the natural wonders of Florida.

done in vain, and that environmental responsibility, through planning, may resume with equal energy to that of the New Deal.

Art also stimulated conservation at the other extreme of the continent. In October 1932, three quarters of a century after art assisted the nation to think of the valley of the Yosemite as common ground, the Director of the National Park Service, Horace Albright, wrote that he had been induced to make a journey to Point Lobos, on the California coast, by "Ferdinand Burgdorff, an artist of Carmel, who has painted some exquisite picture of this extraordinary piece of land. I was so impressed . . . that I was prepared to recommend it for acquisition by the government."[20]

Albright was able to guide the acquisition of this quintessentially Californian point of land into public ownership by the state of California, the way having been made easier by Burgdorff's paintings and etchings, which helped its legislators to see what Albright saw—wondrous shifting interactions of the creatures of sea, shore, and sky. On the shoreward side of Point Lobos is a highway and the usual paraphernalia of development, bearing many resemblances to the borderlands of the Everglades. California and Florida display both the positive and admonitory lessons of protection, planning, and their absence. A park is a place that is to be spared the ordinary vicissitudes of commerce—a place that without protection would be "developed" into something other than what it is. Art often helps us understand what is worth preserving—sometimes to keep before us the evidence of historic events; sometimes to protect natural wonders such as waterfalls, canyons, or geysers; and sometimes to sustain circumstances in which rare creatures live that could not find substitute habitat.

The CCC, the Arts, and the New Deal for Parks

Despite the exhortations of George Biddle and Gutzon Borglum, President Franklin Roosevelt's initial support for artists did not bubble forth from devotion to art but from his devotion to conservation. This self-described "grower of trees" did, in fact, plant thousands of trees, and his retirement plan, he said, was to get back to practicing conservation at Hyde Park—as George Washington had at Mount Vernon (see chapter eight). Roosevelt and Washington both advocated treating the national estate as a responsible owner with a sense of intergenerational trusteeship would treat a personal estate. And both sought to protect special places for "the enrichment of the lives of all of us"—the words are Roosevelt's enunciating his sense of the sentiments of Washington as well.[21]

In the midst of the First Hundred Days of his administration, Roosevelt suggested to Harold Ickes and Horace Albright that they go for a ride in the country. Mrs. Roosevelt would have a picnic prepared, and the expedition would survey Herbert Hoover's fishing camp to determine if it would work as a weekend retreat for the President. Camp Hoover lies west of Washington at the end of ninety dirt-

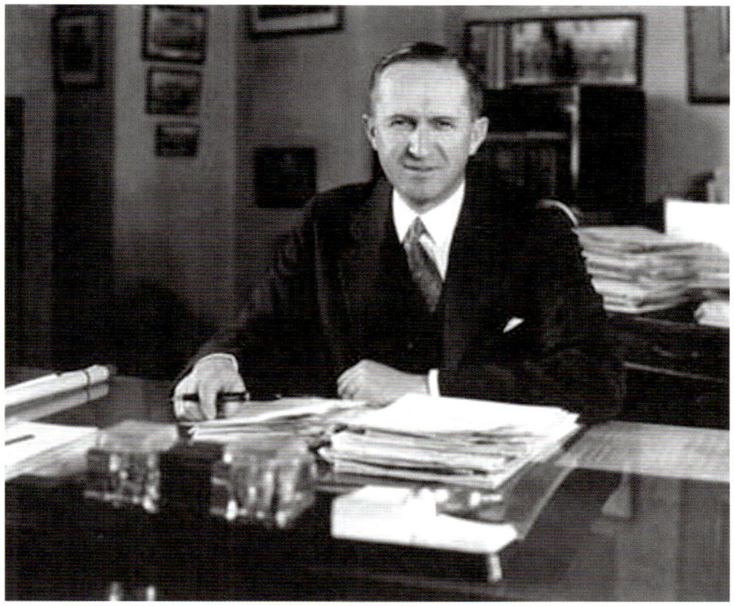

Horace M. Albright, Director, the National Park Service

road miles. It is high in Shenandoah National Park and set amid a grove of old-growth hemlocks above a succession of waterfalls. Although Roosevelt later decided that he preferred the cabin-complex in the Catoctins of Maryland, later named "Camp David" by President Eisenhower, the nation has benefitted immensely from the time Albright and Roosevelt spent sitting next to each other on the drive back to Washington, as the Director poured into the President's appreciative ear accounts of the degradation and the glorious possibilities of the National Park System. It was a mess that could be fixed—a mess with a history that Albright imparted to a history-loving president, together with a set of proposals to make matters better. Albright recalled in later years that Roosevelt "told me—really ordered me—to 'get busy . . . Suppose you do something tomorrow about this.'" Roosevelt often induced someone to undertake a difficult task by convincing them that it was their idea.[22]

Albright got busy. Within two months Roosevelt had issued a presidential order under which the National Park System was doubled in size to gain fifty-six national parks, national monuments, battlefields, national cemeteries, and the District of Columbia parks. The War Department, the Agriculture Department, and the Bureau of Lands (later Land Management) were relieved of managing parks, and through the ECW/CCC the parks were provided an entirely new workforce. More than six hundred CCC camps were placed under Albright's jurisdiction, one hundred eighteen of them in the parks. One hundred twenty thousand young men went to work making parkways and bridges, planting trees, curbing erosion, learning all the while, and in most cases getting the first decent nutrition of their lives.

The New Deal's consolidation of the management of the national parks into a single agency required the National Park Service to become more capable of research and education across academic disciplines ranging from history to soil science. With help from the WPA and CCC, it also became

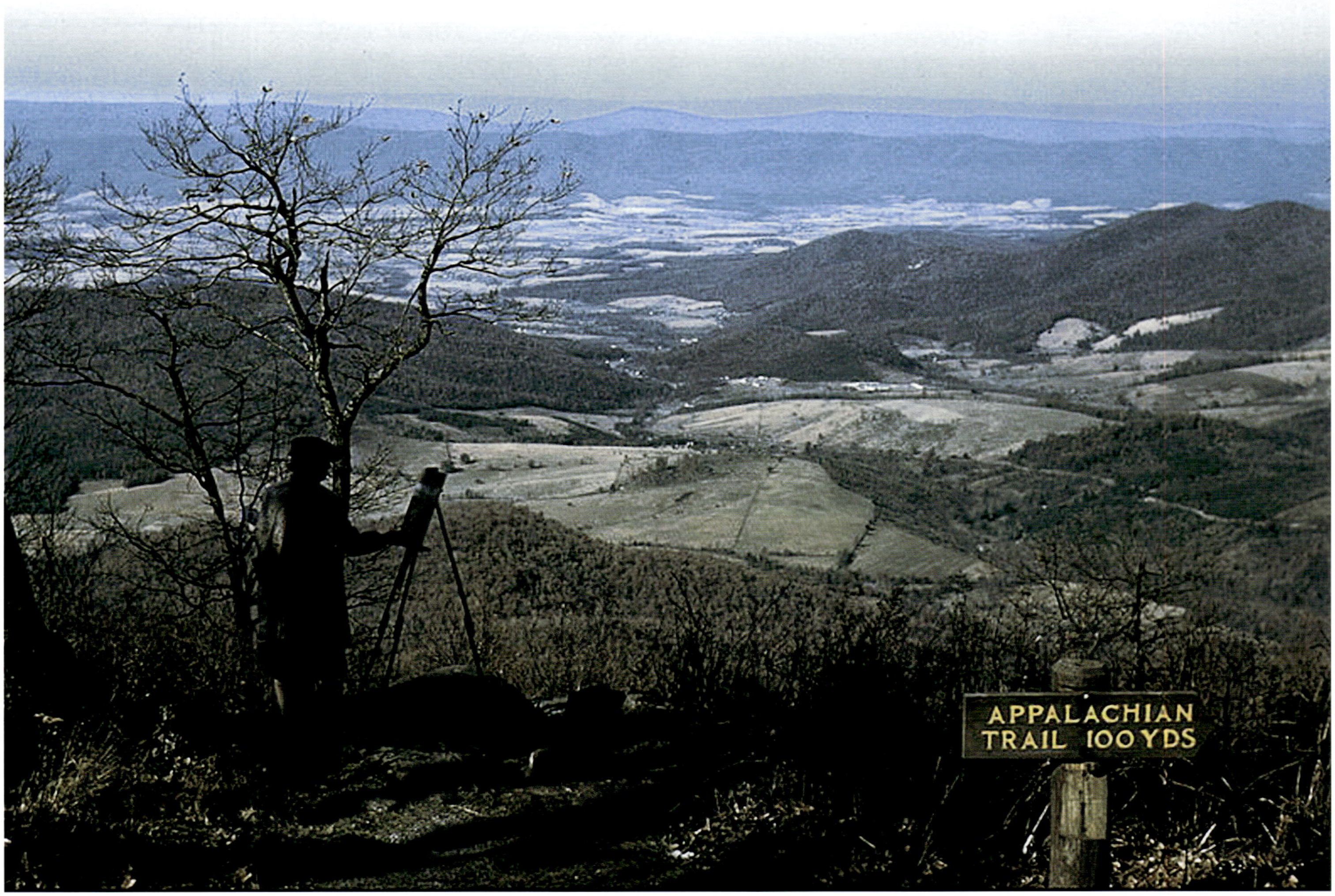

The Blue Ridge Parkway
Historic American Buildings Survey

The Blue Ridge Parkway extends 469 miles from Front Royal, Virginia, to Cherokee, North Carolina; the northernmost 105 miles from Front Royal is called Skyline Drive. It was a WPA and CCC project for which planning commenced in 1933 and construction began following a discussion between President Franklin Roosevelt and the Director of the National Park Service, Horace Albright (see main text). Sections of the parkway were built in the order of greatest need for employment of local people, who were hired whenever possible. Four CCC camps along the route were managed in military style; workers were housed in barracks, marched in formation, and took turns with kitchen duties. The CCC graded the slopes on either side of the roadway; built the guardrails and guard walls; constructed overlooks; planted hundreds of thousands of trees and shrubs and acres of grass to landscape both sides of the parkway roadbed; and built picnic areas, campgrounds, visitor facilities, and maintenance buildings. The original Appalachian Trail had to be relocated away from the parkway route, pressing the wilderness experience downhill (see main text).

responsible for new tasks—some of them outside park boundaries. It administered projects in state parks and trained people in other government agencies, including state park officials and managers in the CCC. Fortunately it could draw into that expanded process the additional educators, historians, and scientists brought to it by the CCC.

In the New Deal's characteristic way, the Park Service learned as it acted, relying upon art to provide discipline, insight, and taste. With history and the natural sciences setting the objectives, landscape architects designed roads, lodges, bridges, trails, gardens, forests, wetlands, ponds, and visitor centers. Not always, nor everywhere, were these undertakings successful, but by the time Roosevelt gave a fireside talk from Two Medicine Chalet, Glacier National Park, on August 5, 1934, he was secure in expressing pride in his new system of "natural and historic treasures." "The present National Park Service stands as an example of efficient and far-seeing governmental administration," he said, as enlarged by "transferring from other departments many other parks, battlefield sites, memorials, and national monuments. This concentration of responsibility has thus made it possible to embark on a permanent park policy as a great recreational and educational project—one which no other country in the world has ever undertaken in such a broad way for protection of its natural and historic treasures and for the enjoyment of them by vast numbers of people."[23]

"Protection" and "enjoyment" were terms derived from the Organic Act of the National Park System enacted during the Progressive Era. The New Deal was providing new emphases upon education and the working arts. The arts of exposition—of that interactive discourse the Park Service traditionally calls "interpretation"—had been customary in national parks through "interpreters" and through sculpture, plaques, and signage. The content of these communications enhanced a sense of common purposes, common heritage, and common destiny on battlefields and in other historic places. After 1933, expository art and interpretation emphasized the themes of the New Deal post office murals, reminding the people of what they had experienced together, some of it pleasant and some of it tragic. The intended result was a more confident citizenship committed to the active pursuit of happiness.[24]

The young men enrolled in the CCC, said Roosevelt, were engaged in that pursuit as they were becoming worthier participants in democracy. His program for the public lands, like his support for the public arts, arose from his sense of a proper solicitude by government for "the enrichment of the lives of all of us." Where better to work at that than in the nation's parks, where, said the President, they would "perform the double function of enjoying much and learning much," building "great public projects for the benefit of the public" with the "definite objective of building human happiness." Reiterating the theme of his "Rendezvous with Destiny Speech" of 1936 and of many fireside talks, Roosevelt urged at MoMA in 1939 that the pursuit of happiness be seen as active citizenship. As young people worked on CCC and WPA projects, whether they thought of themselves as artists or not, they could be "free to be themselves and to be in charge of the discipline of their own energies and ardors" and freely asserting for all "the right of spontaneous life." Those that were artists—including some who did not think of themselves that way—should be free to "express themselves with complete freedom from the strictures of dead artistic tradition or political ideology. While American artists have discovered a new obligation to the society in which they live, they have no compulsion to be limited in method or manner of expression."[25]

As the CCC directly applied many of the arts to conservation," Roosevelt reminded his listeners in New York that "art in America has always belonged to the people and has never been the property of an academy or a class." In accordance with this principle, he said, "the great Treasury projects, . . . our public buildings are being decorated," and as further examples "of the continuity of this tradition. The Federal Art Project of the Works Progress Administration is a practical relief project which also emphasizes the best tradition of the democratic spirit. The W.P.A. artist, in rendering his own impression of things, speaks also for the spirit of his fellow countrymen everywhere."[26]

The CCC artist was speaking for that spirit as well, often working beside a WPA artist to enlarge public understanding of what place-making and conservation could do. The visual arts were put to use in the history and ecology being taught in the parks with the aid of a new cadre of professional scholars, naturalists, and researchers entering the Park Service with the CCC. Kindled by their presence, new energy and broader understanding was brought to the work of the artists of landscape design. Place-based and place-making art in the parks and in other CCC projects enriched and enlivened a nation much in need of enlivening.

For some, park building and landscape restoration were not art. And for others, the filmmaking and photography employed by the CCC to explain its work to the public were not art either. But from the outset of the New Deal's conservation work, place-making was honored as art, and so was verbal and symbolic communication. Constituencies had to be built. The most famous of the New Deal's uses of the arts were for place-making—and thus community sustenance—in post office murals. Parks are even more appropriate for these purposes. They are places selected for their incandescence in teaching and learning, including learning about conservation. So there was high compatibility between the CCC–Park Service programs in the arts and the photography programs administered by Rexford Tugwell and Roy Stryker for the Farm Security Administration and the Resettlement Administration; these were made kinetic in the motion picture documentaries of Pare Lorentz (see chapter seven). The CCC also availed itself of the art of photography, sometimes borrowing FSA photographers, sometimes on its own. It produced more than thirty "conservation films," and participated with the Soil Service in making *The Heritage We Guard*, a full-length feature film. And its "Radio Committee" made full use of the art of the audio documentary.

These efforts were welcomed by the president, who in 1939 said that it was in the nation's interest to "extend the perspective of the general public, which too often has been accustomed to think of the fine arts as painting and possibly sculpture." The needs of the time required that that general public should become "increasingly aware of the enormous importance of contemporary industrial design, architecture, including the great social art—housing—which by its very nature is one of the most formidable challenges to a democracy, as well as photography, the printed book, the illustration, the advertisement, the poster, the theater and the moving picture. Thus, a nation-wide public will receive a demonstration of the force and scope of all these branches of the visual arts." Nationwide, the CCC and WPA had demonstrated that architecture for public use, including landscape architecture, might indeed be "fine art."[27]

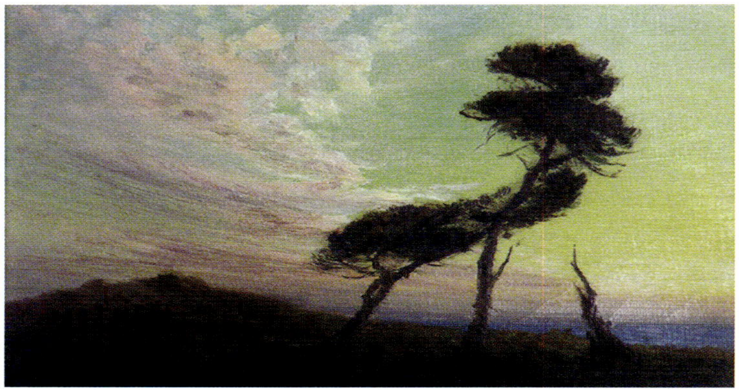

California Coast
Ferdinand Burgdorff, 1911

Ferdinand Burgdorff was born in Cleveland, Ohio. After art studies there and in Paris he lived in boxcars with workers building the railroad between Yuma, Arizona Territory, and Calexico, California, riding away from the rail line to paint the desert "undisturbed by a single human within miles." He sold enough of his desert paintings to finance a tour of Greece and Egypt before settling briefly in Santa Fe and moving on to Pebble Beach, near Carmel, in California. There he built a home designed by Bernard Maybeck, and became an illustrator for *Sunset* magazine, in which many of his paintings were published. He became virtually the painter-laureate of the Monterey Peninsula, working well into his nineties (see main text).

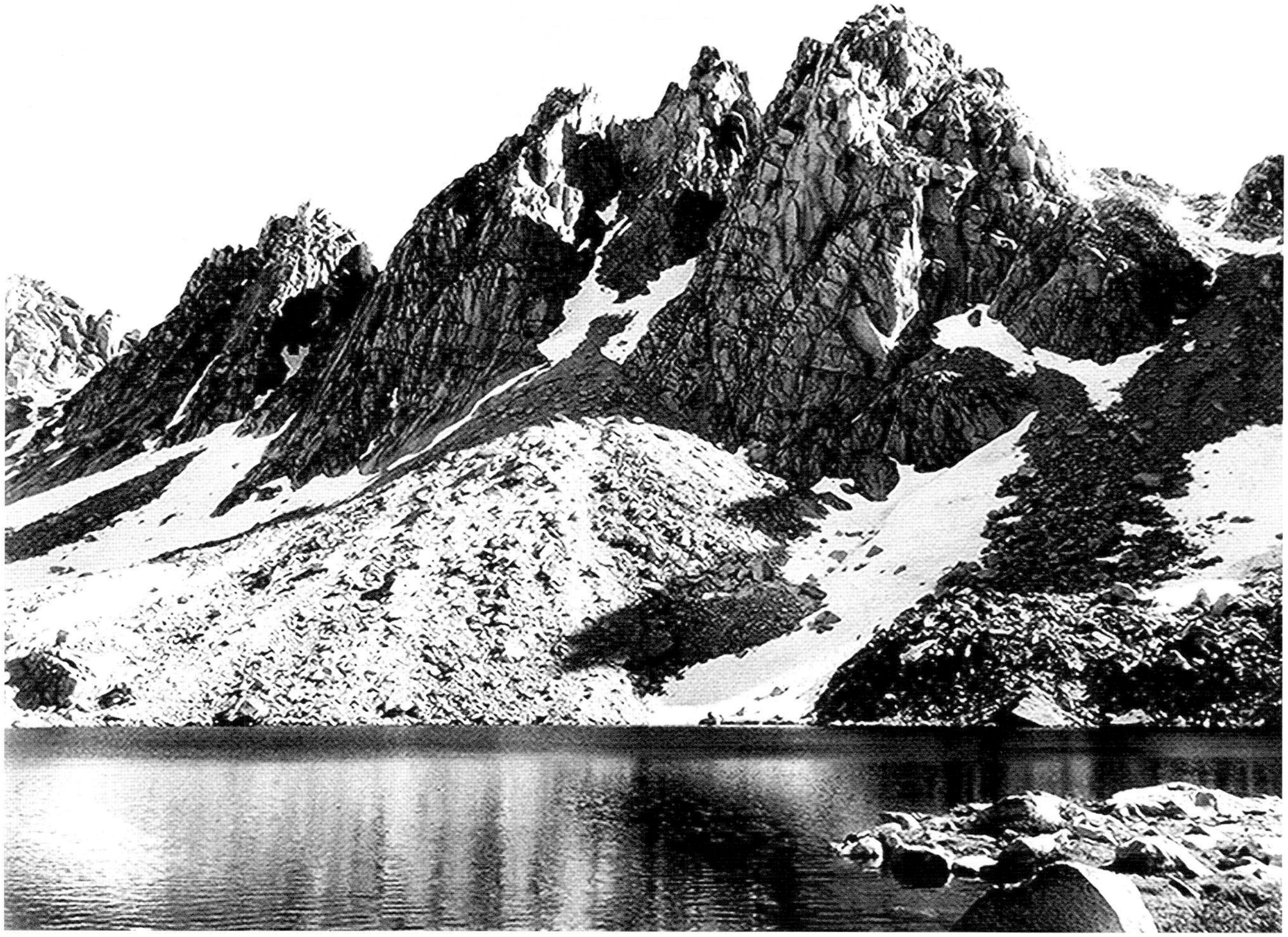

"Kearsage Pinnacles"
Kings River Canyon
(Proposed as a national park)
Ansel Adams, c. 1936

In 1941, after most of the work on Harold Ickes's Department of the Interior Building was done, the National Park Service commissioned Ansel Adams to create for it a photo mural of the National Parks. It was never completed because of wartime exigencies. However, Adams took 226 photographs for the project, adding many of Kings Canyon taken in 1936 when the establishment of the park was being proposed, and one of Yosemite he had presented as a gift to National Park Service Director Horace M. Albright.

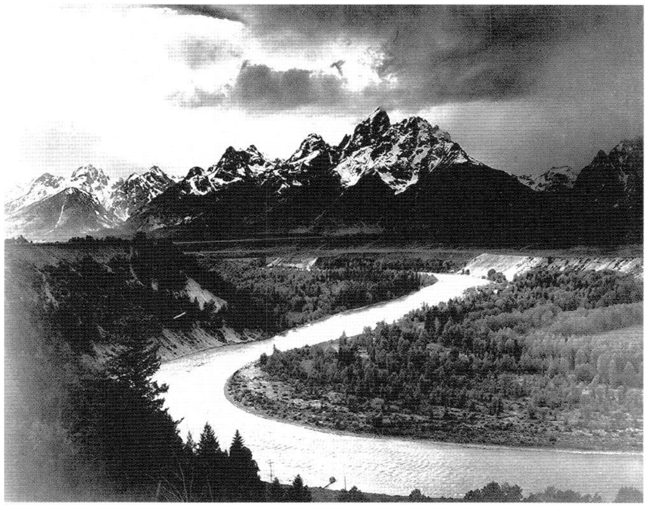

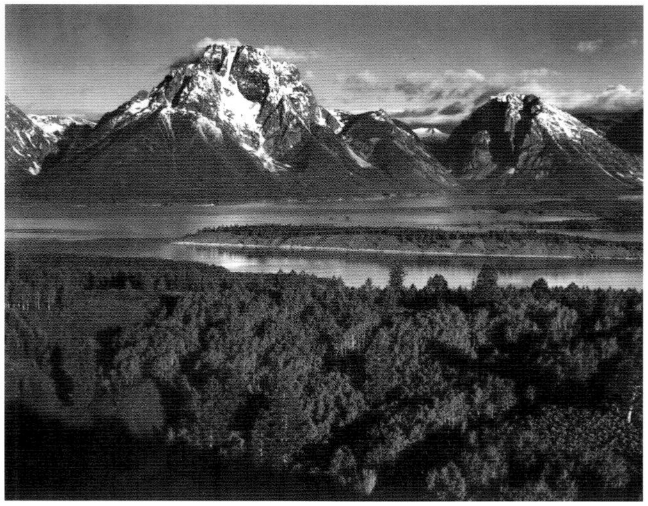

Far left:
"The Tetons—
Snake River"
Grand Teton National Park
Ansel Adams, c. 1933–42

Left:
"View Across the River Toward Mount Moran, Grand Teton National Park"
Ansel Adams, c. 1933–42

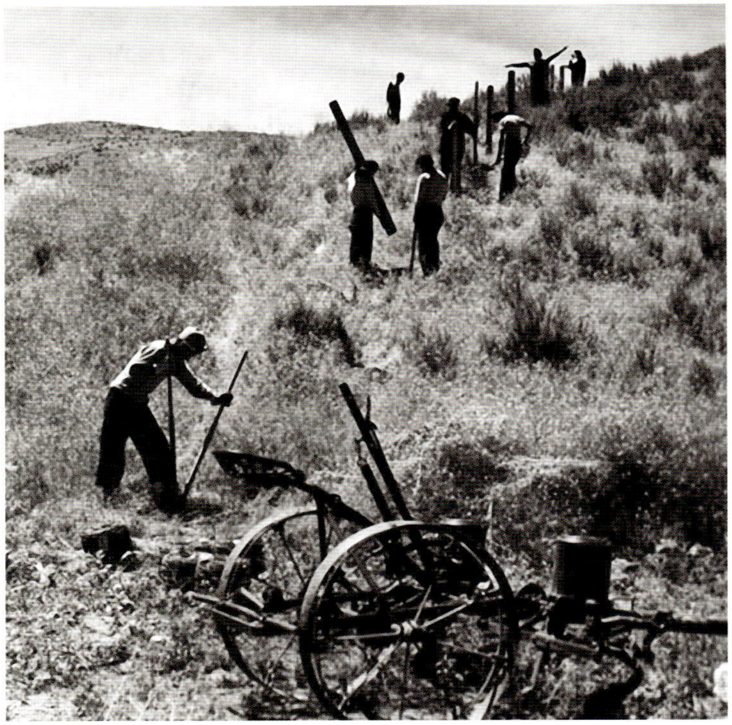

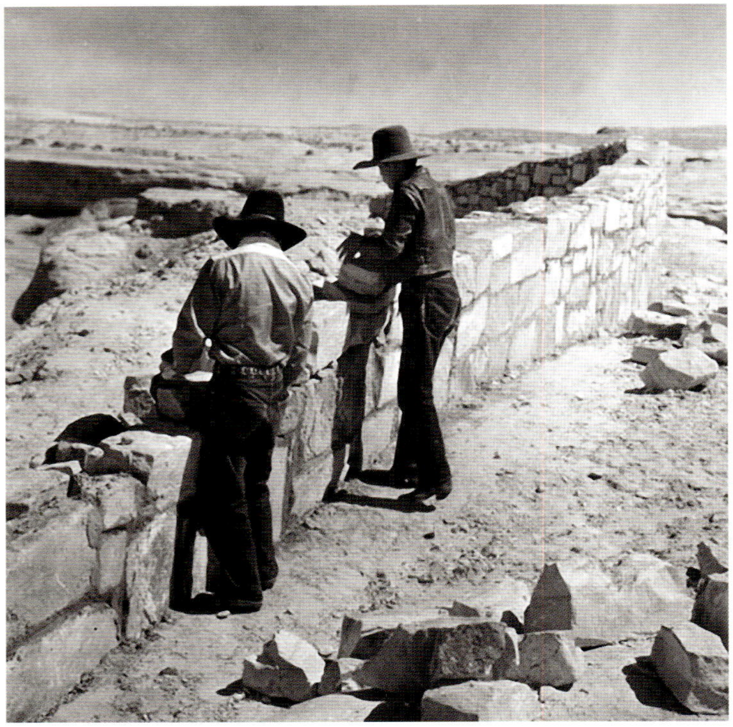

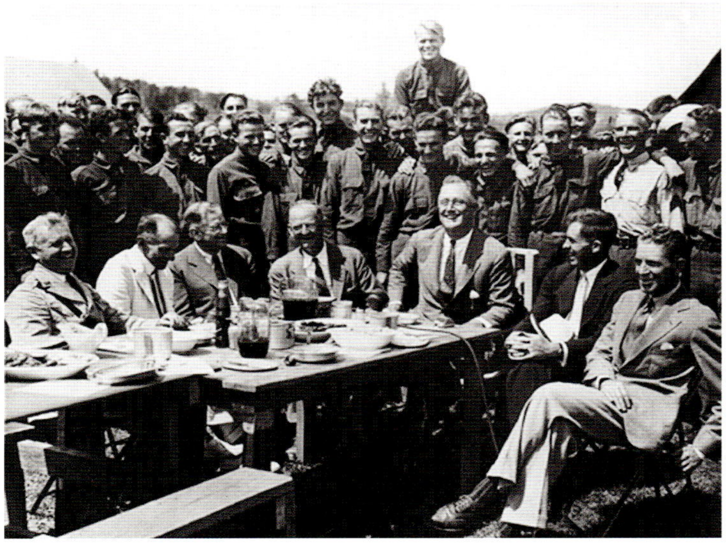

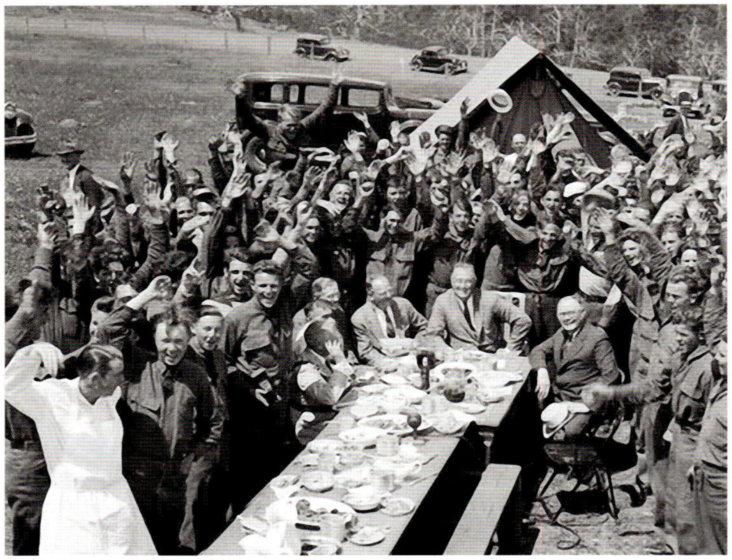

Top left and right:
CCC camps

Bottom left and right:
FDR visits a CCC Camp

President Franklin Roosevelt made his first visit to a CCC camp on August 12, 1933, accompanied by Secretary of the Interior Harold Ickes and Arno Cammerer, who had just succeeded Horace Albright as director of the National Park Service. During the following summer, the President and his family inspected camps in the West, after Eleanor Roosevelt had visited several eastern camps, including the one at Acadia National Park (see main text).

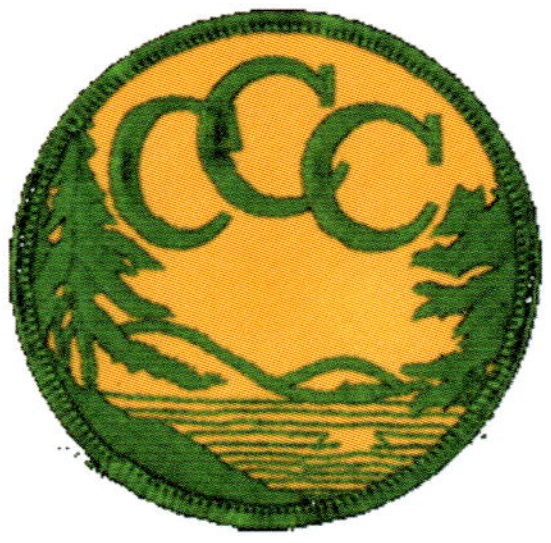

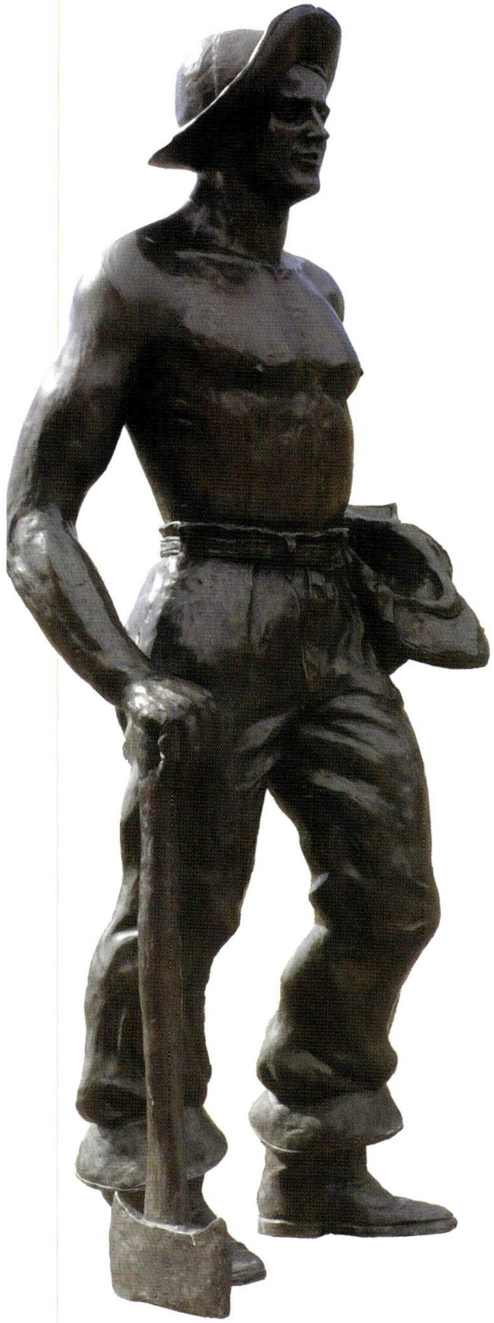

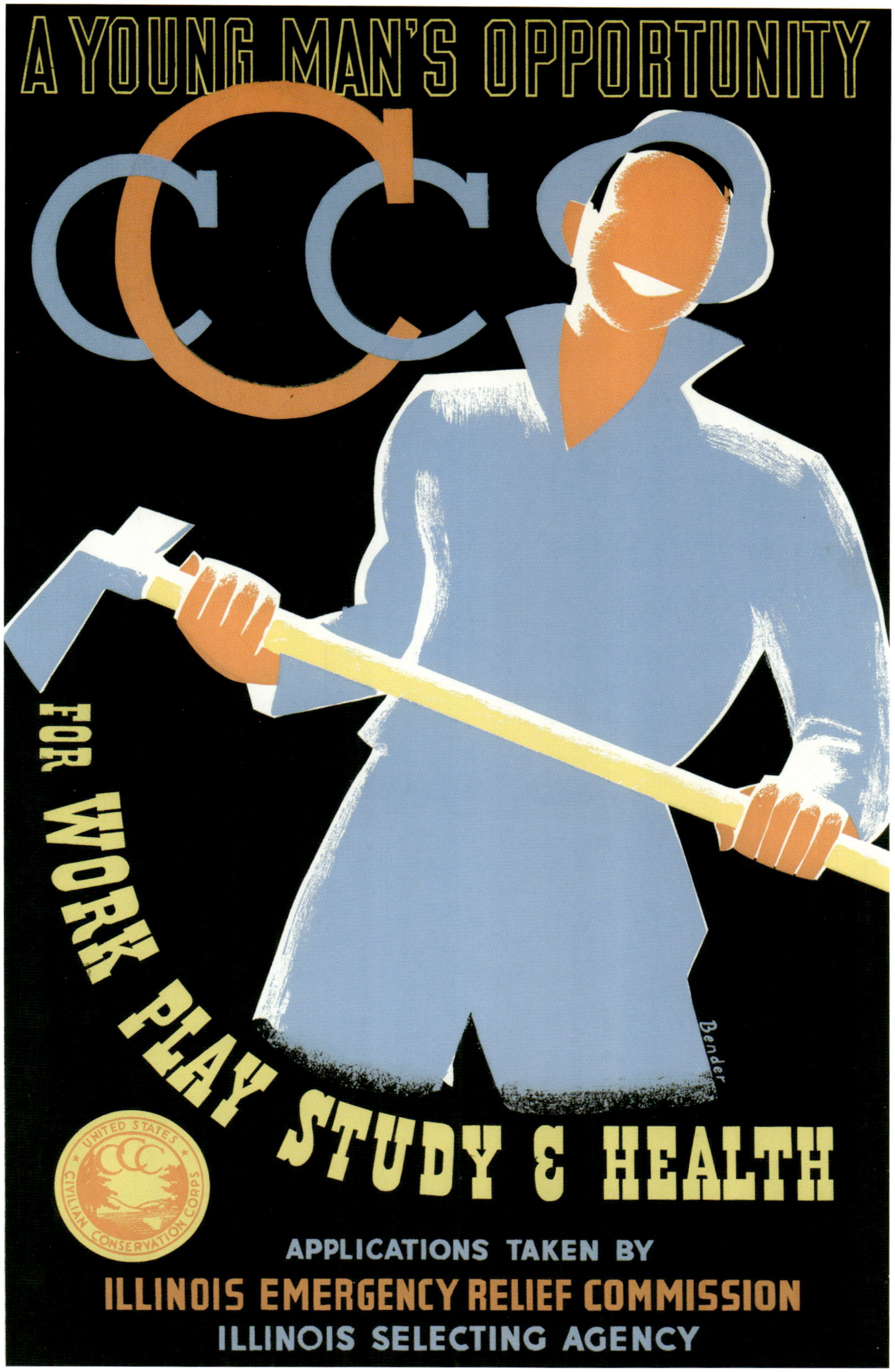

Far left:
CCC Worker statue,
Red Rocks

Left:
"CCC A Young Man's
Opportunity for Work Play
Study & Health"
Albert Bender, c. 1935

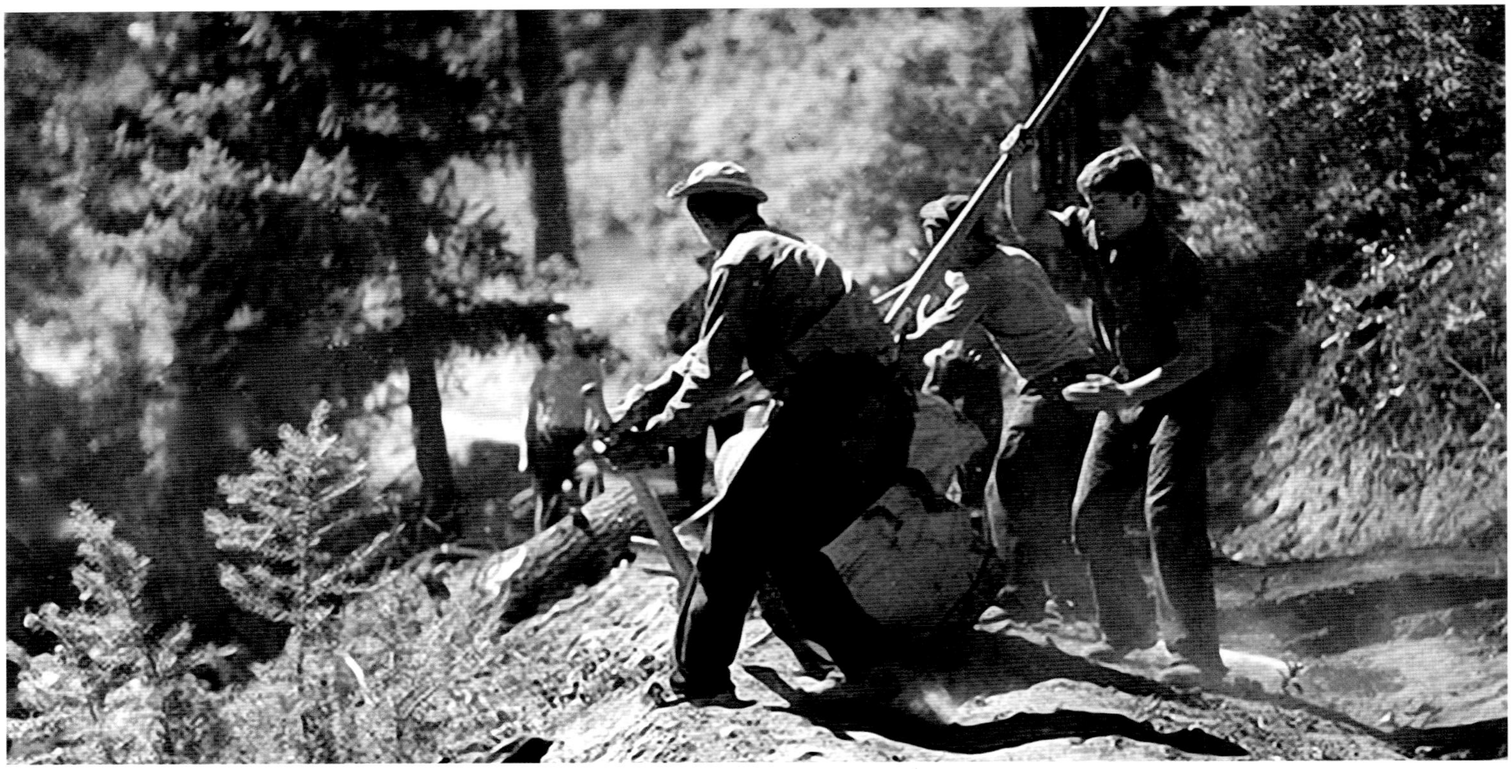

CCC crews clearing a trail in Boise National Forest

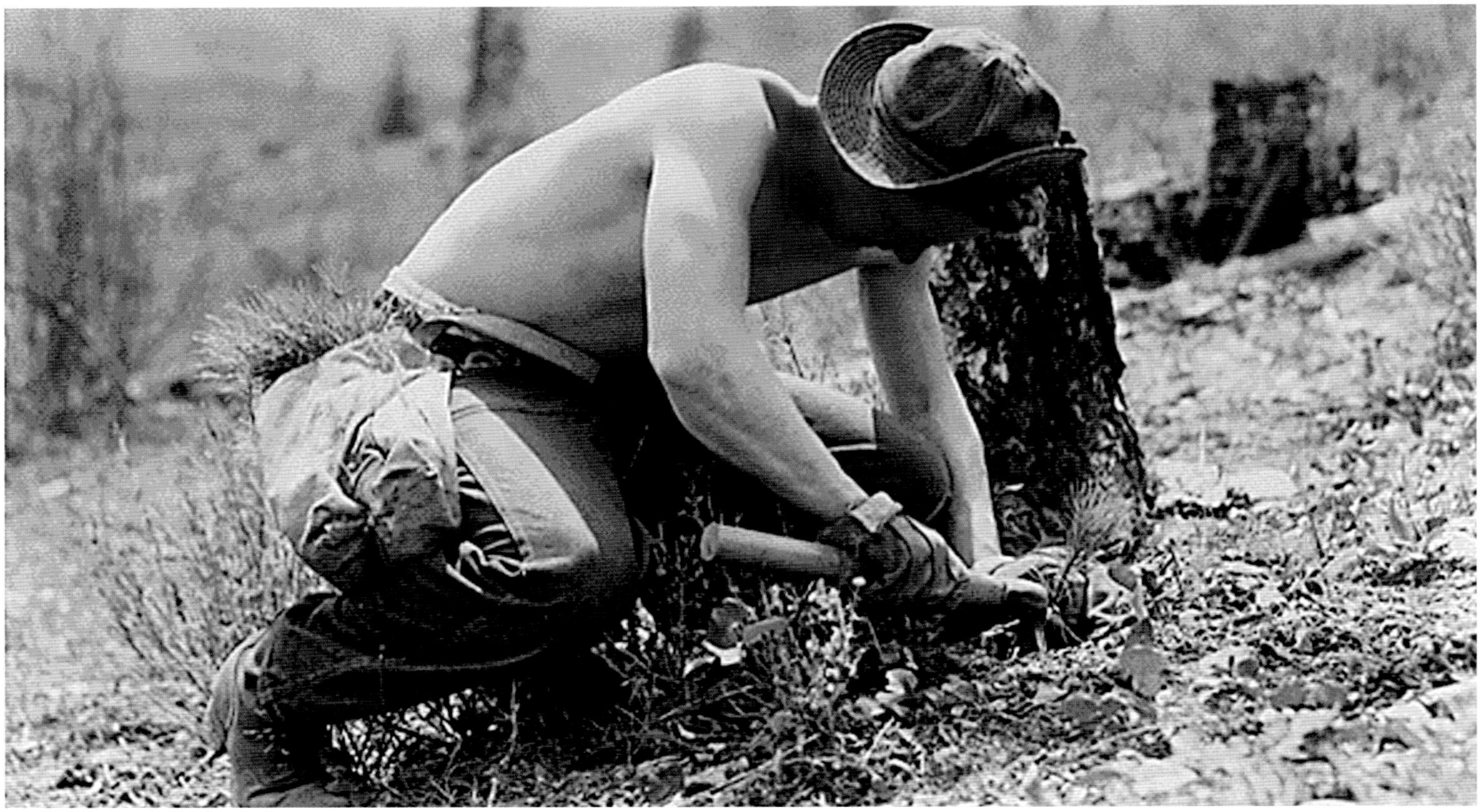

Bottom:
CCC crew planting trees

More than two and a half million young men were enrolled in forty-five hundred camps during the nine years of the Emergency Conservation Work (ECW) and its successor after 1937, the Civilian Conservation Corps (see main text). Pay was thirty dollars per month, and generally twenty-five dollars of that was sent directly to a family member eligible for relief. The CCC troops regularly handled mail service to local residents, and provided the chief market for local food crops. Eventually there were ECW and CCC camps in all states and in Hawaii, Alaska, Puerto Rico, and the Virgin Islands.

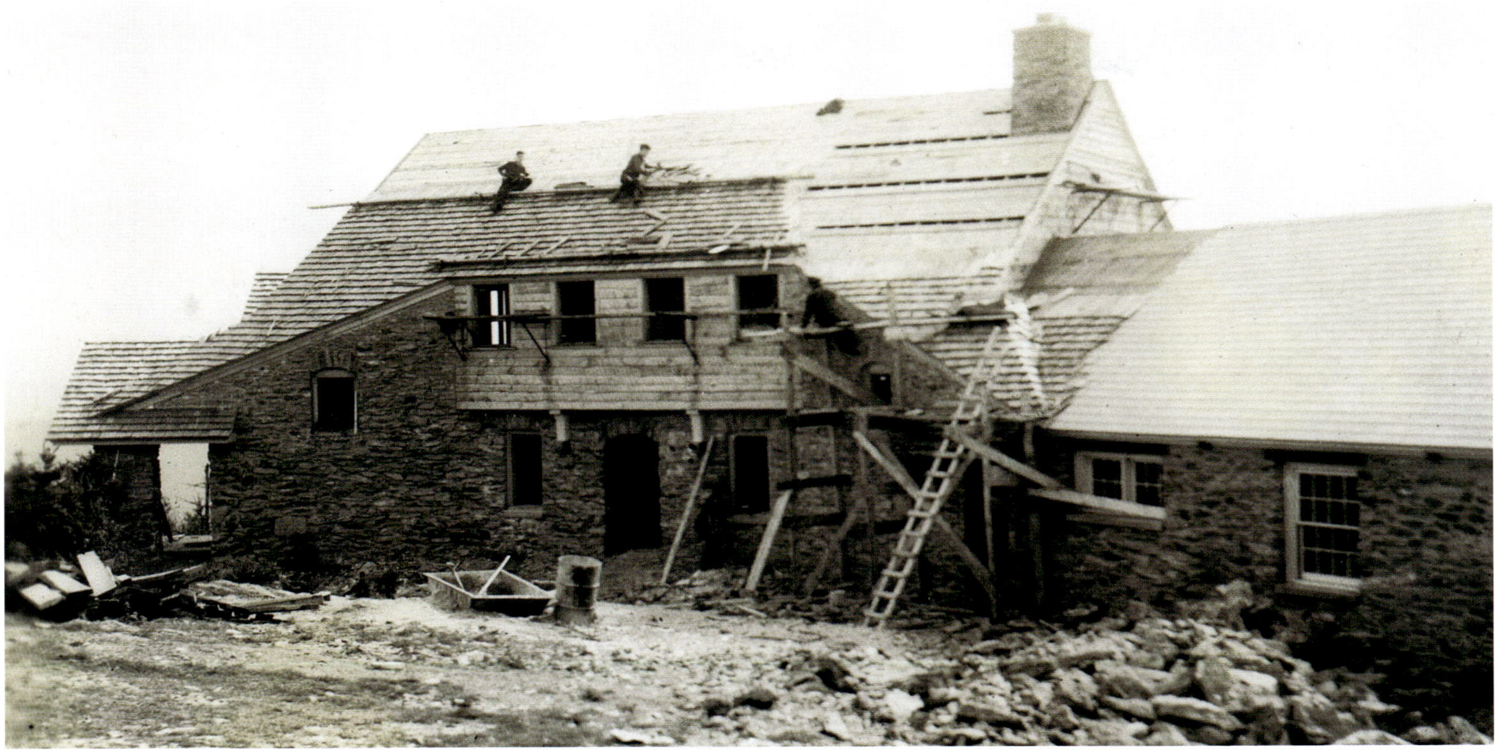

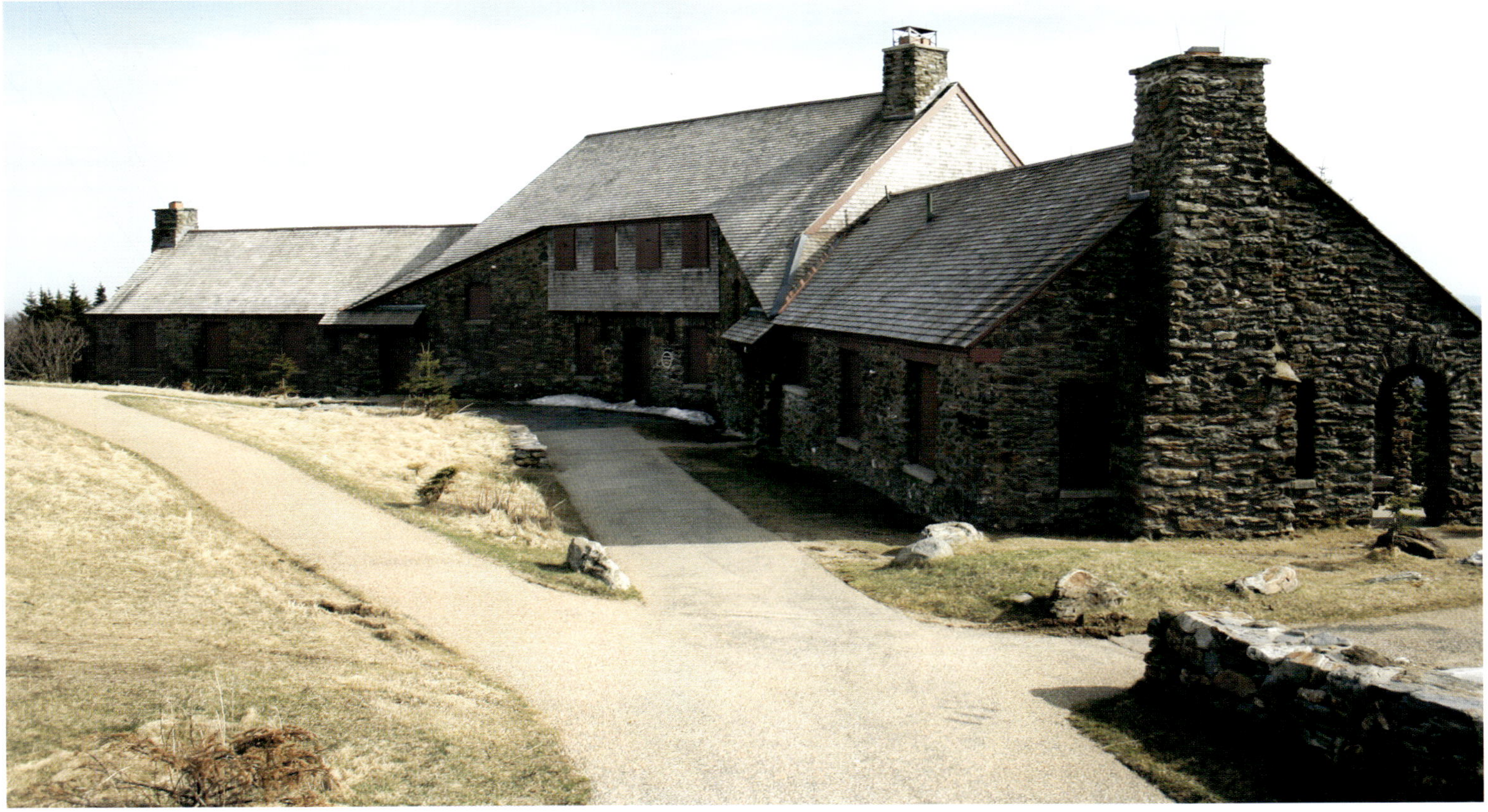

Bascom Lodge, c. 1935
CCC enrollees working local slates onto the roof.

Bottom:
Bascom Lodge today

Below: The plaque fixed to the entrance wall at the lodge.

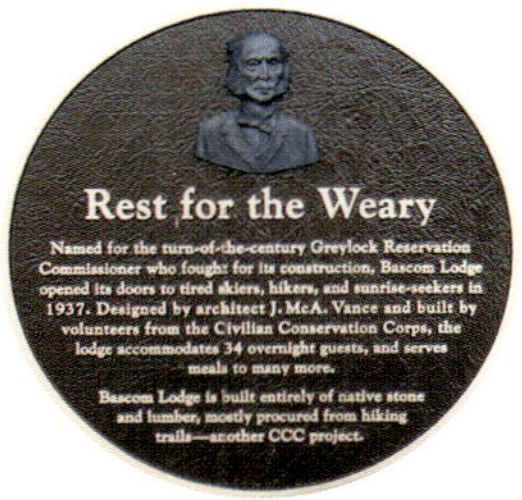

Bascom Lodge was built by the ECW (CCC) between 1933 and 1937 at the summit of Mt. Greylock in the Massachusetts Berkshires to shelter hikers and tourists. It stood in the midst of CCC roads, trails, vistas, firebreaks, forest health programs, and recreation facilities. It was built of local materials such as Greylock schist and red spruce to the plans and specifications of architect James McArthur Vance of Pittsfield, Massachusetts. It replaced a summer hotel that had burned down in 1929 and was named in honor of John Bascom, a Greylock Reservation Commissioner and Williams College professor. Vance also designed the Thunderbolt Ski Shelter, built in 1940 by the CCC as a warming hut for skiers.

Mingus Mill at Smokemont, Shenandoah National Park

In 1937 the CCC restored Mingus Mill, a turbine-driven gristmill that is one of the nineteenth-century structures preserved in the Shenandoah National Park. The mill, built in 1886 by John Mingus, has two water turbines rather than a classic water wheel. The turbines are connected to grindstones on the first floor by an iron shaft and by a series of pulleys to a wheat cleaner and bolting chest on the second floor. Grain goes by bucket belt to the wheat cleaner, which is essentially a fan blowing light dust from the grain; the wheat cleaner then drops it back to the first floor to be ground. The ensuing flour goes back to the second floor and the bolting chest, which uses bolts of progressively courser cloth to separate it into different grades.

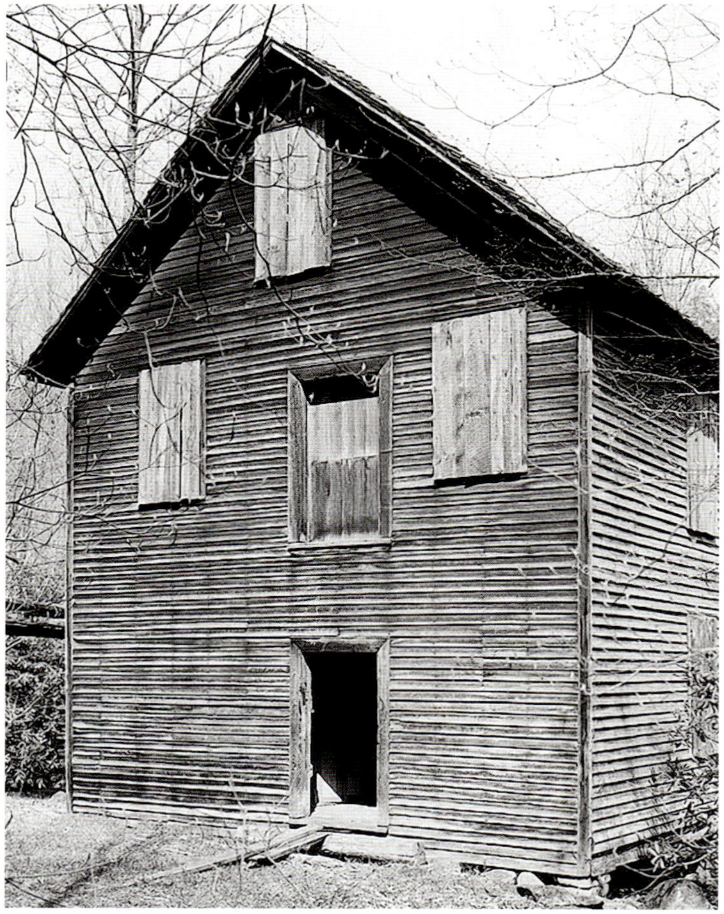

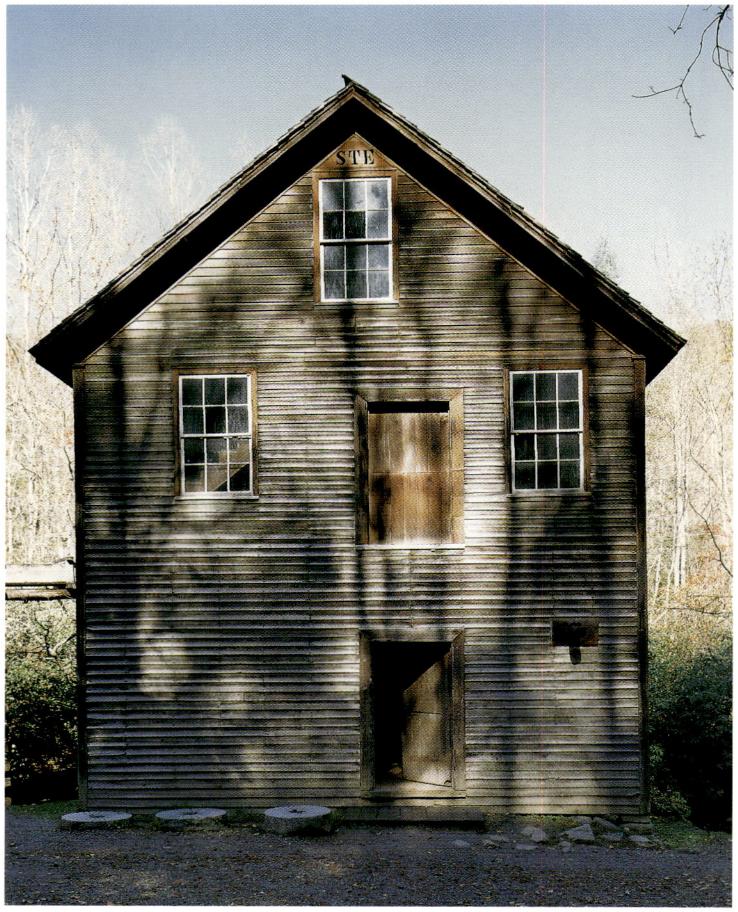

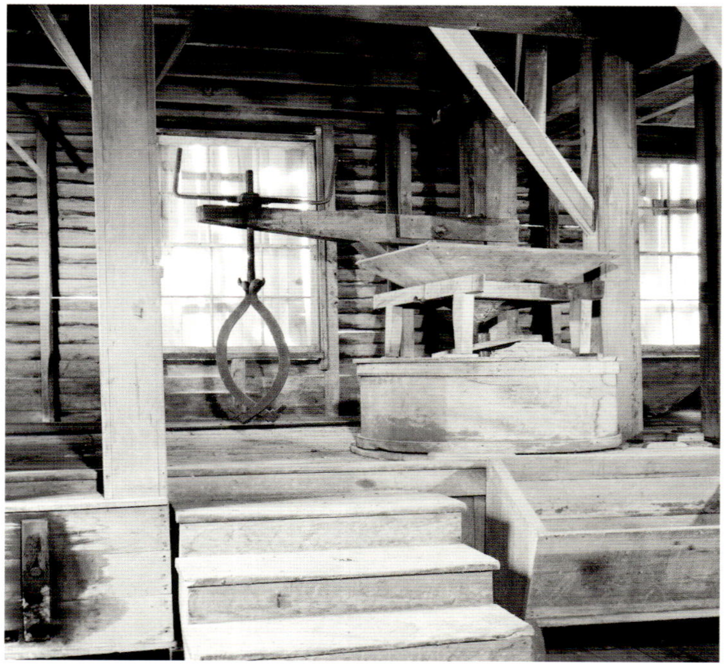

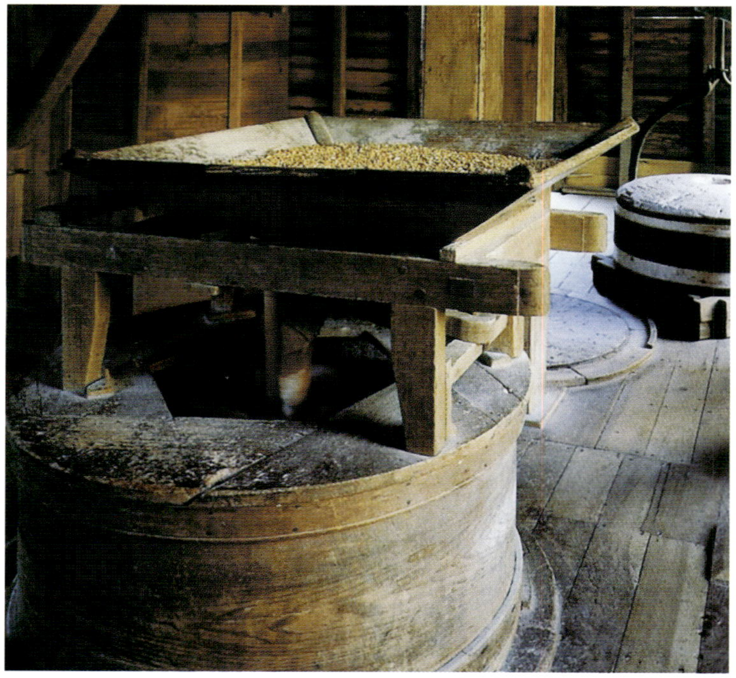

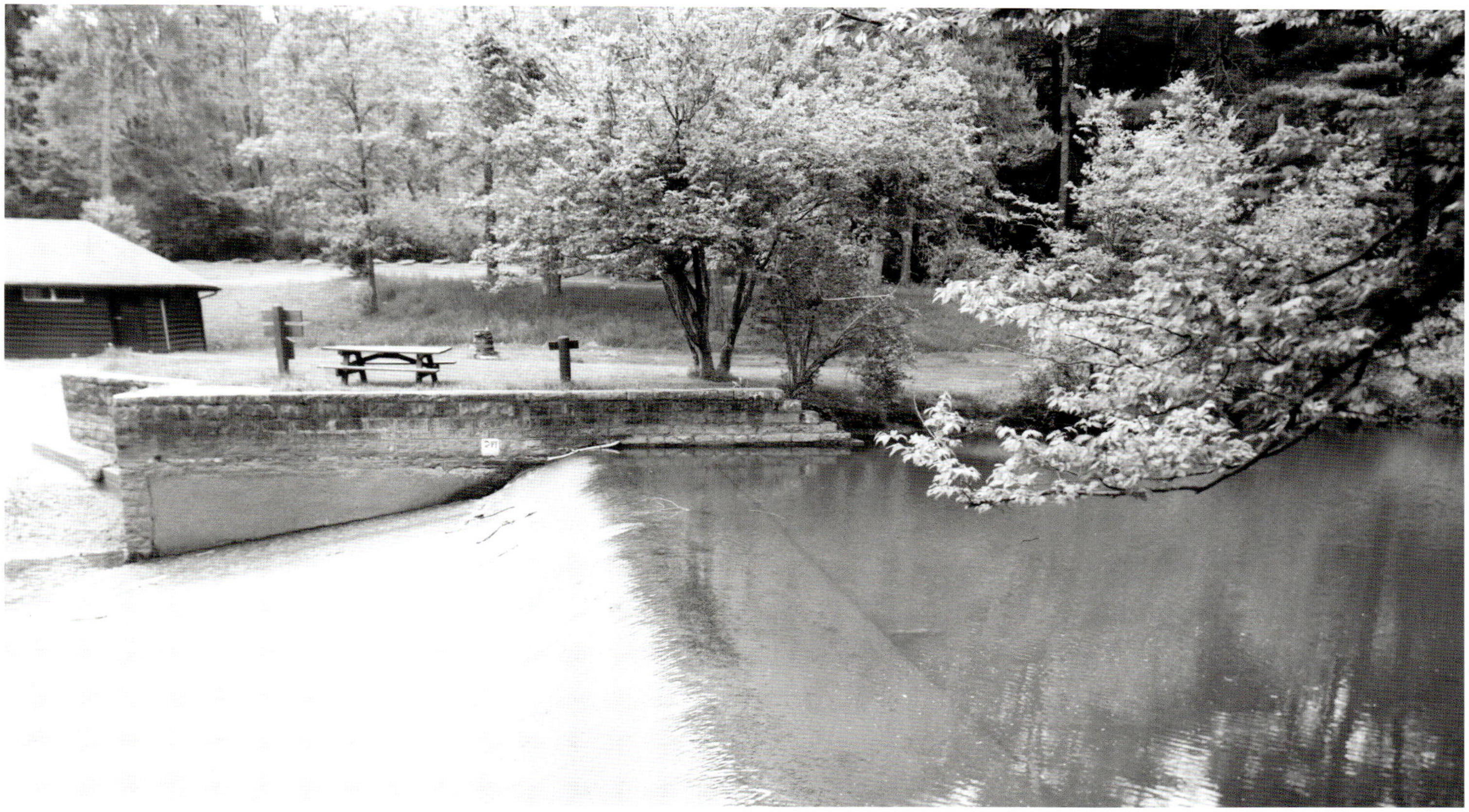

Loleta Recreation Area, Upper Dam, Allegheny National Forest, Elk County, Pennsylvania

The WPA/CCC enlarged the mill pond into a lake by building up the dam on Millstone Creek at the site of the old sawmill town, Loleta. The CCC also cleared land and constructed visitor facilities.

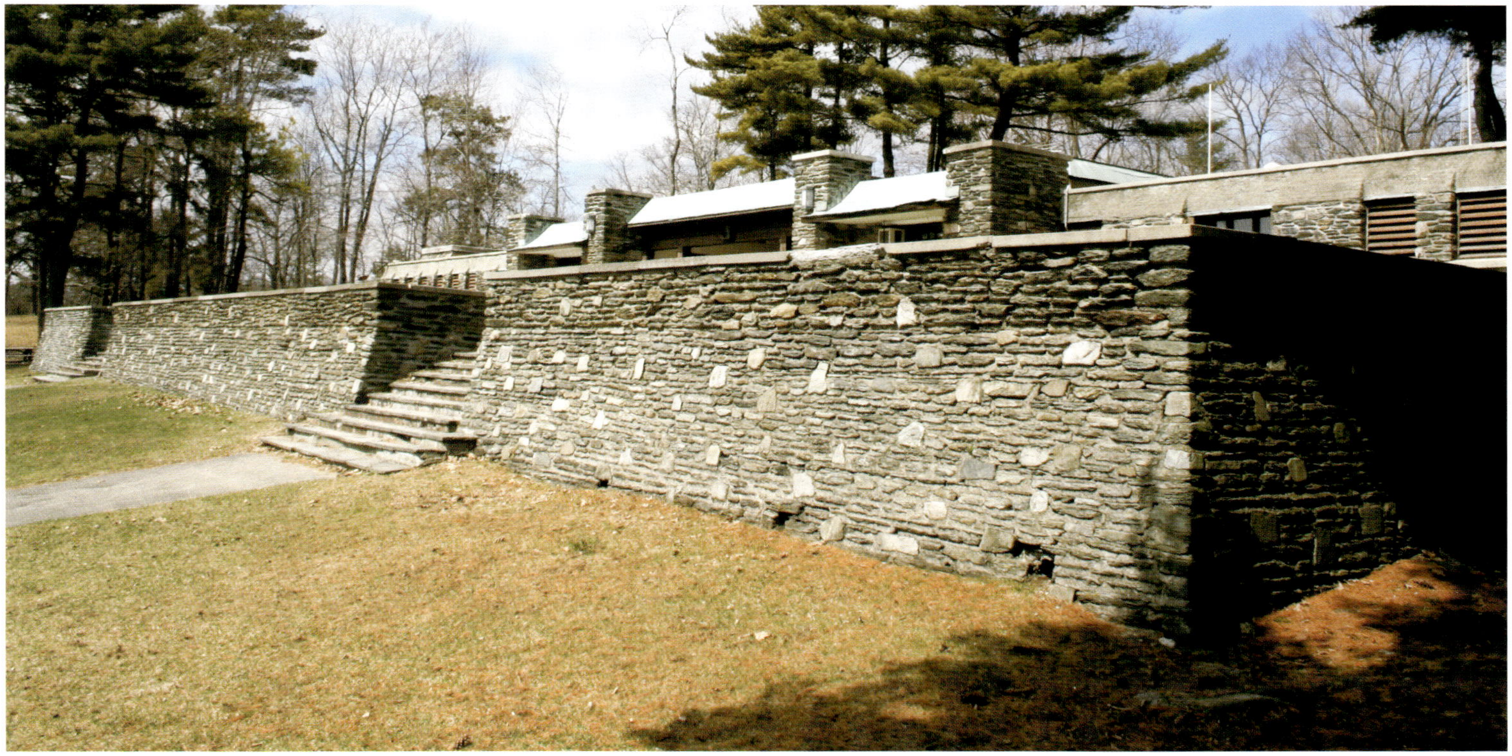

CCC Camp SP-3 constructed the local stone terrace walls fronting the bathhouse at Lake Taghkanic State Park in Columbia County, New York.

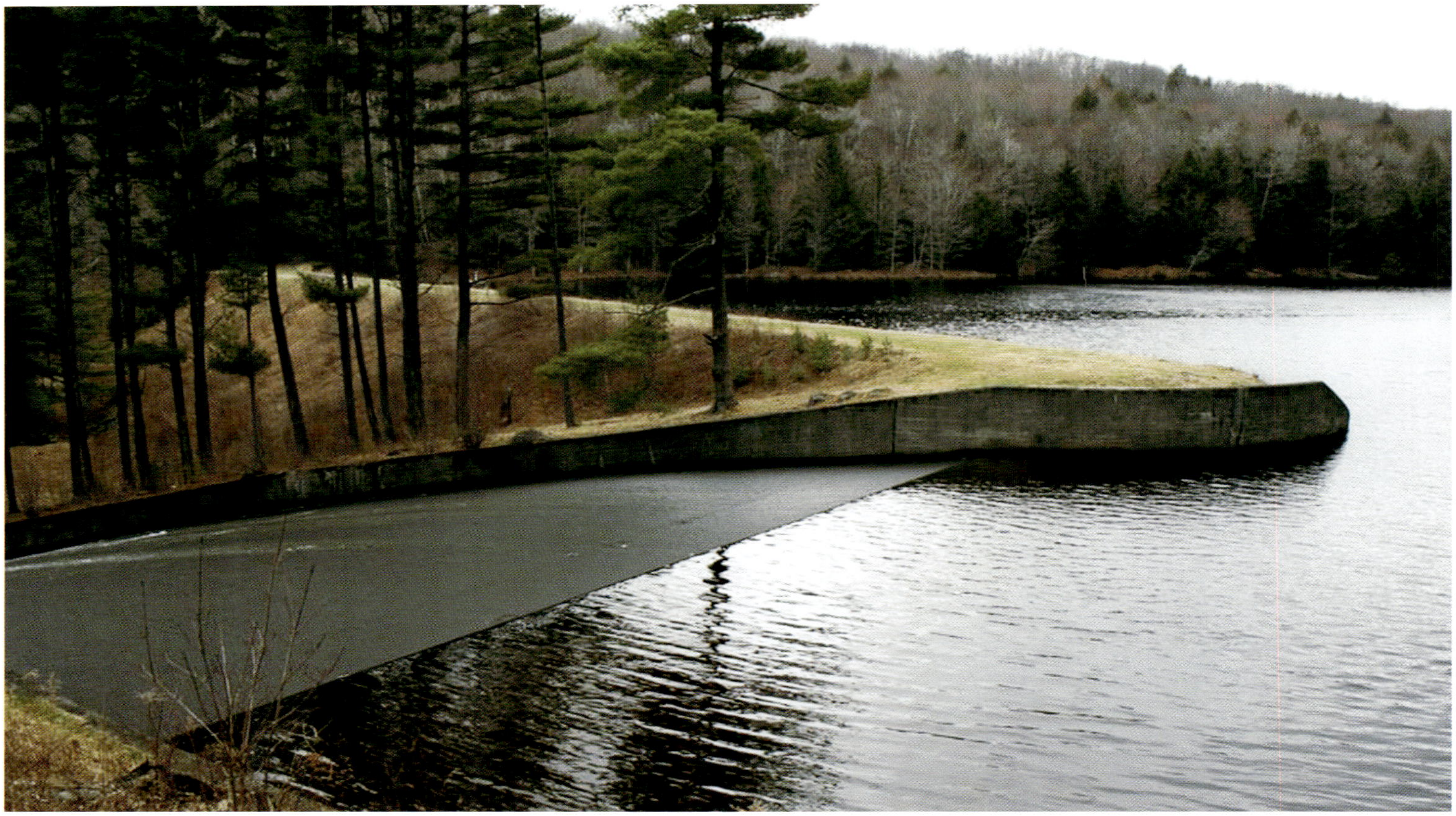

The "CCC Dam"
Cherry Plain State Park,
New York

The CCC built the dam and facilities in the midst of the two-thousand-acre Capital District Wildlife Management Area.

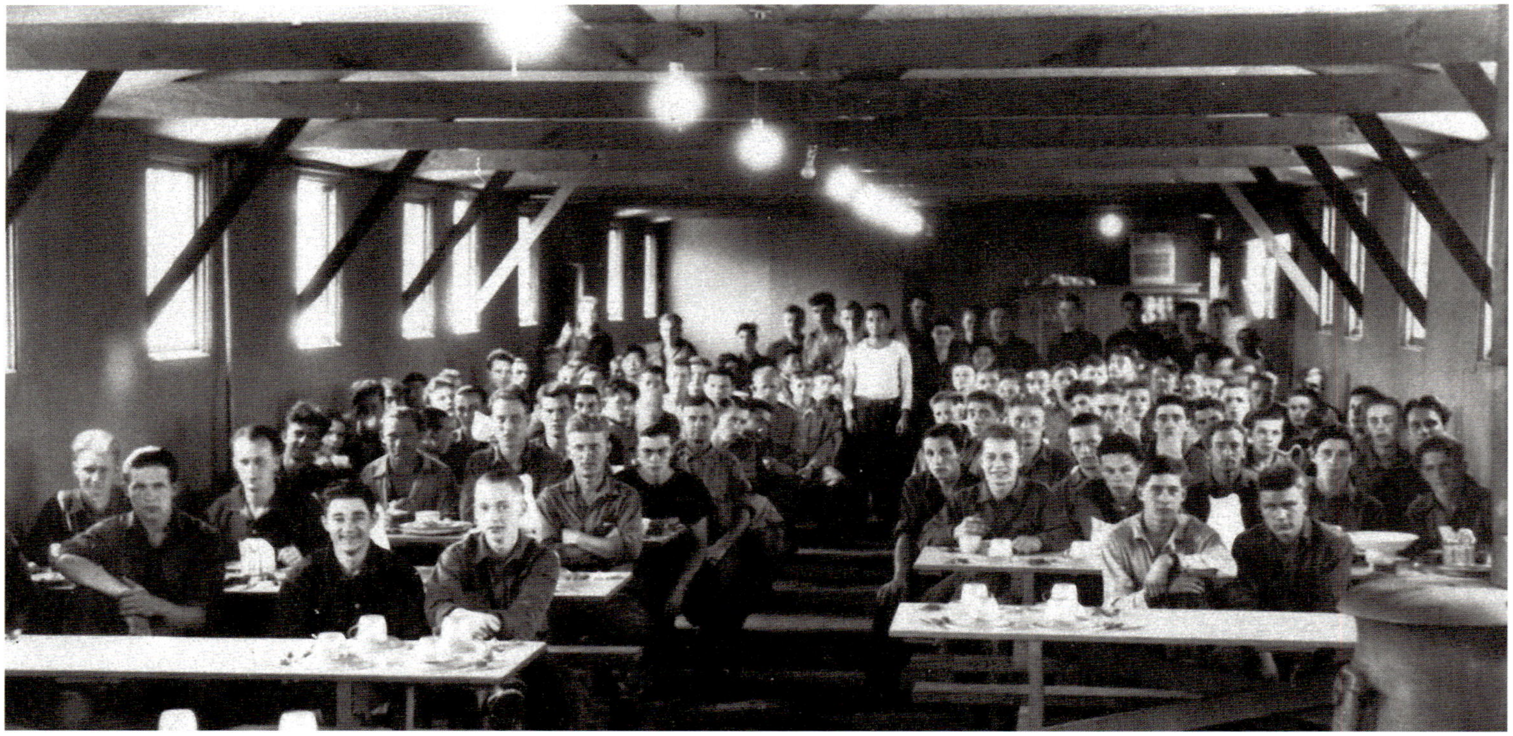

Bottom:
CCC Company 205, which built the dam pictured above, shown in their mess hall in the Cherry Plain State Park.

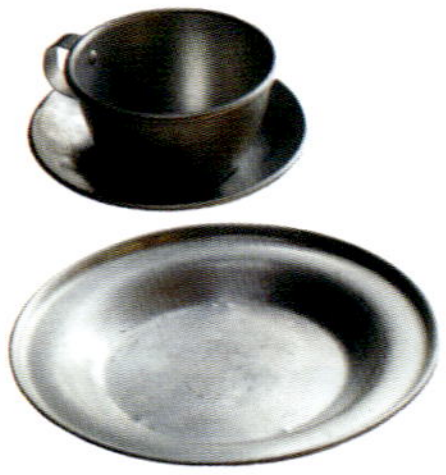

Above: Aluminum cup, saucer, and plate used in the mess hall.

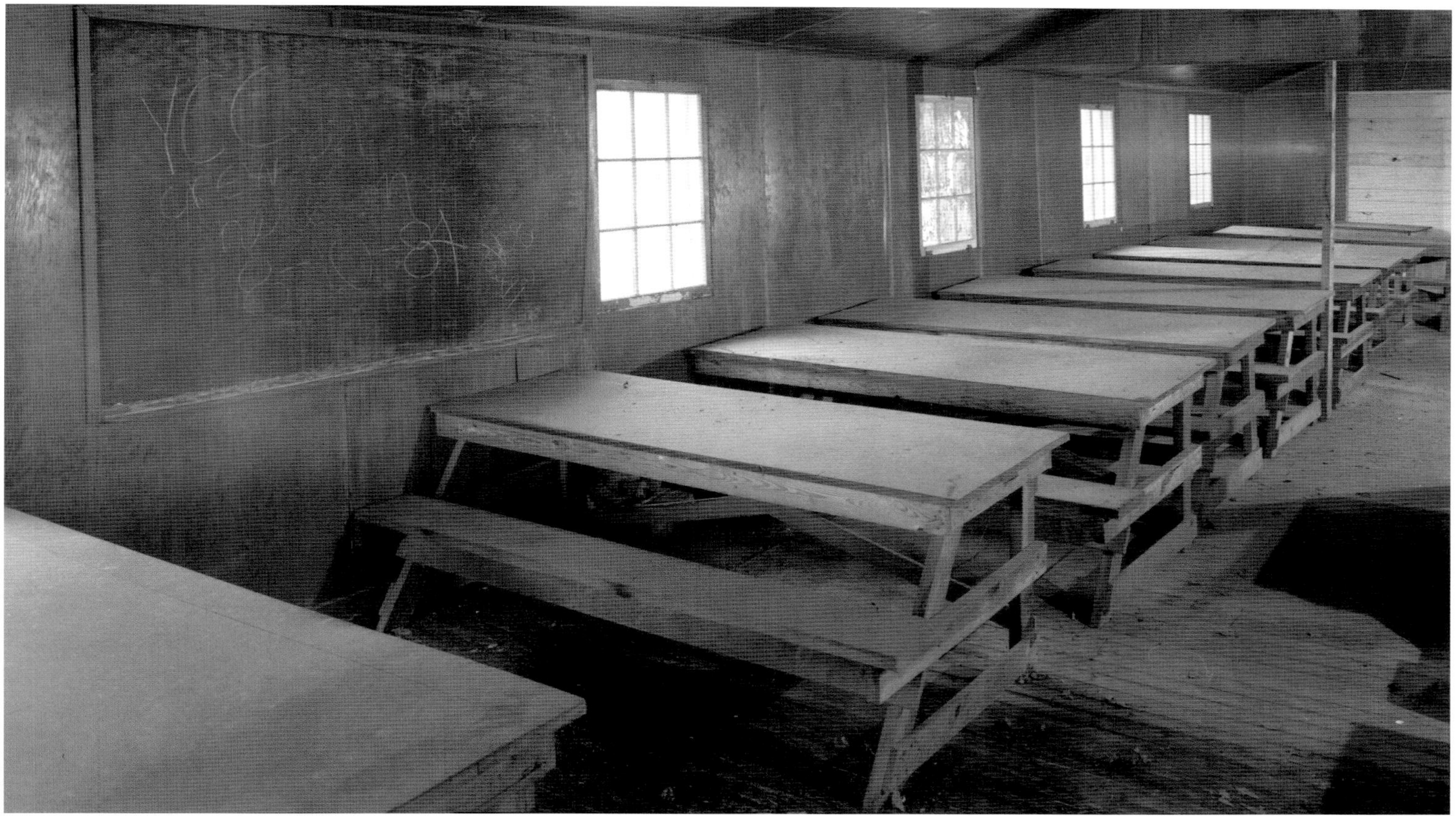

CCC Education Building
Rabideau Camp,
Blackduck, Minnesota

The camp was used by the University of Illinois between 1946 and 1972 for its engineering and forestry schools. It was designated a National Historic Landmark in August 2006 as the CCC campsite in the best condition of the twenty-six that survive. In 1999 the United States Forest Service began restoring the Education Building. Thirteen of the twenty-five original structures of the CCC Rabideau Camp are still standing, including the mess hall, five barracks, three officers' quarters, the recreation hall, the hospital, the laundry building, and the education building.

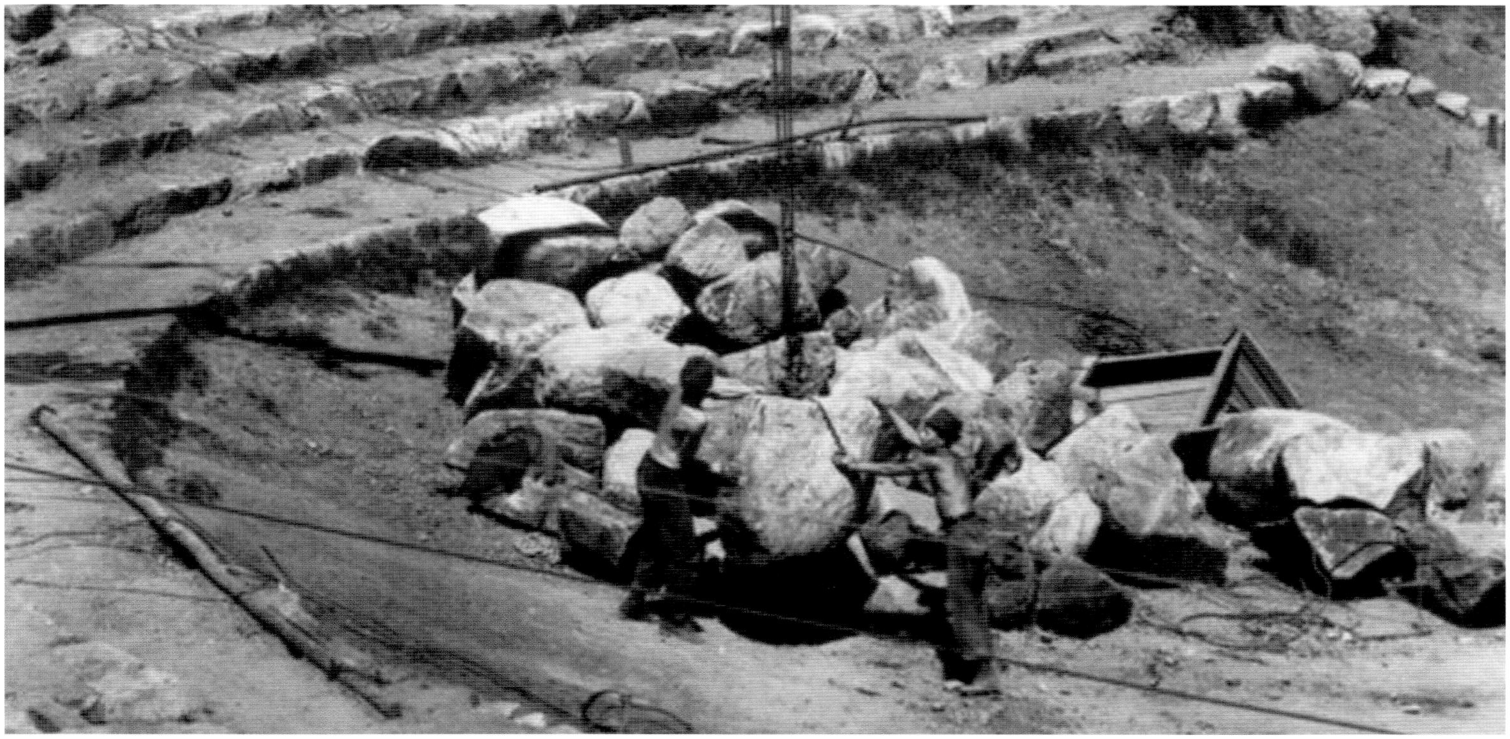

Bottom:
The Mountain Theater at
Mount Tamalpais State Park

Mount Tamalpais State Park, just north of San Francisco's Golden Gate Bridge, offers hiking trails, redwood groves, oak trees, and sweeping grasslands. From the summit one can see the Farallon Islands twenty-five miles out to sea, the Marin County hills, San Francisco, the hills and cities of the East Bay and beyond them, Mount Diablo.

For "the Mount Tam Amphitheater" the CCC crews, supervised by landscape architect Emerson Knight, placed lichen-encrusted boulders in a series of curved terraces to accommodate more than four thousand spectators.

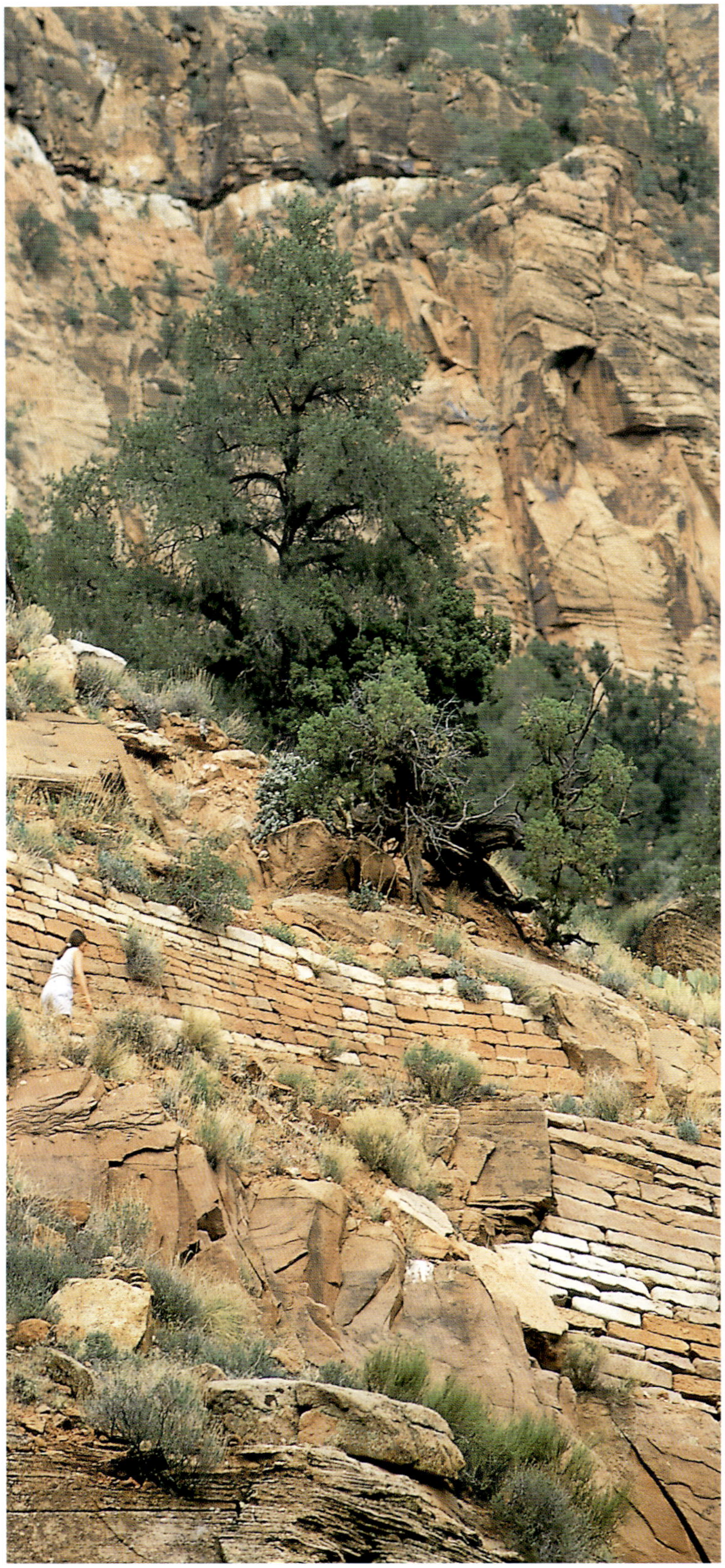

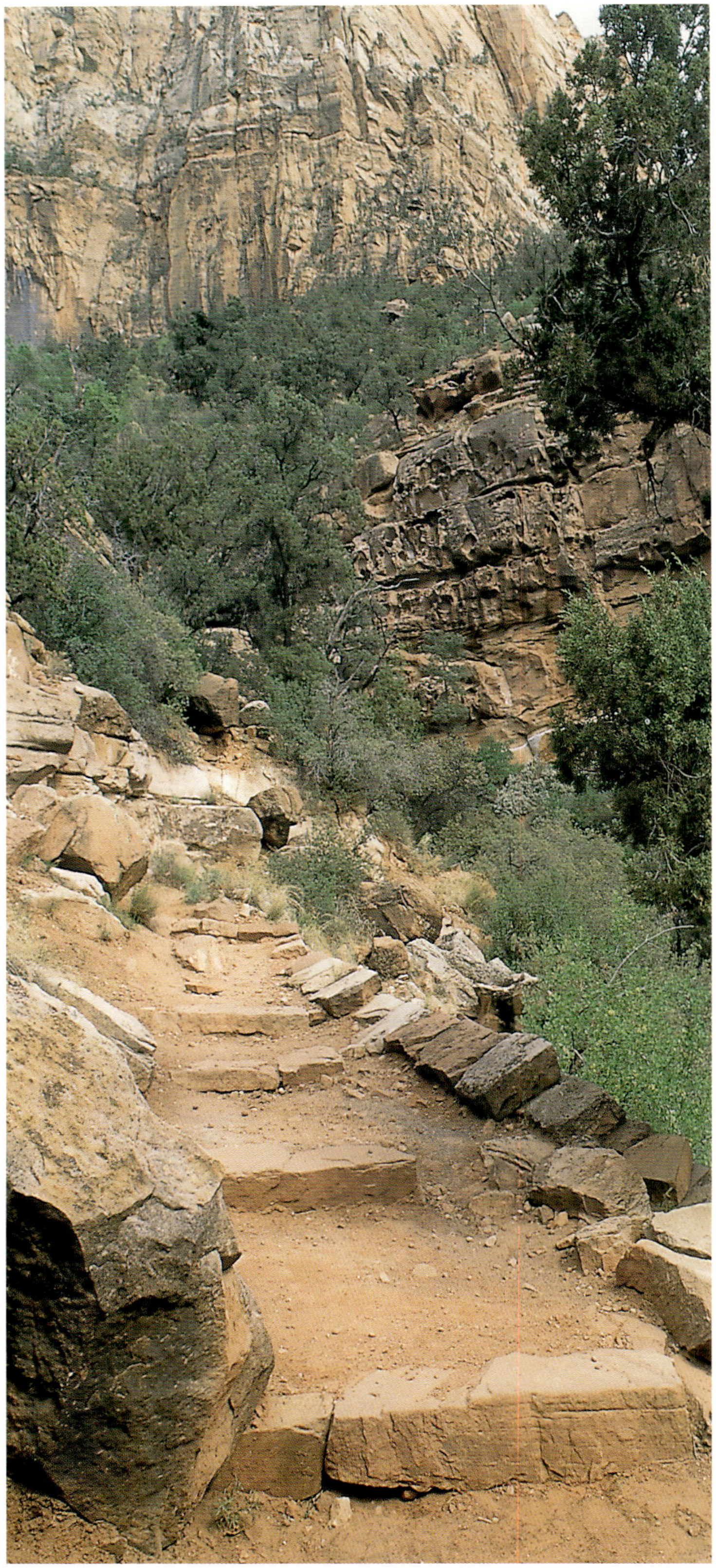

Right, far right:
Zion National Park
Cut-rock buttressing on the
Watchman Trail

The CCC constructed the Watchman Trail and Canyon Overlook Trail in 1933 and 1934, using mules, picks, shovels, and explosives. Water and cement mix had to be carried up the Zion Park trails.

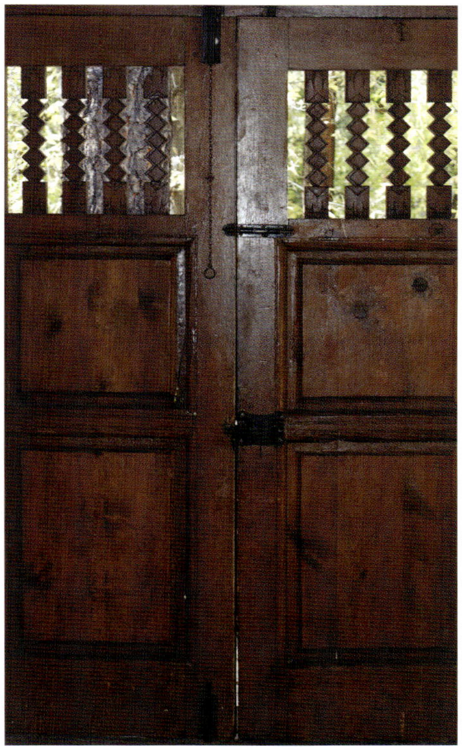

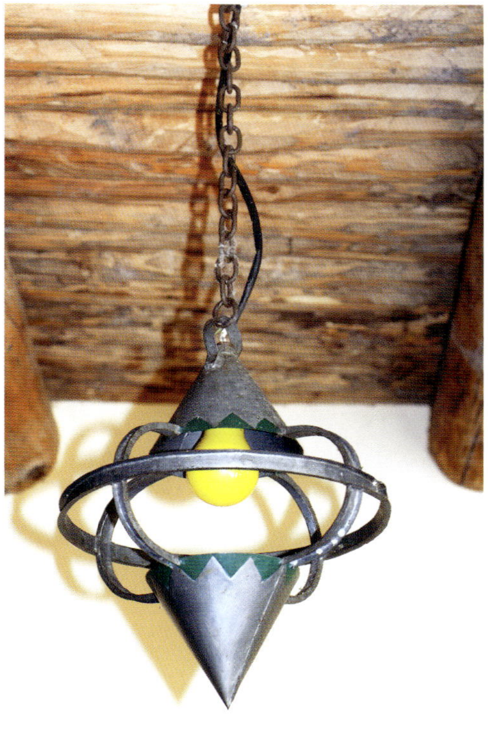

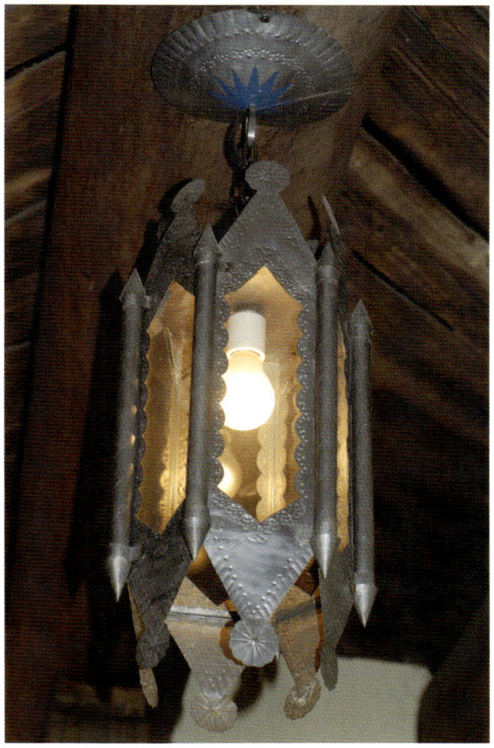

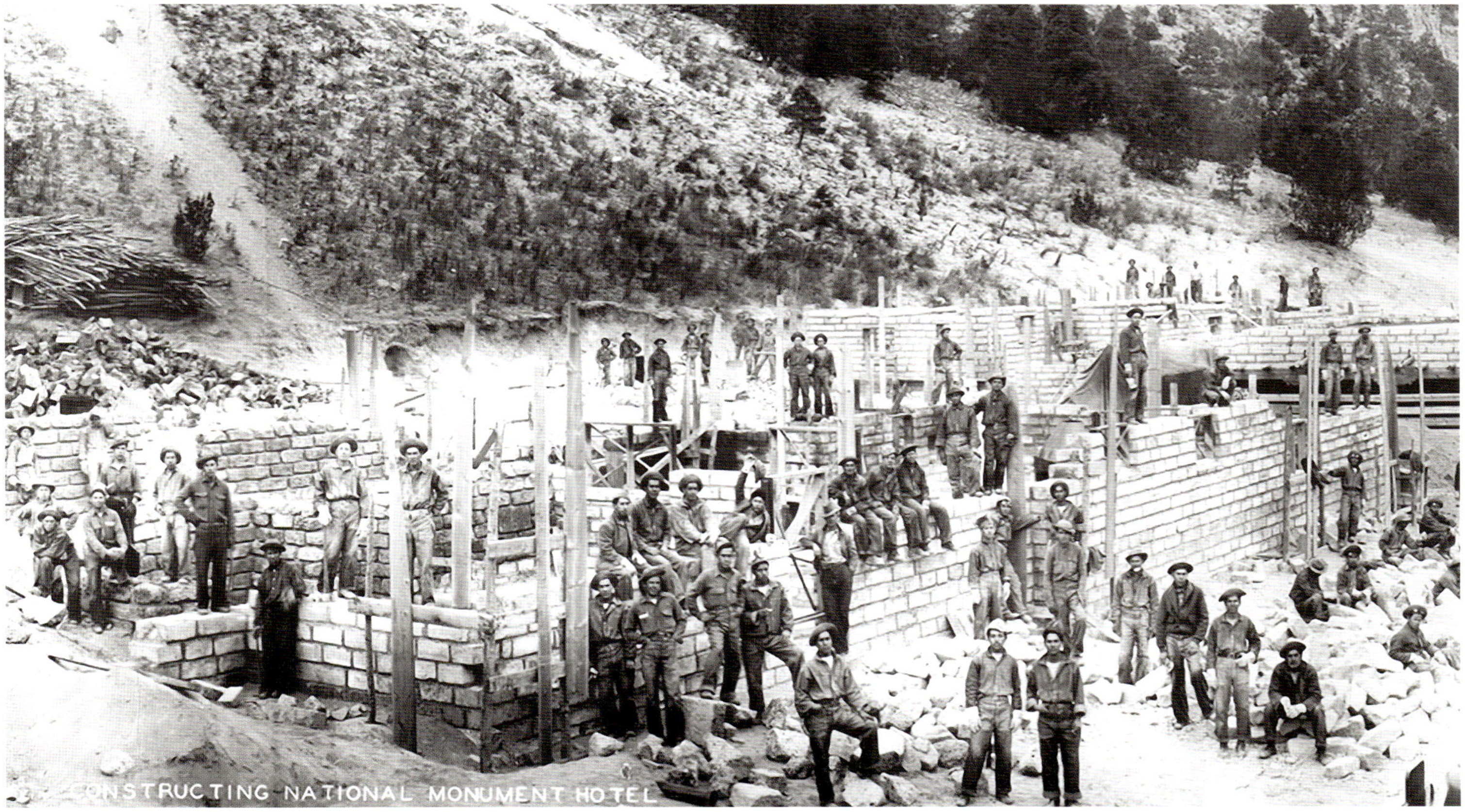

The Bandelier Historic District within Bandelier National Monument includes thirty-one CCC-constructed buildings intended to convey a sense of a New Mexican village, while providing office space and apartments for employees.

The workmanship of everything from the stonecutting to the design and finish of the fittings and furnishings was consistently high. All of the buildings were constructed of stone—Bandelier rhyolite tuff—connected by stone walls, plastered portals, flagstone walkways, and stone-edged planting beds. The entrance road was bordered with a stone guardrail and stone-lined gutter. The woodworkers went on to make the doors for the new museum at Tumacacori National Monument, which replicated the doors of one of the more ambitious Spanish missions.

The Historic American Buildings Survey (HABS)

IN 1933, Charles E. Peterson of the National Park Service proposed a Historic American Buildings Survey (HABS). It would employ out-of-work architects and draftsmen to document systematically "America's antique buildings" before they disappeared, thereby preserving the nation's architectural heritage, which, he wrote, was being destroyed "daily at an alarming rate. The ravages of fire and the natural elements together with the demolition and alterations caused by real estate 'improvements' form an inexorable tide of destruction destined to wipe out the great majority of the buildings which knew the beginning and first flourish of the nation. The comparatively few structures which can be saved by extraordinary effort and presented as exhibition houses and museums or altered and used for residences or minor commercial uses comprise only a minor percentage of the interesting and important architectural specimens which remain from the old days. It is the responsibility of the American people that if the great number of our antique buildings must disappear through economic causes, they should not pass into unrecorded oblivion."[28]

After securing funding from FERA/WPA Administrator Harry Hopkins, the National Park Service started sending its HABS teams out on the road.

The Park Service next organized the Historic American Engineering Record (HAER) and Historic American Landscapes Survey (HALS) arranging with the Library of Congress to keep the records. HAER and HALS have also helped to draw attention to the need to preserve and protect a wide range of building types and engineering technologies as diverse as pueblos, houses, factories, stores, windmills, bridges, railroads, canals, electronic generation and transmission networks, parkways, roads, and dams. Through cooperative agreements with the Library and private philanthropy, the National Park Service has recorded America's constructed heritage in surveys and reports of more than thirty-nine thousand historic structures and sites dating from pre-Columbian times to the twenty-first century, in more than 557,000 measured drawings, large-format photographs, and written histories.

The measured drawings were in black ink on standard sheets supplied by the Washington office, "complete, clear, and accurate and in sufficient detail to serve as a basis for the reconstruction of the building if it were to be destroyed," but they were not necessarily to be thought of as works of art, nor were the HABS photographs. Plans were to be fully dimensioned, showing all wall thicknesses, and were to include a compass. Elevations were to be clearly identified and free of "such extraneous background effects as clouds, trees and bushes, except when such details add to the historical or architectural significance of the drawings." The drawings were to show the existing conditions of the structure at the time of recording and identify any alterations or additions to the original structure. Fanciful "reconstruction" drawings were forbidden. Nonetheless, the district HABS officers in New Mexico and Louisiana supplemented their documentation with watercolor-tinted drawings and renderings, and some districts produced conjectural reconstructions of historic building "cleaned up" by eliminating later additions and alterations from the drawings. At least two photographic views of each building were to be taken using a five-by-seven-inch view camera and were to include the building serial number and a foot rule for scale. In cases of groups of buildings, "buildings of irregular or complicated plan or outline," or "important, exceptional, or particularly interesting details, either exterior or interior," additional photographs were permitted, but HABS stated that it was "more important that they be clear and sharp in their delineation of detail than that they be artistically composed or effective from a pictorial point of view."[29]

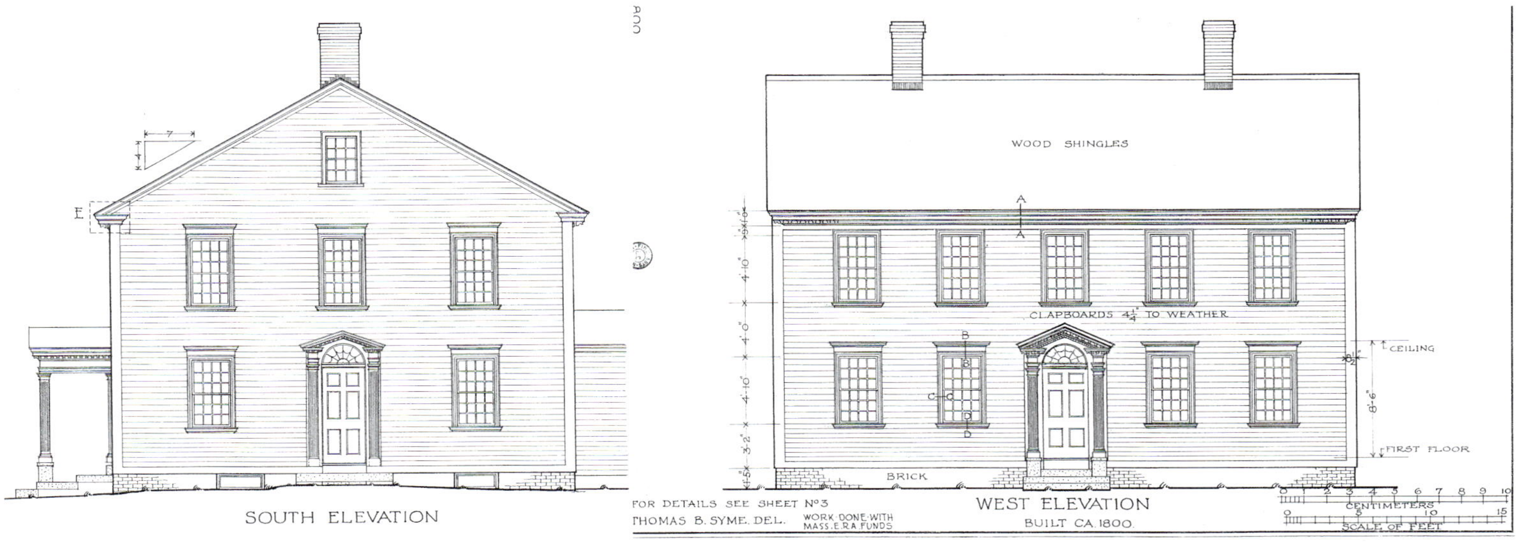

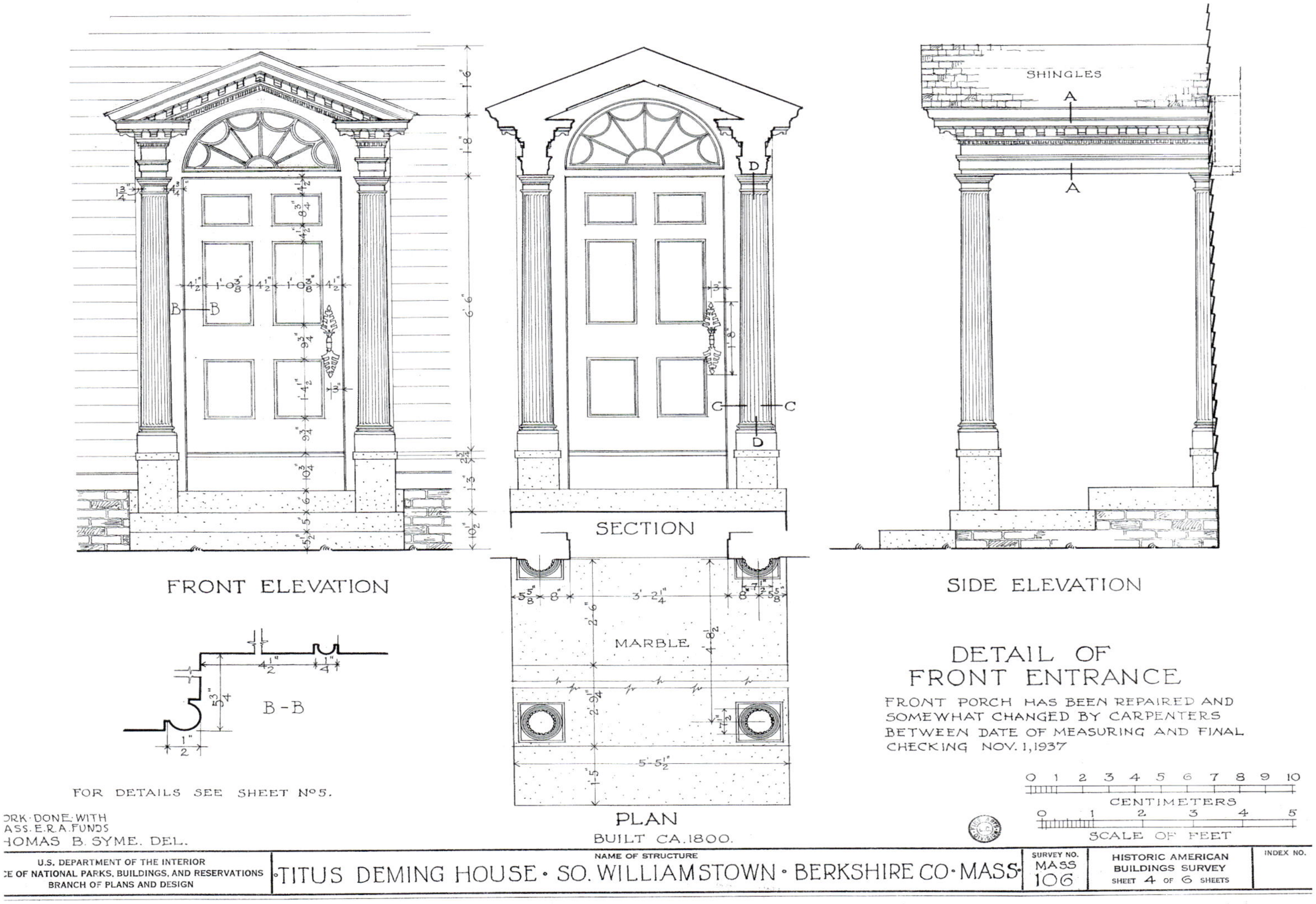

Left, top and bottom; below:
The Titus Deming House, South Williamstown, Massachusetts

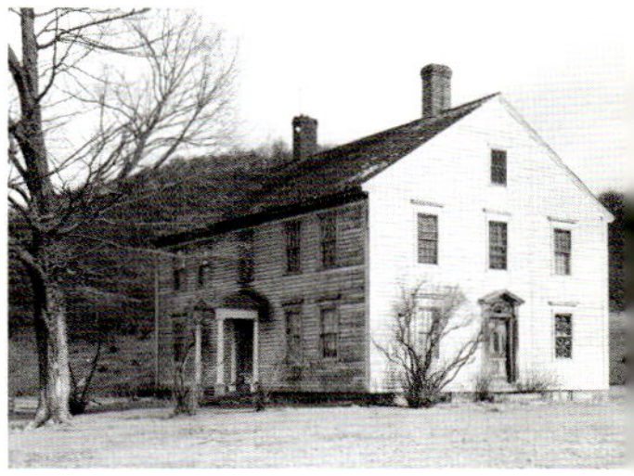

Titus Deming served in the militia during the Revolutionary War and built this house in 1800 in a very conservative community, using a colonial style by then somewhat out of fashion nationally. The chimneys and fireplaces were built from bricks made on the property; the fireplaces and mantles are original, as are the front door with its fanlight, lock, latch and bar, and the exposed beams and exposed walls with boards up to twenty-two inches wide. In 1934 HABS sent two architectural draftsmen to measure and draw the exterior and interior details, and Arthur C. Haskell photographed the house for the survey.

Below:
The Deming House today.

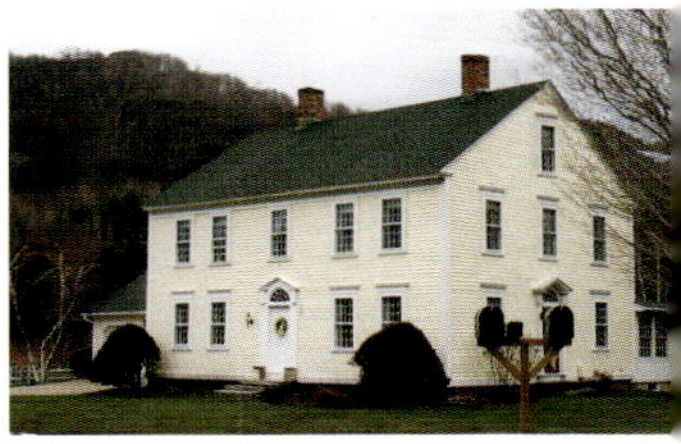

Top and bottom:
St. Nicholas Chapel, Fort Ross, Sonoma County, California

The Russians established their southernmost fort in North America in 1812 at a place they called "Fortress Ross"—there was no person named Ross involved. The manager of the settlement for the Russian-American Company reported that "the Russian, Creole, and Aleut employees . . . expressed their intention to build at their own expense a chapel dedicated to St. Nicholas," and their building fund was augmented in 1823–4 by contributions from officers and crews of three Russian Navy ships visiting San Francisco Bay. Fort Ross was a seal and sea-otter hunting station and a source of food for the Russians in Alaska. The log chapel lay within a stockade with the governor's house, barracks, and magazine, around a small mustering ground. Though completed by 1825, it was never consecrated as a church because the commercial colony had no imperial sanction. According to a visiting priest in 1836, about 15 percent of the settlement's population, then numbering 260, consisted of Indians baptized in the Eastern Orthodox faith; among the residents were also a few Lutherans and Roman Catholics. Other Indians in the area had been proselytized by the Spanish missions to the Roman Catholic faith, and Protestant missionaries became active by the first decades of the nineteenth century.

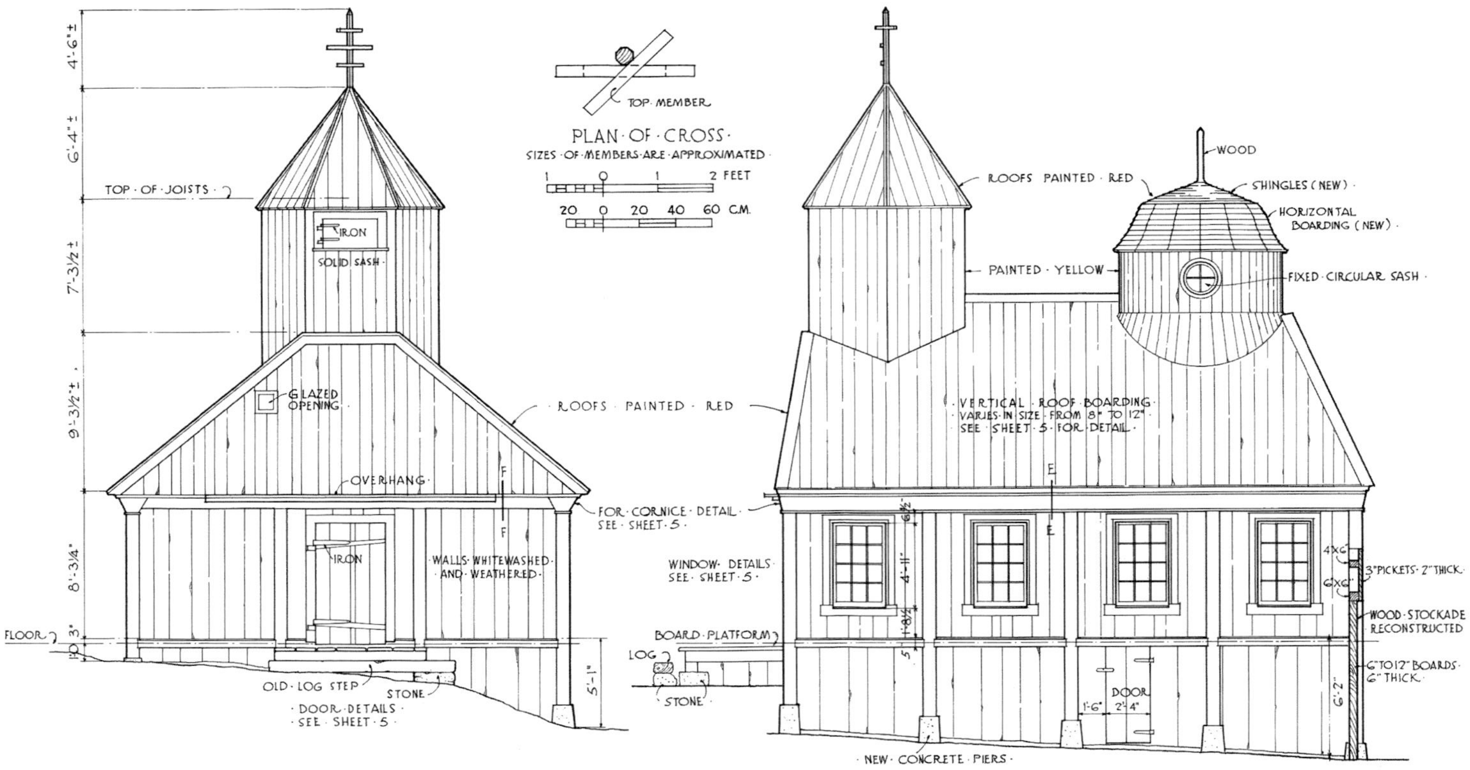

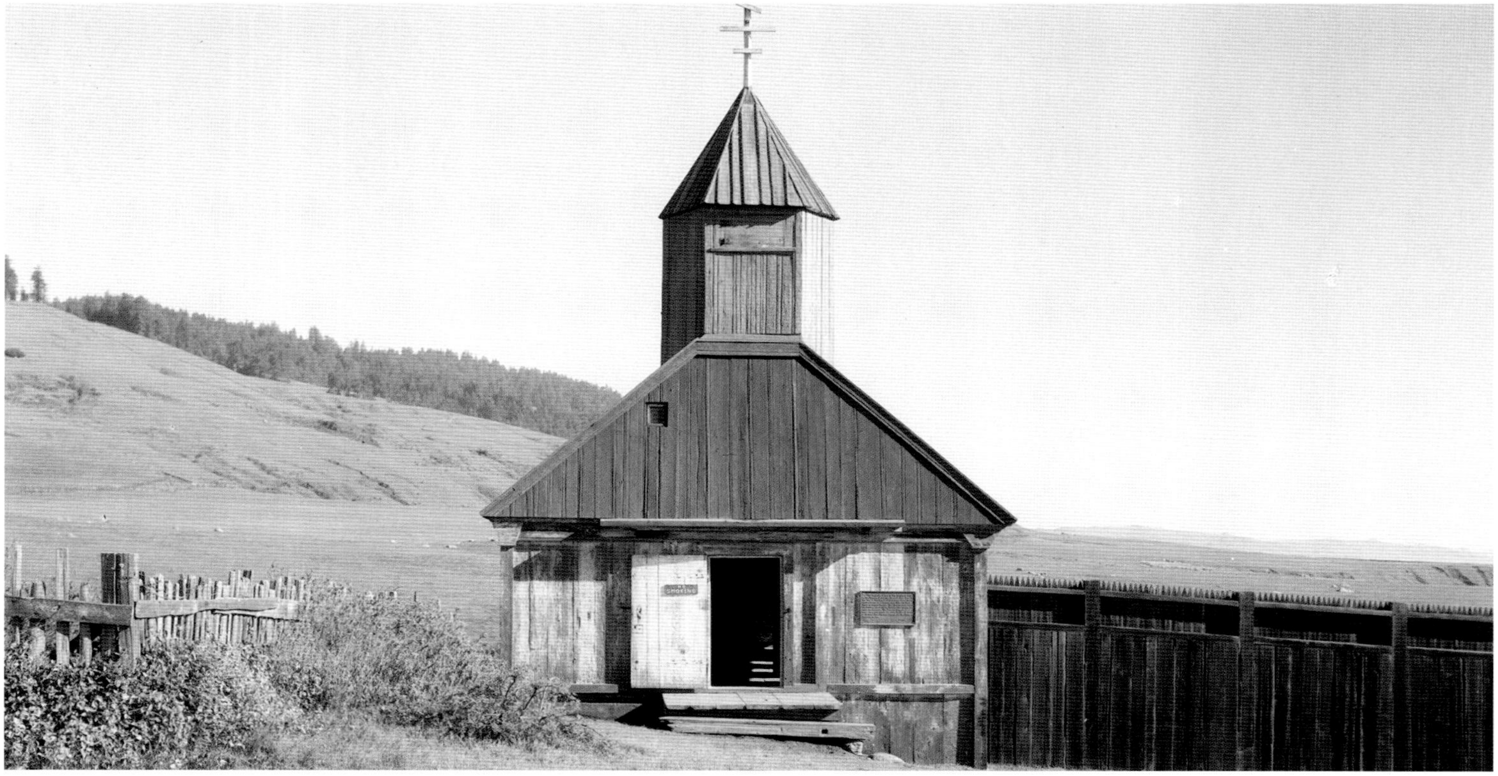

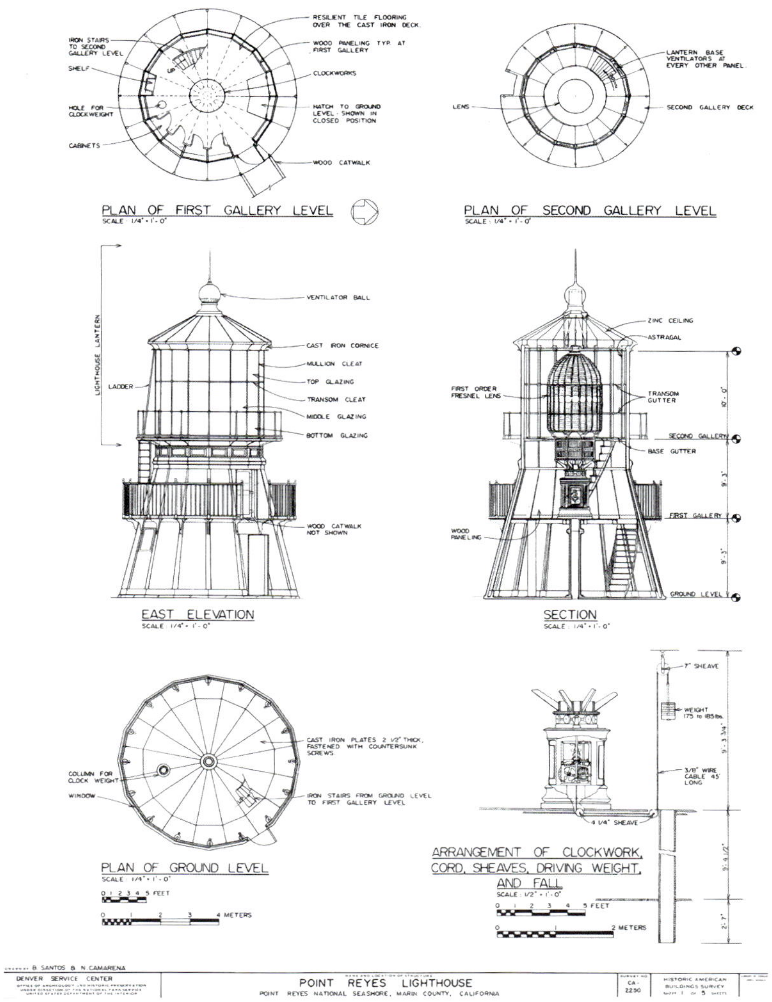

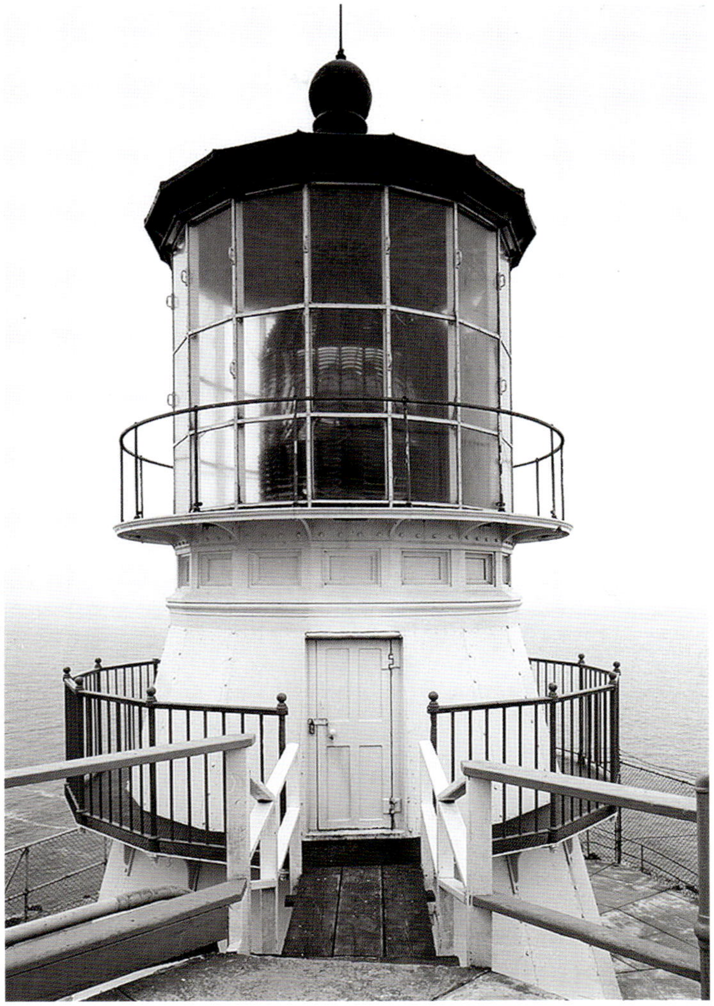

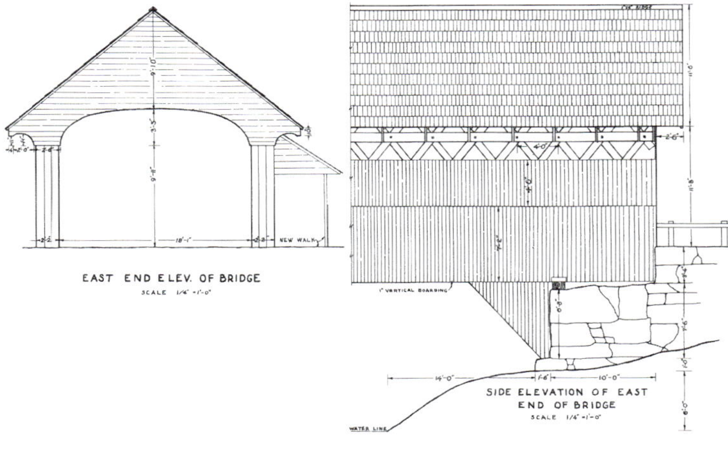

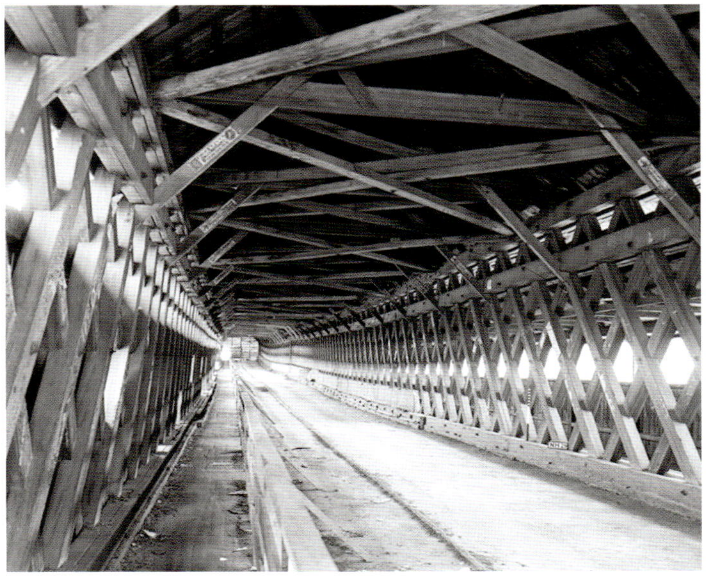

Top far left and left:
Point Reyes Lighthouse

Point Reyes juts ten miles out into the sea lanes to San Francisco Bay. The lighthouse, built in 1870, was retired from service in 1975 when the U.S. Coast Guard installed an automated light and transferred the lighthouse to the National Park Service.

The lighthouse lens and mechanism were constructed in France in 1867 and shipped around Cape Horn to San Francisco, while the components for the cast iron tower were placed on a second ship, which landed on Drakes Bay. From there the parts were hauled by oxcart over the headlands to Point Reyes, six hundred feet above sea level, and over six weeks, lowered from the top of the cliff to the lighthouse platform, put back together, and installed.

Bottom far left and left:
Covered bridge spanning the Connecticut River, Orford, New Hampshire

The 440-foot-long bridge at the Orford crossing, constructed in 1856, employed the lattice truss, a design that was supplanting the older Connecticut River bridges during the mid-nineteenth century because it was strong enough to be supported by a single stone pier in the center of the river. It was damaged in a flood in 1905, and again in 1936, and when replaced by a new steel arched bridge, the wooden bridge was exploded, and allowed to collapse and to float downstream.

Top and bottom:
Mission Santa Bárbara, Santa Barbara, California

The Mission Santa Bárbara Virgen y Mártir was established on the Feast of Saint Barbara, December 4, 1786, as the tenth of twenty-one Spanish California Missions. It is still in use as a parish church and to serve a community of Franciscan friars. Its guest rooms, conference rooms, sanctuary, cemetery, and mausoleum are set within ten acres of gardens. The earthquake of June 29, 1925, occurred during a chapel service. The roof and beams in the front of the church fell, but no one was hurt. Restoration was completed in 1927, and the towers reinforced in 1953.

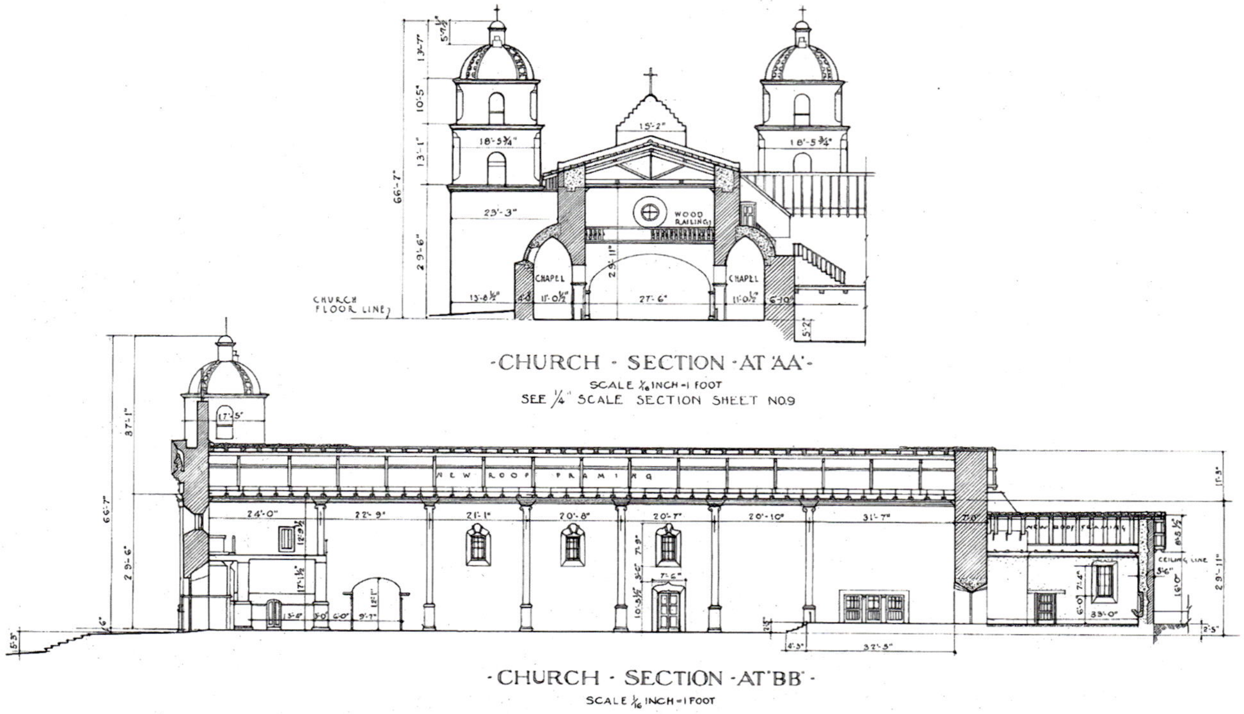

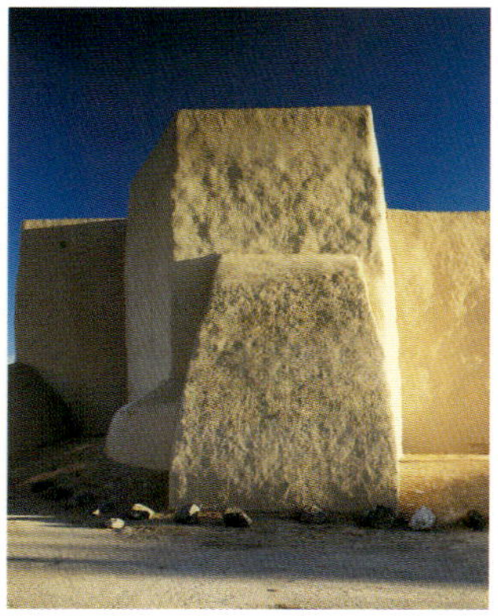

Above:
The church of San Francisco de Asis in the Ranchos de Taos, four miles southwest of Taos, New Mexico, was painted by Georgia O'Keeffe and photographed by Ansel Adams. It is built of adobe, which must be renewed each spring and refreshed after heavy rains, which do occur in Taos.

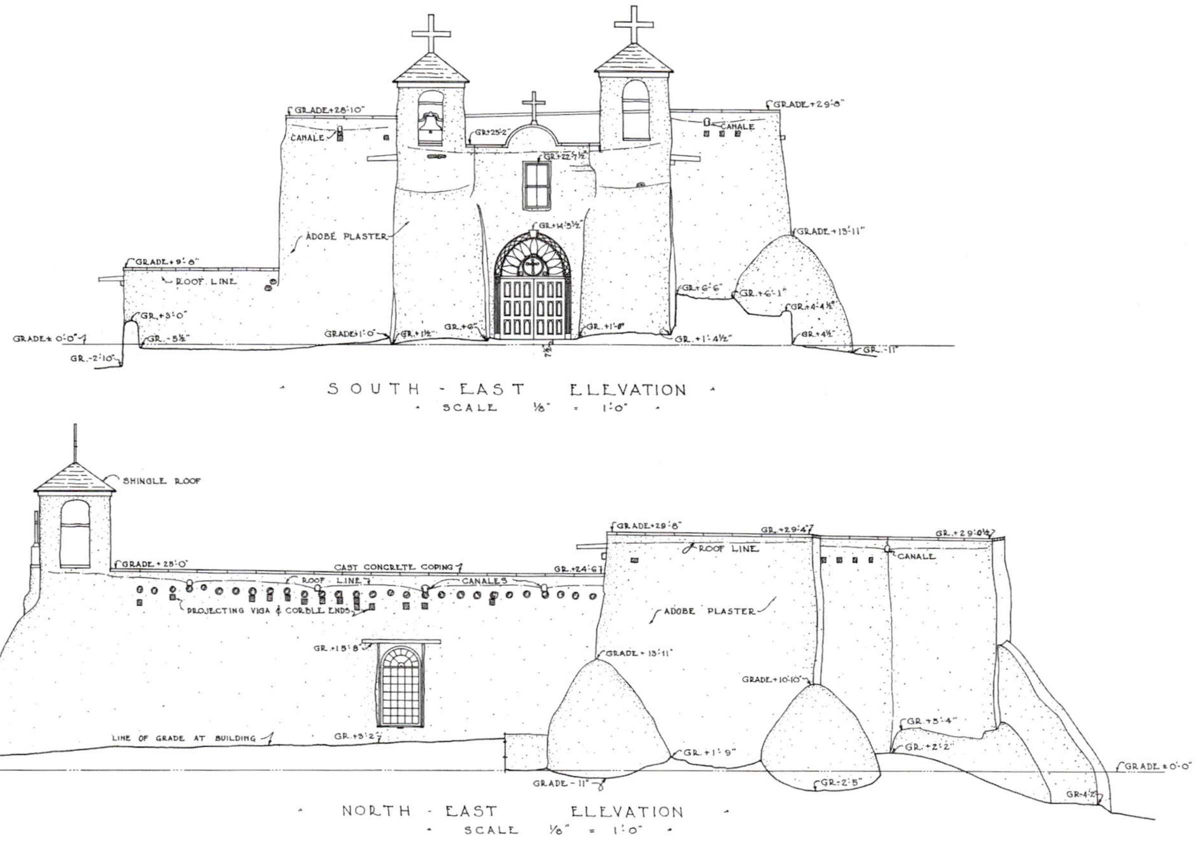

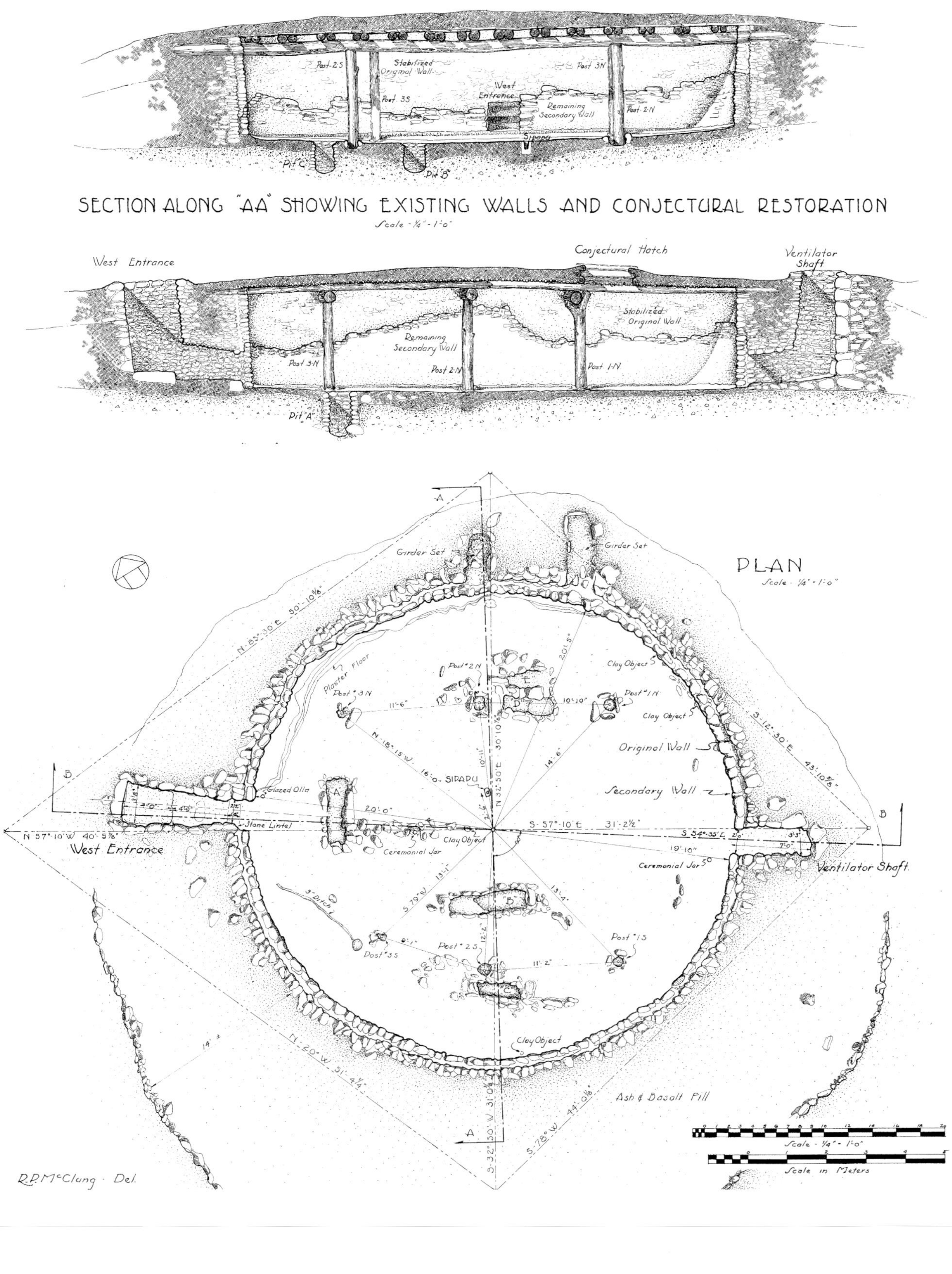

Top and bottom:
Section and plan of the large ceremonial space at Bandelier National Monument, New Mexico, 1939

HABS drawings recorded the appearance and dimensions of Puebloan, Spanish Colonial, and Territorial buildings in New Mexico.

Art at Work on the Park Landscape

The designed landscapes of the national and state parks as works of art directly express the value society invests in preserving and appreciating natural areas. Few other arts, with the exception of landscape painting, more fully explore the leitmotif of American culture. Neither pure wilderness nor mere artifact, the national park is the purest manifestation of the purely American genius which sought to reconcile a people obsessed with progress with the unmatched price paid for that advance: the near total loss of the American wilderness.

—Ethan Carr, *Landscape by Design*

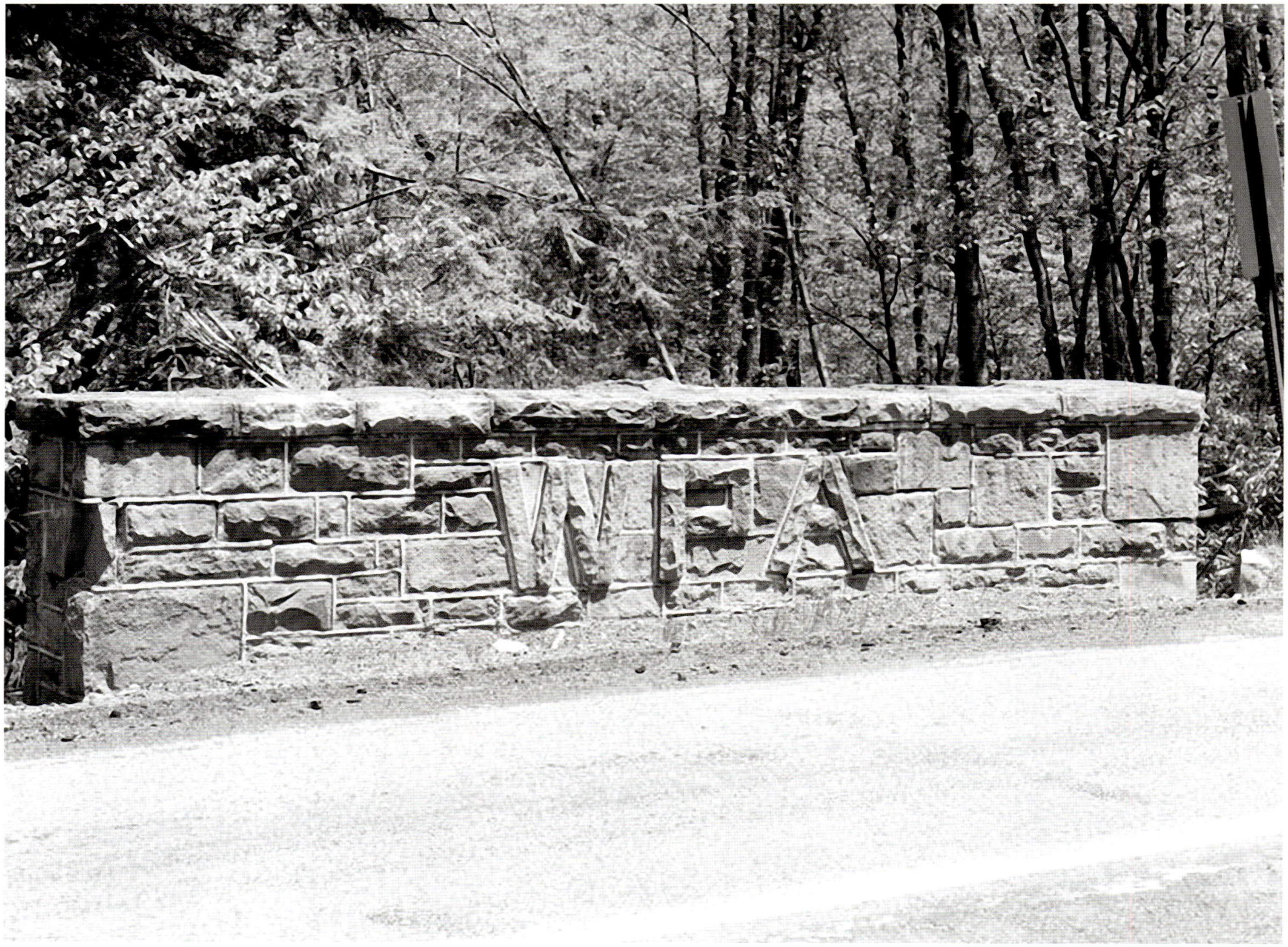

Pond Creek Bridge spanning Pond Creek at Bear Lake Road (State Route 2016), Thornhurst vicinity, Lackawanna County, Pennsylvania

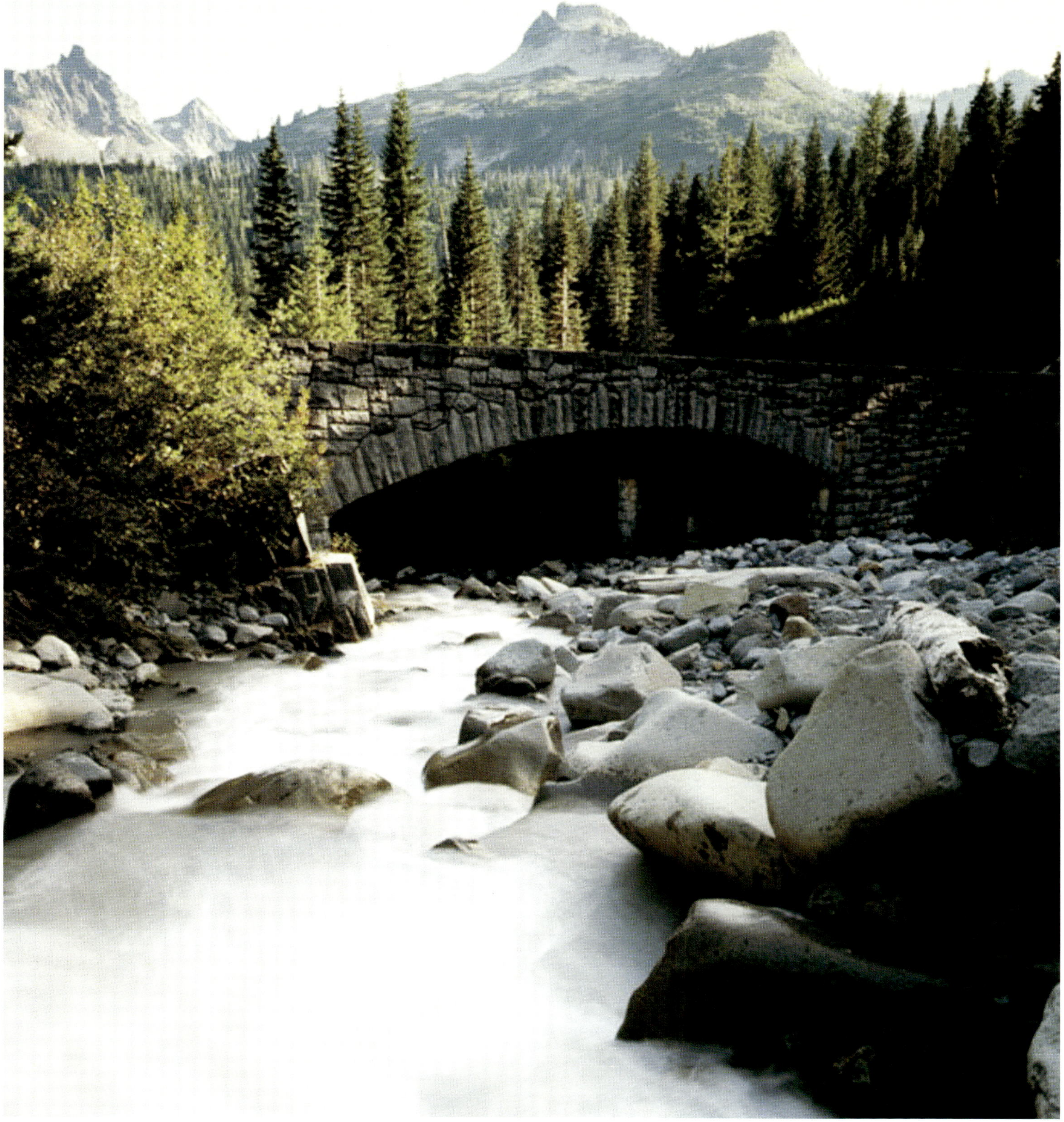

Stevens Creek Bridge spanning Stevens Creek on Stevens Canyon Highway, Mount Rainier National Park, Washington

Stevens Creek flows from the Mount Rainier glacier to the Cowlitz River on the southern boundary of the park, through a canyon carved by glaciers. The bridge, of reinforced concrete faced with stone, was built in 1940 to withstand the intense glacial flow through Stevens Canyon. It was constructed by the Emergency Conservation Work (ECW) program, the proto-CCC.

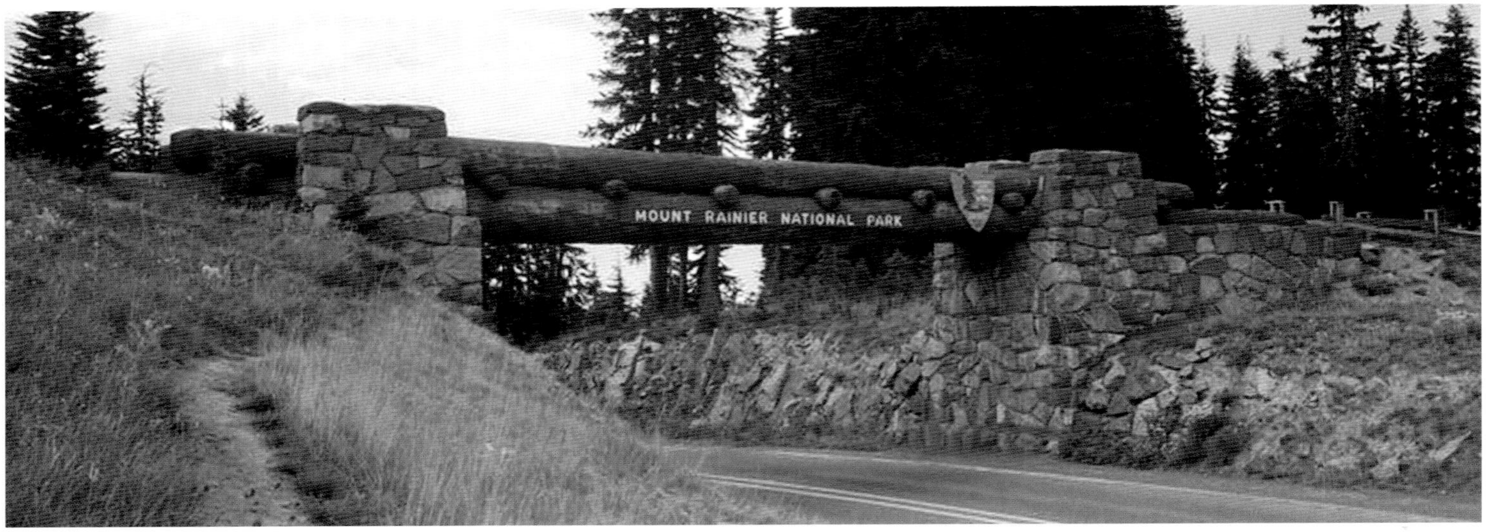

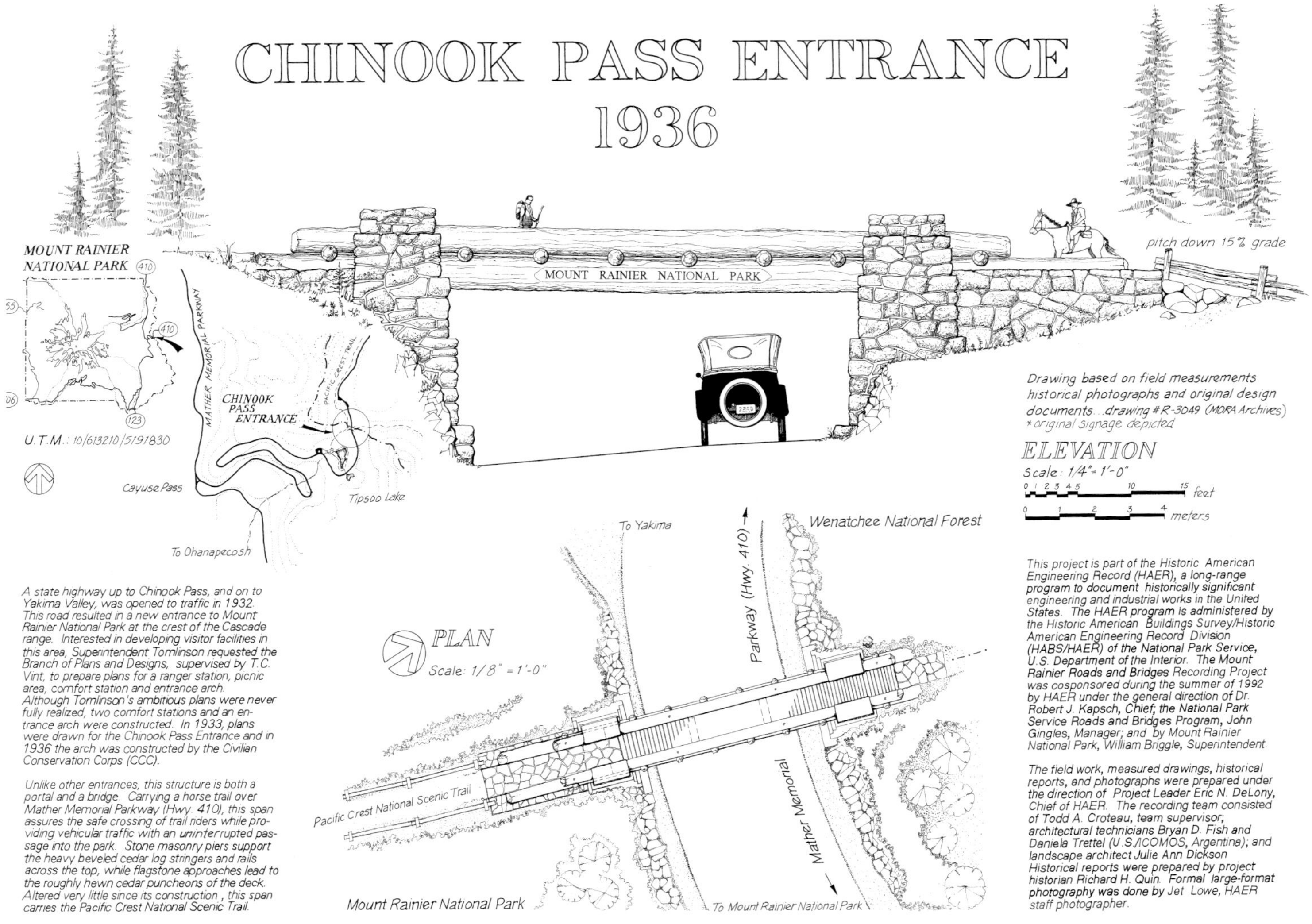

Chinook Pass Entrance on Mather Memorial Highway at Chinook Pass, Mount Rainier National Park, Washington

Bottom:
The log and masonry entrance arch was constructed by the Emergency Conservation Work (ECW) in 1934–36.

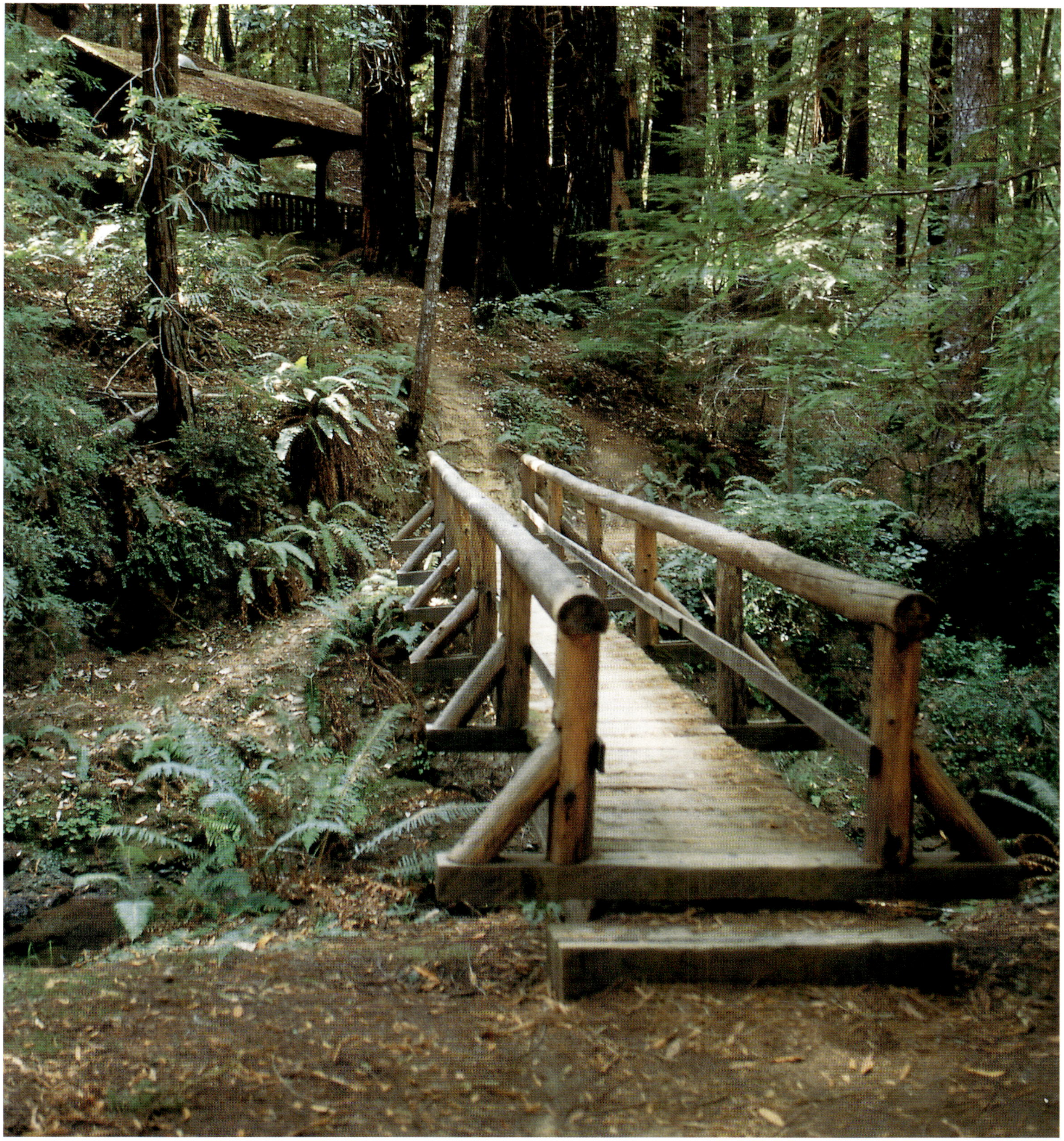

Mendocino Woodlands
CCC Camp
Mendocino, California

Mendocino Woodlands was one of forty-six campgrounds created by the WPA, the ECW, and the CCC (see main text). The rustic wood-and-stone buildings are surrounded by a second-growth redwood forest. The 720-acre Mendocino Woodlands was originally planned as a site for youth summer camps in which the participants would be introduced to the wonders of nature. The two- and four-bedroom cabins, communal shower buildings with hot water and electricity, and a kitchen/dining hall complex in each of the three separate camps are preserved much as they were in the 1930s.

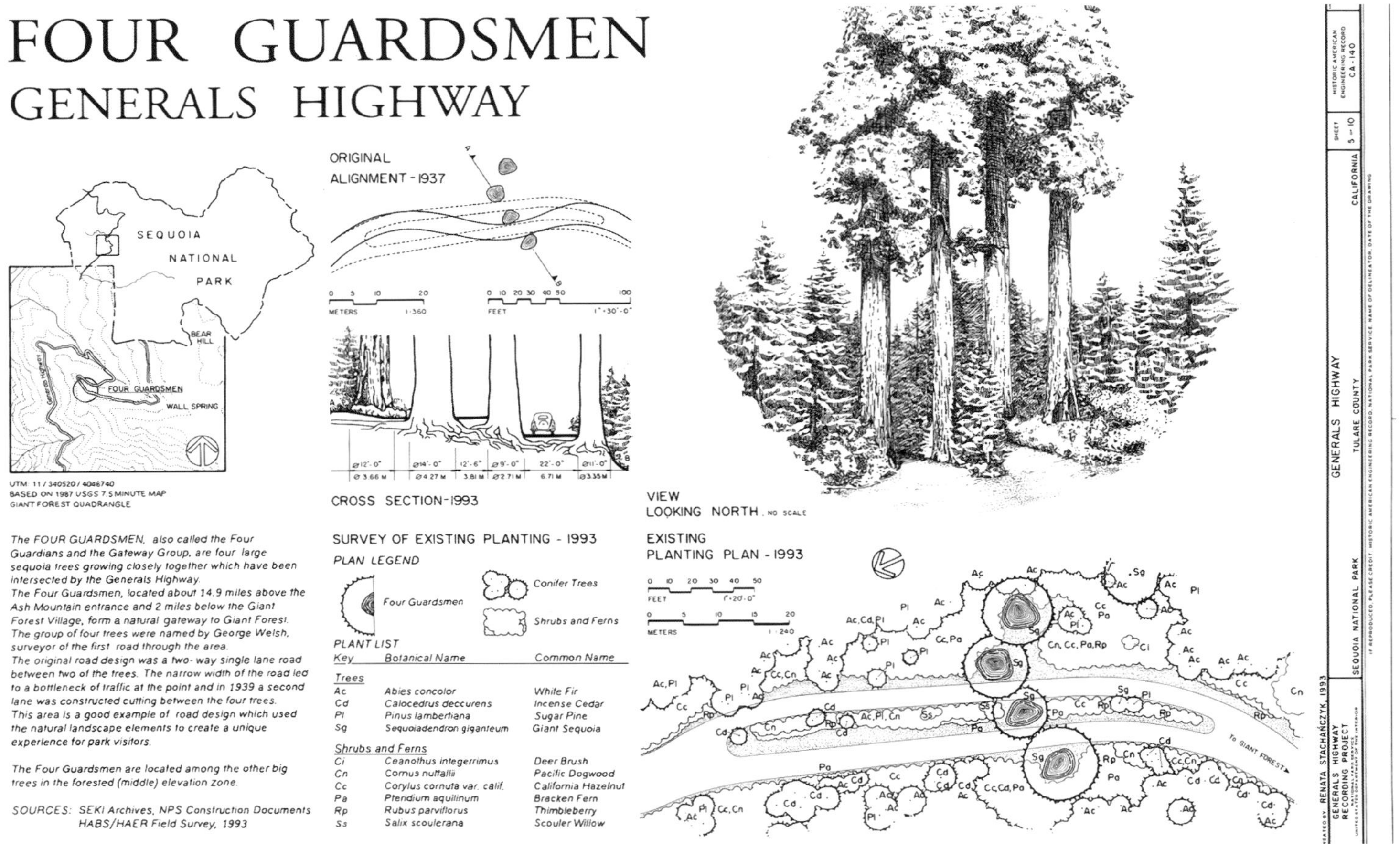

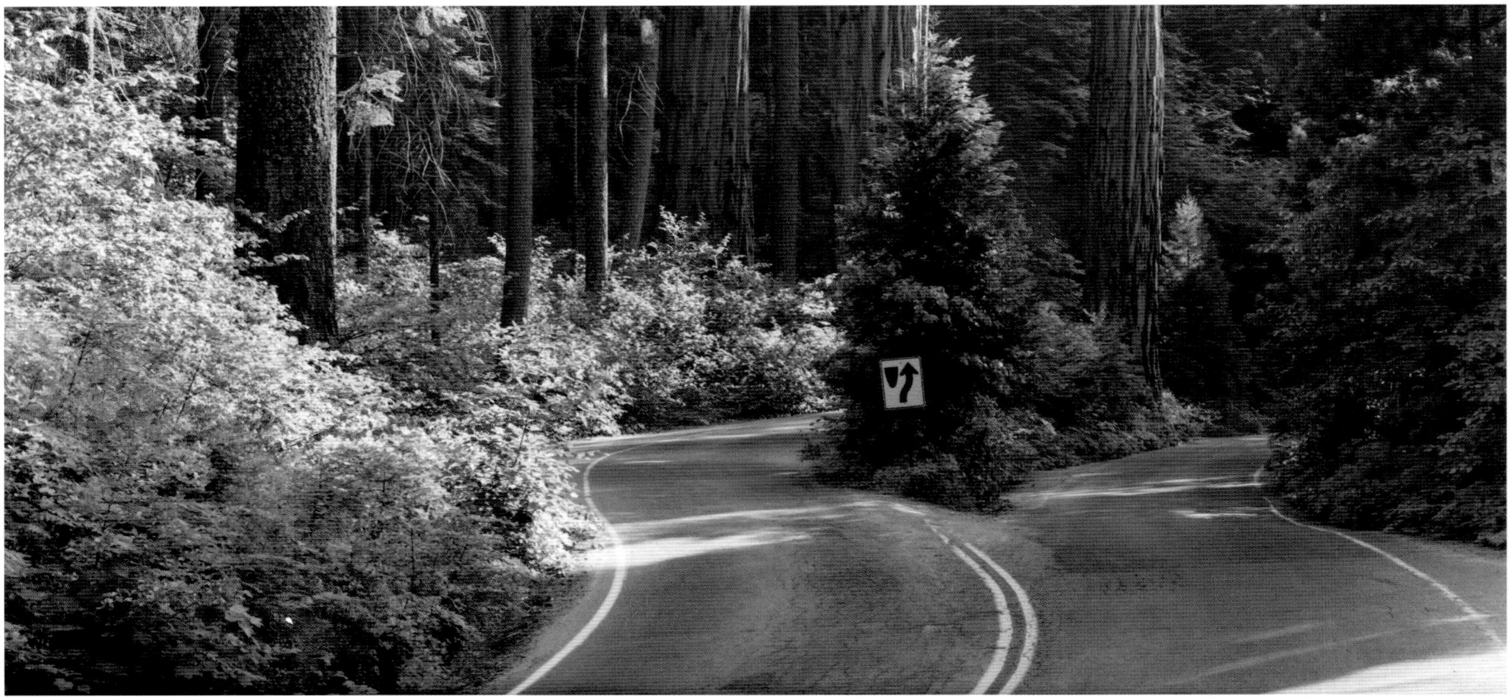

Four Guardsmen
Sequoia and Kings Canyon National Park, California

On the Generals Highway, about fourteen miles from the park entrance, are the Four Guardsmen—four giant sequoias that require that the road divide to pass by them. They serve as a natural gateway to the Giant Forest section of the park. The original single-lane highway had its second lane built by the CCC in 1938.

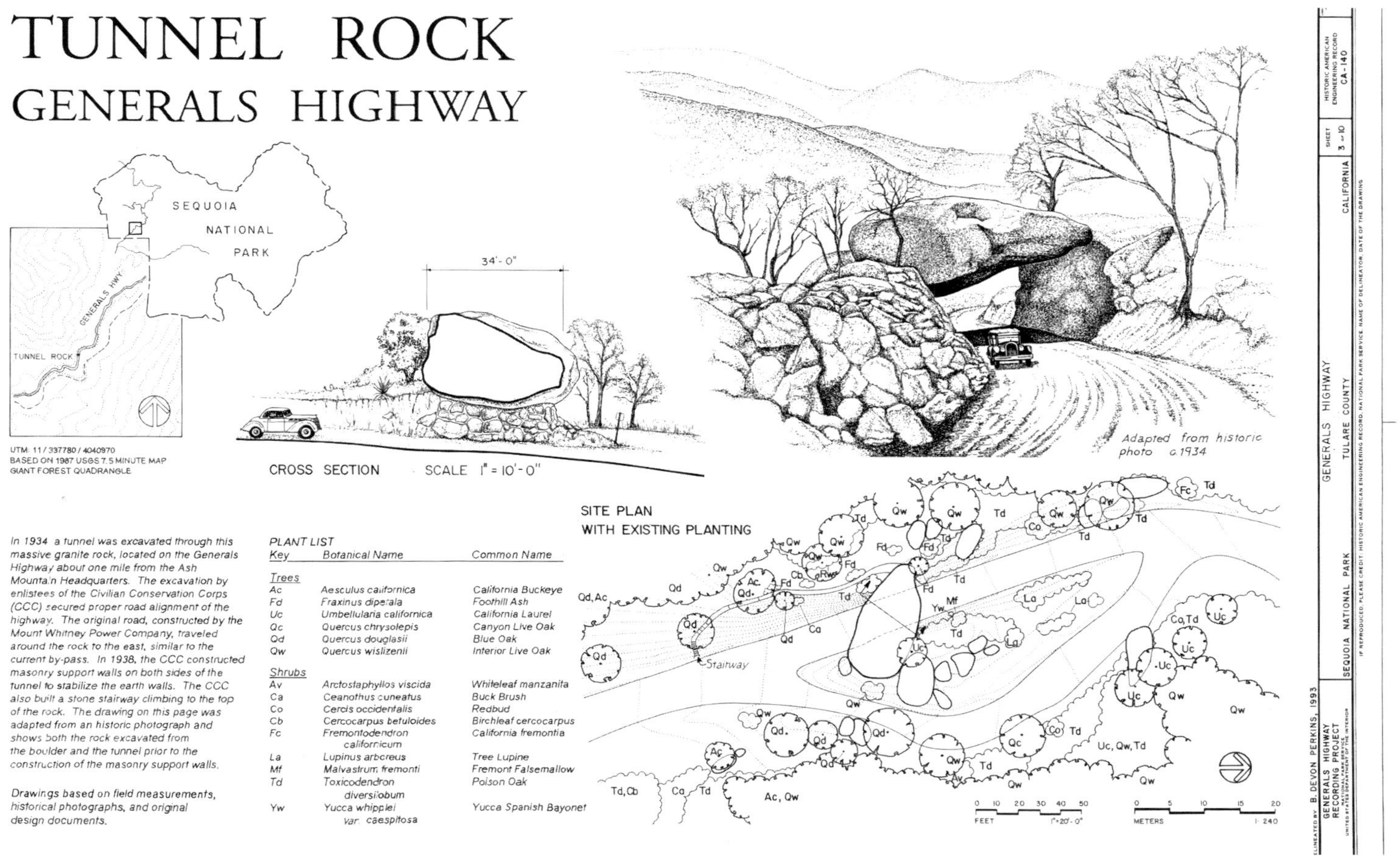

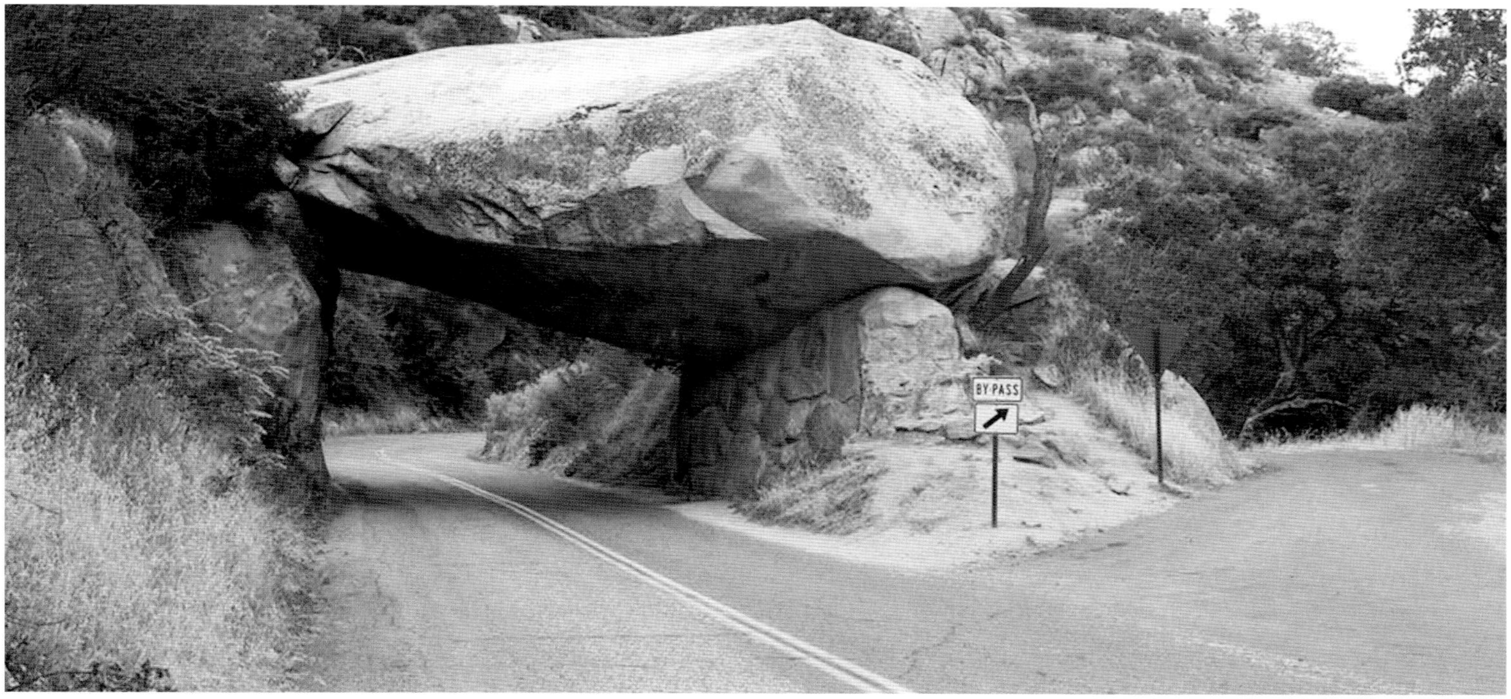

Tunnel Rock
Sequoia and Kings Canyon National Park, California

Tunnel Rock was another feature of the Generals Highway. The original wagon road circumvented the granite boulder, but in 1934 and 1938 the CCC enlarged the passage under it and built support walls to allow the road to pass beneath it.

Top right and far right:
Guernsey State Park,
Wyoming

From 1933 to 1936, on a high cliff, the CCC used hand-hewn timbers and forged iron to build the Guernsey Museum. The floors are made from flagstone quarried in Thermopolis, Wyoming. The arched walkways line up to point to Laramie Peak, the highest peak in the surrounding region.

Middle far right:
CCC stonework
Table Rock State Park,
South Carolina

This three-thousand-acre state park lies along the Blue Ridge Mountains in the northern section of Pickens County, South Carolina, which contains the tallest mountain completely within the state, Pinnacle Mountain.

Bottom far right:
Wyalusing State Park,
Wisconsin

CCC overlook, five hundred feet above the confluence of the Wisconsin and Mississippi Rivers.

Bottom right:
Devil's Den State Park,
Arkansas

In the oak-hickory forest of the Lee Creek Valley in Arkansas' Boston Mountains lies the National Historic District in which the CCC built a native stone dam, a pavilion restaurant, cabins, roads, trails, stone walls, bridges, and the Yellow Rock Overlook.

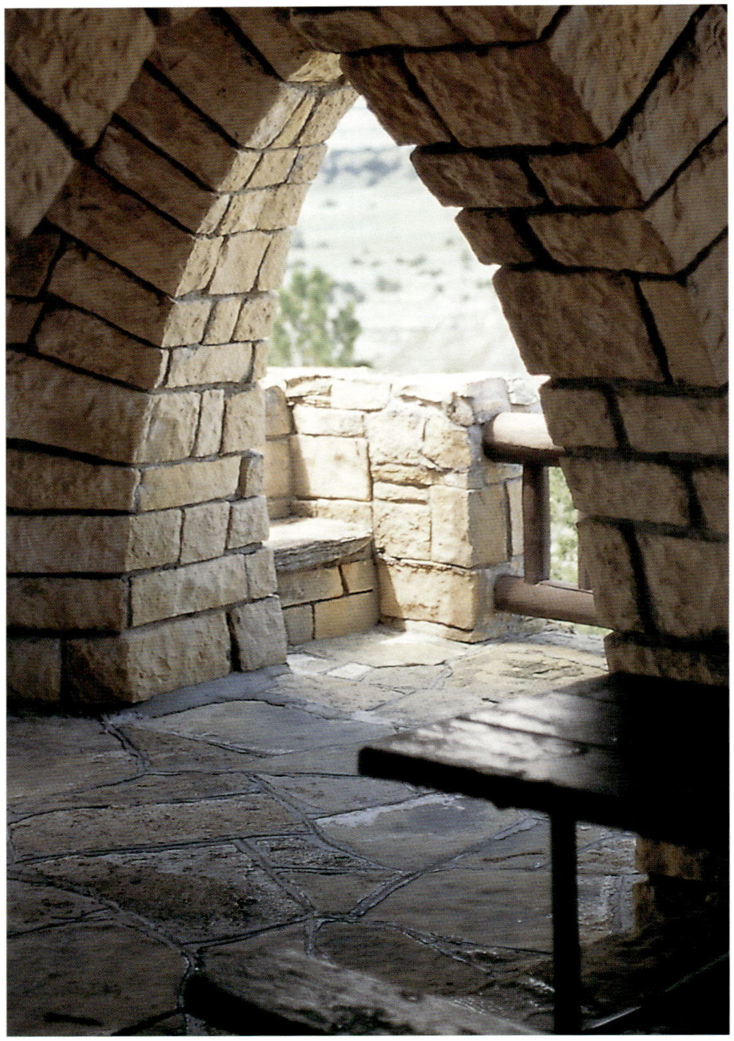

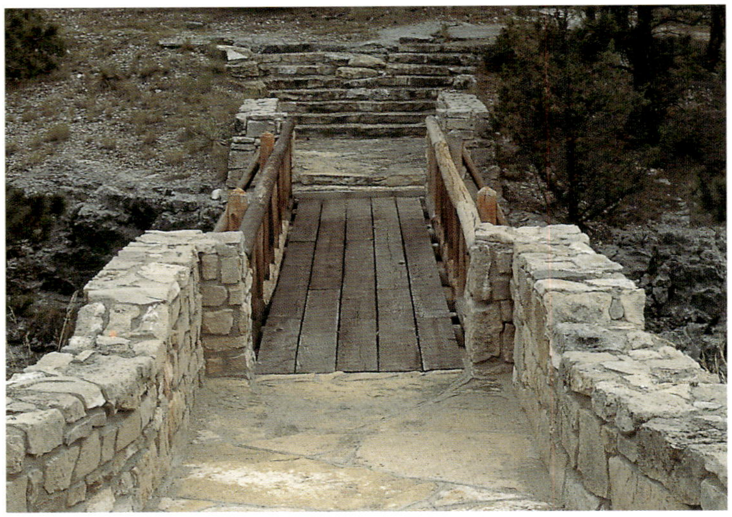

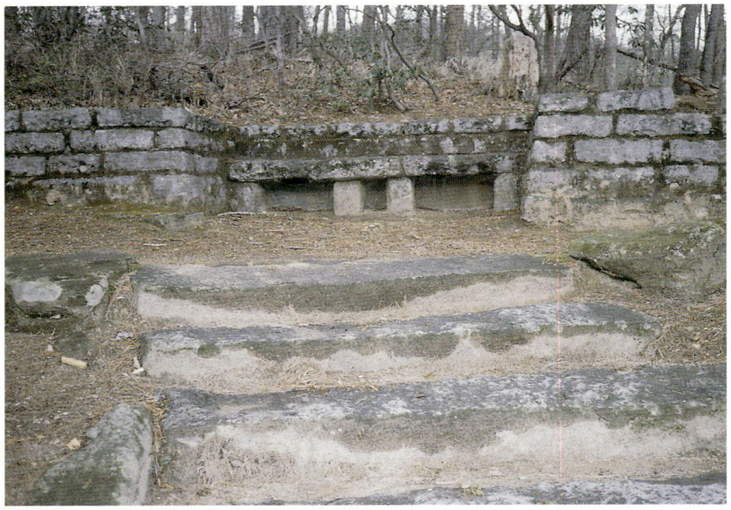

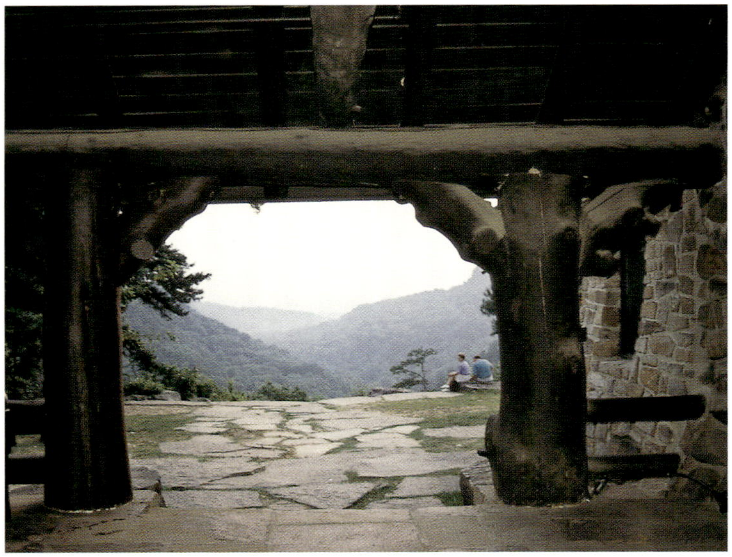

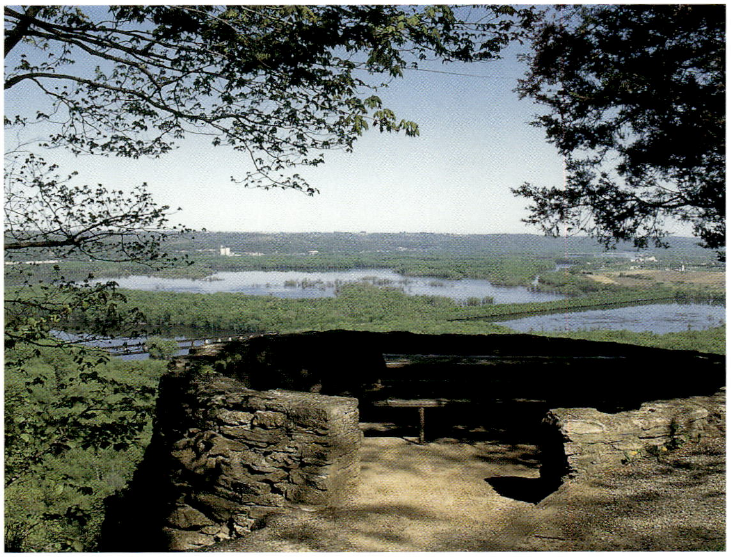

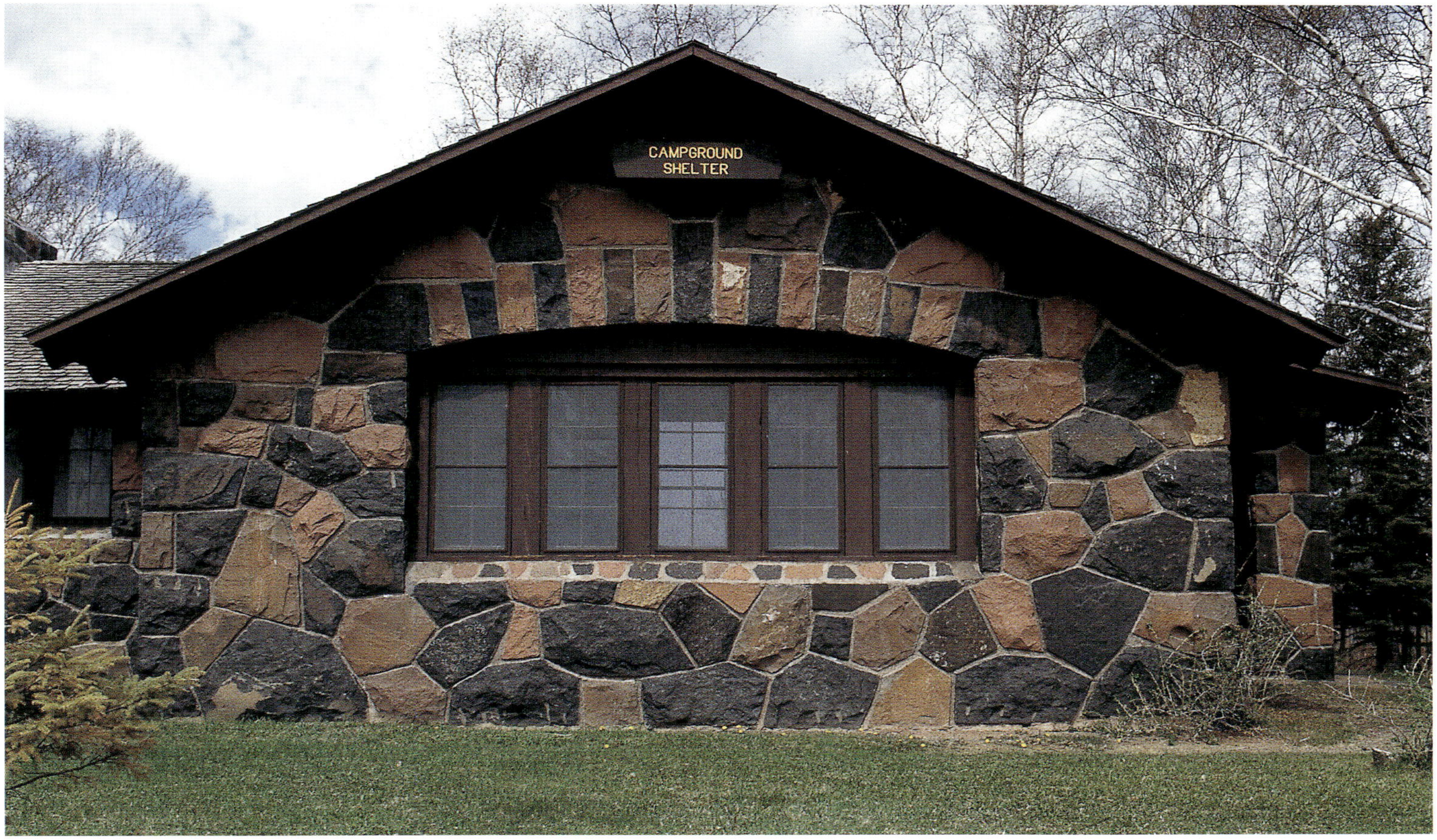

Campground Shelter
Gooseberry Falls State Park, Minnesota

Two Italian stone masons supervised the CCC as the crews built the shelter of red, blue, brown, and black granite. The red granite was quarried in Duluth, while the darker variety was taken from an outcrop near East Beaver Bay, just north of the park. The sand for the mortar was brought from Flood Bay, south of the park, and logs were cut and milled in Cascade River State Park.

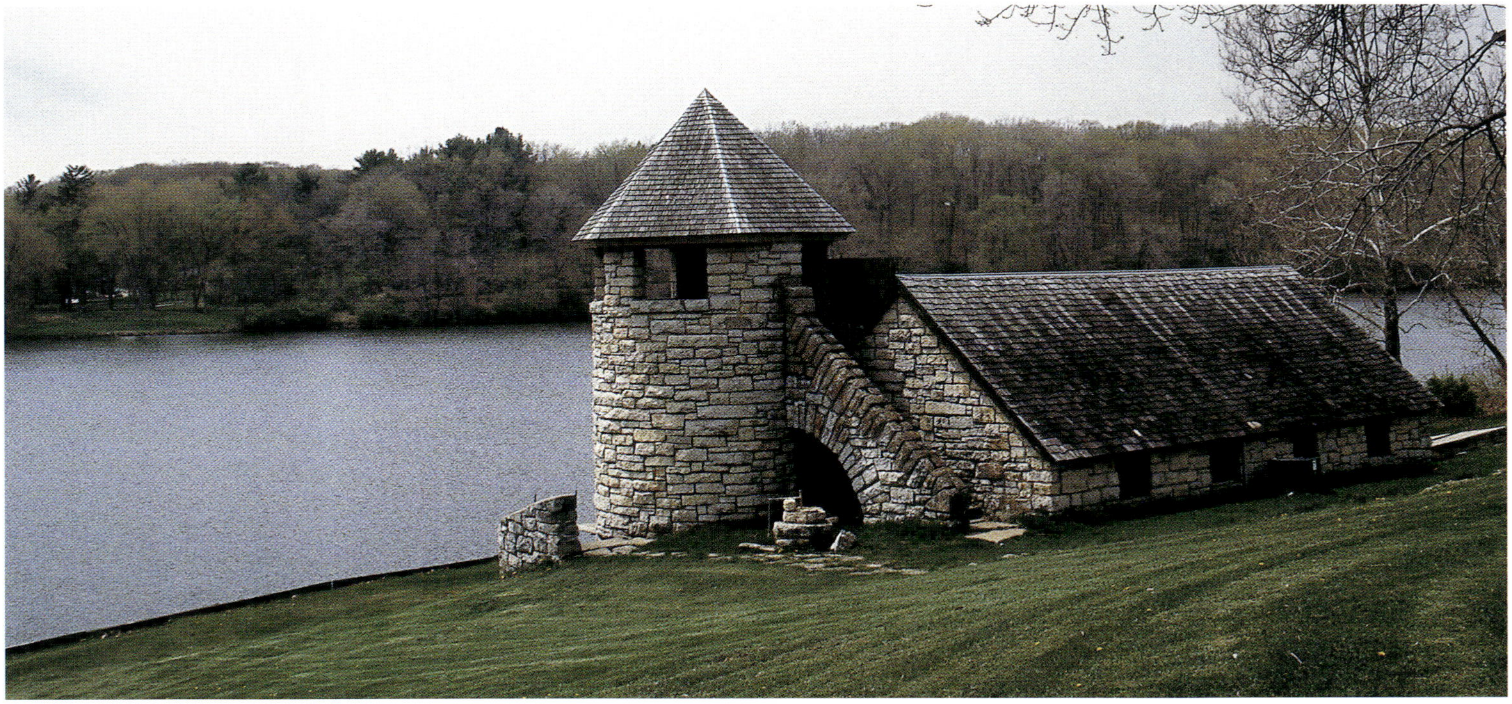

Backbone State Park, Iowa

The dolomite limestone ridge called the "Devil's backbone" was shaped by a loop of the Maquoketa River. The CCC, which had two camps in the park, used the limestone for the park buildings.

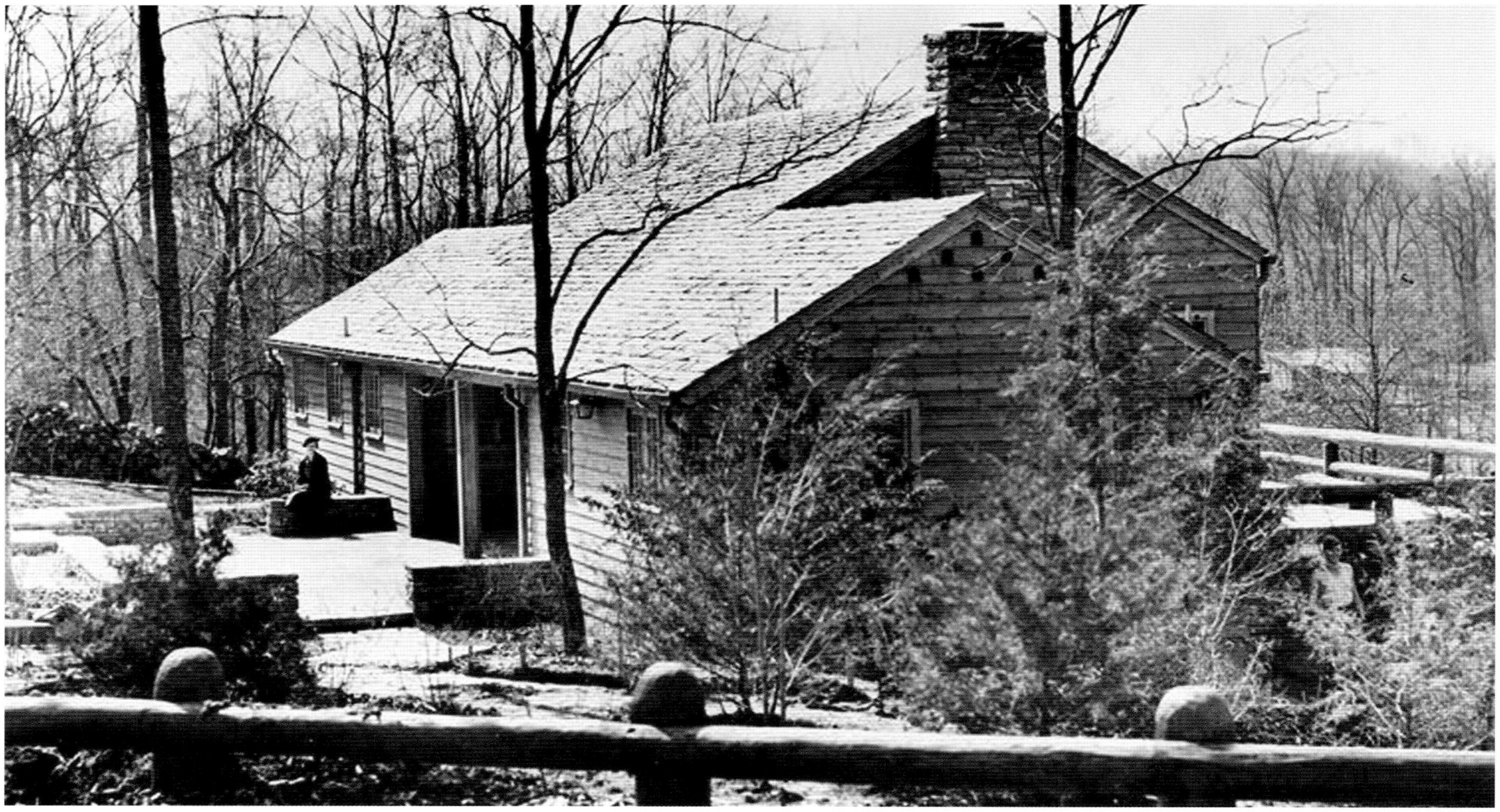

Norris Dam State Park, Tennessee
In cooperation with the Tennessee Valley Authority (TVA) and the National Park Service, the CCC built this restaurant of local timber and stone.

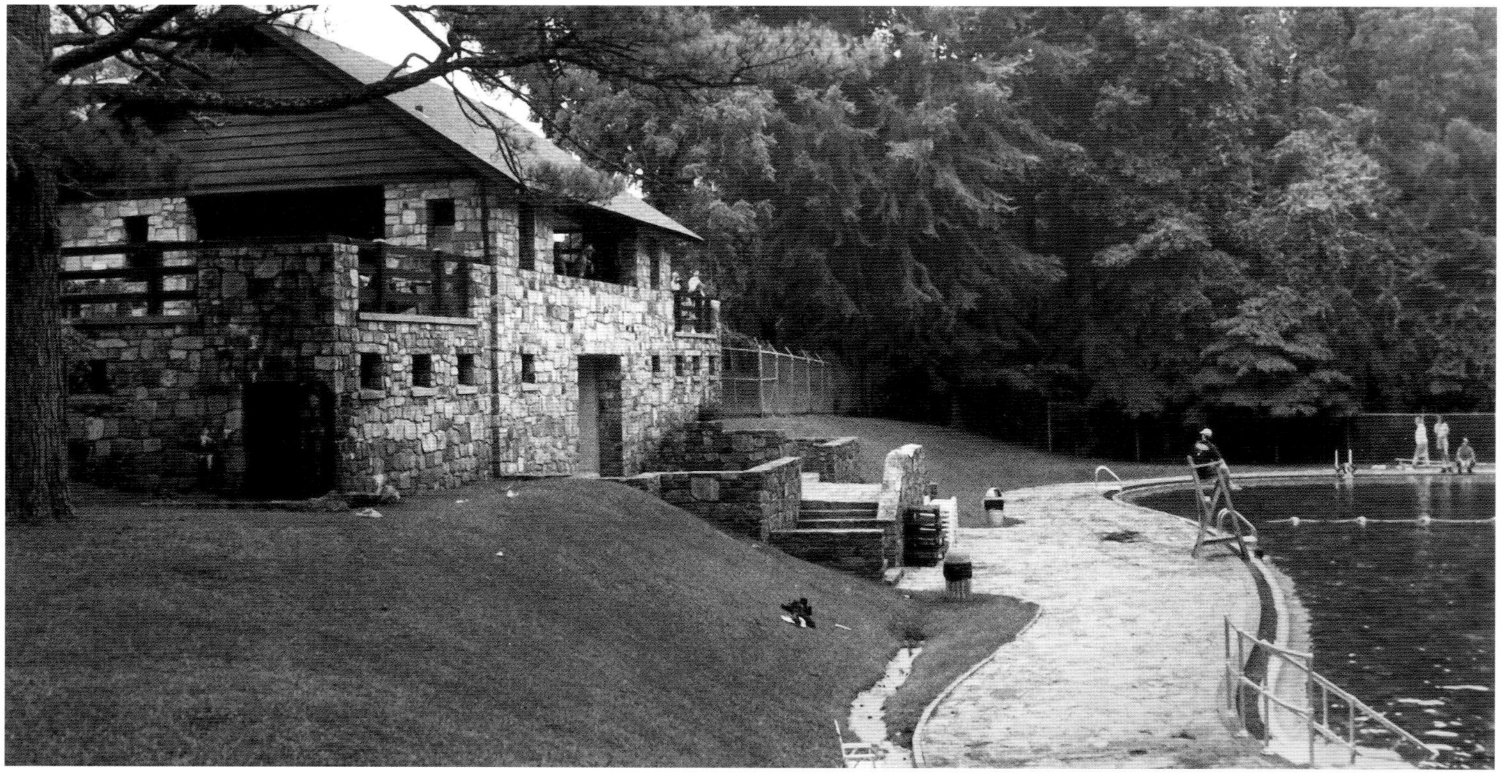

Liberty Bell Pool
Pine Mountain State Park, Georgia, c. 1940

The fifteen-hundred-acre state park was conserved and developed by the CCC, and often visited by President Roosevelt when he was in residence at Warm Springs. Nearby was the Resettlement Administration's agricultural and industrial community of Pine Mountain Valley.

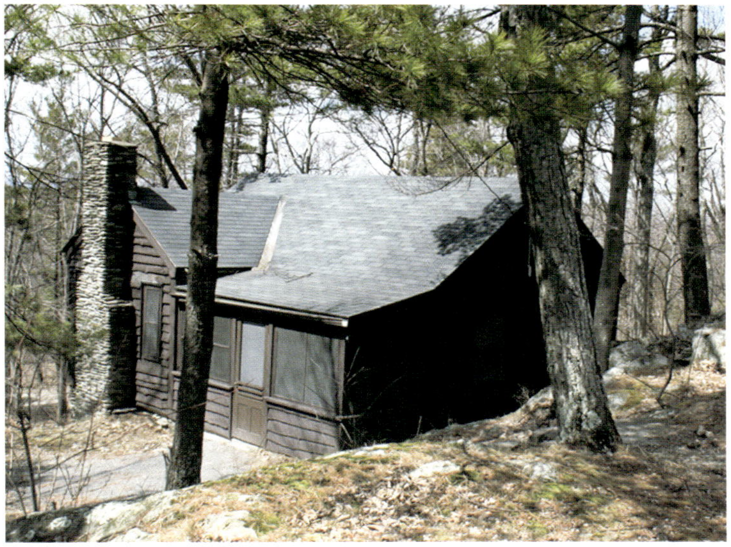

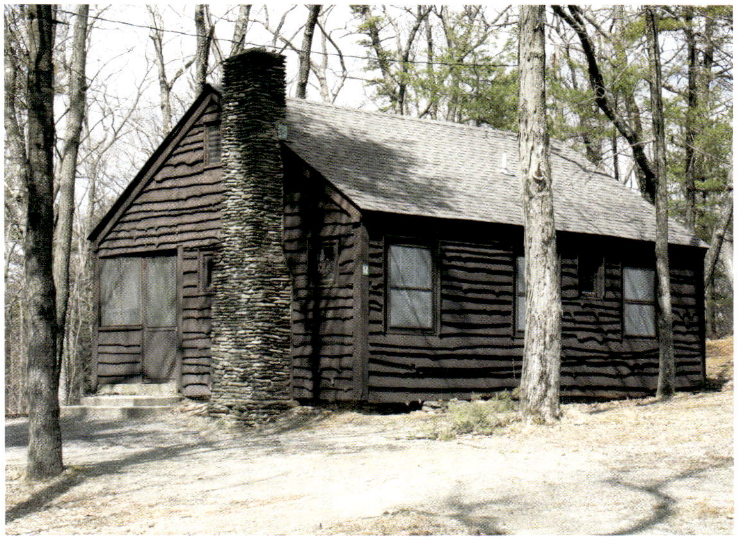

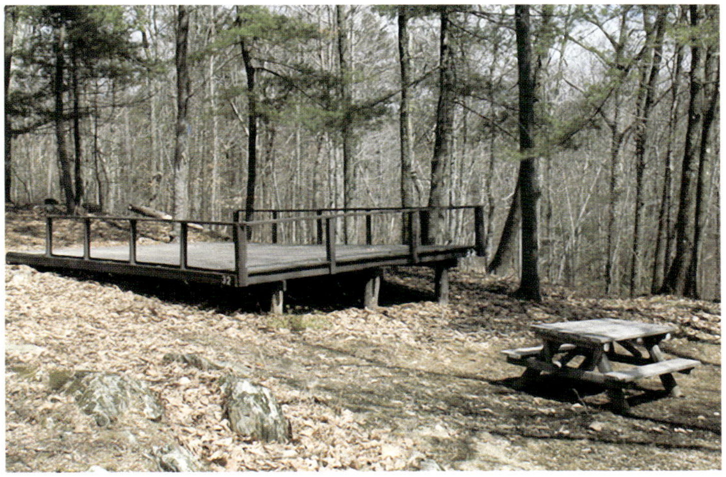

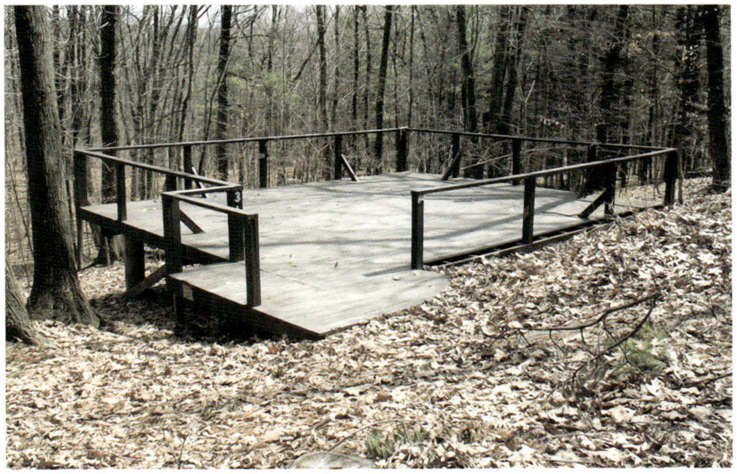

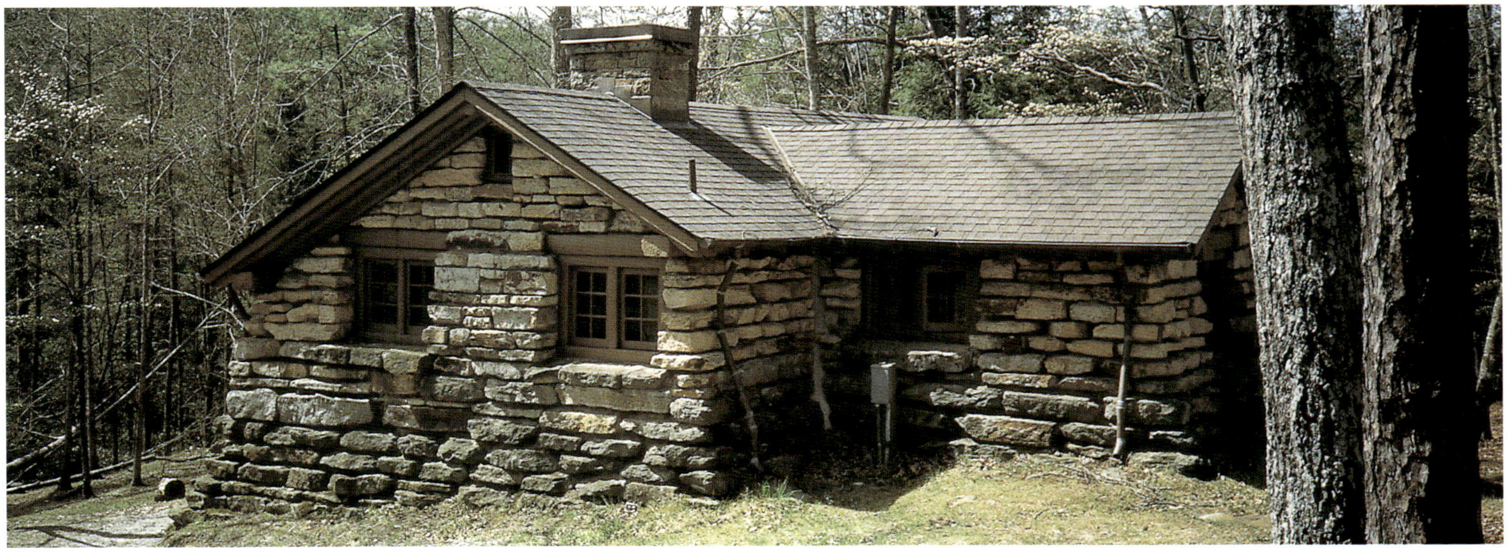

Top and middle:
Cabins and Camping Platforms
Lake Taghkanic State Park, New York

In 1933 a CCC camp was established in the state park, and CCC crews built the East Beach Bathhouse, the East Beach, the cabins, camping platforms, and the water tower.

Bottom:
Cabin 3, Pickett State Park, Jamestown, Tennessee

In 1933 the Stearns Coal and Lumber Company donated nearly twelve thousand acres to the state of Tennessee to be developed as a forest recreational area. The ECW/CCC worked there between 1934 and 1942, building trails, cabins, furniture, a recreation lodge, a ranger station, and a twelve-acre lake. Many of the original buildings were constructed of sandstone quarried locally.

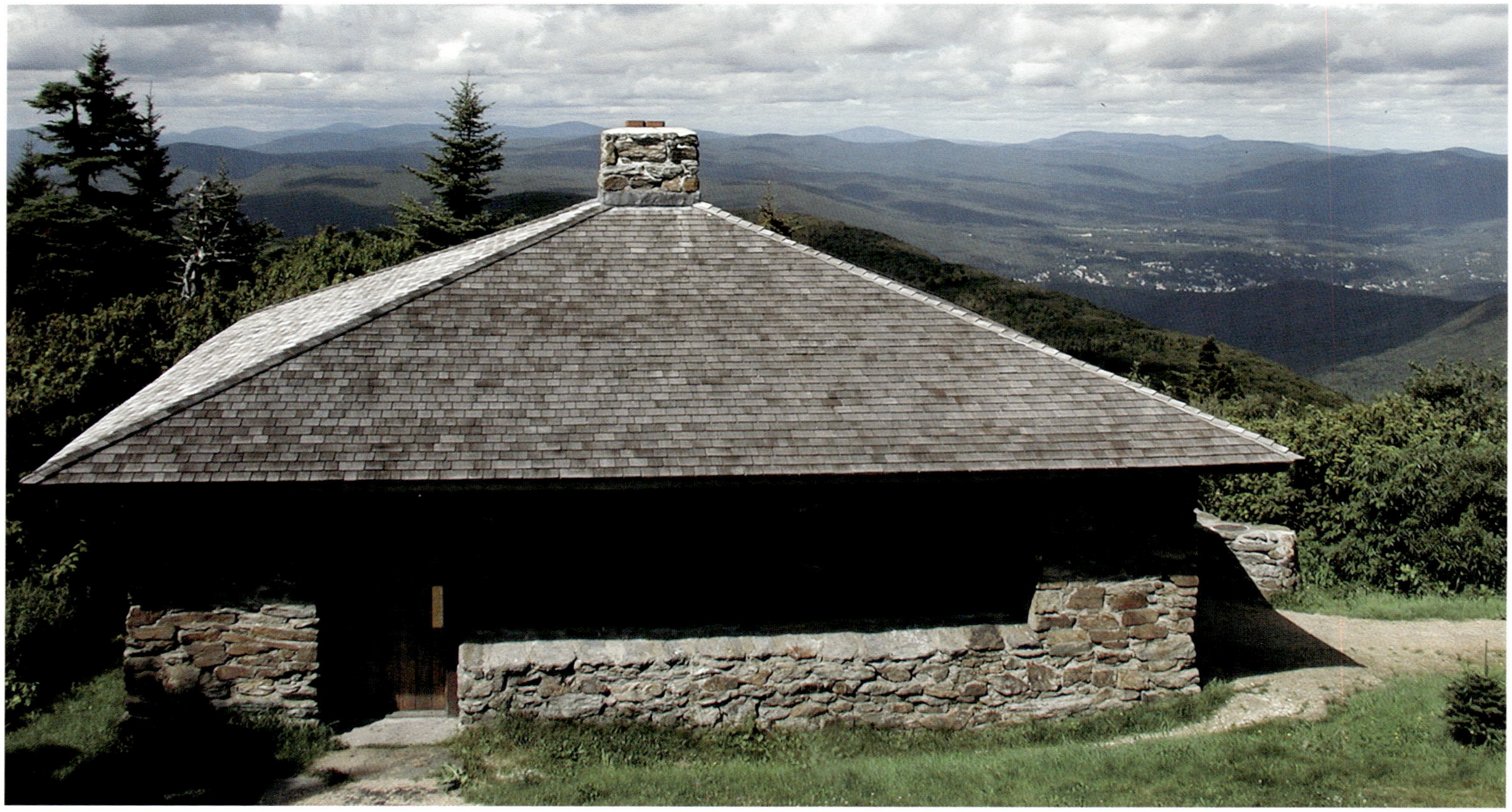

Mount Greylock, Massachusetts
Thunderbolt Ski Shelter
(see also p. 127)

The CCC built Thunderbolt Ski Shelter and Bascom Lodge of local stone and of oak and spruce cut on the mountain. The very steep Thunderbolt Ski Trail was the site of the Massachusetts Downhill championships from 1935 to 1948 and the U.S. Eastern Amateur Ski Association Championships in 1938 and 1940. Many of the local men who skied on the Thunderbolt later served in the 10th Mountain Division during World War II.

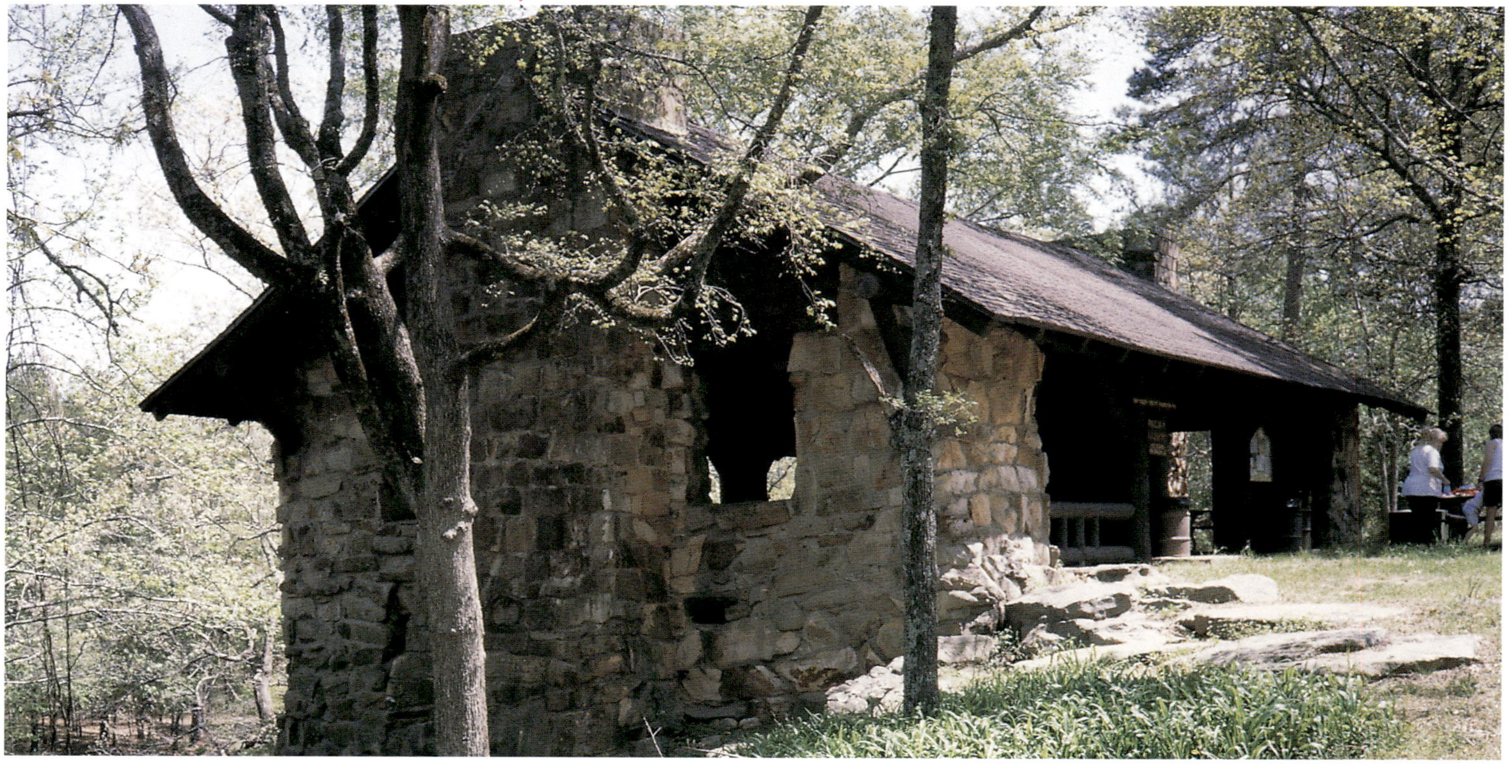

CCC Work, Petit Jean State Park, Arkansas
Petit Jean State Park includes three National Historic Districts containing CCC work on Mather Lodge, on the bluff of Cedar Creek Canyon, and on a dam, lake, cabins, water tower, and bridges.

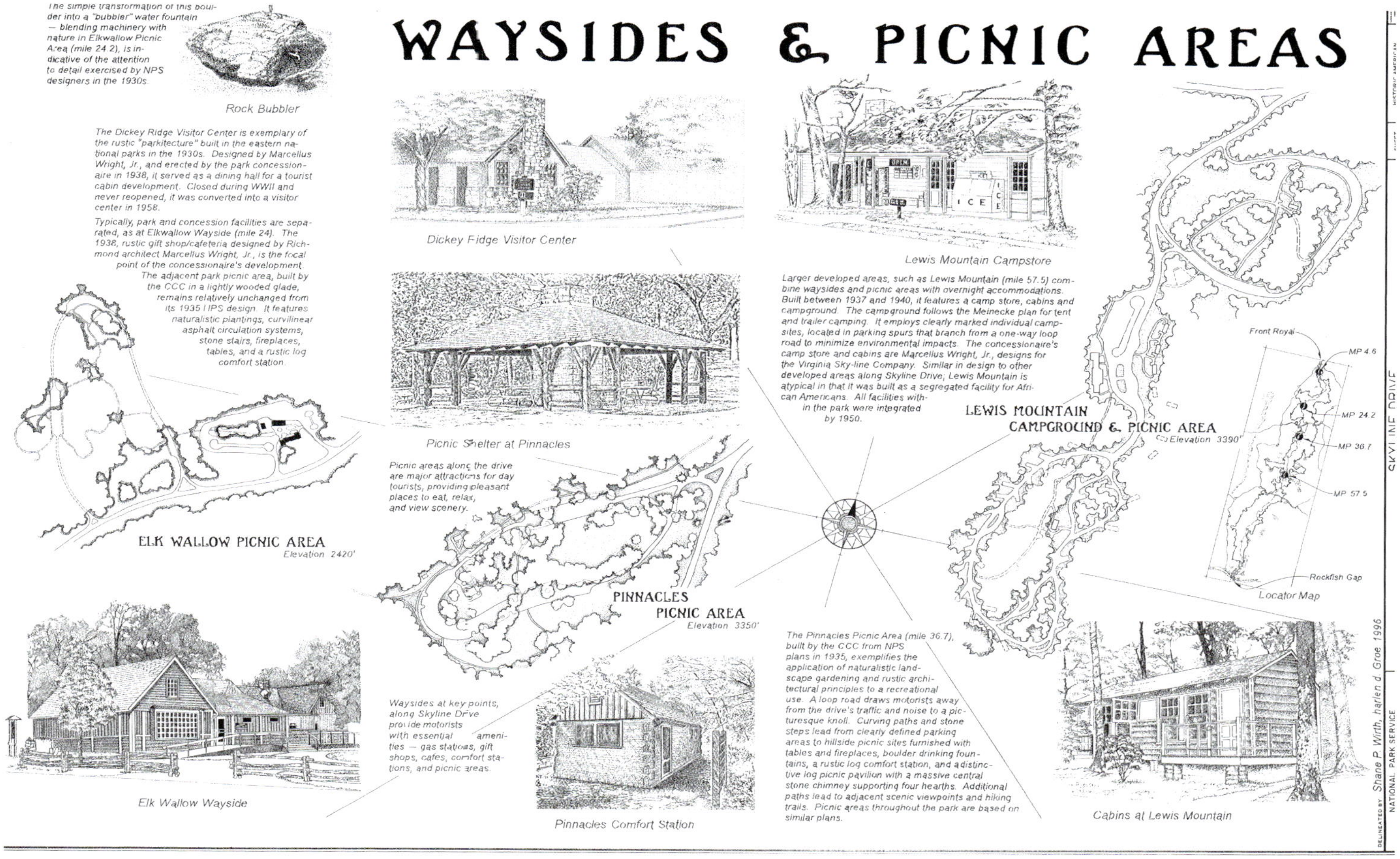

Skyline Drive
Shenandoah National Park
A sheet from the Historic American Engineering Record (HAER) portfolio showing developed areas and structures built during the New Deal.

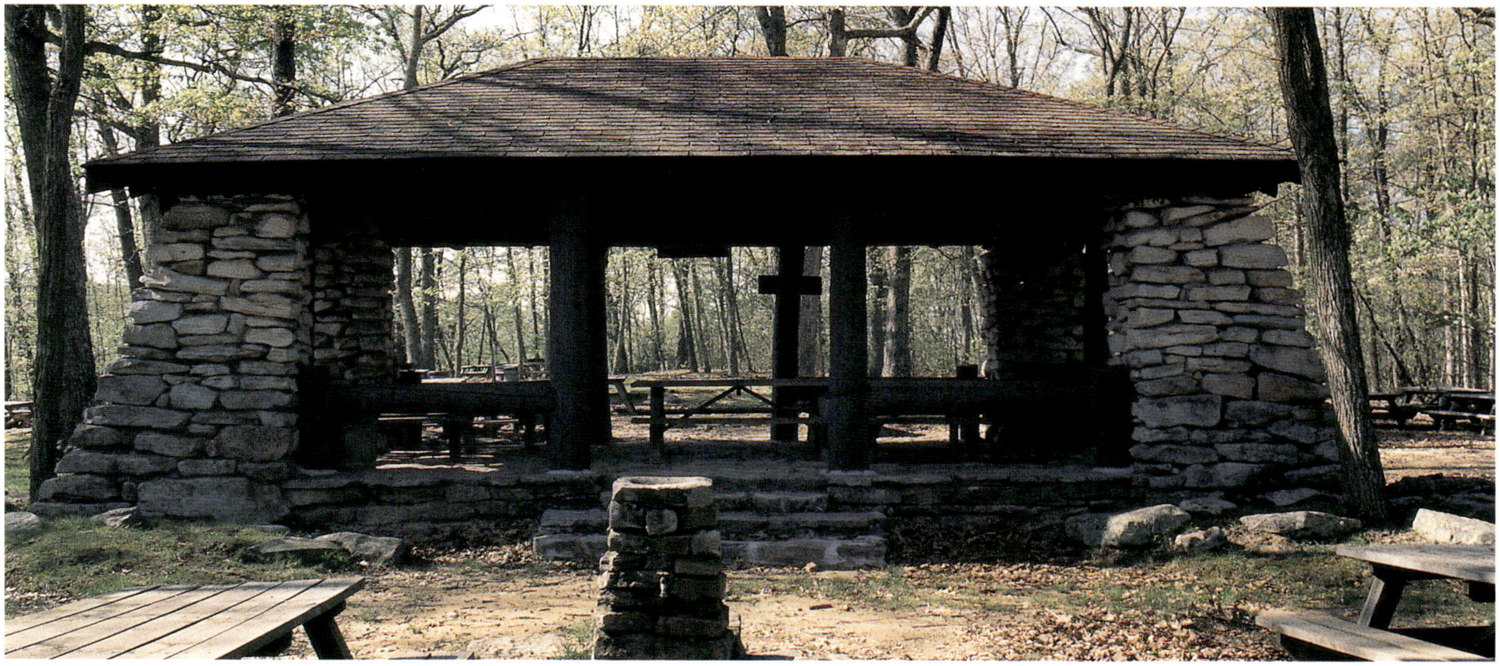

Babcock State Park,
West Virginia
Picnic Shelter, 1937

Most of Babcock State Park's 4,127 lumbered-out acres were purchased in 1934 for two dollars per acre—100 acres cost ten dollars per acre. The CCC planted trees, built trails, roads, cabins, an administration building, and a swimming pool.

On the Road

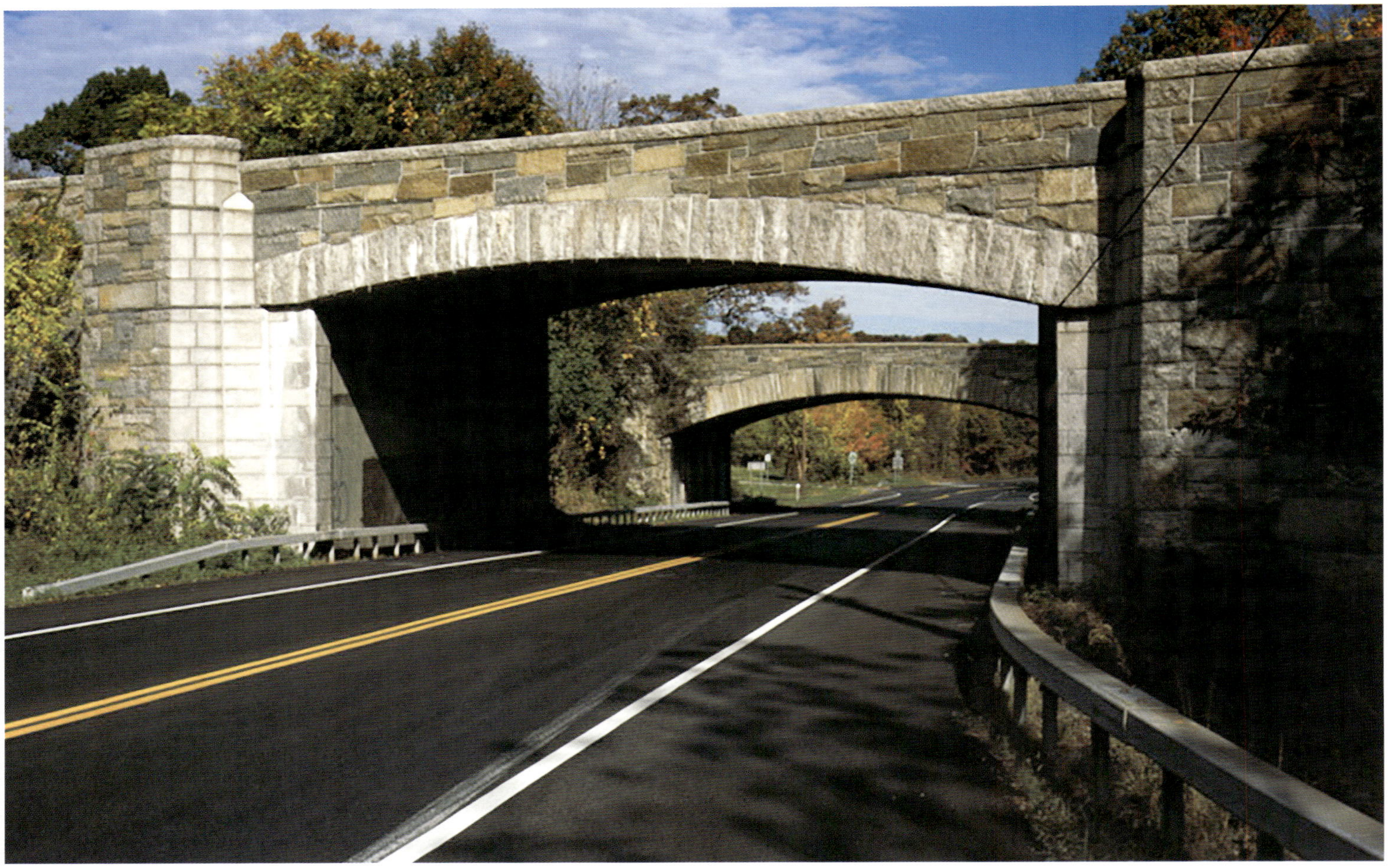

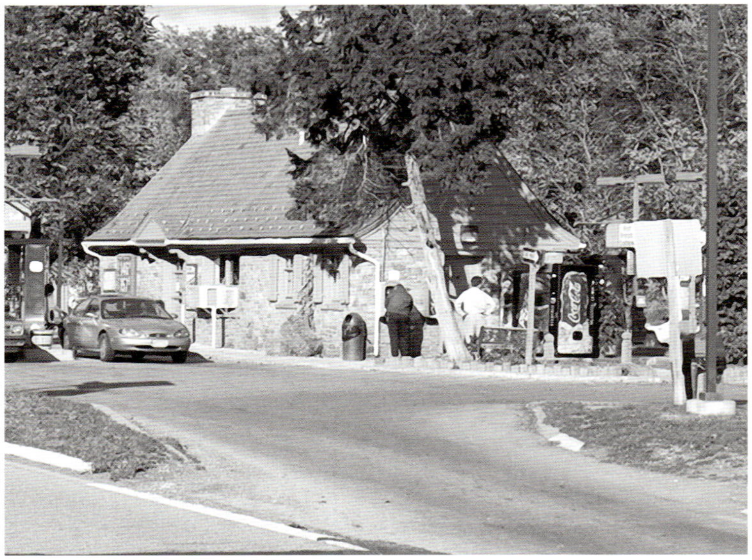

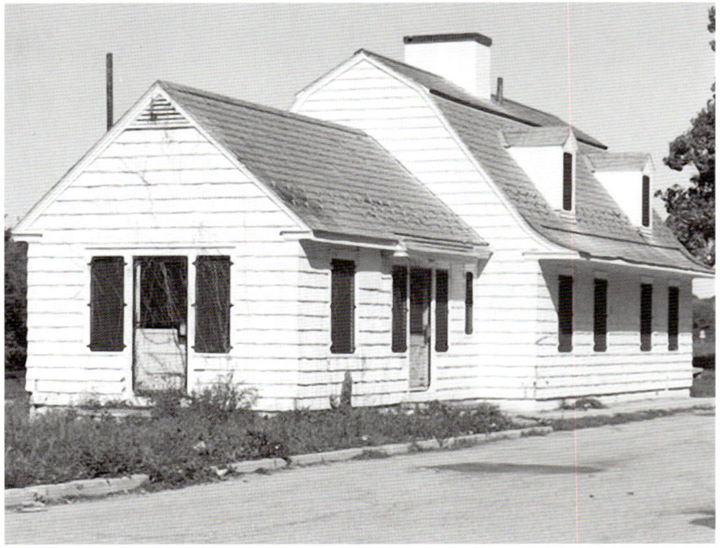

Overpass at route 134 Taconic State Parkway, New York

An early section of the Taconic State Parkway in New York was developed while FDR was Governor. These stone-faced bridges originally spanned two-way traffic.

Bottom right: Shenandoah service station

Bottom far right: Todd Hill service station Taconic State Parkway, New York

In accordance with Franklin Roosevelt's declared preferences for local continuity of style (see main text), these two filling stations on the Taconic State Parkway were designed to represent Dutch architectural traditions.

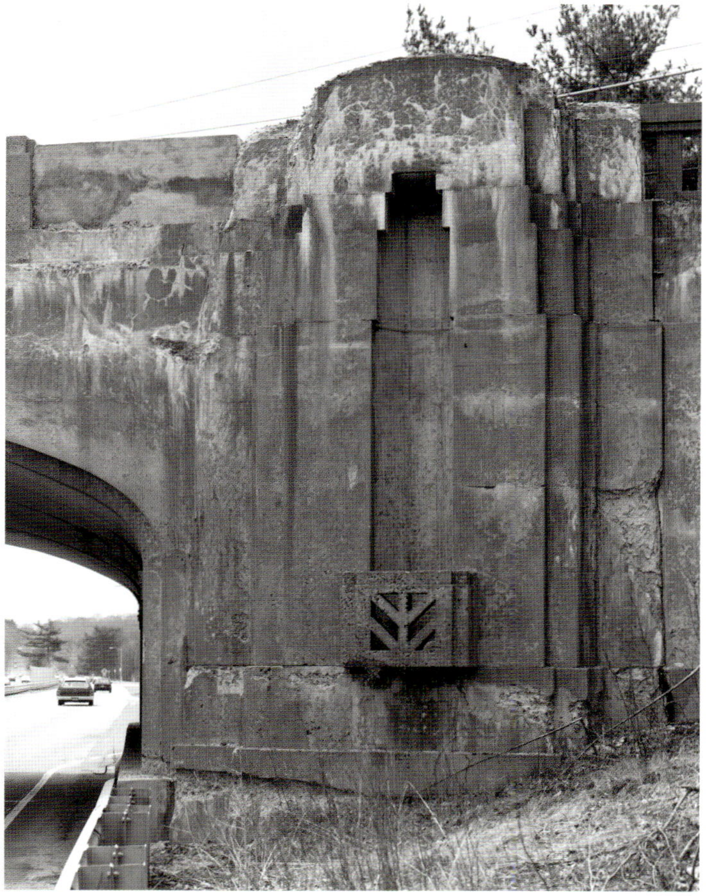

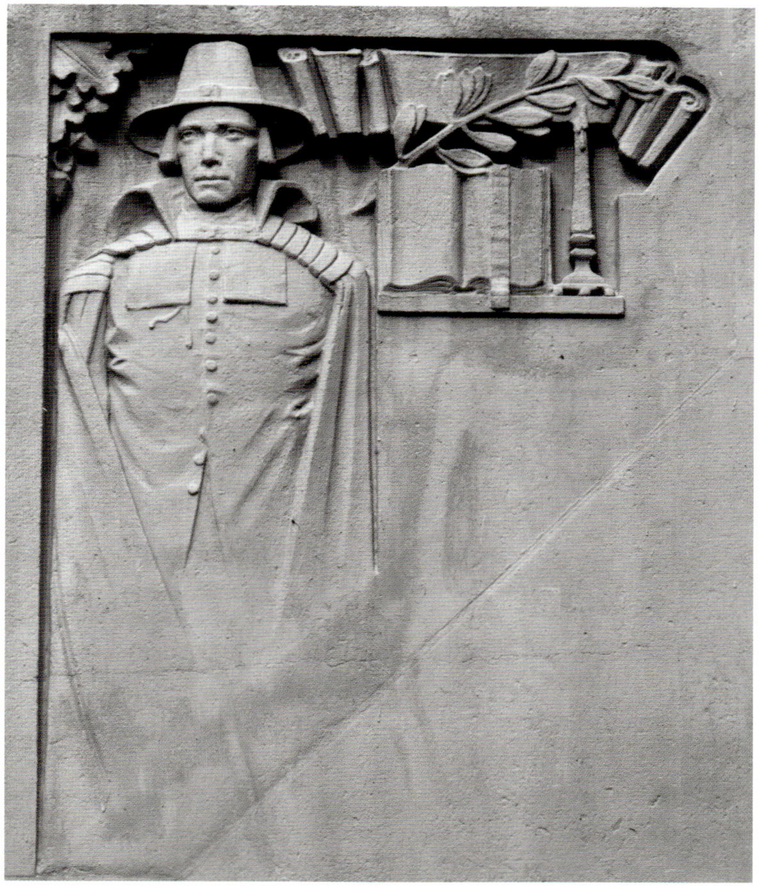

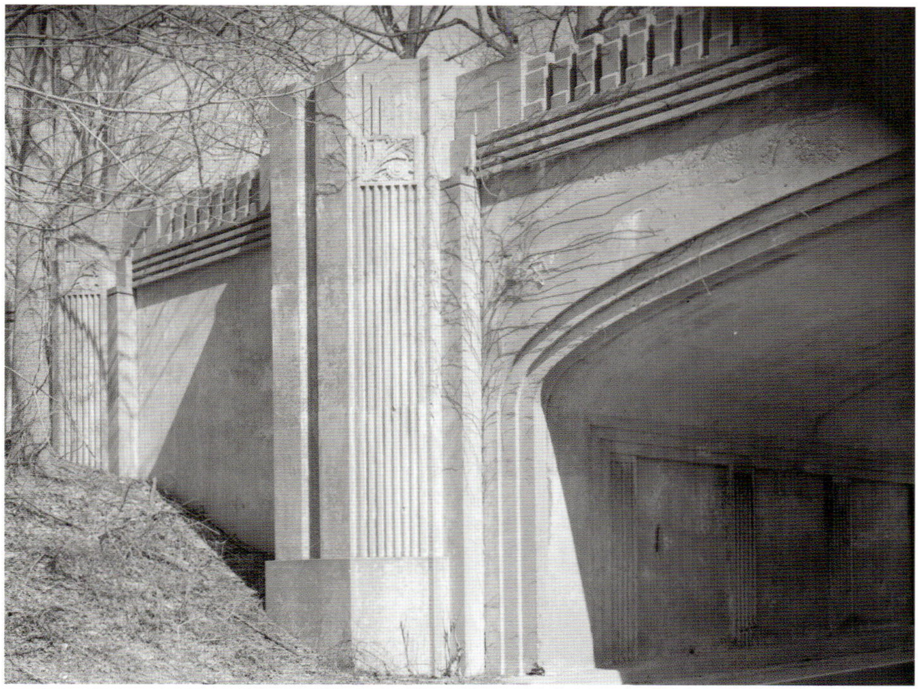

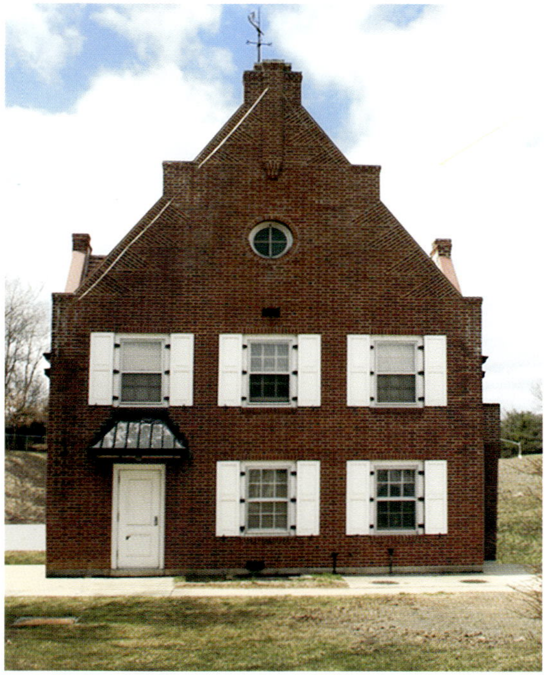

Top far left:
Merritt Parkway,
Bridge No. 744 at
Route 59
Fairfield, Connecticut

Detail of northeast abutment.

Top left:
Merritt Parkway, Comstock Hill Road Bridge, spanning the Merritt Parkway
Norwalk, Connecticut

Pilgrim relief sculpture, detail of abutment.

Bottom far left:
Abutment and Wingwall
Merritt Parkway, Lapham Avenue Bridge, spanning the Merritt Parkway at State Route 165, New Canaan, Connecticut

Bottom left:
Dutch Colonial brickwork, tollhouse of Rip Van Winkle Bridge
Greene County, New York

The tollhouse (now an administration building) of the Rip Van Winkle Bridge opened in summer 1935. The single-stepped gable design was probably drawn from the Luykas Van Alen House of 1737, in Kinderhook, on the other side of the Hudson River.

Civic Parks

Twenty-one bridges, no two alike, and thirty-one stone stairways connect the river level with downtown San Antonio. The San Antonio River was saved from drainage attempts in the 1920s by citizens led by Emily Edwards, wife of the city's planner. Riverwalk was designed by Edwin Arneson and Robert Hugman and developed by the WPA largely of local sand-colored rock. More than eleven thousand trees and shrubs were planted, and seventeen thousand feet of walkways and thirty-one stairs built. Hugman urged such a venture as an alternative to paving over the then-noxious San Antonio River.

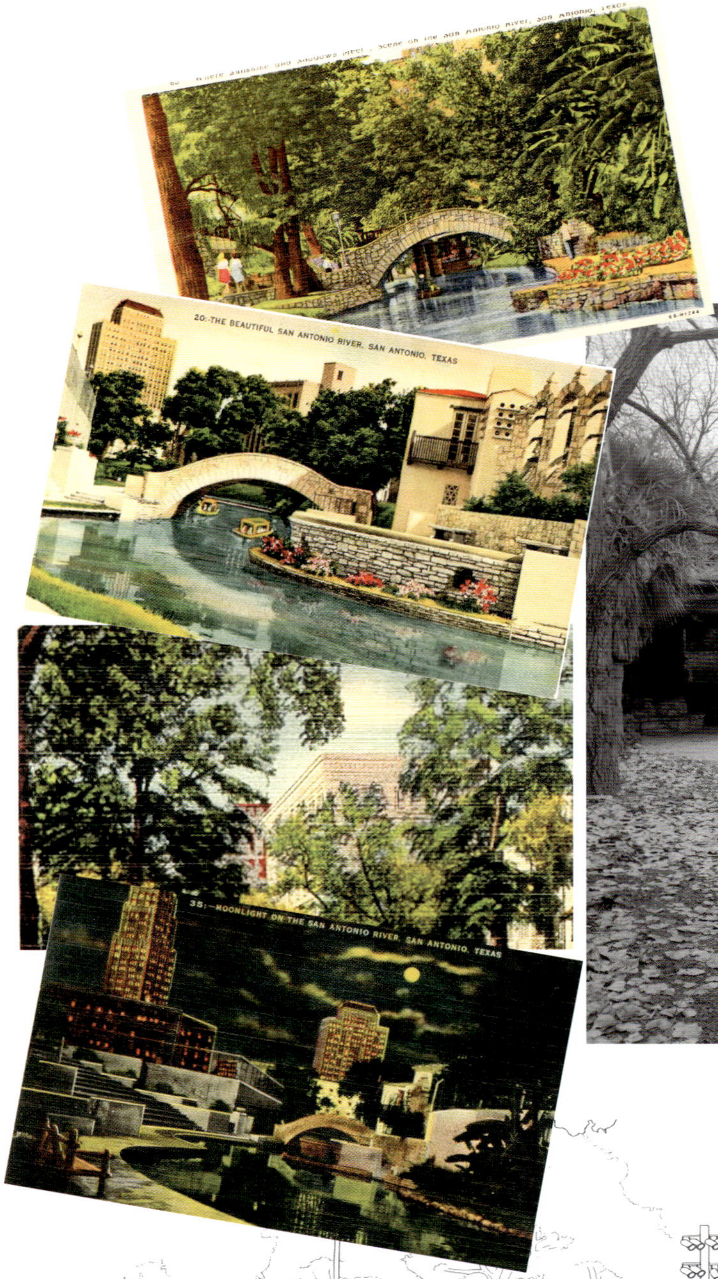

Right, top to bottom:
Postcards from the 1930s depicting views along the Riverwalk.

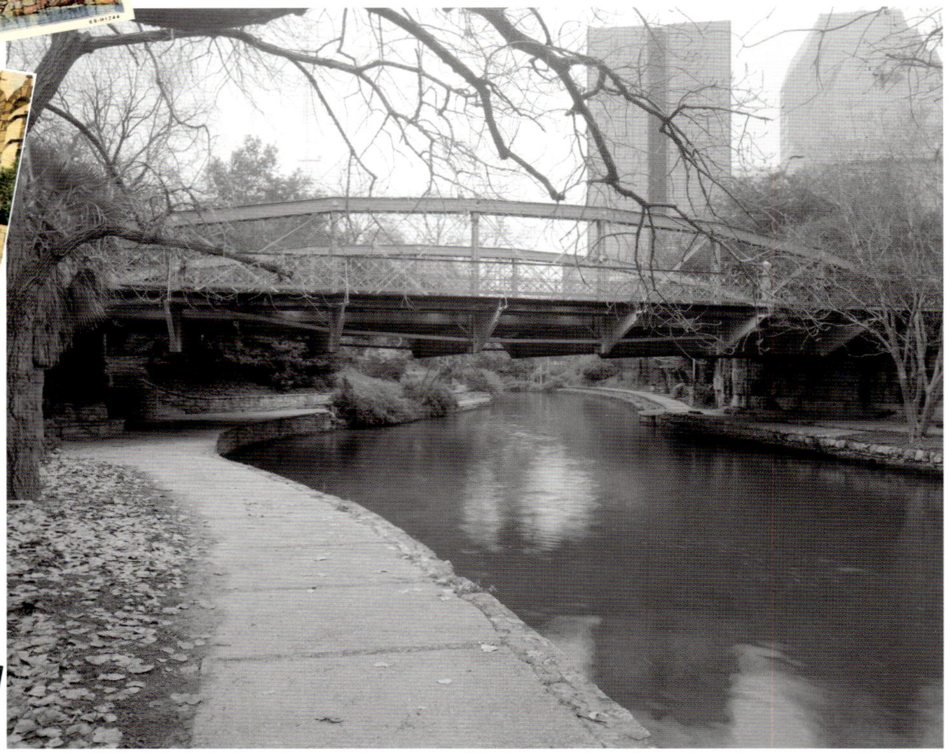

Far right:
Riverwalk,
San Antonio, Texas
The Augusta Street Bridge, 1939

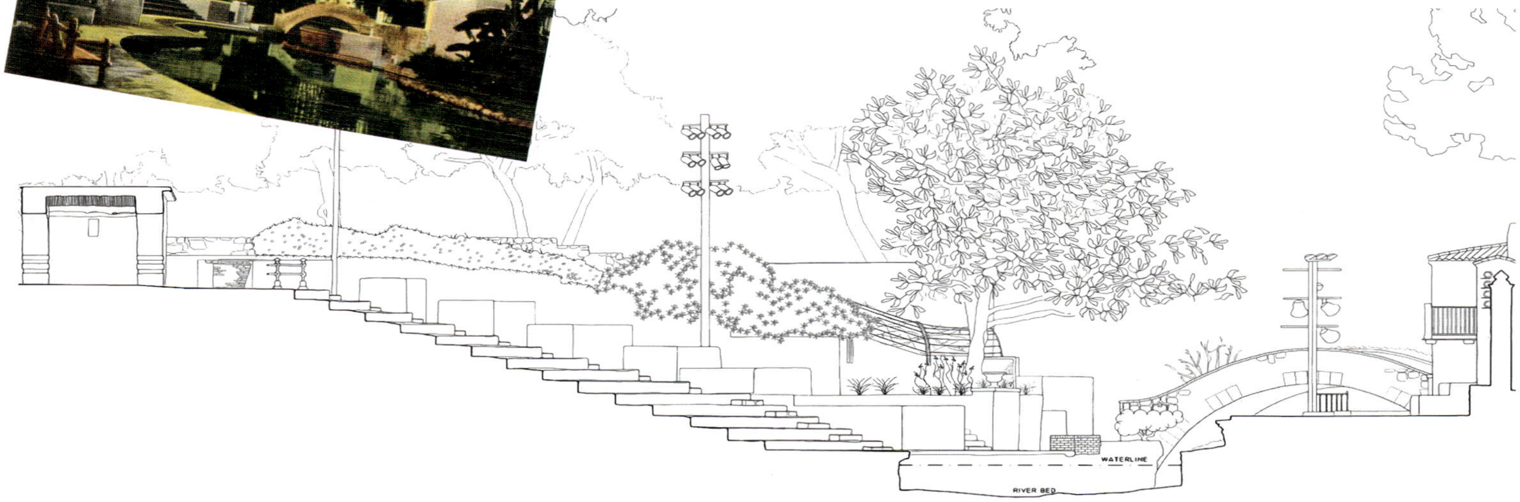

Bottom:
A section from a series of HABS/HAER drawings of the open-air Arneson River Theatre on the Riverwalk at La Villita. Built in 1939, this outdoor amphitheater hosts many exciting events on the Riverwalk. The Arneson Theatre has a unique design: located at the entrance of La Villita, the river separates the audience from the stage. In the summer months there are free dance performances almost every evening.

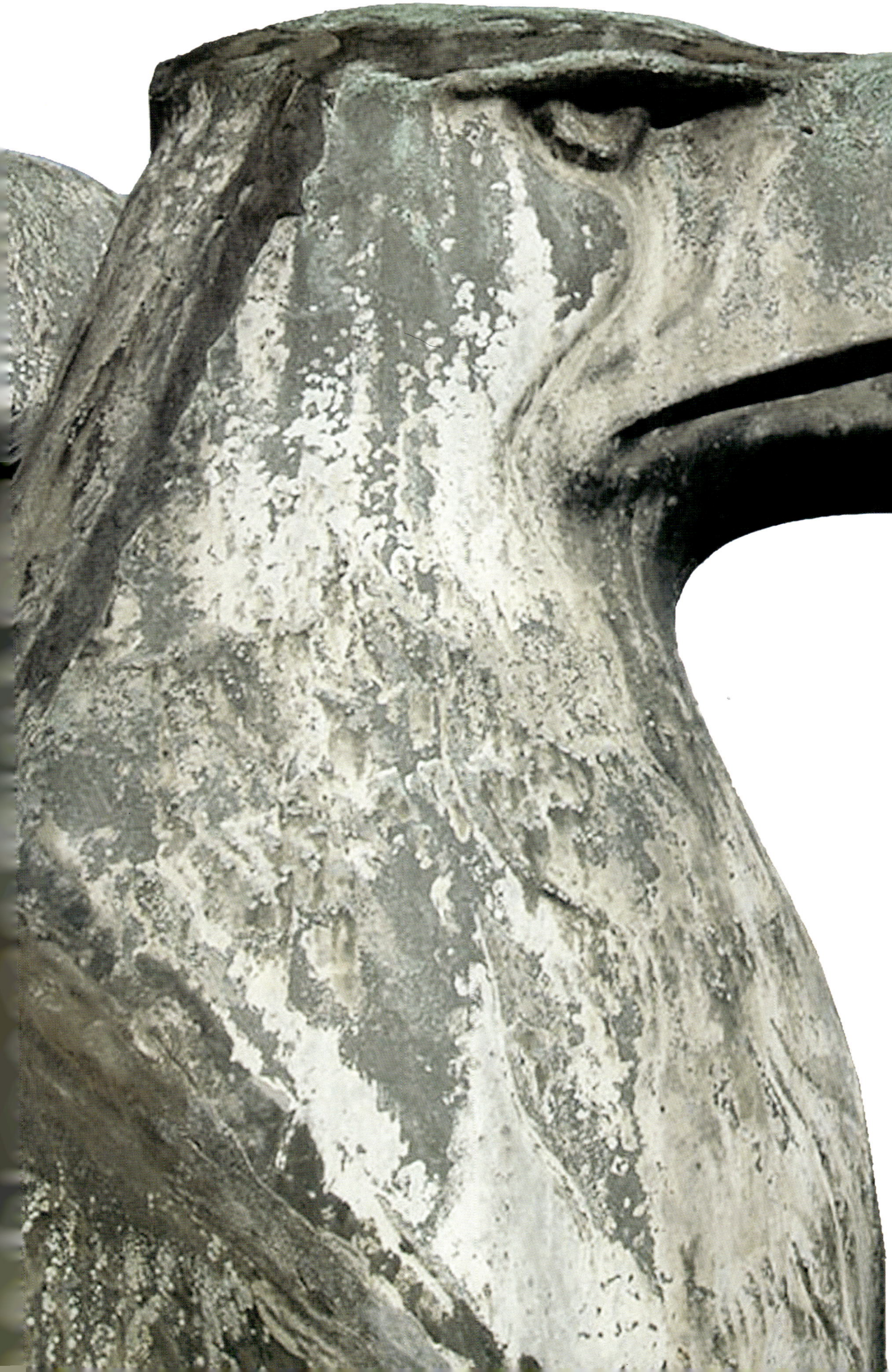

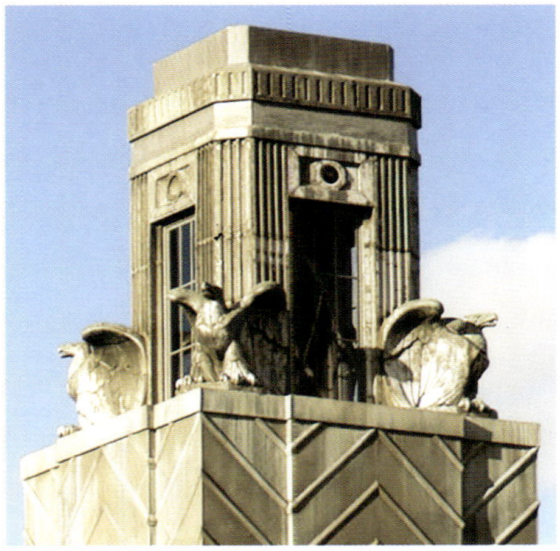

Left and above:
Eagles, Ellis Island Ferry Building
Ellis Island, New Jersey

The Ferry Building was designed by Chester H. Aldrich in the art deco style and built by the PWA—not the WPA—for $133,000. Between 1936 and 1954 eight million immigrants waited in the Ferry Building for passage off the island. It has been restored, including its copper cupola and eagle sculpture.

Hall of State, Fair Park, Dallas, Texas

The Hall of State was the centerpiece for the 1936 Texas Centennial. At the head of the Esplanade, the Hall of State was to represent the legacy for Texas. The 277-acre Fair Park in Dallas, Texas, largely constructed in 1935, is the only pre-1950 world's fair site remaining intact in the United States. It is also a cultural, educational, and sports facility in active use, for the Texas Hall of State, Dallas Museum of Natural History, Dallas Aquarium, Texas Discovery Gardens, D.A.R. Museum, Women's Museum, and the Science Place and Planetarium.

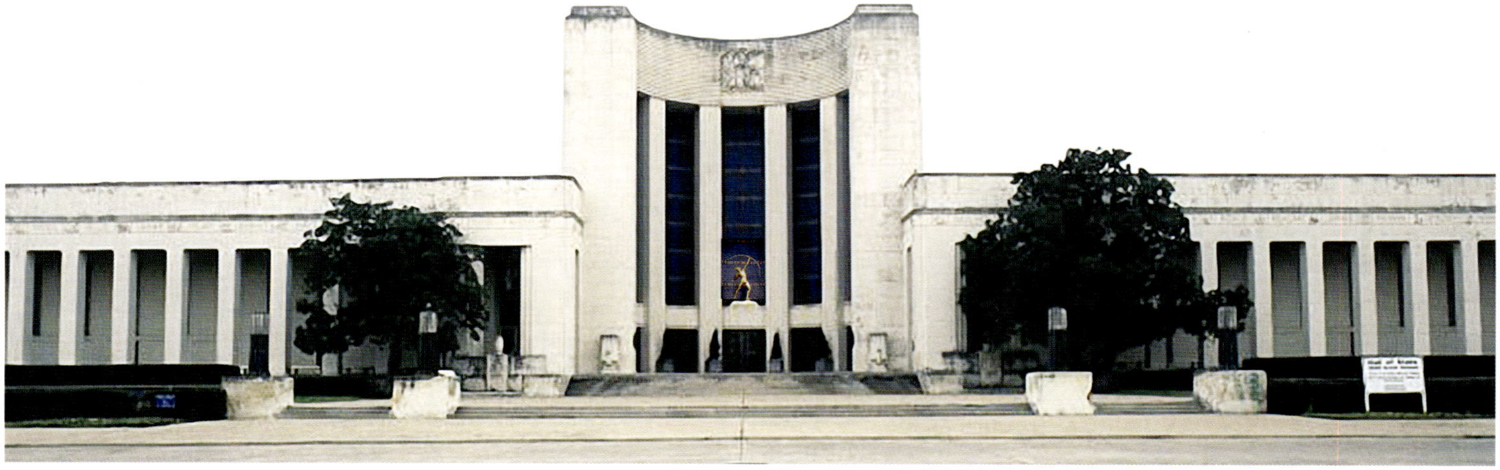

Middle:
"Speed"

Pierre Bourdelle bas-relief symbolizing travel by air.

Pierre Bourdelle was born in Paris and apprenticed with his father, a sculptor and painter, and August Rodin. Bourdelle taught at Long Island University as an artist-in-residence.

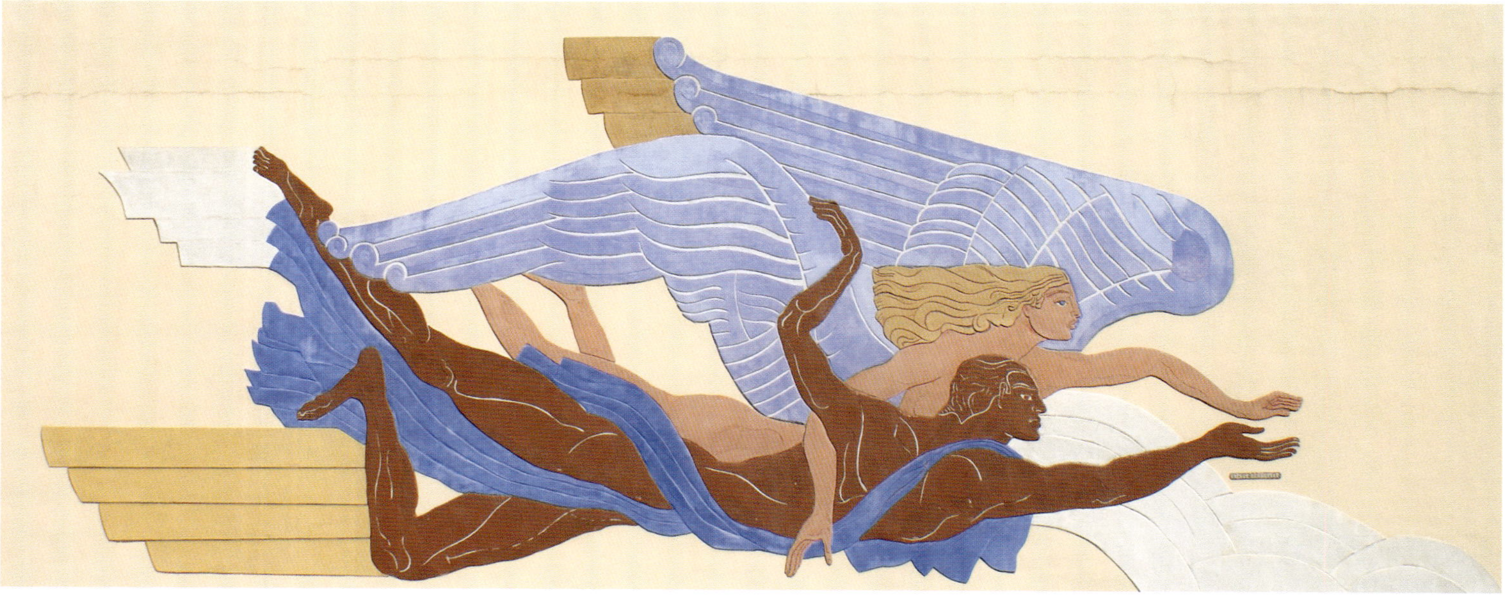

Bottom:
"Streamline"

Bourdelle bas-relief symbolizing travel by land.

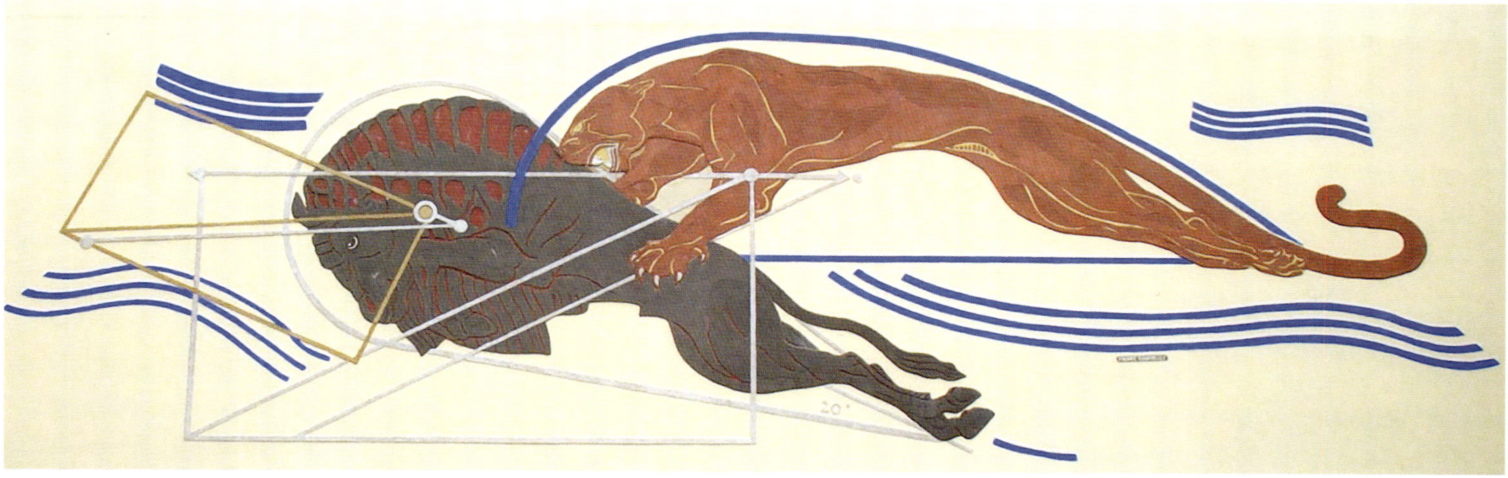

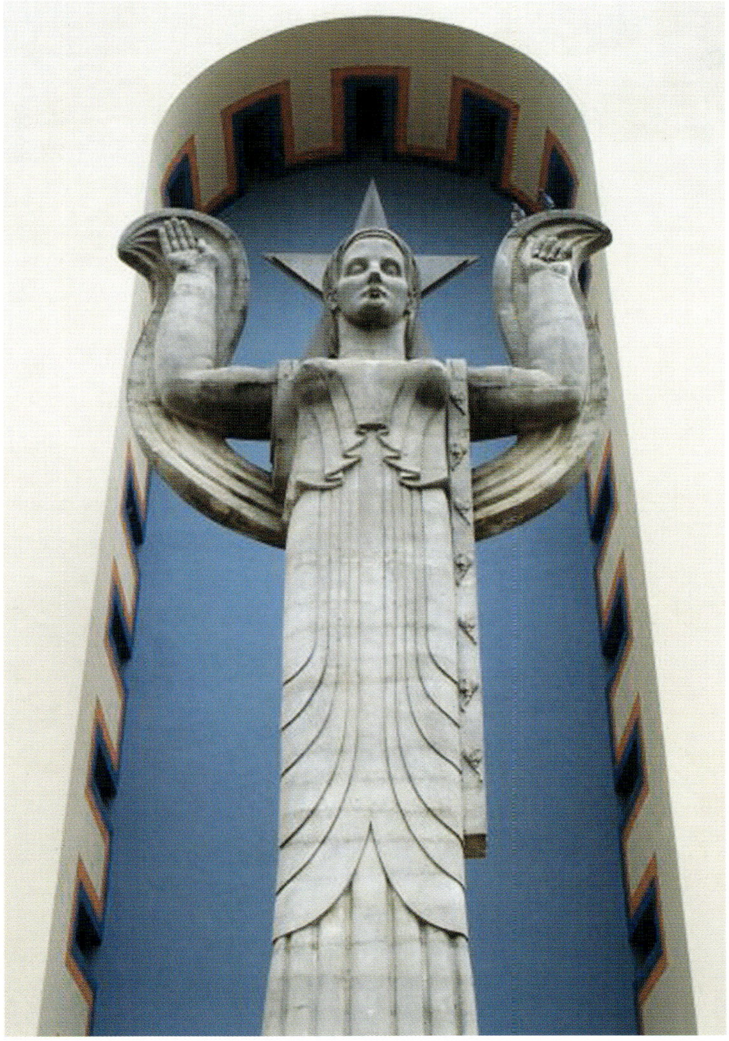

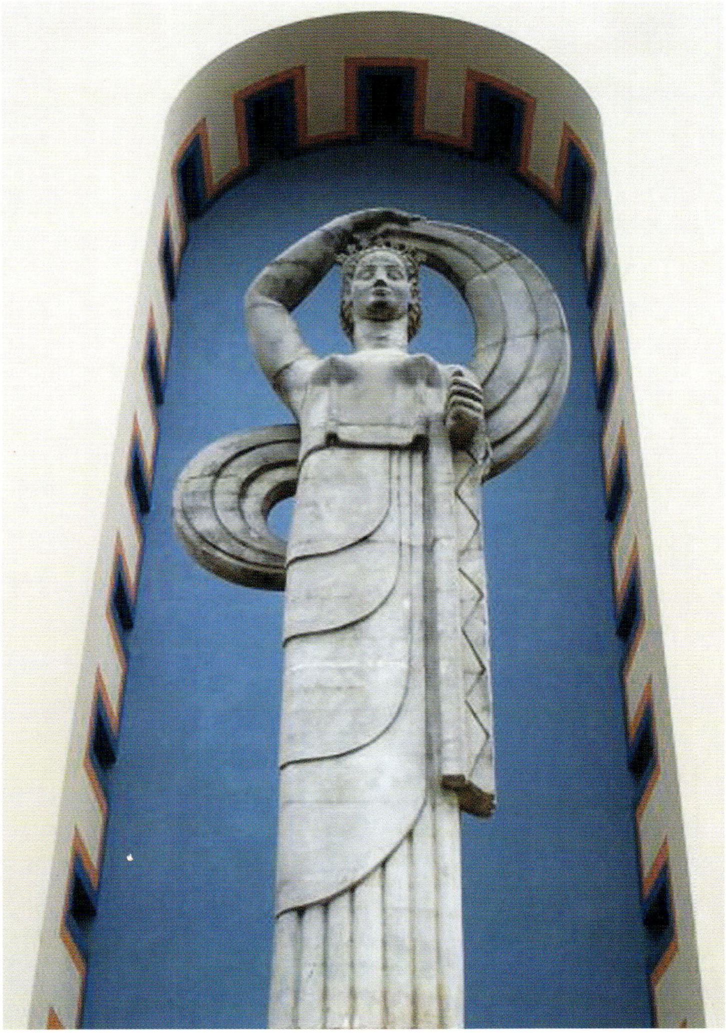

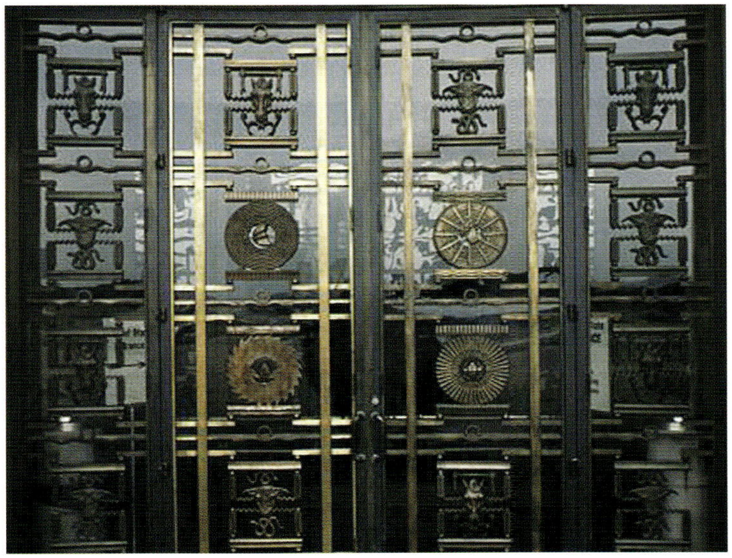

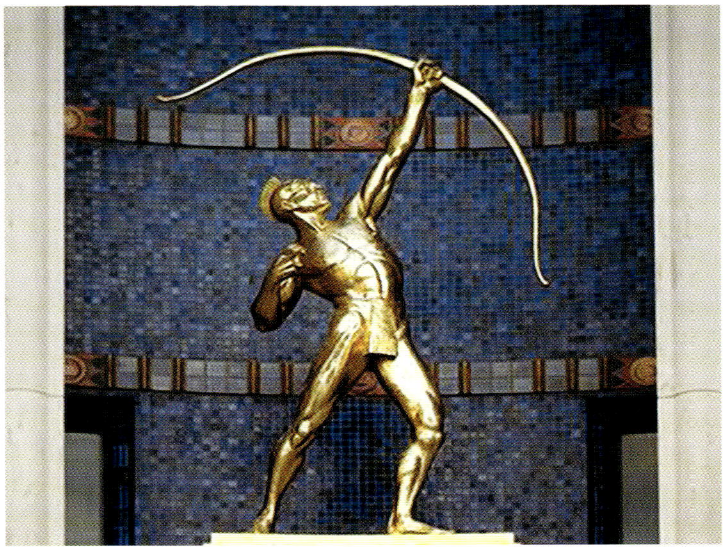

Top far left:
"Texas"
Lawrence Tenney Stevens

The model was Helen Ramsay, a Texas Centennial Rangerette.

Top left:
"Confederacy"
Lawrence Tenney Stevens

The seven stars in the lady's crown represent the seven original seceding states that joined the Confederacy.

Bottom far left:
Doorway of the Hall of State Building
Fair Park, Dallas, Texas

Bottom left:
The entrance is guarded by a gilded "Tejas warrior."

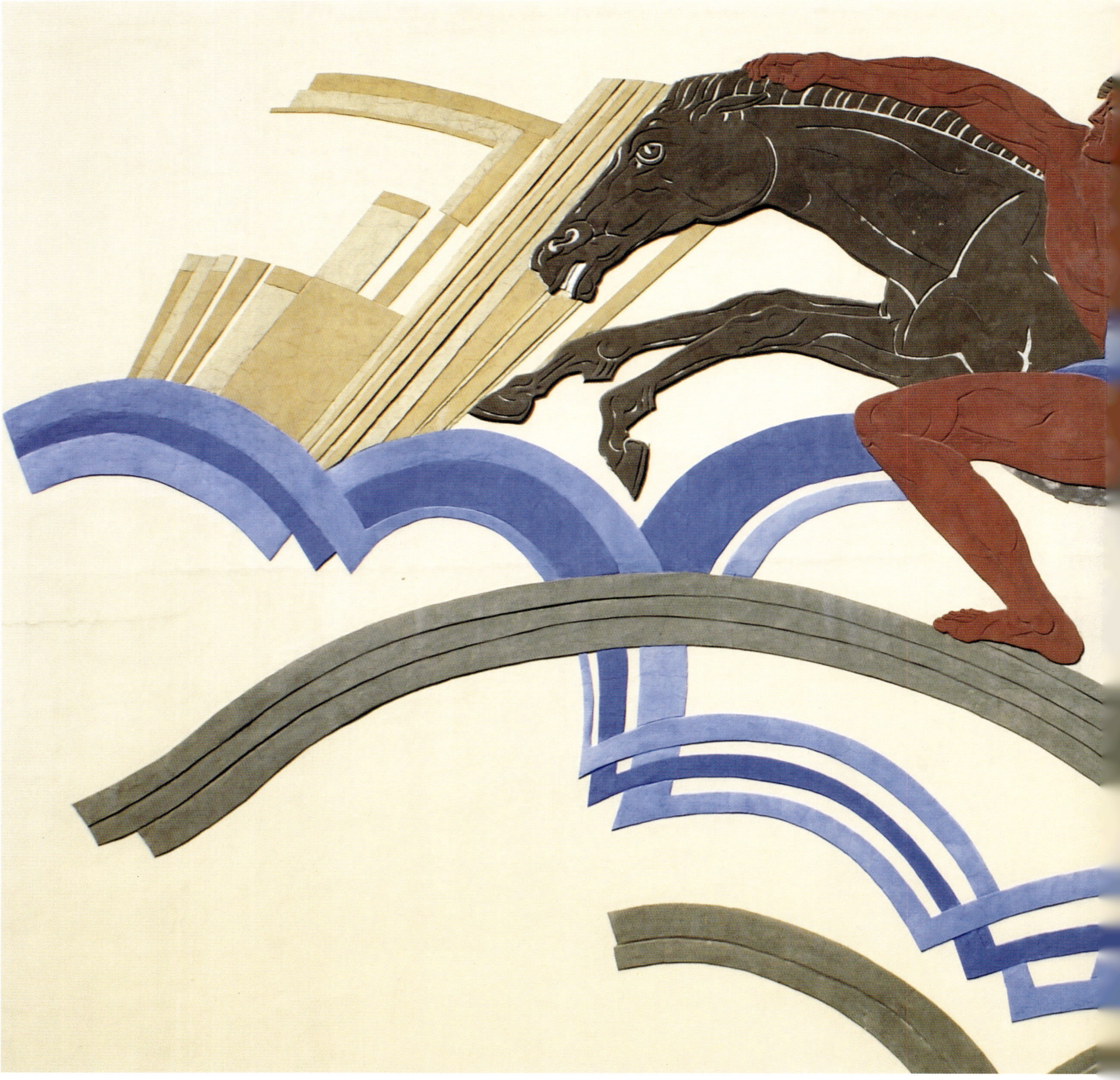

"Man Taming
Wild Horse"

Pierre Bourdelle
bas-relief symbolizing
travel by water.
South end, Centennial
Building, Fair Park,
Dallas, Texas

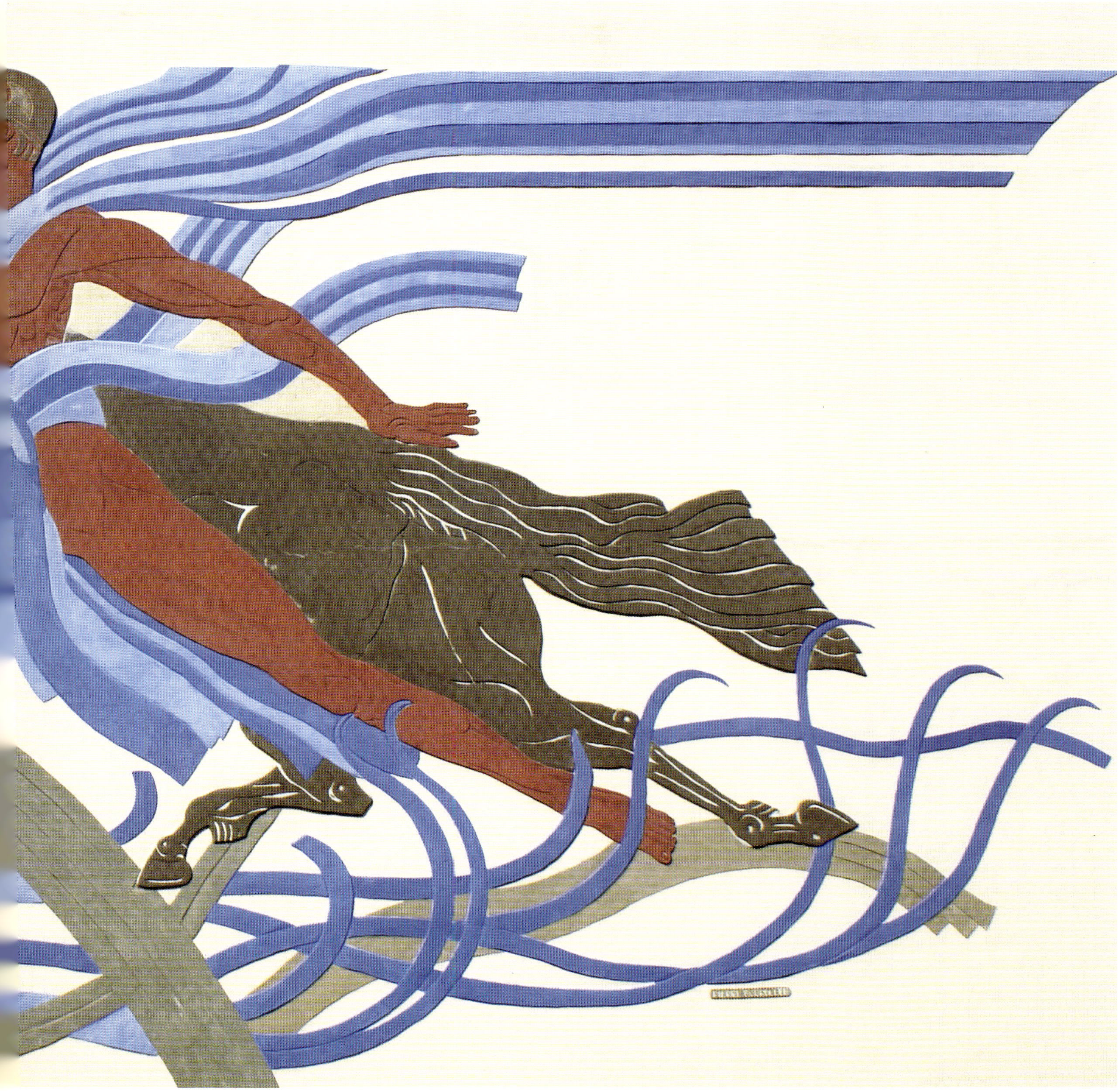

Chapter Five

The WPA/FAP

A few generations ago, the people of this country were taught by their writers and their critics and their teachers to believe that art was something foreign to America and to themselves–something imported from another continent and from an age that was not theirs–something they had no part in, save to go and see it in a guarded room on holidays and Sundays. But recently, within the last few years, they have discovered that they have a part. They have seen in their own towns, in their own villages, in schoolhouses, in post offices . . . pictures painted by their sons, their neighbors–people they have known and lived beside and talked to. They have seen . . . rooms full of paintings by Americans–some of it good, some of it not good, but all of it native, human, eager and alive–all of it painted by their own kind in their own country, and painted about things they know and look at often and have touched and loved.[1]

(President Franklin D. Roosevelt, 1941)

American artists have discovered a new obligation to the society in which they live.[2]

(President Franklin D. Roosevelt, 1939)

IN 1935 FRANKLIN ROOSEVELT LAUNCHED his Emergency Relief Appropriations Act (ERAA), containing the largest peacetime appropriation in the nation's history, of which four billion dollars were to be spent on continuing work relief. Administration of the CCC was folded into the newly formed WPA under the provisions of Federal One. Federal One had five divisions: the Federal Art Project (WPA/FAP), the Federal Music Project, the Federal Theatre Project, the Federal Writers' Project, and the Historical Records Survey. All together they employed more than forty thousand people classified as "artists and other cultural workers." The Federal Art Project (WPA/FAP), managed by Holger Cahill, employed more than five thousand artists when in full swing, providing art for hospitals, schools, and other government buildings. It operated its own mural program, an easel-painting division producing nearly 108,000 paintings, and a sculpture division that made 18,000 pieces. It maintained a graphic arts workshop, a photography project, a scenic-design division (making models of historic stage sets and new architectural models for hopeful start-up ventures), a poster division, and a stained-glass division. Its twenty-two-thousand-plate Index of American Design was a grand catalogue assembled from illustrated reports by artists sent on field trips around the country to record traditional designs in furnishings, ritual pieces, and utilitarian objects—among them axe handles as "comely" as those celebrated by Walt Whitman, weather vanes, and iconic street signs.[3]

Cahill's WPA/FAP Arts Service Division provided illustrative material to the WPA's "writers, musicians and theaters; its Exhibitions Division organized public showings; its Art Teaching Division gave classes in settlement houses and community centers; in the New York City area alone, an estimated 50,000 children and adults participated in classes each week. The FAP also set up and staffed 100 arts centers in 22 states; these included galleries, classrooms and community workshops and served an estimated eight million people." Some are still in business, supported by locally generated budgets.[4]

Established or well-connected artists such as George Biddle and Olin Dows benefited from commissions from the Treasury's TRAP and Section. Many others, then obscure but now celebrated, were happy to get modest stipends from WPA/FAP work-relief, among them Philip Guston, Moses Soyer, Jackson Pollock, Mark Rothko, Jacob Lawrence, Ivan Albright, Marsden Hartley, Philip Evergood, and Mark Tobey. Many of them did so not entirely out of necessity but also because they shared George Biddle's belief that "the artist" should be "conscious of the fact that he is of service to the community."[5]

Holger Cahill and the WPA/FAP

Holger Cahill wrote with satisfaction that his program had "brought the artist closer to the interests of a public which needs him, and which is now learning to understand him. And it has made the artist more responsive to the inspiration of the country, and through this the artist is bringing every aspect of American life into the currency of art."[6]

There was no one better qualified than Cahill to know what "every aspect of American life might be"—unless it be Lorena Hickok (see chapter six). Cahill was born in 1887 as Sveinn Kristjan Bjarnarsson to impoverished Icelandic immigrants, and abandoned eleven years later by his abusive father in rural North Dakota. After a term in an orphanage and speaking only Icelandic, Cahill worked as a farmhand in a Gaelic-speaking prairie village, then as a Nebraska cattle-driver. He went to night school while clerking for the Northern Pacific Railroad in its big brick headquarters opposite the train station in St. Paul, and heaved coal on Lake Superior ore boats and on an ocean liner sailing the Pacific. He jumped ship in Shanghai, got passage home, sold insurance, washed dishes in hotels, and made it to New York to attend night school again, this time in journalism and creative writing at New York University, where he met the editor and future novelist, Mike Gold. Gold gave Cahill a job as a reporter, and a byline as Edgar Holger Cahill, by which he would be known for the rest of his life. When Gold left for Harvard, Cahill took his place as editor and ran two small weekly newspapers for three years before becoming a freelance journalist. He attended Columbia University and The New School for Social Research, and became a figure within the New York art scene. He began writing press releases for the Society of Independent Artists, developing friendships with John Sloan, Robert Henri, George Bellows, Mark Tobey, Walt Kuhn, Jules Pascin, Joseph Stella, William Zorach, and Max Weber, for whose 1930 show he wrote the catalogue. In 1922 he joined the staff of the Newark Museum and thereafter moved both upward and outward to organize exhibitions on American Primitives and American Folk Sculpture.[7]

In 1932 Cahill became acting director of the Museum of Modern Art (MoMA) and organized an exhibition of early American folk art, the catalogue for which bore a title with a New Deal-ish tone: *American Folk Art: The Art of the Common Man in America, 1750-1900*. By then the associations of the Rockefeller family with MoMA and with Mexican mural art had been manifested in the mural commissions at Rockefeller Center. Cahill moved that association ahead with a grand-slam MoMA exhibition in 1933. Entitled *American Sources of Modern Art*, it presented the effects of the pre-Columbian art of Mexico, Peru, and Central America on Gauguin, the fauvists and cubists, and also its more direct influence upon the generation of Latin American muralists who instructed American artists such as George Biddle and Olin Dows.

In 1935, Harry Hopkins convinced Cahill to take the leadership of the WPA/FAP.

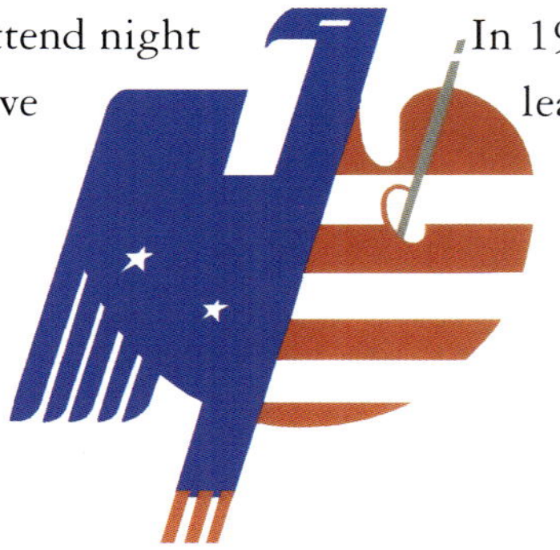

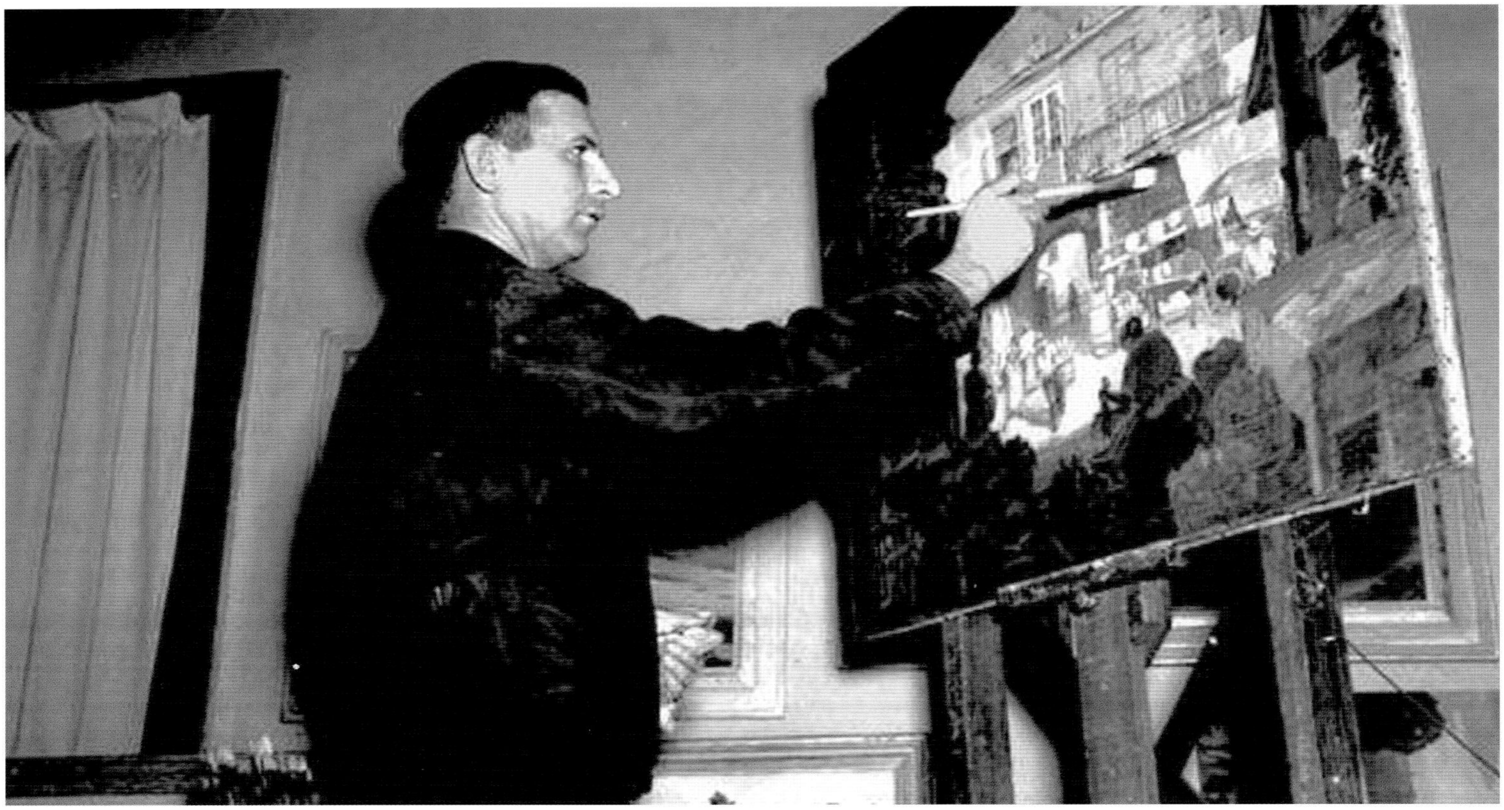

An artist at work on a painting of a New Orleans courtyard scene in 1936.

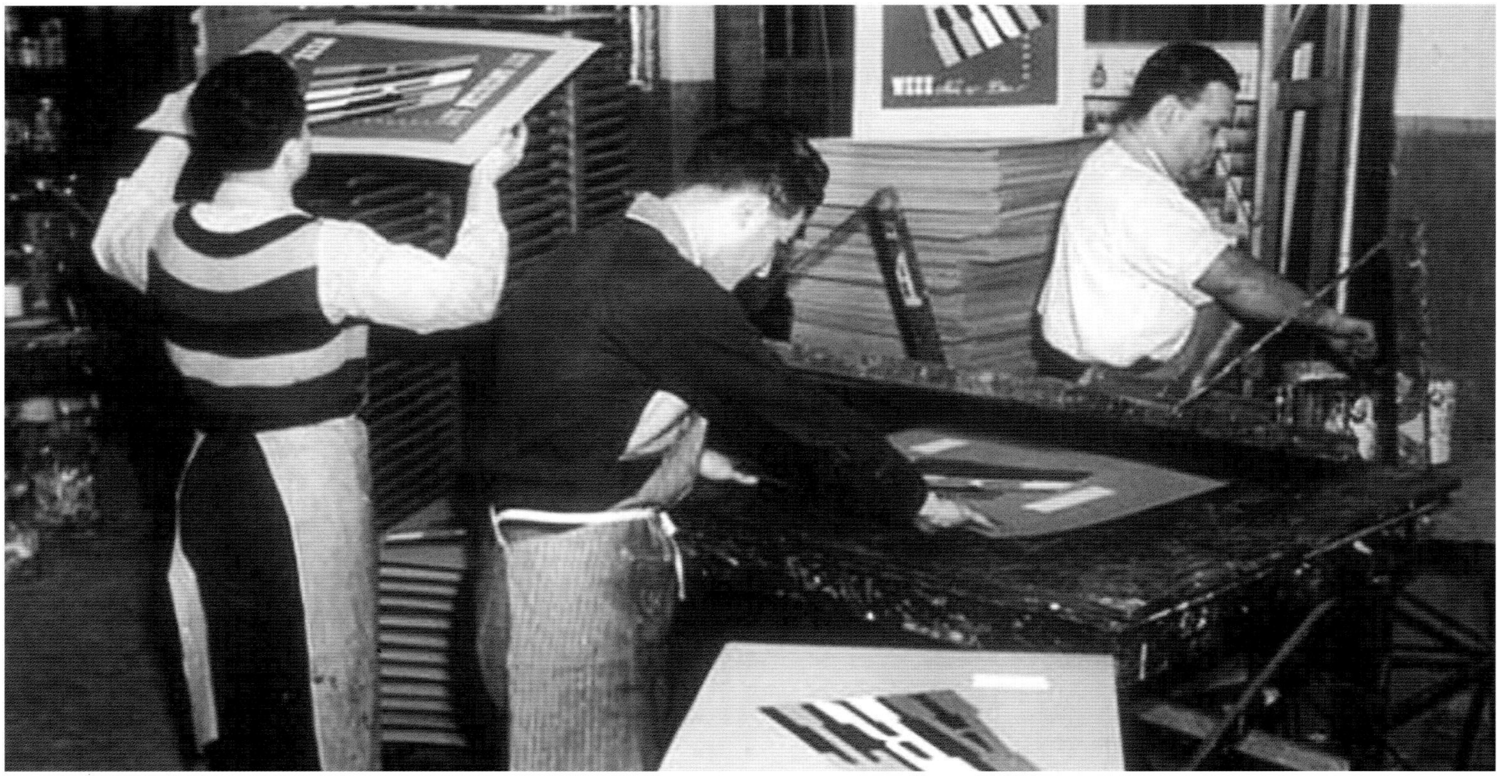

Printers making serigraph posters for New York City, 1940

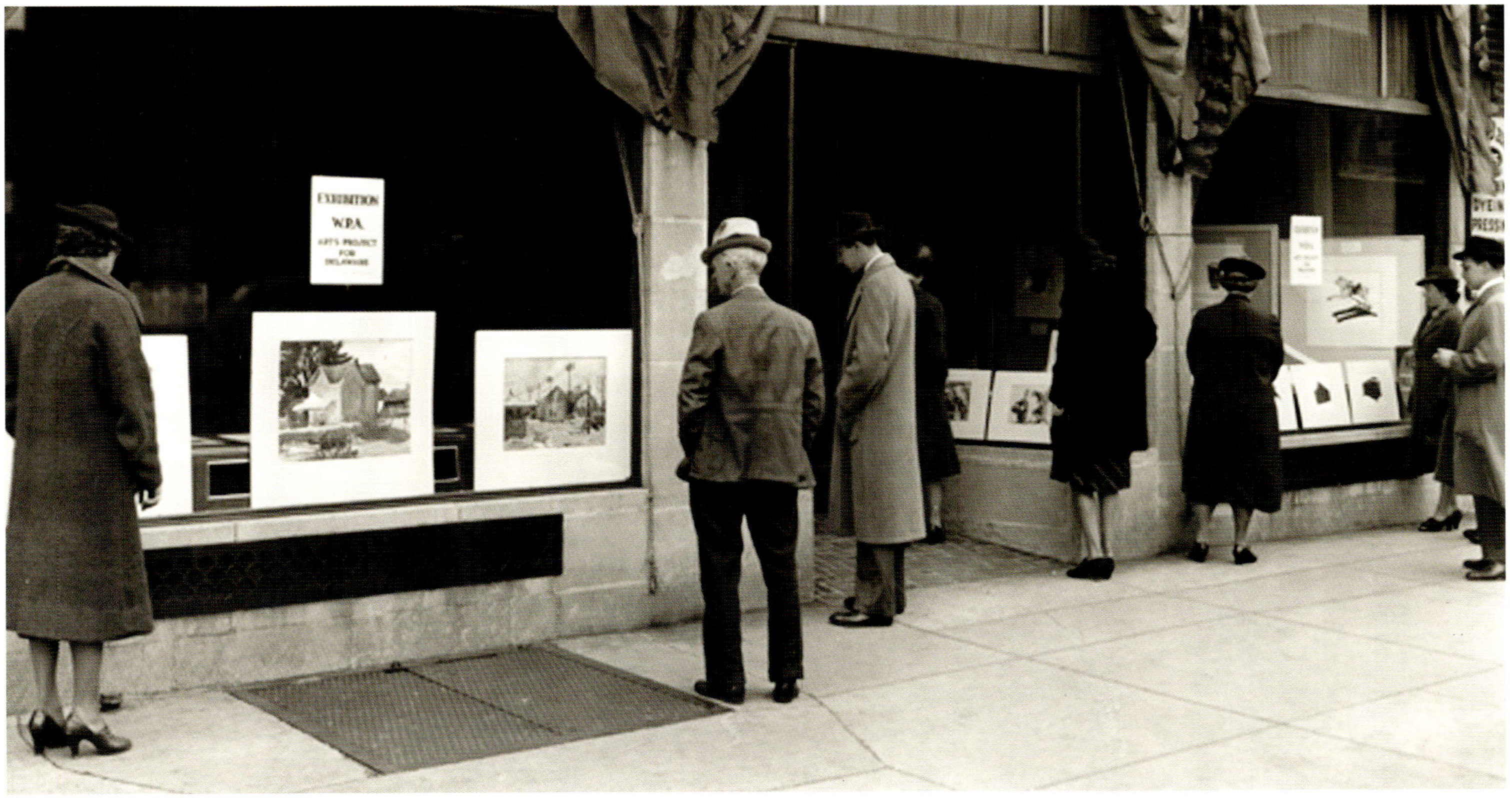

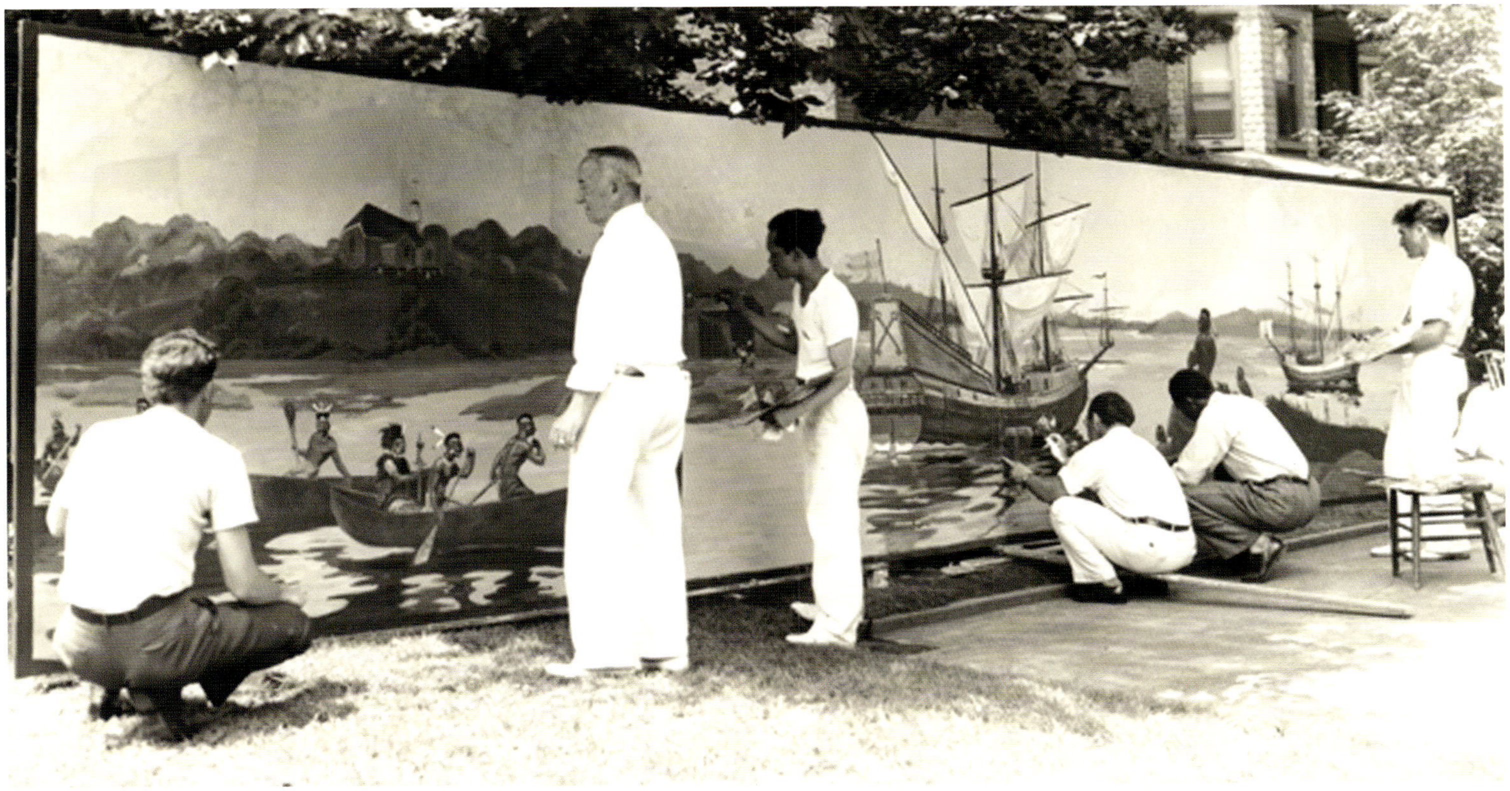

Street-front display of paintings in windows.
Exhibition of WPA/FAP arts project for Delaware
Willard Stewart

Bottom:
WPA/FAP painting in progress on "Mural to commemorate the 300th anniversary of the landing of the Swedes in 1638"
Willard Stewart

Willard Stewart was born in Wilmington, Delaware, and was the primary photographer for HABS and for the Delaware Federal Writers Project. Many of his images were published in *New Castle on the Delaware* and *Delaware: A Guide to the First State, 1651–1936.*

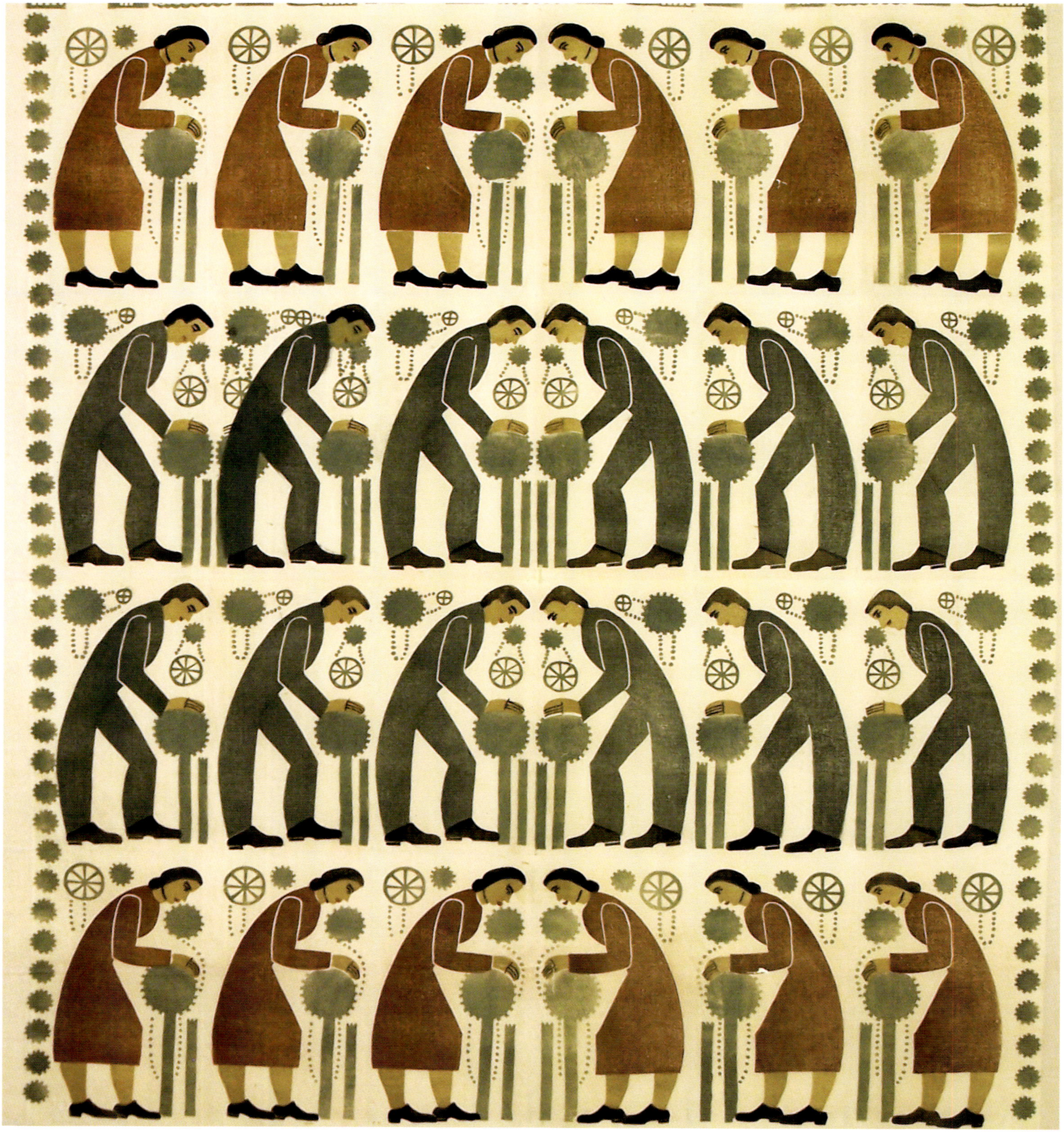

This page and opposite (detail):
Wall Hanging by WPA Handcraft Project, Milwaukee, Wisconsin
Florence Kawa, c. 1935

The Milwaukee Handcraft Project began in 1935 as an experiment, employing nine hundred workers who had been dismissed as unemployable because of age or disability. They produced rugs, draperies, furniture, wall hangings, and toys that were purchased by hospitals and schools. The wall hanging displayed here was given to Eleanor Roosevelt.

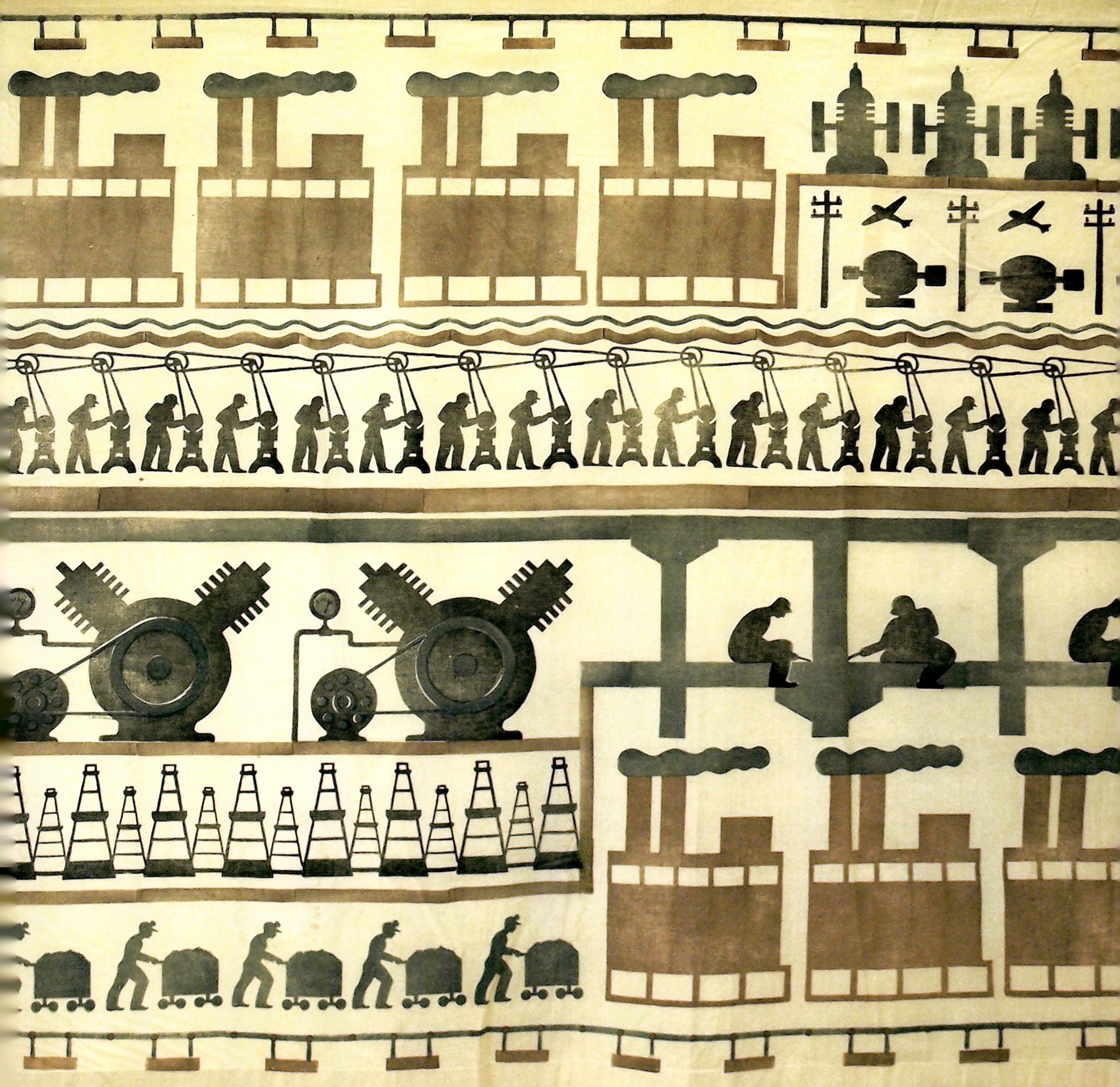

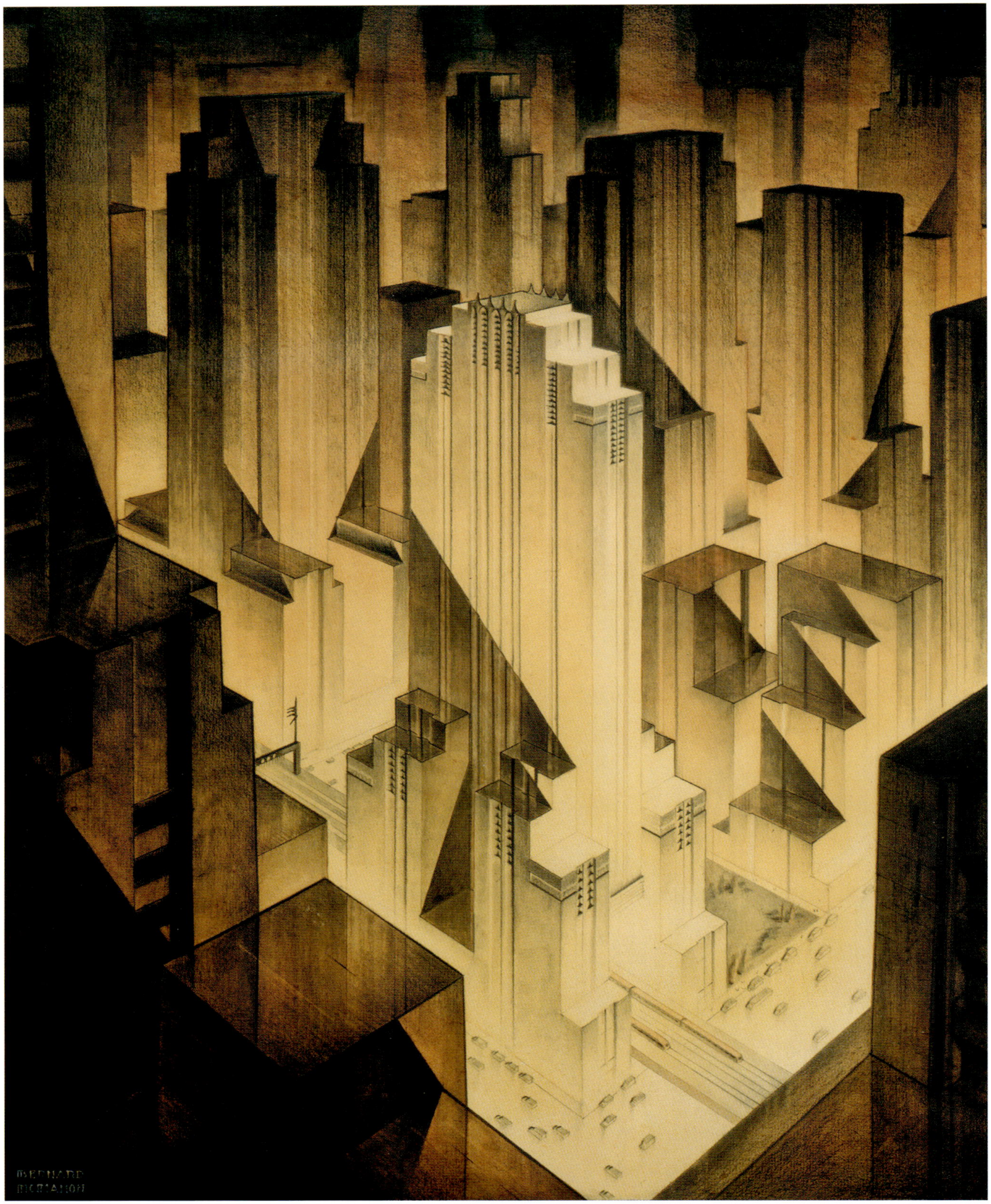

The Skyscraper
Bernard McMahon,
undated

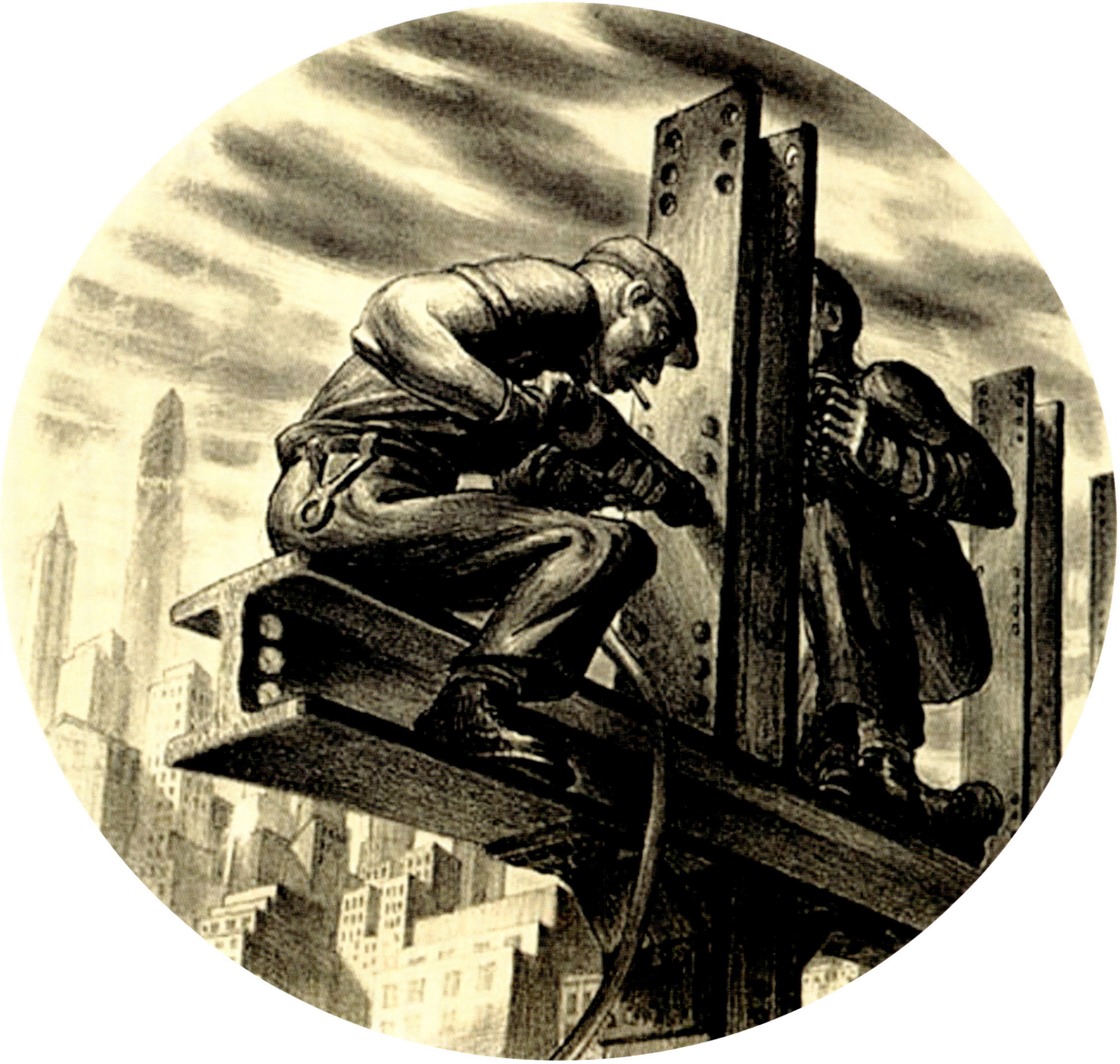

Builders
Harry Sternberg,
1935 or 1936
Lithograph

Harry Sternberg was born and grew up on the Lower East Side of Manhattan. He pioneered the artistic use of screenprinting and offset lithography, and was a leader of the American Artists' Congress and the FAP Graphics Division. He taught graphic arts at the Art Students League in New York.

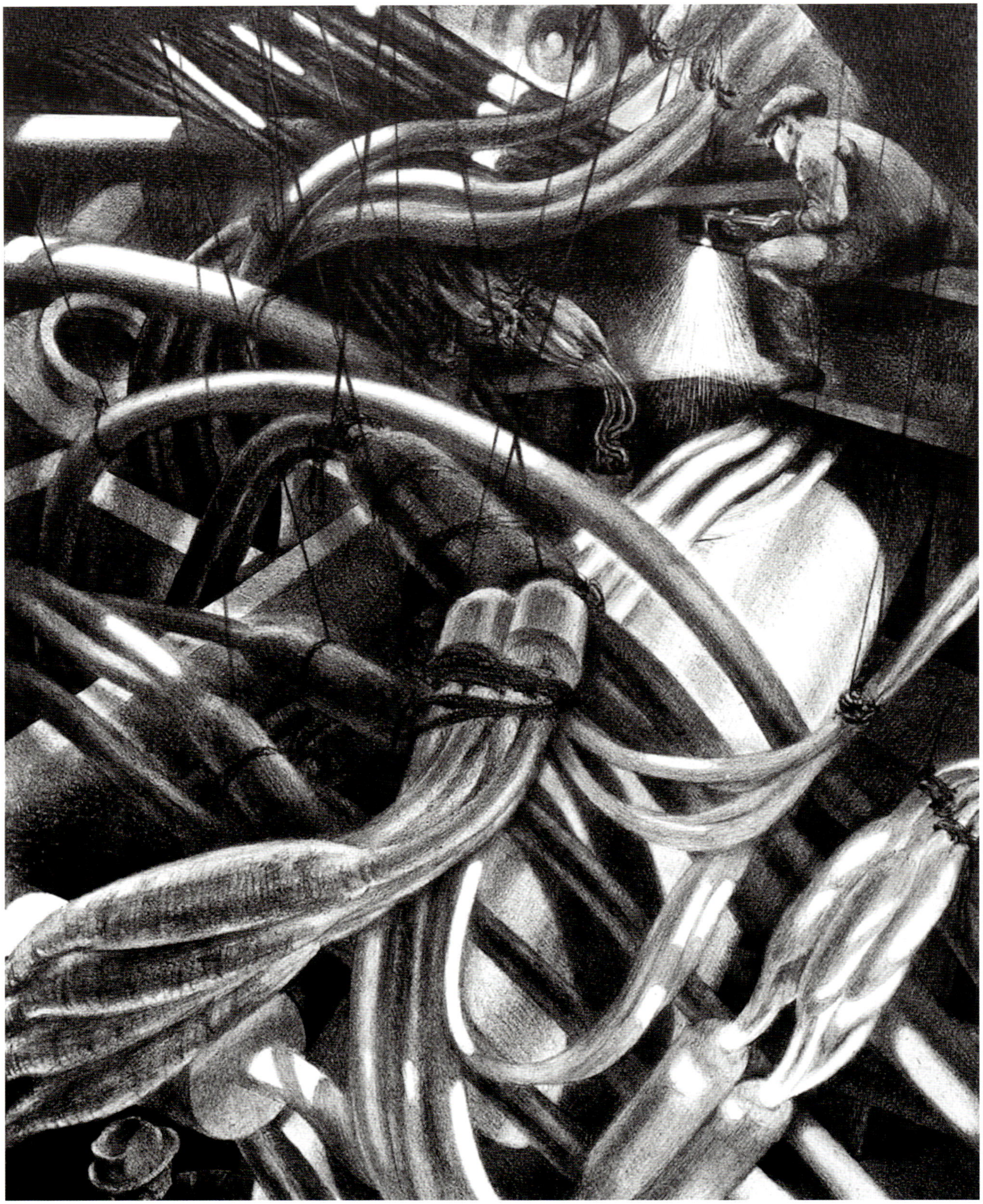

Guts of Manhattan
Louis Lozowick, 1939
Lithograph printed by
George Miller

Louis Lozowick was born in the Ukraine. He attended Kiev Art School before migrating to New York. He studied at the National Academy of Design and at Ohio State University before traveling for five years through Europe. He manipulated the ganglia of construction and utility cables seen through scaffolding during the construction of subway lines.

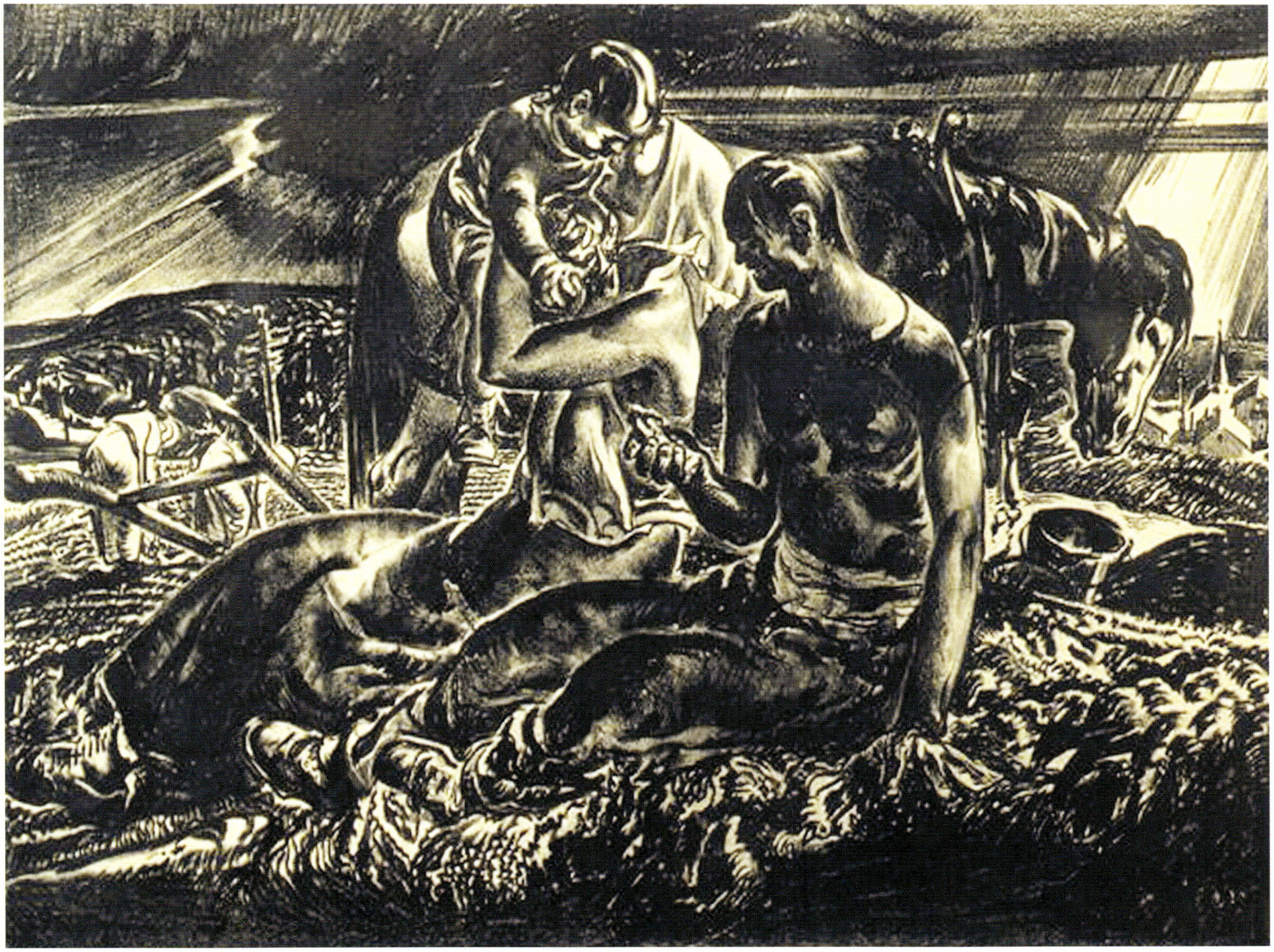

Workers in the Field
John Costigan, 1934
Lithograph on paper

John Costigan was born in Providence, Rhode Island, and was raised in New York by his aunt and uncle, the parents of George M. Cohan. He made theater posters and other prints for a lithography company for twenty-two years, and he worked as a magazine illustrator, landscapist, and figure painter, saying that he disdained portraits because the subjects wanted flattering pictures. He served in the infantry in World War I and supported himself during the Depression with magazine illustration. During World War II he was a machine operator in a defense plant. In the late 1960s, the Smithsonian Institution sponsored a Costigan retrospective that toured nationally.

Right:
Man With Load
(or *The Toiler*)
Robert Blackburn, 1936
Charcoal, ink, and graphite

Robert Blackburn was born in the British West Indies, moved to New York at the age of thirteen, and participated in the Harlem Arts Workshop, the Uptown Art Laboratory, and the Harlem arts salon known as "306." He studied lithography at the WPA-sponsored Harlem Community Art Center and came to be associated with a group of artists including Jacob Lawrence, Romare Bearden, Ernest Crichlow, and Roy DeCarava. He worked in the mural section of the WPA and was a representative of the Harlem Artists' Guild to the New York World's Fair. He became a teacher and a widely celebrated printmaker. The worker bearing a burden appears in other works in this book and frequently in the works of the Mexican muralists.

Far right:
Workers of the World, Unite!
Rockwell Kent, 1937
Wood engraving
(see main text)

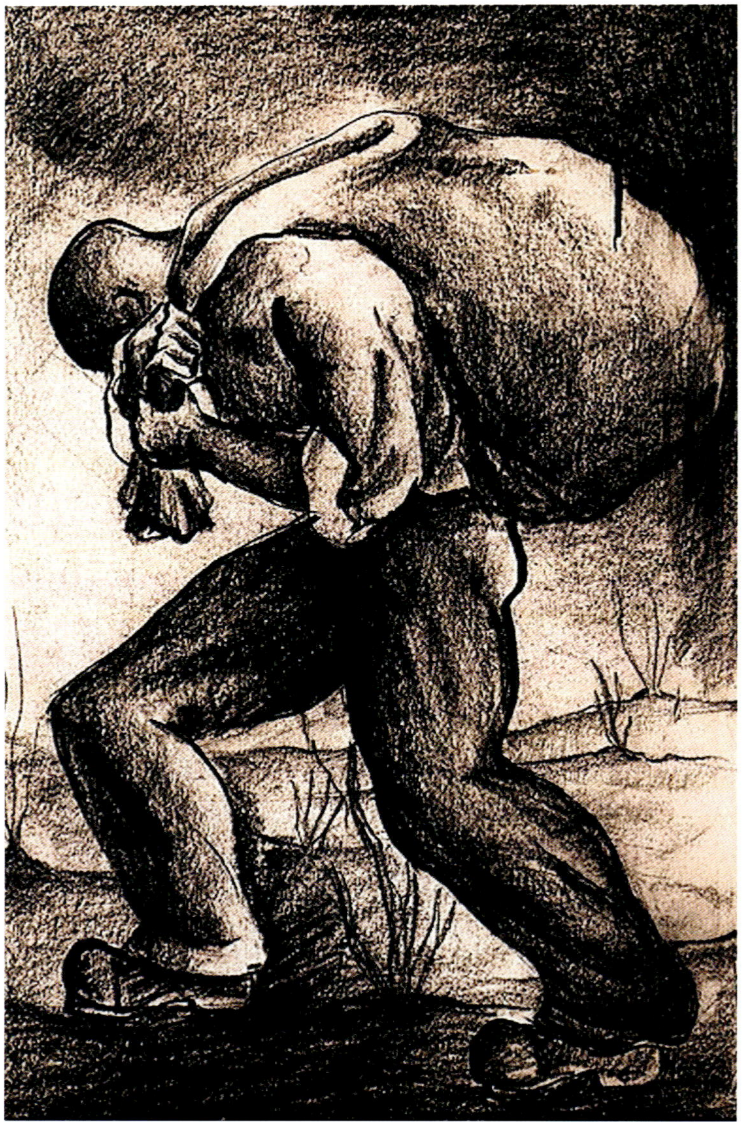

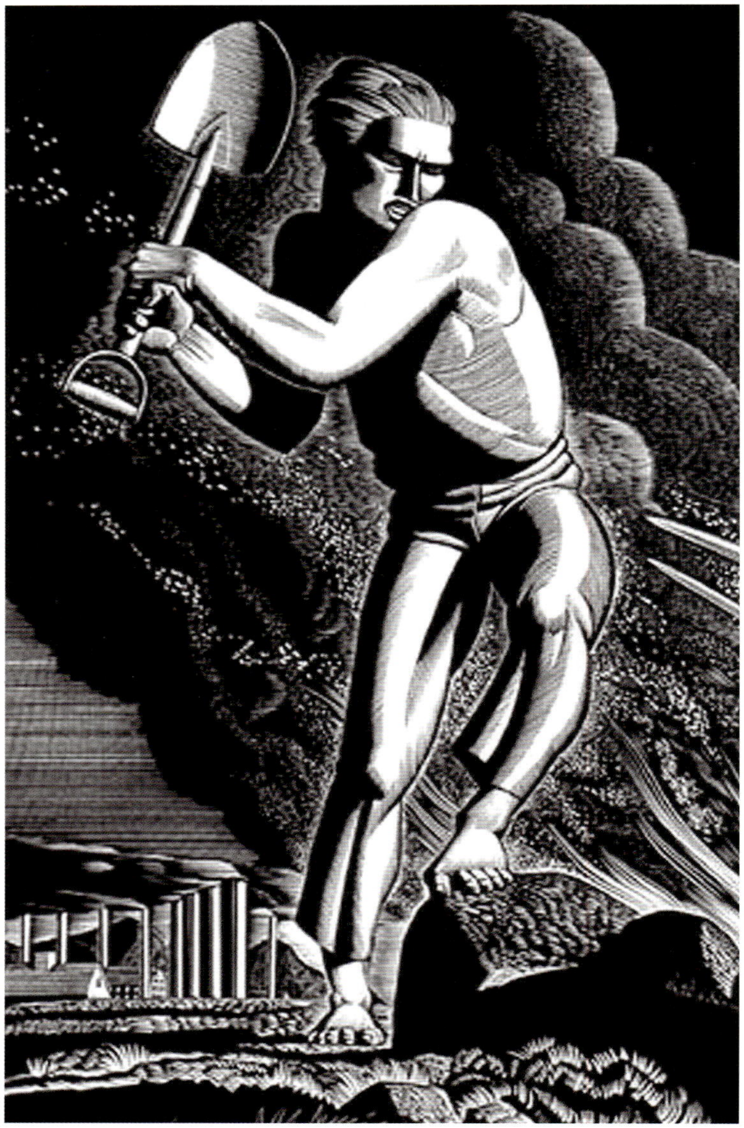

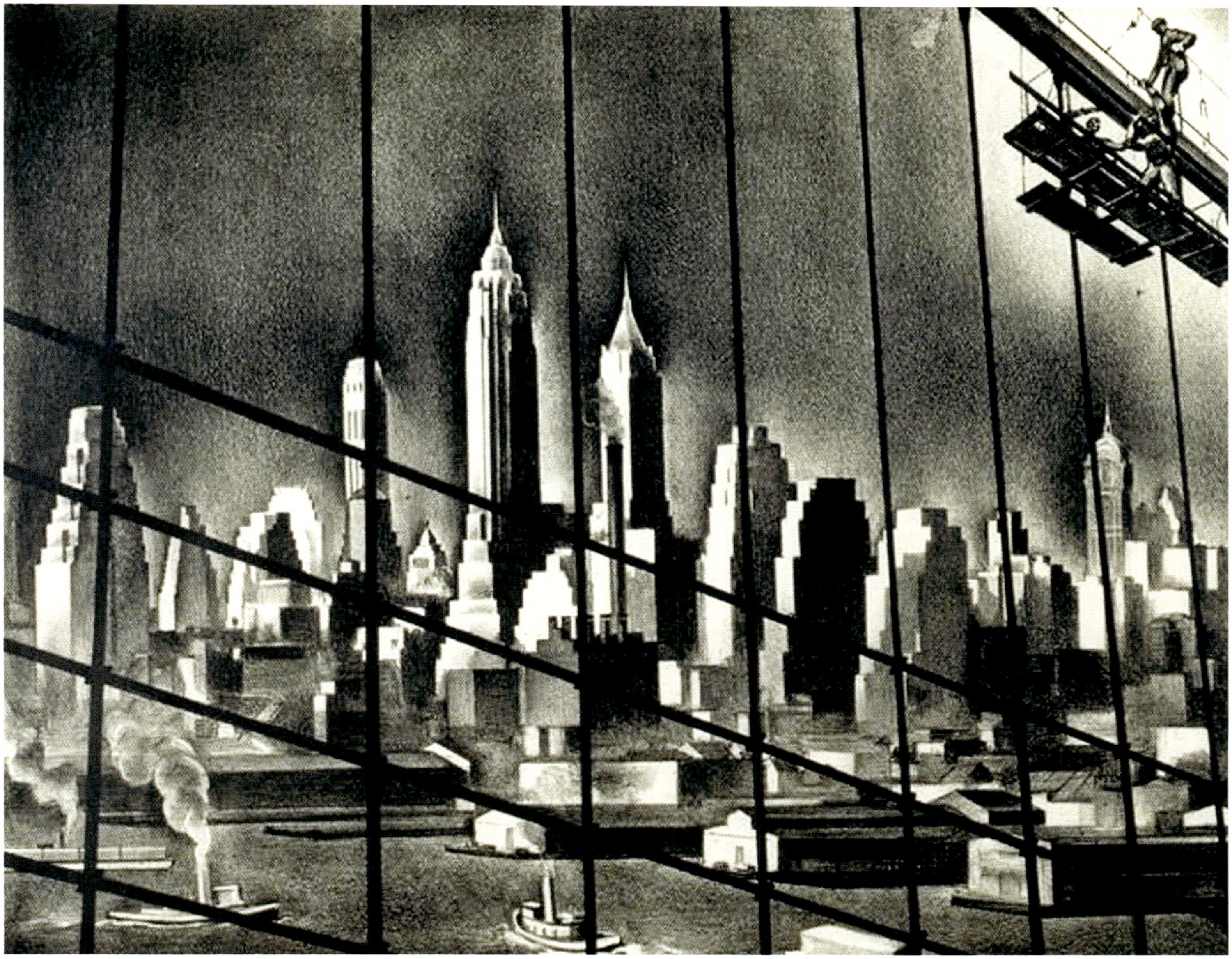

Bridge Repair
Louis Lozowick, 1938
Lithograph on paper

Lozowick worked as an illustrator for magazines and for the WPA/FAP graphics and murals programs. He was aligned with the Russian Constructivist Movement, which used Industrial Age materials to create abstractions, and was best known for his lithographs of skyscrapers.

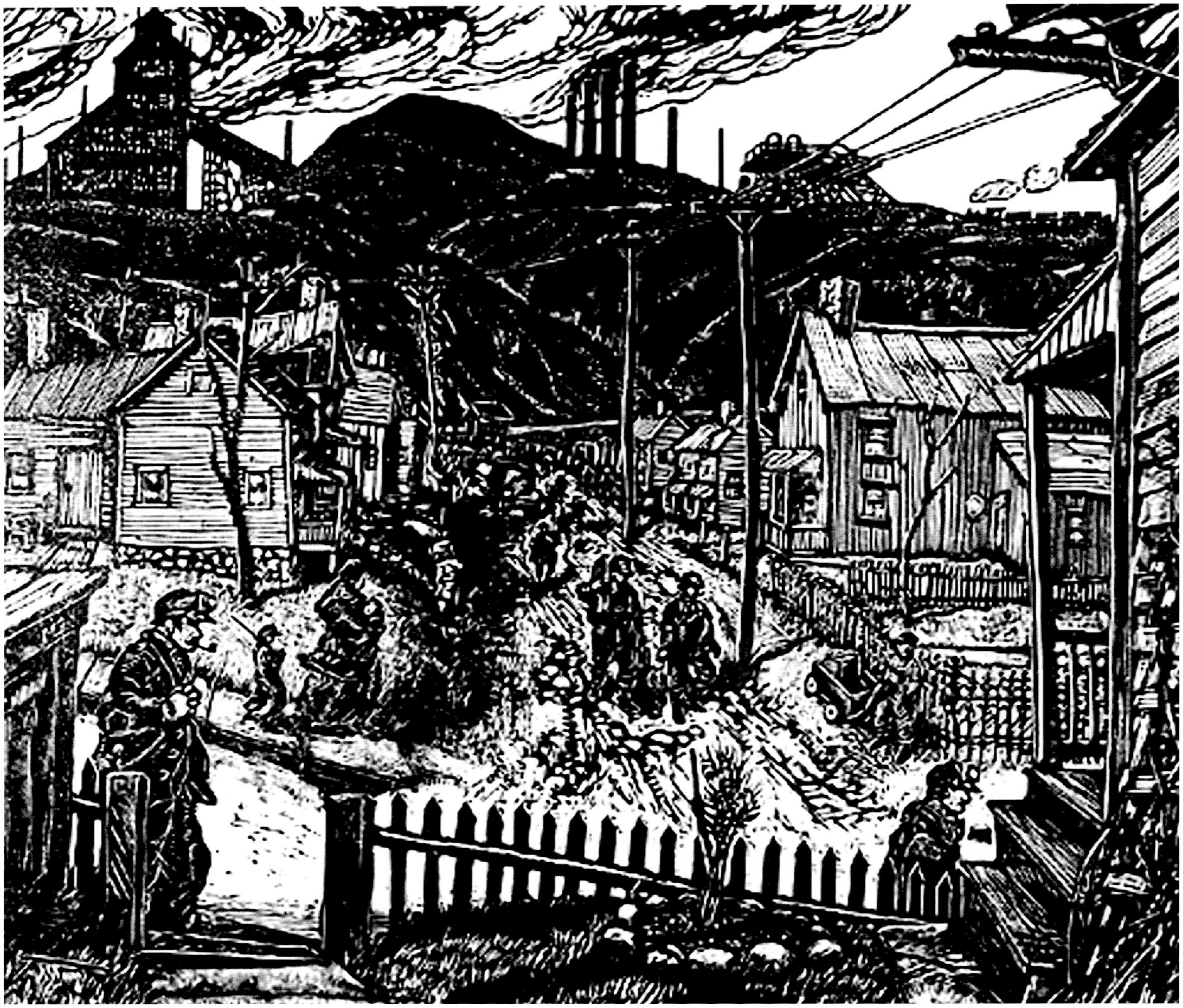

Black Country
Michael Gallagher, 1941
Wood engraving
on paper

Michael Gallagher was co-inventor of the carborundum mezzotint technique. He supervised the Pennsylvania WPA/FAP Graphics Workshop in Philadelphia from 1935 to 1941.

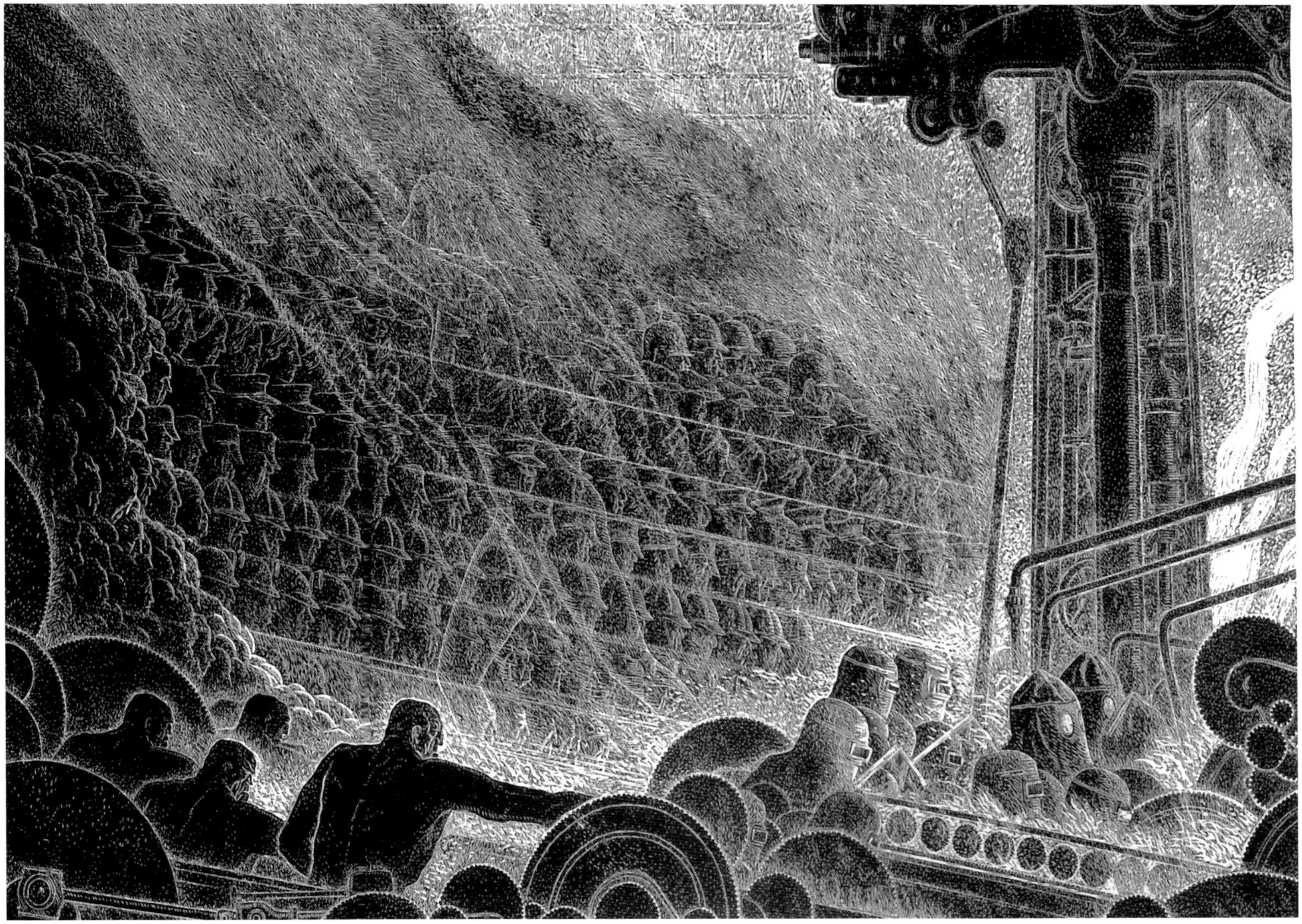

Machine Fodder
Carl Hoeckner, 1940

Carl Hoeckner was a painter, lithographer, landscapist, muralist, and teacher, best known for his "social documents" indicting war and injustice.

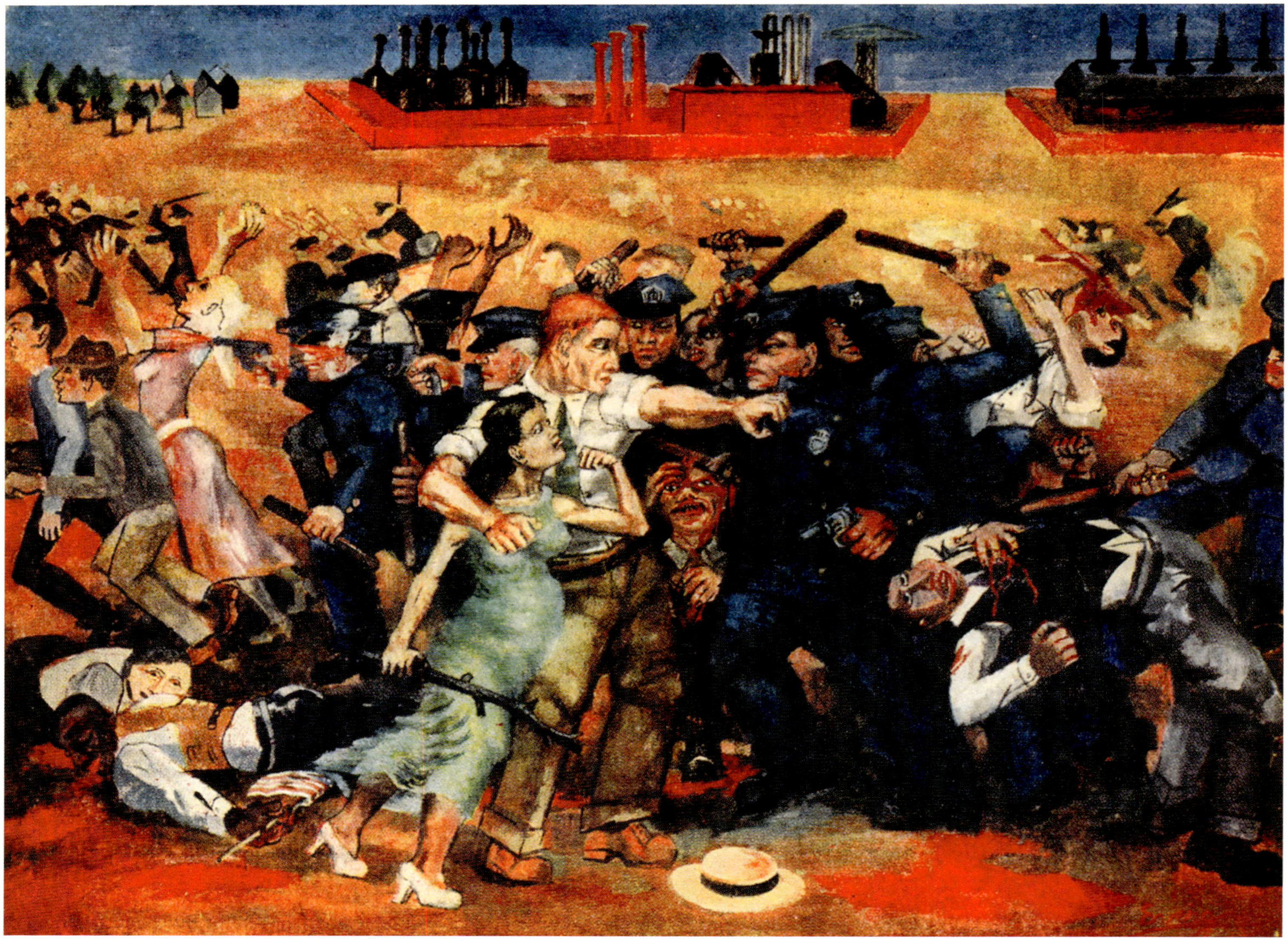

American Tragedy
Philip Evergood, 1937

American Tragedy depicts the 1937 Memorial Day Riot at Republic Steel's South Chicago plant. A worker and his pregnant wife in their best clothing are about to be attacked by the police.

Philip Evergood settled in New York and was the managing supervisor of the New York easel-painting division of the WPA/FAP in 1938, where he made certain that easel painters received their "check of $24 a week . . . and they were given complete freedom of expression." "They brought in paintings of people in the park, or workers on the wharves, or anything that struck their fancy; even a still life, or a cat sitting in a window. I mean anything that they felt that they could express themselves well with as artists." His job was also to see that "they brought a canvas in that was respectably done and craftsmanlike and not just any old sloppy thing. In other words, that they were taking it seriously." He joined the American Artists' Congress and served as president of the Artists Union. His mural, *The Story of Richmond Hill*, completed in 1937 for a public library in Queens, New York, has content as tough as *American Tragedy*.

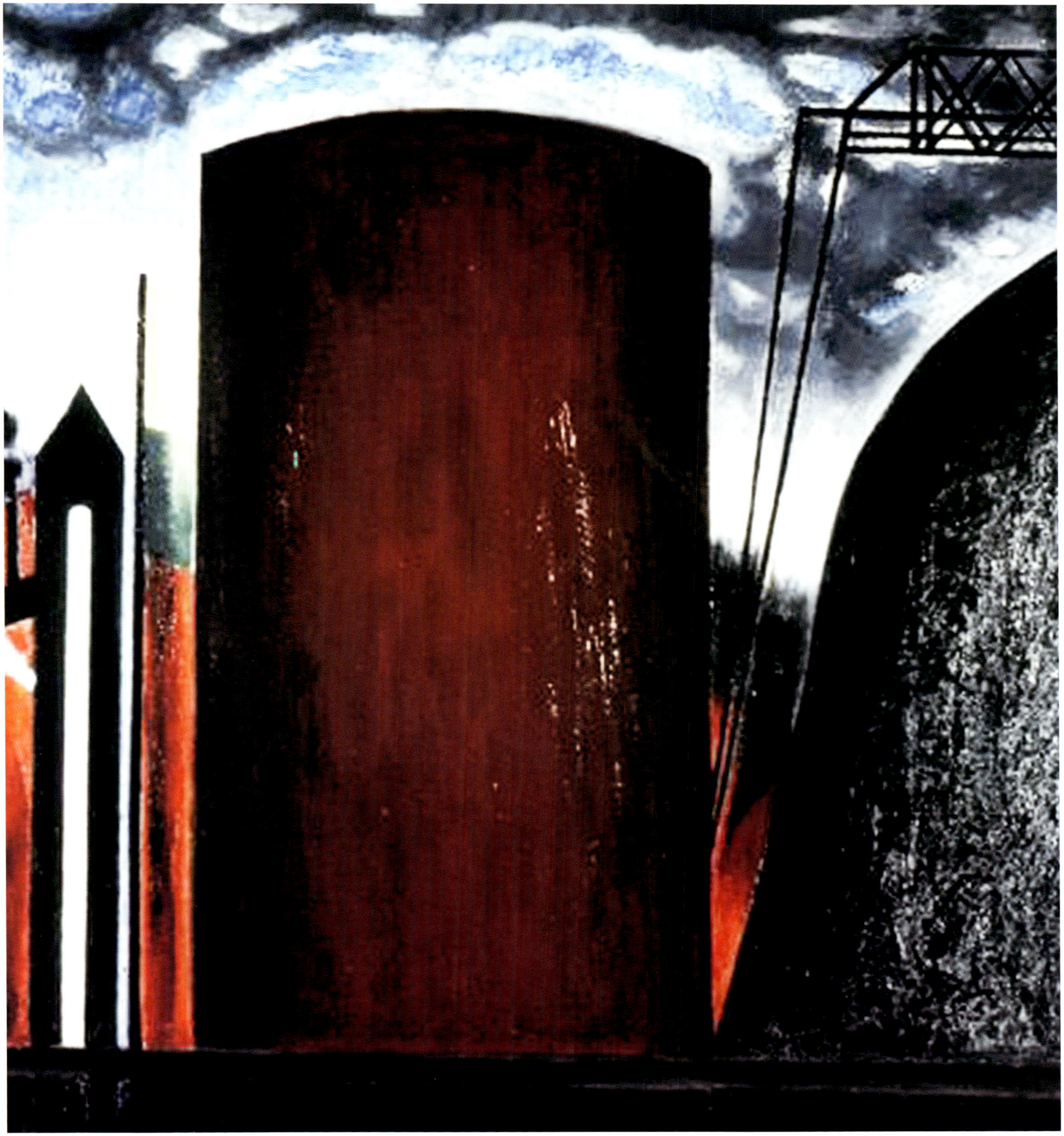

Smoke Stack
Joseph Stella, c. 1935

Joseph Stella was born in Italy and immigrated to New York at the age of nineteen. He studied medicine, but became an illustrator after attending the Art Students League in New York. He studied for three years in Europe, was shown at the 1913 Armory Show, traveled in Europe again from 1927 to 1934, and worked for the New York City WPA/FAP easel program.
"I was greatly impressed by Pittsburgh. It was a real revelation. Often shrouded by fog and smoke, her black mysterious mass—cut in the middle by the fantastic tortuous Allegheny River and like a battlefield, ever pulsating, throbbing with the innumerable explosions of its steel mills—was like the stunning realization of some of the most stirring infernal regions sung by Dante." He went to Pittsburgh in 1908 on an assignment to "draw steel mill workers and miners" for The Survey (1909–14).

American Scene
Oscar Weissbuch, 1939
Wood Engraving on paper

Oscar Weissbuch, known for his figurative work and for townscapes, worked for the New York WPA/FAP graphics program.

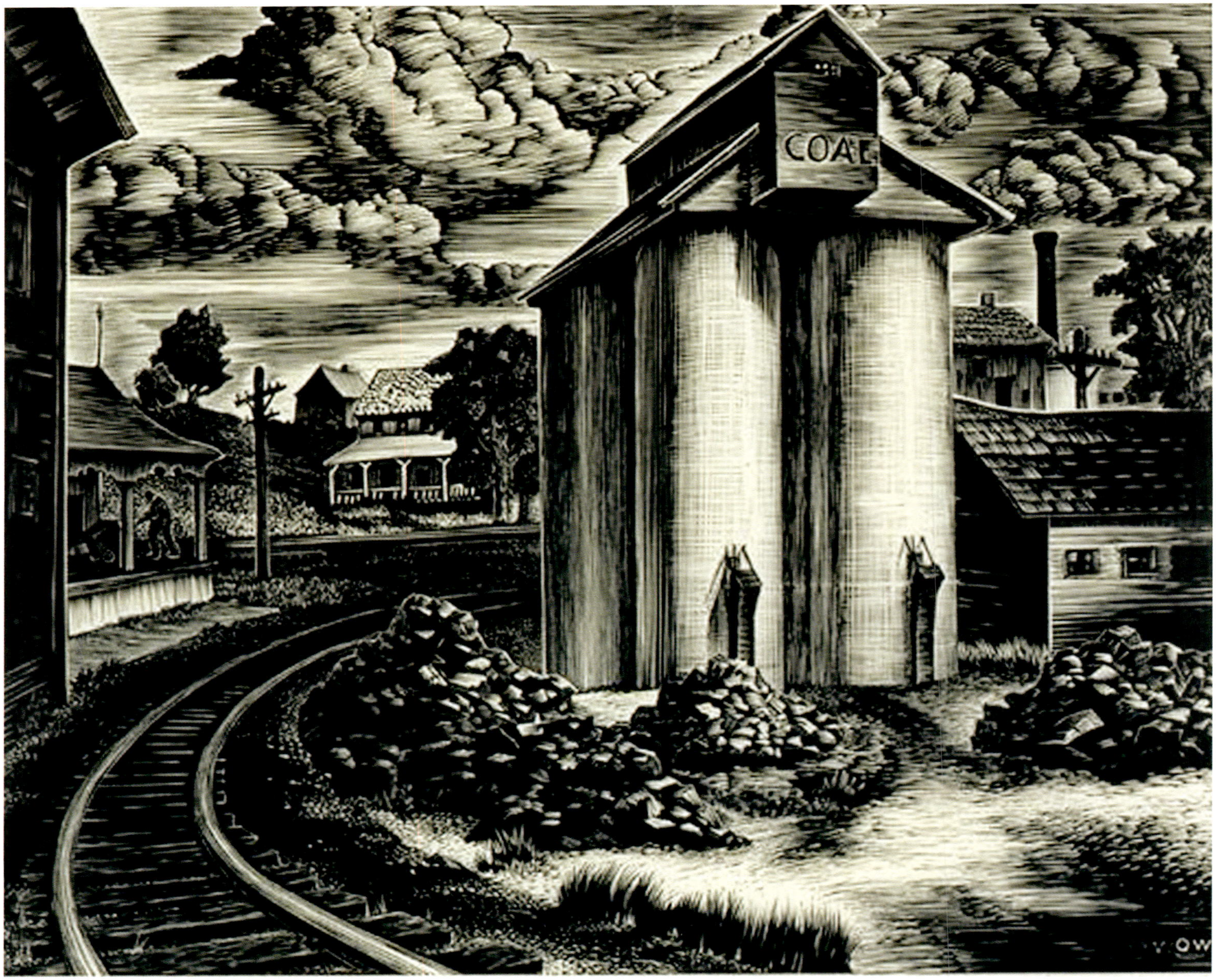

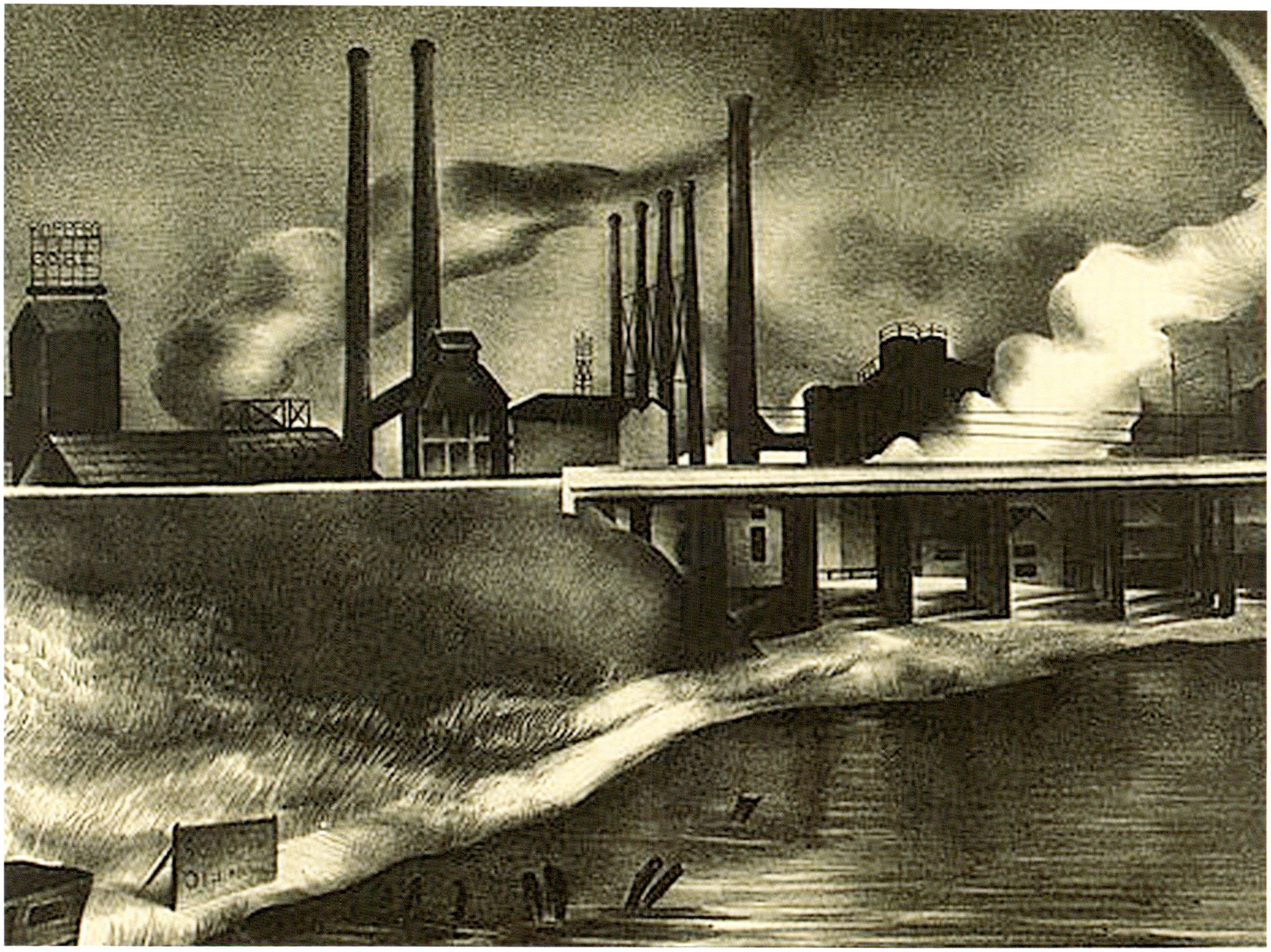

Koppers Coke
Victoria Hutson Huntley,
1932
Lithograph

Victoria Hutson Huntley won first prize at the 1933 Philadelphia Print Club's National Exhibition for *Koppers Coke*, of which she said: "I worked a week just on the sky of Kopper's (sic) Coke and that included nights as well . . . Sometimes I spend days on a relatively small area—putting tone on tone in order to arrive at the richness of value and texture which I find necessary."

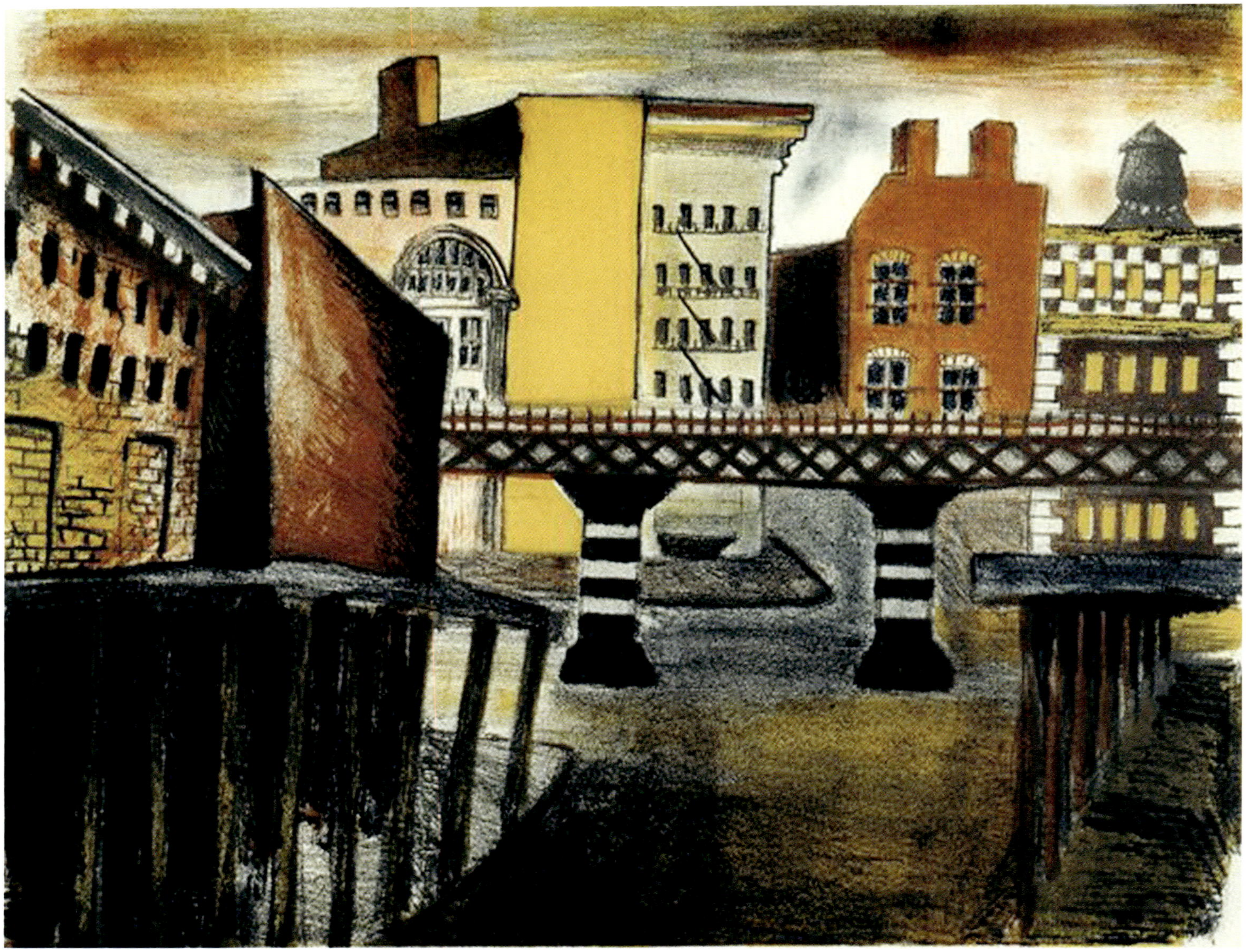

Near Wallabout Market
Ida York Abelman, 1937
Lithograph

Ida York Abelman studied at the National Academy of Design and the Design Laboratory in New York. Her work was collected by the Federal Art Gallery, the Whitney Museum of American Art, the Museum of Modern Art, the Philadelphia Art Museum, and the Corcoran Gallery. Though often said to be a "Social Realist," she incorporated in her designs abstract elements and symbols, often derived from machines. She was a member of the American Artists Congress and produced lithographs for the WPA/FAP.

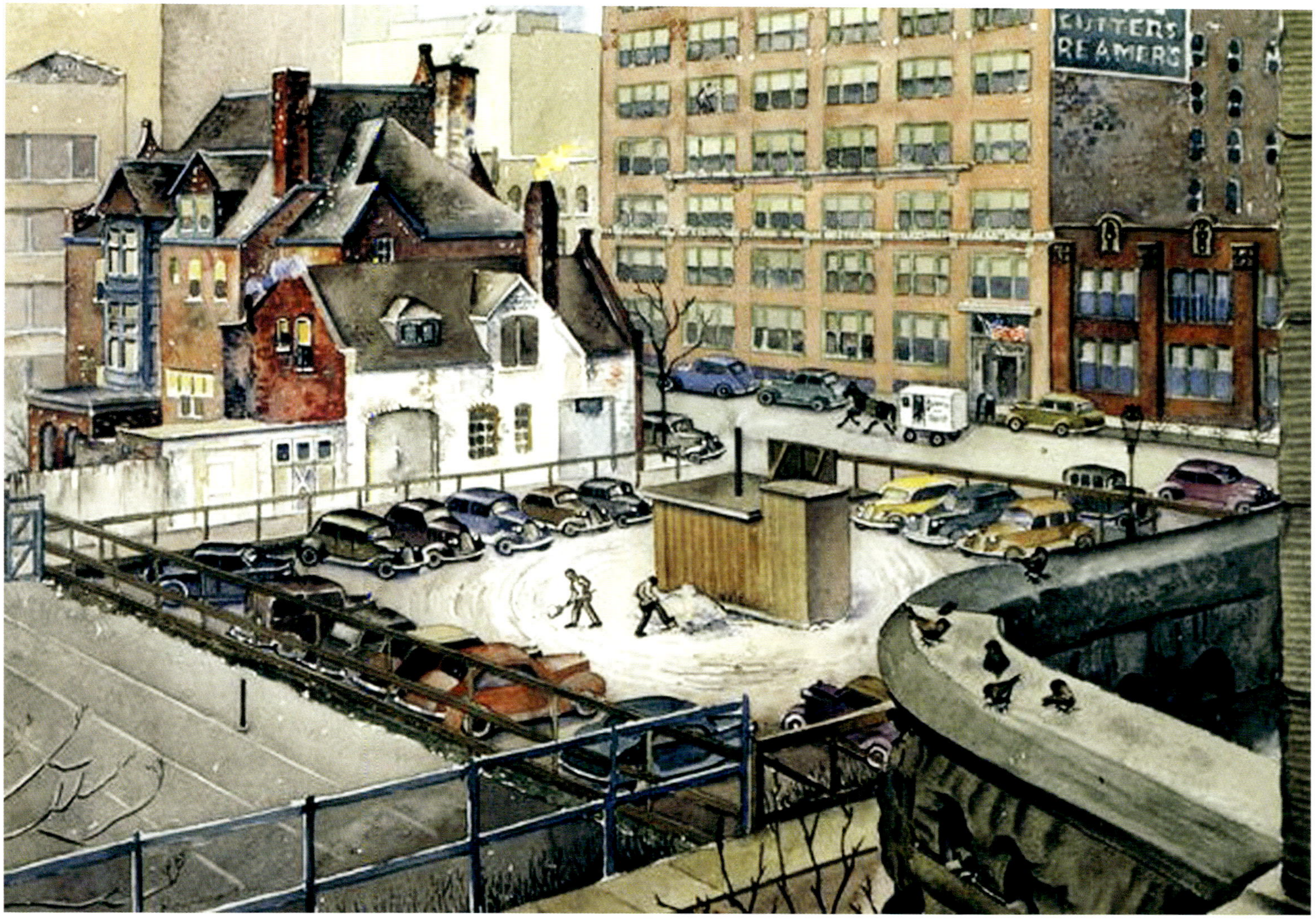

The Parking Lot
Rowena Fry, c. 1939
Watercolor on paper

Rowena Fry was born in Alabama and received her art training at the Watkins Institute in Nashville, Tennessee, The Art Institute of Chicago, and the Hubert Ropp School of Art in Chicago. She worked in oil, watercolor, and printmaking. In 1938–39, she created murals and paintings for the WPA/FAP.

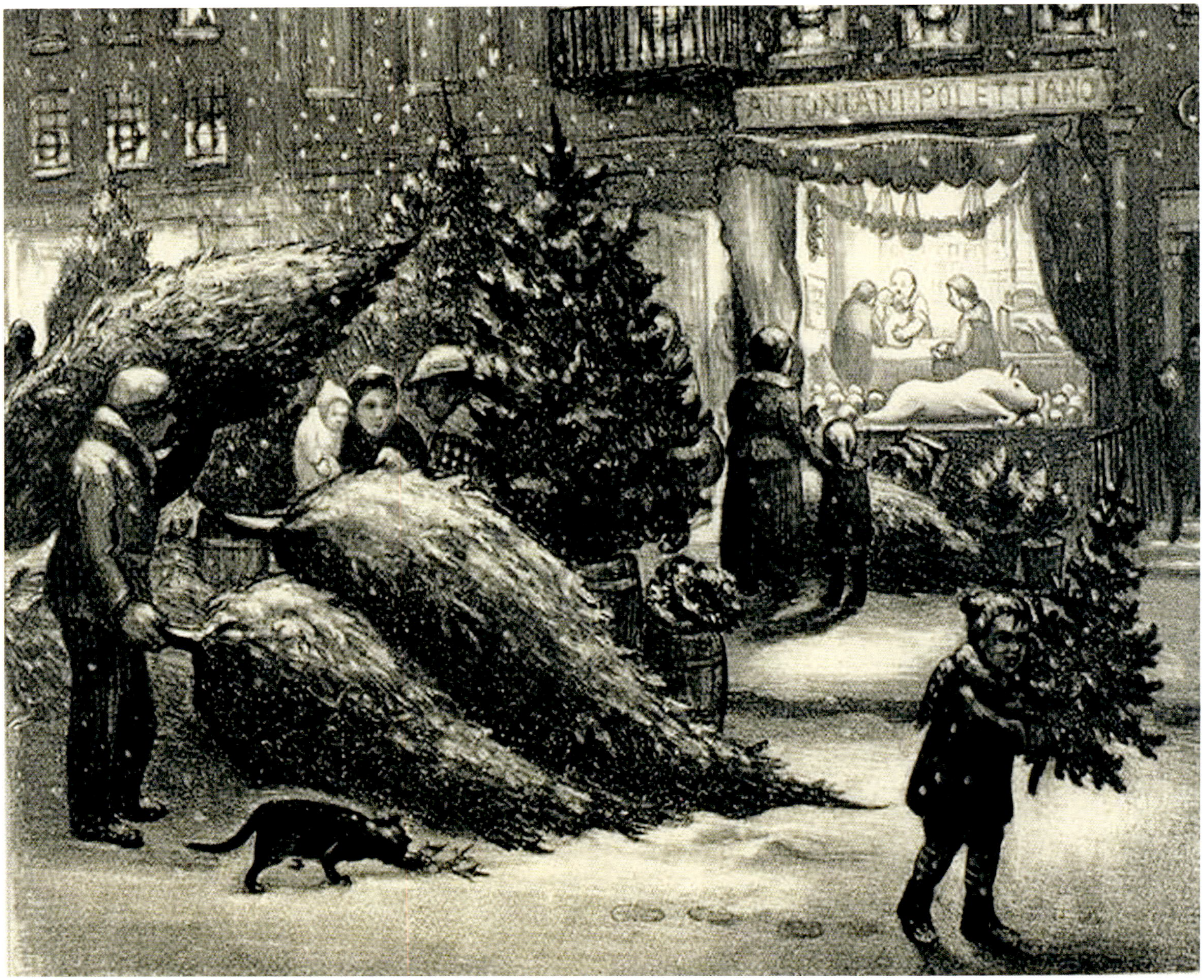

Christmas Trees
Mabel Dwight, c. 1935
Lithograph

Mabel Dwight studied art at the Hopkins Art School in San Francisco and later settled in Greenwich Village. She worked for the New York WPA/FAP between 1935 and 1939. Dwight went to Paris and discovered the medium of lithography. After a short marriage to Eugene Higgins, she changed her name to Dwight, a name she apparently made up for herself (see main text).

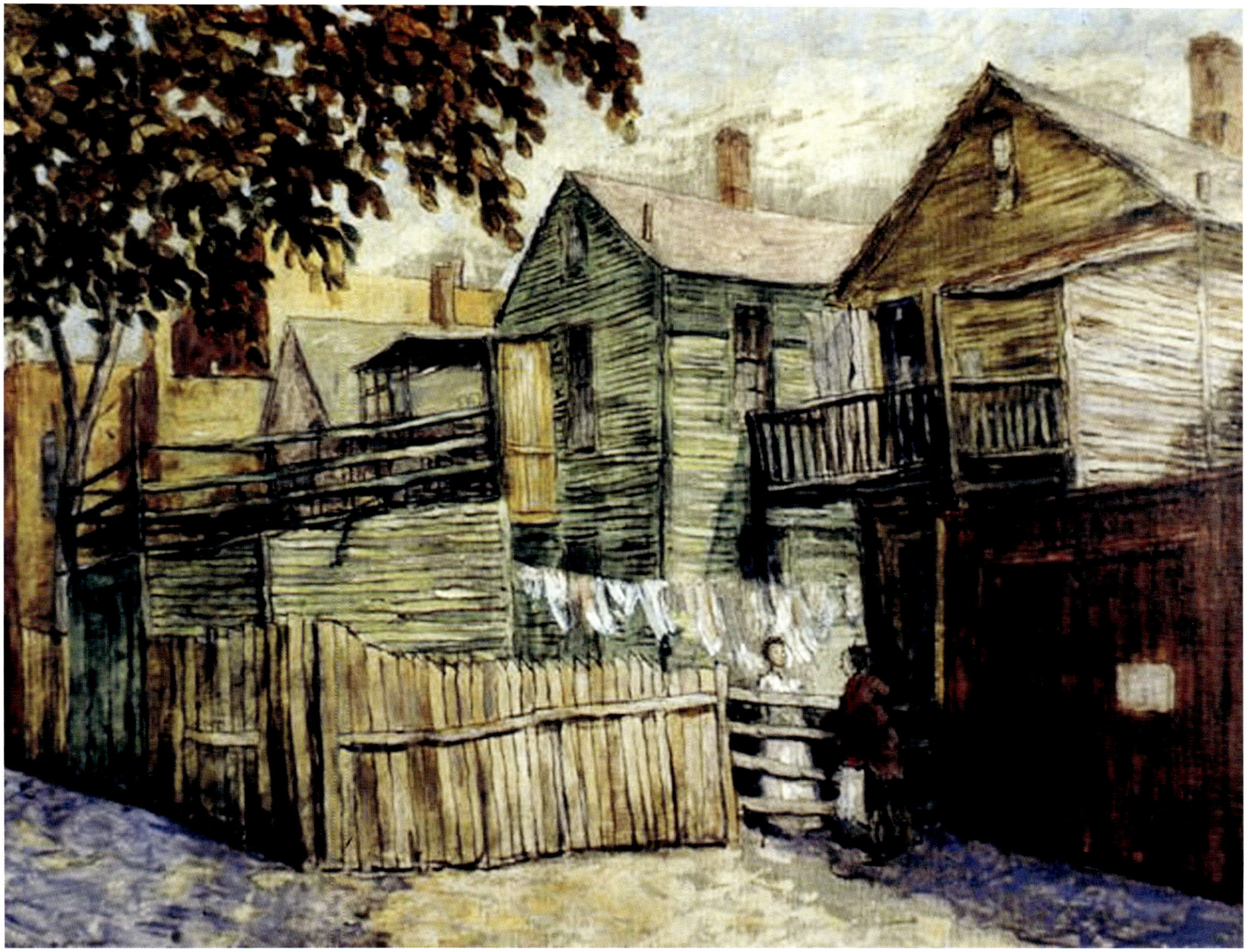

South of Diversey
Marshall Smith, 1937
Oil on canvas

Marshall Smith was a native of Prairie du Chien, Wisconsin. He worked for the Illinois WPA/FAP easel program in Chicago.

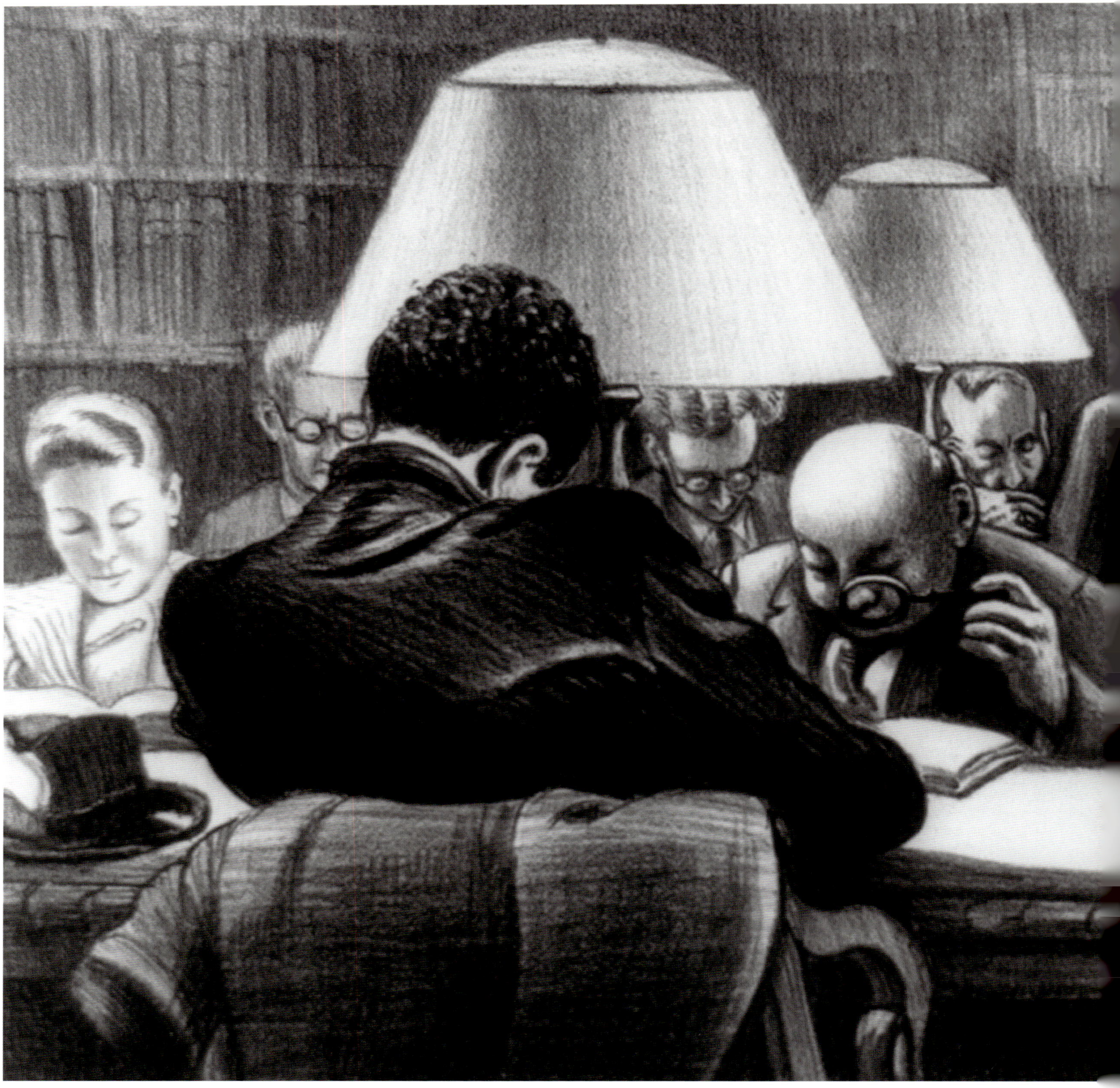

Silence
Mabel Dwight, 1938
Lithograph
(see also page 180)

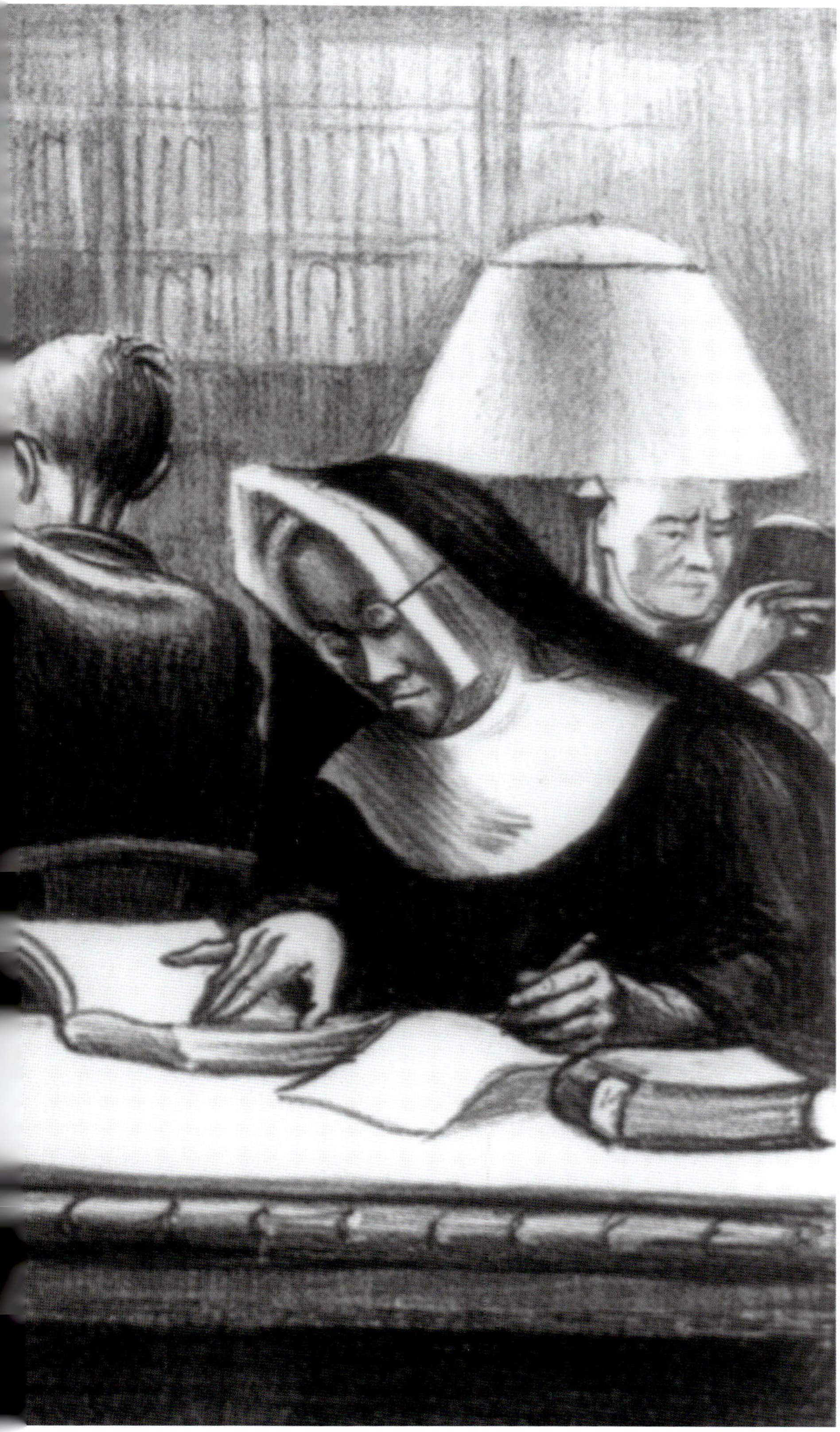

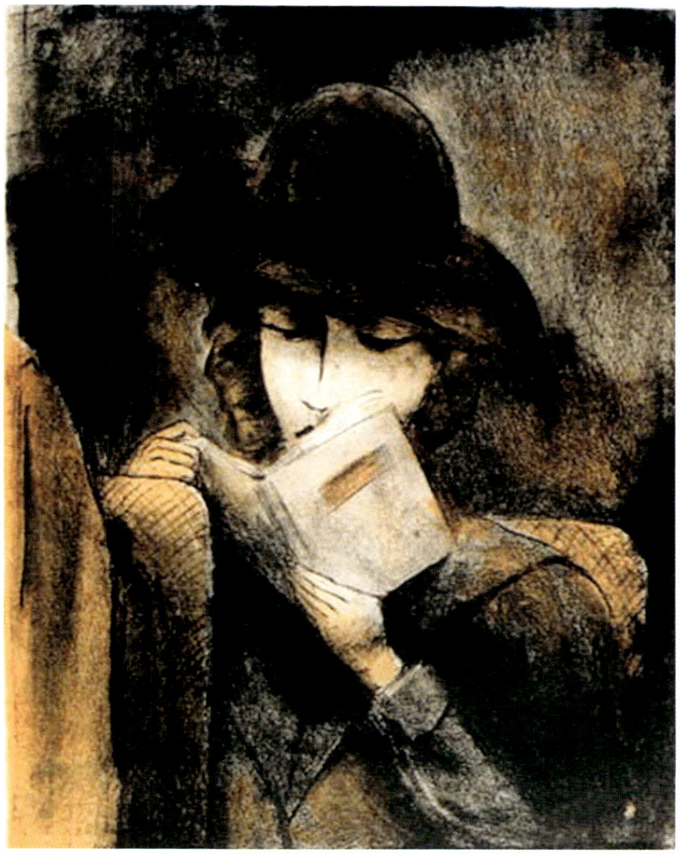

Girl Reading
Isadore Weiner, 1938
Lithograph

Isadore Weiner was born in Chicago and studied at the Art Institute. He worked for the Illinois WPA/FAP graphics program, taught art at Hull House, and exhibited in Chicago.

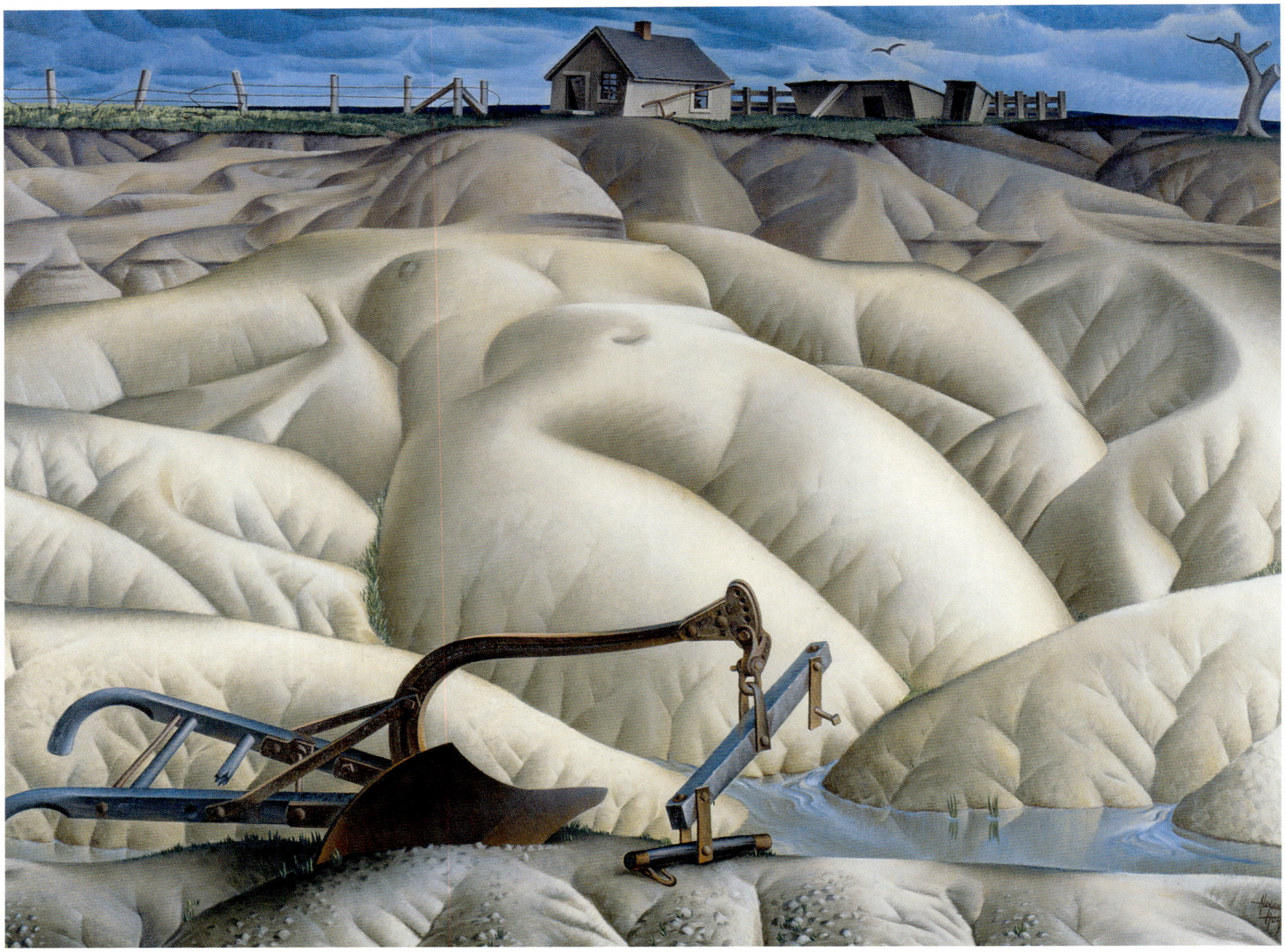

Erosion No. 2-Mother Earth Laid Bare
Alexandre Hogue, 1936
Oil on canvas

Like most of the other works in Alexandre Hogue's Erosion series, *Mother Earth Laid Bare* has a traditional tripartite structure: a sharply observed foreground; a deep, spatially ambiguous middle ground (in this instance, eroded earth); and, at the horizon, a narrow strip of land upon which are silhouetted shambling farm buildings. In each picture there is a prominent mechanical means of sod-busting, usually a tractor or plow. In *Mother Earth Laid Bare*, the cutting edges of the plow threaten the land, which has the shape of a supine, defenseless female figure. Hogue reported later that he saw such a scene near Dallas, where ravaged beds of white clay lay exposed after erosion washed away the plowed topsoil.

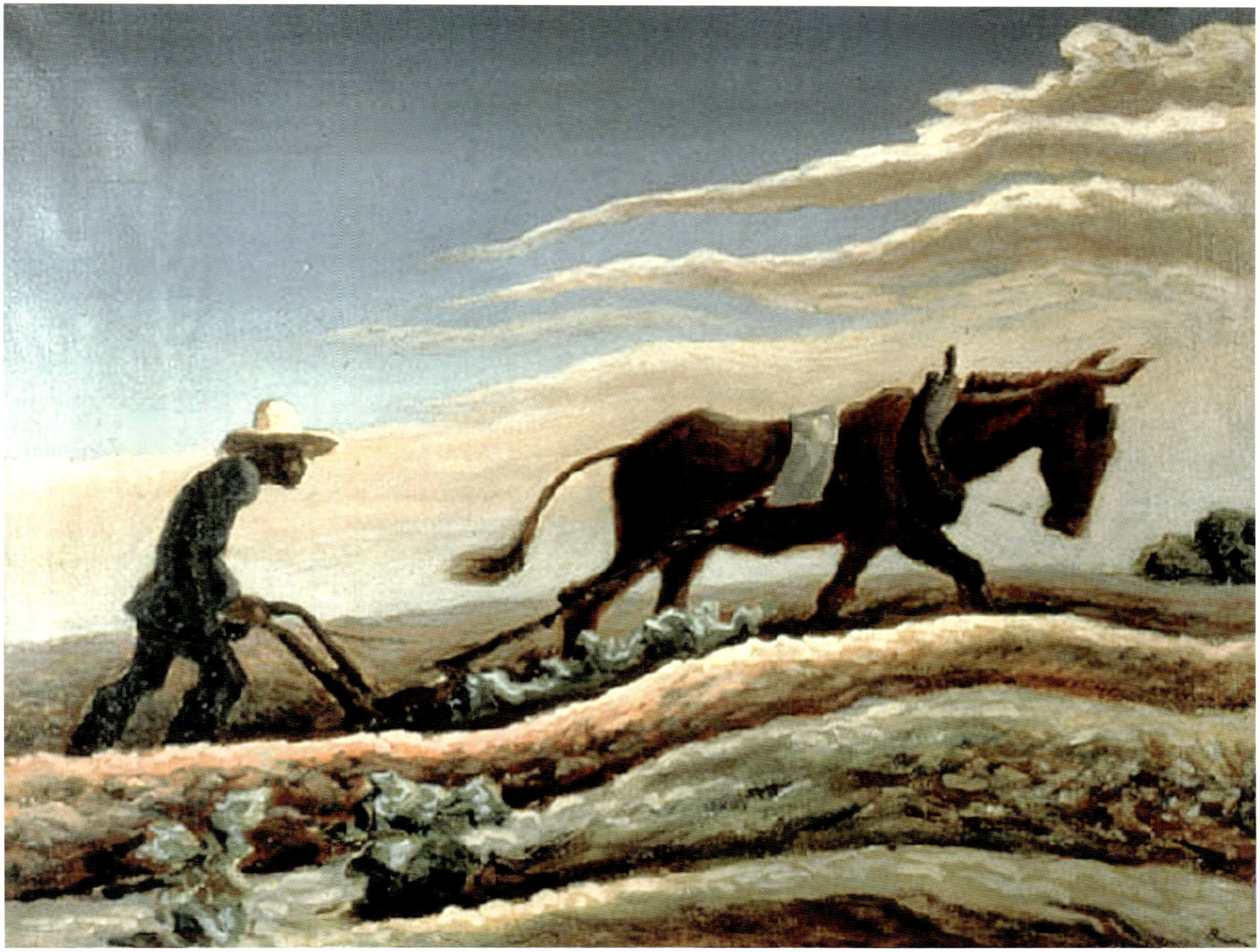

Plowing It Under
Thomas Hart Benton, 1934
Oil on linen
(see main text)

Thomas Hart Benton was born in Neosho, Missouri, studied at the Art Institute of Chicago, went to Paris, studied at the Academie Julian, and began using color for mood rather than verisimilitude, in the "Synchronist" mode. After returning to the United States, he participated in the Forum Exhibition in 1916. He broke with modernism and with the avant-garde in the early 1920s, and adopted an approach that he, and others, called "Regionalism." His murals of the early 1930s included a panorama for the New School for Social Research in New York City. He taught at the Art Students League in New York and privately tutored Jackson Pollock, among others. Though he accepted government commissions, he was able to support himself with private work. In 1935 he became the director of the City Art Institute and School of Design in Kansas City, Missouri, where he lived for the rest of his life. He worked in both mural and easel forms and wrote many articles on art as well as two autobiographies.

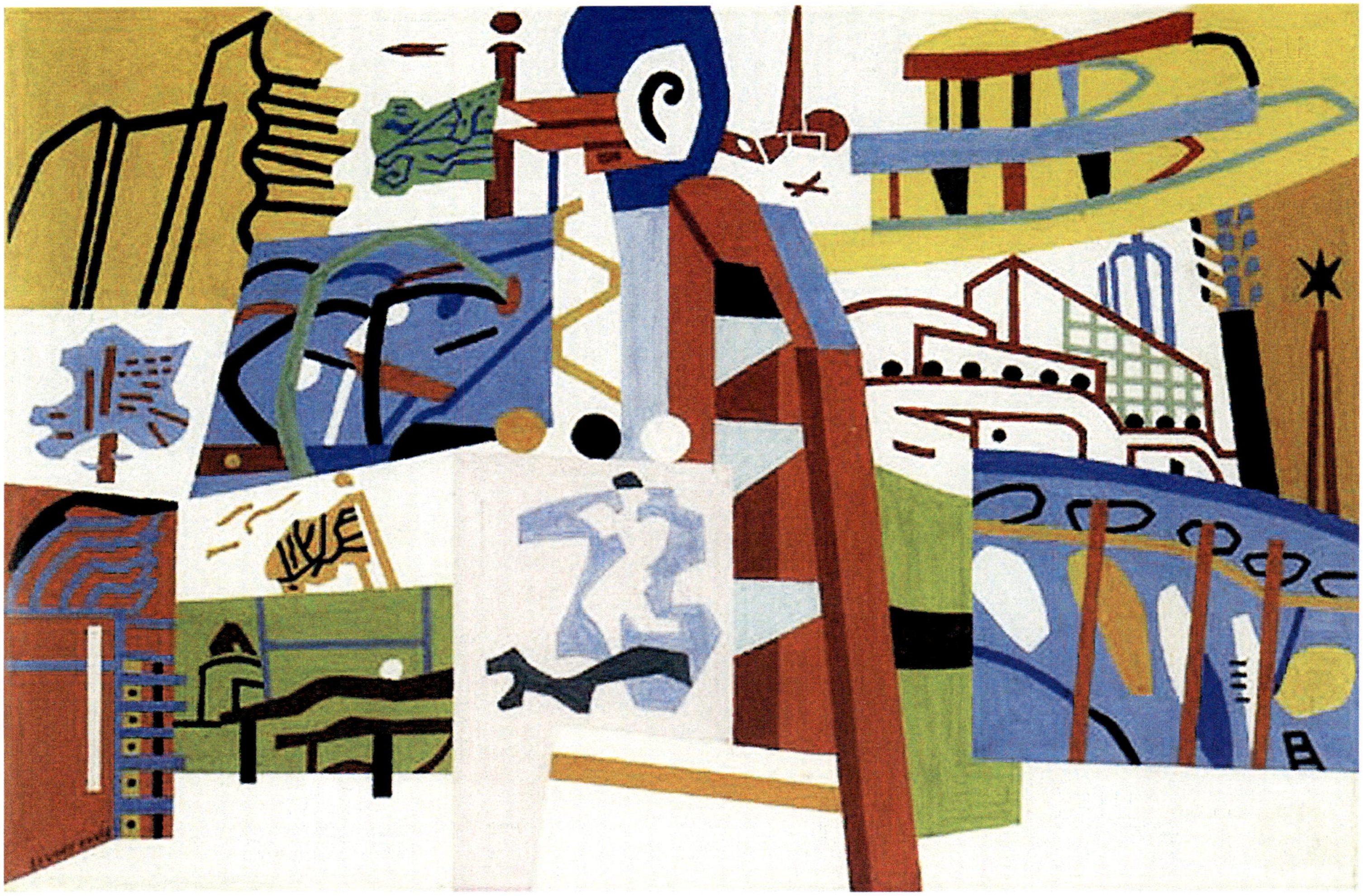

Impression of the New York World's Fair
(Mural study, Communications Building, World's Fair, Flushing, New York)
Stuart Davis, 1938

Stuart Davis came from an artistic family: his father was an art editor and his mother was a sculptor. Both were trained at the Pennsylvania Academy of the Fine Arts. Davis studied under Robert Henri, was a childhood friend of John Sloan, William Glackens, Everett Shinn, and George Luks, and worked as a magazine illustrator. In 1913 he began submitting drawings to *Harper's* and *The Masses*, and five of his paintings were included in the Armory Show.

The New York Federal Art Project

Of the five thousand artists enrolled in the WPA/FAP, half worked in New York, among them Stuart Davis, Willem de Kooning, and Arshile Gorky. Davis, de Kooning, and Gorky produced good work for the WPA/FAP as well-trained and meticulous draftsmen. Jackson Pollock and Mark Rothko had greater difficulty as painters for the WPA/FAP because they could not draw as well as the other three.

By 1915 Davis was experimenting with Cubist abstraction and collage. In his Eggbeater series of the late 1920s, which he later called the basis of everything he subsequently painted, Davis executed still lifes in Cubist geometry and space. He was a frequent companion of Duke Ellington and said that he considered jazz "the only thing that corresponded to an authentic art" in the United States; he introduced billboards, cigarette packages, jazz rhythms, and other symbols of America into his paintings.

Davis was one of the first artists to sign up for the WPA/FAP and the PWAP, and throughout the 1930s and 1940s he taught at the Art Students League and at the New School for Social Research, both in New York. His sense of what he called "Americanness" included enthusiasm not only for jazz but also for colonial architecture. He first went to Gloucester in 1915 with other artists working for *The Masses* and spent most summers there. He referred to himself as an "addict of the New England coast"; fishing schooners share space in his work with fish processing plants, gas pumps, and commercial signs.

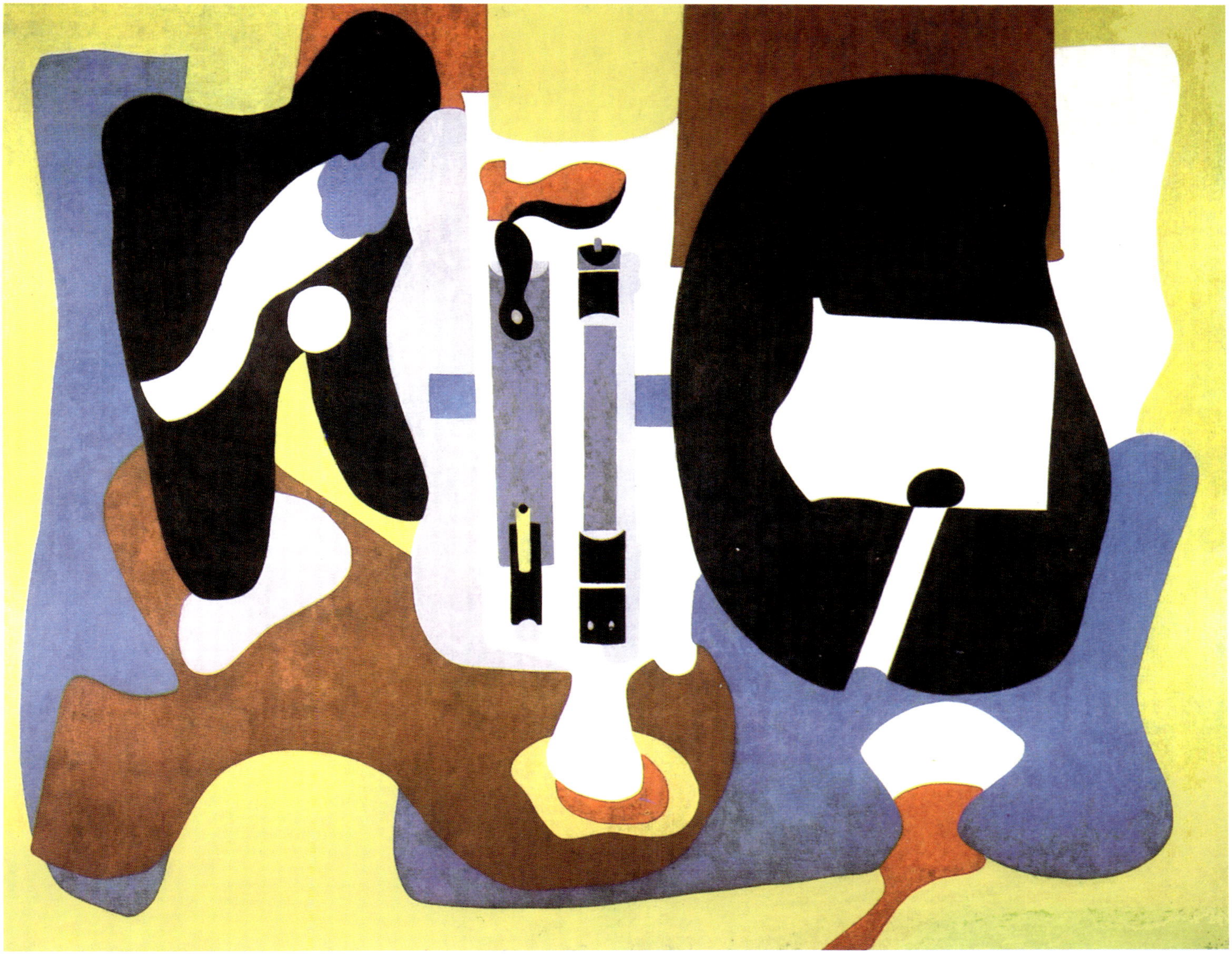

Mechanics of Flying
Arshile Gorky, 1936–37

Arshile Gorky was born in Armenia as Vosdanik Adoian. He immigrated to the United States in 1920, studied at Boston's New School of Design, and moved to New York City in 1925. He was a fine figurative draftsman. In 1930 Gorky's work was included in a group show at the Museum of Modern Art in New York. From 1935 through 1941 he worked with the WPA/FAP. In the early 1940s Gorky began creating abstractions in sly organic shapes and glowing colors. He committed suicide at the age of forty-four.

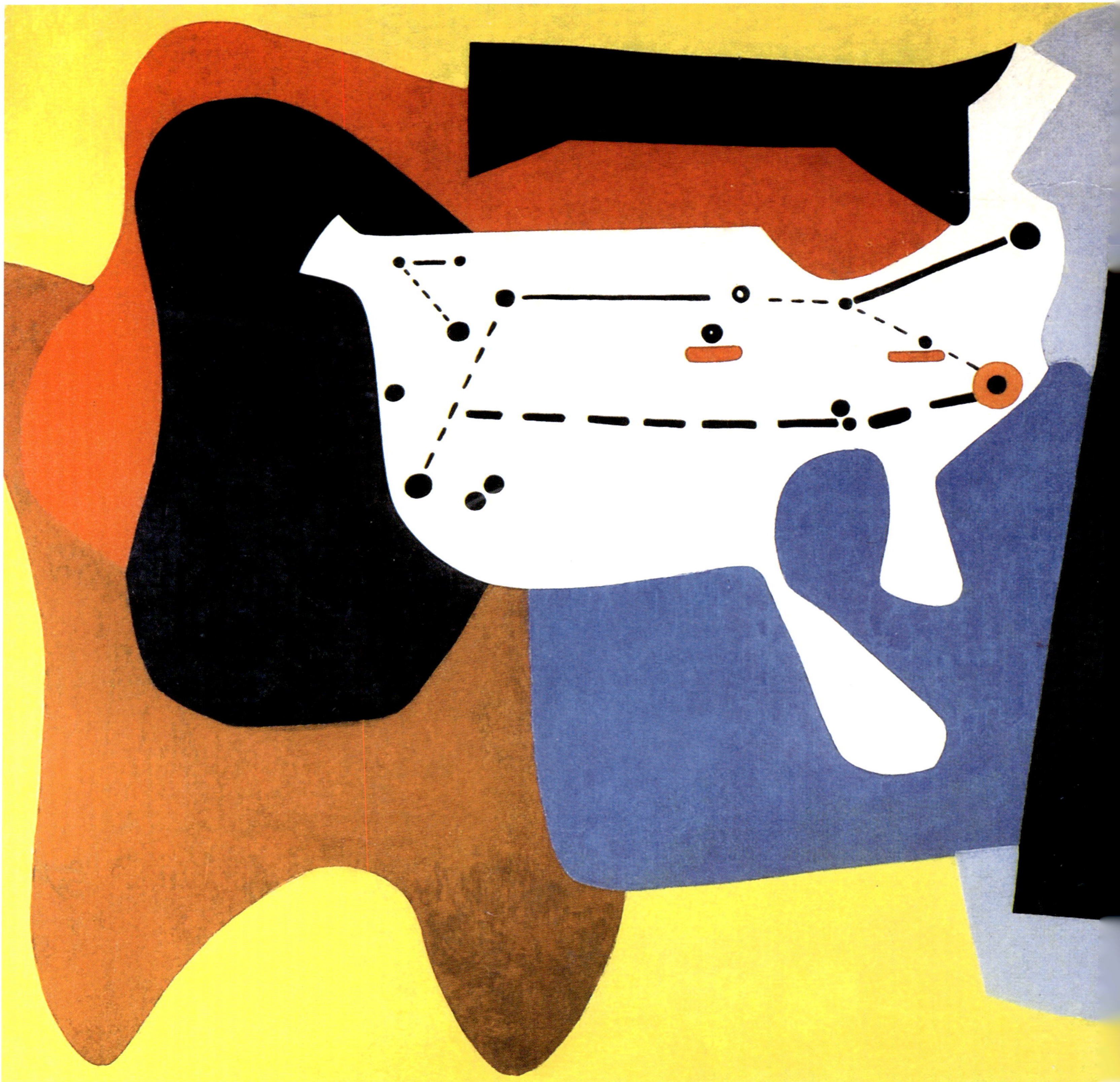

Aerial Map
Arshile Gorky, 1936–37

Below:
Arshile Gorky

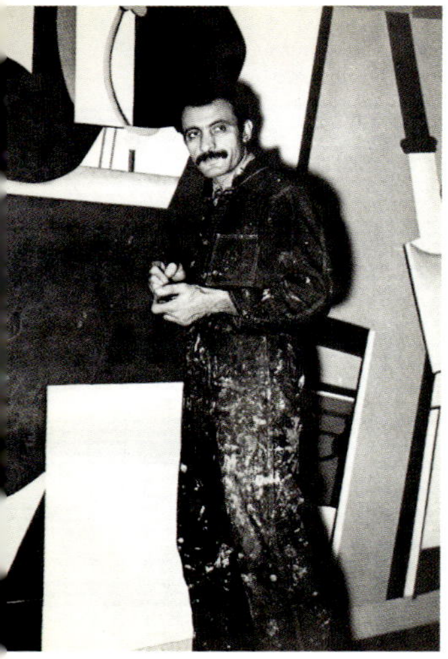

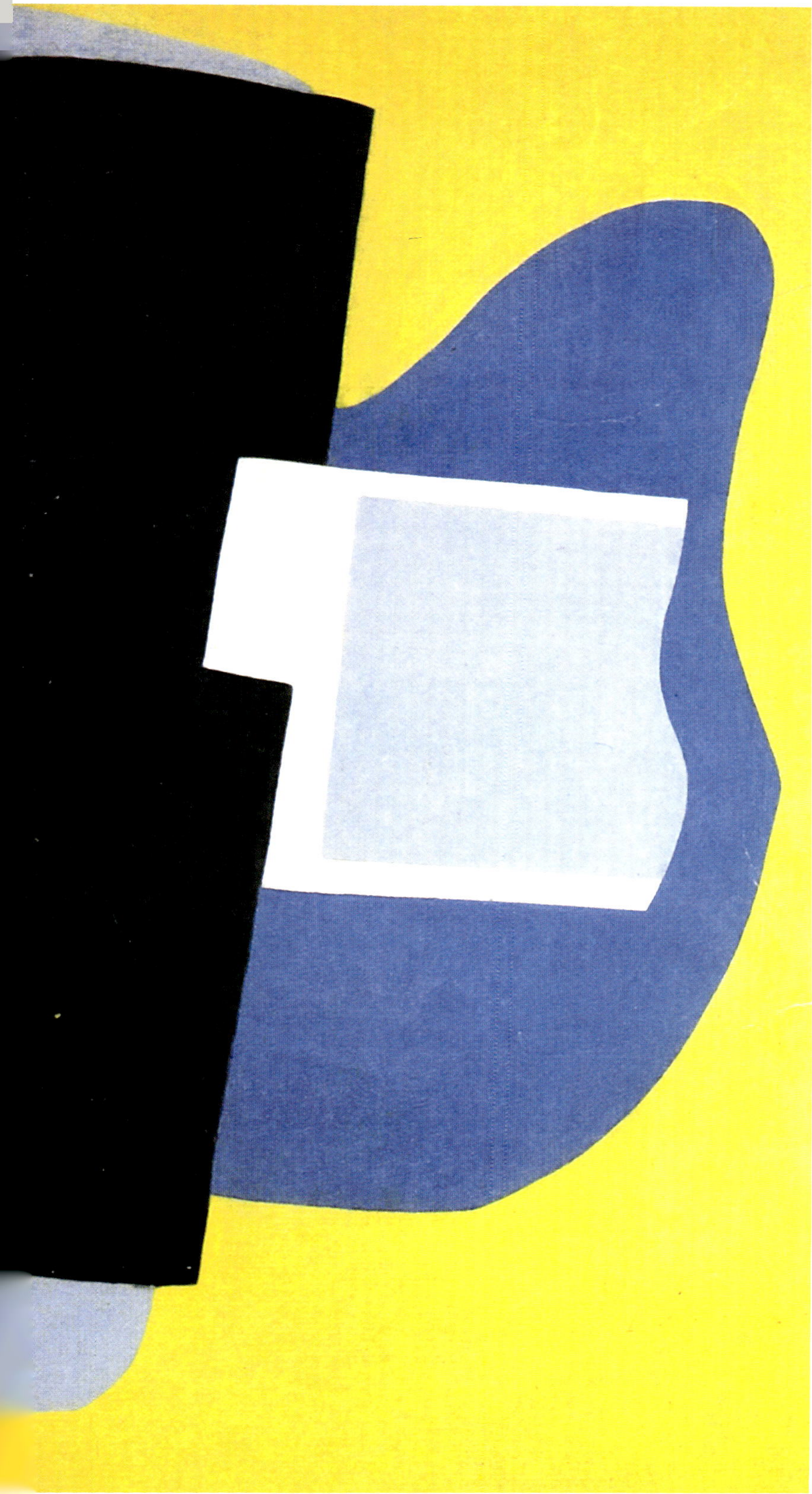

Arshile Gorky executed ten murals for Newark Airport's Administration Building in 1936–37 and only two, *Aerial Map* and *Mechanics of Flying*, have survived, rediscovered under fourteen coats of paint in 1972 by Ruth Bowman. When Gorky explained them to New York's Mayor Fiorello La Guardia, the Mayor responded: "If this is art, then I'm a horse's ass," adding "I am a conservative in art as I am a progressive in my politics. That's why, perhaps, I cannot understand it." Gorky replied, "Mayor, you know about politics. But I know about art!" Gorky said of *Mechanics of Flying* that he had taken a thermometer, hygrometer, anemometer, and an airline map of the United States—important in aviation—and to emphasize that importance he detached them from their environment as shapes. A reporter wrote in 1937: "Visitors to the new Administration Building at Newark Airport were walking around in a daze yesterday trying to decipher a series of startling murals. Equally puzzled were two Russian artists assigned by the WPA to paint the Cubistic brain children of Arshile Gorky, the WPA maestro who conceived the murals. They had a sketch on the floor and were gazing at it in awe. It was a frightening assortment of multi-colored angles and lanes with something that looked like a silhouette of Popeye the sailor on his back eating two telephone poles.

'This is the top,' hazarded the first artist, pointing a tentative finger toward a Japanese sunset.

'No,' said the second artist, turning the sketch around and cautiously touching a character study of Old Faithful. 'This is the top.'"[8]

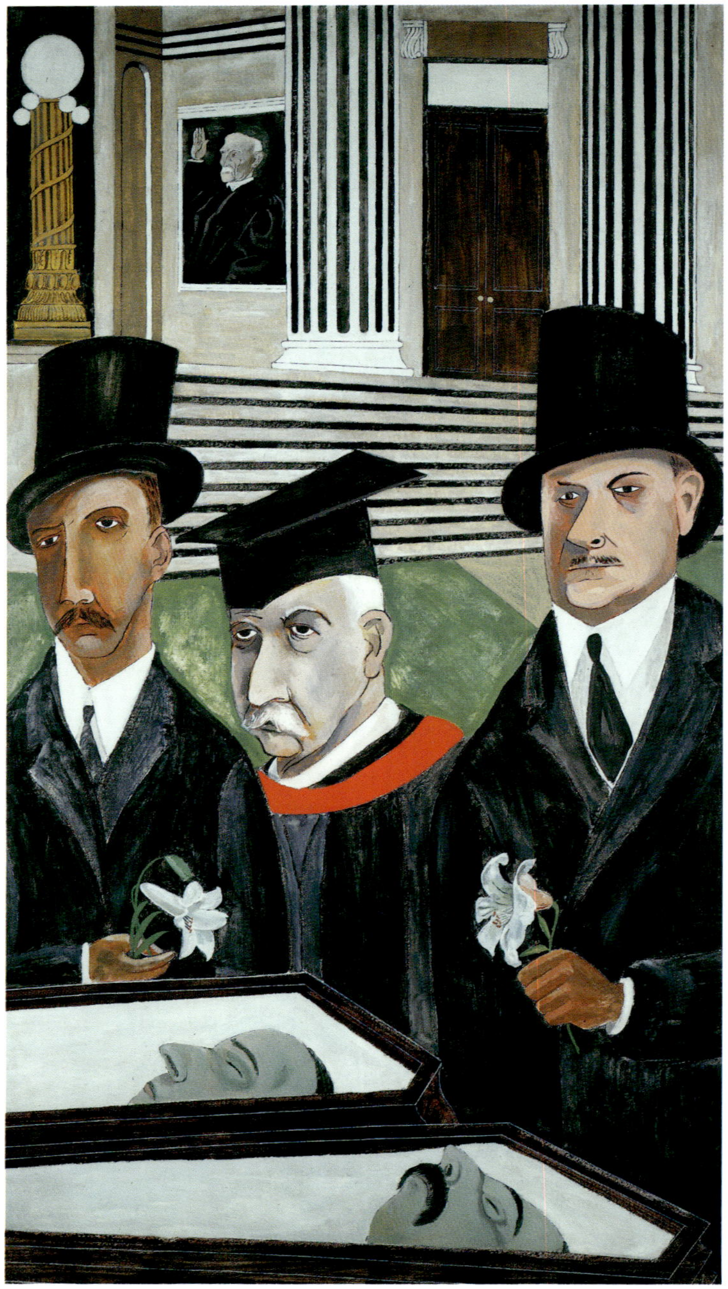

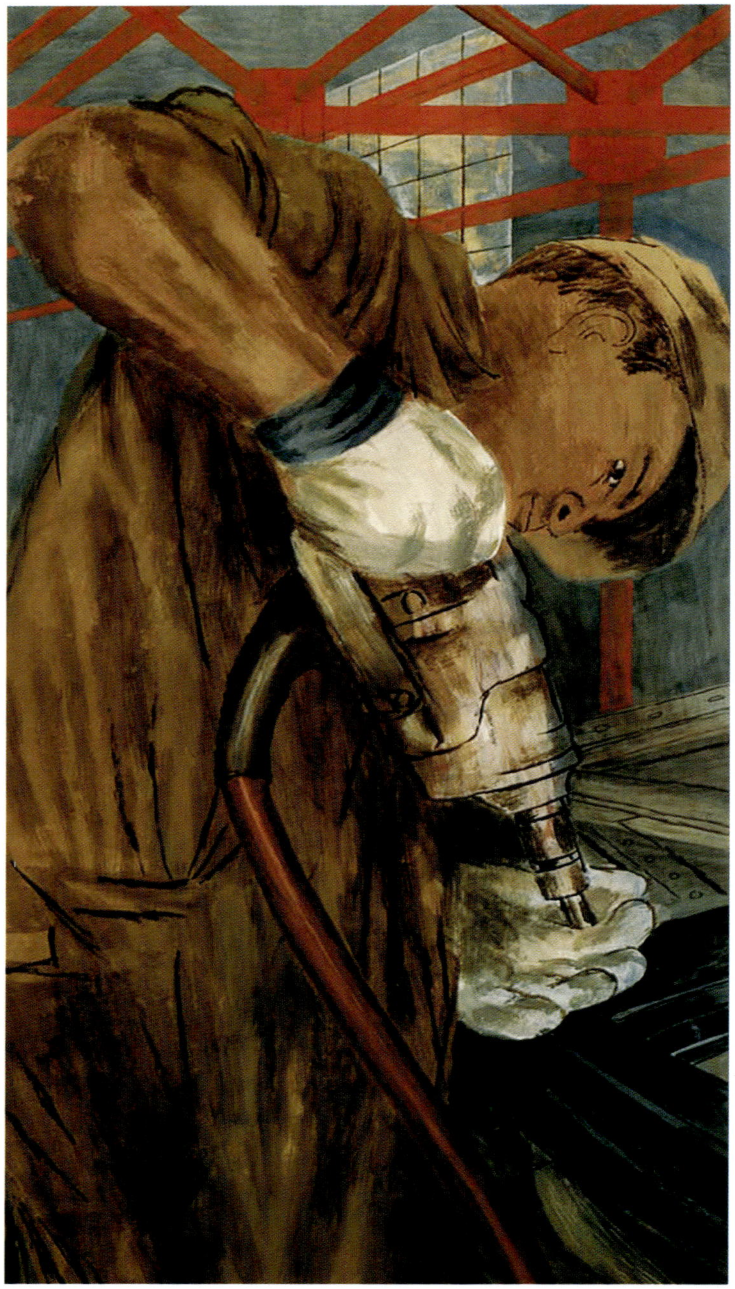

Right:
The Passion of Sacco and Vanzetti
Sacco-Vanzetti series
Ben Shahn, 1931–32
Tempera on canvas

Far right:
The Riveter (mural study, Bronx, New York, central postal station)
Ben Shahn, 1938
Tempera on paperboard

The Riveter was one of two works submitted by Shahn for the Treasury Section competition to decorate the Bronx Central Postal Station in New York. Shahn's theme was that human beings and their talents were as important to preserve as natural resources such as soil and water.

Ben Shahn was born in Lithuania; his family immigrated to Brooklyn when he was six. His early education consisted mainly of studying passages from the Bible by copying texts—and throughout his life his art often included words, names, and quotations. He apprenticed to a lithographer, learning typesetting and composition, and in his art there are also detached letters as shapes in space, and nuances in the thickness of lines. Between 1919 and 1922 he studied at New York University, the City College of New York, and the National Academy of Design in New York. He shared a studio in 1929 with Walker Evans and began making his own photographs of people and street scenes. Much of his work was concerned with the political questions of the time, and also portrayed in solitary figures the loneliness of the city dweller.

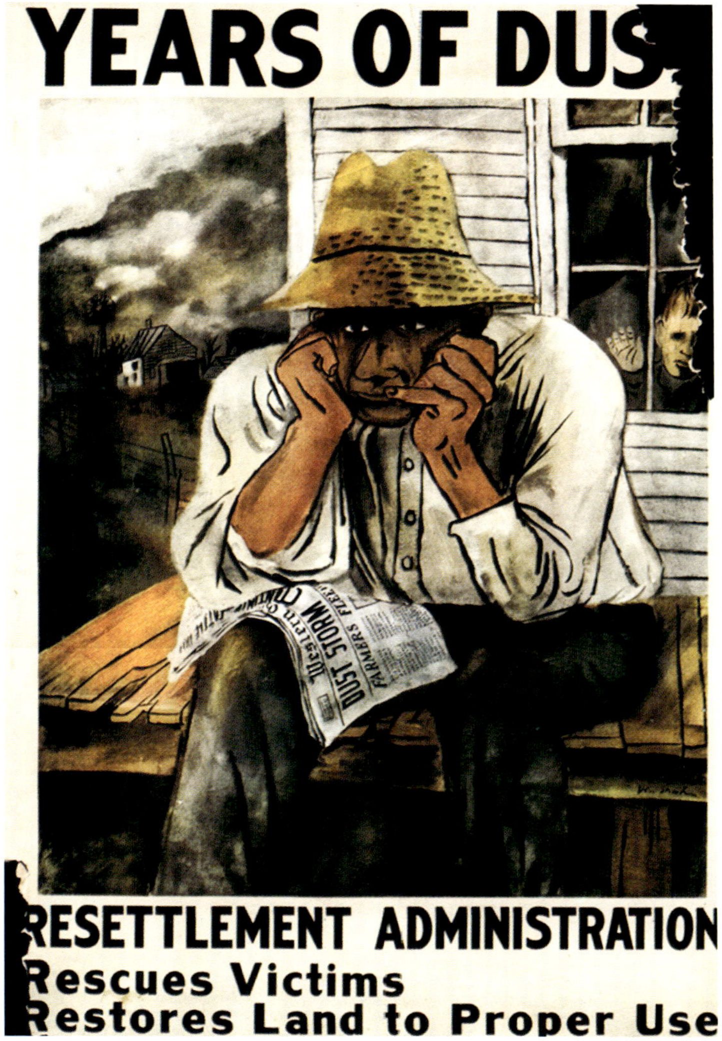

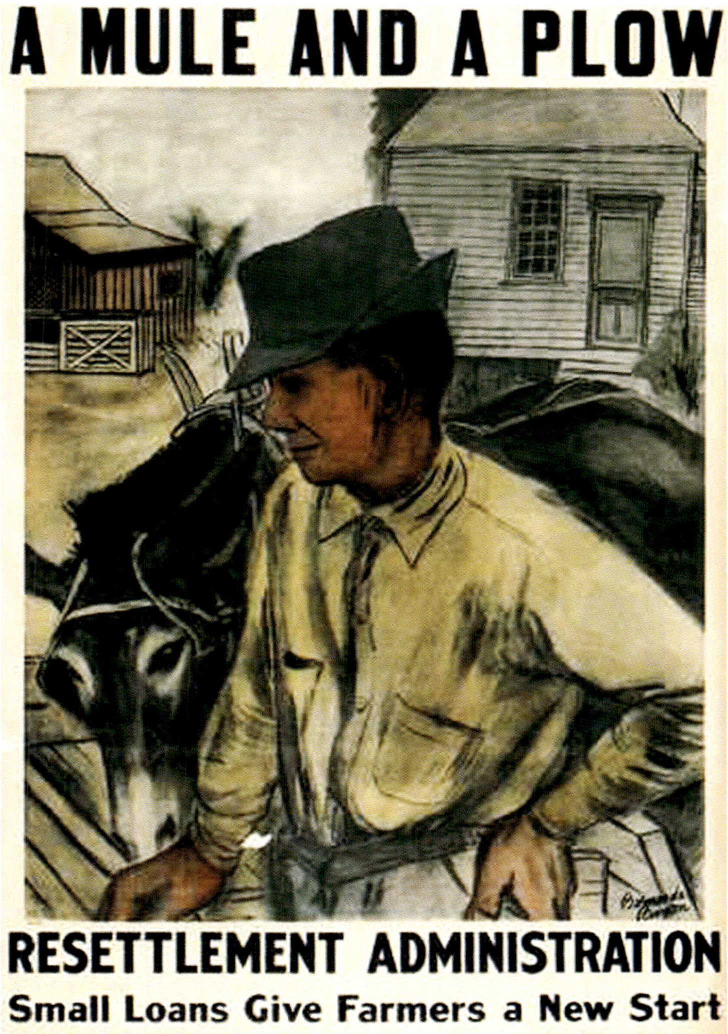

"Years of Dust"
Ben Shahn, 1937
Photolithographic poster

In his 1937 poster *Years of Dust*, Shahn contrasted an image of an impoverished pre–New Deal farmer trapped by years of drought with a listing of the Resettlement Administration's positive actions (see main text).

"A Mule and a Plow"
Bernarda Bryson Shahn, 1937
Photolithographic poster

Bernarda Bryson was a newspaper journalist who in 1933 traveled to New York to interview Diego Rivera for an Ohio newspaper. There she met Ben Shahn, who became her life companion. They married shortly before Mr. Shahn's death in 1969. In the mid-1930s they drove across the country documenting rural life for the Resettlement Administration. Bernarda Bryson's series of lithographs from that trip was published in 1995 as "The Vanishing American Frontier." Later, they collaborated on New Deal–era murals in the Roosevelt Public School in Roosevelt, New Jersey, and the Bronx General Post Office.

In 1932–33, Shahn assisted Diego Rivera on the murals for Rockefeller Center. Thereafter, he worked for the WPA/FAP on many projects including an unrealized mural for a federal prison that addressed social and political questions affecting the poor and disenfranchised; he also worked as a lecturer, teacher, writer, and as active citizen: he served as a city councilman in the model community of Roosevelt, New Jersey, between 1945 and 1948. He died in New York in 1969.

Between 1931 and 1932 Shahn created a series of twenty-three gouaches and temperas about the trial of the anarchists Nicola Sacco and Bartolomeo Vanzetti, who had been arrested and executed for the murder of a guard during a robbery of a shoe factory in Massachusetts. Their radicalism and their immigrant status inflamed the public and the court against them, despite flimsy evidence in the case. Shahn depicted the two in their coffins as those prominent in their conviction and execution stand by, clad in top hats and formal dress; Harvard President Abbott Lawrence Lowell, who chaired the commission that found no evidence of bias in the trial or appeals process, wears academic robes. Behind them, in a courthouse portal, is a portrait of Judge Webster Thayer, who presided over the trial and the appeals process. Shahn returned again and again to this subject about which he produced paintings, an ink drawing, three serigraphs, and a mosaic mural.

Civic Graphics

Graphics for the Rural Electrification Administration
Lester Thomas Beall, 1937

Lester Beall was born in Kansas City, Missouri. He studied at the University of Chicago and, like Harold Ickes, was coached by Amos Alonzo Stagg. He took classes at the Art Institute of Chicago, moved to New York in 1935, and then to Wilton, Connecticut. As a graphic artist he produced designs for the *Chicago Tribune*, Sterling Engraving, The Art Directors Club of New York, Hiram Walker, Abbott Laboratories, *Time, Collier's,* and the Rural Electrification Administration (REA).

The electrification of America was a New Deal priority, raising the standard of living for millions. From 1937 to 1941, Lester Beall's posters for the REA celebrated its bounteous achievements; here, radio waves are depicted as arrows sending information into the farmhouse. Other posters in this series extolled electric lights, plumbing, and electric washing machines. Beall's graphic designs, typically in bright, primary colors, often used interrelated words and images in the manner of the Russian Constructivists.

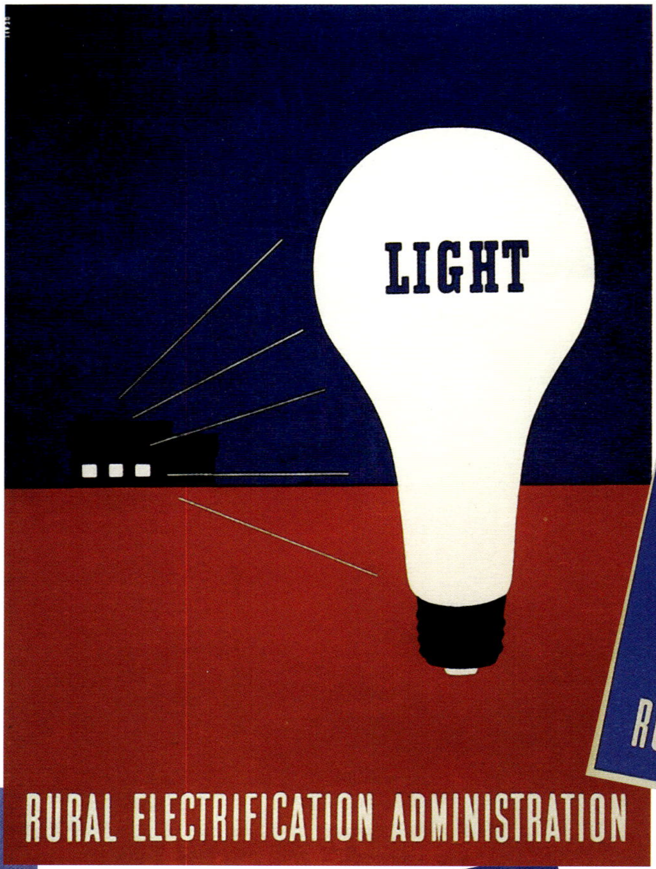

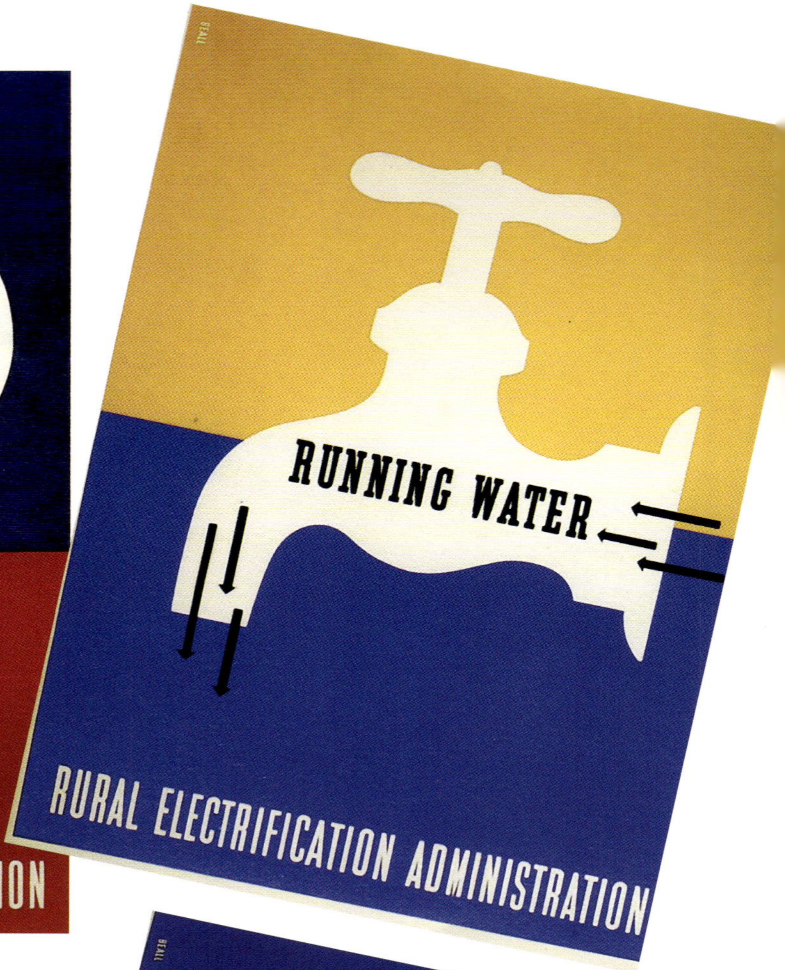

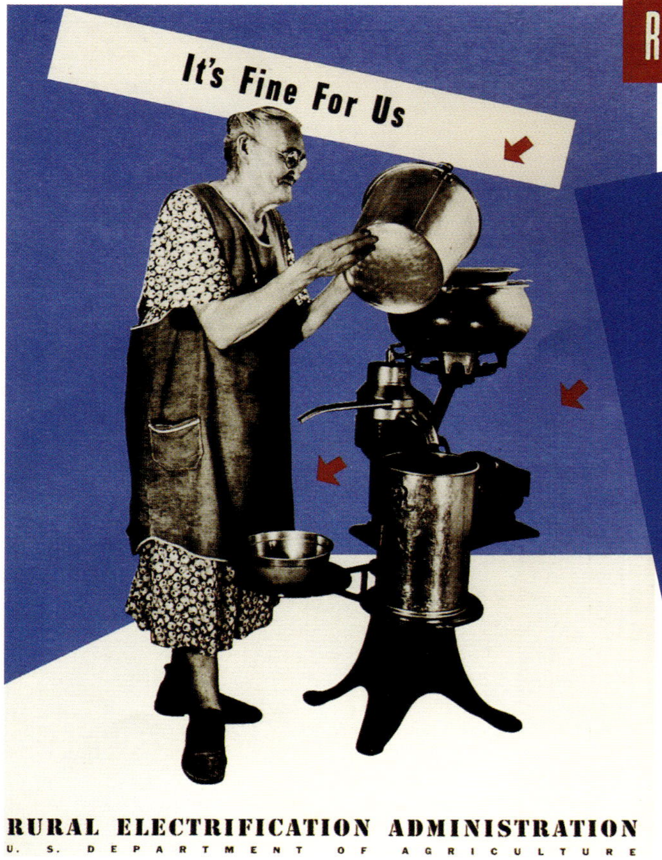

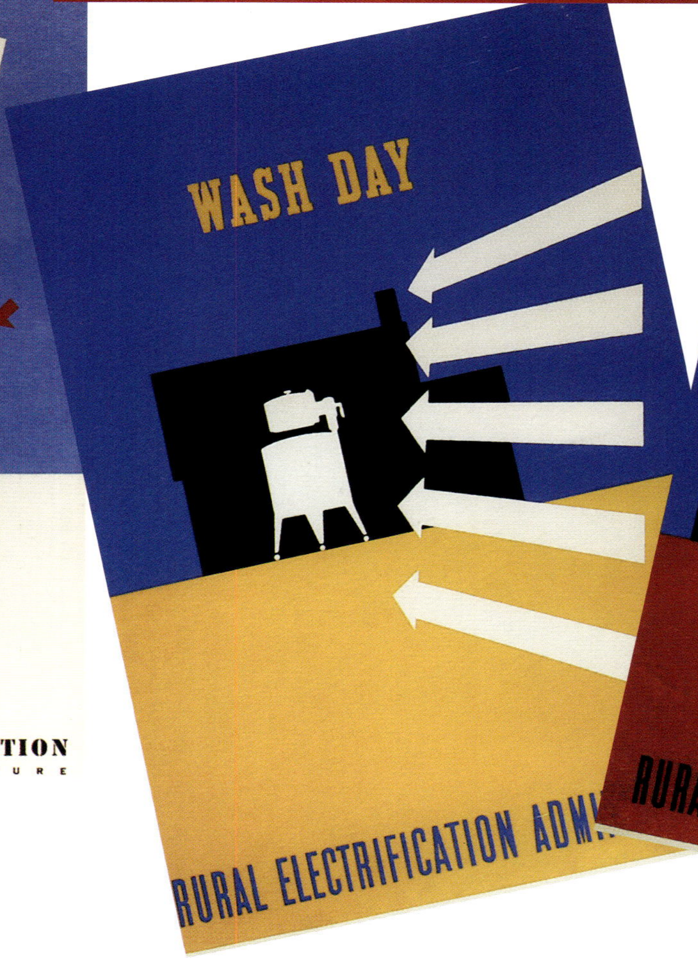

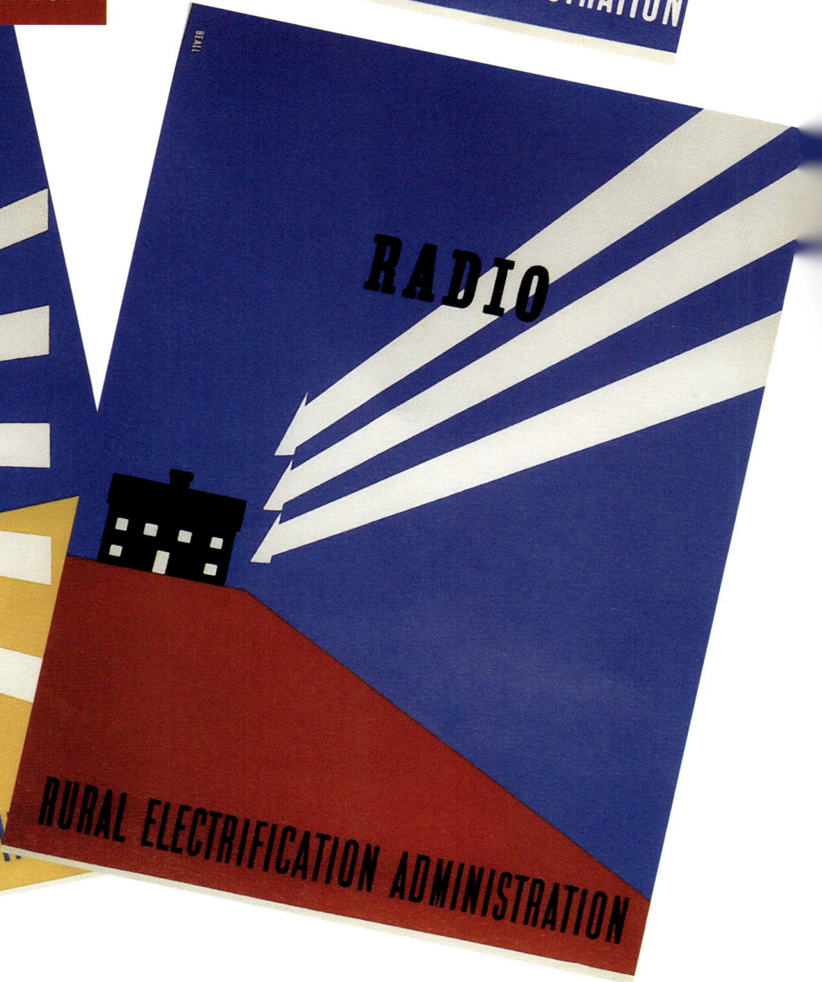

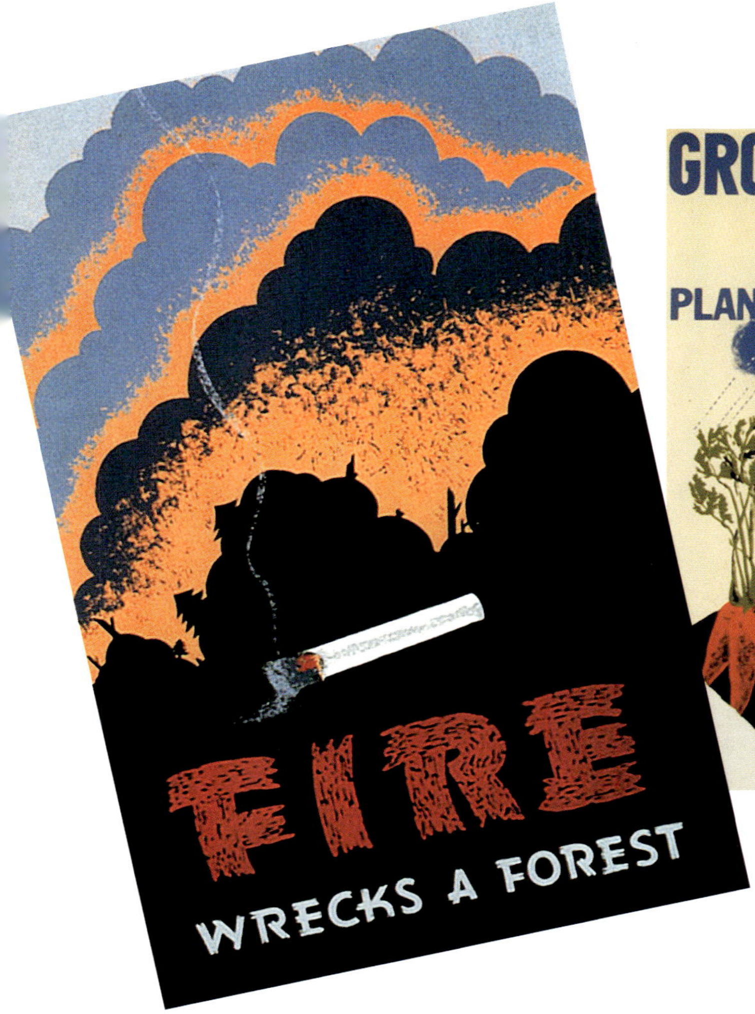

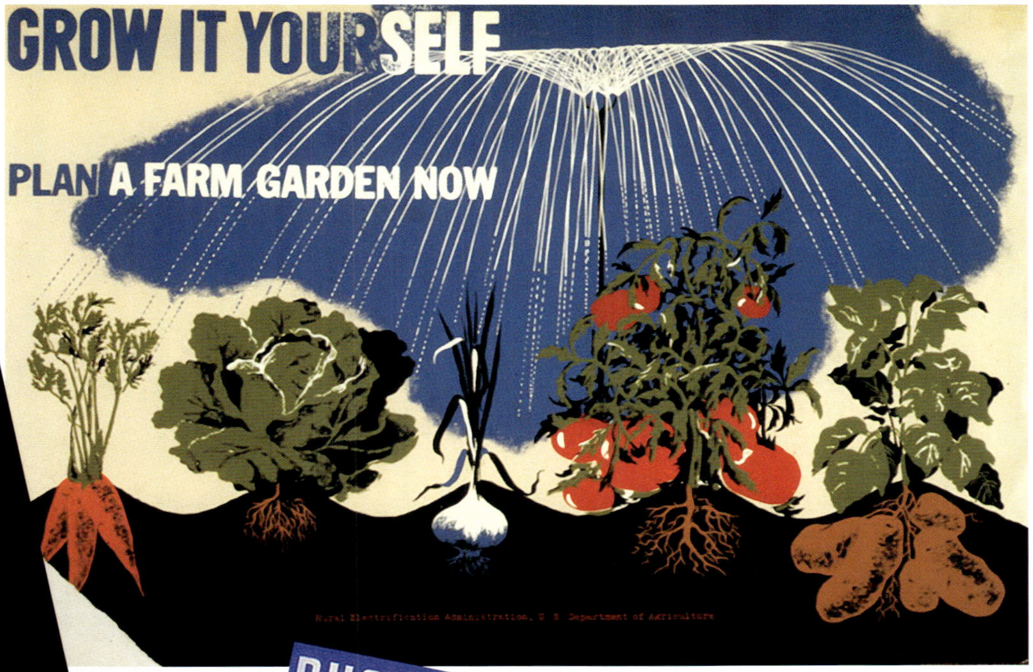

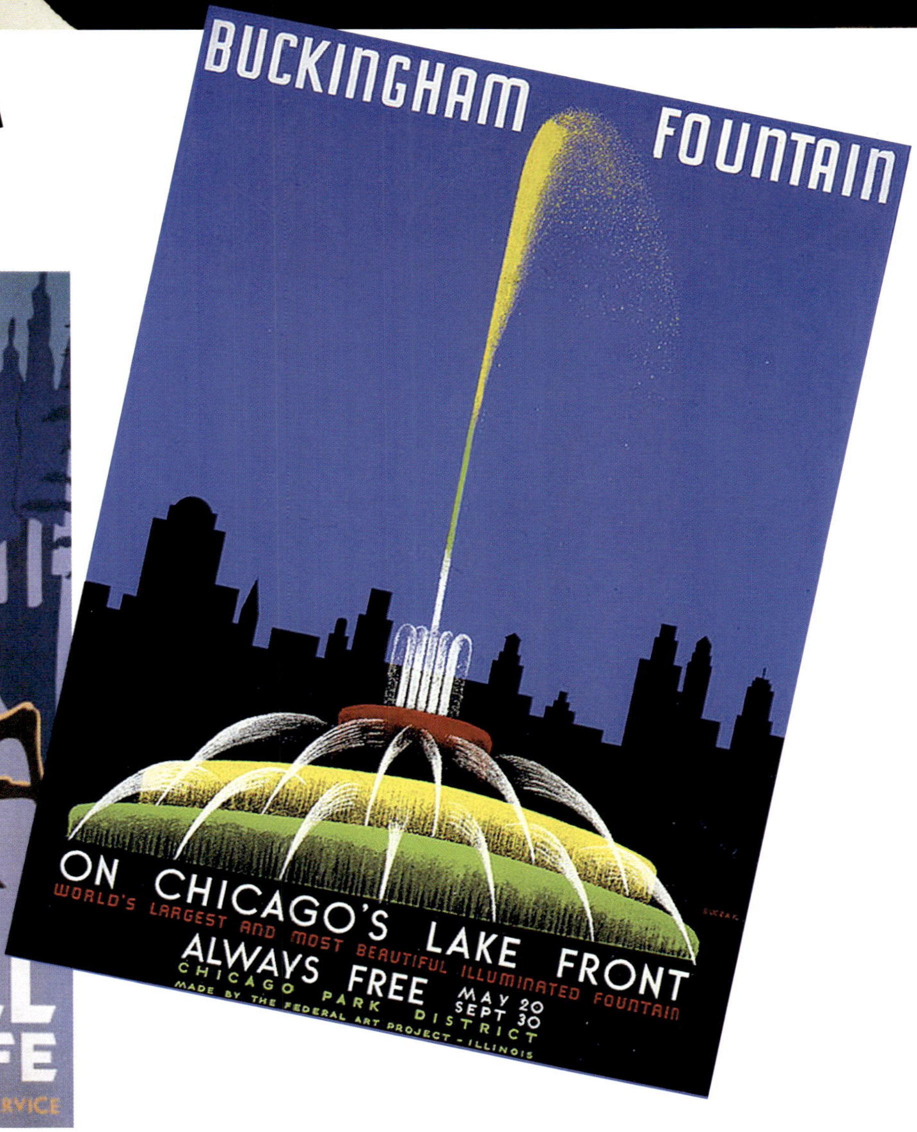

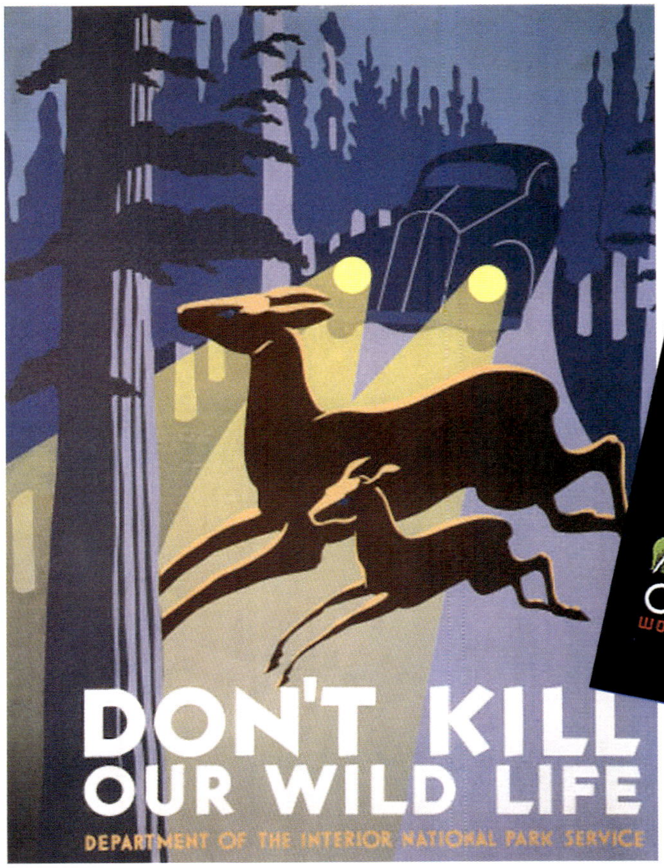

Clockwise from top left:
"FIRE WRECKS A FOREST"
Poster for forest fire prevention showing a burning cigarette and a forest fire.
1939

"GROW IT YOURSELF: PLAN A FARM GARDEN NOW"
Herbert Bayer, 1941
A poster created for the U.S. Department of Agriculture promoting victory gardens: carrots, lettuce, corn, tomatoes, and potatoes.

"BUCKINGHAM FOUNTAIN"
WPA for the Chicago Park District
John Buczak, 1939

"DON'T KILL OUR WILD LIFE"
John Wagner, 1940

The Federal Music Project

Sixteen thousand musicians were given employment when the Federal Music Project was at maximum strength. They performed in orchestras and chamber groups, choruses and opera companies, concert bands, dance bands, and theater orchestras. One estimate is that five thousand performances each week reached three million people, brought together largely by the efforts of local cosponsors. Another study concluded that the music project employed 15,000 artists who gave 225,000 performances. There were WPA concerts in Central Park, and "classes in rural areas and urban neighborhoods; in 1939, an estimated 132,000 children and adults in 27 states received instruction every week. A Composers Forum Laboratory afforded composers in several major cities the opportunity to hear their work performed with complete instrumentation."[11]

At the less formal end of the spectrum, the Project sent forth wise, patient, and respectful listeners with recording devices to seek out "Appalachian banjo pickers, . . . New England gut-bucket strummers, . . . Texas fiddlers, . . . Tennessee yodelers, and Indiana jug bands," providing to the Library of Congress and the Smithsonian Institution the basis for long-lasting (and thoroughly enjoyable) programs in folk life and folk music. The Index of American Composers achieved for music what the Design index did for artifacts, "cataloguing 5,500 works by 1,500 composers; WPA ensembles performed every one of these catalogued works. Extensive recording of folk music was carried out, especially in the Southeast and South Central regions. WPA workers also pioneered in music therapy experimentation. Finally, Music Project workers also served as copyists, arrangers and librarians, expanding the availability of musical work."[12] See also chapter seven.

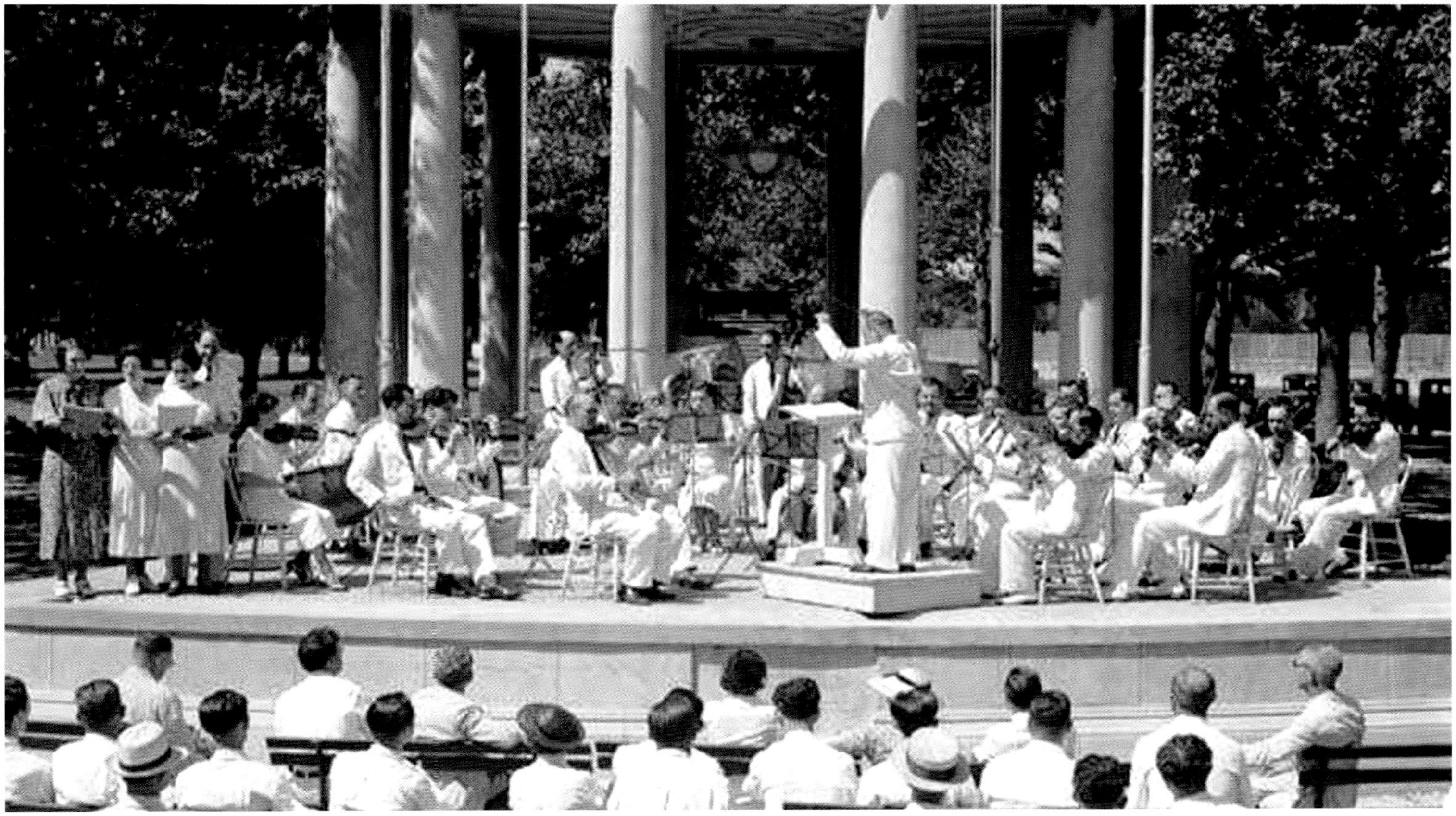

"The Little Symphony Orchestra—E. T. Fontana, Leader," 1936

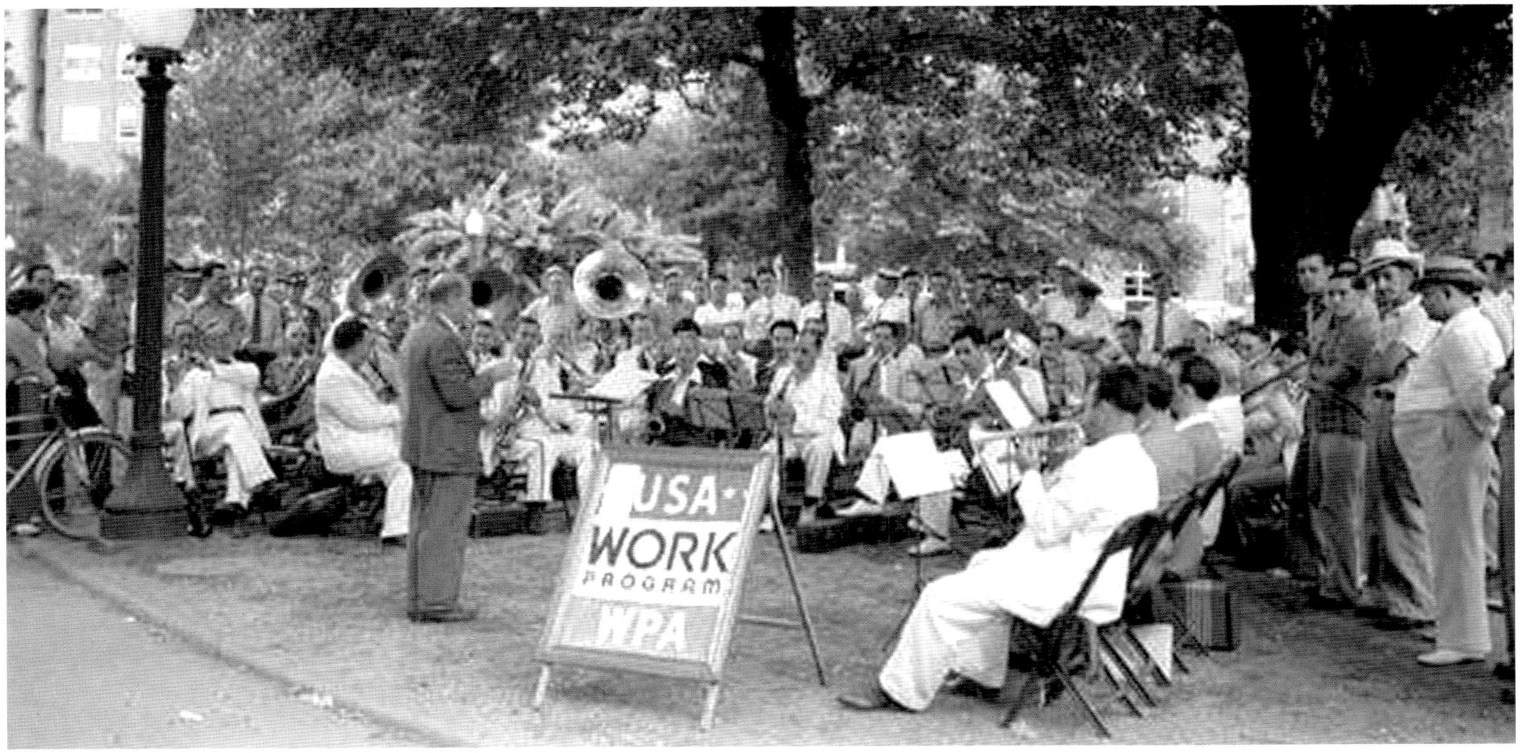

Noon-day concert held by the WPA band at Lafayette Square, 1940

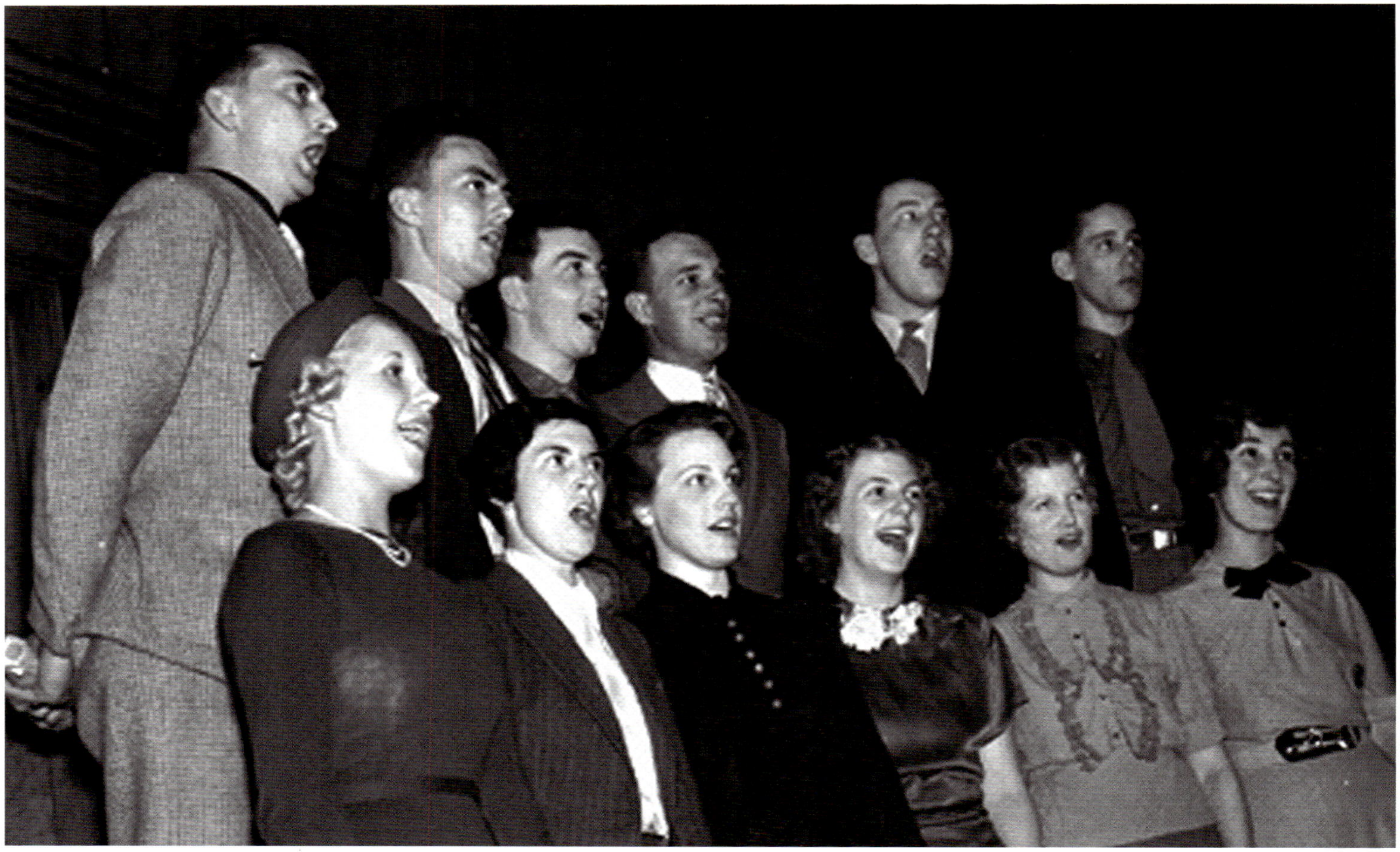

Adult Educational group at WPA Opera Rehearsal, Buffalo, New York

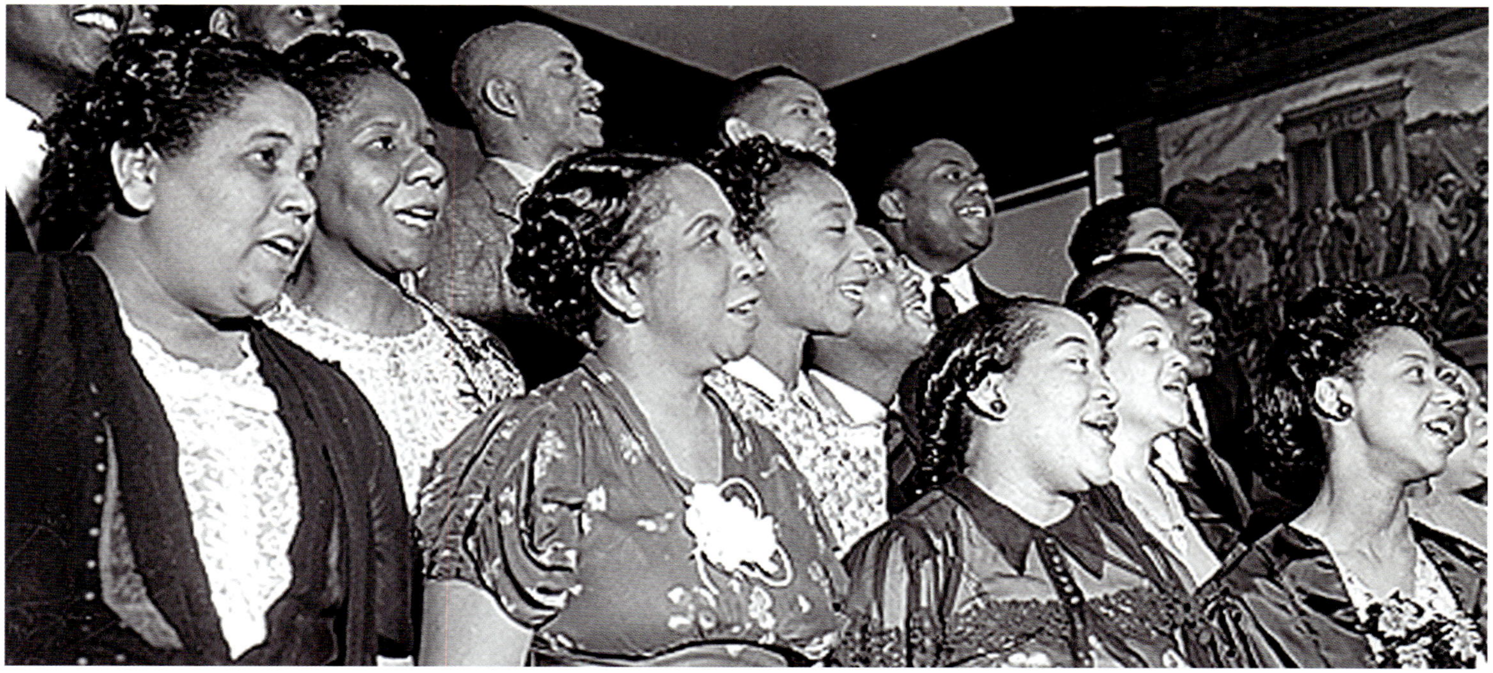

Negro Spiritual Singers

From North Carolina, the singers were trained through a WPA Federal Music Project and participated in the White House program for the King and Queen of England, June 8, 1939.

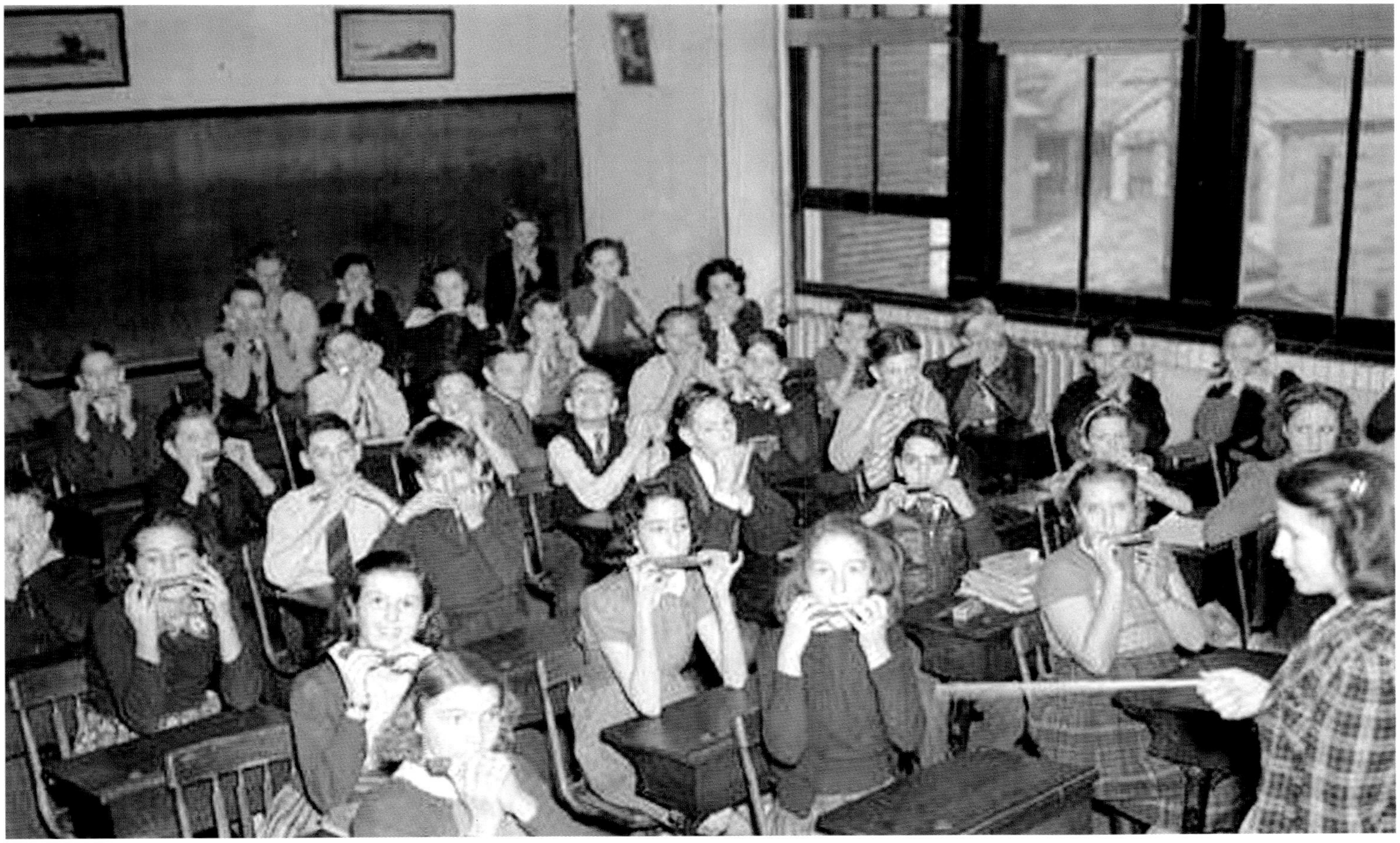

Harmonica class at
Robert C. Davey School,
Louisiana.
1940

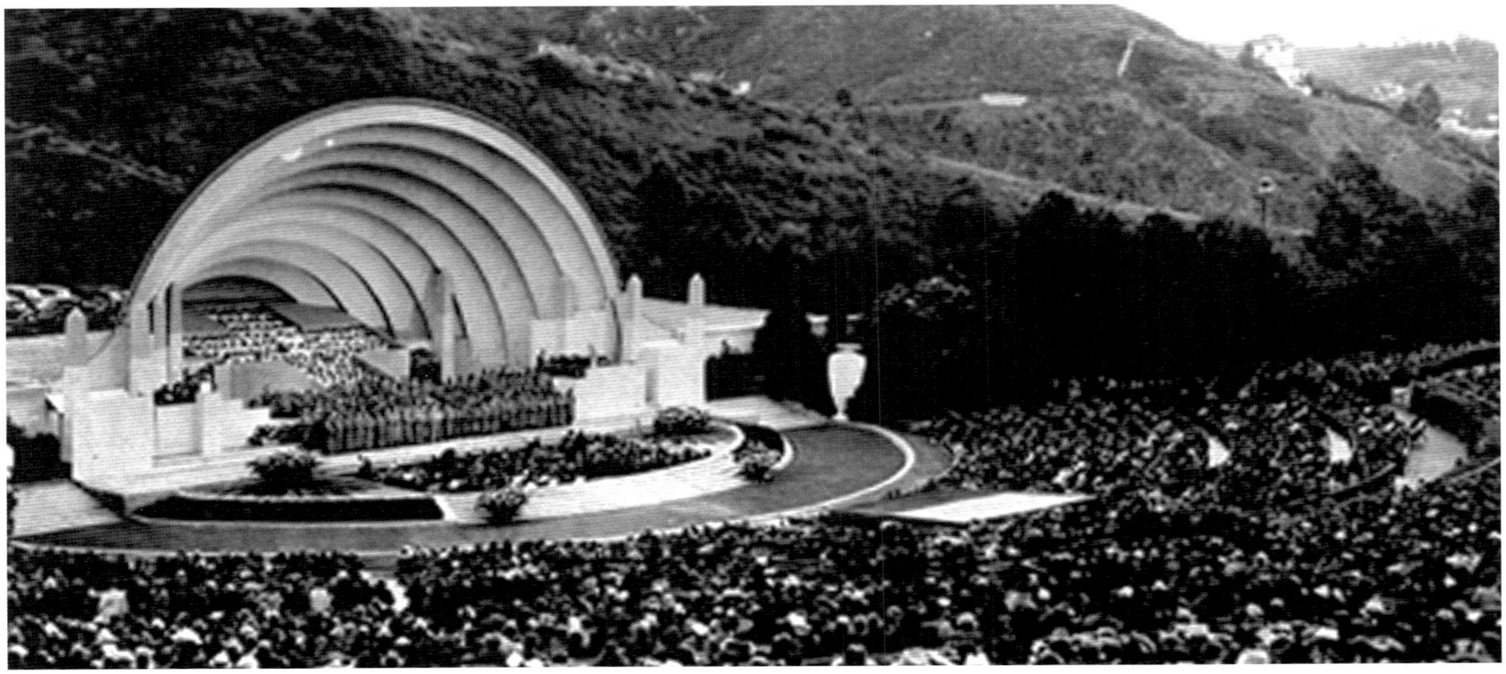

Los Angeles WPA
Symphony

Thirty-five thousand
people attended this 1937
Easter Sunrise Service at
the Hollywood Bowl in
California.

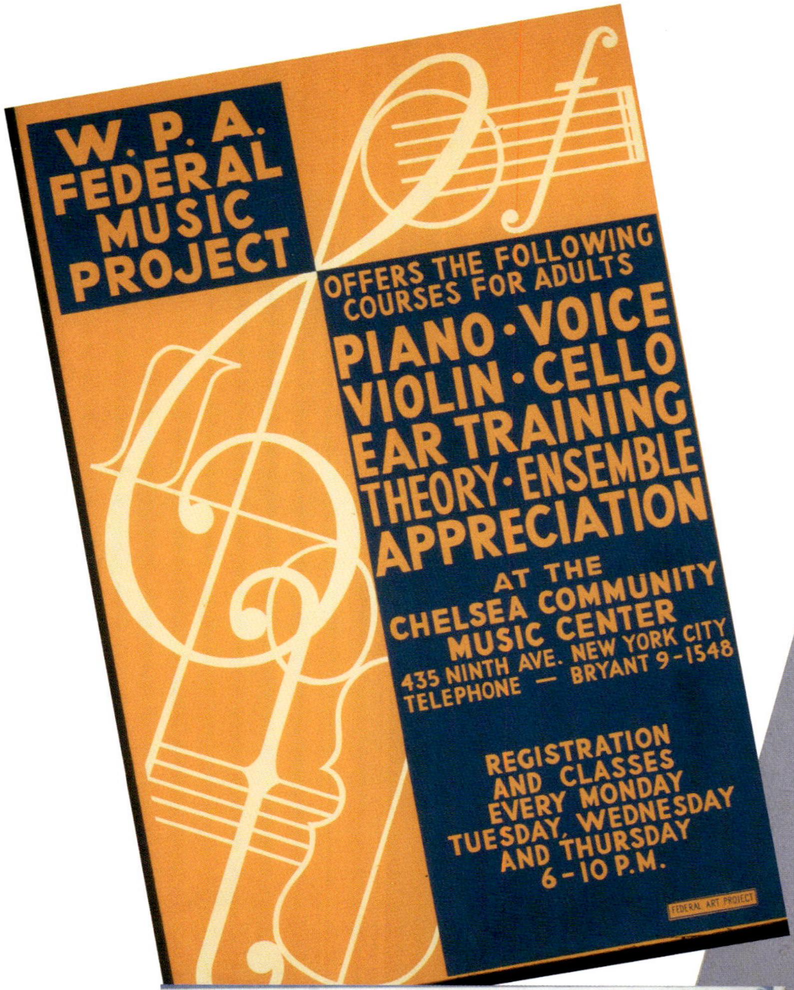

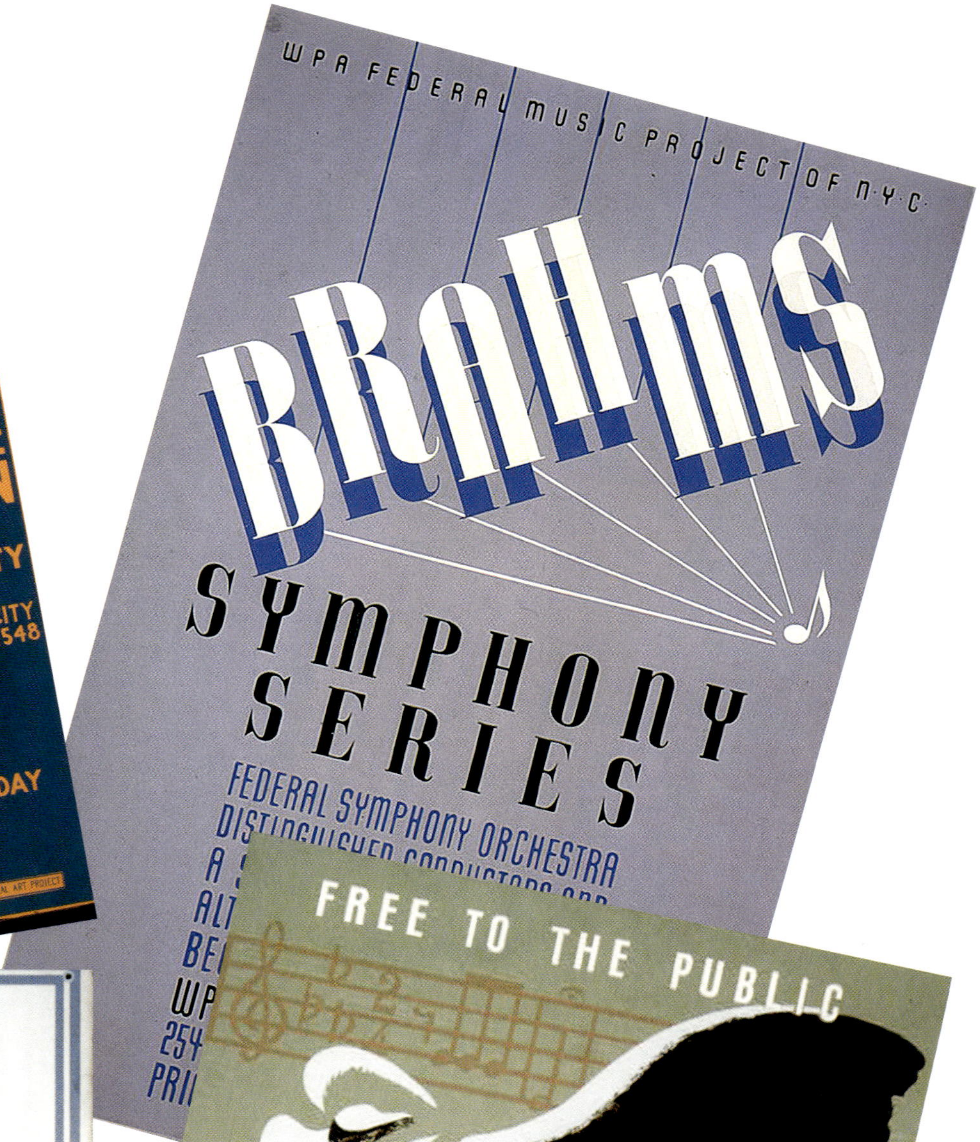

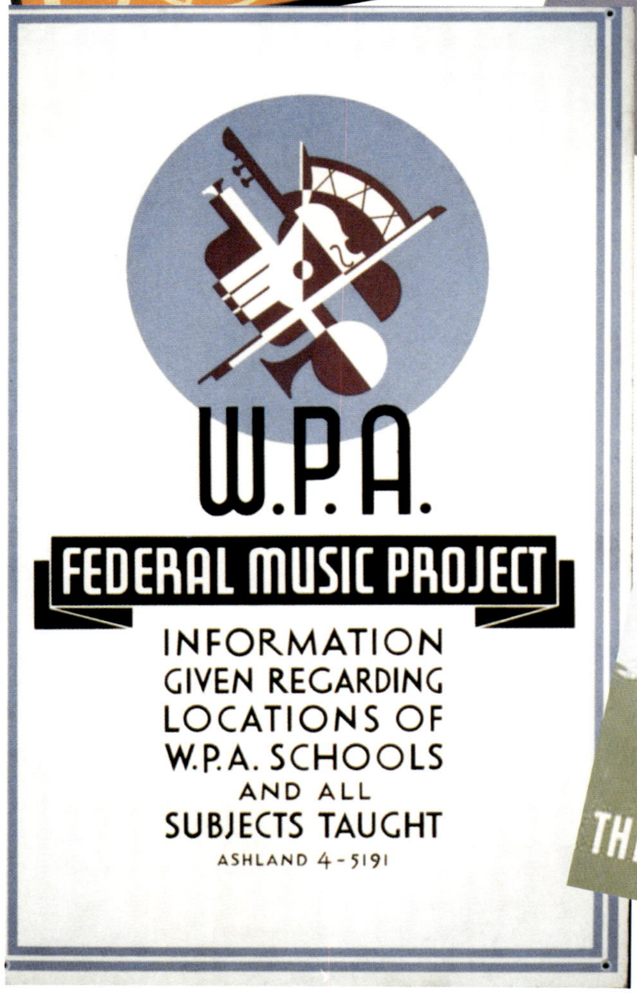

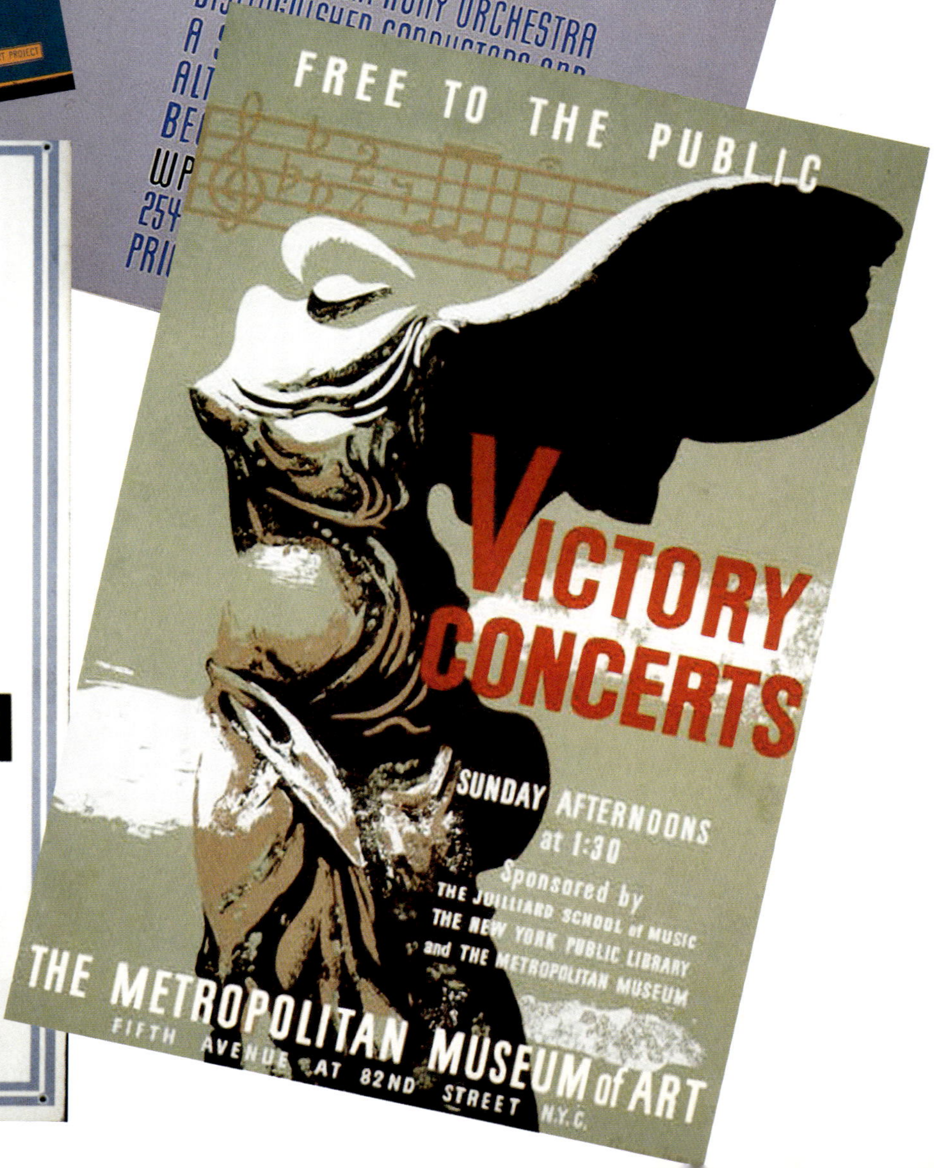

Clockwise from top left:
"W.P.A. Federal Music Project"
Chelsea Community Music Center

"Brahms symphony series"
Poster for WPA/Federal Symphony Orchestra at the WPA Federal Music Theatre, New York City
Jerome Henry Rothstein

Jerome Henry Rothstein designed posters for the WPA poster division. During World War II he flew thirty missions with the 8th Air Force division and was awarded the Distinguished Flying Cross.

"Victory Concerts" at the Metropolitan Museum of Art: Free to the public
Byron Browne

W.P.A. Federal Music Project: schools and classes
Martin Weitzman

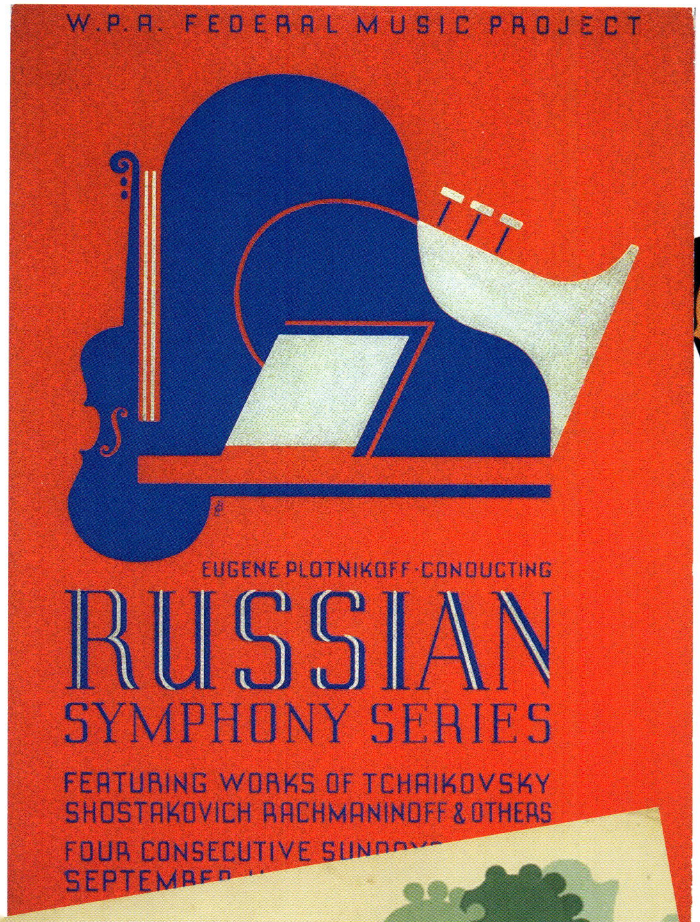

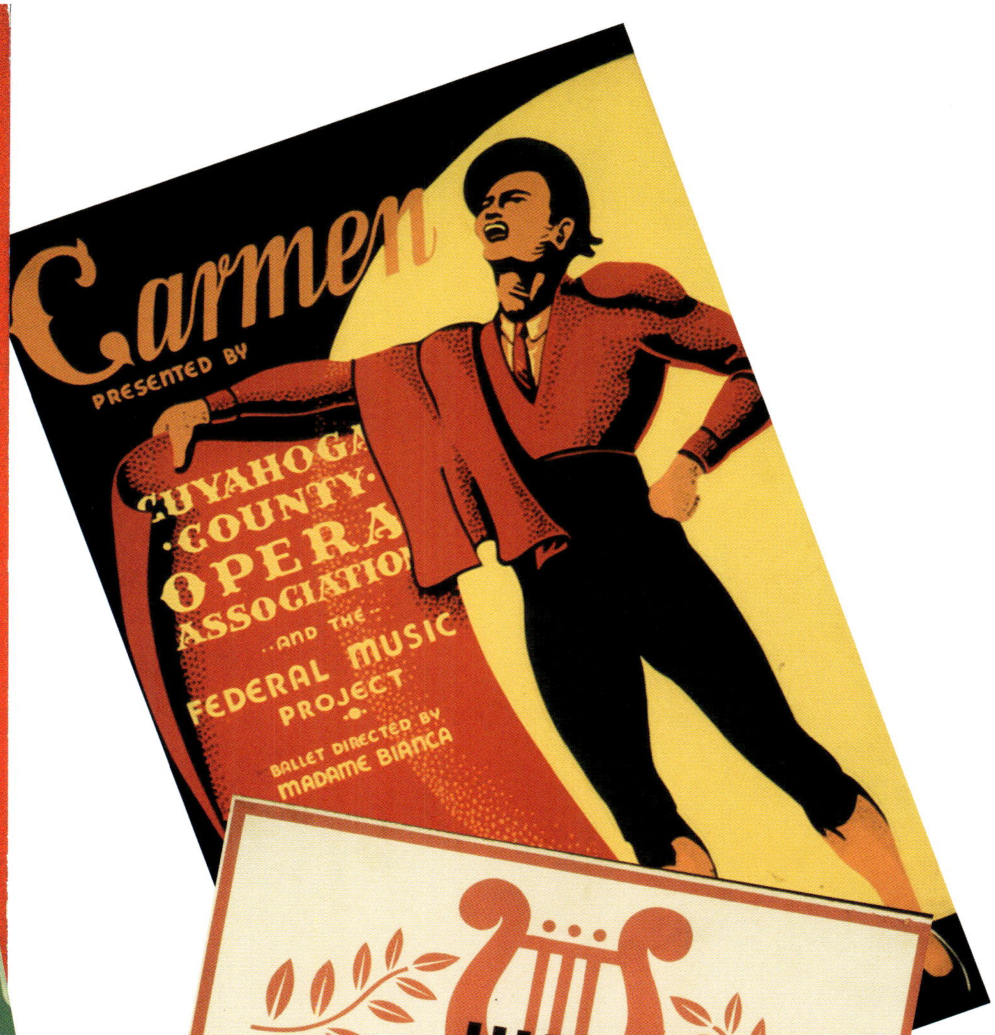

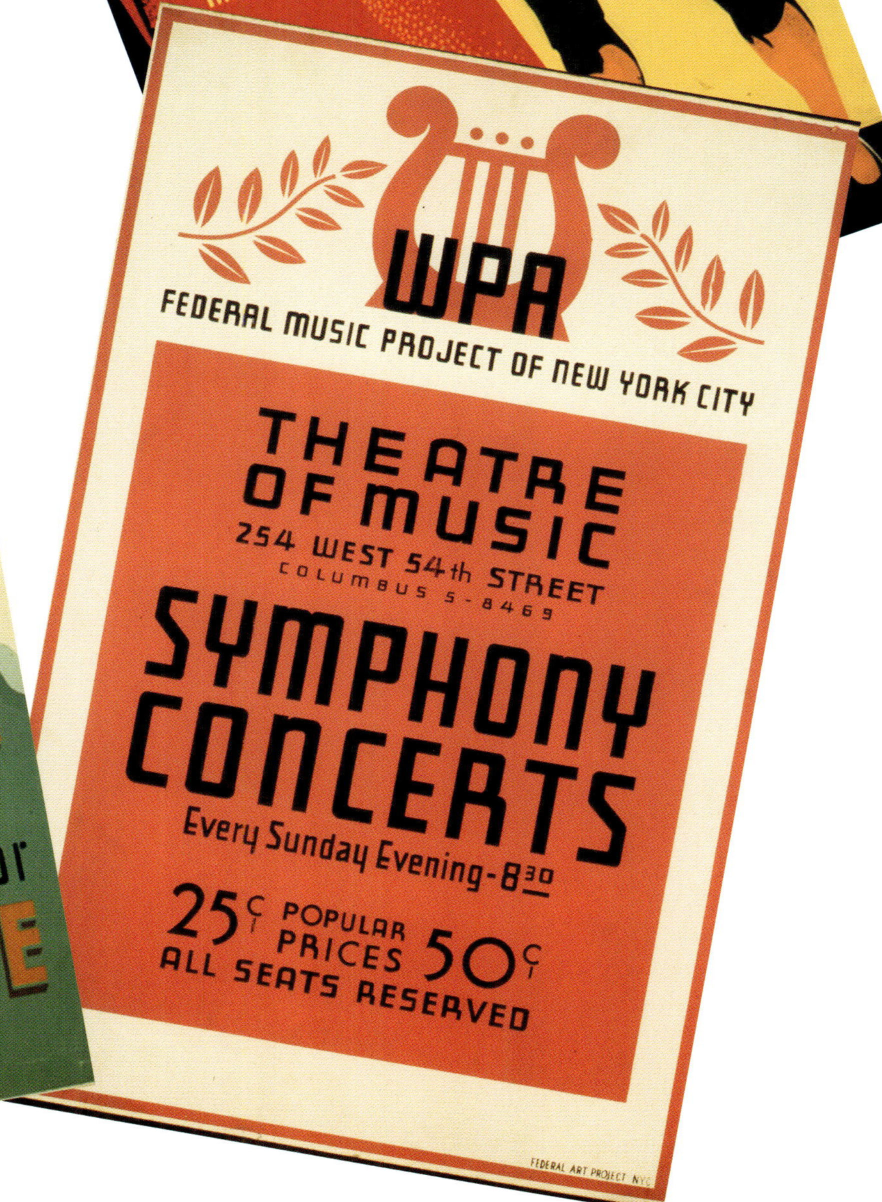

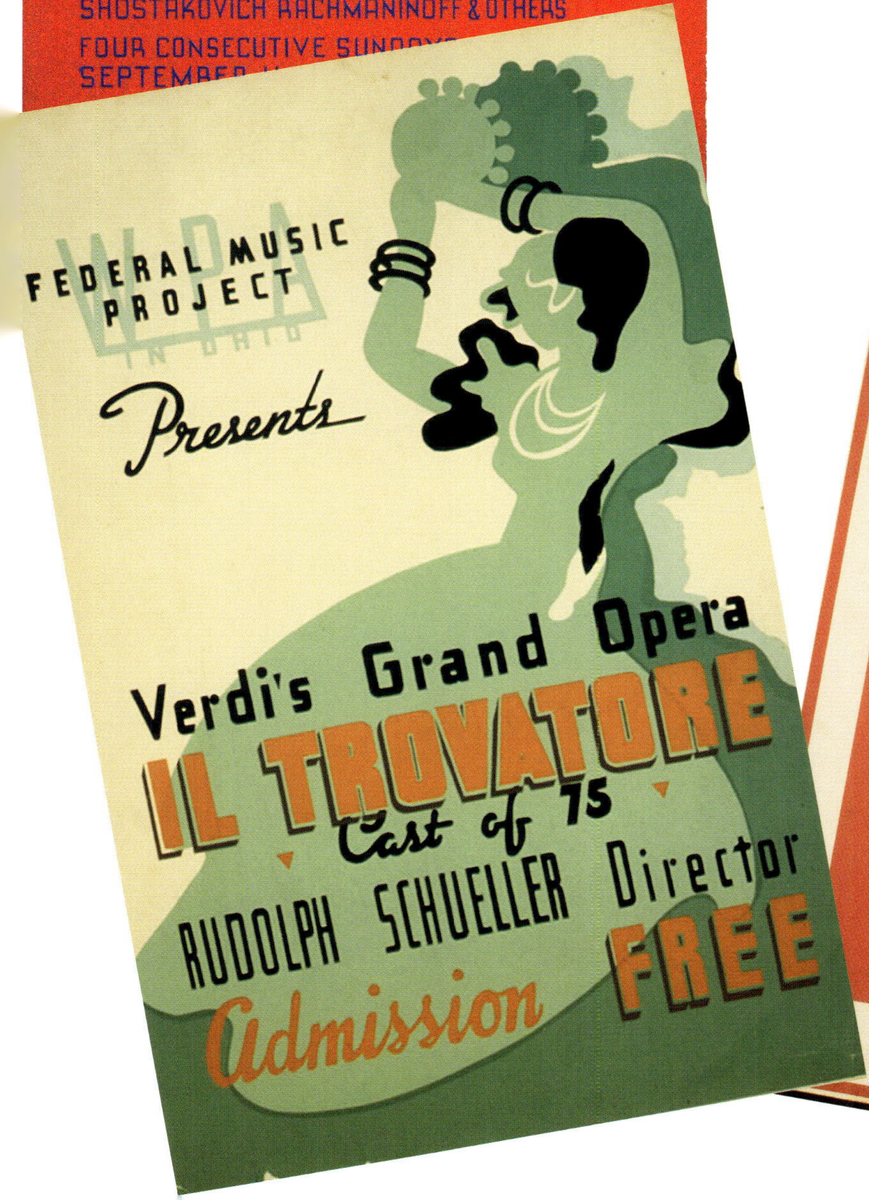

Clockwise from top left:
Russian Symphony Series
Eugene Plotnikoff,
Conducting
Featuring works of
Tchaikovsky, Shostokovitch,
Rachmaninoff, and others.
Leslie Bryan Burroughs,
1939

Carmen Presented by
Cuyahoga County Opera
Association and the
Federal Music Project:
Ballet "directed by
Madame Bianca."
John LaQuatra, 1939

Symphony concerts
WPA Federal Music
Project of the New York
Theatre of Music

Il Trovatore presented by
Ohio Federal Music
Project, Rudolph Schueller,
director.
1937

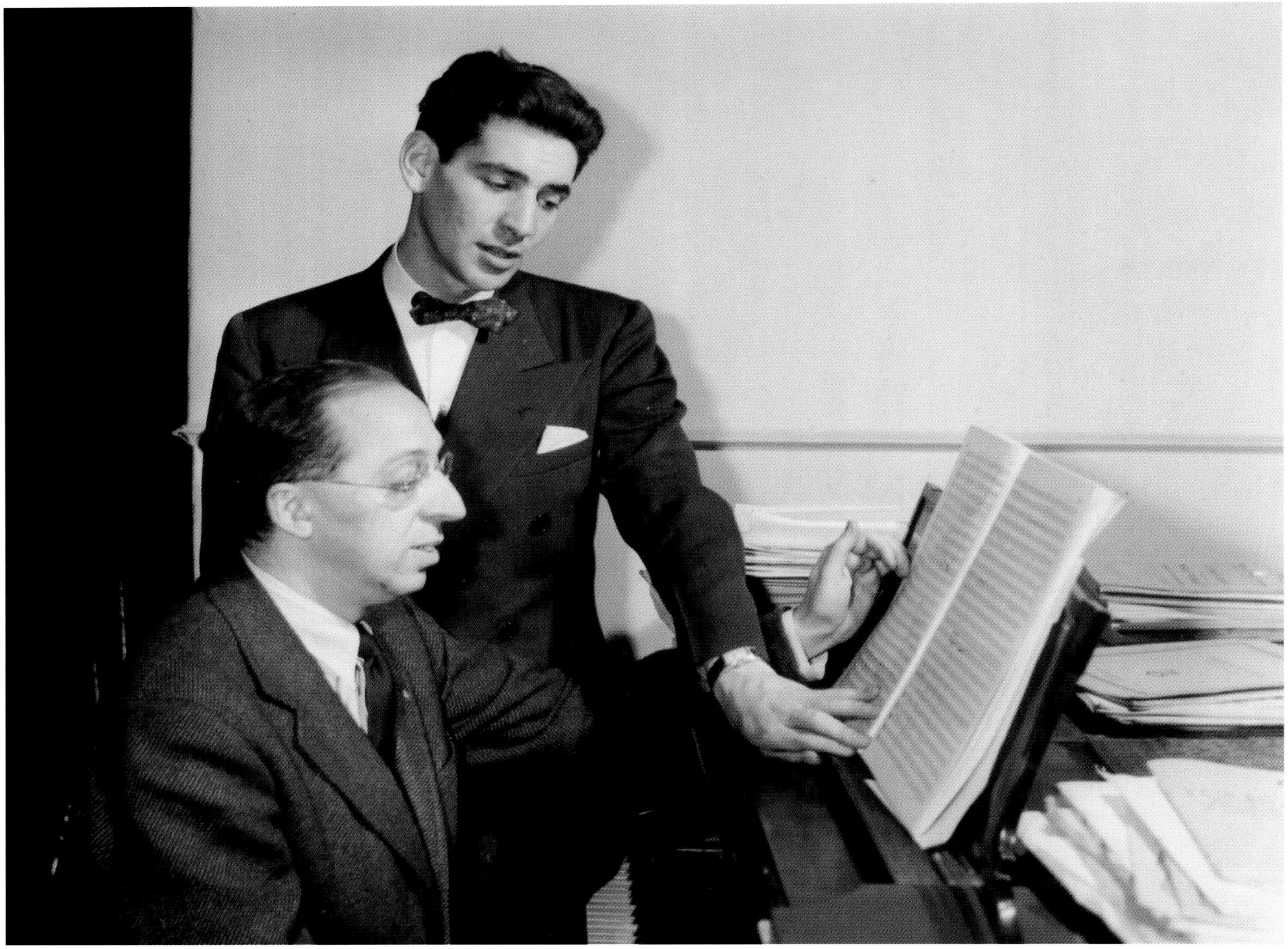

Aaron Copland and Leonard Bernstein in 1940.

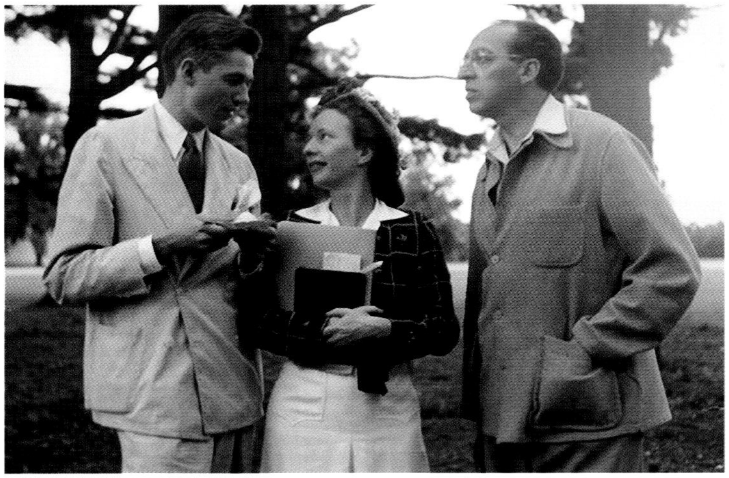

Aaron Copland, Agnes DeMille, and Oliver Smith at Tanglewood, 1942.

The Federal Music Project sponsored free concerts and transcriptions of sea chanteys, cowboy and folk songs, Indian dances, Quaker hymns, and Negro spirituals (see text about Grace Falke Tugwell especially).

Aaron Copland wrote that the rediscovery of folk music by the Federal Music Project and the rise of radio allowed him to "say what I had to say in the simplest possible terms in 'The Second Hurricane,' a children's play opera, 'Music for Radio,' and the ballet scores for 'Billy the Kid,' 'Rodeo,' and 'Appalachian Spring.'" As a film music composer in Hollywood, Copland scored films providing musical images

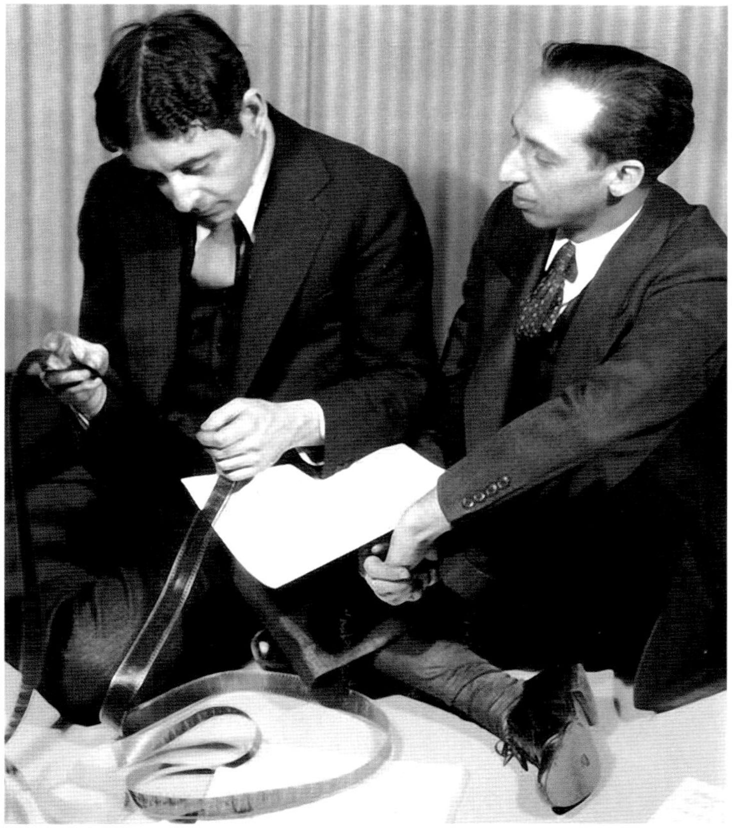

Aaron Copland and Ralph Steiner looking at film, 1932.

that backed the dialogue of John Steinbeck, Thornton Wilder, Lillian Hellman, and Henry James. Scores included those for *Of Mice and Men, Our Town, The North Star, The Red Pony,* and *The Heiress.* In wartime, Copland produced his *Lincoln Portrait.* Many of his themes were borrowed from Mexican tavern songs, cowboy songs, and Shaker hymnody. Copland presented this sort of music directly in Old American Songs.

Marc Blitzstein's agitopera *The Cradle Will Rock* was produced in 1937 by the Federal Theatre Project to support striking garment workers. The sweatshop owners did not like the message, and the New Deal's opponents disliked spending taxpayers' money on support for unions. Just before the premiere, the WPA cut off funding, and the right to use the costumes, the sets, and the orchestra was denied. Rather than call off the performance, Orson Welles (the director) and John Houseman (the producer) transferred the venue to the Venice Theater, twenty-one blocks uptown, rented it for one hundred dollars, and the cast, crew, and audience trekked to Fifty-ninth Street and Seventh Avenue. At 9 p.m., Welles and Houseman stood on the stage to introduce the play and the curtains rose to reveal Marc Blitzstein in his shirtsleeves at his piano, illuminated by a single spotlight operated by Abe Feder. Blitzstein wrote later that "I saw the place was jammed to the rafters. The side aisles were lined with cameramen and recorders. And there was I, alone on a bare stage, perched before the naked piano in my shirt sleeves." The conductor, Lehman Engel, "had rushed home, got his winter overcoat, and returned to smuggle my orchestra score out of one theater and into another." The Federal Theatre Project decided to release the play as it was performed that night, and it played for two more weeks at the Venice to sold-out crowds. It went on a national tour, played on Broadway for thirteen weeks, and became the first original-cast Broadway musical play to be recorded as a complete production.

As a Harvard senior in 1939, Leonard Bernstein organized a student production of Blitzstein's opera in oratorio style, with performers in everyday clothes, seated on a bare stage, stepping forward for their numbers. The Boston police refused permission for the FTP performance of *The Cradle Will Rock*, so Bernstein put it on exactly as it had been done in New York, himself substituting for Blitzstein—the Harvard Campus Police, in Cambridge, were more sympathetic than the Boston constabulary.

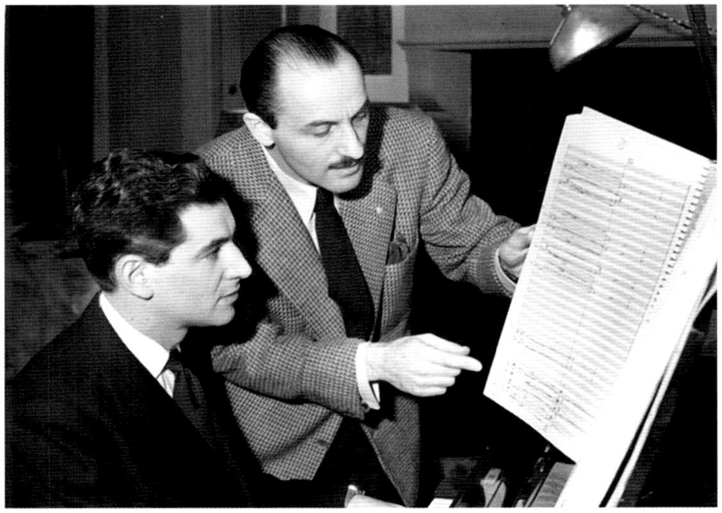

Leonard Bernstein and Marc Blitzstein, March 1946

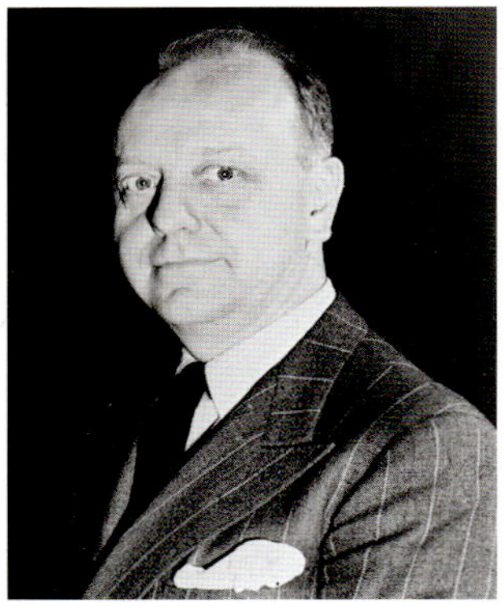

Above:
Portrait of Virgil Thomson

Virgil Thomson's scores for Pare Lorentz's *The Plow That Broke the Plains* and *The River*, and for Robert Flaherty's *Louisiana Story*, have become his best-known works. He had produced an opera based on Gertrude Stein's *Four Saints in Three Acts*, directed by John Houseman. Houseman became co-director with Orson Welles of the WPA Negro Theater Project's *Macbeth*, for which Thomson provided incidental music. Thomson also wrote the music for a production of Hamlet directed by Houseman.

Aaron Copland wrote that Thomson's score for *The River* provided "a lesson in how to treat Americana" and certainly Copland learned from it, as did Roy Harris. In film music Thomson's scores for Lorentz offered a folkish yet astringent alternative to the late–Romantic Germanic scores of Erich Korngold and Franz Waxman.

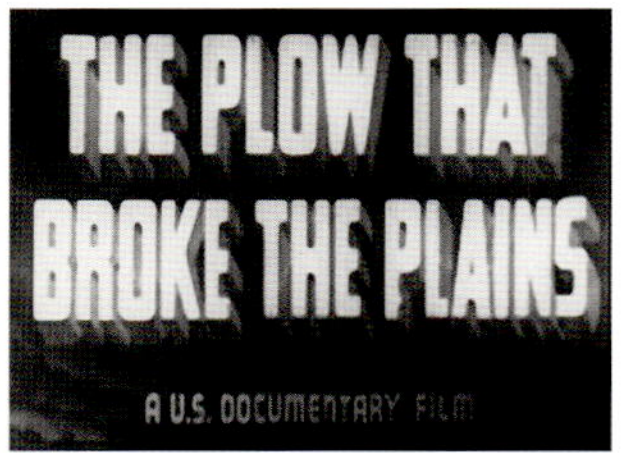

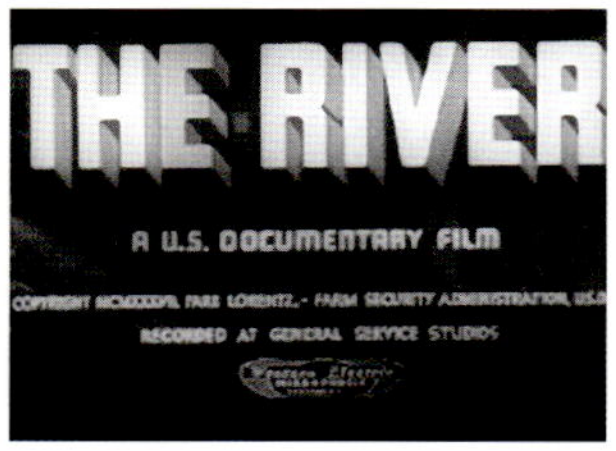

Above:
Main titles of *The Plow That Broke the Plains* and *The River*

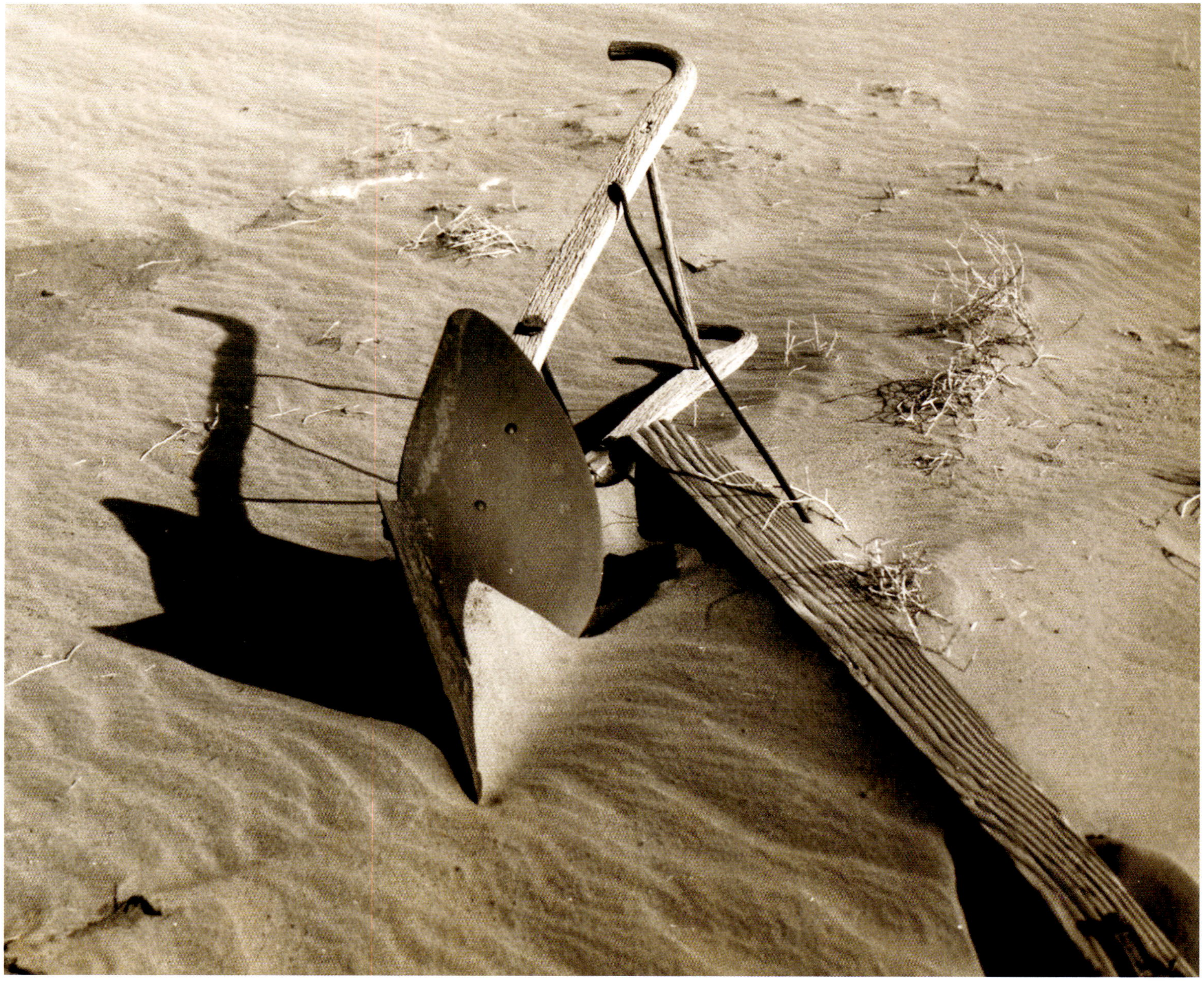

Right:
Plow covered by sand, Cimmaron County, Oklahoma
Arthur Rothstein, 1936

John Avery Lomax began contributing field recordings to the Library of Congress in 1932. During the next ten years, Lomax, his wife Ruby, his daughters Bess and Shirley, and his sons, John Jr. and Alan, recorded some of the most important traditional performers in the history of American folklore, including the African American singer and musician Huddie "Leadbelly" Ledbetter. In 1934, Lomax was named honorary consultant and curator of the Archive of American Folk Song at the Library of Congress and later became an advisor in several capacities to the WPA. John and Ruby Lomax made a famous "Southern States Recording Trip" in 1939, collecting sound recordings, and documents, on a sixty-five-hundred-mile expedition. Approximately twenty-five hours of folk music from more than three hundred performers included ballads, blues, children's songs, cowboy songs, fiddle tunes, field hollers, lullabies, play-party songs, spirituals, prison songs, and work songs.

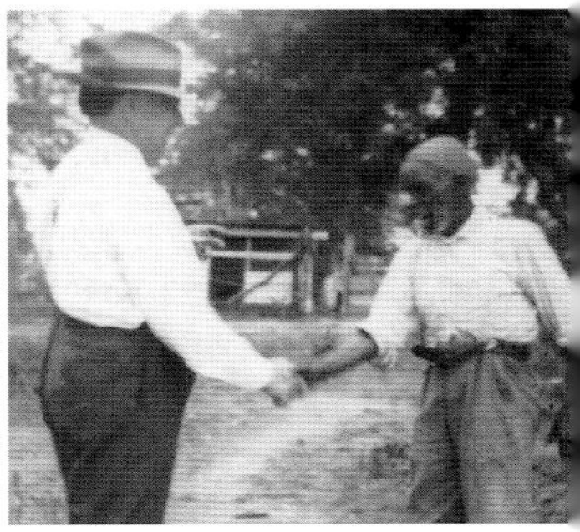

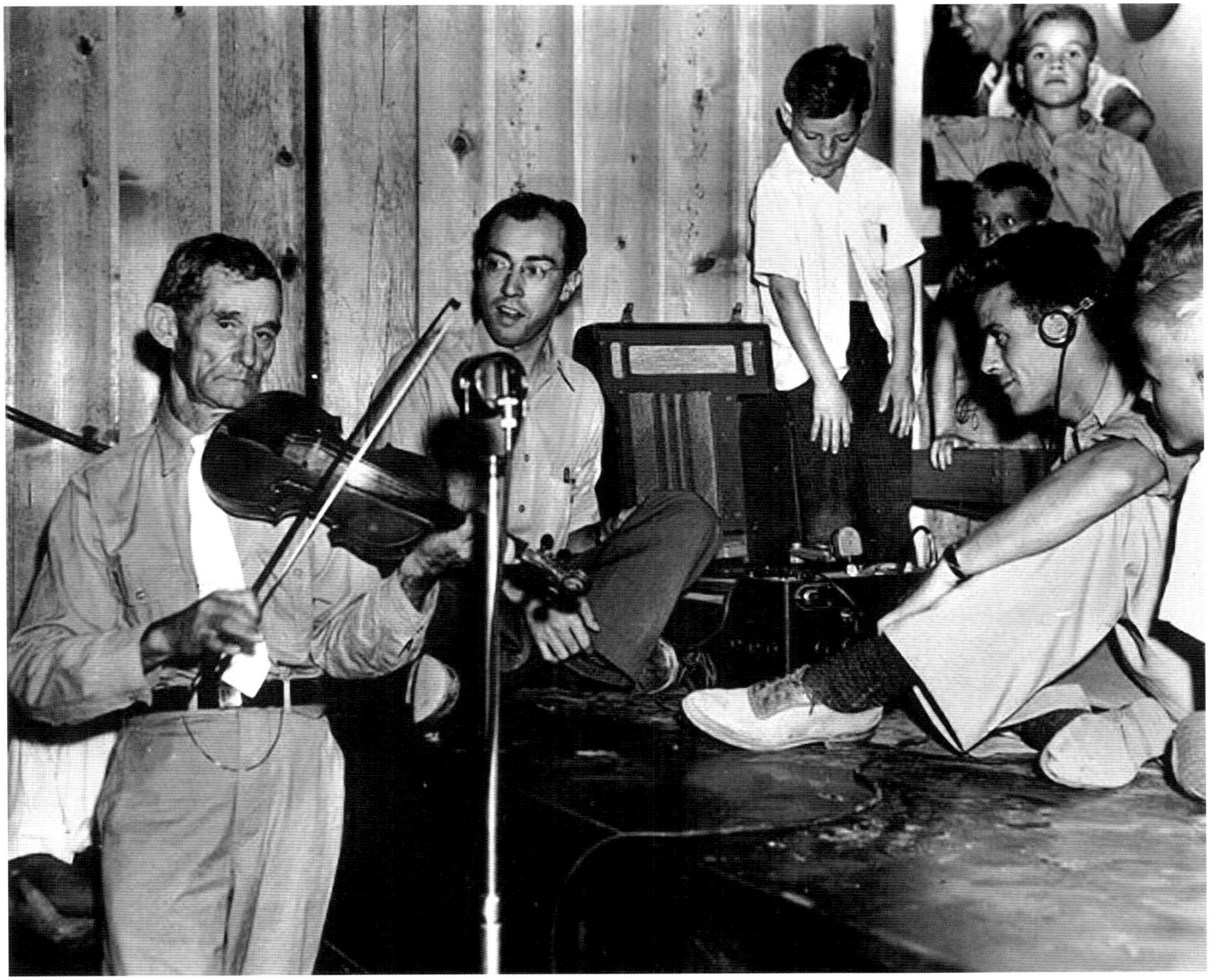

Above:
Uncle Rich Brown and John A. Lomax (*left*) at the home of Mrs. Julia Killingsworth near Sumterville, Alabama, 1940

Left:
Will Neal playing fiddle and being recorded by Charles Todd and Robert Sonkin.
Arvin FSA Camp, 1940

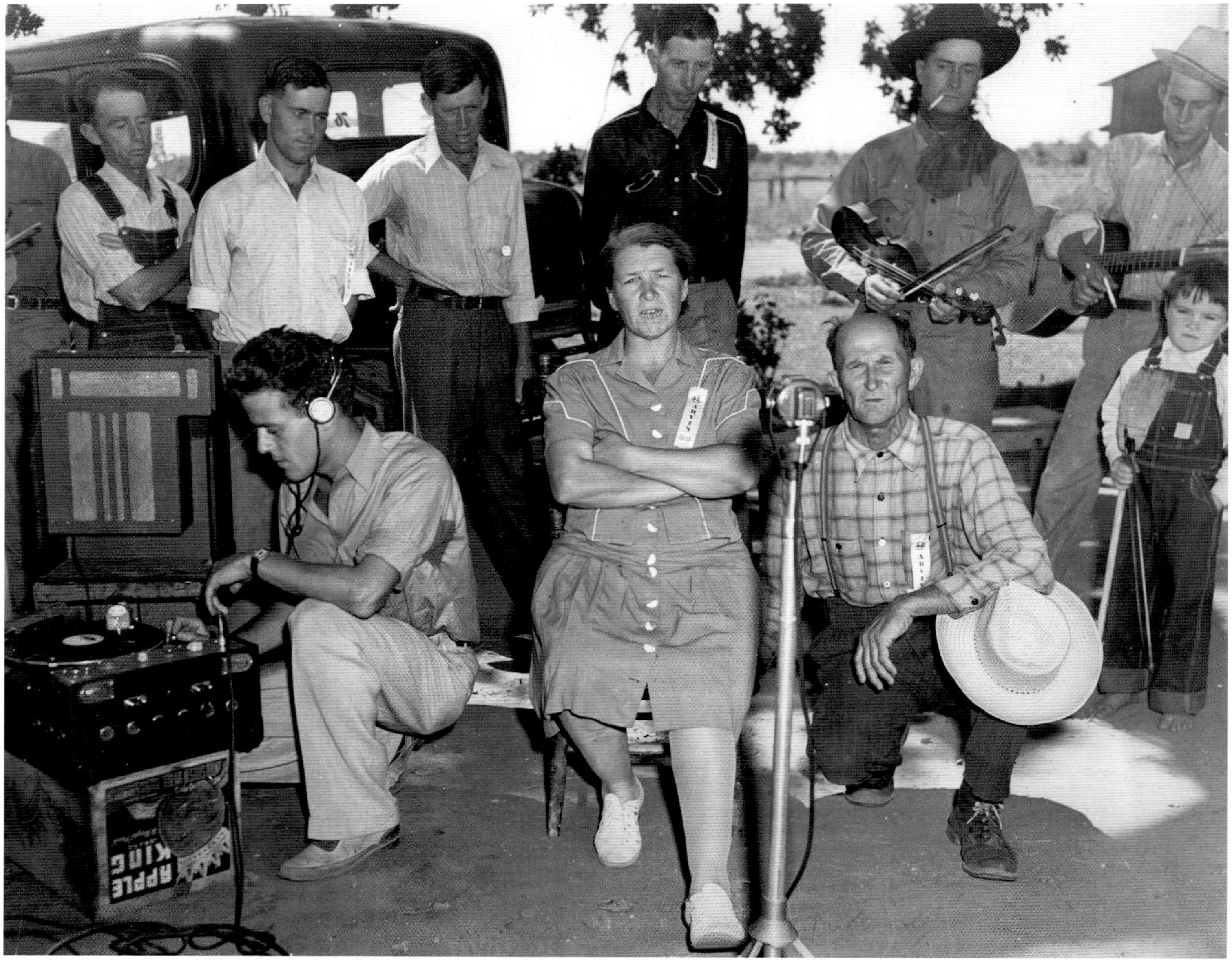

Mr. and Mrs. Frank Pipkin being recorded by Charles Todd with seven men and a little boy in the background.

According to Charles Todd, "Mrs. Pipkin was a gold mine of Old English ballads. Many thought of her as the prototype for Ma Joad in The Grapes of Wrath." When Todd was doing his recording sessions, John Steinbeck was in the same camps doing research for *The Grapes of Wrath.*

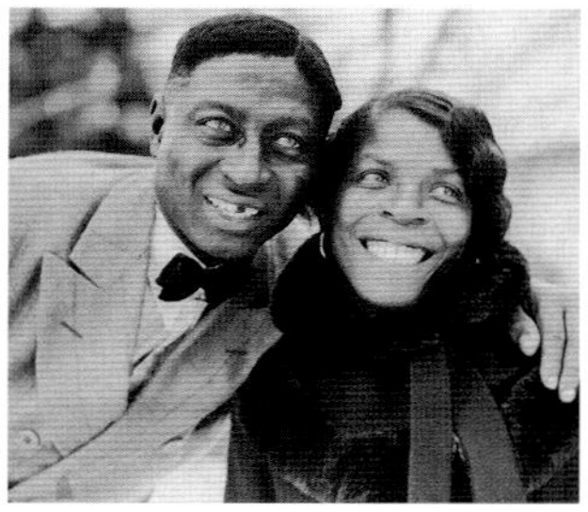

Huddie Ledbetter (Leadbelly) and Martha Promise Ledbetter, Wilton, Connecticut, February, 1935.

Alan Lomax: ". . . the thing that I always tried to do with important singers when I met them was to sit down and record everything they knew, give them a first real run-through of their art. They heard it all back, they listened to it, they rejoiced in it with someone who appreciated it, maybe, as much as they did. And this was a tremendous experience for people who may have been isolated in their own communities. Suddenly they see their thing from a wider perspective . . . I think that's maybe the most important thing that folklorists and people interested in the people's art do in their work. They give music, musicians, talent, an audience that maybe they lost in their own community because times have changed, commercial music has come in and taken the place of what they had. So they get a chance to understand how great they are in that process of listening, recording, and recapitulating their whole artistic heritage.

"My father and I met Lead Belly in the Angola Penitentiary in 1933. We came there looking for the roots of American black song, and we certainly found them with Lead Belly. I'll never forget: He approached us all the way from the

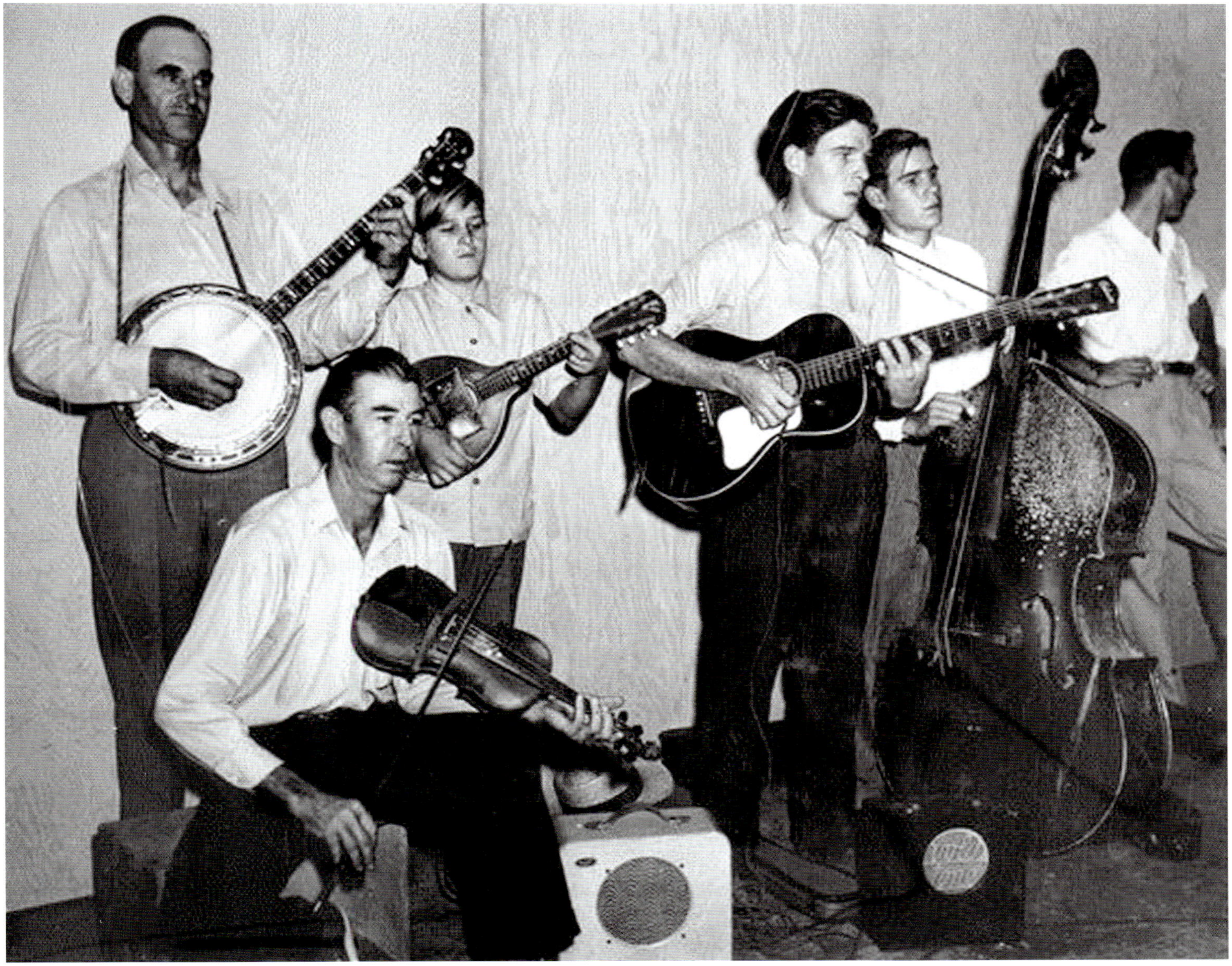

King family playing music

building where he worked, with his big twelve-string guitar in his hand. He sat down in front of us and proceeded to sing everything that we could think of in this beautiful, clear, trumpet-like voice that he had, with his hand simply flying on the strings. His hands were like a whirlwind, and his voice was like a great clear trumpet. You could hear him, literally, half a mile away when he opened up. . . . And I think the thing that he felt in himself and transmitted to his audience, and the thing that has made him a figure that no one can forget, that impressed the whole world, was the fact that he endured this incredible experience of work in the backward, dangerous, reactionary South, prison experiences, and came out of it with a laugh like a boy, with a sense of total joy in himself . . .

"It was this note of triumph, an old note that came from the generations of work-song singers, his ancestors in Africa and in the U.S. who cleared the land for cultivation, that echoed through Lead Belly's voice . . . Lead Belly didn't write many songs. What he did, more remarkably than that—we told him one time, 'Lead Belly, you know, these Yankees

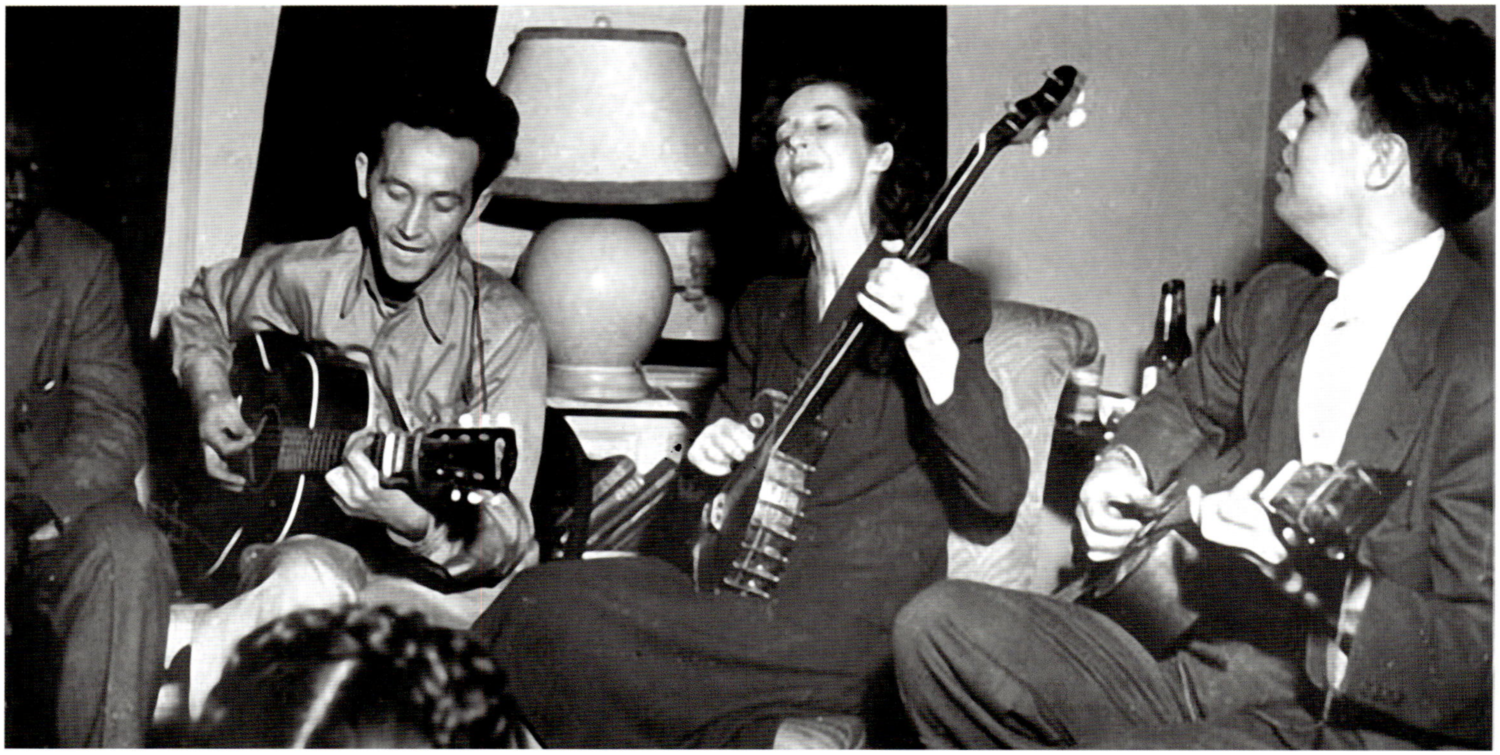

Sonny Terry (obscured), Woody Guthrie, Lilly Mae Ledford, Alan Lomax, New York, 1944.

Alan Lomax began collecting folk music for the Library of Congress at the age of eighteen.

don't understand anything you're singing about.' So Lead Belly said, 'I'll explain it to them.' And he began to annotate his songs with kind of a preacher's chant between every verse explaining exactly what the lyrics were about, what the dialogue in the songs concerned. And by the time he'd finished singing one of these songs, you had experienced a kind of a black drama—you'd been at a happening in a black house, a fight at a country dance, or something like that . . .

"I'll never forget the first time I saw Woody [Guthrie]. We were doing a benefit for this Spanish cause, the Spanish Loyalists who were fighting against Franco, and Woody was on the show. It was one of the first nights he was in New York. He stepped out on the stage, this little tiny guy, big bushy hair, with this great voice and his guitar, and just electrified us all. I remember the first song I heard him sing: 'Mention Dirty to My Heart.' It was a ballad about Pretty Boy Floyd: [singing] 'Come and gather round me children, and a story I'll tell, about Pretty Boy Floyd the outlaw, Oklahoma knew him well.' Well, I realized, listening to this song, that I was meeting a guy who was a ballad maker, in the same sense as the people who made 'Jesse James,' and 'Casey Jones,' and all the ballads that I spent my life trying to find and preserve for the American people. I thought they were from anonymous people. Well, here was Mr. Anonymous singing to me . . . And he did then turn to being a full-time American ballad writer and prose writer. And I think that his model maybe set up many things for writers and ballad makers all over the world."[13]

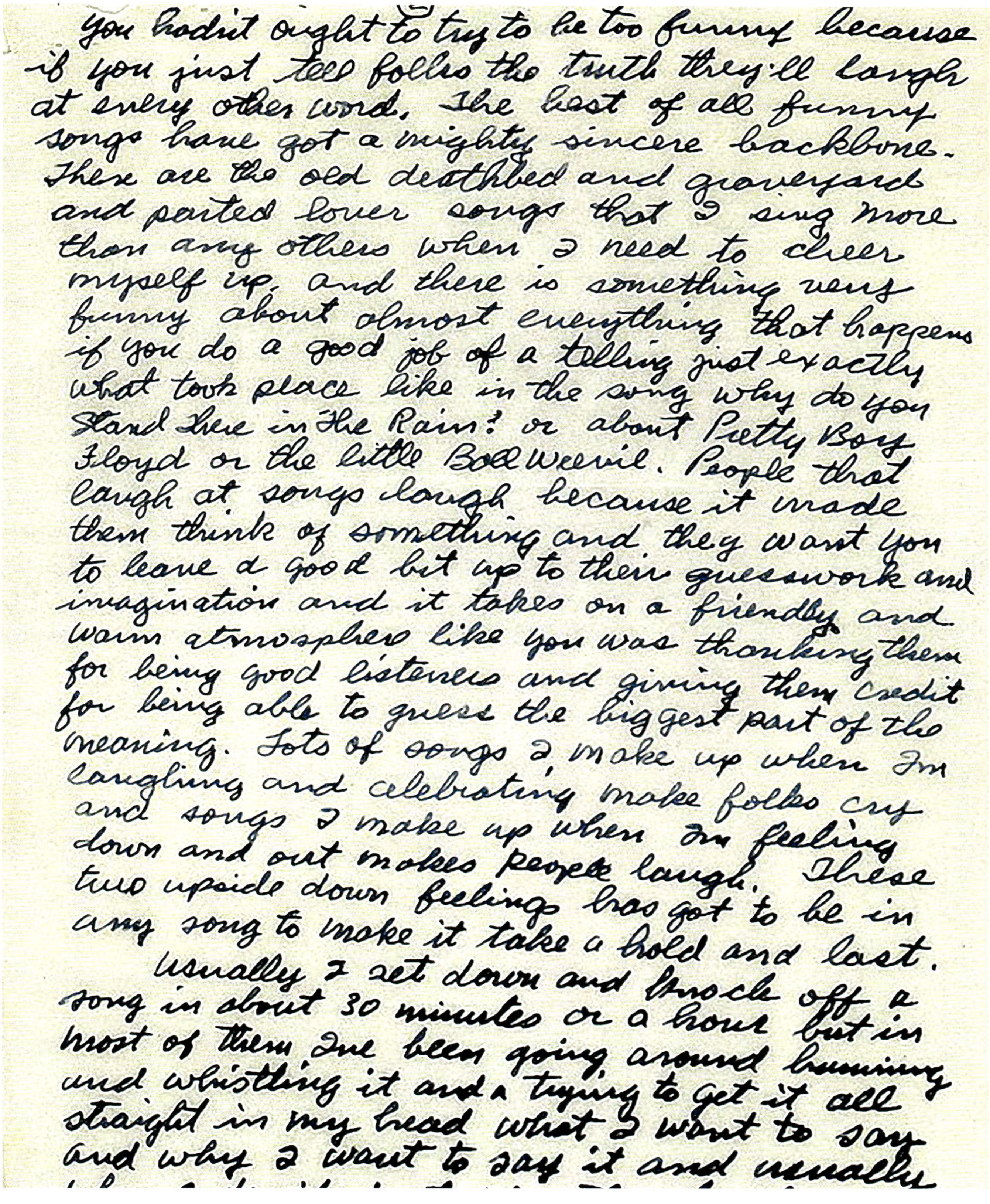

You hadn't ought to try to be too funny because if you just tell folks the truth they'll laugh at every other word. The best of all funny songs have got a mighty sincere backbone. These are the old deathbed and graveyard and parted lover songs that I sing more than any others when I need to cheer myself up, and there is something very funny about almost everything that happens if you do a good job of a telling just exactly what took place like in the song why do you Stand there in The Rain? or about Pretty Boy Floyd or the little Boll Weevil. People that laugh at songs laugh because it made them think of something and they want you to leave a good bit up to their guesswork and imagination and it takes on a friendly and warm atmosphere like you was thanking them for being good listeners and giving them credit for being able to guess the biggest part of the meaning. Lots of songs I make up when I'm laughing and celebrating make folks cry and songs I make up when I'm feeling down and out makes people laugh. These two upside down feelings has got to be in any song to make it take a hold and last.

Usually I set down and knock off a song in about 30 minutes or a hour but in most of them I've been going around humming and whistling it and a trying to get it all straight in my head what I want to say and why I want to say it and usually

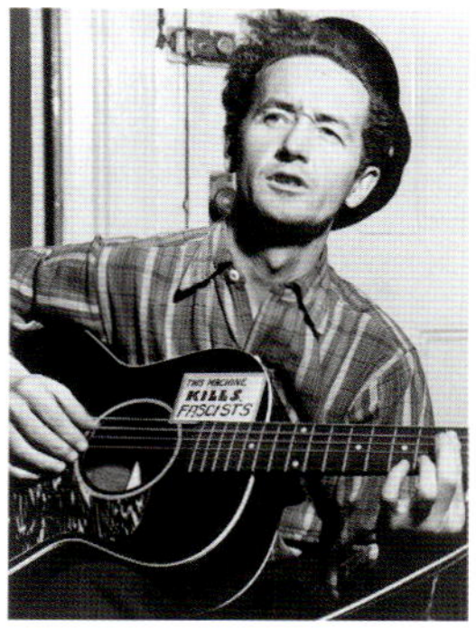

Woody Guthrie, 1943

Left:
A page from a letter by Woody Guthrie to Alan Lomax on songwriting, September 19, 1940

The Federal Writers' Project

In full disclosure, I hereby state that I treasure my association with those "banjo pickers, . . . gut-bucket strummers, . . . Texas fiddlers, . . . Tennessee yodelers, and Indiana jug bands," during my tenure as Director of the Smithsonian's National Museum of American History and its music programs, and further acknowledge a thrill of joyous recollection when I recall working with veterans of the WPA/FAP Writers' Project, when I was editor of the 1983 edition of the 1942 truncated version of the thousand-page, two volume, 1937 draft of the *WPA Guide to Washington*. The weighty original, the first of the *Guides*, had been produced by an array of first-rate writers who put into it some of their best brief work, but bulking it up to a size that made it no longer portable. They seem to have enjoyed themselves, but their work was too argumentative to be acceptable in the changed ideological climate of 1942. The 1983 version recovers some of the feistiness, and makes somewhat more explicit its debt to the then new discipline of oral history, as practiced by Studs Terkel and others, which the New Deal writers had cleverly intertwined with the then equally new statistical "social science," as well as with the older arts of photography and lithography. As the literary critic Alfred Kazin wrote, "road by road, town by town, down under the alluvia of industrial culture . . . {the *Guides* helped} give . . . a foundation in the American inheritance {through} an extraordinary self-scrutiny" providing to the "dispossessed" affirmation that somewhere they belonged.[14]

The WPA/FAP Writers' Project employed nearly sixty-seven hundred writers at its peak, including Terkel, Ralph Ellison, Richard Wright, John Cheever, Saul Bellow, Margaret Walker, Arna Bontemps, and Zora Neale Hurston. Three million copies of eight hundred titles were produced by 1941. Among them were slave narratives, studies in architecture, science, and American Indian cultures, and a great deal of fundamental research, editing, and text for other government agencies.[15]

The Historical Records Survey

Only people who know the struggle to find the truth in history, to understand what people thought was happening to them as it happened, and to convey a sense of such matters can fully appreciate the work of the smallest and least expensive of the components of the WPA/FAP, the Historical Records Survey. All historians, indeed all citizens, are beneficiaries of the archivists who went forth to find the fundamental documents of our history and to preserve them as the written counterparts to the images provided by the Index of Design.

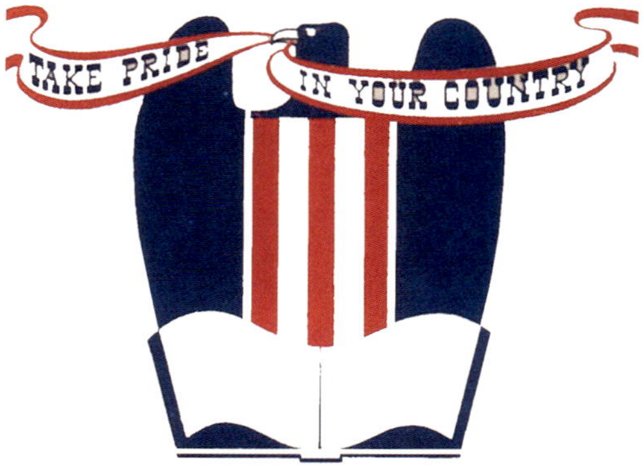

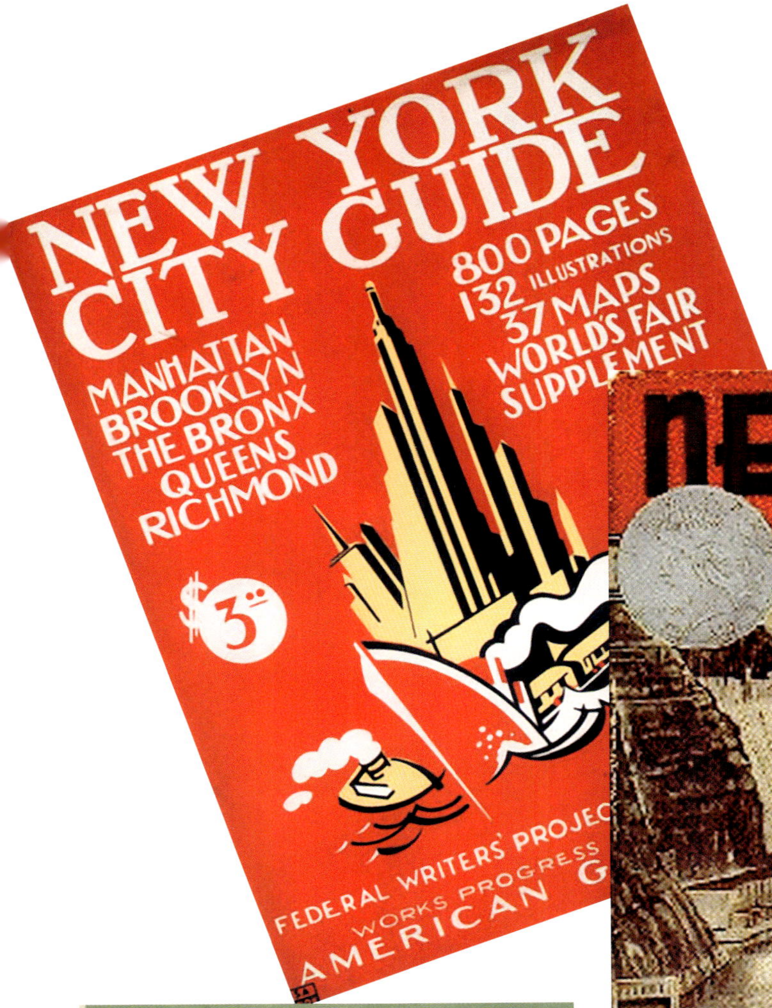

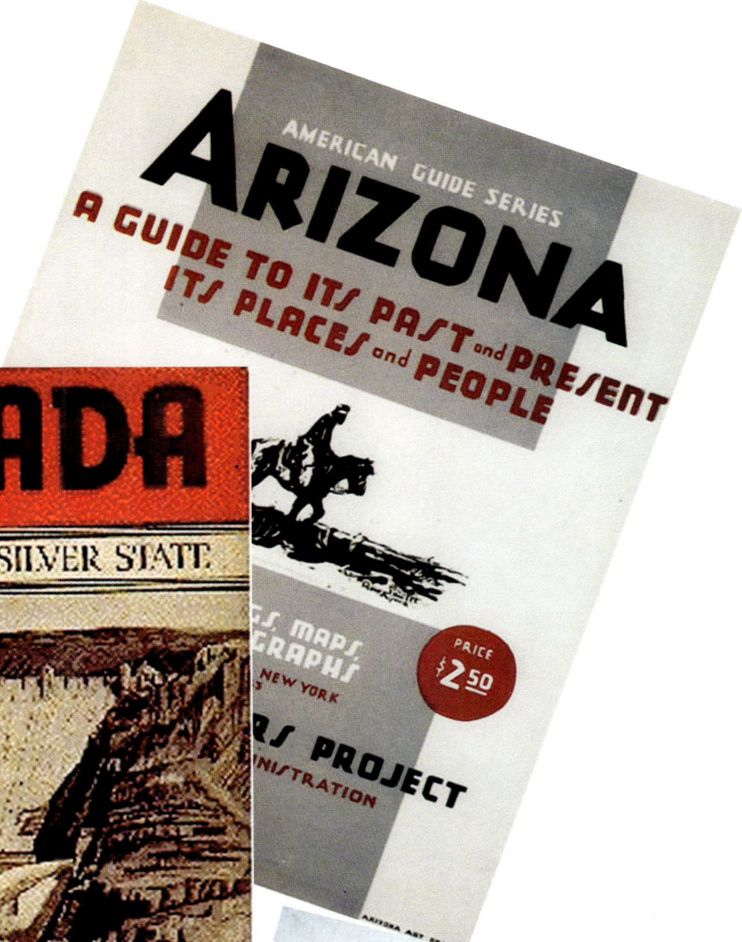

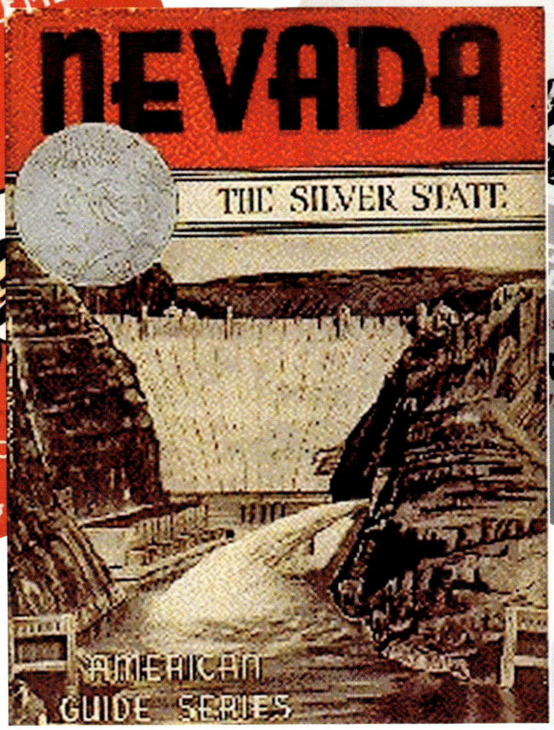

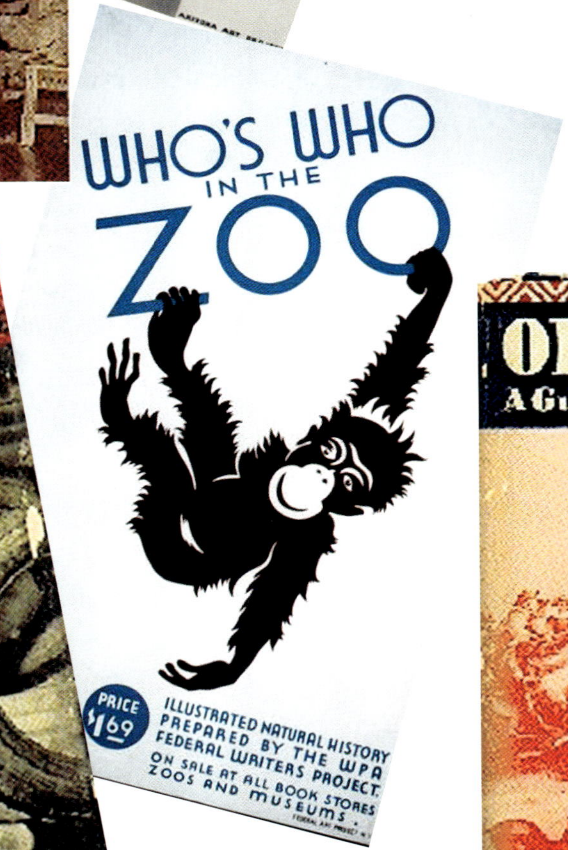

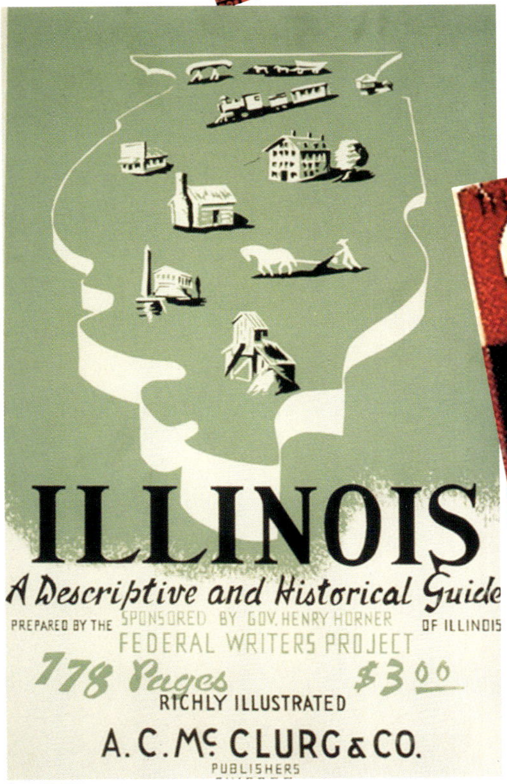

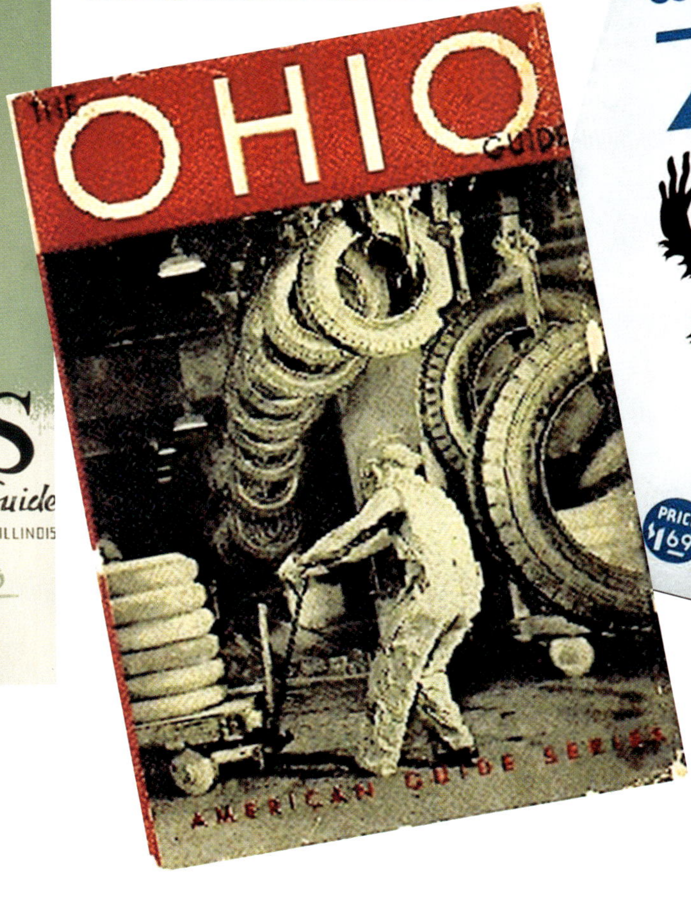

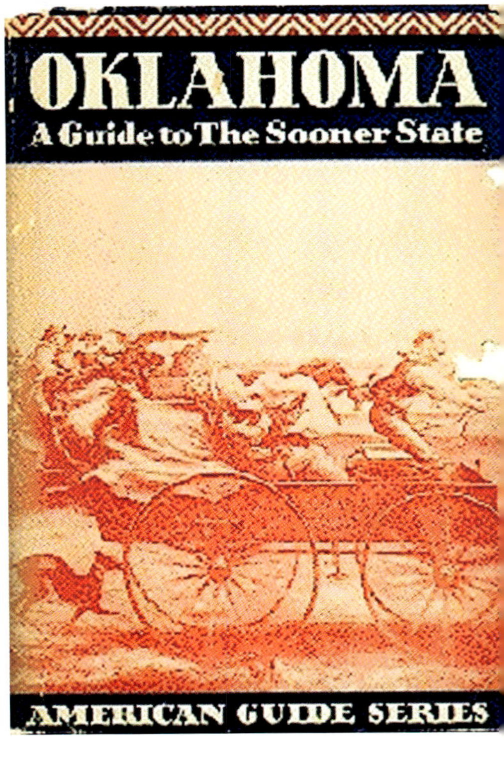

The WPA Guides (see main text)

The American Guides—in part travel guides, in part social commentaries, and in part regional histories—were the great achievement of the WPA Federal Writers Project. The Project at its height employed more than seventy-five hundred men and women. *Time* wrote of it in 1943 that for "a total expenditure of $27,189,370, the Project published enough written matter to fill seven 12-ft. shelves in the library of the Department of the Interior, . . . approximately a thousand publications, including pamphlets; a guidebook for each of the 48 States, the U.S. Territories; 30 book-length city guides; . . . twenty other guides such as U.S. One, Maine to Florida, The Oregon Trail, Here's New England; one hundred fifty volumes in the series Life in America, ranging from Cavalcade of the American Negro to Baseball in Old Chicago." The writers received prevailing WPA wages, averaging ninety-three dollars a month in northern cities, eighty-five dollars elsewhere.

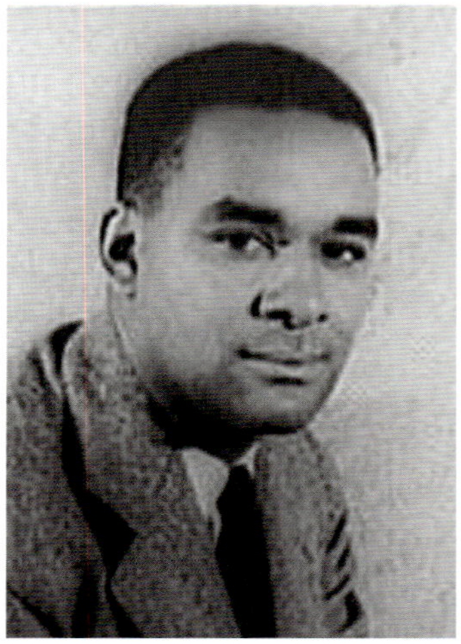

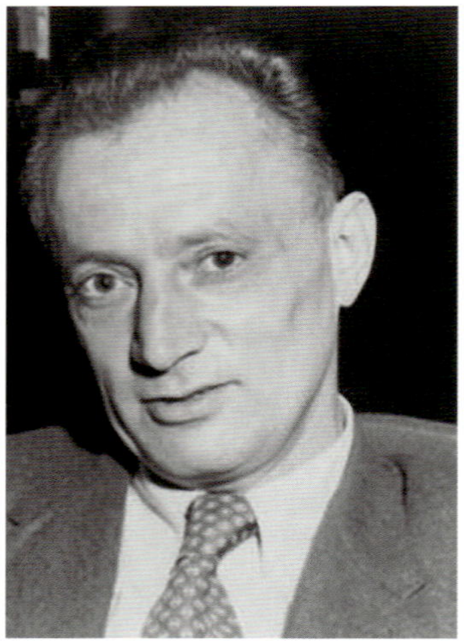

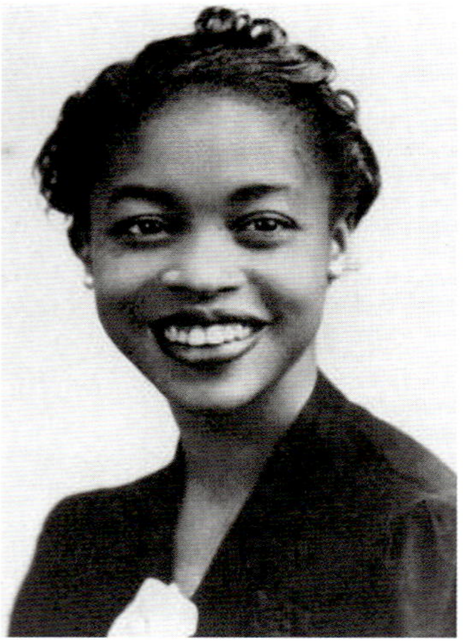

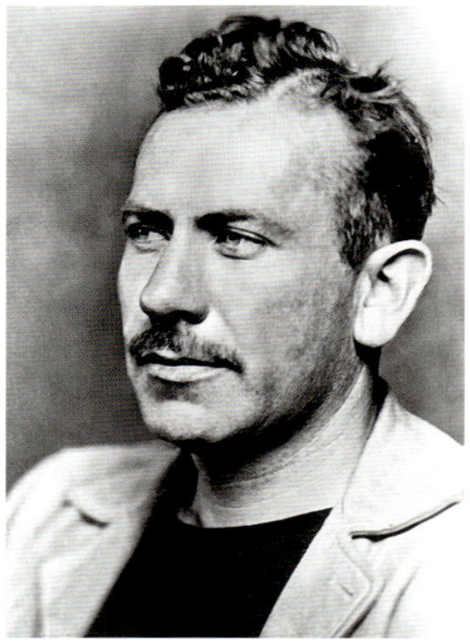

Top, left to right:
Richard Wright
Nelson Algren
Margaret Walker
John Steinbeck

Below:
The Grapes of Wrath original jacket

Steinbeck's novel was banned, burned, denounced, debated, read, and honored, becoming a reality-defining experience for many people. Its political effects were enormous. As art, it worked. The Associated Farmers of California were displeased with the book's depiction of California farmers' attitudes and conduct toward the migrants, and denounced it as "a pack of lies" and "communist propaganda." The John Ford film of 1940 was, in fact, more political and further to the left in its message.

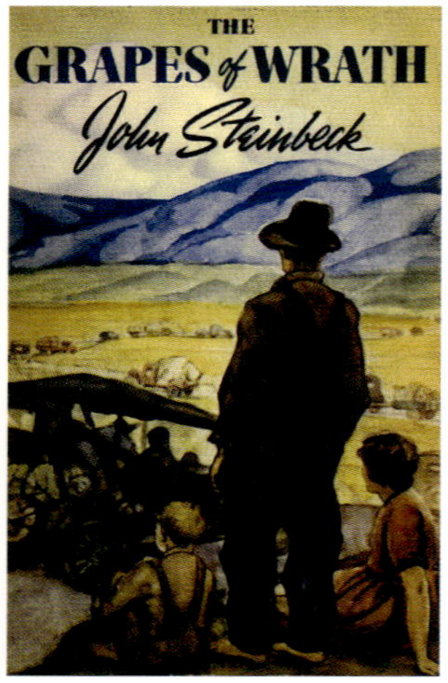

Richard Wright

Richard Wright grew up in Mississippi. In *Native Son* and *The Outsider* he set a tone for African American literature in a "nationalist spirit . . . a new culture in the shell of the old . . . And . . . when a people begin to realize a meaning in their suffering, the civilization that engenders that suffering is doomed." Both he and his African American colleague Zora Neale Hurston worked for the WPA Federal Writers' Project, and took an intense interest in folklore, including folk music, but he derided Hurston and the Harlem Renaissance as too bland, only "worthy of French poodles who do clever tricks."

Nelson Algren

While enrolled in the WPA/Federal Writers' Project, Nelson Algren made the prostitutes and junkies of East St. Louis characters in his novels and short stories. One of his WPA projects was the "America Eats" program to "produce a series of regional guides describing immigration, settlement and customs as these factors related to the universal language of food," ultimately published in 1992.

Margaret Walker

Margaret Walker was born in Birmingham in 1915, attended Northwestern, and became a part of the Harlem Renaissance with Zora Neale Hurston, Langston Hughes, and W. E. B. Du Bois. Her colleagues in the Illinois WPA Writers' Project included Saul Bellow, Studs Terkel, Arna Bontemps, and Richard Wright, whose biography she wrote.

John Steinbeck

John Steinbeck lived in Pacific Grove, California, near Monterey, where much of the material for *Tortilla Flat* and *Cannery Row* was gathered. He said of the WPA that "when it came we were delighted, because it offered work . . . I was given the project of taking a census of all the dogs on the Monterey Peninsula, their breeds, weights and characters. I did it very thoroughly and, since I knew my reports were not likely to get to the hands of the mighty, I wrote some pretty searching character studies of poodles and beagles and hounds. If such records were kept, somewhere in Washington, there will be a complete dog record of the Monterey Peninsula in the early thirties." Maybe, but the WPA made possible his inquiries into conditions in the camps of migrant farm workers, where he found the material—and inspiration—for *The Grapes of Wrath*, which won him the Pulitzer Prize.

The Federal Theatre Project

Alfred Kazin also affirmed the success of the Federal Theatre Project in offering reassurance to "a nation . . . hungry for news of itself." At full tilt, the Theatre Project employed 12,700 people and played to an estimated audience of 30 million people, three-fourths of whom got free admission. Many saw "live theater for the first time." It had units in thirty-one states and New York City, some proliferating into several companies, giving more than one thousand performances each month. Among its twelve hundred productions, there was an all-black *Macbeth* in New York produced by Orson Welles and John Houseman, and Marc Blitzstein's opera, *The Cradle Will Rock*. Sinclair Lewis's admonition against the rise of American fascism, *It Can't Happen Here*, was presented with Lewis playing the lead. Other productions provided paying jobs for E. G. Marshall, Burt Lancaster, Joseph Cotten, Sidney Lumet, Martin Ritt, Elia Kazan, Will Geer, Arthur Miller, Joseph Losey, Canada Lee, and Nicholas Ray, and among composers, both Blitzstein and Virgil Thomson. Radio voices developed by the FTP included that of Welles on the "Federal Theatre of the Air," which reached ten million listeners on all the major networks.

Many offstage people in the theater business needed work as well; thirty thousand musicians—pit organists and pianists among them—were being replaced by recorded music, while motion pictures replaced vaudeville and live theaters closed as movie palaces were built. Loews had thirty-six houses offering live entertainment in 1930; by 1934, Loews was down to three, and live entertainers lost jobs to projected flickers upon a screen. The Living Newspapers presented dramatized newspaper clippings and commentary that was described by the director of the Theatre Project, Hallie Flanagan, as "adult," a term she and Harry Hopkins used to mean provocative of beneficial reform. When interviewed in 1964 for the Archives of American Art, Secretary Morgenthau recalled the friendships of his wife, Elinor, and Eleanor Roosevelt with Flanagan and their rallying behind her embattled program. Flanagan was an Iowan like her boss, Harry Hopkins, and like Hopkins became very sophisticated in urban culture after going to the Theatre Project from a professorship at Vassar. The Living Newpaper was an easy target for those who wanted the whole Theatre Project gutted, especially after it became the largest of the WPA/FAP programs, taking a third of its budget. The ultimate demise of the Theatre Project came from wartime budgetary constraints and as the outcome of congressional aversion to tax support for the Living Newspapers. Testimony had been introduced in Congressional hearings that the Living Newspapers had been invented in the Soviet Union by Jacob Leby Moreno, to provide what the regime of Joseph Stalin wanted the illiterate to know about the daily news; the playwright

Right:
Hallie Flanagan

Hallie Flanagan studied theater production in Europe. After teaching at Yale she became director of the Vassar Experimental Theatre in Poughkeepsie. Among those she put to work in the WPA/FTP were Orson Welles, John Houseman, Burt Lancaster, Joseph Cotten, Canada Lee, Will Geer, Joseph Losey, Virgil Thomson, Nicholas Ray, E. G. Marshall, and Sidney Lumet.

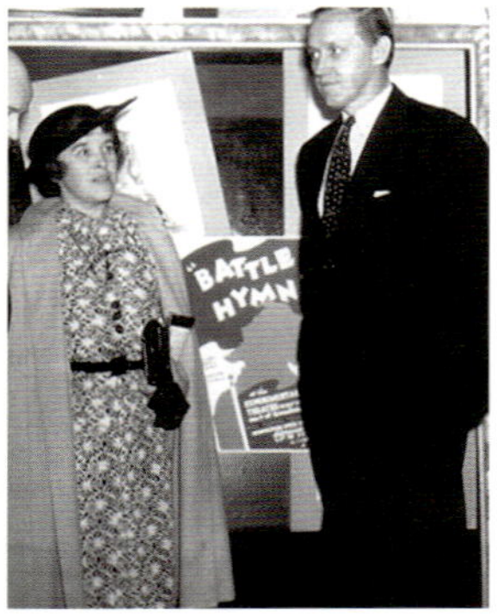

Above:
Hallie Flanagan and Harry Hopkins in the Lobby of the Experimental Theatre

Harry Hopkins was head of the FERA and WPA (see main text), within which Hallie Flanagan directed the Federal Theatre Project.

Bottom right:
"BATTLE HYMN" poster

Bottom far right:
"ONE THIRD OF A NATION"
Leon Carlin, 1936

Elmer Rice had made the concept integral to the Federal Theatre Project in New York City in 1935 when he was its director. Though Rice's Newspapers were without Stalinist messages, they had a distinct leftish tone, and Rice was intransigent: he later resigned when told that current political figures could not be impersonated at public expense on stage. Aside from its anti-fascist messages, it discouraged racial segregation, both on stage and in its audiences.[16]

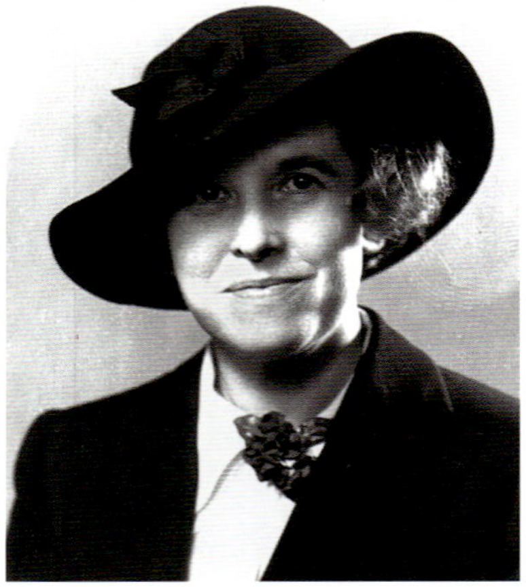

While they lasted, Living Newspapers dealt with syphilis testing, housing discrimination, racial injustice, employer nastiness to unions, and Supreme Court opposition to New Deal farm programs and the Tennessee Valley Authority. *Power* was about electric power and rural electrification; *Triple-A Plowed Under* was about the Supreme Court and the Agricultural Adjustment Act. *One Third of a Nation* was, it must be conceded, a famous phrase of the President, who was the chief executive of the administration paying the bills.

The New Deal produced magnificent art that was managed neither by the Treasury's Section nor by Federal One. There was art in the design of schools, hospitals, the Triborough Bridge, the Oakland–San

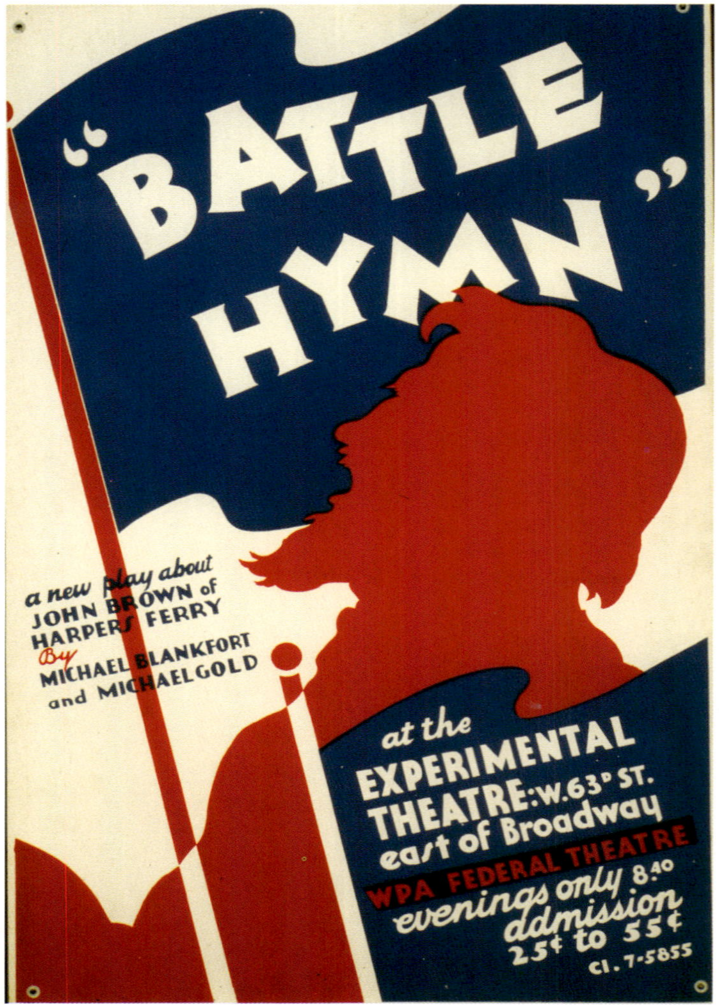

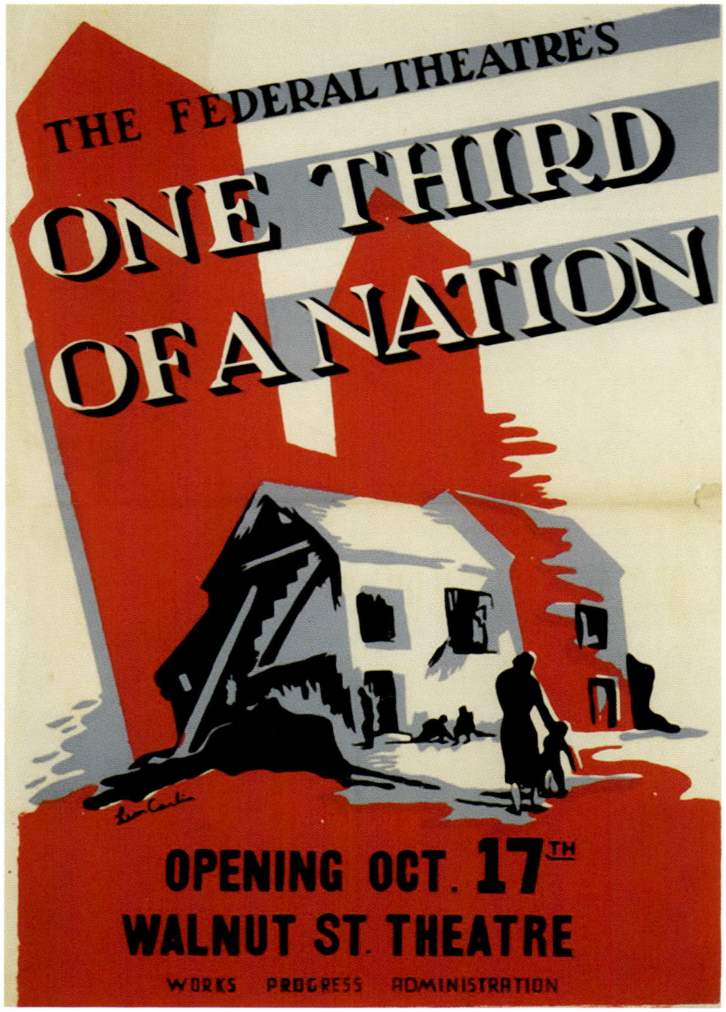

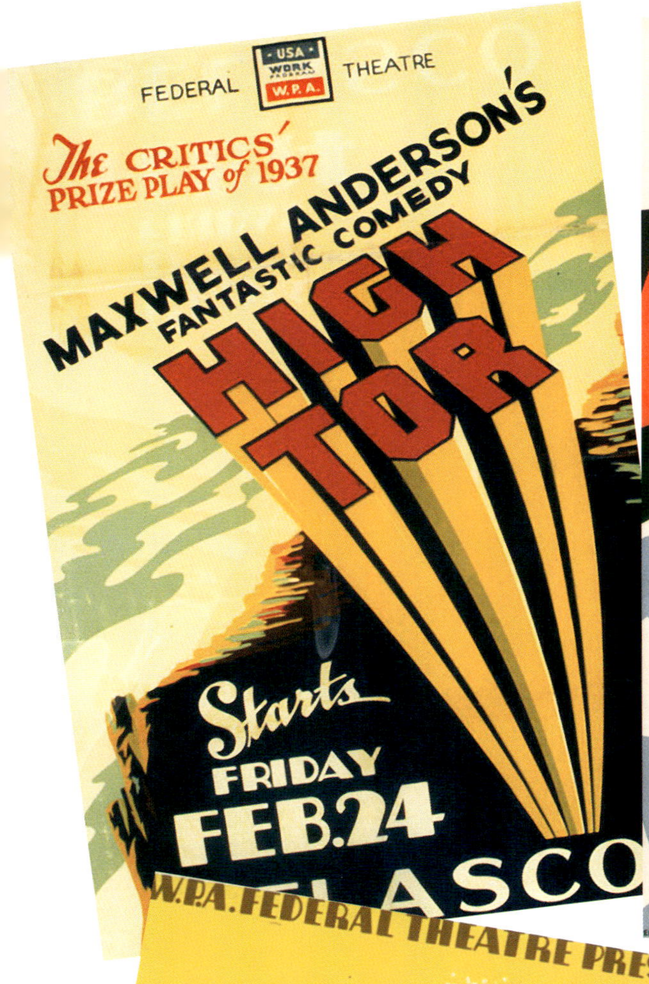

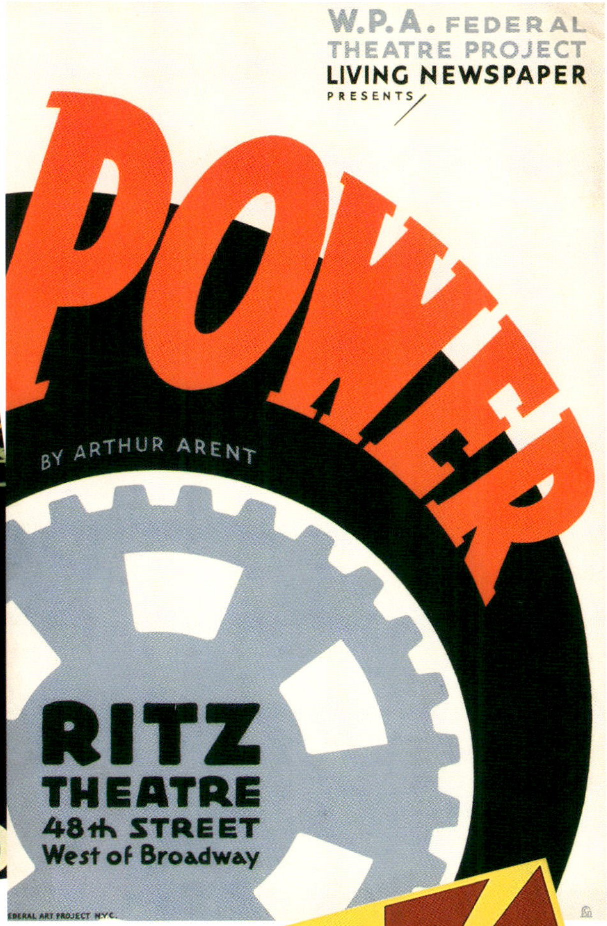

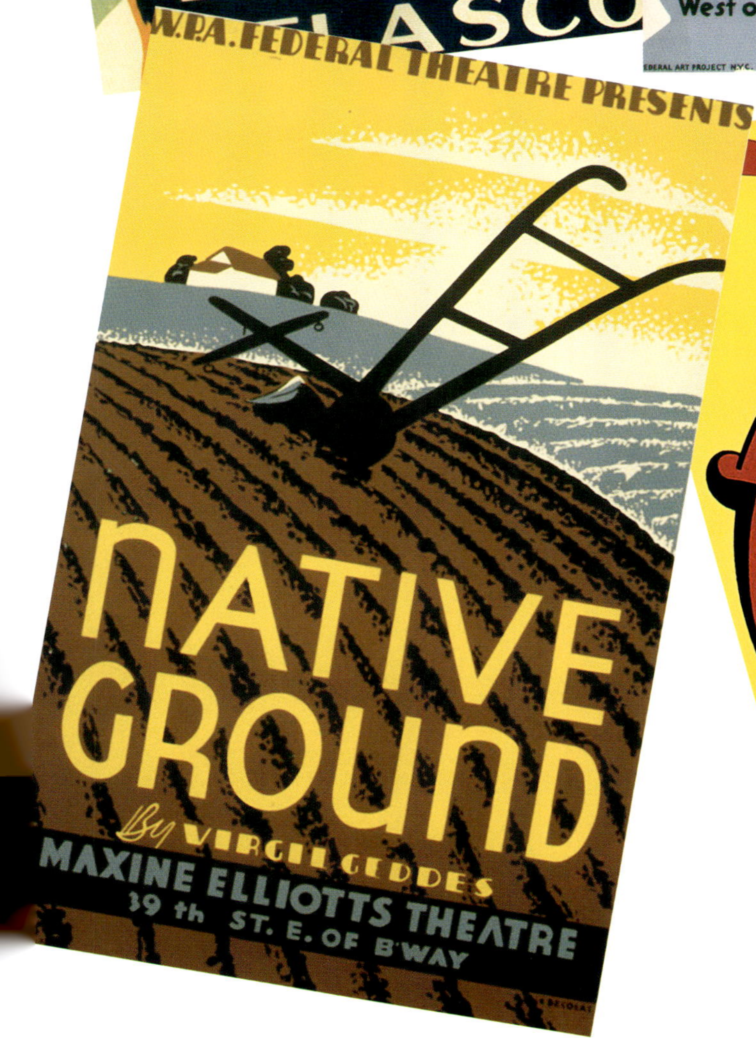

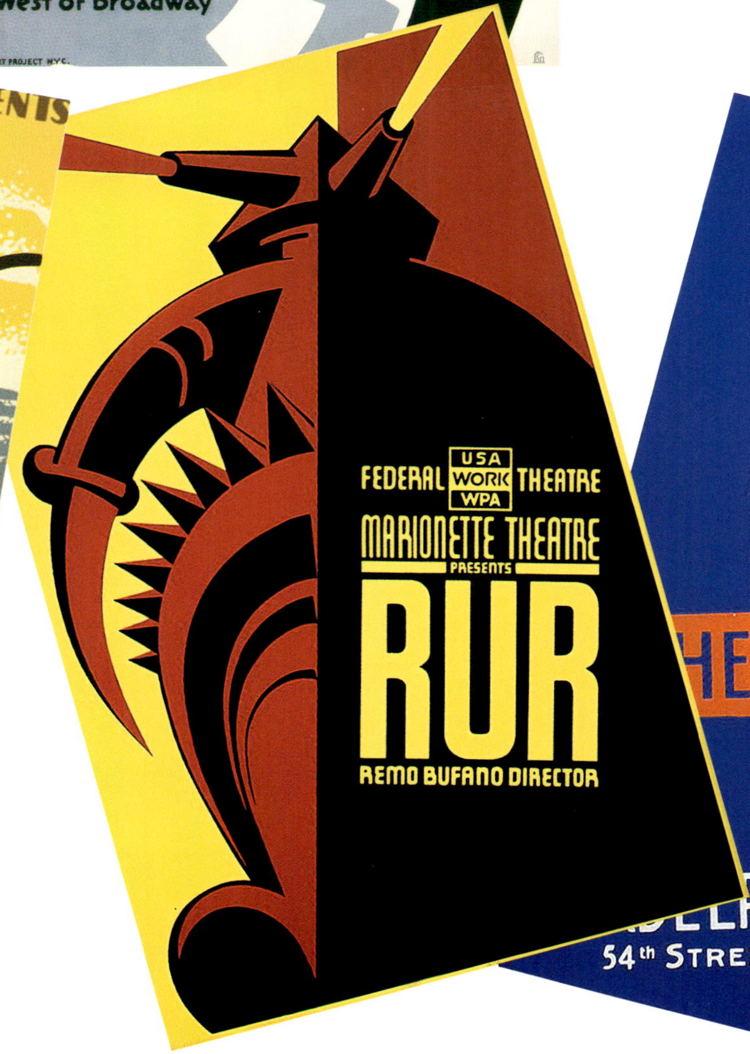

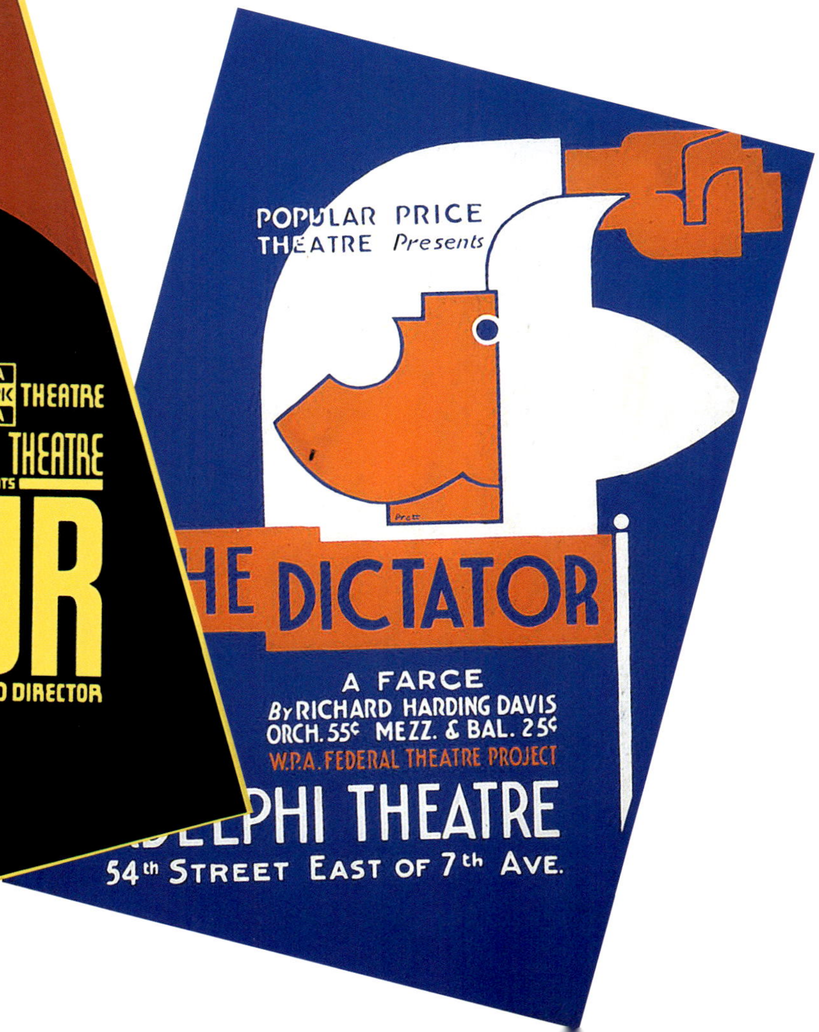

Clockwise from top left:
Maxwell Anderson's fantastic comedy *High Tor*, 1937

Poster for WPA/FTP presentation of *Power* by Arthur Arent, Ritz Theatre, New York City, 1937
A Living Newspaper Production

The concept of a "living newspaper" (see main text) originated in the Red Army's "Zhivaya Gazeta," and German and American agitprop troupes made use of large casts, spectacular sets, and film and vaudeville techniques to substitute for literate expression in illiterate societies. From 1935 to 1939 the Federal Theatre's living newspapers addressed agricultural reform, labor relations, public ownership of utilities, housing problems, and public health—but not race relations.

Popular Price Theatre presents *The Dictator*, a farce by Richard Harding Davis
Poster designed by Herbert W. Pratt

Poster for WPA/FTP presentation of *RUR* at the Marionette Theatre, 1939.
Poster designed by Charles Verschuuren

Native Ground by Virgil Geddes
Poster designed by Emanuel DeColas, 1939

Right:
"Sing for Your Supper: a topical musical revue"
Aida McKenzie, 1939

Far right:
The Cradle Will Rock
Marc Blitzstein
Poster for the 1937 performance
Federal Theatre Project Collection

Bottom right:
"Leaning on a shovel" skit from New York City prodution of *Sing for Your Supper*
New York City Federal Theatre Project, WPA, May 1939

A musical review, *Sing for Your Supper,* satirized the WPA/FTP itself as well as New Deal politicians. In the "leaning on a shovel" skit, WPA workers sang: "When you look at things today
Like Boulder Dam and TVA
And all those playgrounds where kids can play
We did it—by leaning on a shovel!"

Bottom middle:
Marc Blitzstein's *The Cradle Will Rock* in rehearsal

Marc Blitzstein was born in Philadelphia. His agitpr-opera *The Cradle Will Rock* was directed by Orson Welles. His opera *Regina* was adapted as an opera from Lillian Hell-man's *The Little Foxes.* Blitzstein composed music for films such as *Surf and Seaweed* and the docu-mentary *The Spanish Earth.*

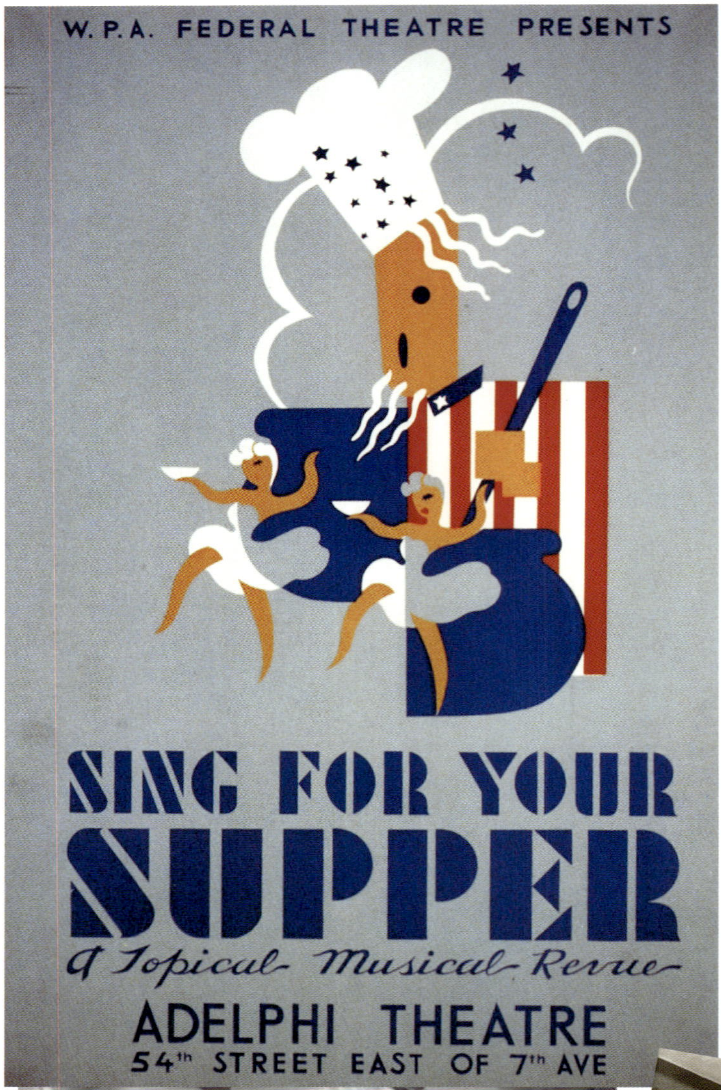

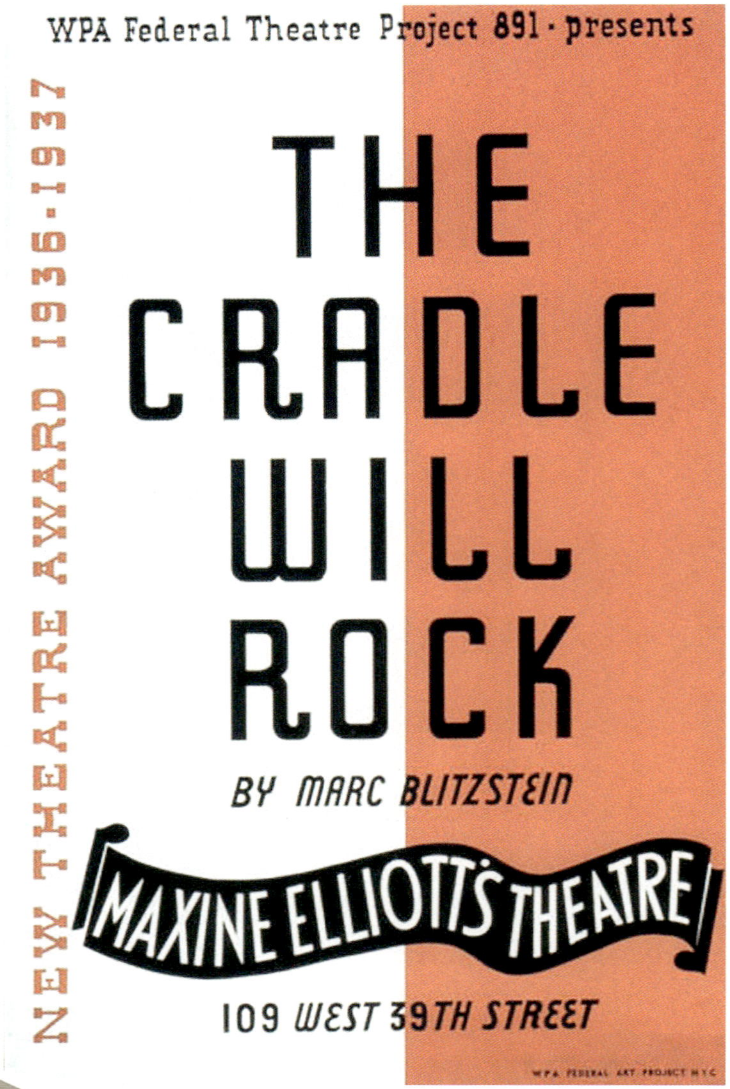

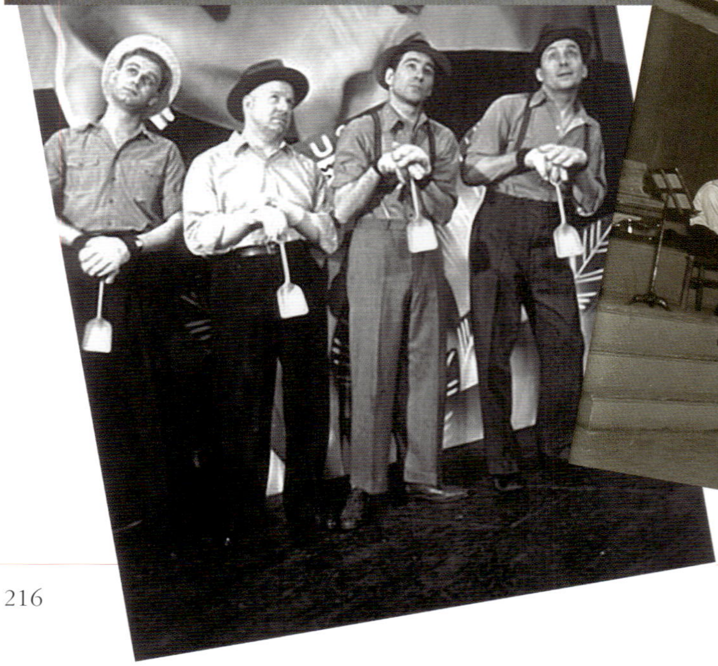

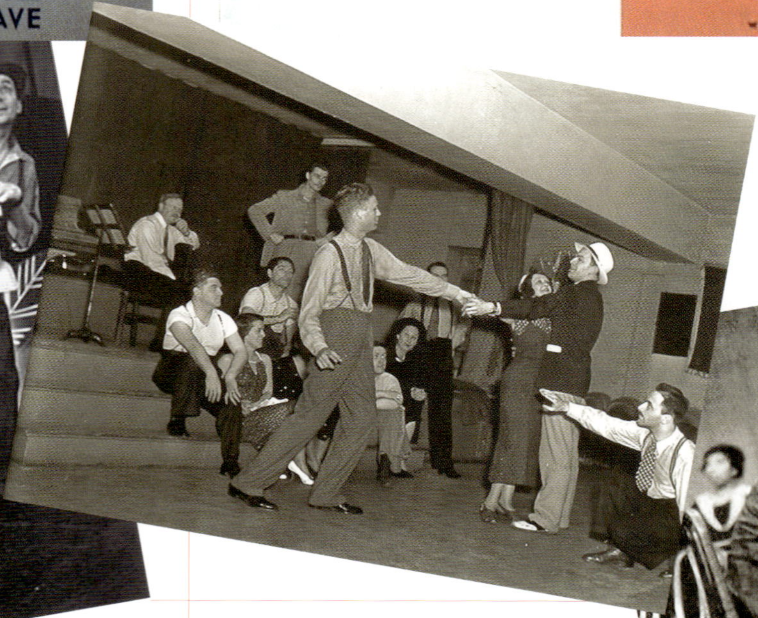

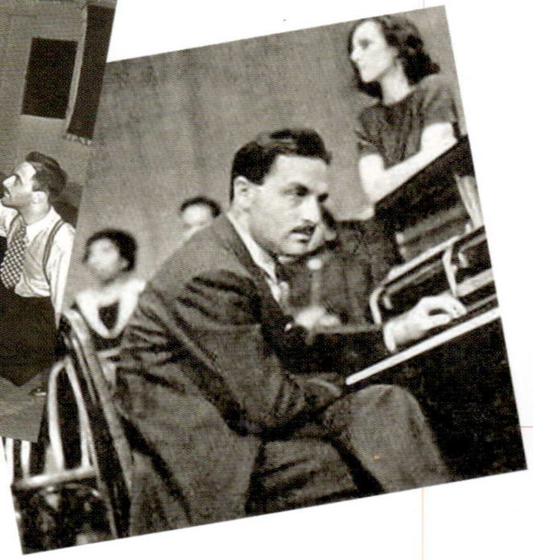

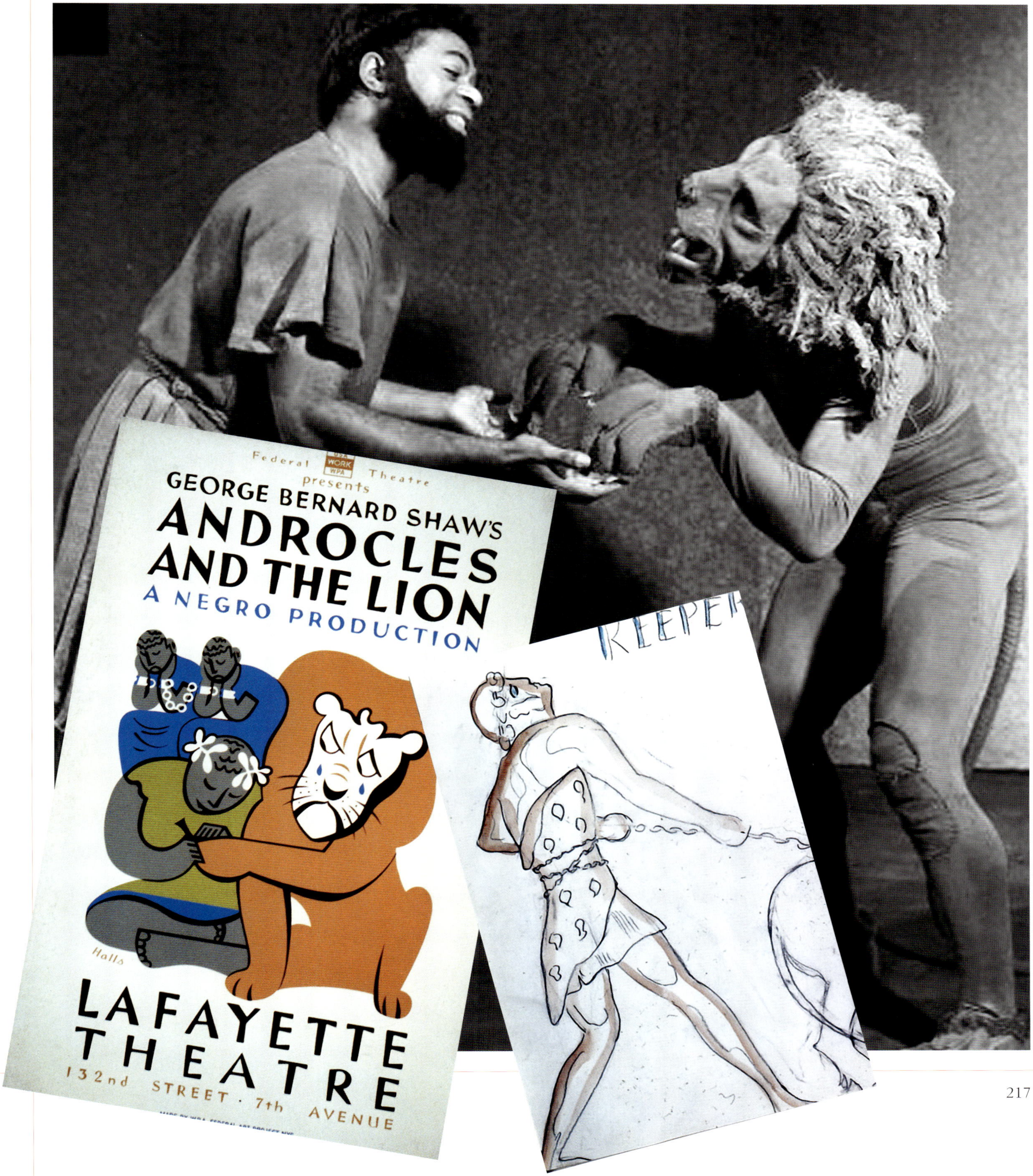

Negro Theatre Project presentation of *Androcles and the Lion* at the Lafayette Theatre, 132nd Street and Seventh Avenue
Poster Designed by Richard Halls
Federal Theatre Project Collection

George Bernard Shaw's *Androcles and the Lion* was a favorite at the WPA/FTP Lafayette Theatre unit in Harlem. This production at the WPA Building of the New York World's Fair featured Arthur Wilson as Androcles and Add Bates as the lion.

Right:
Macbeth
Poster by
Anthony Velonis

Far right:
Macbeth duel scene from the New York production, c. 1935

Bottom right:
Orson Welles and John Houseman

John Houseman hired a twenty-one-year-old Welles to direct productions of Harlem's Negro Theatre Unit of the WPA/FTP. Wanting to give his all-black cast a chance to play classics, he offered them *Macbeth* relocated to Haiti at the court of King Henri Christophe (and with a setting of voodoo witch doctors). Jack Carter was Macbeth.

Bottom far right:
Opening night of *Macbeth*, c. 1936

On the opening night of *Macbeth* in Harlem, ten thousand people were in the streets around the Lafayette Theater; all its 1,223 seats were filled, and curtain time was delayed by forty-five minutes. "After the curtain fell on the final tableau of the witches holding Macbeth's severed head aloft as Hecate intoned ominously, 'The charm's wound up!' cheers and applause filled the auditorium for 15 minutes . . . The 'Voodoo Macbeth' . . . was one of four Manhattan premieres in the spring of 1936 that solidified the shaky reputation of the Federal Theatre Project."[ii]

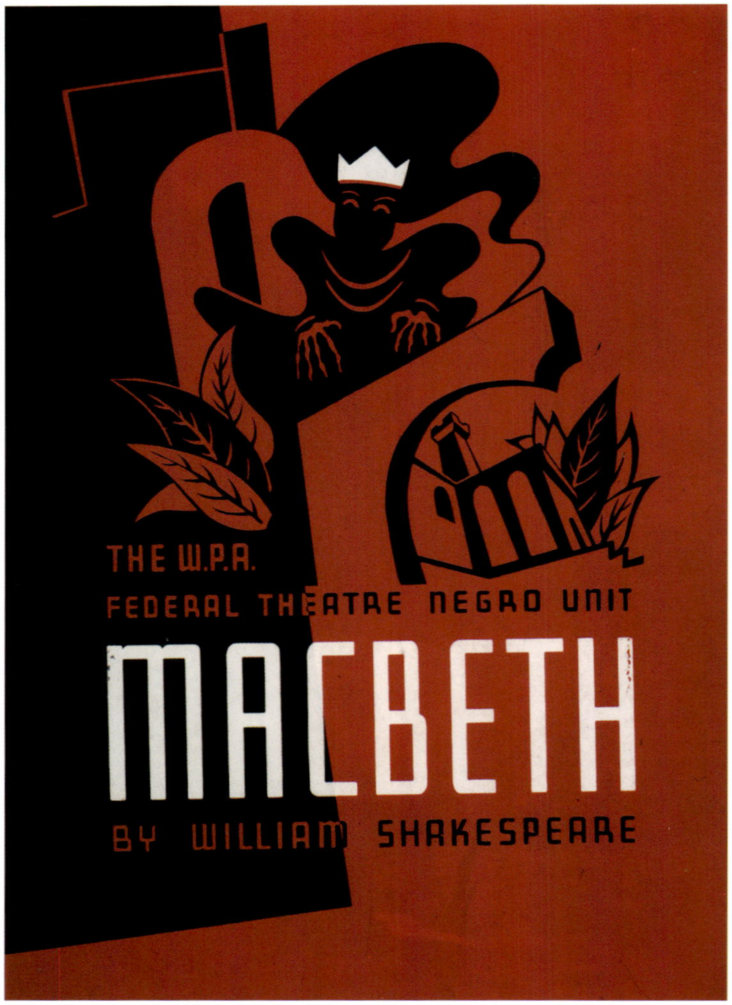

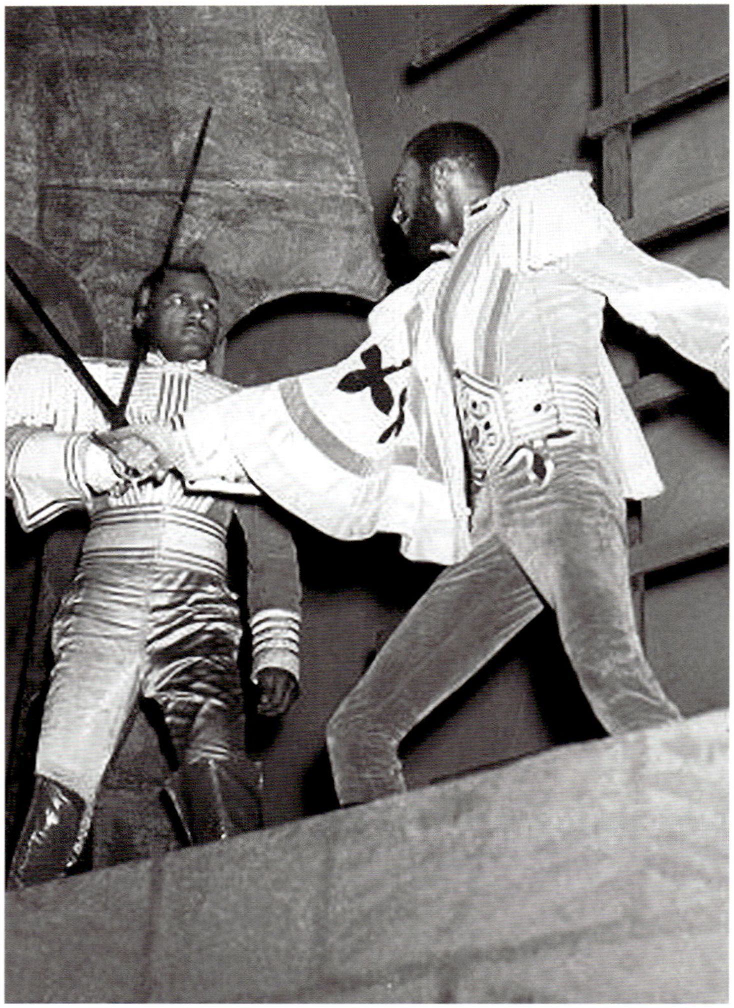

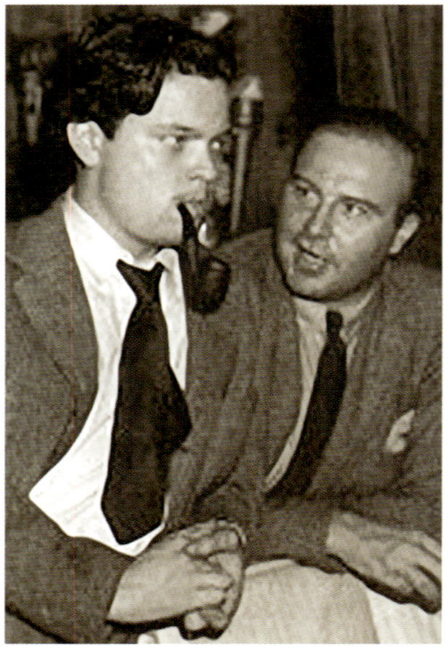

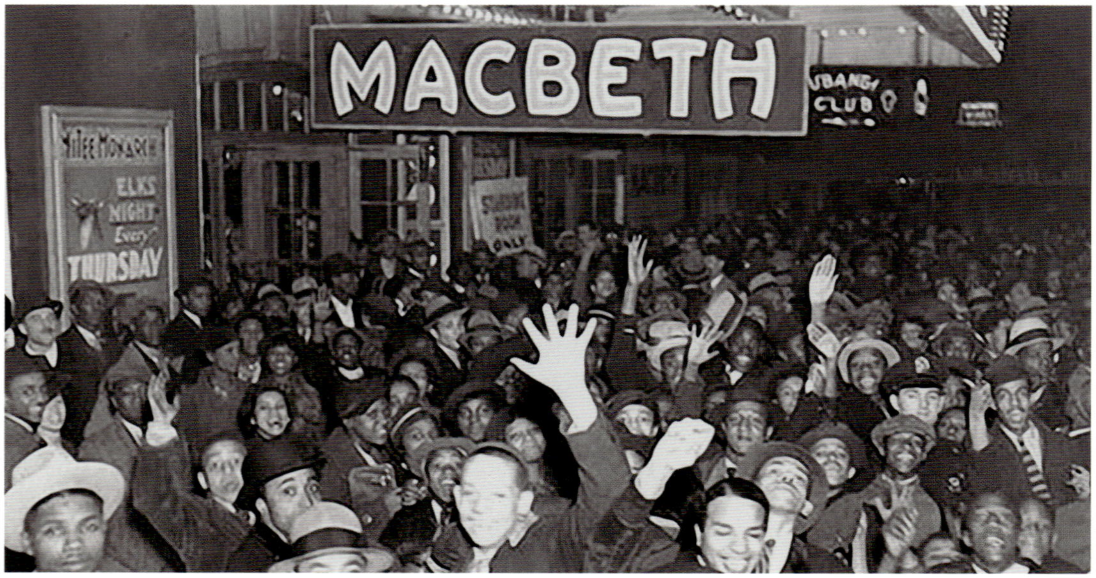

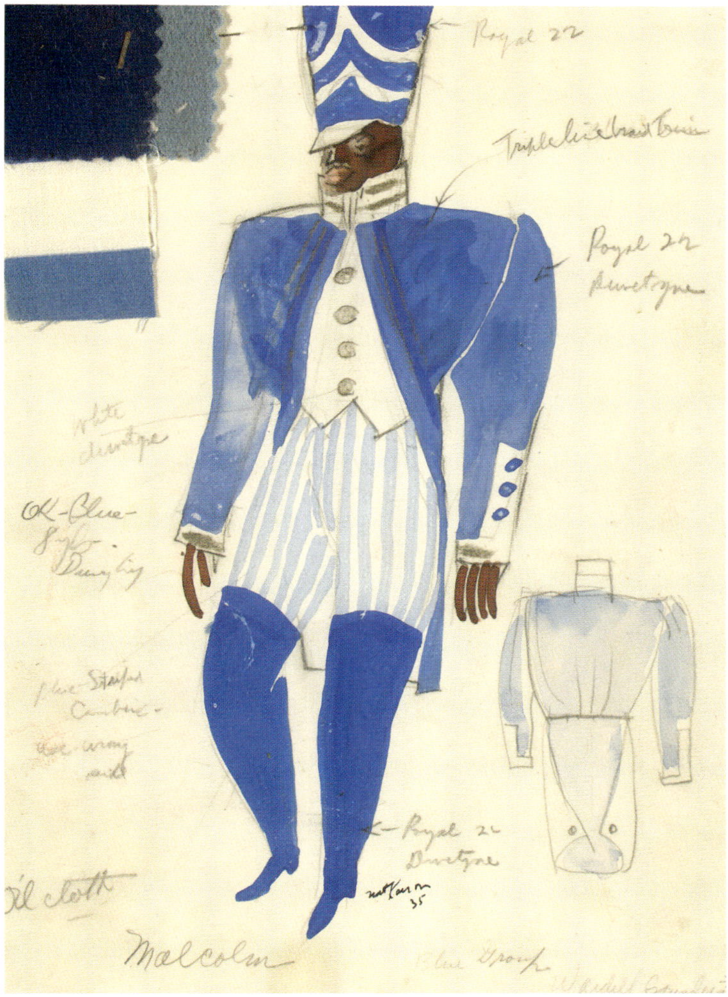

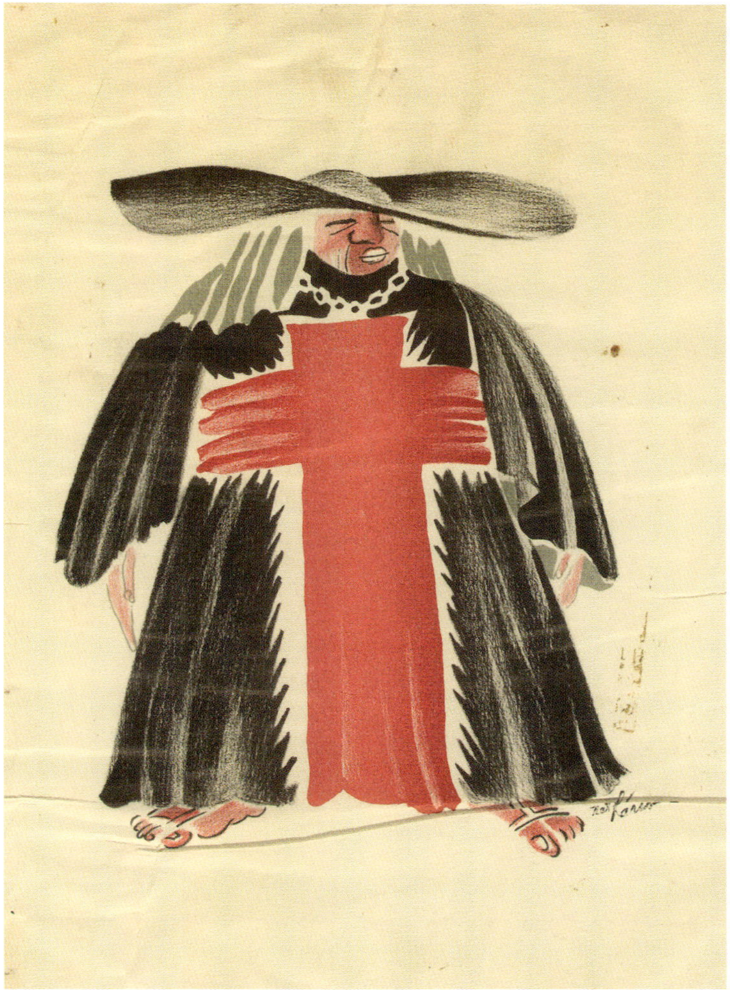

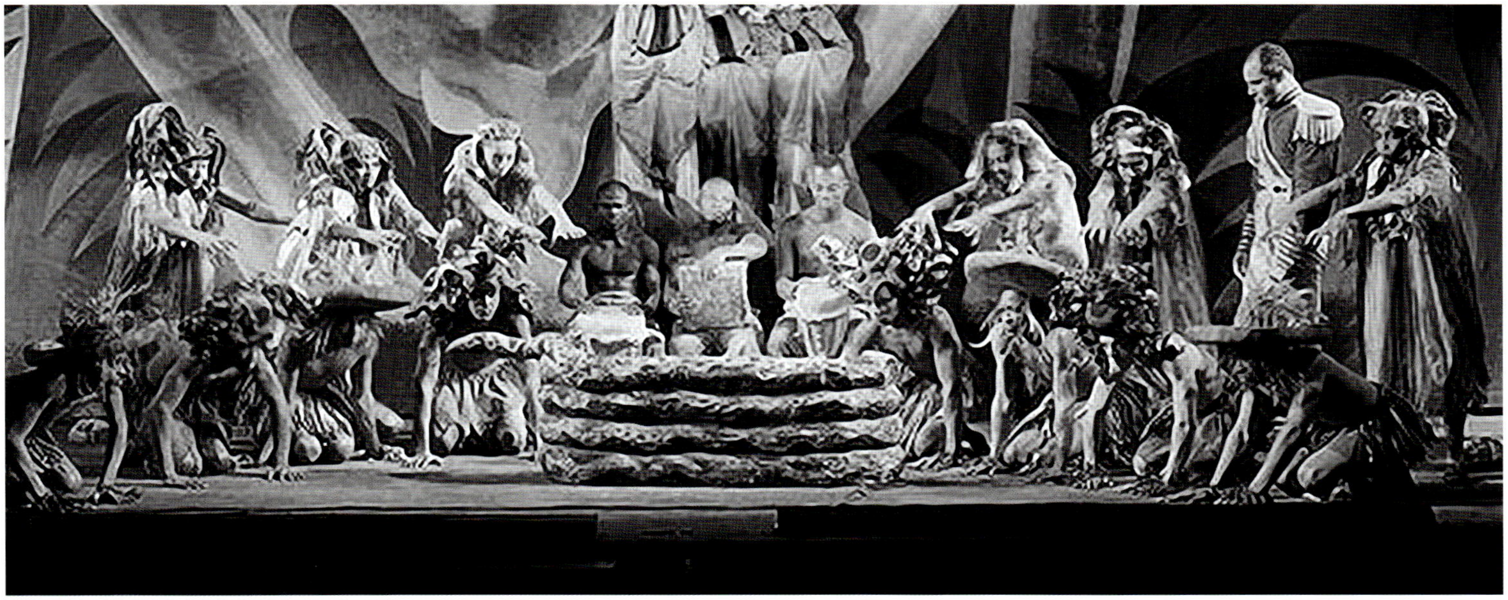

Top far left and left:
Watercolors of costume designs from the New York production of *Macbeth*.

Bottom:
Macbeth voodoo witches and skeleton backdrop.

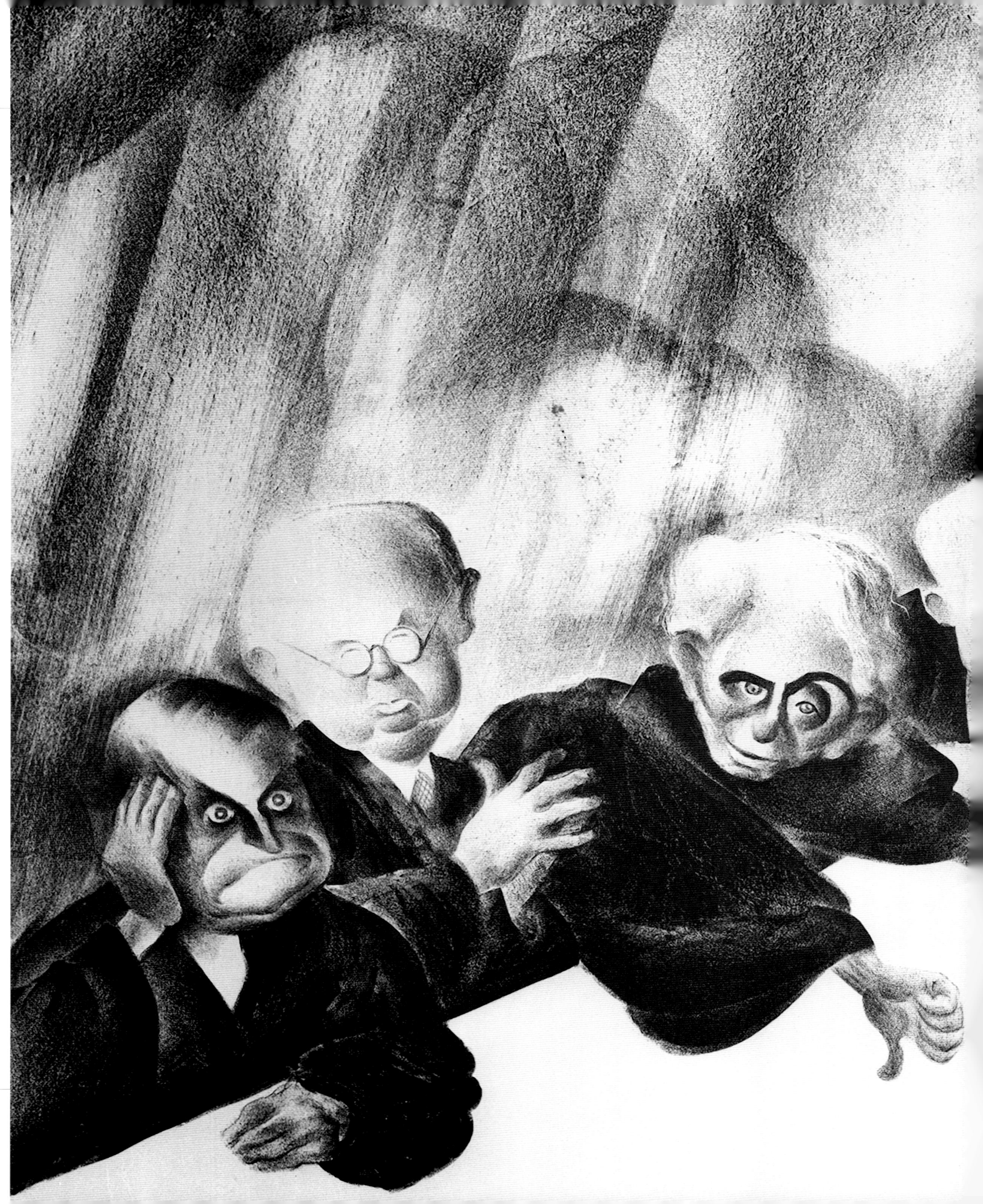

Cartoon of Supreme Court justices *(from left to right)* Roberts, Butler, Brandeis, Van Deventer, Chief Justice Hughes (standing), McReynolds, Sutherland, Stone, and Cardozo in session 1937 (inscribed "To Franklin Delano Roosevelt in appreciation")
Al Hirschfeld, 1937

Al Hirschfeld's cartoon was in its way "combat art" during Roosevelt's campaign to "pack" the Supreme Court with justices friendlier to the New Deal than the current majority of the court. Justices Stone, Brandeis, and Cardozo were more sympathetic to the New Deal—and were depicted by Hirschfeld as looking livelier than the others. They seemed to be a permanent minority until Chief Justice Hughes led the Court into its own accommodations—he is looking stately and shrewd, which he was.

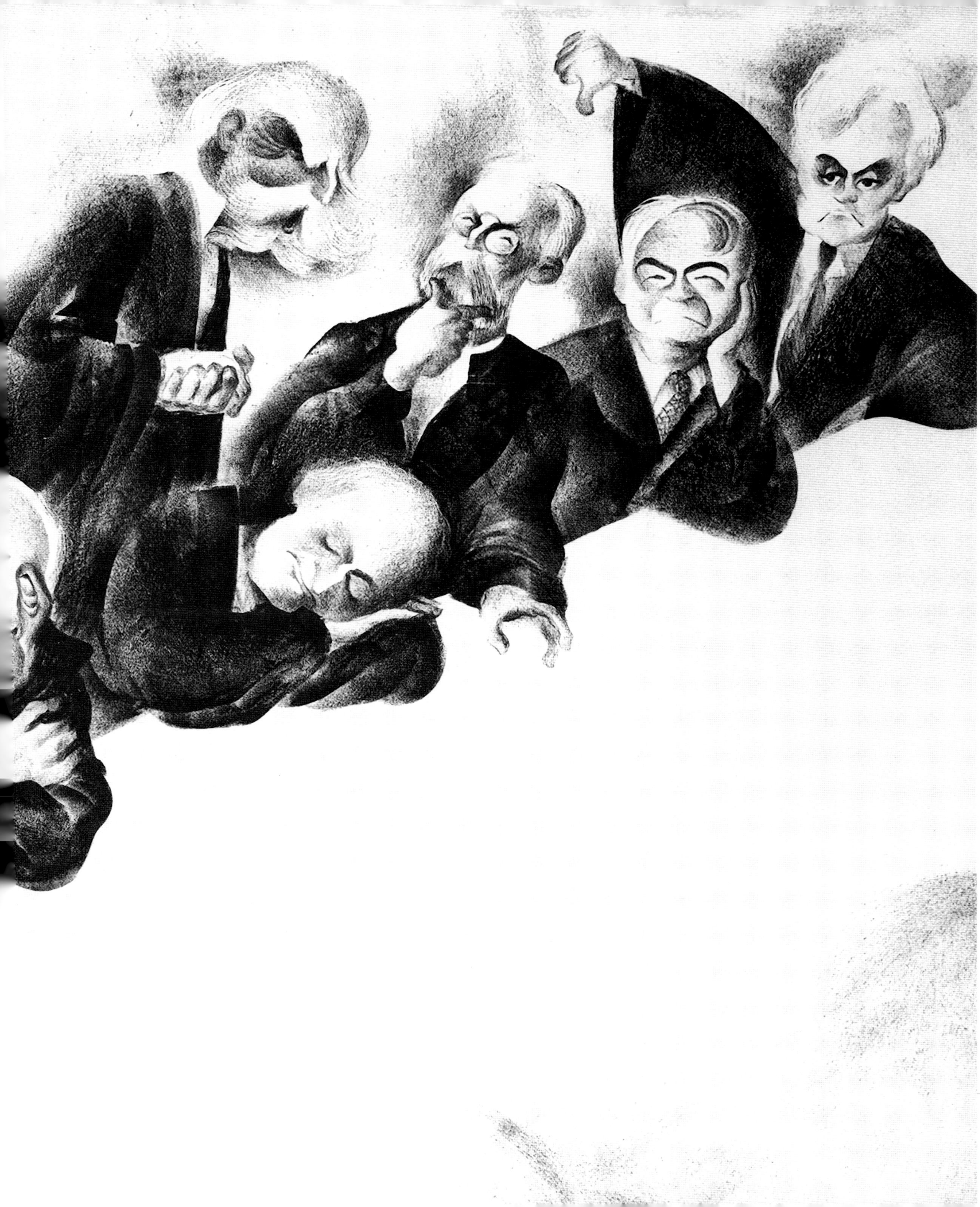

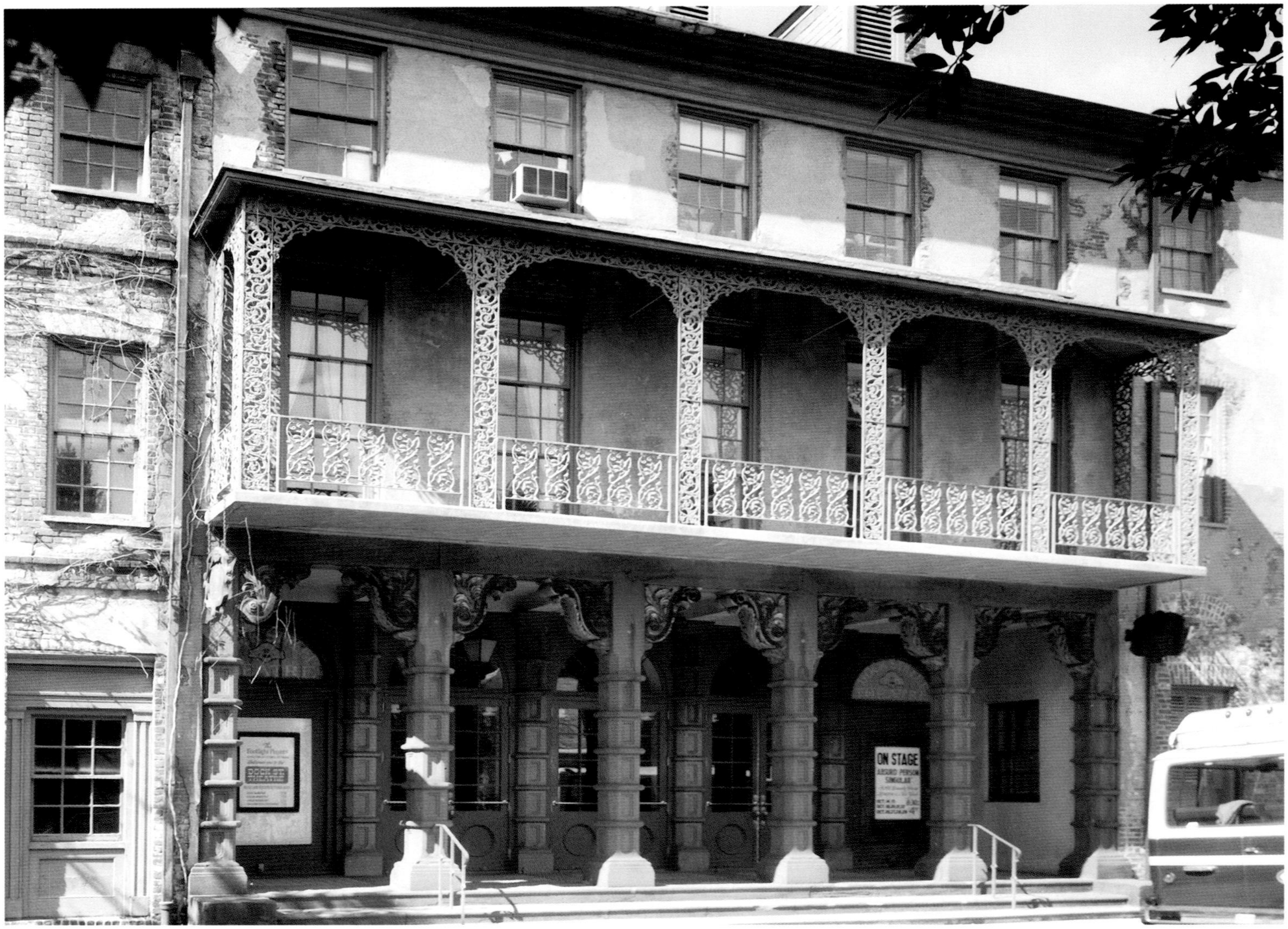

Dock Street Theatre
Charleston,
South Carolina

The building was restored by the City of Charleston in the 1930s, as a Works Progress Administration project. During this project a large section was constructed behind the hotel containing a stage and auditorium characteristic of the eighteenth century. The renovated building took the name of a 1730s theater that stood on the Queen Street (formerly Dock Street) side of the property. This theater is said to have been the first building in America constructed specifically for theatrical performances.

Francisco Bridge, and a thousand other bridges, the "Overseas Highway" to the Florida Keys, and half a million miles of other highways, the Lincoln Tunnel, and many more. Some maritime architects would surely say that there was art in the aircraft carriers *Enterprise* and *Yorktown*—built by the PWA-WPA. Had he lived to see it, Frederick Law Olmsted, artist of the land, unquestionably would have seen the art in the design of the three Greenbelt towns: Greenhills, Greendale, and Greenbelt itself. Eight million people, all endowed with a creative sense, worked for the WPA, some on such manifest masterpieces as the Timberline Lodge on Mount Hood (see pp. 336–343), some on artistically enabling, and handsome, buildings such as the Dock Street Theater in Charleston.[17]

Franklin Roosevelt put artists to work to advance national unity within a capacious covenant, and two of his most eloquent and least formal speeches demonstrate how he put his own arts of persuasion to work for those causes. In the first, delivered at Glacier National Park on August 5, 1934, he associated art and parks in advancing the "the fundamental idea . . . that the country belongs to the people, that it is in the process of making for the enrichment of the lives of all of us." The second was his dedicatory address for the National Gallery of Art in 1941, the theme of which was the achievement of the

New Deal in putting art to work affirming the national covenant. In eight years, he said, Americans had become accustomed to finding in their public buildings works "painted by their own kind in their own country, and painted about things they know and look at often and have touched and loved." It was as if in those works artists had responded to a call to use their skills to enhance a pursuit of happiness for themselves and their fellow citizens—as if Roosevelt had urged them to do as President John F. Kennedy urged the nation two decades later to "ask not what your country can do for you," but to "ask what you can do for your country."[18]

According to Edward Bruce, the New Deal organized its arts programs to take "the snobbery out of art" so that it might become "the daily food of the average citizen." Though they might have a "beneficial effect upon the whole art movement in the country" the primary purpose of those programs was to sustain what Bruce called the "unity movement" in the country. Gutzon Borglum put it a little differently in writing Harry Hopkins that "the real success . . . of aid to the creative ones among us, is in . . . what that does to the nation's mind . . . to coax the soul of America back to life," and George Biddle's letters to Roosevelt (discussed in chapter one) made the point with a little more political emphasis, asserting that art could help in "the social revolution that our country and civilization are going through." Years later, the art historians Marlene Park and Gerald Markowitz said of Bruce and his associates that they "believed that people would naturally like art if it was of high quality" and if it offered subject matter "relevant to their lives: a family enjoying a picnic, a farmer putting cows into the barn, citizens marching in a hometown parade, laborers washing up in the Mississippi, New Englanders maple sugaring, in a winter landscape, glass blowers practicing their craft, women curing tobacco on a small farm, families and friends picking oranges, neighbors talking over the fence, spectators at a stock sale, and children waiting for rural mail delivery." By presenting these common experiences in post office murals "the artist should serve the society as a whole." That was the intention of the New Deal art programs, and that was its achievement.[19]

Art worked—hard—in hard times. Then as the New Deal lost energy, a mass extinction swept away the arts program, the CCC, PWA, and WPA. Their cabinet level champions were removed by Roosevelt himself in 1938–39 when he consolidated most of their functions into the Federal Service Authority, now the General Services Administration.[20]

Nonetheless, by the end of World War II, the role of the arts in uniting the American people was no longer a partisan matter. General Dwight D. Eisenhower had this to say at the Metropolitan Museum of Art in 1946: "[In our] determination to establish and maintain a peace in which the creative and expressive instincts of our people may flourish . . . we will fail unless we consciously appreciate the value of art in our lives and take practical steps to encourage the artist and preserve his works . . . Even for the roughest of soldiers there is more of ancient Egyptian history to be felt and understood in a lonely, graceful column rising against the sky in a naked field than there is in all the descriptive matter that was ever written on the subject."[21]

We return to this passage in Eisenhower's address when we come to the origins and symbolic significance of the Washington Monument—as rediscovered by the New Deal. Here, at the pivot of this book, we come to Eisenhower's subsequent sentence: "It is our privilege to pass on to the coming centuries treasures of past ages, and to add to these the artistic creations of our own." When Eisenhower became president, he took up the mantle of Roosevelt by inviting the Commission on Fine Arts to give him affirmative proposals for federal support for the arts, as Roosevelt had sent scouts to "go out to make me do it."

The Commission sent back a report urging Eisenhower to create a federal cultural center in Washington to complement the National Gallery and the Smithsonian Institution. In his State of the Union Address, Eisenhower advanced the New Deal legacy by proposing a Federal Advisory Commission on the Arts, admonishing the Congress that the federal government "should do more to give official recognition to the arts and other cultural activities."[22]

The Index of American Design

The Index of American Design is a compilation of nearly eighteen thousand watercolor renderings intended to create a pictorial survey of the rise and development of European-American design before 1900, including weather vanes, quilts, toys, tavern signs, figureheads, and stoneware, most of them by anonymous craftsmen. The renderings were created under the auspices of the Index of American Design project, part of the Federal Art Project of the WPA, which operated from 1935 to 1942. It was not a nostalgic or antiquarian enterprise; it was initiated by modernists dedicated to abstract design, hoping to influence industrial design—thus in many ways it paralleled the founding philosophy of the Museum of Modern Art in New York.

The founders of the Index were Ruth Reeves, a textile designer, and Romana Javitz, head of the Picture Collection at the New York Public Library, who convinced Holger Cahill, the Director of the WPA/FAP to engage Constance Rouke, a cultural historian and folklorist, and Adolph Cook Glassgold, a designer, to supervise the work. The Index operated in thirty-four states and the District of Columbia.

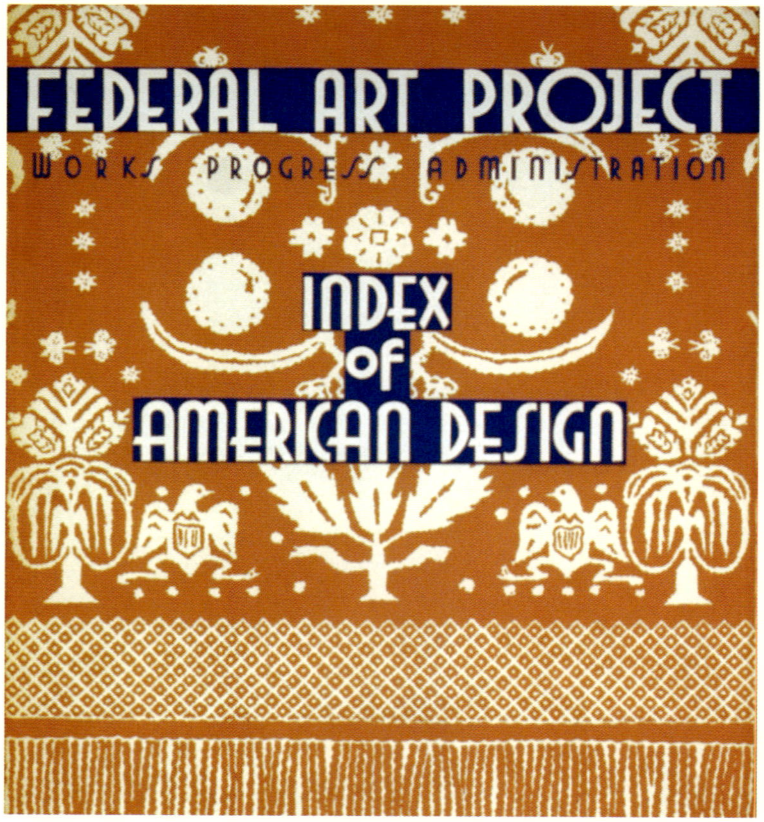

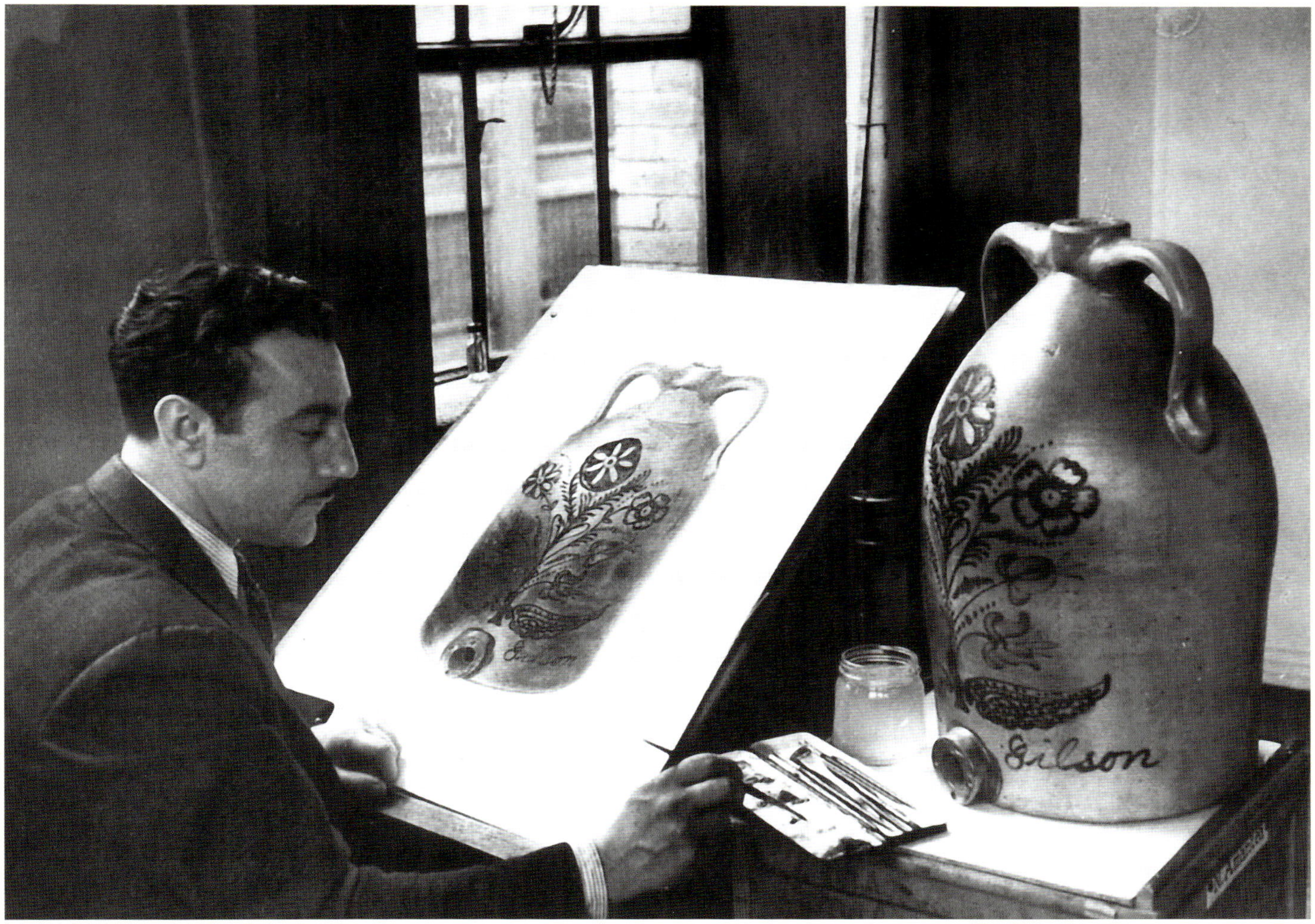

Nicholas Amantea working on a rendering for the Index of American Design project, April 1939.

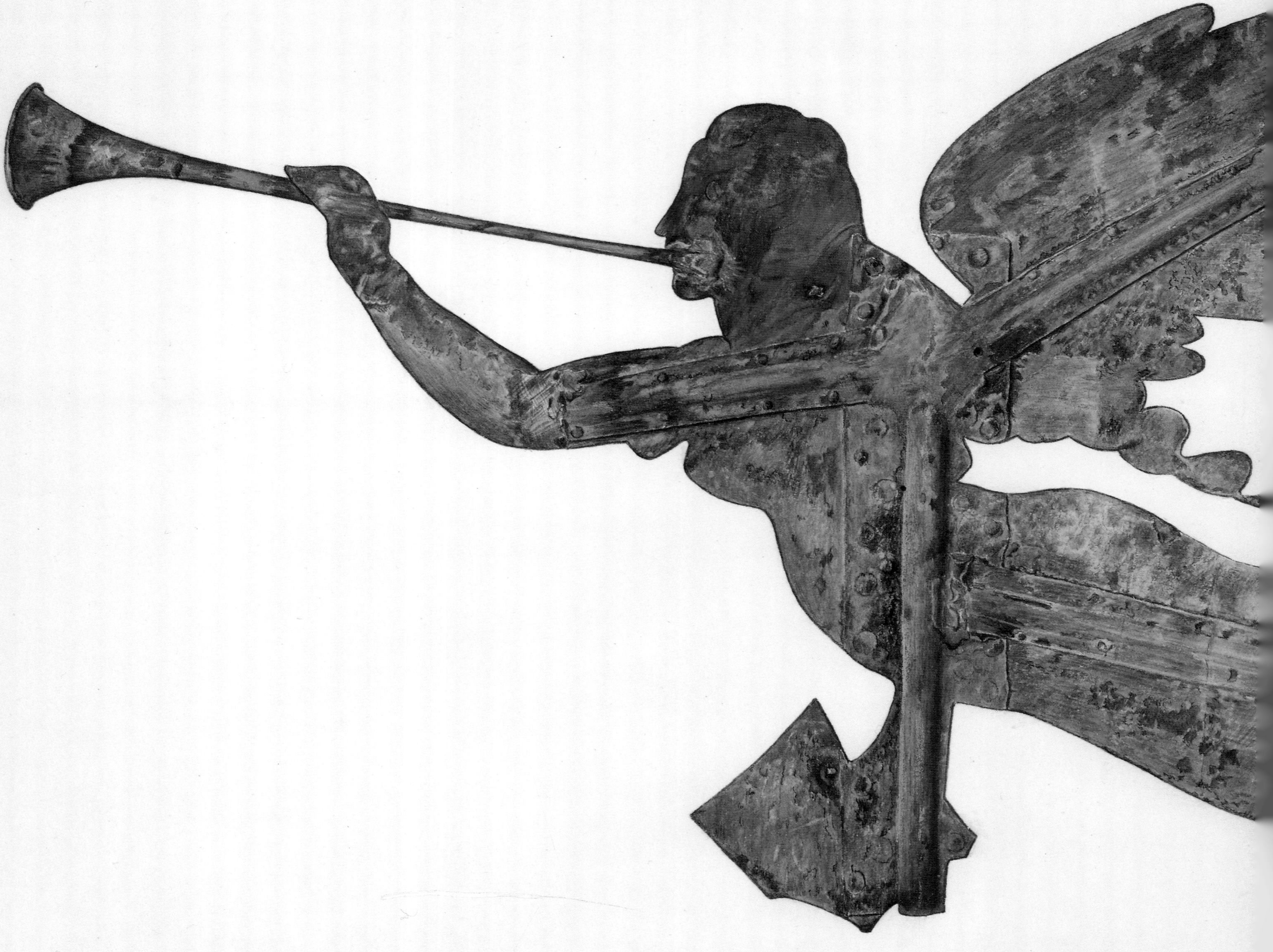

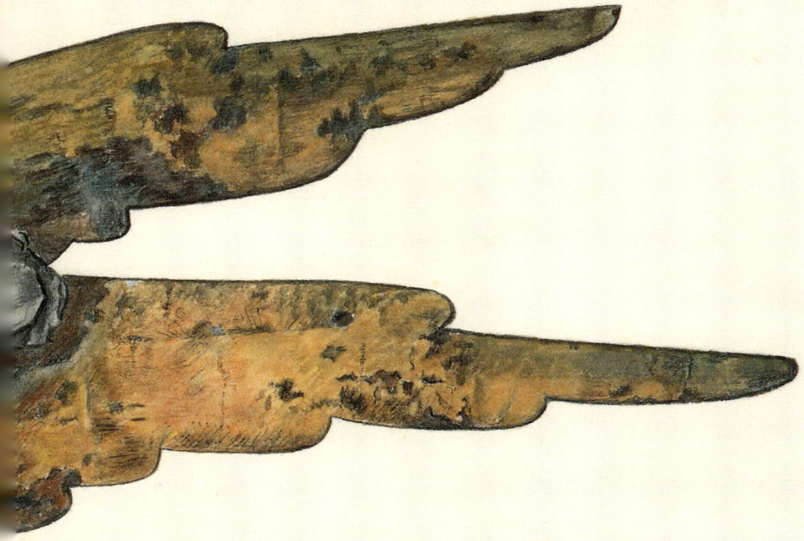

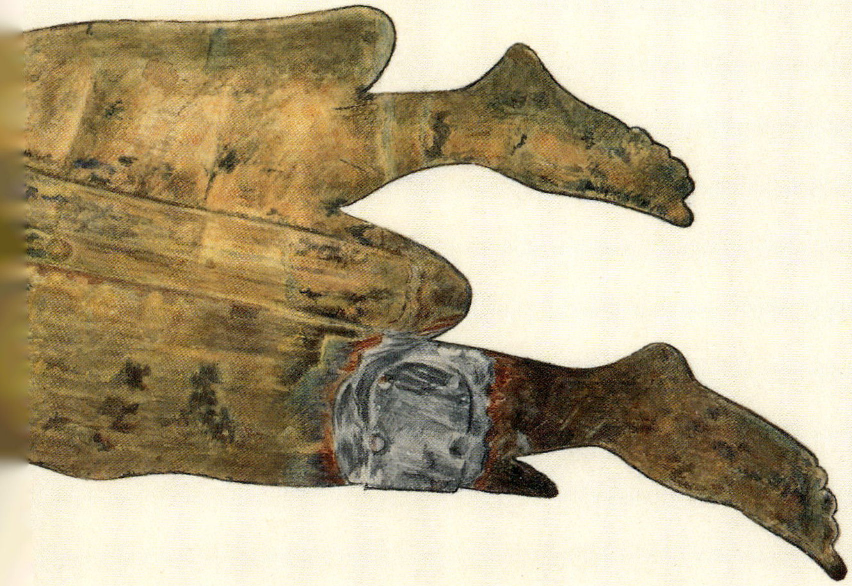

Gabriel Weather Vane
Lucille Chabot, c. 1939
Watercolor on paper

In 1965 Lucille Chabot's Index rendering of this weather vane was reproduced on a United States postage stamp. The high quality of many Index renderings owes much to Suzanne Chapman, an illustrator employed by the Museum of Fine Arts, Boston, who acted as a special supervisor for the project, and prepared a technical guide showing how to render each object: how to apply watercolor over a preliminary pencil drawing, "working in" the light areas first and then building up more intensely colored or darker passages by applying additional layers. In a separate instructional program artists prepared special demonstration drawings to show this process, step-by-step, from a pencil drawing, through the initial layer of paint, and, finally, to the finished watercolor.

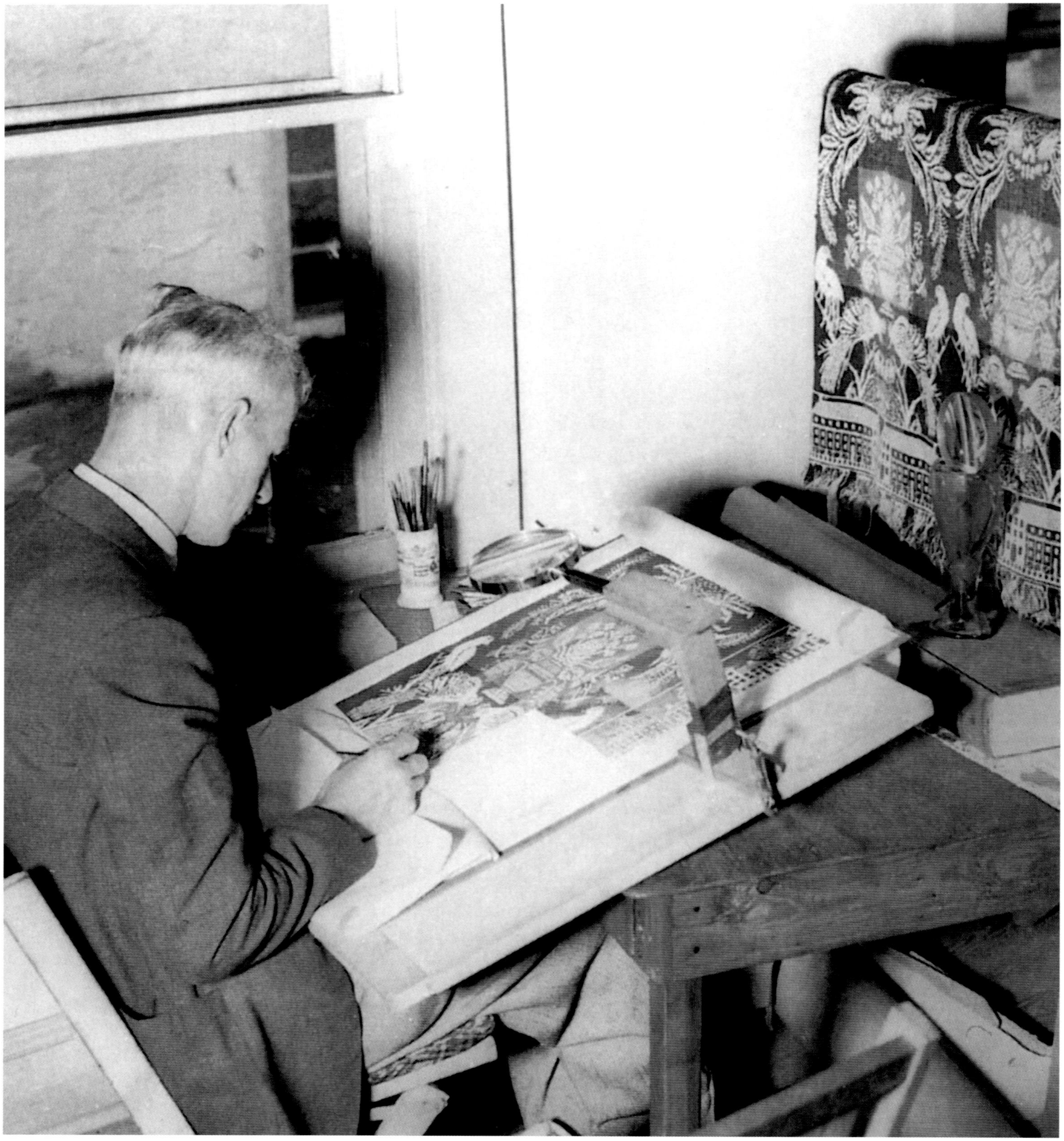

Magnus Fossum, a WPA artist, copying the 1770 coverlet "Boston Town Pattern" for the Index of American Design. Coral Gables, Florida, February 1940

Magnus Fossum was a farmer for twenty-five years, but he was forced to move south during the Depression. When an accident cost him his left hand in 1934, his drawing skills enabled him to be employed on the Index. On nights and weekends, he brought home his work to draw and paint, using drafting instruments and a magnifying glass to ensure fidelity. When he received an insurance settlement in 1937, he acquired ten acres of farmland, left the project, and rarely produced another picture.

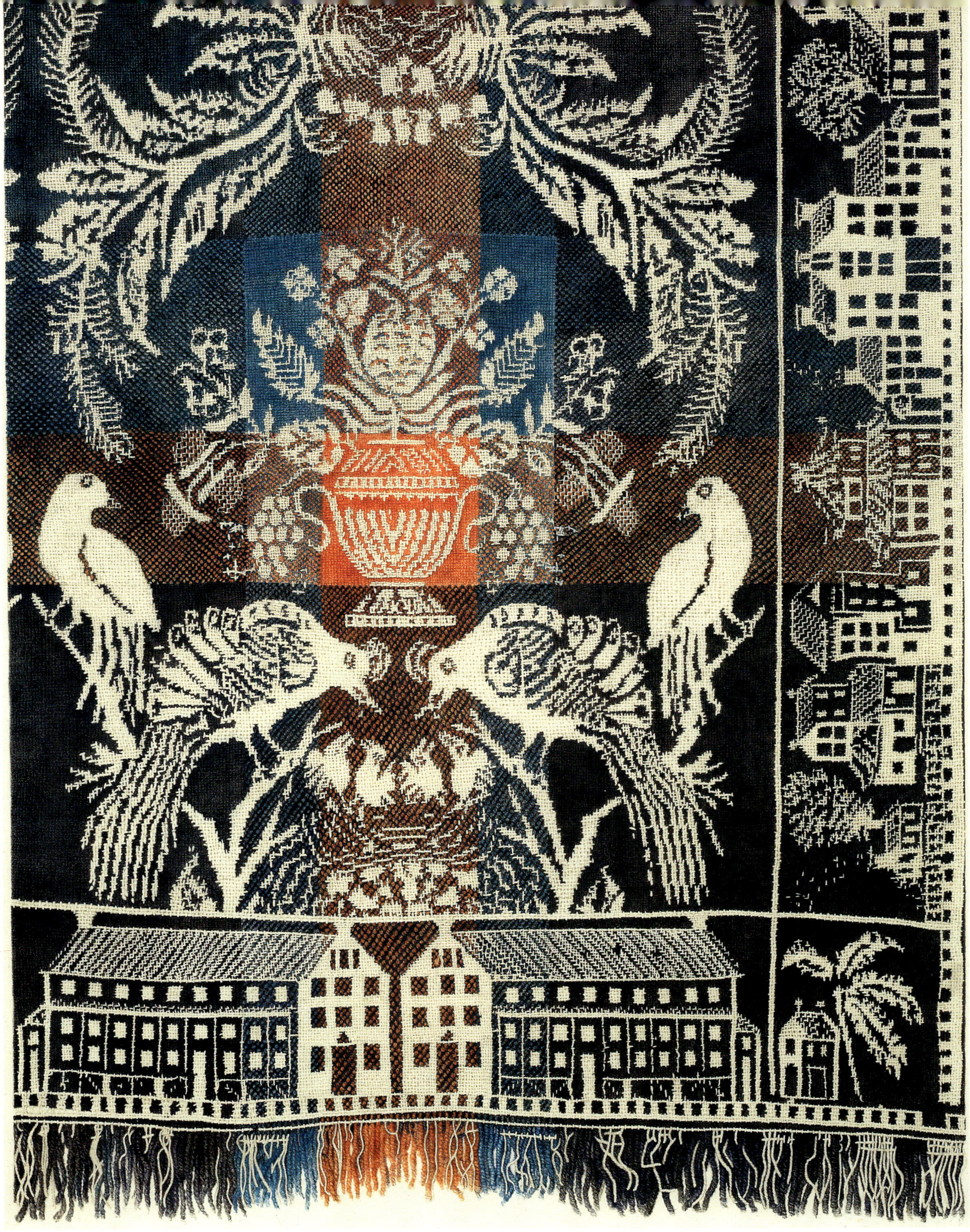

Boston Town Coverlet
Magnus Fossum, 1935–42

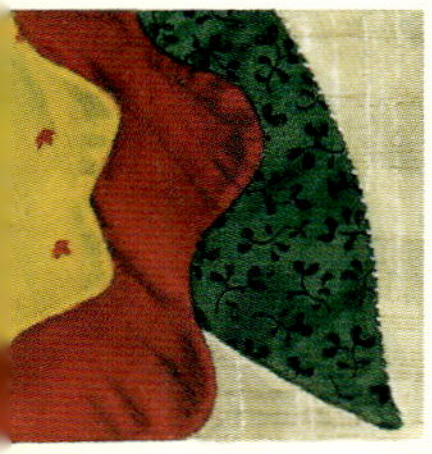

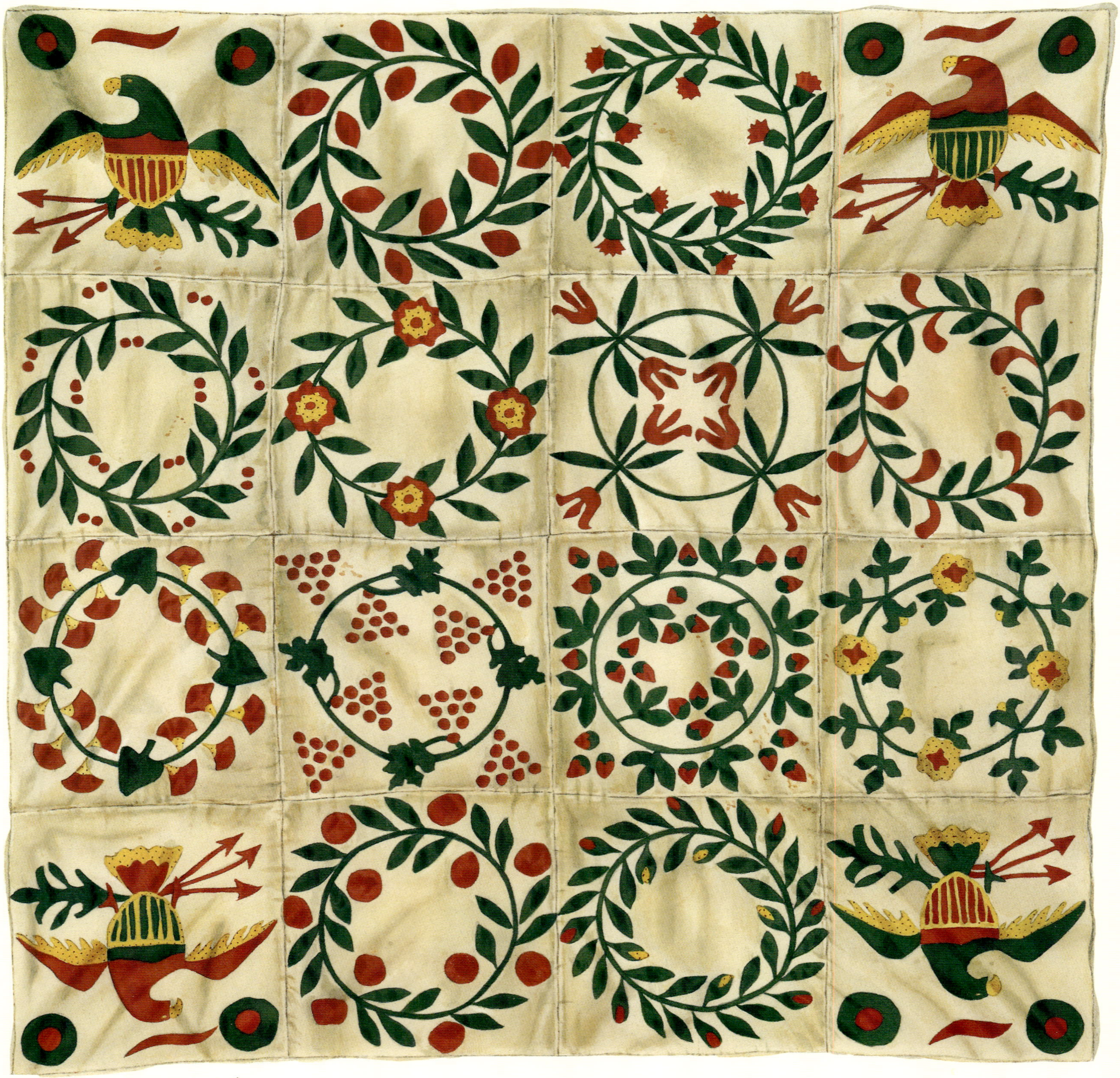

Above (detail) and right: *Quilt* Charlotte Angus, 1935–42 A watercolor rendering of an unattached appliqué quilt top with a detail of one of the square blocks.

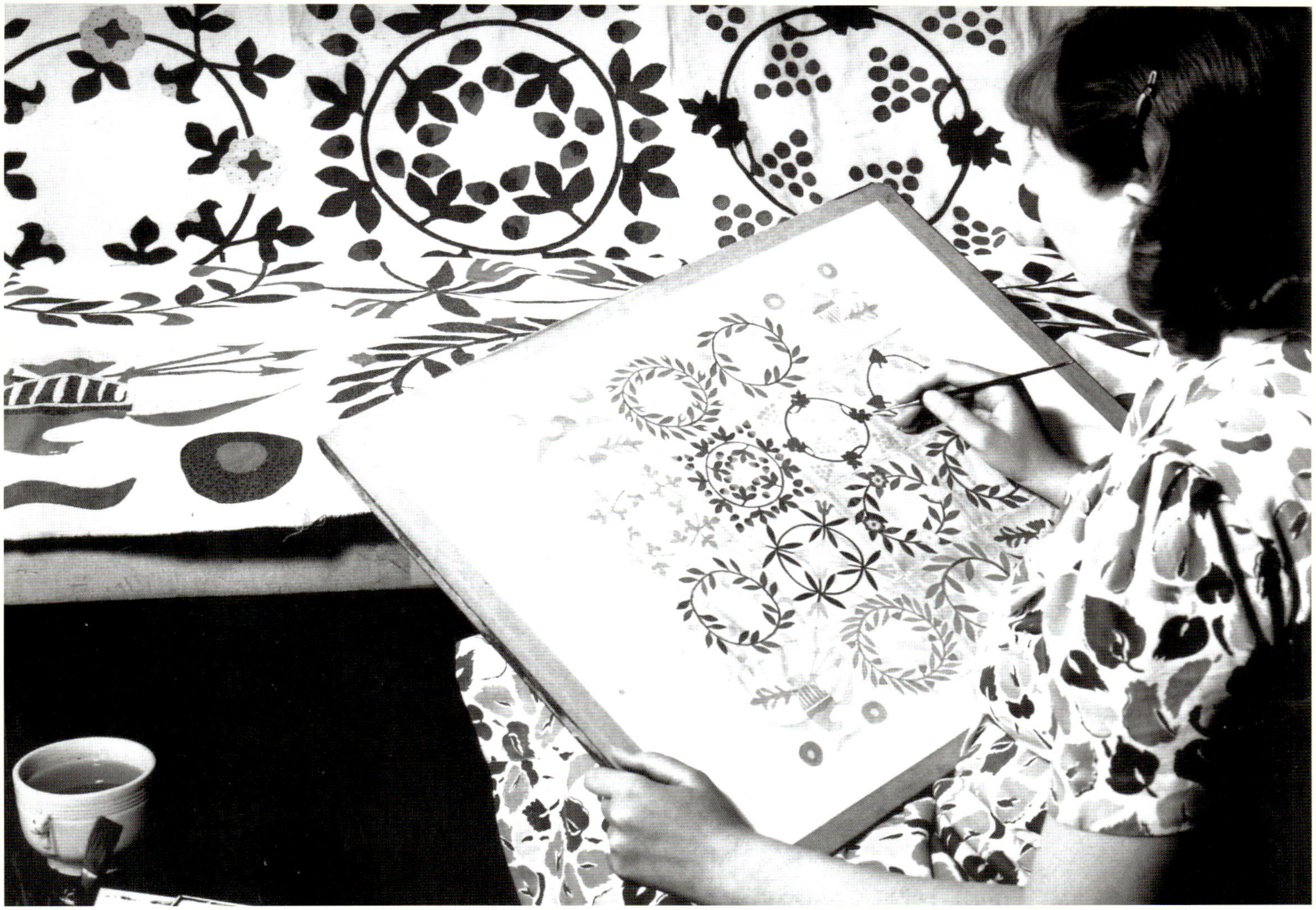

Charlotte Angus working on a rendering (shown on the opposite page) of Appliqué Sampler Quilt Top, 1940.

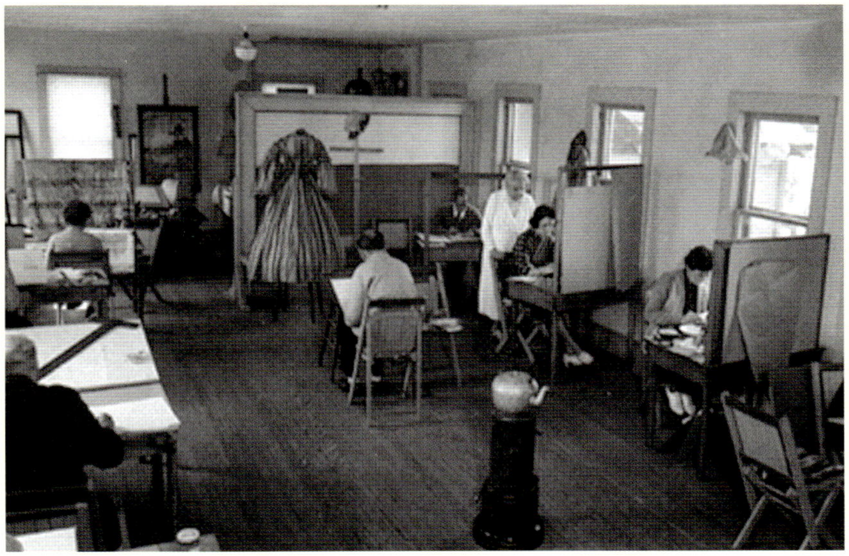

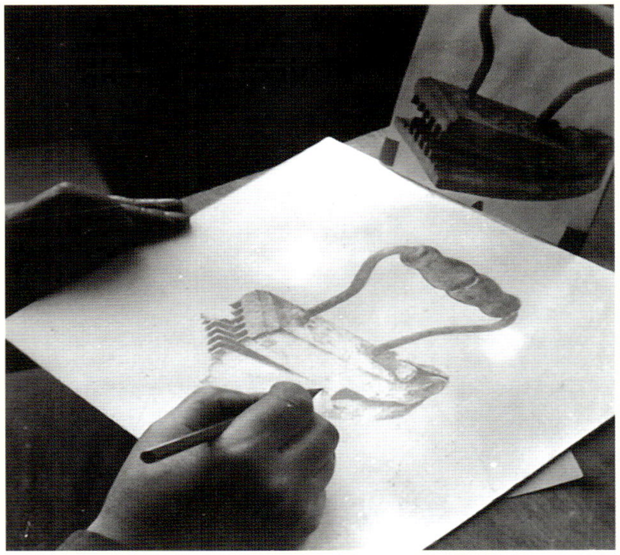

Bottom far left:
Artists at work in the Early American Design Studio at Coral Gables, Florida.

Bottom left:
Drawing a flat-iron in a New York studio.

Part Two

The New Deal,
the Earth, the Arts, and Three Presidents

Chapter Six

The Art of Franklin Roosevelt

"The causes for which he fought are far greater than any individual person."
(Eleanor Roosevelt, as quoted by Robert E. Sherwood)[1]

ROBERT E. SHERWOOD'S FOURTH PULITZER PRIZE came to him for his double biography, *Roosevelt and Hopkins*, an exhilarating account of the high adventure of politics in the 1930s and 1940s. As a screenwriter before he became a speechwriter for President Franklin Roosevelt, Sherwood had provided some of the most memorable lines spoken by Spencer Tracy, Lewis Stone, and Bette Davis, and sung by Clark Gable (in *Idiot's Delight*). In *Abe Lincoln in Illinois* he and Raymond Massey made Abraham Lincoln a folk figure giving a personality to American virtues much in need of affirmation. For those of us who grew up in the 1930s, Sherwood's and Massey's Lincoln was our Lincoln.

In his *Roosevelt and Hopkins*, Sherwood offered some observations about the arts of presidential leadership, selecting "the word artist" to suggest "the quality of Roosevelt's extraordinary creative imagination," and explaining that he had done so because Roosevelt "was an artist and no canvas was too big for him." As Sherwood said, "he was more successful than any previous president in dramatizing and personalizing the processes of government for the people." John Collier, the other member of the New Deal inner circle who knew both art and politics, agreed. Roosevelt, he wrote, was "an *artist* at the core. His medium as an artist was the lives of men and the life of man . . . not poetry, or painting, or music, or physical architecture, but life itself in human society." Roosevelt's political method was to affect "life itself in human society." He brought "the essential problems . . . into the open and gave them a much needed airing," making himself the message as well as the messenger. Franklin Roosevelt was indeed a master artist. Art—as communication—worked for him, with him, and through him. The peril in such a success was, Sherwood admitted, that it served to "increase the solitary power of the president," and presidents and presidential courtiers are prone to tire of the arduous and irritating necessities of creating constituencies and to settle instead for creating a cult.[2]

Mrs. Roosevelt told Harry Hopkins that she did not welcome the exertions of those who would make too much of a hero of her husband: "The causes for which he fought are far greater than any individual person." The New Deal could not become "entirely dependent upon him." It needed instead to build a "foundation" among "the great masses of the people." To which Sherwood added, "I believe that there Mrs. Roosevelt was expressing her husband's point of view as well as her own." Roosevelt's arts programs recruited artists to help build such a foundation. Though the President's own dramatic art could "personalize and dramatize" his "causes," his efforts would be of little lasting effect unless other arts and other artists assisted the people to understand what was at stake and what was required.[3]

Franklin Roosevelt often seemed the only person on stage. He came to power by eclipsing the colorless Herbert Hoover, and from the outset of his first presidential campaign he was able to demonstrate his stage management of such *coups de theatre* as being the first presidential candidate to arrive by airplane to accept his first nomination. Sometimes, however, the theater made its own coups, and the solitary master-player only narrowly escaped a humiliation that could take down the entire cause in a personal fall.

How the New Deal Got Its Capital Letters

When Roosevelt accepted the nomination of his party for the presidency for the first time, his new deal did not yet have capital letters, and Roosevelt's reading of the phrase was so understated as to be almost stealthy. It was neither capitalized in his written text nor emphasized in his delivery, perhaps because it was not original. It had been used by Nicholas Biddle, Henry James, and Mark Twain; as a campaign slogan by David Lloyd George in 1919, and in the title of an article by Stuart Chase. It was almost worn enough to have been a cliché, but its function in Samuel Rosenman's draft had been merely to carry energy across a gap between a ringing invitation to popular support and an invocation of the enduring spirit of Abraham Lincoln. "I pledge you, I pledge myself," Roosevelt read, "to a new deal for the American people."[4]

It was not the newness of his proposed "deal" that mattered, but its restatement of the covenant between president and people within a continuity restored and aspirations renewed. Herbert Hoover would never have extended his expert hands to clasp those of the commonality. Woodrow Wilson never unbent to such populism; he was too chilly, too disdainful of the too-often-uncomprehending masses. Roosevelt loved the crowd, and the crowd loved him. Roosevelt, like Abraham Lincoln, offered mutual pledges with and for the American people, summoning them as co-agents of beneficial change, not hectoring them to comply or acquiesce. Everything Roosevelt did and said after he came of age spiritually, intellectually, and politically in the 1920s manifests a genuine desire for companionship in political adventure with the common man.

The uppercase letters for "New Deal" were bestowed in a cartoon by Rollin Kirby in the *New York World Telegram* on the morning after Roosevelt's speech in Chicago. Roosevelt had arrived in the convention city by air, so the airplane was the news, not the slogan. But that slogan caught on. It was a convenient box-car term of the sort on which journalism dotes for its ease in imparting apparent simplicity to highly complex evolving phenomena. We still use it retrospectively, in its capitalized and by now memorialized form, because we, too, need large categories to save us from bewilderment by an effulgence of related instances. The term "New Deal" implies clarity in what was not a clear set of propositions, and that

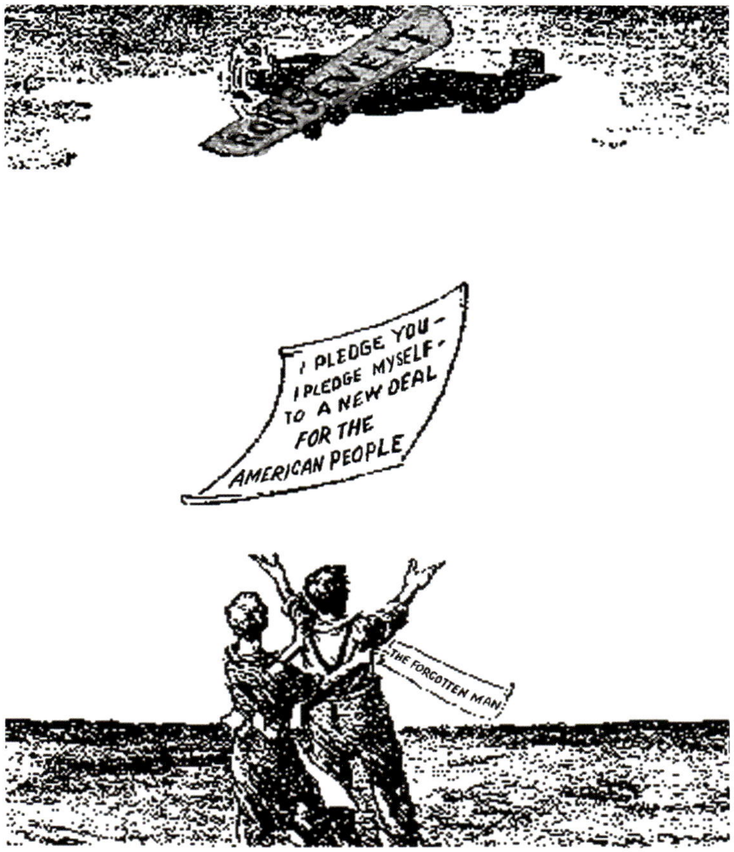

Early mention of the New Deal in a newspaper cartoon.

After studying art in New York and Paris, Rollin Kirby became America's most famous political cartoonist of the 1920s and 1930s. His cartoons first appeared in the *New York Mail, New York World*, and *New York Post*. A strong advocate of civil liberties, Kirby often attacked the Ku Klux Klan and corrupt politicians. He was sympathetic to the women's suffrage movement and contributed art to both *The Women Voter* and *The Suffragist*. Among his friends were his fellow artists Boardman Robinson, Albert Sterner, and Robert Minor. Kirby won three Pulitzer Prizes for cartooning in 1921, 1924, and 1928.

was Rollin Kirby's intention. He was a committed New Dealer. He had studied Daumier and Millet in Paris, before he returned to New York to put his skills to work for the kinds of causes in which he and Franklin Roosevelt believed. Kirby's ferocious anti-Tammany cartoons of the 1920s provided the "graphics" for the young Roosevelt's rhetoric even then, sharpening the edge to the Hudson River squire's previously bland youthful style.

In June 1936, Roosevelt went to Philadelphia to accept the nomination for the presidency by the Democratic Party for the second time. Rejecting the cautious counsel of Raymond Moley and other advisors that he avoid the inflammatory populist rhetoric of his cousin Theodore's final years,

Roosevelt was ready to out-theodore Theodore. Sheer political calculation might have brought him to that position, for otherwise he would have lost ground on his left flank to Huey Long, Floyd Olson, and the followers of Francis Townsend in California. Yet the angry undertones of his voice as he gave his newly radical message suggest that he had been affronted by the refusal of many respectable people, neighbors, and former schoolmates, to understand that his New Deal was saving capitalism from its own excesses. While staving off a Communist threat on the left, he was refusing to give ground to a Fascist threat on the right. Henry Wallace, Roosevelt's Secretary of Agriculture, and in 1940 his running mate for his third term, was wrong about many things, especially in his failure to grasp the danger to democracy posed by Stalinism at home and abroad. Recognizing just in time that Wallace was straying from his competency in domestic matters and had let himself be beguiled into accepting Communist support, Roosevelt dumped him as vice-presidential running mate in 1944 and substituted Harry Truman. It must be said, however, that Wallace was alert to the peril to American democracy from the right—more alert than many who did not trouble themselves to learn about how great that danger was—despite all that Sherwood and Sinclair Lewis tried to tell them.

During the war against Germany, Italy, and Japan, Wallace correctly warned that "the really dangerous American fascists, are not those who are hooked up directly or indirectly with the Axis. The FBI has its finger on those. The dangerous American fascist is the man who wants to do in the United States in an American way what Hitler did in Germany in a Prussian way. The American fascist would prefer not to use violence. His method is to poison the channels of public information. With a fascist, the problem is never how best to present the truth to the public but how best to use the news to deceive the public into giving the fascist and his group more money or more power."[5]

Those of us who had the duty to interview American Fascists and Communists after their release from wartime internment can assert with confidence that many of them were intelligent, resourceful, and in readiness. Lorena Hickok, the best female journalist of the domestic scene in the 1930s, reported that the Stalinists and Trotskyites were very active: "the Communists . . . openly say they hope the Administration will fail. They want bloodshed." The American Fascists released from internment in 1946 were frank to say that they wanted bloodshed also; their chief intellectual, Lawrence Dennis, told me that they believed they had only narrowly missed their opportunity in the 1930s.[6]

There were plenty of home-grown Fuhrers available. Some of them were operating in the Midwest, leading Hubert Humphrey to take the threat presented by Dennis seriously enough to read his *The Coming American Fascism* even before he read *Mein Kampf*. The disaffected had been turning to the Communist Party, to Fascist thuggery such as the German American Bund, to the Ku Klux Klan, and to left-wing and right-wing demagogues and ideologues such as Floyd Olson, Huey Long, Gerald L. K. Smith, and Father Charles E. Coughlin. Some intellectuals took to Marx and Engels; others commended Dennis. In 1936, the Fascist threat at home and abroad had not yet reached its apogee. Stalin was in power, yet the non-Communist left was still willing to blink at much that was horrible in his regime. Roosevelt's primary task was to stand off the extreme left, with its totalitarian aspirations and its violent methods, while reaching out to the moderates who could sustain the New Deal's democratic reforms. His hold on power was tenuous, and his own physical condition far more precarious than he wished the nation to know, as he came to his own personal and physical rendezvous with destiny.

Reaching Out

Roosevelt's second presidential campaign required him to use his dramatic art to present himself with vigor and confidence. On June 27, 1936, he arrived at Franklin Field, a baseball stadium, to make his acceptance speech. At the outset all went well. The presidential limousine circled the field. A hundred thousand loyal Democrats cheered him, heard each other cheering, and many took each others' hands. The car delivered the President to the backstage roost where he was to ready himself to make everybody feel better, to be the voice of hope, of fearless determination, of reinvigoration. Only believe! Do not fear! All will come right!

But he had lost all control of his legs to poliomyelitis. The car could get him to a curtained area, but he could reach the podium only by being carried, using his braces, or using a wheelchair. Then he would have to struggle on those braces from a backstage chair to a rostrum on which he could steady himself with one hand while holding his speech with the other. The speech he had in his pocket was about a "Rendezvous with Destiny" in which his generation would make its own struggle by doing the very best it could. Any show of infirmity would not only betray his personal weakness, but also the very fragility of his experiment in restoring to the nation its confidence. If he could not sustain the mood, "fear itself" would come flooding back.

He had to get to the podium, to the focus of those lights. For the nation's sake, he must radiate confidence and energy, must appear irresistible, invulnerable. There was still much fear, and much to be afraid of. As he readied himself to move from backstage along a short walkway to the rostrum, Roosevelt and his staff saw to it that his hair was right, his glasses were right, his suit was straight, his shirt pulled properly down to let his necktie descend gracefully across an upper body whose muscularity had been developed to compensate for the shriveled weakness of his legs. And his steel braces? Surely somebody had made them secure?

Part way along the walkway, Roosevelt saw the eighty-three-year-old Edwin Markham smiling at him from the edge of the crowd. If Roosevelt were to reach out to him it would be a gesture of explosive symbolic power; Markham was a dangerous "leftie," with a long record of resisting Communism without succumbing to any worshipful illusions about the consequences of unregulated capitalism. He was especially famous as a friend to impoverished farmers, but he was also known to do what he could to bring public understanding of the plight of industrial workers. On the previous night Roosevelt had told his cautious adviser, Raymond Moley, that he was feeling feisty. He was growing angry, he said, at the businessmen who were making it difficult for him to salvage an economic system that had lost the confidence of so many ordinary people. One out of every ten Americans seeking work could not find jobs, and a third of those employed and unionized were on strike for better wages. The two Fisher Body plants in Flint, Michigan, had been occupied by armed strikers for six weeks. Many people were expecting a bloody outcome. It was less than a year before the Little Steel strike, and the turning loose of "security forces" by the South Chicago police and management. After the firing ceased on a crowd of strikers and their families, ten were dead or dying and fifty-eight were wounded. Earlier presidents had called out the National Guard to rout pickets and protect plants; Roosevelt called upon the Congress to pass what became the Wagner Act, to protect union organizers and give federal sanction to a right to strike.[7]

In those inflamed circumstances, Markham was a marked man. His *The Man with a Hoe*, composed as a rumination upon an equally famous painting by Jean-Francois Millet, was a lament for oppressed farmers rather than oppressed industrial workers, but even thirty years earlier, when it was written, there was so much unrest in the countryside that the railroad magnate Collis P. Huntington offered a five thousand dollar award to any writer who could provide a rebuttal. As Huntington understood, both poem and painting were exhortations toward rescue of the exploited and oppressed, and to the work of Millet and Markham, more graphic evidence was added by New Deal photographers, by painters such as George Biddle, and journalists such as Lorena Hickok.

Extending a hand to Markham would have been sufficiently prompted by *The Man with the Hoe*. But he was also the poet of Lincoln, the man with the axe. Although his agrarian poem-manifesto was Markham's most famous work, New Dealers would think of him also as the author of the references to slavery that he insisted upon making at the dedication of the Lincoln Memorial. Roosevelt might have been induced to turn to him for that alone on his way to his own "rendezvous with destiny."

Because Markham was a famously flaming radical, turning to him was risky, and turned out to be more risky than Roosevelt intended, however feisty he felt. Here is the account of the events of the following few minutes given by Mike Reilly, the President's Secret Service agent:

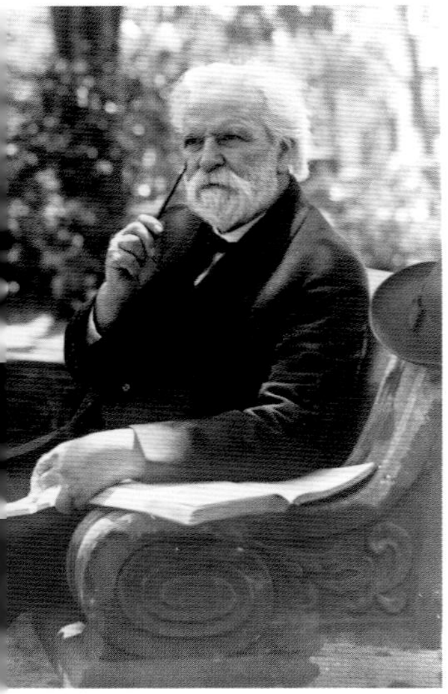

Edwin Markham

> As he neared the platform the Boss saw an old man with a long white beard and a lovely peaceful face. It was the great poet, Edwin Markham. FDR waved to Markham, and the old poet, obviously deeply touched by the salute, pressed forward, his hand outstretched. The President reached out also. As the elderly poet extended his hand, somebody in the crowd pushed him heavily against Jimmy. Jimmy, off balance, fell against his father, and the combined weight of Jimmy and FDR was too much for one of the President's braces. He could only stand when both braces were rigid, and Jimmy's added weight unsnapped the right brace. The President fell. I was walking right behind him and as I saw him go down I dropped and managed somehow to get my shoulder under his right armpit, catching him before he hit the ground. I steadied him for a second and as I straightened up he came up, too, resting on my shoulder. Gus Gennerich, another Detail man, promptly snapped the brace rigid and the Boss was all right, but badly shaken.[8]

Roosevelt managed not to lose his glasses, but he did lose his temper. "Clean me up" he snapped. His companions pulled him to his feet, and he moved to the podium. Steadying himself with a hand on the lectern, he used the other to open his text. Roosevelt had just had a very difficult five minutes. As he acknowledged the cheers, however, his mastery came back to him, his famous smile broadened, and he began, in that incomparable voice: "I thank the millions of Americans who have borne disaster bravely and have dared to smile through the storm . . . To some generations much is given. Of other generations much is expected. This generation of Americans has a rendezvous with destiny."[9]

Those words still echoed in our memories when they were recalled by President Kennedy in 1961—"ask not . . ." Kennedy and Roosevelt reminded us, as Lincoln had reminded his generation, that there is an unbroken sequence reaching us from the founders' bold venture in self government. The New Deal covenant asked us to take our parts in a society in which the pursuit of happiness is possible, and even practical. When Roosevelt said "I believe in my heart that only our success can stir their ancient hope," he was situating himself, and us, in the great American tradition. "Philadelphia is a good city in which to . . . reaffirm the faith of our fathers; to pledge ourselves to restore to the people a wider freedom; to give to 1936 as the founders gave to 1776—an American way of life." Then, in sequence, he invoked the symbols of the place, as any artist would. He was, after all, in Franklin Field, in Philadelphia, William Penn's city of "philanthropy," a word that, Roosevelt reminded his listeners, evoked a spirit of shared suffering and mutual obligation; Roosevelt used it as a synonym for "charity shared—in the true spirit of that grand old word. For charity literally translated from the original means love, the love that understands, that does not merely share the wealth of the giver, but in true sympathy and wisdom helps men to help themselves . . . Liberty requires opportunity to make a living—a living decent according to the standard of the time, a living which gives man not only enough to live by, but something to live for."[10]

Huey Long was making a political program out of sharing the wealth, and not only that of voluntary givers. In his effort to steer public opinion away from extremes of right or left, Roosevelt's success depended upon his skill in conveying to enough of the public, enough of the time, that the New Deal's non-confiscatory schemes could stimulate the economy to generate for most people "not only enough to live by, but something to live for." To rally those who might be willing to abandon fear and dare to hope, he could compete successfully with Long and others by using broadcast radio. The radio networks were more accessible to a President than to Long, Floyd Olson, or even to Wendell Willkie, though Willkie's backers included every major owner of newspaper and broadcasting corporations. Roosevelt had an early advantage, which came from necessity. He could not campaign as they did, but they could not use radio as an art form, as he did. Not until Thomas E. Dewey came along in 1940 did Roosevelt face an opponent who had a radio voice and manner. Long and Olson were camp-meeting, open-air orators, and Willkie was laggard in heeding his media advisers.

Radio—Franklin Roosevelt's Medium

Roosevelt told a traditional story with non-traditional devices, although he also made use of every symbol, every phrase, and every icon at his disposal to stress the continuity of his endeavors with the American covenant of Washington and Lincoln. With his encouragement, the New Dealers reanimated iconographic sculpture and the memorials and monuments to those grand predecessors, reinforcing a message being asserted by contemporary artists and by Roosevelt himself. Soon after his election to the presidency in 1932 he told the *New York Times* that he saw the office as "pre-eminently a place of moral leadership," citing Washington and Lincoln as examples of "our great presidents [who] were leaders of thought at times when certain historic ideas in the life of the nation had to be clarified." He often insisted that he was doing their good work.[11]

Roosevelt's discovery of broadcast radio was essential to his success. His physical infirmity prevented him from traveling widely to make himself heard. Therefore understanding his medium is essential to understanding his artistry. Roosevelt developed a new rhetoric using radio that evolved as radio itself exfoliated from individual stations into networks convenient to personalized persuasion. A president could reach millions if he understood both the ubiquity and the intimacy of the medium. When first invented, the radio was conceived as a super-telephone for person-to-person communication, of no greater use in politics than a walkie-talkie. During Roosevelt's apprenticeship for power, however, new microphones and receivers made radio sound intimate, as broadcast made it ubiquitous. The Communications Act of 1933 was an early New Deal measure setting up the Federal Communications Commission to oversee the allocation of frequencies to avoid "shingling," overlap and overtalk. The FCC did not license networks; it licensed stations. Because the possessors of profitable "owned and operated" stations could save the cost of originating programs in each, by creating studios to serve their own stations and those licensed to others, and because advertisers found buying time on bundles of stations cheaper and more convenient than negotiating with each separately, the networks were ready for Roosevelt. Whenever he asked to chat on their allocation of the nation's airtime, they would assess the value of their station licenses, and then, with expressions of magnanimity, they would accede.

Thus did radio become a means of centralized political persuasion, by which a person chair-bound by paralysis could visit his countrymen in their homes. The trick was in perfecting the rhetoric of intimacy. When the voices of radio's inventors had first been heard bellowing through static, who could have imagined the power of a mellow tenor conversing with the millions? Roosevelt's magic lay in his voice, not in his accent, for he had the wrong way of speaking to take upon himself the role of common man leading common men. By emphasizing that wrong way, he made it the right way. Roosevelt used the exoticism of his speech straightforwardly, making no special emphasis of it nor dissembling it. A man who had never known constricting economic necessity could utter a line such as "necessitous men are not free men" in his "Rendezvous with Destiny" speech with utter conviction, because whatever other inconsistencies there may have been in his life and career no one could doubt the passion with which he sought to be of help to the third of the nation that was "necessitous" and thus "no longer free." For those so afflicted, he said in that aristocratic voice and manner, "liberty [was] no longer real; men could no longer follow the pursuit of happiness."[12]

"Sam Nichols"
Ben Shahn

Speaking for the Man with a Hoe

As Roosevelt addressed the nation, art was providing indelible images confirming what he said and affirming the necessity for remedy. Edwin Markham had offered verses that many people still recalled and John Steinbeck echoed in his descriptive prose in *The Grapes of Wrath*, while the Farm Security Administration photographers made them visual. Eudora Welty made some of the most searing of those pictures as a documentary photographer, and Ben Shahn was both a photographer and painter of dangerous truths about life on the land. Markham had shown the way with his "The Man with the Hoe."

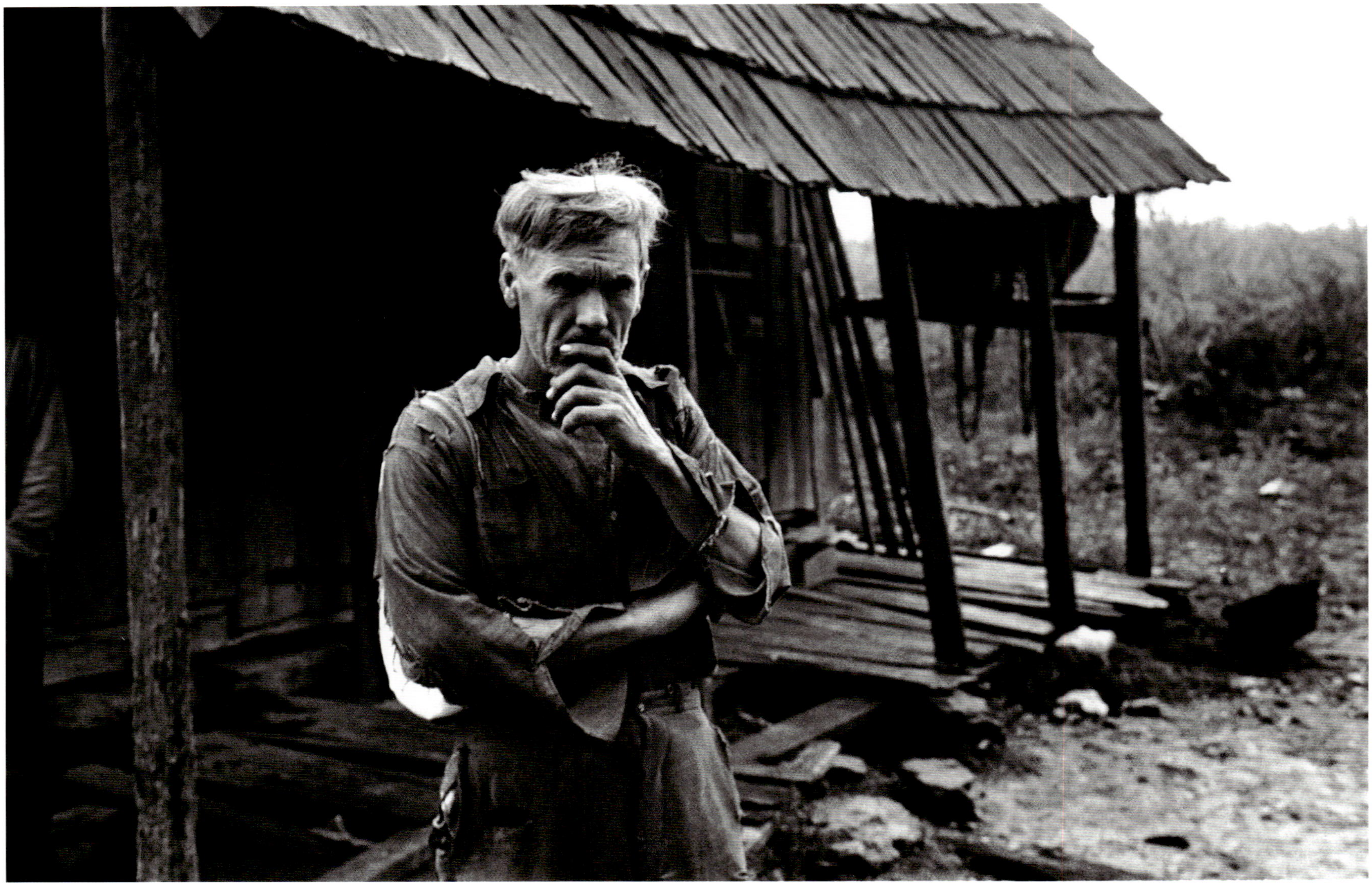

The Man with a Hoe

Bowed by the weight of centuries he leans
Upon his hoe and gazes on the ground,
The emptiness of ages in his face,
And on his back, the burden of the world.
Who made him dead to rapture and despair,
A thing that grieves not and that never hopes,
Stolid and stunned, a brother to the ox?
Who loosened and let down this brutal jaw?
Whose was the hand that slanted back this brow?
Whose breath blew out the light within this brain?
Is this the Thing the Lord God made and gave
To have dominion over sea and land;
To trace the stars and search the heavens for power;
To feel the passion of Eternity?
Is this the dream He dreamed who shaped the suns
And marked their ways upon the ancient deep?
Down all the caverns of Hell to their last gulf
There is no shape more terrible than this—
More tongued with cries against the world's blind greed—
More filled with signs and portents for the soul—
More packed with danger to the universe.
What gulfs between him and the seraphim!
Slave of the wheel of labor, what to him
Are Plato and the swing of the Pleiades?
What the long reaches of the peaks of song,
The rift of dawn, the reddening of the rose?
Through this dread shape the suffering ages look;
Time's tragedy is in that aching stoop;
Through this dread shape humanity betrayed,
Plundered, profaned and disinherited,
Cries protest to the Powers that made the world,
A protest that is also prophecy.
O masters, lords and rulers in all lands,
Is this the handiwork you give to God,
This monstrous thing distorted and soul-quenched?
How will you ever straighten up this shape;
Touch it again with immortality;
Give back the upward looking and the light;
Rebuild in it the music and the dream;
Make right the immemorial infamies,
Perfidious wrongs, immedicable woes?
O masters, lords and rulers in all lands,
How will the future reckon with this Man?
How answer his brute question in that hour
When whirlwinds of rebellion shake all shores?
How will it be with kingdoms and with kings—
With those who shaped him to the thing he is—
When this dumb Terror shall rise to judge the world,
After the silence of the centuries?

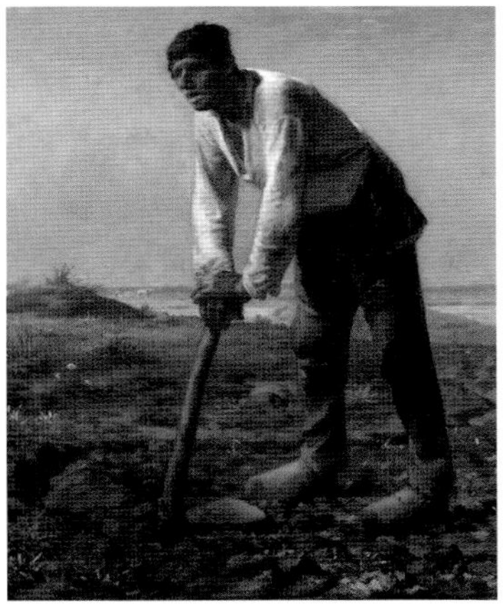

Man with a Hoe
(detail)
Jean-François Millet,
1860–62
Oil on canvas

Millet's *Man with a Hoe* appeared at the Paris Salon of 1863 just as Napoleon III was leading a heedless and vulgar industrializing of France, driving the French peasantry off the land seized from the old aristocracy in the revolutions of the eighteenth century. Millet's peasant is a dirty, brutish toiler, the very antithesis of a free and independent yeoman. His field is hopeless, while the rich man's, next door, thrives.

After many silent centuries, the world was convulsed in terrible judgment in the 1930s. For prophets like Markham, the time finally came when the President of the United States, one of the masters, lords, and rulers of that world, pledged himself to seeking redress of the injuries of the ages, and to seek again the music and the dream. That is what Markham heard in Franklin Roosevelt's peroration in Philadelphia in 1936:

"We seek not merely to make government a mechanical implement, but to give it the vibrant personal character that is the very embodiment of human charity . . . Better the occasional faults of a government that lives in a spirit of charity than the consistent omissions of a government frozen in the ice of its own indifference."[13]

Lorena Hickok Reports

The degradation of the peasant plowman of which Markham had written had become a part of the American story by 1930. The grapes of wrath were being harvested amid drought and insect plagues and depression. Art told the nation what was happening on the farm, sometimes in poetry echoing Markham's in the broken phrases of the time, sometimes in painting, sometimes in the new media of documentary photography and film. Here we turn to the art of Lorena Hickok, who worked in another twentieth-century medium—documentary journalism. A few of Hickok's published reports are set forth here, although unlike much else in this volume they were not intended to work upon a broad audience to support public policy or action. Their audience was not the public, but the senior managers of New Deal policy and action. They are here to provide us with a sense of what was in the mind of Harry Hopkins and Rexford Tugwell as they shaped agricultural policy, and as Tugwell managed the process of providing the public with images that illustrated the reality brought to him and Hopkins—and Eleanor Roosevelt—by Hickok's art.

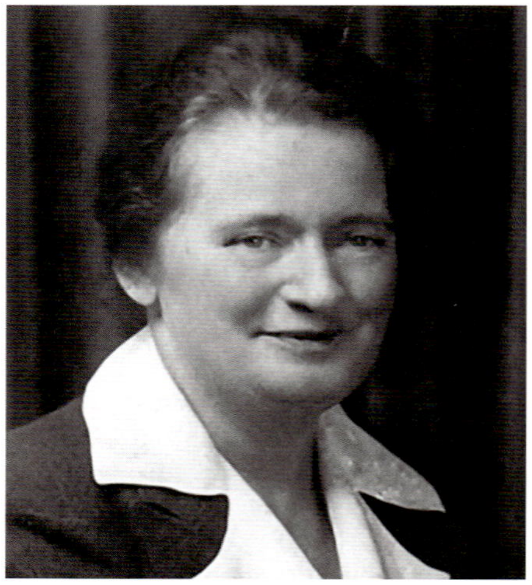

Lorena Hickok

In August 1933 Hickok set out in her old blue Ford, traveling westward from Minneapolis, away from the soothing green of the Big Woods and the cool blue lakes, toward parched and desolate South Dakota, where she had been abandoned by her abusive father when she was fourteen. She had been an ungainly child, nearly six feet tall, big-boned, expecting little and grateful to find work, first as a domestic servant and then as a policewoman. Amid squalor and small-time crime, her grit, intelligence, and steadfastness gained her, as "Hick," the respect of the reporters on the *Minneapolis Tribune*, and a job on the rewrite desk. When her chance came to write "first-cut pieces," she was good enough to merit a byline, and when she went on to the Associated Press, she became the only female journalist in the nation to compete with Edna Ferber and Dorothy Thompson. Uncorruptible and unbeguilable, skeptical of charming strangers, and abrupt in the "listen bub!" (or what she herself described as the "listen girlie") manner, she was an artist of spare, tack-it-down prose. She was also capable of expressive friendship and profound loyalty. Her particular friend, during her mature years, was Eleanor Roosevelt who helped her learn how her art might work for her country.[14]

In 1933–34 she was on assignment, no longer for the *Tribune* or the Associated Press but, instead, for Mrs. Roosevelt, Harry Hopkins, and the New Deal's work-relief programs. She was to "go round the country and look this thing over." She was to report back in simple, direct language, eschewing the tendentious statistics, skewed summaries, and ex parte excuses that too often come from the field agents of disbursers of large sums of money. Her job was to depict accurately the realities of daily life and death among those for whom the relief agencies managed by Hopkins were supposed to provide the necessities.[15]

Hickok became the administration's one-person polling organization, focus-group organizer, and in-house reality check. She loved the work. Although she and Hopkins were precise and powerful writers, neither composed explanations of their lives for posterity. Their lives, their work, ideology, and affection merged in their usefulness to Franklin and Eleanor Roosevelt. They had other friendships, but the centering points of each life was in the White House, where they both lived for long periods, as a convenience for his work with the President, and Hickok with the President's wife. Politics was personal for them, as it was personal for the whole country. The two Roosevelts were at its epicenter, in their inexplicable and immensely kinetic symbiosis. In the anthracite region of Pennsylvania, Hickok had written Hopkins, "you seldom hear the average man say 'I'm a Republican,' or 'I'm a Democrat.' What they do say is: 'I'm for the president.'"[16]

The stock market crashed not once but thrice—in 1929, in 1931, and again in 1937—and each time America tottered back to its feet, as Hickok had risen after her father's final whipping. That was the spirit of Roosevelt himself, after his loss of the use of his legs and after the near-disaster in Philadelphia in 1936. When Hickok went back to South Dakota in 1933, the farmers had been trying to get up and to stay on their feet, over and over again for seven years, with dust and blood in their eyes, through the collapse of markets, and insect plagues, blizzards, and drought. Depression? It was the state of the Union and had been for rural people since 1926. And in the cities, as she reported, in October 1933, people were "entering the third winter of their distress . . . New York City was wholly unprepared to take on this job . . . did not see it coming—any more than did the country at large. It has swept up with the dizzy, terrifying force and speed of a tornado . . . [The people are] all thrown together into a vast pit of human misery, from which a city, dazed, still only half awake to the situation, is trying to extricate them.[17]

In August 1933 she wrote from Pennsylvania: "The Red Cross, I was told, is now down to the point where it is giving out only cloth—and sometimes without thread or buttons. There is a crisis developing over the lack of shoes. School opens early in September, and practically everywhere I went I heard the cry, 'Our children must have shoes, or they can't go to school.' . . . I found one man re-soling shoes for his family with pieces of automobile tire." That October from North Dakota she wrote that she had driven "over a road so full of ruts that you couldn't tell it from ploughed fields up to a shabby little country church, standing bleakly alone in the center of a vast tawny prairie land. Grouped about the entrance to the church were a dozen or more men in shabby denim, shivering in the biting wind that swept across the plain."[18]

Here are a few more of her reports:

North Dakota, 1933: "After a succession of poor crops, this whole area apparently is in the process of drying up and becoming a desert . . . [W]heat in North Dakota last year brought about 30 cents a bushel. It costs 77 cents a bushel to raise it. This year they had no crop at all. I sat in with an investigator who was taking their stories. Again and again on the applications appeared the statement: 'Hailed out. No crop at all.' One man had sown . . . 140 acres of wheat, 25 acres of oats, 20 acres of rye, 30 acres of corn, and 20 acres of barley. All he harvested was a little corn. He was lucky, at that. I drove past cornfields today that had never grown up at all. There lay the immature stalks on the ground as the hail had beaten them down—half-starved cattle rooting around among them . . . Of the men I saw this afternoon none had any income except a little here and there from cream checks. And this will soon be stopped, for their cows are going dry for lack of food . . . For themselves and their families they need everything. Especially clothing. 'How about clothes?' the investigator asked one of them. He shrugged—'Everything I own I have on my back,' he said. He then explained that, having no underwear, he was wearing two pairs overalls, and two, very ragged, denim jackets. His shoes were so far gone that I wondered how he kept them on his feet. With one or two exceptions none of the men hanging about the church had overcoats. Most are there in denim—faded, shabby denim. Cotton denim doesn't keep out the wind very well."[19]

"The women and children are even worse off than the men. Where there has been any money at all, it has gone for shoes for the children and work clothes for the men. The women can stay inside and keep warm, and the children can stay home from school . . . The plight of the livestock is pitiable. All these people have got to keep their stock alive this winter is roughage—and darned little of that. They've even harvested Russian thistle to feed to their horses and cattle. Russian thistle, for your information, is a thistle plant with shallow roots that dries up in the fall and is blown across the prairies like rolls of barbed wire. The effect on the digestive apparatus of an animal, if it were fed the dried plant, would be, I should imagine, much the same as [if] . . . it had eaten barbed wire! However—'We tried to cut it while it was still green,' one of the farmers said."[20]

North Dakota, October 1933: "If I had to live here, I think I'd just quietly call it a day and commit suicide. The people up here—farmers, people on relief, and those administering relief—are in a daze. A sort of nameless dread hangs over the place. Last Summer for the second year the grasshoppers—great big fellows, two or three inches long—came in clouds and ate up their crops. The farmers now say the soil is all full of grasshopper eggs. They feel utterly hopeless . . . What makes it so serious is the climate up here, only 12 miles from the Canadian border. Last Winter the temperature went down to 40 degrees below zero and stayed there ten days, while a 60-mile wind howled across the plains. And entering that kind of a Winter we have between 4,000 and 5,000 human-beings—men and women and children—without clothing or bedding, getting just enough food to keep them from starving. No fuel. Living in houses that a prosperous farmer wouldn't put his cattle in . . . I visited this afternoon one of the 'better' homes of people on the relief rolls. Out on the wind-swept prairie it stood—what had once been a house. No repairs have been made in years. The kitchen floor was all patched up with pieces of tin—a wash boiler cover, ten can lids, some old automobile license plates. You could see daylight through the crack under the door. Great patches of plaster had fallen from the walls. Newspapers had been stuffed in the cracks about the windows. And in that house two small boys . . . were running about without a stitch on save some ragged overalls. No shoes or stockings. Their feet were purple with cold."[21]

"It is the 'Siberia' of the United States. A more hopeless place I never saw. Half of the people—the farmers particularly—are scared to death. I got that feeling this afternoon. They were terrified."[22]

Nebraska, November 1933: "We started out . . . intending to drive up into the Northern part of the country to see some farmers. By that time the whole sky was covered with the haze—the sun just a lighter spot in the brown curtain. I realized then what was happening. Dust storm. We used to have them when I was a child out there, but not quite that bad. If there had been snow on the ground to be blown about, this would have been a blizzard. We'd gone less than ten miles when we had to turn back. It kept getting worse. You couldn't see a foot ahead of the car. It was a truly terrifying experience . . . Like driving in a fog, only worse because of the wind, which, it seemed, would blow the car right off the road. When we stopped we had to put on the emergency brake because the wind, at our backs, actually started the car rolling. We wondered if we were ever going to get back to town. It was as though we were being picked up in a vast, impenetrable, brown cloud, which was whirling us right off the earth. The street lamps were on when we got back to Huron. By noon it was as black as midnight. You couldn't see across the street. It kept it up until sundown, and all Monday morning we drove past drifts of brown sand . . . having these dust storms, less intense, every two weeks or so this fall. All this sort of thing makes for fear—and unrest. Some of the farmers I saw Monday looked like frightened children."[23]

"Another thing that scares them is their debt load. They're afraid to borrow any more money. Their land, their homes, their machinery, their livestock—all mortgaged. They owe for seed loans, and, since they didn't even get seed out of this year's crop, many of them, if they go on, must borrow money for seed again this spring—if they can get it . . . They are afraid of losing their farms . . . their cows have carried them through some bad years in the past. Now, for the first time, they cannot feed their cows. But they are afraid to let them go . . . Therefore, they're turning them out to shift for themselves. During my trip down into Rosebud country and up around Huron, I saw livestock that would make you sick. But we can't feed all the livestock in South Dakota. So—that's that . . . One farmer told me his horses were so weak that, although he lived only 11 miles from town, it took him all day to get to town and back. Relief people told me that a man will show up for work with a team of horses, that the horses will work pretty well during the forenoon, that they'd begin to sag in the early afternoon, were completely exhausted by night, and didn't show up the next day. There have been cases where the horses actually dropped in the harness while at work on the roads . . . I wrote you about how they were feeding Russian thistle to their cattle. Well, did you ever hear of Russian thistle soup? That's what some of those people are eating. They cut the thistles green and stack them up. Inside the stacks the stuff is still green—although perhaps rotted a little. They haul that out, stew it up with a little flour and water, and eat it!"[24]

Georgia, January 1934: "If there is a compulsory school system in the state, it simply isn't functioning. It can't. The children just can't go to school, hundreds of them, because they haven't the clothes. The illiterate parents of hundreds of others don't send them. As a result you've got the picture of hundreds of boys and girls in their teens down here in some of these rural areas who can't read or write. I'm not exaggerating. I've been told that again and again. Why, some of them can barely talk!"[25]

New Orleans, April 1934: "In one county up in Northeastern Alabama you've evidently got a stranded population of several thousand people . . . They're in the mountains, trying to farm. Can't make a go of it. No industries of any kind. Three doctors in the county—one of them the health officer, one practicing without a license, and the third an old man about to die. Not very long ago the county relief director up there got a call out into the country one night. They said a woman was very sick. When they got out there, they delivered a baby—using the headlights on their car for light! In another county up in that vicinity there are 300 displaced tenant farmers. Every now and then one of them will come in and beg the relief director: 'Please buy us a tent, ma'am. We can't find no house.'"[26]

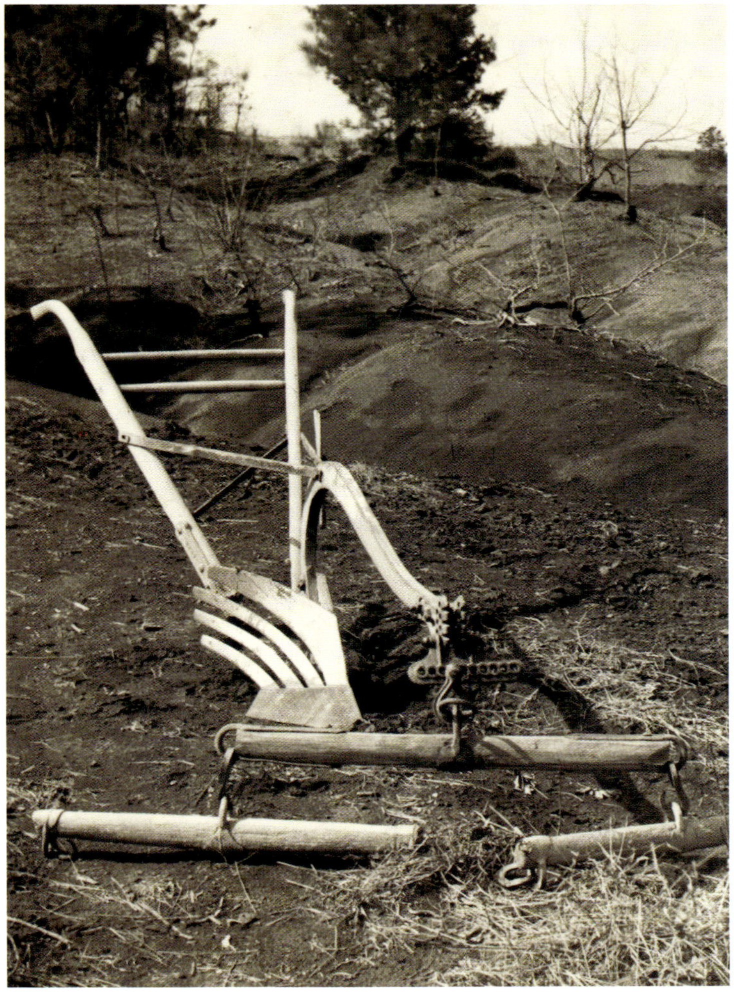

"Erosion, Macon County, Alabama"
Arthur Rothstein, 1937

Chapter Seven

Rexford Tugwell, Roy Stryker, Photographers, Folk Music, and Films

"They seem to be trusting in God–and the Government. There's a chance to create a new kind of industrial life, with decent wages, decent housing. Gosh, what possibilities!"[1]
(Lorena Hickok, reporting from Alabama, April 1934)

"A love of people and a love of life. And those things were contagious."[2]
(Roy Stryker on the art of Carl Mydans, interview with Richard Doud for the Archives of American Art)

THE MOST WIDELY KNOWN WORKS OF ART sponsored by the New Deal are the post office murals; the photographs of Ben Shahn, Eudora Welty, Walker Evans, Dorothea Lange, Arthur Rothstein, Gordon Parks, Carl Mydans, Russell Lee, Jack Delano, and Marion Post; and the documentary motion pictures of Pare Lorentz. The work of all the artists of film was under the aegis of Rexford Tugwell and Roy Stryker and was for the purpose of building public support for the work of the Resettlement Administration, the Farm Security Administration, the Soil Erosion Service (later the Soil Conservation Service), the WPA, the TVA, and the CCC. Tugwell has been less discussed among art historians than Stryker—but as Stryker acknowledged, Tugwell was not only the man who hired him, but the man who managed him, set his course, and protected him, while adding his own powerful ideas to the selection and deployment of the people who worked for him. Perhaps most important, Tugwell had direct access to the Roosevelts, and used it, although on the chart of the Department of Agriculture he reported to Henry Wallace.

Tugwell was born in 1891 near Sinclairsville, a hamlet in the fruit-growing flatland corner of western New York between Erie and Buffalo. He grew up in the nearby town of Wilson where his father, a fruit farmer, had a small cannery. The cannery paid for his tuition at the University of Pennsylvania's Wharton School of Finance and Commerce, where his parents' Social Gospel convictions and his own experience with the shadow side of capitalism were reinforced by Social Gospel intellectuals led by Simon Patten and Adolph Adolphus ("A.A.") Berle, whose father was a Social Gospel minister. Tugwell was hired by the University of Washington to teach marketing, a proficiency he pronounced to be "dreary" but which became of great importance to him, to art, to the New Deal, and to the nation a few years later. While studying labor conditions in lumber camps, he accepted a summons from Felix Frankfurter to help the war effort by managing the American University Union in Paris, a leave center for American officers serving in France. He returned home to teach economics at Columbia University and to advise governors, including Frank Lowden of Illinois, and in New York both Al Smith and Franklin Roosevelt.

In 1927 Tugwell refused to heed advice to abstain from going to Russia to study collective farming, an error for which he was dogged for the rest of his life by charges that he was "Rex the Red." In fact, he deplored Stalin's brutality and consistently opposed Communism's "iron logic" and "mechanistic doctrines." In some ways he was not a New Dealer; he disliked welfare spending and advocated a balanced budget. He was, however, an advocate of state planning, as were his colleagues A. A. Berle and Raymond Moley, with whom he formed the core of Roosevelt's "Brain Trust" during the campaign for the presidency in 1932.

Tugwell was as good-looking as a movie star, impeccable in grooming and dress, cool, sophisticated, urbane, and aloof. To many he struck as arrogant, he became known as "Tugwell Rex." When President Franklin Roosevelt nominated him to be Undersecretary of Agriculture in 1934, he went to his confirmation hearing wearing white buckskin shoes, a perfectly creased, tailor-made suit, and each hair on his magnificent head in place, prompting Senator Murphy of Iowa to demand: "Did you ever follow a plow?" "Yes, sir." "Did you ever have mud on your boots?" "Yes, sir." "Do you know how hard it is to get a dollar out of the soil?" "Yes, sir." He was confirmed 53 to 24, despite Senator Dickinson's reading to the Senate a self-description written by Tugwell when he was twenty-four: "I am strong, I am big and well-made, I am muscled and lean and nervous . . . I am sick of a nation's stenches, I am sick of propertied Czars. . . . I have dreamed my great dream of their passing, I have gathered my tools and my charts; My plans are fashioned and practical; I shall roll up my sleeves—make America over!"[3]

It was easy to make a joke of somebody like that, and Tugwell's style did not change much as he got older, although with Henry Wallace taking the heat and the bows as Secretary, Roosevelt could name Tugwell Assistant Secretary of Agriculture and then Undersecretary. His rewriting of food and drug laws affronted the drug makers and the publications carrying drug advertising, and he also got into trouble with many industrial-scale farmers who objected to the diminution of a ready supply of cheap labor as the result of his efforts toward resettlement of their distressed neighbors. Furthermore, Tugwell shared Eleanor Roosevelt's enthusiasm for resettlement not only of rural populations into collective farms, but also of some of the urban poor into model towns such as Homestead, New Jersey (for which Ben Shahn painted his famous murals).[4]

Resettlement was the most radical reconsideration of American rural life since the onset of privatization of the public domain through land grants, sales to land companies, and homesteading. The assumption behind this experiment in the creation of a widespread class of independent small proprietors, by now so familiar as to obliterate recollection of its novelty among land systems worldwide, was that once on their plots of ground the farmers could take care of themselves. Some could. Many could not. On the edges of the arable, the previously public lands had come into the hands of people who could not make decent lives upon them, but struggled along even when prices for commodities such as wheat and corn were artificially elevated. Land even less hospitable to farming was put under cultivation to meet demand when Europe went to war and could not produce

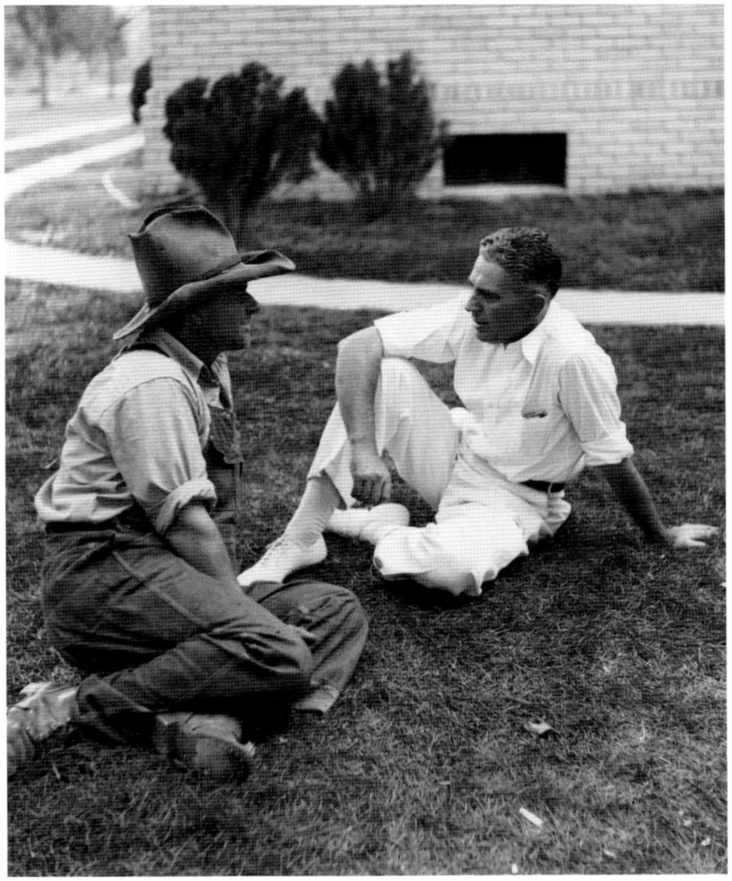

Rexford Tugwell confers with a farmer in Springfield, Colorado. Arthur Rothstein, 1936

Forest fire
Paul Landacre, c. 1937
Wood engraving
on paper

Paul Landacre was born in Columbus, Ohio, attended Ohio State University, worked for the California WPA graphics program, and later taught at the Otis Art Institute in Los Angeles. He became a successful illustrator of books, such as *The Natural History of Trees*, published in 1953.

enough for itself. On Appalachia's slopes, on its sandy lowlands and its leached-out, thin-soiled escarpments, as on the High Plains, prices fell, the insects invaded, the droughts came, and people grew poorer and more hopeless even before the general Depression. That additional catastrophe further shriveled demand for their meager crops. Resettlement meant getting these suffering people off the land or supporting them on it with government handouts. Farm security, broadly considered, included soil conservation, better erosion control, crop rotation, better use of the land as it was, and better prices.

Rexford Tugwell was a major force advancing these efforts in concert with the leaders of rural electrification, the TVA, the WPA, and the CCC. Many of the specific ventures of the agencies under his leadership did not survive the New Deal, but David Kennedy has justly written of the lasting consequences of the full panoply of these endeavors that to "tens of millions of rural Americans, the New Deal offered the modern comforts of electricity, schools, and roads, as well as unaccustomed financial stability.[5]

In the end, resettlement occurred as much through individual exertion as through government programs. People got jobs in war work in the cities. Some stayed in the localities where they were but "resettled" by working their way out of tenancy into ownership of their own small farms, where rising prices in wartime helped them make ends meet. The government-sponsored resettlement advocated by Tugwell also meant dispersing industry into planned communities to which immigrants in the larger older cities might be encouraged to move, once they knew that jobs awaited them. Urban resettlement produced greenbelt model communities, but became successful only when World War II increased demand for the products those factories produced.

Resettlement had the effect of evacuating large areas of the West and Southeast. It finally worked out when prices rose and the numbers of rural people needing employment fell in wartime. Meanwhile it gave greater impetus to the efforts of the Soil Conservation Service to make farming on marginal lands possible by encouraging contour plowing, erosion control in gullies, crop rotation, and efforts to substitute orchards for corn plots. Apple trees do not leach out nutriments as do corn and tobacco plants.

Grace Falke, later Mrs. Rexford Tugwell, was often the companion of Lorena Hickok on her travels through Appalachia to report on conditions in the leached-out slopes and eroded "coves" between hard-scrabble ridges where there was little sentimentality left about free and independent yeomanry. Falke and Hickok also wrote to Harry Hopkins and Tugwell about what they saw in the shacks of the played-out people on the played-out land of the share-cropping Black Belt and Delta of the South, in the Dust Bowl of the High Plains, and in the migrant camps of California. These grim lives were revealed in Hickok's letters and also in the photographs taken at the direction of Tugwell and Roy Stryker and to a considerable extent managed by Grace Falke. Both in literary and pictorial form, these documents explained the need for the work of Tugwell's Resettlement Administration, Farm Security Administration, and Soil Erosion Service (later Soil Conservation Service, and now Natural Resources Conservation Service).

Grace Falke reported directly to Tugwell, Hickok to an initial readership of two, Eleanor Roosevelt and Harry Hopkins, but her terse, precise, edged, and actionable prose carried consequences for millions. In a letter to Hopkins, written from Florence, Alabama, on June 6, 1934, Hickok wrote of "table land. Thin soil. Terrible housing. Illiteracy. Evidence of prolonged undernourishment. No knowledge of how to live decently or farm decently or farm profitably if they had decent land." That was the point. They needed help in farming better and help in getting better land to farm.[6]

Hickok reported that Tennessee was worse: "There you can see constantly evidence of what happens when you cut timber off mountain sides and plant crops there. There are great patches of rock." And upon those eroded and rocky hills people were trying to farm. Perhaps, she wrote, if they were to be given new land "with careful and authoritative supervision they might eke out a living." Perhaps the TVA could bring factories to the valleys where the mountain

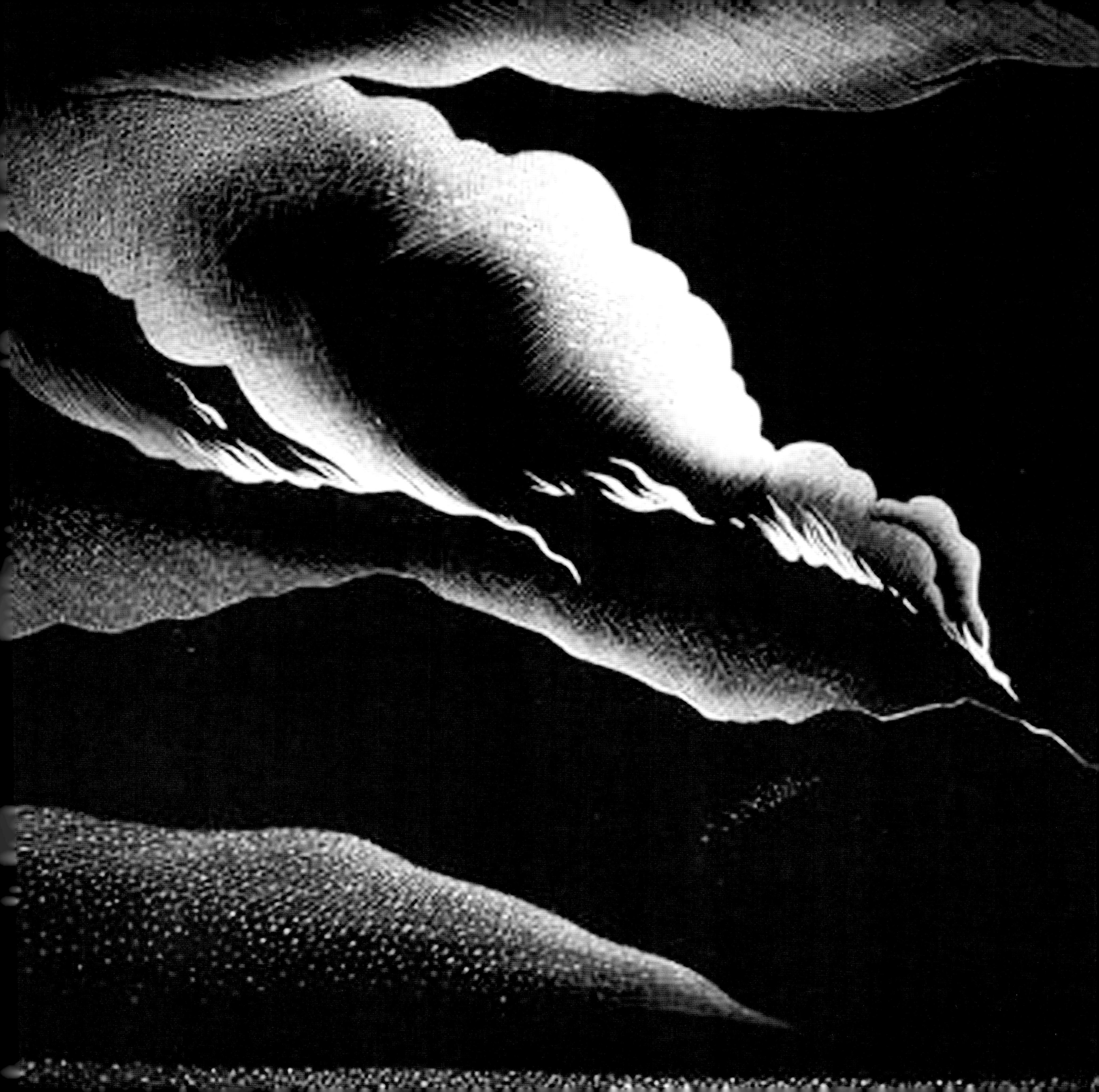

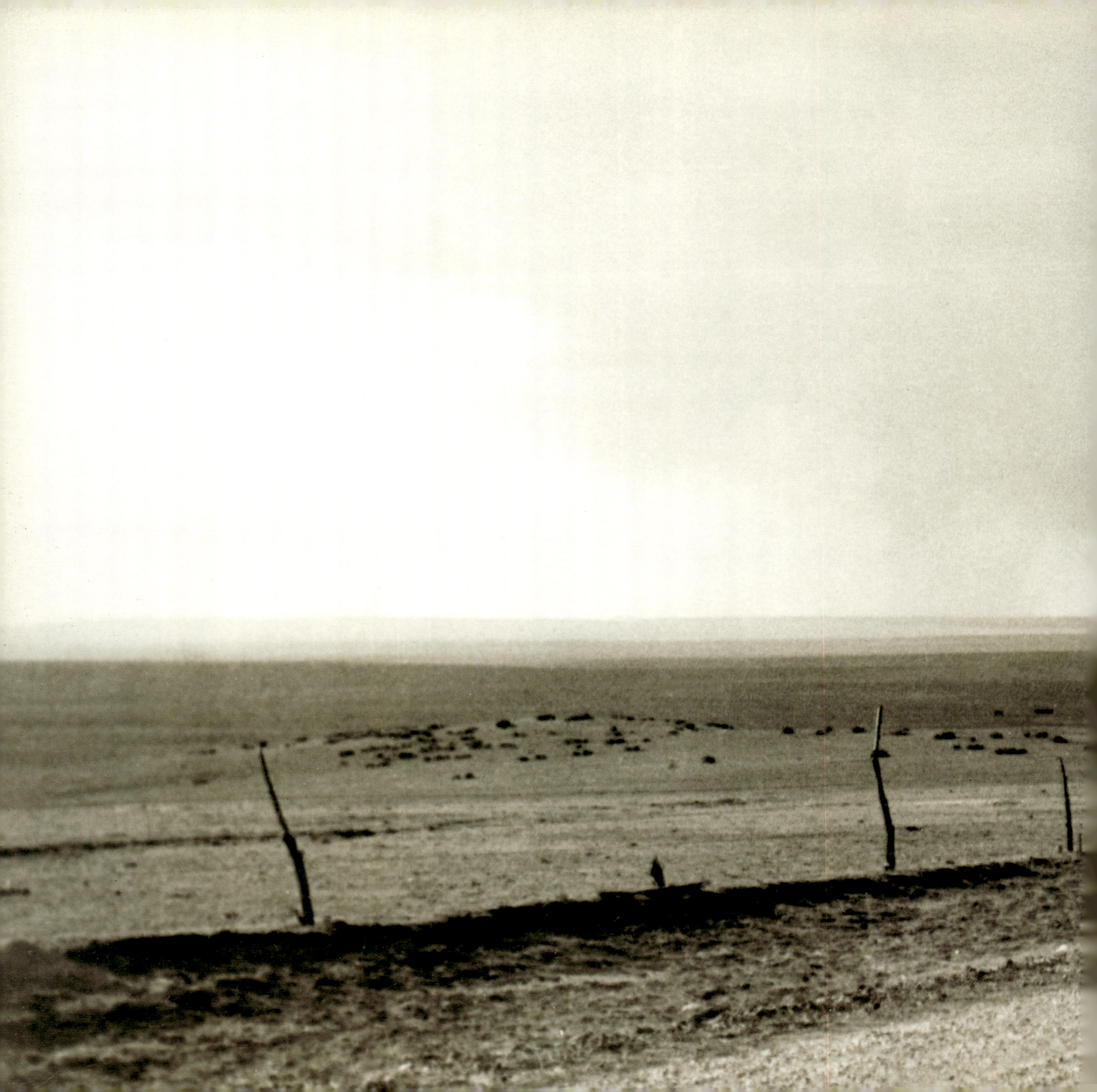

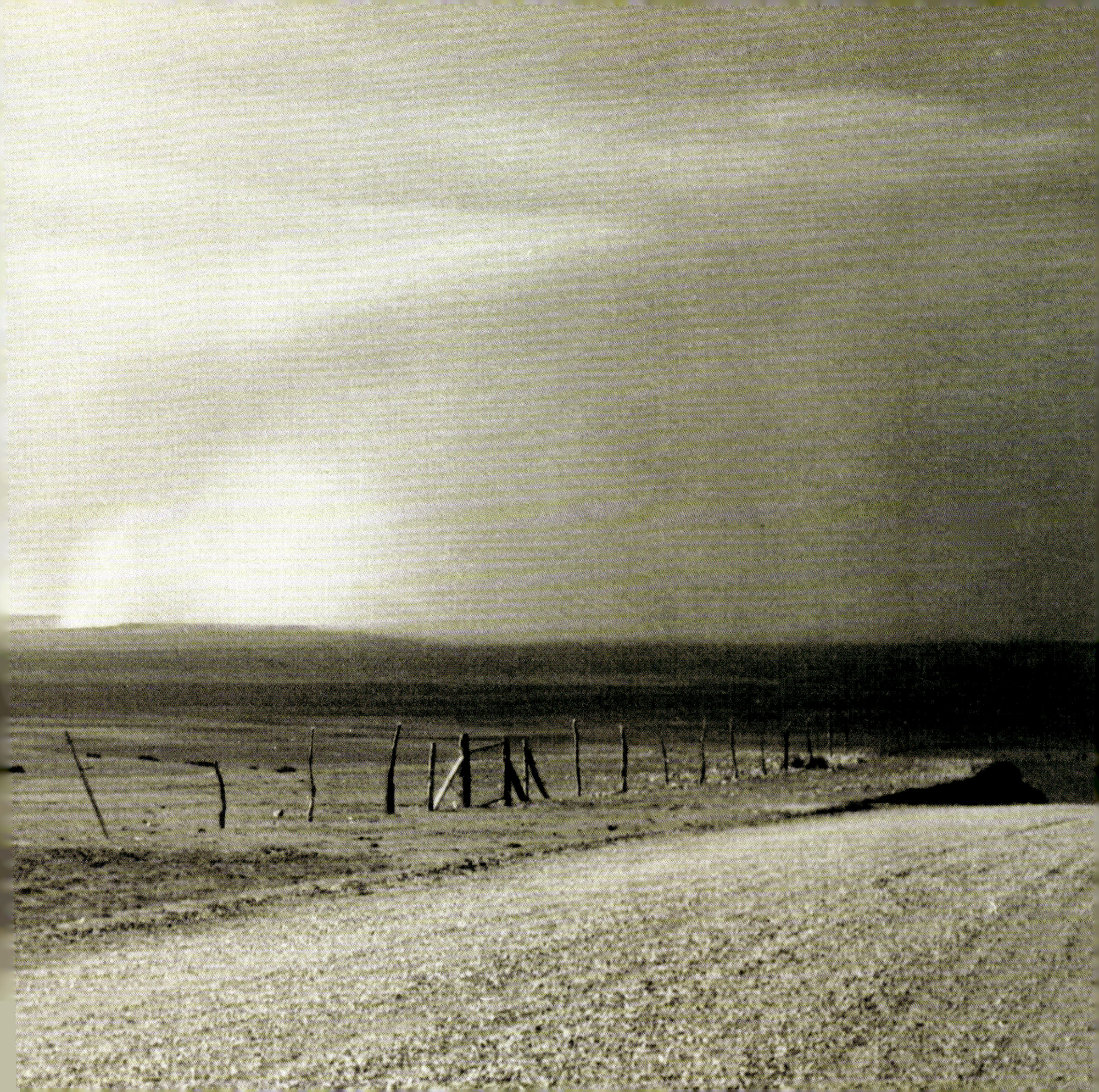

Previous pages:
"A dust storm near Mills, New Mexico"
Dorothea Lange, 1935

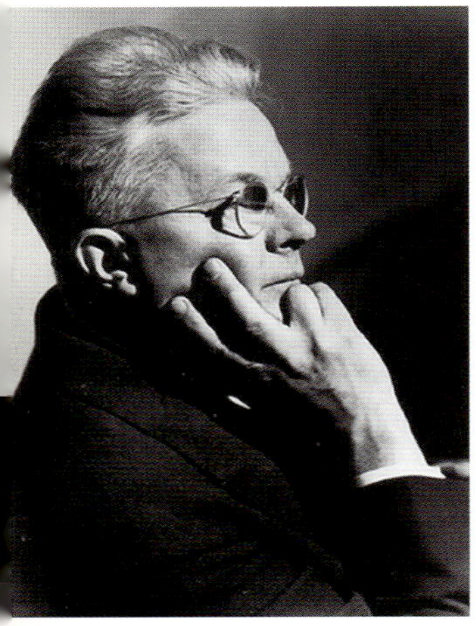

"Roy Emerson Stryker"
Gordon Parks, 1947

"We had to help make a country conscious of the Dust Bowl, the migrants, the sharecroppers, and the difficulties that had beset the country."
Roy Stryker, letter to Helen Hill Miller, October 11, 1960[iii]

people might be "absorbed in the industries." Then—perhaps—the Resettlement Administration might "rehabilitate the present adult generation where they are. Try out orchards instead of corn on the table land, for instance." Hickok wrote Hopkins that several ideas along these lines had been "advanced by Grace Falke . . . who has joined me on this trip. Help the parents to get at least a fairly decent living now and do a bang-up job of public health and education on the children." And build subsistence housing, like that Hickok said had "the nicest houses I've seen anywhere. They are building them of a beautifully colored rock found on the place." Though the people were deep in debt, "they seem to be trusting in God—and the Government. There's a chance to create a new kind of industrial life, with decent wages, decent housing. Gosh, what possibilities!"[7]

Some of those possibilities were fulfilled within the viewshed of those visitors who look forth from the little windows at the top of the Washington Monument. We urge that perspective in the next chapter, in which George Washington is presented as our first conservationist president. Here what is seen through those windows permits some suggestions of the effects of New Deal agricultural policy led by Rexford Tugwell. To the west, southwest, and northwest one can glimpse the wondrous results of soil conservation and farm resettlement as they led to the recreational reuse of thin-soiled marginal lands. Prince William Forest, once a wasteland eroded by growing corn and tobacco and by overgrazing, is a retreat for picnickers and backpackers who seldom notice the foundations of slave cabins. The parklands of the Catoctins now include not only Camp David but many places of recreation for the public. Beyond the horizon to the south, the Great Smoky Mountains no longer hide from view a national rural slum. Resettlement was not popular there, nor was it popular among the people displaced to create Acadia National Park, Shenandoah National Park, and the flanks of the Blue Ridge Parkway. Yet if one considered what happened to the children and grandchildren of those who took government checks and moved out, often to jobs provided by other government checks, the outcome was humane. In Minnesota, Wisconsin, and Michigan, soil conservation and farm resettlement worked together to make what could be farmed farmable, and what could not enjoyable—out of black fly season.[8]

Roy Stryker

Roy Stryker was born in 1893 on a farm near the center point of Kansas, around which the Arkansas River struggles in a great bend through dusty, short-grass plains, seeking the Mississippi and the Gulf. Stryker was a rangy young man who loved reading. On weekends and summers, while he studied chemistry at the Colorado School of Mines, Stryker sweated as a cowhand, saving enough of his wages to buy with his brother a "couple of thousand acres of grassland." Then, "for seven years, I . . . looked after the cows. In the winter time I grub staked out, worked for a cattle outfit or a mining outfit or some other place . . . very rich experience . . . in the hard rock mines . . . But I did read all the time." World War I came along, and the cowhand/chemist became an infantryman. In France, he decided to sell his "cattle outfit" and studied economics at Columbia. He needed a little more cash, and a job on the side, which came to him through introductions arranged by George Collins, a Social Gospel clergyman/economist whom he had met at the School of Mines. Collins also acquainted him with "the New Republic, the Nation, [Walter] Rauschenbusch, the very famous theologian from Rochester Seminary," and the Union Settlement (part of Union Seminary). The loan came from Wills William Sweet of the Y.M.C.A., "a very, very liberal man" and one of the leaders of the application of Social Gospel theology to social work. Sweet's example and settlement work were, said Stryker, "an imprint."[9]

During his first year at Columbia he met Tugwell, who was "giving courses in Utopian Socialism and various things . . . a magnificent teacher when he felt like it. I had another very fine professor, William Weld, who had been a missionary . . . in the Near East and India. He had a great deal of interest in visual things. And I found myself making charts, helping him [Weld] out . . . And I suppose that was a contribution to my visual interest." And Tugwell, basically a descriptive economist, often said "'how can you talk about the economic system if you don't know what a bank looks like?'" So Stryker was not surprised when Tugwell called him one day and said, "'We're doing a book called *American Economic Life*, and I want it illustrated . . . The book came out. I had my name on it. I wrote nothing; but I must say I am proud of the job of illustration that we did." Margaret Bourke-White's pictures of industry in Cleveland had been discovered by Tugwell, who had given examples to Stryker as potential illustrations. When she first came to New York, he went to the station to meet her and their friendship began.[10]

While at Columbia, Stryker had also thought of producing a *Pictorial Sourcebook of American Agricultural History* with "a hell of a lot of pictures." He had seen Dorothea Lange's images of migrant farm workers, which reminded him of his own work for the YMCA with the migrants in Colorado, and he began thinking of her as a potential partner. Then Stryker met Walker Evans, who "was working for The Rehabilitation Division of the Department of Interior" and also "got acquainted with Ben Shahn." They too saw life as he did. Shahn had returned from "a trip down through the South" making pictures of poor farmers that provided Stryker a "great . . . education." By then Stryker had joined Tugwell in Washington, and their urgent projects together eclipsed all thought of a private venture in illustrated economics. The plight of all the nation's farmers was growing worse, and they were "getting a lot of pictures in. The newspapers were coming over; we were peddling pictures; we were pushing them. Still unsophisticated, still pretty disorganized, we were learning fast."[11]

Tugwell's invitation to Stryker, "Why don't you come down?" was about as passionate an expression of affinity as he displayed in all their years together. "It wasn't cussedness, it wasn't superciliousness, it was a peculiar shyness." He was "not a very communicative person." When Stryker had "a feeling of insecurity" he sometimes asked "'Rex, are we doing all right?' And Tugwell would look up and say: 'I don't know, I guess you are. I haven't any complaints. Why in the hell don't you go back to work. I don't like to hold hands.'" He was not "a demonstrative person. [Once] he had had a very bad strep throat, and he damn near died. And I rushed down to him. He was so pleased to see me, so deeply pleased to see me. And he suddenly pulled the blind up for a moment and let his emotions out. Then bang! went the curtain down."[12]

Stryker and Tugwell agreed on the essentials: the primary intention of the famous photography program they managed was not to encourage art or artists. Although the program was "really doing art projects," said Tugwell, "we didn't have any idea it was going to become an art form. No. We knew that these were awfully good photographers and that they were something more than just the kind of people that the newspapers would send out. I don't know anything about aesthetic theory and I am not an artist. [Nonetheless] to me, they [the FSA photographs] are very tender and touching things—very sensitively done. To me it is still marvelous that a fellow like Rothstein would sit a woman in a doorway and tell such a big story—that is a genuine artist who can do that. It is the kind of touch that Wyeth has. He paints someone at a window, and a flower, and you see the whole world in it."[13]

"Most of our people were interested in art, had some art training, had desires to be artists," said Stryker, but had "discovered photography offered them something." He and Tugwell were looking for people with "curiosity," "a desire to know," and "the eye to see the significance around them." He wanted a "journalist or a good artist" who could "read." The qualifying question was "what interested him? . . . How sharp was his mental vision as well as what he saw with his eyes?" Could they be good at "communicating" through being "intelligent enough to sense what they were doing. They were trying to tell us, tell the public, make pictures that were genuine, that recognized . . . the pertinent things." That would require of them that they take the time to "understand why they were at that place, and what they were going to do . . . We looked at them in terms of what did they have to say about this little group of people, this particular

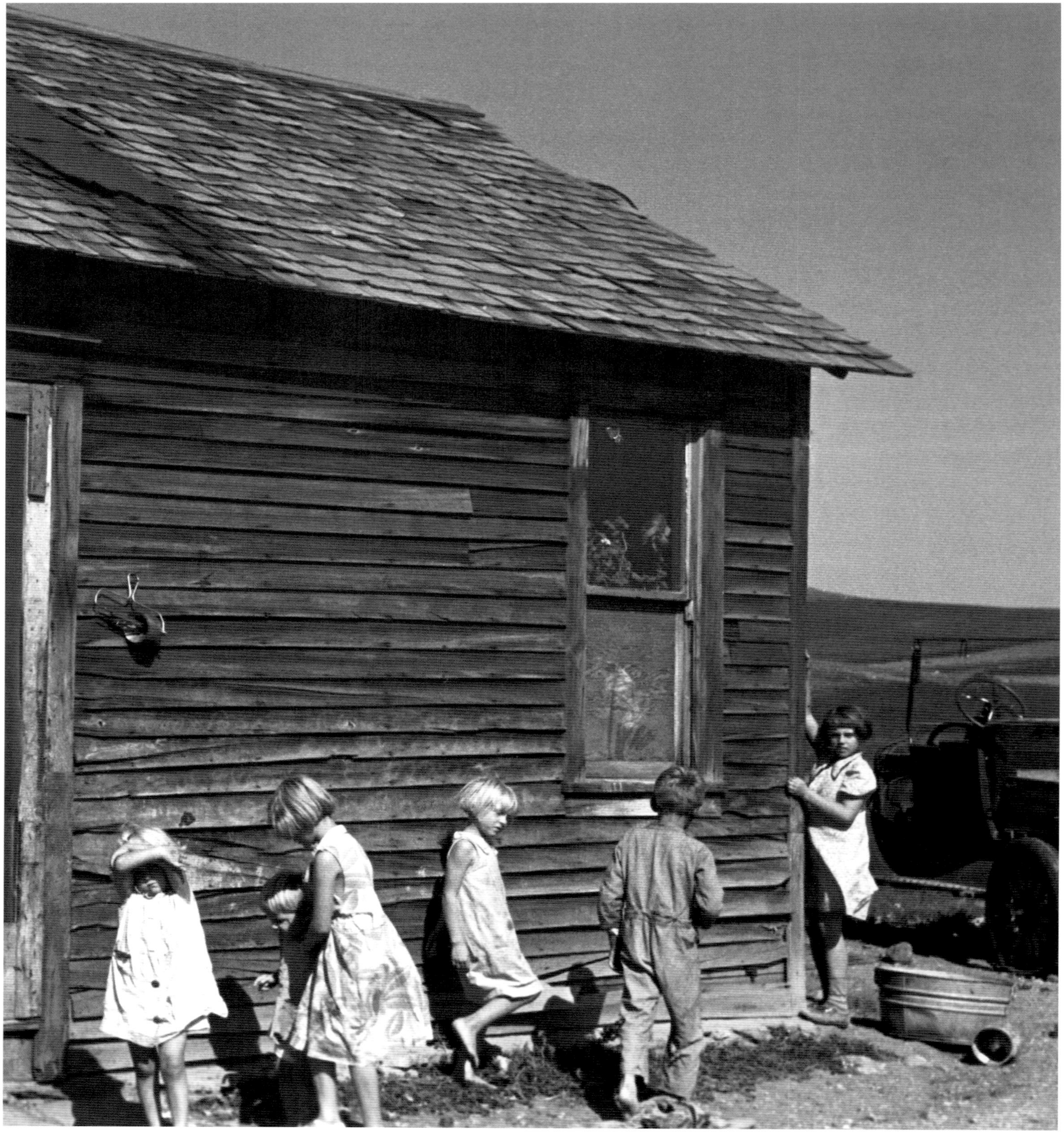

"Children in front of Olaf Fugelberg's farmhouse, Williams County, North Dakota"
Russell Lee, 1937

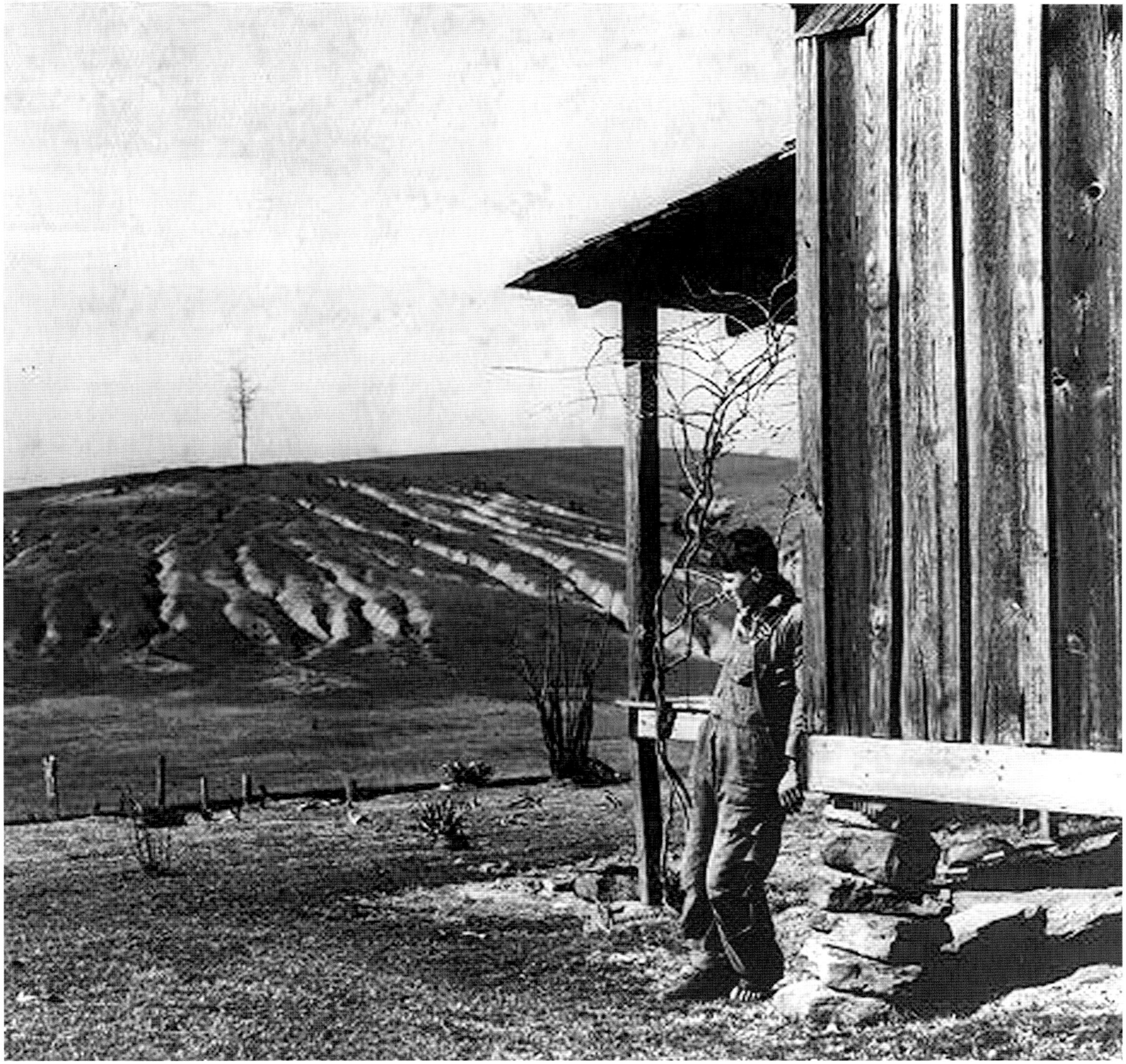

"Eroded land on tenant's farm. Walker County, Alabama"
Arthur Rothstein, 1937

village, this particular dust area." Above all else Tugwell and Stryker sought "a sincere, passionate love of people, and respect for people." That was because "Farm Security was an action program. They were going to help move people out of depressed areas—primarily rural . . . to help people get back into a going-concern situation, to be able to make a living on their places, and to help straighten out their debt difficulties, to help them get better practices." Photography was useful for supplying Tugwell's "field people with tools to make the program clear" and, of course, for informing "the American people about some of these 'lower third' and their problems."[14]

Recent scholars of the New Deal have stressed the importance of the Social Gospel in motivating Tugwell, Stryker, and many of the photographers who used art to strengthen public support for programs to help meet those problems, though in their interviews with Richard Doud of the Archives of American Art in the 1960s, neither Tugwell nor Stryker offered fulsome statements of Christian faith. That was not the way of the time. Religiosity was not yet in vogue, nor were there television interviewers ragging public officials for scriptural references or theological distinctions that would have baffled the Council of Trent. A reporter once asked the impertinent questions by now tolerable on television, to which Roosevelt, according to Secretary of Labor Frances Perkins, our witness to the occasion, replied as if he were "puzzled" rather than annoyed: "Philosophy? Philosophy? I am a Christian and a Democrat—that's all." And that was all that he and his colleagues were likely to aver in the matter. Their actions were their professions of faith. As Perkins wrote, they were "willing to do experimentally whatever was necessary to promote the Golden Rule." For someone like Perkins, "steeped in the Social Gospel tradition" that was indeed "all" that needed to be said theologically.[15]

The rest was implementation and technique. Among the things necessary to promote the Golden Rule was to gain public assent for doing more. That was the work of Roy Stryker's photographers, each in his or her own way. He said: "Walker Evans's pictures are . . . not the accident, he plans them, he walks around, he looks, and all of a sudden—his is a composed job. Walker walks around and all of a sudden sees . . . the tombstone in the cemetery, the street, the houses. It's an interesting picture, because you know that he planned it. That's not 'composed' in the sense that that word is so badly used at times, but he hunts till he finds the right viewpoint, the right place to stand . . . Walker was apt to stand back and see a static relationship in most of his pictures . . . Ben Shahn is there at the moment, he helps, perhaps, to set up some by his conversation, but he sees the faces, he sees the juxtaposition of faces; a second later it's too late. He had to hit it right. Some of that is accident, but he knows what he's after, he sees—you see, he sees a whole concept there. Ben . . . was never on our payroll but was assigned to other organizations within Resettlement and Farm Security, known as Special Skills—they were largely artists, craftsmen, and designers . . . Ben . . . did an extended photographic trip, and contributed . . . some of the most exciting . . . human documents in the whole file . . . Dorothea Lange had done a good deal of work on the immigrants in California . . . Marion Post . . . has particularly a great sense of our land, of our terrain and a feeling of people on the land, probably more than some of the others. A great love of people, a great warmth and understanding of people . . . Jack Delano came in from a WPA project . . . he was a musician and a very good one, an artist by training. And very successful . . . John Collier was . . . son of the old Indian Commissioner. He had very little schooling but in some ways was one of the most sophisticated of all of our people, in that strange unsophisticated manner that . . . added zest and glamour to the place . . . Walker Evans would do it one way, Ben Shahn had quite different way . . . sometimes you look at Ben's pictures and you think you see the consternation, the irritation, the frustrations of these men; but Ben stirred up some of that . . . And Arthur [Rothstein], naïve little Bronx boy that he is . . . stayed within that naiveté of the city boy . . . Carl Mydans . . . had some of the same thing. Some people would call it bumptiousness. I wouldn't. A love of people and a love of life. And those things were contagious."[16]

"The *Times* could stand pictures, we were a year ahead of *Life* and *Look*, ferment was on, we came at the right time . . . We were in a period of hard times in this country, a very disturbing time. Even people who weren't hungry . . . were distressed, disturbed, worried . . . So, as these things were picked up by the newspapers, picked up by the magazines later on, and seen in various ways, I suspect that a lot of the public . . . found . . . a rapport with some of the faces they saw. Photographs were fresh then, so maybe we had more impact because of their freshness, because of photographs' newness. *Life* didn't cover many of our stories; *Look* didn't. So it was done by an enormous number of small magazines. We got into the local presses out through the fields, where field people used the material. We rode that wave and . . . we then began to broaden our scope . . . We began to . . . cover the main street of America . . . Photographers took pictures of filling stations, a wonderful picture that Walker Evans took of old tires that had been piled, not like they are today, they were piled on posts. Migrants came in and bought these old tires. These things all begin to stir, you tasted this, let's have some more of it . . . And it wasn't long before the pictures began to arrive and they were good."[17]

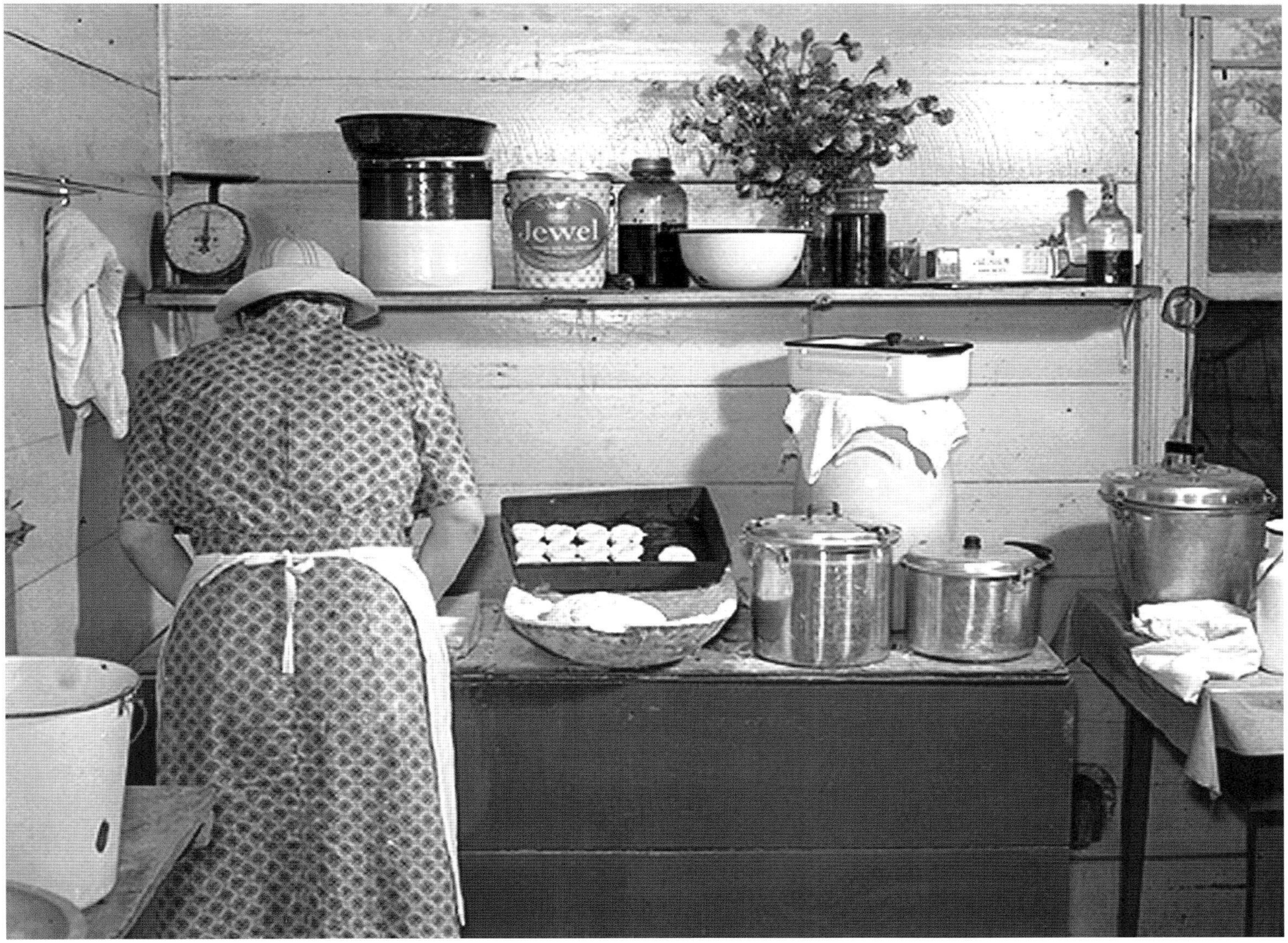

"One of the Wilkins family making biscuits for dinner on cornshucking day at Mrs. Fred Wilkins' home near Tallyho, Granville County, North Carolina"
Marion Post Wolcott, 1939

As chief of the Farm Security Administration's Historical Section, Roy Stryker directed the acquisition of photographic documentation that presented the need for the New Deal's programs and depicted some of their early successes (see main text).

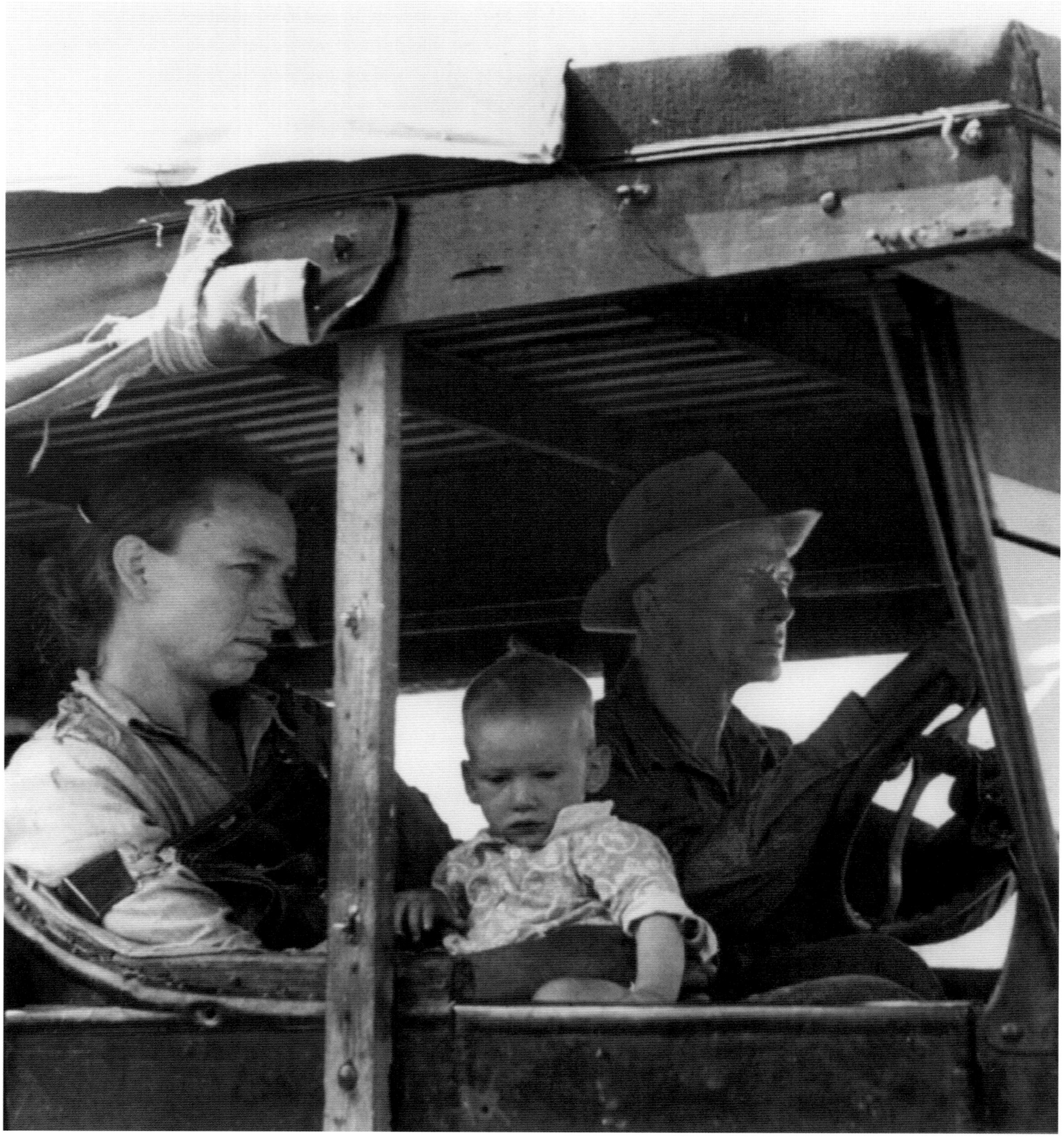

"White migrant family in their automobile east of Fort Gibson, Muskogee County, Oklahoma"
Russell Lee, 1939

Opposite:
"Man standing by car door, stalled on the desert, facing a future in California. No money, ten children, from Chickasaw, Oklahoma. Southern California"
Dorothea Lange, 1937

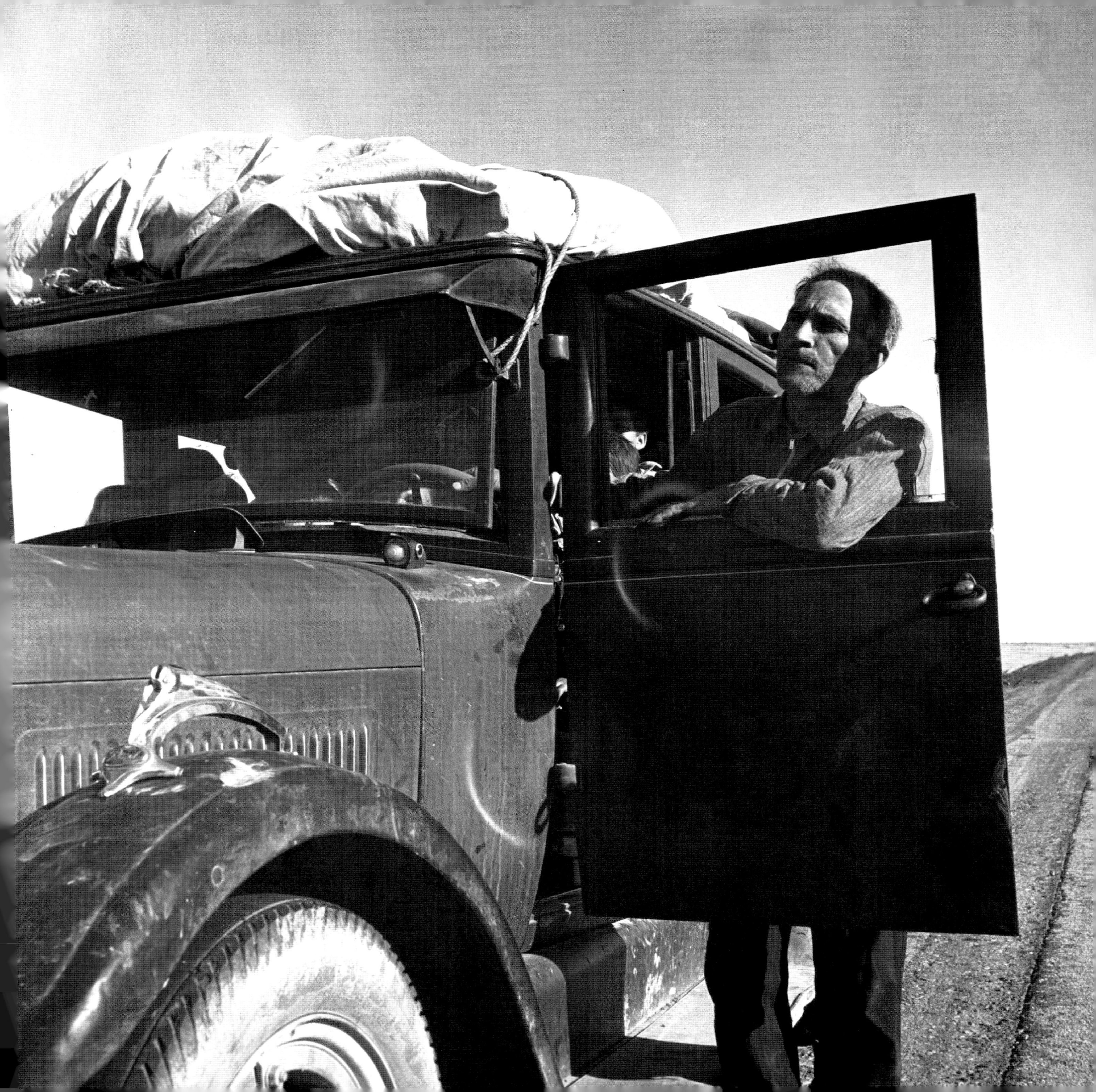

Dorothea Lange

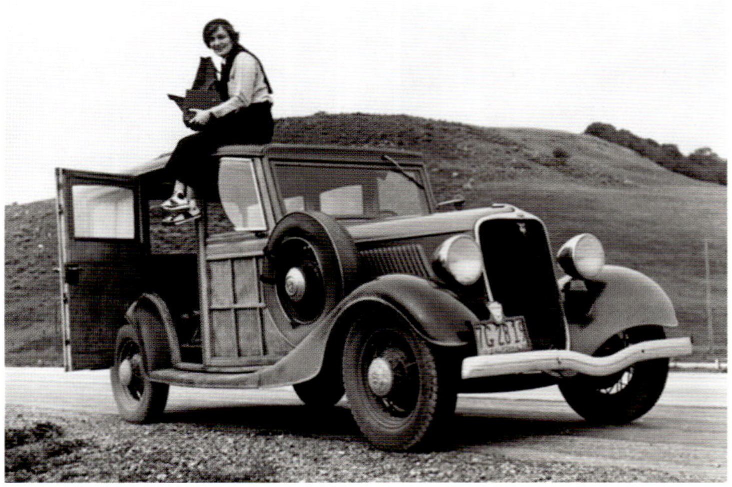

Dorothea Lange with camera on the road in California February, 1936

Dorothea Lange was forty years old when she made the photograph "Migrant Mother." In 1933, on her first day away from fashionable portrait photography—her first "on the street" where the Depression was "beginning to cut very deep" she made "White Angel Breadline" (see pp. 22–23). In an interview during the 1960s, she told of watching from the upstairs window of her studio as the unemployed drifted past, and of deciding to take her camera to "concentrate upon people, only people. All kinds of people, people who paid me and people who didn't." She photographed men sleeping on sidewalks, leaning against storefronts; one man sat slumped, head bowed, next to an overturned wheelbarrow.

Before the San Francisco general strike broke out, on July 16, 1934, Lange had already photographed men with fists raised, mouths open, shouting, and she left indelible images of the violence of the longshoremen's strike. Paul Taylor, who was teaching economics at Berkeley, saw an exhibit of her work and asked for one of her pictures to illustrate his work. Taylor became field director for rural rehabilitation, and in the belief that "words alone could not convey the conditions," he hired Lange. And ten months later he married her. When she met the first Dust Bowl migrants, "I went home that day a discoverer, a real social observer." She was also a social persuader—her captioned photographs convinced the California authorities to seek federal money to house migrants in camps.

Lange went on to photograph "drought refugees" from Texas, Oklahoma, and Arkansas, and tell their stories in sequences of pictures. In "First Rural Rehabilitation Colonists, Northern Minnesota to Matanuska Valley, Alaska," Lange told the story of resettled farmers en route to Alaska in eleven pages of photographs with no captions.

Among the first administrators who heeded Rexford Tugwell's call to Washington to staff the Resettlement Administration was Lewis Hewes, who took along copies of Lange's and Taylor's reports to show to Tugwell and Eleanor Roosevelt. Lange was hired as "field investigator, photographer" in the agency's Information Division, based in California and with responsibility for five states.

On assignment for Tugwell and Roy Stryker, Lange photographed by day, and at night wrote letters, clipped stories from local newspapers, and gathered research reports, pamphlets, and memos written by local FSA staff. Although she sometimes stayed in one place for several days, she often had to travel several hundred miles in a day. If an assistant was along, they might travel all night, taking turns driving and sleeping, or sleeping in a single room in an auto court [motel], like those in California's Central Valley between U.S. 99 and the railroad tracks, where the roar of trucks and the clanking of trains resounded throughout the night. "[It] was hard, hard living," Lange recalled, ". . . not too far away from the people we were working with."[18]

Roy Stryker said of her that she "was the real matriarch of our organization. If you look at the pictures she did of the immigrants, hers was the greatest collection of migrants. They all did them, but Dorothea—I guess, is the mother; I said the matriarch; she is the mother. The photographers . . . conquered [resistance] by . . . honesty, . . . forthrightness, sympathy, and a certain warmth that they all had . . . Dorothea . . . because of . . . her mother instincts, would warm up anyone. And if you look at the captions—she wrote the best captions of all . . . you see what she had people say to her, it must have been that she sparked a great deal of . . .

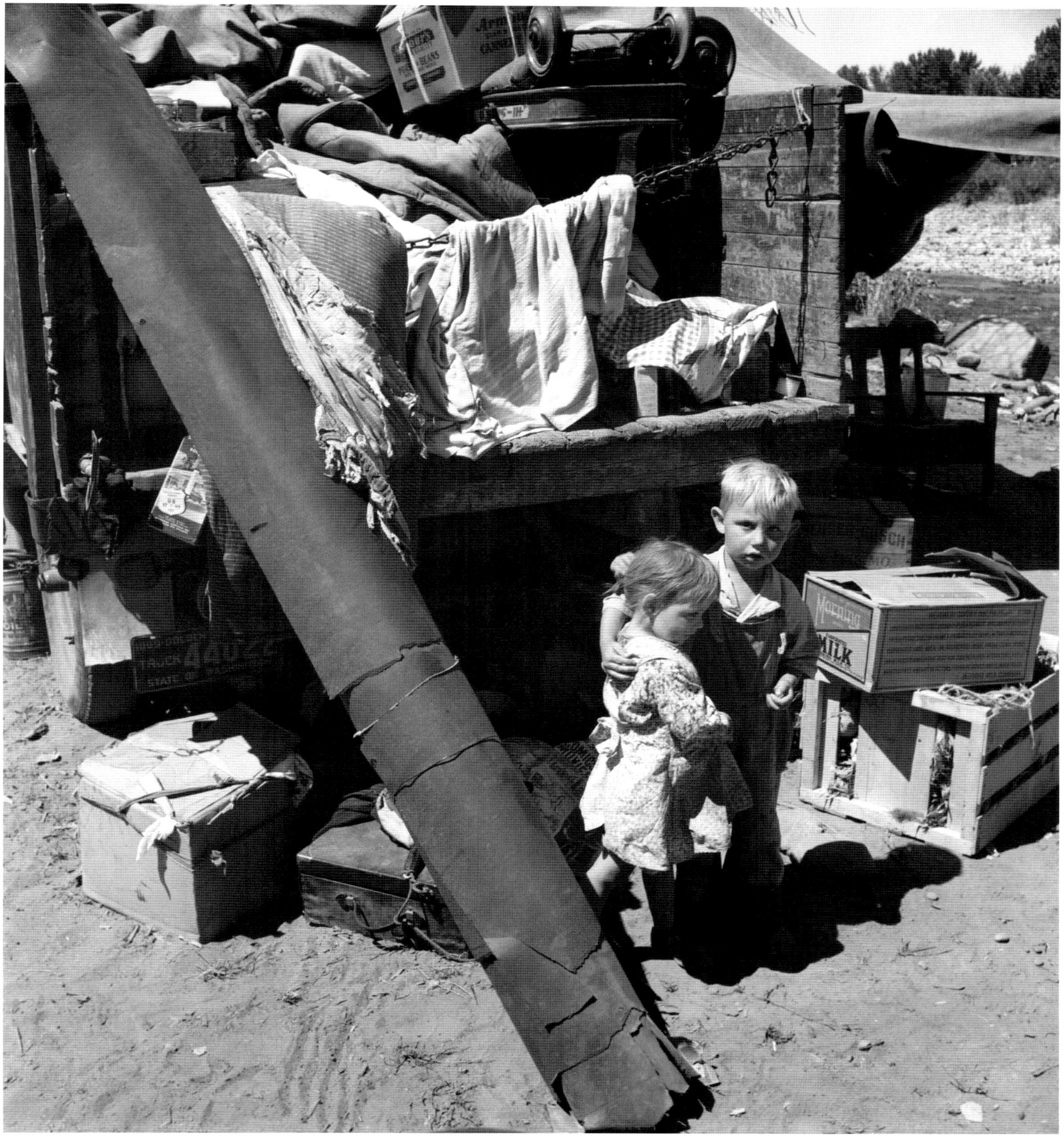

"A young brother and sister from a family of nine in 'Rambler's Park' in Yakima, Washington. From Oklahoma, they have all lived on the road for three years. The roll of kitchen linoleum diagonally in the foreground carries the hope of being unfurled in a settled new home some day" Dorothea Lange, 1939 rapport." She explained in an interview that "often it's just sticking around and being there, remaining there, not swooping in and swooping out in a cloud of dust; sitting down on the ground with people, letting the children look at your camera with their dirty, grimy little hands, and putting their fingers on the lens, and you let them, because you know that if you will behave in a generous manner, you're very apt to receive it . . . I have asked for a drink of water and taken a long time to drink it, and I have told everything about myself long before I asked any question. 'What are you doing here?' they'd say. 'Why with your camera? What do you want to take pictures of us for? Why don't you go down and do this, that, and the other?' I've taken a long time, patiently, to explain, and as truthfully as I could."[19]

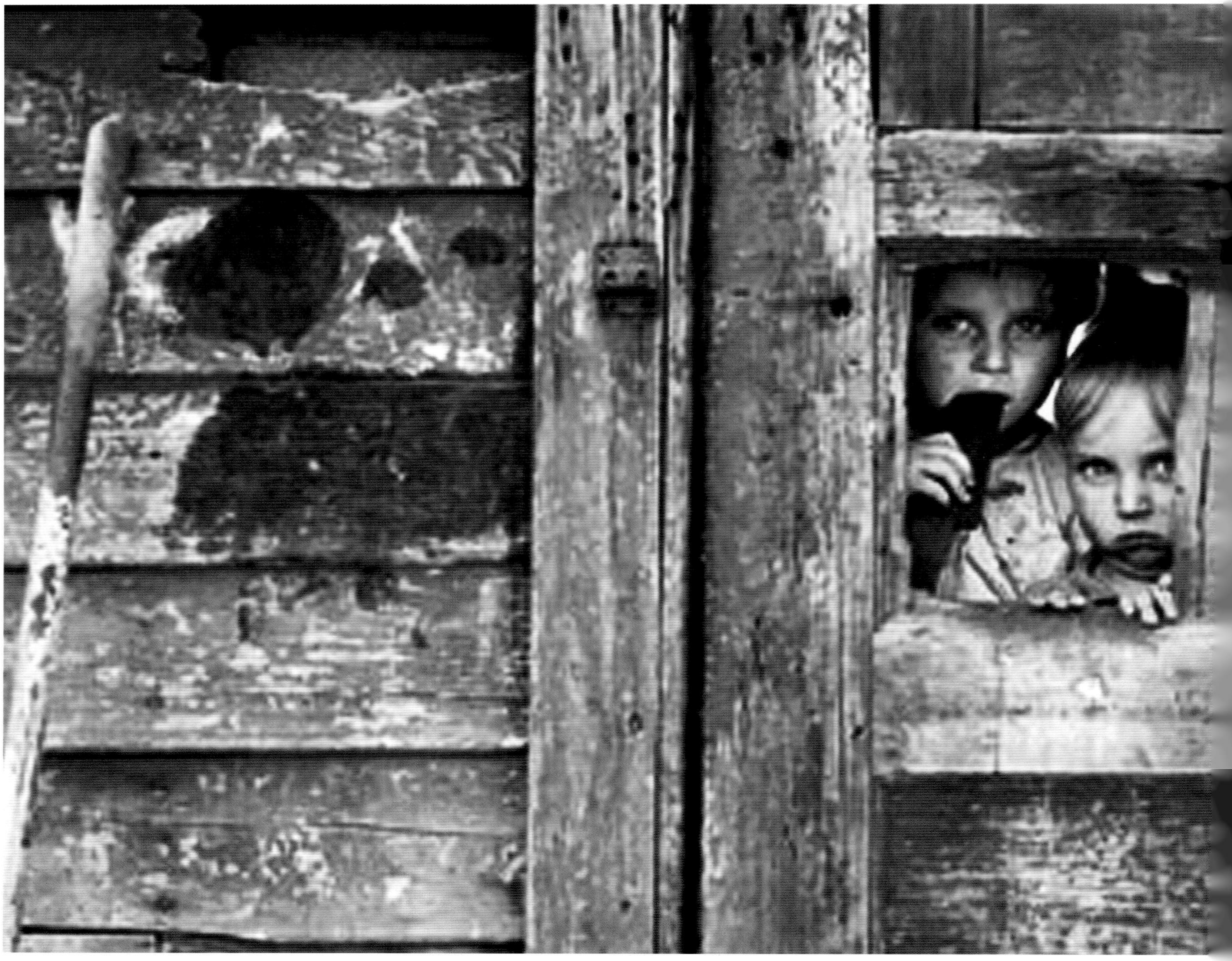

"Between Weedpatch and Lamont, Kern County, California. Children living in camp"
Dorothea Lange, 1940

Lange listened to the people she photographed and tried hard to remember their exact words until she could write them down in her looseleaf "daybook," "often with great excitement . . . just hoping that I could hold on to them until I got back to the car". "I am writing captions until my fingers ache to say nothing of my head," Lange told Stryker in 1937. "This is no small job . . . Am not sending it on to you in sections, as I had originally planned, because I am making cross-references . . . It's not the individual captions that [take] the time but it's the arrangement and grouping. If this is not done I believe that half the value of fieldwork is lost."[20]

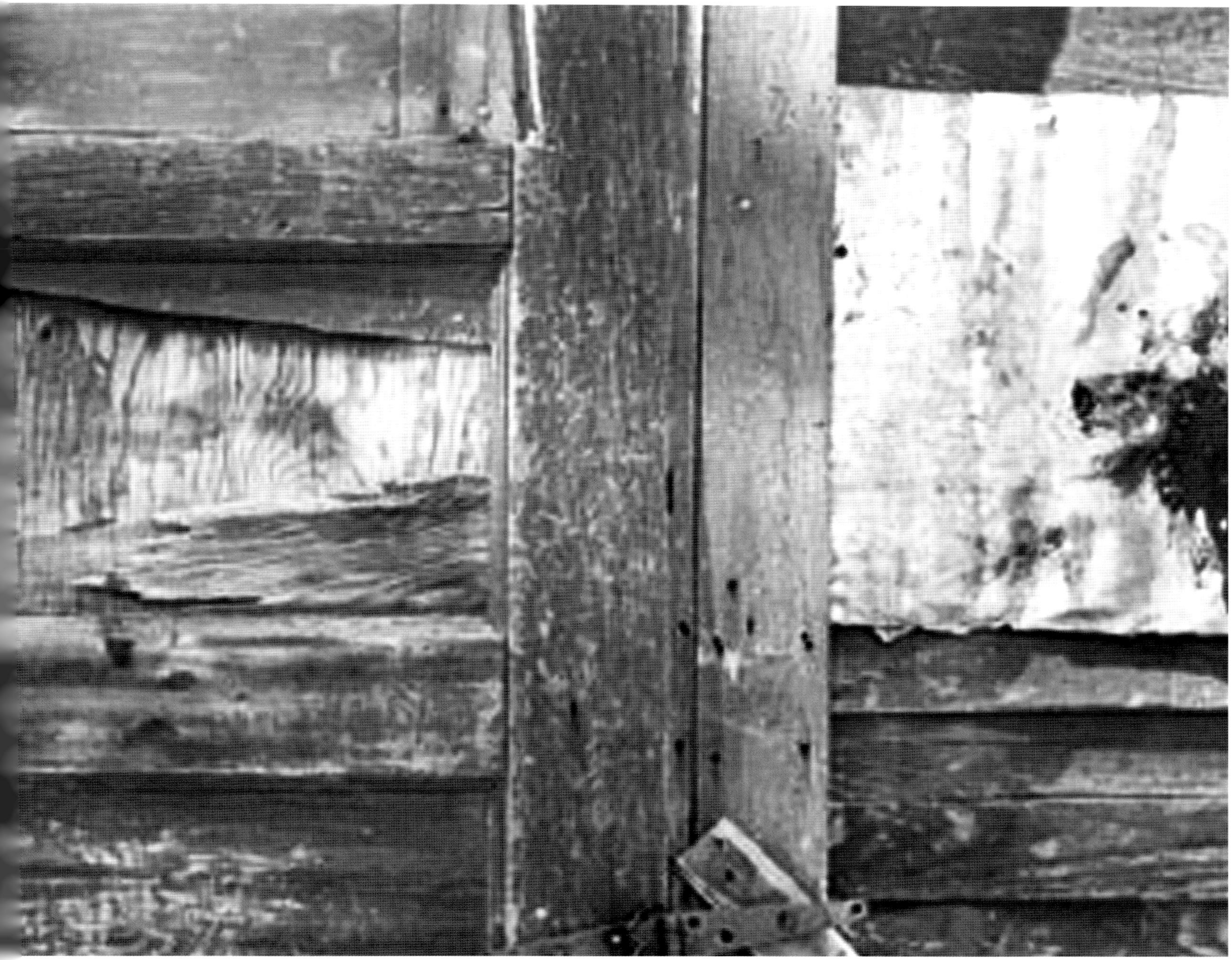

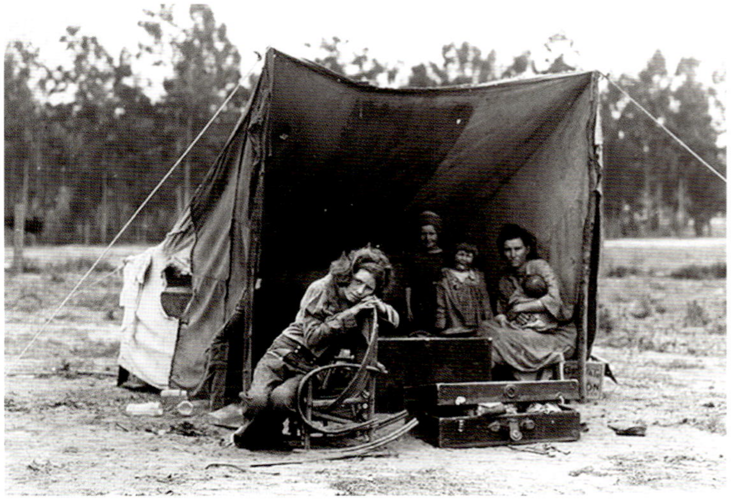

"Migrant agricultural worker's family. Seven hungry children. Mother aged thirty-two. Father is native Californian. Nipomo, California"
Dorothea Lange, 1936

The woman in this picture—the migrant mother, Florence Owens Thompson—was born in Oklahoma in 1903 "in a tepee," she said. Her father died when she was thirteen months old, but her mother lived to be 108. Even before the Depression, Florence, her husband Cleo, and their growing family left Oklahoma for California. For a time they found work around Shafter, California. But as the Depression settled in, they were forced to become migrant farm workers. They followed the harvests until the war created jobs.

Opposite: "Migrant Mother, 1936"

Lange had just completed a month-long photographic assignment and was driving back home in a wind-driven rain when she came upon a sign for the Pea-Pickers Camp. Something beckoned her to postpone her journey home and enter the camp. She took a series of six shots—the only photos she took that day. The woman in "Migrant Mother" had seven children and was on the brink of starvation.

In 1960, Lange described her experience in an interview in *Popular Photography*: "It was raining, the camera bags were packed, and I had on the seat beside me in the car the results of my long trip, the box containing all those rolls and packs of exposed film ready to mail back to Washington. It was a time of relief. Sixty-five miles an hour for seven hours would get me home to my family that night, and my eyes were glued to the wet and gleaming highway that stretched out ahead. I felt freed, for I could lift my mind off my job and think of home.

"I was on my way and barely saw a crude sign with pointing arrow which flashed by at the side of the road, saying PEA-PICKERS CAMP. But out of the corner of my eye I did see it. I didn't want to stop, and didn't. I didn't want to remember that I had seen it, so I drove on and ignored the summons. Then, accompanied by the rhythmic hum of the windshield wipers, arose an inner argument:

"'Dorothea, how about that camp back there? What is the situation back there? Are you going back? Nobody could ask this of you, now could they? To turn back certainly is not necessary. Haven't you plenty of negatives already on this subject? Isn't this just one more of the same? Besides, if you take a camera out in this rain, you're just asking for trouble. Now be reasonable, etc., etc., etc.

"Having well convinced myself for 20 miles that I could continue on, I did the opposite. Almost without realizing what I was doing I made a U-turn on the empty highway. I went back those 20 miles and turned off the highway at that sign, PEA-PICKERS CAMP.

"Destitute in a pea-pickers camp, because of the failure of the early pea crop. These people had just sold their tent in order to buy food. I was following instinct, not reason; I drove into that wet and soggy camp and parked my car like a homing pigeon. I saw and approached the hungry and desperate mother, as if drawn by a magnet. I do not remember how I explained my presence or my camera to her but I do remember she asked me no questions. I made five exposures, working closer and closer from the same direction. I did not ask her name or her history. She told me her age, that she was thirty-two. She said that they had been living on frozen vegetables from the surrounding fields, and birds that the children killed. She had just sold the tires from her car to buy food. There she sat in that lean-to tent with her children huddled around her, and seemed to know that my pictures might help her, and so she helped me. There was a sort of equality about it.

"The pea crop at Nipomo had frozen and there was no work for anybody. But I did not approach the tents and shelters of other stranded pea-pickers. It was not necessary; I knew I had recorded the essence of my assignment."[21]

After returning home, Lange alerted the editor of a San Francisco newspaper to the plight of the workers at the camp, presenting him with two of her photos. The editor informed federal authorities and published an article that included Lange's images. As a result, the government rushed a shipment of twenty-thousand pounds of food to the camp.

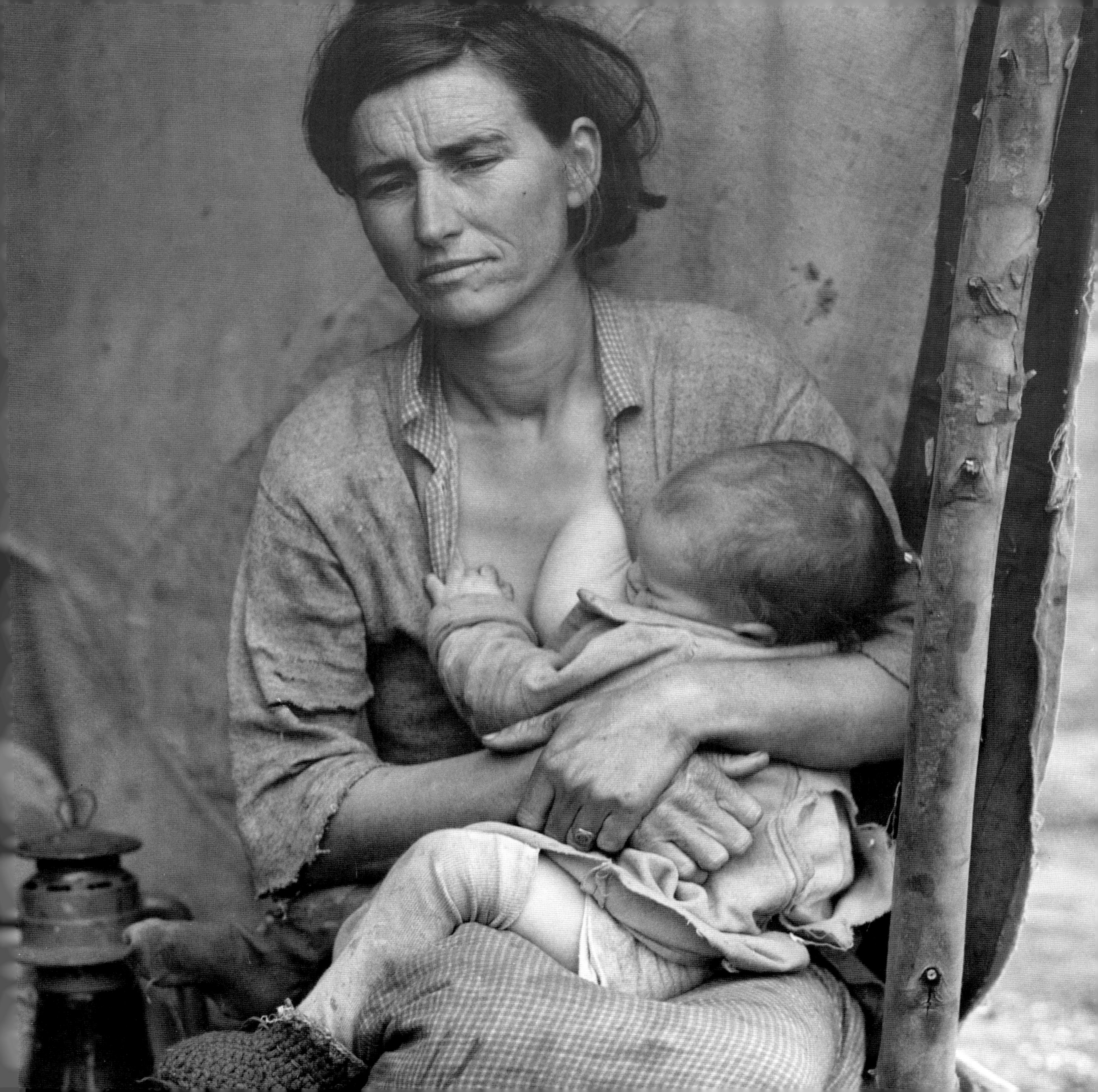

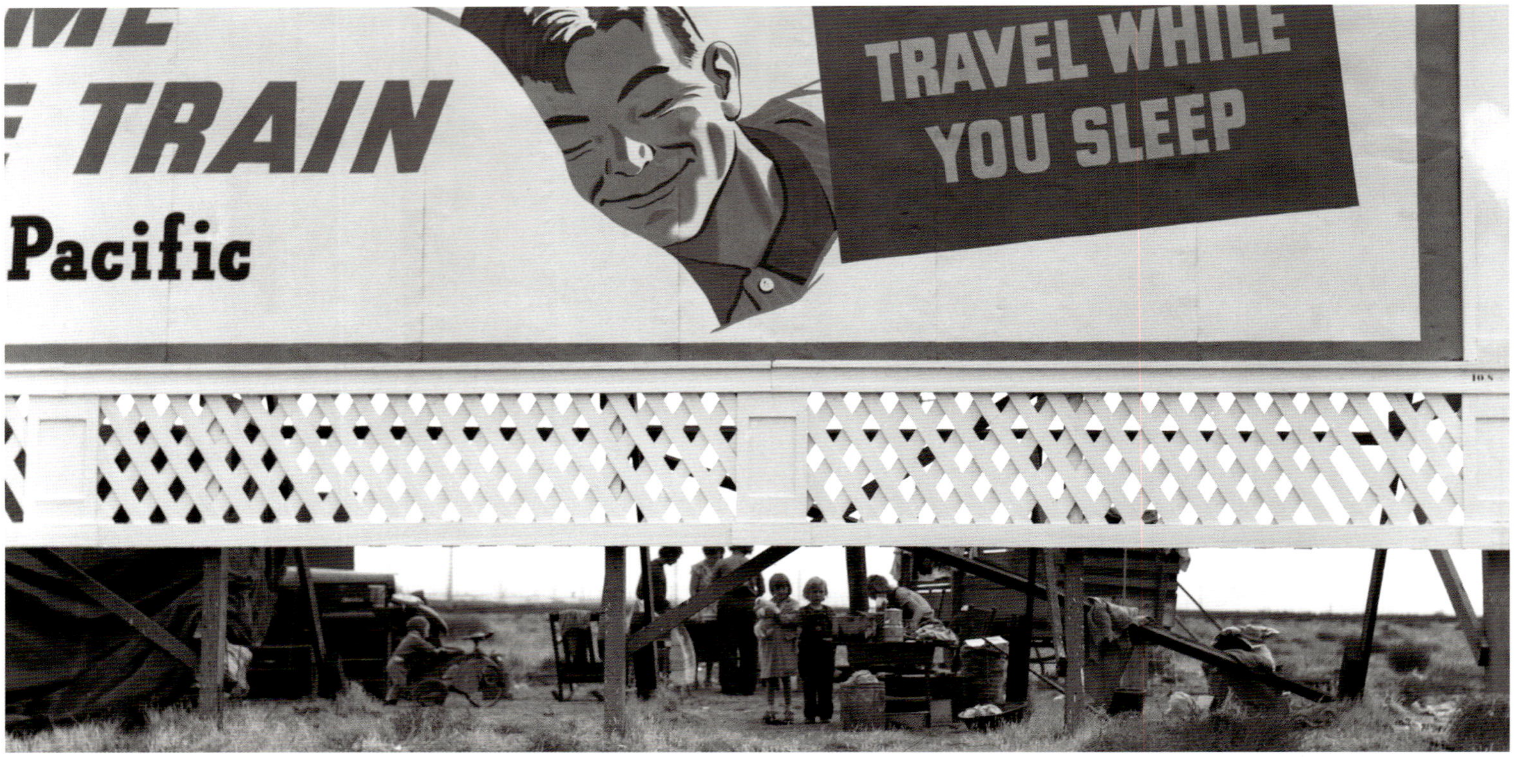

"Billboard along U.S. 99 behind which three destitute families of migrants are camped. Kern County, California"
Dorothea Lange, 1938

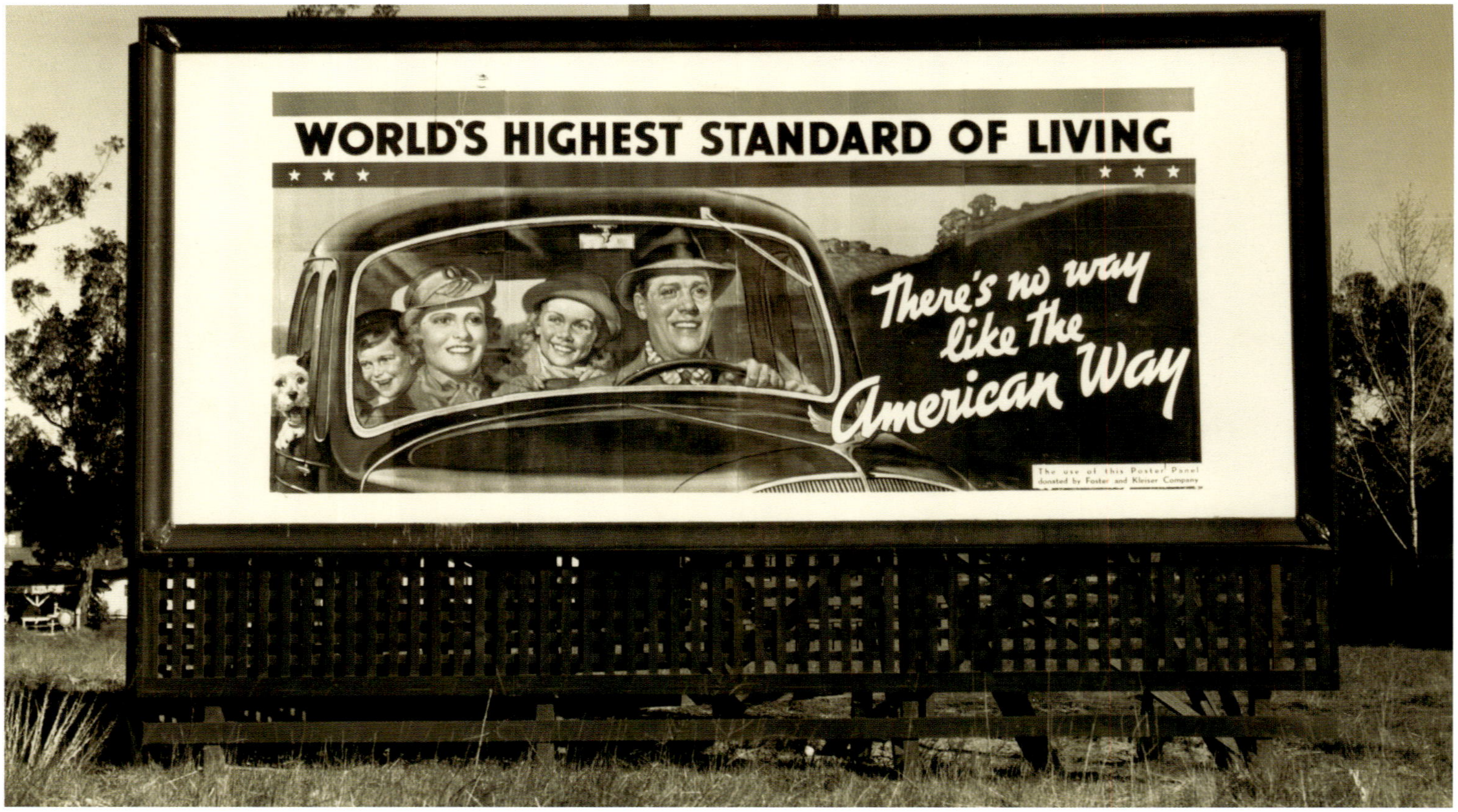

"Billboard on US Highway 99 in California. A national advertising campaign promoting the National Association of Manufacturers"
Dorothea Lange, 1937

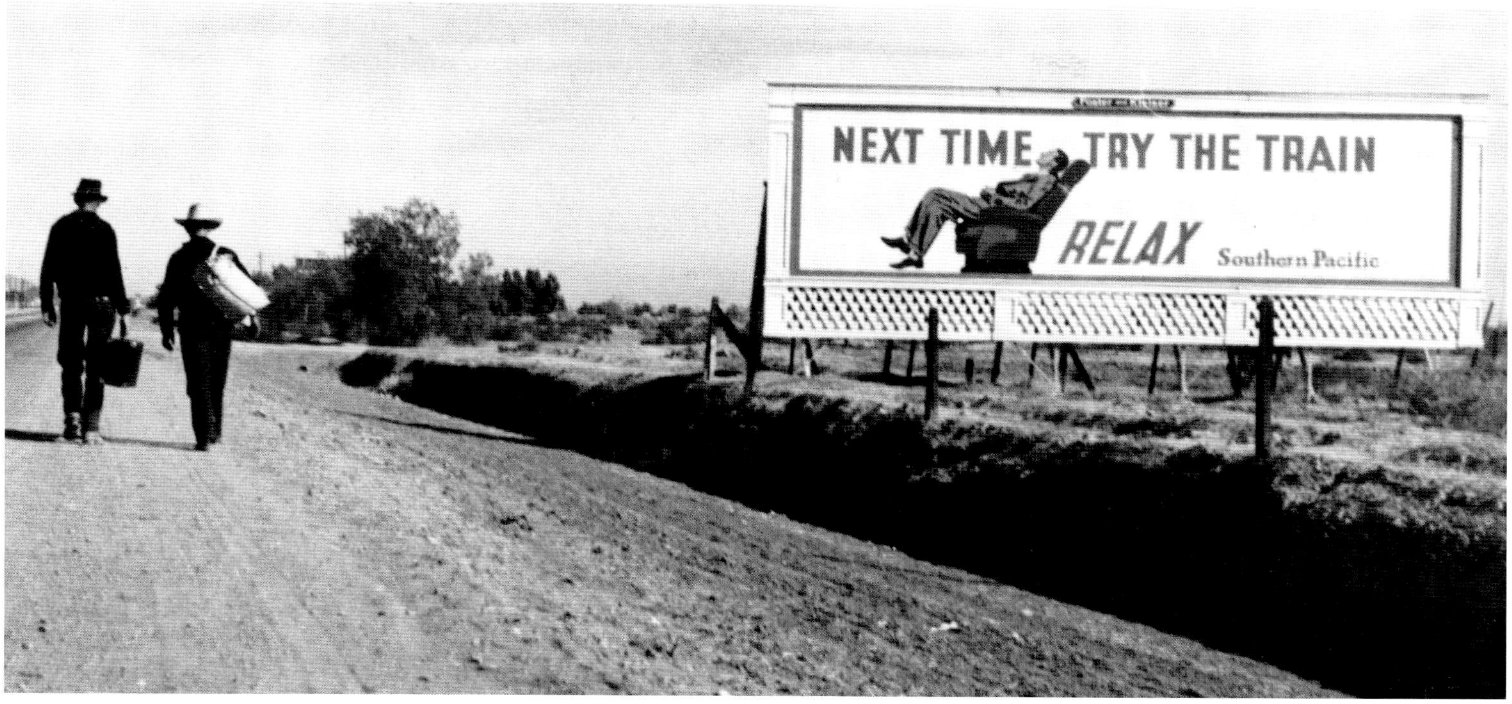

"Toward Los Angeles, California"
Dorothea Lange, 1937

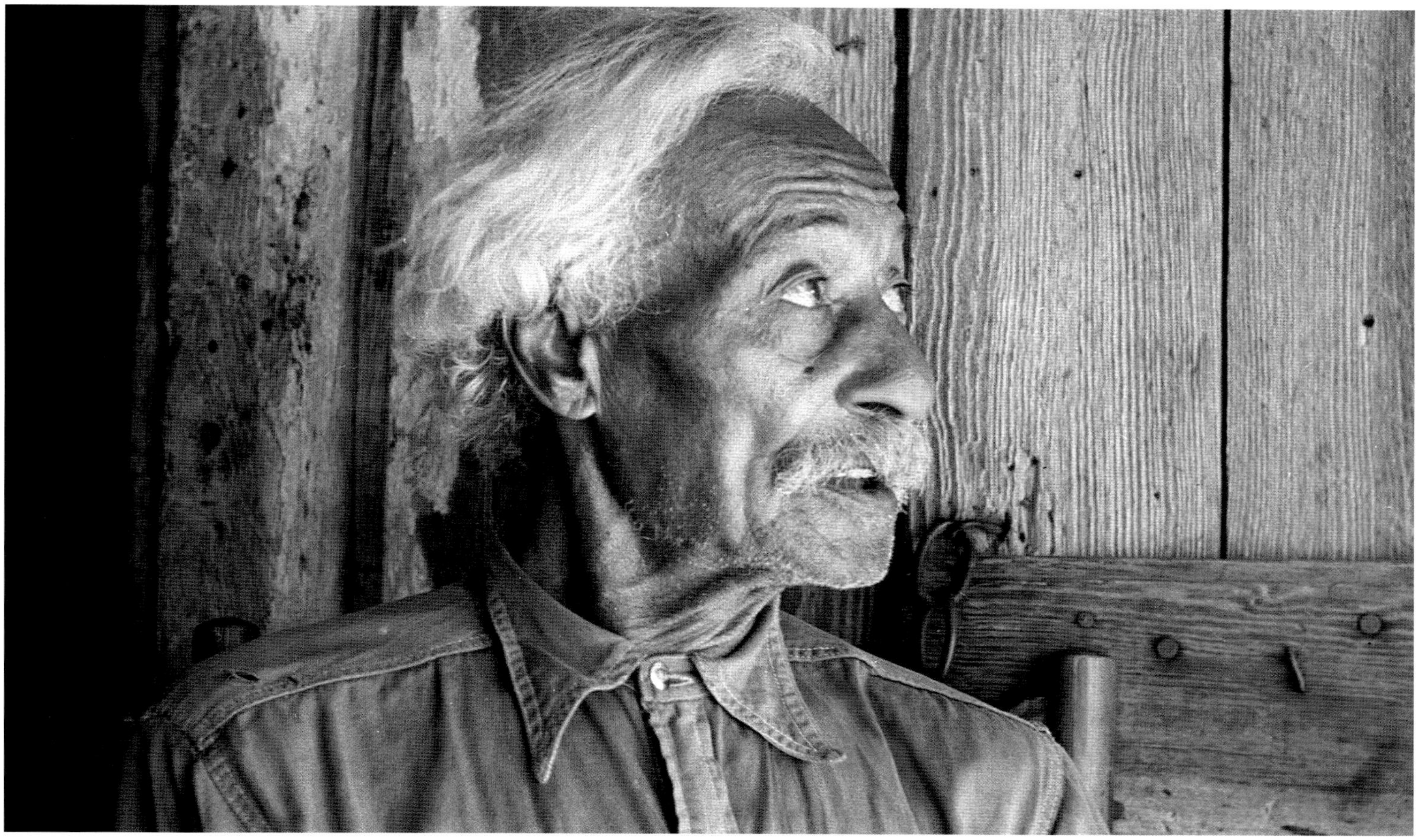

"Bob Lemmons, Carrizo Springs, Texas. Born a slave about 1850, south of San Antonio, Texas. Came to Carrizo Springs during Civil War with white men seeking new range for their cattle. In 1865, with his master, was one of the first settlers. He knew Billy the Kid, King Fisher, and other noted bad men of the border"
Dorothea Lange

Arthur Rothstein

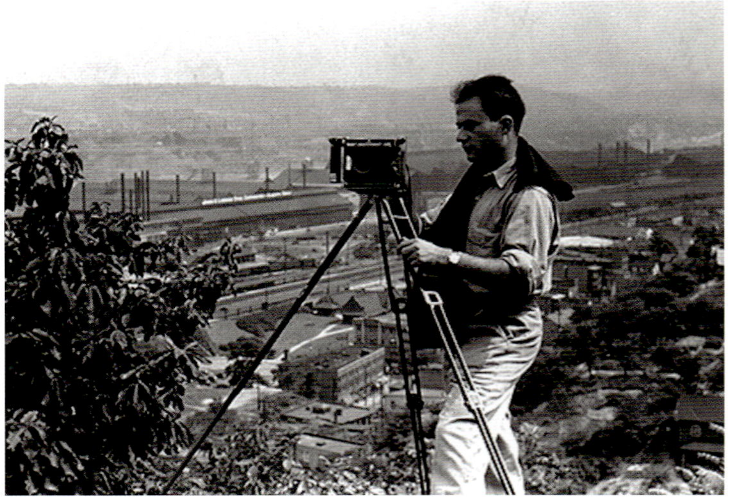

Arthur Rothstein, 1938

Arthur Rothstein was born in New York in 1915. He was the first photographer hired by Roy Stryker for the RS/FSA. His first assignment was to document the lives of some Virginia farmers who were being evicted to make way for the Shenandoah National Park and relocated by the Resettlement Administration. Subsequent trips took him to the Dust Bowl and to cattle ranches in Montana, to build constituencies for the Bankhead-Jones Farm Tenant Act, which gave Rexford Tugwell's Resettlement Administration new life as the Farm Security Administration. In 1940 he was hired as a staff photographer for *Look* magazine; he became its director of photography. He then went to *Parade* where he remained until his death in 1985.

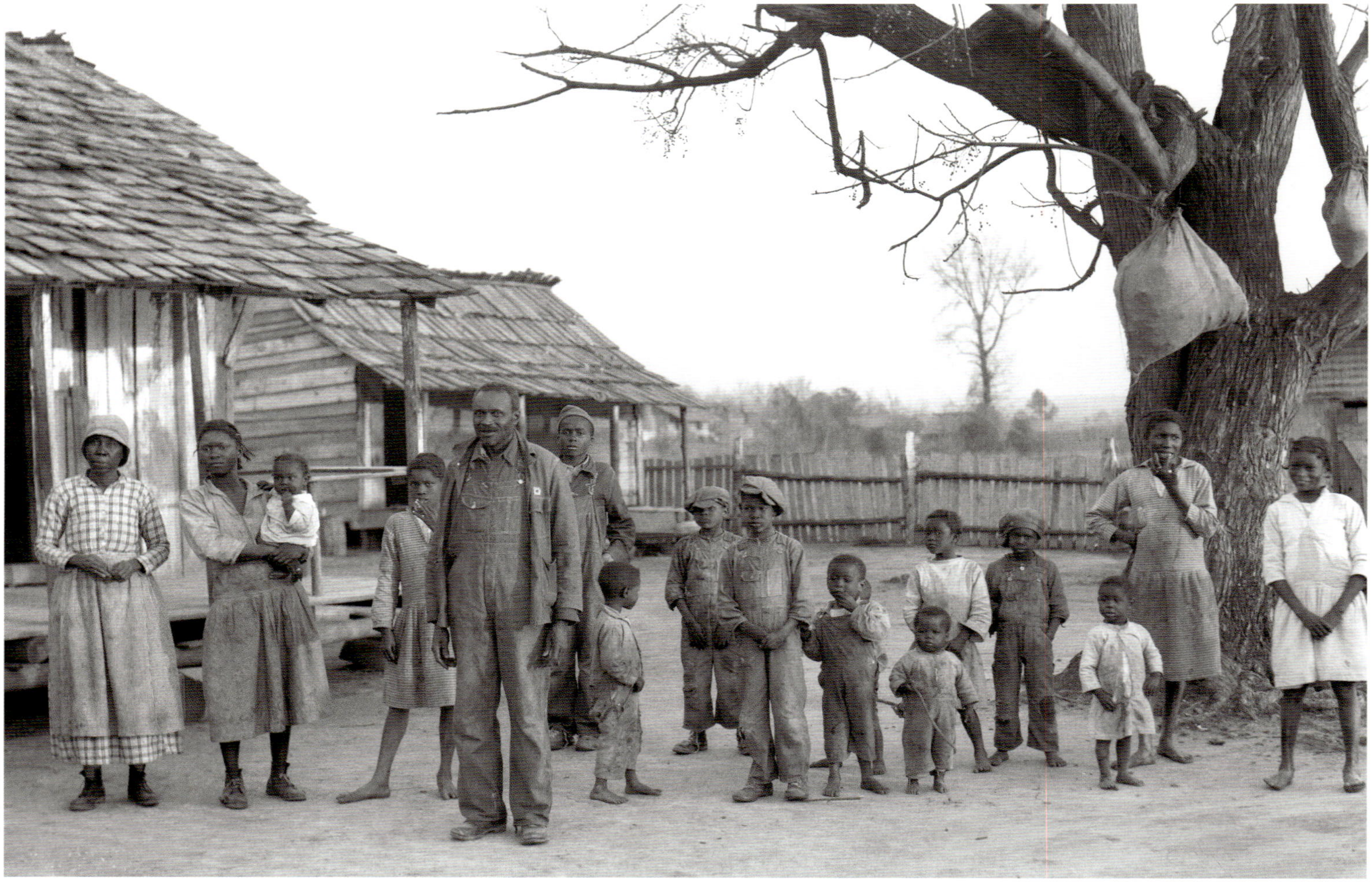

"Negroes, descendants of former slaves of the Pettway Plantation. They are living under primitive conditions on the plantation. Gees Bend, Alabama"
Arthur Rothstein, 1937

Opposite:
"Artelia Bendolph of Gees Bend, Alabama"
Arthur Rothstein, 1937

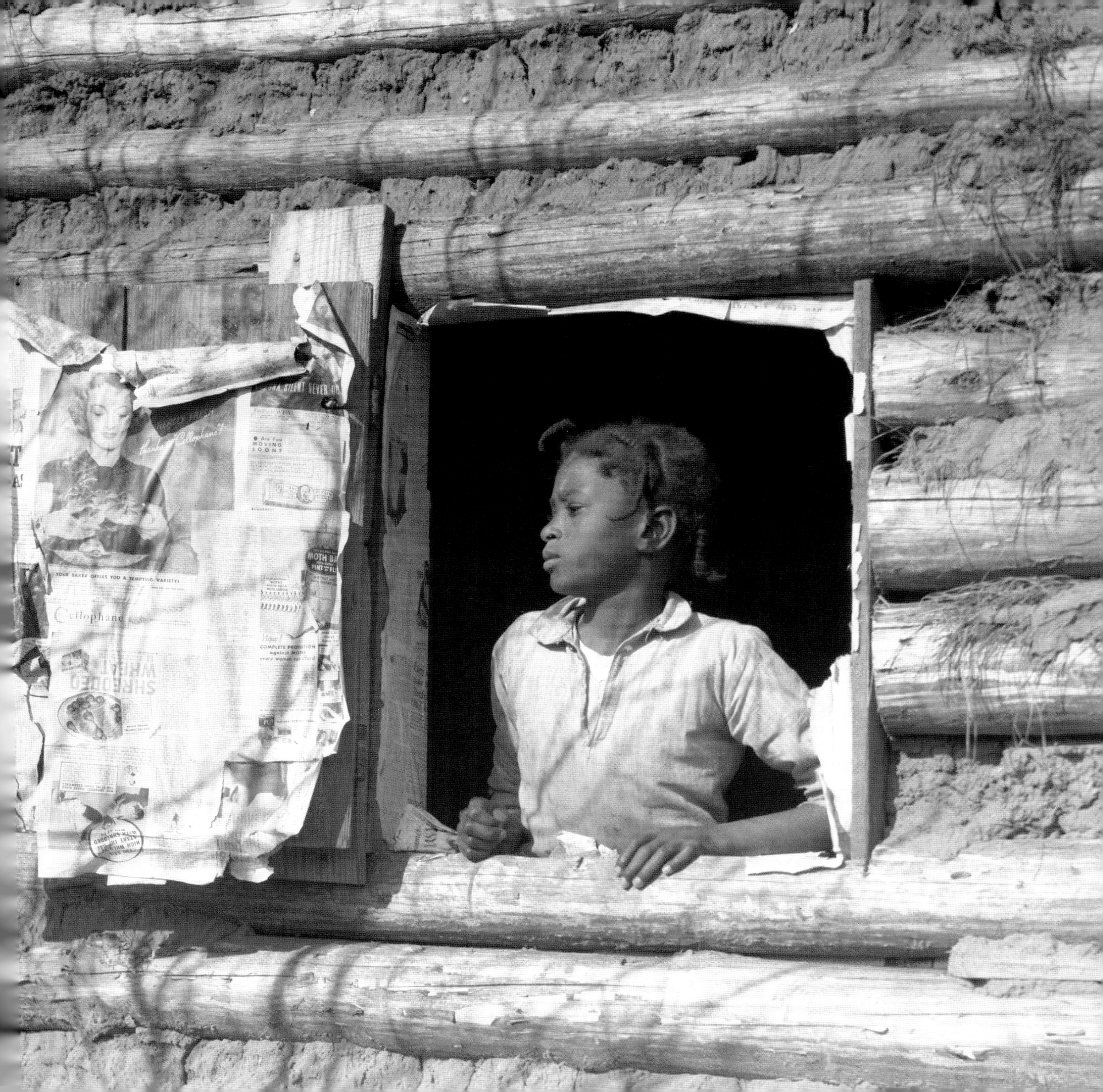

YOUR BAKER OFFERS YOU A TEMPTING VARIETY!
Cellophane
Are You MOVING SOON?
COMPLETE PROTECTION against MOTHS every woman can afford

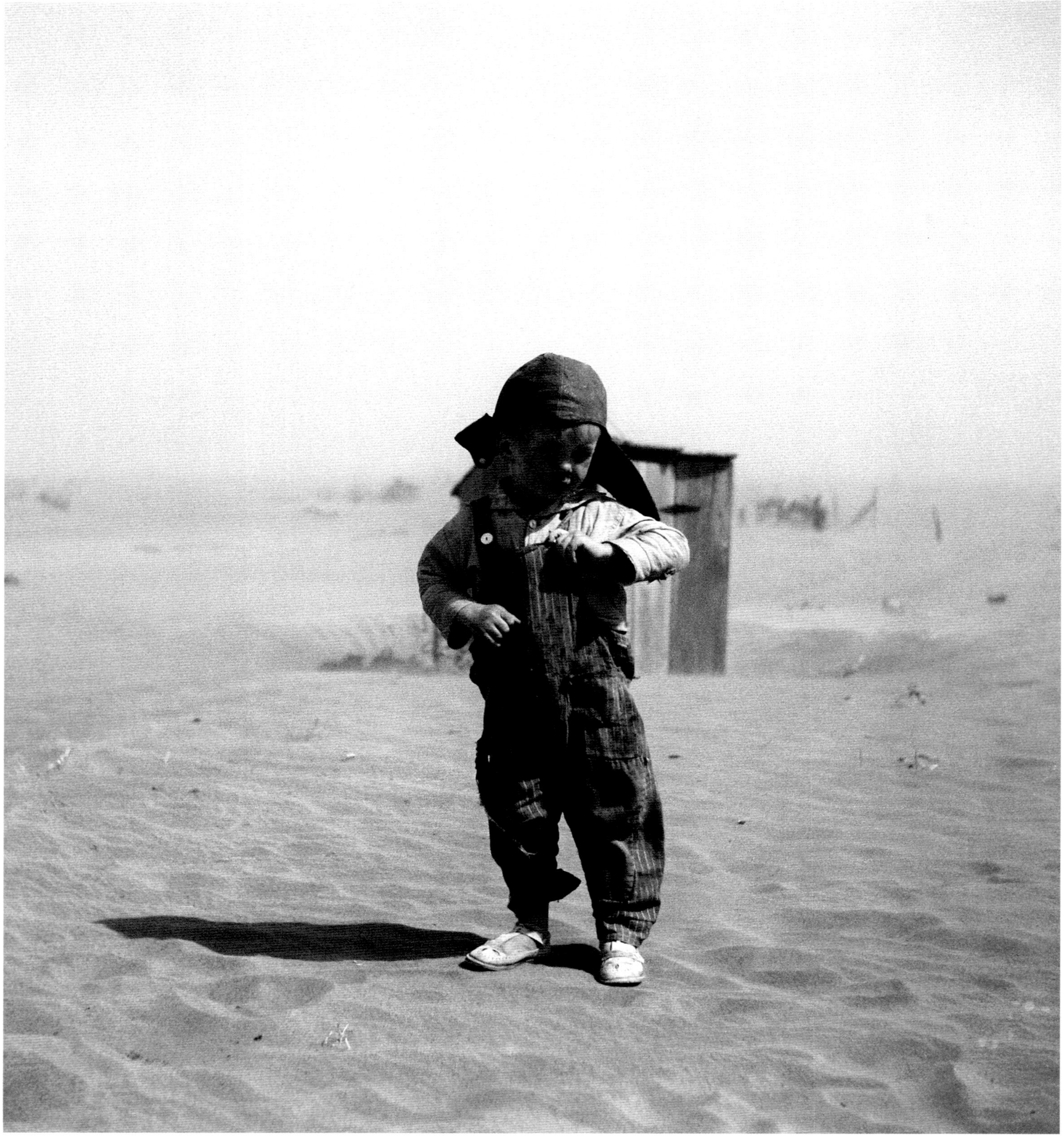

"Dust is too much for this farmer's son in Cimarron County, Oklahoma"
Arthur Rothstein, 1936

Opposite:
"Fleeing a dust storm"
Arthur Coble and his sons walking in the face of a dust storm, Cimarron County, Oklahoma.
Arthur Rothstein, 1936

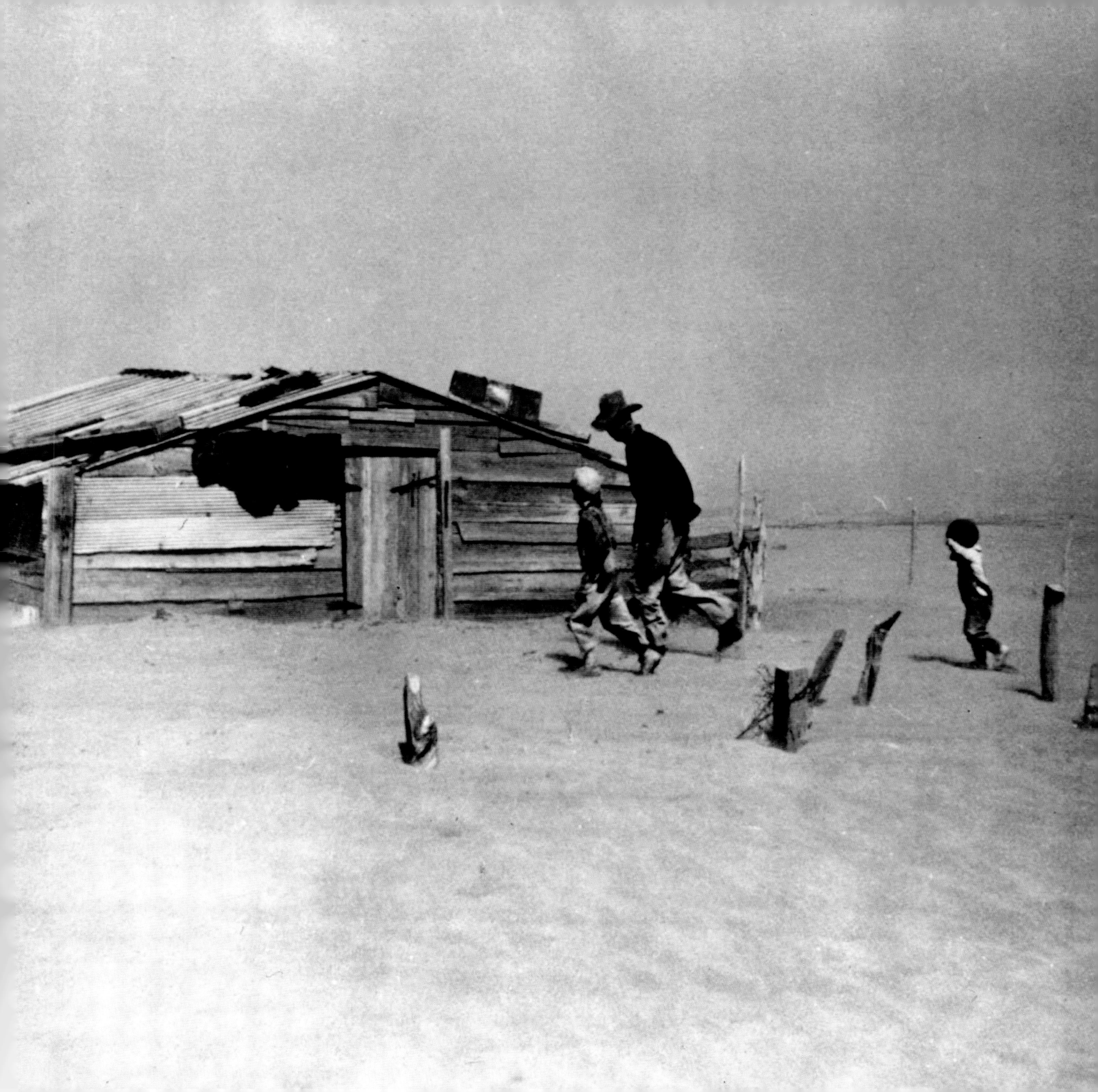

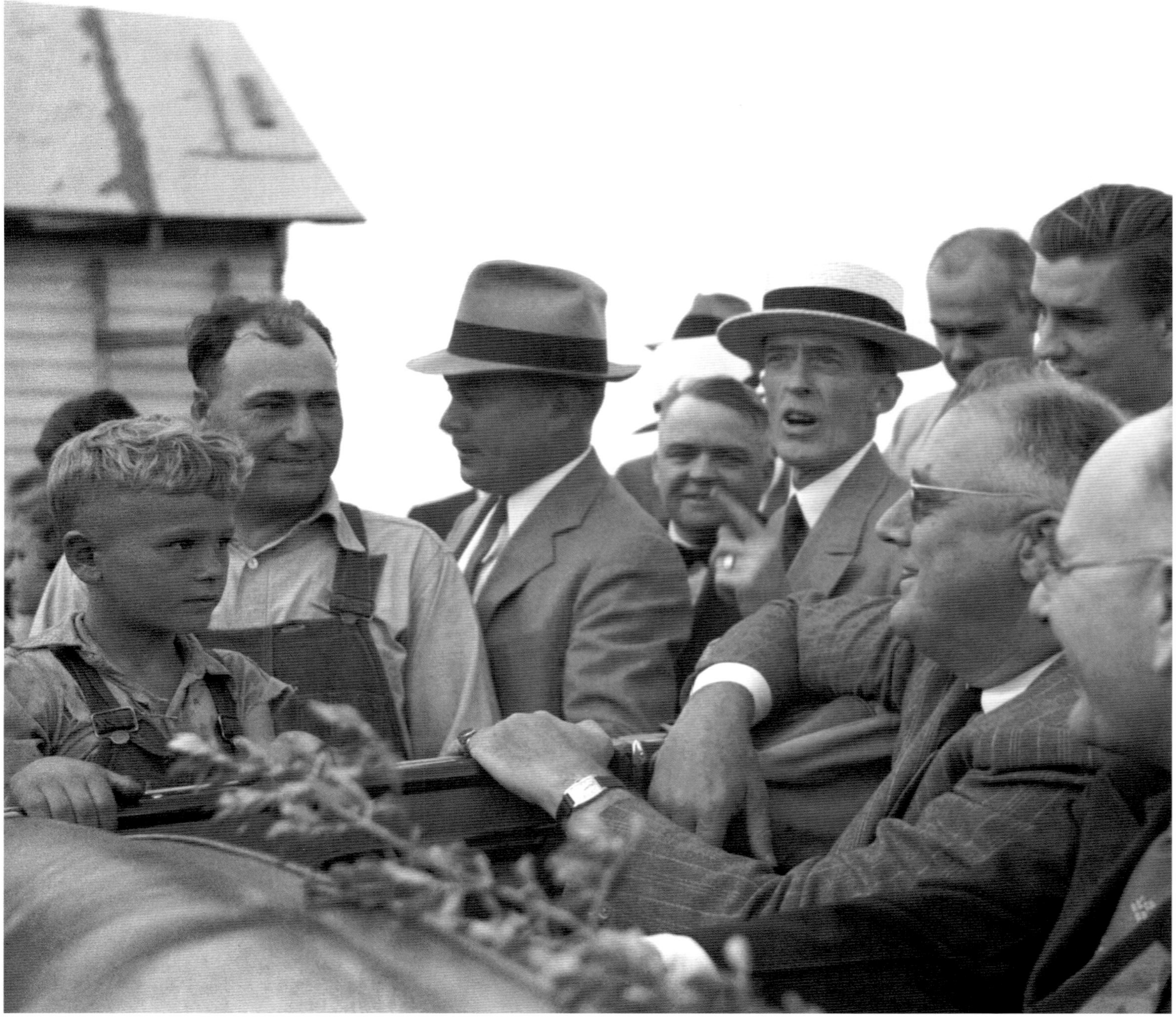

"President Roosevelt visits farmer who is receiving drought relief grant. Mandan, North Dakota"
Arthur Rothstein, 1936

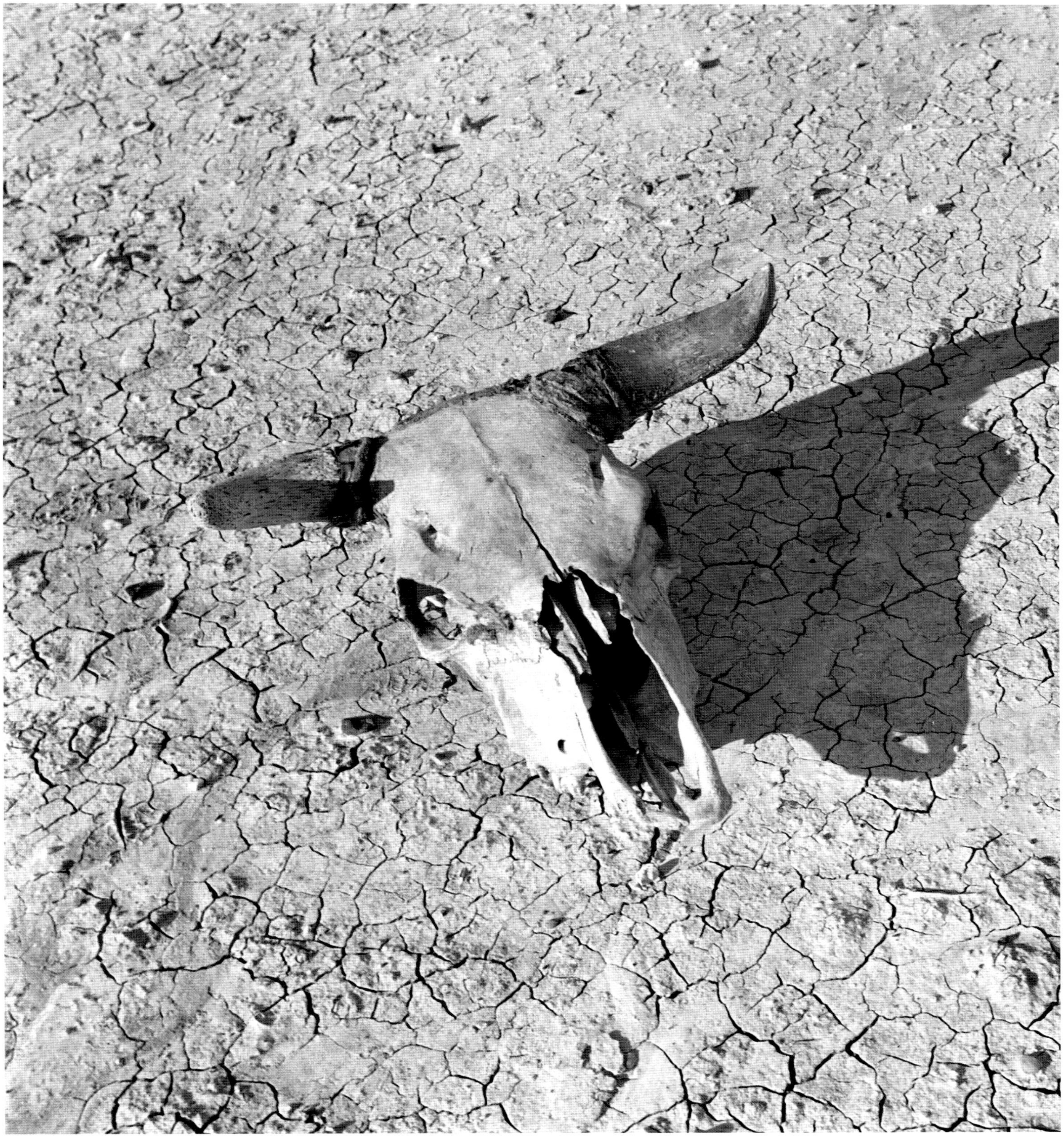

Skull
Arthur Rothstein, 1936

Rothstein photographed the same steer's skull twice, having moved it about ten feet. The different backgrounds led critics to call the skull a prop—and to attack the credibility of all the FSA photographs. Rothstein expressed regret for his breech of photographic ethics—and for the subsequent damage done to the FSA.

"American Gothic"
Gordon Parks

Born in Kansas, the youngest of fifteen children, Gordon Parks moved to Minnesota after his mother died, dropping out of high school just short of graduation. He found work as a Pullman dining car waiter, met the photographers Bernard Hoffman and Robert Capa, worked as a freelance fashion photographer, spent a year as an FSA photographer, and made his famous "American Gothic," an interpretation of Grant Wood's painting, but with a black cleaning woman, Ella Watson, standing in front of an American flag holding a mop and broom rather than Wood's pitchfork-wielding Iowans.

Gordon Parks

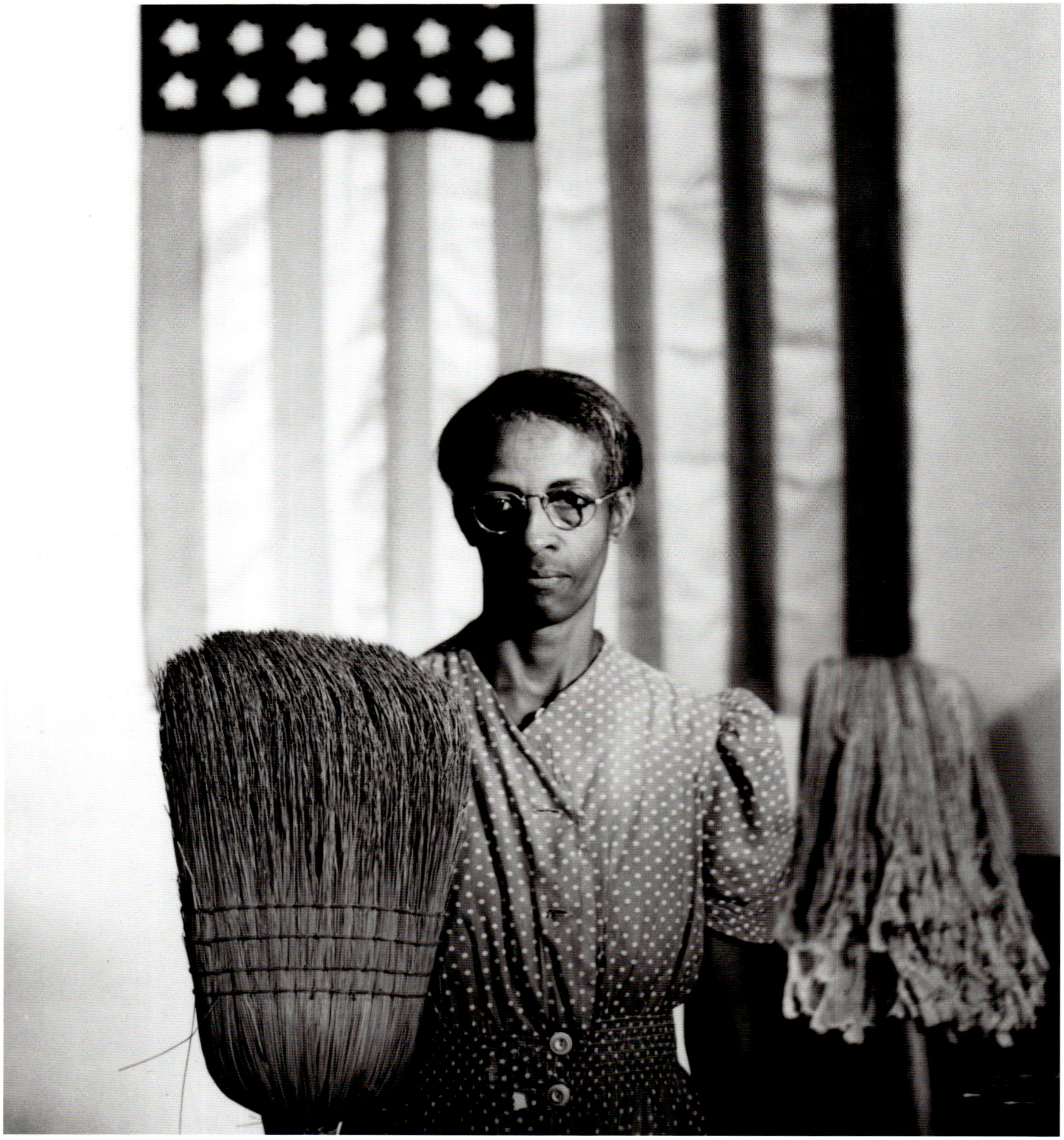

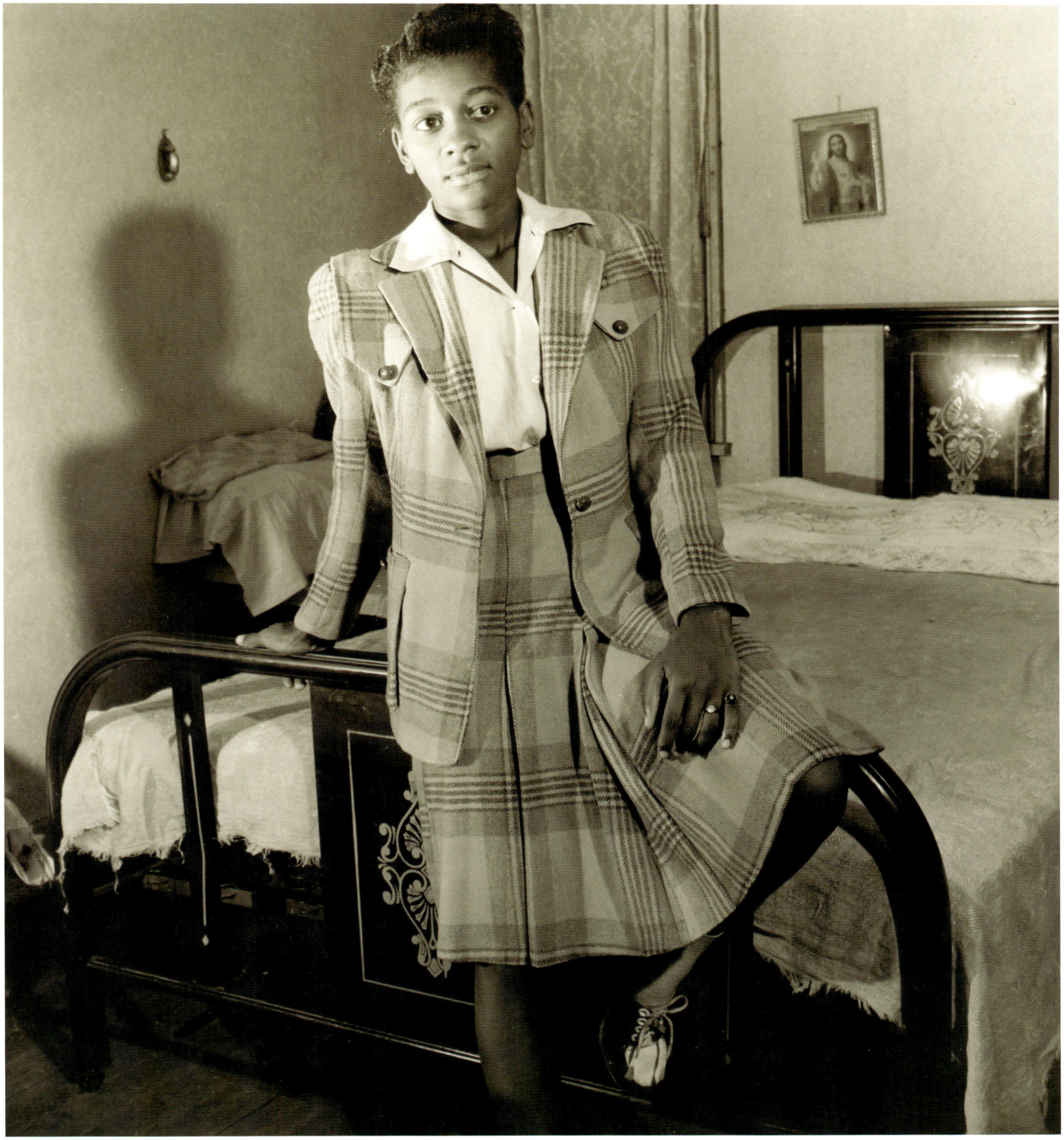

"Ella Watson's daughter"
Gordon Parks

Walker Evans

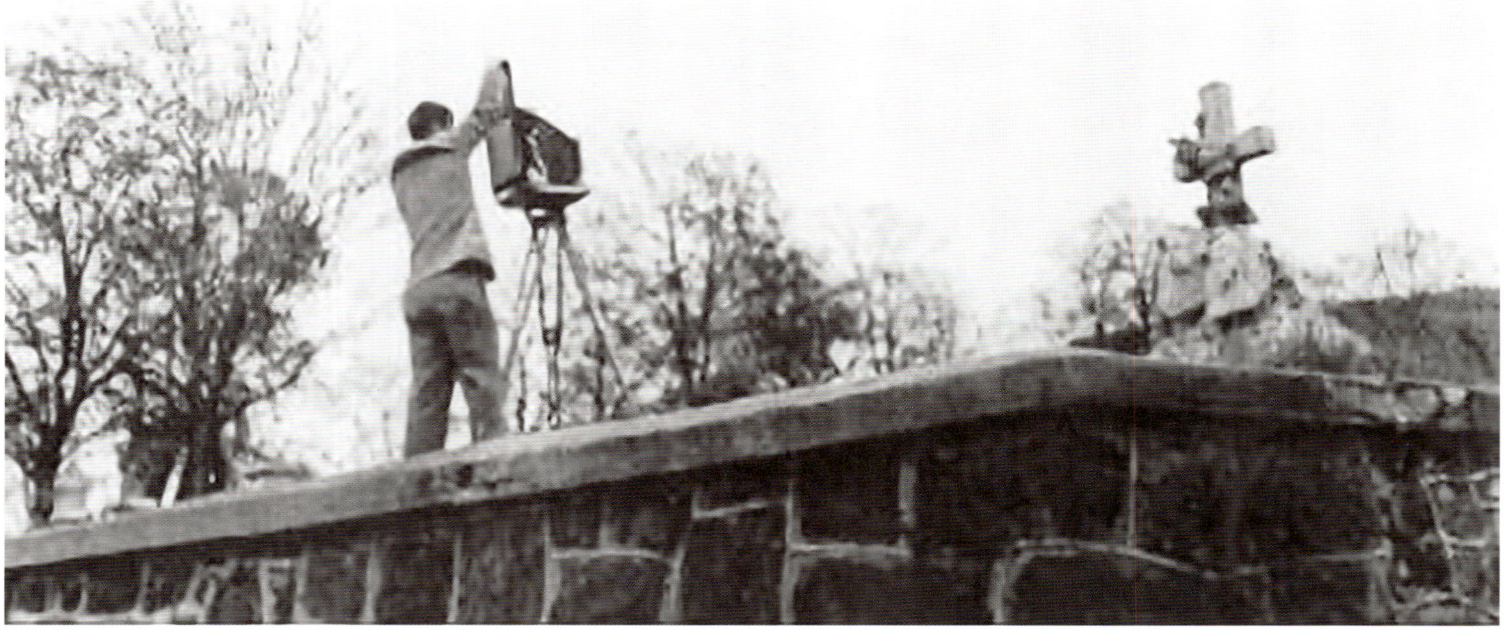

Walker Evans preparing to photograph a cemetery from the bottom of Fourth Street, Bethlehem, Pennsylvania, 1935

Walker Evans was born in St. Louis, Missouri, educated at Andover and Williams, and lived for a time in Paris pursuing his love of contemporary literature—especially for Joyce, T. S. Eliot, Baudelaire, and Flaubert. He returned to New York at the end of the 1920s and became a writer and advertising photographer. On his own he made semi-abstract geometric photographs of electric signs, sidewalk displays, and elevated train platforms; illustrated a documentary book attacking Cuba's Machado regime; and photographed African sculpture for the Museum of Modern Art. He was hired by Roy Stryker in October 1935, after he had done some work at the Department of the Interior. During the eighteen months or so that he worked for Stryker, he photographed in West Virginia, Pennsylvania, Louisiana, Mississippi, Georgia, South Carolina, Alabama, Arkansas, and Tennessee. His best-known work, however, was produced for *Fortune* magazine during a leave of absence: a series of photographs of Alabama sharecroppers. Though *Fortune* published neither the photographs nor the text that James Agee wrote to accompany them, their work did appear in 1941 in *Let Us Now Praise Famous Men*.

Roy Stryker said of Evans's work that his pictures were "not the accident, he plans them, he walks around, he looks, and all of a sudden—his is a composed job. Walker walks around and all of a sudden sees . . . the tombstone in the cemetery, the street, the houses. It's an interesting picture, because you know that he planned it. That's not 'composed' in the sense that that word is so badly used at times, but he hunts till he finds the right viewpoint, the right place to stand."[22]

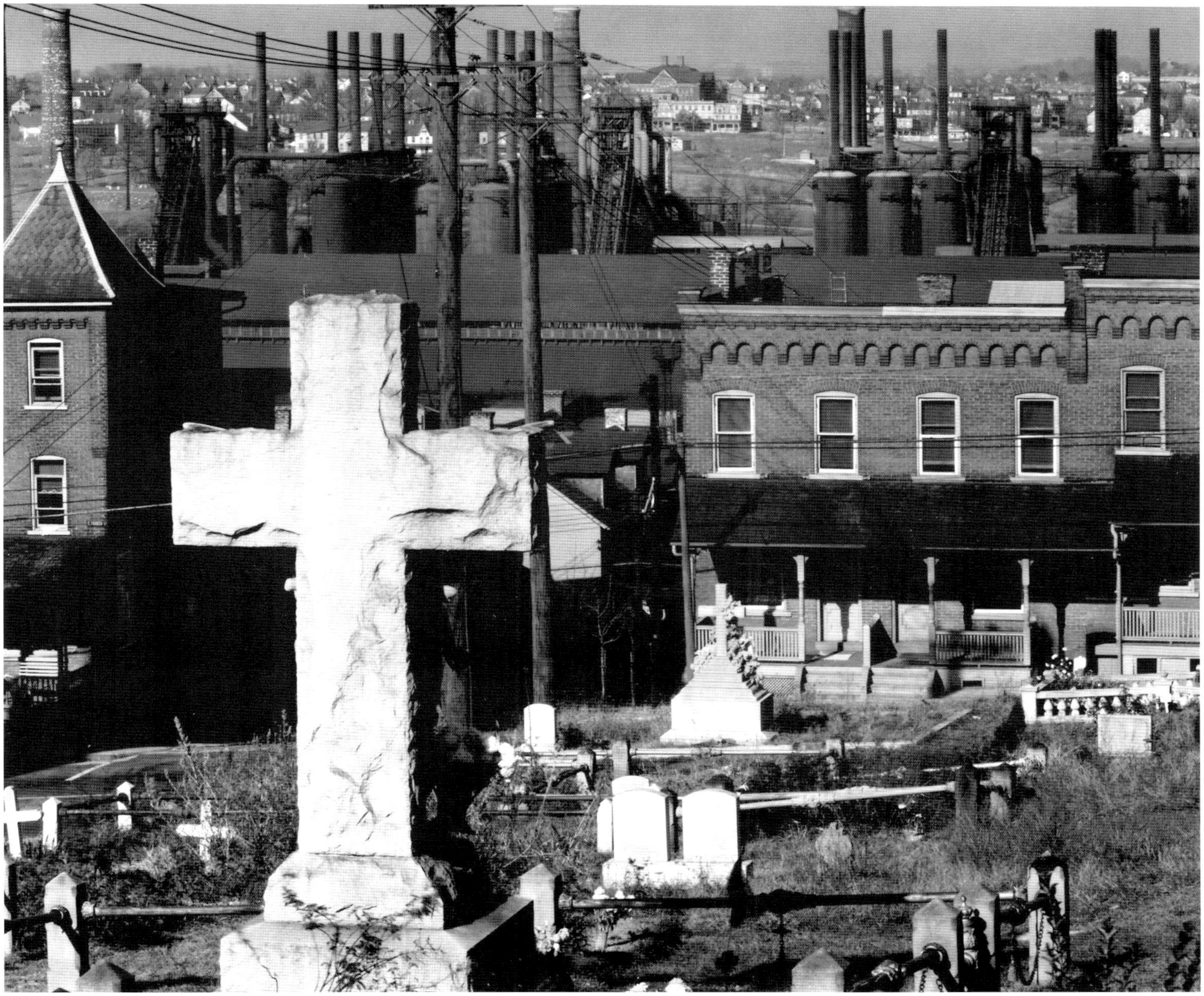

"Bethleham steel mill and graveyard. Pennsylvania"
Walker Evans, 1935

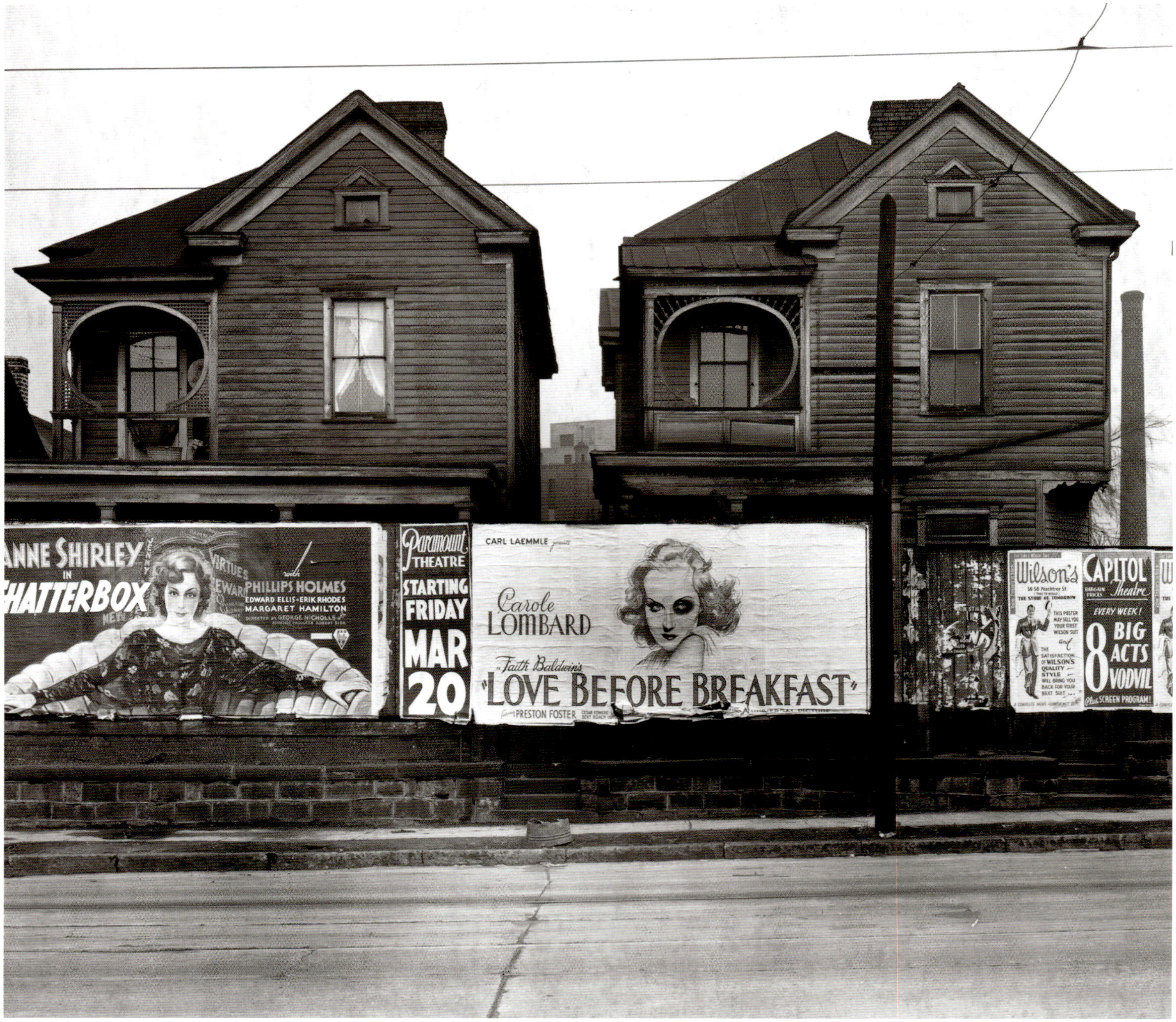

"Frame houses and a Bill-board, Atlanta, Georgia"
Walker Evans, 1936

The black eye that Carole Lombard sports in one billboard echoes the oval frames on the porches of the two houses. Glamour contrasts with squalor.

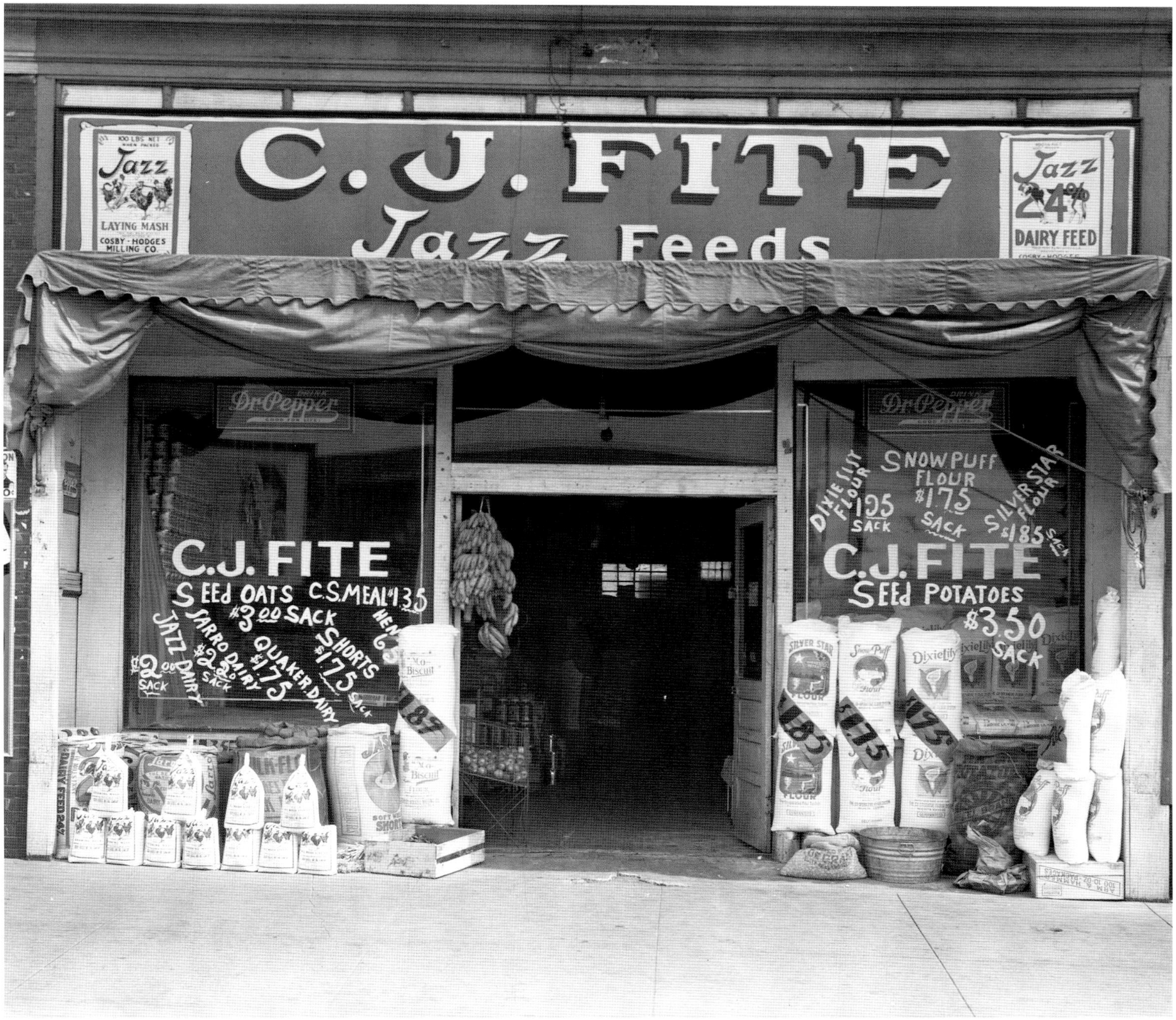

"Feed store, Alabama"
Walker Evans, 1936

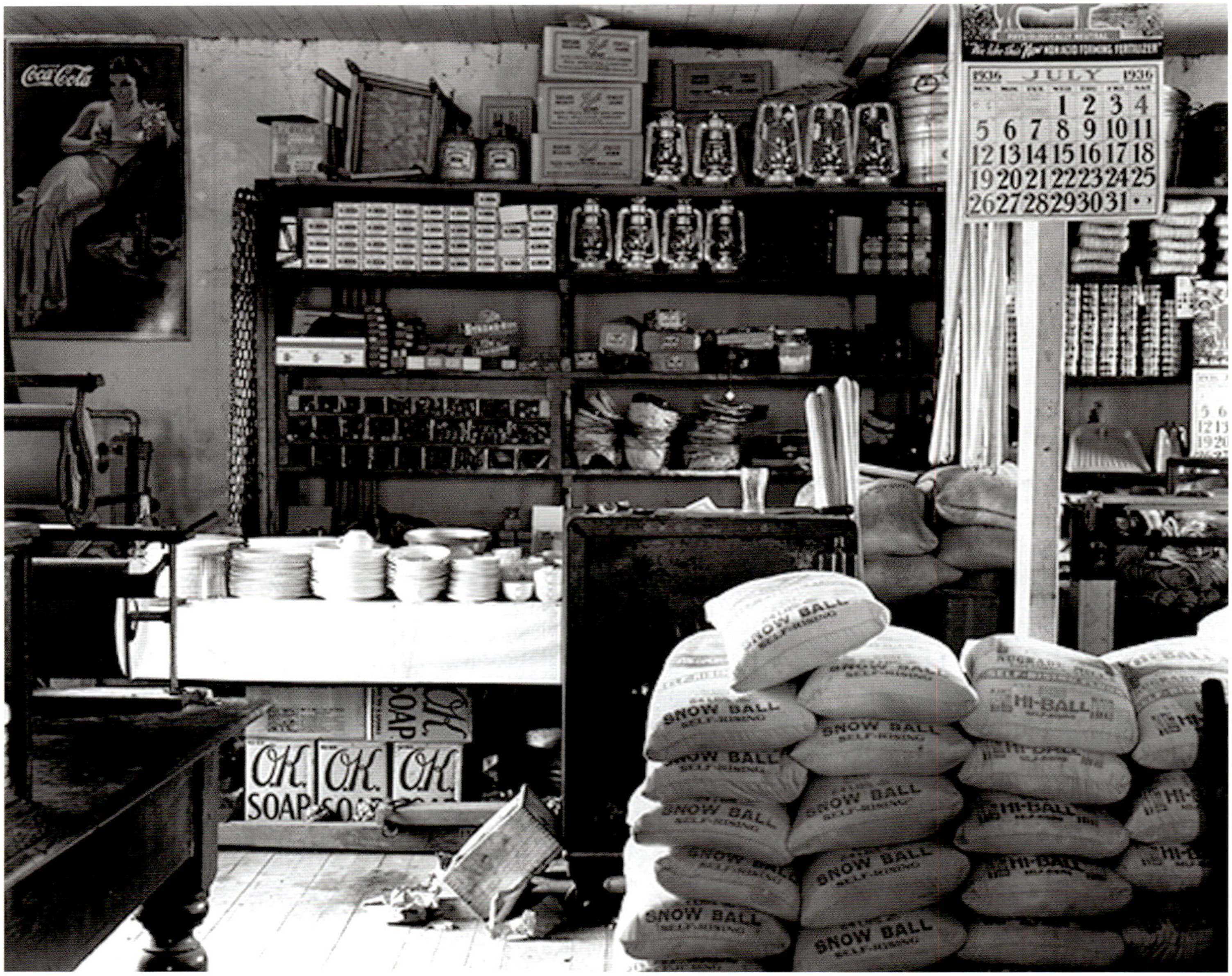

"General store interior, Moundville, Alabama"
Walker Evans, 1936

Moundville, near a complex of Mississippian (thirteenth- to fourteenth-century) mounds set about a vast plaza, was incorporated in the early 1900s.

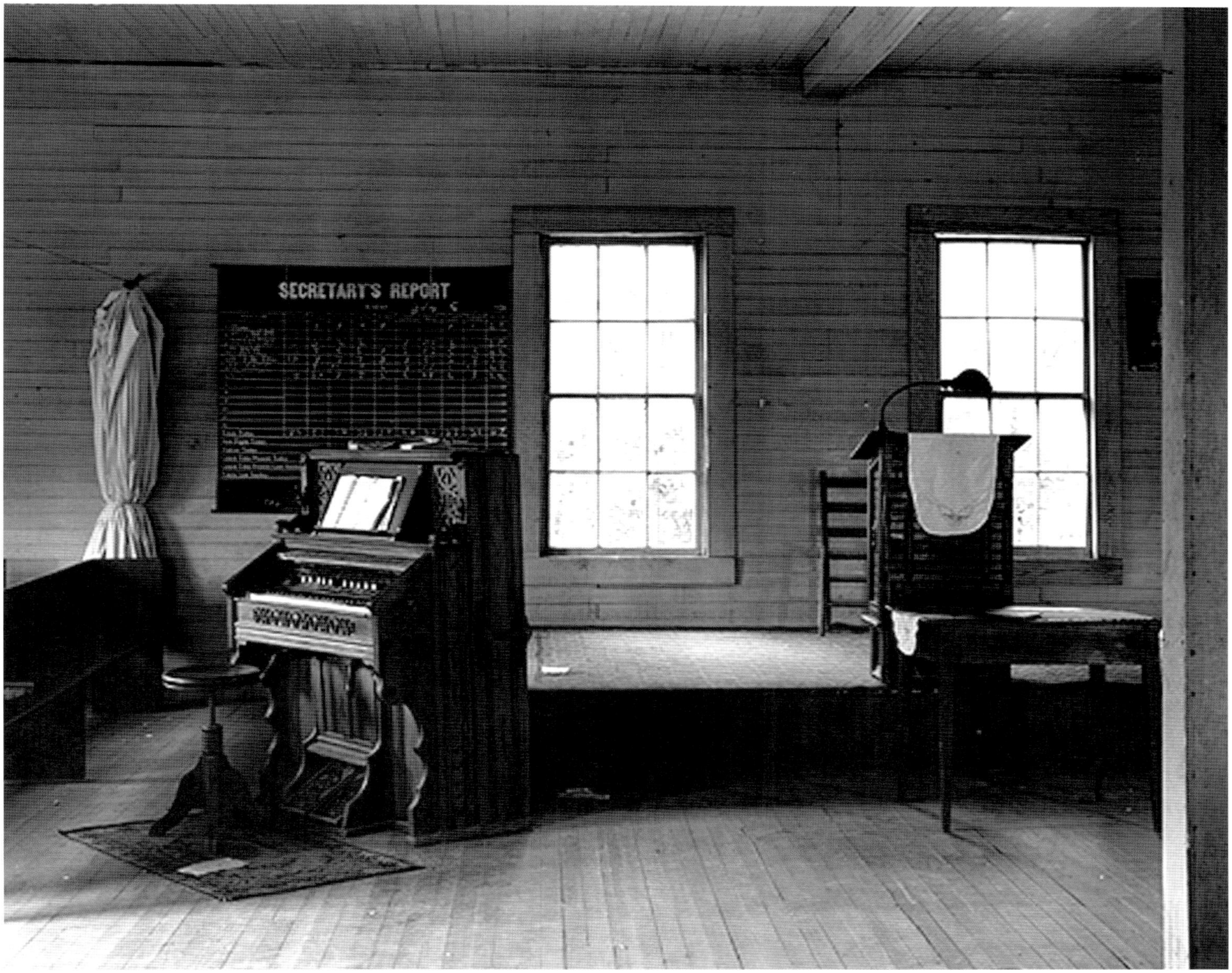

"Church interior with Pump Organ, Alabama"
Walker Evans, 1936

Evans once said:
"I am for man's work, nature bores me as an art form."

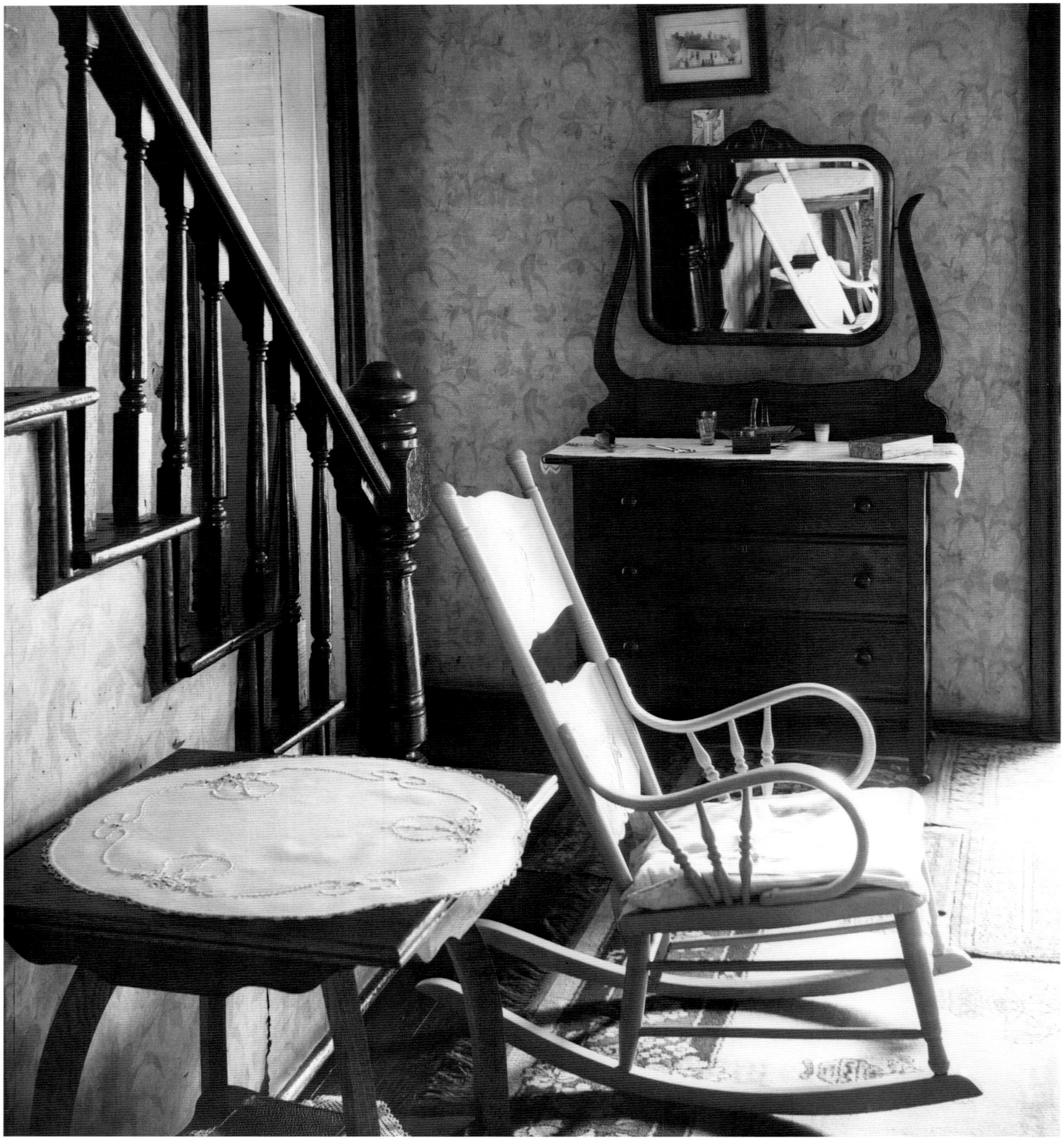

"Interior of unemployed man's house, Morgantown, West Virginia"
Walker Evans, 1935

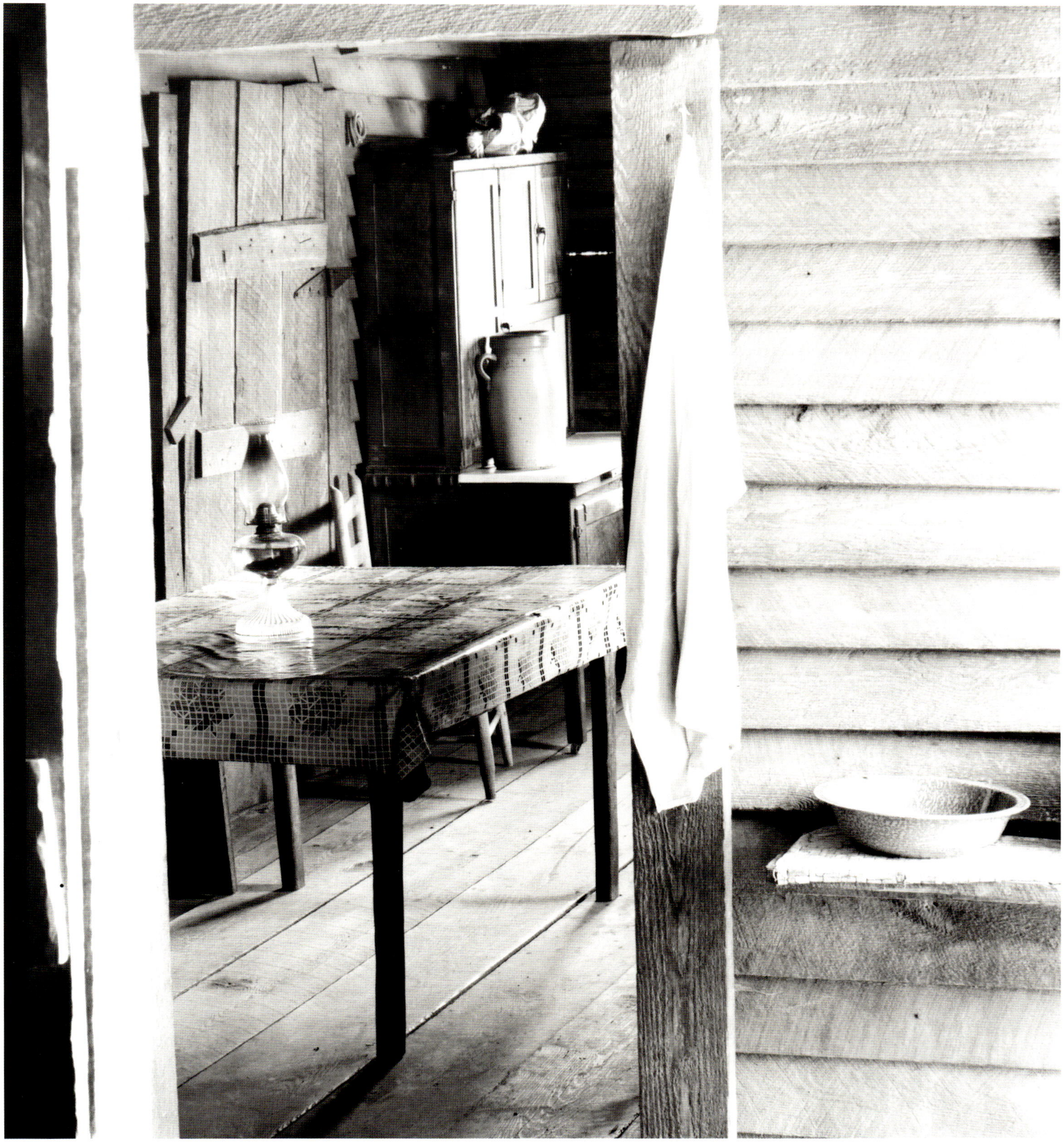

"Washstand in the dog run and kitchen of Floyd Burroughs's cabin, Hale County, Alabama"
Walker Evans, 1936

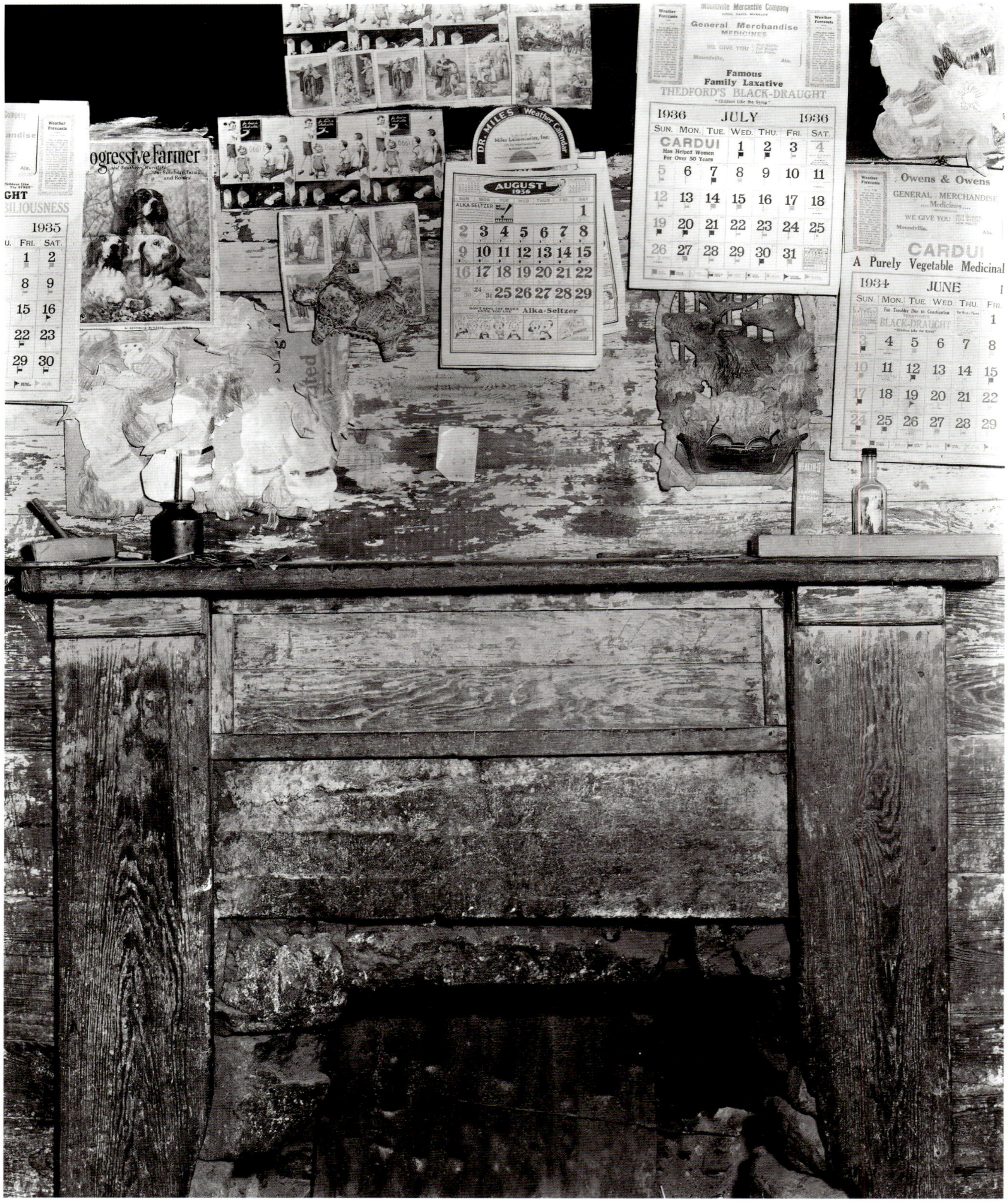

"Fireplace in Frank Tengle's home, Hale County, Alabama"
Walker Evans, 1936

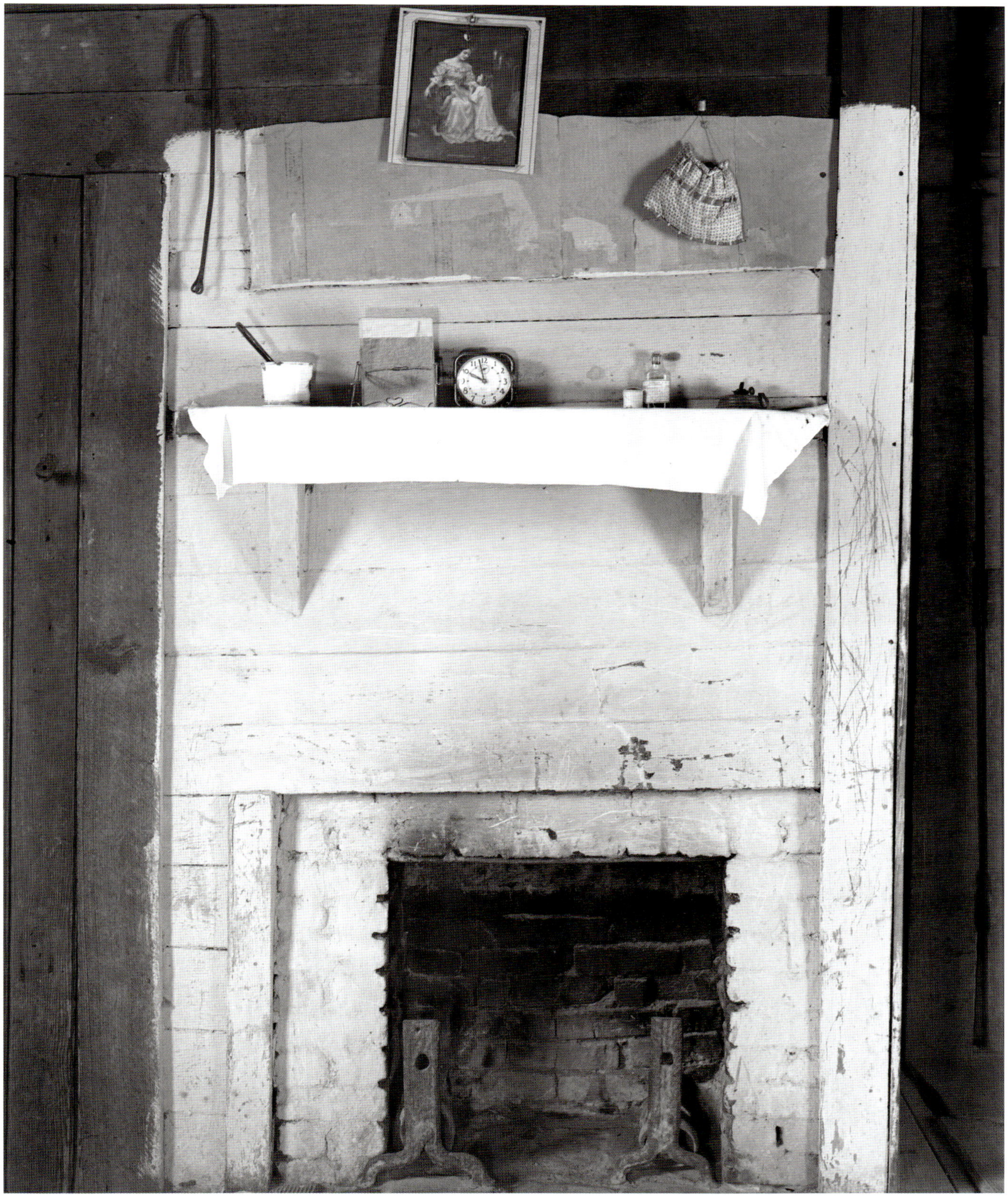

"Fireplace in bedroom of Floyd Burroughs's cabin, Hale County, Alabama"
Walker Evans, 1936

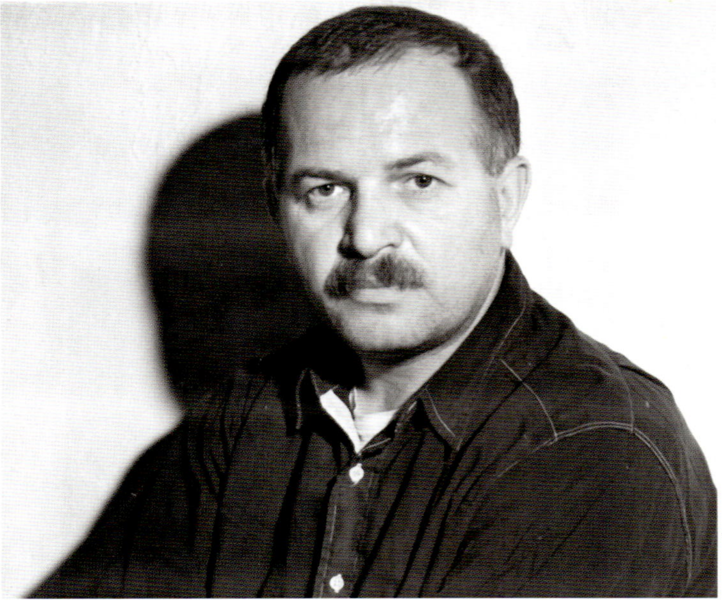

Ben Shahn
Arthur Rothstein, 1938

Ben Shahn

Roy Stryker said of Shahn's way of working that he was "there at the moment. He helps . . . to set up some by his conversation, but he sees the faces, he sees the juxtaposition of faces; a second later it's too late. He had to hit it right. Some of that is accident, but he knows what he's after, he sees . . . a whole concept there." Though his studio-mate, Walker Evans, had given him technical instruction in photographic technique, Shahn asserted that his photographs were "the raw materials of painting" and that he used his compact 35-mm Leica as a mechanical sketchpad. Shahn moved through and around the scene as he made a set of exposures, and he once likened his photography of a country auction to the creation of a movie script.[23]

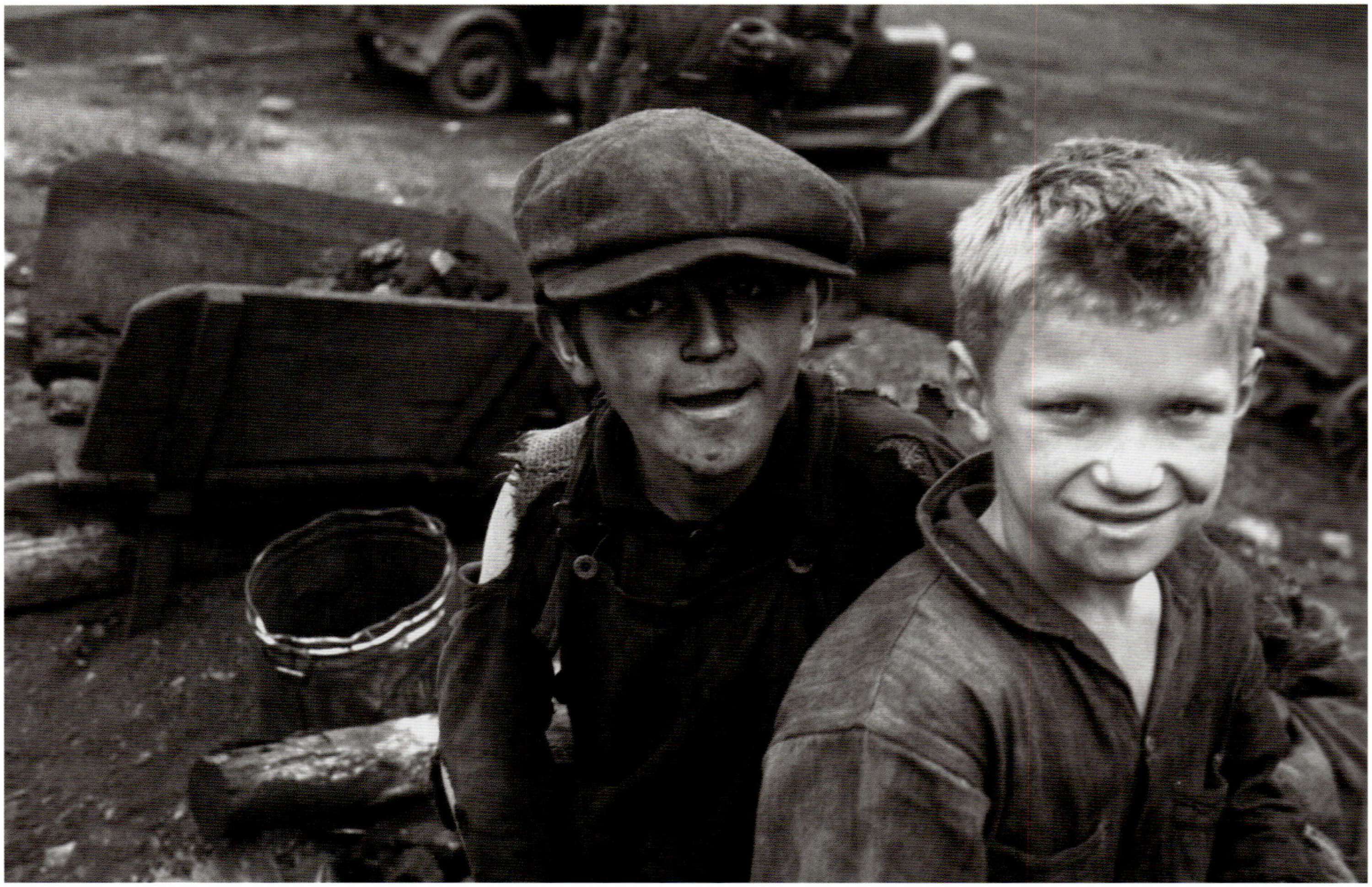

"Boys who salvage coal from the slag heaps at Nanty Glo, Pennsylvania, salvaging coal from the rock dumps . . . receive 10 cents per hundred pound sack or two dollars a ton. One man can fill from ten to twenty sacks a day"
Ben Shahn, 1935

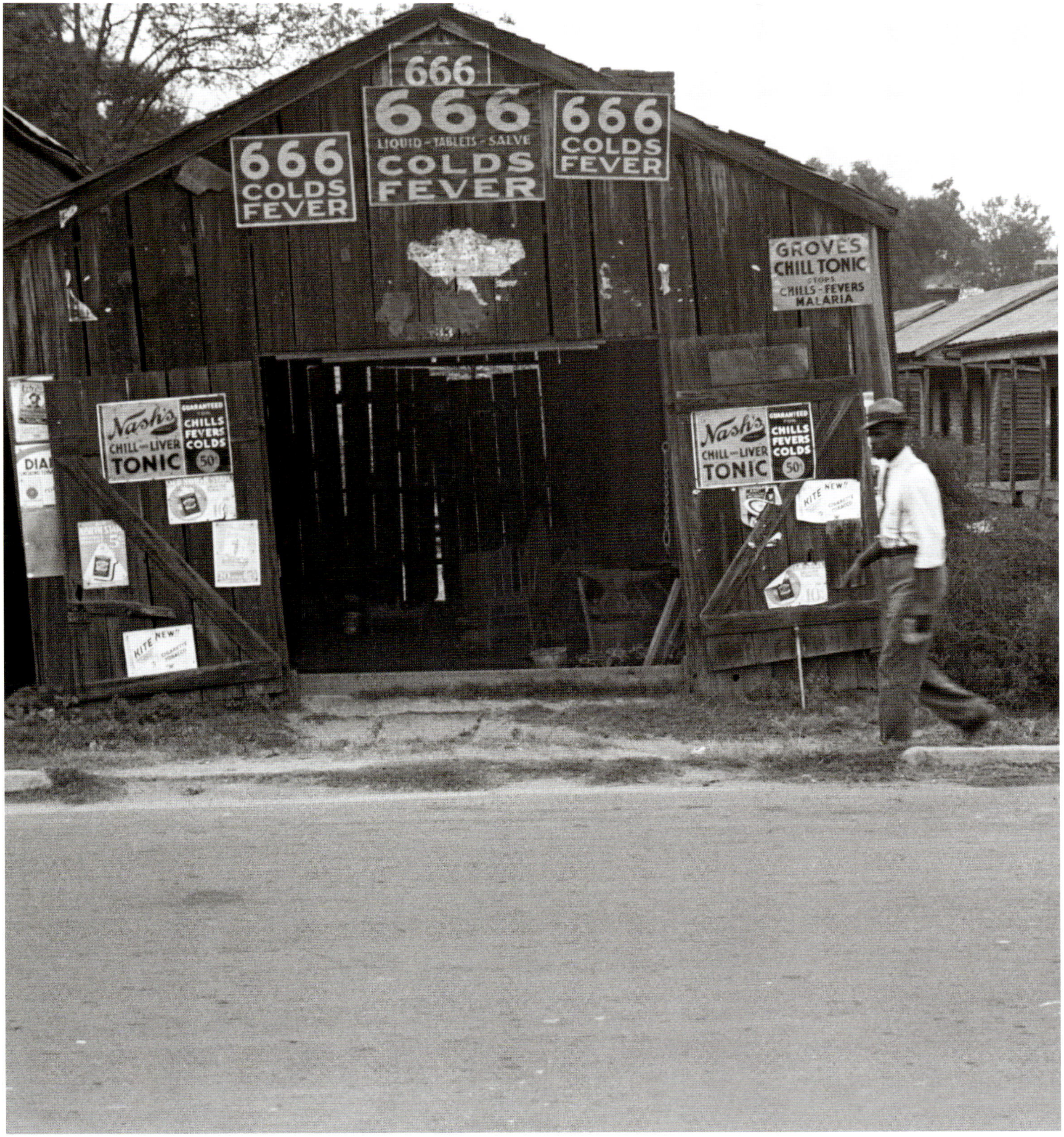

"Advertisements for popular malaria cure, Natchez, Mississippi"
Ben Shahn, 1935

Top:
"Cotton pickers, Pulaski County, Arkansas"
Ben Shahn, 1935

Shahn arrived in Pulaski County at harvest time.

Bottom:
"Cotton pickers, Pulaski County, Arkansas, at the end of the day—60 cents a day"
Ben Shahn, 1935

"Oh, listen, I saw things when I made arrangements to meet with a group of cotton pickers and they'd leave at, say, 5:30 in the morning and I had a lot of photographs of them actually gathering . . . steam rising out of their breath. That's because it was early and cold. They'd take along those huge cans of water, the kind that milk used to come in, you know those big milk cans that farmers use . . . and by the time it was nine o'clock, that thing was just as warm as anything you want to call it, and those poor people were there, say twelve hours, at 5 cents per hour, and then come back—we drove them back to the company store and drink three cokes, one after another. Drink up in one swoop one quarter of their earnings . . . For instance I was stopped one day by a colored man and he saw DC plates on the car and he told me a heart-rending story. He was a sharecropper. And I said, 'Why don't you go and complain . . . We have this board and so on.' He says, 'The man I work for is on the board.'"[iv]

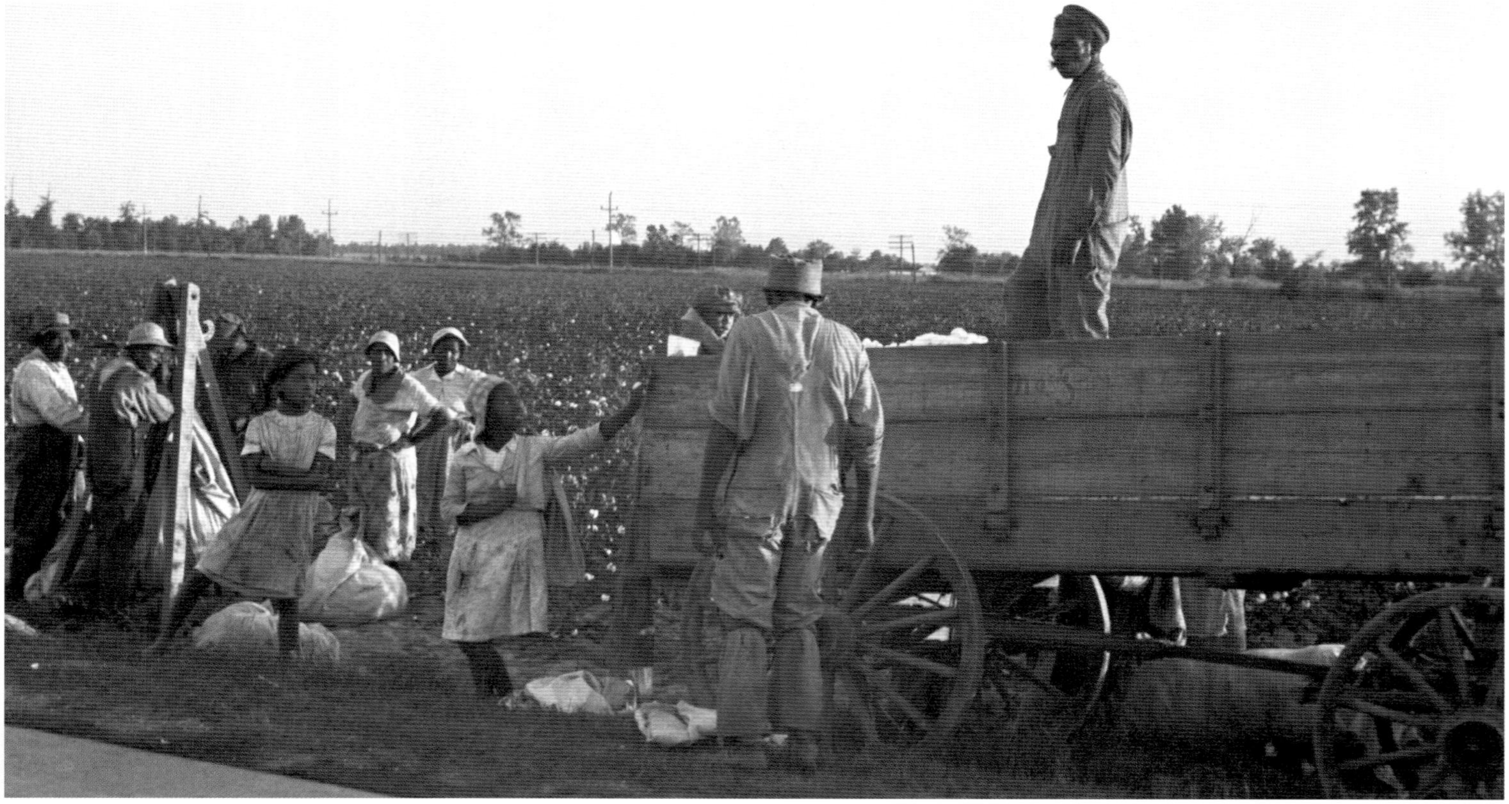

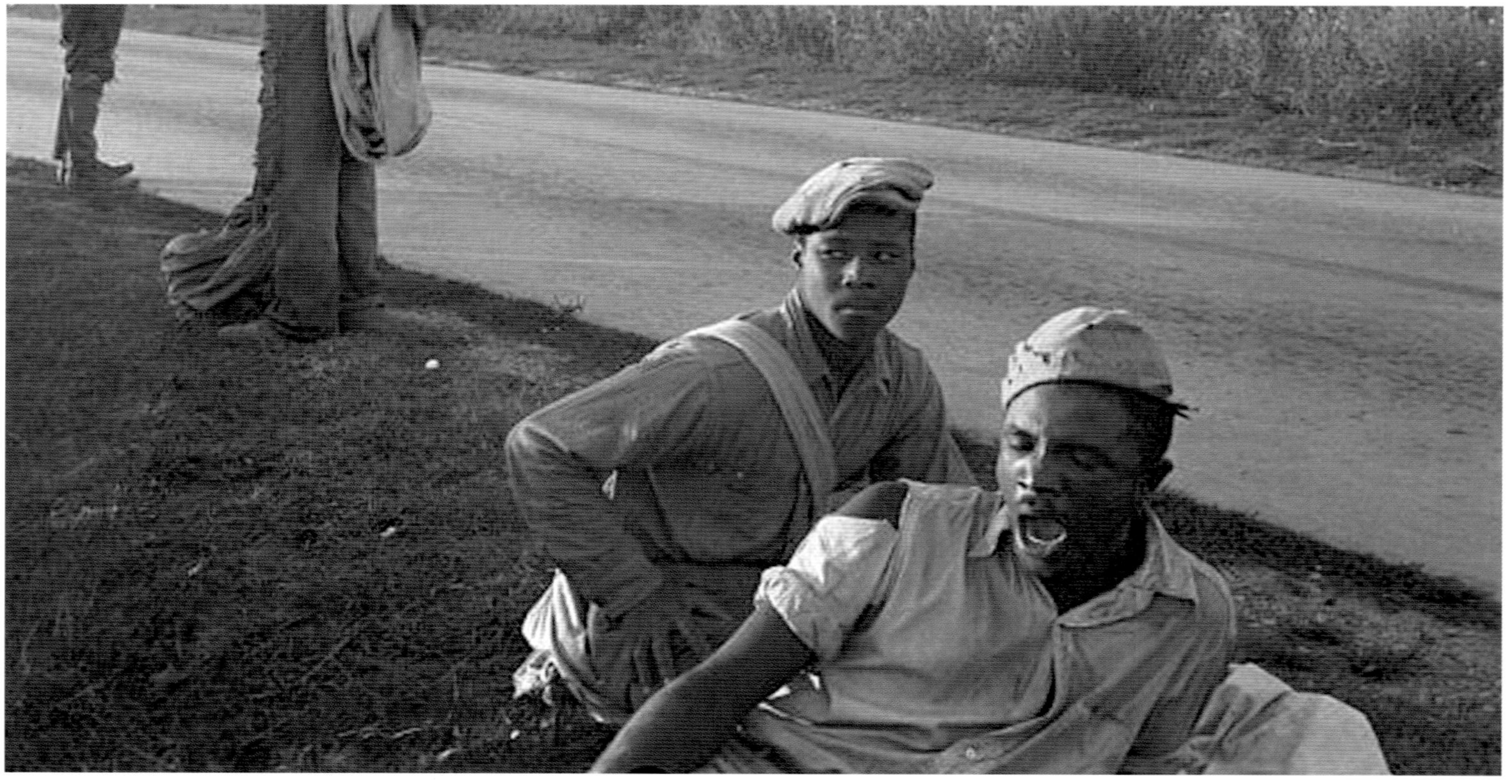

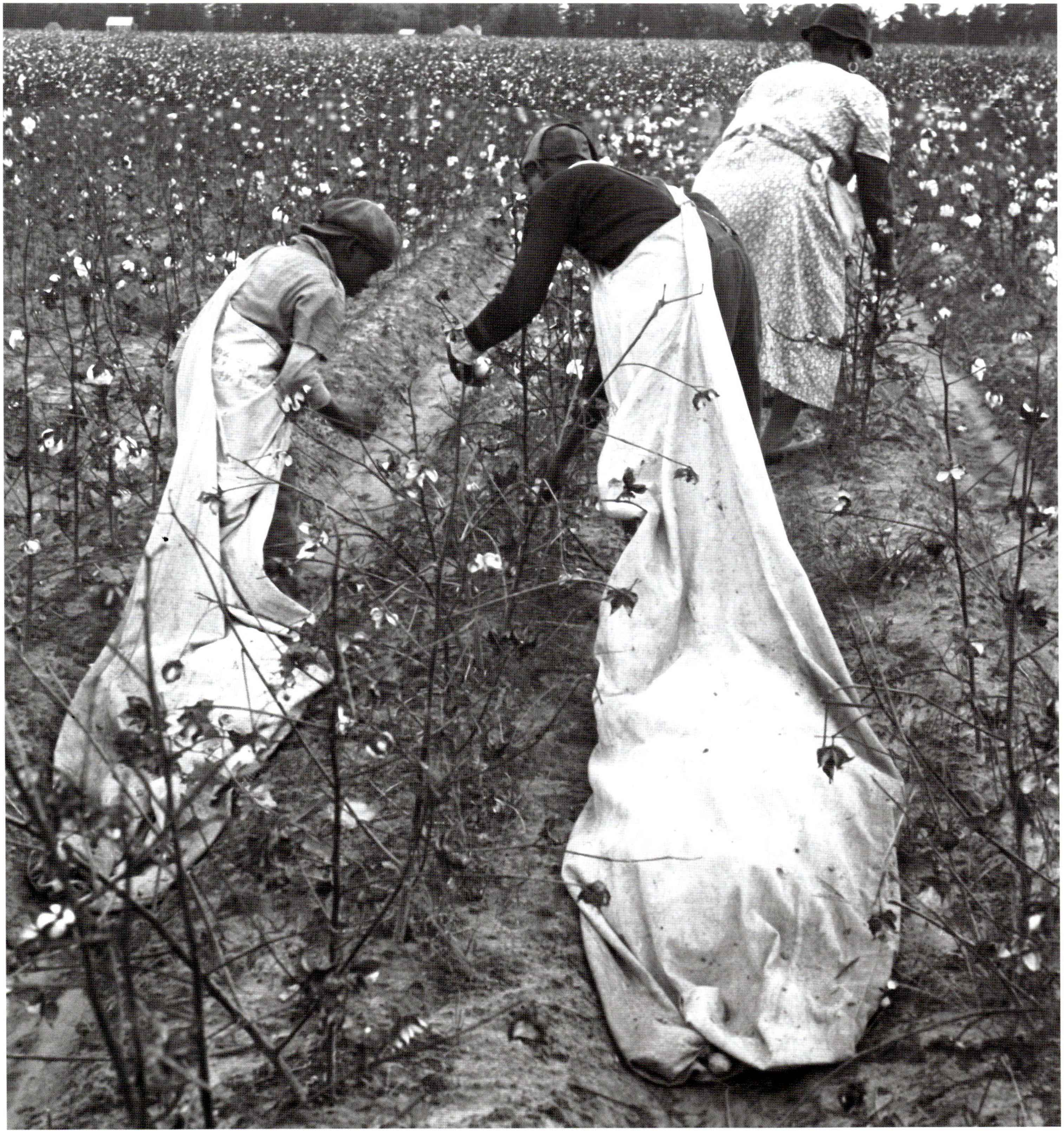

"Cotton pickers, Pulaski County, Arkansas"
Ben Shahn, 1935

"I had then [in the late 1930s] crossed and recrossed many sections of the country, and had come to know well so many people of all kinds of belief and temperament, which they maintained with a transcendent indifference to their lot in life. Theories had melted before such experience. My own painting then had turned from what is called 'social realism' into a sort of personal realism . . . There were the poor who were rich in spirit, and the rich who were also sometimes rich in spirit. There was the South and its storytelling art, stories of snakes and storms and haunted houses, enchanting; and yet such talent thriving in the same human shell with hopeless prejudices, bigotry, and ignorance."[v]

Marion Post Wolcott

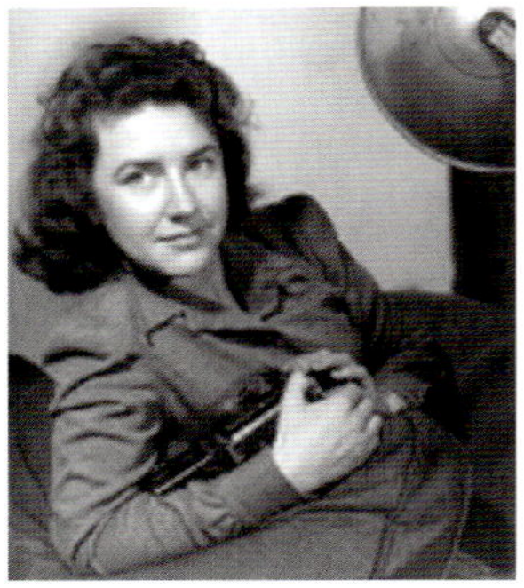

Marion Post Wolcott

Marion Post grew up in Montclair, New Jersey, attended the Edgewood School in Greenwich, Connecticut, and worked with her mother for Margaret Sanger's birth control clinic in "The Village," in New York City, where their companions were musicians, artists, writers, and actors. She studied early childhood education at the New School for Social Research, and then at New York University, taught children in a Massachusetts mill town, studied dance in Paris, and later, child psychology at the University of Vienna. After returning to the United States, she taught at a progressive school, and began taking photographs of her friends in the WPA Group Theatre, published her first work in *Stage Magazine*, and worked with Elia Kazan on *People of the Cumberlands*, a film about union organizing in the South. She left teaching to become a staff photographer for the *Philadelphia Evening Bulletin*, and was introduced to Roy Stryker by Paul Strand and Ralph Steiner. Stryker hired her, and she was one of his FSA photographers from 1938 through 1941.

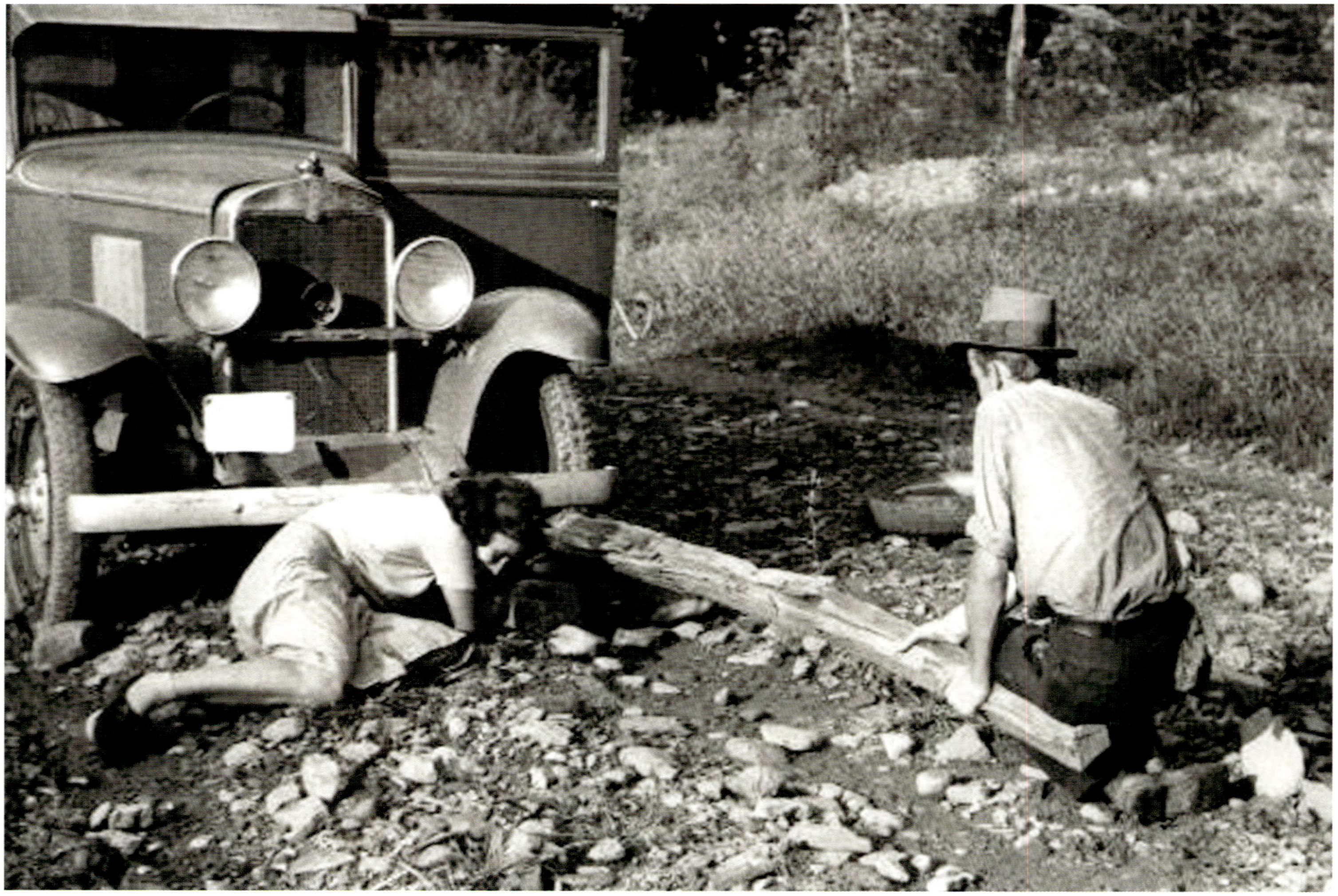

"MPW helping to change tire, Up Creek Road. Breathitt County, Kentucky, 1940"

"Mountaineer and Marion Post Wolcott changing a tire with a fence post as a jack. On assignment up South Fork of Kentucky River, Breathitt County—MPW's Borrowed Car in Creek, Pulled up by Mule. Kentucky"
Marion Post Wolcott, 1940

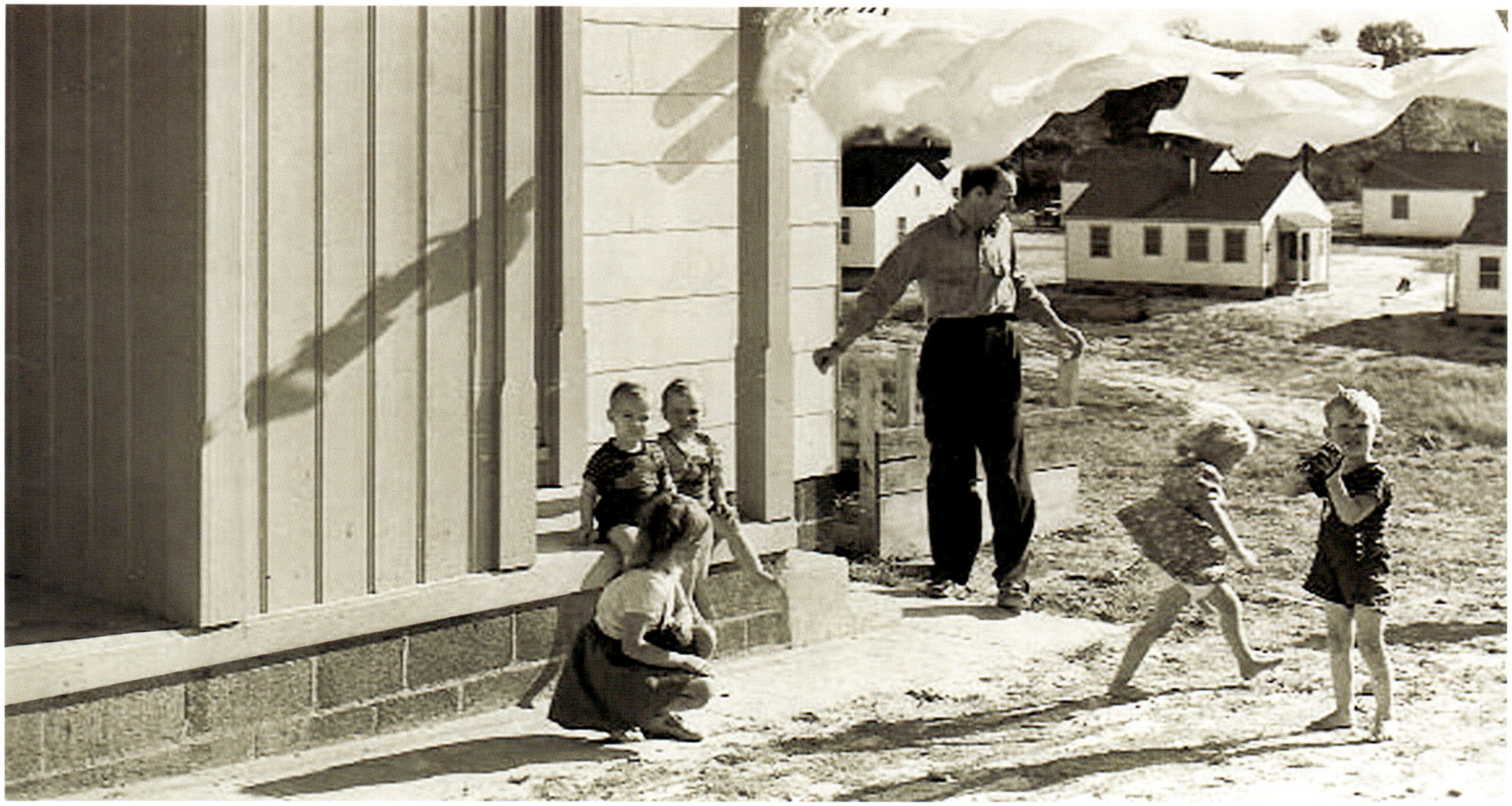

"Sunset Village; New Housing for Migrants. Bellegrade, Florida"
Marion Post Wolcott, 1940

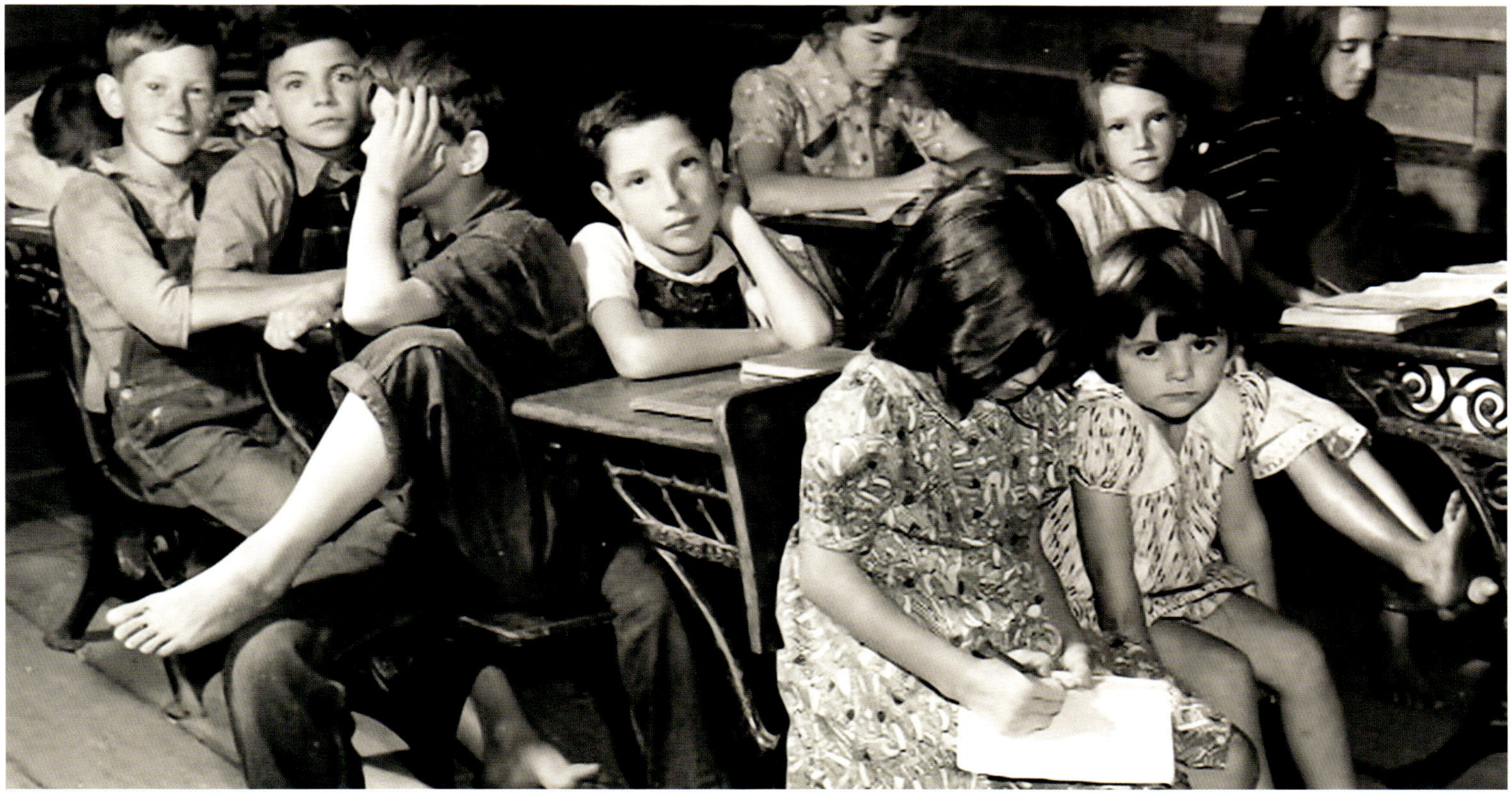

"Children at Desks, One Room School House. Breathitt County, Kentucky"
Marion Post Wolcott, 1940

Rexford Tugwell and Grace Falke Tugwell

When Richard Doud interviewed Rex Tugwell after talking with Roy Stryker, he asked about the origins of resettlement. Tugwell responded that he "conceived the idea of the Resettlement Administration and Roosevelt set it up by executive order, and we operated with emergency funds. It was the companion piece really to the WPA with Hopkins" but with the emphasis upon "rural areas" where government aid would help in "the rehabilitation of the poor farmers" after "two very serious years of drought, which created what was then called the Dust Bowl, and blew away a lot of soil in the West which had come into use unwisely during the [First World] war, and left the people really stranded, and they began to drift away." Since they "simply couldn't all leave," there were "millions of them on relief, on account of the drought, and this was quite aside from our problem of rehabilitation, and resettlement."[24]

And how could there be a need for photography—for art—amid all this distress? Could art work? "Because this was so dramatic, and because it meant misery and tragedy for so many families, and because we hoped it would never happen again, at least, not in the same way, we thought not only that we ought to have a record of it, for future generations—that is the historical part—but also to show people who weren't involved in it, how extremely serious it was. Then, of course, there was the other part, that these people who had all these skills in order to" take those photographs "were mostly unemployed themselves and they were delighted to get the opportunity to work . . . it wasn't any soft job for them, either. They had very small allowances and quite small pay, and yet they did this enormous, wonderful job—record making. I know we were all very proud of them later."[25]

They had reason for pride, for they had helped a nation understand itself. Tugwell recalled that he and Stryker met when he was chairman of the economics department at Columbia, Stryker was one of his instructors, and they "worked together in a number of ways; not only was he teaching, but we had written a textbook together . . . It was so good, and had taken hold so well, that when I went to Washington and conceived of the necessity for making some record of this [the Depression] and using these pictures to convince people that what we were doing needed doing, I sent for Roy. Grace had charge of that division."[26]

One can picture him turning to her, for she added that Stryker was "very reluctant . . . because he thought his future was in teaching." But after "we"—an interesting plural—"explained to him what we . . . were interested in doing . . . he finally became so excited by the excitement around us that he couldn't resist." In his own interview with Doud, Stryker said that the form of Tugwell's invitation was: "Well, damn it, make up your mind. If you want to come, come. If you don't, don't. I just want to tell you one thing. You may do far more education here than you'll ever do if you stay at Columbia . . . You may not make much money, we may both be out on the street, but we can drink our soup together."[27]

Tugwell said only that Stryker "plunged in and got all these people, and began to take pictures and every once in a while he would come in and . . . say, 'Now, I want you to explain to me what I am doing.' Once again, Grace Tugwell intervened: 'I would say, "Look Roy, you are doing exactly what he wants." About five years ago, he called me up and he said . . . he still wanted to know what he was supposed to have been doing, and apparently he was under the impression that since he enjoyed this so much, he was not doing the correct thing." To which Tugwell added: "He still doesn't know. . . . This amused us so much that we talked about it many times and just decided to put him off, because what he was doing was all right and whether he understood it or not didn't matter to us."[28]

And did Grace Tugwell "understand"? That she did, though she insisted thirty years later that she "didn't attempt to do anything but try to interpret policy and to cooperate with the regional people when they indicated an interest or a willingness to use this material. I would just put it in Roy's lap. 'Roy, rush out there and see what you can do . . .' I would tell him, 'Roy, that last batch of pictures was absolutely wonderful. This is exactly what we want.' Of course, in between he would be getting directions about what areas needed attention and so on, but not specific directions. We would just say, 'Roy, this is the situation here or there; can Dorothea [Lange] or so on go in there easily?' That was all the direction he needed." Perhaps, but not all he desired, for Stryker told Doud that "[Rex] Tugwell's only advice to me, only direction to me [was] . . . 'We need pictures.' He never said how to take them. He said, 'Remember that the man with the holes in his shoes, the ragged clothes, can be just as good a citizen as the man who has the better shoes and the better clothes.'"[29]

Stryker and both Tugwells expressed pride in having provided the American people with "a chance to see for the first time" the human consequences of the Depression, "such a tragedy and so wide-spread. To go and analyze it and explain it to people through pictures was really a thrilling experience." The artists, recalled Rexford Tugwell, "got very stirred up about this material," and "this enthusiasm . . . built itself up." And, as Grace Tugwell added: "It was the only way to do it. Words were simply not adequate."[30]

Doud then shifted the conversation to power relationships: "Roy keeps saying . . . that you protected him—you held an umbrella over him all the time you were there and your successors continued this protection . . . I was wondering who you protected him from." Tugwell responded characteristically that Stryker "was extremely conscious of the kind of criticism that might come from yokel congressmen." Tugwell could offer little protection from such "yokels," so it was no wonder that "Stryker felt that he was very vulnerable, because he had people out taking pictures, and taking lots of pictures too." With Tugwell, who was often derided as a mere "braintruster" without everyday, manure-on-the-boots experience, as his only insulator from what Tugwell persisted in calling "carping criticism" it became essential that they have "one great protection—the President. If we got into any particular criticism, all I had to do was go and tell the President, 'You are going to hear something bad.' He would laugh." The arts projects were no laughing matter to the "yokels" however, for "Harry Hopkins people" included some in the "Theater Project" who were thought to be redder than "Rex the Red" and they "became very conspicuous. Then he had the artists and then Harry was kind of belligerent about it too. We just tried to keep out of sight."[31]

Grace Tugwell had been Hopkins's employee in the National Youth Administration, and she knew that its work, the folklorists, and the Theatre Project were "not something that you could hide, you see. A good deal of the documentary films you could hide very well, because it wasn't on the wall of a post office." Her husband agreed and added that "a photograph—it was a photograph, it was a picture. This was something that you couldn't deny." The public would take its reality from a truth it thought "was evident."[32]

Though Tugwell appraised Stryker's program as "tremendously effective," it aroused Congressional fury at the effectiveness of "all this fancy propaganda." By the time the Tugwells were interviewed by Doud, the onus of propaganda had been erased by patriotic art during World War II. So Grace Tugwell plunged ahead: "Which was exactly what we were trying to do —propaganda . . . tell the story, so that we would get more cooperation and help."[33]

In his own interview Stryker said that Tugwell was there "to protect me . . . in a few instances" but generally when he was embattled, he turned to Grace Falke. One day, when he was on vacation in Vermont, his deputy "called me long distance, he got me on the phone and said, 'Roy, you're going to get your throat cut, they're taking you on again.' So I came down and . . . went to see Grace Falke—and it was stopped." Later, he was in trouble again and "walked into Miss Falke's office to see Tugwell and said to her 'Well, Grace, it's been fun.'" To his interviewer Stryker said that she "had a strange way of watching us." So she watched, and responded: "Well I don't know that you're right about that." Tugwell came in and Grace said to him, "Dr. Tugwell, I think the Photographic Section is in a bad position, a bad situation right now." Tugwell did not say anything to Stryker, but responded to her: "Tell Ken Clark I want to see him this afternoon." Stryker had been reminded that "we were watched over. We did survive." When Tugwell himself became too much a "lightning rod" and was on his way out, Stryker recalled,

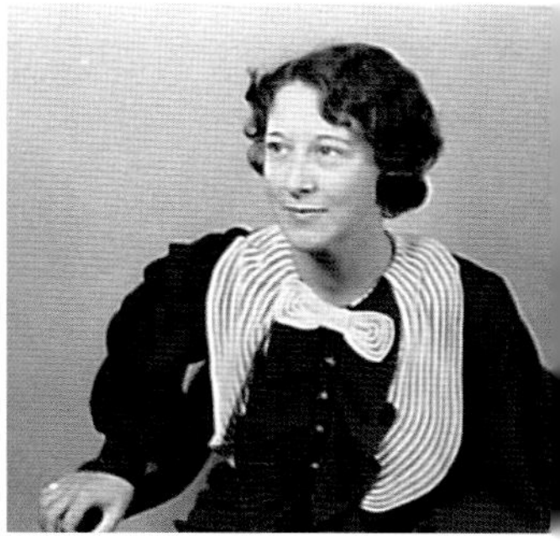

"Grace E. Falke"
Arthur Rothstein, 1935

"he came over to the office for a visit, walked around, pulled out drawers, asked a few questions, looked more than I realized, turned to me and said, 'We did better than we thought, didn't we?' That's all, virtually all, I ever heard from him after that time."[34]

Nonetheless, when in 1964 Stryker wrote the Tugwells about his interviews with Richard Doud, knowing that Doud was on his way to talk with them as well, he addressed them as "Dear Folks," and went on to say "it was the two of you who did the important things at the important times, which made the difference," and "you may not like the word Grace—but you did mother us. I so often think of that operation as a family of birds growing up in a healthy, happy home."[35]

When the end came, it was both because opposition had grown against "the story" being told in major measure because Tugwell was telling it, and, as he said, he had become "a favorite target quite early." He admitted later that he was afraid that he "was more to blame for everybody's difficulties in Resettlement than anybody else . . . I thought the program would go on better if I left." His old foes in the drug and advertising business mobilized the newspapers against him. His drug law reforms "hit them in their advertising, you see, and this together with the congressmen who wanted to criticize Roosevelt was enough. I was a notorious character. There is no secret about that." Nor was there any secret in the animosity of the big farmers and their representatives to resettlement.[36]

Folk Music and Eleanor Roosevelt

After his dismissal from the Agriculture Department, Tugwell put in a stint in the molasses business and then became Chairman of Mayor Fiorello La Guardia's New York Planning Commission. Once again, he found himself in a political cul-de-sac, at the end of which stood Park Commissioner Robert Moses, who had powerful friends in the press, as Tugwell did not. When he and Grace Falke were married by La Guardia in 1938, *Time* gave the occasion this acrid notice: "Married. Rexford Guy Tugwell, 47, most handsome original Brain Truster, now chairman of New York City's Planning Commission; and his onetime assistant, Grace Falke, 30, director of National Youth's art projects; by Mayor La Guardia; in Manhattan. Mr. Tugwell's first wife, Florence, mother of his two grown daughters, divorced him three months ago."[37]

When he had had enough of Moses, Tugwell accepted Roosevelt's appointment as governor of Puerto Rico, where his molasses expertise made it a little easier for him to undertake diversifying Puerto Rican agriculture to lessen its blighting dependence on sugar. Ten years later, when Eleanor Roosevelt visited the Tugwells in Puerto Rico, Grace Tugwell took her to Arecibo to view what was described in "My Day" as "a new experiment" providing sugarcane workers with shares in the profits that came from working a common piece of land, around which they would build homes "and have a garden and a small crop of their own."[38]

Collective farming was one project of Mrs. Roosevelt's. Another was the National Youth Administration and a third was folk music. Grace Falke Tugwell's "National Youth art projects" depended upon the support of Mrs. Roosevelt, who wrote in her autobiography that early in the New Deal "one of the ideas I agreed to present to Franklin was that of setting up a national youth administration . . . It was one of the occasions on which I was very proud that the right thing was done regardless of political consequences." The President's executive order establishing the National Youth Administration (NYA) in 1935 stipulated that it pay high school and college students to stay in school and work part-time, with on-the-job training in federally funded work projects. The NYA included a program for African Americans headed by Mary McLeod Bethune, among the many New Deal administrators who emerged from the Social Gospel Movement and carried its vocabulary of ideas into the Civil Rights movement of the 1960s (see chapter ten).[39]

Grace Falke Tugwell served as the liaison between the National Youth Administration's art projects and the Joint Committee on Folk Arts of the WPA Federal Writers' Project, under John A. Lomax, Benjamin Botkin, and Charles

Seeger (father of Pete Seeger), as they rediscovered a legacy of music including the dozen folk songs recorded by Zora Neale Hurston. As a recording angel, as well as a great prose writer, Hurston gave voices to poor rural people given faces in the photographs—and prose—of Eudora Welty. While Grace Tugwell was working with the Joint Committee, Botkin was urging that it and the Writers' Congress give the public "a point of view" the "integrity" of which would derive "from its nature as a direct response of the artist to a group and group experience with which he identifies himself and for which he speaks." Like photography, the folk music they advocated and discovered could "make the inarticulate articulate and above all, to let the people speak in their own voice and tell their own story." It also provided the basic material for Virgil Thomson's soundtracks for Pare Lorentz's *The Plow That Broke the Plains* and *The River*.[40]

Rexford and Grace Tugwell told their story, as did Stryker, in interviews with Richard Doud for the Archives of American Art in the 1960s. They explained to Doud how documentary film accompanied by folk-music-derived scores came to help forgotten people "find their own voice and tell their story." Tugwell said that Pare Lorentz came to them through Robert Flaherty, the famous documentary film-maker, who had made the *Men of Ireland* and *Nanook of the North*. Tugwell and Stryker "had conceived the idea of having a motion picture showing what had happened to the soil in the Dust Bowl" and the masterpiece of Pare Lorentz, *The Plow That Broke the Plains*, depicted people left behind after "the extension of agriculture in a dry-land country where it never should have been extended to. The story was that the Indians had always warned the white men that they shouldn't break the plains. Pare Lorentz was a young fellow who wanted to undertake this."[41]

According to Tugwell, "Grace had charge of all that," to which she replied: "My having charge of it was second hand, you see. They came to me only when they had problems, or when they couldn't get along with each other, or when they needed money." She was Tugwell's assistant in charge of the three divisions, among them "information" and "getting out all of the directives, all the paper work . . . centered in my office and my real job was to keep everybody happy." Doud reported that "Roy [Stryker] mentioned one time that there were some very good disc recordings made for radio to be played in local areas" and asked "Do either of you know anything about those?" Rexford Tugwell responded: "Would this be the folk songs? We had a whole division for that."

Pare Lorentz, Art, Land, and People

Pare Lorentz was born in Clarksburg, West Virginia, in 1905, the son of a publisher and a professional singer. In 1925, after college, he decamped to New York City where he wrote commercial copy for electric bulbs before finding a better métier as a film critic for *Judge*, *The New York Evening Journal*, *Vanity Fair*, *Town and Country*, *McCall's*, *Fortune*, *Harper's*, *Scribner's*, *Forum*, and *Story*. Then he turned to politics, and wrote an admiring portrait, *The Roosevelt Year: 1933*, which he tried to make into a documentary film. He found no backers, so he took a job writing a political column for the Hearst newspapers. It did not last long; Lorentz was fired for writing too enthusiastically about Henry Wallace. For *Newsweek*, Lorentz wrote an article on the Dust Bowl, and for a second time unsuccessfully attempted to find backers to turn his prose into film. Then he was introduced to Tugwell and Stryker.

In 1935 they commissioned Lorentz, a film critic who had never made a film, to create documentary films to support their endeavors to help "suffering human beings that were caught and trapped in the devastation caused by soil erosion." Lorentz bestowed upon them, and posterity, *The Plow That Broke the Plains* and *The River*, which provided narrative lines to the messages imparted, instance by instance, in the still photographs of Stryker's Resettlement and Farm Security program.

The score by Virgil Thomson for *The Plow That Broke the Plains* included many references to the folk music being rediscovered by the folklorists of the WPA. Its budget of six thousand dollars included recording Thomson's score by the New York Philharmonic, though in the end the total cost of Lorentz's masterpiece rose to twenty thousand dollars.

Tugwell and Stryker were pleased by the public response to *The Plow That Broke the Plains*. One day in Tugwell's office, they had finished telling Lorentz so when Lorentz turned to a topographic map of the Mississippi River on the wall and told them that they were "missing the biggest story in the world." He was still earning his living as a movie critic for *McCall's*, whose editor had permitted him space for a five-thousand-word story on the great Mississippi flood of that year. Lorentz turned a pedestrian committee report into a prose poem, much of which he used for the narration for *The River*, his next film, for which Tugwell found the five thousand dollars to start him out by asking the President to see to it that it was provided, saying of Lorentz "he's my shooter. He photographs America to show what it's like to our people." The Pare Lorentz Film Center is at the Franklin D. Roosevelt Presidential Library and Museum, appropriately set in the compound in which they first met after Lorentz found a friend who could secure an invitation to Hyde Park. Following a showing of Sonja Henie in *Thin Ice*, the after-dinner group watched *The River*. The President pronounced it good, and asked what more he could do to help. The problem was distribution, so the first public showing was held at the White House and the United States Film Service was created, with Pare Lorentz as its chief. Its first distributed film was *The River*. Lorentz made two more films, *Ecce Homo!* and *The Fight for Life*, and oversaw production of two others, *Power and the Land* for the Rural Electrification Administration, and *The Land* for the Agriculture Department. During World War II he served in the Air Corps, producing training films for pilots, and in 1946, he produced the filming of the Nuremberg Trials, as Chief of Motion Pictures, Music and Theatre in the Occupied Areas of Germany. He made no more films, but helped others as a consultant. He died in 1995 at the age of eighty-six.

Lorentz lived in great comfort in his latter years, having married one of the heiresses of the *Washington Post*. His youthful struggles for political independence while employed by William Randolph Hearst were far in the past as his sponsors, the Rexford Tugwells, returned to academic life. In 1946, Tugwell found New York politics too much for him, and acceded to an offer from the Chancellor of the University of Chicago, Robert Maynard Hutchins, to become a professor of political science. Tugwell gave his next ten years to teaching and writing in Chicago before following Hutchins to the Center for the Study of Democratic Institutions in Santa Barbara, California. He died in 1979.

Roy Stryker's Last Career

When Tugwell's Farm Security program, including Roy Stryker's photography operation, was coming to an end, Stryker received a telephone call from Ed Stanley. Stanley, one of his "old mentors," told him that he had gone to work for "Earl Newsom, a big public relations firm" and had a job for Stryker. They met "on Madison Avenue and I guess up on the twenty-second floor. I sat there . . . looking out the window at the lights, it was cool and very pleasant." Stanley said in the warm tones I recall from a similar experience, "Roy, wouldn't it be wonderful to be able to hire photographers, pay them a good salary, send them around all over the world? American Locomotive wants a story done on locomotives in China." Stryker responded "Get thee behind me, Satan, but don't push too hard." The next day Earl Newsom interviewed him. Newsom "was a Missouri boy and he found that I was a country boy, so he said, 'Roy, you and I have a great deal in common.'" With that on the table Newsom went on, "'Our big account is Standard Oil.'" Stryker explained that his father, "having been a Populist . . . thought there were great evils in the world: railroads, Wall Street, and the greatest of these three was Standard Oil" and took his leave. The next day he changed his mind, having taken counsel with his friend Jonathan Daniels.[42]

From 1943 to 1950, Stryker produced photographic projects for Newsom's client Standard Oil, providing steady employment to Berenice Abbott, Gordon Parks, Todd Webb, Esther Bubley, Harold Corsini, Russell Lee, Arnold Eagle, Elliott Erwitt, and Sol Libsohn. Several of them also joined him in documentary work for more clients, including the Jones & Laughlin Steel Corporation. In Pittsburgh he established the Pittsburgh Photographic Library—now at the Carnegie Library of Pittsburgh. Roy Stryker died in 1975, thirty-three years before Jeanine Isabel Butler's *Documenting the Face of America*, the first documentary film about his putting art to work, was broadcast on PBS. And what of Stryker's great "file" for the New Deal—a few samples of which appear in this book? It was saved, barely, he said, by his having sought again the aid at "the right time" or from "the right people . . . We got our file transferred to the Library of Congress thanks to Jonathan Daniels, thanks to "Mr. Big," the President, and Bob Sherwood . . . Archie MacLeish was there at the time {as Librarian of Congress} and he had quite a respect for it. Mr. Roosevelt said, 'Talk to the archives . . . talk to Archie MacLeish.' It was transferred {to the Library} Bob Sherwood finally came home from abroad—Paris or London. It had his approval. Otherwise it would be scattered to the four winds today."[43]

There is a direct line from George Washington, who sketched his own illustrations for his treatise on soil conservation, to Roy Stryker, Pare Lorentz, and the Farm Security Administration photographers. That line connecting our first conservation president to the New Deal came through the great environmental philosophers of the mid-nineteenth century, especially the most systematic and actionable of them, George Perkins Marsh. In the New Deal years, the Marshian tradition was best expressed by Walter Lowdermilk, another of the astonishing talents who worked under Rexford Tugwell at the Department of Agriculture. Lowdermilk and his colleague Hugh Bennett were artists in public presentation, using photographs and radio to present the message that Lorentz wrote for his narrator in *The River*: "Poor land makes poor people and poor people make poor land." Roy Stryker gave faces to these ideas, the faces that we see in these pages. Art in his hands explained the work of Rexford Tugwell's resettlement and restoration by giving evidence that, in the words of Lorentz: "it's the geography that makes the people, and underneath it all . . . the land and its geographical structure and so on, but after all, when all is said and done, the problem of the Depression of that period was the suffering human beings that were caught and trapped in it. So obviously we were concerned with people. We had no other choice."[44]

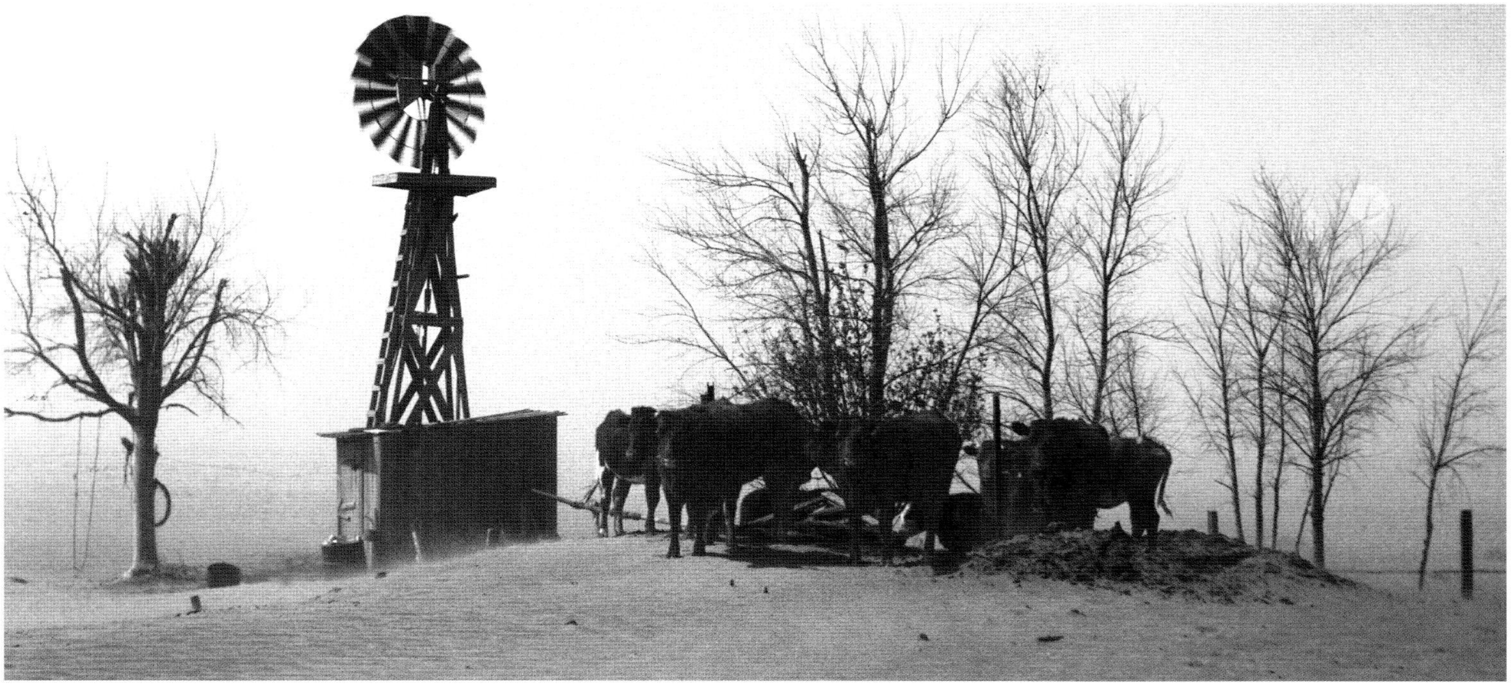

"Stock watering hole almost completely covered by shifting topsoil. Cimarron County, Oklahoma" Arthur Rothstein, April 1936

Chapter Eight

Presidents and Monuments

"How much more delightful . . . is the task of making improvements on the earth, than all the vainglory which can be acquired from ravaging it, by the most uninterrupted career of conquests."
(George Washington, December 4, 1788)

"There is more of . . . history to be felt and understood in a lonely, graceful column rising against the sky . . . than there is in all the descriptive matter that was ever written on the subject."
(Dwight D. Eisenhower, April 2, 1946)

"Let us hope . . . that . . . [our descendants] will believe we have honestly striven every day and generation to preserve a decent land to live in and a decent form of government to operate under."
(Franklin Roosevelt at Mount Rushmore, 1936)

THE NEW DEAL MOBILIZED ART to serve a nation in need. As a result that nation was provided a glory of documentary films and photographs, radio programs, paintings, cartoons, poetry, fiction, folk music, and both newspaper and magazine writing that qualified—and is collected—as literature. The New Deal also renewed acquaintance with how great presidents had "dramatized and personalized the processes of government for the people"—in the words of Robert Sherwood. One of the means Franklin Roosevelt employed for that purpose was calling attention to the monuments and memorials to George Washington and Abraham Lincoln, the two predecessors to whom he most often referred. Roosevelt was profoundly a man of tradition who learned much from Washington and Lincoln. As Sherwood also pointed out, "the word artist," rightly applied to Roosevelt, may be used with equal efficacy of all three.[1]

Washington inspired awe and deference so successfully that we may forget how assiduously he worked as an artist to produce that effect, which was essential to the success of his endeavors on behalf of his country and on behalf of the land. Those artists who best understood Washington's intentions and best honored his legacy designed the Washington Monument as a six-hundred-foot abstract form encouraging meditation upon his example. In 1936 at Mount Rushmore, Roosevelt was moved to such a meditation by an image of Washington that brought forth from him profound deliberations upon intergenerational trusteeship.

After watching the sunlight shift across the faces carved into the mountain, Roosevelt said that the "importance of the work" lay in the power of those iconic images to induce sober consideration of "what our descendants . . . will think about us." He hoped, he said, "that they will believe we have honestly striven every day and generation to preserve a decent land to live in and a decent form of government to operate under." That was one of the "historic ideas in the life of the nation" that Roosevelt had set out to "clarify" in his presidency, which, he told the *New York Times*, he saw as "pre-eminently a place of moral leadership," citing Washington as his exemplar.[2]

In his first Inaugural Address, Roosevelt set forth his famous invocation of moral qualities associated with Washington in combating fear itself: "confidence . . . thrives only on honesty, on honor, on the sacredness of obligations, on faithful protection, on unselfish performance; without them it cannot live." The thriving of confidence was essential to "recovery" and then to "restoration" to which Roosevelt often referred in his fireside chats, as he had in his "Rendezvous with Destiny" speech. It is noteworthy that Roosevelt chose to use Lincoln's term "recovery" rather than "reconstruction," which had come into use with Herbert Hoover and his Reconstruction Finance Corporation [RFC].[3]

The Washington Monument imparts a moral of recovery and restoration. It does so not only because Washington's career in public life required him to achieve a series of magnificent recoveries and restorations of confidence, but also because it urges the attentive to consider its relationship both to its site and to Mount Vernon, across the Potomac River. The Monument is interesting for what it is not, and might have been—a huge equestrian statue, only distinguishable by its size from the lapidary encomia to other generals strutting and gesturing around the capital city. The makers of the Washington Monument assumed that the public knew that Washington was a general and that he was a president. They chose to provide an invitational symbol instead of a declamatory one, so that people who came into its presence might be encouraged to meditate—think harder—about Washington as the man he was before and after he was a general and a president, to recall that he was bent upon fulfilling commitments as a citizen of the earth before and after his commitments to his nation.

The Monument evokes recollection of the endeavors of Washington's final years at Mount Vernon, as a private person engaged in environmental restoration. That legacy was rediscovered by the New Deal as its leaders were also discovering the symbolic resonances of the Monument they rescued from decay—restoring it physically and ideologically at the same time. We may share in the New Deal's achievement as we too give heed to the circumstances of its creation, including the redemption of its site in the middle of the nineteenth century to the environmental convictions of its re-creators and to the desires expressed by Washington as to how he wanted to be remembered.

The Monument memorializes Washington as a public figure—it is in a public place. It also celebrates the Washington who is buried on his estate at Mount Vernon "without parade or funeral oration" in accordance with his instructions in his will, as "a man close to mother earth" in Franklin Roosevelt's description. James Thomas Flexner, one of Washington's most comprehending biographers, concluded that his burial instructions showed that the "old warrior, the old President, the great hero wanted no marching troops, no solemn dignitaries, no American Westminster Abbey. He wanted to be buried quietly, beside his own relations, on a hillside of the childhood home he had always loved."[4]

Washington's Monument—Mount Vernon

Mount Vernon is an estate, a work of art, and a monument to Washington's efforts in conservation. Washington loved that land. "How much more delightful," he said, "is the task of making improvements on the earth, than all the vainglory which can be acquired from ravaging it, by the most uninterrupted career of conquests." Franklin Roosevelt honored that expression on April 14, 1939, when he spoke at Mount Vernon of Washington's desire to be remembered for his reverence for the earth: "His early training on a plantation, his profession of surveyor, his studies in agriculture and the development of farm lands were never replaced by his outstanding military service . . . [W]hen Mount Vernon came to him by inheritance, here his heart was planted for all time. Here he could talk with his neighbors about . . . improvement . . . , about gristmills on the creeks, . . . about the top soil, which even then had begun to run off to the sea, about the planting of trees, new varieties of food and fodder crops, new breeds of horses and cattle and sheep." Washington could only give it his full attention when he was a private citizen between the Seven Years' War and the Revolution, and during the three years between his retirement and his death in 1799. When he was in command or in office, he instructed his overseers in the management of Mount Vernon.[5]

In 1796, when he was readying himself to leave the presidency and resume the management of his estate, Washington wrote Alexander Hamilton of the usual planters' cycle of heedless exploitation and desolation of the land, followed by migration out of places where plantation agriculture was no longer possible into new places where it could not be long sustained—then new desolation, then new migration, again and again. "It must be obvious to every man who considers the agriculture of this country," wrote Washington, "how miserably defective we are in the management of [our lands] . . . [A] few years more of increased sterility will drive the Inhabitants of the Atlantic States westward for support; whereas if they were taught how to improve the old, instead of going in pursuit of new and productive soils, they would make these acres which now scarcely yield them anything, turn out beneficial to themselves." Lamenting slavery's abuse of the earth, as well as its abuse of people, Washington wrote his nephew Lawrence Lewis on August 4, 1797: "I wish from my soul that the Legislature of this State could see the policy of gradual abolition of slavery."[6]

Washington was too wise to think that would happen soon. He consulted with the British agronomist Arthur Young about the improvement of his estate so that it might become attractive for sale in smaller parcels to "real farmers," the class of yeomen later called "family farmers." His experience with such people in Pennsylvania had taught him that farmers working their own land without slaves would be more likely to diversify their crops and would thus prevent its degradation. Washington's "real farmer" plan was a private anticipation of Lincoln's Homestead Act and of the New Deal's endeavors through Rexford Tugwell to achieve resettlement of independent family farmers and rescue them from tenancy. And Washington's most extensive and ambitious literary work, a forty-thousand-word, illustrated treatise on the rotation of crops, was a private prototype in "visualization and concentration" (in Flexner's description) of the educational materials of the land-grant institutions encouraged in Lincoln's administration by the Morrill Act; this act provided grants to states to establish universities and colleges to give instruction in sound agronomy. Despite all Washington could do, however, few Virginia landowners were persuaded—with few exceptions they continued to keep their land under constant cultivation of soil-exhausting crops and did little to retard erosion.[7]

Washington was not victorious in that last campaign. He was able only to arrest further degeneration of the fertility of the land at Mount Vernon, and after his death in 1799, the erosive damage resumed until his heirs were forced to sell

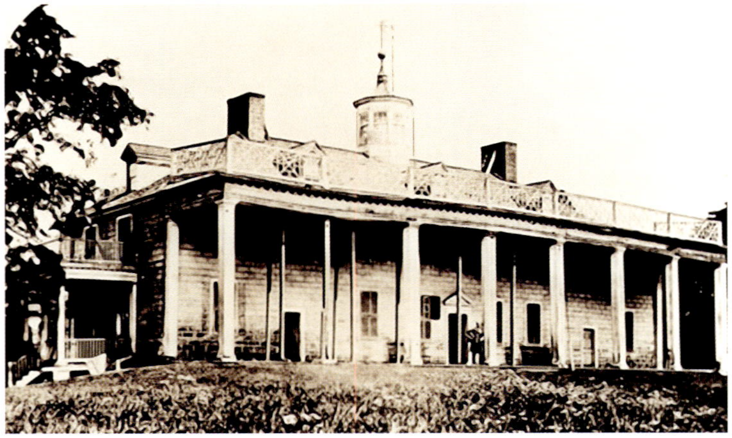

Early stereograph showing Mount Vernon in need of repair.

what was left of his estate in 1860. The purchaser, the Mount Vernon Ladies Association, resumed his conservation program as they restored the Mount Vernon mansion. Elsewhere in the valley of the Potomac, obsessive reliance upon growing corn and tobacco continued to wreak desolation until the New Deal, which took Washington's example seriously. On the day Harold Ickes assumed the leadership of the Public Works Administration, he announced his determination to rehabilitate the Washington Monument, telling the press on May 20, 1934, that he hoped immediately to be "able to finance . . . a thorough cleaning and renovation" so that one might look down "without shame" at its setting. Once that was accomplished, the shame of the neighboring landscape might be addressed, including the rutted track to Mount Vernon upon which many visitors got lost even in daylight. Work began on the George Washington Memorial Parkway. Scaffolding went up on the Monument, and the tennis courts and asphalt roads were taken out of the grounds around it. Today, visitors looking forth from the top of the Washington Monument can observe the wondrous results of stewardship by the New Deal. The thin-soiled tobacco lands to the west and south are now showing signs of recovery. In the foreground lies the once fertile island in the Potomac reduced to eroded desolation by the Mason family's tobacco cultivation, but recovered in the 1930s by the National Park Service, CCC, and WPA. Now reforested, restored, and thriving as the Theodore Roosevelt Island National Memorial, it has become an assembly point for battalions of bicyclists setting forth on the asphalt trail to Mount Vernon, paralleling the George Washington Memorial Parkway between landscapes dedicated to two conservation presidents.[8]

When Franklin Roosevelt assumed management of the estate at Hyde Park in 1910, he knew that it had once produced award-winning crops of corn but now was a dismaying spectacle of gullies and bare clay. Writing in 1937, two years before he made his pilgrimage to Mount Vernon, Roosevelt told the historian and artist Hendrik Willem Van Loon that despite his tree-planting, "I can lime it, cross-plough it, manure it, and treat it with every art known to science, but it has just plain run out." That was true of much of the corn- and wheat-growing land along the Hudson. By the 1930s, that region, like Virginia by the 1830s, had lost much of its farming population. Many of New York's small proprietors, like their counterparts in Virginia a century earlier, had no other recourse than to abandon the "ruined" land and start again "beyond the mountains." Under the auspices of the New Deal, Eudora Welty wrote accounts of how painful this ripping up and moving out of the South continued to be in the twentieth century, although advances in soil conservation under the New Deal made it more likely that "cultivation" would replace "locomotion"—as Abraham Lincoln said he, too, hoped would happen.[9]

Washington, Man and Monument

George Washington was himself a work of art. He created a man-monument requiring no classical references like those later sculptors and painters imposed upon their images of him. In Robert Sherwood's terms, Washington "personalized" and "dramatized" the nobility, steadfast courage, dignity, and strength required of him as general, constitution-maker, and president. Washington made of himself the embodiment, as well, of the restorative energy he brought to his service of the earth in his post-presidential years. The English historian of American politics and art, Marcus Cunliffe, applied Sherwood's concept to Washington as "man and monument," showing how he became fully useful to his country through the art of personalized policy, managing the affects of how he stood in public, walked, rode a horse, talked, and shaped his countenance. Having mastered dancing, horsemanship, and clothing, he also prepared himself for selection to lead an army by having himself painted to emulate the figure of a British officer in a portrait he admired. Even when his army was in full retreat, he stage-managed his white campaign tent as his power center and power symbol. It went up every night, in the best and worst of circumstances. Using no more stagecraft than the producer-actor David Garrick might have used for any traveling production, Washington came to personify recovery as he led the army back from its humiliations and led his country from the embarrassments of its first sputtering experiment in self-government under the Articles of Confederation.[10]

As he presided over the writing of the Constitution, wrote Sherwood, "Washington personified the ideal of federal union. The Founding Fathers established the office of President with the knowledge that Washington was there to fill it. They fitted the office to his tremendous measurements." Sherwood's judicious use of the term "measurements" reminds us that public necessity required Washington to pay more attention to the tailoring of his military uniform and his presidential quasi-uniform than has any subsequent commander-in-chief or president. To dramatize and personalize his commanding roles, when it was not at all clear that there was much that was substantial behind him, he had to dress the part. It was much in his country's interest that he give confidence to a rag-tag army and a parvenu government. Franklin Roosevelt had broadcast radio; Washington had tailoring, tent-making, oil portraiture, sculptured likenesses, flags, trumpets, and drums. In a pre-electronic age, he put the arts to work by welcoming to Mount Vernon portrait painters, sculptors, and even contrivers of life-casts with their suffocating plaster. He seems to have had infinite patience for posterity's agents: the sculptor Auguste Houdon was his house guest for two weeks, and he welcomed extended stays by unknown artists such as Benjamin Henry Latrobe, who would come for tea and might stay for a week or so. Charles Willson Peale painted him seven times from life after his first visit to Mount Vernon in 1772. While Peale served in the Continental army, he was a one-man Office of War Information, producing nineteen versions of a military Washington portrait before it went into lithographed versions, some of which were still hanging in remote post offices in the Midwest in the 1930s.

In 1795 Peale's seventeen-year-old son Rembrandt Peale was at Mount Vernon, making his own first version of Washington, with his father painting beside him "to calm my nerves" and Gilbert Stuart standing by to paint on alternate days to those assigned to the two Peales. The apparently tireless subject thus provided material for seventy painted copies by Stuart and ten by the younger Peale, who even then was not fully satisfied. In 1824 Rembrandt Peale's twice-life-sized portrait of Washington, embellished by symbols of Roman deities and bearing the inscription "Pater Patriae," went on display in the U.S. Capitol on Washington's birthday and became so evocative of the pre–Civil War, imperial pride of "Young America" that public demand required nearly eighty copies. Peale "used the resulting publicity to lobby Congress, unsuccessfully, for a commission to paint an equestrian portrait of General Washington." His lack of success with the Congress may be attributed to those who knew that the father of his country disliked being discussed with references to Romans more exalted than the citizen-farmer-general Cincinnatus, and had explicitly opposed equestrian statuary in his honor since he scotched that notion in 1783 when it was proposed by the Continental Congress.[11]

Washington was clear that he did not wish to be thought of as imperial in his pretensions nor to be enveloped in what he called "vainglory." He chose to have himself painted in retirement by Gilbert Stuart in the simple black velvet suit of a squire, with his right hand extended as if to greet a visitor. Here was the man who made Latrobe feel at ease in 1796, the country gentleman who could talk with a young artist "with ease and attention," laughing "heartily" at "good humored" jokes—some of them Latrobe's and some his own. In 1800 Latrobe dismissed the notion of commemorating such a man with any statue, equestrian or otherwise, as "folly."[12]

If not some huge statue of a general on horseback, then what should be an appropriate monument for a general, a president, and a conservationist? In one of history's generous moments, the opportunity to make that recommendation fell to George Perkins Marsh, who in 1865 published his masterpiece *Man and Nature.* As soon as his role was recognized, Marsh began his effort to induce his fellow citizens to rescue the site of the Washington Monument from the squalor into which it, like the Mount Vernon estate, had fallen. And the first systematic American advocate of active conservation was not compelled to act alone, for the Army Corps of Engineers, which was to do the monument-building, was in the hands of a sympathetic general, and Marsh could call upon the aid of Hiram Powers and Larkin Goldsmith Mead, two sculptors experienced in symbolic expression of moral ideas. They were triumphantly successful in honoring Washington's ways of thinking—and writing—as the Mount Vernon restoration was also under way. By 1930 a new generation, led by Franklin Roosevelt, came to Mount Vernon and to the Washington Monument, imbued with Washington's conviction that humans have created most environmental problems and humans must find means to make matters better—precepts stated by Marsh in an injunction that man must "become a moral agent; to build where he had destroyed, to replace where he had stolen."[13]

Marsh and his colleagues were able to make that more likely by seeing to the restoration of the site of the monument, and then by placing upon it a monumental symbol appropriate to Washington—as moral agent. The site itself was symbolic: it was a disgrace typical of a disgraceful national condition. In 1850, Henry Adams could make his way to it only by shooing aside the cattle roaming the site and finding his way past the piles of dung they had left along their paths to the tidal creek that bordered the site. Adams's great-grandfather, the president succeeding Washington, had once safely bathed in "the Tiber," as it was called, but it had since become a fetid open sewer down which passed the wastes of a third of the city. Sheds on the monument grounds housed a slaughterhouse and rendering plant turning those cattle into beef and hides, amid racks used to cure tobacco. A recent study of the site states that "the Monument Grounds [had] acquired names such as 'Beef Depot,' the 'Cattle Meadow,' and the 'Washington National Cattle Yard' . . . the buildings were 'surrounded by offal rotting two or three feet deep.'" The stench carried for a half mile, bearing on the wind testimony to that sordid epoch in the nation's life in which, wrote the art critic, urban theorist, and conservationist Lewis Mumford in 1931, man "had played the part of an irresponsible, destructive being—as he had, to his own misfortune, in classic times." Marsh was Mumford's instructor in what had been learned "in classic times" and long forgotten—to be rediscovered again by the New Deal's chief exponent of Marshian doctrine, Walter Lowdermilk.[14]

Adams described what he saw of the desolated shores of the Potomac in terms like those used by Marsh and Lowdermilk of the shores of the Mediterranean: all seemed to "belong to the dead, and not to the living." That disgrace affronted Marsh and all other seekers after "permanence of . . . relations to the fields, the meadows, and the pastures, to the rain and the dews of heaven, to the springs and rivulets with which it waters the earth." In the midst of the squalor stood the ruined site and the shambles about the failed monument—now a symbol of the nation's failure to build a memorial to a founder who had given much of the energy of his last years to reconciliation with nature. At the center of that desolation was the stub of a monument left unfinished in 1860 by the parsimony of the preceding two generations, whose indifference was expressed in the casual strewing of marble blocks amid the offal. Robert Mills's original proposal would have had that stub emerge from a Babylonian base surrounded by a Greek temple, housing Washington in a Roman toga and seated in a Greek chariot drawn by Arabian steeds driven by an Etruscan Winged Victory. Marsh could take some satisfaction in not having to demolish that "sort of temple-like excrescence from the base." Mills's stub was there, however, and Marsh's Yankee frugality ordained that it establish the height of any obelisk to be built upon it—according to what he had learned to be proper proportions.[15]

Mills had accommodated the taste of America's imperial age of the 1830s and 1840s, when bronze equestrian generals were set gesturing toward victories in public parks, and generals were being honored in most of the paintings purchased by Congress, such as those by John Trumbull (1756–1843): the *Surrender of Cornwallis at Yorktown* (1817–1820), the *Surrender of Burgoyne at Saratoga* (1817–1821), and the *Resignation of Washington at Annapolis* (1824). Only one presented a relatively peaceful topic: the *Signing of the Declaration of Independence* (1818). As Marsh's biographer, David Lowenthal, wrote: "Much art commissioned for the U.S. Capitol was blatantly jingoist, American Manifest Destiny lording it over vanquished lesser breeds." Mills's design for the Washington Monument had proclaimed a bellicose imperial vision like Emanuel Leutze's *Westward the Course of the Empire*, which still presents to visitors to the Capitol an allegory of Indian replacement, in which crossing the Appalachians to fight Indians and acquire an empire was the Jacksonian equivalent of crossing the Delaware to establish a republic.[16]

Marsh, Powers, and Mead

After the Civil War a new national mood was represented by Marsh and Powers. Like Lincoln, they had opposed the military adventures of the slave-owning and Indian-exterminating Jacksonians. Having argued against the imperial war against Mexico, they rallied to the Union, and shared the nation's sorrow in the terrible price paid for victory in the Civil War. "Public art in the United States," wrote Powers, should not "glorify martial force and victory in battle." Instead, "it was the artist's sacred duty, especially if American . . . to

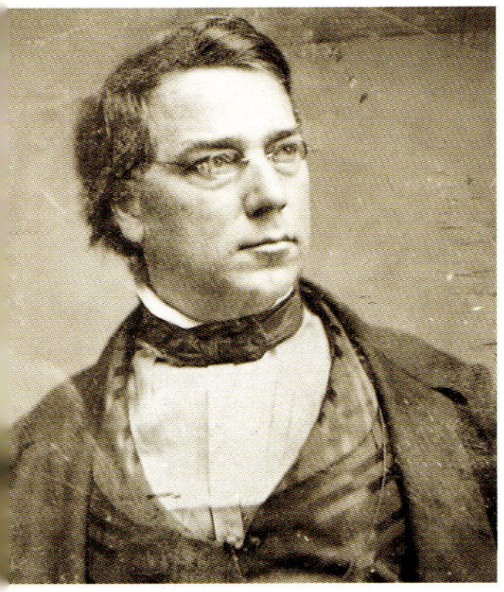

"George Perkins Marsh"
Mathew Brady, c. 1860

celebrate amity and promote peace . . . [rather than] an armed conqueror—for surely ours is not a military people—our mission is to persuade, and not coerce mankind." No wonder Marsh and Powers agreed that Mills's proposal for bullying sculptures to accompany the Washington Monument was "highly objectionable." Powers was drawn therefore to that other Washington who had sought "to persuade" his contemporaries toward "amity." Nor did Mills's bellicose trumpery commend itself to Mead. His tomb for Abraham Lincoln in Springfield, Illinois, was guarded by squads of sculptured soldiery, and for a time he suggested something similar for Washington. But he had designed his Lincoln tomb in 1865, immediately after Lincoln's death, while many thought of him as commander-in-chief, and he soon abandoned the notion of putting figures of men or horses around a Washington Monument.[17]

As Marsh, Powers, and Mead began in the 1870s to provide instruction to the Corps of Engineers for a new design for the Washington Monument, the site required a massive effort toward recovery and restoration. Marsh knew that the man to whom that monument was to be dedicated had worked at conservation up to the day he suffered his fatal illness. Marsh himself had grown up in Vermont's overgrazed and over-lumbered landscape. After Dartmouth College and a career as a lawyer, artist, inventor, Vermont Congressman, and foe to railroad rapacity, he became Minister to Turkey in 1849. After returning to Vermont, he was so effective a campaigner for Abraham Lincoln that he was made Minister to Garibaldi's new Italian government in 1861 and held that post for more than twenty years. In both of his ambassadorial posts he toured the eroded shores of the Mediterranean and described in essays and dispatches how "destructive man" had degraded places revered as seats of learning in classic times. Sicily had once been forested. Desolate North Africa had once been graced with fields of grain. By 1860, Italy had become a sad spectacle of loss and shame. Marsh integrated these Mediterranean experiences with what he knew of New England and with what had been reported by the explorers of the American West, explaining to his countrymen that their homeland was unlikely to tolerate further abuse without permanent damage. Marsh's literary art warned of dust bowls, predicting that they would bring the high, dry North American plains to the condition of Spain, Palestine, and North Africa, as, in fact, they did. Seven decades later they were photographed and filmed by the New Deal.

When he began his consideration of what might be a fitting monument to George Washington in the 1860s, Marsh shared his environmental lessons and concepts of public sculpture with Mead and Powers. Both had experience in conveying messages about public policy through symbolic art. Powers was celebrated as the creator of *The Greek Slave*, an antislavery manifesto in white marble and the most famous political sculpture of the age. It depicted a "chained female nude," a white woman in white alabaster, ostensibly a captive taken by the Turks in the recent Greek war of independence, but in everyone's minds, a slave, of any race, anywhere. *The Greek Slave* advanced the cause of emancipation by calling attention to the horrors of slavery imposed upon anyone, white or black—a disagreeable message for those seeking to justify the "institution" by arguing that dark-skinned people were born to be slaves. The power of that image cost Powers his grandest commission, *America*, intended for the Capitol but denied its place because *The Greek Slave* had infuriated the slave owners who were in charge of the building until the victory of the party of Lincoln in 1860. Powers's statues of Franklin and Jefferson were, finally, installed in the Capitol and his *America* was shipped to the U.S. with Lincoln's encouragement, only to be lost in a warehouse fire in 1865.

Thanks to Marsh, Mead was famous also as a creator of conspicuous sculptural symbols. After a fire destroyed the Vermont State House, Marsh convinced the state legislature to rebuild its dome in the shape of the United States Capitol and to give it, like the Capitol, a sculptural climax—but not one with military overtones. Instead, Vermont was provided a statue of *Ceres*, the Roman goddess of good environmental practice.[18]

So—what would Marsh, Powers, and Mead believe to be appropriate for Washington, the founder of American conservation? Horatio Greenough had carved from white marble a huge Washington as Jove, and had thereby embarrassed those who had known that Washington had made plain his desire to go to his grave as a man dedicated not to personal glory but to redemptive husbandry. Marsh was imbued with the same passion even as a youth in erosion-ravaged Vermont. That passion grew stronger as he traveled under the unrelenting sun along the once fertile fringes of the Nile Valley, observing and measuring many ancient obelisks, some lying prostrate under the unrelenting sun, some still vertical but half engulfed by sand as brown as seeds of grain but sterile. The indelible lesson of his observations was that desolation may come after improvidence, and sterility may ensue even where there had once been flourishing agriculture. Abandoned obelisks showed that Man had failed Nature, each a harsh but necessary lesson. Might an obelisk not be made both instructive and hopeful? Marsh measured the proportions of obelisks as he recorded his thoughts about how the environmental history of the Mediterranean lands might impart lessons to his own countrymen.

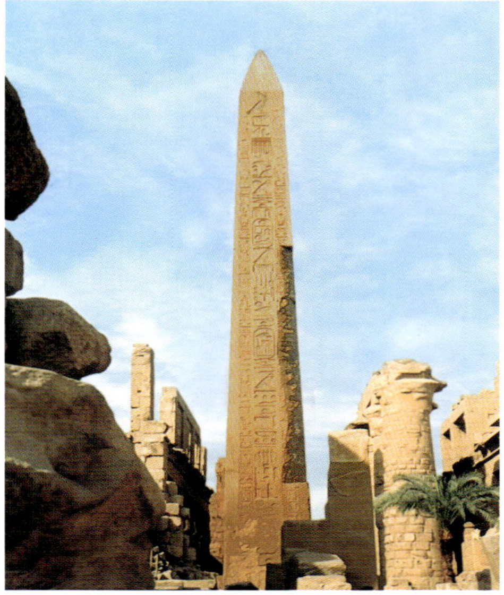

Obelisk at Karnak

In the fifth century, the city was sacked by the Vandals, who failed to maintain the irrigation system that had sustained the grain-growing region around it. In 535, when conquered by the Byzantines, it was still a city; a century later it was briefly repopulated before being sacked by the Berbers in the seventh century; they wholly destroyed the irrigation works and the city was abandoned, partially preserved under sand.

For a pharaoh, an obelisk might be only a statement of pride and power, intended to overawe but not to exhort. If associated with George Washington it might bespeak majesty and at the same time impart a moral imperative. Washington often urged intergenerational stewardship of the land in words very similar to those of Marsh: "Man has too long forgotten that the earth was given to him for usufruct alone, not for consumption, still less for profligate waste." There had been much haste in Washington's time. Land seemed plentiful, opposition weak, and labor—cheap. Few of his contemporaries were willing to pause to give heed either to him or to the damage they were inflicting, since they could buy a new acre more cheaply than they could restore an old one. The ill-effects of their profligacy were becoming manifest in Marsh's generation.[19]

Marsh, Powers, and Mead designed a Washington Monument as an abstract form but also a form so exotic as to require meditation if it were to induce an observer to recapture the set of associations with Washington that were in the minds of those who designed it. It is an Egyptian obelisk—without the encrustations and inscriptions the ancient Egyptians associated with their obelisks. Marsh and his colleagues sought to make sure that the monument would not suffer from intrusive transitory propaganda. Therefore, they permitted no sculptured groups around it to invoke the topical, or limit the range of associations that its pure abstract form draws forth. Thanks to their wisdom, the monument speaks for itself as great music speaks for itself. The Washington Monument says what it has to say, unmediated. General Dwight D. Eisenhower was justified in his view that "there is more of . . . history to be felt and understood in a lonely, graceful column rising against the sky . . . than there is in all the descriptive matter that was ever written on the subject."[20]

Marsh and his colleagues were not seeking to create another symbolic invocation of Washington's Olympian gravitas. The soaring obelisk they designed has very different implications. For Marsh especially, as for Franklin Roosevelt, Washington was a son of the earth as well as the father of his country. On February 9, 1879, Marsh wrote his kinsman and political ally, Senator George Edmunds of Vermont, that "by a letter from the sculptor Mead to Mrs. Marsh, I understand that the main feature of the Washington Monument is to be an obelisk of great height," and staked out his claim to be an expert on the form: "I believe I have not only seen but sketched every existing genuine—that is, Egyptian—obelisk, for no other can fairly be said to be genuine. The obelisk is not an arbitrary structure which everyone is free to erect with such form and proportions as suit his taste and convenience, but its objects, form, and proportions were fixed by the usage of thousands of years; they satisfy every cultivated eye, and I hold it an esthetical crime to depart from them."[21]

On March 31 Edmunds forwarded Marsh's letter to General Thomas Lincoln Casey of the Corps of Engineers, who was to direct the project. Edmunds endorsed Marsh's views; "our minister at Rome," he wrote, was qualified to settle "the Washington Monument question . . . [since he was] among the most learned and accomplished of those in any country who have given the subject of architecture and monumental art attention." Thereafter Casey was able to assure all who inquired that "the proportions of the parts of this obelisk are in exact accordance with the classic proportions of parts of this style of architecture, as determined after careful research by the Hon. George P. Marsh, American minister at Rome."[22]

Mills's incomplete stub might now be incorporated economically as well as appropriately into a symbolic obelisk. Marsh, a man of poetic genius, had made possible through art a meditation upon Washington's role as a hero who would look to the sun, but remain close to the earth; whatever bold new achievements might be accomplished by the nation of which Washington was the first president, they would be grounded in a respect for nature. That message the New Deal found completely compatible, and, furthermore, actionable.

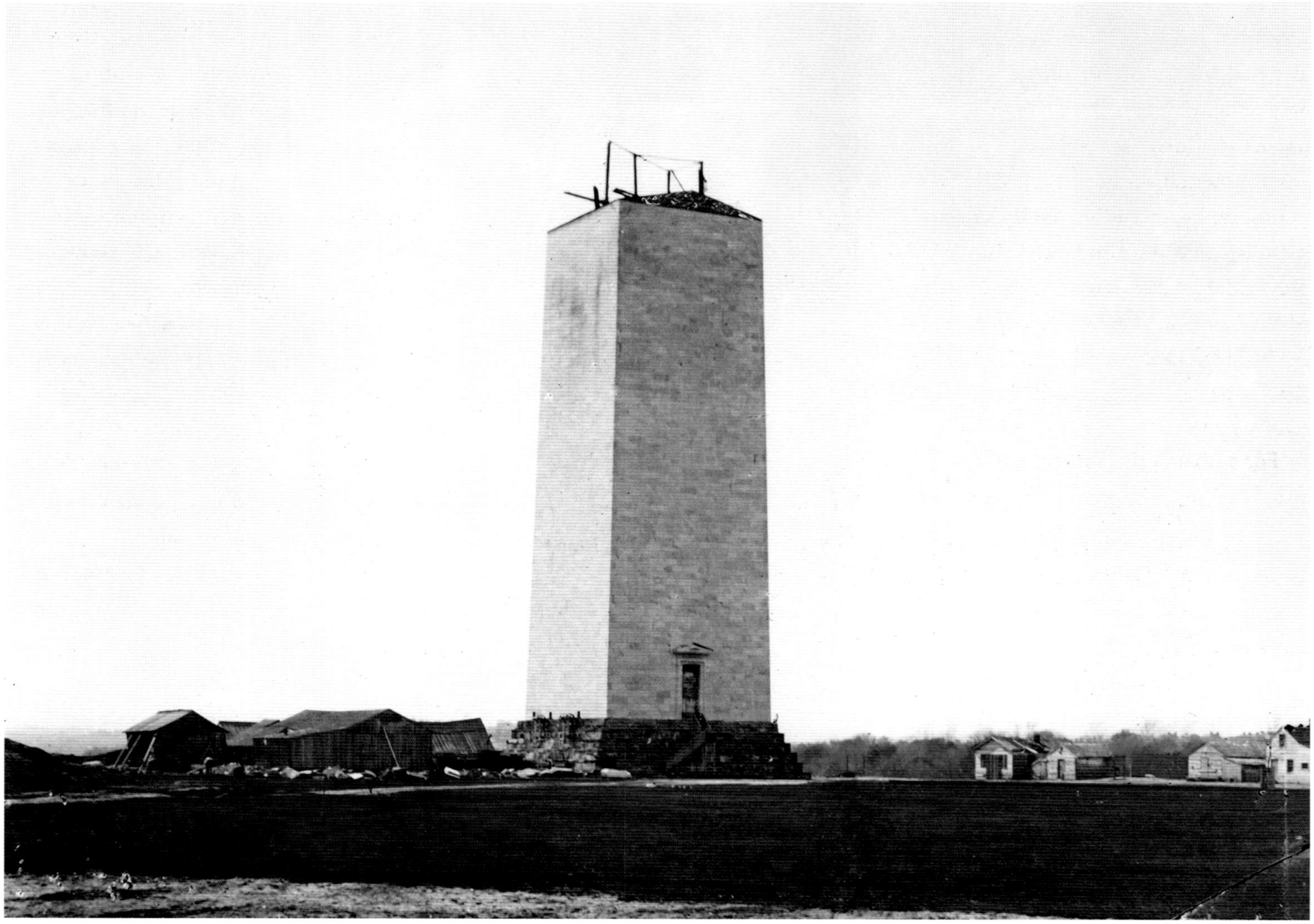

The stump of the Washington Monument under construction

By the time Franklin Roosevelt visited Mount Vernon, the example of Washington and the doctrines of Marsh were firmly embedded in New Deal programs managed by Harold Ickes, Rexford Tugwell, Hugh Bennett, and Walter Lowdermilk—the programs explained to the American people by Pare Lorentz and by the photographers managed by Roy Stryker.

George Marsh had predicted the desolation described and pictured by New Deal writers and visual artists—some of whom, like Eudora Welty, were both. The work of Marsh's life was making more likely the stability that the New Deal began to make possible through resettlement and the efforts of such soil scientists as Bennett and Lowdermilk under the aegis of Rexford Tugwell. At Columbia in the 1920s, Stryker and Tugwell had shown how to use art to illustrate—and stimulate—environmental action. In the 1930s, photography, including Welty's documentary pictures, illustrated among the New Deal's work that of the Soil Erosion Service (Soil Conservation Service) led by Bennett and Lowdermilk, as it published illustrated manuals for crop rotation, providing modern graphics as Washington had provided his own sketches for his treatise on the subject. The purpose of the Service was the same as his: to make the work in the fields "less harassing to those who labor and more beneficial to those who employ them." In the 1860s Marsh had renewed the struggle for a "stability of existing arrangements and accommodations" in human interaction with the natural world. For Lowdermilk and Bennett in the 1930s, that meant the achievement of "a permanent agriculture." Today's term is "sustainability"—for which a fitting symbol still is a great, stable, soaring obelisk set where once there had been flux and desolation.[23]

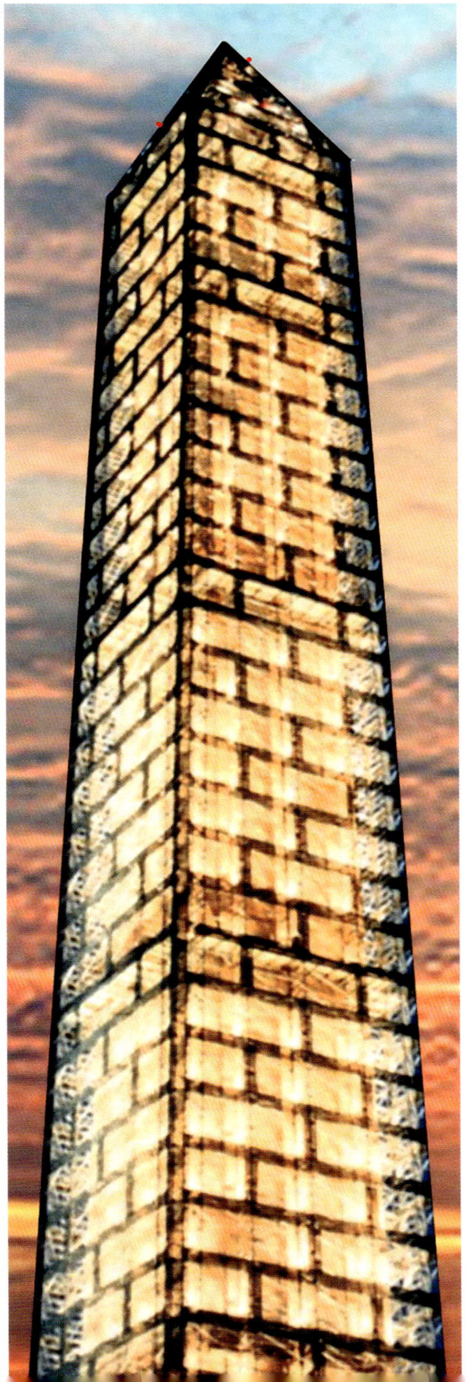

The history of conservation theory in America had begun with the environmental awakening of the early eighteenth century to which Jonathan Edwards gave a voice and a basis in science. In the next generation, George Washington made environmental theory practical by adding to its message the specifically agricultural science developed by British agronomists such as Arthur Young. Washington's ethic-and-practicum was reasserted in the Age of Lincoln by George Marsh, reanimated in the Progressive Era by Theodore Roosevelt, Gifford Pinchot, and the elderly Carl Schurz, and asserted again in the 1930s by the New Deal. All along, the arts were allies in the cause, calling focused attention to what might otherwise be only dimly perceived. Then, with recognition, restorative action became possible. Even Pinchot, no natural showman, came to employ photographs and slides to make his points—as he did on behalf of Governor Franklin Roosevelt's conservation programs in New York in the 1920s.[24]

The Washington Monument remains an invitation to pause to consider its context, its origin, and its intended message. At Mount Rushmore, Franklin Roosevelt showed how fruitful such a pause might become. The presence of a symbol open to broad interpretation in Washington City elicits both understanding and action. The memory of Washington inspires such meditation upon Marsh's "great question . . . whether man is of nature or above her."[25]

The history of the Monument enables us to understand why Harold Ickes was so

The Washington Monument was restored in the 1990s, clad in scaffolding designed by Michael Graves (a rendering is shown here).

eager to rehabilitate it, and to tell the press that he hoped not only to be "able to finance . . . a thorough cleaning and renovation" of the symbolic sculpture itself but also to undertake sufficient conservation work in the neighborhood so that one might look down "without shame" at its setting. Ickes began that work as, according to Lewis Mumford, "the moral" of *Man and Nature* was reappearing in "the conservation movement and the parks movement," and was "never so important before as they are in our own day." The conservationists of the generation that redesigned and completed the monument were imbued with the same spirit as Washington himself, which is why the work of art they created to serve his memory became so important to kindred spirits in the New Deal. The restored estate at Mount Vernon and the restored Washington Monument were symbols of good stewardship. In 1937 Harold Ickes bought a version of the Mount Vernon mansion on a property of 250 acres in Montgomery County, Maryland, to which President Roosevelt often drove when the CCC-redeemed slopes of the Catoctins seemed too distant. On his "Headwaters Farm," Ickes began his own work in the art of landscape restoration, like those undertaken by George Washington, by Franklin Roosevelt, and by Henry Morgenthau, and as advocated by George Marsh and Walter Lowdermilk.

Marsh has his own monument, a handsome house built on the property where he was born in Woodstock, Vermont. His home has been twice expanded and is now the centerpiece of a restored landscape from which the scars of fire, overgrazing, and erosion have long ago disappeared. Its recovered woodlands and experimental forests of pine, larch, and fir make it a conservation park as Mount Vernon is a conservation park, although in a different climate with different topography and a different kind of ownership. The house is now presented as it was when it was dedicated as a national park in 1998, after remodeling by Frederick Billings and later by Laurance and Mary Rockefeller. The Marsh-Billings-Rockefeller National Historical Park in Woodstock, Vermont, is a counterpart and complement to Franklin Roosevelt's Hyde Park National Historic Site and to Mount Vernon. Yet for Roosevelt, Washington, and Marsh, the greater legacy is the entire national park system, together with the national forest system, and every acre that bears the beneficial effects of the agency that in the New Deal was first called the Soil Erosion Service. Truly, Rexford Tugwell, Roy Stryker, Hugh Bennett, and Walter Lowdermilk have earned somewhere a tablet like that placed upon the grave of Sir Christopher Wren in Westminster Abbey: "Lector, si monumentum requiris, Circumspice" ("Reader, if you seek his monument, look around you.")

The Franklin D. Roosevelt Memorial occupies a quiet corner of Potomac Park in Washington. It does not call attention to itself. On its walls are quotations from some of Roosevelt's best-known speeches, and a very effective sculptural summoning of the man himself, at human scale, in a wheelchair. Eastward through the foliage and high on the Capitol dome is Thomas Crawford's *Freedom*. Roosevelt needed nothing grand in marble, no outsized statuary. At Mount Rushmore, he showed his understanding of the dramatic and personalizing possibilities of very large works of art, but he did not seek to have any made to dramatize himself. His only request was for a simple marble slab, with a brief inscription to be placed outside the National Archives.

Chapter Nine

Hugh Bennett, Walter Lowdermilk, and the Eleventh Commandment

"Walter Lowdermilk . . . is the man out here with the grey matter."
(Rexford Tugwell to President Franklin Roosevelt, according to Inez Lowdermilk)

"We weren't beaten. But all we had to fear 'is fear itself.' . . . And people–sure, they were downtrodden, beaten, but . . . damn it all, if you . . . look at some of the pictures . . . some of those guys said, 'We still can carry on.'"
(Roy Stryker interviewed in 1964)

THE AMERICAN CONSERVATION MOVEMENT began in the Age of Lincoln. The New Deal acknowledged the prototypical roles in that period of George Perkins Marsh, Carl Schurz, Frederick Law Olmsted, and Lincoln himself. Franklin Roosevelt's associates respected George Washington's earlier efforts on behalf of the earth and sorrowed with him in his disappointments in failing to convince more than a few of his contemporaries to heed the lessons of his written work and his example. Yet the thinking of such writers as Lewis Mumford and such practitioners as Rexford Tugwell, Hugh Bennett, and Walter Lowdermilk owed a direct debt to the legislation brought forward by Lincoln and to the scientific inquiries of Marsh and his philosophy of active conservation. Bennett and Lowdermilk were grounded in Marsh's research and his recommendations.

Even in the nineteenth century, when the only systematic efforts toward soil conservation had come from Horace Cleveland's advocacy of planting trees in the West, Mumford credited Marsh with getting Cleveland started. In Lincoln's administration, wrote Mumford, "Marsh's book . . . marked a turning point in public policy; the National Government ceded Yosemite, on condition that it be maintained as a public park . . . Yellowstone was set aside . . . the Sequoia Park . . . established, and the dedication of wild lands to forestry and recreation went on with gathering acceleration." Before that, public land policy had been a promiscuous privatizing of the public domain that Mumford called "disastrous."[1]

Cleveland, Schurz, and Olmsted became the great nineteenth-century expositors of Marsh's doctrines. President Rutherford Hayes made Schurz Secretary of the Interior in 1877, with a single ranger to police the Yellowstone. Schurz recruited General Philip Sheridan to help prevent lumbering in parks and in forest reserves where the trees were old and large, brought a forest reserve act to enactment by Congress on the tenth try, and had the satisfaction of seeing a million acres go into the first reserve (the Shoshone). Ickes had a portrait of Schurz placed outside the door to the office of the Secretary of the Interior. A portrait of Ickes has been placed next to that of Schurz during the tenure of all subsequent Secretaries familiar with the history of the department. The legacy of New Deal policy is also commemorated in portraits, but not portraits of the great and famous. It appears in the faces of humble people in the films of Pare Lorentz and in the photographs commissioned by Rexford Tugwell and Roy Stryker that rallied the public to support the work of Hugh Bennett and Walter Lowdermilk.

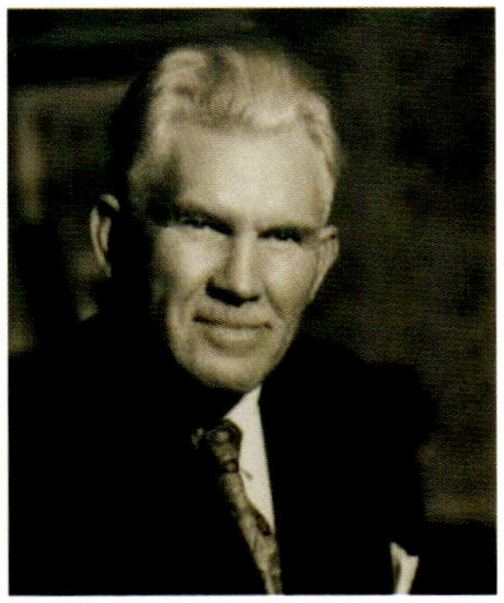

Walter C. Lowdermilk

Bennett and Lowdermilk were two North Carolina country boys who in the first days of the New Deal founded the Soil Erosion Service in the Department of the Interior.† When Bennett was young, "he rode a mule to school using a fertilizer sack for a saddle. Sometimes when the mules were needed in the field, the brothers would walk to school and back, a distance of seven miles." After graduating from the University of North Carolina in 1903, Bennett went to work as a soil surveyor for the Agriculture Department's Bureau of Soils at one thousand dollars a year. Maynard Cook, his biographer, asserted that Bennett "liked the work from the start, particularly because it was about 95 percent outdoor activity. He loved the land—the smell of it, the feel of it, its beauty, its variety." He also loved rallying public support. To the wonderment of his fellow soil scientists, his byline began to appear in *Country Gentleman*, *Scientific Monthly*, *The North American Review*, *American Game*, *Nature*, and *Farm Journal*. Bennett became famous for his term "sheet erosion," as the co-author of *Soil Erosion: A National Menace*, and as a storyteller.[2]

> "Bill McClendon of Bishopville, South Carolina, and I were stirring through the woods down there in middle Virginia when we noticed two pieces of land, side by side but sharply different in their soil quality. The slope of both areas was the same. The underlying rock was the same. There was indisputable evidence that the two pieces had been identical in soil makeup. But the soil of one piece was mellow, loamy, and moist enough even in dry weather to dig into with our bare hands. We noticed this area was wooded, well covered with forest litter, and had never been cultivated. The other area, right beside it, was clay, hard and almost like rock in dry weather. It had been cropped a long time. We figured both areas had been the same originally and that the clay of the cultivated area could have reached the surface only through the process of rainwash—that is, the gradual removal, with every heavy rain, of a thin sheet of topsoil. It was just so much muddy water running off the land after rains. And, by contrast we noticed the almost perfect protection nature provided against erosion with her dense cover of forest."[3]

Lowdermilk was fifteen years older than Bennett. His family had joined the rural trek from North Carolina to Arizona, where he attended the University of Arizona before a Rhodes Scholarship took him to Oxford, and then to Germany. His religious principles led him to go to work assisting Herbert Hoover's Commission on Relief in Belgium after World War I. After doing erosion research in Montana, he went to China with his wife, Inez Marks, a Methodist missionary and teacher. China was in the grip of an erosion-produced famine so dramatic that Lowdermilk was able to add confirmation on a grand scale to Bennett's insights, and "the full and fateful significance of soil erosion was burned into . . . [his] consciousness."[4]

In *Man and Nature* George Marsh had written of the devastation of the ancient grain-growing regions of Europe and North Africa. Lowdermilk photographed these scenes and applied to them conclusions drawn from the circumstances he encountered in China. He saw abandoned Chinese walled cities evidencing "former grandeur" teetering along the edges of the "colossal erosion" of gullies six hundred feet deep, amid sandy wastes left where once were forests and cultivated fields. Amid similar wastes in North Africa lay columns and obelisks, providing symbols of human improvidence to eyes trained in what Lowdermilk called "agricultural archaeology." Lowdermilk's accounts of the Chinese experience confirmed Mumford's references to European "classic times," when Seneca had compared the erosion of the overplanted and overgrazed landscapes lying beyond the walls of the Romans' sacred groves to the fertility within those walls.

Meanwhile, Bennett had published an illustrated report on 136,000 acres of formerly cultivated land ruined by erosion in Fairfield County, South Carolina. A decade before Roy Stryker's FSA photography, Bennett's report included photographs of steep hillsides that had been cleared, planted to cotton, and had become as deeply eroded as Lowdermilk's Shansi Province. Bennett also offered images showing how a

†As noted earlier, in 1935 it became the Soil Conservation Service, and in 2008 the Natural Resources Conservation Service.

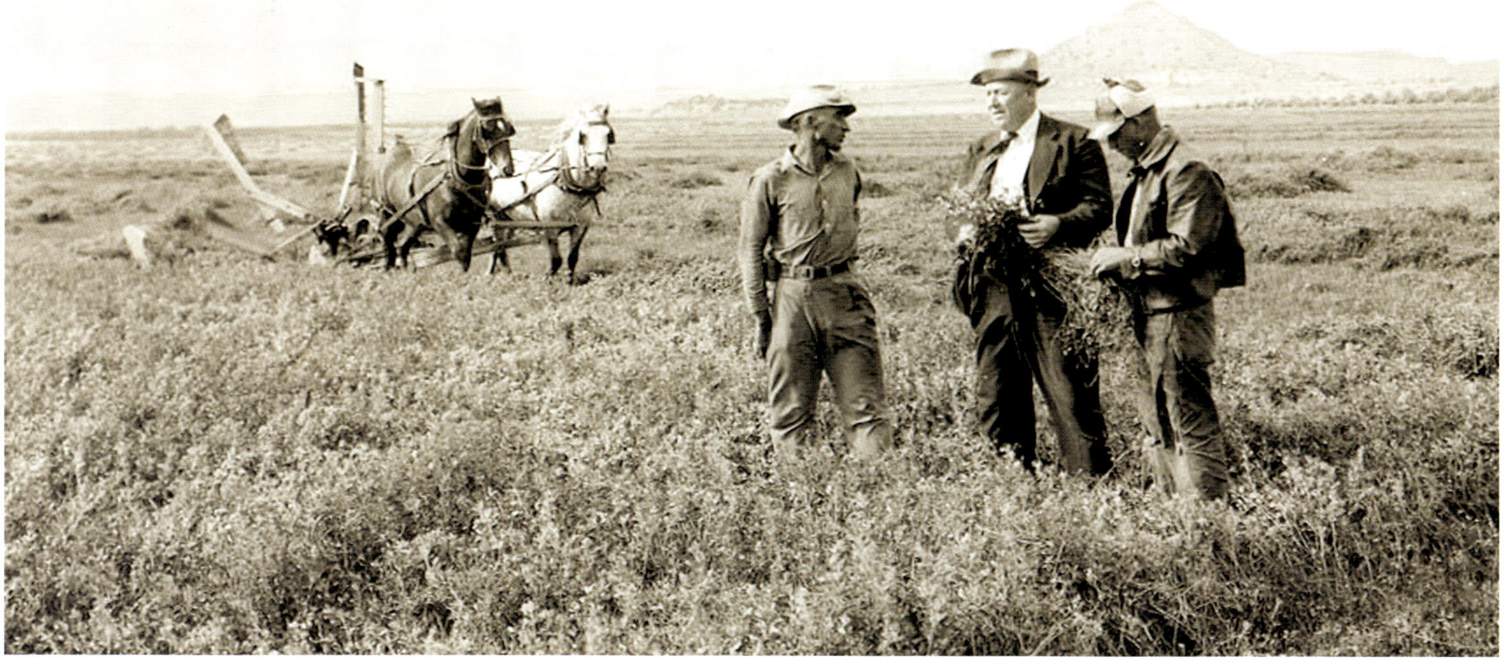

Hugh Bennett with Oklahoma Farmers

field might be reclaimed by contour cultivation and terracing, convincing Congress to add soil erosion research to the Agriculture Department budget in 1929. That appropriation provided funds for two erosion study stations, which soon became ten, among them Lowdermilk's in the San Dimas watershed of California, where he had settled after the Chinese Communist uprising in 1927.[5]

In 1933 the New Deal sent two hundred "CCC boys" to help him. Inez Lowdermilk reported that "many scientists and government people came to see what he was doing." Among them was Rexford Tugwell. Inez Lowdermilk reported that while he was inspecting the work "the President phoned Tugwell, asking if he recommended that the job of Chief of the new Soil Conservation Service be given to Hugh Bennett. 'Do so only if you appoint Walter Lowdermilk as Associate Chief. He is the man out here with the grey matter,'" was Tugwell's reply according to Mrs. Lowdermilk, who added that "President Roosevelt personally asked for Walter's immediate release from the Forest Service."[6]

Roosevelt also intervened personally to put soil science to work in aid of John Collier's Indian programs. Earlier leaders of the Bureau of Indian Affairs had dumped fifteen thousand sheep and goats on the Navajo Reservation. These voracious exotic animals had increased to more than a million by 1933, until most of the Reservation's once grassy sixteen million acres came to look like Attica or Sicily. Collier's eldest son was his assistant in the Bureau of Indian Affairs, and a younger son was one of Tugwell's and Stryker's photographers. The three Colliers asked for help for the Navajo and for the Sioux on their equally devastated Rosebud and Pine Ridge Reservations, on the understanding that Bennett adopt Collier's hypothesis that erosion work should be done with "local leadership among the Indians themselves." An "Erosion Control Station" was established among the Navajo after the Tribal Council declared that "unless sound plans for the control of this erosion are developed and carried into practice without further delay, the greater portion of the reservation will be damaged beyond repair." CCC crews were summoned to start fencing, and Stryker's photographers arrived soon afterward to start recording the results. Collier assured Congress that he had "developed the highest regard for [Bennett] . . . He sees the matter steadily and whole, and is not an engineering fanatic nor . . . an animal husbandry fanatic."[7]

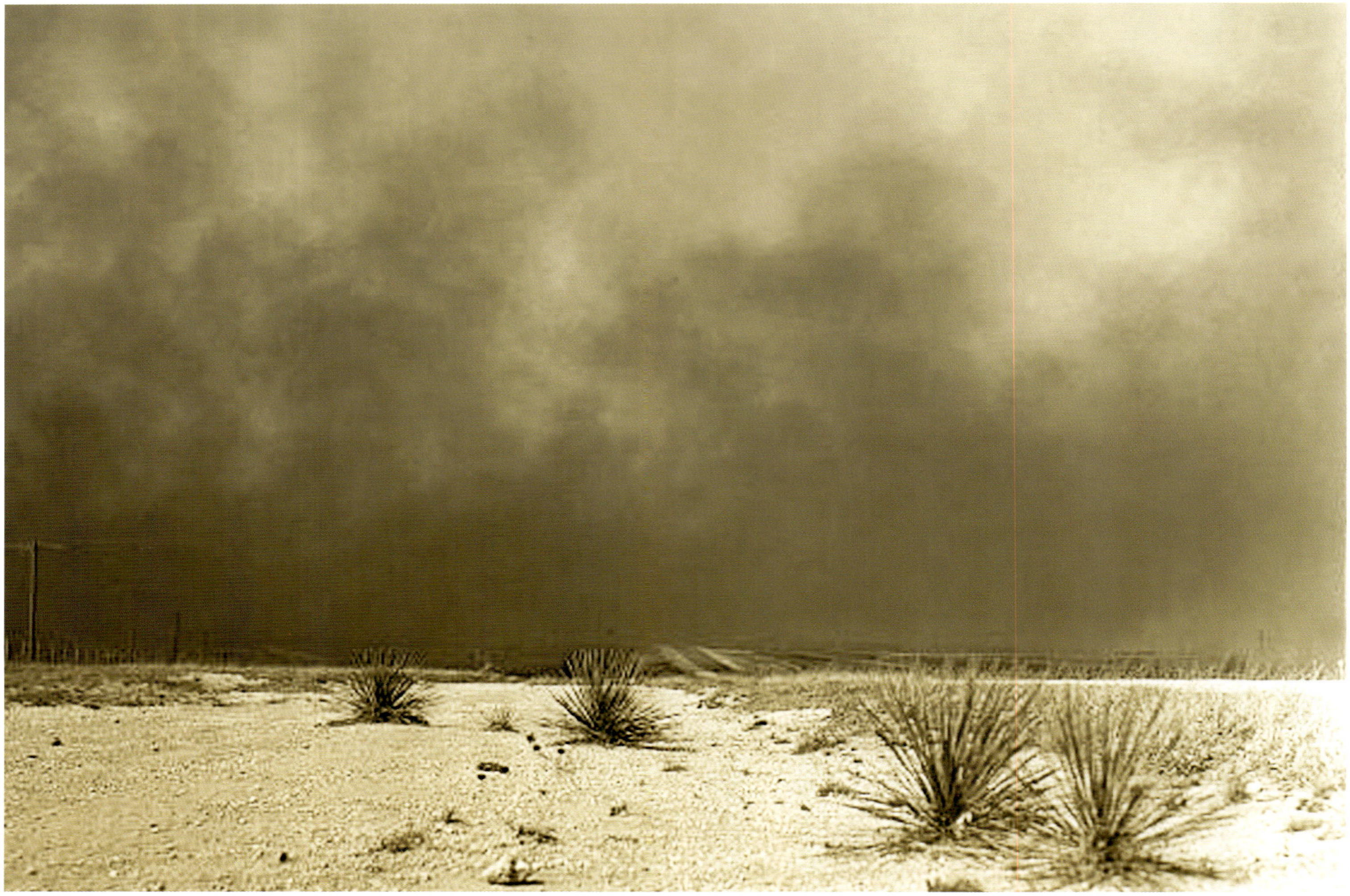

Heavy black clouds of dust rise over the Texas Pandhandle. Arthur Rothstein, 1936

As Pare Lorentz showed the nation, the high, dry plains were suffering drought. Dust was flying up from fields once covered by a poultice of short grass but grazed down to its roots and ripped apart by disc plows. The Soil Erosion Service had an immense job to do. In April 1935, Hugh Bennett had Senate hearings coming up. His field agents told him that a dust cloud was forming up also. So he dithered, dallied, and found reasons to be required urgently in the field, while those agents tracked the cloud's eastward movement, billowing bigger and bigger as it gained reinforcement with each mile from new updrafts of dust from drought-stricken barren land and smoke from wild fires. Bennett became available to testify when the dust cloud reached the Appalachians. The hearing began. When his testimony reached its most urgent, he asked for a recess, suggesting they all go to the windows. The storm struck; the sky turned an ugly orange-brown and hid the sun.[8]

As Bennett wrote: "This particular dust storm blotted out the sun over the nation's capital, drove grit between the teeth of New Yorkers, and scattered dust on the decks of ships 200 miles out to sea. I suspect that when people along the seaboard of the eastern United States began to taste fresh soil from the plains 2,000 miles away, many of them realized for the first time that somewhere something had gone wrong with the land." The expansion of the Soil Erosion Service began with that realization and was accelerated by the release of Stryker's photographs and Lorentz's films. The first of many soil conservation districts in the nation was established near the Bennett homestead in Anson County, North Carolina, in August 1937.[9]

Lowdermilk, Marsh, and the Promised Land

From August 1938 through November 1939, Walter and Inez Lowdermilk traveled more than twenty-five thousand miles along the routes taken by George Marsh around the Mediterranean and the Middle East, "reading the land" and reading as well the ruins of civilizations that had been based on a prosperous agriculture. He wrote many magazine articles, often illustrated by Stryker's photographs, about erosion in the United States. The Annual Report of the Smithsonian Institution carried his "Lessons from the Old World to the Americas in Land Use" as its title article (the Soil Conservation Service published a summary, "Conquest of the Land Through 7,000 Years" in 1953—and printed more than three million copies). The Lowdermilks visited Palestine following George Marsh's route (Marsh had been ambassador to Turkey when the Turks ruled Palestine). The once "promised land" had become so eroded that Lowdermilk was moved to urge—successfully—a Jordan Valley Authority to follow the TVA's lead, fighting erosion, assisting irrigation, and generating power. With enough water and proper soil management, he insisted, Israel could accept at least four million more European Jews.[10]

Lowdermilk's "agricultural archaeology" was reinforcing Marsh's—with contemporary implications. Three million people had inhabited Palestine in Roman times, climatic conditions had not much changed, restoration of the soil was possible, and the climate and terrain were similar to those around Lowdermilk's station at San Dimas. Lowdermilk enlivened his lectures with his own photographs of poverty-stricken people living in clusters of huts amid the ruins of antiquity, including columns, colonnades, and obelisks. He grew a Van Dyke goatee like that of the popular travel lecturer Burton Holmes. His wife wrote later of listening to his broadcasts "telling of the tragedy of land despoliation and consequent dead civilizations he had seen in North Africa and in Mesopotamia." Inez Lowdermilk also became an increasing force on her own as a radio commentator and lecturer. A British diplomat reported to the Foreign Office that she "obviously sees herself in the role of a modern Old Testament Prophet." The Lowdermilks' theme was Marsh's theme: "overgrazing . . . [had] laid bare the soil to the winds, and the careful agriculture that had supported millions vanished. Like Timgad . . . Leptis Magna had been swallowed by sand . . . Walking among these ruins, we pondered the sense of might and power the Romans must have felt . . . Would our civilization have the same end?"[11]

After World War II, Lowdermilk returned to China, but his passionate support for the Zionist cause kept drawing him back to Israel, where his work became "a dream come true" because, wrote his wife, "the Bible presents the most authentic and longest-written record of any nation except China." Lowdermilk became a leader of the American Palestine Committee and of the Christian Council on Palestine, which also included the Social Gospel theologian Reinhold Niebuhr, the philosopher Carl Friedrich, and Senator Owen Brewster of Maine. After he published *Palestine: Land of Promise* in 1944, American Zionist rabbis appearing in Congressional hearings to argue the case for increased Jewish immigration into Palestine often cited his work. After he retired from the Soil Conservation Service, he worked with the Israelis to implement some of the measures outlined in the book, leading some Israeli leaders to favor technical assistance for agricultural development even more than direct food assistance. Minister of Development Mordecai Bentov was quoted as saying: "We don't need powdered milk; we need Lowdermilk." They got him and they got The Lowdermilk School of Agricultural Engineering at Haifa.[12]

Social Work and the Social Gospel

"Poor land makes poor people and poor people make poor land." That good Marshian doctrine might have come from a lecture by Walter Lowdermilk; it was spoken by the narrator in Pare Lorentz's *The River*, a film about human welfare and about the welfare of the earth. The New Deal was led by people whose environmental philosophy was inextricable from their social philosophy, as they sustained the Social Gospel of their parents and grandparents. In its political expressions in the Progressive Era and the New Deal it did not trumpet its theological precepts nor did it parade its religiosity. But it put conviction to work for distressed people and for a distressed countryside. A commitment to aid the less fortunate and also to attend respectfully to a created world were twin aspects of the Social Gospel as it shone through the sometimes gray technocratic language of the Progressives and blazed forth in the New Deal.

It came to Rexford Tugwell from his parents, who were Social Gospel Congregationalists who supported William Jennings Bryan primarily for religious reasons. Roy Stryker, Hugh Bennett, and Walter Lowdermilk all were advanced in their careers because people committed to the Social Gospel helped them. Lowdermilk married a missionary and joined with Reinhold Niebuhr in causes larger than the battle against soil erosion. Stryker's career was built on the principles of Niebuhr's predecessor, Walter Rauschenbusch, and made possible by evangelists. He and Tugwell were economists and Bennett and Lowdermilk were scientists, and they were also religious people who used art to serve a social mission—helping the rural poor through alleviating soil erosion. Even when writing science and economics, their intensity of expression was often so eloquent that it could provide captions for the photographs taken for the agencies they administered. Lowdermilk's lectures were illustrated by his photographs of ragged people and environmental degradation, like the scenes presented in Marsh's elegiac prose-poetry, by Stryker's FSA photographers, and in his own pictures of environmental loss in Palestine and North Africa. When Marsh saw the evidence in the 1850s, there were plenty of American artists painting ruins; Marsh made the associations of those images to conservation policy, and his genius extended to knowing how also to use powerful symbols such as obelisks lying upon desolate ground. Lowdermilk, Rexford Tugwell, and Roy Stryker had other devices as well, for they could summon photography to help in the good work.

Lowdermilk was the link between Marsh and the New Dealers. The growth of the movement called "the Social Gospel" in the intervening years provided additional fervor to the work of Tugwell, Stryker, Bennett, and Lowdermilk. They came to conservation from religious conviction. Religious dedication to the suffering earth and to less fortunate people sprang from that movement, which was by no means limited to people of a Christian tradition, and reaffirmation of religious principals was supported by contemporary scientific research, including Lowdermilk's illustrated reports of watershed conservation in California, China, and Israel, and Bennett's descriptions of conditions in Virginia and Florida. Lewis Mumford, who shared their regard for Marsh, wrote in 1931 that the Dust Bowl and desolated Appalachia should be seen not as technocratic problems, but as places in which people were suffering. New Deal agricultural policy was people policy, and at its core was religious conviction. Henry Wallace, for example, had "absorbed his family's . . . conception of the farmer as God's chosen servant and environmental steward." His grandfather had taught that "those who cultivated the earth had 'a sacred duty to maintain the stored energy of the farm.'" Wallace was therefore the right leader for a department in which Stryker, Tugwell, Lowdermilk, and Bennett could work comfortably.[13]

Many of Roosevelt's associates were trained in Christian and Jewish settlement work, an urban ministry that informed the rural work given a similar name—resettlement—driven by similar motivations. Settlement-house experience was a crucial formative experience for the Morgenthaus, Harold Ickes, and Harry Hopkins, confirming the Social Gospel convictions of Roy Stryker, Rexford Tugwell, A. A. Berle, Walter Lowdermilk, and Frances Perkins. They all rolled up their sleeves to help "make America over" for the better, as that better was perceived in their fundamental faith.

Roy Stryker was justified in being "very proud" of the ways in which his photographers acted upon the same convictions to call the people together in the common endeavor on behalf of "a country . . . in turmoil, a country in trouble.

We weren't beaten. But all we had to fear 'is fear itself.' . . . And people—sure, they were downtrodden, beaten, but . . . damn it all, if you . . . look at some of the pictures . . . some of those guys said, 'We still can carry on.' . . . Sometimes it's well for us all, a family to see itself with problems, instead of everything easy. All of a sudden there's cohesiveness, they're pulled together suddenly because they have to—they're like cattle suddenly attacked by the wolves, the cows all circle around and the calves all come to the middle . . . [T]hat's what happened. Life isn't all a series of pools, and television sets . . . There's some trouble in the world . . . That's what we . . . believed." Franklin and Eleanor Roosevelt imparted a powerful sense that—as Stryker said—"we belonged to our organization and a President who was trying to give hope and faith . . . We were part of that . . . And our photographers . . . weren't interested in going out and just holding their camera up and shooting. They knew what they were doing."[14]

Tugwell permitted himself a rare show of enthusiasm when he talked of helping people: "Nobody was interested in these people. They didn't belong to any farm organization and usually their better-off neighbors either used them for part-time help or sharecroppers or some such way as this, and they were simply not interested in their welfare. They were an abandoned lot of people . . . The trouble usually was . . . his land, because it had eroded . . . worn out." As was the farmer. "Nobody wanted to help these people. [They] . . . were the most friendless, hopeless people there were in the whole country. Nobody wanted to see them."[15]

The photography programs of the Resettlement Administration and Farm Security Administration made "them" visible—"the migratory laborers who came out . . . from Oklahoma and for them we set up work camps, so that they would have means of shelter." And for those who might be somehow insulated from the effects of the Depression, the photographs forced a clear-eyed recognition that a "neighbor who was always so well-to-do was suddenly selling apples."[16]

Although raised in the country, Roy Stryker learned about "settlement" in a city, as did Perkins, Morgenthau, Ickes, and Hopkins. Tugwell had became acquainted with "the best and worst of industrial America" when he lived during his high-school years in a boarding house in Buffalo. Their urban settlement work and the alliance of the Social Gospel to Jewish liberal theology explain the evangelical tone of much New Deal prose, the camp-meeting theatricality of Hugh Bennett's famous management of a dust storm to testify for him and for better budgets for soil conservation. That was also the tone of the Lowdermilks' evangelical style on the platform.

In a Soil Conservation Service report still in print by that agency, Walter Lowdermilk set forth the New Deal's "Eleventh Commandment":

> Thou shalt inherit the Holy Earth as a faithful steward, conserving its resources and productivity from generation to generation. Thou shalt safeguard thy fields from soil erosion, thy living waters from drying up, thy forests from desolation, and protect thy hills from overgrazing by thy herds, that thy descendants may have abundance forever. If any shall fail in this stewardship of the land, thy fruitful fields shall become sterile stony ground and wasting gullies, and thy descendants shall decrease and live in poverty or perish from off the face of the earth.[17]

In her memoirs, Inez Marks Lowdermilk recorded that "Walter closed every talk he gave with this commandment, dramatizing it with color slides taken on our trip through Roman lands showing vividly the results of man's abuse of his natural resources." By then he and she were on the air regularly with the same message, and she was lunching with Mrs. Roosevelt. At the end she could proudly state that "when President Roosevelt died, Walter's book, *Palestine, Land of Promise*, was found open on his desk, about halfway read."[18]

Roy Stryker retired in 1952 and died in 1960. Walter Lowdermilk died in 1974, and Inez Marks Lowdermilk in 1989.

Chapter Ten

Lincoln and Roosevelt

"One fire was on his spirit, one resolve–to send the keen ax to the root of wrong, clearing a free way for the feet of God."
(Edwin Markham on Abraham Lincoln, 1922)

"It is the main duty of government, if it is not the sole duty of government, to provide means of protection for all citizens in the pursuit of happiness against the obstacles, otherwise insurmountable, which the selfishness of individuals or combinations of individuals is liable to interpose to that pursuit."[1]
(Frederick Law Olmstead, 1865)

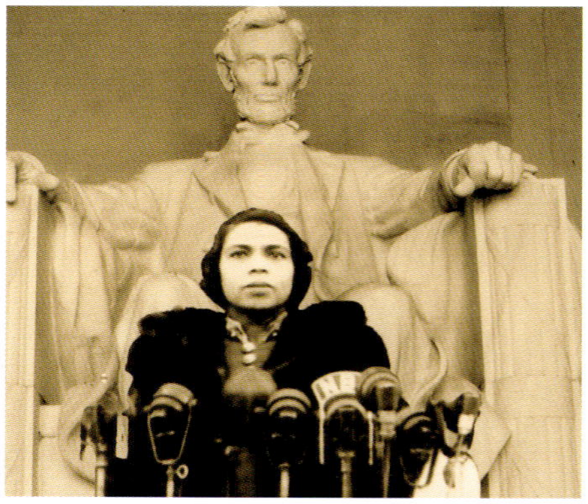

Marian Anderson

After seventy vocal recitals across the United States in 1938, the great contralto Marian Anderson was refused the use of Constitution Hall in Washington, D.C., by the hall's owners, the Daughters of the American Revolution–she was African American and would not sing to segregated audiences. The Secretary of the Interior, Harold L. Ickes, invited Anderson to perform instead at the Lincoln Memorial. On Easter Sunday, April 9, 1939, she sang on the Mall. The police estimated that the audience numbered more than seventy-five thousand people; millions more listened on the radio (see main text).

THE LINCOLN MEMORIAL WAS DEDICATED IN 1922 in a segregated ceremony in which nothing was said about freeing slaves. An allegorical scene in the murals painted by Jules Guerin alluded to the subject and Edwin Markham included in his dedicatory poem these lines: "One fire was on his spirit, one resolve—to send the keen ax to the root of wrong, clearing a free way for the feet of God." That was it. The building had been constructed during the administration of Warren Harding, the president who promised a return to "normalcy" leaving discrimination enforceable by law throughout the nation. Harding's predecessors, Woodrow Wilson and William Howard Taft, were not of Lincoln's mind on racial matters, so the Lincoln Memorial was presented as a shrine not to emancipation but to the reconciliation of North and South—reconciliation without redemption, leaving unaddressed the original sin of slavery and its lingering effects.

Marian Anderson acknowledged Lincoln's emancipating role when she sang at the Memorial to an unsegregated audience of seventy-five thousand people, yet both she and that audience asserted that disadvantaged people had all along been forcing the larger society to include them within the covenant—and must continue to do so until it was truly inclusive of all. That was the message of the Reverend Martin Luther King, Jr., at the Memorial in 1963 in his "I Have a Dream" speech. During the 1920s and the New Deal period, demonstrations at the Memorial by African Americans had shown their determination to clear their own "free way," but the predominant culture seemed to take little notice. Nor was there much outcry when in 1939 Anderson sought to give a concert in the Washington auditorium of the Daughters of the American Revolution, and was refused that venue because she was "a Negress" who would not perform to a segregated audience. Seeking help, Walter White of the National Association for the Advancement of Colored People met with Assistant Secretary of the Interior Oscar Chapman to find an alternative. "Wouldn't it be a good idea," suggested Chapman, "if we used the Lincoln Memorial?" White caught the idea and caught his breath: "if we could have her sing at the feet of Lincoln!" And on Easter Sunday she did. Chapman later reported that when Franklin Roosevelt was asked to approve, he replied: "She can sing from the top of the Washington Monument if she wants to."[2]

Anderson was introduced by Harold Ickes, who began by directing the eyes of the audience to "this wonderful outdoors and the moon and the stars" granted by God, he said, "with no distinction of race, creed, or color." He then gestured upward, proclaiming that the Memorial stood for the "principle of equality of opportunity which Abraham Lincoln believed so explicitly . . . genius draws no color line . . . had it not been for [his] . . . great heart" Anderson would not be able to stand where she did as "a free individual in a free land." That was probably true to some extent, but after the passage of another three-quarters of a century, because of the transforming effects of Anderson, King, and countless other people of color, the Lincoln Memorial has become a place to think of insisting upon the full rights of citizens as well as emancipation.[3]

When Anderson sang and Ickes spoke, segregation still reined, as Anderson reminded her audiences by altering the lyrics of the anthem "My country 'tis of thee, Sweet land of liberty": she did not sing "*Of* thee I sing," but "*To* thee we sing." America was not yet a wholly "free land"—to that ideal "we" sang, and toward it many struggled. Scott Sandage, a historian and essayist writing in 1993, noted that her "change made the national hymn subtly political, painting 'land of liberty' as more aspiration than description." Six years after Ickes delivered his introduction of Anderson at the Lincoln Memorial, he placed a magnificent portrayal of the scene of the Anderson concert by Mitchell Jamieson in a conspicuous position in the Interior Department building. Jamieson's painting *really* works because its surprise—its intended shocker—is that Anderson is barely perceptible within the portico of the memorial, and that what counts is the assembly of civil rights leaders in the foreground, centering upon the figure of Mary McLeod Bethune. On the day after the concert, Bethune had said: "We are on the right track," and she wrote later: "Through the Marian Anderson protest concert we made our triumphant entry into the democratic spirit of American life."[4]

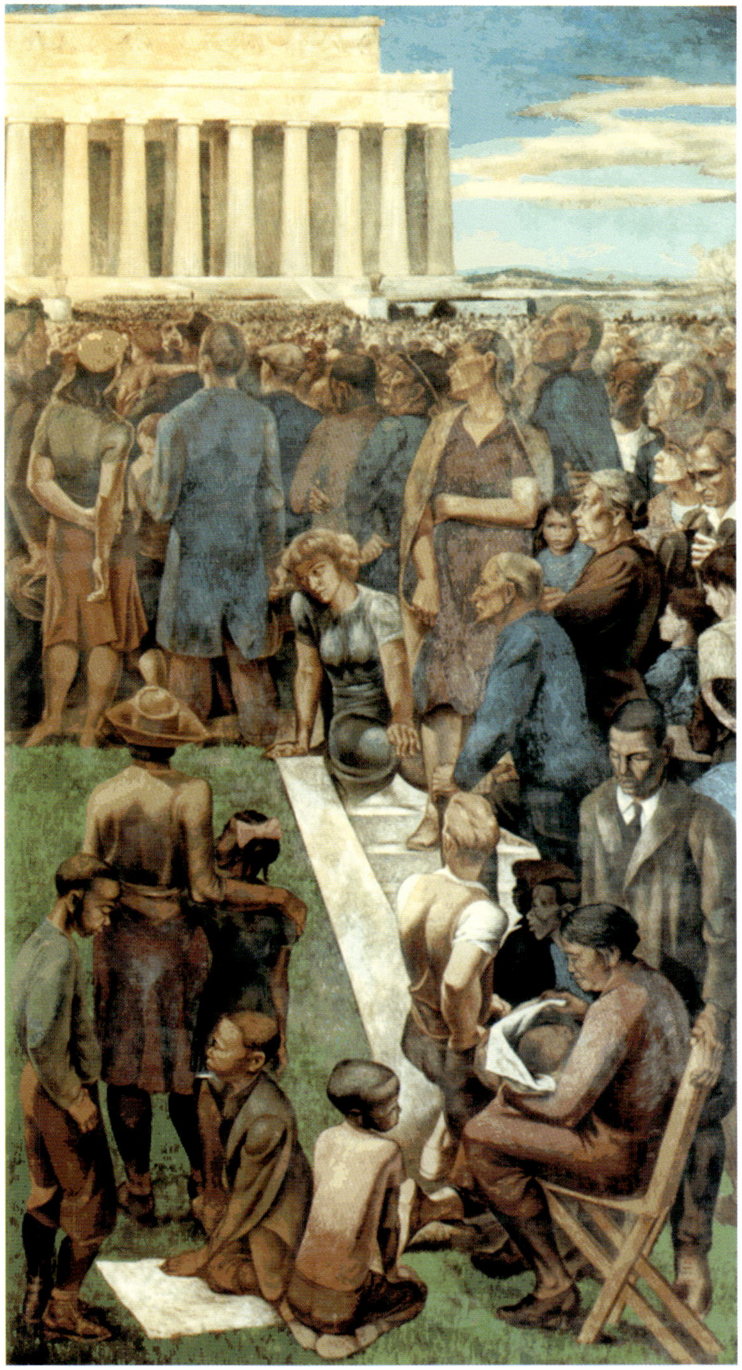

An Incident in Contemporary American Life
(Marian Anderson performing at the Lincoln Memorial)
Mitchell Jamieson, 1942

Born in Kensington, Maryland, Mitchell Jamieson studied art at the Corcoran College of Art and Design in Washington, D.C., and in Mexico. The Treasury Section commissioned him to paint post office murals in Willard, Ohio, and in both Laurel and Upper Marlboro, Maryland. His Willard mural was executed for a railroad town and is a Mexican-style paean to big machines and brawny workers.

Then in 1941–2 came his commission to provide a mural for the Interior Department Building. It is a miracle of subtlety and resonating overtones (see main text). The message is as much about the consequences of Anderson's concert as about the event itself. Anderson's concert at the Lincoln Memorial is seen as another opportunity for self-emancipation of African Americans by their own exertions, rather than as a reiteration of their having been liberated. It is about the present rather than the past.

Jamieson served as a combat artist in Normandy and on Iwo Jima and was awarded a Bronze Star for valor. He taught, painted for *Life* magazine, and was the first official artist of the NASA Mercury Project. After service as a combat artist in Vietnam, he painted scenes of domestic protest against the Vietnam War. He taught at the University of Maryland until his death in 1976.

As Sandage also pointed out, the modern civil rights movement "came of age on Easter Sunday 1939 . . . The concert was not the first African-American political use of Lincoln's memory, nor even the first civil rights gathering at his memorial. But it was . . . the first black mass action to evoke laudatory national publicity and earn a positive place in American public memory . . . [B]lack organizers transformed a recital of sacred music at a national shrine into a political rally. In an era obsessed with defining Americanism, activists successfully portrayed their adversary as un-American. It was a formula civil rights activists and other protesters would repeat at the Lincoln Memorial in more than one hundred big and small rallies in subsequent decades—most notably in the 1963 March on Washington for Jobs and Freedom when Martin Luther King, Jr., proclaimed his Dream from the steps where Marian Anderson had sung."[5]

Lincoln's Symbolic Genius

Like the best of New Deal art, the Lincoln Memorial has induced action as well as feeling. From Edwin Markham through Marian Anderson and Martin Luther King, artists (and King was certainly that) have found at the memorial a field of force upon which they could draw as they called forth from the nation a fresh commitment to Lincoln's "new birth of freedom."

Soon after the death of Franklin Roosevelt, Robert E. Sherwood was moved to consider afresh how similar were the ideals of Franklin Roosevelt and Lincoln as each sought to achieve national recovery and reconciliation. Sherwood's best known scripts had been for the play and motion picture *Abe Lincoln in Illinois*. During the New Deal years in which he was at the side of Franklin Roosevelt, he had come to perceive powerful bonds between the two great redemptive presidents. Roosevelt restored the nation with the aid of art—his own and that of others. So did Lincoln—and on the ample scale described by Frederick Law Olmsted, a man who understood scale.

Olmsted made his life—and his living—working as an artist of landscapes and ecosystems. That was why, he said, he ventured to assume "the title of artist." Although his countrymen may not have been quite ready to "fully estimate the merit of the park as a work of art," Lincoln was, and therefore Olmsted perceived in him a fellow artist capable of "natural, spontaneous, individual action of imagination—*creative*." Having shown what art could achieve in New York's Central Park, with the 250,000 acres of George Vanderbilt's Biltmore Estate, and along Boston's necklace of green, Olmsted discerned "creative genius" in Lincoln that comprehended park-making on an even larger scale, and knew the symbolic power of public architecture and monumental sculpture.[6]

During the Civil War, wrote Olmsted, "Lincoln drew forth from the people "a livelier susceptibility to the influence of art . . . and greater progress in the manifestations of artistic talent . . . than in any similar period before in the history of the country . . . It was during one of the darkest hours, before Sherman had begun the march upon Atlanta or Grant his terrible movement through the Wilderness, when the paintings of [Albert] Bierstadt and the photographs of [Carleton Emmons] Watkins, both productions of the War time, had given to the people on the Atlantic some idea of the sublimity of the Yosemite, and of the stateliness of the neighboring Sequoia grove, that consideration was first given to the danger that such scenes might become private property and . . . their value to posterity be injured." In June 1864, "to secure them against this danger," Lincoln endorsed an action by the Congress that set the Yosemite aside to be "devoted forever" to the common use. (The Yosemite Valley was placed under the care of the state of California until it became a national park.)[7]

When Lincoln took office, two more of the nation's unifying symbols, the Capitol and the Washington Monument, were as yet unfinished. In the previous chapter we have seen how the monument was rescued, at his urging, by artists closely associated with him. The interior of the Capitol was, in 1860, a warren of cubicles, pipes-without-outcomes, curtains where walls should be,

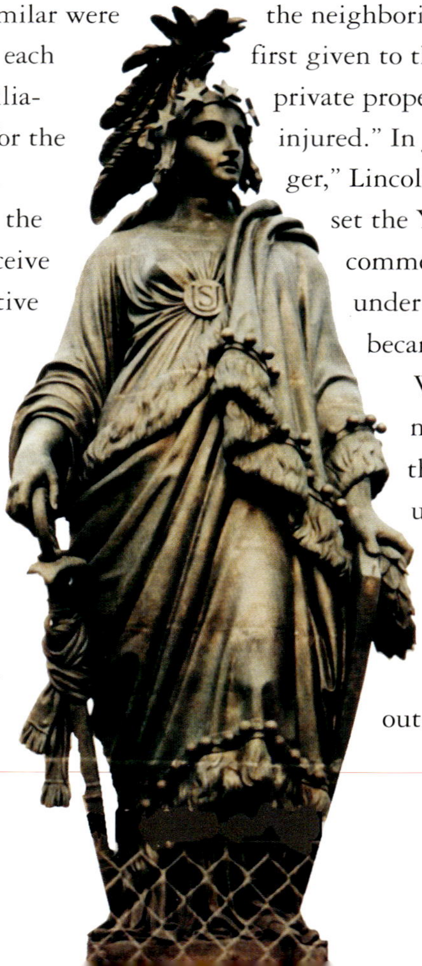

Freedom
Thomas Crawford, 1865
U.S. Capitol

graffiti, and trash. The President saw to it that the building was cleaned and its public spaces provided with new ceremonial canvases that put history painting to work in the Capitol, as two generations later WPA artists put it to work in thirteen hundred murals for post offices. Next, Lincoln ordered that the Capitol dome be finished and surmounted with Thomas Crawford's *Freedom*, a bronze statue nineteen and a half feet tall, weighing seven tons, its crest 288 feet above the Capitol's east plaza. "The forces of the insurgents watched [the dome] rounding upward to completion for nearly a year before they were forced from their entrenchments . . . [until *Freedom*] was poised upon its summit in the year that President Lincoln proclaimed the emancipation of the slaves." Doubters such as John Eaton of Toledo, Ohio, grumbled to the President that "people were saying" that "hoisting the statue . . . over the Capitol dome . . . was an extravagance during wartime." Lincoln's response was that art should do its work. "If people see the Capitol going on," he told Eaton, "it is a sign we intend the Union shall go on."[8]

Among the Confederates who learned that Crawford's *Freedom* was going into place was Jefferson Davis, commander in chief of the army then threatening the defenses of the city of Washington. Davis had been Secretary of War in James Buchanan's administration before Lincoln took office. When Crawford's design had to be approved, Davis, as Secretary, forced a change in the headgear of *Freedom*. Crawford had drawn a liberty cap, a symbol of freedom for slaves since 1789; Davis had it replaced with a Roman helmet. The helmet is still there, even though Lincoln, in effect, put the liberty cap back in place with the Emancipation Proclamation. Rescuing the Yosemite for the nation and installing the statue of *Freedom* were symbolic acts honoring an inheritance in places and in ideas to be shared for the nourishment of the spirit of the nation. As if preparing a draft for Roosevelt's "Rendezvous with Destiny" speech, Olmsted explained: "It is the main duty of government, if it is not the sole duty of government, to provide means of protection for all citizens in the pursuit of happiness against the obstacles, otherwise insurmountable, which the selfishness of individuals or combinations of individuals is liable to interpose to that pursuit." And as if composing the charter for the New Deal reorganization of the National Park System, he urged "government to withhold . . . from the grasp of individuals, all places favorable . . . to the recreation of mind and body."[9]

Franklin Roosevelt and Personalizing the New Deal

Franklin Roosevelt appears to have had little desire to become a cult figure nor had his wife that desire for him. He did not surround himself with phalanxes of uniformed minions nor did he encourage the arts to manufacture millions of posters of his visage, to make counterparts to the epic films of Leni Riefenstahl for the Nazis or to the huge sculptures of Stalin cluttering the Russian landscape. Roosevelt's manner of speech, like the jaunty face bearing his uptilted cigarette-holder, became familiar enough, but not because cartoonists or photographers were subsidized to make them known. In his speech about a rendezvous with destiny, Roosevelt did not offer himself as an embodiment of that destiny, invoking instead a covenant of reciprocity with citizens in the mutual pledges of 1932 and the refreshed compact of the rendezvous of 1936. Those were the causes "for which he fought . . . far greater than any individual person."[10]

In wartime Roosevelt became more than a political leader, more even than a commander in chief of the armed forces. As the editors of the soldiers' magazine, *Yank*, wrote: "he was the Commander in Chief, not only of our armed forces, but of our generation." In that role, Winston Churchill wrote of him that he "altered, decisively and permanently, the social axis, the moral axis, of mankind by involving the New World inexorably and irrevocably in the fortunes of the Old. His life must therefore be regarded as one of the commanding events in human destiny." Roosevelt's indispensability does not seem to have inflated his ego toward the madness of great ones, although he was human. Being admired gave him pleasure, but he did not solicit or encourage adulation. When it appeared, it was not welcomed by his wife, by Harry Hopkins, his closest aide, or by Sherwood, his colleague and chronicler.[11]

It is noteworthy that there are few Roosevelt images among the thousands of commissioned works of the New Deal—only the three in the group that Olin Dows painted for Roosevelt's local post office at Hyde Park. Three—among the thousands of murals commissioned by the Treasury Arts Project for more than eleven hundred post offices. One shows Roosevelt in his car looking at blueprints as a designer of that post office. Fair enough: he had been active in working with Henry J. Tombs on the concept sketches and working drawings for four Hudson Valley post offices, for buildings on his estate, for the James Roosevelt Library built by his mother in his father's memory, and for his own Georgia vacation retreat.

The second of Dows's "Roosevelt panels" shows the President as host to the King and Queen of England at lunch. The third presents him as a vigorous young man before he needed that automobile to get around, joining his neighbor Archibald Rogers in clearing dead wood to prepare for the planting of new trees. He might be permitted this very delicate reference to his stated profession, and also to his affinity, otherwise cloaked in class distinctions, to Abraham Lincoln the rail-splitter. He was only implied in a fourth panel, in which Dows showed local apple pickers resting in the afternoon shade to listen to the radio. There was no doubt as to the implication; a local historian consulted by Dows had reported that when she asked the President who he had in mind when he spoke into the microphones at his desk to deliver a "fireside chat," he replied that among those he visualized was the "kind of individual citizen he had known so well in Dutchess County all my life."[12]

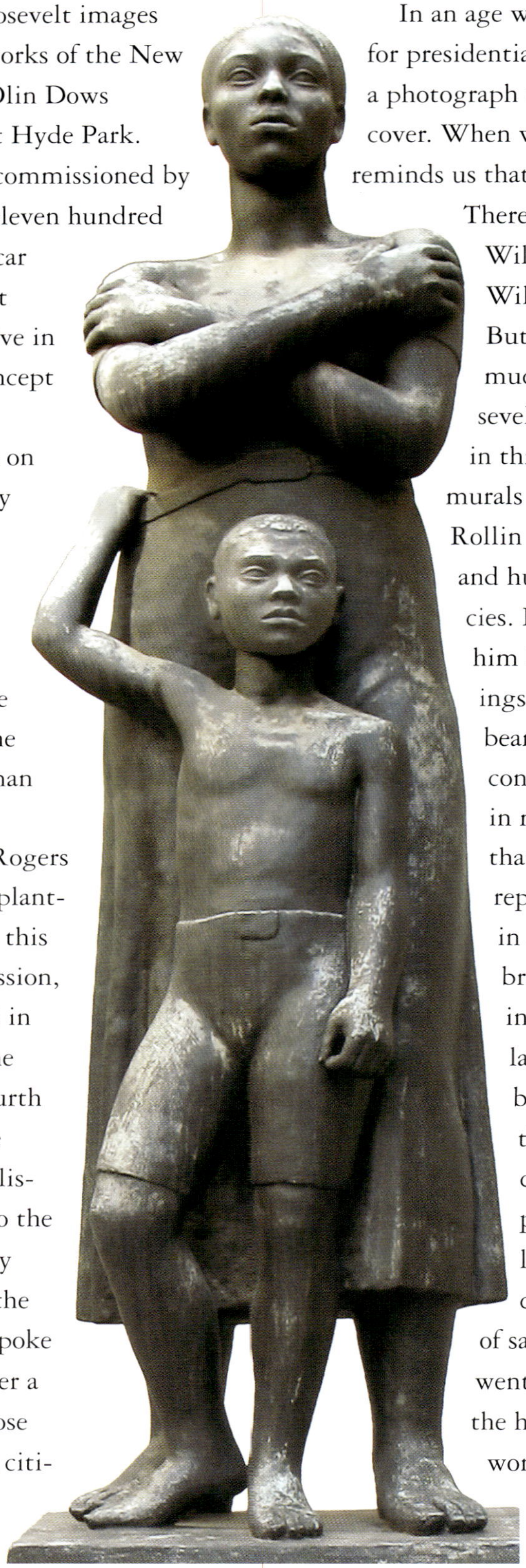

Negro Mother and Child
Department of the Interior Courtyard
Maurice Glickman, 1940

Maurice Glickman was born in Romania, immigrated to New York, studied at the Art Students League in New York, trained many other sculptors, including Leonard Baskin, and received commissions from the Treasury Section for the post offices at South River, New Jersey, and Northampton, Pennsylvania. His work has been exhibited at the Whitney Museum, the Museum of Modern Art, the Metropolitan Museum of Art, and the Hirshhorn Museum.

In an age when engineering supplanted sculpture for presidential monument-making, *Life* magazine put a photograph of the Hoover (Boulder) dam on its first cover. When we see that famous picture today it reminds us that there is no Franklin Roosevelt dam. There is a Theodore Roosevelt Dam, a William Howard Taft Dam, a Woodrow Wilson Dam, and a Calvin Coolidge Dam. But for the patron-president of the TVA and much other dam-building—nothing. Roosevelt certainly encouraged being included in three murals in the Hyde Park post office murals and evidenced delight in the cartoons of Rollin Kirby and Bill Mauldin depicting him and humanizing the abstractions of his policies. He was well aware that photographs of him had iconic power as apertures to meanings transcending personality, and posters bearing his likeness were displayed to invite confidence in a caring president—yes, and in more than a president—in a government that cared about its people. Lorena Hickok reported from dismal, squalid Pennsylvania in August 1933 that Roosevelt's picture brought hope—and faith in democratic institutions. "It is the tremendous popularity of the President that undoubtedly brings the Federal government [into the hopes of the people.] . . . The soft coal miners; for instance . . . carried his picture in their picket lines and in their little patriotic parades—with an American flag and queer little bands made up of saxophones and accordions—when they went back to work. Stuck up in a window of the home of a miner who had been out of work and nearly starving on inadequate relief for more than a month, I saw a newspaper clipping, apparently out of an advertisement, of the President's picture . . ." But when Eleanor Roosevelt wrote of "the causes for which he fought" that she believed—and he believed—to be "far greater than any individual person," she was alluding to a cluster of purposes, not to any indented paragraphs in the creedal statement of an ideology. That cluster formed the nucleus of a capacious covenant in which every American had a respected place.[13]

Two Works of Art in a Courtyard

Art worked to advance that covenant in many post office murals, in many a performance of the Living Newspapers, throughout the Interior Building, and, with quiet intensity, through two statues placed by Harold Ickes in its courtyard: Maurice Glickman's *Negro Mother and Child* and Louis Slobokin's *Abe Lincoln*. They are just outside the cafeteria, accessible to those seeking a little sunlight and quiet to think about why they come to work. These two statues summarize the New Deal aspiration to offer all Americans equal access to the pursuit of happiness. While Edward Bruce and Olin Dows were in charge of the Federal Art Project (FAP), it commissioned *Negro Mother and Child* from the Romanian-born sculptor Maurice Glickman. In the spring of 1934 Bruce presented its model to the President, Mrs. Roosevelt, Ickes, Hopkins, and Morgenthau in the agency's final exhibition in which it presented its best work.[14]

The other great statue in that courtyard, Louis Slobodkin's *Abe Lincoln*, supplements the theme of a shared citizenship within the covenant with another concept, the shared relationship of the people to the earth: a polity grounded in a shared home. Slobodkin's figure of the young Lincoln is somewhat larger than life-size, but it is not the monumental Lincoln by Daniel Chester French enshrined in the Lincoln Memorial, nor that of Larkin Mead in the Lincoln Tomb in Springfield, Illinois, nor that granite portrait carved by Gutzon Borglum on Mount Rushmore. Slobodkin's figure is of a young man making use of the tools of a manual trade, a citizen *from* the nation commissioned by fate to lead it, emerging as organically as a young tree from the soil of his country. This was the uncommon man who became assiduous in assuming the demeanor of a common man, one of the most successful corporate lawyers of his age who became better known as a rail-splitter than a parser of precedents: Slobodkin's title for his work was "mender of rails." As a rising politician, Lincoln successfully presented himself as ordinary though "presidential," a difficult exercise in dramatic art achieved by encouraging the press, and by courtesies to poets, photographers, and cartoonists. Having studied the example of Lincoln, Roosevelt achieved his own triumphs of communication with a demeanor in which Robert Sherwood discerned a "strenuous avoidance of solemnity."[15]

The portraits of Lincoln painted in his lifetime to satisfy presidential tradition are earnest formalities memorable only as interesting transcriptions of more evocative black-and-white photographs by Mathew Brady, which are as intimate, unpretentious, and deliberate in avoidance of monumentality as the Roosevelt of the fireside chats. Roosevelt's conversational radio manner was like Lincoln's sidelong approach to the camera. Roosevelt was handsome, but the example of Warren Harding had made that almost a

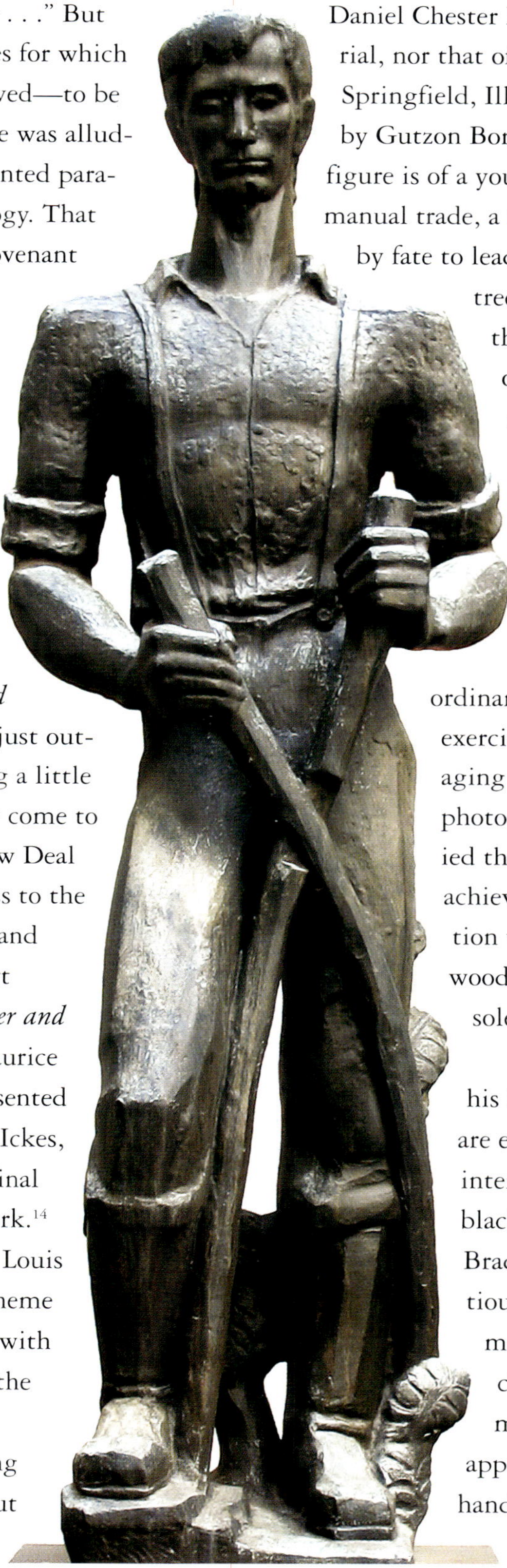

Abe Lincoln
Louis Slobodkin, 1940
Cast made by order of the Treasury Section for Secretary of the Interior Harold L. Ickes. The original bronze was destroyed (see main text).

liability. Lincoln made *not* being handsome an advantage, as he presented himself as a plain person emerging from plain people. As his quest for the presidency required him not only to ready himself for it, but to ready his countrymen for him in it, Lincoln made a virtue of his asymmetrical face, and his humble birth and upbringing. The young Lincoln in the Interior Department courtyard is Lincoln as Everyman, such a one as might have to strive mightily to become a Great Emancipator. Slobodkin was trained at the École des Beaux Arts, won many prizes, and received commissions from the Section for post offices in Washington and at Madison Square Garden in New York, but his best work is his *Lincoln*.[16]

Art and the Soul of a Nation

Although Franklin Roosevelt permitted himself to show vulnerability no more often than did Lincoln, they were both "acquainted with grief," in the words of the Prophet Isaiah—their own and the grief of others—and sought to alleviate the suffering of others without being either patronizing or fatuous. They were able to do so because they were willing to measure success by what was done, not by what they wished to have done. In 1940, when the programs of the second term were decomposing and the Depression had returned, when a third of the nation was still ill-housed, ill-clothed, and ill-fed, when Hitler was triumphant in Europe and the Japanese apparently irresistible in China, Mrs. Roosevelt invited a delegation from the American Youth Congress to talk with the President in the East Room. With the simplifying radicalism of youth, they wanted to know why he was paying so much attention to events abroad and so little to pursuing domestic reform, including desegregation of the armed forces. One assertive young man rose to admonish him, saying that they were all "a little bit angry" with him.[17]

Easily virtuous folk still get "a little bit angry" at Lincoln for settling for an Emancipation Proclamation as a military measure only, with its effects limited to the areas still controlled by the Confederacy. Why didn't he wave a magic wand to ordain instant and universal emancipation of the slaves? Was Roosevelt equivalently culpable for failing to desegregate fully the armed forces? Probably. And he probably knew it, for his response to his questioner was an inquiry of his own: had the young man read Carl Sandburg's *Lincoln*? And then he added: "I think the impression was that Lincoln was a very sad man, because he could not do all he wanted to do at one time, and I think you will find examples where Lincoln had to compromise to gain a little something." Lincoln, said Roosevelt, was "called a politician . . . but he was a politician who was practical enough to get a great many things done for this country. He was a sad man because he couldn't get it all done at once. And nobody can."[18]

Roosevelt himself certainly could not. Those who worked most closely with him admired his high idealism about ends and his refusal to capitulate to despair when he could not bring results close to those ends. John Collier wrote of him that "his self-controlling intention could not, in the political-social nature of things in his epoch, move unmixed and undiluted to ends quickly attainable . . ." But he did not quit. And he did not turn bitter. Instead, he embraced what he called "cheerfulness"—a kind of quiet joy in endeavoring toward the good without always knowing the outcome. He had a card posted on his wall bearing a statement of Lincoln made in the midst of the Civil War: "I do the very best I know how—the very best I can; and I mean to keep on doing that until the end. If the end brings me out all right, then what is said against me won't amount to anything. If the end brings me out wrong, 10,000 angels swearing I was right would make no difference."[19]

The many Lincoln statues in small-town parks, some of which were depicted in New Deal murals, often carry inscriptions celebrating Lincoln as the Great Emancipator, and with justice. Emancipation, like desegregation, ensued from the courage and pertinacity of many brave uncelebrated people, and from great presidents doing the best they could when they could and training the next generation to finish the job. Without Lincoln, there might have been no victory for the United States over the slave-owners' confederacy, no re-united states dedicated not merely to "propositions" but to aspirations to achieve those propositions in practice.

The fact that every president who served under Lincoln—Grant, Garfield, Harrison, and even McKinley—included the struggle for racial justice in their inaugural addresses shows the power of his example. Similarly, without Franklin and Eleanor Roosevelt, until the nation as a whole had paid a still higher price for its injustices, there would have been no grand redeeming moment for Dwight Eisenhower at Central High School in Little Rock, and the way would have been far harder for John F. Kennedy at the end of his life, and for Lyndon Johnson to press ahead toward a Civil Rights Act and a Voting Rights Act. All along, the practitioners of moral leadership asked the people, and the people's artists: "what can you—each of you—do for your country?" "Will you join with Lincoln's 'better angels' and the higher aspirations of Franklin Roosevelt's New Deal, to join in the work of renewing the American covenant?"

In its place of honor in the Interior courtyard, Slobodkin's *Lincoln* reminds us of those angels and those aspirations, to inspirit the struggle for a "more perfect union" with each other and with nature. Throughout the long chronicle of redemption of the American dream, artists have often been summoned "to coax the soul of America back to life." In the New Deal period, that was their most important work.[20]

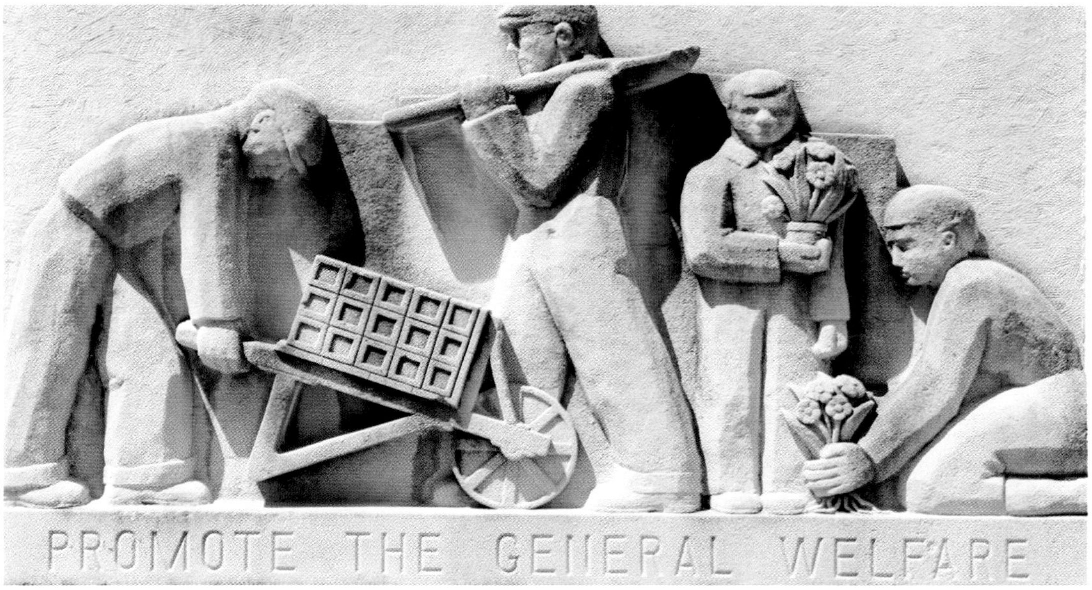

One of the five bas reliefs by Lenore Thomas, 1937. Mounted on the base of an exterior wall of The Greenbelt, Maryland, Community Center

How Art Worked

The next thirty-one pages are devoted to three examples of the redemptive power of art, as it served the American polity during the New Deal period. In each case the materials were at hand, but like the land itself, had been abused, neglected, or insufficiently appreciated; in each, a program of public works provided jobs and occasions for gifts of genius toward the public good.

Within Colorado foothills sculpted by wind and water, the CCC created the Red Rocks Amphitheatre—a work of sculpture that was also a performing arts theater and rallying ground for community action for people of all classes and of many traditions.

At Timberline Lodge, near Portland, Oregon, the WPA brought together a grand assemblage of works of art within a work of art, in another spectacular mountain setting. The Portland, Oregon, metropolis, burgeoning nearly as rapidly as the Front Range communities rejoicing in Red Rocks, was provided not only a magnificently romantic hostelry but also a synthesis of Wild West and Old Alpine symbols—with subtle reminders of Native American precedents thrown in.

At La Purísima, near Lompoc, California, CCC workers rescued a ruined and morally ambiguous religious site that had been allowed to decay by the cattle barons who had come into its possession after it ceased to be a place of worship. Teams of young Angelenos not only brought back to life a building, but because the CCC was not only a construction agency but an educational one as well, the restoration provided explanation that made its ambiguities candid. An invitation was thereby provided to meditate upon the bright and the shadowy aspects of a state-supported imperial religion that brought both sacrificial service and exploitation into an existing culture. Architecturally, a tradition was sustained and renewed by restoration that was continuous from the dry-land Middle East and North Africa to the dry-land Southwest and central California. In the end, the buildings became ruins and stables, and the people and their culture had been all but eradicated. Then the WPA and CCC appeared to restore the buildings, grounds, and memories.

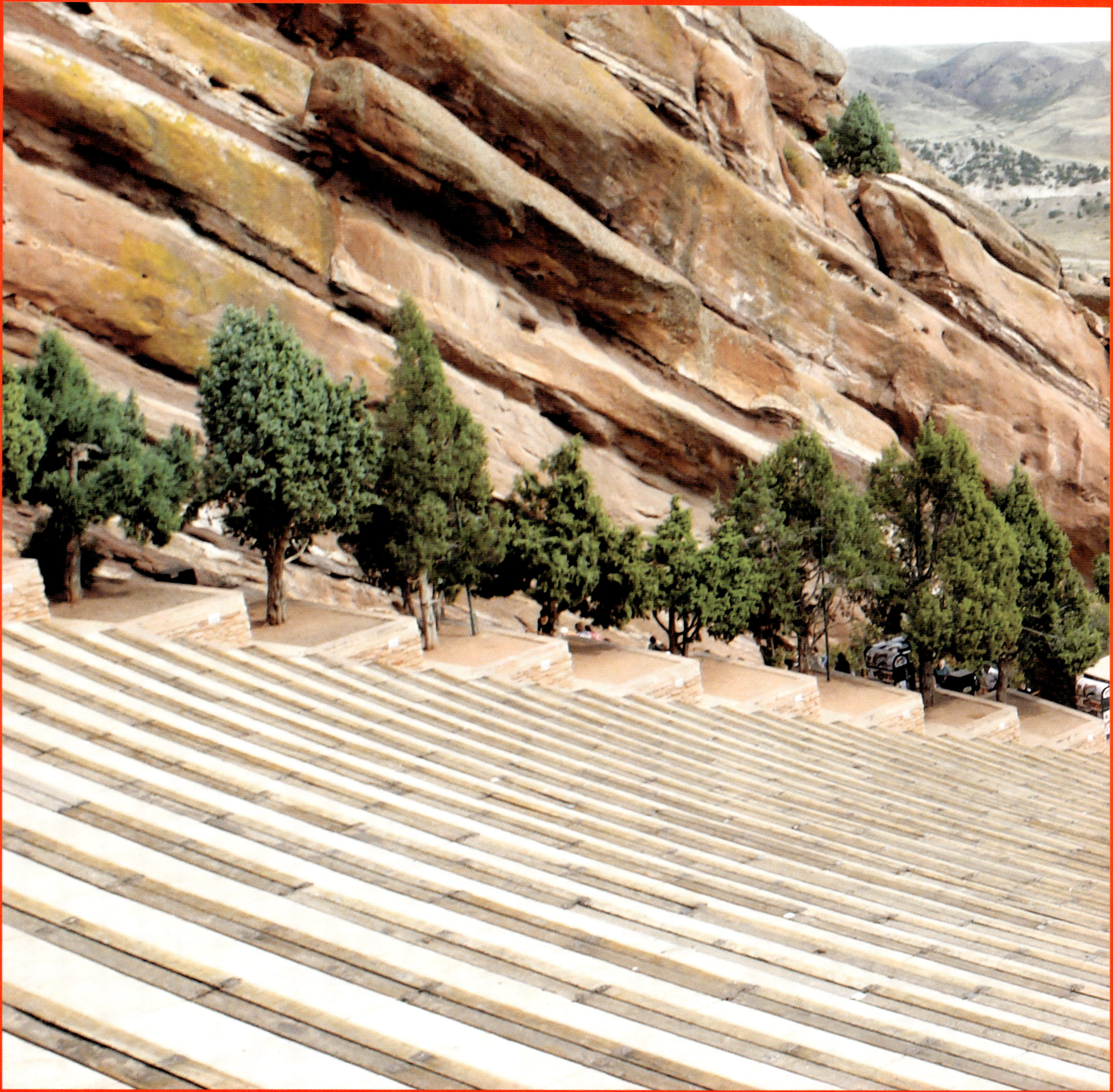

Red Rocks Amphitheatre

Ship Rock and Creation Rock, each three-hundred-foot sandstone monoliths, stand guard over an erosion-sculpted bowl fifteen miles west of Denver. The acoustics within the bowl are remarkably good; even before the CCC came to the scene, performers had been making music there—perhaps for several thousand years. A promoter, John Brisben Walker, produced concerts between 1906 and 1910 on a temporary platform in the bowl. In 1927 George Cranmer, manager of Denver Parks, convinced the city government of Denver to purchase the area from Walker. The CCC and the WPA provided labor and materials to complete a design by Burnham Hoyt, which was dedicated on June 15, 1941. It has been the venue for thousands of performances and video recordings, including those of U2, Moody Blues, Widespread Panic, and Dave Matthews.

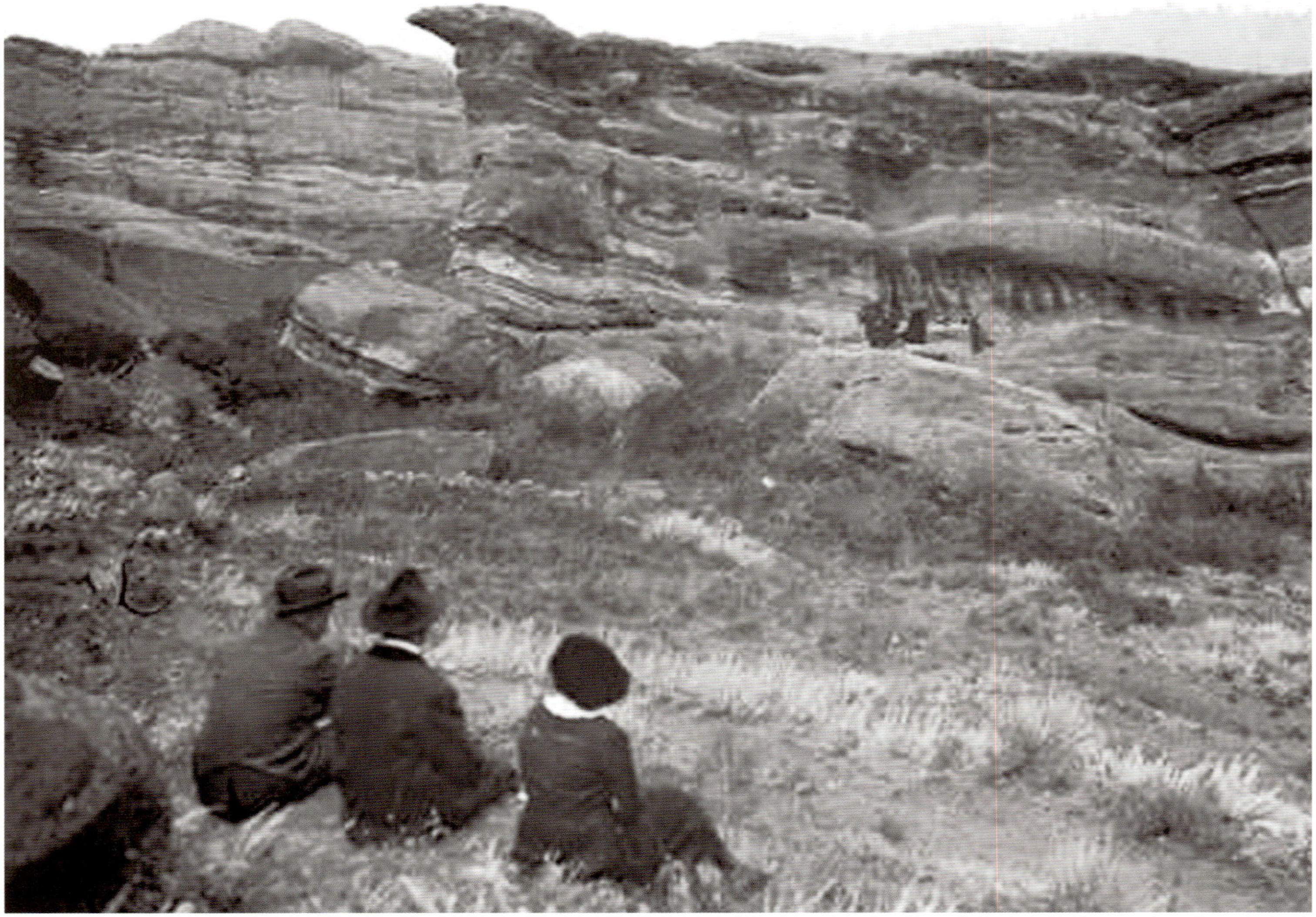

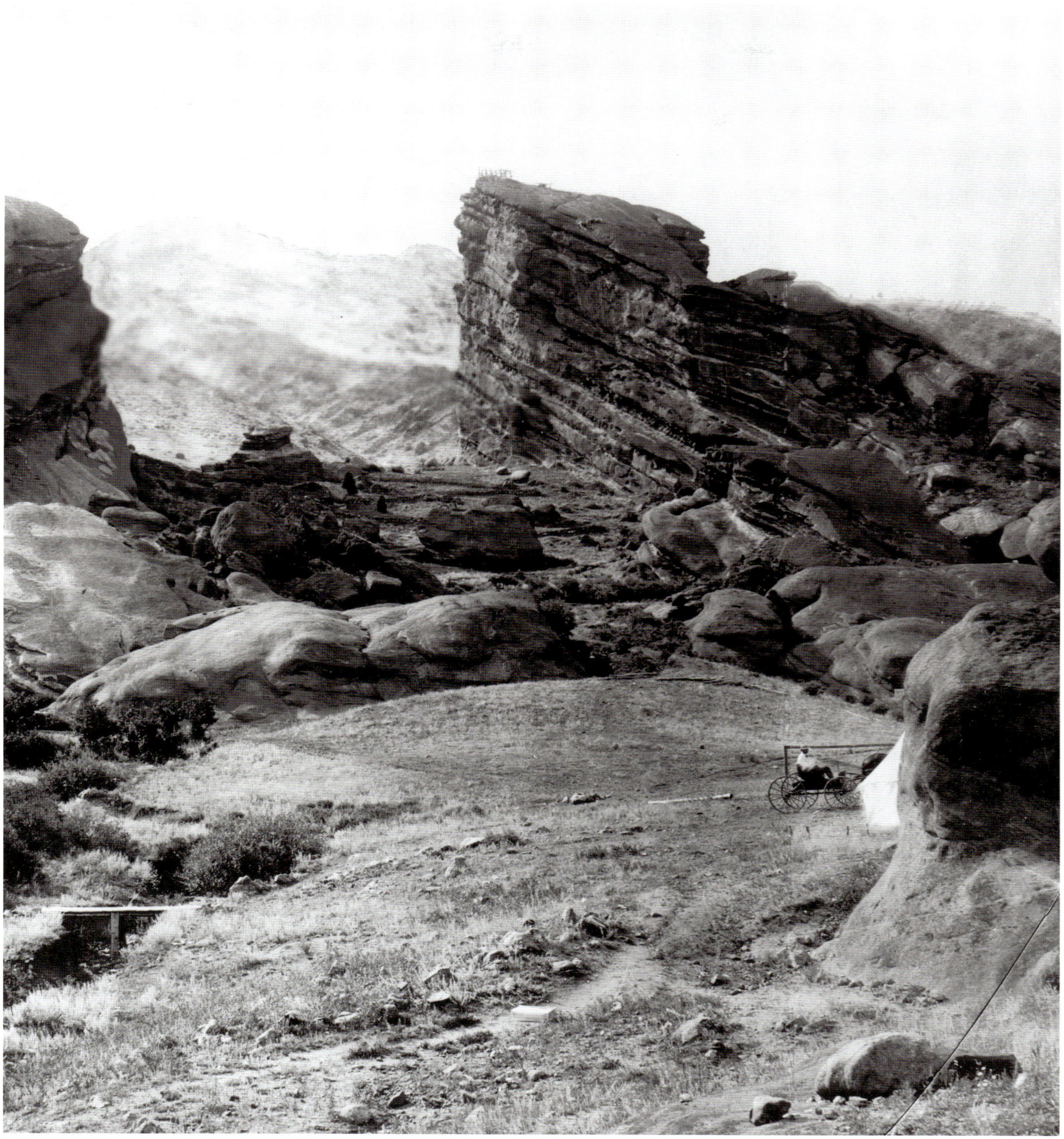

Previous page:
Red Rocks Amphitheatre

Opposite:
Picnickers amid the Red Rocks Park, between 1910 and 1920

This Page:
A lonely camper with horse, buggy, and tent in Red Rocks when it was privately owned. It was sometimes called "The Garden of the Titans" and sometimes "the Garden of the Angels."
c. 1900

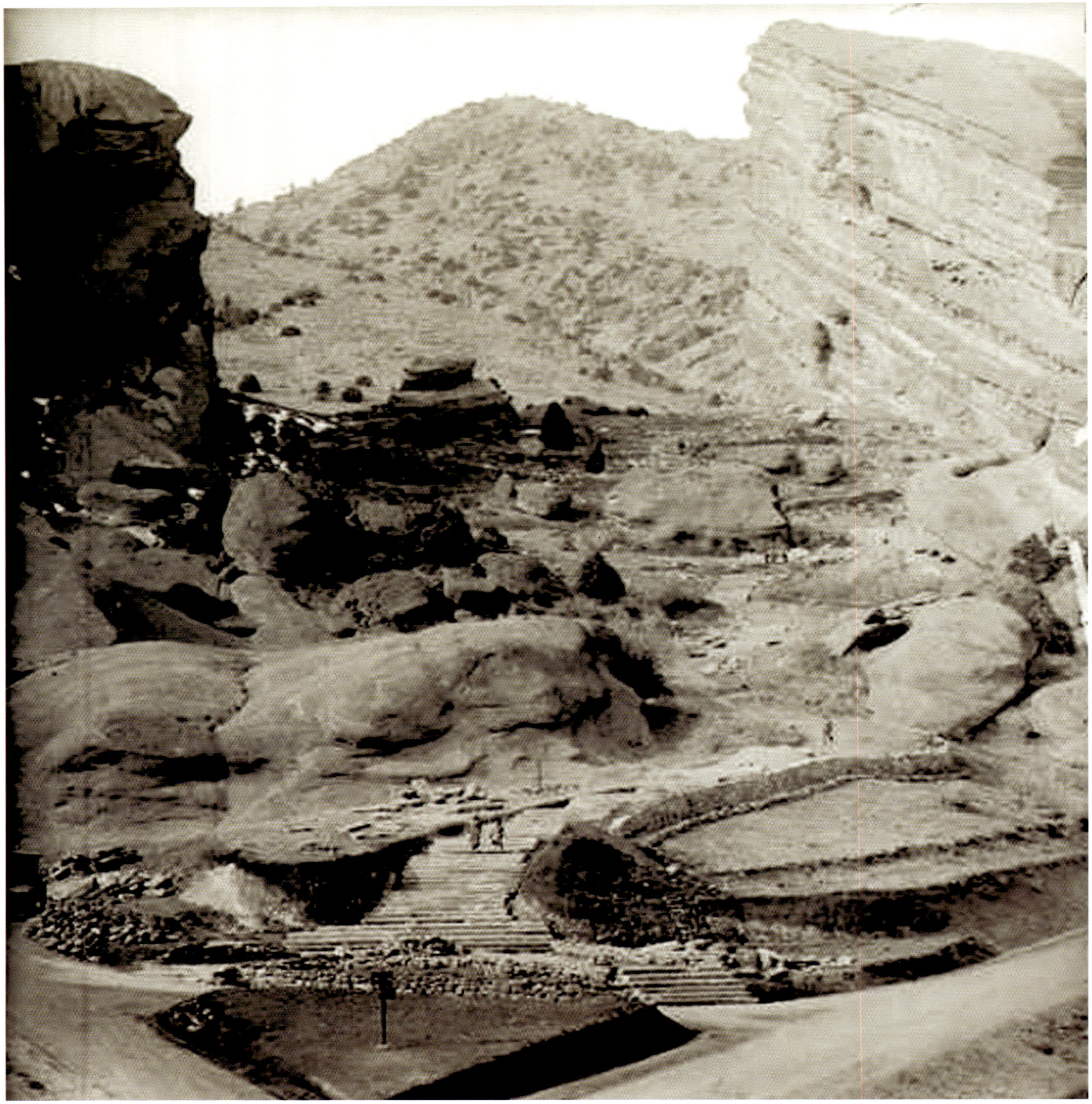

View of Red Rocks

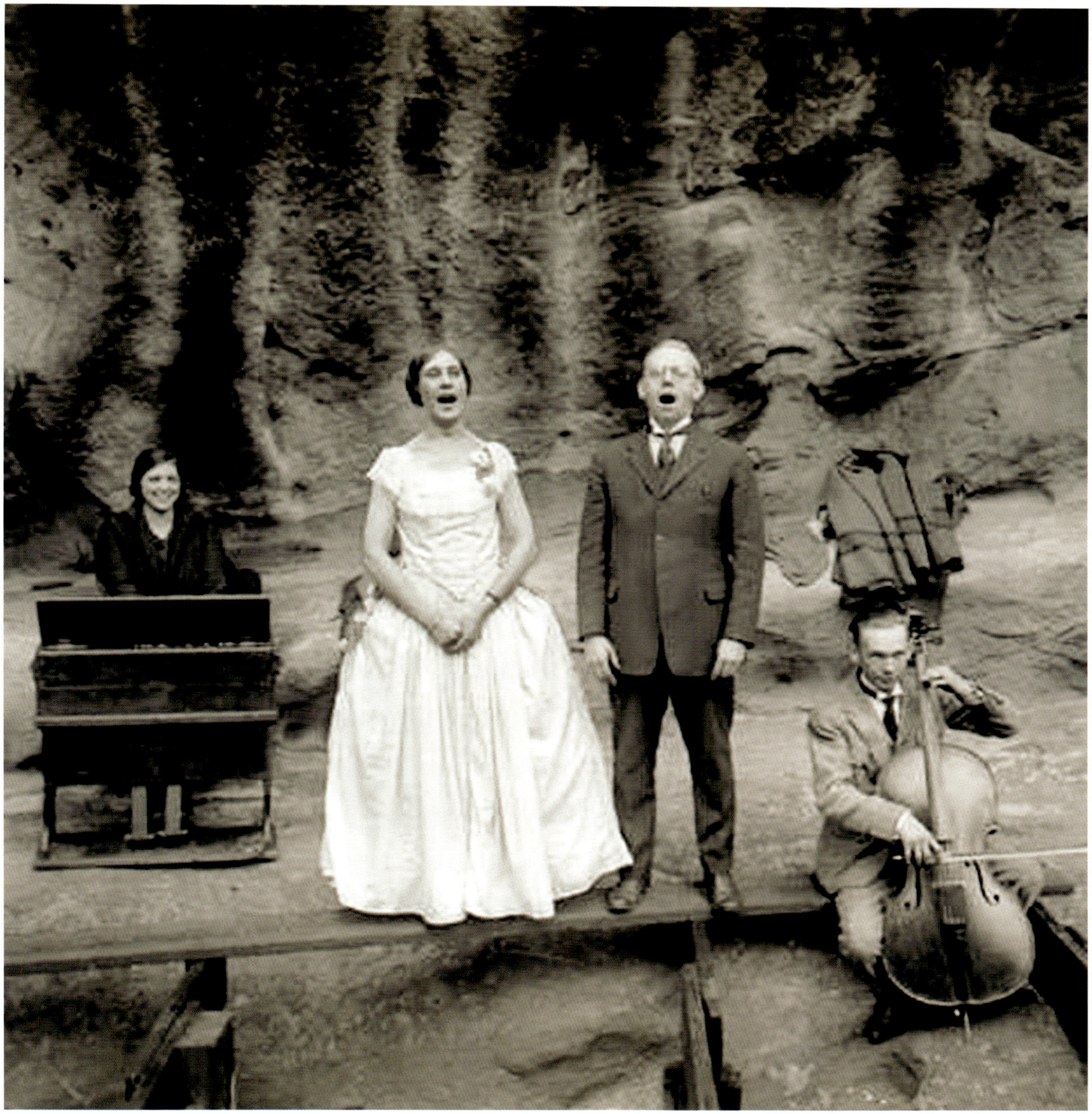

Four musicians from Signor Ferrulo's band check the acoustics, August 1910

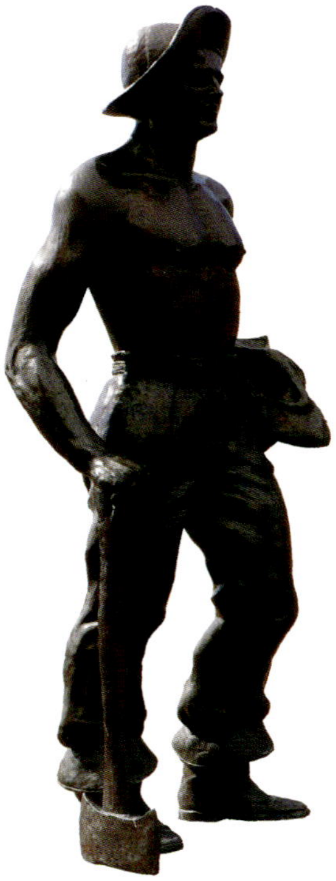

Statue of a CCC worker,
Red Rocks

CCC Company No. 1848 worked for five years at Red Rocks. Their camp is now the headquarters for the Denver Mountain Parks District. Company 1848 had approximately 175 members, each paid thirty dollars per month, twenty-five dollars of which was sent to their families. The amphitheatre project required them to remove twenty-five thousand cubic yards of rock and dirt, and put in place ninety thousand square feet of flagstone, ten carloads of cement, eight hundred tons of quarried stone, and thirty-thousand pounds of reinforced steel.

Right:
Red Rocks, curved rows of seating

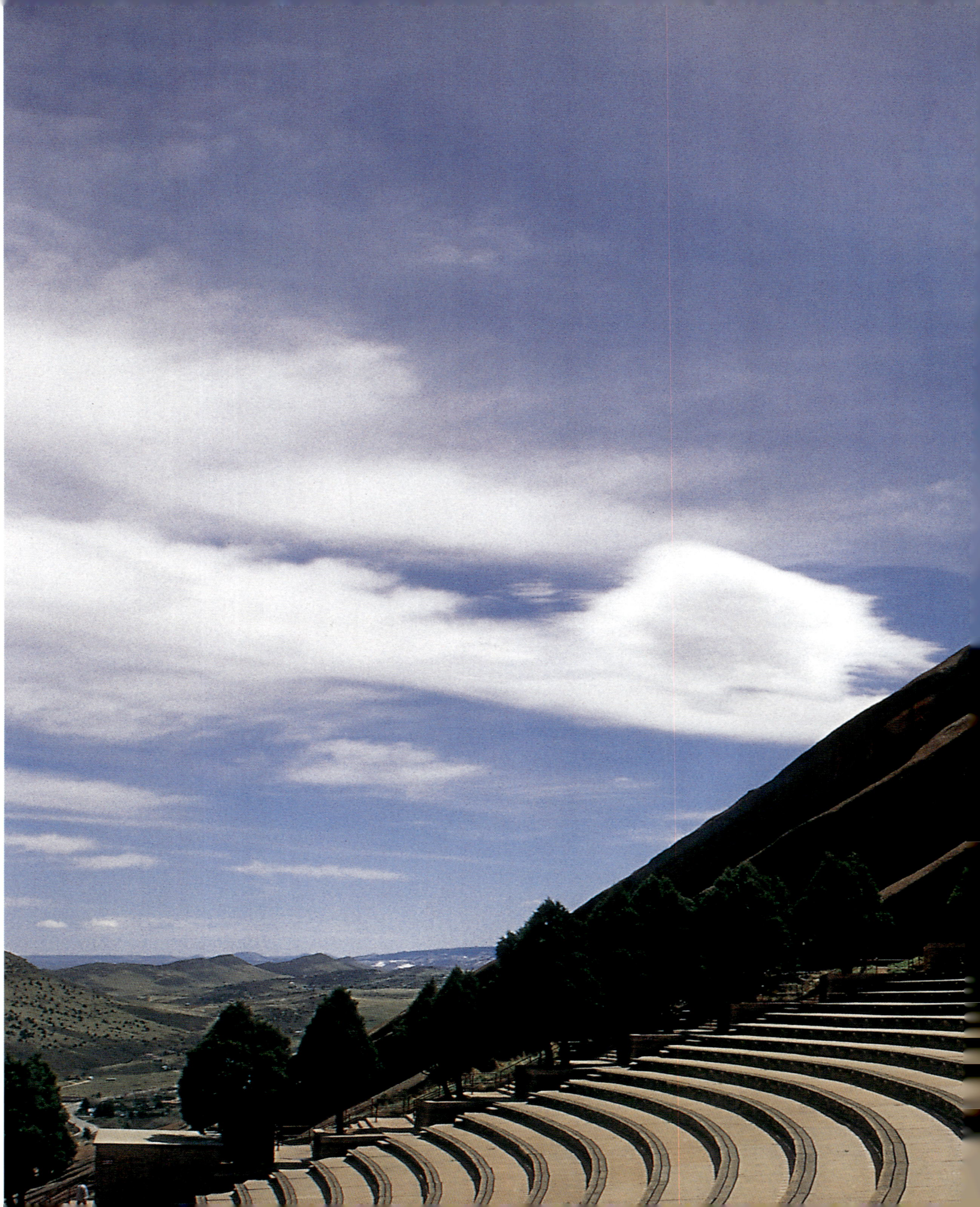

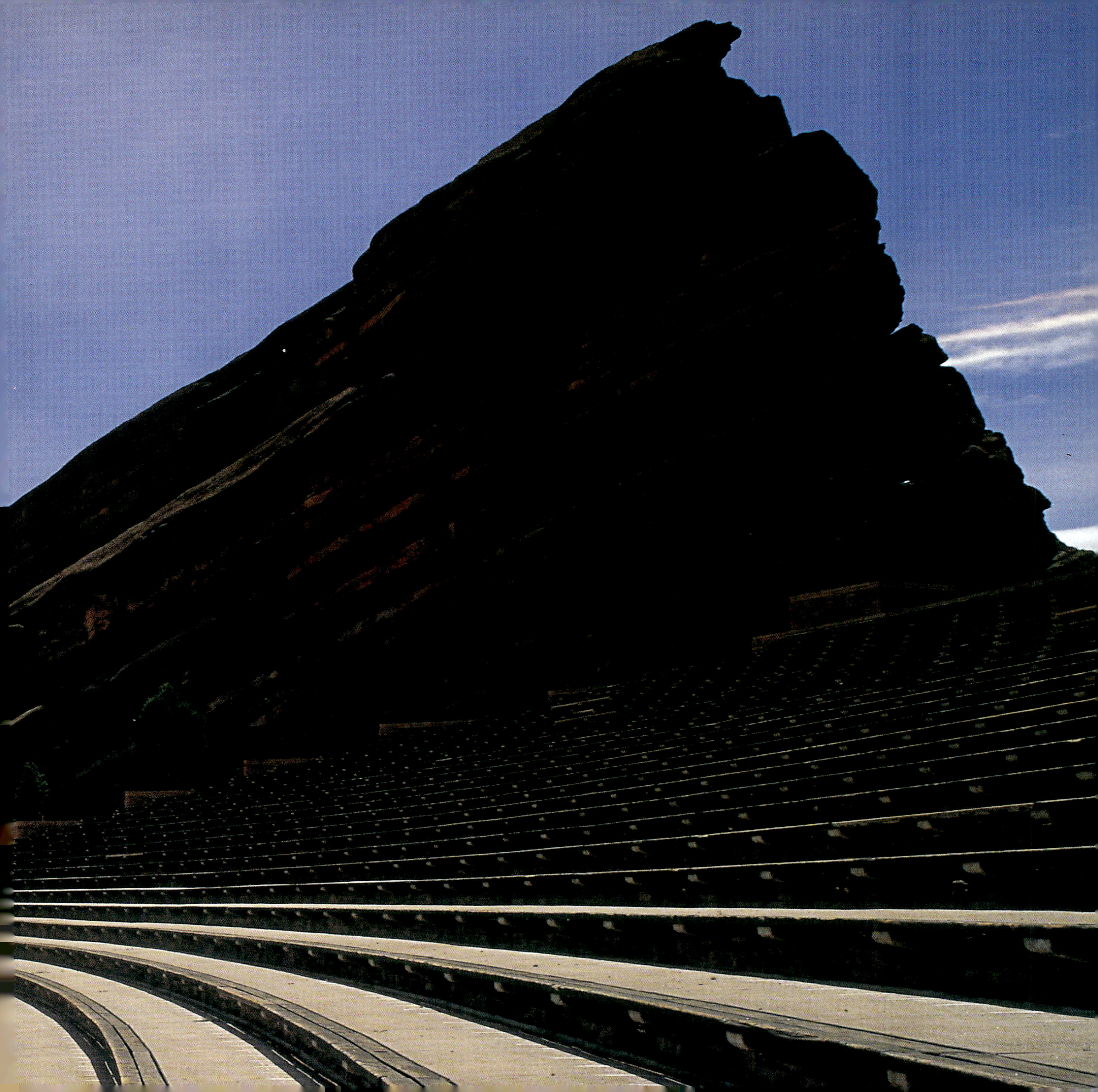

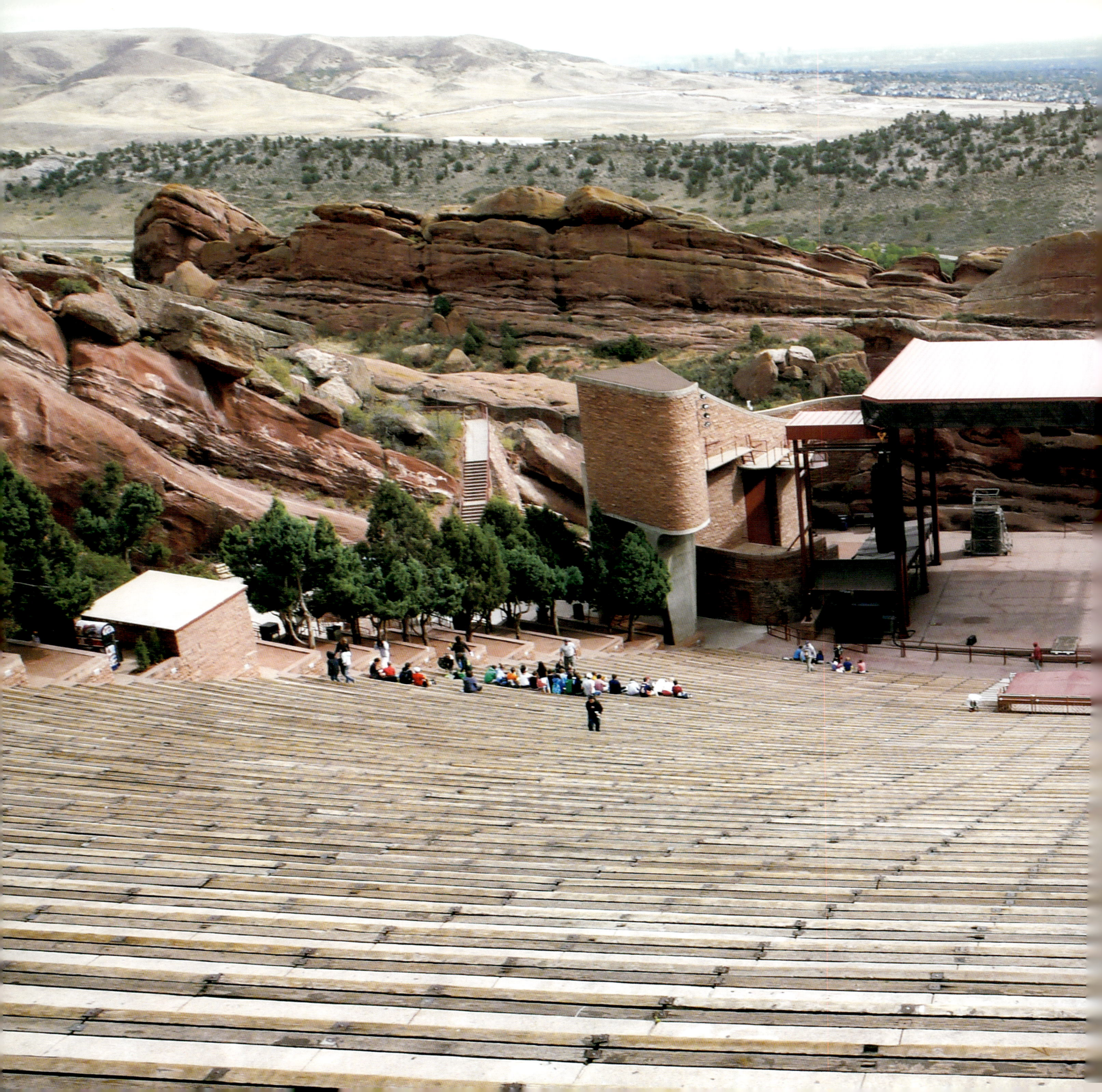

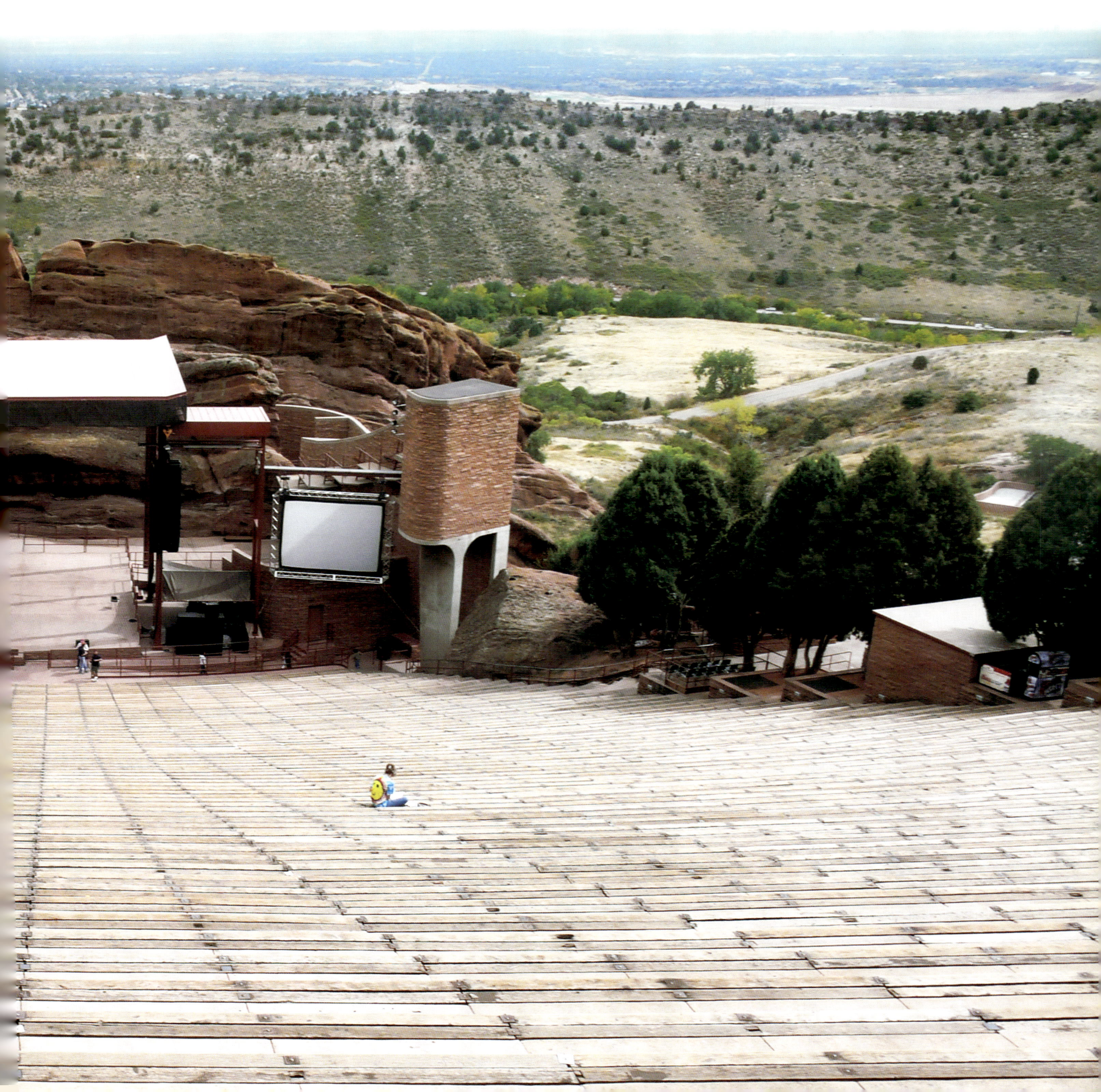

Previous pages:
Performance area with Stage Rock behind it and Denver in the distance.

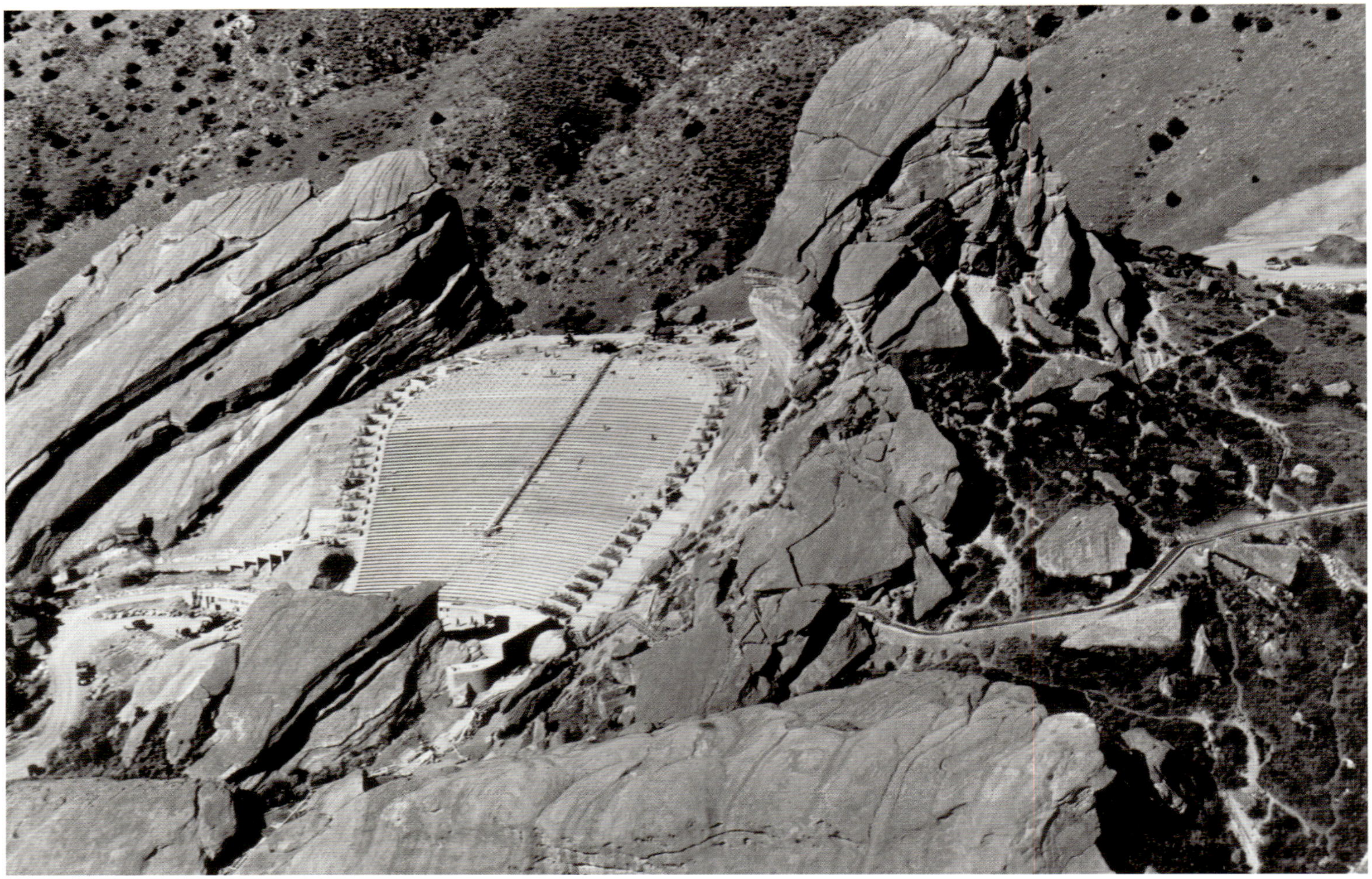

Top:
An aerial view from June 1941. Note the necessary asymmetry demanded by the rock formation. The black line going through the seating is the construction conveyor belt.

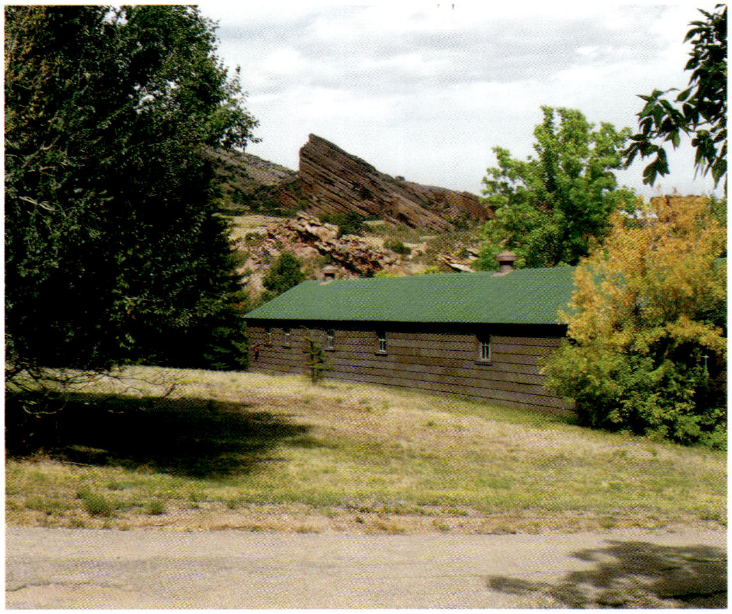

Bottom right:
Red Rocks seen to the north from CCC camp buildings.

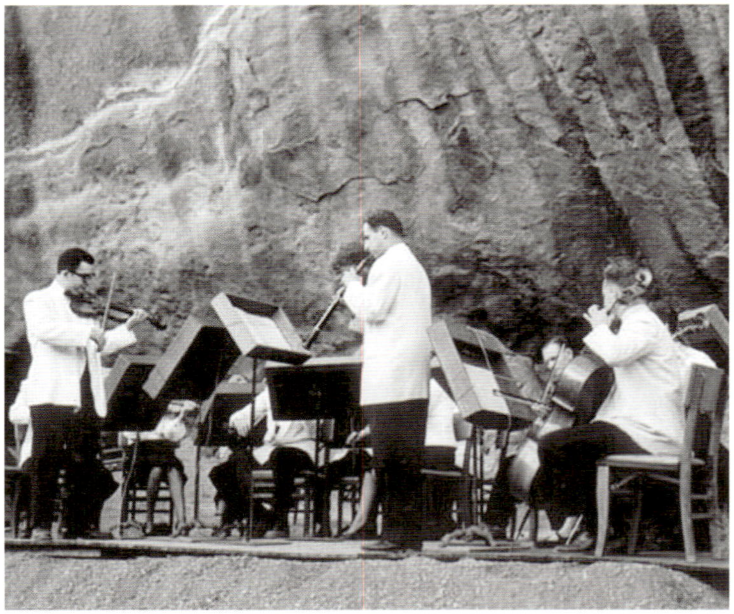

Bottom far right:
Concert by the Denver Chamber Music Society at Red Rocks Park in 1940.

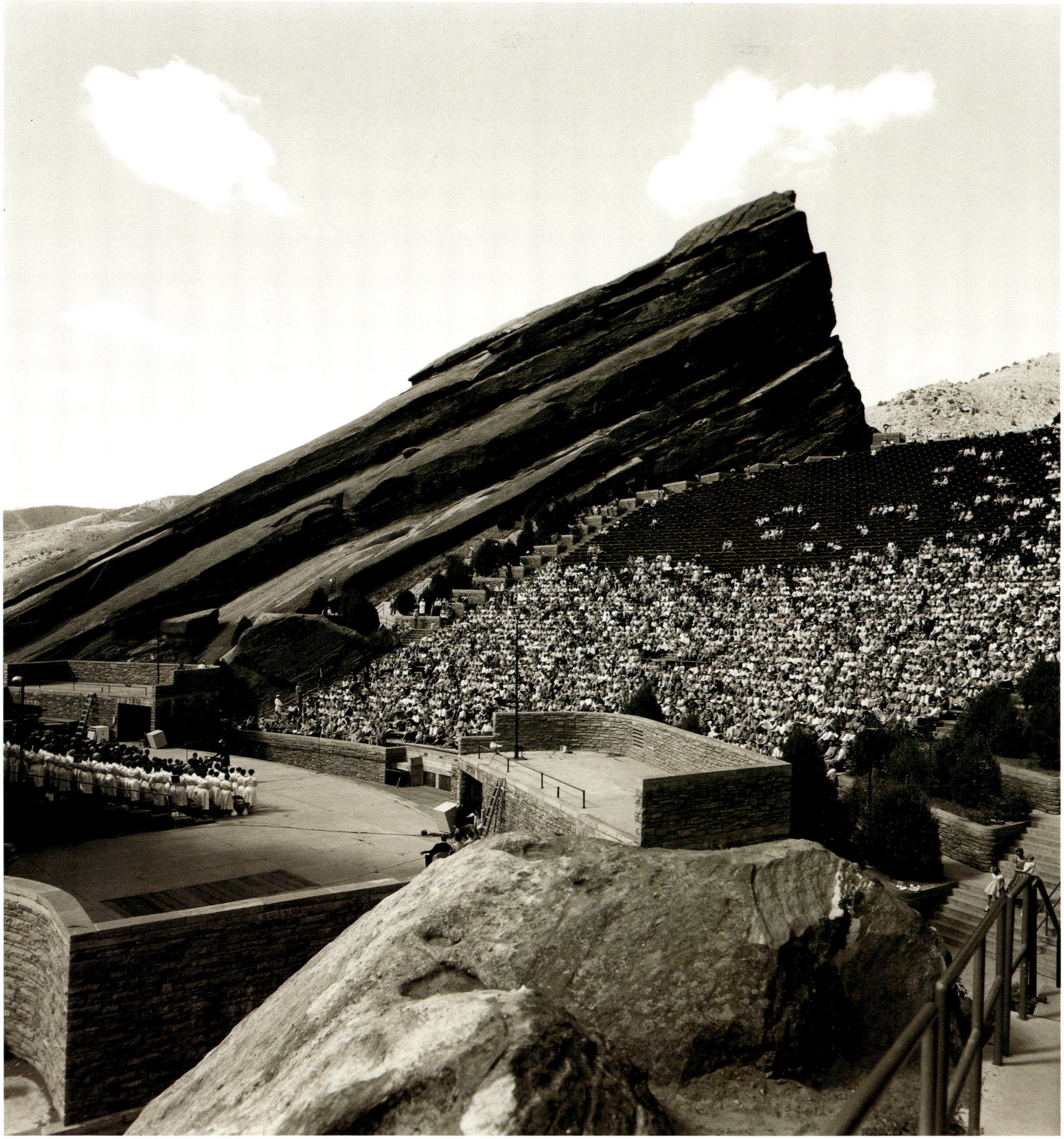

The first event at the park was the Easter Sunday Sunrise Service, 1947. The sun rises directly behind the stage.

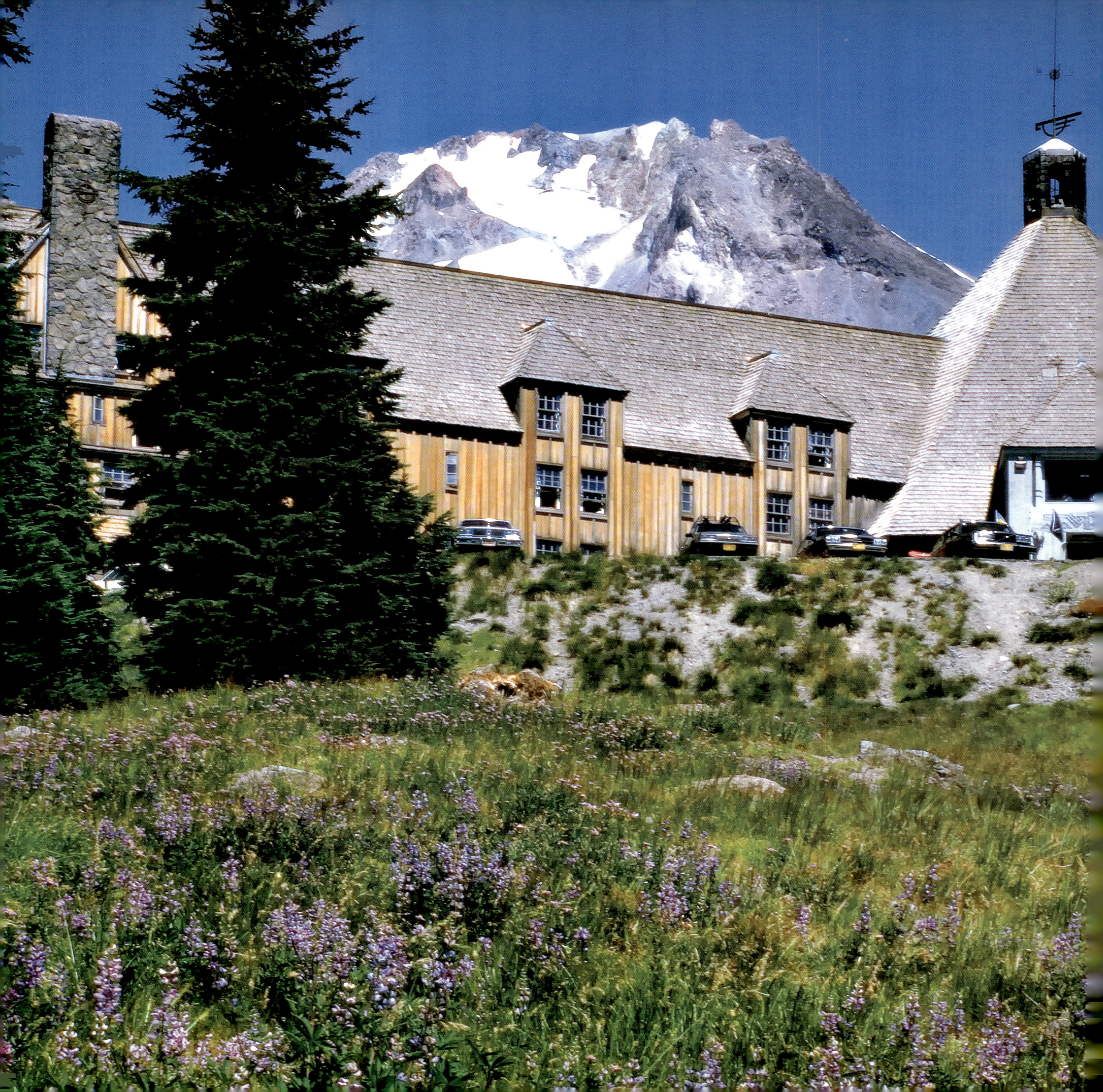

Timberline Lodge

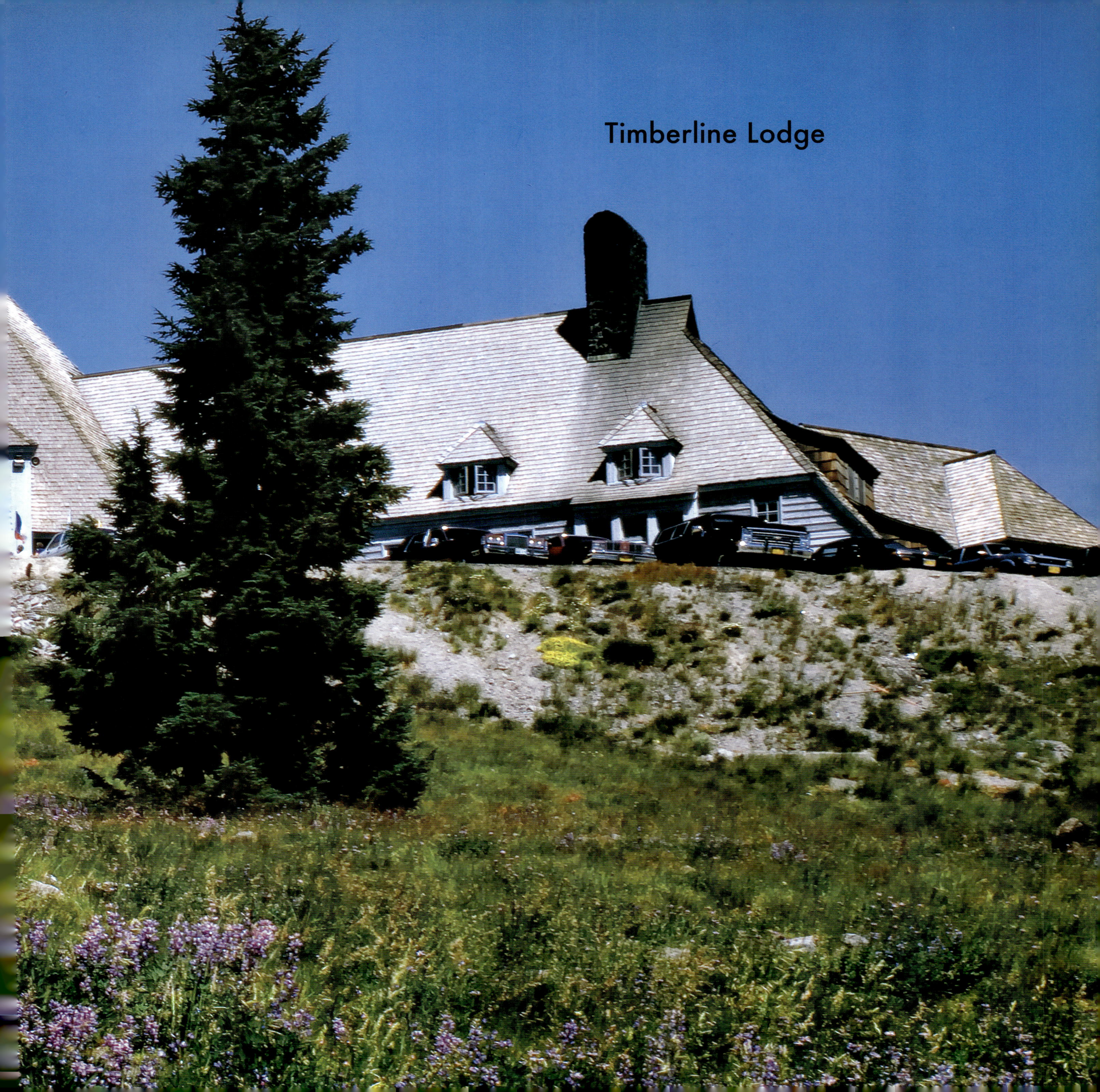

Previous pages:
Timberline Lodge in the spring.

This page:
A rendering of the final design of the south side and main entrance of Timberline Lodge.

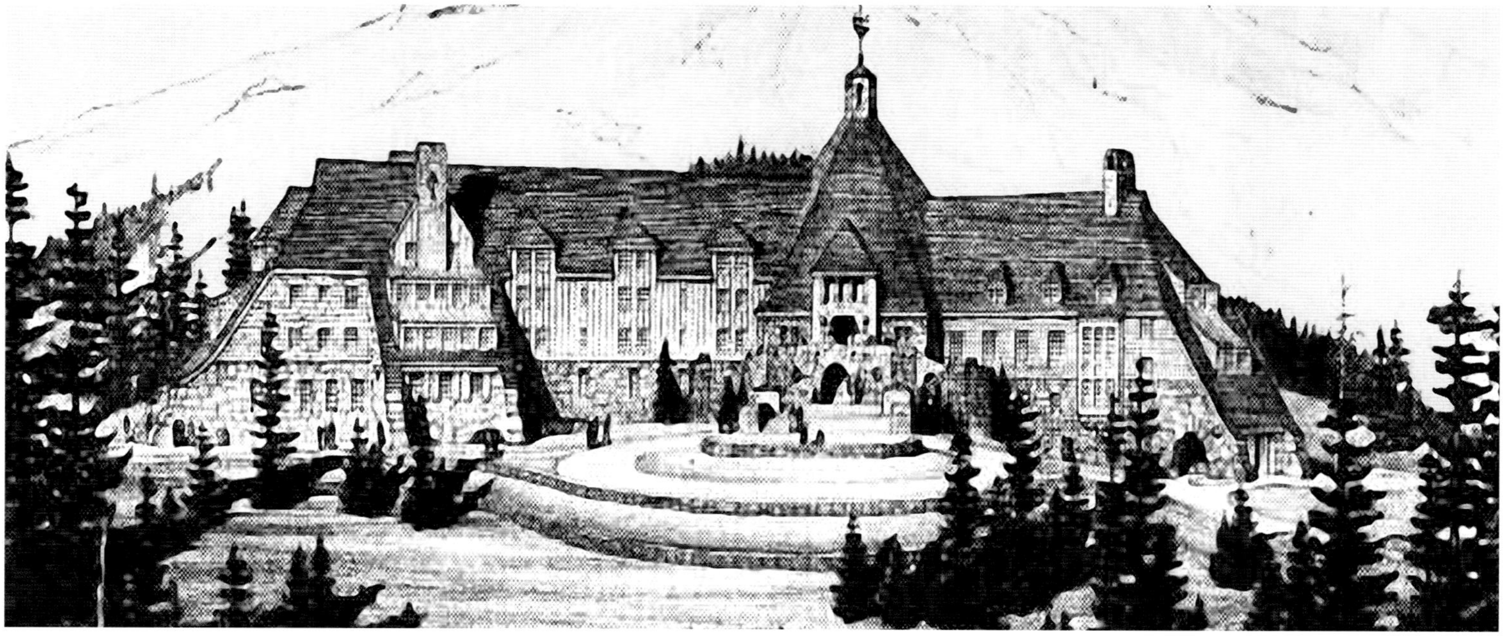

Timberline Lodge is six thousand feet up on the south slope of Mount Hood. According to WPA records, its building costs totaled $695,730 in 1936–38; 20 percent of the cost was for materials and the remainder for labor, 90 percent of which was from the WPA (the workers lived nearby in a tent city). Building trade laborers received the top rate of ninety cents per hour, and unskilled laborers fifty-five cents per hour. The price of materials was kept down by using recycled goods. Women wove upholstery, drapes, and bedspreads, and hand-hooked rugs from cut-up CCC blankets and other scraps. Newell posts were fashioned from cedar utility poles, their crowns carved into bears, seals, and other animals. The screens hanging in front of the fireplaces were made from the tire chains of the trucks that carried materials and workers up the mountain, and the fireplace andirons were forged from old railroad rails. Rocks used in the fireplace and foundation were taken from the site. It was derelict during World War II and steadily deteriorated through the late 1940s. By 1955 the firm operating the lodge was shut down by the IRS, and the structure so dilapidated that the U.S. Forest Service, which owns it, considered demolition. Timberline was saved by Richard Kohnstamm, a twenty-nine-year-old social worker. The Forest Service leased the derelict building to him, and some years later began to offer some assistance. A full-tilt recovery was launched by the Friends of Timberline, making use of funds contributed from the Comprehensive Employment and Training Act (CETA).[21]

Some of the skilled masons "were Italians who had come to this country in more prosperous times. Their beautiful work may be seen not only at Timberline, but also along the old Columbia River Highway and other Oregon highways. Construction workers at the lodge probably numbered about one hundred at any given time, but the jobs were rotated (except for highly skilled workers) in order to give work to as many of the unemployed as possible." President Franklin D. Roosevelt dedicated the completed building on September 28, 1937. Gilbert Stanley Underwood was the architect of record. Underwood was already renowned for his work on the Ahwahnee Lodge in the Yosemite Valley and other lodges in the national parks, but there seem to have been inter-agency rivalries at work, for Underwood's octagonal central "head house" was modified to a hexagon by W. I. "Tim" Turner, a U.S. Forest Service architect, and his USFS team of Linn A. Forrest, Howard L. Gifford, and Dean R. E. Wright.
E. J. Griffith was Director of the WPA for Oregon. Many of the designs for textiles and rugs were created by Margery

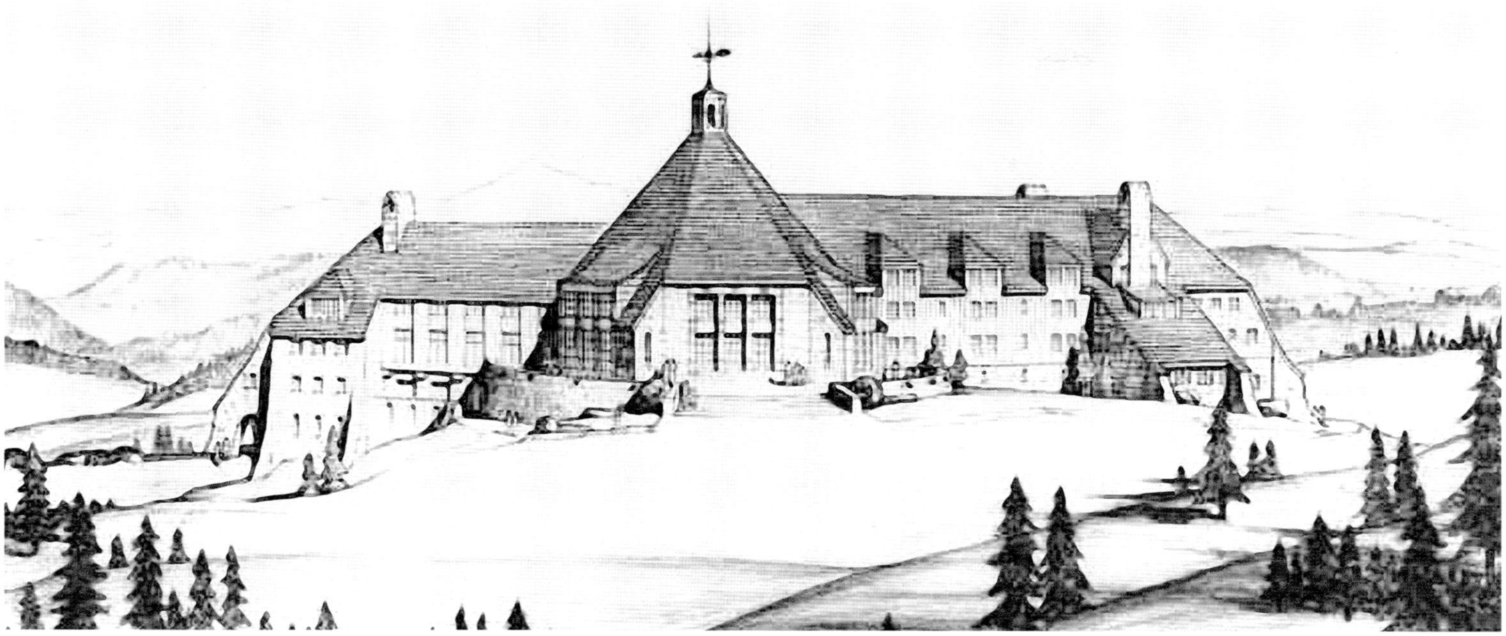

A rendering of the north side of Timberline Lodge.

Hoffman Smith of Portland, who was State Fine Arts Administrator for the WPA/FAP. A local tradition says that her 750-pound "snow goose" bronze weather vane above the head house was suggested by the "April Moon sign" in a "Campfire Book" being read by the daughter of a WPA worker, though Smith's abstract forms etched into the Lodge's chimney are taken from motifs in the art of the local Warm Springs Indians: the compass-like image is called "Working Hands"; the bird flying over three mountains is called "The Return of Spirit"; and the bird-headed man holding a staff is a shaman. Smith's mother was an early Oregon Arts and Crafts designer, and it is likely that both generations were acquainted with the Prairie School architect William Gray Purcell, who carried into his work in Portland in the 1920s the motif system of Louis Sullivan, George Maher, George Elmslie, and Frank Lloyd Wright, and followed by Smith in Timberline's draperies, bedspreads, rugs, tables, columns, sectional sofas, lampshades, and hanging lights. Smith also commissioned mosaics, murals, carvings, and paintings from Oregon artists including C. S. Price, Darrel Austin, and Charles Heaney.

In a still unpublished essay, "The Builders of Timberline Lodge," members of the WPA/FWP wrote of the work of the WPA/FAP at Mount Hood as arising from a "mystic strength that lives in the hills . . . captured in wood and stone, and in the hands of laborer and craftsman . . . presented as man's effort at approximating an ideal in which society, through concern for the individual, surpasses the standard it has unconsciously set for itself . . . All classes, from the most elementary hand labor, through the various degrees of skill to the technically trained were employed. Pick and shovel wielders, stonecutters, plumbers, carpenters, steam-fitters, painters, wood-carvers, cabinet-makers, metal workers, leather-toolers, seamstresses, weavers, architects, authors, artists, actors, musicians, and landscape planners, each contributed to the project, and each, in his way, was conscious of the ideal toward which all bent their energies." The *Oregon Journal* declared that "the reason for this enthusiasm might have been found in the fact that many of the men who were employed were those who, a few months previously, opened listless and discouraged eyes each morning, to confront a cheerless and foodless day . . . Each workman on Timberline Lodge gained proficiency in manual arts. He was a better workman, a better citizen, progressing by infinitely slow steps to the degree above him."[22]

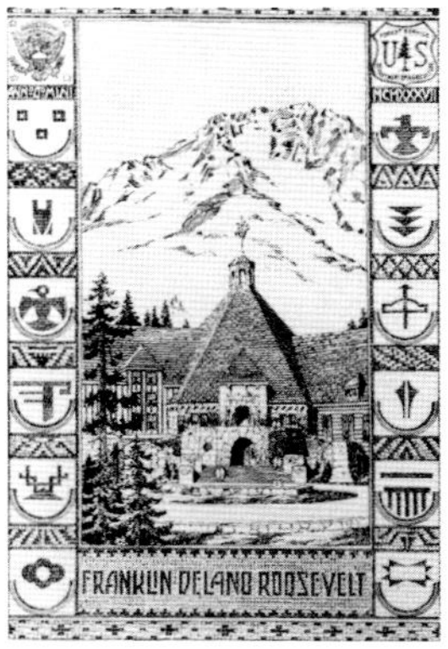

Celebratory Timberline Lodge menu cover

President Franklin Roosevelt and Eleanor Roosevelt dedicated Timberline Lodge on September 28, 1937. The feast included salmon and huckleberry pie.

Top:
Doorway and lintel of the front entrance of the lodge, flanked by two rams' heads The lodge's ten-foot-tall main door was hand-hewn and weighs over eleven hundred pounds.

Bottom right:
Curved posts form an arch framing the stairway. This theme is repeated in doorways and in the furniture.

Bottom far right:
The dining room at Timberline Lodge.

Opposite:
Looking down at one of the fireplaces in the Head House. The hexagonal theme is repeated in the table designs and the layout of the floorboards.

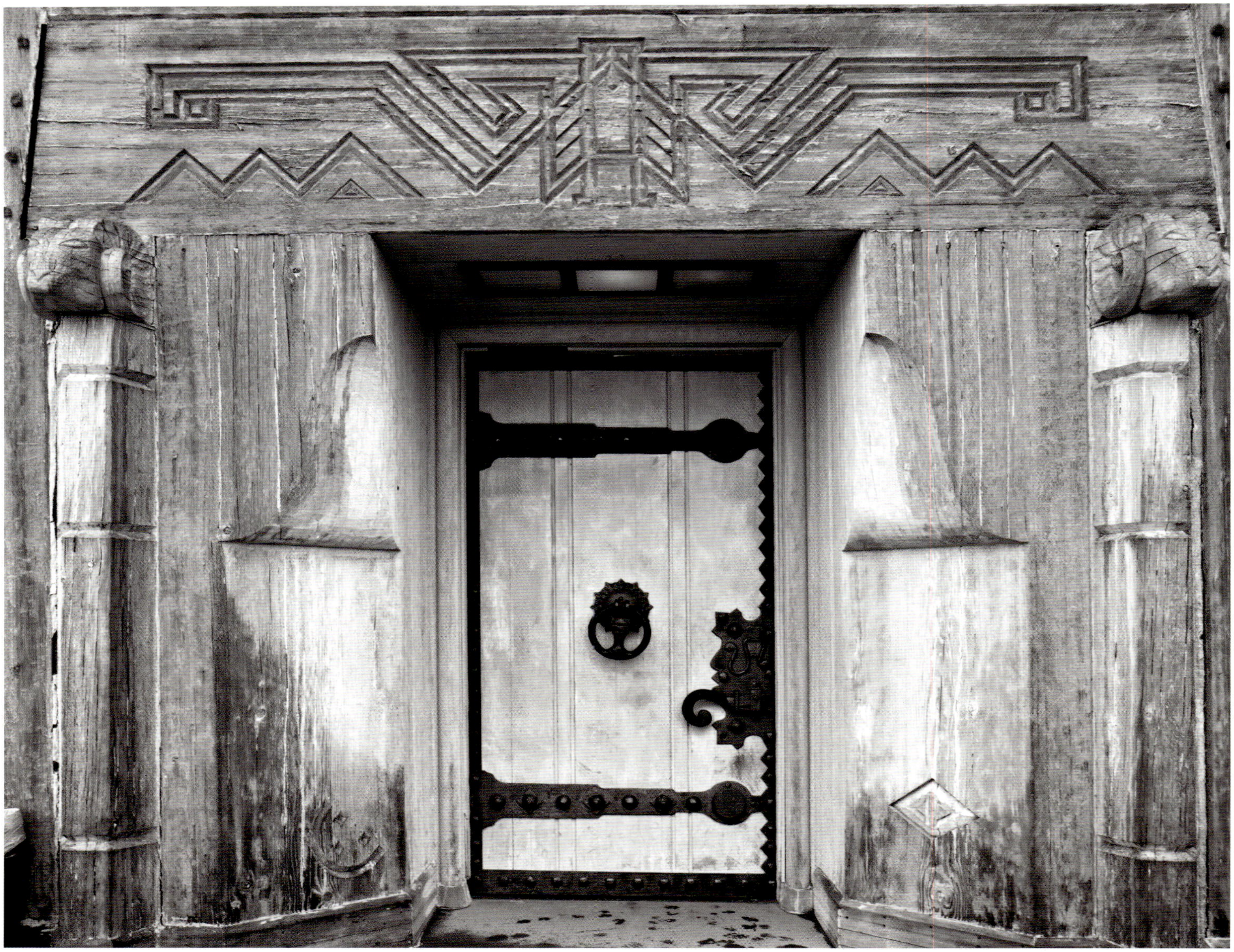

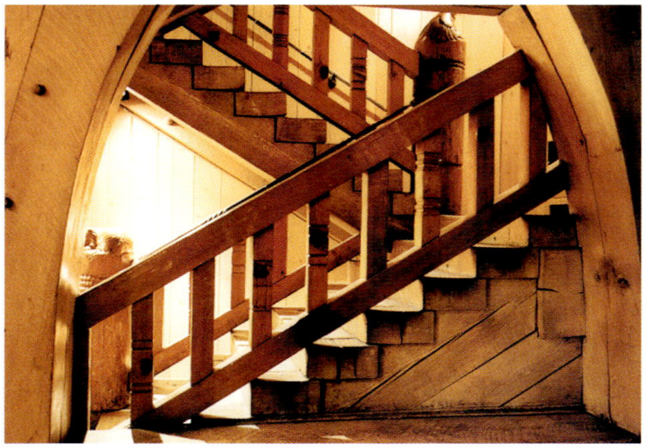

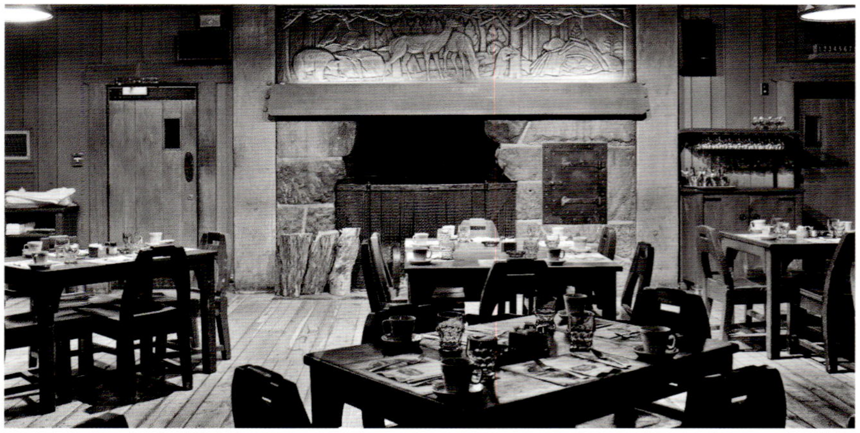

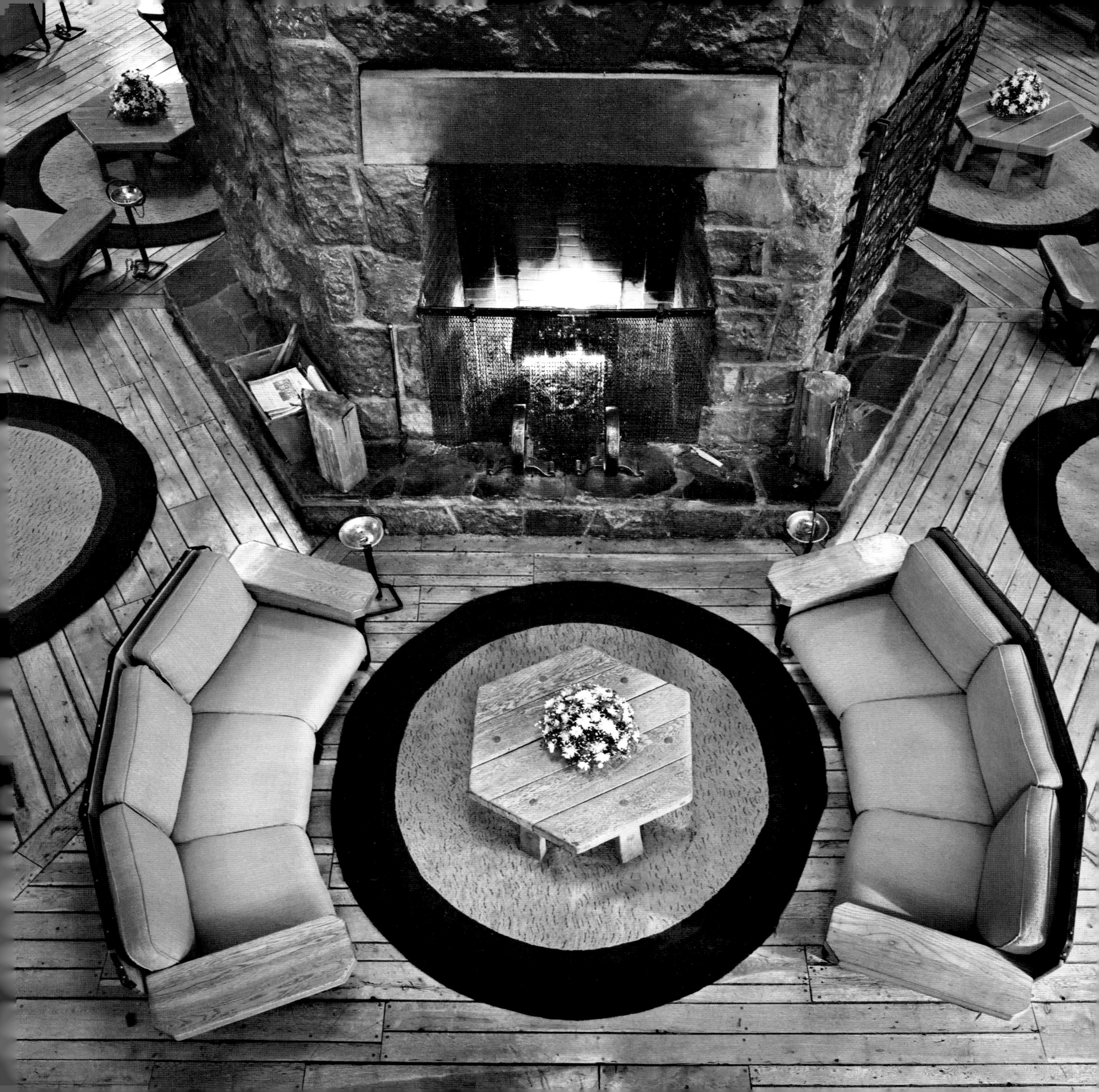

Carvings, clockwise from top left: An owl, a hawk, a bear cub, and a duck. There are nineteen carvings atop newel posts in the lodge interior. The posts were made from rescued utility poles purchased at $2.10 each. The carvings, representing the wildlife around Mount Hood, are now smoother after years of touching. They were designed in a free and informal style, allowing the chisel marks to be clearly visible.

Bottom right: A section of the main lounge at Timberline Lodge.

Far right top and bottom: The hexagonal "head house" is four stories high around a ninety-eight-foot-tall chimney stack.

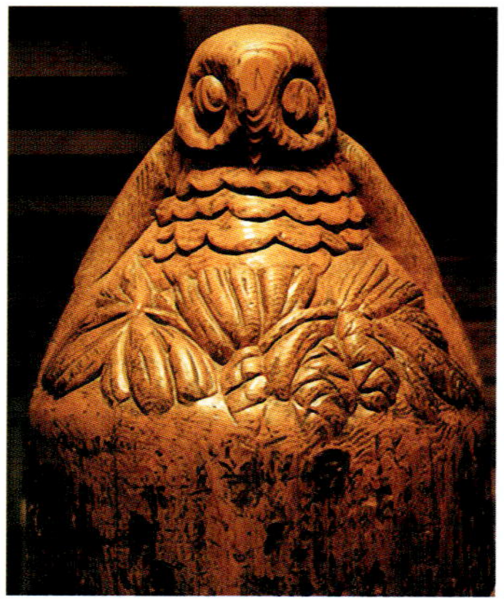
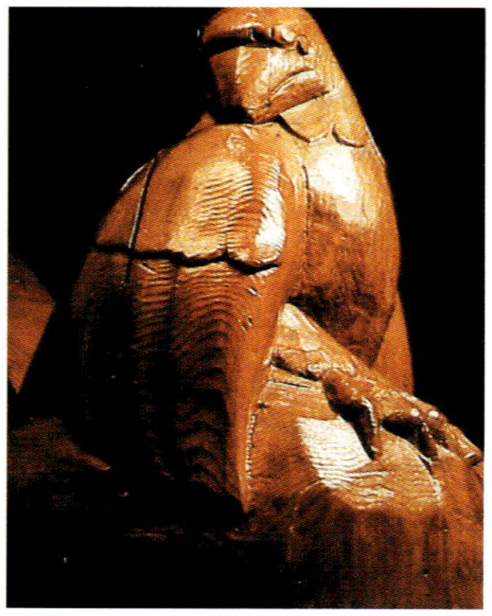
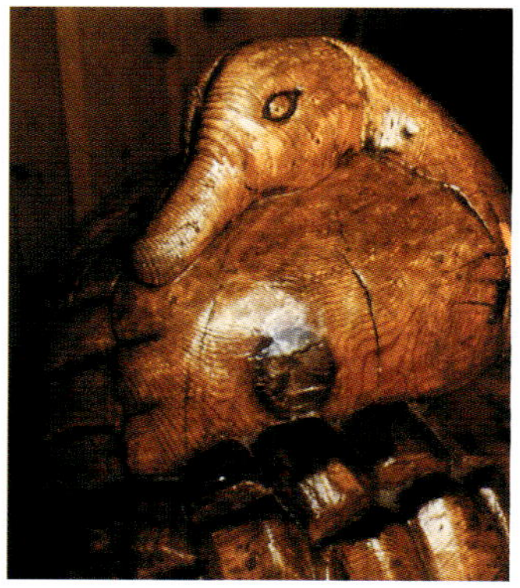
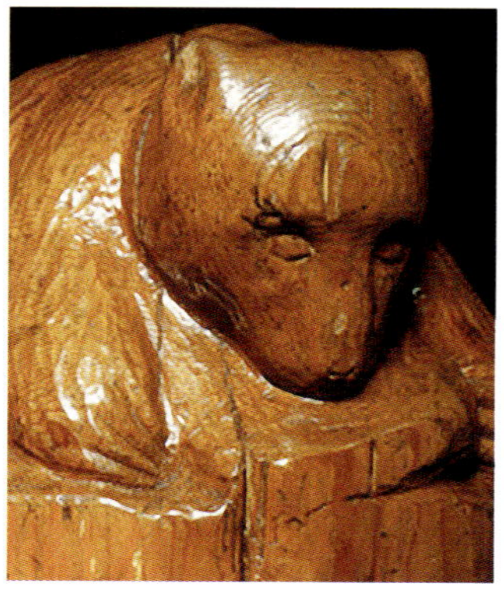
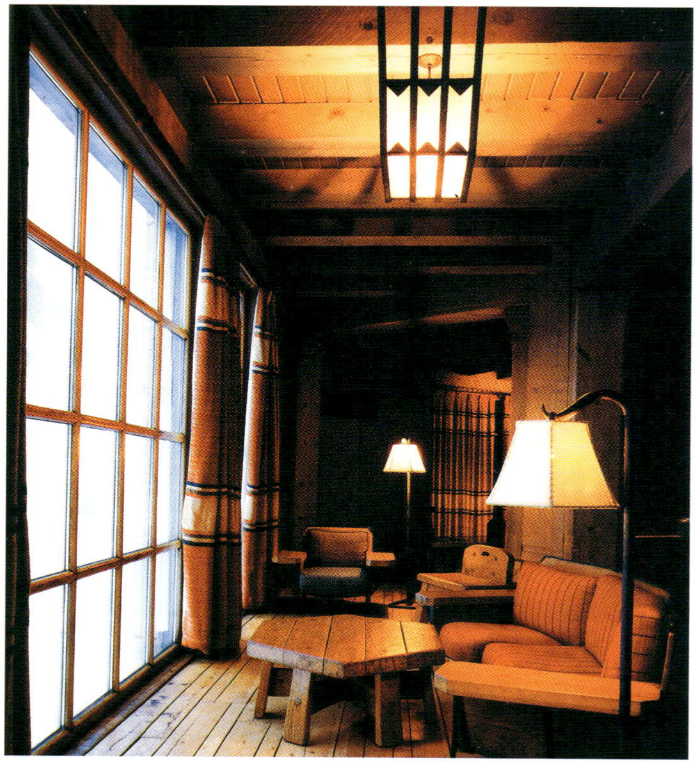
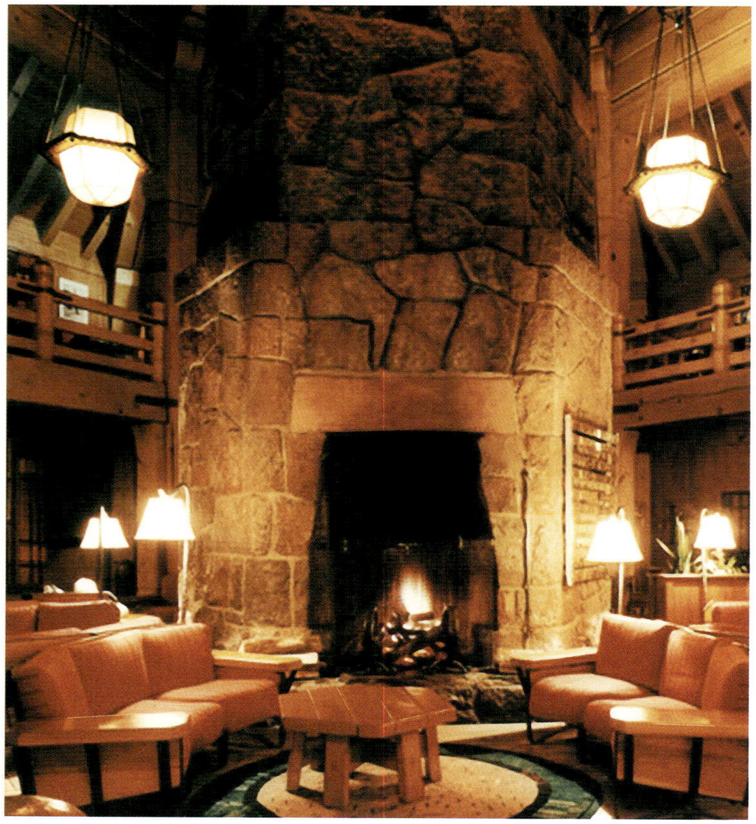
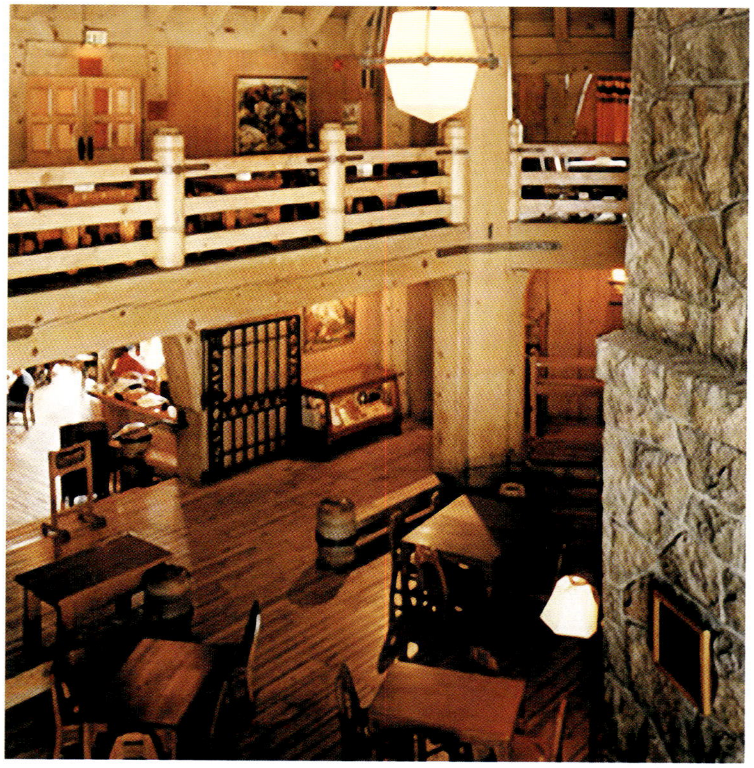

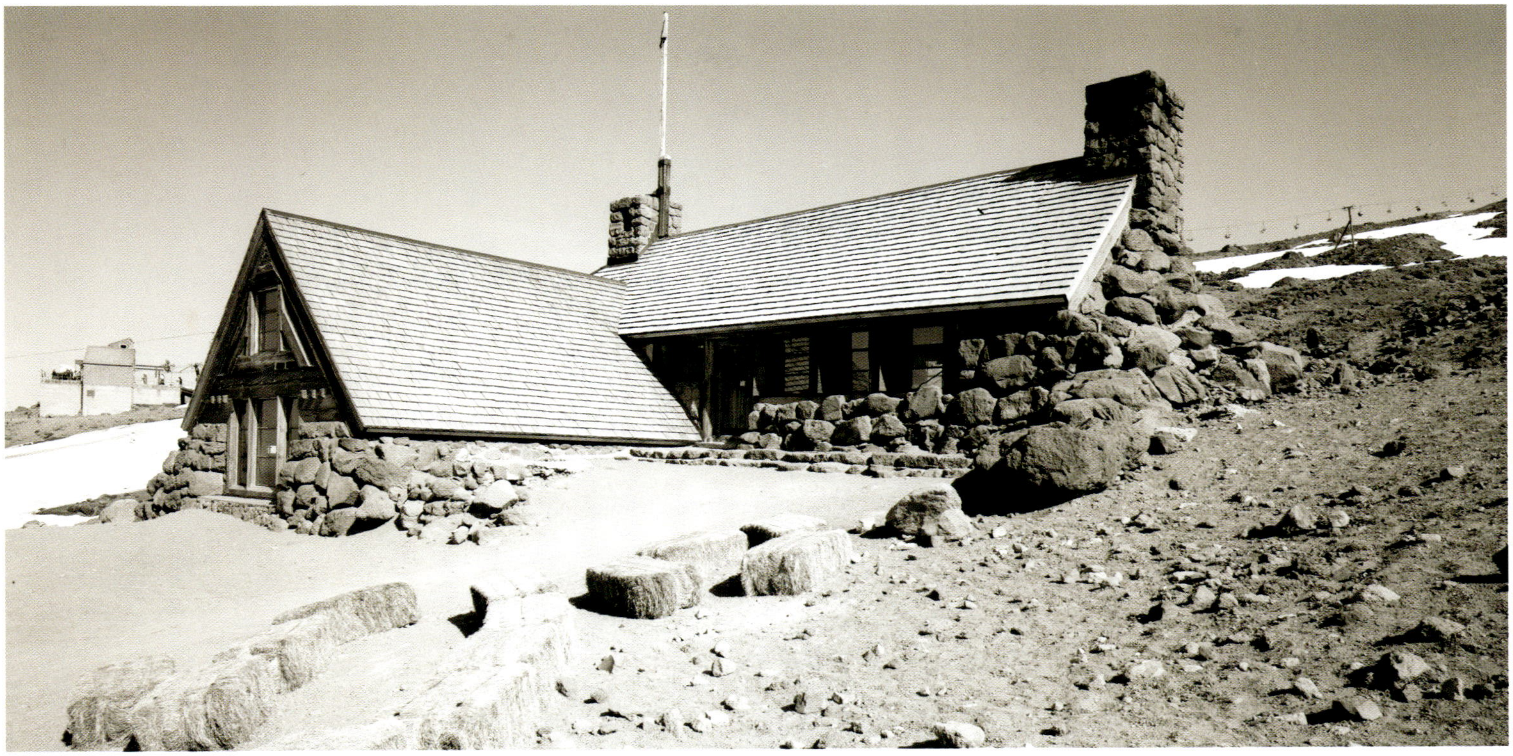

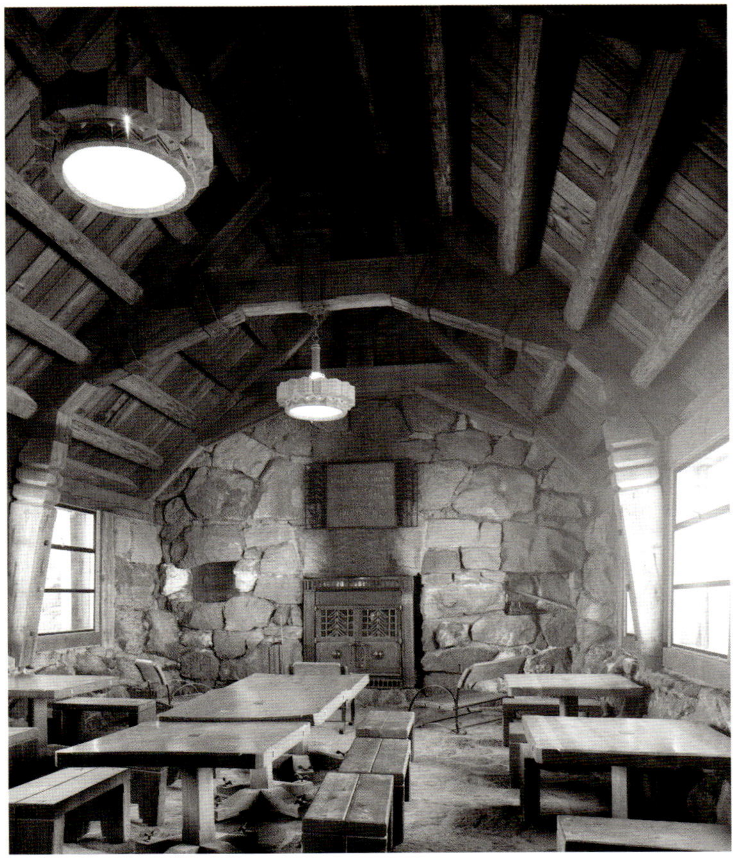

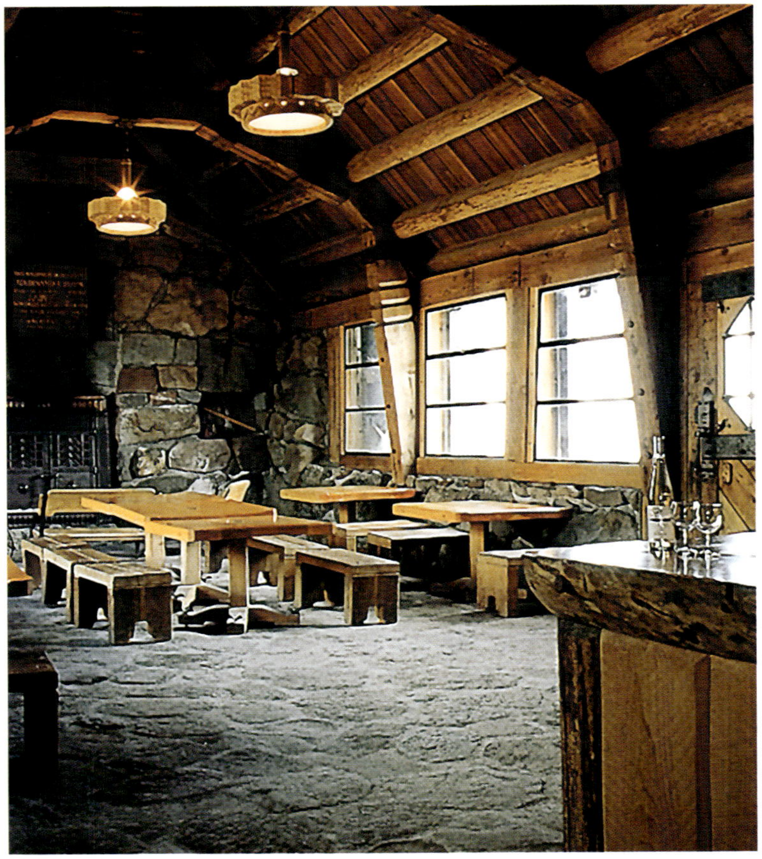

Top:
The exterior of the Silcox Hut looking northwest.

Bottom far left:
Interior of the Silcox Hut.

Bottom left:
Interior of the Silcox Hut today.

"The movement to restore the Silcox Hut to its New-Deal glory germinated in 1986 when a cadre of climbers, intent on saving a structure the Forest Service threatened to tear down, formed a non-profit group called The Friends of Silcox Hut. Over an eight-year period, hundreds of volunteers poured $400,000 of donated funds and an equal dollar figure of donated materials and services into the structure. They constructed bunk rooms capable of housing 24 overnight visitors, dug drain fields, laid water pipes, installed bathrooms and showers, built a modern kitchen, replicated the wood and iron work of the original hut, wired the structure, and refurbished vintage furniture and fixtures."[vi]

La Purísima

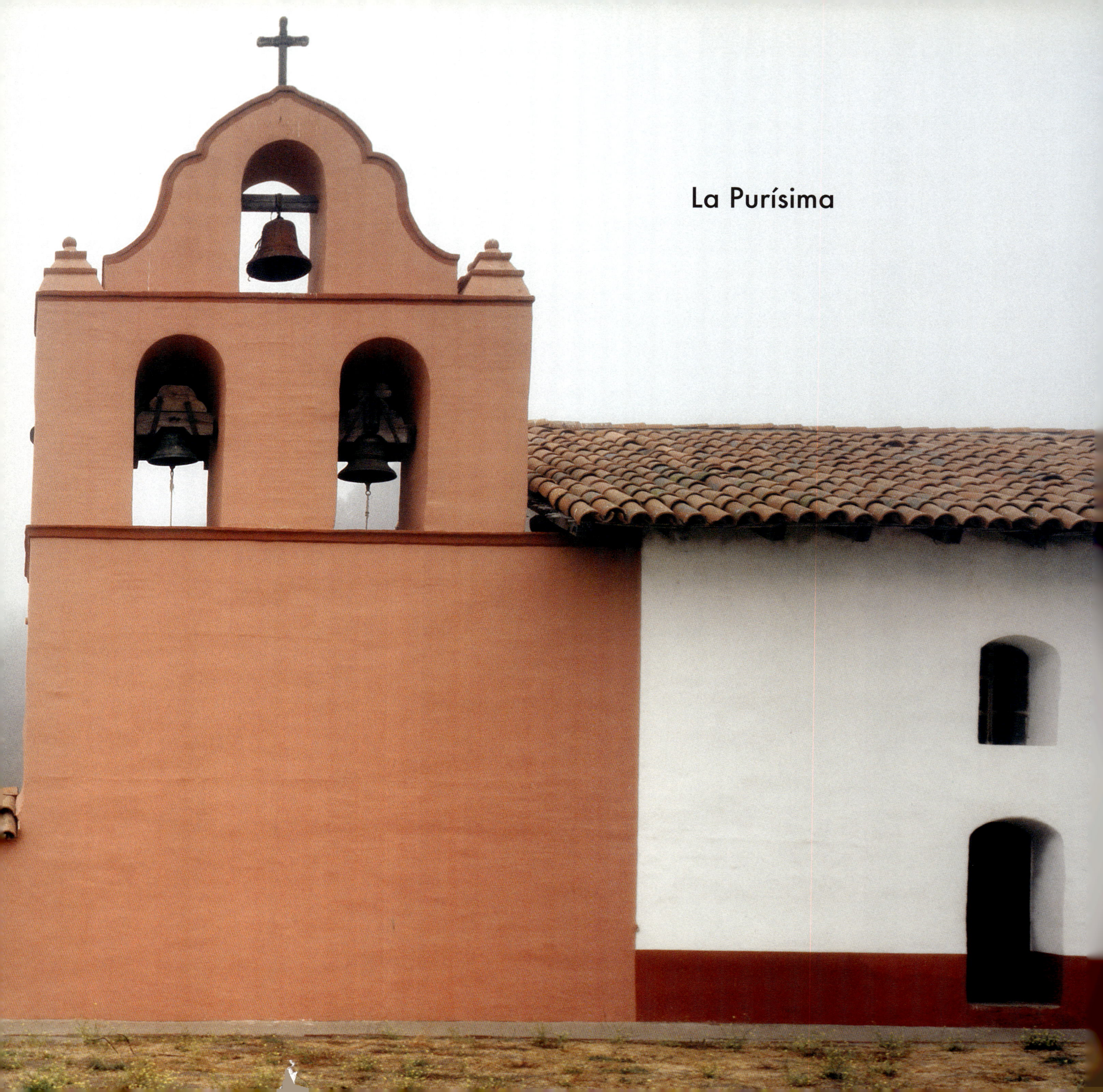

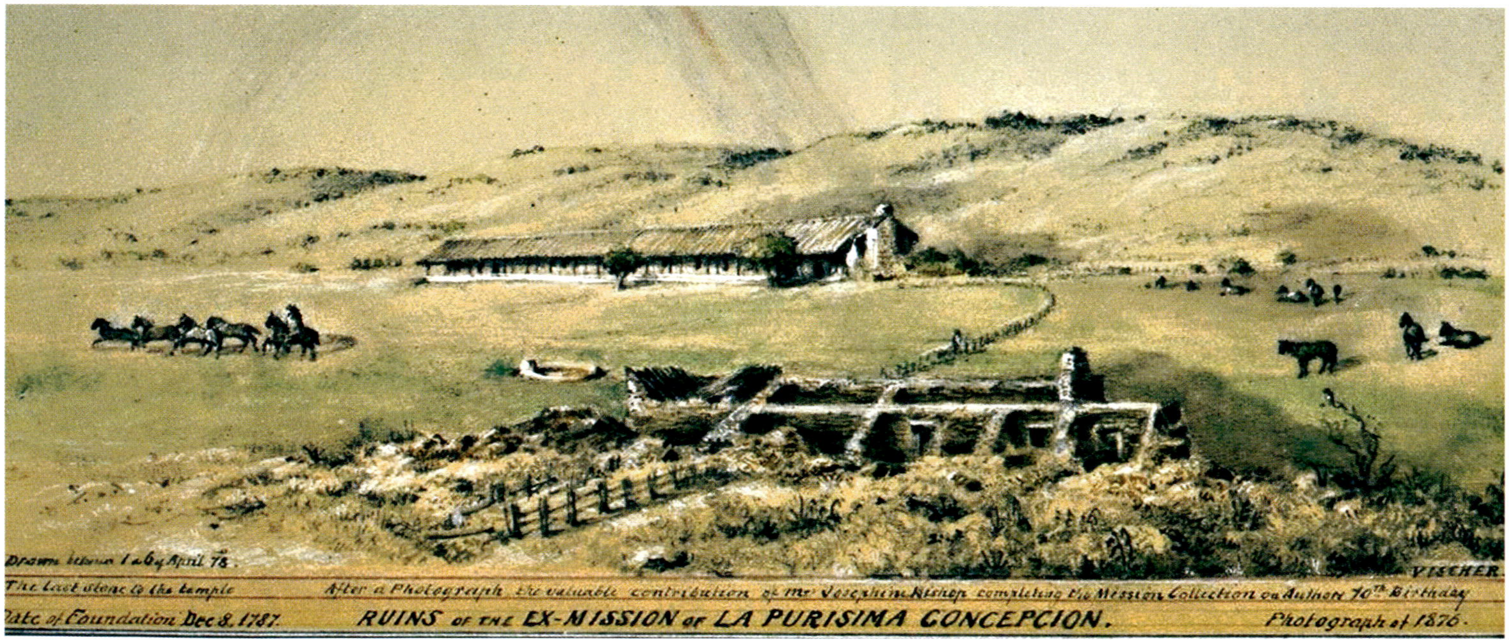

Opposite:
The campanario. One of La Purísima's original bells, forged in Lima, Peru, survived the destruction of the mission and was transported to nearby Guadalupe. It was brought back in 1941.

This page:
A watercolor based on a late-nineteenth-century photograph of the mission ruins.

La Purísima Mission was founded in 1787 by Fray Fermín Francisco de Lasuén as the eleventh California mission. It lies four miles east of Lompoc below a red-sand California hillside covered with trees that survive with little water. In 1804 smallpox, measles, and other health problems began to take a heavy toll on the mission Indians. Between 1804 and 1807 there were about five hundred deaths (one death for every three Indians living at the mission) and the total population of mission Indians began a decline throughout California. On December 21, 1812, a succession of earthquakes brought down the old church and damaged most of the other mission buildings. Heavy rains followed the quake and completed the destruction. A new La Purísima Mission was built in a small canyon northeast of the original founding site and directly on the Camino Real. It became the control point of the mission's two hundred thousand acres, including eleven ranchos, two vineyards, and an anchorage at Cojo Bay. The new mission complex included a large residence building, a church, and many utility buildings including a warehouse, an Indian barracks, a blacksmith shop, and a small hospital.

After 1834, Mexico secularized the missions, and La Purísima was sold to a succession of cattle ranchers. The mission buildings were abandoned and fell into ruin. As the buildings became shapeless jumbles of brown adobe overgrown with weeds and brush, only a few broken walls remained. By 1933, the ranchers had departed, and the Union Oil Company, their successor, was a willing seller of 507 acres to the State of California.

In April 1934, a CCC camp inspector saw the possibilities for a reconstruction. The necessary new materials were careful facsimiles of the original bricks, floor tiles, and other structural elements. The project architect, Fred Hageman, and his team developed the plans from which CCC Companies 2950 and 1951 rebuilt the mission under the supervision of the National Park Service. The first major project, the residence building, was completed in 1936; the water system, fountains, and cistern were in place by 1938, the church in 1939, the shops and quarters building in 1940, and, finally, the residences and interior decoration of the church in 1941. CCC enrollees made by hand 110,000 adobe bricks, 31,000 roof tiles, and 15,000 floor tiles for the residence building alone. The first religious services in more than a century were held in the church on December 7, 1941. When completed, the mission was turned over to the State of California to administer.

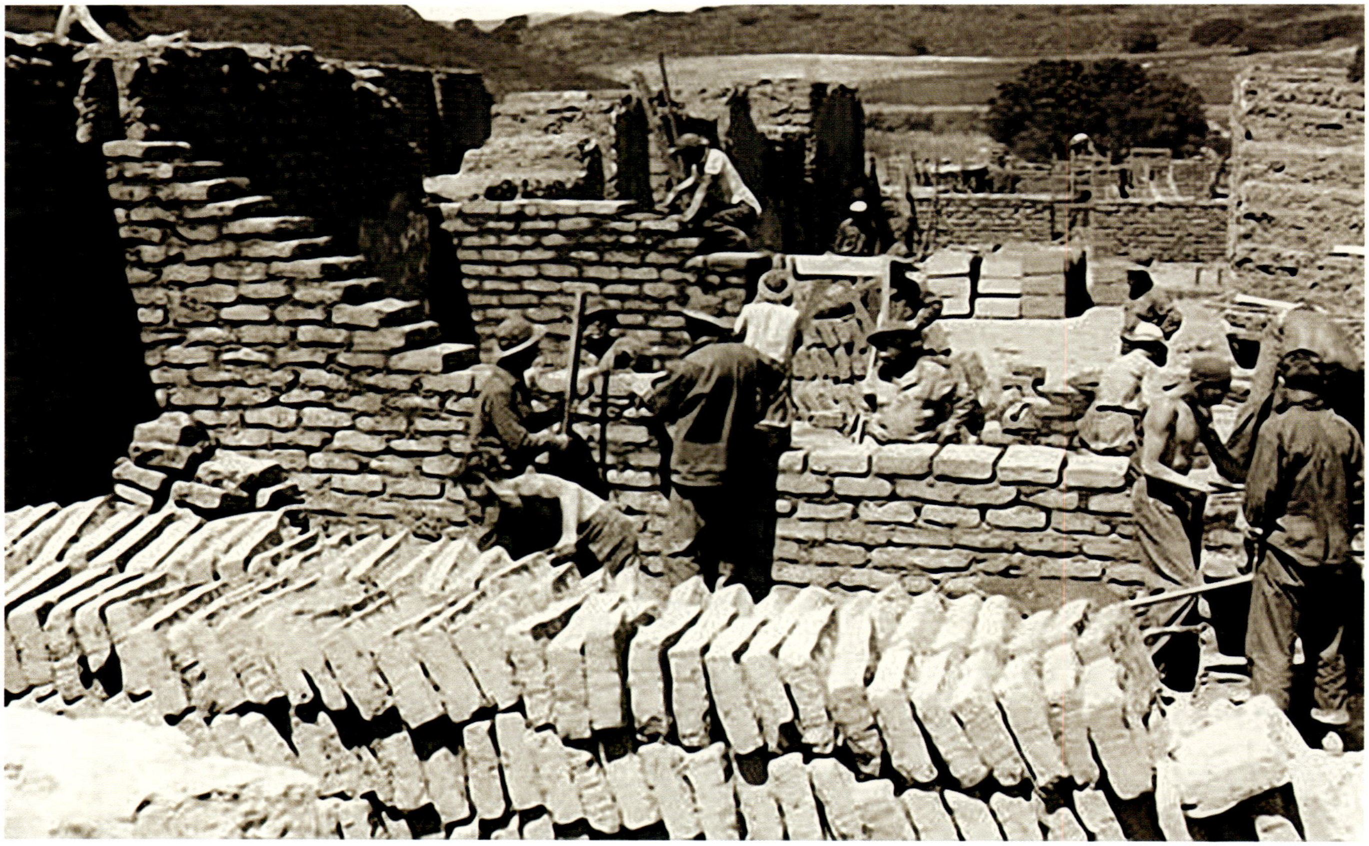

CCC enrollees working with some of the sixty-five-pound adobe bricks handmade on the site.

Fred Hageman wrote of the completed reconstruction: "We have an imposing row of long, low, white adobe buildings, surmounted by broad expanses of red tiled roofs extending nearly a thousand feet along a northeast-southwest axis, facing across the little canyon of Los Berros . . . in front of the Church and beside the Shops and Quarters building is the hard bare plaza where Padre Payeras once assembled his hundreds of dusky children and instructed them in the orders of the day. While in front of the Residence Building the perfume from myriad flowers hangs heavy in the air, and the only sound we hear in the hush of an evening is the tinkling splash of water in the fountains or perhaps the whirring wings of the hummingbird . . . Should we wonder, then, that we find this line written in the Visitors' Register by a descendant of a Spanish pioneer? 'Gracias a Dios. La memoria vivira.'"[23]

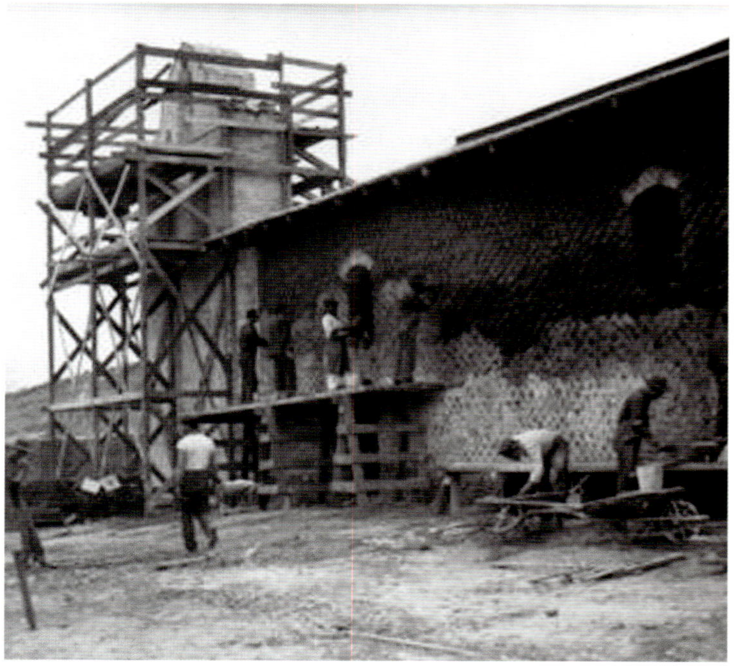

Teams work on the exterior, smoothing over a coating of adobe with small metal trowels the architect designed, simulating the texture of handwork. Some of the old mission's exterior walls were originally tinted pink or purplish red. A geologist identified a sample of the raw material as diatomite and pointed out a vein of it in the ground. CCC crews excavated it and ground it into the pigment in the finishing coats.

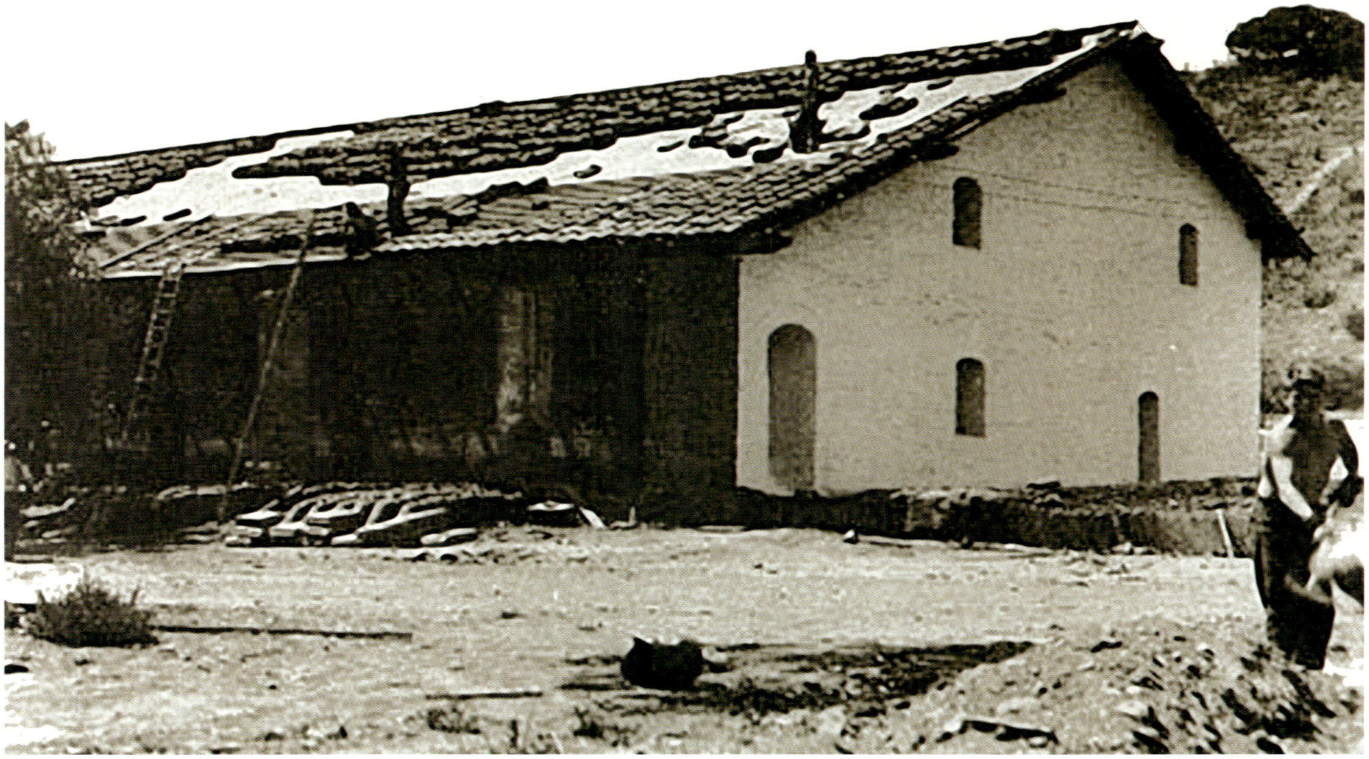

At work on the roof

The clay for the sixteen-pound rounded red roof tiles and the flat floor tiles were made from a nearby vein, and dried and fired in the CCC's own kiln.

Another perspective is offered by Nicolasa I. Sandoval (Chumash):

"I come here often with friends. Starting at the interpretive center, we consider the perspectives of people who walked before us in this place—first known as Amúu. Through the thirteen reconstructed buildings, we learn about how Chumash people lived, labored, and died here in the years between 1813 and 1834. In the infirmary, we imagine those who succumbed to unknown diseases. The infirmary chapel reminds us of the lives that symbolically began and abruptly ended here. Exploring the gardens, we think about the hearts and hands of people who spent countless hours turning the earth. Their work to plant and reap food sustained life in this community. We visit the spare monjerio (dormitory) where Native girls and unmarried women were required to live, sleeping on pallets far from the warmth of their families. In the padres' residence, we witness the strength and artistry of the carpenters who built the chairs, benches, and beds that offered comfort and rest to the priests.

In this place we remember people who made irrevocable choices of great consequence. We honor the genius of our first people and their continuing legacy. As I walk here, I feel the gravity of a catastrophic past. I fill my lungs with the fresh air of hope—glad to be alive, triumphant that we are still here."[24]

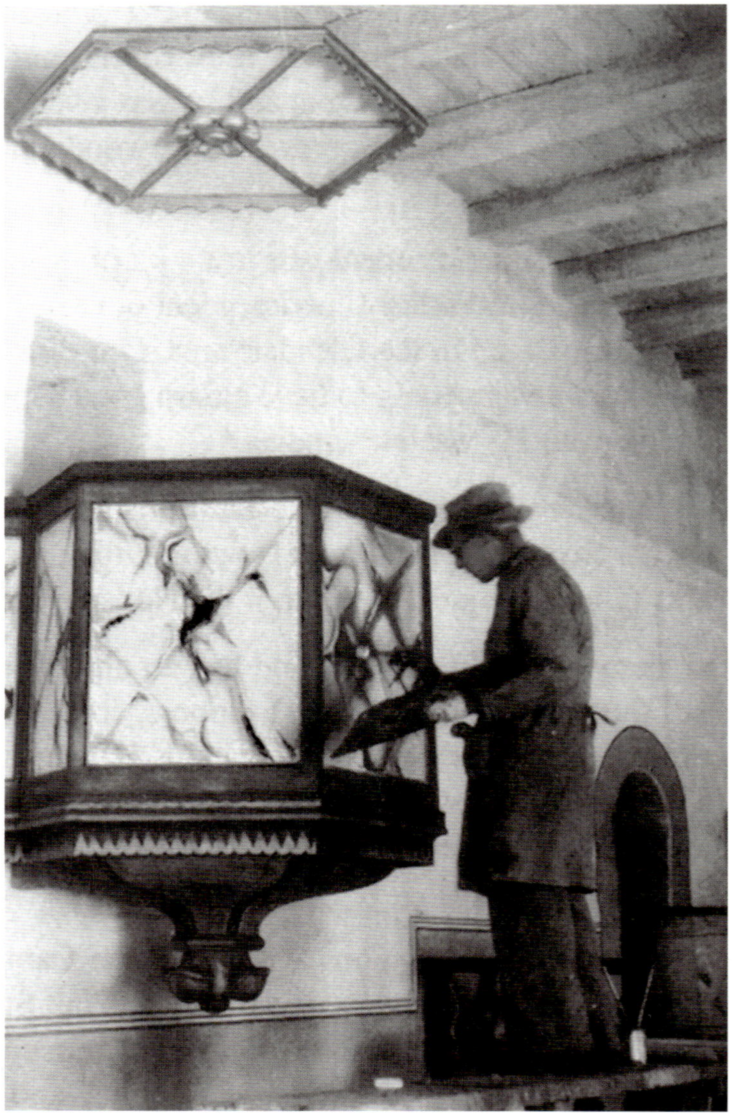

A WPA artist painting the rostrum in the chapel of the residence building.

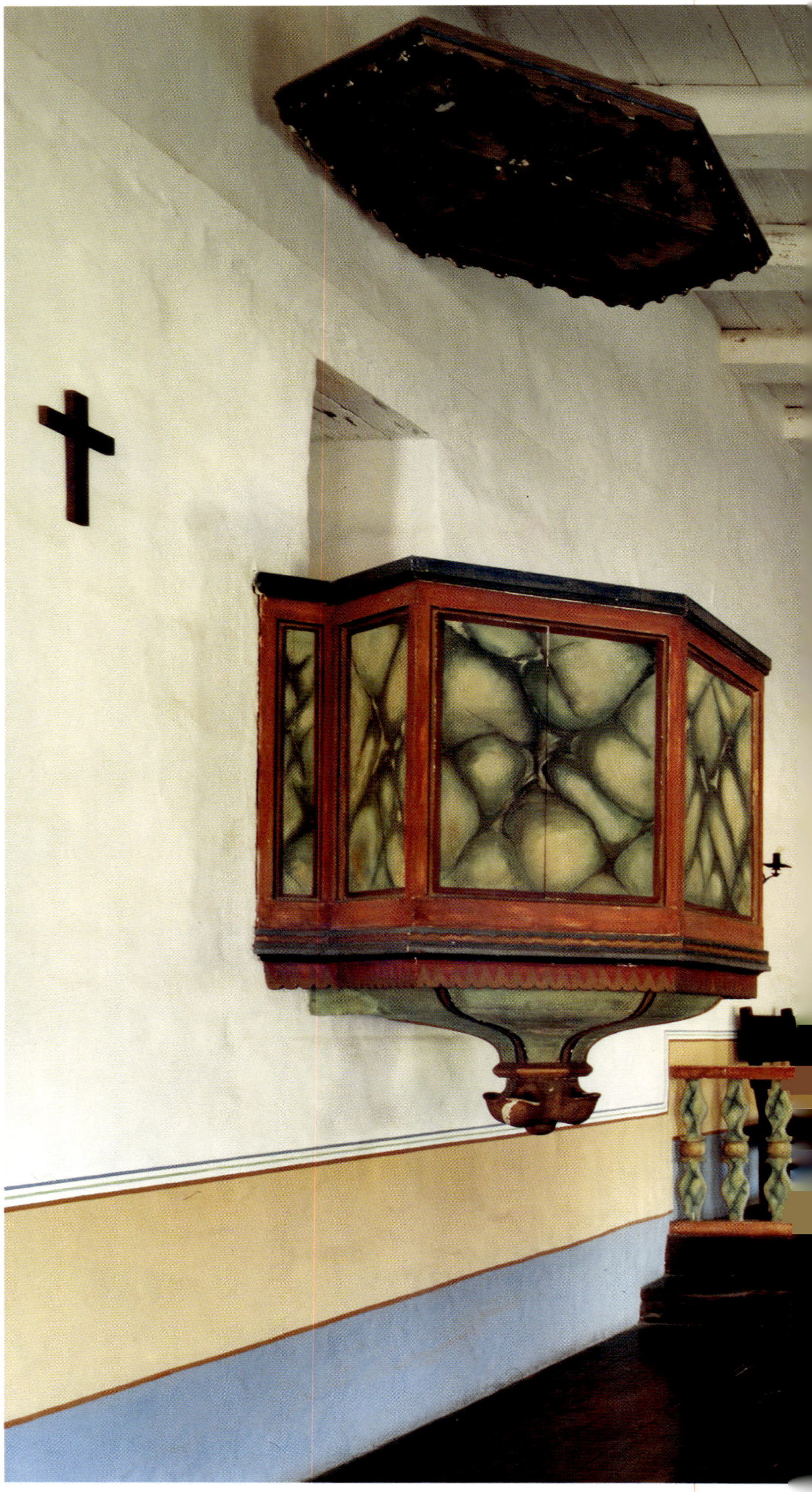

A former CCC enrollee wrote: "Today I take my grandchildren there and show them the altar. I used an adze on the wood that got placed on the altar. I remember we tied cut-up pieces of tires around our ankles for protection." Some of the boys got so good at adzing that they made them a little too smooth. The project architect, Fred Hageman, said, 'No, I want more tool marks.'"

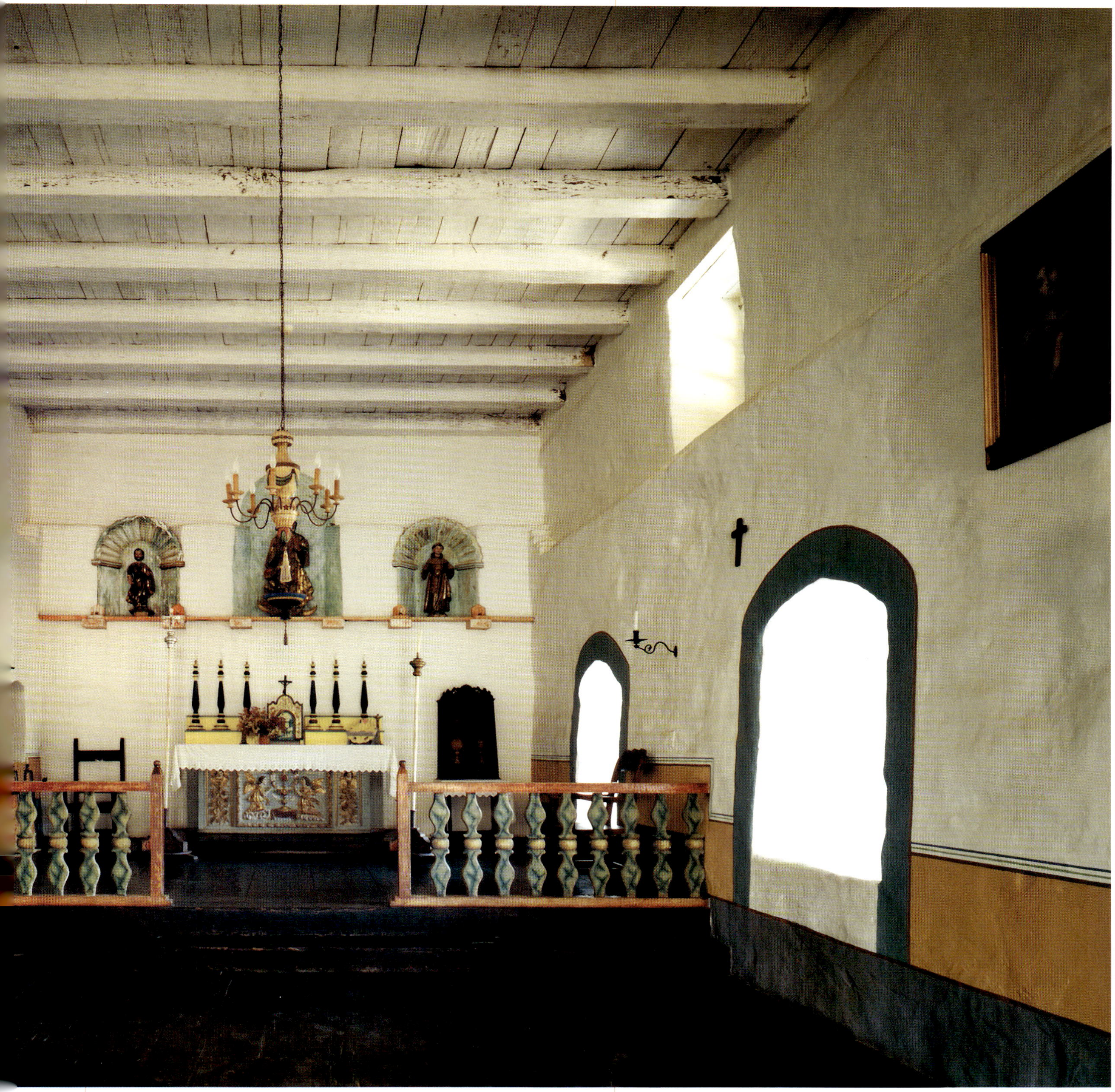

The chapel

Right:
Two enrollees holding up replicated mission chairs.

According to the project architect Fred Hageman, "The material for making the furniture was harvested from local pine forests by enrollees. The logs were transported to camp, placed over a saw-pit, and whipsawed into crude planks, one at a time. Only by this method could the character of the old articles be reproduced. A few pieces were made of mahogany and magnolia, as were the originals."

Opposite:
La Sala, where the business of the mission was conducted.

Following pages:
The Sanctuary of La Purísima. While there are chairs along the sides, it was customary for the congregation to stand, as it is in many churches in the Mediterranean tradition.

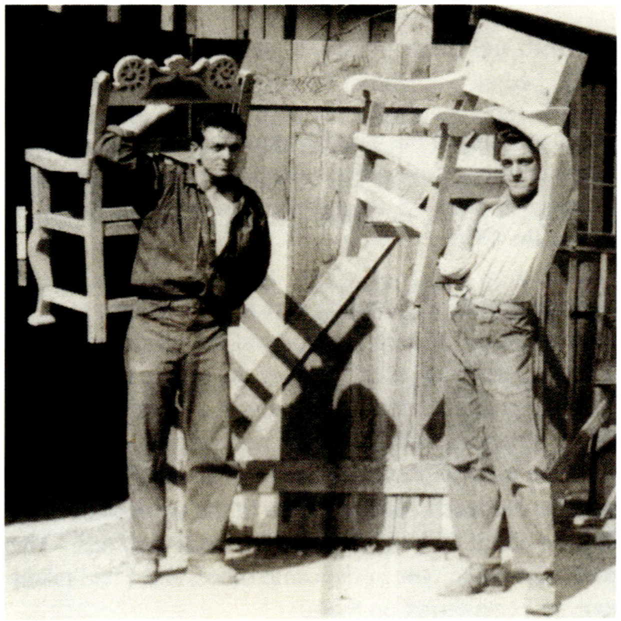

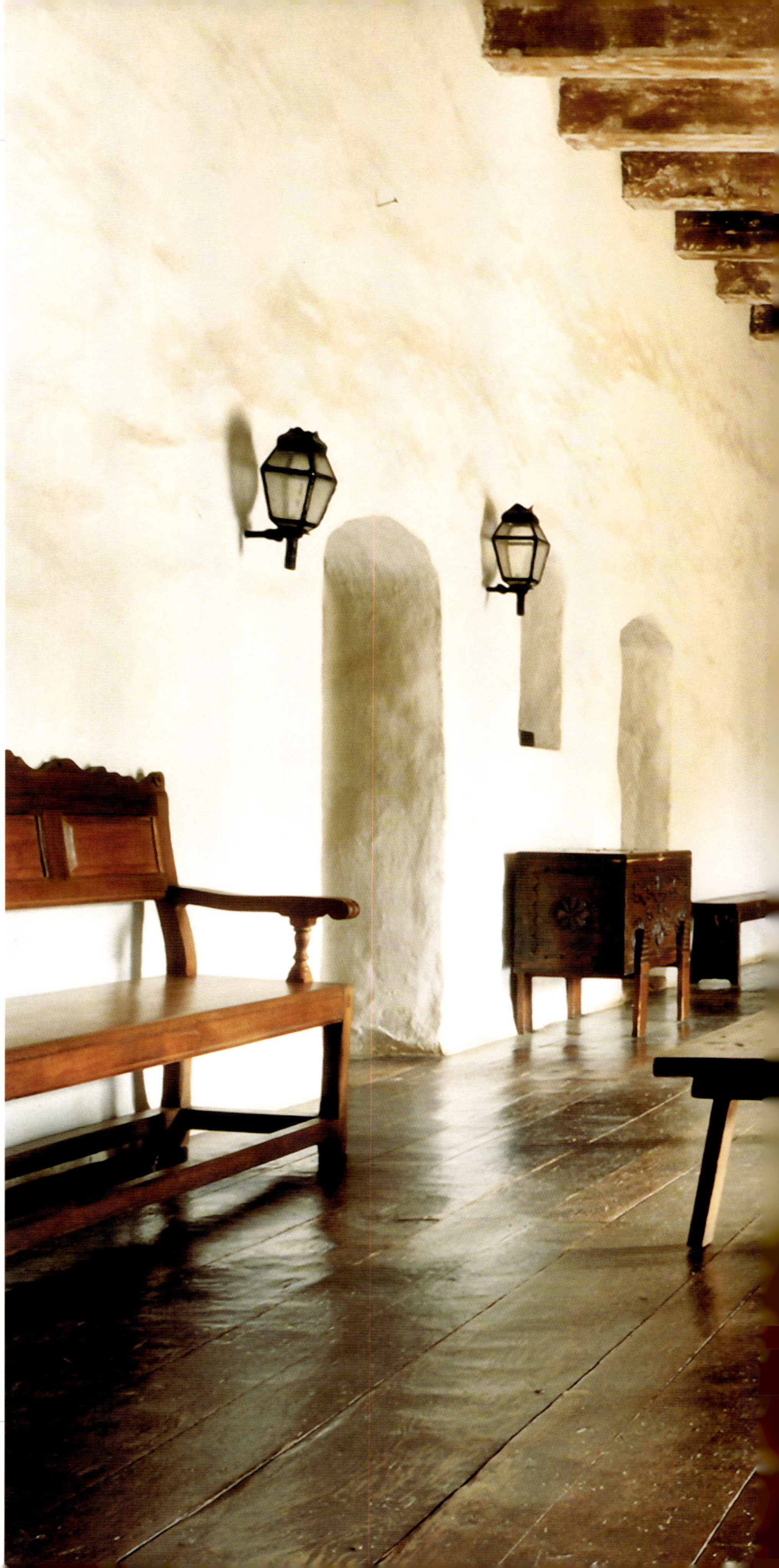

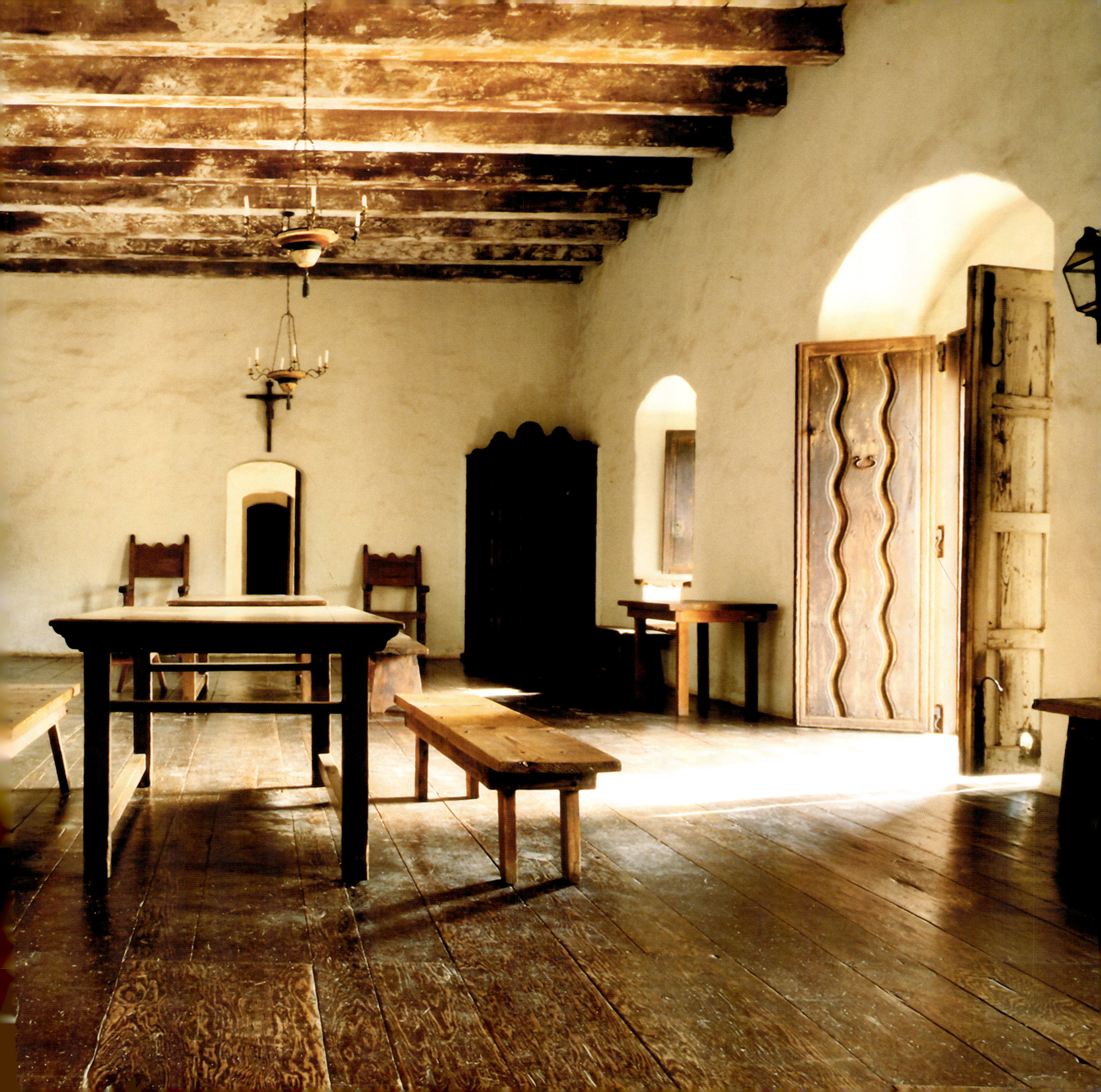

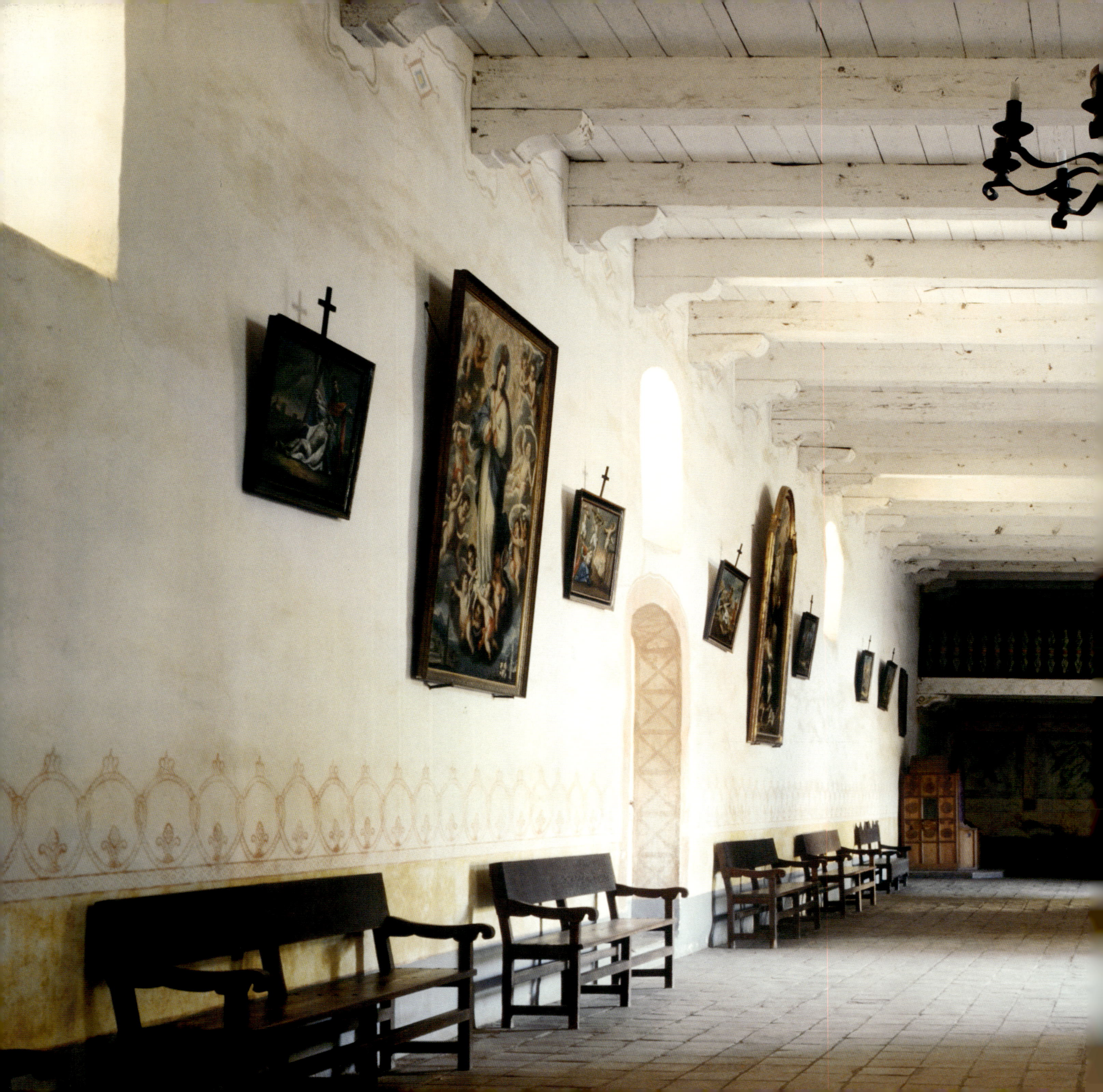

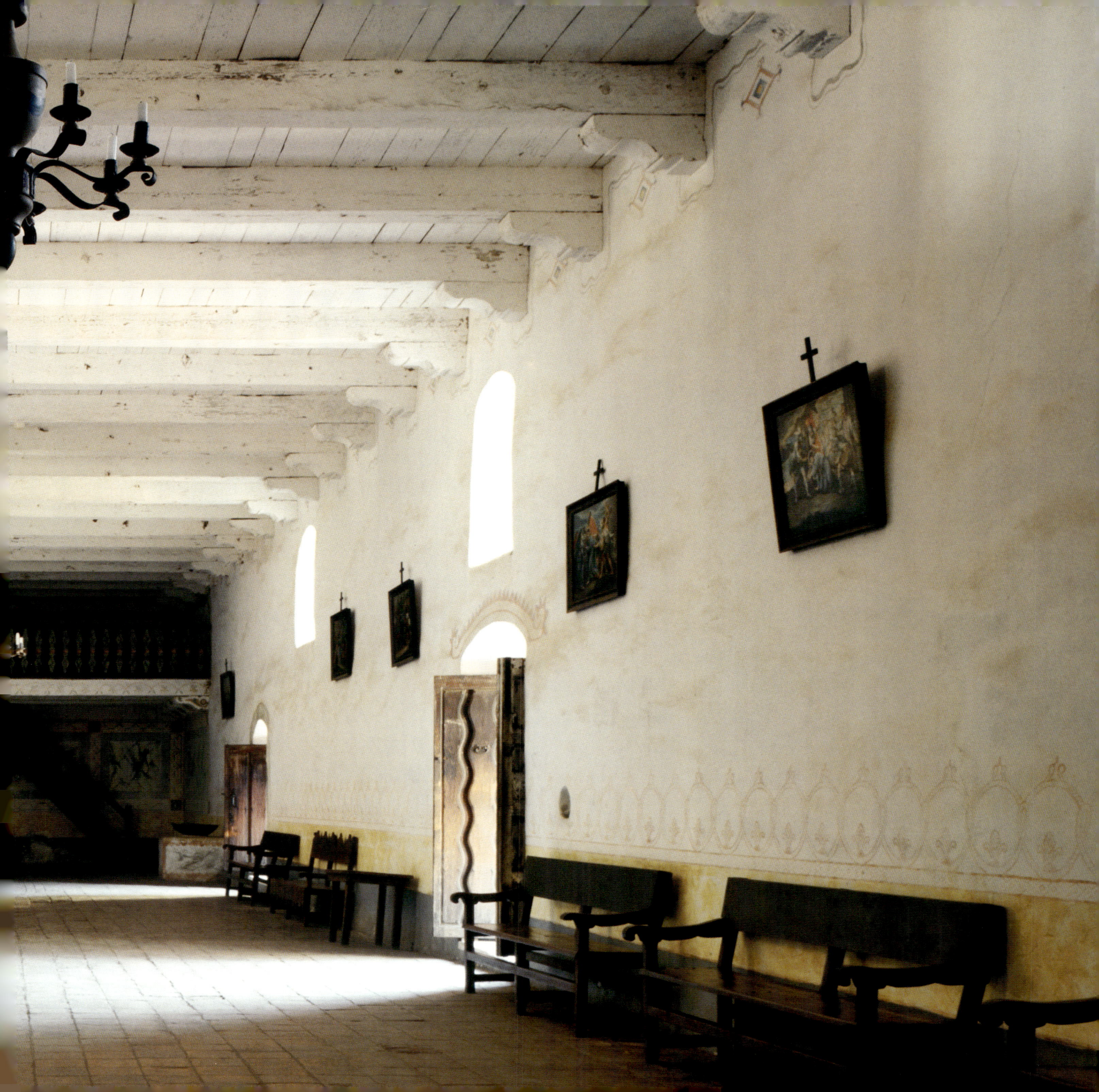

Sources of Quoted Passages

The endnotes in the text are intended to permit the reader to situate quotations in their context by identifying the sources from which those quotations are taken. I began with the intention of giving credit in endnotes for ideas as well, with bibliographic references to authors—and direct sources—who led me toward assertions and conclusions. However, as I went along I found that after more than sixty years of writing for publication, and seven and a half decades of being influenced by reading and conversation on political subjects, I was producing more notes than text—a book in effect thicker in reassertion than in assertion. This is not that kind of book. I have settled instead for giving the references for quotations, assuming the risk that in failing to give credit to ideas or even, in some cases, to chains of ideas, I will be found to have assimilated in school or college, law school or life, much that emerges here without attribution. Accordingly the following list of sources for quoted passages does not purport also to be a list of sources of ideas. I have done the best I can to give true accounts of people and events, having listened to and/or read accounts of them from people I have learned to trust, or having been present and awake when the matters described transpired.

As I have reviewed the list of sources, it also functions quite well as a set of suggestions for further reading.

Books:

Alter, Jonathan. *The Defining Moment: FDR's Hundred Days and the Triumph of Hope.* New York: Simon & Schuster, 2006.

Brinkley, Alan. *The End of Reform.* New York: Vintage, 1996 edition.

Burns, James M. *The Lion and the Fox.* New York: Harcourt Brace, 1984 edition.

Carlisle, John C. *A Simple and Vital Design: Indiana Post Office Murals.* Indianapolis: Indiana Historical Society, 1995.

Carr, Ethan. *Wilderness by Design: Landscape Architecture and The National Park Service.* Lincoln and London: University of Nebraska Press, 1999.

Collier, John. *From Every Zenith.* Denver: Sage Books, 1963.

Dos Passos, John. *The Ground We Stand On: Some Examples from the History of a Political Creed.* New York: Harcourt Brace, 1941.

Dows, Olin. *Franklin Roosevelt at Hyde Park.* New York: American Artists Group, 1949.

Dunaway, Finis. *Natural Visions: The Power of Images in American Environmental Reform.* Chicago: University of Chicago Press, 2005.

Ernst, Joseph W., ed. *Worthwhile Places: Correspondence of John D. Rockefeller, Jr., and Horace M. Albright.* New York: Fordham University Press, 1991.

Heacox, Kim. *An American Idea, The Making of the National Parks.* Washington, D.C.: National Geographic, 2001.

Hickok, Lorena. *One Third of a Nation.* Edited by Richard Lowitt and Maurine Beasley. Urbana: University of Illinois Press, 2000 edition.

Hirschfeld, Fritz. *George Washington and Slavery: A Documentary Portrayal.* Columbia, MO: University of Missouri Press, 1997.

Ickes, Harold. *Back to Work: The Story of the PWA.* New York: Macmillan, 1935.

James, George Wharton. *Harry Cassie Best: Painter of the Yosemite Valley, California Oaks, and California Mountains,* **c.** 1930.

Jefferson, Thomas. *Writings.* New York: Library of America, p. 959.

Kennedy, David M. *Freedom from Fear, The American People in Depression and War, 1929-1945.* New York: Oxford University Press, 2005.

Kennedy, Roger G. *Greek Revival America.* New York: Stewart Tabori & Chang, 1989.

——. *Architecture, Men, Women and Money in America, 1600-1860.* New York: Random House, 1985.

——. *Mr. Jefferson's Lost Cause: Land, Farms, Slavery and the Louisiana Purchase.* New York: Oxford University Press, 2003.

——. *Rediscovering America.* Boston: Houghton Mifflin, 1990.

——. *Wildfire and Americans: How to Save Lives, Property, and Your Tax Dollars.* Lincoln, NE: Bison Books, 2008.

Larkin, Oliver. *Art and Life in America.* New York: Holt, Rinehart, and Winston, 1960 edition.

Leuchtenburg, William. *Franklin D. Roosevelt and the New Deal.* New York: Harper, 1963 edition.

Lieberman, Robbie. *My Song Is My Weapon: People's Songs, American Communism, and the Politics of Culture, 1930-50.* Champaign-Urbana: University of Illinois Press, 1989.

Look, David W., and Carole L. Perrault. *The Interior Building: Its Architecture and Its Art.* Washington, D.C.: National Park Service, 1986 (quoting critic in *The Skylight*, vol. 2, no. 1, May 1939, p. 1).

Lowdermilk, Inez. *All in a Lifetime: An Autobiography.* Berkeley, CA: The Lowdermilk Trust, 1986.

Lowenthal, David. *George Perkins Marsh.* Seattle: University of Washington Press, 2000.

Marling, Karal Ann. *Wall to Wall America: Post Office Murals in the Great Depression.* Minneapolis: University of Minnesota Press, 2000 edition.

Marsh, George P. *Man and Nature.* Edited by David Lowenthal. Cambridge, MA: Harvard University Press, paperback edition, 2000.

McKinzie, Richard. *The New Deal for Artists.* Princeton, NJ: Princeton University Press, 1975.

Morgenthau, Henry III. *Mostly Morgenthaus.* New York: Ticknor and Fields, 1991.

Mumford, Lewis. *The Brown Decades. A Study of the Arts in America, 1865-1895.* New York: Harcourt Brace, 1931.

Noel, Thomas J. *Sacred Stones: Colorado's Red Rocks Park and Amphitheatre.* Denver: City and County of Denver Division of Theatres and Arenas, 2004.

Parisi, Philip. *The Texas Post Office Murals.* College Station: Texas A & M University Press, 2004.

Park, Marlene, and Gerald Markowitz. *Democratic Vistas: Post Offices and Public Art in the New Deal.* Philadelphia: Temple University Press, 1984.

Perkins, Frances. *The Roosevelt I Knew.* New York: Harper Colophon, n.d.

Peterson, Merrill. *Lincoln in the American Memory*. New York: Oxford University Press, 1994.
Reilly, Mike. *Reilly of the White House*. New York: Simon and Schuster, 1947.
Savage, Christine E. *New Deal Adobe. The Civilian Conservation Corps and the Reconstruction of Mission La Purísima*. Santa Barbara: Fithian Press, 1991.
Schlesinger, Arthur Jr. *The Coming of the New Deal*. Boston: Houghton Mifflin, 1958.
Sherwood, Robert E. *Roosevelt and Hopkins*. New York: Harpers, 1950 edition.
Smith, Richard Norton. *Patriarch: George Washington and the New American Nation*. Boston: Houghton Mifflin, 1993.
Thomas, Bernice L., *The Stamp of FDR: New Deal Post Offices in the Mid-Hudson Valley*. Fleischmanns, NY: Purple Mountain Press, 2002.
Watkins, Thomas H. *Righteous Pilgrim: The Life and Times of Harold Ickes, 1874-1952*. New York: Henry Holt, 1990.
——. *The Great Depression: America in the 1930s*. Boston: Little, Brown and Company, 1993.
WPA Guide to Washington. Edited by Roger G. Kennedy. New York: Pantheon, 1983, p. 222.

Magazine articles:

Biddle, George. "The Artist Serves His Community." *American Magazine of Art* 27, no. 9, part 2 (September 1934): 32.
Helms, Douglas. "Hugh Hammond Bennett and the Creation of the Soil Erosion Service." *National Resources Conservation Service, Historical Insights*, no. 8 (September 2008).
——. "Conserving the Plains: The Soil Conservation Service in the Great Plains." *Agricultural History* 64 (Spring 1990): 58–73.
——. "Walter Lowdermilk's Journey: Forester to Land Conservationist." *Environmental Review* 8 (1984): 132–145.
Langa, Helen. "Two Antilynching Exhibitions." *American Art* (Spring 1999): 11 ff.
Lange, Dorothea. "The Assignment I'll Never Forget: Migrant Mother." *Popular Photography* (February 1960).
Lowdermilk, Walter C. "Terracing Land Use Across Ancient Boundaries." Washington, D.C.: Soil Conservation Service, 1940: mimeographed.
Marontate, Jan. "Technical Standards and Institutionalization Processes in New Deal Art Projects." *The Journal of Arts Management, Law, and Society* 33, no. 4 (Winter 2004): 281–297.
Rosenzweig, Roy, review essay on the "Papers of F. L. Olmsted." *Journal of Social History* 18, no. 2 (Winter 1984).
Sandage, Scott. "A Marble House Divided: The Lincoln Memorial, the Civil Rights Movement, and the Politics of Memory, 1939–1963." *The Journal of American History* 80, no. 1 (June 1993): 135–167.
Sarton, George. "George Catlin's Obsession." *Isis* 2, no. 1 (1934): 74 ff.
New York Times Magazine, September 11, 1932.
New York Times, April 9, 1944.
Time, Monday, March 2, 1936.

Private letters, unpublished manuscripts, and some useful Web sites:

Adams, Don and Arlene Goldbard. "New Deal Cultural Programs: Experiments in Cultural Democracy," http://www.wwcd.org/policy/US/newdeal.html
Albright recalls FDR: Shenandoah National Park Administrative History, National Park Service Web site, http://www.nps.gov/history/history/hisnps/NPSHistory/adminhistory.htm
Bernstein, Peter L., private letter, August 2007.
Cahill: The New York Public Library has the Cahill Papers and maintains a very useful Web site at http://www.nypl.org/research/chss/spe/rbk/faids/cahill.html#biog
Eisenhower at the Metropolitan Museum of Art, April 2, 1946, National Endowment for the Arts Web site.
Farr, William E. "Julius Seyler Biography." Center for the Rocky Mountain West, Missoula: The University of Montana, http://www.umt.edu/montanamuseum/paint/seybio.htm
For Collier: Records of the Bureau of Indian Affairs, Record Group 75, Washington, D.C., National Archives and Records Administration, Washington, D.C., filmed from Records of the Office of the Commissioner of Indian Affairs, Entry #178: Office File of Commissioner John Collier.
For the texts for Roosevelt's speeches, including Roosevelt before the 1936 Democratic National Convention, Philadelphia, Pennsylvania, June 27, 1936, the best source on the web is http://www.feri.org/archives/speeches/jul0232.cfm
Franklin D. Roosevelt, Glacier National Park, August 5, 1934, National Park Archives, available as part of the administrative history of Glacier National Park on the National Park Service Web site, http://www.nps.gov/history/history/hisnps/NPSHistory/adminhistory.htm
Lincoln on the dome, quoted on the National Capitol Web site.
Mackintosh, Barry. *The National Park Service, the Early Years*, National Park Service Web site.
Benjamin West quoted in Web page provided by Nelson-Adkins Museum of Kansas City, http://www.tfaoi.com/aa/4aa/4aa189.htm
Miesse, William C. *The Significance of Mount Shasta as a Visual Resource in 19th and Early 20th Century California: Art and Artists 1841-1941*. Unpublished manuscript found on the web, 1989.
Morgenthau interview with Erica and Lewis Rubenstein, November 9, 1964, Archives of American Art.
Olin Dows, interview by Dr. Harlan B. Phillips, October 31, 1963, Records of the Archives of American Art (not on Web).
Olmsted, Frederick L. *Yosemite and the Mariposa Grove: A Preliminary Report*, 1865, available in full at http://www.yosemite.ca.us/library/olmsted/report.html
The Peales' Washingtons: Web site of the United States Senate. With ample bibliographic references, http://www.senate.gov/artandhistory/art/artifact/Painting_31_00001.htm
Presidential inaugurals: http://www.bartleby.com/124/index.html; http://avalon.law.yale.edu/subject_menus/inaug.asp
President Ronald Reagan in Remarks at a Luncheon for Recipients of the National Medal of Arts, June 18, 1987, National Medal of Arts Web site, http://www.nea.gov/honors/medals/index.html
Rexford and Grace Tugwell, interview by Richard Doud, January 21, 1965, Archives of American Art, http://www.aaa.si.edu/collections/oralhistories/transcripts/tugwel65
Roosevelt at Rushmore, National Park Service Web site for Mount Rushmore, http://www.nps.gov/archive/moru/park_history/carving_hist/carving_history.htm
Roy Stryker, interviews by Richard Doud, Archives of American Art, Smithsonian Institution,

October 17, 1963; June 13, 1964; January 23, 1965, http://www.aaa.si.edu/collections/oralhistories/transcripts/stryke63.htm#october_17,_1963_

Springwood: http://www.nps.gov/history/nr/twhp/wwwlps/lessons/82springwood/82springwood.htm

Washington to Continental Congress, New York, July 10, 1776, to be found on the Library of Congress Web site, http://memory.loc.gov/learn/features/timeline/amrev/north/independ.html

Kansas State Historical Society Web site, http://www.kshs.org/portraits/curry_john.htm

Additional references:

America from the Great Depression to World War II: Photographs from the FSA-OWI, 1935-1945. American Memory, the Library of Congress.

Anderson, James C., ed. *Roy Stryker: The Humane Propagandist*. Louisville: University of Louisville, 1977.

Brannan, Beverly W. and Carl Fleishhauer, eds. *Documenting America: 1935-1943*. Los Angeles: University of California Press, 1988.

Bustard, Bruce I. *Picturing the Century: One Hundred Years of Photography from the National Archives*. Washington, D.C.: National Archives and Record Administration, 1999.

Carlebach, Michael and Eugene F. Provenzo, Jr. *Farm Security Administration Photographs of Florida*. Gainesville: University Press of Florida, 1993.

Davis, Allen F. *Mind's Eye, Mind's Truth: FSA Photography Reconsidered*. Philadelphia: Temple University Press, 1989.

Featherstone, David, ed. *Observations: Essays on Documentary*. San Francisco: The Friends of Photography Bookstore, 1984.

Johnson, Brooks. *Mountaineers to Main Streets: The Old Dominion as seen through the Farm Security Administration Photographs*. Norfolk, VA: The Chrysler Museum, 1985.

McDannell, Colleen. *Picturing Faith: Photography and the Great Depression*. New Haven: Yale University Press, 2004.

Smith, Terry. *Making the Modern: Industry, Art, and Design in America.* Chicago: University of Chicago Press, 1993.

Spirn, Anne Whiston. *Daring to Look: Dorothea Lange's Photographs and Reports from the Field.* Chicago: University of Chicago Press, 2008.

Stott, William. *Documentary Expression and Thirties America*. Chicago: The University of Chicago Research Press, 1986.

Welty, Eudora. *One Time, One Place: Mississippi in the Depression: A Snapshot Album*. Jackson: University Press of Mississippi, 1996.

Endnotes

Chapter One

1. Gutson Borglum, to Harry Hopkins, quoted in Robert E. Sherwood, *Roosevelt and Hopkins*, p. 59.
2. "New deal" speech, quoted in Burns, pp. 139–140.
3. Kennedy "ask not" in his first inaugural address. One of the pleasures of the Internet is that all the presidential inaugurals are to be found on the Web (see listing of useful Web sites).
4. Ibid., so to speak.
5. It is good to be able to state that the Mayflower Compact and the Declaration are also easily accessible on the Web.
6. Roosevelt, First Inaugural Address (see notes 4 and 5).
7. Bernstein private letter, August 2007.
8. FDR First Inaugural Address, inaugurals Web site.
9. Eliot quoted in Brinkley, p. 246.
10. Franklin D. Roosevelt as quoted by Henry Morgenthau, Jr., in an interview with Erica and Lewis Rubenstein for the Archives of American Art, November 9, 1964.
11. Extract of address by FDR at the dedication of the National Gallery of Art on March 17, 1941, as cited and more fully quoted in Park and Markowitz, p. 6.
12. Hopkins quoted ibid., p. 5.
13. Biddle in Biddle, George, "The Artist Serves His Community," p. 32.
14. Borglum to Hopkins, in Sherwood, p. 59.
15. *Time*, Monday, March 2, 1936.
16. Biddle in Biddle, p.32.
17. Schlesinger on the Morgenthaus, in Morgenthau, pp x, xi; Henry Morgenthau III on Jewish refugees, ibid. pp. 118 ff.
18. Photograph inscription in Morgenthau, opposite p. 169; Schlesinger on p. x. Morgenthau interview, supra. Morgenthaus, father and son, on Roosevelt, Morgenthau, p. 431.
19. Schlesinger in *The Coming of the New Deal*, p. 266.
20. Quoted in Sherwood, pp. 61–2.
21. Ibid.
22. Dows on meeting with Bruce and Mrs. FDR, Records of the Archives of American Art, Interview with Olin Dows by Dr. Harlan B. Phillips, October 31, 1963, Tape 2, pp. 3–7.
23. Dows on Marsh, Ibid. p. 80.
24. Ickes to Hopkins to Morgenthau for Bruce, McKinzie, p. 9.
25. Dows, Ibid. pp. 36–38; Rothstein quoted in McDannell, p. 35.

Chapter Two

1. Morgenthau interview with Erica and Lewis Rubenstein for the Archives of American Art, November 9, 1964.
2. Dows in Interview, Tape 2, p. 80.
3. Adams quoted by President Ronald Reagan in Remarks at a Luncheon for Recipients of the National Medal of Arts, June 18, 1987.
4. Roosevelt in his Rendezvous with Destiny Speech. See http://www2.austincc.edu/lpatrick/his2341/fdr36acceptancespeech.htm; Roosevelt and war, First Inaugural, quoted in Burns, p. 164, and inaugurals Web site.
5. I am quoting and following the lines of William Leuchtenburg's account, pp. 162 ff.
6. Leuchtenburg, ibid.; Indians, McKinzie, p. 28.
7. Ibid. See also McKinzie, pp. 8 ff.
8. Hickok quoted in Kennedy, *Freedom,* p. 250.
9. Roosevelt and crackpots, quoted in Kennedy, *Freedom*, p. 242.
10. Ickes as quoted in Watkins, p. 371.
11. Watkins, pp. 370 ff.
12. Ibid.
13. Ibid.
14. Ickes vs Hopkins, Leuchtenburg, p. 129, Leuchtenburg on Ickes, pp. 70–71; Sherwood in *Roosevelt and Hopkins*, p. 70.
15. The quoted bit on ward halls etc., comes from a Watkins caption, after p. 276.
16. Roosevelt at Interior cornerstone laying, *WPA Guide to Washington*, p. 277.
17. Ibid.
18. Because they were subject to the same rules as any other relief recipients, the artists to whom TRAP delivered monthly paychecks had to put up with procedures better adapted to furnishing underwear to the CCC than paintings: their materials had to be requisitioned from a central warehouse in New York; they were required to submit time sheets to prove they had "put in their hours"; and those without much experience or reputation were placed under foremen called "master artists," and supervised by committees made up of an architect, the "master artist," and an eminent art professional in the area, generally a museum director.
19. Ibid.
20. Hauser in Park and Markowitz, p. 14.
21. No mythology and Bruce, ibid., p. 8.
22. Ibid., pp. 12–13; Dows in Interview, Tape 2, p. 80.
23. Story of Ickes's appointment in Collier, pp. 160 ff.
24. Collier Records. Bureau of Indian Affairs.
25. Navajo Reservation, quoted in Helms, *Hugh Hammond Bennett.*
26. The Early Renaissance origins of the "BuRec" murals was suggested to me, along with much else of value, by Kim Sullivan, who is chief curator, keeper, and expositor of the art in the Interior Building.
27. *WPA Guide*, p. 278. (The Guide says Auchea of the Kiowa Five was "Pueblo"—he was Kiowa).
28. Ibid., except for Bruce to Mechau, which is in Marling, p. 252.
29. Curry quoted on Kansas State Historical Society Web site, http://www.kshs.org/portraits/curry_john.htm
30. Quotations from Watkins, pp. 450–451.
31. Look and Perraeult, p. 127.

Chapter Three

1. Eleanor Roosevelt, in "My Day" at http://www.gwu.edu/~erpapers/myday/displaydoc.cfm?_y=1949&_f=md001230
2. John Dos Passos, *The Ground We Stand On: Some Examples from the History of a Political Creed* (New York: Harcourt, Brace, 1941), p.3.
3. Stone, in Park and Markowitz, p. 11.
4. FDR to Peoples, Bernice Thomas, p. 17.
5. Dows, p. 180.

6. Dows on Mrs. Roosevelt, p. 180.
7. See discussion in Thomas, supra.
8. Tender purity from Southlands Foundation Web site.
9. See discussion in Thomas, supra.
10. See Dows in his discussion of the post offices, interview cited, supra.
11. Ibid.
12. Marling on Robinson, p. 37; then came Depression and in the 1950s and 1960s, the gutting of Pittsburgh by "urban renewal" as Colorado enjoyed the benefits of the deliberate dispersal of the old industrial cities after World War II—and the Kaufmann's murals were purchased for installation in Colorado Springs.
13. Biddle in Biddle, p.32.
14. FDR to Norman Thomas, quoted in Kennedy, *Freedom from Fear*, p. 211.
15. The definitive account of the "Two Antilynching Art Exhibitions" is by Helen Langa in *American Art*, Spring 1999, pp. 11 ff.
16. Biddle as quoted in Marling, ibid., pp. 30–31.
17. Story of Rockefeller Center mural in Dows, pp. 180 ff. Rivera's explanation quoted in Marling, p.31.
18. FDR quoted in Marling, p. 42; Biddle, ibid., pp. 30–31.
19. Benton in Marling, p. 41.
20. Causes, ER in Sherwood, p. 833; ER in "My Day" quoted in Ross, p. 228.
21. Extract of address by FDR at the dedication of the National Gallery of Art, on March 17, 1941, as cited and more fully quoted in Park and Markowitz, p. 6.
22. Dows on abstraction, quoted in Marontate, pp. 281–297; FDR quoted in Ross, p. 278; Bruce on American scene, ibid., p. 44.
23. Marling, ibid.
24. John C. Carlisle, *A Simple and Vital Design: The Story of the Indiana Post Office Murals.*—D.L.
25. The description of Kent's technique comes to us from Cecilia Esposito, Director of the Plattsburgh State Art Museum, State University of New York, except for the reference to Harvey Ellis, which comes from my own inquiries.

Chapter Four

1. Available on the National Park Service Web site.
2. Lincoln, quoted by Collier, p. 157.
3. Collier in the First Annual Report of the Department of the Interior under Secretary Harold Ickes, cited in Watkins, pp. 534–535.
4. Catlin, George, *Last Rambles*, London, 1868, quoted in Sarton, George, "George Catlin's Obsession," *Isis*, Vol. 2, No. 1, (1934), pp. 74 ff.
5. Ibid.
6. Catlin, quoted by Barry Mackintosh in his *The National Park Service, the Early Years* on the National Park Service Web site; West quoted in Web page provided by Nelson-Adkins Museum of Kansas City, http://www.tfaoi.com/aa/4aa/4aa189.htm; Olmsted, *Yosemite and the Mariposa Grove: A Preliminary Report*, 1865, available in full on http://www.yosemite.ca.us/library/olmsted/report.html
7. For Long and the Byronesque and willful Constantino Beltrami, please see my *Men on a Moving Frontier* and *Rediscovering America.*
8. Stanley's images of the Casa Grand adobe platform mound in Arizona provided evidence to support its selection as one of the nation's first national monuments protected by the Antiquities Act.
9. Whittredge quoted on Wikipedia.
10. Olmsted on Yosemite, http://www.tfaoi.com/aa/4aa/4aa189.htm; Olmsted, *Yosemite and the Mariposa Grove: A Preliminary Report*, 1865, available in full on http://www.yosemite.ca.us/library/olmsted/report.html
11. I am quoting from an account by Hal Schindler of the *Salt Lake Tribune*, to be found at http://historytogo.utah.gov/salt_lake_tribune/in_another_time/021697.html
12. Moran and cavalry escort, quoted in Heacox, *An American Idea*, p. 170.
13. Ibid., p. 171.
14. Ibid.
15. For reasons too complex and conjectural for discussion here, the expedition of Lewis and Clark, and the other Jeffersonian voyages of discovery, failed to include artists, and the camera obscura sent along on one of them does not appear to have been used. I have set out my own thoughts about such reasons in my discussion of the relationship of James Wilkinson to Thomas Jefferson in *Mr. Jefferson's Lost Cause* and in *Burr, Hamilton, and Jefferson.* I do not think Wilkinson wanted precise records kept of where the "exploring" and provocative explorations authorized by Jefferson actually went.
16. William C. Miesse, *The Significance of Mount Shasta as a Visual Resource in 19th and Early 20th Century California: Art and Artists 1841-1941*, 1989, Unpublished manuscript to be found on the Web. TR to Harrie Cassie Best, dated Nov. 12, 1908, in: George Wharton James, *Harry Cassie Best: Painter of the Yosemite Valley, California Oaks, and California Mountains*, **c.** 1930, p. 18.
17. Louis Hill as quoted in Farr, on http://www.umt.edu/montanamuseum/paint/seybio.htm, n.p.
18. The art and science of the American Bonapartes is its own fascinating tale, the frontispiece for which might be H. Avery Johnson's "Skating at Bonaparte's Pond," painted for the Bordentown, N.J., post office during the New Deal. In its background is the New Jersey mansion of Carlo Bonaparte's Uncle Joseph, once King of Spain, whose summer hunting lodge in the Adirondacks became the core of an artists' colony.
19. For three centuries, the Everglades had been thought to be the swampy equivalent in ugly uselessness to the Great American Desert, or the West Texas plateau. The interior of South Florida was too *wet* to seem of much interest when first assessed for acquisition by Thomas Jefferson in 1805, just as the 800,000 acres of the Texas Big Bend were deemed too dry. Painting, photography, and some splendid nature writing brought respect to the Everglades and Big Bend, and they are now National Parks, although neither is among the most visited, and neither contain famous hostelries or tourist "wow-spots."
20. Albright to John D. Rockefeller, Jr., Ernst, pp. 128–9.
21. Franklin D. Roosevelt, Glacier National Park, August 5, 1934, National Park Archives available as part of the administrative history of Glacier National Park on the National Park Service Web site.
22. Ickes was aware that although Roosevelt could not walk, he could "motor"—and he loved well-built parkways, with fine stonework bridges and abutments. Roosevelt and Ickes did not agree on the subject of road building in national parks. Even before the CCC came along to build most of the Blue Ridge Parkway past Camp Hoover and along the crest of the Shenandoahs, the Park Service was already "slowly and carefully building up the finest system of scenic roads of any

nation on earth, and the cream of them all is in the national parks." (That statement did not please wilderness lovers, and still does not.) (Arno Cammerer on best roads, quoted in Watkins, p. 553)
Roosevelt's personal enthusiasm for road-building was clear enough, so it required political courage for Ickes on February 25, 1935, to stand in the auditorium of the old Interior Building "to defy his president and [incidentally] his own director of the National Park Service," saying: "I am not in favor of building any more roads in the National Parks than we have to build. I am not in favor of doing anything along the lines of so-called improvements that we do not have to do. This is the automobile age, but I do not have patience with people whose idea of enjoying nature is dashing along a hard road at fifty or sixty miles an hour. I am not willing that our beautiful areas ought to be opened up to people who are either too old to walk, as I am, or too lazy to walk, as a great number of young people are who ought to be ashamed of themselves." (Ickes on Skyline Drive, Watkins, pp. 471–2.)
Ickes did not live long enough to experience snowmobiles. (Albright recalls FDR, in Shenandoah National Park Administrative History, available on the National Park Service Web site.)

23. Franklin D. Roosevelt, Glacier National Park, August 5, 1934, National Park Archives available as part of the administrative history of Glacier National Park on the National Park Service Web site.
24. Ibid.
25. President Franklin D. Roosevelt, speaking at the dedication of a new building for The Museum of Modern Art, N.Y., as printed in the *Herald Tribune* on May 11, 1939. The Museum of Modern Art Archives, New York: Monroe Wheeler Papers.
26. Ibid., MoMA Speech. Franklin D. Roosevelt, Glacier National Park, August 5, 1934, National Park Archives available as part of the administrative history of Glacier National Park on the National Park Service Web site.
27. Ibid., MoMA Speech.
28. Charles A. Peterson, *The Historic American Buildings Survey*, 1933.—D.L.
29. Ibid.—D.L.

Chapter Five

1. Extract of address by FDR at the dedication of the National Gallery of Art, on March 17, 1941, as cited and more fully quoted in Park and Markowitz, p. 6.
2. President Franklin D. Roosevelt, MoMA Speech cited previously.
3. In this paragraph I am following the outline of, and quoting from, an elegant summary entitled "New Deal Cultural Programs: Experiments in Cultural Democracy" by Don Adams and Arlene Goldbard to be found on the Web.
4. Ibid.
5. Biddle in George Biddle, "The Artist Serves His Community"; I am continuing to paraphrase or quote from the exemplary summary of Adams and Goldbard, supra.
6. The New York Public Library has the Cahill Papers and maintains a very useful Web site at http://www.nypl.org/research/chss/spe/rbk/faids/cahill.html#biog, from which the chronology of my account comes; Adams and Goldbard, ibid.
7. I am using the friends and painters list of the New York Public Library culled from Cahill's correspondence. Ibid.
8. From Gerard Sullivan, "Mr. Gorky's Murals and the Airport They Puzzle," Newark *Star-Ledger* (June 10, 1937).
9. From "Content is a Glimpse." *Location* Vol. 1, no. 1 (spring 1963): 45–53, an artist's statement composed of excerpts from a 1960 interview of Willem de Kooning by David Sylvester for the B.B.C.—D.L.
10. Irving Sandler, *A Sweeper-up After Artists* (London: Thames & Hudson, rev. ed. 2009); *Strokes of Genius* (film).—D.L.
11. Adams and Goldbard, supra., and sources cited by David Kennedy in *Freedom from Fear*, p. 255.
12. Adams and Goldbard, supra. My quotation about folk music comes from David Kennedy, *Freedom*, ibid.
13. Interview text, pp. 206–208. Alan Lomax interview with Jim Brown, American Roots Music. Permission granted.
14. Kazin quoted in David Kennedy, ibid., pp. 255–6
15. Kazin, ibid.
16. I am continuing gratefully to paraphrase Adams and Goldbard, supra, and use the statistics to be found therein.
17. Some of these examples come from David Kennedy's treatment of the WPA in *Freedom from Fear*, pp. 251 ff.
18. Franklin D. Roosevelt, Glacier National Park, August 5, 1934, National Park Archives available as part of the administrative history of Glacier National Park on the National Park Service Web site; extract of address by FDR at the dedication of the National Gallery of Art, on March 17, 1941, quoted in Park and Markowitz, p. 6. Kennedy's admonition in his Inaugural Address.
19. Park and Markowitz, p. 9; for Borglum and Biddle, see Chapter One.
20. In 1947, President Harry Truman asked Former President Herbert Hoover to lead a commission to consider greater efficiencies in federal construction and building management. The "Hoover Commission" urged creation of an "Office of the General Services" as a holding company for the exhausted dreams of the past and the pedestrian necessities of the present, including the Treasury Department's Bureau of Federal Supply and Office of Contract Settlement, with whatever shred remained of its once-celebrated Section on Fine Arts, and the remnants of both Harry Hopkins's WPA/CWA and Ickes's PWA. The General Services Administration—the GSA—became an independent agency in July 1949.
21. Eisenhower at the Metropolitan Museum of Art, April 2, 1946, as reported on the National Endowment for the Arts Web site.
22. Eisenhower quoted on NEA Web site.

Chapter Six

1. Eleanor Roosevelt and Sherwood, Sherwood, p. 933.
2. Ibid., pp. 72–73 and 932–3.
3. Ibid.
4. We owe the research on the provenance of the term New Deal to Jonathan Alter in his *The Defining Moment.* For the texts for Roosevelt's speeches the best source on the web is http://www.feri.org/archives/speeches/jul0232.cfm
5. Henry Wallace quoted in the *New York Times*, April 9, 1944.
6. Communists. Hickok, p. 12. As to Fascists: I interviewed Lawrence Dennis at his home and wrote a report filed in the Yale University Library.
7. I am following the outline of labor conditions in the mid-1930s in Park and Markowitz, p. 4.
8. Reilly, pp.98–99. I am grateful to Robert Clark

of the Franklin D. Roosevelt Presidential Library for this useful reference, and correction of fallacious accounts published elsewhere.

9. Speech before the 1936 Democratic National Convention, Philadelphia, Pennsylvania, June 27, 1936.
10. Ibid.
11. Roosevelt as reported by the *New York Times Magazine*, September 11, 1932, p. 2.
12. FDR, Philadelphia Speech, cited supra.
13. Ibid.
14. Hickok, learning and as self-described in Hickok, xxvi–xxvii.
15. Ibid.
16. Hickok report, *One Third of a Nation*, p. 9.
17. Ibid., p.45.
18. Ibid., pp. 11 and 55.
19. Ibid., p.56.
20. Ibid., p. 57.
21. Ibid., p. 60.
22. Ibid., p.83.
23. Ibid., p.93.
24. Ibid., pp. 94–96.
25. Ibid., p.159.
26. Ibid., p. 212.

Chapter Seven

1. Hickok report, *One Third of a Nation*.
2. Interviews with Roy Stryker by Richard Doud, for Archives of American Art, October 17, 1963, June 13, 1964, and January 23, 1965.
3. *Time*, June 25, 1934.
4. Oral history interview with Rexford and Grace Tugwell by Richard Doud, Jan. 21, 1965, Archives of American Art, Smithsonian Institution. http://www.aaa.si.edu/collections/oralhistories/transcripts/tugwel6. Resettlement may not have been initially Tugwell's idea. He said to Doud that it had been given him to manage: "Harry Hopkins . . . who had begun his operations early in 1933, almost at once after the President's inauguration. He had begun a certain number of communities. He had set up a section for this, and he had begun a certain number of communities, which were spread mostly throughout the South and West. As I recall, there were about one hundred of those . . . [They were placed in an] organization called Subsistence Homesteads, which was in the Department of the Interior, and which had been a favorite project of President and Mrs. Roosevelt and Louie Howe. This is the one that came under so much criticism in the newspapers and magazines at that time. Arthur Dale was the favorite target. This was one of Mrs. Roosevelt's favorite projects down in West Virginia near Morgantown . . . When we organized the Resettlement Administration, I discovered that the President put in the executive order setting up the Resettlement Administration that this group was transferred to us in Resettlement, so that we had to try and do the best we could with what was really a failing project. I was always a little resentful that I got blamed for what the newspapers insisted on calling "subsistence homesteads."
5. Kennedy, *Freedom from Fear*, p. 378.
6. Hickok, Florence, Alabama June 6, 1934 to Harry Hopkins, pp. 270–271.
7. Ibid.
8. In the Midwest the states had been anticipating resettlement since the 1860s—please see my *Wildfire and Americans*—as did Vermont and New Hampshire after the passage of the Weeks Act in the Progressive Era.
9. Interviews with Roy Stryker by Richard Doud, for Archives of American Art, October 17, 1963, June 13, 1964, and January 23, 1965.
10. Stryker, ibid.
11. Stryker, ibid.
12. Stryker, ibid.
13. Tugwell interview, cited supra.
14. Stryker, cited supra.
15. Frances Perkins, *The Roosevelt I Knew* (New York: Harper Colophon, n.d.), p. 330. For Social Gospel, social action, and art in the New Deal, see Colleen McDannell, *Picturing Faith: Photography and the Great Depression* (New Haven: Yale University Press, 2004); Finis Dunaway, *Natural Visions: The Power of Images in American Environmental Reform* (Chicago: University of Chicago Press, 2005). "Steeped in the Social Gospel tradition" is David Kennedy's phrase in *Freedom from Fear*, p. 146.
16. Stryker, cited supra. http://www.aaa.si.edu/collections/oralhistories/transcripts/stryke63.htm#october_17,_1963_
17. Ibid.
18. Anne Whiston Spirn, *Daring to Look: Dorothea Lange's Photographs and Reports from the Field* (Chicago: University of Chicago Press, 2008).—D.L.
19. Stryker, from Archives of American Art interview.—D.L.
20. Anne Whiston Spirn, cited supra.—D.L.
21. Dorothea Lange, "The Assignment I'll Never Forget: Migrant Mother," *Popular Photography* (February 1960).
22. Stryker, supra.
23. Stryker, ibid.
24. Tugwell, interview cited supra.
25. Ibid.
26. Rexford G. Tugwell, Thomas Munro, and Roy E. Stryker, *American Economic Life and the Means of Its Improvement*, 3d ed. (New York: Harcourt, Brace and Company, c. 1930).
27. Stryker interview, cited.
28. Stryker, ibid; the Tugwells interview cited supra.
29. Stryker and Tugwell interviews cited supra.
30. Ibid.
31. Rexford and Grace Tugwell, interview cited.
32. Ibid.
33. Ibid.
34. Stryker interview, cited above.
35. Stryker to the Tugwells, July 24, 1964, FDR Library, Tugwell Papers, Box 25.
36. Tugwell in interview with Doud, cited supra.
37. *Time*, December 5, 1938.
38. I am grateful to Mary Jo Binker of the Eleanor Roosevelt Papers for this reference.
39. Eleanor Roosevelt, *This I Remember* (New York: Harper, 1949), pp. 162–163. The NYA was abolished, with so much else of the New Deal, in 1943.
40. Lieberman, p. 34.
41. Interview with Rexford and Grace Tugwell by Richard Doud, cited supra.
42. Stryker, interview cited supra. So Stryker went to work for Ed Stanley fifteen years before I did. Ed Stanley was my boss at the National Broadcasting Company in the mid-1950s, as he invented "Meet the Press" for television and a forerunner of "All Things Considered" called "Collector's Item," a two-hour weekly assemblage of short pieces for radio from many correspondents, for which he chose me as host.
43. Ibid.
44. Lorentz quoted by Phillips, p. 75; Stryker, Interview cited supra.

Chapter Eight

1. Sherwood, pp. 82–83 and 932–3.
2. Roosevelt at Mount Rushmore, cited supra; Roosevelt at Mount Vernon, April 14, 1939,

http://www.presidency.ucsb.edu/ws/index.php?pid=15742. And on moral leadership, as reported by the *New York Times Magazine*, September 11, 1932, p. 2.

3. Greenough on morality in art, Oliver Larkin, p. 180.
PWA Press Release 695, May 20, 1934; Roosevelt at Mount Vernon, April 14, 1939, http://www.presidency.ucsb.edu/ws/index.php?pid=15742. And on moral leadership, as reported by the *New York Times Magazine*, September 11, 1932, p. 2. FDR First Inaugural and Fireside Chat, available on the Roosevelt Speeches Web site (see below); Roosevelt as reported by the *New York Times Magazine*, September 11, 1932, p. 2; Sherwood on Roosevelt's dramatizing, *Roosevelt and Hopkins*, p. 933.
4. Roosevelt at Mount Vernon, April 14, 1939, cited supra; Flexner at p. 455.
5. Washington and improvements, December 4, 1788, in Smith, p. 63; FDR at Mount Vernon, available on both the Mount Vernon Web site and the Roosevelt speeches Web site.
6. Washington's rotation plan, Flexner, p. 453; Washington to Young, quoted in Smith, p.138; Washington on yeomen and small lots, quoted in Hirschfeld, Washington, p. 76. Jefferson quoted in larger context in my *Mr. Jefferson's Lost Cause*, pp. 12 ff.
7. Washington to Young, quoted in Smith, p. 138.
8. PWA Press Release 695, May 20, 1934.
9. FDR to Van Loon, February 2, 1937, President's Personal File, FDR Library.
10. Sherwood, pp. 933–4; Washington to Continental Congress, New York, July 10, 1776, to be found on the Library of Congress Web site; Washington in Sherwood, p. 932.
11. Senate history, ibid.; Washington's interment, in Flexner, p. 455.
12. Washington and improvements, December 4, 1788, in Smith, p. 63; Latrobe in Edward C. Carter, John C. Van Horne, and Charles E. Brownell, *Latrobe's View of America, 1795-1820* (New Haven: Yale University Press, 1985), pp. 94–5.
13. Marsh on the question, p. 465. See Lowenthal, and other relevant quotations from Marsh, pp. 154, 192 ff., 280–1; McCosh quoted p. 303.
14. Marsh writing in a letter to Gen. T. L. Casey from Rome, April 25, 1879, reprinted in Harvey, pp. 291–307. Description of site from a planning document for the National Museum of African American History to be found on http://www.louisberger-nmaahceis.com/NMAAHC%20archaeology%20presentation%20Jan%2030as%20delivered.pdf; Mumford quoting Marsh, and on his own in *Brown Decades*, pp. 76–77; Walter C. Lowdermilk, pp. 1–133, quoted in Helms, "Walter Lowdermilk's Journey: Forester to Land Conservationist."
15. Marsh on excrescence, Marsh to George F. Edmunds and Gen. T. L. Casey, from Rome, April 25, 1879, reprinted in Harvey, pp. 291–307. That letter from Marsh to Edmunds is interesting. Did Marsh only "understand" that the obelisk form had been chosen, or had he reached some sort of understanding that it should be chosen? Had he, Mead, and Powers discussed the matter? Had they agreed on how "the Washington Monument question" should be settled, and had they done so before or after Marsh had "not only seen but sketched every existing genuine—that is, Egyptian—obelisk"? And why refer to "the sculptor Mead"? Perhaps because Mead had used an obelisk for his most celebrated commission, the tomb of Lincoln in Springfield, Illinois. He had won that competition in 1865, the year in which Marsh published *Man and Nature*, while Mead was with him in Italy. They would hardly have missed occasions to discuss the theme of restoration, central to that book, and the impact of witnessing obelisks lying amid desolation too far advanced to permit restoration.
16. Lowenthal in "Flesh," pp. 17–28.
17. Lowenthal, Ibid.
18. The gold on the dome is a twentieth-century addition, as is the replacement in 1938 of my kinsman Larkin Meade's *Ceres* by a work by Dwight Dwinell, who was an octogenarian Sergeant-at-Arms of the legislature. Mead initially went to Italy with his brother-in-law William Dean Howells, the grandson of William Dean, as was my own grandfather. Mead's son, Larkin, married Edwina Winter, daughter of the Vermonter Edwin Winter, of Mount Rainier National Park (see p. 113). Her sister was my grandmother.
19. These quotations and others of a similar tone are taken from pp. 124–128 in my *Wildfire and Americans*.
20. Eisenhower at the Metropolitan Museum of Art, April 2, 1946, as reported on the National Endowment for the Arts Web site.
21. Letters, in Harvey, pp. 291–307.
22. Ibid.
23. Washington, on migrancy, Washington to Young, quoted in Smith, p. 138.
24. Edwards as conservationist and scientist is the subject of the final chapter in my *Wildfire and Americans*.
25. Marsh on the question, p. 465. See Lowenthal, and other relevant quotations from Marsh, pp. 154, 192 ff., 280–1; Lowdermilk's text is on Lester Brown's "Earth Policy" Web site: http://www.earth-policy.org/Books/PB/PBch3_ss7.htm; Mumford, pp. 79–80.

Chapter Nine

1. Mumford in *Brown Decades*, pp. 76–77.
2. Maurice Cook, "Hugh Hammond Bennett: the Father of Soil Conservation." North Carolina State University Web site, http://www.soil.ncsu.edu/about/century/hugh.html
3. Bennett quoted ibid.
4. Inez Lowdermilk, *All in a Lifetime*, p. 198.
5. I am grateful to John Elder for the references to Plato and Seneca.
6. Inez Lowdermilk in *All in a Lifetime*; Wallace's note appears in Helms on Bennett, cited supra.
7. Navajo Tribal Council Resolutions, p. 151, quoted in Helms on Bennett; .John Collier to William Hastings, July 28, 1933, Chronological File, John Collier Papers, Microform of the original papers in Yale University Library. Sanford, N.C.: Microfilming Corp. of America, 1980, cited in Helms, "Hugh Hammond Bennett."
8. Helms, in "Conserving the Plains" pp. 58–73.
9. Cook, supra.
10. Lowdermilk, *All in a Lifetime*, p. 198.
11. Ibid., p. 164.
12. Ibid.
13. Wallace quoted in Phillips, pp. 68–9.
14. Stryker interview, cited supra.
15. Tugwell interview, cited supra.
16. Ibid.
17. Lowdermilk's text is on pages 198 and 199 of Inez Lowdermilk's *All in a Lifetime*.
18. Mumford, ibid., p.229.

Chapter Ten

1. Mumford, ibid.
2. Chapman quoted in Peterson, Lincoln, p. 352;

FDR quoted in Sandage, pp. 135 ff.
3. Ickes speech in Watkins, p. 652.
4. Sandage, pp. 135–167.
5. Ibid.
6. Olmsted as artist, quoted in Roy Rosenzweig, in a review essay on the "Papers of F. L. Olmsted," *Journal of Social History*, Vol. 18, No. 2. (Winter 1984), pp. 289–295. At Biltmore Olmsted worked with Gifford Pinchot, Vanderbilt's chief forester and later Franklin Roosevelt's guide to forestry as well as the organizer of the U.S. Forest Service. Olmsted and Pinchot were important transmitters of the doctrines of George Perkins Marsh to such New Deal conservationists as Walter Lowdermilk.
7. Olmsted, *Yosemite and the Mariposa Grove: A Preliminary Report*, 1865, available in full on http://www.yosemite.ca.us/library/olmsted/report.html
8. Olmsted, Ibid; Lincoln on the dome, quoted on the National Capitol Web site.
9. Ibid.
10. Sherwood, ibid.
11. Sherwood and the verdict of Yank, Sherwood, p. 882; Churchill quoted by Sherwood, pp. 933–4.
12. Dutchess county farmer, ibid., p. 63.
13. Hickok, p. 9.
14. Edward Bruce's account of the work of FAP (June 22, 1935) says that the plaster model of Glickman's work was "one of the most interesting pieces of sculpture done for the project" and that it was "ordered to be cast in bronze by the President" himself. Not quite. The President remarked that Glickman's evocation of the mother-and-child icon of two millennia of European art, but with African features, was "worthy to be in bronze." Someone, probably Bruce, ordered that it be cast—and sent it to the White House. The President turned it over to the National Museum, which in turn passed it back to Bruce, who offered it as part of the package of works he and the Section presented to Ickes for the Interior Building. Glickman was later commissioned by the Section for sculptures for the post office in Northampton, Pennsylvania, and a Treasury Building in Saddle River, New Jersey. (The elegant short histories of the Slobodkin and Glickman sculptures, and references to Bruce's final report for the PWAP, are to be found in Look and Perraeult, pp. 116 ff, quoting critic in *The Skylight*, Vol. 2, no. 1, May 1939, p. 1.)
15. Sherwood on solemnity, *Roosevelt and Hopkins*, p. 219.
16. Slobodkin's masterwork suffered many indignities. The casting in Harold Ickes's courtyard is not the original bronze. That had been smashed by order of Edward J. Flynn, Tammany boss of the Bronx. For early favors to Roosevelt, Flynn had been elevated to the chairmanship of the Democratic National Committee and also of the Committee in charge of the New York World's Fair of 1939, giving a Tammany boss power over the arts of the kind feared all along by Harold Ickes, Harry Hopkins, and Edward Bruce. Five years earlier, they had sought to convince Roosevelt that commissions for important works of art should be made on merit, despite the importunings of Postmaster-General James A. Farley on behalf of the spoils system. When asked why patronage-bound procedures produced no respectable art, Morgenthau said later that "formerly the ward bosses picked artists for murals [and sculpture] and gave as an example Ed Flynn the boss of the Bronx."
In a contest at the World's Fair, Bruce contended against Flynn beyond the protective reach of Morgenthau, and lost: Flynn's men dominated the jury selecting art for the Fair, and they eagerly sought commissions for themselves and their friends. Bruce attempted to deprive one of Flynn's lieutenants of the commission for the interior of the United States Pavilion, insisting instead upon a competition managed by the Section. Flynn pushed Bruce aside. George Biddle remonstrated that Bruce was too timorous. Bruce went to the press with attacks on both Biddle and Flynn, and Flynn lay in wait for Bruce's next project, which was putting Slobodkin's fifteen-foot *Lincoln* statue amid a garden and water courses, in the "culminating statement of the Treasury's art program." The critics saw the model and rejoiced in it as "a unique symbol of American unity." Flynn declared it "too big, far too high, and hid all the lighting" of his United States Pavilion. Just before the Fair opened to the public, the Boss had his work crew destroy it and hide the pieces. Ickes had another casting made and gave it sanctuary in his courtyard a year later. There it remains, a relic of a controversy over local control, patronage, professionals, and the inherent difficulties of governmental support for the arts in a democratic system. The pieces were never found, so I presume they were deliberately hidden. A narrative of this affair appears in McKinzie, p. 69. My further details are from the somewhat more sanitized version in Look and Perraeult, pp. 118–119.
(See Morgenthau interview, November 9, 1964, cited supra.) Morgenthau had good cause to know Flynn, for, as noted above, the Bronx had provided his only direct, personal exposure to public or private finance before being elevated to the command of the United States Treasury. Morgenthau proceeded to tell his questioners with pride that in the work of his and Bruce's Section with Roosevelt's help, a competitive method for commissioning . . . was established and . . . much better work . . . .obtained.")
17. Lincoln sad, in Burns, p.423.
18. Ibid.
19. John Collier, in his memoir, *From Every Zenith*, Denver: Sage Books, 1963, pp. 294–5; Best I can, Burns, p. 246.
20. Borglum to Hopkins, in Sherwood, p. 59.
21. Susan Baker Munro, "The Seventy-fifth Anniversary of the New Deal" (Oregon Historical Quarterly, Vol. 109, No. 2, Summer 2008), www.historycooperative.org/journals/ohq/109.2/munro.html.—D.L.
22. "The Builders of Timberline Lodge," part of an unpublished collection "Art for the Millions" by the Federal Writers' Project, to support the WPA/FAP.
23. Frederick C. Hageman and Olaf T. Hagen, *Mission La Purísima Concepcion: A Glance Through Its History and The Story of Its Restoration* (National Park Service, undated).—D.L.
24 Nicolasa I. Sandoval, in *American Indian Places*, Frances H. Kennedy, ed. (Boston: Houghton Mifflin, 2008), pp. 250–251. Reprinted by permission of Houghton Mifflin Harcourt Publishing Company. All rights reserved.

CAPTION ENDNOTES

i. John James Audubon, *Birds of America*.—D.L.
ii. *Civilization* January–February 1996.
iii. Stryker, in Tugwell Papers, Box 25, FDR Library.
iv. Ben Shahn interview, Archives of American Art, Smithsonian Institution, April 14, 1964.—D.L.
v. Ben Shahn, *The Shape of Content* (New York: Vintage Books, 1957).—D.L.
vi. Andy Dappen, *Backcountry Magazine*.—D.L.

Art Sources and Credits

Pages 1, 20, 25, 27, 36, 86–87, 164, 165, 166, 182–183, 218 (far right, top and bottom), 242: Courtesy Franklin D. Roosevelt Presidential Library

Pages 2–3, 6–7, 83, 204, 240, 245, 247, 250–251, 252, 254, 255, 257, 258, 259, 260, 261, 262–263, 264, 265, 266, 267, 268, 269, 270, 271, 272, 273, 274, 275, 276, 277, 278, 279, 280, 281, 282, 283, 284, 285, 286, 287, 288, 289, 290 (bottom), 291, 293, 297, 312:
Library of Congress, Prints & Photographs Division, FSA/OWI Collection

Pages 4–5, 76–77, 78–79, 80, 81, 82–83, 84–85:
Photographs by Wyatt McSpadden
Post Office™ Murals reprinted with the permission of the United States Postal Service. All Rights Reserved. Written authorization from the Postal Service is required to use, reproduce, post, transmit, distribute, or publicly display these images.

Pages 8–9, 125 (poster), 194, 195, 200, 201, 214 (bottom), 215, 216 (top), 218 (top right):
Library of Congress, Prints & Photographs Division, WPA Poster Collection

Page 23: © The Dorothea Lange Collection, Oakland Museum of California, City of Oakland. Gift of Paul S. Taylor.

Page 24: Associated Press

Pages 27 and 28: © Condé Nast

Page 29: Smithsonian American Art Museum, Gift of the Museum

Pages 30, 39, 40, 124 (top, bottom right), 126, 162, 216 (bottom right):
National Archives and Records Administration

Page 31: Archives of American Art, Smithsonian Institution

Page 32: Smithsonian American Art Museum, Gift of Mr. and Mrs. Moses Soyer;
Art © Estate of Moses Soyer/Licensed by VAGA, New York, NY

Page 34: Photograph by Maurice Constant, Library of Congress, Prints and Photographs Division

Pages 37, 45 (bottom), 120, 128 (bottom, b/w), 129 (top), 131 (top), 135 (top, bottom, top margin), 136, 137, 138, 139, 140, 141, 142, 144, 145, 146 (top right), 148 (top), 151 (top), 152, 153 (b/w), 154 (b/w), 222:
Library of Congress, Prints & Photographs Division, Historic American Buildings Survey/Historic American Engineering Record

Pages 41, 42: University of Washington Libraries, Special Collections, UW20938z (Book mending), UW20941z (Clothing outlet), UW20914z (Sewing center), UW20953z (High School library)

Page 42: FDRL, Harry Hopkins Papers: Box 50

Pages 44, 123, 128 (top, b/w), 133 (bottom), 199, 306, 307:
Courtesy of the National Park Service

Page 45 (top):
Secretarial Portrait of Harold L. Ickes
By Henry Salem Hubbell
Oil on Masonite
INTR 1636
Credit Line: Interior Museum, U.S. Department of the Interior

Page 46: Smithsonian American Art Museum, Transfer from the U.S. Department of the Interior, National Park Service
© 2009 Estate of Reginald Marsh / Arts Students League, New York / Artists Rights Society (ARS), New York

Page 47: Photographs by Jena Pike, Park Rapids Enterprise; Post Office™ Carvings reprinted with the permission of the United States Postal Service. All Rights Reserved. Written authorization from the Postal Service is required to use, reproduce, post, transmit, distribute, or publicly display these images.

Page 49: Photograph by Lucy Wood Collier, 1907; John Collier papers, 1910–1987 (inclusive), Manuscripts and Archives, Yale University Library

Page 50: Library of Congress, Prints & Photographs Division

Pages 51–54, 57, 64, 88–89, 90–91, 317, 320, 321:
Courtesy of the U.S. General Services Administration, Fine Arts Program

Pages 58–60: Photographs by Ted Spiegel; Post Office™ Murals reprinted with the permission of the United States Postal Service. All Rights Reserved. Written authorization from the Postal Service is required to use, reproduce, post, transmit, distribute, or publicly display these images.

Page 62: Courtesy of National Farmers' Bank, Owatonna, Minnesota

Page 63: Manhunt, John Steuart Curry © Mrs. Kathleen Curry, Ben and Beatrice Goldstein Collection, Library of Congress

Pages 68–71: Gift of Edsel B. Ford, Photographs © 2001 The Detroit Institute of Arts
© 2009 Banco de México Diego Rivera Frida Kahlo Museums Trust, Mexico, D.F. / Artists Rights Society (ARS)

Pages 72–73: Courtesy Indiana University Archives; Art © T.H. Benton and R.P. Benton Testamentary Trusts/UMB Bank Trustee/Licensed by VAGA, New York, NY

Pages 74–75: Photo courtesy of the Pettaquamscutt Historical Society; Post Office™ Murals reprinted with the permission of the United States Postal Service. All Rights Reserved. Written authorization from the Postal Service is required to use, reproduce, post, transmit, distribute, or publicly display these images.

Pages 86–87: Photographs by Darryl Jones; Courtesy of the United States Postal Service; Post Office™ Murals reprinted with the permission of the United States Postal Service. All Rights Reserved. Written authorization from the Postal Service is required to use, reproduce, post, transmit, distribute, or publicly display these images.

Pages 92, 93: "Mail Service" Smithsonian American Art Museum, Transfer from the General Services Administration; "Self-Portrait" Smithsonian American Art Museum, Museum Purchase; "Study for U.S. Post Office Mural, Alaska" Plattsburgh State Art Museum; 170 (far right) Library of Congress Courtesy of the Plattsburgh State Art Museum, Plattsburgh College Foundation, Rockwell Kent Collection. Bequest of Sally Kent Gorton.

Page 94: Courtesy of Roosevelt Public School, Roosevelt, New Jersey
Art © Estate of Ben Shahn/Licensed by VAGA, New York, NY

Page 95: Smithsonian American Art Museum, Transfer from the General Services Administration

Page 97: Independence National Historical Park, Philadelphia, NPS

Page 99: Paul Mellon Collection, Image courtesy of the Board of Trustees, National Gallery of Art, Washington, 1844/1845, oil on canvas, .710 x .580 (28 x 22 x ⅞)

Pages 101, 167, 168, 193 (far right), 209, 219: Library of Congress

Page 103: Smithsonian American Art Museum, Gift of Mrs. Joseph Harrison, Jr.

Page 104: Smithsonian American Art Museum, Gift of the Misses Henry

Page 106: National Cowboy and Western Heritage Museum, Oklahoma City, OK

Page 108: Collection of The Butler Institute of American Art, Youngstown, Ohio

Pages 110–111: Smithsonian American Art Museum, Lent by the Department of the Interior Museum

Pages 116–117: Group of people at Red Rocks, Courtesy Colorado Historical Society (Lillybridge Collection, CHS-L2387). All Rights Reserved

Page 118: Courtesy of Gilcrease Museum, Tulsa, OK

Page 122: Courtesy of Bodega Bay Heritage Gallery

Page 124 (bottom far right): © Bettmann/CORBIS; bottom: Civilian Conservation Corps Museum

Pages 127, 150 (top): Massachusetts Department of Conservation and Recreation, CCC Archives

Pages 125 (statue), 127 (bottom), 129 (bottom), 130 (top), 135 (bottom margin), 149 (top, middle), 153 (color), 323, 325, 330, 332–333, 334 (color):
Photographs by David Larkin

Page 128 (color): Photographs by Paul Rocheleau

Page 130 (margin, bottom): Photographs by Sharon Klein, Berlin, New York, Historical Society

Page 131 (bottom): Mill Valley Public Library

Pages 132, 330–331, 344, 348–349, 350–352, 352–353:
Photographs by Michael Freeman

Page 133 (top): Photographs by Sally King, National Park Service

Pages 143, 146 (bottom, far right top, middle, bottom), 147, 148 (bottom), 149 (bottom), 150 (bottom), 151 (bottom):
Photographs by Ethan Carr

Page 155: Photograph by Kevin Daley, National Park Service

Pages 156, 157, 158–159:
Photographs by Steven Butler

Pages 167, 168: Library of Congress, Prints and Photographs Division, Ben and Beatrice Goldstein Foundation Collection (Library of Congress)

Pages 169, 171, 172, 175, 176, 177, 178, 179, 180, 181, 183, 248:
Collection of the Illinois State Museum/Courtesy of the Fine Arts Program, Public Buildings Service, U.S. General Services Administration. Commissioned through the New Deal art projects.

Page 170 (right): © Estate of Robert Blackburn, used with permission

Pages 170 (far right), 173, 185, 197, 198, 199, 203 (bottom), 205, 206, 211, 217, 304:
Library of Congress

Page 184: © 2009 The Philbrook Museum of Art, Inc., Tulsa, Oklahoma

Page 185: Art © T.H. Benton and R.P. Benton Testamentary Trusts/UMB Bank Trustee/Licensed by VAGA, New York, NY

Page 186: Smithsonian American Art Museum, Transfer from the United States Information Agency through the General Services Administration; Art © Estate of Stuart Davis/Licensed by VAGA, New York, NY

Pages 187, 188–189:
Reproduced courtesy of The Port Authority of New York and New Jersey
Arshile Gorky, "Aerial Map" and "Mechanics of Flying" © 2009 Artists Rights Society (ARS), New York

Page 190 (right): Sacco-Vanzetti series
Tempera on canvas, Unframed:
84½ x 48 in. (214.6 x 121.9 cm)
Whitney Museum of American Art, New York;
Gift of Edith and Milton Lowenthal in memory of
Juliana Force 49.22
Art (c) Estate of Ben Shahn/Licensed by VAGA,
New York, NY

Page 190 (far right): Courtesy of Smithsonian American Art Museum, Transfer from the General Services Administration

Page 191 (left): Courtesy Franklin D. Roosevelt Presidential Library;
Art © Estate of Ben Shahn/Licensed by VAGA, New York, NY
Page 193 (right): Courtesy Franklin D. Roosevelt Presidential Library;
Art © Estate of Bernarda Bryson Shahn/Licensed by VAGA, New York, NY

Pages 202, 203 (top): Photographs by Victor Kraft; Aaron Copland Collection, Music Division, Library of Congress © Mrs. Rheba Kraft

Page 204 (top): J. Warren Perry Collection of Photographs, Music Library, State University of New York at Buffalo (C17-013)

Page 205 (margin): Photograph by Ruby T. Lomax, Library of Congress, Prints & Photographs Division, Lomax Collection

Pages 205, 206, 207: Photographs by Robert Hemmig, Library of Congress, Prints and Photographs Division

Page 206 (Mr. and Mrs. Pipkin): Todd and Robert Sonkin Migrant-Worker Collection. American Folklife Center

Page 206 (bottom): Library of Congress, Prints & Photographs Division, Lomax Collection

Pages 206–208: Alan Lomax interview with Jim Brown, American Roots Music. Used by permission.

Page 208: Library of Congress, Prints & Photographs Division, Lomax Collection

Page 208 (letter): Woody Guthrie Manuscript Collection, American Folklife Center, Library of Congress.
Woody Guthrie letter, copyright Woody Guthrie Publications, Inc. Used by permission.

Page 209 (margin): Library of Congress, Prints & Photographs Division, photograph by Al Aumuller, New York World-Telegram and the Sun Newspaper Collection

Page 212: Richard Wright, photograph by Carl Van Vechten: Prints and Photographs Division, Library of Congress; Nelson Algren, photograph by Walter Albertin, Library of Congress; John Steinbeck, photograph by Sonya Noskowiak, Courtesy of Department of Special Collections and University Archives, Stanford University Libraries

Page 212: *The Grapes of Wrath*, John Steinbeck, original 1939 edition, courtesy Penguin Group (USA), Inc.

Pages 216 (bottom middle, bottom far right), 218 (bottom right, bottom left): Federal Theatre Project Collection, Special Collections & Archives, George Mason University Libraries

Page 219: Courtesy Franklin D. Roosevelt Presidential Library
© Al Hirschfeld, Reproduced by arrangement with Hirschfeld's representative, the Margo Feiden Galleries, Ltd., New York, www.alhirschfeld.com

Pages 226–227: Paul Mellon Collection, Image courtesy of the Board of Trustees, National Gallery of Art, Washington, 1844/1845, oil on canvas, .710 x .580 (28 x 22 x ⅞)

Page 229: Index of American Design, Image courtesy of the Board of Trustees, National Gallery of Art, Washington, 1935/1942, watercolor, pen and ink, and graphite paper, .673 x .542 (26½ x 21 5/16)

Page 230: Index of American Design, Image courtesy of the Board of Trustees, National Gallery of Art, Washington, 1935/1942, watercolor on graphite paper, .427 x .506 (16 13/16 x 19 15/16)

Page 228: Nicolas Amantea, Photograph by Herman; National Gallery of Art, Washington, D.C., Gallery Archives

Page 231: Charlotte Angus, National Gallery of Art, Washington, D.C., Gallery Archives

Page 235: Rollin Kirby, By permission of Rollin Kirby Post

Page 238: Photograph by Underwood & Underwood, Library of Congress

Page 241: Courtesy of J. Paul Getty Museum, Los Angeles, Oil on canvas, unframed: 31½ x 39 in (80 x 99 cm)

Page 290 (top): Photograph by Trude Fleischmann

Page 300: Courtesy of Mount Vernon Ladies Association

Pages 310, 311: National Resources Conservation Service

Pages 326, 327: Courtesy of Colorado Historical Society

Pages 328, 329, 334 (b/w), 335:
Courtesy of Denver Public Library, Western History Collection (Aerial: Z8890; Singers: Rhoads, RH 45; Singers: Rhoads; RH 102; Symphony: Z 8891)

Pages 336–337, 340 (b/w), 341, 342 (owl): Photographs by Lawrence Hudetz

Pages 338, 339:
Oregon Historical Society

Page 339 (margin): Friends of Timberline

Pages 340 (color), 342 (hawk, duck and bear; bottom), 343:
Courtesy of Timberline Lodge

Page 345: Courtesy of The Brancroft Library, University of California, Berkeley (BANC PIC 19xx.039:23—ALB)

Pages 346, 347, 348, 350:
Courtesy La Purísima Mission, SHP

Index

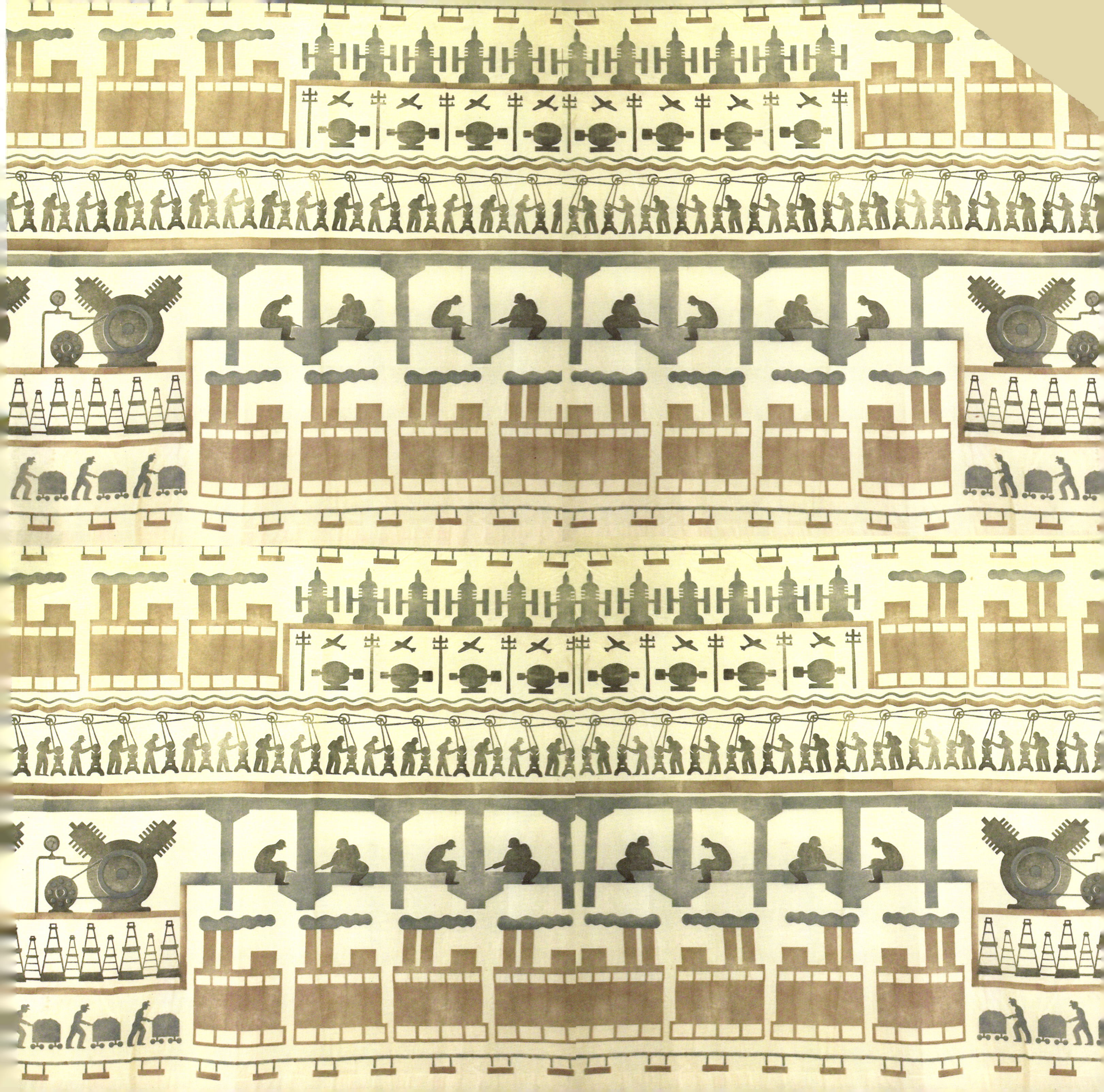

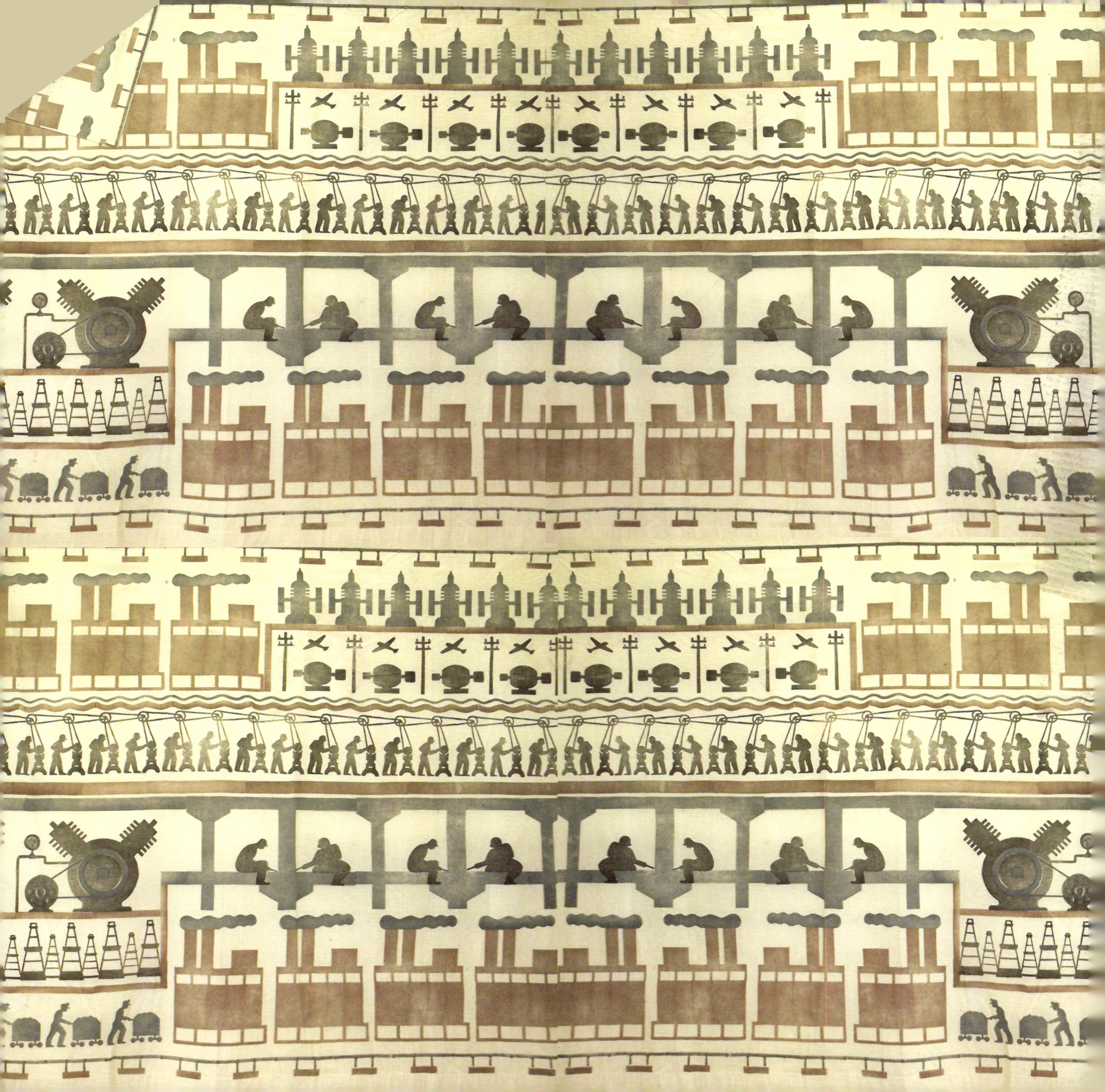